Mastercam Version 8 Mill

Su-Chen Jonathon Lin, Ph.D.
Professor of Computer-Aided Manufacturing
College of Technology
Eastern Michigan University

F.C. Tony Shiue, Ph.D.
Professor of Computer-Aided Design
College of Technology
Eastern Michigan University

Scholars International Publishing Corp.
Ann Arbor, Michigan

Mastercam Version 8 Mill
Scholars International Publishing Corp., 2001

Scholars staff:
Marketing manager: Grace Lin
Chief editor: Jonathon Lin
Project editor: Karen L. Sterzik
Project manager: Mei-Shan Lin
Illustrator: Mei-Shan Lin, Maggie Yan
Cover designer: Joshua Chen
Printer/Binder: Sheridan Books, Chelsea Michigan
Printed and bound in the United States of America

To request more information on this publication, contact:

Scholars International Publishing Corp.
605 Green Road
Ann Arbor MI 48105
Phone: (734) 930-0813 or FAX:(734) 741-1927
Internet: WWW. Scholarsbook.com

Lin, SuChen Jonathon, and F.C. Tony Shiue
Mastercam Version 8 Mill
Includes index.
ISBN 1-886552-15-0

Mastercam Version 8 Mill

Preface

CAD/CAM technology has emerged as one of the major driving forces in our modern manufacturing industry. Due to increased computer power and the advancement of CAD/CAM software, manual CNC programming has been replaced by CAD/CAM programming in recent years. Mastercam CNC programming software has become the leading PC-based CAM software due to its power and ease of use.

Mastercam software is widely used in industry and schools. It has become a leading tool for teaching CNC programming. Additionally, there is a need for a comprehensive text to teach students of all skill levels to effectively use Mastercam. This text is intended to be used to teach CAD/CAM/CNC with Mastercam software in schools and in industrial training classes. It is also a valuable reference for all levels of Mastercam users.

This book is one of a series of three Mastercam books. Our previous version, "Mastercam Version 7", is very comprehensive in content and very large in size. Adding the new features in Mastercam 8 to this already huge book becomes impossible. We split the new version into two books: "Mastercam Version 8 Mill" and "Mastercam Lathe". "Mastercam Solids" is still a separate third book. "Mastercam Version 8 Mill" covers most of the important features and functionalities of Mill for Version 8.

One new chapter in reverse engineering has been added in addition to many significant changes throughout the book to reflect the new features in Version 8. The reverse engineering in Chapter 20 was written by Mr. Braxton Carter of HighRES, Inc. This chapter describes how to perform 3D digitizing, then use Mastercam to convert digitized data to a surface model and generate toolpaths to produce the part.

This book is suited for a two-semester course. It is appropriate for industrial technology, engineering technology, and engineering courses at many levels; universities and colleges, junior colleges, trade schools, high schools, as well as for courses offered by industry. The first semester covers 2D toolpath programming and the second semester presents 3D toolpath programming.

Su-Chen Jonathon Lin

Mastercam Version 8 Mill

Acknowledgements

The author is indebted to many persons and organizations for their help and contributions in making this book into a reality. First, I wish to express my sincere appreciation to Iven May of CNC Software, Inc. He is the person who initiated the book idea and gave numerous suggestions toward making it possible. His three colleagues in the Educational Division of CNC Software, Dan Newby, Rick Meyers, and Mike Freimann, also provided a lot of assistance and especially helped by reviewing the manuscript.

Special thanks are due to Jack, Brian and Mark Summers who provided Mastercam software and helped tremendously in marketing the book to Mastercam users. Because they are so friendly and easy to work with, they make the project progress smoothly.

Thanks are extended to Scholars staff. Mei-Shan Lin and Maggie Yan prepared several hundred illustrations using AutoCAD and Mastercam. Without their great skill and care, the book would never have been finished. Joshua Chen, art and cover designer, created artworks and provided assistance to develop chapter 19. His work is very appreciated. I greatly appreciate the excellent work Ms. Karen Sterzik has contributed to this book in editing and using PageMaker to do the page layout design.

I am greatly indebted to my dear wife, Grace, for her patient and continuous support. Your great skill in running the business has made Mastercam books widely distributed. I am also grateful to my son, Andrew, and daughter, Carol, for their support. I will do my best to stay at home more and to enjoy time with you while you are young.

A credit needs to be given also to Delmar Publishers, Inc. for granting me their permission to use the following twelve figures and tables:

Figure 1.2 Direct numerical control
Figure 1.3 Distributive numerical control
Figure 2.6 Toolholder system for machining centers
Figure 2.11 Insert identification system
Figure 2.20 Drilling
Figure 2.21 Milling
Figure 2.22 Turning
Figure 2.9 Unit horsepower required for drilling AISI 1112 steels
Figure 2.10 Approximate conversion factor for unit horsepower required to drill other materials
Figure 2.11 Unit horsepower for milling
Figure 2.12 Unit horsepower for turning various materials
Figure 7.39 Pocket cutting direction

All the above illustrations are Reproduced by Permission.
COMPUTER NUMERICAL CONTROL: FROM PROGRAMMING TO NETWORKING

Mastercam 8

Table of Contents

Chapter 1 CNC Programming Fundamentals

1.1	NC, CNC and DNC, What are they ?	1-1
1.2	Advantages and Limitations of CNC	1-3
1.3	CNC Operations	1-4
1.4	Career Opportunities	1-4
1.5	CNC System Elements	1-6
1.6	CNC Applications and Machines	1-8
1.7	NC Coding Systems	1-12
1.8	NC Addresses	1-13
1.9	NC Words	1-15
1.10	NC Functional Blocks	1-21
1.11	NC Programming Methods	1-21
1.12	CNC Control Systems	1-22
1.13	CNC Drive Systems	1-25
1.14	CNC Interpolations	1-27
1.15	Machine Axes Designation & Direction	1-30
1.16	Reference Zero Points	1-32
1.17	Positioning Systems	1-35

Chapter 2 Machining Fundamentals

2.1	CNC Milling Processes	2-1
2.2	CNC Turning Processes	2-1
2.3	Cutting Tool Materials	2-6
2.4	Tooling for Milling	2-10
2.5	Tooling System for Turning	2-13
2.6	Inserts Identification and Selection	2-16
2.7	Toolholders	2-21
2.8	Machining Parameters	2-24
2.9	Face Milling	2-32
2.10	End Milling	2-33
2.11	Milling with Ball End Mills	2-36
2.12	Drilling Operations	2-37
2.13	Boring Operations	2-39
2.14	Tapping Operations	2-41
2.15	Turning Operation	2-44

Chapter 3 Mastercam Environments

3.1	Launching Mastercam (Windows 98)	3-1
3.2	Changing the Size of the Window	3-2
3.3	Mastercam Screen	3-3
3.4	Exiting Mastercam	3 6
3.5	Using Mastercam Navigation Commands	3-6
3.6	Getting Help	3-8
3.7	Setting System Configuration	3-10
Ex	Exercises	3-21

Chapter 4 3D Toolpaths I:Generated from Wireframe Models

4.1	CAD/CAM NC Programming Process	4-1
4.2	Mastercam Process Overview	4-2
Ex	Exercises	4-14

Chapter 5 Basic (2-D) Geometry Construction

5.1	Create Menu	5-1
5.2	Point and the Point Submenu	5-2
5.3	Line and Its Submenu	5-6
5.4	Arc and the Arc Submenu	5-13
5.5	Fillet and the Fillet Submenu	5-20
5.6	Spline and the Spline Submenu	5-23
5.7	Curve and Surface	5-26
5.8	Rectangle and the Rectangle Submenu	5-27
5.9	Chamfer and the Chamfer Submenu	5-29
5.10	Letters and the Letter Submenu	5-31
5.11	Ellipse and Ellipse Submenu	5-35
5.12	Polygon and Polygon Submenu	5-36
5.13	2-D Geometry Construction Project	5-37
Ex	Exercises	5-50

Chapter 6 Modify Existing Geometry

6.1	Delete Function	6-1
6.2	Modify Functions	6-2
6.3	Xform Functions	6-12
Ex	Exercises	6-44

Chapter 7 2D Toolpath Generation: From Print to Part

7.1	2D Toolpath Modules	7-1
7.2	Tool Definition	7-3
7.3	Operations Manager	7-15
7.4	Backplot Function	7-15
7.5	Verify	7-20
7.6	Job Setup	7-24
7.7	Contour definition	7-27
7.8	Coordinate Setting	7-34
7.9	Contour Module	7-38
7.10	Pocket Module	7-66

7.11	Drill Module	7-99
7.12	Circle mill Module	7-122
7.13	Point Module	7-127
7.14	Engraving Letters	7-127
Ex	Exercises	7-143

Chapter 8 Associativity and its Applications

8.1	Associativity	8-1
8.2	Job Setup, Tool Manager, Define Tool, and Tool Parameters	8-2
8.3	Operations Manager	8-2
8.4	Chain Manager	8-24
Ex	Exercises	8-35

Chapter 9 2D Toolpath Editing

9.1	File Structure of Toolpaths	9-2
9.2	Deleting Toolpaths using Operations Manager	9-6
9.3	Transform Toolpaths	9-10
9.4	Translating Toolpaths	9-12
9.5	Rotating Toolpaths	9-24
9.6	Mirroring Toolpaths	9-35
Ex	Exercises	9-43

Chapter 10 Mastercam Process and Toolpath Planning

10.1	Part and Raw Material Drawings	10-1
10.2	Part Features Geometry creation	10-5
10.3	Toolpath Modules Selection	10-6
10.4	Tooling Data and Machining Data	10-8
10.5	Process Plan Sheet Preparation	10-8
10.6	Post Processor Selection	10-12
Ex	Exercises	10-15

Chapter 11 Constructing 3D Wireframe Models

11.1	Wireframe Modeling Fundamentals	11-1
11.2	Wireframe Model Construction Examples	11-5
Ex	Exercises	11-94

Chapter 12 Surface Modeling I: Fundamentals and Creation

12.1	Surfaces	12-1
12.2	Surface Mathematics	12-2
12.3	Surface Types	12-3
12.4	Mastercam Surfaces	12-6
12.5	Ruled Surfaces Modeling	12-7
12.6	Loft Surfaces Modeling	12-16
12.7	Coons Surfaces Modeling	12-24
12.8	Revolved Surfaces Modeling	12-44
12.9	Draft Surfaces Modeling	12-46
12.10	Swept Surfaces Modeling	12-54
Ex	Exercises	12-61

Chapter 13 Surface Modeling II: Derived & Composite Surfaces

13.1	Derived surfaces Modeling	13-1
13.2	Trim/Extend Surfaces Modeling	13-23
13.3	Composite Surfaces Models	13-63
Ex	Exercises	13-111

Chapter 14 3D Toolpaths I:Generated from Wireframe Models

14.1	Two Surface Toolpath Generation Methods	14-1
14.2	3D Toolpaths Common Parameters	14-2
14.3	3D Toolpath Modules	14-7
14.4	Ruled Toolpath Module	14-7
14.5	Loft Toolpath Module	14-18
14.6	Coons Toolpath Module	14-21
14.7	Swept Toolpath Module	14-32
14.8	Surface of Revolution Toolpath Module	14-42
Ex	Exercises	14-47

Chapter 15 3D Toolpaths II: Generated from Surface Models

15.1	Surface Toolpath Functions	15-1
15.2	Rough Functions	15-2
15.3	Common Parameters	15-2
15.4	Rough Specific Parameters	15-8
15.5	Cut Depths, Gap Settings and Edge Settings	15-12
15.6	Rough Parallel Function	15-20
15.7	Rough Radial Function	15-26
15.8	Rough Project Function	15-31
15.9	Rough Flowline Function	15-36
15.10	Rough Contour Function	15-44
15.11	Pocket Rough Function	15-50
15.12	Rough Plunge Function	15-59
15.13	Finish Functions	15-63
15.14	Parallel Finish Function	15-65
15.15	Parallel Steep Finish Function	15-70
15.16	Finish Leftover Function	15-71
15.17	Finish Radial Function	15-73
15.18	Project Finish Function	15-81
15.19	Flowline Function	15-91
15.20	Contour Function	15-95
15.21	Finish Shallow Function	15-97
15.22	Finish Pencil Function	15-104
15.23	Finish Scallop Function	15-105
Ex	Exercises	15-123

Chapter 16 Multiaxis Machining

16.1	Rotary Axes and Directions	16-1
16.2	4-Axis and 5-Axis Machines	16-2
16.3	Part Features for 4th and 5th Axis Machining	16-3
16.4	Rotary 4-Axis Function	16-3
16.5	5-Axis Toolpath Functions	16-12
16.6	Curve 5-Axis Common Parameters	16-13
16.7	Drill 5-Axis Function	16-32
16.8	Swarf 5-Axis Function	16-43
16.9	Flowline 5-Axis Function	16-54
Ex	Exercises	16-59

Chapter 17 3D Toolpath Editing

17.1	Project Function	17-1
17.2	Trim Function	17-8
Ex	Exercises	17-13

Chapter 18 3D Toolpath Planning

18.1	Identifying Features and Surfaces	18-1
18.2	Wireframe Model Construction	18-3
18.3	Surface Module Selection	18-4
18.4	Toolpath Modules Selection	18-4
18.5	Toolpath Planning	18-4
18.6	Tooling	18-5
18.7	Accuracy Requirement	18-6
18.8	Toolpath File Management	18-6
Ex	Exercises	18-13

Chapter 19 Engraving Artworks

19.1	Artworks and Bitmap Images	19-1
19.2	Vector Formats	19-2
19.3	Adobe Streamline Program	19-3
19.4	Importing Vector Drawings to Mastercam	19-14
19.5	InterFlux Program	19-20
Ex	Exercises	19-28

Chapter 20

20.1	Reverse Engineering	20-2
20.2	Square up Digital Part for Digitizing	20-3
20.3	3D Manual Digitizer Usage	20-4
20.4	Creating Revolve Surfaces Using 2D Digitized data	20-4
20.5	Extruded Solids	20-6
20.6	Loft Surfaces	20-7
20.7	Coons Surfaces	20-8
20.8	Generating Toolpaths	20-8
Ex	Exercises	20-8

Chapter 1

CNC Programming Fundamentals

Objectives:

1. Understand the basic concepts required in CNC programming and operation.
2. Be aware of the career opportunities in NC related jobs.
3. Know NC programming words and commands.
4. Be familiar with CNC machines and their axes designation.
5. Know various reference zero points in CNC programming.

1.1 NC, CNC and DNC, What are they ?

Four terms are often used in describing the emerging technology dealt with in this book:

- numerical control (NC)
- computer numerical control (CNC),
- direct numerical control (DNC)
- distributive numerical control (DNC).

Numerical Control (NC)

Numerical control (NC) is a technique for controlling machine tools or processes by using coded command instructions. The NC controller interprets these instructions and then converts them into two types of control signals: **motion control signals** and **miscellaneous control signals** (Figure 1.1).

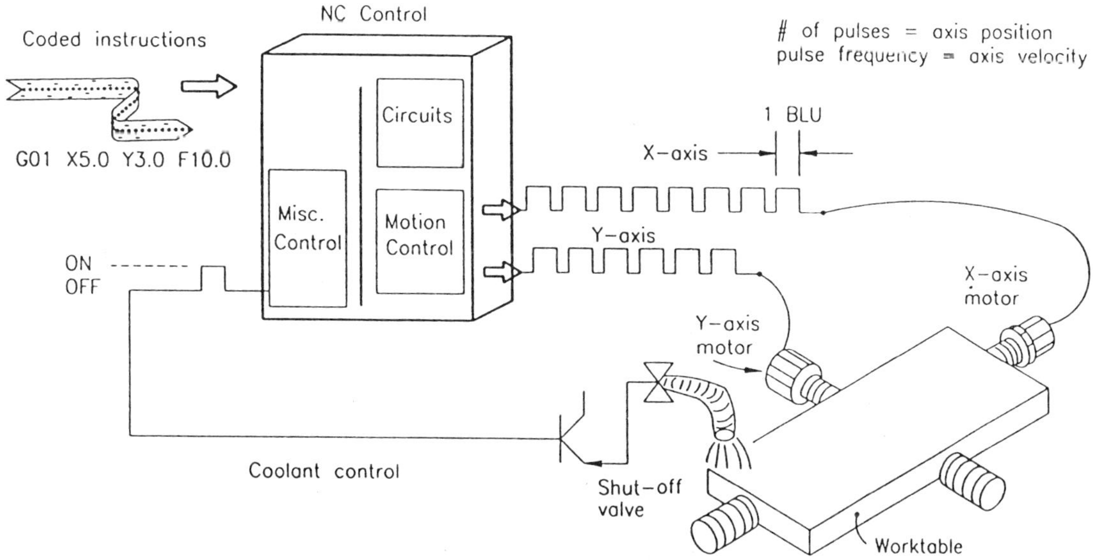

Figure 1.1 Numerical control

Motion control signals are a series of electric pulse trains that are used to control the position and the speed of the machine table and spindle. Each pulse activates a motion of one basic length-unit (BLU) which is the minimum increment size of the NC control system. The typical increment for one BLU in the old generation of NC controls is 0.001in. (or 0.01 mm), while in modern CNC controls, the increment resolution can reach 0.0001 in. (or 0.001 mm). The number of pulses transmitted to each axis determines the incremental axis position, and the frequency of these pulses regulates the axis speed.

Miscellaneous control functions are a set of on/off signals to implement the control of the speed and direction of the spindle rotation, control of coolant supply, selection of cutting tool, automatic clamping and unclamping, etc.

NC is often referred to as the older generation of numerical control technology. NC systems are hard-wired controls in which most functions are implemented by electronic hardware based upon digital circuit technology.

Computer Numerical Control (CNC)

Computer numerical control (CNC) is the numerical control system in which a dedicated, stored program computer is built into the control to perform basic and advanced NC functions. CNC controls are also referred to as soft-wired NC systems because most of their control functions are implemented by the *control software programs.* All numerical control machines manufactured since the seventies are of CNC type. The control signals in CNC systems are in the form of binary words. Each word contains a fixed number of bits, 32 bits or 64 bits are commonly used. Each bit of data produces one BLU motion in the controlled axis. Theoretically a 32-bit word could represent one of up to $2^{32} = 4,294,967,296$ different axial positions. If the system resolution is, for example, BLU = 0.0001 in., this number can represent up to 429,969 in. possible motions, which is more than enough for all types of applications.

Direct Numerical Control (DNC)

Direct numerical control uses a shared computer to simultaneously control the operation of a group of NC machine tools (Figure 1.2). The main tasks performed by the computer are to program and edit part programs as well as download part programs to NC machines. The idea of direct numerical control began in the mid-1960s in Cincinnati Milacron and General Electric. In 1970 about a half-dozen vendors marketed their DNC systems.

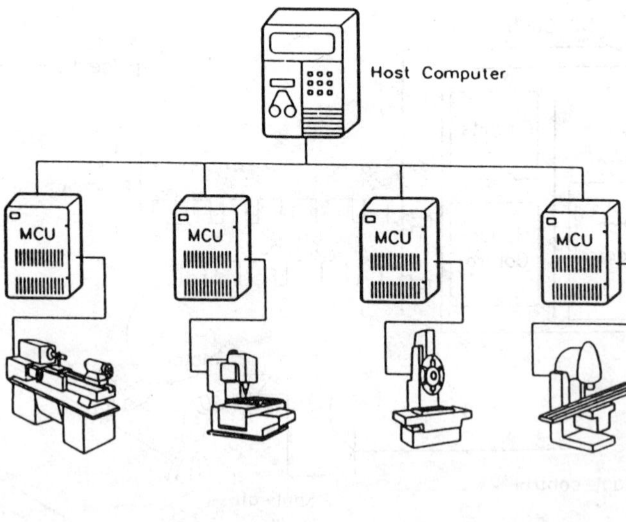

Figure 1.2 Direct numerical control (Source; S. C. Jonathon Lin, Computer Numerical Control: From Programming to Networking, 1994.Courtesy of Delmar Publishers, Inc.)

Direct numerical control was not widely used in industry mainly due to two reasons. The industry could not afford the expensive mainframe computers which could cost as much as a million dollars each. The other reason was the introduction of CNC in 1970s. The capacity of stored memory and enhanced intelligence of the built-in low cost dedicated computer replaced the desirable features of the DNC systems.

Distributive Numerical Control (DNC)

The main concept of distributive numerical control is to use a network of computers to coordinate the operation of a group of CNC machine tools (Figure 1.3). This new form of DNC systems began to evolve in the early 1980s and grew with the development of computer and communication technologies. Today many CNC machines, together with robots, programmable logic controllers and other computer-based controllers, have been integrated into DNC systems to make automated manufacturing systems possible.

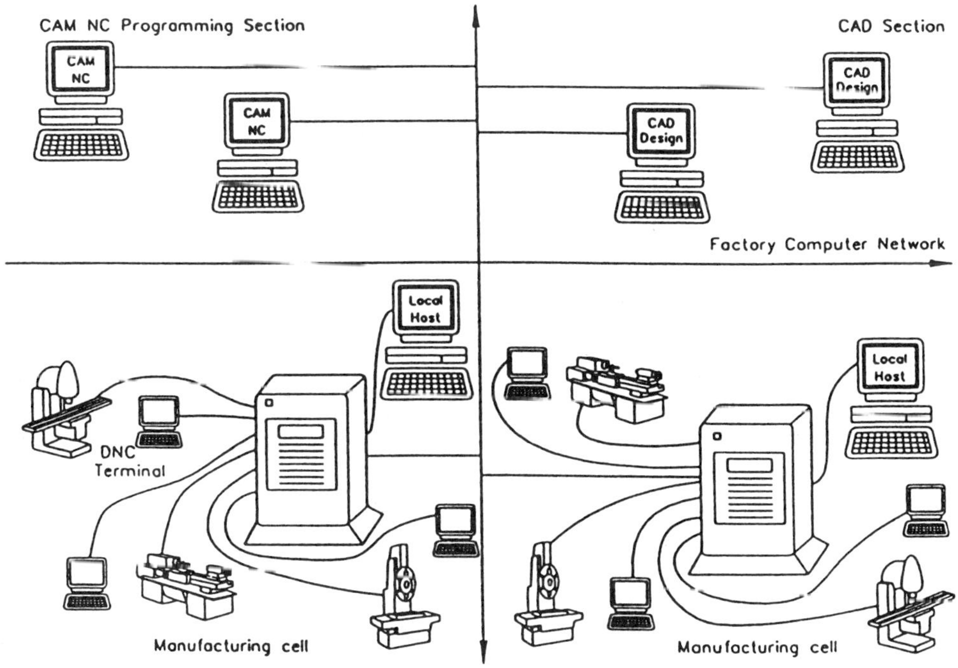

Figure 1.3 Distributive numerical control (Source: S. C. Jonathon Lin, Computer Numerical Control: From Programming to Networking, Courtesy of Delmar Publishers, Inc.)

1.2 Advantages and Limitations of CNC

The main advantages of using CNC technology are to **reduce product cost, improve product quality, and facilitate production planning and control**. These can be realized through these **nine** causes:

	•Facilitation of flexible automation
•Increased productivity	•High accuracy and repeatability
•Reduced production costs	•Reduced indirect operating costs
•Facilitation of complex machining operations	•Greater flexibility
•Improved production planning and control	•Lower operator skill requirement

Three main drawbacks of using CNC technology include **high initial investment, high maintenance requirement, and not cost-effective for low productions runs**.

1.3 CNC Operations

The organizational structure for implementing computer numerical control operations varies throughout the industry. The larger the operation, the greater the need for organization. The functions found within a CNC group are the same no matter how large the group is; the only difference is how those functions are delegated. A small shop might have only one or two people performing all of the NC department functions, while a medium to large operation will divide the NC functions into groups or even assign them to departments (Figure 1.4):

- NC shop management
- NC part programming
- Tool and fixture design
- Machine maintenance
- NC machine operation

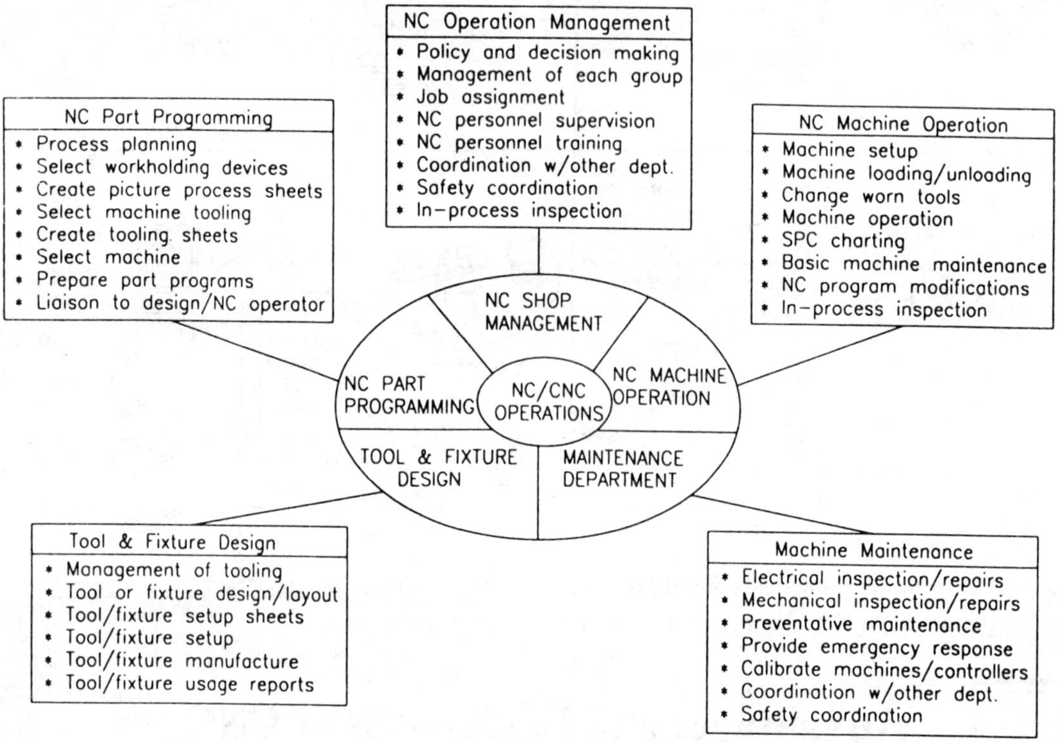

Figure 1.4 NC/CNC operations

1.4 Career Opportunities

There are about three hundred thousand NC related jobs available to service 170,000 NC/CNC machine tools in the U.S. industry today. The demand for NC related personnel has increased in a very steady pace as industry moves further into automated manufacturing. The job titles associated with NC personnel may appear as NC manager or supervisor, process planner, part programmer, tool designer, tool maker, machine setup person, machine operator, or maintenance person. The major responsibilities, required job skills, as well as education and experience of each job title are summarized in Table 1.1.

Table 1.1 CNC Career Opportunities

Job Title	Responsibility	Required Job Skills	Education/Experience
NC manager or supervisor	• Oversee NC operations • NC personnel hiring, training and job assignment • Coordination with other departments • Evaluate and acquire new CNC machine tools and CAD/CAM software	— Management skills — Machining knowledge — NC programming and operation background	4-year college degree with several years of manufacturing experience
Process planner	• Determine what machining processes to be used, with what sequence, and in what machines • Select cutting tools and workholders and fixtures • Prepare operation sheets and tooling sheets	— Overall knowledge of machining, tooling, and capability of available equipment — Good background in manufacturing and CNC	At least 2-year college degree, 4-year college degree preferred
Part programmer	• Prepare part programs • Prepare NC documents concerning setup instructions • Prepare process plan if needed	— Good command at math, geometry and trigonometry — Sound knowledge of machining — Blue-print reading — Computer skills — Use of CAD/CAM software	2-year college degree or vocational technical school
Tool designer	• Select standard tooling • Design special-purpose tooling	— Good command at locating and clamping knowledge — Knowledge of tool making — Understanding of standard tooling and fixturing	At least 2-year college degree with tool and machine experience 4-year college degree preferred
Tool maker	• Assemble and preset standard tooling • Make special-purpose tooling • Repair damaged tooling items	— Highly skilled in machining — Knowledge in CNC — Print reading and making	4-year apprenticeship program
Machine setup person	• Set up fixture and cutting tools on the machine • Coordinate the machine • Determine and enter offset and compensation values • Correct errors in tooling and program • Tryout run the program	— Good knowledge in machining and tooling — Understanding of part program and machine functions	Machinist experience with extensive CNC knowledge
Machine operator	• Load and unload workpieces • Monitor machining in progress • Finished part inspection • SPC charting • Regular check-up	— General knowledge of machining	Technical programs in vocational technical school, area occupational school, community college

1.5 CNC System Elements

A typical CNC system consists of the following **six** elements shown in Figure 1.5:

- Part program
- Program input device
- Machine control unit
- Drive system
- Machine tool
- Feedback system

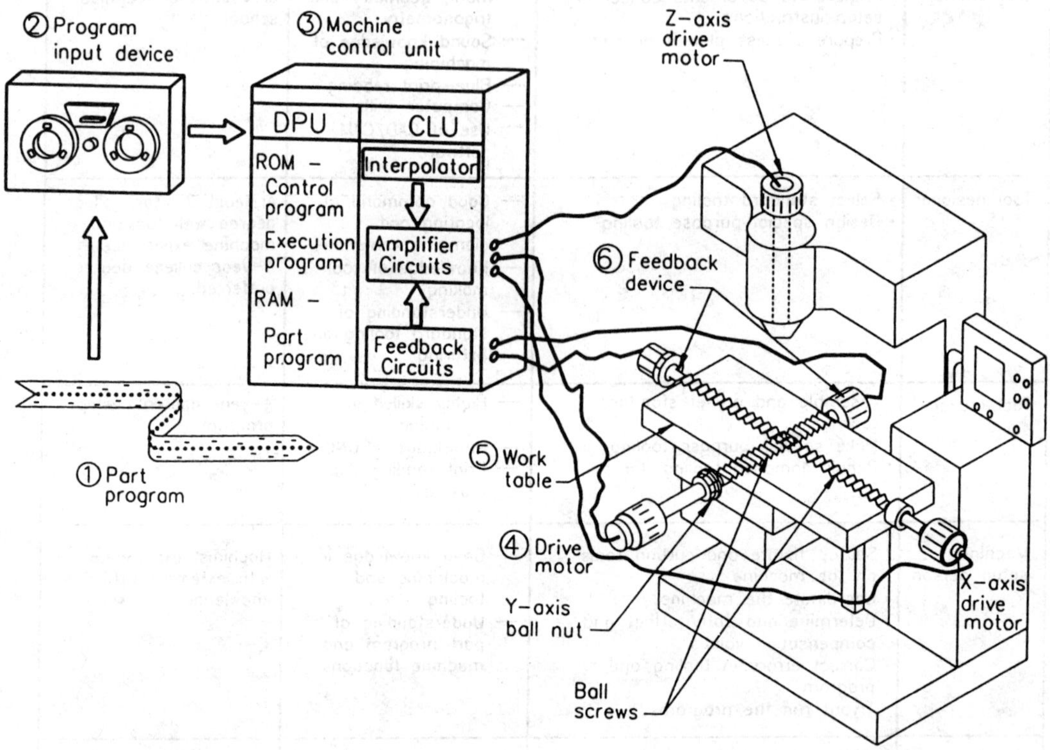

Figure 1.5 CNC system elements

Part Program

A part program is a series of coded instructions required to produce a part. It controls the movement of the machine tool and the on/off control of auxiliary functions such as spindle rotation and coolant. The coded instructions are composed of letters, numbers and symbols and are arranged in a format of functional blocks as in the following example.

```
N10 G01 X5.0 Y2.5 F15.0
```

- N10 — Sequence number
- G01 — Linear interpolation mode
- X5.0 — X-coordinate (5.0")
- Y2.5 — Y-coordinate (2.5")
- F15.0 — Feed rate (15 in/min)

Program Input Device

The program input device is the mechanism for part programs to be entered into the CNC control. **Three** commonly used program input devices are **punch tape reader, magnetic tape reader, and computer via RS-232-C communication.**

Machine Control Unit

The machine control unit (MCU) is the heart of a CNC system. It is used to perform the following functions:

- Read coded instructions
- Decode coded instructions
- Implement interpolations (linear, circular, and helical) to generate axis motion commands
- Feed axis motion commands to the amplifier circuits for driving the axis mechanisms
- Receive the feedback signals of position and speed for each drive axis
- Implement auxiliary control functions such as coolant or spindle on/off, and tool change

Drive System

A drive system consists of **amplifier circuits, drive motors, and ball lead-screws**. The MCU feeds control signals (position and speed) of each axis to the amplifier circuits. The control signals are augmented to actuate drive motors which in turn rotate the ball lead-screws to position the machine table.

Machine Tool

CNC controls are used to control various types of machine tools. Regardless of which type of machine tool is controlled, it always has a **slide table and a spindle to control of position and speed.** The machine table is controlled in the X and Y axes, while the spindle runs along the Z axis.

Feedback System

The feedback system is also referred to as the *measuring system*. It uses position and speed transducers to continuously monitor the position at which the cutting tool is located at any particular time. The MCU uses the difference between reference signals and feedback signals to generate the control signals for correcting position and speed errors.

1.6 CNC Applications and Machines

CNC technology has been successfully applied to almost every aspect of the manufacturing industry. Their applications are often classified in these **five** categories:

- Chip removal (metal cutting)
- Grinding
- Unconventional machining
- Fabrication
- Special-purpose applications

The machines controlled by CNC can be classified into the following **eight** categories:

- CNC mills and machining centers
- CNC lathes and turning centers
- CNC EDMs
- CNC grinding machines
- CNC cutting machines (laser, plasma, electron, or flame)
- CNC fabrication machines (sheet metal punch press, bending machine, or press brake)
- CNC welding machines
- CNC coordinate measuring machines

Figures 1.6 to 1.14 show some typical CNC controlled machine tools used in industry.

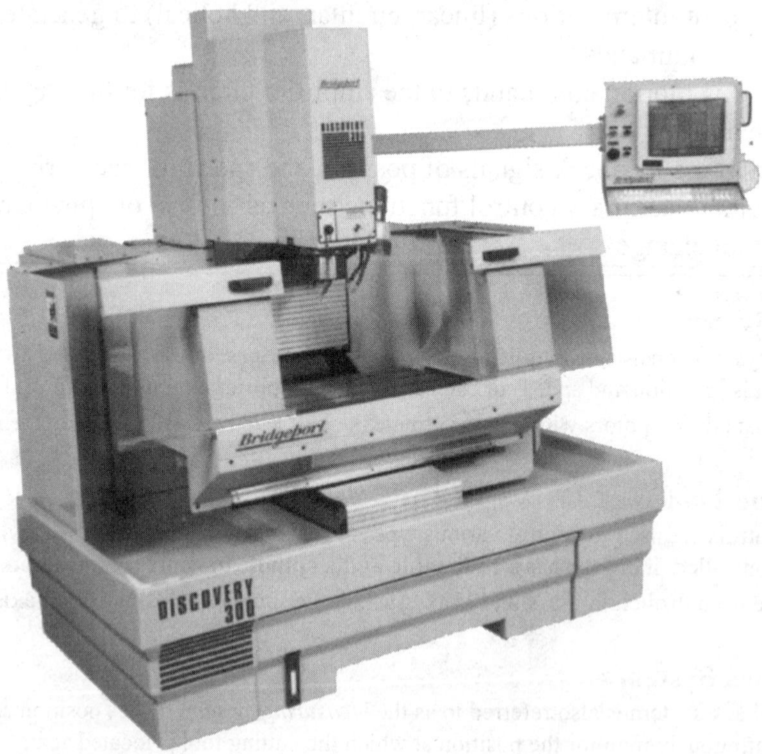

Figure 1.6 CNC milling machine (Courtesy of Bridgeport Machines, Inc.)

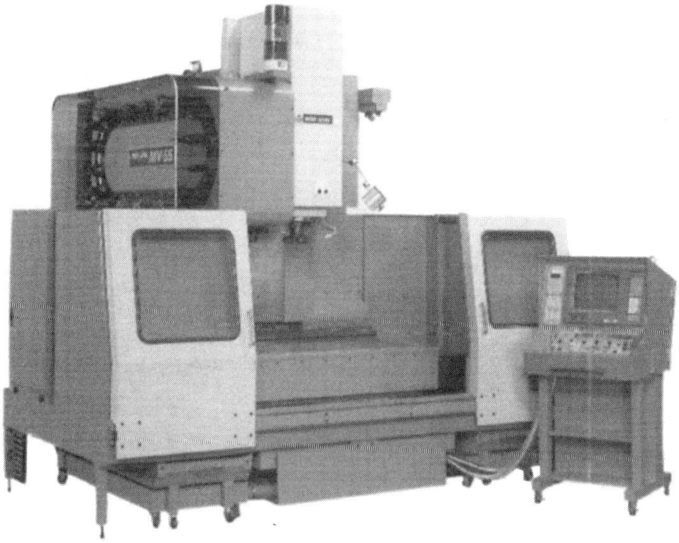

Figure 1.7 CNC Vertical machining center (Courtesy of Mori Seiki Co., LTD.)

Figure 1.8 CNC Horizontal machining center (Courtesy of Mori Seiki Co.,LTD.)

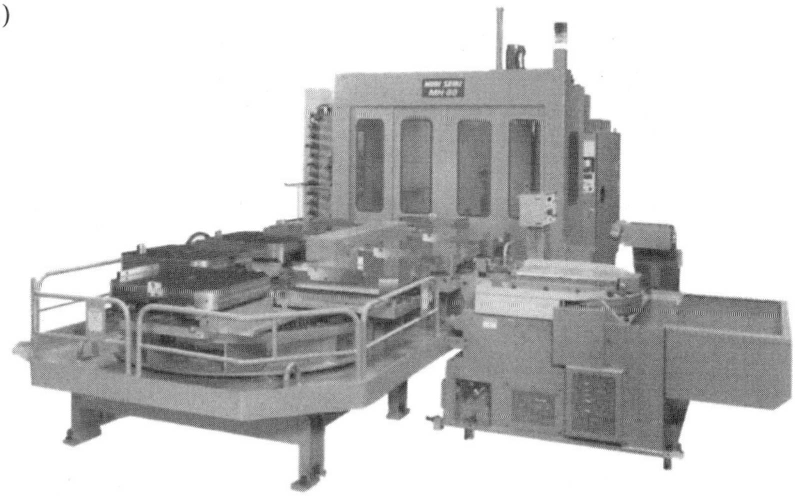

Figure 1.9 Double-column machining center (Courtesy of Okuma Machinery, Inc.)

Figure 1.10 CNC Turning center (Courtesy of Leadwell CNC Machines Mfg. Corp.)

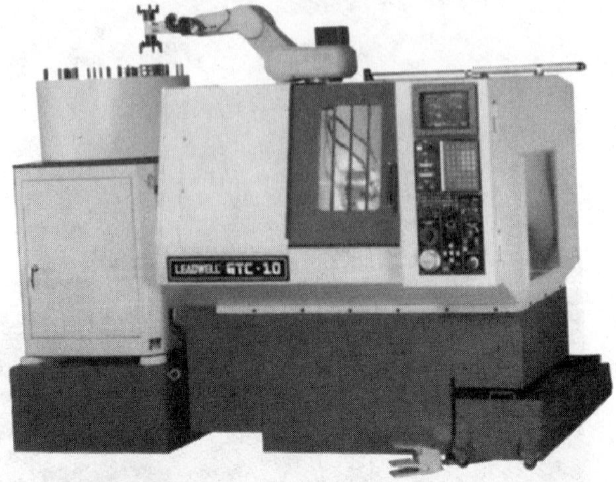

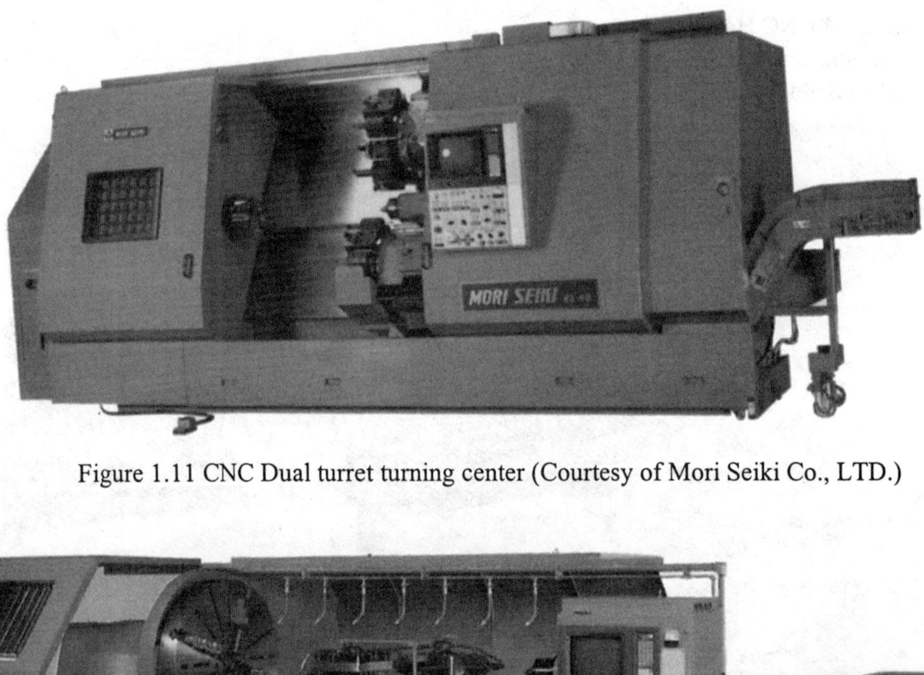

Figure 1.11 CNC Dual turret turning center (Courtesy of Mori Seiki Co., LTD.)

Figure 1.12 Heavy-duty CNC lathe (Courtesy of Mori Seiki Co., LTD.)

Figure 1.13 CNC Measuring machine (Courtesy of Okuma Machinery, Inc.)

Figure 1.14 CNC fabrication machine (Courtesy of Peddington Corp.)

1.7 NC Coding Systems

There are **two** coding systems used in NC/CNC controls: **EIA and ASCII standards.** The EIA coding system is established by the EIA standard 244-B. This code was widely adopted in North America before the ASCII code was established. The hole pattern assignment of EIA codes is given in the **left column** of the Figure 1.15.

ASCII is an acronym for the American Standard Code for Information Interchange. It refers to the code used to represent common keyboard characters. The ASCII NC code for punched tape was established by the RS-358-B standard. It is also referred to as the ISO code. The hole pattern of ASCII codes is given in the **right column** of Figure 1.15.

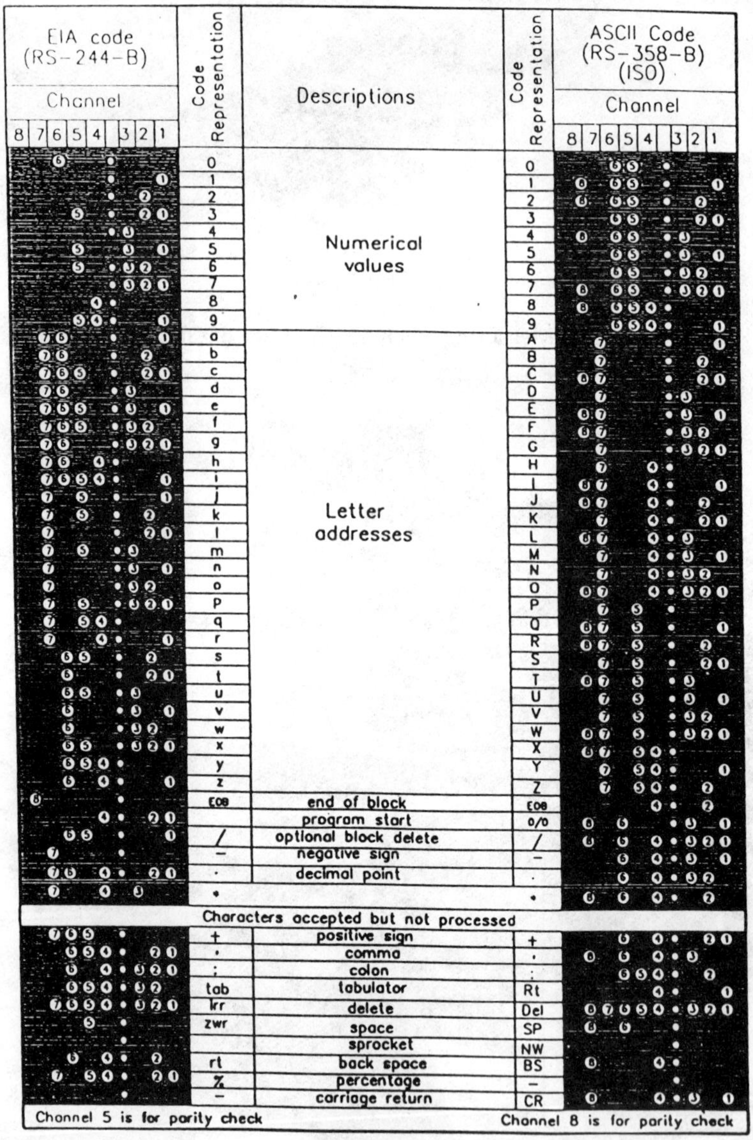

Figure 1.15 EIA and ASCII NC Coding systems

1.8 NC Addresses

An address is the letter at the beginning of each word which defines the meaning or purpose of the numerical data. The addresses used in NC programming have been specified by ANSI's EIA RS-274-B standard. Most of the letters are assigned to a unique function, but some have two functions. The NC addresses can be classified into the seven groups according to their functionality; refer to Table 1.2.

Table 1.2 NC Addresses

Address Type	Description	Illustration
1. Dimension		
a. Primary linear dimensions		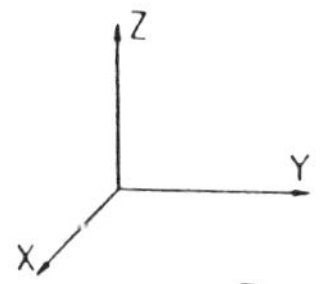
X	Primary X motion dimension	
Y	Primary Y motion dimension	
Z	Primary Z motion dimension	
b. Secondary linear dimensions		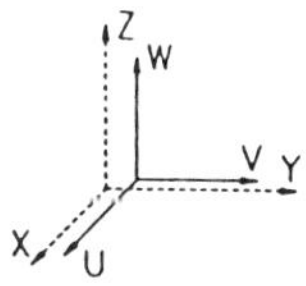
U	Secondary dimension parallel to X axis	
V	Secondary dimension parallel to Y axis	
W	Secondary dimension parallel to Z axis	
c. Tertiary linear dimensions		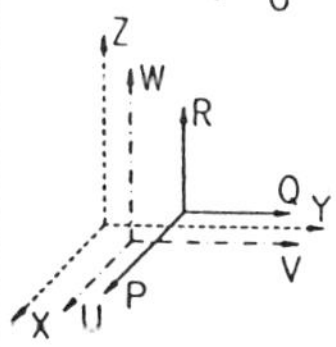
P	Third dimension parallel to X axis	
Q	Third dimension parallel to Y axis	
R	Third dimension parallel to Z axis	
d. Primary rotary dimensions		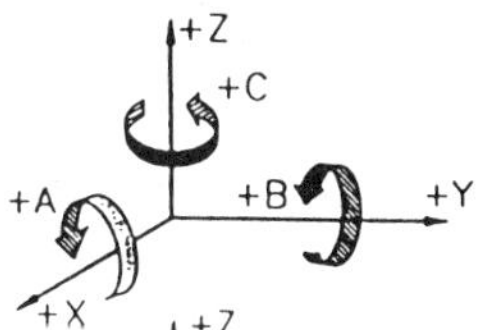
A	Angular dimension around X axis	
B	Angular dimension around Y axis	
C	Angular dimension around Z axis	
e. Special rotary dimensions		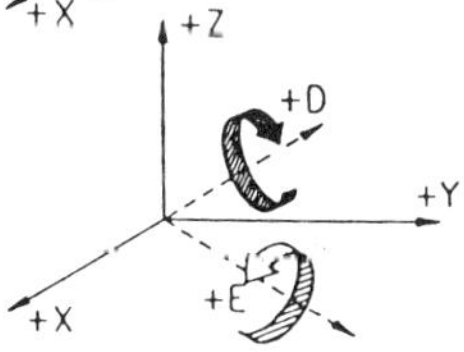
D	Angular dimension around a special axis or line	
E	Angular dimension around a special axis or line	
2. Arc center		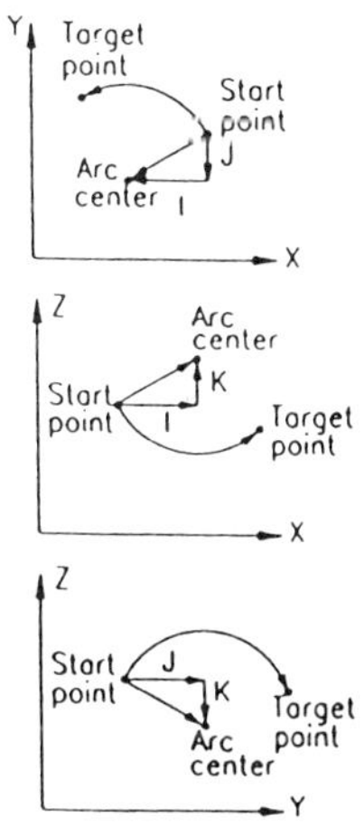
I	X dimension for circular arc center	
J	Y dimension for circular arc center	
K	Z dimension for circular arc center	

Table 1.2 (Continued)

Address Type		Description	Illustration
3. Feed			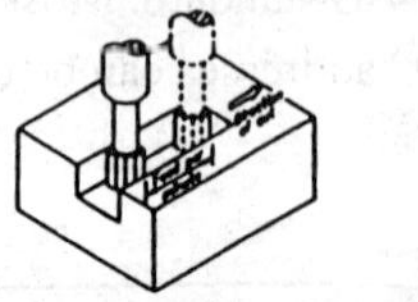
	F	Primary feed function (applied to the main slide table)	
	E	Secondary feed function (applied to the second slide table)	
	D	Third feed function (applied to the third slide table)	
4. Thread pitches			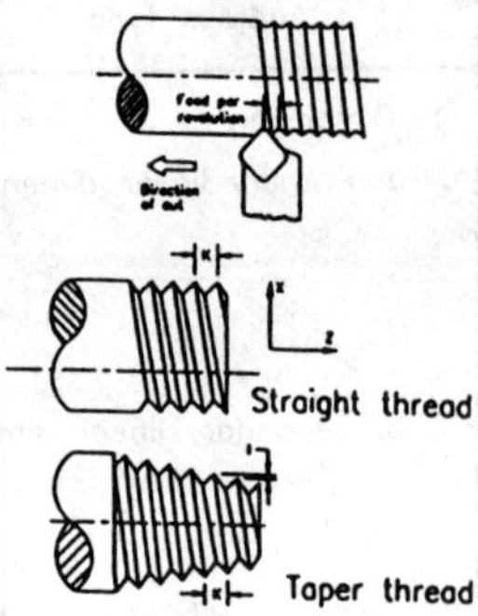
	I	Thread pitch in the X axis	
	J	Thread pitch in the Y axis	
	K	Thread pitch in the Z axis	
5. Preparatory functions	GXX		A preparatory function is defined by the address G followed by two digits to specify the control mode of the operation. (see Tables 1.4 and 1.5 for detail)
a. Motion commands		G00, G01, G02, and G03	
b. Plane selection commands		G17, G18, and G19	
c. Cutter compensation commands		G40, G41, and G42	
d. Tool length offset commands		G43–G49	
e. Fixed cycle commands		G80–G89	
f. Unit selection commands		G20 (or G70) and G21 (or G71)	
g. Positioning system commands		G90 and G91	
h. Coordinate system setting commands		G92, G54–G59	
6. Miscellaneous function	MXX		A miscellaneous function is defined by the address M followed by two digits to specify the type of machine control. (see Table 1.6 for detail)
a. Program stop		M00 and M01	
b. End of program		M02 and M30	
c. Spindle rotation		M03, M04, and M05	
d. Tool change		M06	
e. Coolant control		M07, M08, and M09	
7. Other functions			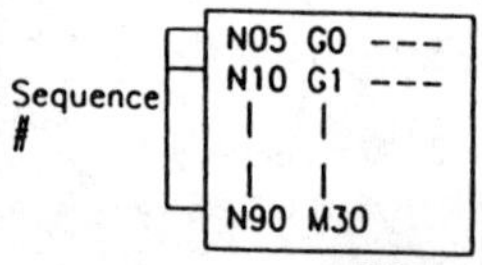
	N	Sequence number of program block	
	S	Spindle speed function	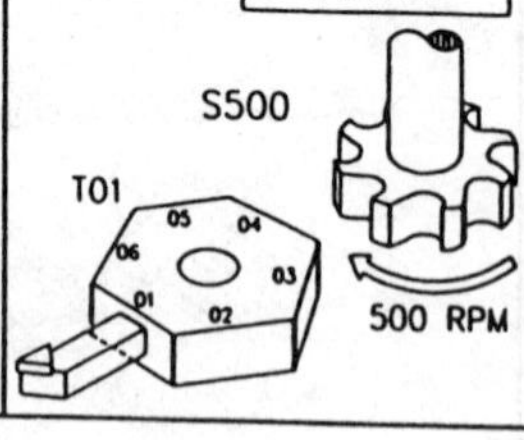
	T	Tool function	

1.9 NC Words

NC part programs are coded instructions that are organized into functional blocks. Each **block** consists of one or more NC words. An **NC word** is a collection of characters that begins with an address followed by numbers. A **character** is one byte (8 bits) of information representing a number, letter, or symbol. The sequence and arrangement of NC words in part programs must follow a certain pattern that is called the **tape format** or program format.

An NC word is the collection of characters arranged in a certain order to cause a special action by an NC machine. NC words always begin with a letter address followed by a numerical value. Table 1.3 lists **seven groups** of NC words.

Table 1.3 NC words

NC Words	Description	Typical Examples
1. **Dimension words**	Specify coordinates of a tool path.	X10.5 Y4.5 Z-1.0
2. **Arc center words**	Indicate coordinates of an arc center.	I3.0 J1.5 or R3.5
3. **Feed word**	Specify the feed rate of machining.	F15.0
4. **Preparatory words**	Specify command modes, the information of the block to be executed.	G90 G1 G2 G43
5. **Miscellaneous words**	Indicate control modes such as program stop, spindle rotation, tool change, coolant control, end of program, etc.	M0 M3 M6 M7M30
6. **Spindle words**	Specify spindle rotation speed in RPM	S3000
7. **Tool words**	Indicate the tool number to be selected	T5

Preparatory Words

The term "preparatory" in NC means that it "prepares" the control system to be ready for implementing the information that follows in the next block of instructions. A **preparatory function** is designated in a program by the word address G followed by two digits. Preparatory functions are also called **G-codes** and they specify the control mode of the operation. On the next page, Table 1.4 illustrates **eight groups** of commonly used G-codes in CNC milling machines. Following that, Table 1.5 lists the G-codes for CNC turning machines.

Table 1.4 G-Codes for Milling

Command Group	G-code	Function and Command statement	Illustration
Tool motion	G00	Rapid traverse G00 Xx Yy Zz	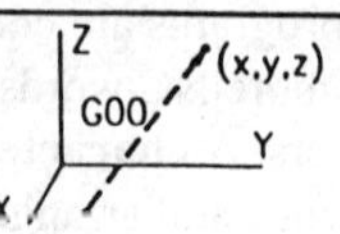
	G01	Linear interpolation G01 Xx Yy Zz Ff	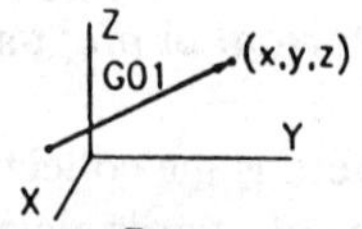
	G02	Circular interpolation in clockwise direction G02 Xx Yy Ii Jj G02 Xx Zz Ii Kk G02 Yy Zz Jj Kk	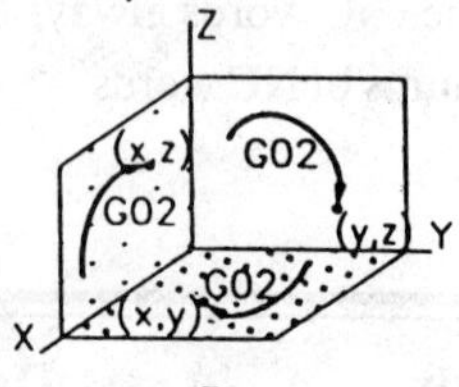
	G03	Circular interpolation in counter-clockwise direction G03 Xx Yy Ii Jj G03 Xx Zz Ii Kk G03 Yy Zz Jj Kk	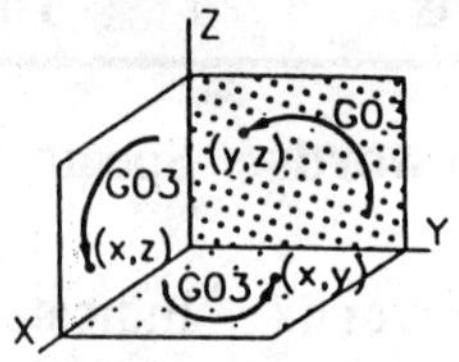
Plan selection	G17	XY-plane selection	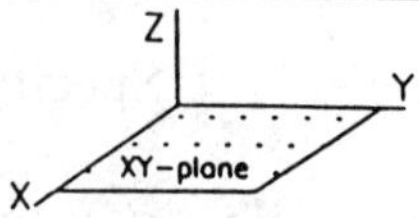
	G18	ZX-plane selection	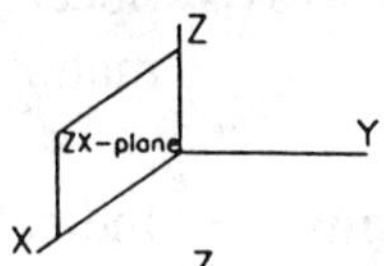
	G19	YZ-plane selection	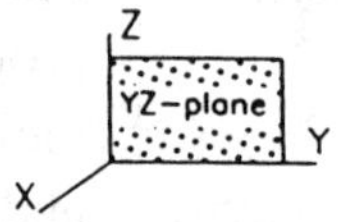
Unit selection	G20 or G70	Inch unit selection G20 or G70	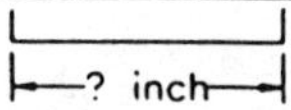
	G21 or G71	Metric unit selection G21 or G71	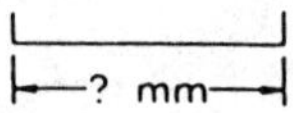
Offset and compensation	G40	Cutter diameter compensation cancel G40 G0 (or G1) Xx Yy	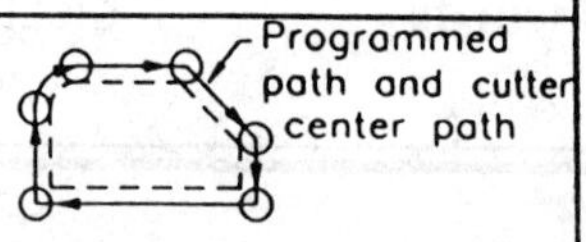
	G41	Cutter diameter compensation left G41 G0 (or G1) Xx Yy Dd	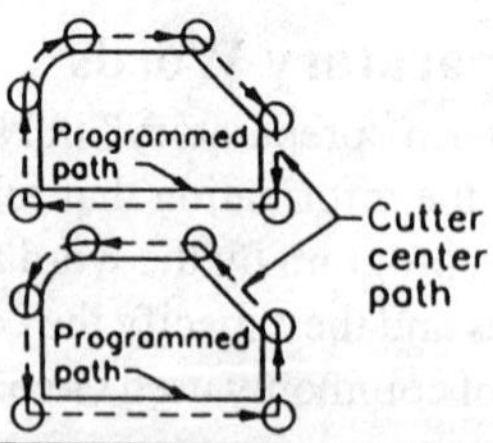
	G42	Cutter diameter compensation right G42 G0 (or G1) Xx Yy Dd	

Table 1.4 (Continued)

Command Group	G-code	Function and Command statement	Illustration
	G43	Tool length offset G43 Hh	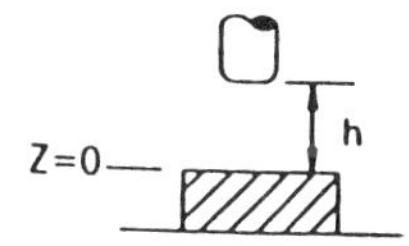
Positioning system	G90	Absolute positioning system G90 Xx Yy Zz	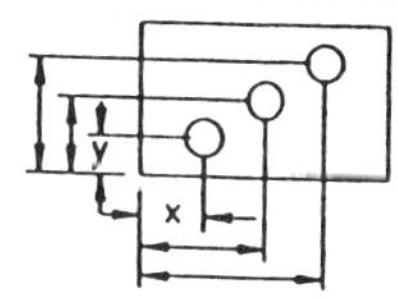
	G91	Incremental positioning system G91 Xx Yy Zz	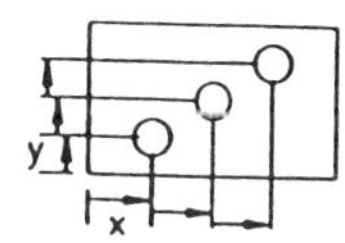
Feed unit selection	G94	Feed per minute system G94 Ff	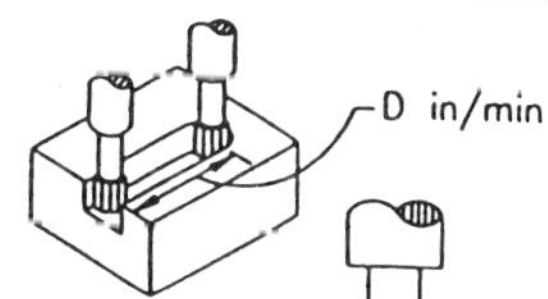
	G95	Feed per revolution system G95 Ff	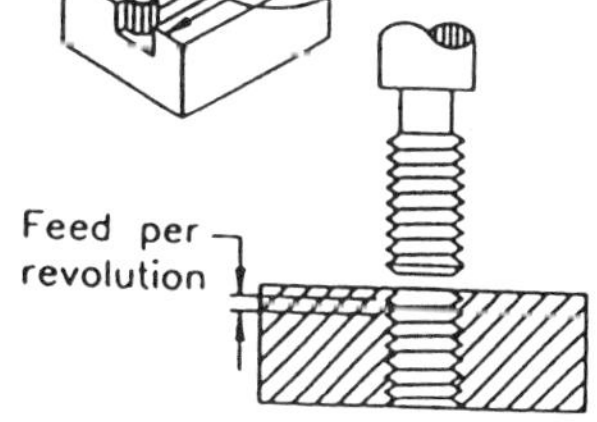
Work Coordinate Definition	G92	Absolute zero setting G92 Xx Yy Zz	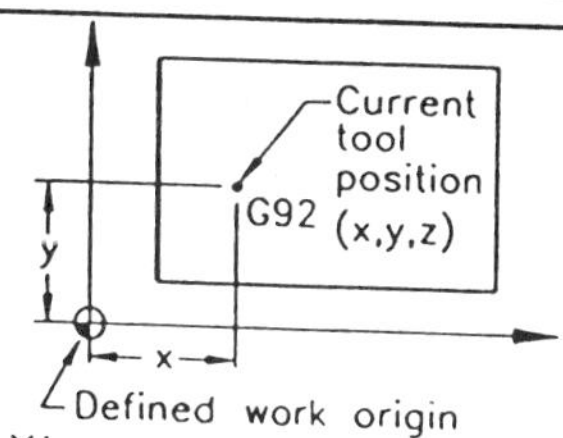
	G54 – G59	Work Coordinate setting G54 Xx Yy Zz	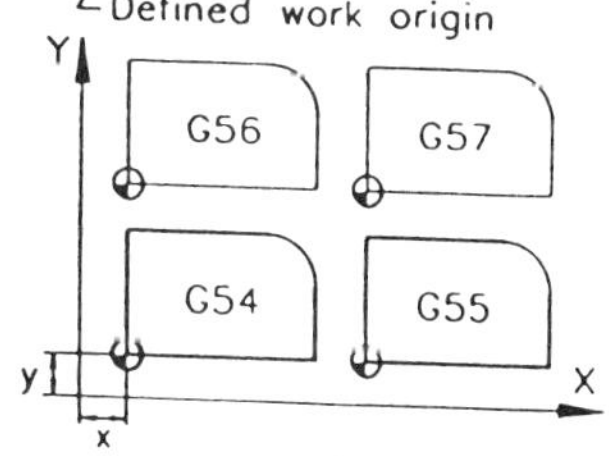
Fixed cycles selection	G80 –	Fixed cycle cancel	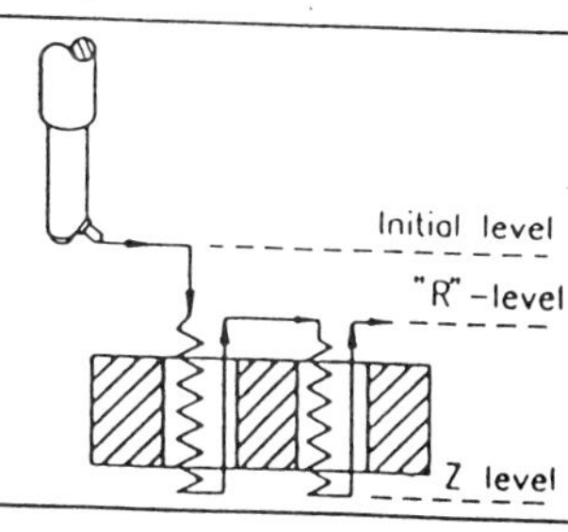
	G81 – G89	Fixed cycle G99/G98 G8_ Xx Yy Zz Rr Ff Qq Pp	

Table 1.5 G-Codes for Turning

Command Group	G-code	Function and Command Statement	Illustration
1. Tool motion	G00	Rapid traverse G00 Xx Zz	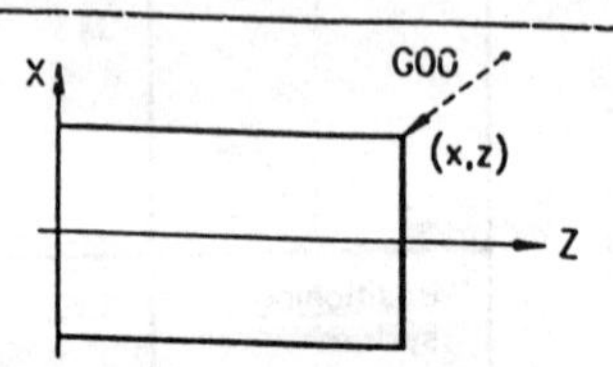
	G01	Linear interpolation G01 Xx Zz	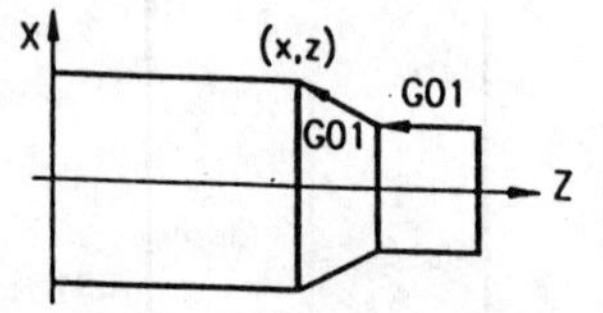
	G02	Circular interpolation in clockwise direction a. IJK method G02 Xx Zz Ii Kk b. R–method G02 Xx Zz Rr	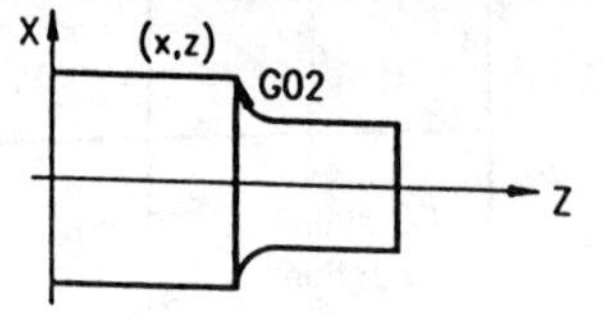
	G03	Circular interpolation in counter–clockwise direction a. IJK method G03 Xx Zz Ii Kk b. R–method G03 Xx Zz Rr	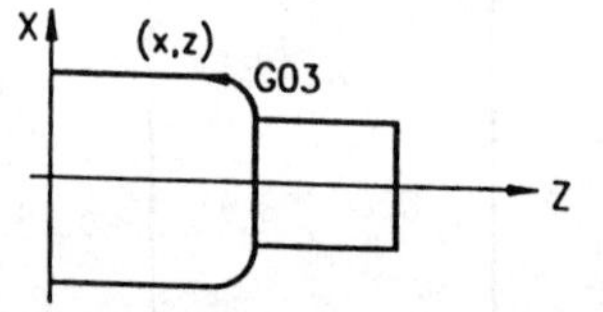
2. Work coordinate definition	G50 or G92 in some controls	(Work zero setting) G50 Xx Zz	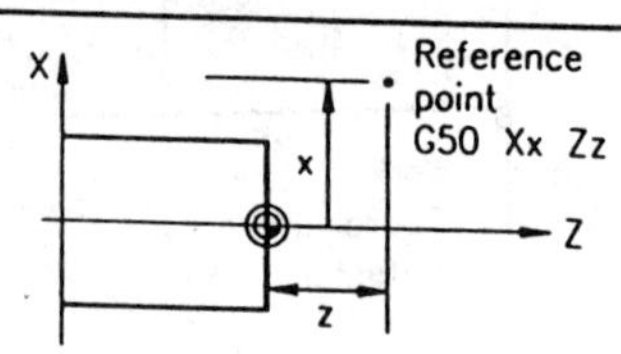
3. Spindle speed control	G50 G96 G97	Maximum spindle speed G50 Ss in RPM Constant surface speed setting G96 Ss in FPM Fixed spindle speed G97 Ss in RPM	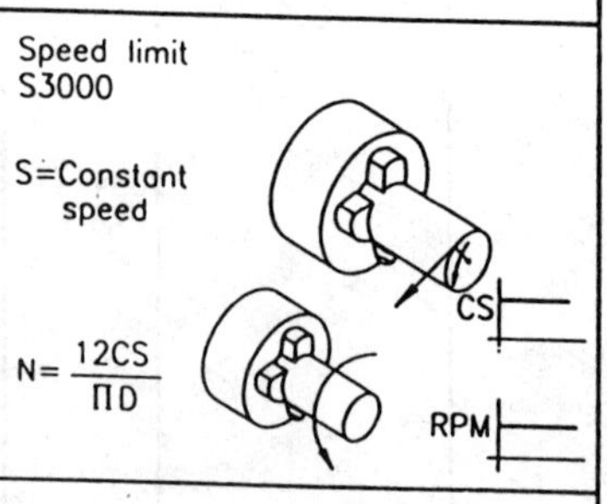
4. Unit selection	G20/G70 G21/G71	Inch unit selection Metric unit selection	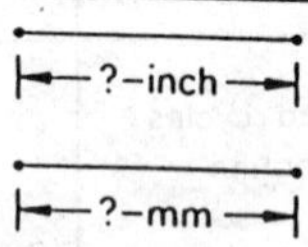

Table 1.5 (Continued)

Command Group	G-code	Function and Command Statement	Illustration
5. Feed Unit Selection	G98	Feed per minute	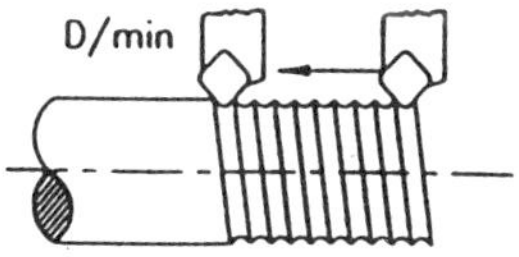
	G99	Feed per revolution	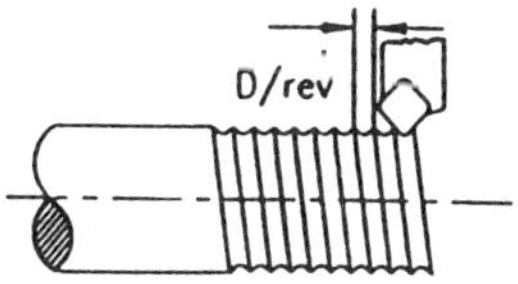
6. Tool nose radius compen-sation	G40	Tool nose radius compensation cancel G40 G0/G1 Xx Zz	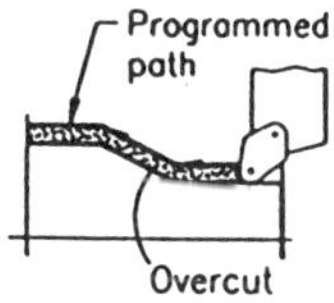
	G41	Tool nose radius compensation left G41 G0/G1 Xx Zz Txxxx	
	G42	Tool nose radius compensation right G42 G0/G1 Xx Zz Txxxx	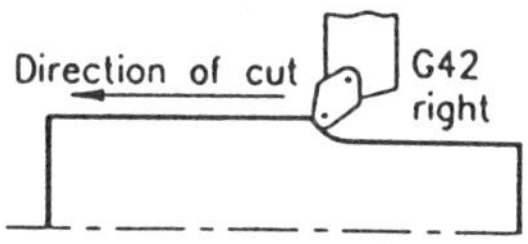
7. Fixed cycles A. Single cycles	G90 G94	Generate one pass of four toolpath moves	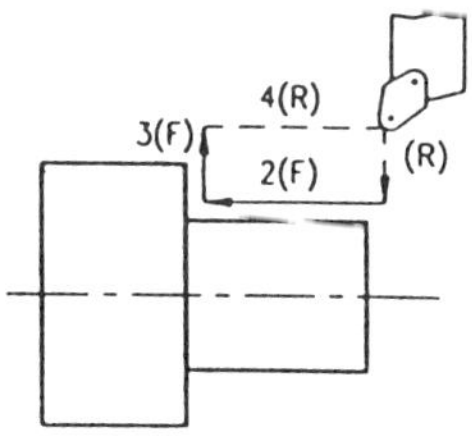
B. Multiple-pass cycles	G71 G72	Generate multiple passes of four toolpath moves	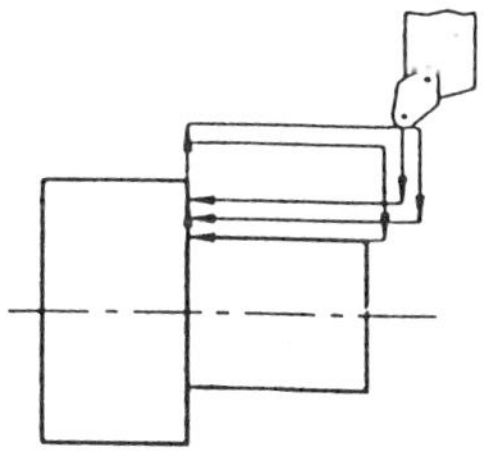

Miscellaneous Words

Miscellaneous functions use the address letter M followed by two digits. They perform a group of instructions such as coolant on/off, spindle on/off, tool change, program stop, or program end. They are often referred to as machine functions or **M-functions**. Table 1.6 illustrates common M-functions used in both milling and turning machines.

Table 1.6 Miscellaneous Functions

Function Group	M-function	Function and Command statement	Illustration
Program Stop	M00	Program stop	
	M01	Optional stop	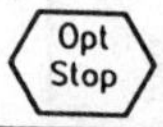
Spindle Control	M03	Spindle on (rotation in clockwise direction)	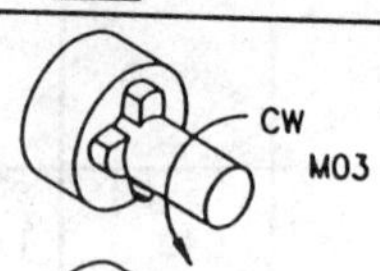
	M04	Spindle on (rotation in counter-clockwise direction)	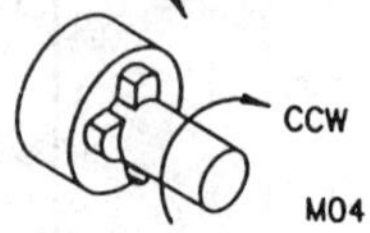
	M05	Spindle off	
Tool Change	M06	Too change to the specified tool number T__ M06	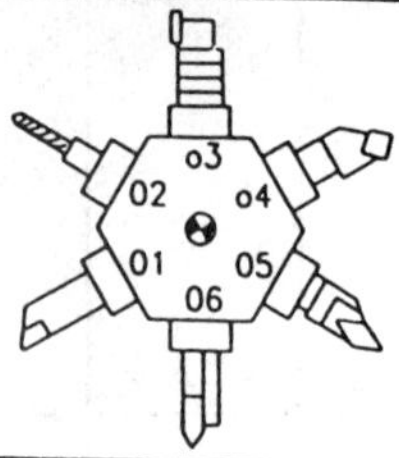
Coolant Control	M07	Coolant on (midst)	
	M08	Coolant on (flood)	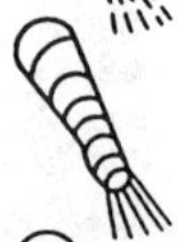
	M09	Coolant off	
End of Program	M02	End of program and tape rewind	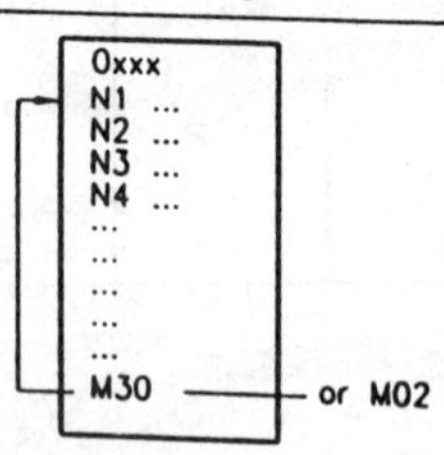
	M30	End of program and memory return	

1.10 NC Functional Blocks

NC controls simultaneously execute **all NC words contained in a block**. Therefore, NC blocks are normally organized according to their tasks. Table 1.7 gives some common functional blocks used in part programming.

Table 1.7 CNC functional blocks

Functional Block	Explanation	Typical Examples
1. Safety feature	Set the control to proper operating modes at the beginning of a part program. This block is also used after a tool change.	G90 G80 G40 G17
2. Coordinate system setting	Define the work zero point.	G92 Xx Yy Zz G54
3. Tool length offset	Offset the difference between the programmed tool length and the acutal tool length.	G43 Hh
4. Tool motion	Generate tool paths to machine the workpiece.	G0 Xx Yy Zz G1 Xx Yy Zz G2/G3 Xx Yy Zz
5. Cutter diameter compensation	Offset the cutter in a specified direction by a given amount of distance.	G41/G42 Xx Yy Hh/Dd G40 Xx Yy
6. Fixed cycle	Generate a series of tool paths to perform hole operations.	G8_ Xx Yy Zz Rr Ff
7. Tool change	Select a tool and cause a tool change.	Tt M6
8. Spindle control	Command spindle rotation speed and direction.	Ss M3/M4 M5
9. Reference point return	Return the tool to the machine home position.	G91 G28 Z0 G91 G28 X0 Y0
10. Program end	Specify the end of part program	M2 M30

1.11 NC Programming Methods

NC part programming methods can be classified into two main categories: **manual programming and computer-assisted programming**. In the manual method, a part program is prepared by manually inputting the coded instructions into the controller by either using a tape-punching unit, via manual data input (MDI) mode on the CNC unit, or using a computer with a text editor.

The computer-assisted NC programming method uses a computer to help automatically generate the tool path for producing a part. It can appear in one of the following three forms:

- NC processor languages (APT, Compact II, etc.)
- CAD/CAM NC software systems
- Conversational programming software as part of the CNC unit

Using NC processor languages to generate part programs is gradually being replaced by CAD/CAM software. More than one-third of the plants use CAD/CAM software systems to generate part programs. This approach is gaining ground and eventually will become the major method of NC programming. Conversational programming, also referred to as interactive programming, has found use in about one-fifth of plants. This type of programming software is provided by the CNC unit builder and is part of the CNC unit. This method is adequate for programming simple workpieces.

1.12 CNC Control Systems

CNC controls can be either a **point-to-point system or a continuous path system.** The point-to-point (PTP) control moves the tool to the programmed point, normally in rapid traverse, without engaging the workpiece. Once the programmed point is reached, machining is then executed in the Z axis direction.

The PTP system is also called the positioning system because its exact tool path normally cannot be controlled. Depending on the control type, the PTP tool path (Figure 1.16) may follow one of the following three modes:

- Axial path (Figure 1.16a)
- 45° line path (Figure 1.16b)
- Linear path (Figure 1.16c)

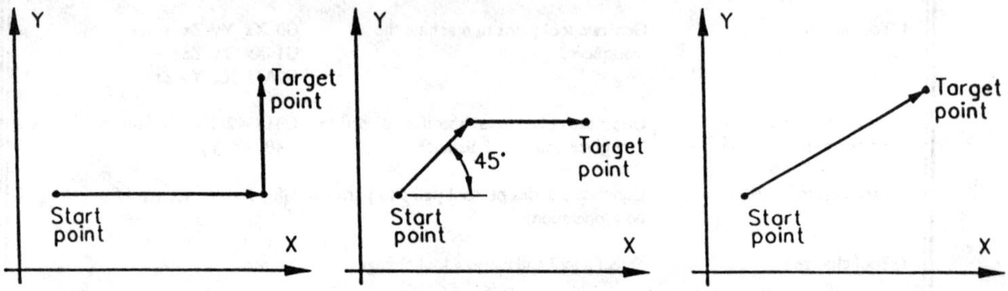

a. axial path b. 45° line path c. linear path

Figure 1.16 PTP tool path

PTP systems are typically used in drilling machines, punch presses, and spot welders which require positioning in the XY-plane in rapid traverse mode while executing machining in the Z axis (see Figure 1.17). PTP control systems are less expensive and are simple in control structure. They are also easy to maintain.

The continuous path control system is also called the contouring system. A **contouring system** is capable of synchronizing two or more axial drives to produce a prescribed path. Depending on the control type, a contouring system can be one of these four types: **2-D contouring, 2½-D contouring, 3-D contouring and 4-D contouring.**

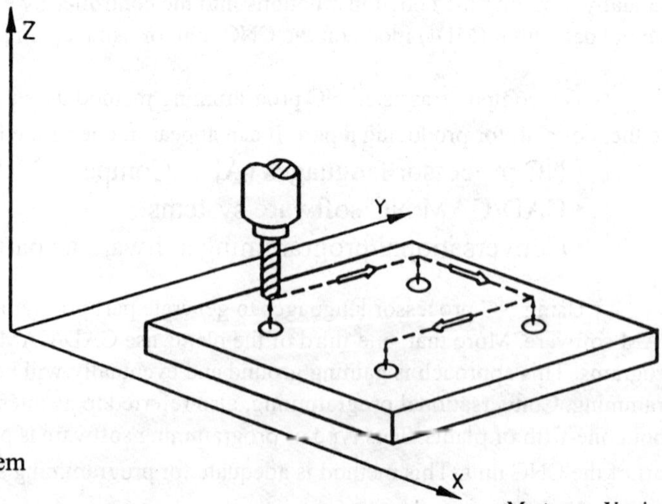

Figure 1.17 Application of a PTP system

2-D Contouring Control

A 2-D contouring system implements linear and circular tool paths in the two-axis (XY-) plane (Figure 1.18). The third (Z) axis is controlled independently of the other two axes. Contouring can be implemented in only one plane, in most cases the XY-plane (in a 2-D system). In other words, a 2-D contouring system can synchronize the feed of only two axes simultaneously. In practice, the feeding to desired depth in the Z axis should be made before contouring in the XY-plane.

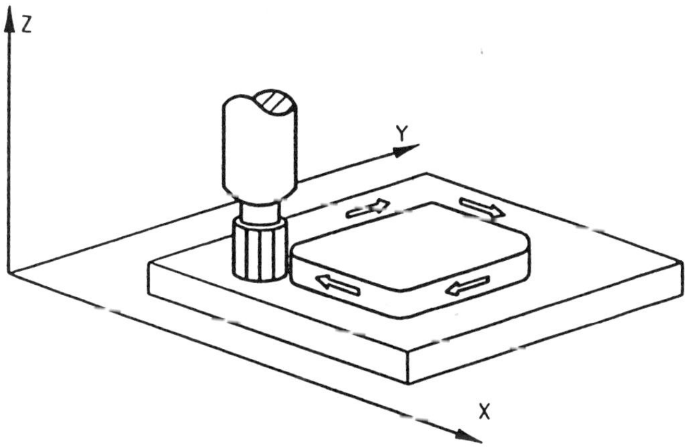

Figure 1.18 2-D contouring

2½-D Contouring Control

In a 2½-D contouring system, **any two** of three axes can be controlled simultaneously. Thus, the contouring can be implemented either in the XY-plane, ZX-plane, or YZ-plane. In practice, the feed can be executed in any one of the three axis, then followed by contouring in any two-axis plane. Figure 1.19 shows contouring in the ZX- and YZ- planes, respectively.

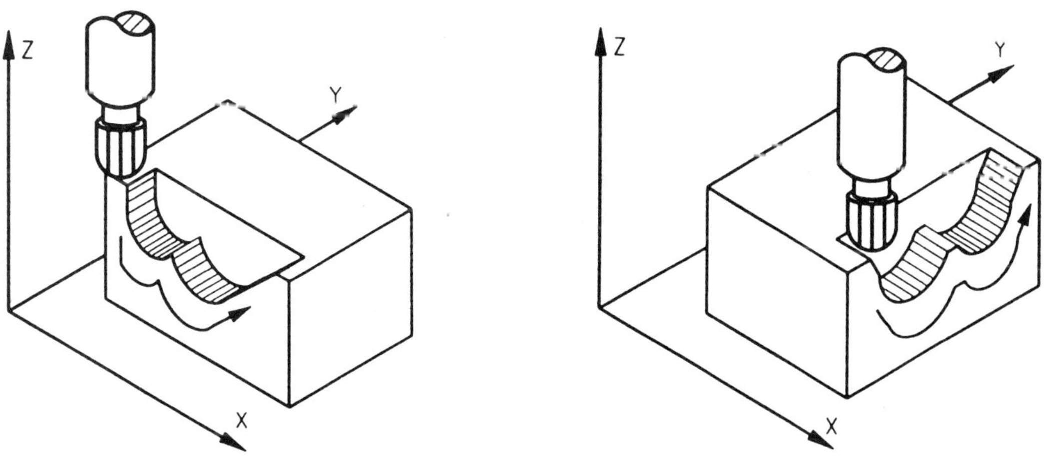

a. in the ZX- plane

b. in the YZ- plane

Figure 1.19 2 ½-D Contouring

3-D Contouring Control

A 3-D contouring system is capable of synchronizing **three axes** simultaneously to produce linear and circular tool paths in 3-D space. It can be used to produce any 3-D surface as shown in Figure 1.20.

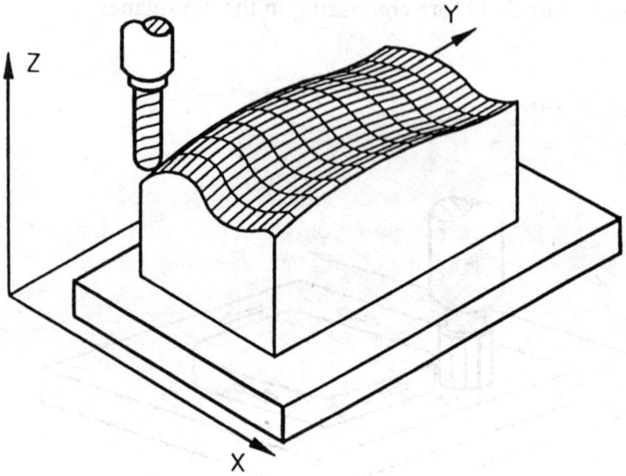

Figure 1.20 3-D contouring

4-D Contouring Control

Some controls furnish an additional axial control for the regular 3-axial control system. The fourth axial control is normally the **rotary axis** which is used for indexing the rotary table. Figure 1.21 shows a 4-D contouring example.

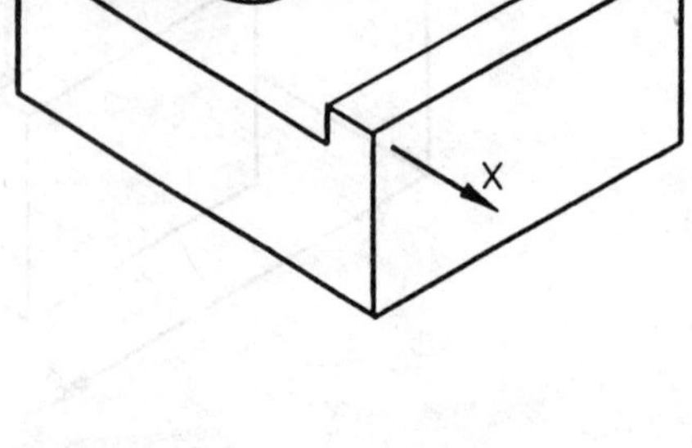

Figure 1.21 4-D contouring

1.13 CNC Drive Systems

The CNC drive systems can be either **open loop or closed loop** type. The main difference between the two systems depends on whether the system has a **feedback loop** to insure the accuracy of system performance.

Open Loop System

No feedback loop is used in open loop drive systems. The drive motor acts upon the control commands from the machine control unit (MCU). The system simply assumes the machine table will reach the target position. There is no way for the MCU to know the actual performance of the system. An open loop system is very sensitive to the load resistance. Position and velocity error may occur when a heavy cutting resistance is encountered. Figure 1.22 shows an open loop CNC drive system. Open loop drives are typically used in PTP systems in which the cutting tool does not engage with the workpiece during positioning. They can also be used in light-loaded cutting machines. Open loop systems are less expensive, but they are prone to load resistances during machining.

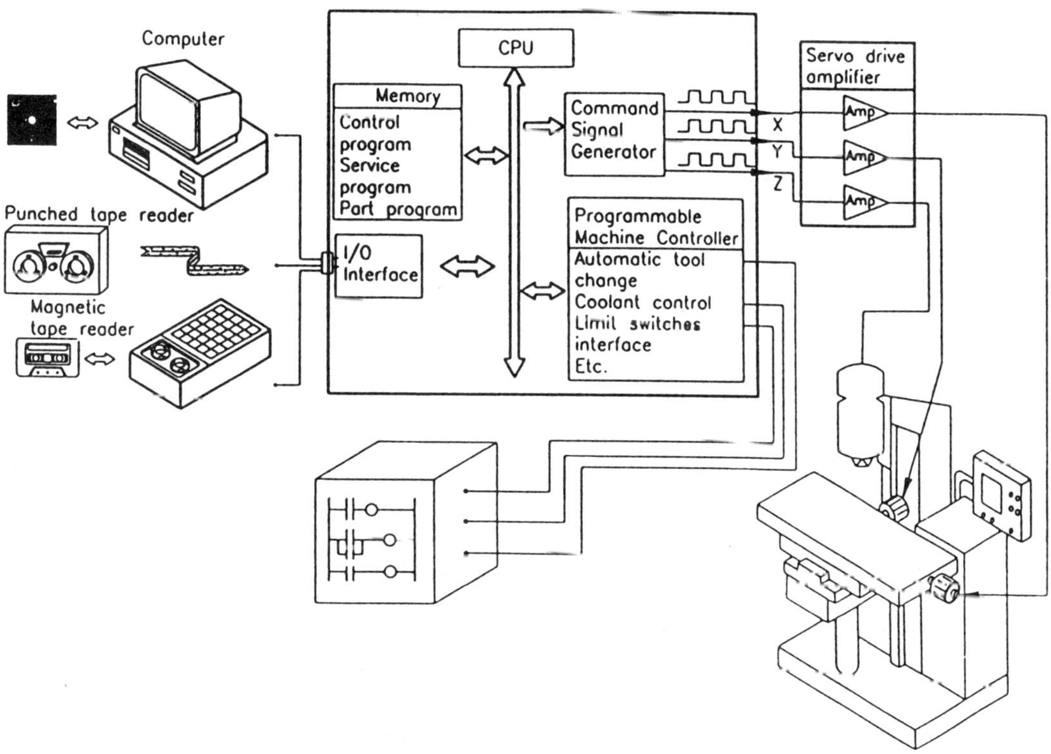

Figure 1.22 An open loop CNC drive system

Closed Loop System

With closed loop drive systems, feedback sub-systems are used to monitor the actual output and correct any discrepancy between desired and actual system performance. Feedback sub-systems may be either an analog or digital type. **Analog systems** measure the variation of physical systems such as position and velocity in voltage level. Tachometers are typically used to measure the velocity, while resolvers for position.

There are two feedback loops in CNC drive systems: **position loop and velocity loop** (Figure 1.23). The **position loop** is the outer loop that consists of a comparator, an amplifier circuit, a velocity loop, a resolver, and a resolver interface. In operation, the comparator receives the reference signal from CNC control and the position feedback signal from the resolver. The difference of these two signals represents the existing positional error. The comparator produces the positional error signal and feeds this signal to the amplifier to drive the servo motor for correcting the error.

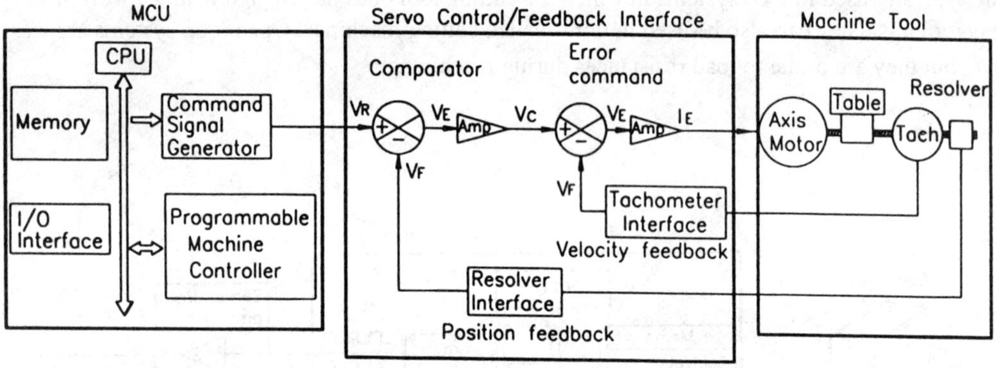

Figure 1.23 Analog type closed loop CNC drive system

The **velocity loop** is the sub-loop within the position loop. It consists of a comparator, an amplifier circuit, a tachometer attached to either the leadscrew or the servo motor, and a tachometer interface.

Digital feedback systems (Figure 1.24) use a digital position transducer to measure the position. Encoders are popular digital position transducers. An up-down counter and a digital-to-analog converter are used in place of the comparator and amplifier. The velocity loop in a digital feedback system is the same as that found in the analog feedback system.

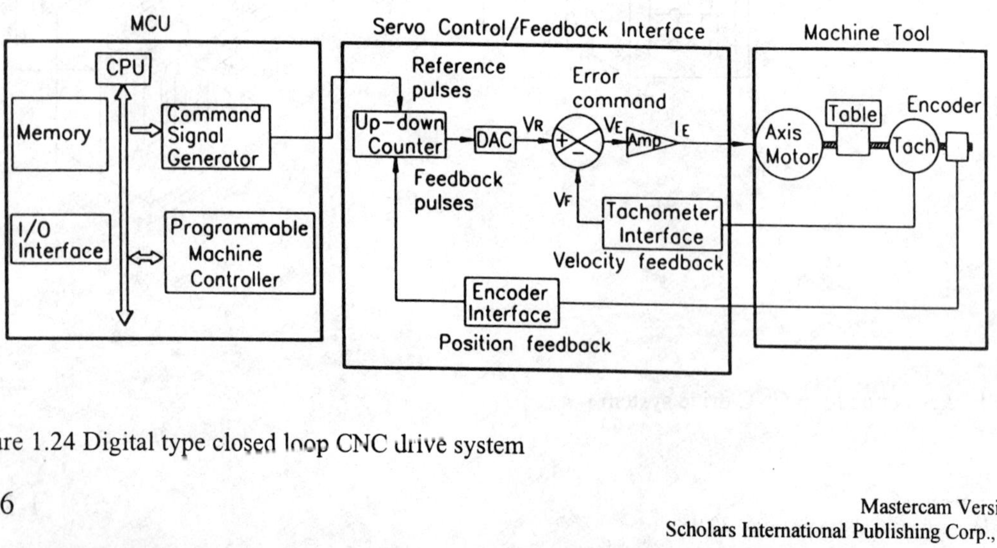

Figure 1.24 Digital type closed loop CNC drive system

1.14 CNC Interpolations

CNC controls use various forms of interpolation to execute contouring tool paths. **Interpolation** is the process of producing a series of intermediate data points between given coordinate positions. The interpolation points are implemented by various types of CNC control interpolators.

The **two** main functions provided by an interpolator are:

Compute intermediate coordinate positions along the programmed path

Compute the axial velocity of an individual axis along the contour path

CNC controls furnish the following **five** possible types of interpolations:

- Linear interpolation
- Circular interpolation
- Helical interpolation
- Parabolic interpolation
- Cubic interpolation

All modern CNC controls furnish linear, circular, and helical interpolation; very few controls support parabolic and cubic interpolations.

Linear Interpolation

Linear interpolation moves the tool from the starting point to the target point along a straight line. Linear interpolation can be implemented in a 2-D plane or 3-D space. It is used in two categories of applications: machine lines (Figure 1.25) and on the following page, approximate irregular curves (Figure 1.26) and surfaces (Figure 1.27).

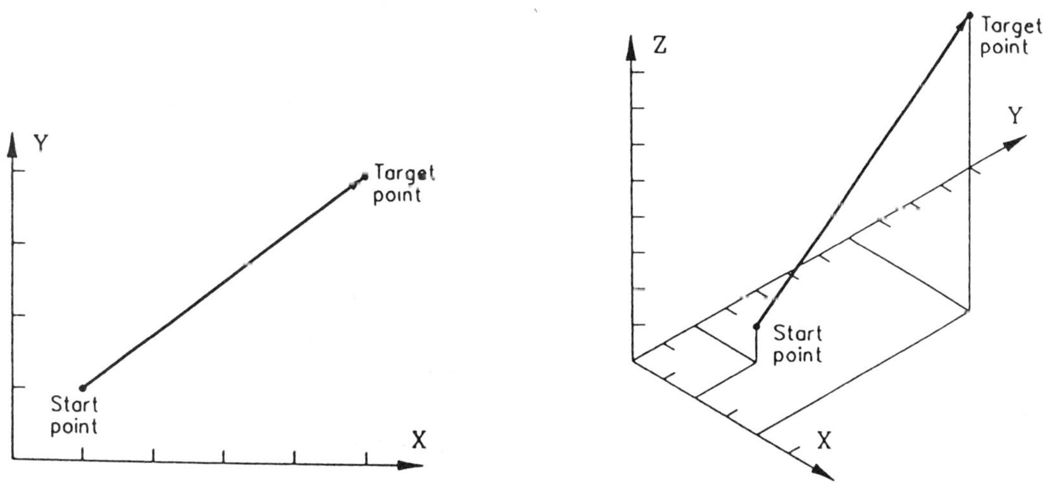

a. in 2-D b. in 3-D

Figure 1.25 Straight line cutting

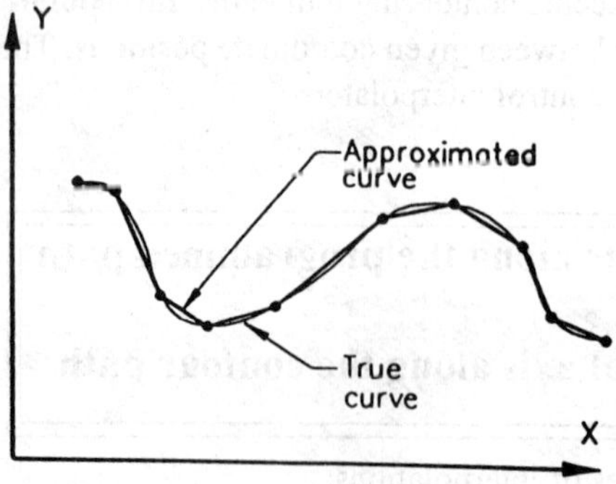

Figure 1.26 Cutting irregular curve

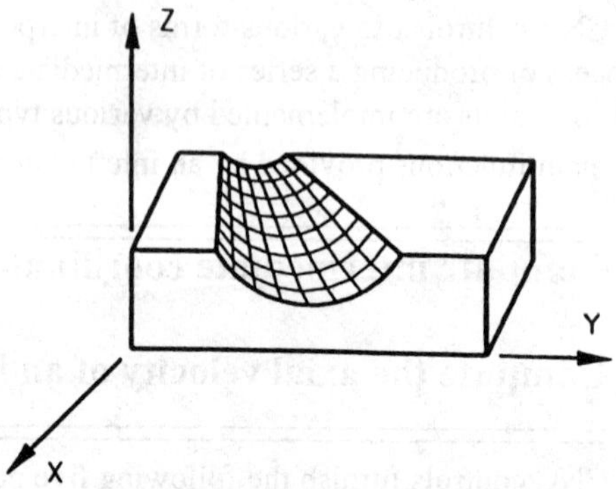

Figure 1.27 Surface cutting

Circular Interpolation

Circular interpolation is programmed to cut circular arcs in one of three principal planes (XY-plane, ZX-plane, or YZ-plane) (Figure 1.28).

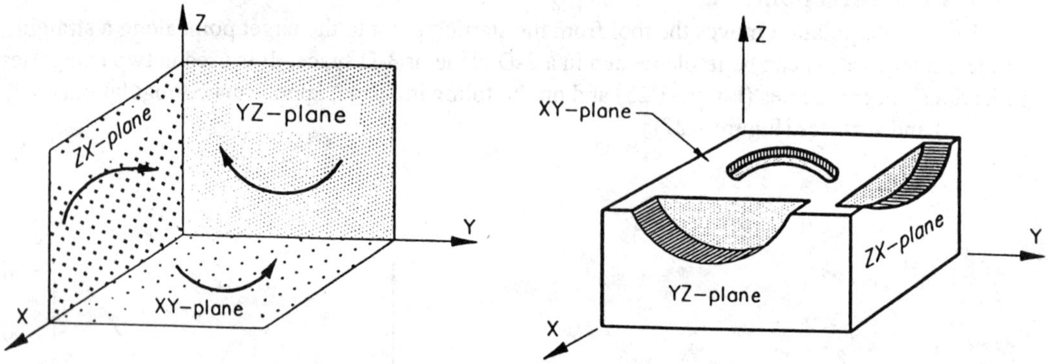

Figure 1.28 Circular interpolation

Helical Interpolation

Helical interpolation combines the two-axis circular interpolation and a linear interpolation in the third axis. It can be used in the following three configurations:

- Circular arc in XY-plane and linear interpolation in Z axis (Figure 1.29**a**)
- Circular arc in ZX-plane and linear interpolation in Y axis (Figure 1.29**b**)
- Circular arc in YZ-plane and linear interpolation in X axis (Figure 1.29**c**)

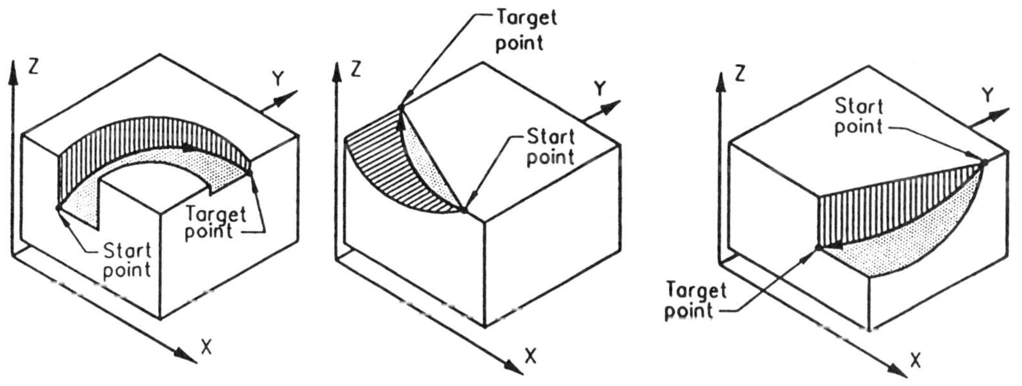

a. Arc in the XY-plane b. Arc in the ZX-plane c. Arc in the YZ-plane

Figure 1.29 Helical interpolation

Parabolic Interpolation

Parabolic interpolation uses three non-collinear points to approximate curves that are of free form (Figure 1.30). It is mainly used in mold and die making where free form designed, rather than precisely defined shapes, are preferred. The use of two or more successive parabolic interpolations can approximate higher-order curves (Figure 1.31). The advantage of using parabolic interpolation is the reduction of programmed points by as much as 50 times that required by the linear interpolation mode.

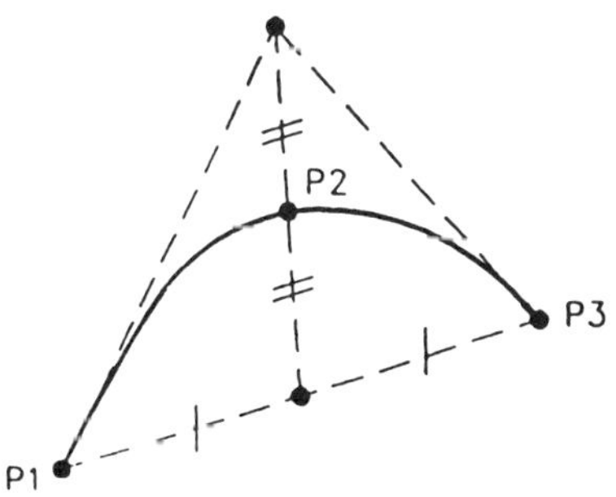

Figures 1.30 Parabolic interpolation

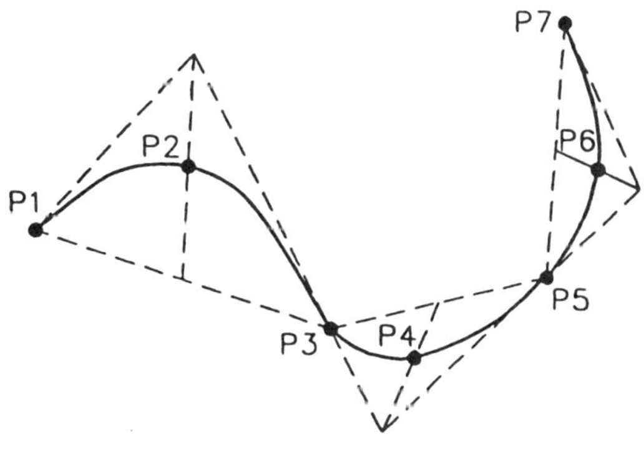

Figure1.31 Parabolic interpolation of a higher order curve

Cubic Interpolation

Cubic interpolation approximates the surfaces defined by third-order geometry. It involves the motion of three axes to machine complex shapes such as automobile sheet metal dies.

1.15 Machine Axes Designation & Direction

The EIA-267-B standard specifies fourteen axes for describing the linear and rotary motions of CNC machines. This includes nine linear axes and five rotary axes. The nine linear axes are further divided into the following three groups: (Figure 1.32)

- Primary linear axes (X,Y, and Z)
- Secondary linear axes (U, V, and W)
- Tertiary linear axes (P, Q, and R)

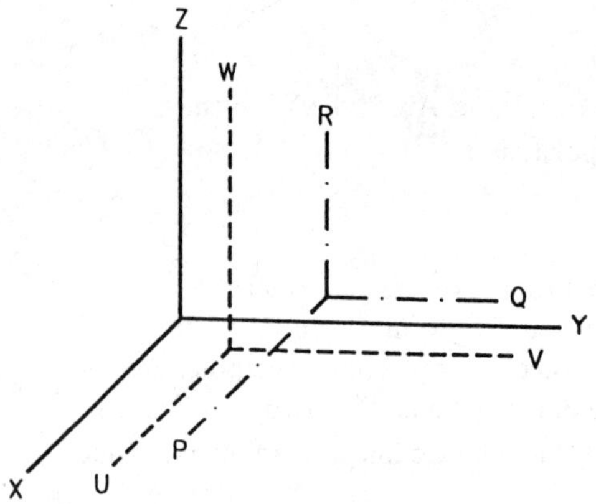

Figure 1.32 Nine linear axes

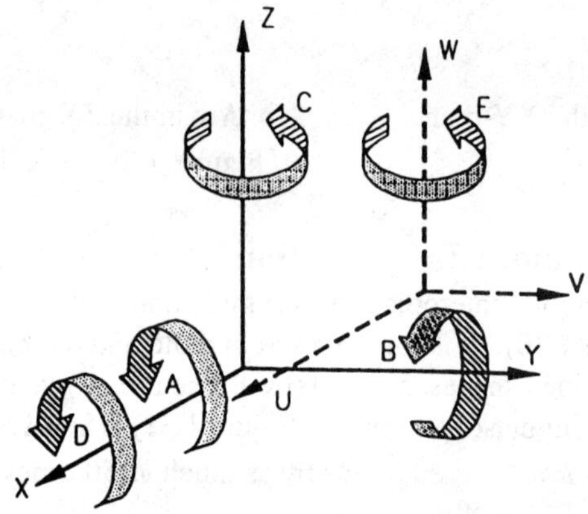

Figure 1.33 Five rotary axes

The primary axes (X, Y, and Z) are assigned to the primary slide table. The secondary linear axes (U, V, and W) are added to the primary axes for defining the movement of the second moving slide or spindle. Similarly, the tertiary linear axes (P, Q, and R) are used to represent the linear motion of the third slide or spindle.

The five rotary axes consist of three primary rotary axes (A, B, and C) and two special axes (D and E) (Figure 1.33). Their definitions are:

Axis A:	**rotary motion around the primary linear axis X**
Axis B:	**rotary motion around the primary linear axis Y**
Axis C:	**rotary motion around the primary linear axis Z**
Axis D:	**rotary motion around any linear axis**
Axis E:	**rotary motion around any linear axis**

Machine Axes Designation

Machine axes are designated according to the "right-hand rule". When the thumb of right hand points in the direction of the positive X axis, the index finger points toward the positive Y axis, and the middle finger toward the positive Z axis. Figure 1.34 shows the right-hand rule applied to vertical machines, while Figure 1.35 applies to horizontal machines.

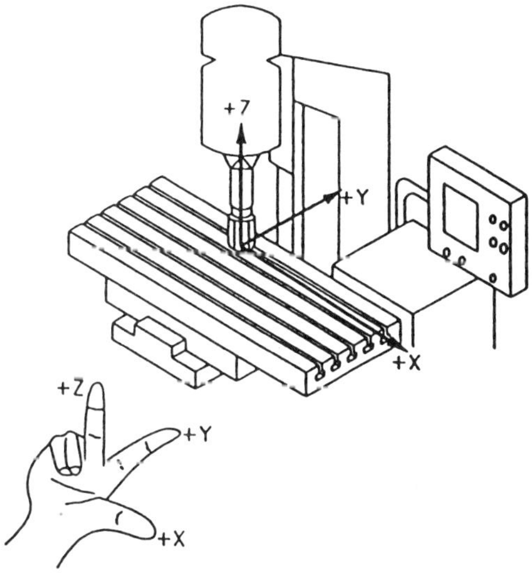

Figures 1.34 Right hand rule: vertical machine

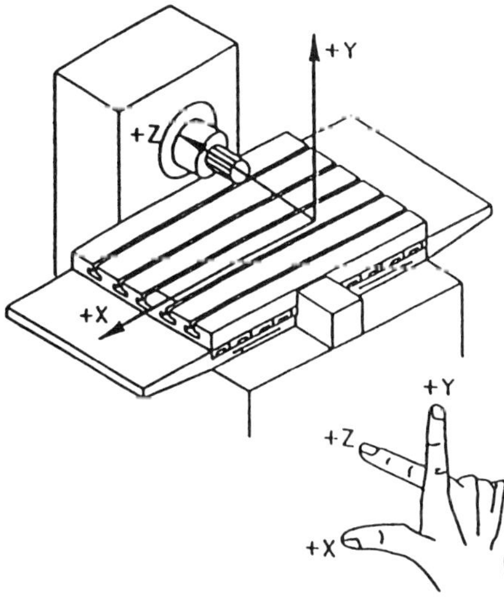

Figure 1.35 Right hand rule: horizontal machine

Direction of Machine Axes

CNC controls use the positive (+) and negative (-) sign to indicate the motion direction of the machine axes. This is how we define the directions.

+Z direction:	is the direction which increases the distance between the workpiece and the cutting tool.
-Z direction:	is in the opposite direction of +Z.
+X direction:	(a) In vertical machines, it is the direction to the right when observed *from* the spindle *toward* its supporting column. (b) In horizontal machines, it is pointed to the right when viewed *from* the spindle axis *toward* the workpiece.
-X direction:	is in the opposite direction of +X.
+Y direction:	follows the right-hand rule: when the thumb points *toward* the +X axis and the middle finger is directed *toward* the +Z axis, the index finger points in the direction of the +Y axis.
-Y direction:	is in the opposite direction of +Y.

1.16 Reference Zero Points

Reference zero points are the base or starting points that are chosen as the reference for calculating the coordinates of the other points. Also, reference zero points are called the **zero points**. CNC controls use the following **four** types of reference zero points to facilitate the programming of tool paths:

- Machine zero point
- Reference return point
- Work zero point
- Program zero point

Machine Zero Point

The machine zero point is the origin of the machine coordinate system. It is set by the machine tool manufacturer and can not be changed.

The machine zero is labelled with an **M** and represented by this symbol:

The location of the machine zero point varies from manufacturer to manufacturer. For turning machines, the machine zero is normally located at the center of the spindle end face (Figure 1.36). In milling machines, the machine zero is usually at the extreme limit of each axis travel (Figure 1.37).

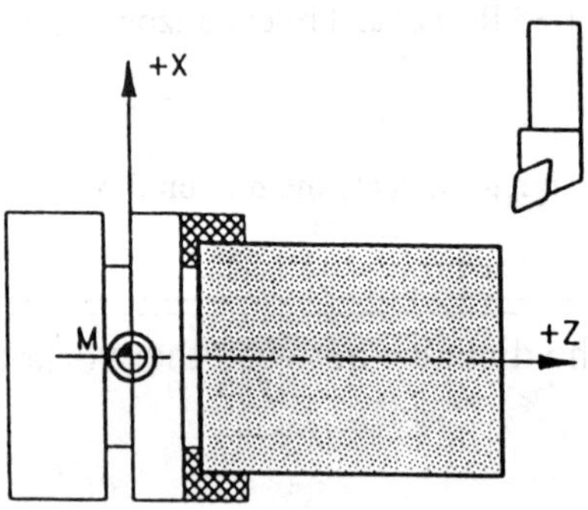

Figures 1.36 Machine zero point of a turning machine

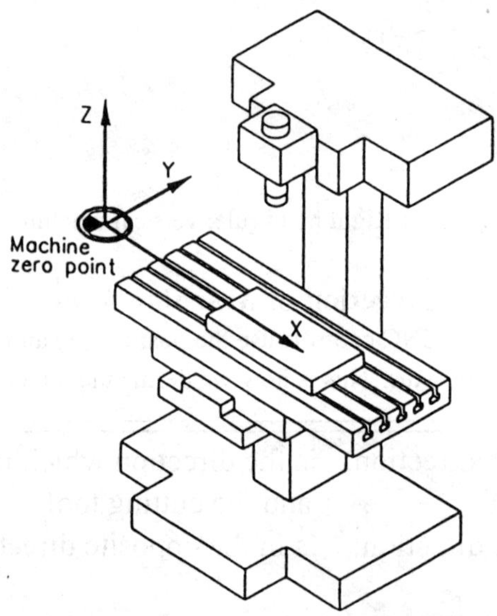

Figure 1.37 Machine zero point of a milling machine

Normally the machine zero is not directly used as the reference point for writing part programs. It may be used in one of the following **three** applications:

- **Initial setup of the machine**
- **As the reference point for other reference points such as reference return points, work zeros, and program zeros**
- **As the tool change position**

Reference Return Point

Reference return points are the locations to which the machine table or the spindle is returned. They are identified by the letter **R** and are represented by the symbol: 

Some CNC controls allow defining up to four reference return points. Normally, the machine zero is set to be the first reference return point in milling machines (Figure 1.38). The second, third, and fourth reference return points are specified by setting their parameter values. They can be set at any convenient location within the work envelope. In turning machines, the reference return point is located in the extreme end of the work envelope (Figure 1.39)

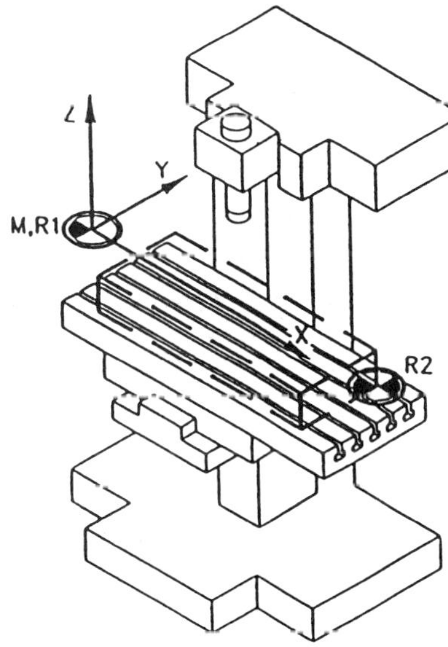

Figures 1.38 Reference return point of a milling machine

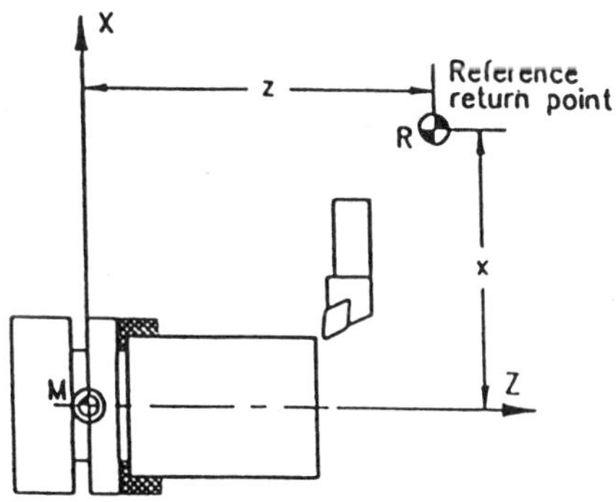

Figure 1.39 Reference return point of a turning machine

The location of the first reference return point is precisely predetermined in each moving axis in relation to the machine zero point. Because of this, it can be used for **calibrating and regulating** the measuring system of the slide table and spindle.

Specifically, the reference point is used in **four** situations:

1. **When the control is powered up, all axes <u>always</u> must be positioned at the reference return point to calibrate the measuring system.**
2. **The machine must be repositioned to the reference return point for reestablishing the proper coordinate values in situations such as losing the current position data due to electrical failure or improper operation.**
3. **All axes must be retracted to the reference point before the tool change can take place.**
4. **At the end of the part program, all axes must be retracted to the reference return point to reset the control system for rerunning the part program or running a new part program.**

Work Zero Point

A work zero point is the origin of the workpiece's coordinate system. It is used to determine the work's coordinate system in relation to the machine zero point. The work's zero points are often referred to as setup points because they are the locations for setting up the workpiece on the machine table. Some CNC controls allow the use of multiple work zero points in one machine setup or operation. The work zero point is labelled by **W** and represented by the symbol: 

The work zero point can be chosen by the programmer at any convenient location within the working envelope of the machine. It is recommended that you place the work zero point in a way that it can be easily located and measured on the workpiece. Figure 1.40 shows two common methods of choosing the work zero point for turnings and Figure 1.41 shows milling examples.

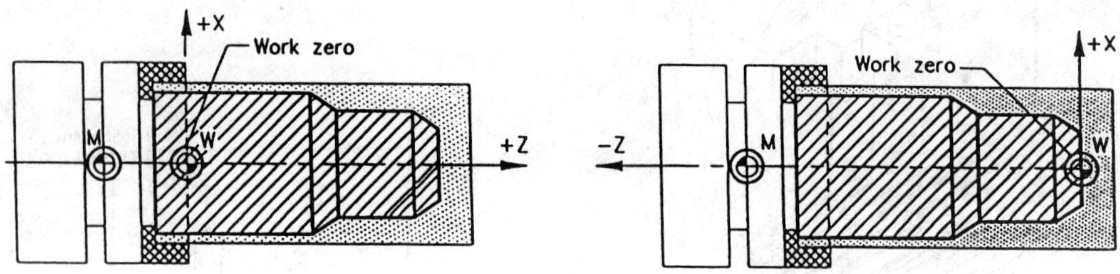

a. located at the chuck face   b. located at right workpiece face

Figures 1.40 Selecting work zero for turning

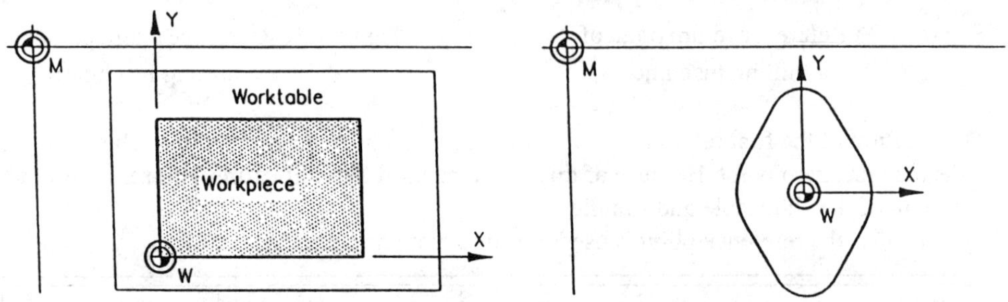

a. located at intersecting point of two datum surfaces b. located at workpiece center

Figure 1.41 Selecting work zero for milling

Program Zero Points

A program zero point is the **origin** of the part program. It is used to locate all other points in the part program. Therefore, it must be chosen before any programming can proceed. The program zero point is labelled by P and represented by the symbol: 

The program zero point normally coincides with the work zero point. However, it can be located at any convenient position. On the next page, Figure 1.42 shows the situation of the program zero point and the work zero point coinciding, while these two points are located separately in Figure 1.43.

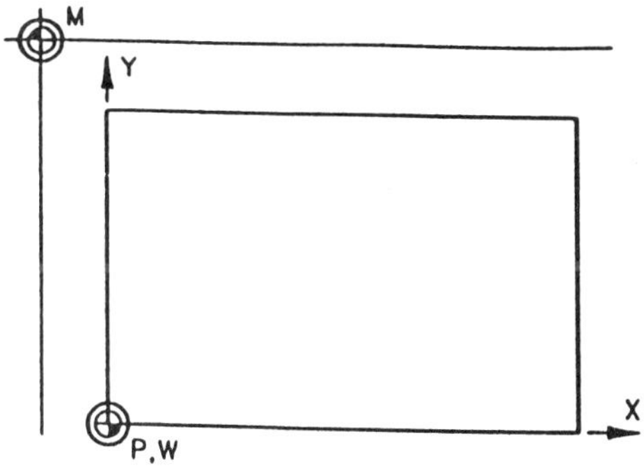

Figures 1.42 Program zero point and work zero point coincide

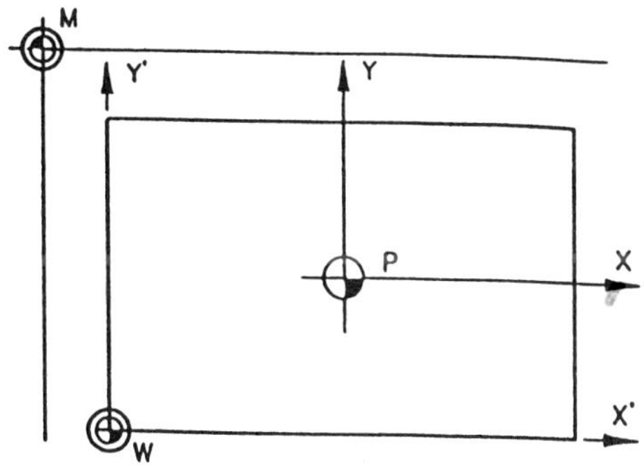

Figure 1.43 Separate program zero point and work zero point

It is possible to define multiple program zero points to facilitate the programming of workpieces with complex features. The **first** program zero point is the **program zero** and the **second** program zero point and **all succeeding points** are referred to as the **local zero point**. Figure 1.44 illustrates using two zero points to write a part program.

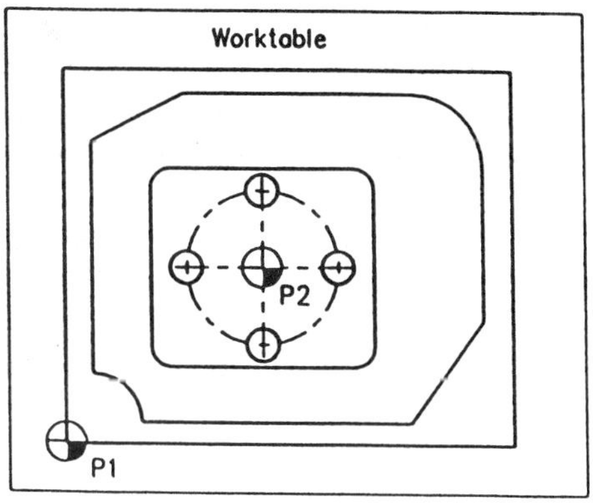

Figure 1.44 Multiple program zero points

1.17 Positioning Systems

We use a positioning system to determine the locations of the positioning points on the workpiece to which the cutting tool is moved. Two methods of positioning systems are used in NC part programming:

- **absolute positioning system and**
- **incremental positioning system.**

Absolute Positioning System

We always measure the dimension data of all positions from a **fixed reference point** in the absolute positioning system. In fact, this point is the program zero point. The absolute positioning system is sometimes referred to as the reference positioning system. Figure 1.45 shows an example using absolute positioning system.

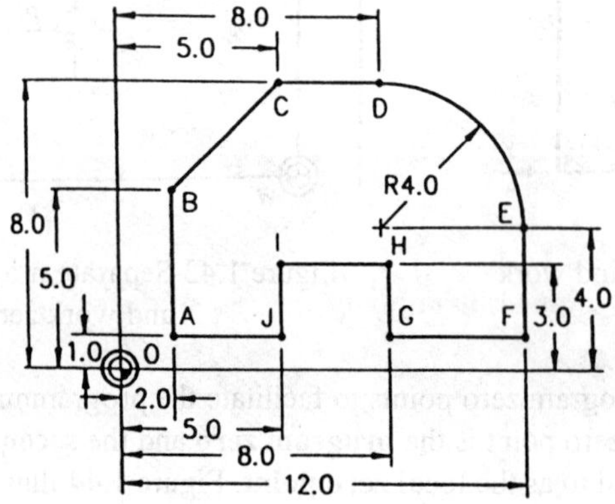

Figure 1.45 Absolute positioning system

Incremental Positioning System

When using the incremental positioning system, the dimension data of a point always refers to the immediately **preceding** point. Each position is measured in relation to the previous one and the coordinate system shifts from point to point. Some important features of the incremental positioning system are given below:

> **a. The program zero point is used as the reference point only for the first programmed point.**
> **b. The plus (+) and minus (-) sign should be used to indicate the direction of tool motion even though points may be located only in the first quadrant.**
> **c. The positioning sequence of the tool path affects the dimension data of a point. This feature is illustrated in Figure 1.46.**

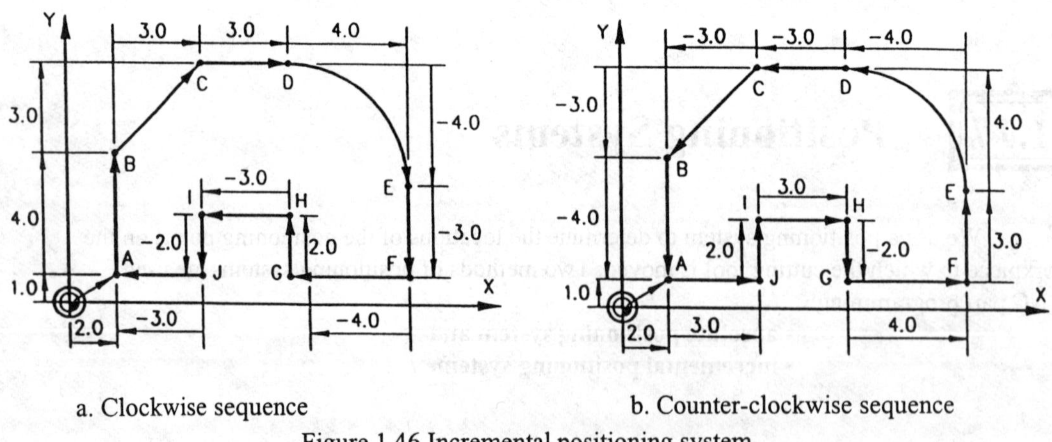

Figure 1.46 Incremental positioning system

Selection of the Positioning System

Using the **absolute positioning system** in part programming is recommended for the following **two** reasons:

1. **The positioning error encountered with an individual point has no effect on subsequent positions.**
2. **The absolute system is easier to use to trace the cutter locations for checking errors because all dimensions are referenced to the same fixed point.**

The **incremental positioning system** is preferred when common patterns (holes, pockets, or contour patterns) in a workpiece are repeated several times. **Three** main disadvantages of using the incremental positioning system are:

1. **Any positioning error will be continued throughout the rest of the program. A positioning error of 1.0" in H1 as shown in Figure 1.47 below, for example, is carried to all succeeding programming positions.**
2. **A compound error is progressively accumulated if more than one error is encountered in a part program. Figure 1.48 below depicts this feature. A positioning error of 0.5" in H1 continues on to H2. An additional error of 1.5" is encountered in H3, the accumulated error of 2.0" then appears throughout the rest of the program.**
3. **It is very difficult to check for any position error, especially in large part programs.**

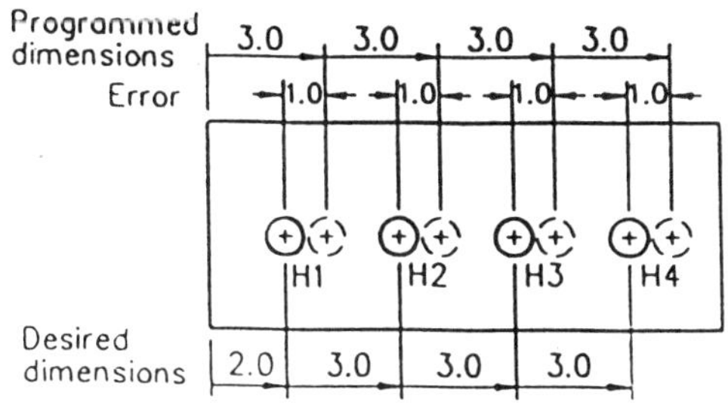

Figure 1.47 A position error is extended to all succeeding programming positions

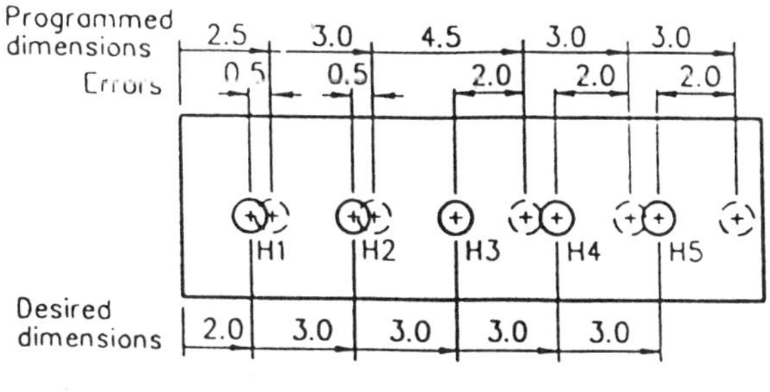

Figure 1.48 Accummulated errors

Chapter 2

Machining Fundamentals

Objectives:

1. Be familiar with the machining processes performed by CNC milling and turning machines.
2. Know cutting tools and tooling systems for CNC machines.
3. Select machining parameters for various machining processes.
4. Provide useful tips for various machining processes.

2.1 CNC Milling Processes

CNC milling machines and machining centers are used to perform **six** types of machining processes. Table 2.1 illustrates these six types of machining processes on the following two pages.

- Facing
- Profiling
- Pocketing
- Slot cutting
- Hole machining
- 3-D surface machining

2.2 CNC Turning Processes

CNC turning machines and turning centers implement the following **ten** types of machining processes:

- Facing
- Profiling
- Drilling
- Threading
- Cutting off
- Turning
- Grooving
- Boring
- Chamfering
- Milling

All ten processes are illustrated in Table 2.2 on the following pages 2-4 and 2-5.

Table 2.1 Milling Processes

Process Type	Tool	Illustration
1. Facing Producing flat surfaces	Face mill for larger surfaces End mill for small surfaces	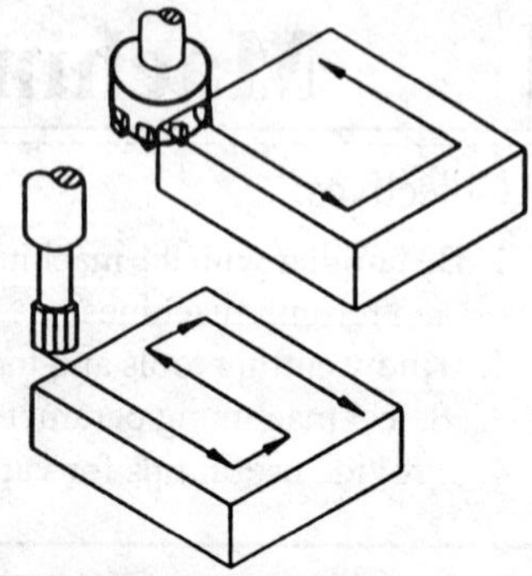
2. Profiling Producing part contours	End mill	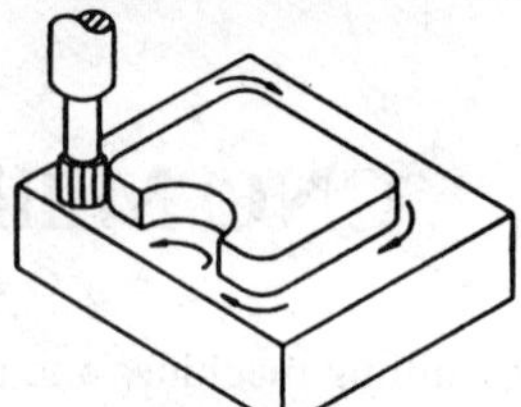
3. Pocketing Removing the material enclosed by a closed boundary	End mill	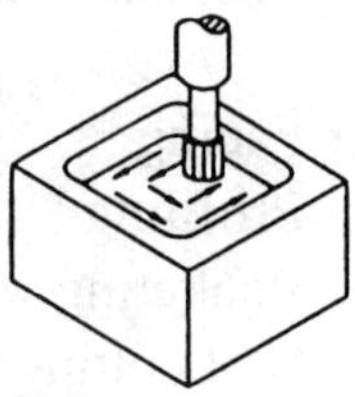
4. Slot cutting Producing various types of slots	End mill	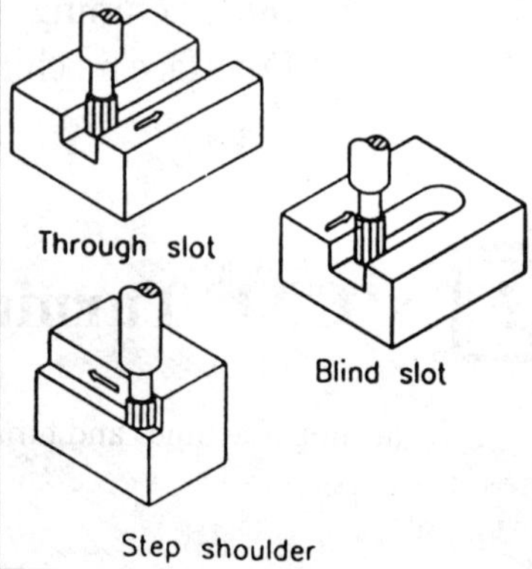
5. Hole machining a. Drilling	Drill	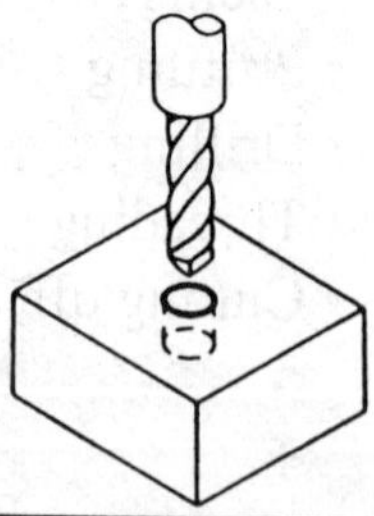

Table 2.1 (Continued)

Process Type	Tool	Illustration
b. Countersinking	Countersink tool	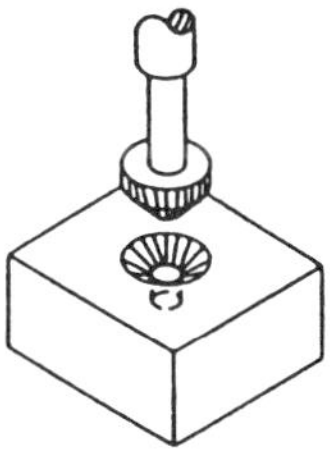
c. Counterboring	Counterbore tool	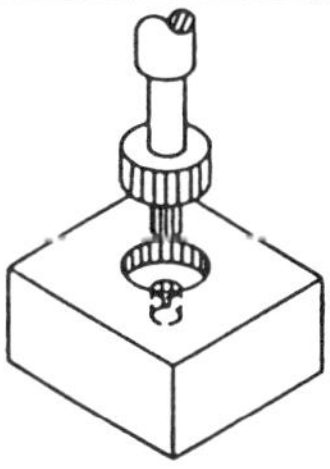
d. Boring	Boring tool	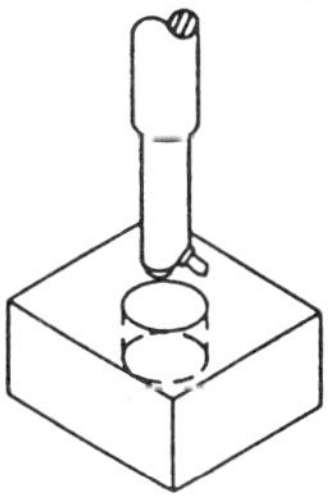
e. Tapping	Tap	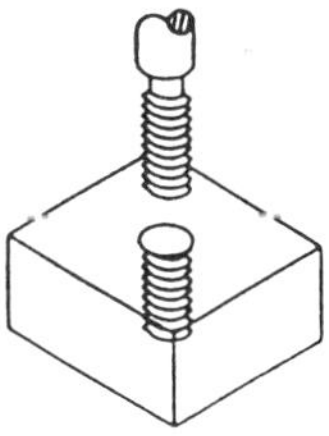
f. Reaming Producing smooth and precise holes	Reamer	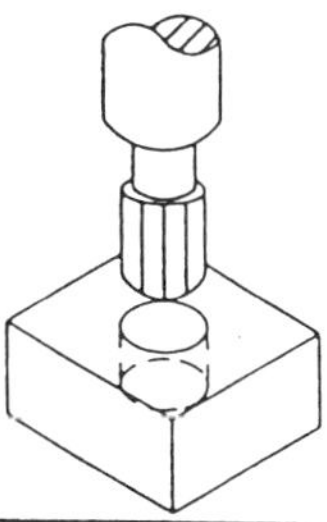
6. 3-D Surface machining Cutting various types of surfaces	Ball-end mill	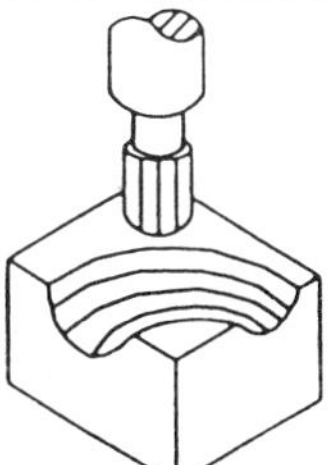

Table 2.2 Turning Machining Processes

Process Type	Tool	Illustration
1. Facing: Producing flat end face a. Facing to center b. Facing to shoulder	Facing tool	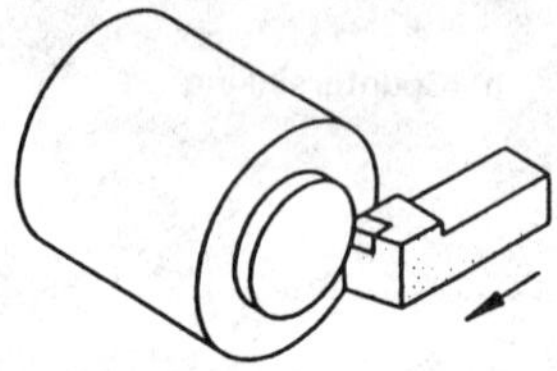
2. Turning: Producing line profiles a. Straight turning	Turning tool	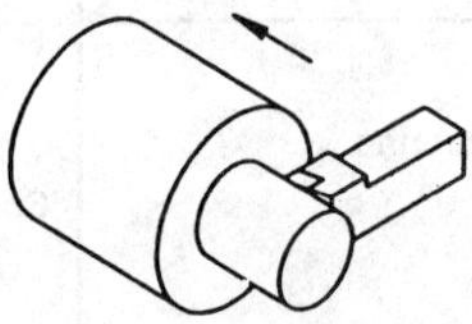
b. Taper turning		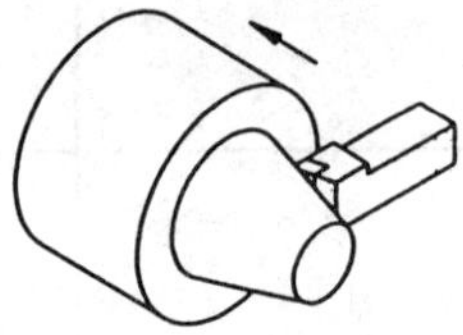
3. Profiling Producing external line and circular profiles	Profiling tool	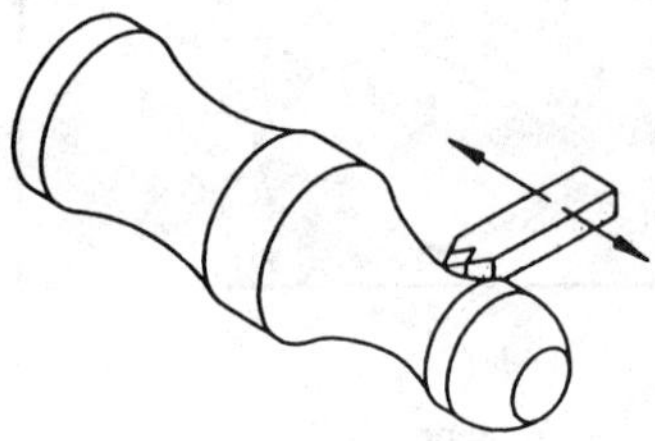
4. Grooving: Cutting various forms of grooves a. Side grooving	Grooving tool	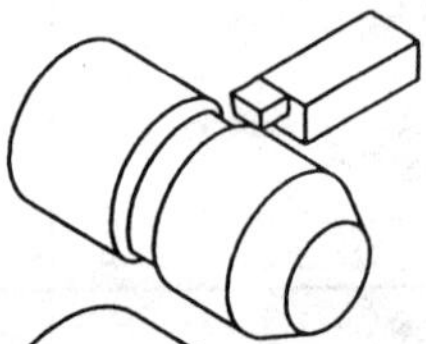 Side grooving
b. Face grooving		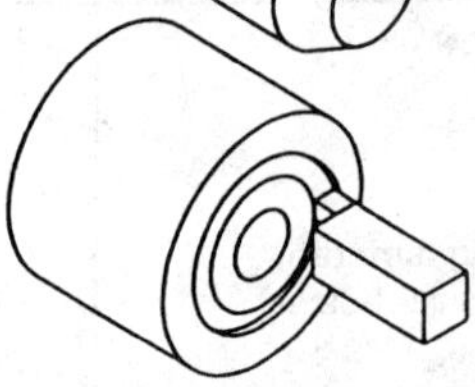 Face grooving
5. Drilling Producing holes in the spindle axis	Drill	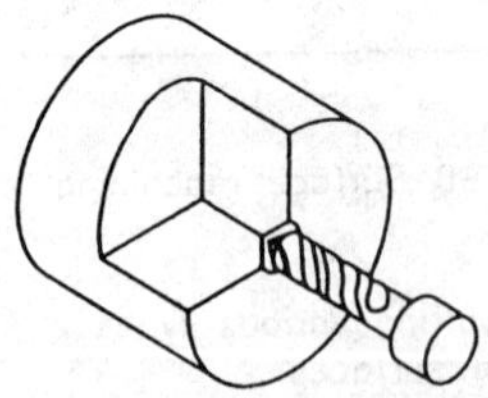

Table 2.2 (Continued)

Process Type	Tool	Illustration
6. Boring Producing internal line and circular profiles	Boring tool	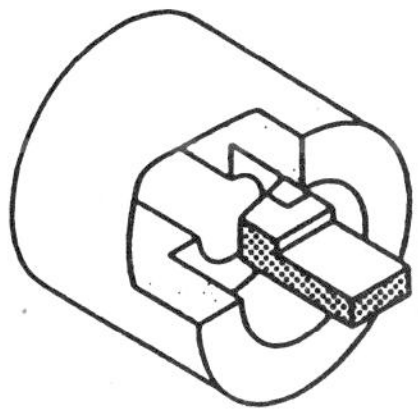
7. Threading: Cutting various thread forms a. External thread	Threading tool	External thread 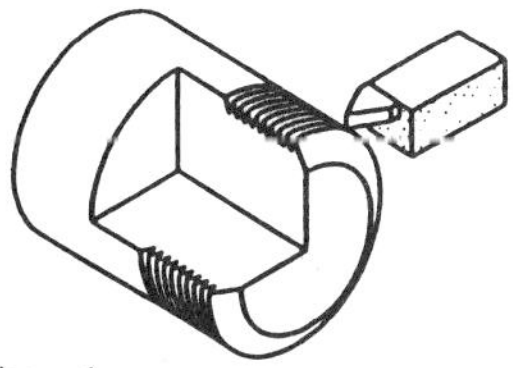
b. Internal thread		Internal thread 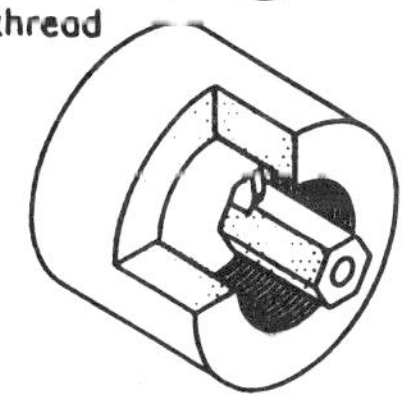
8. Chamfering Generating chamfers at sharp corners	Chamfering tool	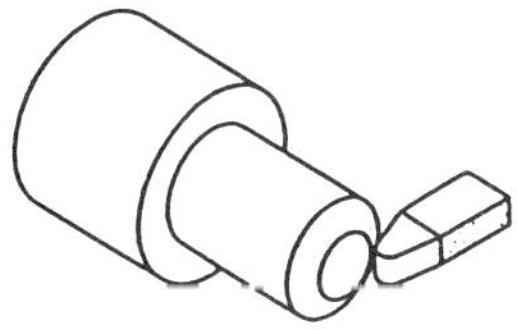
9. Cutting off Separating the workpiece from the stock	Cut-off tool	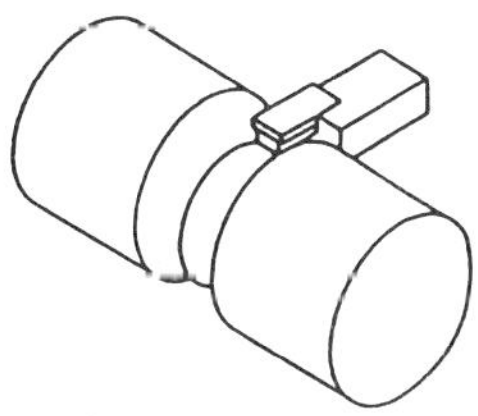
10. Milling Producing slots and surfaces	End mill	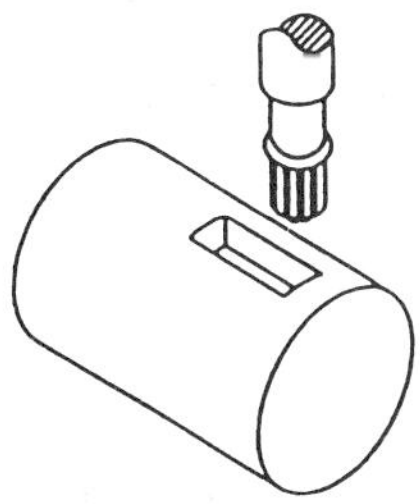

2.3 Cutting Tool Materials

Required Properties of Cutting Tool Materials

Three important properties of any cutting tool material are:

1. Wear resistance (resistance to the various wear mechanism)
2. Toughness (the ability to absorb energy and withstand plastic deformation without fracturing under compressive loading)
3. Hot hardness (the ability to resist stresses and maintain hardness and cutting efficiency at elevated temperatures)

Cutting Tool Materials

The common cutting tool materials used for CNC machining are **high speed steel (HSS), tungsten carbides, cermets, ceramics, and polycrystalline.** Table 2.3 summarizes the characteristics and applications of various cutting tool materials.

Table 2.3 Characteristics and applications of various cutting tool materials

Material	Principal Characteristics	Typical Applications	Advantages
HSS	Tougher than carbides	Low speed machining, and interrupted cuts.	Lower cost than carbide, longer tool life, better surface finish.
Uncoated carbide	Very tough, excellent edge wear resistance.	Roughing to finishing virtually any material including iron, steel, stainless steel, high temperature alloy, non ferrous metals and non- metallic materials.	Higher cutting speed than HSS and tougher than coated carbides.
PVD coated carbide	Very tough, good thermal shock resistance and crater resistance. High retained edge strength. Excellent resistance to buildup on the cutting edge.	Machining of steels, high temperature alloys, stainless steels, difficult to machine materials, aluminum, carbon and alloy steels.	Permit speeds to be increased up to 15% when compared to uncoated with no loss of tool life.
Cermet	Excellent resistance to wear, shock and heat.	Finishing operations on malle able cast irons, carbon steels, alloy steels, stainless steels, and aluminum alloys.	Up to 20 times the tool life of conventional carbide grades.
Ceramics (alumina base)	High hardness, excellent chemical wear resistance.	For high speed rouging and finishing of cast irons and steels.	Better finishes at higher machining rates.
Ceramics (silicon base)	High hardness plus high fracture toughness and thermal shock resistance.	Roughing and finishing operations on cast irons.	Machining speeds up to 5000 sfm and beyond.
Polycrystalline diamond (PCV)	Hardness of diamond plus toughness, excellent wear resistance.	Roughing to finishing operations on aluminum and other soft or abrasive non-ferrous or non-metallic materials.	Better than 30 times the tool life of carbide, even on high silicon aluminum.
Cubic born nitride (CBN)	Exceptional hardness, excellent wear resistance and mechanical shock resistance.	High speed machining on hardened ferrous materials in the 50 65 Rc (480 740 Bhn) range.	Provide many times the edge life of carbide, eliminate the need for costly alternative grinding operations.

ANSI and ISO Carbide Grade Classifications

There are two commonly used classification systems for carbide cutting tools:

ANSI system and ISO system.

ANSI System

The ANSI carbide classification system was initiated in the U.S. automotive industry and more commonly used in the United States. It is also called U.S. **C-system** because it uses the letter C with a numeric digit ranging from 1 to 8 to indicate the carbide grade (Table 2.4)

Table 2.4 ANSI Carbide Classification System

Class	Class	Material to be cut	Application	Characteristics of cutting	Characteristics of carbide
C1	Tungsten	Cast iron, nonferrous metals, and nonmetallics	Roughing cuts	Increasing cutting speed ↓ / Increasing feed rate ↑	Increasing hardness & wear resistance ↓ / Increasing strength ↑
C2	Tungsten		General–purpose		
C3	Tungsten		Finishing		
C4	Tungsten		Roughing cuts		
C5	Tungsten	Steels and steel alloys	Tungsten	Increasing cutting speed ↓ / Increasing feed rate ↑	Increasing hardness & wear resistance ↓ / Increasing strength ↑
C6	Titanium		General–purpose		
C7	Tungsten Titanium and Tantalum in varying amounts		Finishing		
C8			Fine finishing		

Carbide tools are classified into two major categories. One category is composed of the **straight tungsten carbides** (classes 1 to 4), which are hard and have very good wear resistance. They are best suited to machining cast iron, non-ferrous metals, and some nonmetallic materials that are abrasive. The second category (classes 5 to 8) includes the combinations of **tungsten and tantalum or titanium carbide**. These carbides are generally used for machining steels. They are resistant to cratering, which is a serious problem when tungsten carbide is used to machine steels.

ISO System

The ISO (International Organization for Standardization) system is based on the ISO Standard 513-1975(E) which is widely used in Europe. It uses **three** main categories: **P, M, and K** (Table 2.5 on the next page).

P category:	**for machining**	**ferrous metals with long chips**
M category:	**for machining**	**(1) ferrous metals with long or short chips** **(2) non-ferrous metals**
K category:	**for machining**	**(1) ferrous metals with short chips** **(2) non-ferrous metals** **(3) non-metallic materials**

Table 2.5 ISO Carbide Classification System

Symbol and color	Broad material categories to be cut	Class	Application	Characteristics of cutting	Characteristics of carbide
P (Blue)	Ferrous metals with long chips	P01	Finish turning and boring under vibration free operations	↑ Increasing cutting speed ↓ Increasing feed rate	↑ Increasing wear resistance ↓ Increasing toughness
		P10	Turning, copying, threading and milling of light roughing and finishing		
		P20	Turning, copying and milling at medium cutting speeds		
		P30	Turning and milling under heavy feeds and shocks		
		P40	Turning, planning and milling under unfavorable conditions		
		P50	Machining operations demanding very tough carbide		
M (Yellow)	Ferrous metals with long and short chips	M10	Finish turning alloy steels and cast iron	↑ Increasing cutting speed ↓ Increasing feed rate	↑ Increasing wear resistance ↓ Increasing toughness
		M20	General grade for machining of alloy steels and gray cast iron		
	Nonferrous metals	M30	Rough machining of tough materials		
		M40	Turning and parting off of mild steel, nonferrous metals and light alloys		
K (Red)	Ferrous metals with short chips	K01	Finish turning, boring and milling of very hard materials, abrasive plastics and ceramics		
	Nonferrous metals	K10	Turning, milling, drilling, and boring of malleable cast iron, nonferrous alloys, plastics, rubber, etc.		
	Nonmetallic materials	K20	Machining of copper, brass, and aluminum demanding tough carbide		
		K30	Rough machining of soft cast iron, low tensile steel in unfavorable conditions		
		K40	Machining of wood and nonferrous metals in unfavorable conditions		

Table 2.6 Relationship between ANSI and ISO Carbide Classification Systems

	Carbide grade		
ISO	P01 P05 P10 P20 P25 P30 P40 P50	M10 M20 M30 M40	K01 K05 K10 K20 K30 K40
ANSI	C8 C7 C6 C5		C4 C3 C2 C1

Increasing toughness →

← Increasing hardness

Note that both ISO and ANSI designation systems for various types and grades of cutting tool materials are not precise. They can only serve as a general guide in selecting cutting tool materials for specific applications. Cutting tool manufacturers often use their own classification systems with ANSI and ISO equivalent grades for their products.

Cutting Tool Material Selection

Selecting proper cutting tool materials for a specific machining application can provide significant advantages including **increased productivity, improved quality, and reduced costs**. The following factors should be carefully considered in selecting cutting tool materials:

1. Type of material to be machined (ferrous or non-ferrous type)

Select grade C5 - C8 for steel materials

Select grade C1 - C4 for cast iron, non-ferrous metals, and non-metallic materials

2. Machining types

Roughing:
C1 for non-steel materials
C5 for steel materials

General Purpose:
C2 for non-steel materials
C6 for steel materials

Finishing:
C3 for non-steel materials
C7 for steel materials

Precision boring and fine finishing:
C4 for non-steel materials
C8 for steel materials

Figure 2.1 is a comparision chart of the cutting speed range for various cutting tool materials for machining different metals.

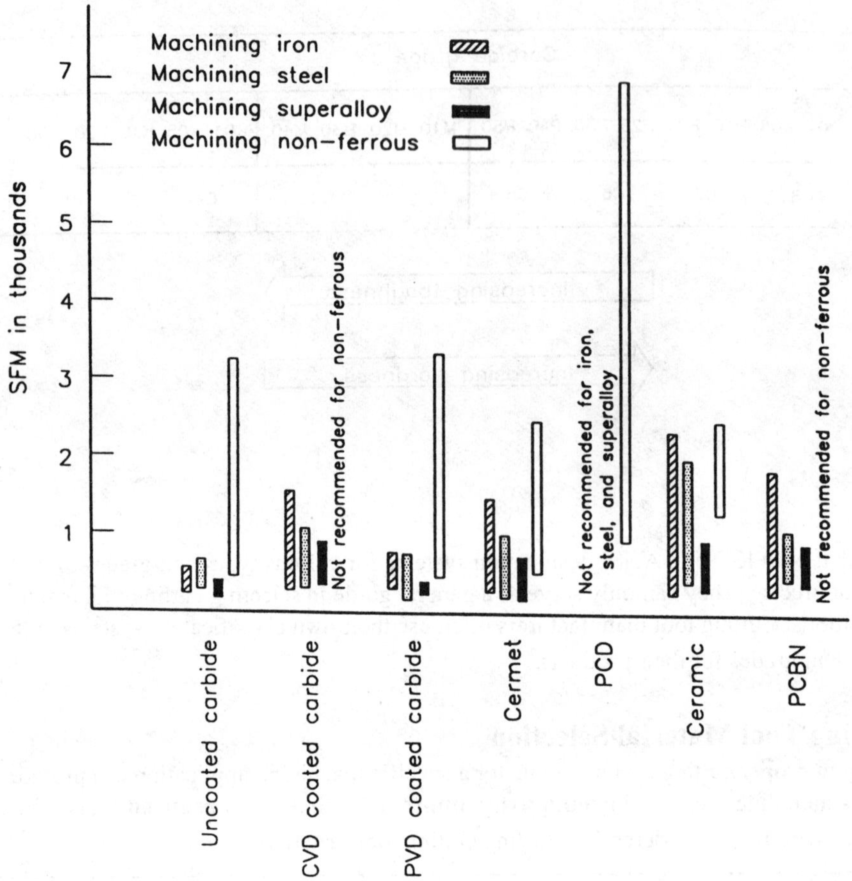

Figure 2.1

2.4 Tooling for Milling

A typical tooling system for machining centers consists of the **four** major components; **automatic tool changer, toolholders, adaptors, and cutting tools.** Any tooling system for CNC machine tools must meet the following **three** requirements:

- capable of holding multiple tools
- automatic tool change to shorten tool change time
- interchangeability

Automatic Tool Changer

An automatic tool changer (ATC) facilitates the quick change of tools in and out of the machine spindle. The tools are stored in the **automatic tool magazine** which is an indexed storage component part of the machine tool. The tools can be selected and changed under the control of the part program. Figure 2.2 on the following page shows a machining center with a chain type of ATC.

Figure 2.2 A chain type of automatic tool changer

Toolholders

Toolholders are used to facilitate the switching of a broad range of cutting tools in and out of the spindle automatically. A toolholder consists of **five** basic components (Figure 2.3):

1. Tapered shank
2. Flange
3. Retention knob
4. Opposed slots
5. Adaptor

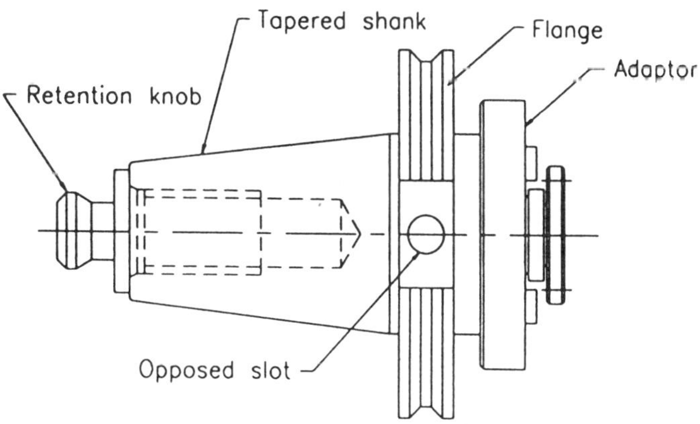

Figure 2.3

Tapered Shank

The tapered shank fits the toolholder to the spindle. The ANSI standard defines **six basic taper shank sizes** including #30, #35, #40, #45, #50, and #60. Larger machines use toolholders that have larger shank taper numbers. The taper of the shank is made to 3.5 in./ft (or a ratio of 7:24).

Taper Shank No.	Type of Machine
#60	**Very large machines**
#50	**Medium size machines (20 to 50 HPs)**
#40	**Small size machines**
#30	**Very small machines**

Flange Type

The flange allows the toolholder to be grabbed by the tool gripper or the machine spindle. There are **two** commonly used flange types: **V-flange and BT-flange** (Figure 2.4). V-flanges are often referred to as Caterpillar V-flanges. They use inch threads for the retention knob and are used to hold inch-dimensioned cutting tools. BT-flanges have metric threads for the retention knob, but their adaptors can be designed to accommodate a wide range of inch-dimensioned cutting tools. BT-flange holders are widely used in Japanese and European made machining centers.

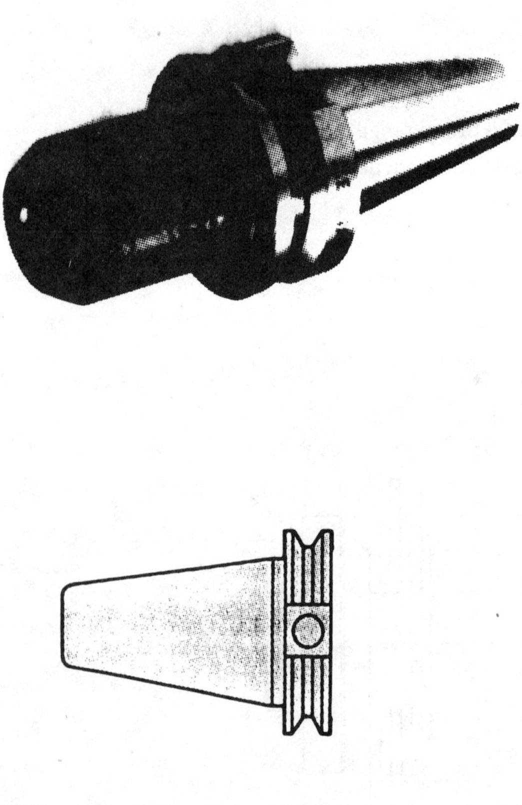

Figure 2.4a V-flange

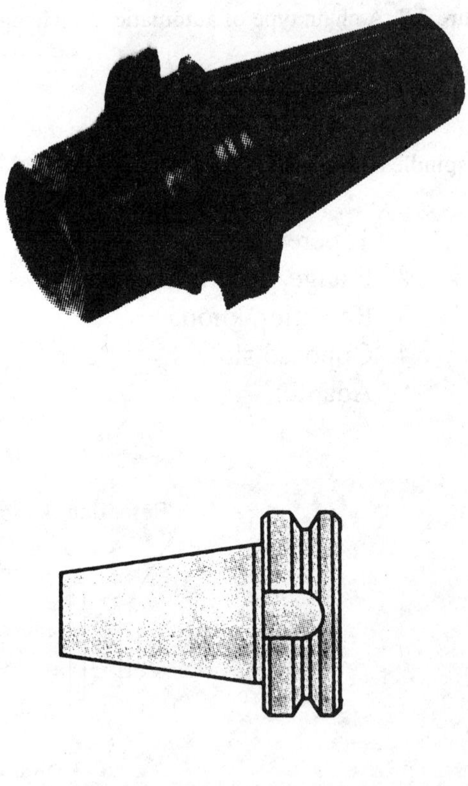

Figure 2.4b BT-flange

Retention Knob

The retention knob allows the locking drawbar of the spindle to pull the toolholder firmly into the spindle and to release the toolholder automatically (Figure 2.5). Retention knobs are made in various styles and sizes. They are not necessarily interchangeable. Only use the retention knobs that are specified by the machine tool manufacturer.

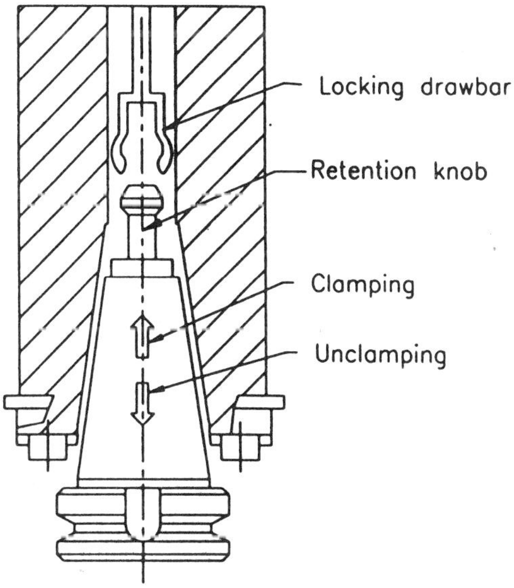

Figurc 2.5

Adaptors

Adaptors are designed with various configurations to accommodate different types and sizes of cutting tools. Toolholders are often named according to their adaptor type. Commonly used adaptors include; **end mill holders, face mill holders, tap holders, collet holders, boring bar holders, Morse taper holders, Jacob taper holders, and straight shank holders.** Figure 2.6 on the next page shows a toolholder selection chart. There is no established standard for specifying the configuration and size of adaptors.

2.5 Tooling System for Turning

The tooling system for turning centers consists of **six** basic components (Figure 2.7):

1. Turret head
2. Mounting blocks
3. Mounting plates
4. Tool holders
5. Sleeves and sockets
6. Inserts or cutting tools

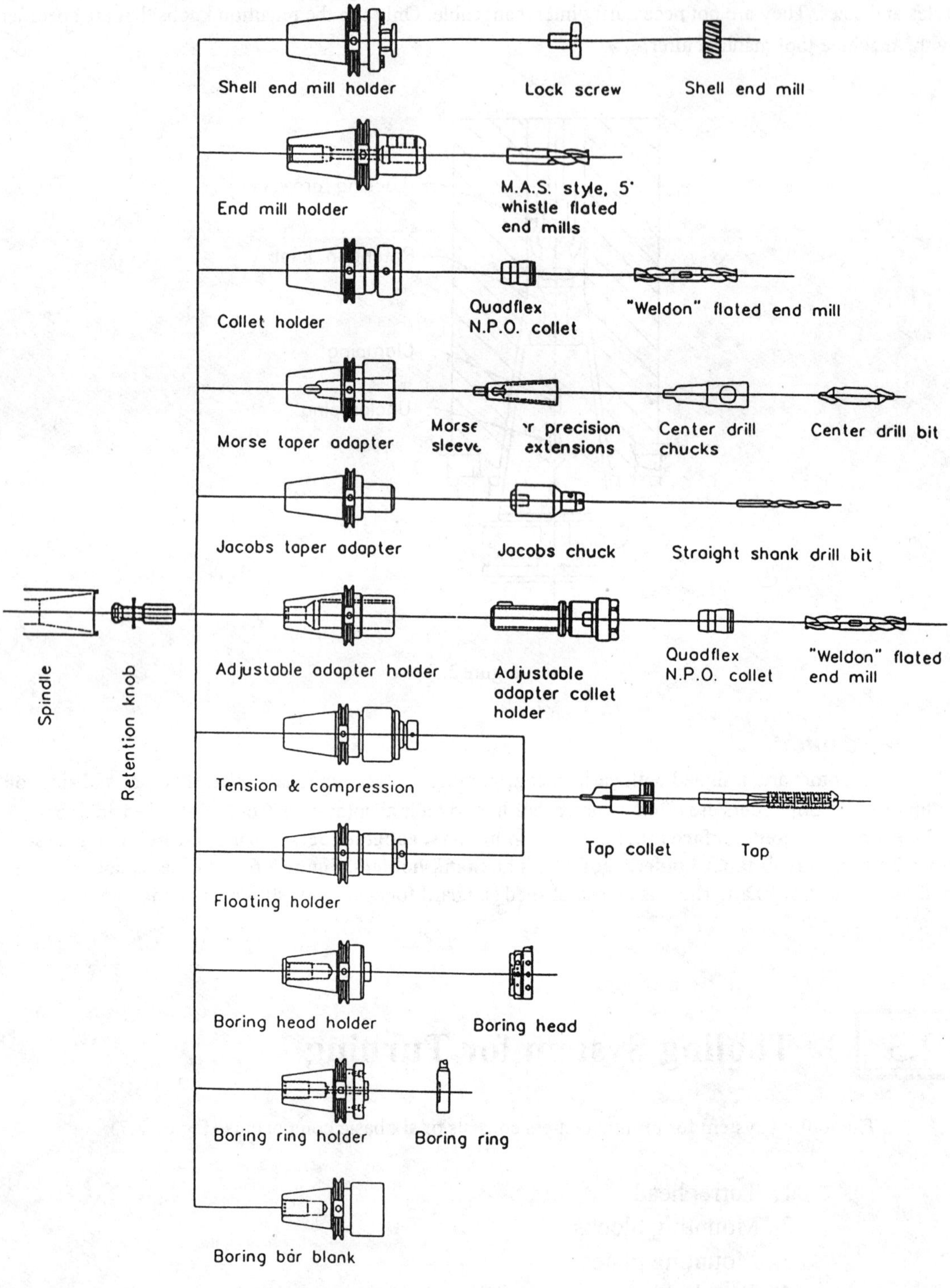

Figure 2.6 Tooling system for milling machines (Source: S.C. Jonathon Lin, Computer Numerical Control: From Programming to Networking, 1994. Courtesy of Delmar Publishers, Inc.)

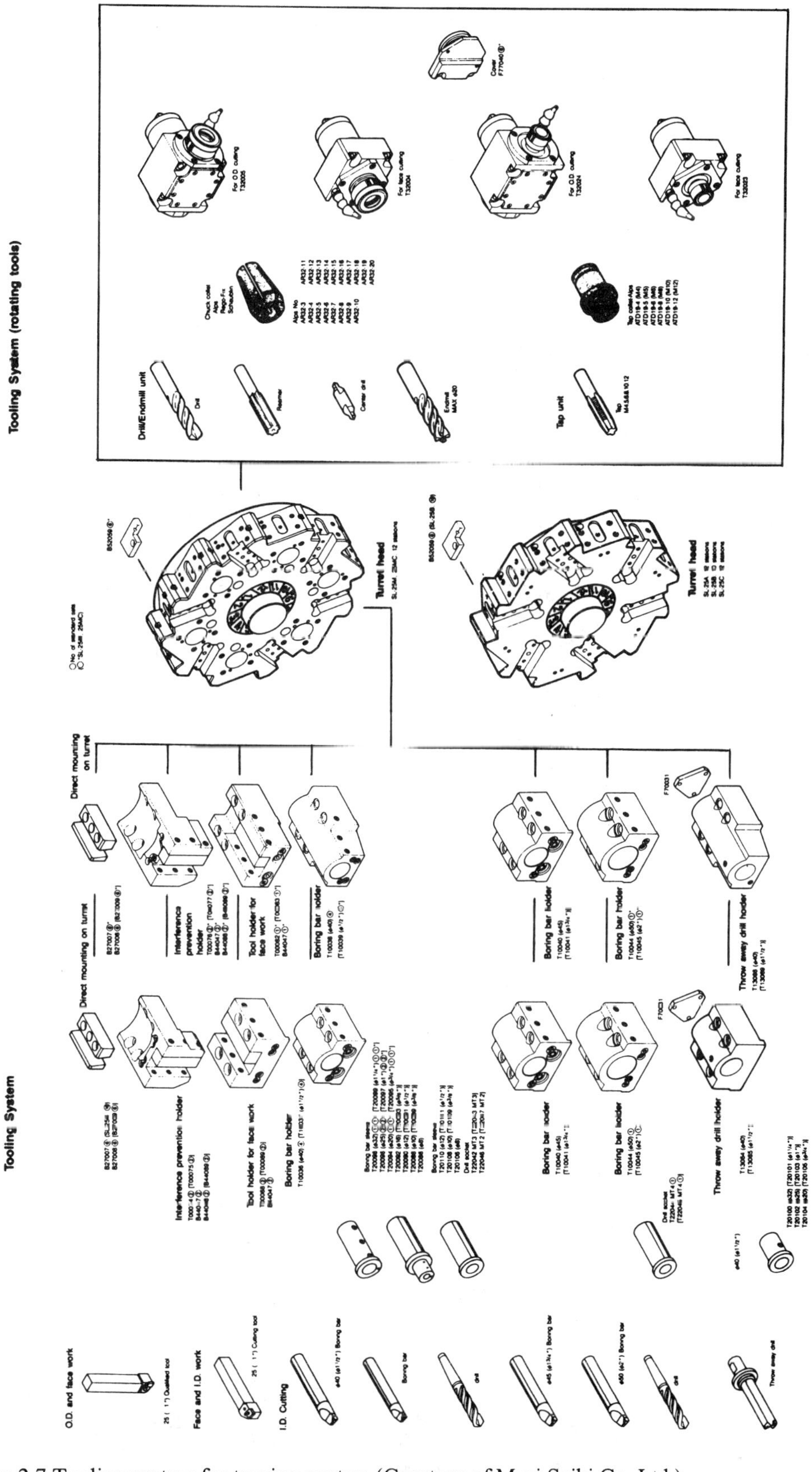

Figure 2.7 Tooling system for turning centers (Courtesy of Mori Seiki Co. Ltd.)

A turret head provides from 6 to 12 tool stations that can be automatically indexed by the control. Depending on the type of cutting tool used, mounting plates or mounting blocks are needed to attach the cutting tools to turret head. Normally, tools for OD turning and facing operations use mounting plates. Boring tools and drills use mounting blocks. Usually sleeves or sockets are needed to allow for different tool shank size. Figure 2.8 shows a 12-station turret head with a variety of cutting tools. Some turning centers provide simultaneous 3-axis control (X, Z, and spindle angular orientation). The spindle C axis can give as small as 0.001° of spindle rotation. Spindle axis control combined with rotating tools allows the machine to turn, bore, drill, mill, tap, and ream the workpiece in any direction in one machine setup. These turning centers have simultaneous 3-axis control which allows the machining of the rotating tools and they are often referred to as mill-turn. Figure 2.9 shows a turret used in a mill turn.

Figure 2.8

(Source of Photographs: Mori Seiki Co. Ltd.)

Figure 2.9

2.6 Inserts Identification and Selection

Indexed inserts are widely used in CNC machines. They are made with various shapes and sizes (Figure 2.10). The ANSI standard provides an identification system to describe the features of inserts. The identification consists of up to 10 symbol codes. Each code defines a feature of the insert (Figure 2.11). The first 7 symbols are mandatory, the following 2 symbols are optional, and the last symbol is for the manufacturer's use. The ISO standard basically follows the ANSI standard except the dimensions are specified in millimeters.

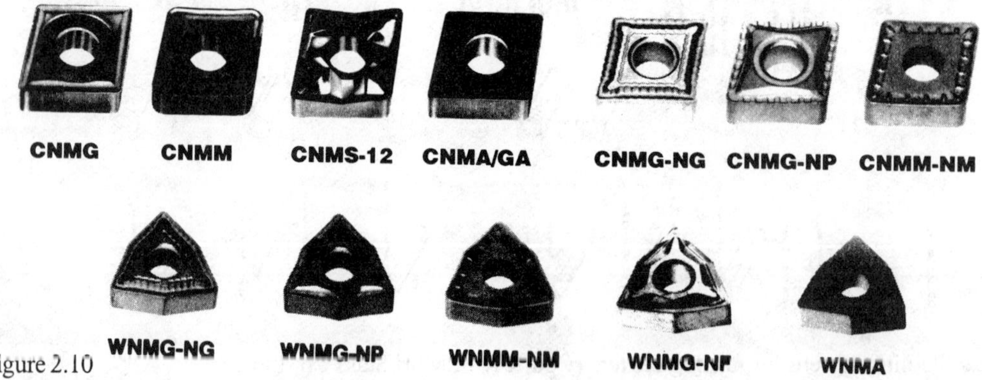

Figure 2.10

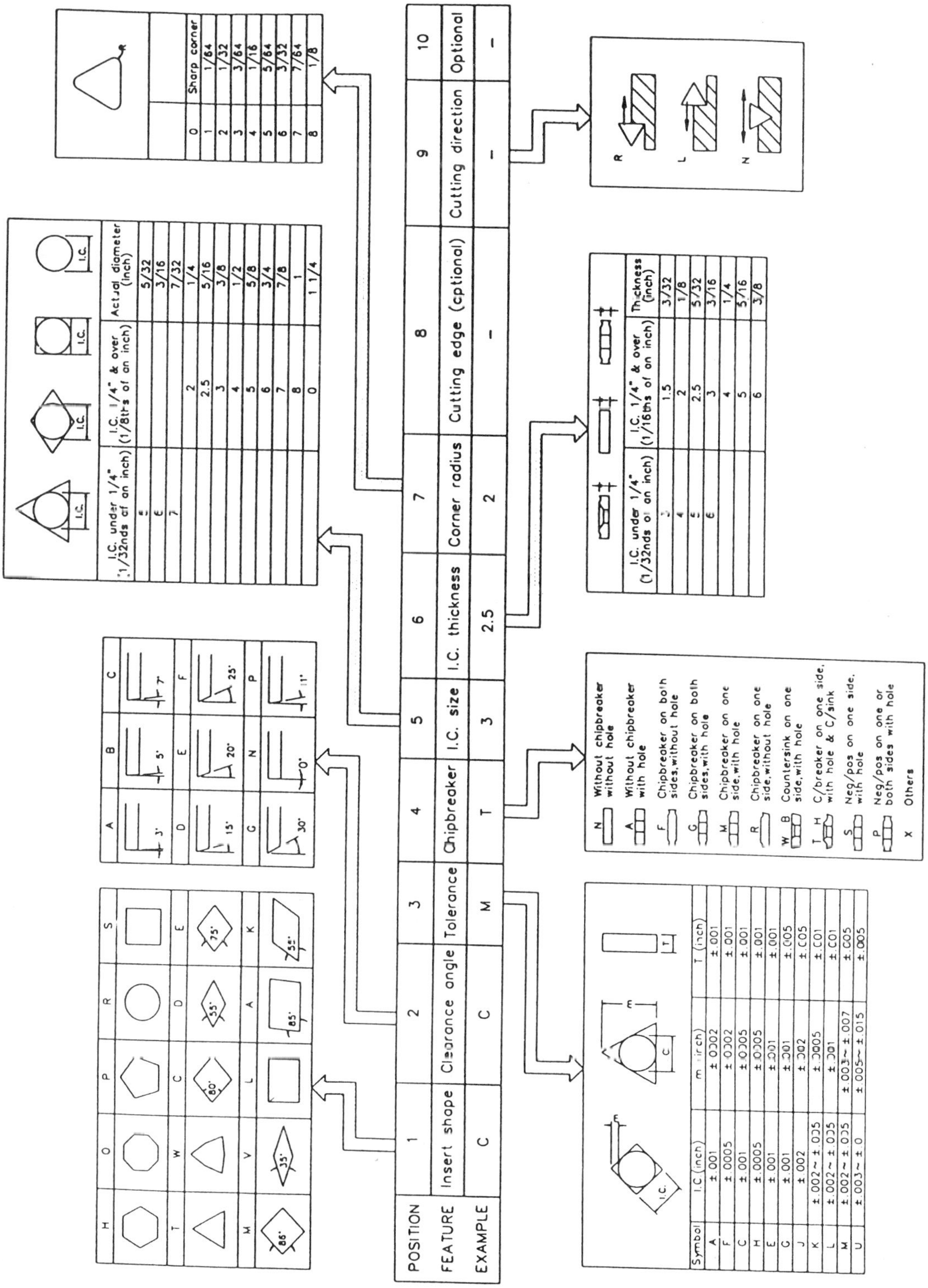

Figure 2.11 Insert identification system (Source: S.C. Jonathon Lin, Computer Numerical Control: From Programming to Networking, 1994. Courtesy of Delmar Publishers Inc.)

Insert Selection

Several factors must be carefully considered in selecting proper inserts for specific applications. These factors include **insert shape, insert size, and chip breaker.**

Insert Shape

Inserts are made in various shapes. The insert shape affects **insert strength, insert angle, maximum number of cutting edges available, power consumption, and versatility**. The larger the included insert angle, the stronger the insert. A round insert is the strongest, while the 35° diamond insert is the weakest type.

The inserts with more sides provide a greater number of cutting edges. A hexagonal shaped insert has six cutting edges, while a triangle shape only furnishes three edges. The cutting edges of those inserts with a zero clearance angle are twice those with a non-zero clearance angle. The zero clearance triangle inserts, for example, have 6 possible edges.

The more commonly used insert types in turning applications include:

80° diamond shape:	**for OD turning, ID boring, and facing**
55° diamond shape:	**for OD turning, profiling, and ID boring**
35° diamond shape:	**for OD profiling and ID profiling**
60° shape:	**for OD turning, ID boring, and facing**
Round shape:	**for OD turning, and ID boring**

Insert Size

Three dimensions used to describe the insert size are the **inscribed circle (IC), thickness (T), and nose radius (R)** (Figure 2.12).

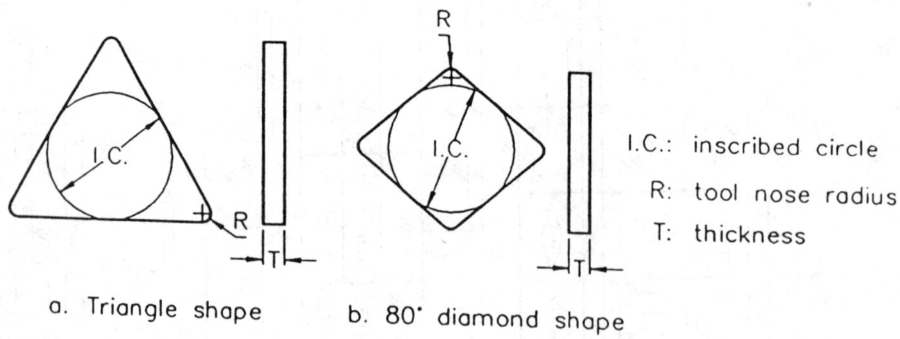

Figure 2.12

The selection of IC size depends on the maximum depth of cut to be taken. The rule of thumb is that the maximum cutting edge engagement is one-half the insert edge length. The cutting edge length is normally longer than the IC size except for square and round inserts as shown in Figure 2.13. The cutting edge length of commonly used inserts can be computed from the formulas given in Table 2.7.

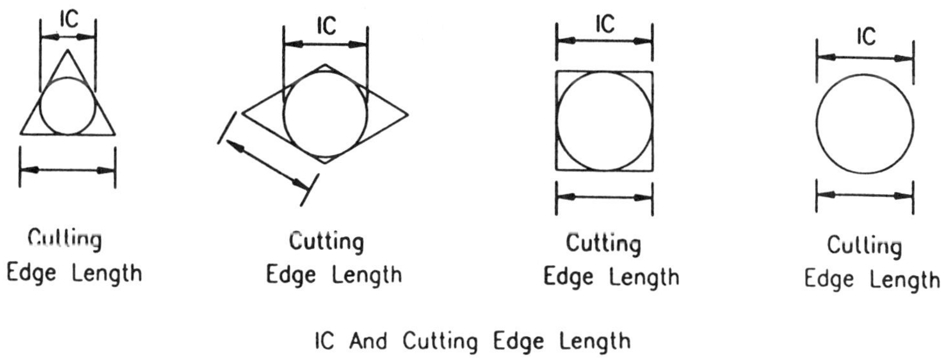

Figure 2.13

Table 2.7 The cutting edge length of various insert shapes

Insert Shape	Cutting Edge Length (L)
Square	L = IC
Round	L = IC
Triangle	L = 1.732 IC
80° diamond	L = 1.015 IC
55° diamond	L = 1.221 IC
35° diamond	L = 1.744 IC

Insert Thickness

The factors affecting the selection of insert thickness are the **feed rate** and the **cutting edge engagement**. The nomograph shown in Figure 2.14 provides a reference guide for selecting the insert thickness to meet the strength requirement. To use this nomograph, connect a line between the selected feed rate and the actual maximum cutting edge engagement. This line intersects with the insert thickness line at one point which is the proper insert thickness. Two scales are given in the insert thickness line, one for regular cuts and the other for interrupted cuts.

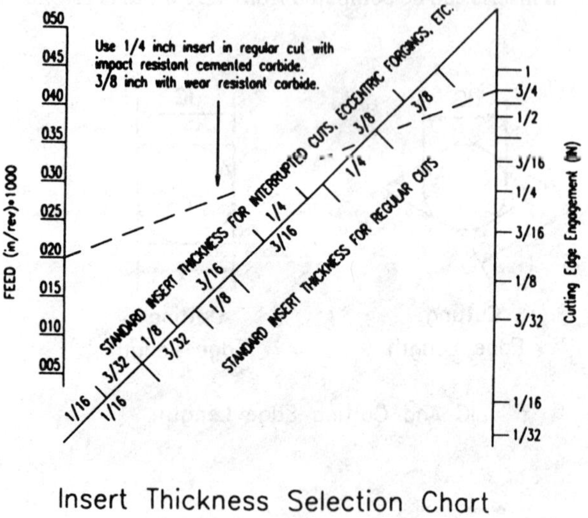

Figure 2.14

Insert Nose Radius

The selection of insert nose radius for an operation is mainly determined by two factors: **feed rate and required surface finish.** The surface finish (or roughness) is normally expressed by an arithmetic average (AA) value or the root mean square (RMS) value. Figure 2.15 provides a nomograph for selecting the proper insert nose radius based on the given feed rate and the required surface finish either in AA or RMS value.

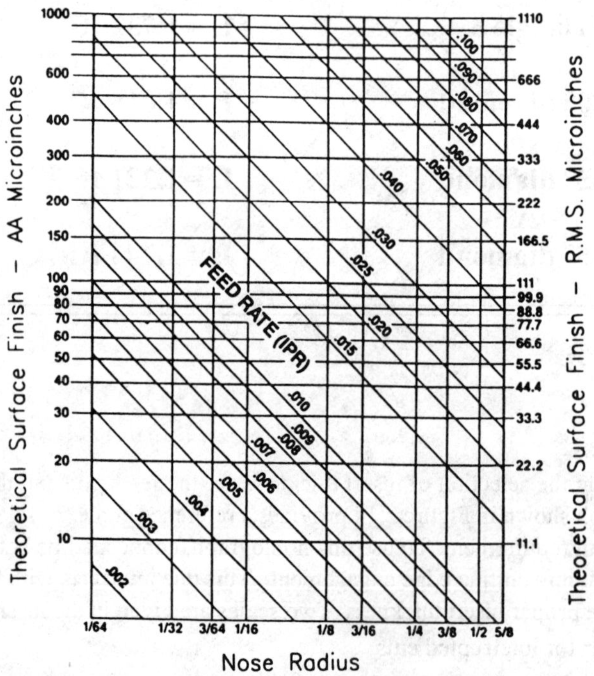

Figure 2.15

Follow these steps to select the nose radius using the nomograph:

1. Locate the required surface finish (AA or RMS) on the vertical line.
2. Follow the horizontal line corresponding to the desired surface finish to the point at which the line intersects the diagonal line representing the feed rate.
3. Project a line from this point downward to the nose radius scale.
4. If this line falls between two values, select the larger value.
5. If no available nose radius generates the required finish, reduce the feed rate.

Chip Breakers

Follow these **two** guidelines when selecting the proper chip breaker:

a. No chip breaker is required for:
   - interrupted cuts
   - turning brittle materials such as cast iron

b. Chip breakers are needed for turning tough, stringy materials such as steels, aluminum, and non-ferrous materials.

2.7 Toolholders

The ANSI standard for insert toolholder identification system is given in Figure 2.17 on the next page. The ANSI identification system describes the following features of an insert toolholder:

1. Clamping method
2. Insert shape
3. Holder style
4. Rake angle
5. Hand of tool
6. Shank size
7. Insert IC size
8. Qualified condition

An insert toolholder is specifically designed to match only one insert shape and size. Therefore, it is very important to choose the right insert toolholder for a particular job. There are **five factors** to be considered in selecting an insert toolholder. They are:

1. Holder style
2. Insert shape and size
3. Rake angle
4. Shank dimension
5. Hand type

The **lead angle** defines the style of the insert toolholder. The lead angle is also referred to as the side cutting edge angle. It is formed between the side cutting edge and one of the principal axis (Figure 2.17). **Three** types of lead angle are **negative lead angle, zero lead angle, and positive lead angle** (Figure 2.18 on page 2-23).

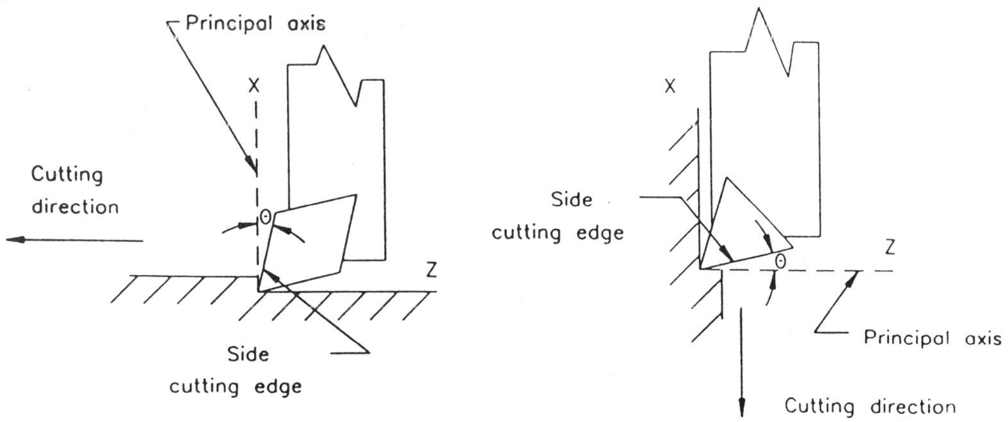

Figure 2.16 Definition of lead angles

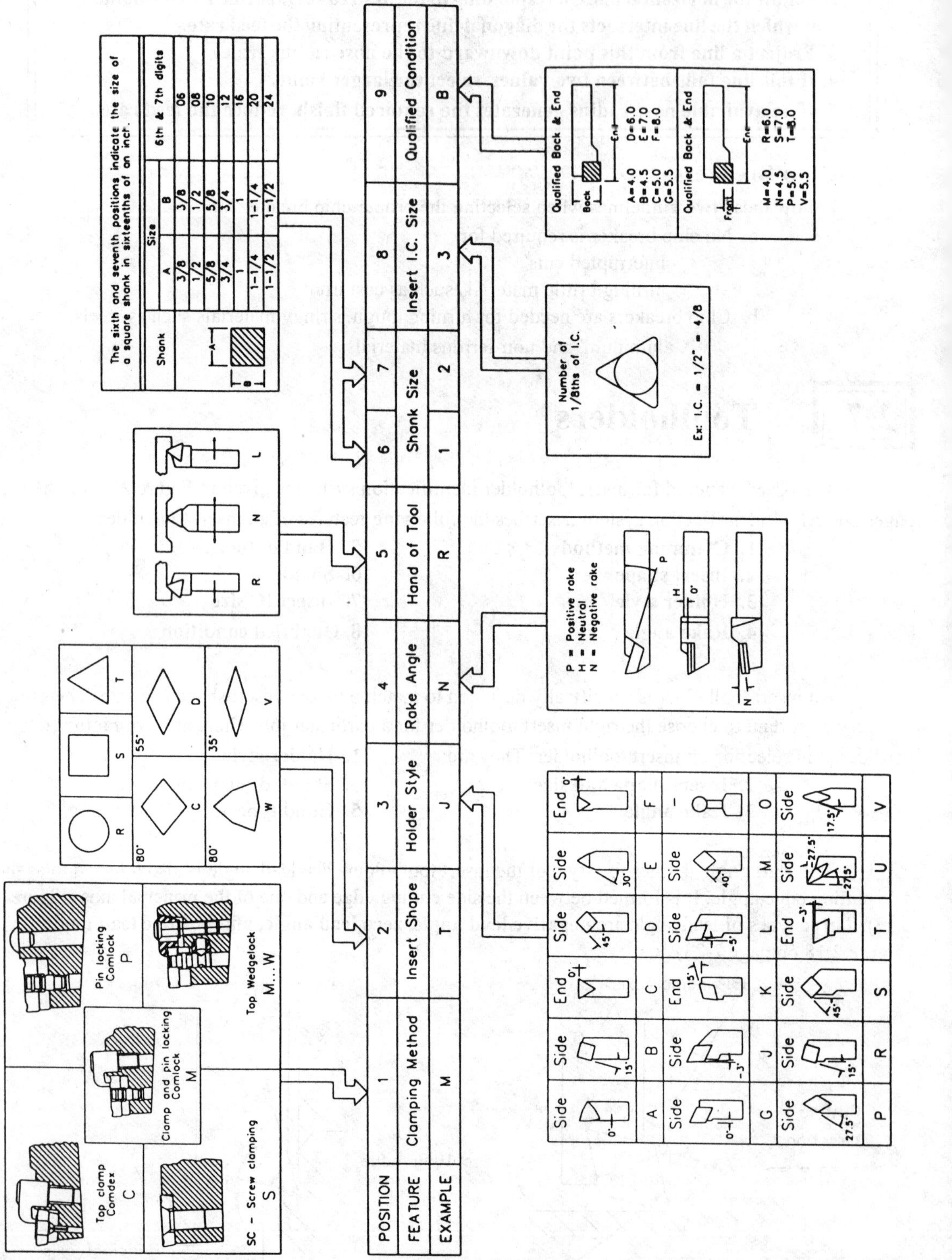

Figure 2.17 Insert toolholder identification system

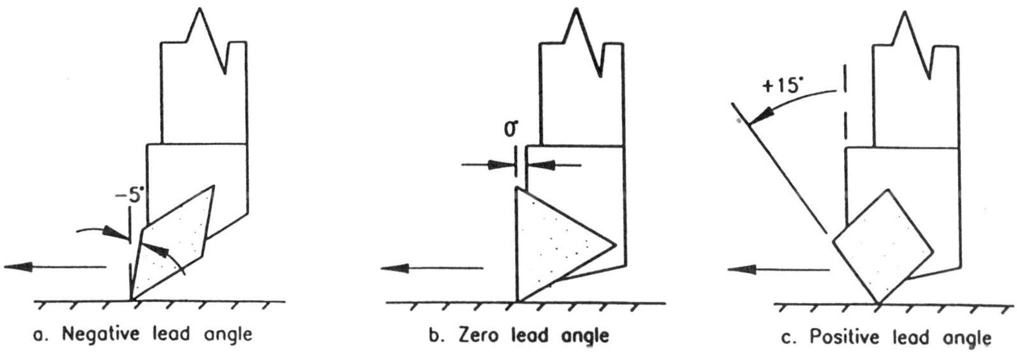

Figure 2.18 Three types of lead angles

The other important angle to be considered in selecting a toolholder type is the **profile** angle. The profile angle is the maximum slope angle that the combination of insert and toolholder can produce in profiling (Figure 2.19). A profile angle can be calculated from the following formula:

Profile angle = 90° + lead angle - insert angle

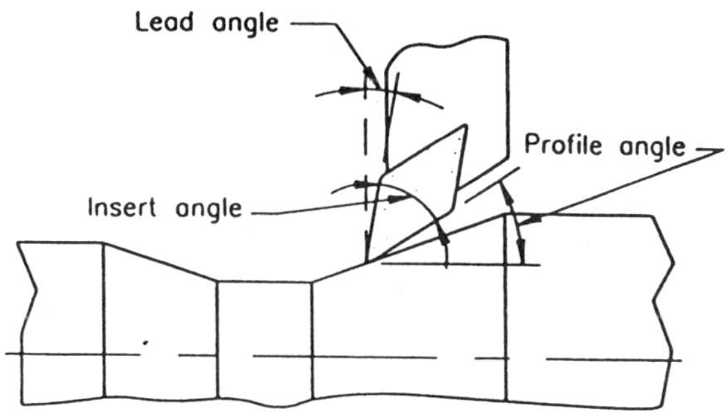

Figure 2.19

In practice, the maximum profile angle to be produced should be at least *2° smaller* than the computed profile angle.

Boring Bar Identification System

A boring bar identification system is actually very similar to that of regular toolholders. The main difference is that a bar composition code is added to the beginning of the identification codes. The bar composition indicates what materials are in the boring bar. Two common boring bar materials are **steel (S)** and **carbide (C)**. The sixth and seventh positions specify the cross section of the shank for regular toolholders, and they are used to represent the bar diameter for boring bars.

The selection of boring bars for specific applications depends on the following seven factors:

1. Bar composition
2. Boring bar style
3. Minimum bore diameter
4. Bar diameter
5. Insert shape and size
6. Hand type
7. Rake angle

Table 2.8 on the next two pages presents a list of combinations of toolholder styles and inserts commonly used in industry. Their typical applications are also included.

2.8 Machining Parameters

Three variables that dictate the efficiency of a machining process include **cutting speed, feed rate, and depth of cut**. These three variables are often referred to as machining parameters. The following factors should be carefully considered in selecting machining parameters:

- Operating capacity of the cutting tool
- Machine's available spindle horsepower
- Machinability of the workpiece material
- Rigidity of the part and fixture

Cutting Speed and Spindle Speed

Cutting speed, also called surface speed, refers to the speed at which the cutting edge of the tool passes over the surface of the workpiece. The cutting speed of a machining operation can be determined by the following two formulas:

$$CS = \frac{\pi \cdot D \cdot N}{12} \quad \text{(unit: FPM in inch units)}$$

$$CS = \frac{\pi \cdot D \cdot N}{1000} \quad \text{(unit: MPM in metric units)}$$

where CS = surface cutting speed, feet/minute (FPM) or meter/minute (MPM)
D = diameter of the rotating part, either the cutting tool or workpiece, in. or mm
N = RPM (rotation speed at which workpiece or cutter will turn)

In drilling (Figure 2.20) and milling (Figure 2.21), the diameter of the rotating part refers to the cutter diameter. In turning (Figure 2.22), the diameter represents the workpiece major diameter.

Table 2.8 Selection of Indexable Insert Holders

Operation Pattern	Holder Illustration	Holder Style	Insert Shape	Applications
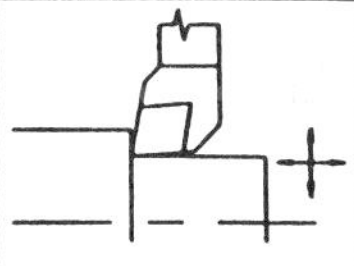	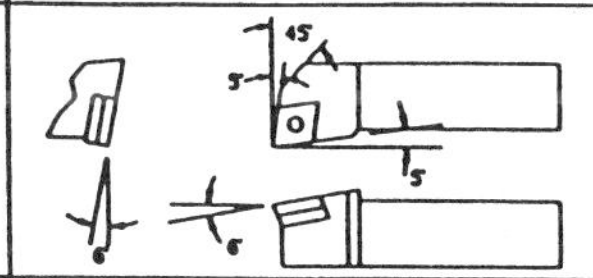	L -5°	C 80° diamond	• OD turning • Facing
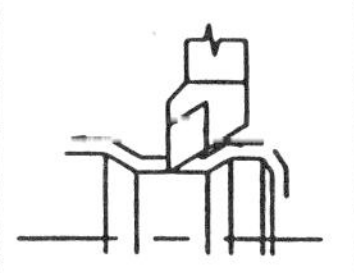	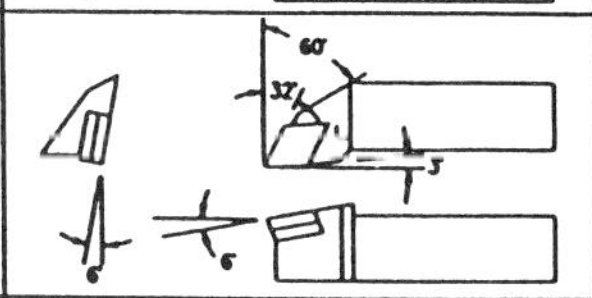	J -3°	D 55° diamond	• OD turning • Profiling with a max. of 30° profile angle
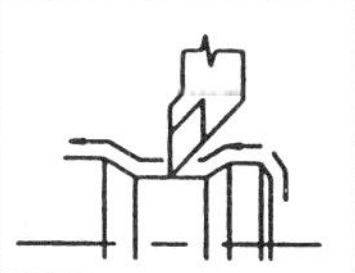	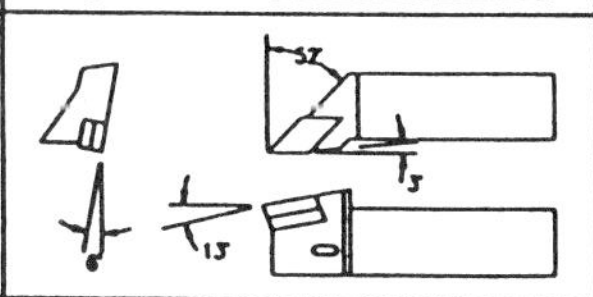	J -3°	V 35° diamond	• OD Profiling with a max. of 50° profile angle
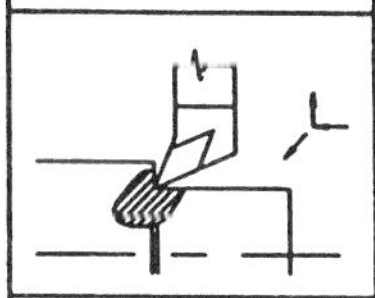	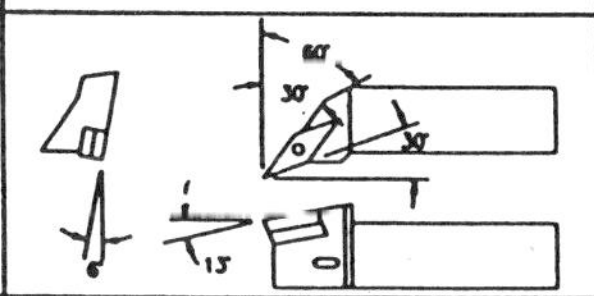	T	V 35° diamond	• Turning and undercutting
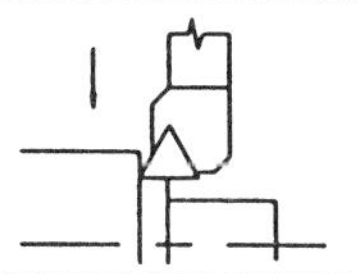	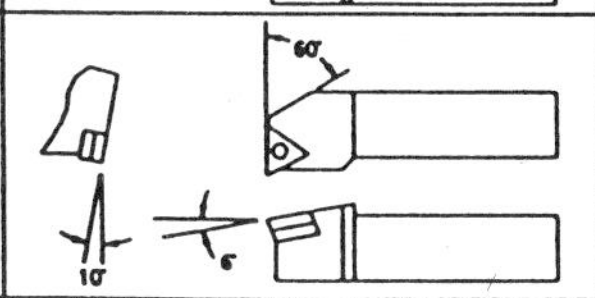	F 0°	T 60°	• Facing with square shoulder cutting
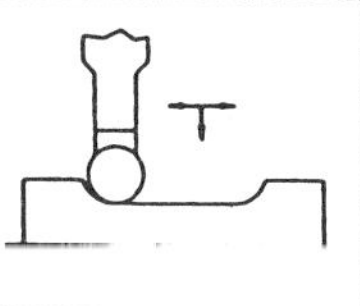	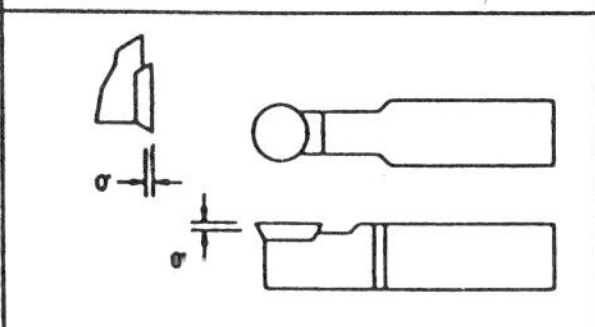	N	R round	• Profiling
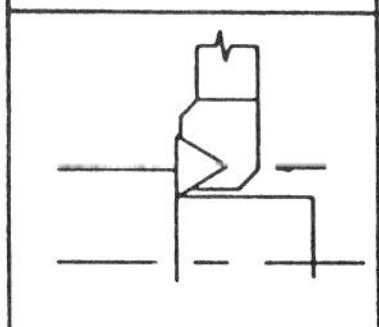	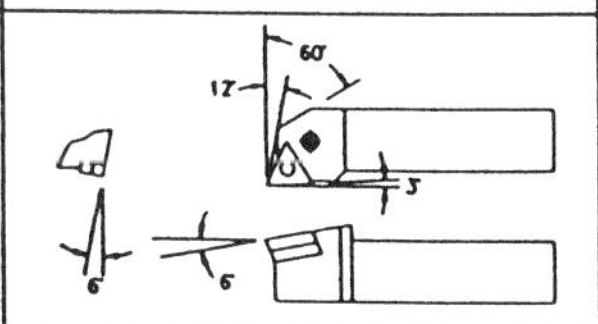	J -3°	T 60°	• OD turning with Square shoulder cutting
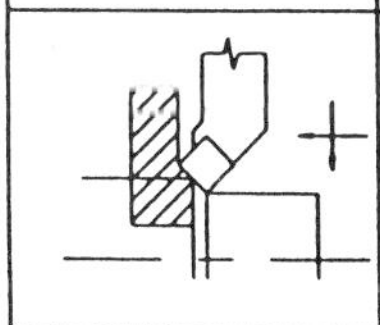	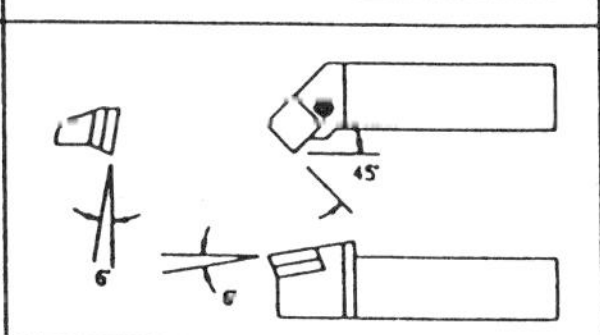	D 45°	T 90° square	• OD turning Facing
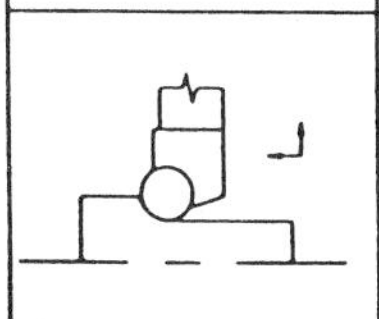	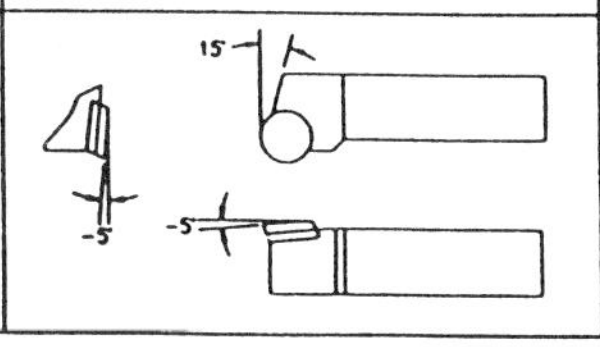	G 0°	R round	• OD turning Facing

Table 2.8 (Continued)

Operation Pattern	Holder Illustration	Holder Style	Insert Shape	Applications
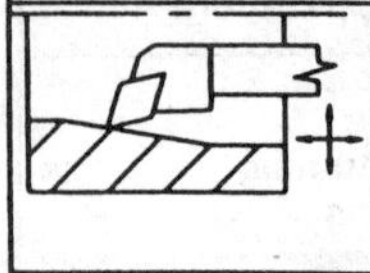	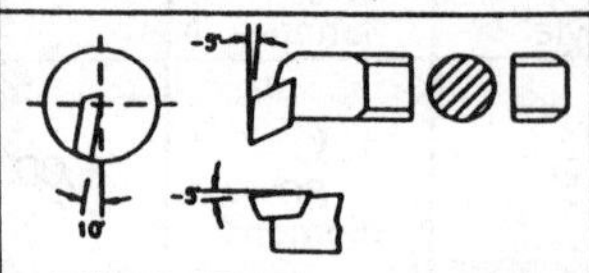	L −5°	C 80° diamond	• Straight surfaces and boring profiles positive
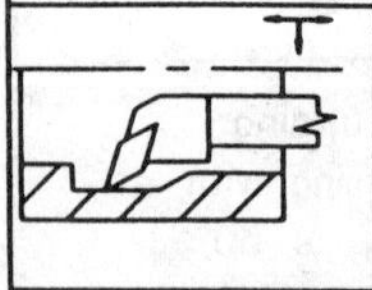	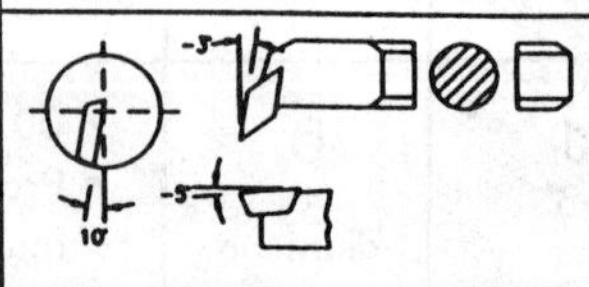	J −3°	D 55° diamond	• Boring internal profiles with the max. profile angle of 30°
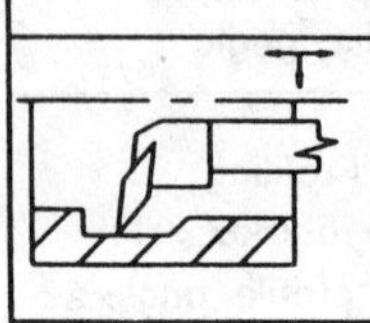	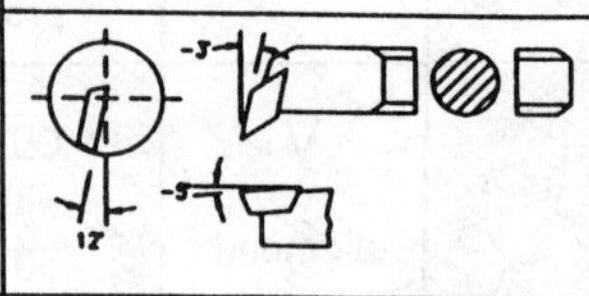	J −3°	V 35° diamond	• Boring internal profiles with the max. profile angle of 50°
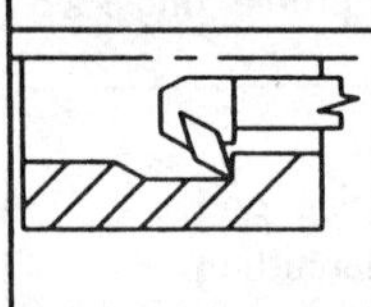	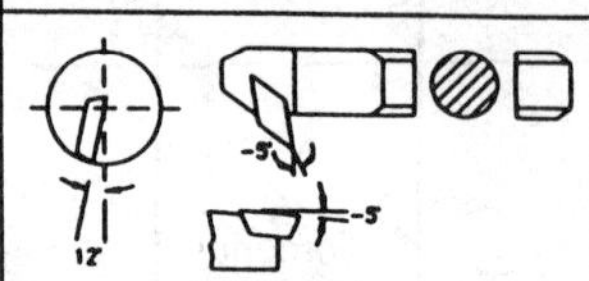	L −5°	V 35° diamond	• Back boring internal profiles
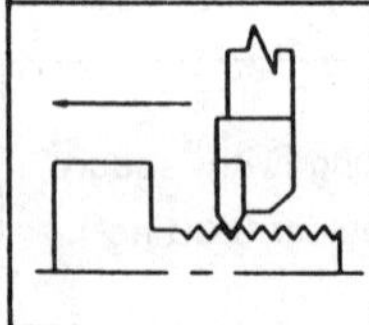	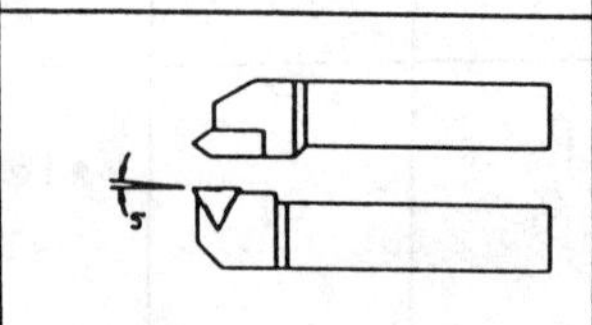	Vertical	Threading insert	• External threads cutting
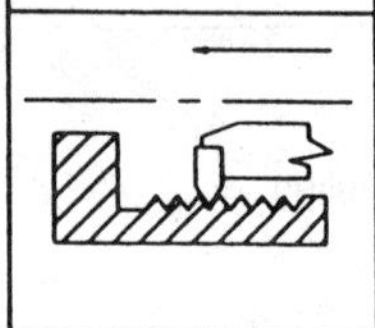	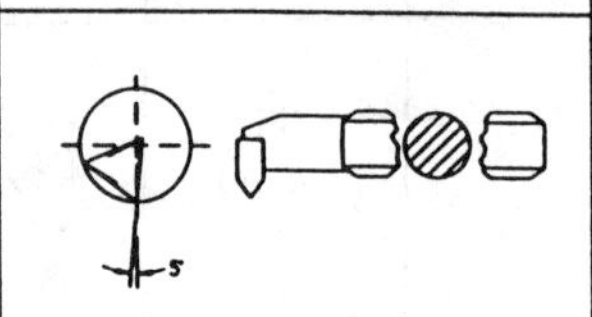	Horizontal	Threading insert	• Internal threads cutting
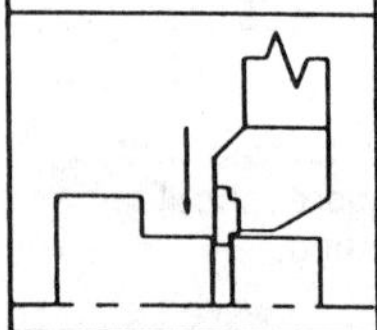	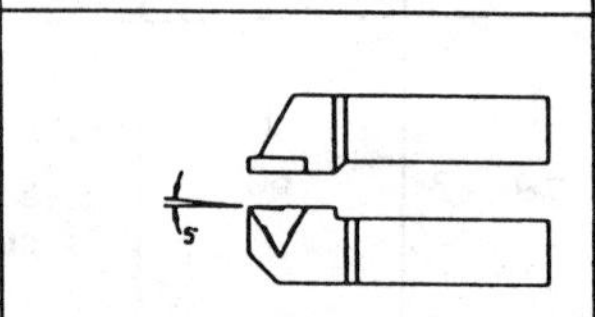	Vertical	Grooving insert	• External grooves cutting
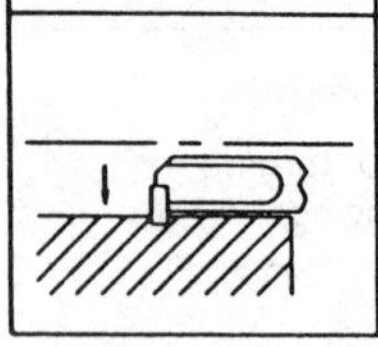	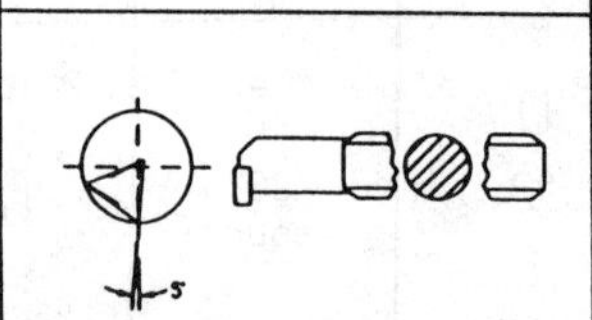	Horizontal	Grooving insert	• Internal grooves cutting

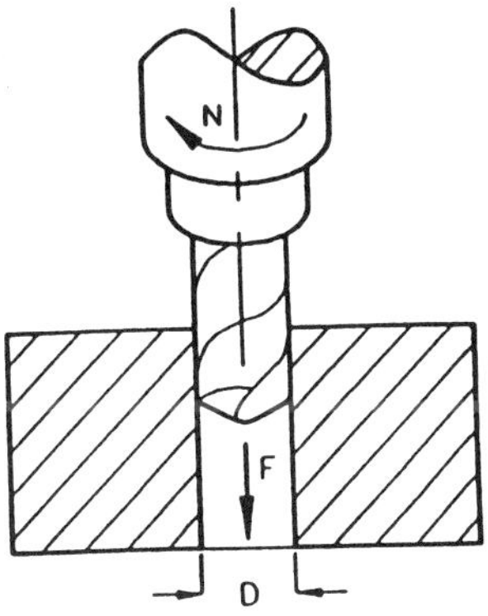

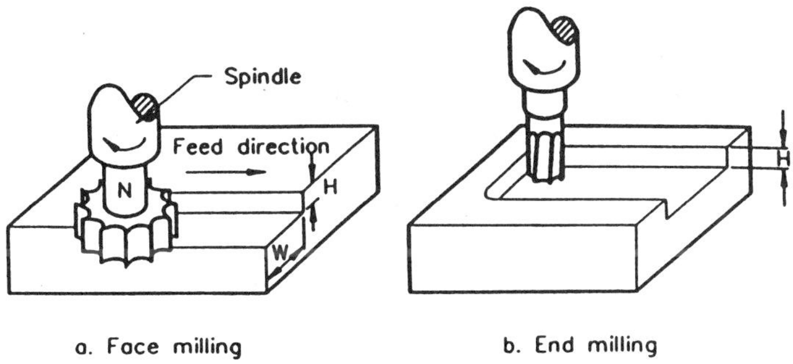

Figure 2.20 Drilling Figure 2.21 Milling
(Source: S.C. Jonathon Lin, Computer Numerical Control: From Programming to Networking, 1994. Courtesy of Delmar Publishers, Inc.)

The surface cutting speed at which a material is machined is a given quantity and is normally obtained from a machining data handbook or experience. We can use the given surface cutting speed value to find the spindle speed by rearranging the above two formulas as follows:

$$N = \frac{12 \cdot CS}{\pi \cdot D} \quad \text{(Inch unit)}$$

$$N = \frac{1000 \cdot CS}{\pi \cdot D} \quad \text{(Metric unit)}$$

where N = rotation speed in RPM

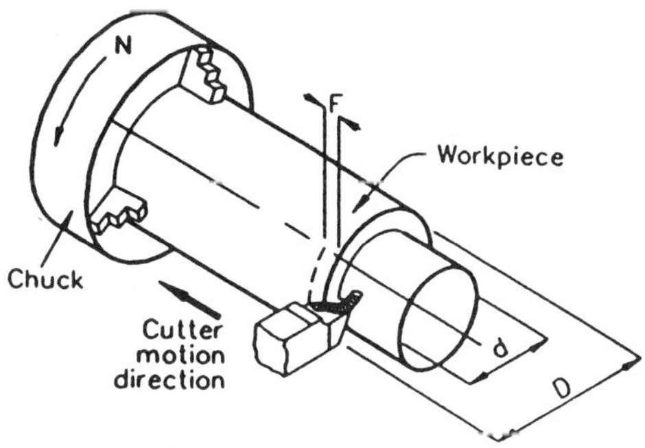

Figure 2.22 Turning (Source: S.C. Jonathon Lin, Computer Numerical Control: From Programming to Networking, 1994. Courtesy of Delmar Publishers, Inc.)

Feed Rate

The **feed** is the movement of the cutting tool in the cutting direction. The **feed rate** is the speed of feed that is normally specified by the following **three** units:

- **Feed per tooth, inches per tooth (IPT) or millimeters per tooth (MMPT)**
- **Feed per revolution, inches per revolution (IPR) or millimeters per revolution (MMPR)**
- **Feed per minute, inches per minute (IPM) or millimeters per minute (MMPM)**

The feed rate *recommended* by machining handbooks or cutting tool manufacturers is normally given in feed per tooth. However, the feed is *programmed* in the units of feed per revolution or feed per minute in NC machines.

The following three formulas can be used to convert the feed rate from feed per tooth to feed per revolution or feed per minute:

$$f_r = f_t \cdot T$$

$$f_m = f_r \cdot N$$

$$f_m = f_t \cdot T \cdot N$$

where f_r = feed per revolution (unit: IPR or MMPR)
f_t = feed per tooth (or flute) (unit: IPT or MMPT)
f_m = feed per minute (unit: IPM or MMPM)
T = number of teeth (or flutes) of the cutter
N = RPM

Depth of Cut

Depth of cut is the distance the cutter penetrates into the workpiece and is measured in the direction perpendicular to the cutter motion direction. The depth of cut is mainly determined by two factors: **available spindle horsepower and rigidity of cutter and machine.**

Material Removal Rate

The material removal rate refers to the amount of material removed per unit time. It is normally expressed in the units of **cubic inch per minute** or **cubic meter per minute**. The formulas to compute the material removal rate for three commonly used machining processes are given below:

1. **For Drilling** (see Figure 2.20):

$$MRR = \frac{\pi \cdot D^2 \cdot f_r \cdot N}{4}$$

where MRR = material removal rate, in^3/min.
D = drill diameter, inches
f_r = feed rate, IPR
N = spindle speed, RPM

2. **For Milling** (see Figure 2.21):

$$MRR = W \cdot H \cdot f_m$$

where W = width of cut, inches
H = depth of cut, inches
f_m = feed rate, inches/minute

3. **For Turning** (see Figure 2.22):

$$MRR = \frac{\pi \cdot (D^2 - d^2) \cdot f_r \cdot N}{4}$$

where D = original (major) diameter of workpiece
d = diameter after cut
f_r = feed (IPR)
N = revolutions per minute

Horsepower Requirement

It is important to know the required power for machining a workpiece under a set of machining conditions. The required horsepower in machining can not exceed the machine spindle power rating. The unit horsepower concept is widely used to calculate the required power for machining a workpiece. The amount of power needed to remove 1 cubic inch per minute of a certain material is called the **unit horsepower** (UHP). It is determined experimentally and is provided in tables for practical use.

The required horsepower can be obtained from the following formula:

$$HP_c = UHP \cdot MRR \cdot C$$

where HP_c − required horsepower at cutter
UHP = unit horsepower
MRR = material removal rate
C = feed correction factor

Tables 2.9 and 2.10 give the unit horsepower for drilling various materials. Tables 2.11 and 2.12 on the next page provide unit horsepower for milling, and turning operations, respectively.

Drill Size, in.	Feed, ipr										
	0.001	0.002	0.004	0.006	0.008	0.010	0.013	0.016	0.020	0.025	0.030
1/8	1.63	1.63	1.22	1.22							
1/4	1.43	1.32	1.17	1.02	0.94	0.86					
3/8	1.40	1.22	1.09	1.02	0.91	0.85					
1/2	1.38	1.07	1.03	0.98	0.86	0.83	0.78	0.75	0.71		
3/4	1.36	1.13	1.02	0.94	0.90	0.86	0.78	0.74	0.70		
1	1.27	1.08	0.99	0.89	0.83	0.82	0.74	0.72	0.70	0.66	
1 1/4	1.22	1.06	0.92	0.87	0.80	0.77	0.72	0.69	0.65	0.62	
1 1/2	1.24	1.02	0.88	0.83	0.78	0.74	0.70	0.67	0.62	0.59	
1 3/4	1.25	1.04	0.85	0.83	0.78	0.71	0.70	0.65	0.62	0.58	
2	1.18	0.99	0.88	0.80	0.76	0.70	0.66	0.64	0.61	0.57	0.55
2 1/2	—	—	—	—	0.71	0.67	0.63	0.61	0.54	0.56	0.53
3	—	—	—	—	—	—	—	0.61	0.57	0.52	0.52

Table 2.9 Unit horsepower required for drilling AISI 1112 steels (Source: S.C. Jonathon Lin, Computer Numerical Control: From Programming to Networking, 1994. Courtesy of Delmar Publishers, Inc.)

Table 2.10 Approximate conversion factor for unit horsepower required to drill other materials (Source: S.C. Jonathon Lin, Computer Numerical Control: From Programming to Networking, 1994. Courtesy of Delmar Publishers, Inc.)

Material	Factor
AISI 1020	1.6
AISI 1035	1.3
1.99% C Tool Steel	1.7
AISI 3150	1.6
Gray Cast Iron	0.5
Malleable Iron	0.6
Stainless Steel	
AISI 416 free-machining martensitic	1.2
AISI 303 free-machining austenitic	1.6
AISI 304 austenitic	1.8
17-7 PH precipitation-hardened austenitic	2.0
4340 Steel heat-treated to 240,000-260,000 psi	2.3

Material	UHP	Material	UHP
Magnesium	0.25	Stainless	
Aluminum	0.25	Free machining	1.0
Copper	0.5	Other	1.7
Brass	0.4	Titanium	
Bronze	0.5	Under 100,000 psi	1.3
Malleable iron	1.0	100,000–135,000 psi	1.7
Cast iron		135,000 and over	2.5
Ferrite	0.7	High–tensile alloys	
Pearlitic	1.0	180,000–220,000 psi	2.0
Chilled	0.7	220,000–260,000 psi	2.5
Steel		260,000–300,000 psi	3.3
Up to 150 BHN	1.4	High–temperature alloys	
300 BHN	1.7	Ferritic low alloys	1.7
400 BHN	2.0	Austenitic alloys	2.0
500 BHN	2.5	Nickel–based alloys	2.5
		Cobalt–based alloys	2.5

Table 2.11 Unit horsepower for milling

(Source: S.C. Jonathon Lin, Computer Numerical Control: From Programming to Networking, 1994. Courtesy of Delmar Publishers, Inc.)

(a) Ferrous Metals and Alloys

Materials	BHN					
	150–175	176–200	201–250	251–300	301–350	351–400
	Unit Horsepower (UHP)					
AISI						
1010–1025	0.58	0.67				
1030–1055	0.58	0.67	0.80	0.96		
1060–1095			0.75	0.88	1.00	
1112–1120	0.50					
1314–1340	0.42	0.46	0.50			
1330–1350		0.67	0.75	0.92	1.10	
2015–2115	0.67					
2315–2335	0.54	0.58	0.62	0.75	0.92	
2340–2350		0.50	0.58	0.70	0.83	1.00
2512–2515	0.50	0.58	0.67	0.80	0.92	
3115–3130	0.50	0.58	0.70	0.83	1.00	
3160–3450		0.50	0.62	0.75	0.87	1.00
4130–4345		0.46	0.58	0.70	0.83	1.00
4615–4820	0.46	0.50	0.58	0.70	0.83	0.87
5120–5150	0.46	0.50	0.62	0.75	0.87	1.00
52100		0.58	0.67	0.83	1.00	
6115–6140	0.46	0.54	0.67	0.83	1.00	
6145–6195		0.70	0.83	1.00	1.20	1.30
Plain cast iron	0.30	0.33	0.42	0.50		
Alloy cast iron	0.30	0.42	0.52			
Malleable cast iron	0.42					
Cast steel	0.62	0.67	0.80			

(b) High–Temperature Alloys

Material	BHN	UHP	Material	BHN	UHP	Material	BHN	UHP
A286	165	0.82	Hastelloy B	230	1.10	Ti–150A	340	0.65
A286	285	0.93	Inco 700	300	1.12	U–500	375	1.10
Chromoloy	200	0.78	Inco 702	230	1.10	4340	200	0.78
Chromoloy	310	1.18	M–252	230	1.10	4340	340	0.93
			M–252	310	1.20			

(c) Nonferrous Metals and Alloys

Material	UHP	Material	UHP	Material	UHP
Brass		Bronze		Aluminum	
Hard	0.83	Hard	0.83	Cast	0.25
Medium	0.50	Med.	0.50	Hard	0.33
Soft	0.33	Soft	0.33	Monel	1.00
Free–machining	0.25	Copper	0.90	Zinc(die cost)	0.25

Table 2.12 Unit horsepower for turning various materials

(Source: S.C. Jonathon Lin, Computer Numerical Control: From Programming to Networking, 1994. Courtesy of Delmar Publishers, Inc.)

The feed correction factor C is used to compensate for the effect of feed on horsepower because **high** feed rates require **less** unit horsepower. Figure 2.23 shows the feed correction factors.

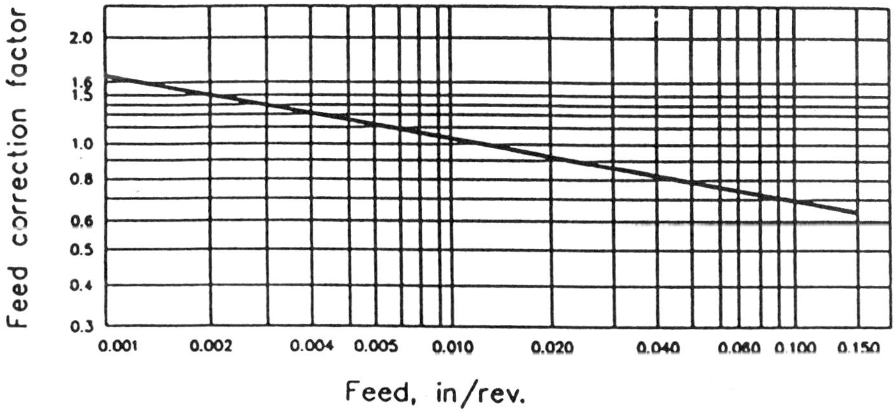

Adjustment for lead angle as follows:

If tool cuts with a lead angle of	Reduce the actual feed by this amount and use the feed correction factor for the finer feed
30°	10%
45°	30%
60°	50%
If the depth of cut is less than the nose radius	30%

Figure 2.23 Feed conversion factor
(Source: Application Data Manual, Courtesy of Carboloy Inc., a Seco Tools Company)

The efficiency of the machine must be considered when calculating the required horsepower because power is needed to overcome friction in the machine. The formula for calculating the required horsepower at the spindle motor is:

$$HP_m = \frac{HP_c}{E}$$

where HP_m = required horsepower at the spindle motor
E = machine efficiency

2.9 Face Milling

Face milling is normally used in two situations:

1. where a large amount of material must be removed in a short period of time
2. a good surface finishing is required.

Cutter Size

When possible, use a larger effective diameter to shorten the machining time. The larger the flat surface to be machined, the larger the effective diameter should be used.

The cutter height determines the allowable maximum depth of cut. The depth of cut should be smaller than the cutter height.

Cutting Width Selection

The selection of cutting width is dictated by two considerations, **tool life and machining efficiency**. The *larger* the cutting width, the *shorter* the tool life and the *better* the machining efficiency. Cutting width must be chosen in such a way that it produces efficient machining, yet tool life is not significantly sacrificed. The engage angle, the angle between the initial contact point and the exit point (Figure 2.24), is often used to relate the cutting width to tool life.

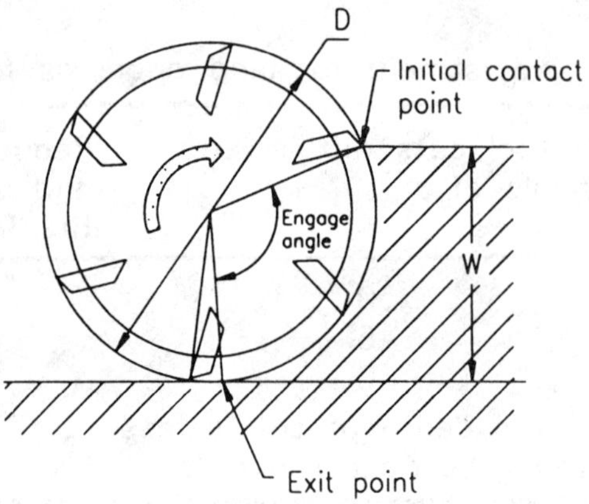

Figure 2.24 Engage angle

Figure 2.25 shows the relationship between the **ratio of W/D to the engage angle.** The engage angle ranges from 0 to 180° depending on the amount of cutting width. The engage angle is 180° for W/D = 1, and 90° for W/D = 0.5.

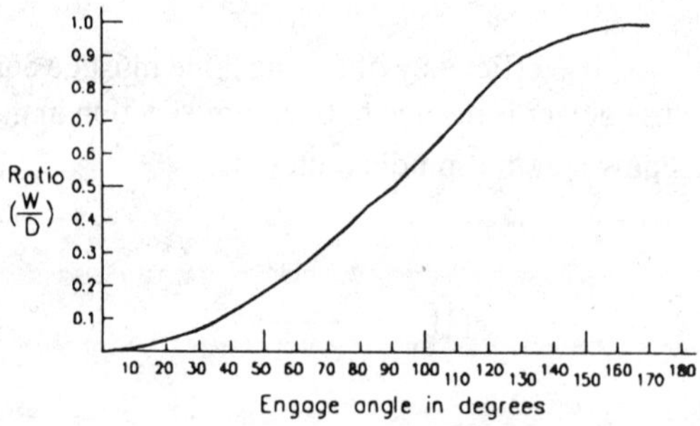

Figure 2.25

Figure 2.26 shows how the engage angle affects the tool life. Tool life decreases drastically after the engage angle exceeding 105°. Also, note that the relationship between the tool life and the engage angle varies from one material to another.

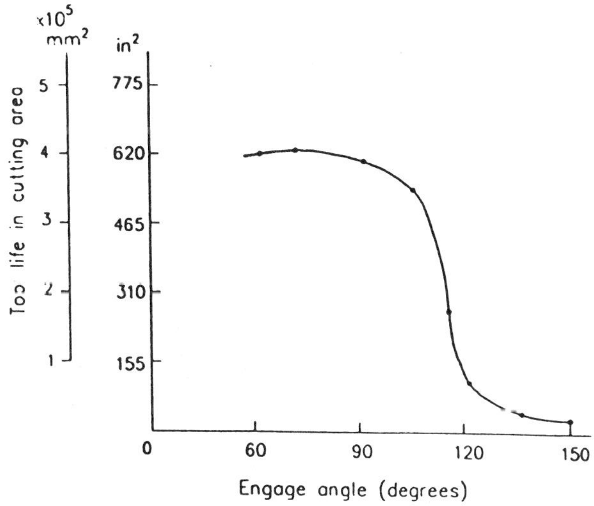

Figure 2.26

The following two rules are used to determine the maximum cutting width in face milling:

W = (.6) D (for face milling steels)

W = (.75) D (for face milling cast irons)

where W = cutting width
D = diameter of face mill

The maximum depth of cut for most face milling operations is **0.1 in.** and the feed rate is approximately **0.001 - 0.01 in./revolution.**

2.10 End Milling

End mills can be used to perform five types of operations: plunge milling, peripheral shoulder milling, slot milling, pocket milling, and profile milling (Table 2.13) on the next page.

Table 2.13 End Milling Operations

Operation Type	Features	Application	Illustration
1. Plunge milling	Repeatly plunges to a predetermined depth retracts, then advances and plunges again. The maximum cutting force acts in the axial (Z) direction where the machine is strongest.	Rapidly remove large quantity of material.	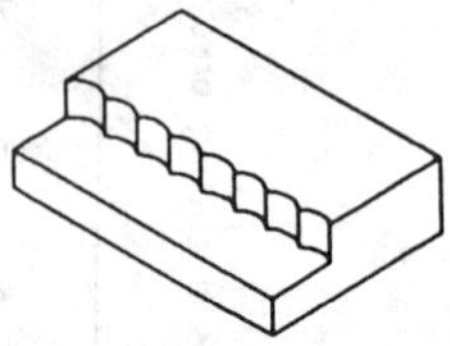
2. Peripheral shoulder milling	Uses end mill's to produce side edges shoulders or steps.	The maximum width of cutter engagement is 3D/4 where D is the cutter diameter.	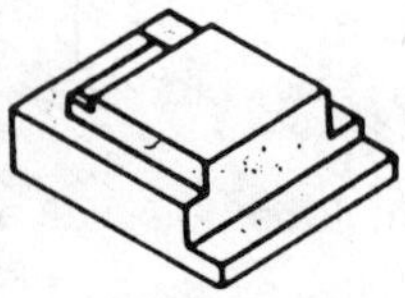
3. slot milling	Uses cutter's side edges to produce blind slot and through slot.	To cut various forms of slots.	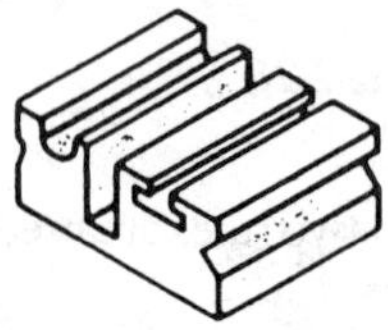
4. Pocket milling	Takes a zig zag or spiral out pattern of cuts in sequence.	To produce a deep cavity.	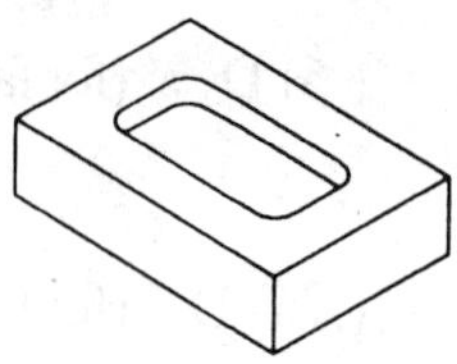
5. Profile milling	Takes the cutter along a predetermined contour.	To machine part profiles that consist of a series of lines and arcs.	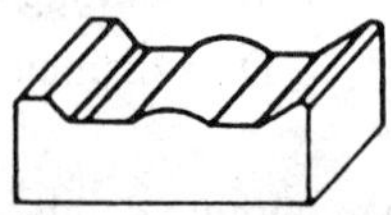

End Mills Selection

End mills are made in various forms, configurations, number of flutes, and end face center types. End mills are available in three forms: **solid end mills, carbide-tipped end mills and indexed inserts.** Solid end mills are made from high speed steel or sintered carbide. They are double or single ended. Carbide-tipped end mills have carbide inserts brazed on the tool body to form the cutting edges. In CNC applications, the end mills with indexed inserts are the most widely used.

End mills are made in a variety of configurations including straight end mills for general purpose applications, waved-formed end mills for roughing operation, ball end mills for machining dies, molds, and surfaces, and shell end mills for producing deep slots, shoulders, or profiles (Figure 2.27 on the next page)

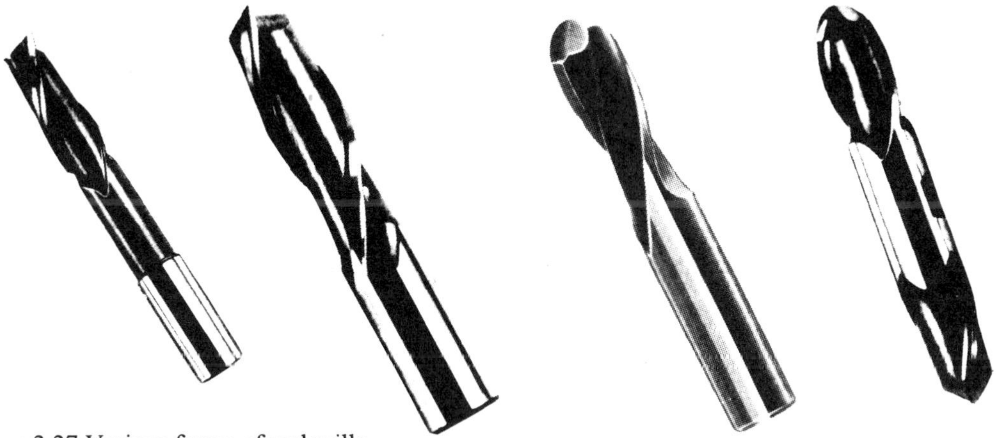

Figure 2.27 Various forms of end mills

End mills have two, three, four, or more flutes to allow for the removal of chips. The fewer the number of flutes means the bigger the cutting pocket.

The end face center of an end mill can be made as either a cutting type or hole type. End mills with a **center cutting** type, have one or two end-cutting edges extending past the center of the cutter (Figure 2.28) so that they can be used for plunging purposes. With the **center hole** type (Figure 2.29), no end-cutting edge is extended to the center of the cutter, therefore, they can not be used to perform plunging operations.

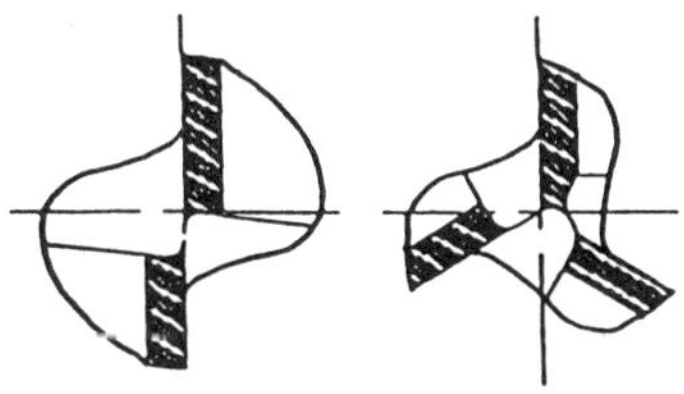

Figure 2.28 Center cutting type

Figure 2.29 Center hole type

The following criteria are used to select end mills for a particular application:

1. **Use end mills with 30° helical angle for general applications. Use 40°-45° helical angle and 15° of axial helical angle at the end face to perform heavy cuttings.**
2. **Use end mills with waved-shaped cutting edges for roughing cuts to obtain rapid metal removal.**
3. **Select end mills with a smaller number of flutes for roughing cuts because they provide larger cutting pockets. Tools with a larger number of flutes are used for finishing cuts.**
4. **Choose tools with the end face of center cutting type for cutting involving plunging. Tools with the end face of center hole type can perform only side cutting.**

The **width of cut** for end milling operations affects the tool life. The maximum width of cut is 75 percent of the cutter diameter (or 3D/4).

2.11 Milling with Ball End Mills

A ball end mill, also known as spherical end mill or ball nose end mill, has a semi-sphere at the tool end. Ball end mills are used extensively in the machining of dies, molds, and workpieces with complex surfaces in the automotive, aerospace, and defense industries.

Effective diameter is the main factor used in the calculation of the required spindle speed. Effective diameter is defined as the **actual diameter of the cutter at the axial depth-of-cut line** (Figure 2.30). The effective diameter is affected by two parameters: **tool radius and axial depth of cut**.

The effective diameter can be calculated from:

$$D_E = 2[R^2-(R-H)^2]^{1/2}$$

where D_E = effective diameter
R = tool radius
H = axial depth of cut

The **effective** radius replaces the cutter radius when calculating the cutting speed for ball end milling. The formula becomes:

$$CS = \frac{\pi \cdot D_E \cdot N}{12}$$

where D_E = effective diameter (in.)
CS = cutting speed (feet/minute)
N = rotation speed (revolution/minute)

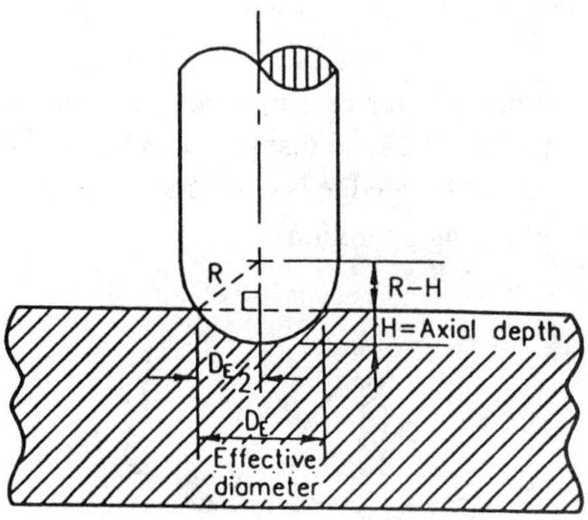

Figure 2.30

When a cutter with a non-flat end, such as a ball end mill, is used to cut a surface in a zigzag pattern, an uncut strip is created between the two cutting passes (Figure 2.31). The height of these undesirable strips is called cusp height.

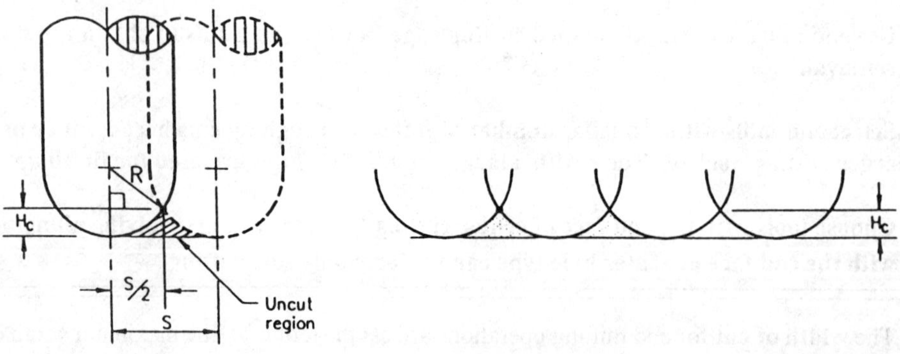

Figure 2.31

The cusp height can be calculated from

$$H_C = R - [R^2 - (S/2)^2]^{1/2}$$

or

$$S = 2[R^2 - (R - H_C)^2]^{1/2}$$

where H_c = cusp height (in.)
R = tool nose radius (in.)
S = stepover value between two cutting passes (in.)

2.12 Drilling Operations

Drilling is the process to produce holes or enlarge existing holes. Commonly used drilling operations include drilling, center drilling, countersinking, and counterboring.

Factors to Be Considered in Drilling

1. Initial condition of holes:

The initial state of holes may have one of three forms:

- Casted holes or forged holes in which rough hole dimension has been formed. These holes can be produced by using a correct-size drill or a two-flute end mill
- Pre-drilled holes in which holes, normally of large diameter, have been drilled by a small drill. The final drilling is done by using a correct size of drill.
- Blank stock. Drilling holes on blank stock may require using more than one drill depending on the size, accuracy, and surface roughness of the holes.

2. Required accuracy of holes

Drilling tends to produce oversized holes with a dislocation of hole centers. Hole oversize and runout are two parameters in measuring the hole accuracy. When the required accuracy of hole, with respect to diameter and runout, is within ±0.005 in., a center drilling is required to locate the hole center.

3. Hole size

The hole **diameter** decides the number of drillings required to produce the hole. Generally speaking, a 1 in. diameter is used as the critical dimension. Only one drilling is required for any hole size that is smaller than **1 in.** of diameter. To drill a 1¼ in. hole, for example, requires two drillings, first drilling with a 3/8 in. drill and then a final drilling with 1¼ in. drill to produce the finished size.

4. Hole depth

Only one drilling pass is required to drill shallow holes. As the depth of hole **increases**, peck drilling is used to clear chips and avoid packing. Peck drilling is recommended when the depth of hole is greater than three to four times the diameter of drills. The distance (depth) of each peck ranges from ½ to 1½ times the drill diameter,depending upon the chip formation and rate of drill breakage encountered.

Note: that the cutting speed and feed rate for drilling deep holes should be reduced according to the ratio of hole depth to drill diameter.

Safety, drill lip, and penetration distance

In drilling with NC machines, the tool moves rapidly to the reference level (**R**) and then feeds into the workpiece until it reaches the hole bottom. **Three** distances should be carefully determined to optimize NC use: **safety, drill lip, and penetration distance** (Figure 2.32).

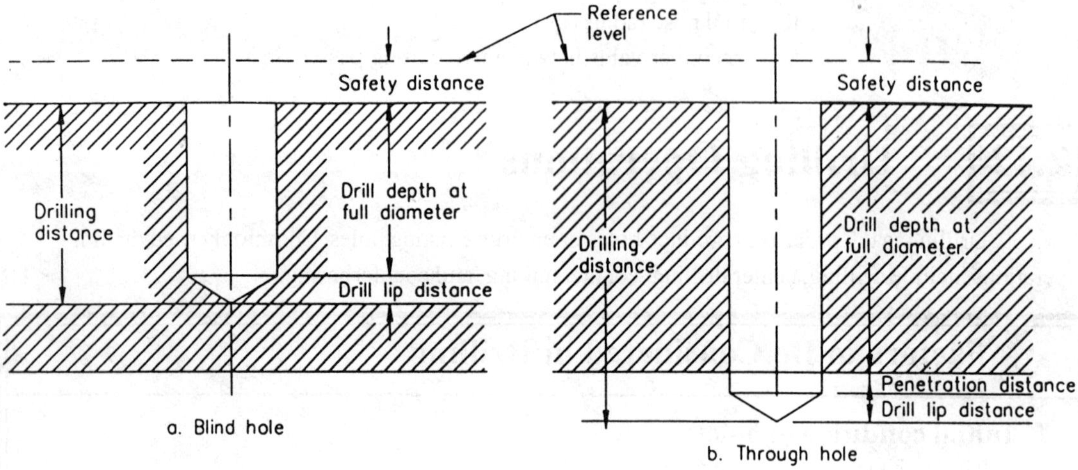

Figure 2.32 Drilling distances

Safety distance

The safety distance is measured from the reference (R) level to the work surface and should be as short as possible to increase NC efficiency. The safety distance is determined by the surface condition of the workpiece and is calculated as follows:

$$L_S = 0.15 \text{ in. (or 4 mm)} \text{ for flat casted, and machined surfaces}$$

$$L_S = 0.2 \text{ in. (or 5 mm)} \text{ for rough surfaces}$$

Drill lip distance

The drill point angle is generally ground to 118° or 59° on each side of the center line. The drill lip distance can be calculated from:

$$L_L = \frac{D}{2(\tan 59°)}$$

or $L_L = 0.3\ D$

where D = drill diameter (in. or mm)
L_L = drill lip distance (in. or mm)

Penetration distance

Penetration distance is the allowance that permits the drill to move to extra depth to remove the burs produced during the time when the drill penetrated through the hole. Generally speaking, the penetration distance is equal to the safety distance that is:

L_P = 0.15 in. (or 4 mm) for flat casted, and machined surfaces

L_P = 0.2 in. (or 5 mm) for rough surfaces

The drilling distance of a blind hole consists of **three** components: **safety distance, depth at full diameter, and depth of drill lip** (Figure 2.32a).

$$L = L_S + L_D + L_L$$

where L = drilling distance
L_S = safety distance
L_D = drill depth at full diameter
L_L = depth of drill lip

The drilling distance for a through hole is the sum of **four** components (Figure 2.32b) and can be found from:

$$L = L_S + L_D + L_P + L_L$$

where L_D = depth of hole

L_P = penetration distance

2.13 Boring Operations

Boring is a precision machining process for producing internal holes by removing metal with single-point tools or tools with multiple cutting edges. Common applications for boring include the enlarging or finishing of existing holes that were drilled, pierced, casted, or forged. Boring operations can be of **two** categories; **single-stage** (Figure 2.33) **and multiple-stage** (Figure 2.34).

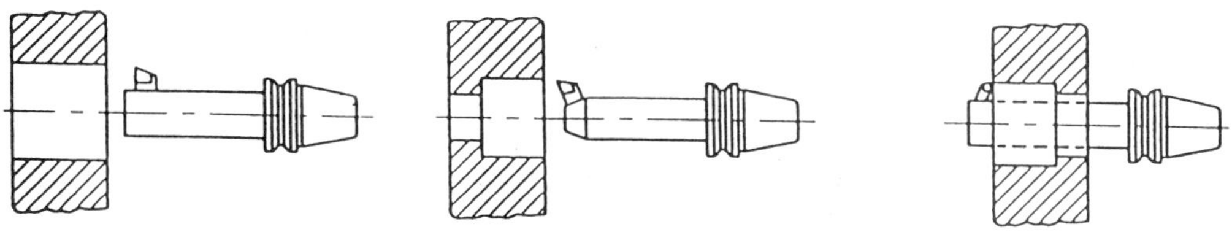

a. through hole b. Blind hole c Back hole

Figures 2.33 Single stage boring operations

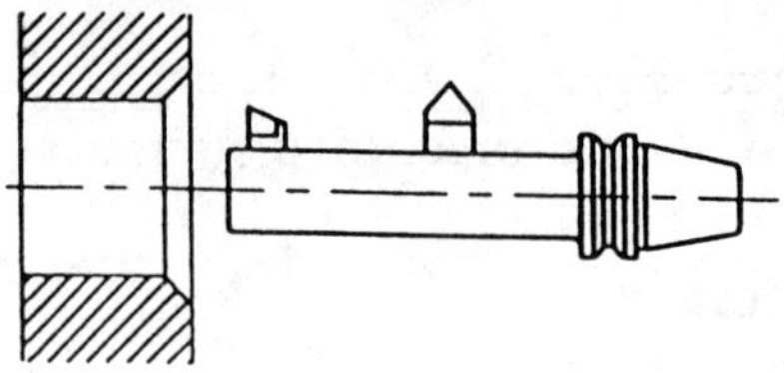

a. Boring and chamfering

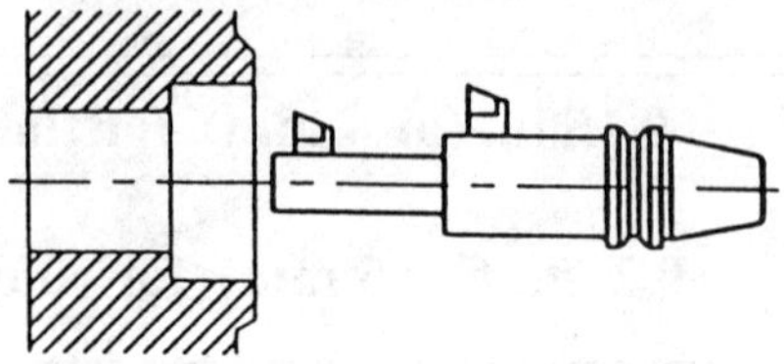

b. Boring two-step hole

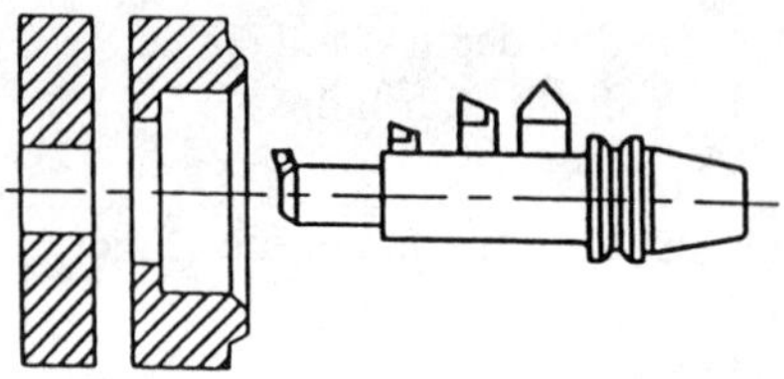

c. Boring three-step hole and chamfering

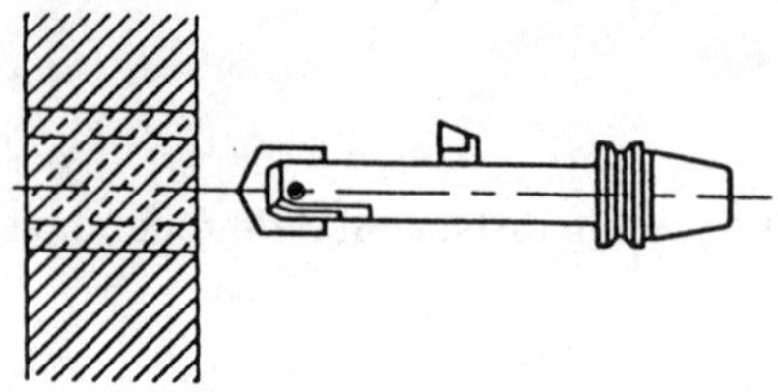

d. Spade drilling and boring

Figure 2.34 Multiple stage boring operations

Boring bars are made of various sizes and types. The most common type is the single-stage boring bar that is a round boring bar with one cutting edge mounted at the end of the bar to perform a single-diameter boring operation. The ratio of length to diameter of the shank (L/D) is the main measure of the boring capability for a boring bar. As a general rule, a L/D ratio of 4 - 5 would provide a stable machining under normal boring conditions. Chatter may occur when this ratio is larger than 5. Actually, chatter results from the deflection of the boring bar that is subjected to the cutting resistant force. The larger the cutting resistant force, the larger the deflection results. In some critical applications, this deflection must be kept within an allowable limit.

Selection of Feed and Depth of Cut

The selection of feed and depth of cut depends on the following factors:

1. Deflection should not exceed 0.001 in. (or 0.02 mm).

2. Use the formula, $F = (8HR)^{1/2}$
to determine the feed for the required surface roughness,
where H = surface roughness (in.),
R = tool nose radius (in.)
F = feed (in./rev).

3. Depth of cut for rough borings ranges from 0.04 - 0.24 in. (1 - 6 mm).
Use 0.02 - 0.04 in. (0.5 - 1 mm) for finish borings.

2.14 Tapping Operations

Tapping is a process of using a tap to produce internal threads in existing holes by a combination of axial and rotary motions. CNC milling machines use hand taps, spiral-pointed taps, spiral-fluted taps, and metric taps for cutting straight threads.

Tap selection

Several types of taps are used in CNC machines to produce internal threads. Table 2.14 on the next page summarizes various tap types and their applications.

Tap drill selection

A tap drill is used to produce the minor diameter of the internal threads. The percentage of thread engagement, or thread height, is an important factor in determining the tap drill size. Figure 2.35 illustrates the definition of thread height percentage. Table 2.15 gives a range of thread height percentage for general applications of classes 1B and 2B.

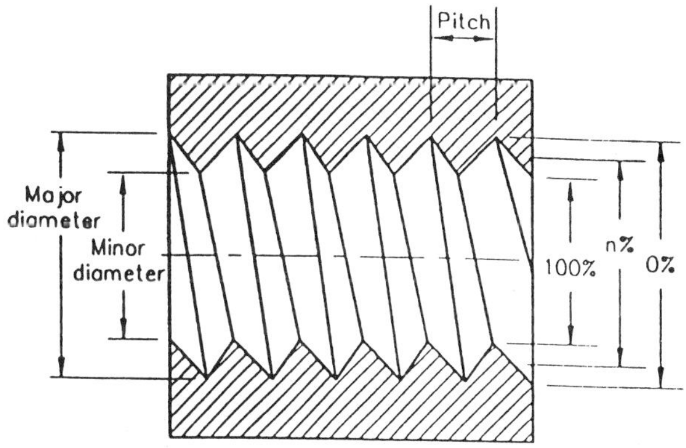

Figure 2.35

Table 2.15 Thread height percentages for various thread sizes

Thread Size	Thread Height, %
#0 to #12	53 to 65
1/4 to 1/2"	64 to 66.5
1/2 to 1"	64 to 67
1 to 2"	66 to 71

Note that the **tougher** the material, the less percentage of thread should be produced. The **closer** the tolerance, the greater percentage of thread is required.

The tap hole diameter can be roughly calculated by the formula:

$$D = D_M - P$$

where D = tap hole diameter
D_M = tap major diameter
P = thread pitch

Table 2.14 Tap Types and Their Applications

Tap Type	Feature	Application	Illustration
A. Hand Tap			
1. Taper Tap	Having first 8 to 10 threads chamfered.	For starting the threads in a deep hole or for tapping through holes.	
2. Plug Tap	Having a 3 to 5 thread chamfer length.	Tapping through holes, general tapping application.	
3. Bottoming Tap	Having only 1 thread chamfer length.	Tapping blind holes where limited lengths of imperfect threads are allowed. They should be used only a taper or plug tap has been used to thread a blind hole as far as possible.	
B. Spiral–pointed tap	Having a left–hand spiral flute at the point to force the chips ahead of the tap. More rigid than conventional taps. Low cutting resistance.	Tapping short through holes in mild steel and stainless steel where chips do not easily break. Produce high precision threads.	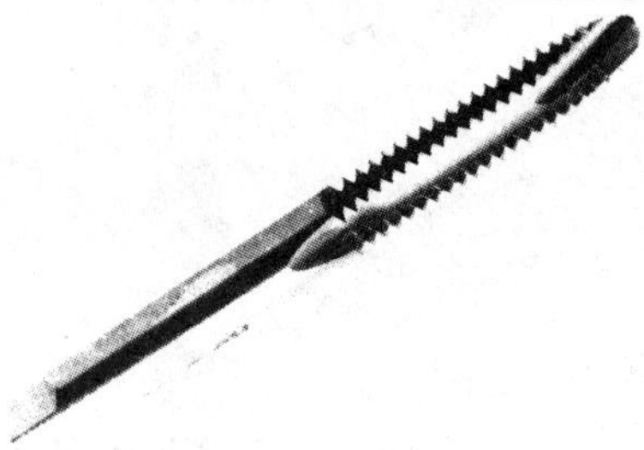
C. Spiral–fluted taps			
1. Spiral–flute taps	Having right hand helical flutes with a helix angle ranging from 25° to 35° to increase lifting action in ejecting chips backward.	Tapping blind holes where chips have to be ejected backward through the open end of the hole.	
2. Fast spiral–flute taps	45°–60° helix angle to increase lifting action in ejecting chips backward.	Tapping deep blind holes in materials that produce long curling chips.	

The following formulas are used to calculate the tap drill size when the thread height percentage is considered:

Unified Threads:

$$D = D_M - \frac{2 \cdot H \cdot Q}{100}$$

$$H = 0.6495\ P$$

$$P = 1/N$$

or $$D = D_M - 0.01299 \times (Q/N)$$

where D = tap drill size (diameter)
D_M = major diameter of tap (threads)
H = thread height
P = thread pitch
Q = thread height percentage
N = number of threads per in.

Metric threads:

$$D = D_M - \frac{2 \cdot H \cdot Q}{100}$$

$$H = 0.6403\ P$$

or $$D = D_M - 0.01281\ P \cdot Q$$

Depth of tap holes

The depth of tap holes must be deep enough to allow the tap to produce threads to the desired depth. In tapping blind holes, the depth of holes is the sum of the **four** distances: **thread length, deceleration length, clearance length, and drill tip length** (Figure 2.36).

$$L = L_l + L_d + L_c + L_t$$

$$L_t = 0.3\ D$$

where L = depth of tap hole
L_l = thread length
L_d = deceleration length (1 -2 thread pitch)
L_c = clearance length (0.5 thread pitch)
L_t = drill tip length
D = tap drill diameter

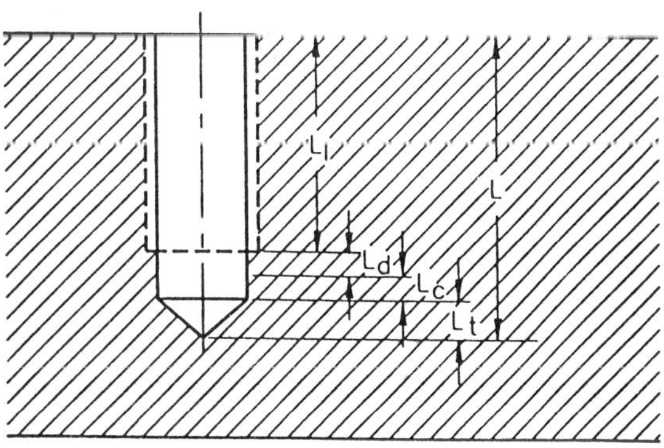

Figure 2.36

2.15 Turning Operation

Turning is an important machining process for producing external and internal profiles and surfaces on a turning machine. Several important factors should be considered in turning operation are presented in this section. They include **feed selection, depth of cut, error resulting from off center of the cutter, and chip breaker.**

Feed selection and surface roughness

Feed is one of important factors in determining the machining efficiency. The selection of feed for turning is mainly governed by the required surface roughness. The theoretical formula for calculating the roughness is: (Figure 2.37):

$$H = R - (R^2 - (F/2)^2)^{1/2}$$

where H = surface roughness (in. or mm)
R = tool nose radius (in. or mm)
F = feed (in./rev or mm/rev)

This equation can be expanded as:

$$H^2 - 2RH = -F^2/4$$

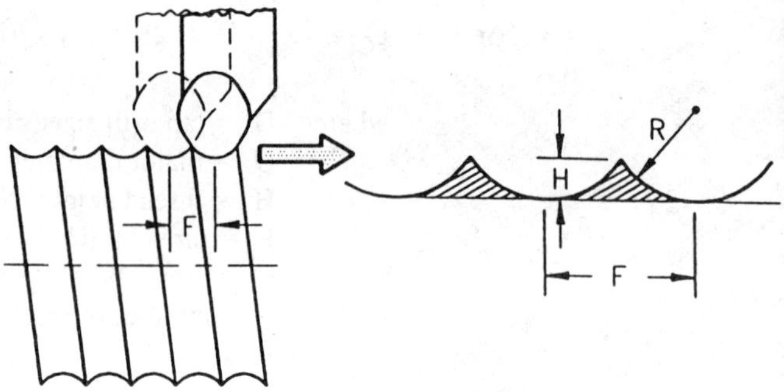

Figure 2.37

Since the value of H is very small, the term H^2 can be overlooked and the equation becomes:

$$H = \frac{F^2}{8R}$$

or $$F = (8RH)^{1/2}$$

The surface roughness can be improved either by **reducing** the feed rate or by **increasing** the tool nose radius. It is preferred to use a larger tool nose radius to obtain better roughness than to reduce the feed rate because chips may congest on the insert tip and cause damage to the surface when too small a feed is used.

Depth of cut and deflection

Generally speaking, the depth of cut for roughing all materials, excluding stainless steels, is about 0.15 in. (4 mm). Roughing stainless steels uses 0.1 in. depth of cut.

The deeper cut requires a larger cutting force. The cutting resistant force causes the workpiece to be deflected. This deflection produces chatter when the workpiece rotates at a relatively high speed. When this deflection is greater than 0.001 in. (or 0.02mm), chatter may be severe enough to make the surface finish requirements impossible to obtain.

Error resulted from off center of the cutter

In most cases, we like to have the cutter tip located at the center in turning operations. The turned diameter is slightly larger than the programmed dimension when the tip of the cutter is off center by a distance (Figure 2.38 on the next page).

The resultant diameter error can be calculated from:

$$\Delta X = (X^2 + Y^2)^{1/2} - X$$

where ΔX = error amount
X = X-coordinate of the programmed point
Y = amount of center offset

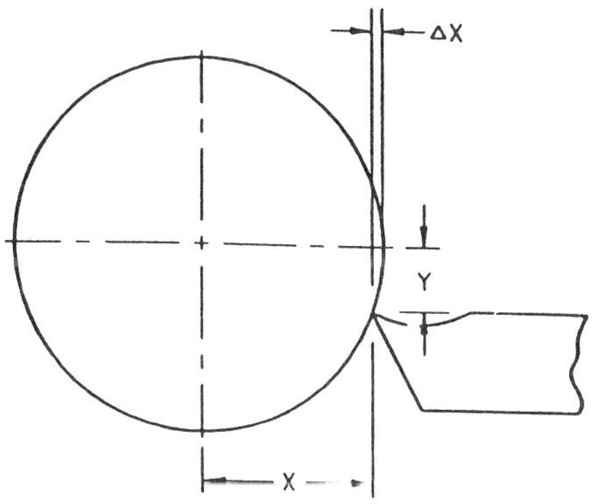

Figure 2.38

Chip breaker

Chips should be broken into pieces or curled into small coils to facilitate the removal from the workpiece and the cutter. When turning brittle materials such as cast iron and intermittent cuttings, the chips are automatically broken, so no chip breaker is required. A chip breaker must be given to the cutter which is used to turn the stingy, tough materials such as steels, aluminum, and so on. Chip breakers can appear in various forms. Figure 2.39 illustrates the basic principle of a chip breaker.

The theoretical radius of curled chips can be determined by two variables: **width of the chip breaker (W) and depth of the chip breaker (H)**, and can be calculated by using the relationship of two similar triangles ABD and ACB.

$$\frac{AC}{AB} = \frac{AB}{AD}$$

Since $AC = 2R$, $AD = H$, and $AB = (H^2 + W^2)^{1/2}$

Therefore, $2RH = H^2 + W^2$

or

$$R = \frac{W^2}{2H} + \frac{H}{2}$$

where W = width of the chip breaker
H = depth of the chip breaker
R = radius of curled chips

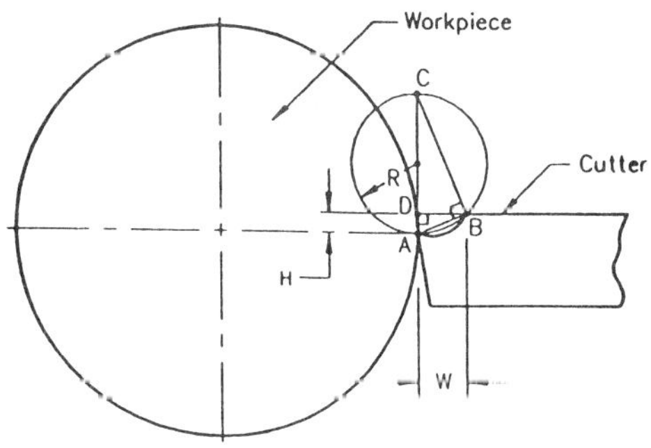

Figure 2.39

The actual chip size is also affected by the feed used in cutting. Larger feed causes chips to be broken easily, whereas smaller feed reduces the effect of chip breaking.

Chapter 3

Mastercam Environments

Objectives:

1. Start the Mastercam program.
2. Understand screen menus and how to move from one screen to another.
3. Know the function of the SAVE, FILE and EXIT commands.

3.1 Launching Mastercam (Windows 98)

There are only **two steps** needed to start Mastercam Mill Version 8 running under Windows 98.

Step 1. If you have created a shortcut icon on the screen, double click on it.

Figure 3.1

Step 2. Click on the Start box, then Programs, Mastercam 8 and finally Mill 8

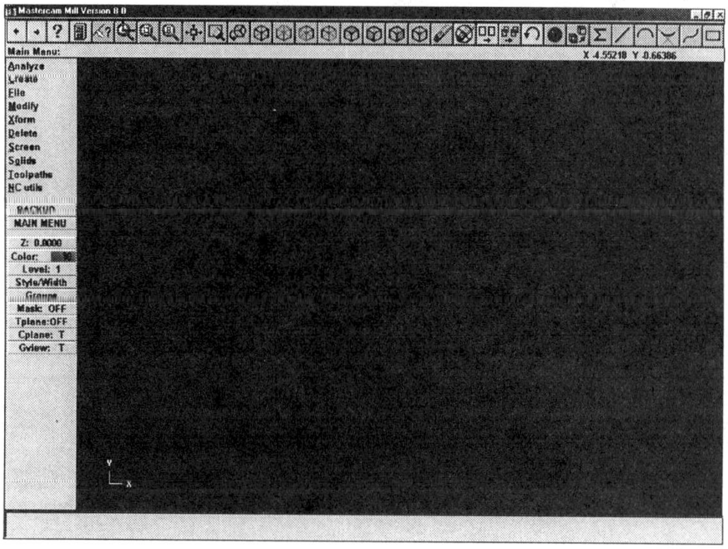

Figure 3.2

3.2 Changing the Size of the Window

Maximize the window

To maximize the Mastercam window to the full screen, click the maximize button on the title bar as shown in Figure 3.3.

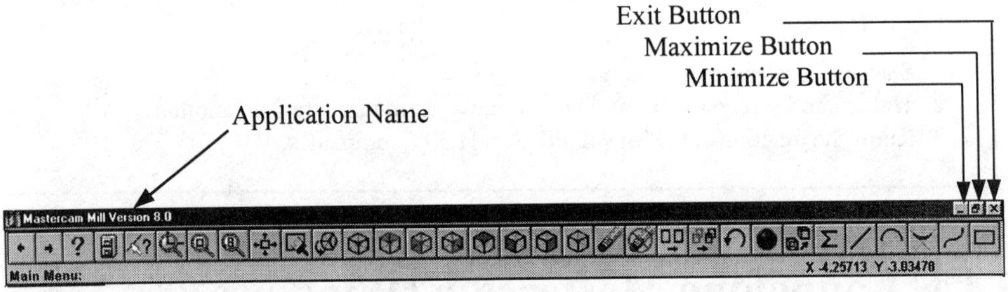

Figure 3.3 The Title Bar of Mastercam

Minimize the window

To minimize the Mastercam window to an icon, click the minimize button on the title bar shown in Figure 3.3 above.

Change the size of the window

<u>**Follow this three step procedure:**</u>

1. Point to the Mastercam border, or corner, and the pointer will change to a two headed arrow.
2. Press and hold the pick (left) mouse button while dragging the corner or border of the Mastercam screen.
3. Release the pick button when you have the desired window size.

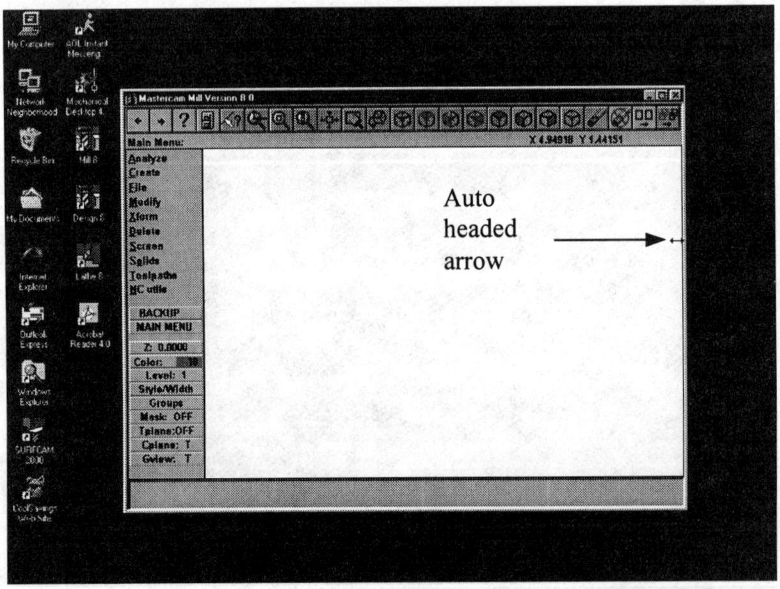

Figure 3.4

Moving a Window

To move a window, position your mouse pointer in the bar at the top of your window that contains the application name (or the title bar), press the pick button, and keep the button down. Drag the window to its new position, and release the pick button.

3.3 Mastercam Screen

After you enter Mastercam, the system will display the Mastercam screen which is divided into **four sections**: a graphics display, a tool bar, a screen menu and a system response area (see Figure 3.5).

Graphics Display Area

This is the working area where your drawing geometry can be created, retrieved or modified.

Toolbar Area

The toolbar is a row of buttons across the top of the screen. These buttons either have an icon or a number to identify them. To get a description of a toolbar icon, move your mouse cursor onto the button, or let the mouse cursor rest over the icon and Mastercam will automatically identify the button. Click any mouse button to activate the icon command.

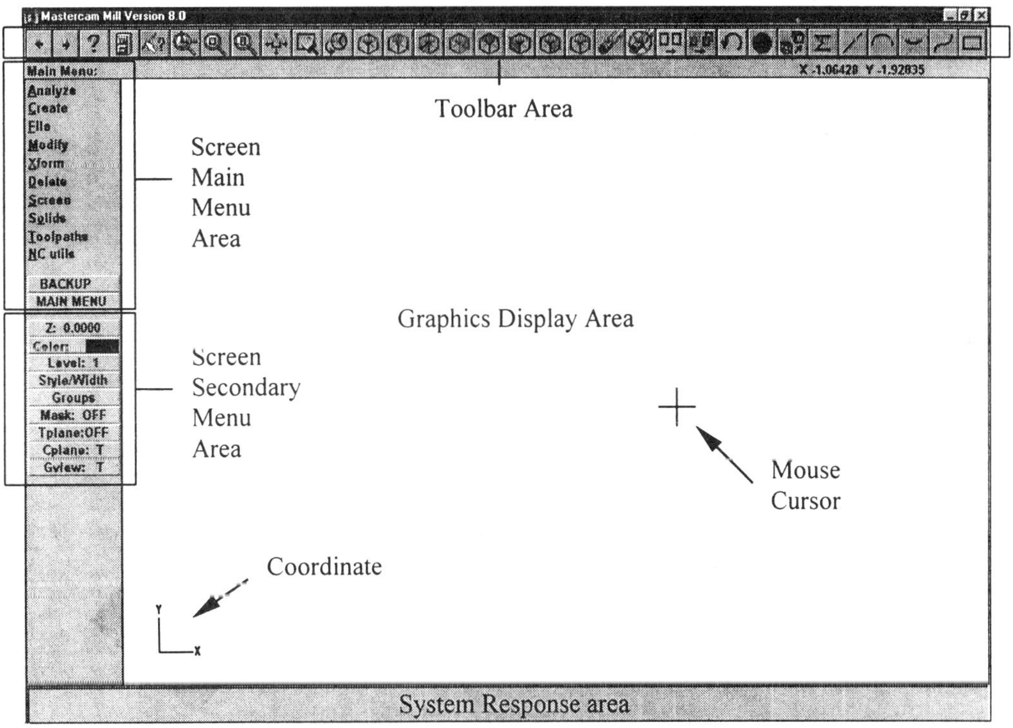

Figure 3.5 Mastercam Screen Display

Screen Menu Area

This area is located at the left of the screen and consists of a main menu and a secondary menu. The **main menu** is used to select the system's main functions such as create, modify, or toolpaths. The **secondary menu** is used to change the system's parameters such as the Z depth or color which is frequently revised by the user. All the commands used in Mastercam can be selected from this area.

System Response Area

One or two text lines at the bottom of the screen indicate the status of the commands. This is where you will receive messages from Mastercam. **Watch this area carefully**; it might require some input from the keyboard.

Selecting a Menu Option

In Mastercam, there are **two** ways to select a menu option from the Screen Menu area:

1. Moving the mouse or pointing devices into the menu area. After the desired menu box is highlighted, press any mouse button to activate the command.

2. Pressing the first capital letter of the command.

The first menu to appear on the Mastercam main menu screen is the Mastercam **Root Menu**. It is shown in the previous Figure 3.5. Some of these menu items have a more detailed submenu from which an item must be selected. A brief description of the commands available from the main menu and secondary menu is listed on Table 3.1 and 3.2.

Table 3.1 The Main Menu

Main Item	Description
Analyze	Displays coordinate and database information for selected object such as point,line, arc, spline, surface or dimension on the screen. It is helpful to identify objects that had already been created. For example, it can be used to determine the angle of an existing line or the radius of a specified circle.
Create	Creates geometry to the drawing database and draws it on the Graphics Display Area. These geometries include line, arc, circle, rectangle, etc.
File	Manipulates disk **files** such as SAVE, GET, CONVERT, TRANSMIT, or RECEIVE.
Modify	Modifies screen geometry with the fillet, trim, break and join commands.
Xform	Transforms already created geometry with the mirror, rotate, scale, and offset commands.
Delete	Deletes an entity or group of entities from the screen and the system's database.
Screen	Plots or views the drawing geometry, shows the number of drawing entities, zooms in and out, changes the viewport number and configuration.
Solids	Construct solid models
Toolpaths	Creates NC toolpaths using drill, contour, pocket, etc.
NC utils	Manipulates and processes NC toolpaths.
BACKUP*	Brings the main menu item to its upper level.
MAIN MENU*	Brings the main menu item to its root page.
*	Refer to section 3.5 for short-cut keys.

Table 3.2 The Secondary Menu

Main Item		Description
Z:	0.0000	Displays and changes the current working depth.
Color:	10	Sets the current system default color.
Level:	1	Sets the current system active level.
Style/Width:		Sets the line style and line width.
Groups:		Select any number of entities and associate them together by name.
Mask:	OFF	Sets the system masking level.
Tplane:	OFF	Sets a tool plane.
Cplane:	T	Sets a construction plane.
Cview:	T	Changes the graphic view. Note that the graphic view can be independent of the construction plane.

The menu, command, and option structure of Mastercam is a **tree** (or *hierarchy*) arrangement. For example, the actual tree arrangement to Create a Rectangle using the 2 points option is shown in Figure 3.6.

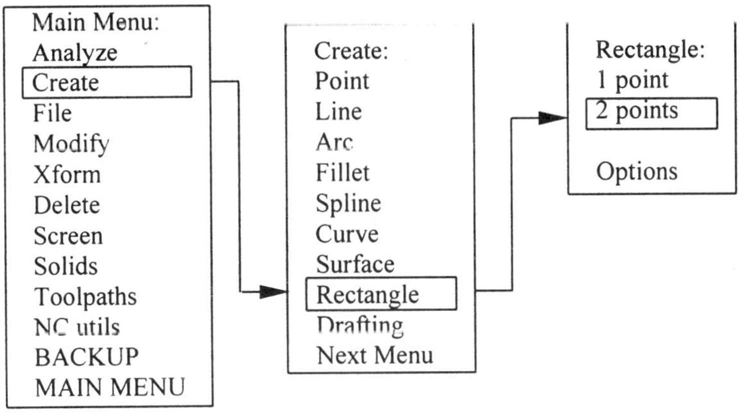

Figure 3.6 The tree arrangement of the CREATE menu

Select the **Create** menu with your mouse pointer. The menu changes and now consists of the submenu of **Create**. Select **Rectangle** and the menu changes to the submenu of **Rectangle**. Select **2 points** to activate the option. Notice the prompts in the system response area. It provides important information for you to follow through.

To conserve space and still allow you to access the commands properly, the convention used in this book for the command selections shown in Figure 3.6 will be indicated as,

Create → Rectangle → 2 points

↵ indicates the **Enter key** should be used

The entire Mastercam command hierarchy is organized systematically. Take your time to review it. You will have more opportunities to learn and practice some of the screen commands in the upcoming chapters.

3.4 Exiting Mastercam

To exit Mastercam, follow the steps shown here. The same steps also apply to the DOS version.

Step 1. Go to the root page of the main menu.
Select MAIN MENU → File → Next Menu

Step 2. Select the Exit option.
Select Exit

Step 3. Confirm to exit Mastercam.
Select Yes

3.5 Using Mastercam Navigation Commands

Understanding Mastercam navigation commands is essential to operating the system effectively. In section 3.3, we explained how to select a menu option from the Screen Menu Area. To speed up the drawing construction, other commands such as accepting the default value and short-cut keys are described as follows:

Default Values

In Mastercam, the **default value** set up by the system (or from previous user input) is indicated in a dialog box in the system response area, e.g.,

Enter the radius
0.5

If you decide to use this default value, you don't have to re-type it and the value can be **accepted** in two ways: (a) press the (Enter) key, or
(b) press the left mouse button.

If you want to **change** the default value at any time, you don't have to erase the old value, just type the new value in its place.

BACKUP and MAIN MENU

BACKUP backs up one menu level at a time and **MAIN MENU** jumps back to main menu. These options are used constantly and are available from every menu option. You can use mouse to select the option or use the following **short-cut keys.**

Menu option	Key(s)
BACKUP	Esc
MAIN MENU	Press Esc key continuously

Mastercam short-cut keys

Short-cut keys have special uses in Mastercam.

Alt + 0	Set Z depth for Cplane
Alt + 1	Set main color
Alt + 2	Set main level
Alt + 3	Set mask level
Alt + 4	Set tool plane
Alt + 5	Set Cplane
Alt + 6	Set Gview
Alt + A	Open the AutoSave window
Alt + B	Toggle the toolbar on/off
Alt + C	Run C-Hook application program
Alt + D	Drafting global parameters
Alt + E	Hide/unhide geometry
Alt + F	Set menu fonts
Alt + G	Selection grid parameters
Alt + H	Display on-ling help
Alt + I	List open files
Alt + J	Job setup
Alt + L	Set current line style and width
Alt + M	List the Mastercam memory allocations
Alt + N	Edit named views
Alt + O	Operation manager
Alt + P	Toggle Mastercam prompt area on/off
Alt + Q	Undo last operation
Alt + R	Edit last operation
Alt + S	Full-time shading on/off
Alt + T	In the toolpath menu, turn toolpath display on/off
Alt + U	Undo
Alt + V	Mastercam version number and SIM serial numver
Alt + W	Set viewport windows
Alt + X	Set main color, level, line style and width from selected entity
Alt + Z	Set visible levels
Alt + '	Create two-point circle
Alt + Tab	Switch between applications
Alt + -	With hidden entities, select additional entities to hide
Alt + =	Unhide selected entities
Tab/Shift + Tab	Navigate between controls in dialog box
Esc	System interrupt or menu backup
Page Up/Page Down	Zoom in/ Zoom out
Cursor Arrows	Pans over geometry
Ctrl + E	In Operation Manager, expand or collapse all operations

Mastercam function keys

Nineteen function keys have special uses in Mastercam. Using Mastercam's short-cut commands and function keys is a fast way to step into an operation and can reduce your drawing time remarkably.

	Function Key	Alt + Function key
F1	Zoom	Fit to extents of the screen
F2	Zoom Previous or Scale by 0.5	Scale by 0.8
F3	Repaint	Cursor Tracking on/off
F4	Analyze	Exit Mastercam
F5	Delete	Delete Window
F6	File	Edit File
F7	Modify	(Blank)
F8	Create	Configuration
F9	Part Information on/off	Draw Axes
F10	Display execute function window	Display execute function window

3.6 Getting Help

If you need help for a Mastercam function key, use the **Alt-H** keys, select **Help Topics → Find**, type **Shortcut Key Reference**, click the topic and click **Display**. A detailed help screen is displayed. See Figure 3.7.

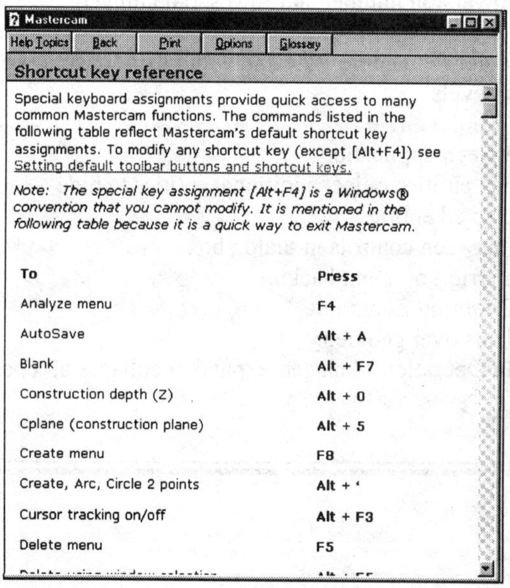

Figure 3.7 Mastercam Shortcut Key Help Screen

In Mastercam Version 8.0, you will notice that the on-line help screen can be accessed by pressing Alt-H. This on-line help, shown in Figure 3.8 is related to the Mastercam Help Index, and provides you with information in great detail. Therefore, it is highly recommended to step into this utility. You can select a topic with the mouse or double-click the control-menu box at the upper-left corner to exit the Mastercam Help. An example showing help on Xform → Translate is shown in Figure 3.9 .

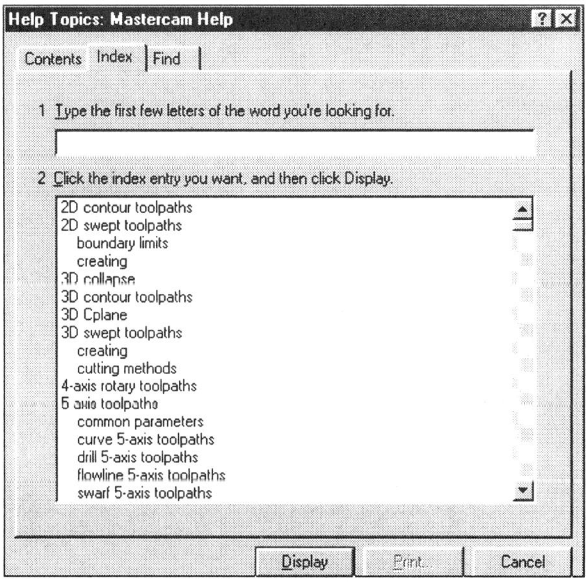

Figure 3.8

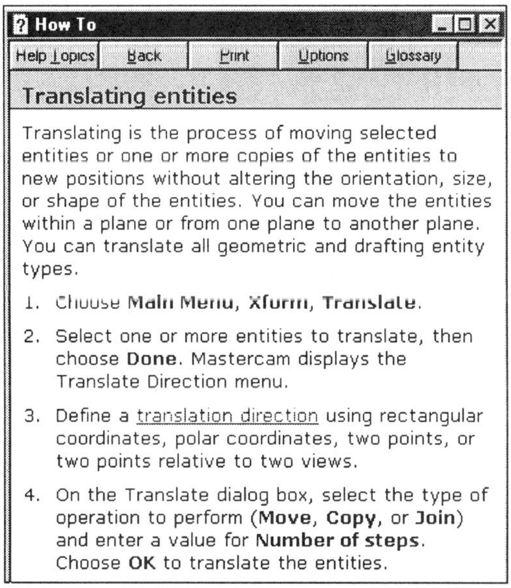

Figure 3.9

3.7 Setting System Configuration

In Mastercam, common system's default values such as Allocations, Tolerances, NC settings and CAD settings are stored in a configuration file (*.CFG). This configuration file is either MILL8.CFG for English units or MILL8M.CFG for metric units. If you want to customize these default startup settings for Mastercam, use the following command sequences:

MAIN MENU → Screen → Configure

The System Configuration dialog box appears as Figure 3.10.

Tip Backing up all the configuration files (*.CFG) to a floppy will help you to recover the original settings.

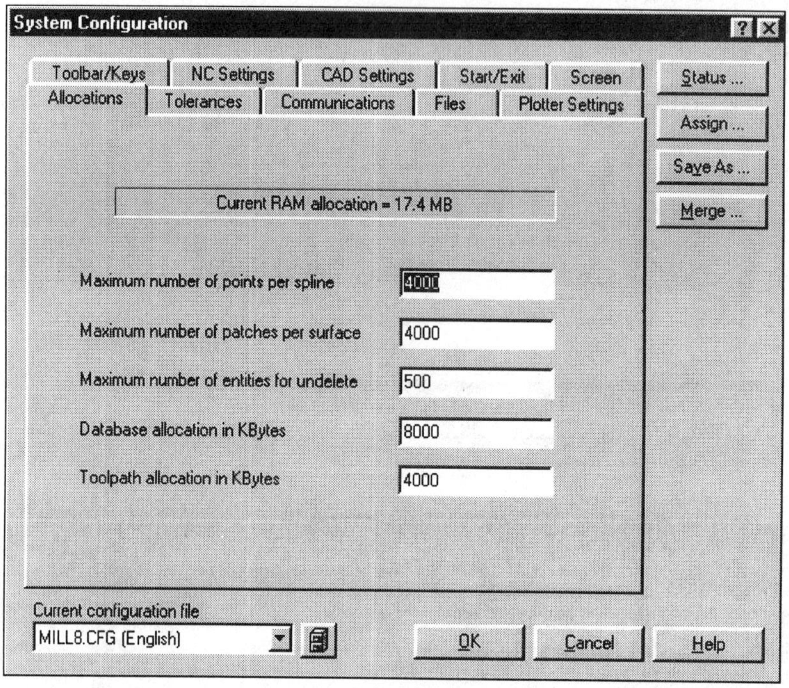

Figure 3.10

The above dialog box is divided into three sections: **button options, tab options** and **current configuration file** options. Next, each section and their options are explained in more detail.

Button Options

OK Located at the bottom, this button closes the System Configuration dialog box to implement the updates. When you choose this option, the system prompts the following message:

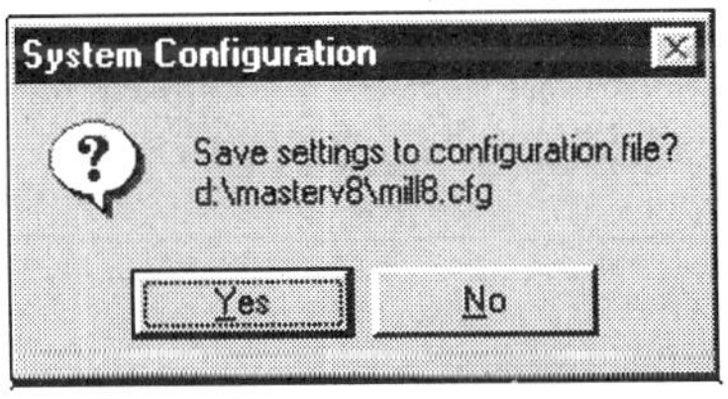

Choosing **Yes** will implement the changes and save them to the current configuration file.

Choosing **No** will implement the changes for the current Mastercam session only, but not save them to the configuration file.

Cancel Exit the System Configuration dialog box without saving or implementing the changes.

Help Opens the help files.

Status In the upper-right corner, this button lets you view which sections of the configuration information have been modified. The modified section has a mark in the check box. Deselecting the check box will undo the changes in that section. See Figure 3.11.

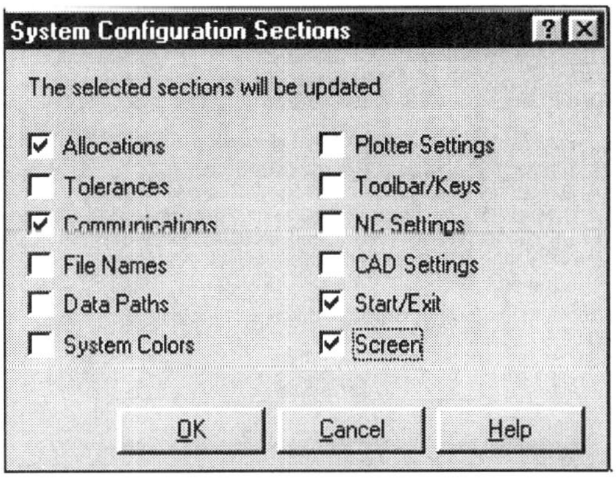

Figure 3.11

Save As Saves the current project, allowing you to select a name for the file.

Assign Assign any configuration file to a post (*.PST) file. The default post processor file is MILL8.CFG for English units or MILL8M.CFG for metric units.

Merge Merge configuration information from other files with the current configuration file.

Tab Options

There are **ten** tabs in the dialog box, each representing a page of configuration parameters.

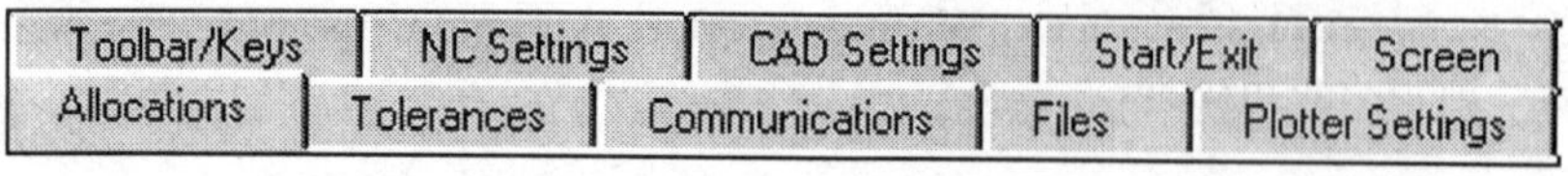

Allocations Set maximum values for certain Mastercam features such as number of points per spline, number of points per surface, number of entities for undelete, database allocation in Kbytes and toolpath allocation in Kbytes. (Figure 3.12.)

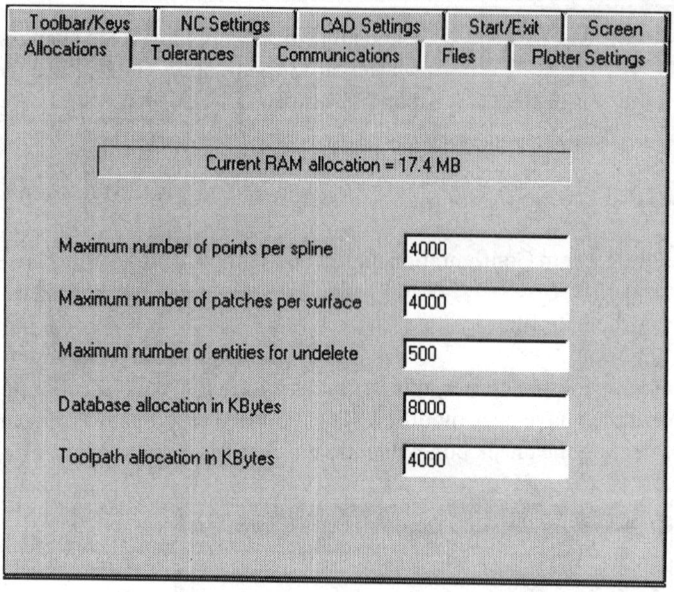

Figure 3.12

Tolerances Set the default tolerances values for different areas of Mastercam.

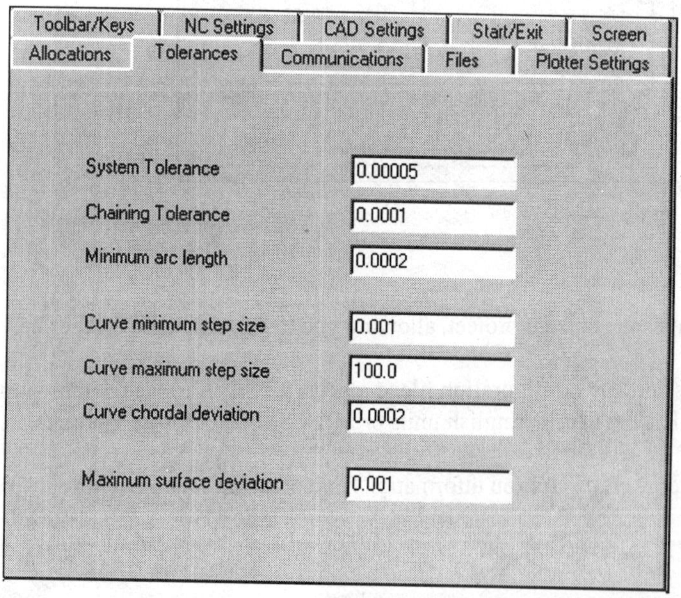

Figure 3.13

Communication Set the default communication settings with CNC control and other peripheral devices as shown here.

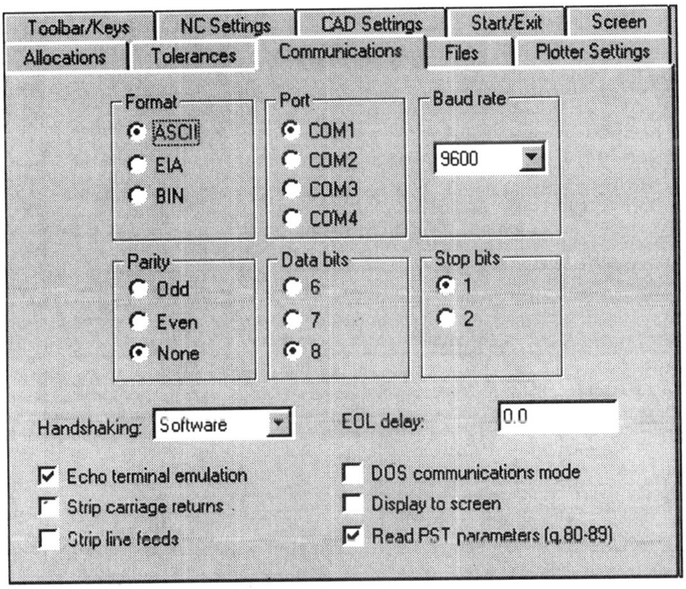

Figure 3.14

Files Set the default values for files and directories used by Mastercam. See Figure 3.15.

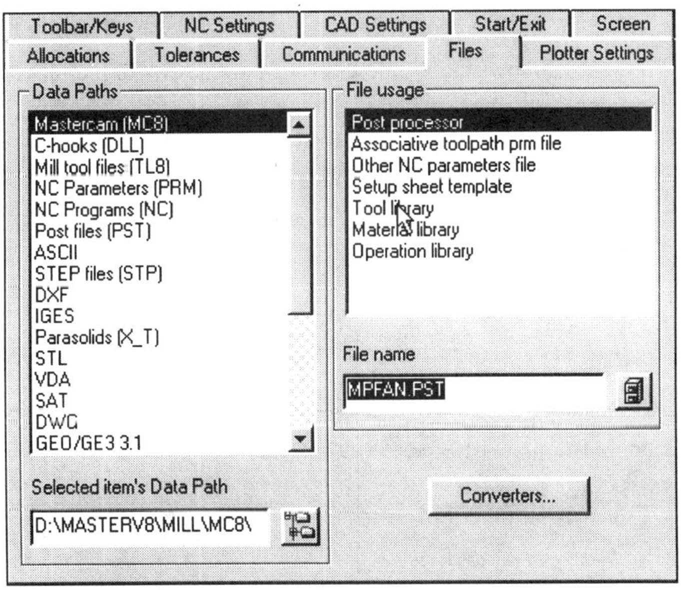

Figure 3.15

Plotter Settings Set default values for plotter parameters. When selected, it opens a page of non-Windows driver parameters. If you select the Use Windows driver check box at the lower-left corner of the dialog box, the dialog box updates to the Windows driver parameters. The following Figure 3.16 shows the non-Windows driver parameters for plotter settings.

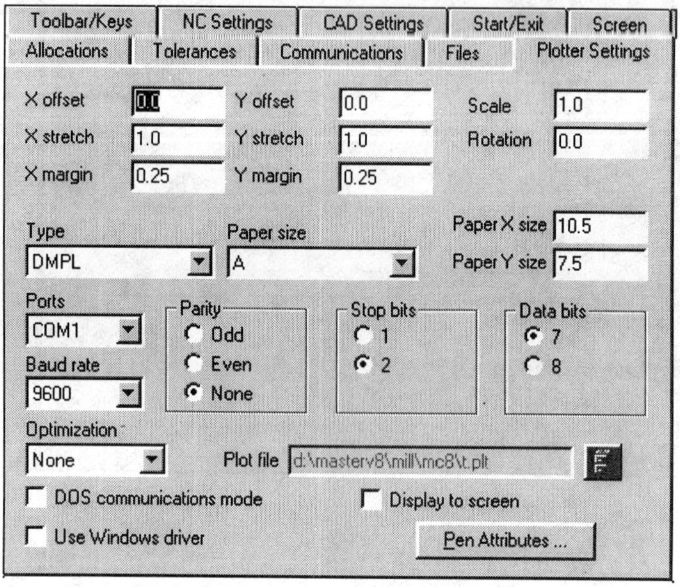

Figure 3.16

The following Figure 3.17 shows the Windows driver parameters for plotter settings.

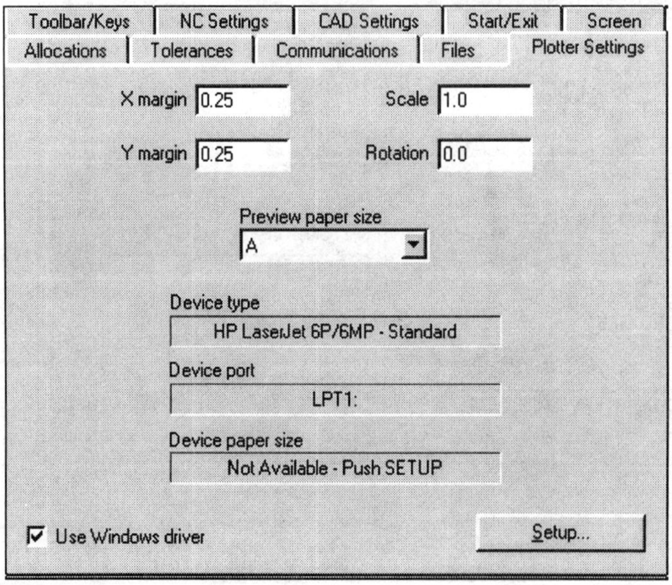

Figure 3.17

Toolbar/Keys Assign function keys (F1 – F12), Alt keys (excluding the standard Windows combination such as Alt + F4), or toolbar buttons to functions, C-hooks, and macros. A maximum of 66 key combinations and 99 buttons can be assigned. See Figure 3.18.

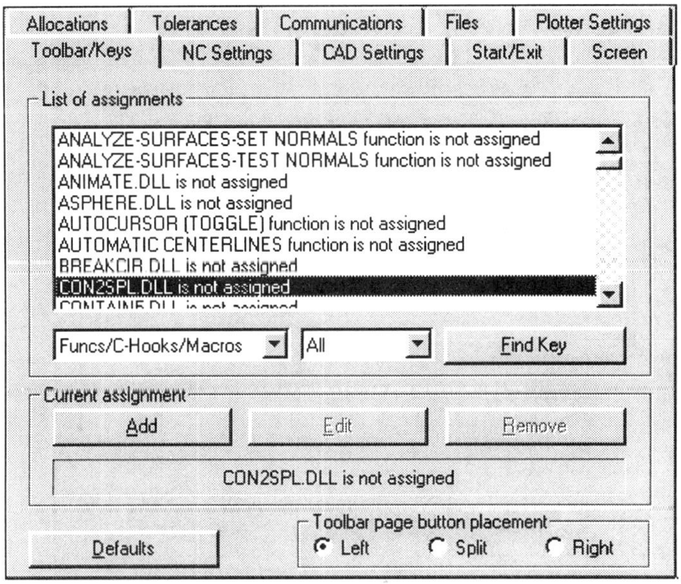

Figure 3.18

NC Settings Set parameters for generating NC data through Mastercam. See Figure 3.19.

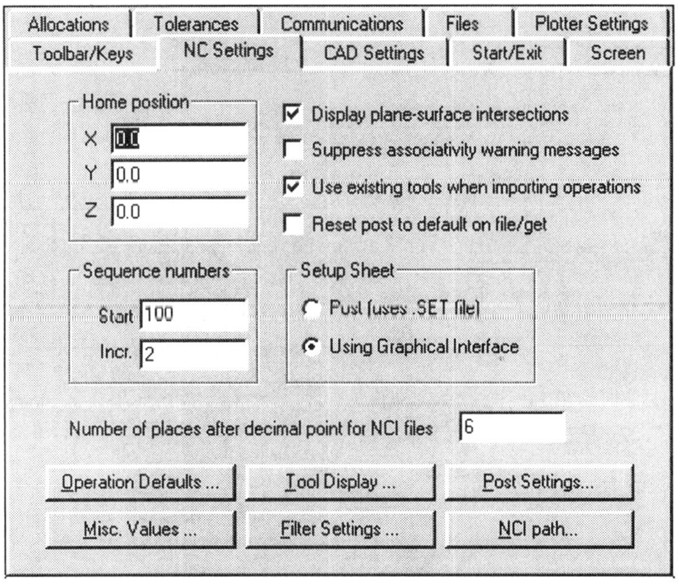

Figure 3.19

CAD Settings Set the default Design parameter values such as Spline/Surface creation type, Drafting settings, IGES write setting, etc. Refer to Figure 3.20.

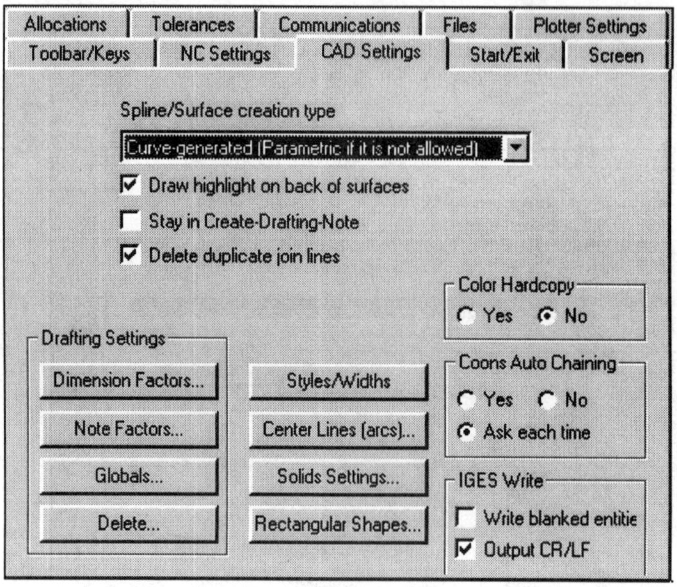

Figue 3.20

Start/Exit Set the default values that the system uses when you start and/or exit Mastercam. These default values include startup configuration file, default construction plane, editor name, C-hooks settings and autosave setting. See Figure 3.21.

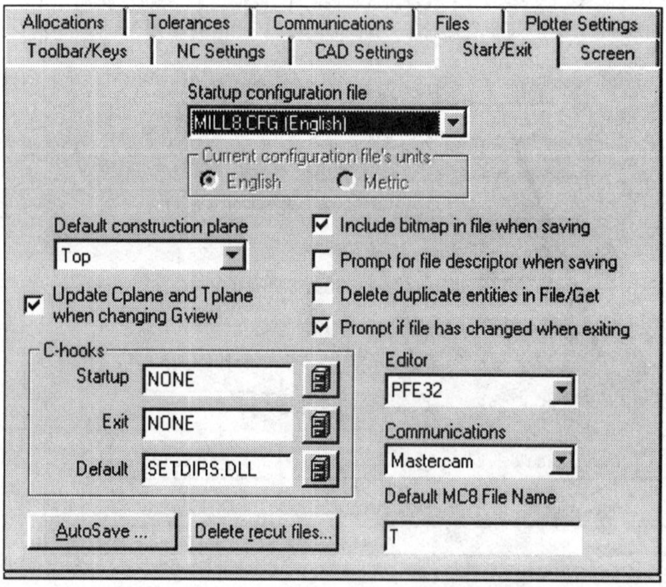

Figure 3.21

Screen Set the appearance of different areas of Mastercam's screen display. It includes menu font, default view configuration, default point entry mode, toolbar visible at system startup, etc.

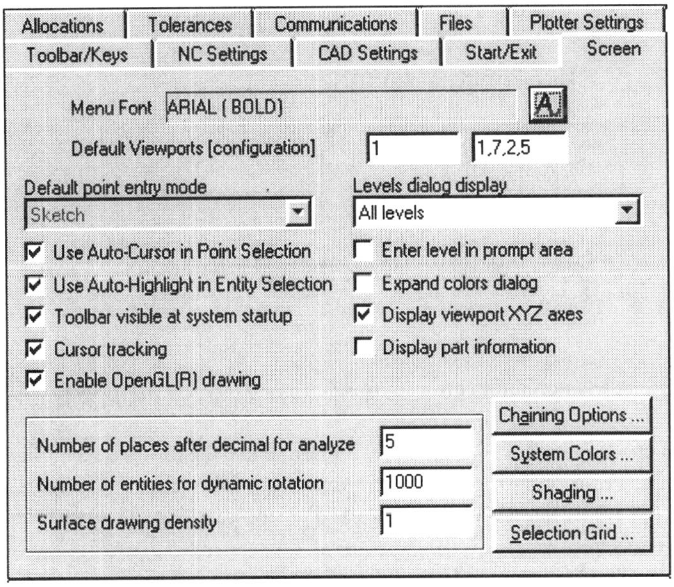

Figure 3.22

Current configuration file options

By selecting the drop-down check mark, you can select the current configuration file for Mastercam. For example, you can select MILL8M.CFG if you are using metric units. See Figure 3.23.

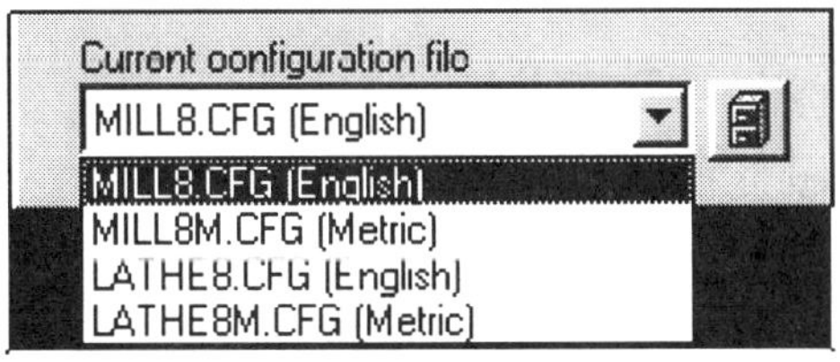

Figure 3.23

Example

In the following example, you will practice the essential commands introduced in this chapter to work with Mastercam. You will enter the Mastercam environment, complete a simple drawing as shown in Figure 3.24, save the drawing and retrieve it. Don't worry about exact sizes or dimensions, but do try to make them look as much like the drawing as possible.

Figure 3.24 Example drawing: Mastercam to go

In the process of creating this drawing, you will learn to use the mouse, select the screen menu commands and enter other input from the keyboard. This hands-on experience is important for you to be familiar with Mastercam and its applications. The learning objectives can be itemized as:

- Entering Mastercam
- Analyzing the drawing entities
- Creating a simple geometry
- Saving to a file
- Exiting Mastercam
- Restarting Mastercam
- Retrieving previous file

Step 1. Entering Mastercam

Follow the procedures shown in Section 3.2.

Step 2. Analyzing the drawing entities

In order to construct the drawing, the first procedure is to identify the drawing entities as shown in Figure 3.25, and the construction sequences. Although this chapter does not cover this procedure, it is important to include it in your practice before you start constructing your drawing.

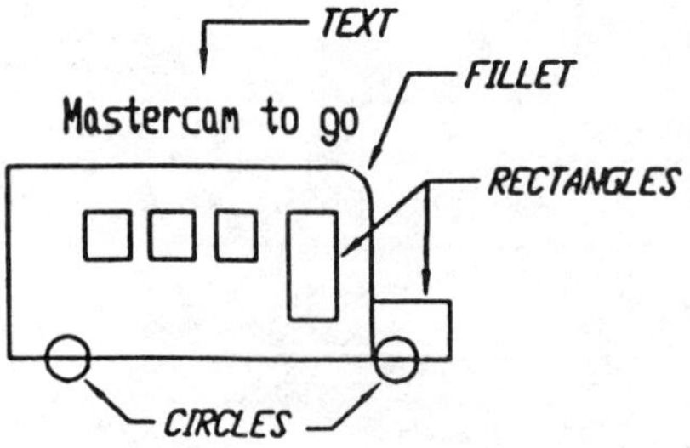

Figure 3.25

Step 3. Creating a simple geometry

For steps 4 through 9, you should refer to the pick points shown in Figure 3.26.

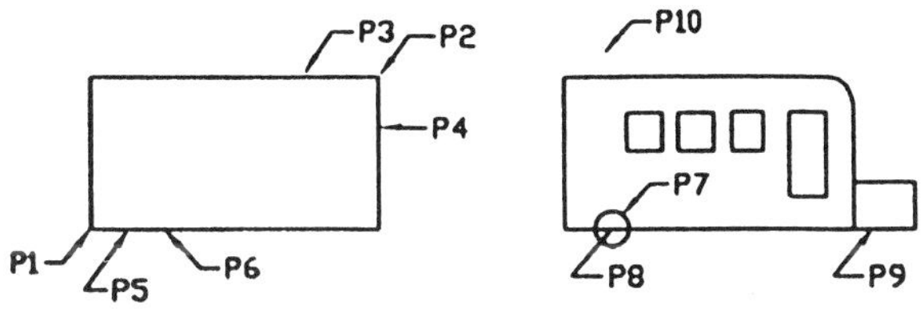

Figure 3.26 Pick points for the example drawing

Step 4. Create a rectangle

Select the menu items:

Main Menu → Create → Rectangle → 2 points

(Notice and switch to the prompt in the System Response Area)

Enter the lower left corner: Pick **P1**

Enter the upper right corner: Pick **P2**

Step 5. Create a fillet

Select the menu items:

Main Menu → Create → Fillet

(Notice the default values in the System Response Area)

Select an entity: Pick **P3**

Select another entity: Pick **P4**

Step 6. Create a circle

Select the menu items:

Main Menu → Create → Arc → Circ 2 pts

(Notice the prompt in the System Response Area)

Enter the first point: Pick **P5**

Enter the second point: Pick **P6**

Step 7. Create rectangles

Follow Step 4 and create the rest of the five rectangles using rectangle commands.

Step 8. Copy a circle

Select the menu items:

Main Menu → Xform → Translate

Select an entity: Pick **P7**

Select the menu items:

Done → Between pts

(Notice the pop-up dialog box on screen)

Enter the points to translate from: Pick **P8**

Enter the points to translate to: Pick **P9**

Set the Translate menu as shown:☞

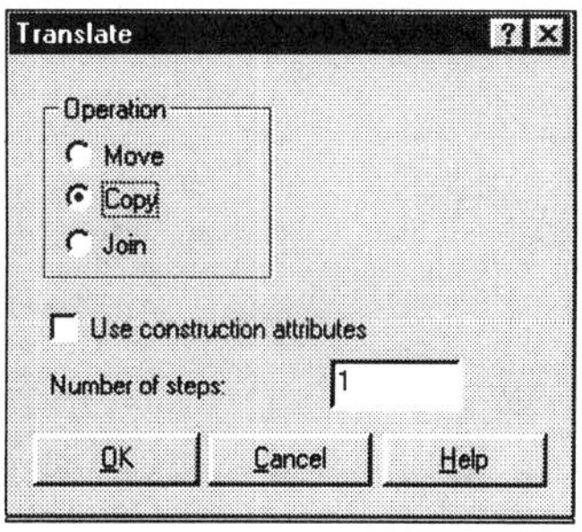

Select **OK** to return from the Translate menu.

Step 9. Create a text note

Select the menu items:

Main Menu → Create → Drafting → Note

(Notice the dialog box appears as below:)

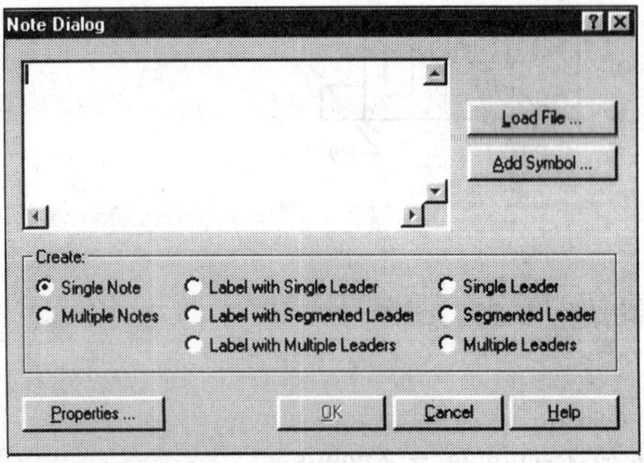

Enter **Mastercam to go**

Select **OK**

Create note: Indicate text position: Pick **P10**

Press **Esc** to end this function

Step 10. Saving to a file

Main Menu → File → Save

Enter file name (Drive:\MILL\MC8\T.MC8): Enter **BUS**

Step 11. Exiting Mastercam

Main Menu → Exit → Yes

Step 12. Restarting Mastercam

Follow the procedures outlined in Section 3.2.

Step 13. Retrieving previous file

Main Menu → File → Get

Enter file name (Drive:\MILL\MC8\T.MC8): Enter **BUS**

Note: The drawing you just created in this example should appear much like Figure 3.24. at the top of page 3-18.

Ex Exercises

Review and practice the essential commands presented in the previous example.

1. Turn on your computer and load Mastercam to access the drawing editor.

2. Begin a new drawing using your own variables.
   Draw six connected lines. (Hint: Create → Line → Multi → Sketch)
   Draw two rectangle boxes.
   Draw four circles.
   Draw two text notes.
   Delete a line, a rectangle box, a circle, and a text note.

3. Save the drawing as **EX** and exit Mastercam.

4. Enter Mastercam and load **EX**.

5. Explain the overall purpose of the Graphics Display Area, Toolbar Area, System Response Area and Screen Menu Area in Mastercam.

6. Briefly describe the ways to select a menu option.

7. What is the short-cut function key for DELETE?

8. Briefly explain the purpose of the following commands: Create, Modify, Xform

Chapter 4

Mastercam Process Overview

Objectives:

1. Provide an overview of CAD/CAM NC programming.
2. Use a simple example to step through the main tasks of CAD/CAM NC programming.
3. Be familiarized with the process of CAD/CAM NC programming.

4.1 CAD/CAM NC Programming Process

The intent of this chapter is to provide an overview of the processing steps required to generate NC codes in a CAD/CAM system. CAD/CAM NC programming involves **three** major components: **CAD, CAM, and a postprocessor**. Figure 4.1 illustrates the CAD/CAM NC programming steps. Each step indicates the input data and output data. Studying the part drawing is the first step of the process. We need to identify what part features need to be produced and determine the size of the raw material. From these, we should be able to determine how much material needs to be removed. The next step is to create a CAD drawing. The main task of the CAD program is to create the part geometry of the final finished part and its raw material shape if necessary.

The CAM program requires **two** types of input data, **part geometry and machining data**, to generate the tool path to machine the part. The output of the CAM program is a generic file called a cutter location data file (NCI) which contains the coordinate values of a series of cutter paths, machining information such as feed rate, spindle speed, coolant control command, etc. The postprocessor converts the NCI file into NC codes readable to CNC controllers. Since CNC controllers vary from vendor to vendor, this requires us to create a dedicated postprocessor for a particular CNC controller/machine combination. We need to know which CNC machine will be used for machining the part in order to select the appropriate postprocessor.

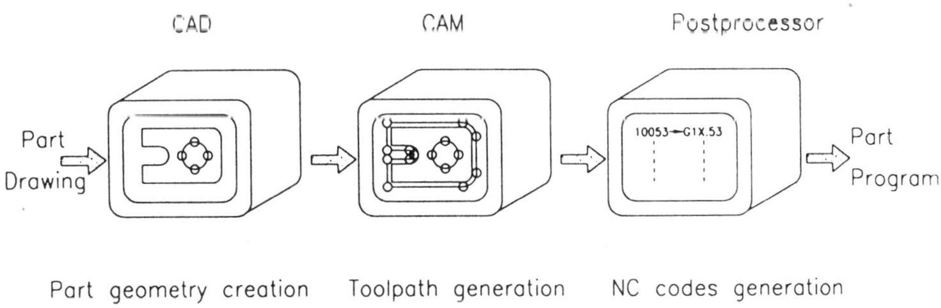

Figure 4.1

4.2 Mastercam Process Overview

This section presents the step-by-step procedure that generates the toolpath to machine a simple part shown in Figure 4.2. This exercise will help you to understand the overall process of CAD/CAM NC programming.

The project involves creating a 6" x 4" rectangle, a blind slot, and four holes. The contour module is used to generate the toolpaths for the outer profile, and the drill module is used for generating the toolpaths for drilling four holes.

Note: If the working envelope of your machine is smaller than 6" x 4", scale all the dimensions by one-half.

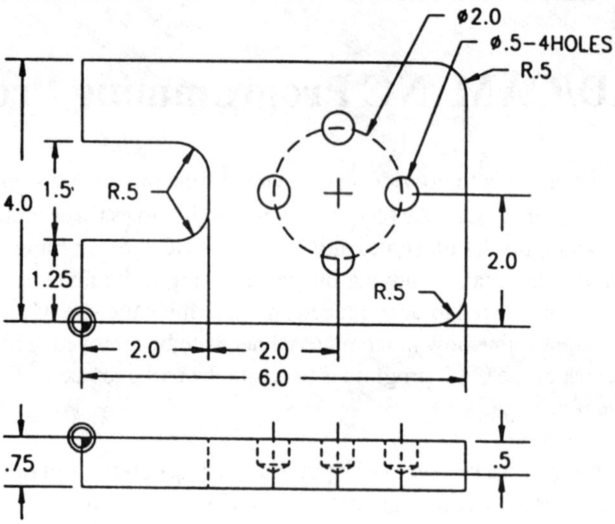

Figure 4.2

⌛Tips: Creating part geometry

1. Create a rectangle with 6" x 4" dimensions.

2. Create two horizontal lines and one vertical line.

3. Break the left vertical line of the rectangle into two pieces. This allows the line to be trimmed.
4. Add four fillets.

5. Trim the left vertical line of the rectangle and two horizontal lines.

6. Create four circles.

7. Define material stock toolpaths → Top setup → select by selecting any material you want or accept the default material.

Tips: Generating toolpaths

1. Use the contour module to generate the toolpaths for the outer profile with a 1" end mill.

2. Use the drill module to generate the toolpaths for drilling four holes with a 0.5" drill.

3. Set the NC parameters according to the following tooling and machining specifications:

Tool No.	Tool Dia.	Feedrate	Plunge Rate	Spindle Speed
1	1.0"	15.0 ipm	10.0 ipm	3000 rpm
2	0.5"	15.0 ipm	-	1500 rpm

Step 1. Enter Mastercam Mill. Following the procedure given in Chapter 3.

Step 2. Create a rectangle.

Select **MAIN MENU →Create → Rectangle → 1 point**
Enter the width: **6** ↵
Enter the height: **4** ↵
Select the **lower left corner → OK**
Enter coordinate: **0.0**
Press **ALT + F1** simultaneously,
then press **F2** to fit the drawing
to the screen as in Figure 4.3.

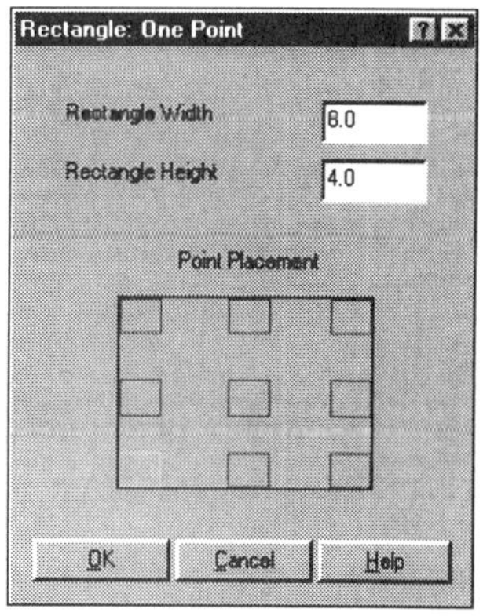

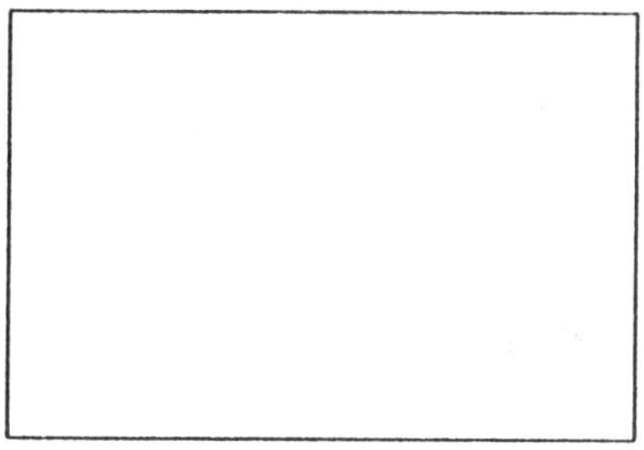

Figure 4.3

Step 3. Create two horizontal lines and one vertical line.

Select **MAIN MENU → Create → Line → Endpoints**
Specify the first endpoint: **-0.5, 2.75** ↵
Specify the second endpoint: **2.5, 2.75** ↵ *to complete the first line*
Specify the first endpoint: **-0.5, 1.25** ↵
Specify the second endpoint: **2.5,1.25** ↵ *to complete the second line*
Specify the first endpoint: **2.0, 3.0** ↵
Specify the second endpoint: **2.0, 1** ↵ *to complete the third line*
The three lines should add to the drawing as shown in Figure 4.4.

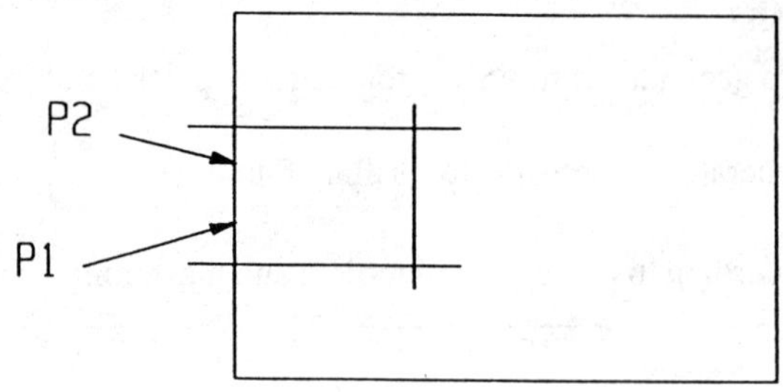

Figure 4.4

Step 4. Break the left vertical line of the rectangle into two pieces.

Use the pick points in Figure 4.4.

Select **MAIN MENU → Modify → Break → 2 pieces**

Select an entity: pick **P1** ↵

Enter the breakpoint: pick **P2** ↵

The left vertical line is broken into two pieces, but you may not see this on the screen. The new drawing should look identical to Figure 4.4 which is redrawn in Figure 4.5.

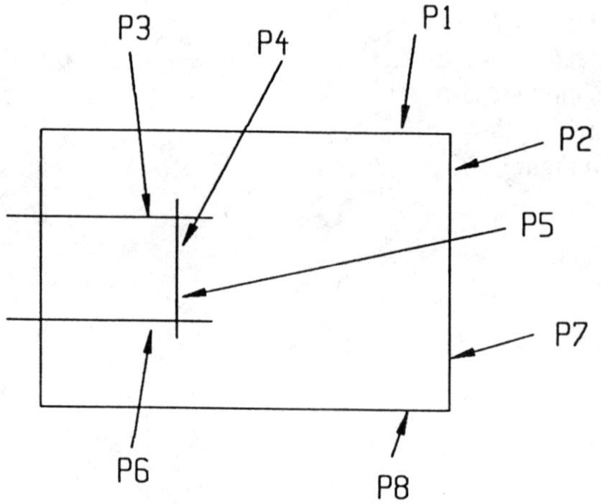

Figure 4.5

Step 5. Add four fillets using the pick points in Figure 4.5.

Select **BACKUP → BACKUP → Fillet → Radius**

Enter the fillet radius: **0.5** ↵

Pick points **P1** and **P2** to complete the first fillet

Sequentially pick points at **P3 - P8** to complete the three remaining fillets

The four fillets should appear as in Figure 4.6.

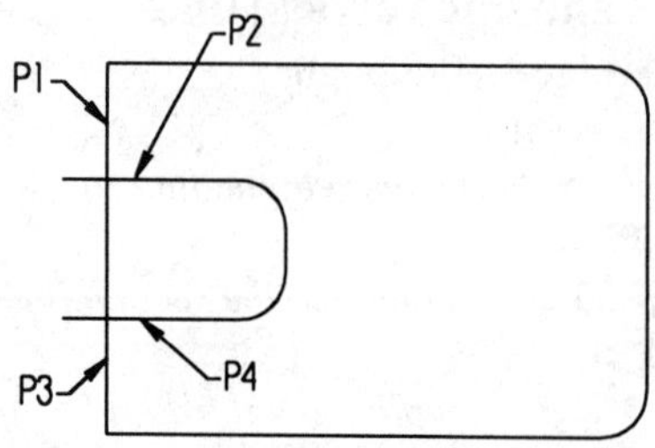

Figure 4.6

Step 6. Trim the left vertical line of the rectangle and two horizontal lines using the pick points in Figure 4.6.

Select **BACKUP** → **Trim** → **2 entities**
Select the entity to trim: pick **P1**
Select the entity to trim to: pick **P2** to trim the upper half of the vertical line
Select the entity to trim: pick **P3**
Select the entity to trim to: pick **P4** to complete the trimming
The trimmed drawing should look like Figure 4.7.

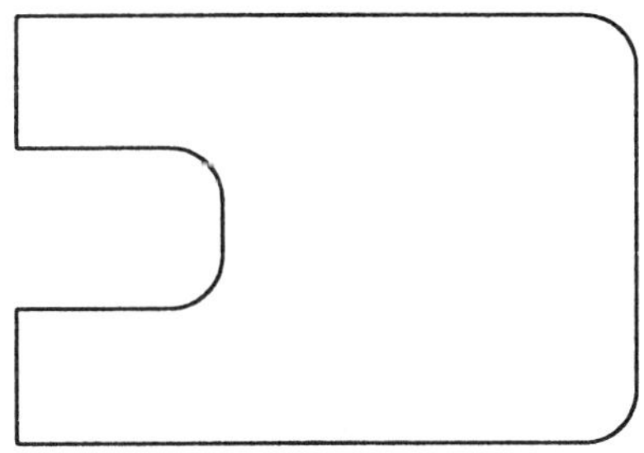

Figure 4.7

Step 7. Create four circles.

Select **MAIN MENU** → **Create** → **Arc** → **Circ pt + dia**
Enter the diameter: **.5** ↵
Enter the center point: **5,2** ↵
Enter the center point: **4,3** ↵
Enter the center point: **3,2** ↵
Enter the center point: **4,1** ↵
The four circles are added to the drawing as shown in Figure 4.8.

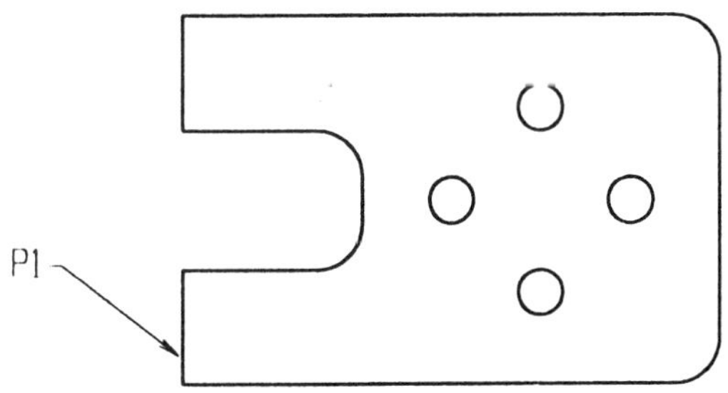

Figure 4.8

Step 8. Initiate the Contour module to generate the toolpath for the outer profile.

Select **MAIN MENU** → **Toolpaths** → **Contour**
Define contour 1: select **Chain** from the chaining method menu
Select the first entity in the contour: pick **P1**
Note: The chaining diamond will go in the clockwise direction
Select **Done** to complete the contour chaining
Use the pick point in Figure 4.8.

Step 9. Select a 1" end mill.

Click the right mouse button, then select **Get tool from library**
The tool manager dialog box with a list of tools should appear as below.

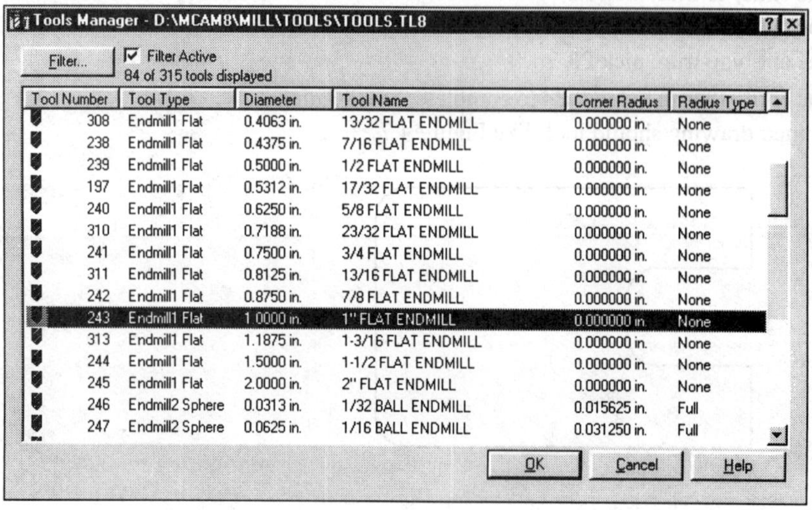

From the Tool Manager list, select **243 Endmill1 Flat**
Select **OK**

Step 10. Select a material.

Click on the right mouse button, then select the "Job setup" option
The Job Setup screen will appear as below

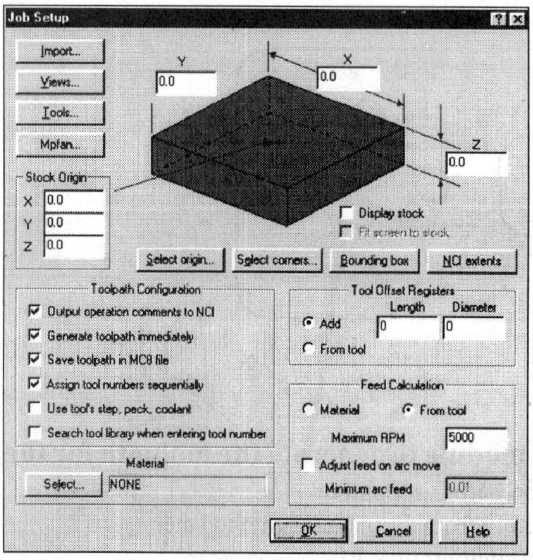

Click **Select** from the bottom of the Material Selection: menu.

The Material list screen is shown below
Select **ALUMINUM inch - 2024 → OK → OK**

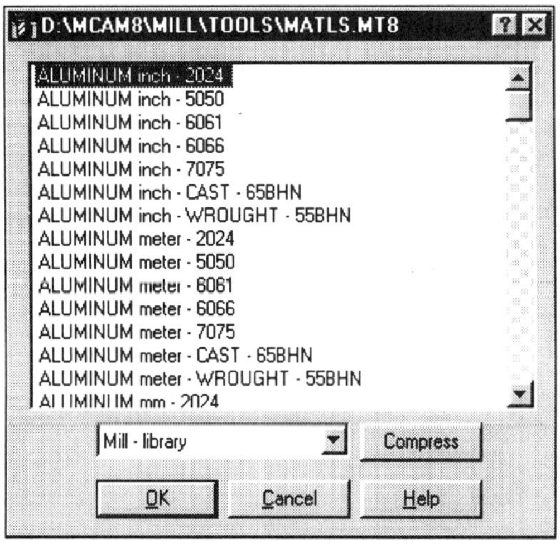

Step 11. Define the tool holder.

Use the right mouse button to click on the **tool icon** of "Endmill"
Set the parameters as below

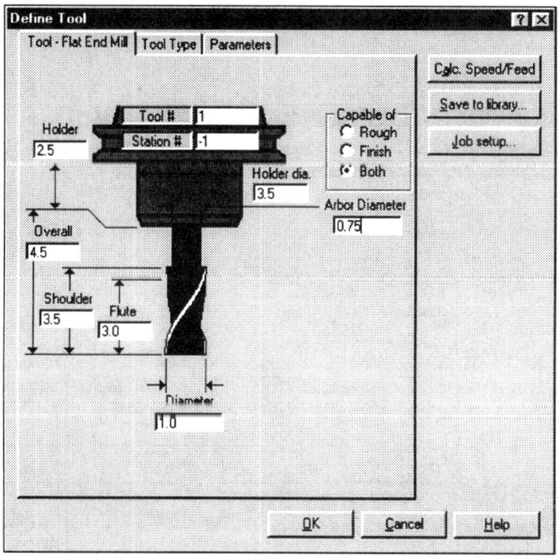

Step 12. Define the tooling and machining parameters.

Select the **parameters button** to open the parameters menu.
Set the parameters as below

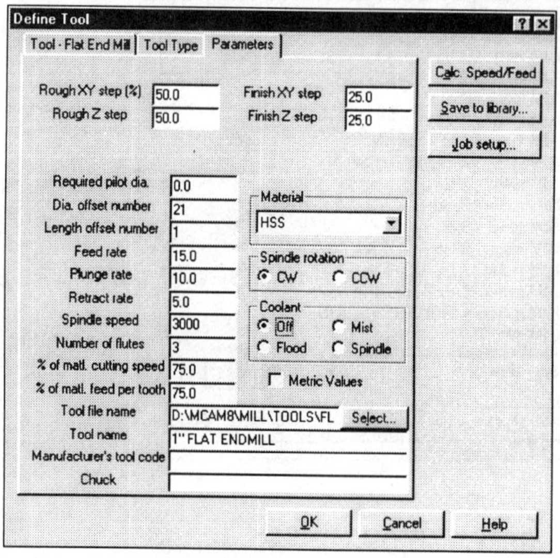

Select **OK**

Step 13. Define tool parameter.

Set the tool parameters as below

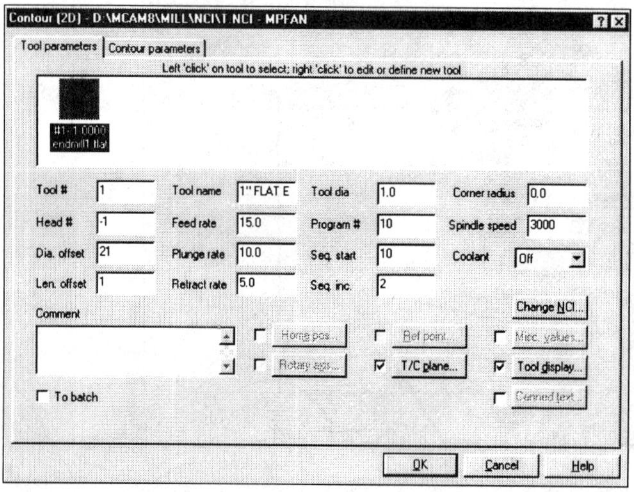

Step 14. Define the contour parameters.

Select the **Contour Parameters** button
Set the parameters as shown next

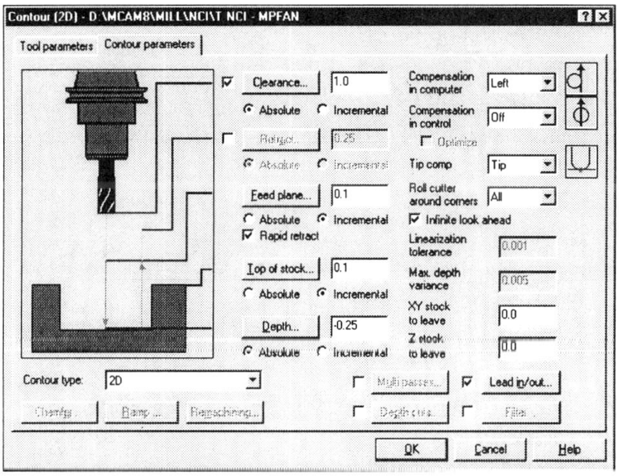

Step 15. Define lead In/Out parameters

Select the **Leadin/out** button
Set the parameters as below

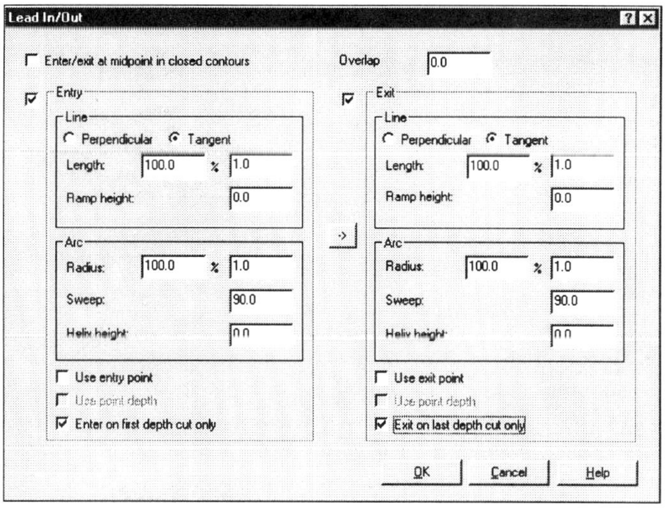

Select **OK → OK**
The toolpaths should appear as in Figure 4.9.

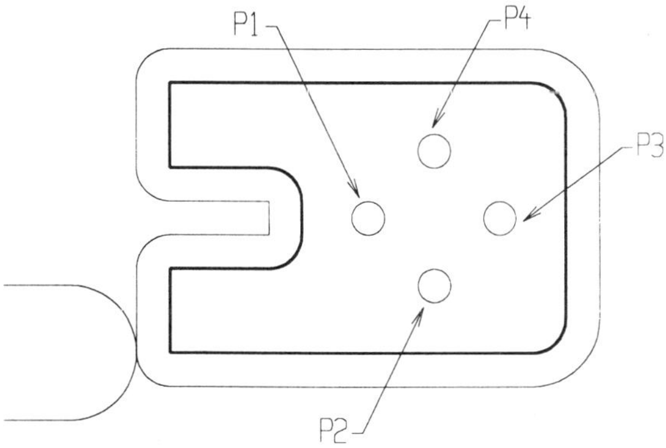

Figure 4.9

Step 16. Initiate the Drill module.

Use the pick points in Figure 4.9.
Select **Drill**
Select **Manual** from the Select points menu
Select **Center** from the point menu
Sequentially pick **P1, P2, P3,** and **P4,**
then press **Esc** to complete the points selection
Select **Done**

Step 17. Set a 1/2" Drill.

Click the right mouse button, then select **Get tool from library**
Select **tool #141** (1/2" drill) as shown below.
Set the Drill parameters to the following settings:

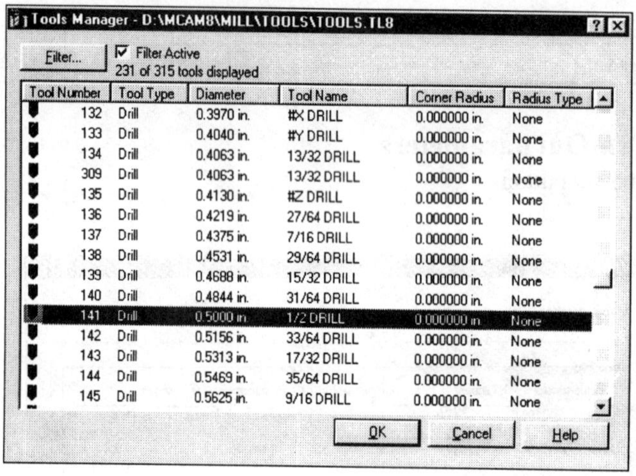

Select **OK**

Step 18. Define the tool holder.

Use the right mouse button to click on the tool icon of the drill
Set the Define Tool parameters as below:

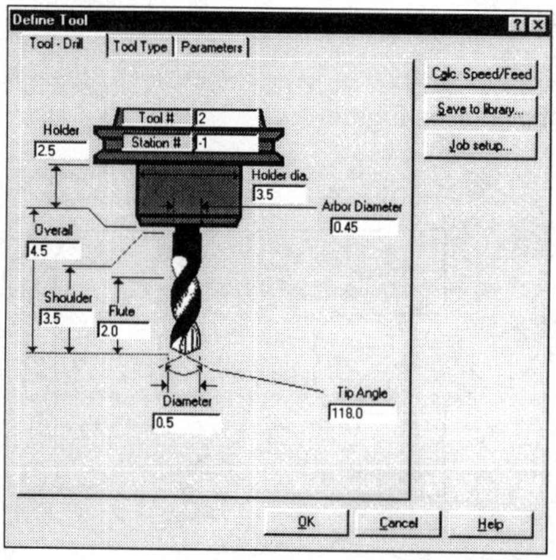

Step 19. Define the machinery parameters

Select the **parameters** button
Set the parameters as below.

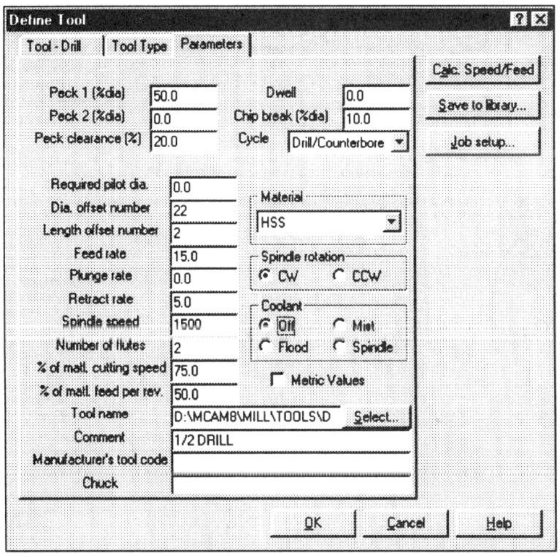

Select **OK**

Step 20. Set the tool parameters as below.

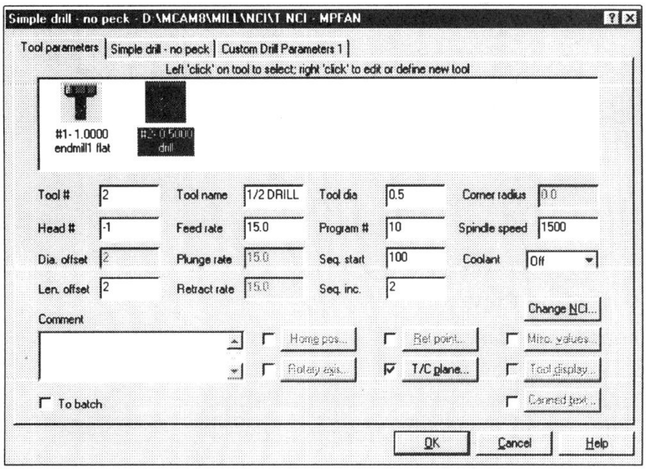

Step 21. Define the drill parameters

Click on the **Simple drill-no peck** tab

Set the parameters as below

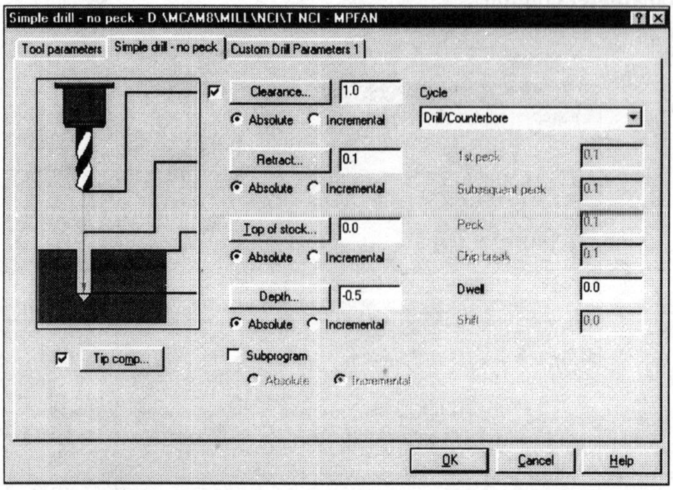

Select **OK**

The drilling toolpaths are added to the drawing as shown in Figure 4.10.

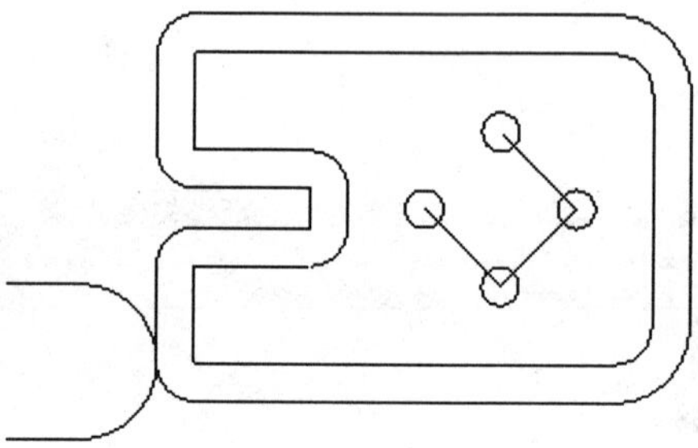

Figure 4.10

Step 22. Change to isometric view

Select **Gview** from the Secondary menu

Select **Isometric** from the Gview menu

Press **Alt** + **F1** simultaneously

then press **F2** to fit the drawing on the screen if necessary.

The drawing should look like Figure 4.11.

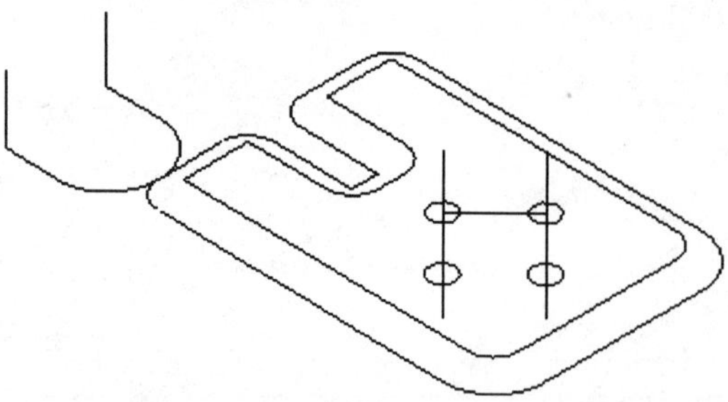

Figure 4.11

Step 23. Select the post processor.

Select **MAIN MENU → NC utils → Post Proc → Change**
Filename: **Mpfan.pst**
Select **Open**

Step 24. Run the post processor to convert toolpath file (.NCI) into NC codes(.NC).

Select **Run**
Select **Yes** to *"Operations have been modified. Create the NCI text file? "*
Select **No** to *"File already exists, overwrite?"* → **Open** (T.NCI)
Filename: **Overview → Save**

The part program should appear on the screen

Exit the list program by clicking the Close box **[X]**

Step 25. List the NC codes

Select **MAIN MENU → File → Edit →NC**
File3name: **Overview**
The program generated from this process is listed below.
Note: Due to different configurations in post processors, your program may be slightly different.

The part program generated from this process is listed below:

```
%
O0010
(PROGRAM NAME - OVERVIEW)
(DATE=DD-MM-YY - 20-06-00 TIME=HH:MM - 15:31)
N10G20
N12G0G17G40G49G80G90
(1" FLAT ENDMILL TOOL - 1 DIA. OFF. - 21 LEN. - 1 DIA. - 1.)
N14T1M6
N16G0G90G54X-2.5Y-1.A0.S3000M3
N18G43H1Z1.
N20Z.2
N22G1Z-.25F10.
N24X 1.5F15.
N26G3X-.5Y0.R1.
N28G1Y1.25
N30G2X0.Y1.75R.5
N32G1X1.5
N34Y2.25
N36X0.
N38G2X-.5Y2.75R.5
N40G1Y4.
N42G2X0.Y4.5R.5
N44G1X5.5
N46G2X6.5Y3.5R1.
N48G1Y.5
N50G2X5.5Y-.5R1.
N52G1X0.
N54G2X-.5Y0.R.5
N56G3X-1.5Y1.R1.
N58G1X-2.5
N60G0Z1.
N62M5
N64G91G28Z0.
N66G28X0.Y0.A0.
N68M01
(1/2 DRILL TOOL - 2 DIA. OFF. - 2 LEN. - 2 DIA. - .5)
N70T2M6
N72G0G90G54X3.Y2.A0.S1500M3
N74G43H2Z1.
N76G98G81Z-.7502R.1F15.
N78X4.Y1.
N80X5.Y2.
N82X4.Y3.
N84G80
N86M5
N88G91G28Z0.
N90G28X0.Y0.A0.
N92M30
%
```

Ex Exercises

1. What are the three major components involved in CAD/CAM NC programming?

2. What should be included in generating CAD drawing?

3. What are the two types of data that should be entered into any CAM program to generate NC toolpath?

4. Describe the output of the CAM program.

5. Explain the main task performed in a postprocessor.

6. Explain why a dedicated postprocessor is needed for a unique combination of CNC controller/machine.

Chapter 5

Basic (2-D) Geometry Construction

Objectives:

1. Understand the function of POINT, LINE, ARC, CIRCLES, RECTANGLE, CHAMFER, SPLINE, ELLIPSE, POLYGON and LETTERS commands.
2. Practice using Mastercam **CREATE** commands to construct entities on screen.
3. Construct part geometries using basic create commands.

Overview

The part geometry of the final finished part and its raw material shape should be defined in the CAD program. This geometric file is then used in the CAM program to generate the toolpaths for producing the part. An accurate and complete CAD geometry model is very essential in implementing any CAD/CAM software for producing a part program. The focus of this chapter is to show how to use Mastercam's CAD functions to create basic 2-D part geometries. The commands presented in this chapter include Point, Line, Arc, Circles, Rectangle, Chamfer, Spline, Ellipse, Polygon and Letters. Advanced geometry modification functions are presented in chapter 6. Three-D wireframe geometric model construction is covered in chapter 11.

5.1 Create Menu

Mastercam groups geometry entity construction functions under the Create menu. To create a geometric entity, we have to follow a proper cascaded menu sequence which starts at the MAIN MENU, followed by the Create menu and necessary sub-menus. Figure 5.1 shows a cascaded sequence for the Create function.

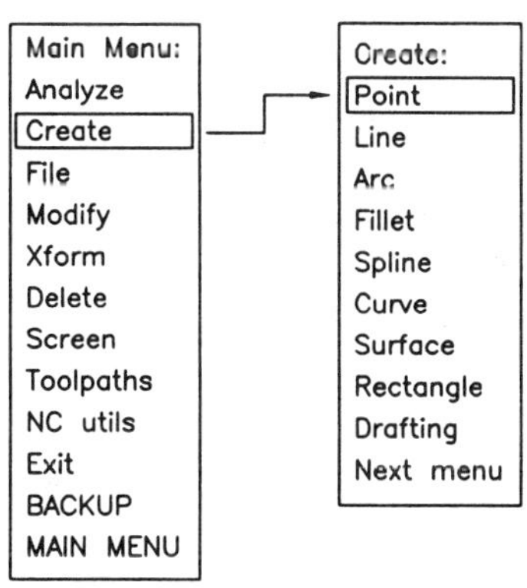

Figure 5.1: Menu for Create

5.2 Point and the Point Submenu

The **Point** command marks points on the drawing with a plus (+) mark. These points can be used as reference points for other geometric constructions when needed.

Select **Create → Point** from the main menu and you will see the following options (Figure 5.2).

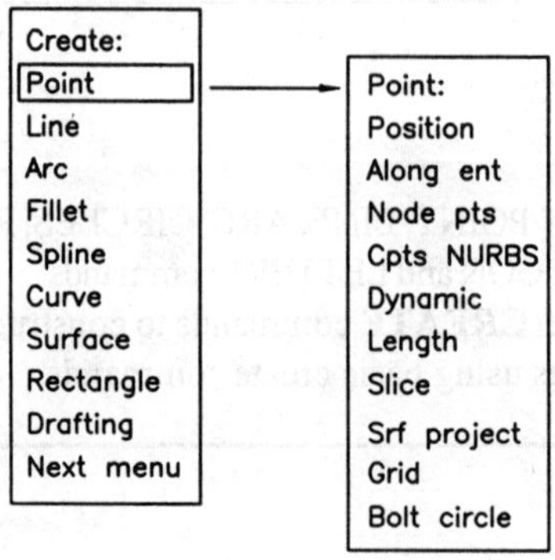

Figure 5.2: Menu for Point

A brief description for the POINT options follows:

Point option	Description
Position:	Create a point by selecting from the following submenu Origin: <Refer to the next table for detailed descriptions of these options.> Center: Endpoint: Intersec: Midpoint: Point: Last: Relative: Sketch:
Along ent:	Create a series of points along an entity with equal distance
Node pts:	Recall the node points used to create a parametric spline curve
Cpts NURBS:	Recall the control points of NURBS curve or 3-D surface
Dynamic:	Create points along an existing entity using the pointing device
Length:	Create a point on an entity by a given distance from the end point.
Slice*:	Create points at intersections of planes with non-coplanar lines, arcs and splines.
srf project*:	Create points on a surface by projecting them directly onto the surface.
Grid*:	Create a grid array of points.
Boltcircle*:	Create points in a bolt circle *Note: * indicates this topic will not be discussed in this chapter.*

Create → Point → Position

Use the Position command to create points on the screen. As shown in Figure 5.3, there are **ten** options available and they will be referred as the **<using position menu>** in the future.

Position	Description
Origin:	Creates a point at the origin.
Center:	Select an entity which has a geometric center, e.g., arc, circle.
Endpoint:	Select an entity which has end points, e.g., line, arc, spline, etc. Pick a location closest to the end point you intend to select.
Intersec:	Select two entities which have an intersection point, e.g., line-line, line-arc, etc.
Midpoint:	Select an entity which has a midpoint.
Point:	Select an existing point.
Last:	Select the last point created.
Relative:	Create a point by giving a relative distance to an existing point. Input the distance as either Rectangular or Polar coordinates.
Quadrant:	Create a point by picking a quadrant position on an existing arc.
Sketch:	Use the mouse to pick the point to be created.

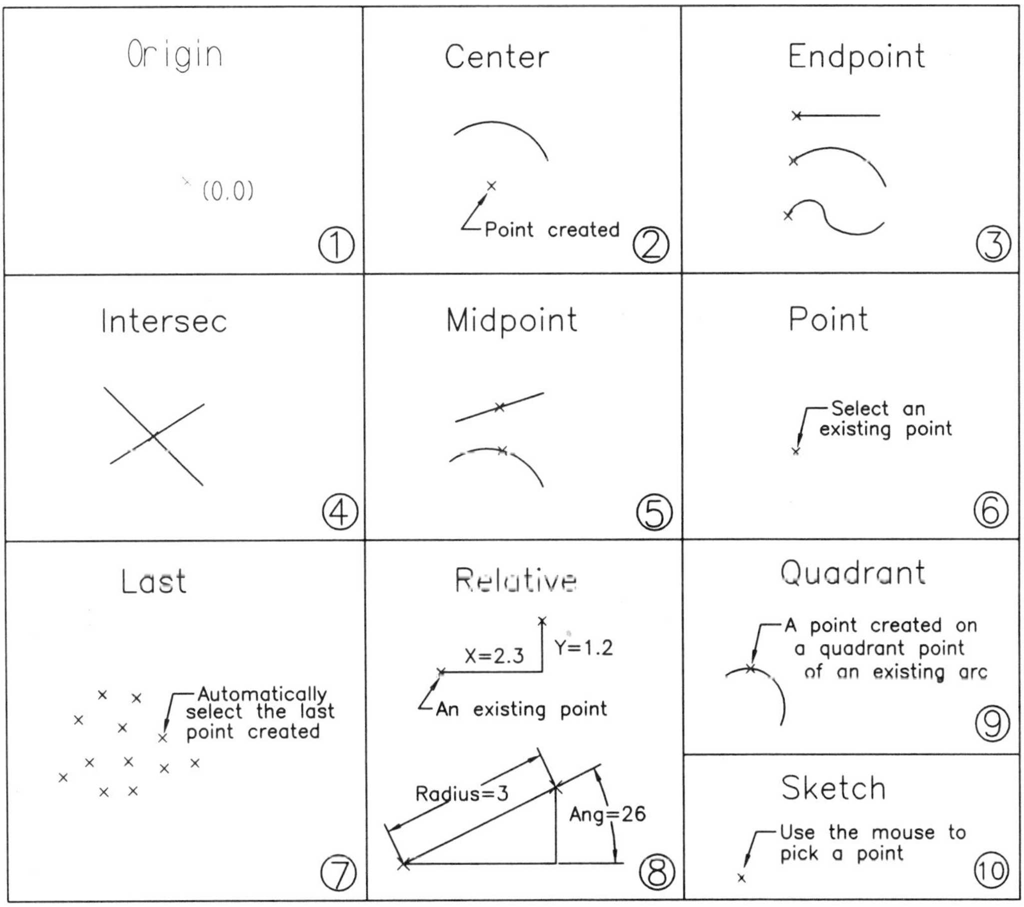

Figure 5.3 Mastercam position menu

Create → Point → **Along ent**

Create a series of points along an entity with equal distance between the points.

Procedure:

Create an entity such as line, arc, circle, fillet or spline.

Select an entity

Use the mouse to select an entity including line, arc, circle, fillet or spline.

Enter the number of points to create (def val): **6** ↵

Note: **def val** stands for default value from the system, see section **3.5** for more detailed information. The points created are spaced at an equal distance along the entity selected as shown in Figure 5.4.

> **Tip** If you want to break an entity into 3 equal sections, this is the command you can use. The number of points to create should be set to 4.

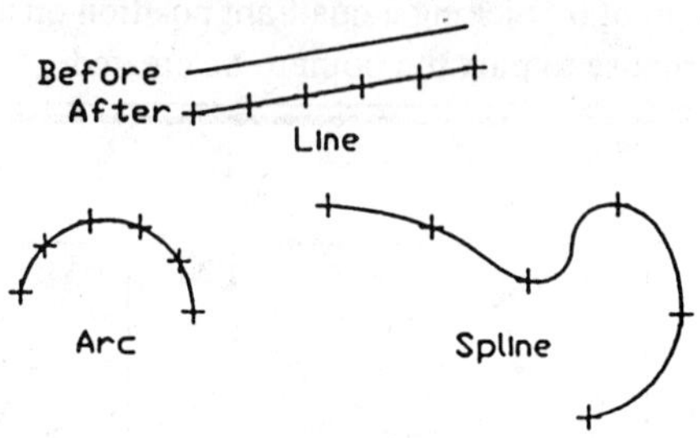

Figure 5.4

Create → Point → **Node pts**

Recall the node points used to create a parametric spline curve (Figure 5.5).

Procedure:

Create a parametric spline curve. Refer to Section 5.6 for the steps in the construction of a parametric spline curve.

Select a parametric spline.

> **Tips** 1. These points are the node points used to define the spline.
>
> 2. If a wrong entity is selected, (other than parametric spline), the system will respond "try again". Use the **Esc** key to quit the selection.

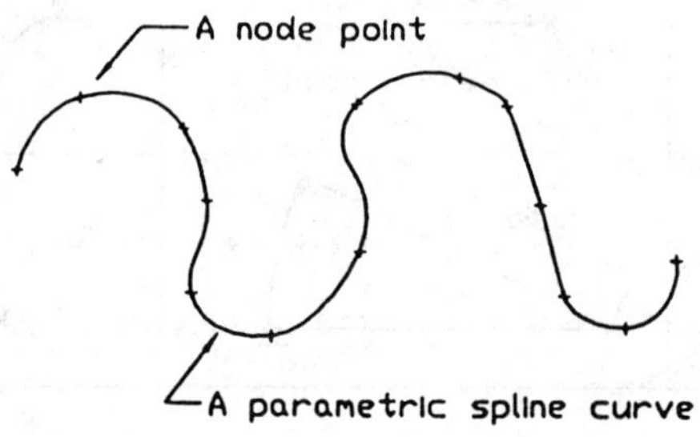

Figure 5.5

Create → Point → **Cpts NURBS**

Recall the control points of NURBS curve or 3-D surface.

Procedure:

Create a NURBS spline.
Refer to Section 5.6 for the construction of a NURBS curve.
Select a NURBS curve (or a 3-D surface).

Tips 1. These points are the control points used to define the curve or surface (Figure 5.6).

2. If you select a wrong entity (other than NURBS curve or surface), the system will response "try again". Use the Esc key to quit the selection.

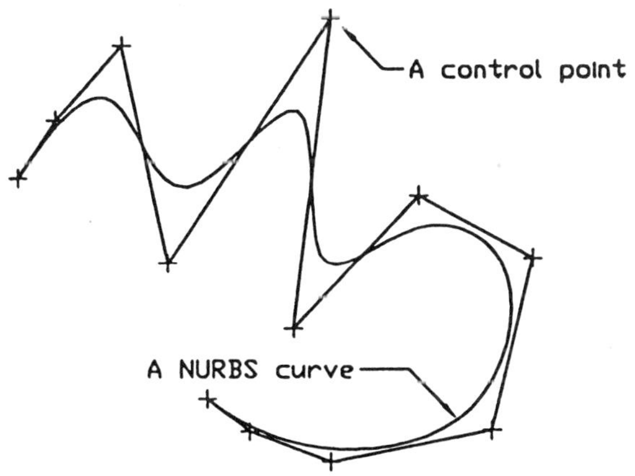

Figure 5.6

Create → Point → **Dynamic**

Create points along an existing entity with the mouse or pointing device (Figure 5.7).

Procedure:

Select an entity such as line, circle or spline.
Move the mouse around the entity and then click the left mouse button to create a point (press Esc when done).

Tip You can use this function to create as many points as you want in any position along the entity selected.

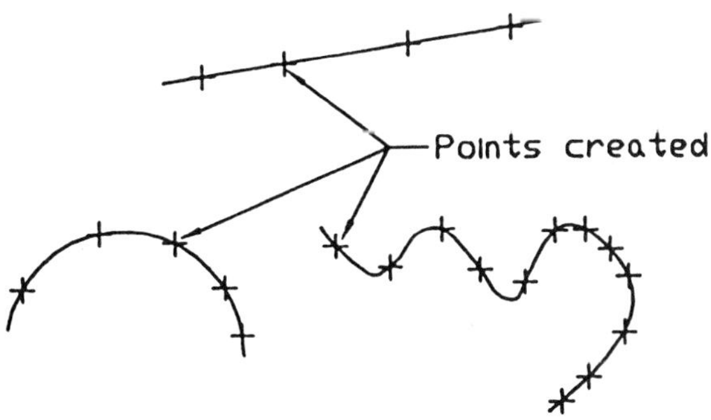

Figure 5.7

Create → Point → **Length**

Create a point on an entity at given distance from the end point. (Figure 5.8).

Procedure:

Create an entity such as a line, arc, etc.

Select an entity: Pick any entity

Length = **1.5↵**

Press **ESC** to quit

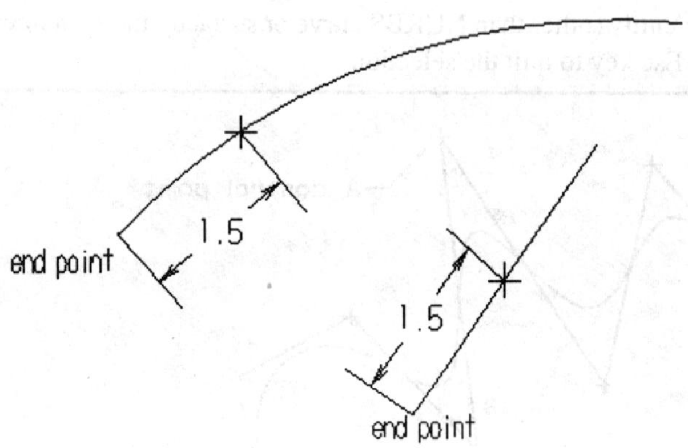

Figure 5.8

5.3 Line and Its Submenu

The **Line** command draws lines on the screen. These lines can be horizontal, vertical, or with any other orientation. It can be used to construct geometries such as those shown in Figure 5.9.

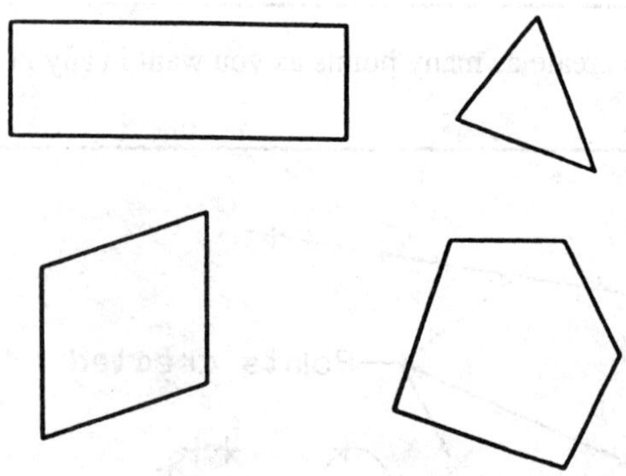

Figure 5.9

Select **Create → Line** from the main menu and you will see the following submenu options.

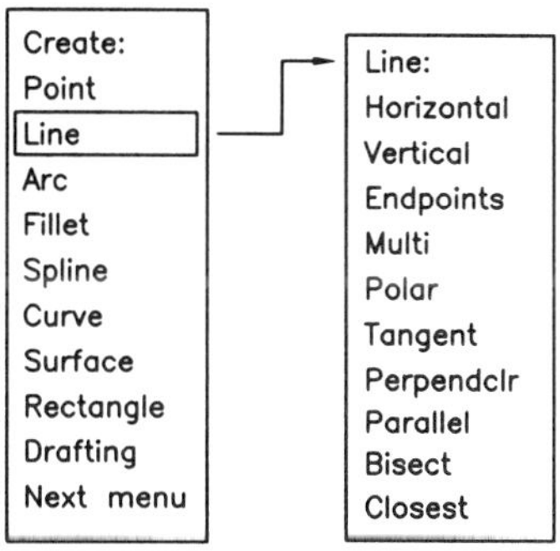

Figure 5.10: Submenu options for Line

In the LINE submenu, there are **ten** options. A brief description of each option is given below and its examples are provided in Figure 5.11.

Line option	Description
Horizontal:	Create a horizontal line.
Vertical:	Create a vertical line.
Endpoints:	Create a line by specifying its two endpoints.
Multi:	Construct multi-line segments by specifying segment endpoints.
Polar:	Create a line using polar coordinate.
Tangent:	Create a line which is tangent to an arc or arcs.
Perpendclr:	Create a line which is perpendicular to a line or an arc.
Parallel:	Create a line that is parallel to reference a line.
Bisect:	Create a line that bisects the angle formed by two intersecting lines.
Closest:	Create a line that is closest to the next entity.

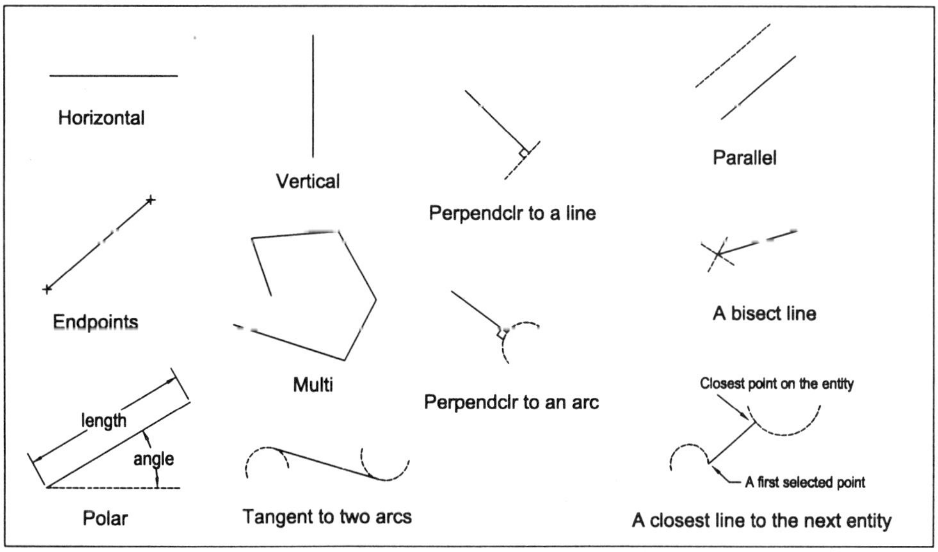

Figure 5.11

Note: The default line style and line width can be changed by picking the Style/Width button from the Menu Area (See Figure 3.3). The available line styles are solid, hidden, center, phantom and Zbreak.

Create → Line → **Horizontal**

Create a horizontal line (Figure 5.12).

Procedure:

Specify the first endpoint <using position menu>: Pick **P1**
Specify the second endpoint <using position menu>: Pick **P2**
Enter the y coordinate (def val): **3.0** ↵
(Press Esc to quit this procedure.)

Note: The default value inside the dialog box is the Y coordinate of the first selected endpoint.

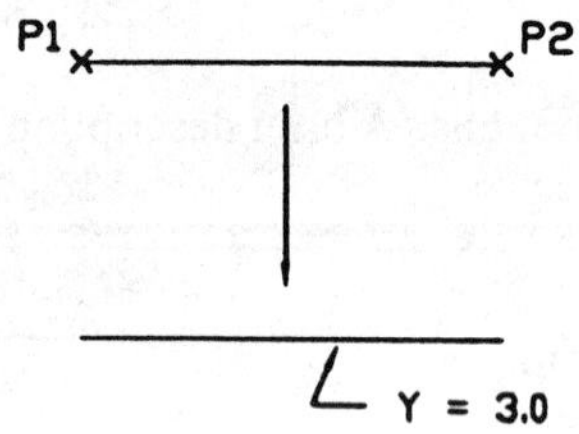

Figure 5.12

Create → Line → **Vertical**

Create a vertical line (Figure 5.13).

Procedure:

Specify the first endpoint <using position menu>: Pick **P1**
Specify the second endpoint <using position menu>: Pick **P2**
Enter the x coordinate (def val): **3.0** ↵
(Press Esc to quit this procedure.)

Note: The default value inside the dialog box is the X coordinate of the first selected endpoint.

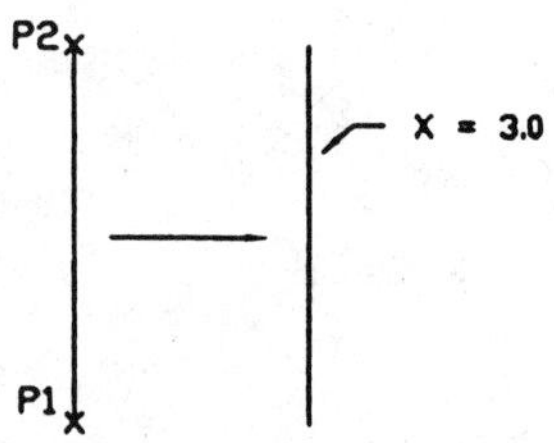

Figure 5.13

Create → Line → **Endpoints**

Create a line by specifying its two endpoints (Figure 5.14).

Procedure:

Specify the first endpoint <using position menu>: Pick **P1**
Specify the second endpoint <using position menu>: Pick **P2**

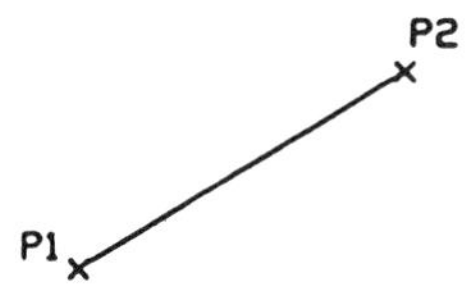

Figure 5.14

Create → Line → **Multi**

Construct multi-line segments by specifying their segment endpoints (Figure 5.15).

Procedure:

Select endpoint 1 <using position menu>: Pick **P1**
Select endpoint 2 <using position menu>: Pick **P2**
Select endpoint 3 <using position menu>: Pickt **P3**
Continue with endpoint selection(s): Pick **P4**, **P5** and **P6**
Select **BACKUP** or press **Esc** key to exit the selection.

Note: As of Mastercam V8.0, the **UNDO** key will undo only the last line segment created.

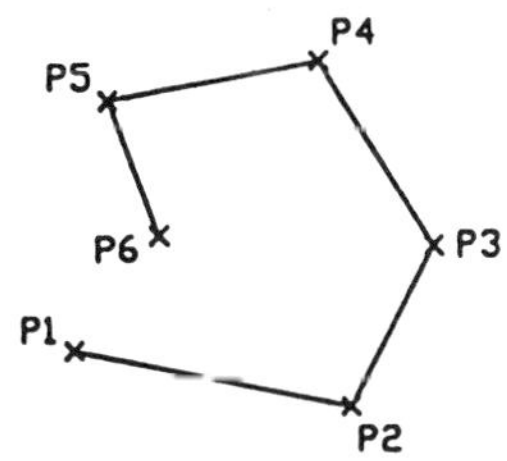

Figure 5.15

Create → Line → **Polar**

Create a line using polar coordinate (Figure 5.16).

Procedure:

Specify an endpoint <using position menu>: Pick **P1**
Enter the angle in degrees (def val): **30**↵
Enter the line length (def val): **2.5** ↵

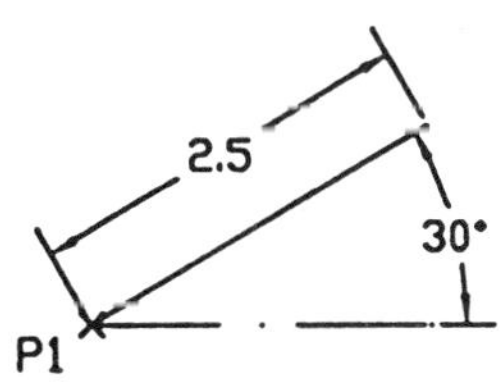

Figure 5.16

Create → Line → **Tangent**

Create a line which is tangent to an arc or arcs. It has **three** options:

Angle:	Create a line with a specified angle and length and tangent to an arc.
2 arcs:	Create a line tangent to two arcs.
Point:	Create a line tangent to an arc through a specified point.

Create → Line → Tangent → **Angle**

Create a line with a specified angle and length tangent to an arc.

Procedure:

Create an arc or a circle similar to the one shown in Figure 5.17.
(Refer to section 5.4 for the construction of arcs.)
Select an arc: Pick **P1**
Enter the angle in degrees (def val): **30**↵
Enter the line length (def val): **2.0** ↵
Select line to keep: **Pick** the correct line segment.

Note: There are two line segments created in this procedure. Choose the one you want to keep.

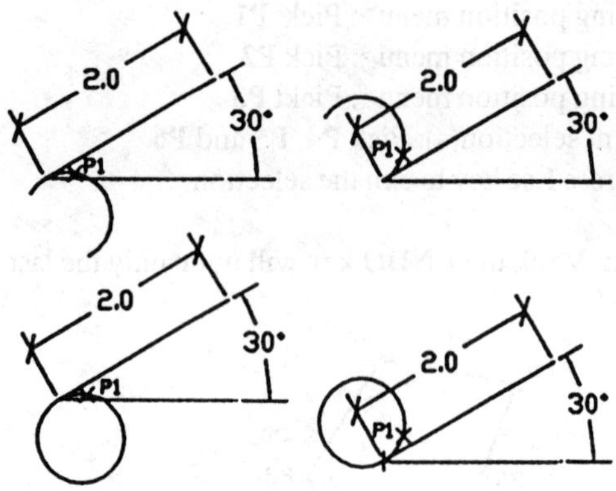

Figure 5.17

Create → Line → Tangent → **2 arcs**

Create a line tangent to two arcs (Figure 5.18).

Procedure:

Create two arcs.
Select an arc: Pick **P1**
Select another arc: Pick **P2**

Tip	There are several possibilities when a line is tangent to two arcs. In procedure 1 and 2, choose the points close to the arcs where you want the line to be created.

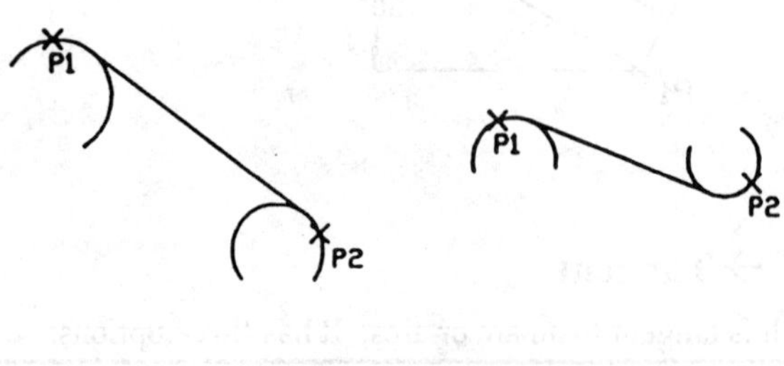

Figure 5.18

Create → Line → Tangent → **Point**

Create a line tangent to an arc or a spline through a specified point (Figure 5.19).

Procedure:

Create an arc.
Select arc or spline: Pick **P1**
Specify an endpoint <using position option>: Pick **P2**
Enter the line lenght (def val): ↵

Note: The default value is calculated automatically from the tangent point to P2.

> **Tip** Generally speaking, there are two possibilities in this case. In procedure 1, choose the points close to the arcs where you want the line to be tangent to.

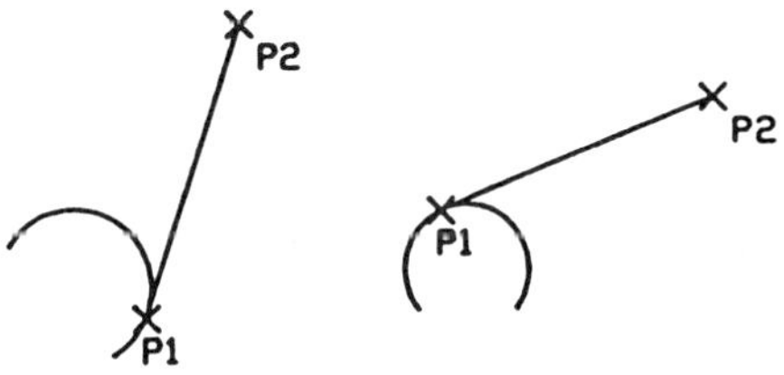

Figure 5.19

Create → Line → **Perpendclr**

Create a line which is perpendicular to a line, arc, spline, or NURBS curve through a point.

It has **two** options:

Point:	Create a line perpendicular to another line, arc, spline NURBS curve through a point.
Arc:	Create a line perpendicular to an existing line and tangent to an existing arc.

Create → Line → Perpendclr → **Point**

Create a line perpendicular to another line, arc, spline, or NURBS curves through a point (Figure 5.20a).

Procedure:

Create a line or an arc.
Select a line or an arc: Pick **P1**
Specify an endpoint <using position menu>: Pick **P2**
Enter the line length (def val): ↵

Note: As shown in Figure 5.20a, in some cases the line created does not have an explicit intersection with the line or the arc selected. Mastercam will automatically extend the line or the arc to calculate intersected point.

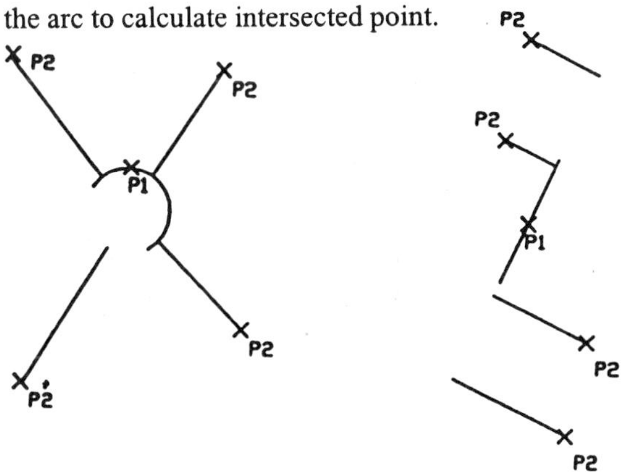

Figure 5.20

Create → Line → Perpendclr → **Arc**

Create a line perpendicular to an existing line and tangent to an existing arc. (Figure 5.20b)

Procedure:

Create a line and an arc.

Select a line: Pick **P1**

Select an arc to place a perpendicular line tangent to: Pick **P2**

Enter the length of the perpendicular line (def val): ←

Select which line to keep: Pick **P3**

Tip Again, there are two possibilities. Mastercam will ask you to choose the one you want to keep.

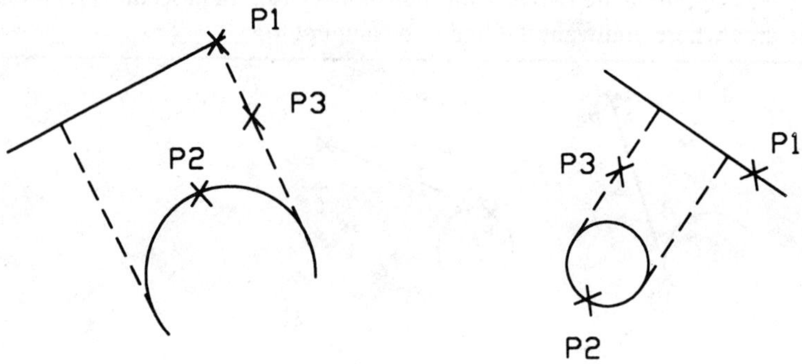

Figure 5.20b

Line Exercise

Using the LINE Command and your mouse, draw each of the following objects as shown in Figure 5.21. Don't worry about exact sizes, but do try to make them look like these drawings as much as possible. Practice the various options covered in this section.

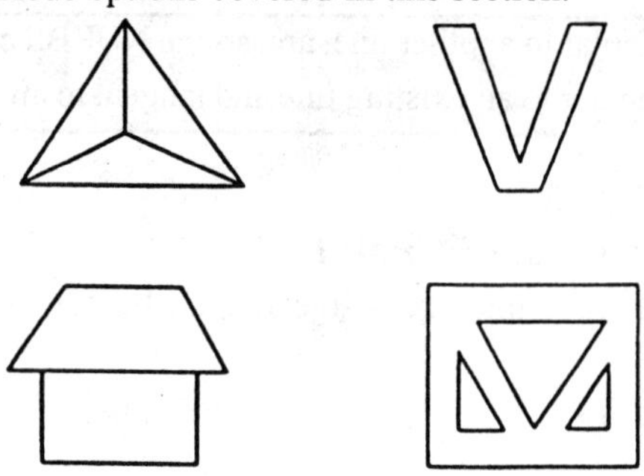

Figure 5.21

Practice LINE commands to draw the the objects shown in Figure 5.22.

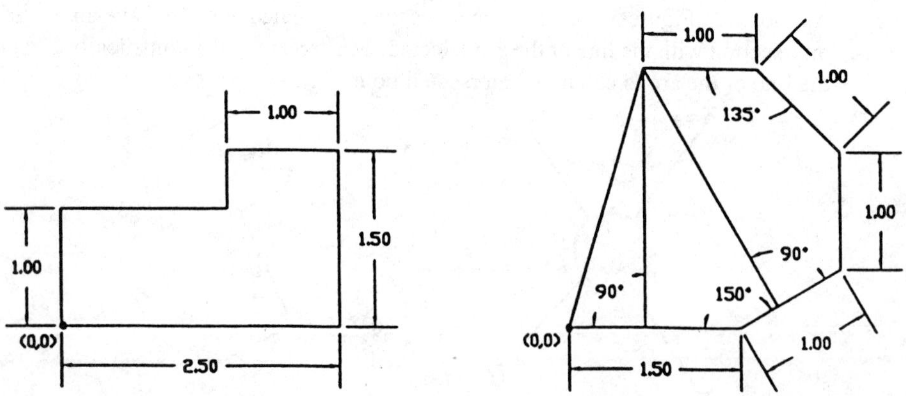

Figure 5.22

5.4 Arc and the Arc Submenu

The Arc command is used to create arcs and circles. Figure 5.23 shows some of the arcs and circles that will be created in this section. Mastercam provides **four** methods to create arcs and **five** methods for drawing circles.

Figure 5.23

In Mastercam, these arcs and circles can be created using several options. Select **Create → Arc** from the main menu and you will see the following **Arc submenu**. A short description of each menu item follows.

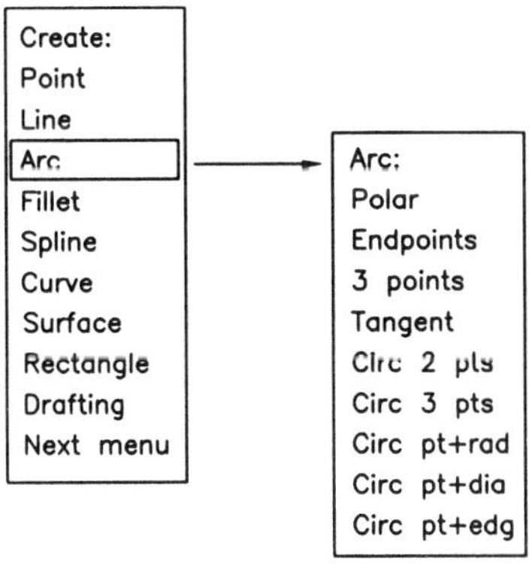

Figure 5.24 Submenu for arc

Arc option	Description
Polar:	Create an arc using polar coordinates
Endpoint:	Create an arc with known two endpoints and its radius.
3 points:	Create an arc with known 3 points
Tangent:	Create an arc that passes through tangent points of select entities
Circ 2 pts:	Create a circle by giving two diameter points
Circ 3 pts:	Create a circle that passes through 3 known points
Circ pt+rad:	Create a circle with a given center point and a radius
Circ pt+dia:	Create a circle with a given center point and a diameter
Circ pt+edg:	Create a circle with a given center point and a point on the circumference

Create → Arc → Polar

Create an arc using polar coordinates. In Mastercam, there are **four** options under polar. These are explained in the following procedures. They are:

Center pt	Sketch	Start pt	End pt

Create → Arc → Polar → **Center pt**

Create an arc with a given center point, radius, initial and final angles. The angles are entered from the keyboard.

Procedure:

Enter the center point <using position menu>: **0,0** ↵
Enter the radius (def val): **1.5** ↵
Enter the initial angle (def val): **30** ↵
Enter the final angle (def val): **280** ↵

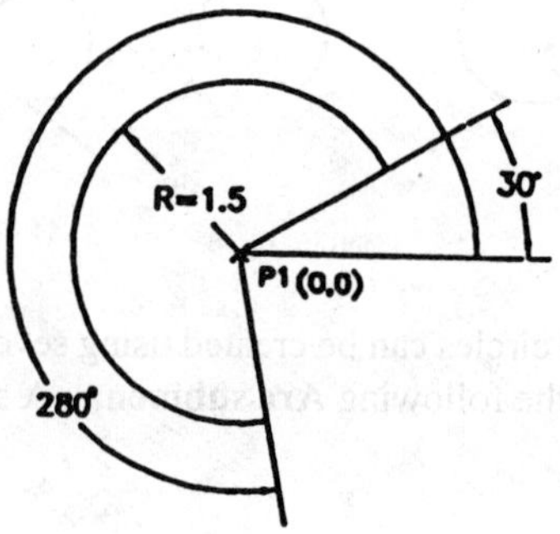

Figure 5.25

Create → Arc → Polar → **Sketch**

Create an arc with a given center point, radius, initial and final angles. The angles are selected by the mouse.

Procedure:

Enter the center point <using position menu>: Pick **P1**
Enter the radius (def val): **1.5** ↵
Sketch the initial angle: Pick **P2**
Sketch the final angle: Pick **P3**

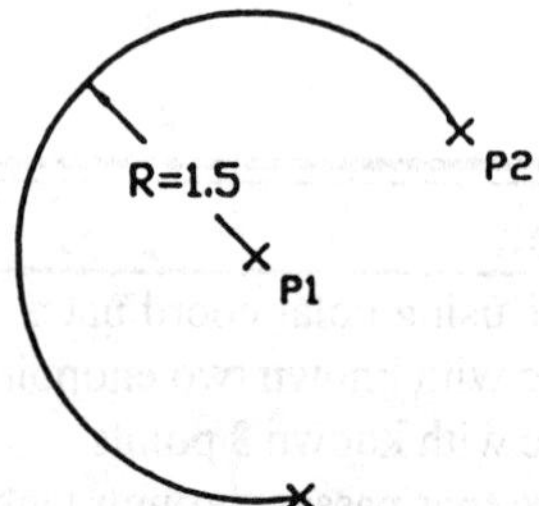

Figure 5.26

Create → Arc → Polar → **Start pt**

Create an arc with given starting point, radius, initial and final angles. The angles are entered from the keyboard.

Procedure:

Enter the start point <using position menu>: Pick **P1**
Enter the radius (def val): **1.0** ↵
Enter the initial angle (def val): **30** ↵
Enter the final angle (def val): **280** ↵

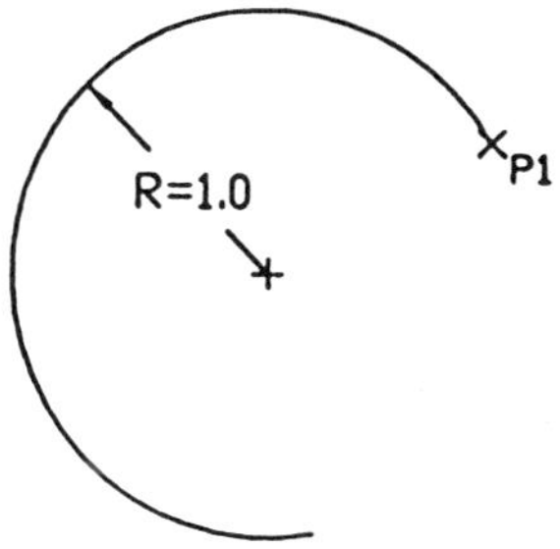

Figure 5.27

Create → Arc → Polar → **End pt**

Create an arc with a given end point, radius, initial and final angles. The angles are entered from the keyboard.

Procedure:

Enter the end point <using position menu>: Pick **P1**
Enter the radius (def val): **1.0** ↵
Enter the initial angle (def val): **30** ↵
Enter the final angle (def val): **280** ↵

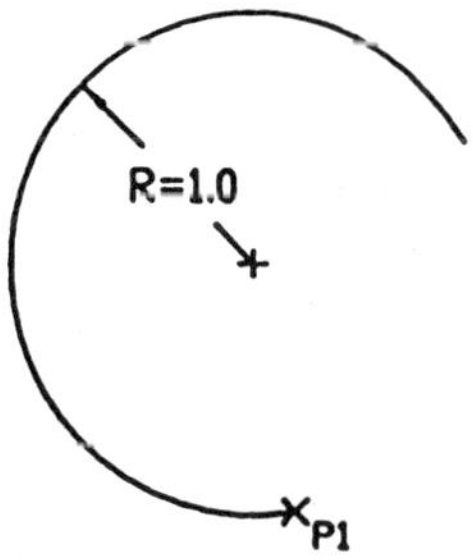

Figure 5.28

Create → Arc → **Endpoints**

Create an arc with two given endpoints and a radius. In general, there is more than one possible choice for the arc. You will have chance to pick the desired one.

Procedure:

Enter the first point <using position menu>: Pick **P1**
Enter the second point <using position menu>: Pick **P2**
Enter the radius (def val): **1.0** ↵
Select an arc: Pick **P3** <pick the desired arc>

> **Tip** In this example, there are four possible arcs to be selected. To pick the desired arc, you need to use the mouse to select a point closest to the arc.

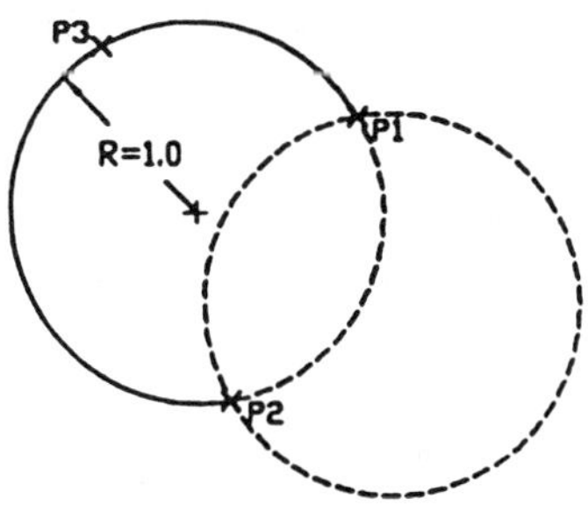

Figure 5.29

Create → Arc → **3 points**

Create an arc that passes through three points selected. The first and third points become the endpoints of the arc.

Procedure:

Enter the first point <using position menu>: Pick **P1**
Enter the second point <using position menu>: Pick **P2**
Enter the third point <using position menu>: Pick **P3**

Note: These three points should not be on the same line.

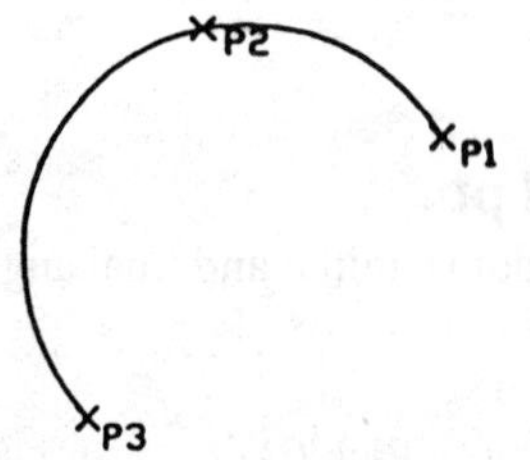

Figure 5.30

Create → Arc → **Tangent**

Create an arc tangent to one, two, or three lines or arcs. There are **six** options under tangent:

1 entity:	Create a 180-degree arc which is tangent to a selected entity.
2 entities:	Create a 360 degree arc that is tangent to two selected entities.
3 ents/pts:	Create an arc that passes through three tangent points of three selected entities.
Center line:	Create a 360 degree arc that is tangent to a line and has its center point on another line.
Point:	Create an arc that is tangent to an entity through another entity.
Dynamic:	Create an arc that is tangent at a selected point on an entity.

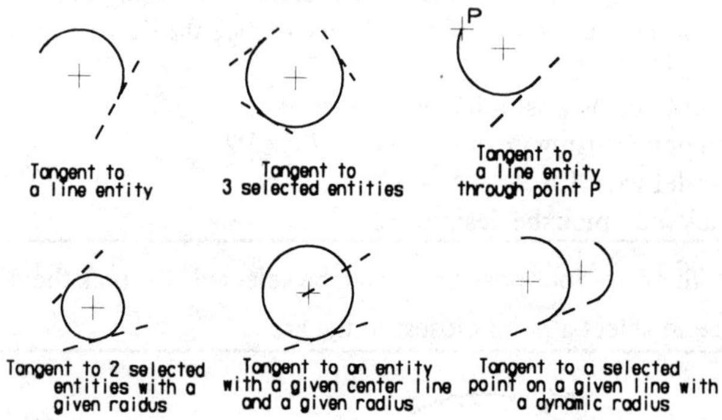

Figure 5.31

Create → Arc → Tangent → **1 entity**

Create a 180-degree arc which is tangent to a selected entity.

Procedure:

Create a line entity.
Select the entity that the arc is to be tangent to: Pick **P1**
Specify the tangent point: Pick **P2**
Enter the radius (def val): **1.0** ↵
Select an arc: Pick **P3**

Tip In this example, there are four possible choices. To pick the desired arc, you need to use the mouse and pick on the desired arc.

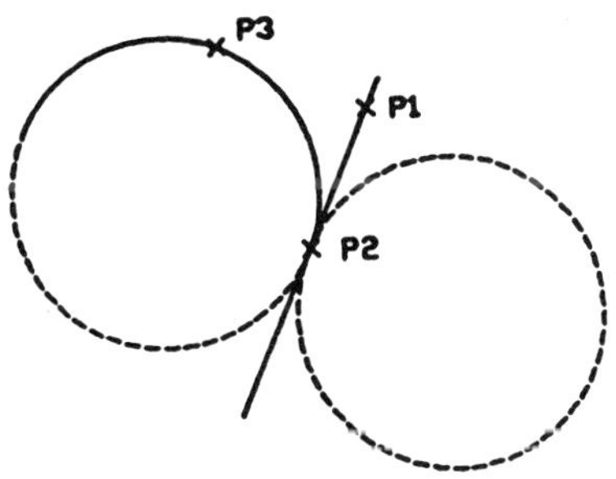

Figure 5.32

Create → Arc → Tangent → **2 entities**

Create an arc that is tangent to two selected entities.

Procedure:

Create 2 lines and/or two arcs.

Enter radius: **1.0** ↵

Select the first entity: Pick **P1**

Select the second entity: Pick **P2**

Tips 1. Select each entity near its tangent point.

2. If the entered radius value is too large, Mastercam displays multiple circular arcs so that you can select the desired one.

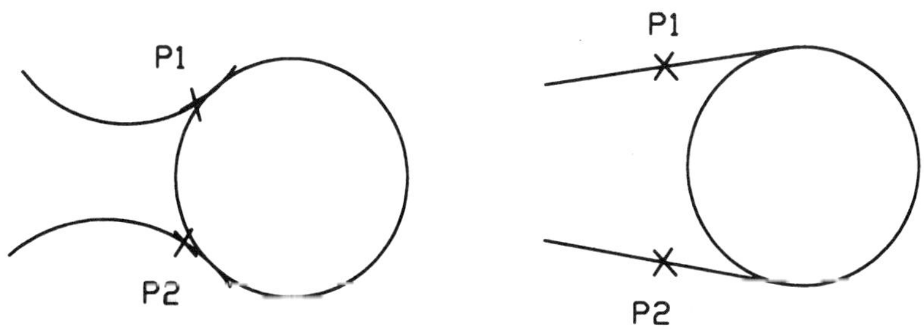

Figure 5.33

Create → Arc → Tangent → **3 entities**

Create an arc that passes through three tangent points of three selected entities. The arc will start at the first entity and end at the third entity.

Procedure:

Create 3 lines and/or three arcs.

Select the first entity: Pick **P1**

Select the second entity: Pick **P2**

Select the third entity: Pick **P3**

> **Tips** 1. Select each entity near its tangent point.
>
> 2. The order of the selection will determine the arc direction.

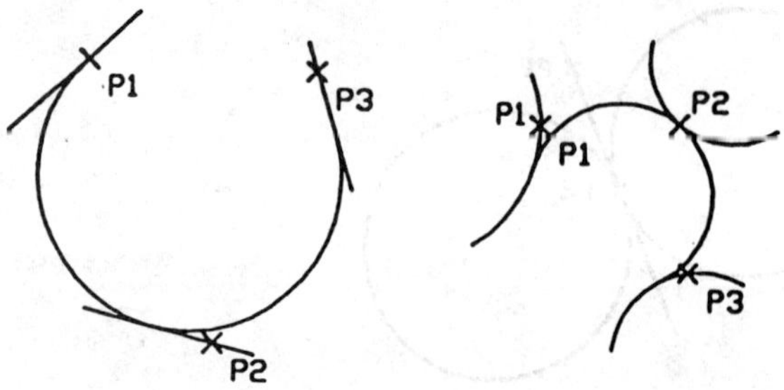

Figure 5.34

Create → Arc → Tangent → **Center line**

Create a 360-degree arc that is tangent to one line with its centerpoint on another line.

Procedure:

Create two non-parallel lines.
Select a line that will be tangent to the circle: Pick **P1**
Select the line to contain the center of the circle: Pick **P2**
Enter the radius of the circle: **2.0** ↵
Select which arc to keep: Pick **P3**

> **Tips** 1. In this example, there are two choices. Pick on the desired arc to keep at the last step.
>
> 2. The tangen line and the center line cannot be parallel.

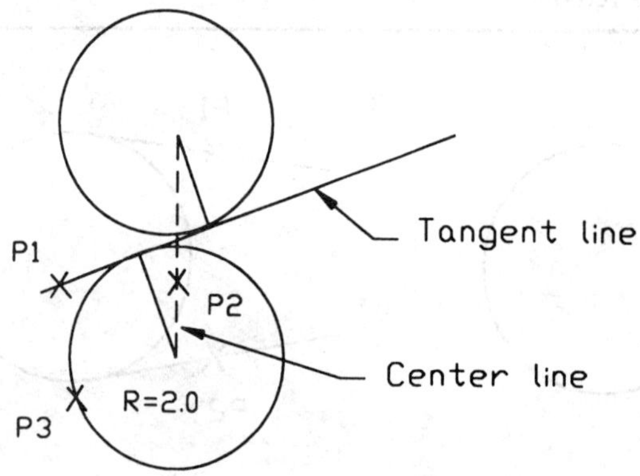

Figure 5.35

Create → Arc → Tangent → **Point**

Create an arc that is tangent to an entity and passes through a point.

Procedure:

Create a line and/or an arc.
Select the entity that the arc is to be tangent to: Pick **P1**
Enter the thru point: Pick **P2**
Enter the radius (def val): **1.0** ↵
Select an arc: Pick **P3**

Tips 1. Select each entity near its tangent point.

2. If there is more than one possible choice, use the mouse to select a point on the closest arc.

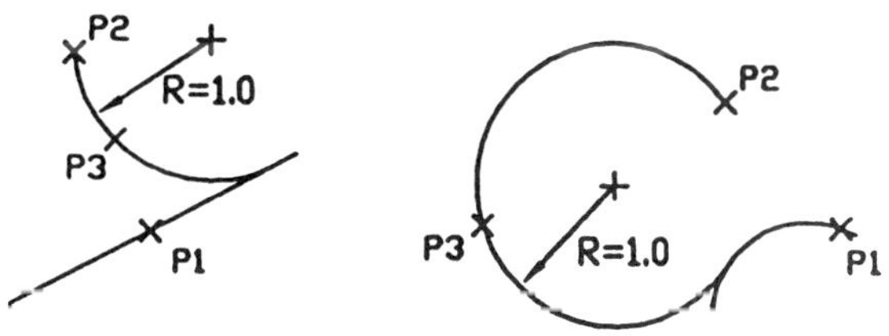

Figure 5.36

Create → Arc → Circ 2 pts

Create a circle by giving two points which lie 180-degree apart on its circumference; or in other words, pick the endpoints of the circle's diameter.

Procedure:

Enter the first point <using position menu>: Pick **P1**

Enter the second point <using position menu>: Pick **P2**

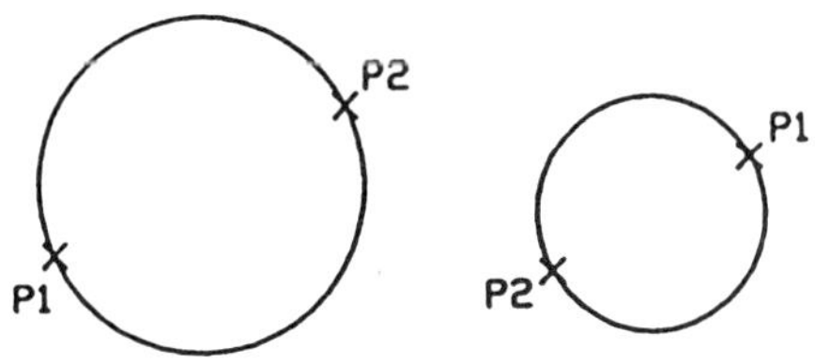

Figure 5.37

Create → Arc → Circ 3 pts

Create a circle by specifying three points on its circumference. These three points should **not** be in a straight line. The selection order is not important.

Procedure:

Enter the first point <using position menu>: Pick **P1**

Enter the second point <using position menu>: Pick **P2**

Enter the third point <using position menu>: Pick **P3**

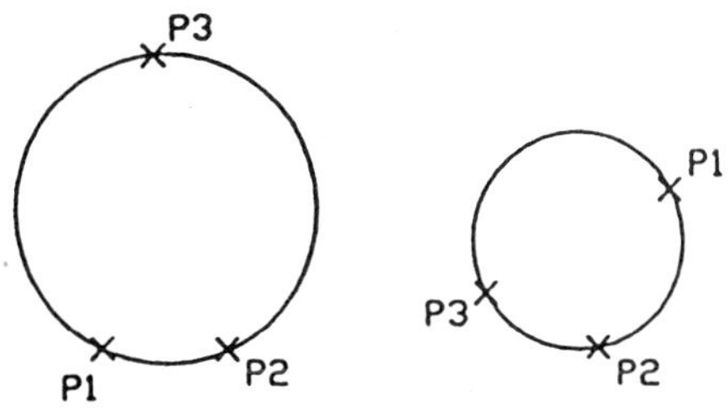

Figure 5.38

Create → Arc → Circ pt + rad

Create a circle with a given center point and a radius.

Procedure:

Enter the radius (def val): **1.0** ↵

Enter the center point <using position menu>: Pick **P1**

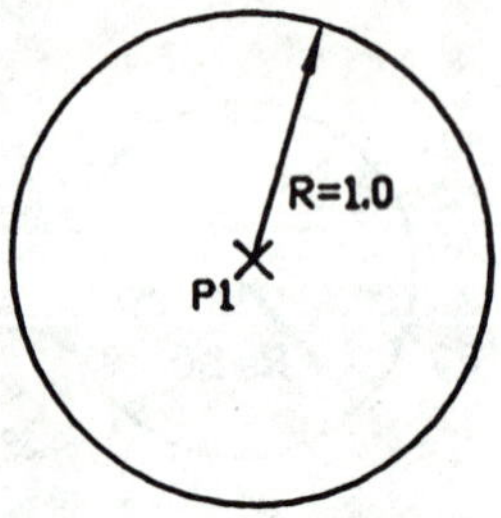

Figure 5.39

Create → Arc → Circ pt + dia

Create a circle with a given center point and a diameter.

Procedure:

Enter the diameter (def val): **2.0** ↵

Enter the center point <using position menu>: Pick **P1**

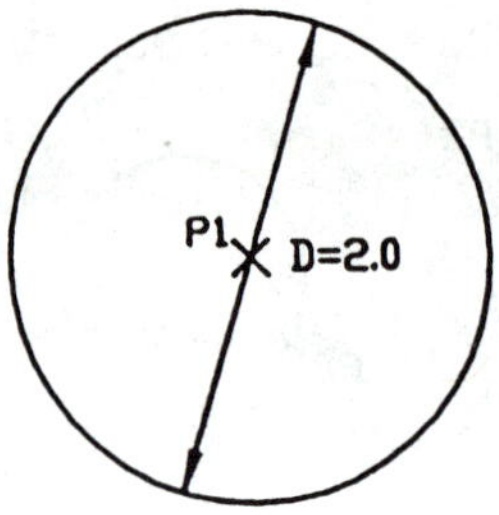

Figure 5.40

Create → Arc → Circ pt + edg

Create a circle with a given center point and a point on the circumference.

Procedure:

Enter the center point <using position menu>: Pick **P1**

Enter the edge point <using position menu>: Pick **P2**

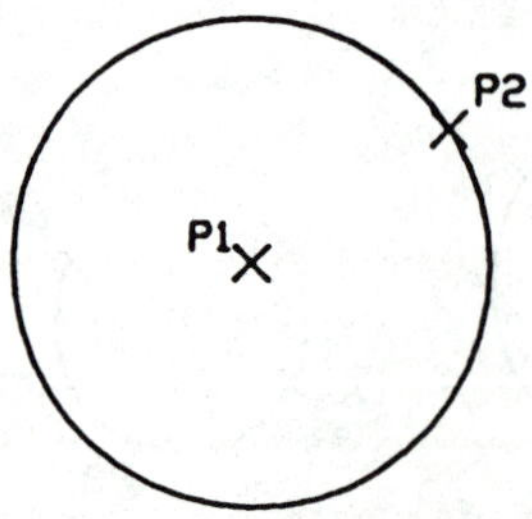

Figure 5.41

Example: Arc and Circle Exercise

Using the ARC Command and your mouse, draw each of the following objects. Don't worry about exact sizes, but do try to make them look as much as these drawings as possible. Practice the various options covered in this section.

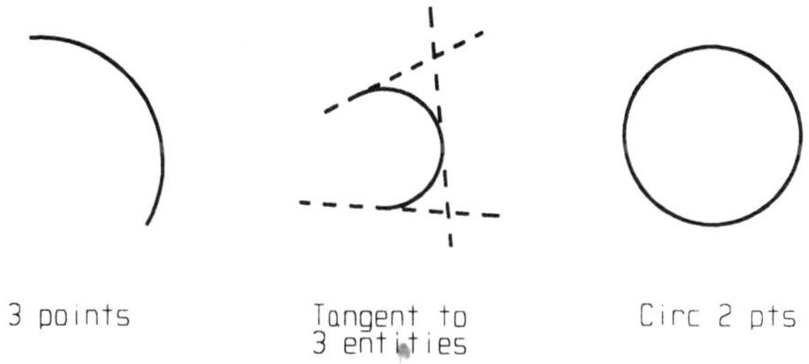

Figure 5.42

Practice using ARC command to draw the following objects.

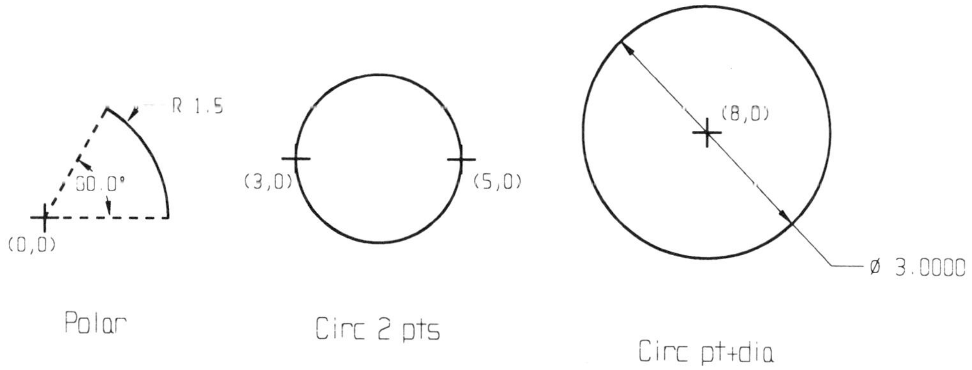

Figure 5.43

5.5 Fillet and the Fillet Submenu

The menu sequence for Fillet command is **Create → Fillet.**

Create one or more fillets for two or more entities by specifying the following **four** fillet parameters:

Radius:	Change to a new radius.
Angle<180:	Toggle the angle option. The angle options can be greater than 180-degrees (L), less than 180-degrees (S), or a full circle (F).
Trim:	Toggle the trim option to either keep (N) or delete (Y) the trimmed line after filleting.
Chain:	Create one or more fillets by chaining several entities at once.

The submenu for fillet is shown here.

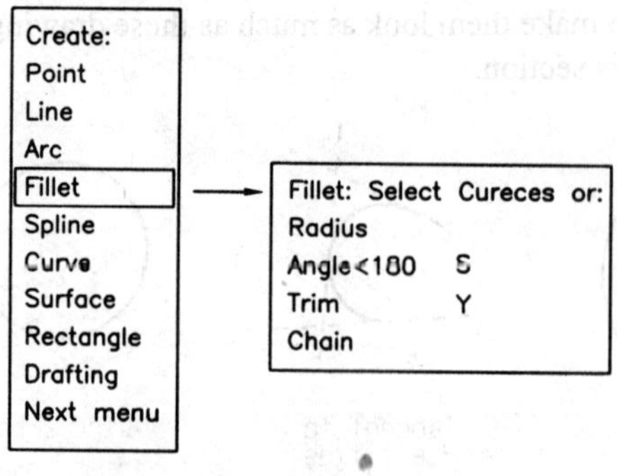

Figure 5.44: Submenu for Fillet

Create a fillet between two lines.

Procedure:

Create two lines.

Choose and change fillet parameters (radius, angle and trim options) if needed.

Select the first entity: Pick **P1**

Select the second entity: Pick **P2**

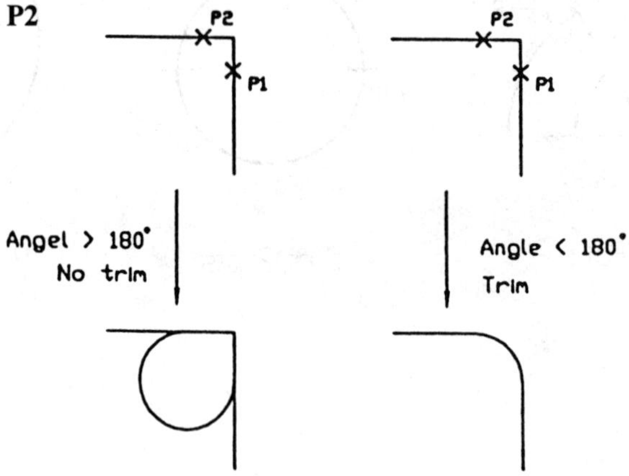

Figure 5.45

Create several fillets by chaining several entities at once.

Procedure:

Create several lines using **Create→ Line→ Multi.**

Choose and change fillet parameters (radius, angle and trim options) if needed.

Select **Chain**

Select the first entity in the chain: Pick **P1**

Select **Done**

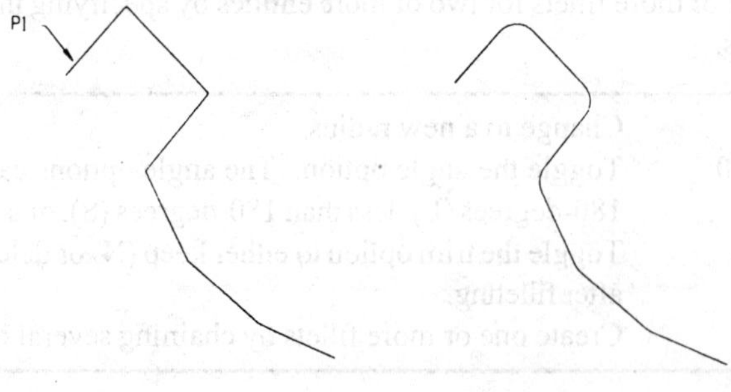

Figure 5.46

5.6 Spline and the Spline Submenu

In Mastercam, the Spline command creates a smooth spline curve that passes through all the node points selected, and there are **two** spline curve options: **Parametric spline** (Type P) and **NURBS spline** (Type N). The user is able to toggle this option by selecting the first option (Type) in the menu (Figure 5.47).

A parametric spline curve is a flexible strip which can be held by weights so that it passes through each of the given points. Corresponding to a draftman's spline, the present mathematical procedure requires that both the slope and the curvature be the same on both sides of the node points.

NURBS is abbreviated from Non-Uniform Rational B-Spline curve or surface. In general, NURBS is smoother than the regular spline curve and may be edited more easily by pulling its control points (see section 6.2.6 and Figure 6.14). It is a useful tool to generate curves and surfaces for the automotive industry.

There are four ways to generate a spline curve:

Manual:	Manually select all the points for the spline curve.
Automatic:	Automatically select the points for the spline curve.
Curves:	Create a spline from existing entities.
Blend:	Create a spline that smoothly joins two arcs, curves, or lines.

The menu sequence for spline is **Create → Spline.**

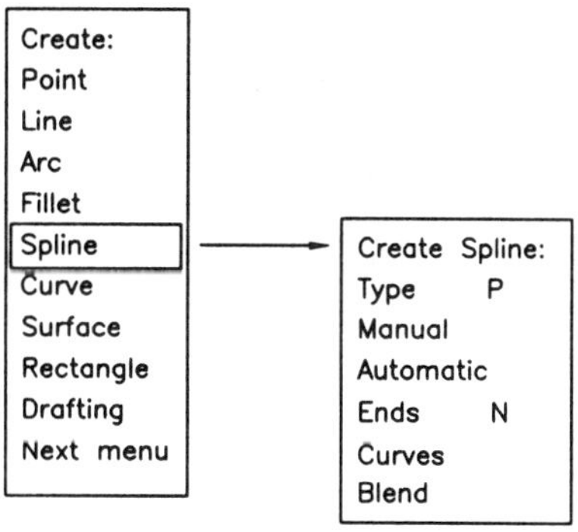

Figure 5.47: Submenu for Spline

The **Ends** option in the menu allows you to modify the slope of the spline at the start and end points. The default value is **N.**

Tips 1. Default maximum value of 1000 node points can be changed in the MILL8.CFG file using **Screen → Configure → Allocations → Maximum number of points per spline.**

2. To generate a closed spline curve, pick the same point for the first and last node points for the curve.

Create → Spline → **Manual**

Manually select all the points for the spline curve. The user needs to select all the points in a proper order.

Procedure:

Select all the node points <using position menu>: Pick **P1**, **P2**, **P3**, etc.
Select **BACKUP** or Press **<ESC>** to finish selection.
Select **Do it** to create the spline.

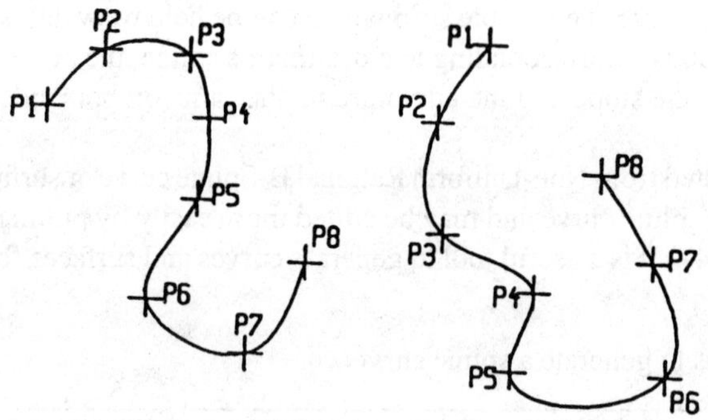

Figure 5.48

Create → Spline → **Automatic**

Automatically select the points for the spline curve. The user needs to select the first, second, and last point on the curve. The system will automatically select other points which stay within the system's curve tolerance.

1. The first, second and last point should be existing points created by the **Create → Point** command.
2. Use the **Create → Spline → Manual** option if it doesn't work as you desired.

Procedure:

Create several points as shown in Figure 5.49
Select the first point: Pick **P1**
Select the second point: Pick **P2**
Select the last point: Pick **P3**
Select **Do it**

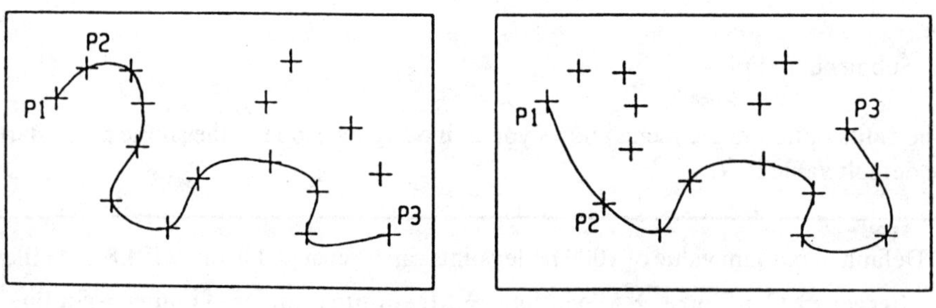

Figure 5.49

When a curve's geometry changes dramatically, create more points around that area to better control the direction of the spline. This is shown in Figure 5.50 on the next page.

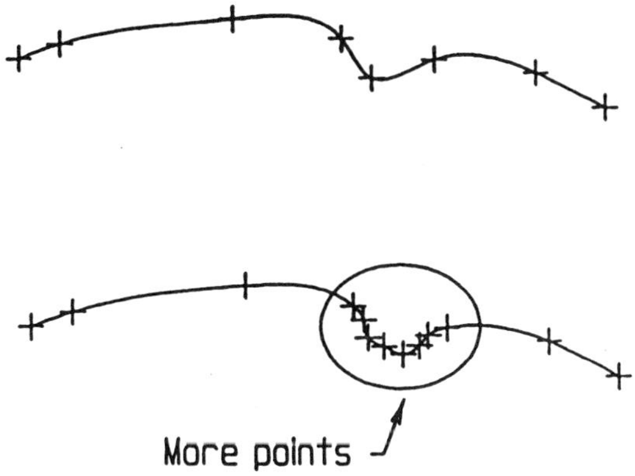

Figure 5.50

A comparison of a NURBS and a parametric spline curve created by the same points are shown in Figure 5.51. Notice the difference at the beginning and ending point.

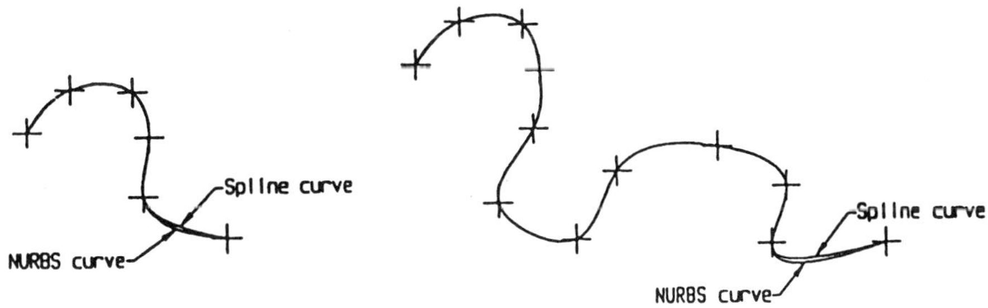

Figure 5.51

Create → Spline → **Curves**

Create a spline from existing entities. You can create a spline from any existing curve or combination of curves; including arcs, lines or splines. If you want to create a spline from only one entity, click the **Single** option. Click **Chain** if you want to create a spline from several entities connected to each other at their endpoints.

> **Tip** You can use Analyze (F4) to check on the new curve.

Create → Spline → Curves → **Chain**

Create a spline from several entities connected to each other at their endpoints.

Procedure:

Create multi-line segments shown in Figure 5.52 using

Create → Line → Multi→ Sketch

Select Curve(s) for spline creation: Pick **P1**

Select **Done → Do it**

<the original line segments are converted to a NURBS curve.>

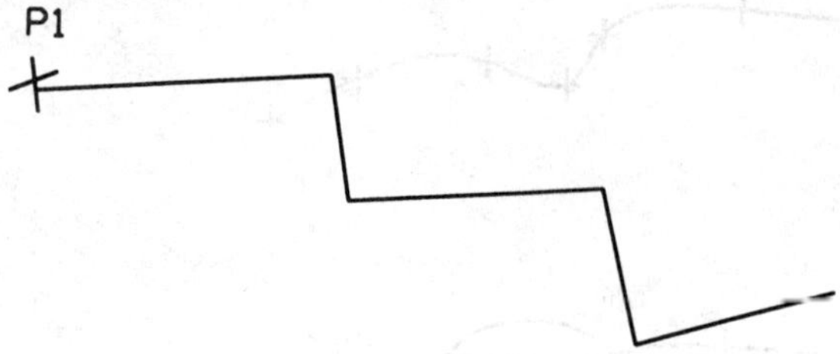

Figure 5.52

Create → Spline → Curves → **Single**

Create a spline from a single entity such as an arc or a line.

Procedure:

Create an arc or line as shown in Figure 5.53.

Select curve(s) for spline creation: Pick **P1**

Select **Done** → **Do it** <The original arc or line is converted to NURBS>

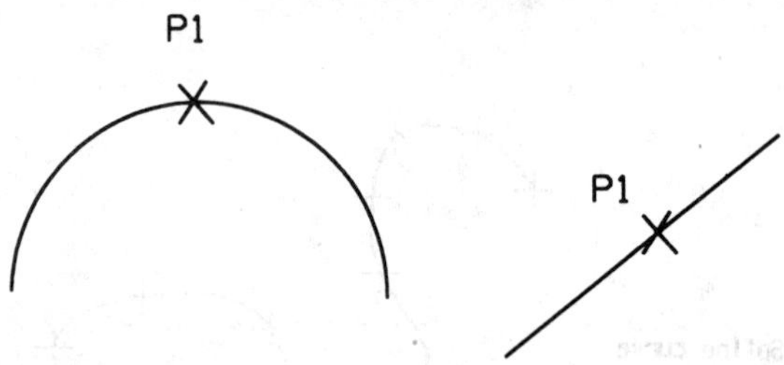

Figure 5.53

5.7 Curve and Surface

Figure 5.54 shows the submenus of the Curve and Surface options. The Curves feature in Mastercam can be used to create a number of curve types on surfaces of existing entities. The Surface function will be covered in chapters 11 and 12.

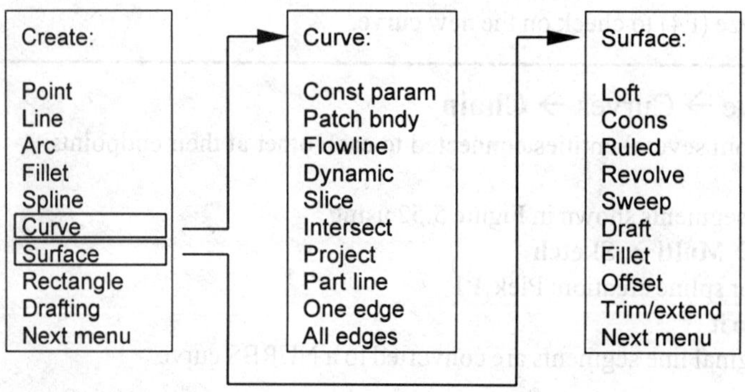

Figure 5.54 Submenus for Curve and surface

5.8 Rectangle and the Rectangle Submenu

The rectangle menu sequence is **Create → Rectangle.**

In Mastercam, there are **three** options to generate a rectangle:

1 point:	Create a rectangle by giving corner point, the width and the height.
2 points:	Create a rectangle by giving its two corner points.
Options:	Enables you to select Rectangular shape, turn on rotation, make corner fillets, create center point and create rectangular surfaces.

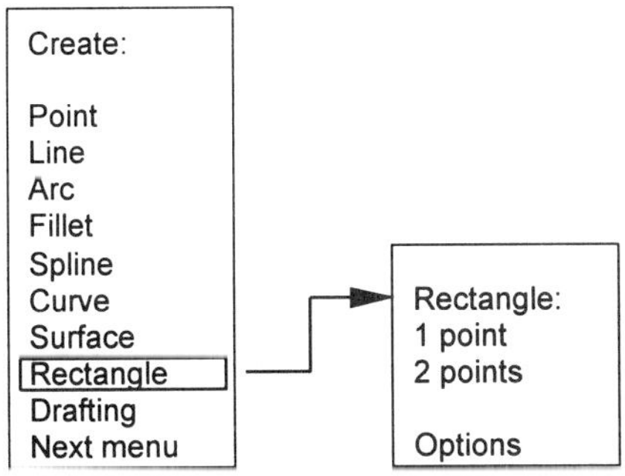

Figure 5.55: Submenu for Rectangle

Create → Rectangle → 1 point

Create a rectangle by giving corner point, the width and the height.

Procedure:

Enter the lower left corner <using position menu>: Pick **P1**
Enter the width <def val>: **3.0** ↵
Enter the height <def val>: **2.0** ↵
Give a coordinate or use the mouse to place the rectangle.

> **Tip** The width and the height can be negative values. If both of them are negative, the point selected in Procedure 1 becomes the upper right corner.

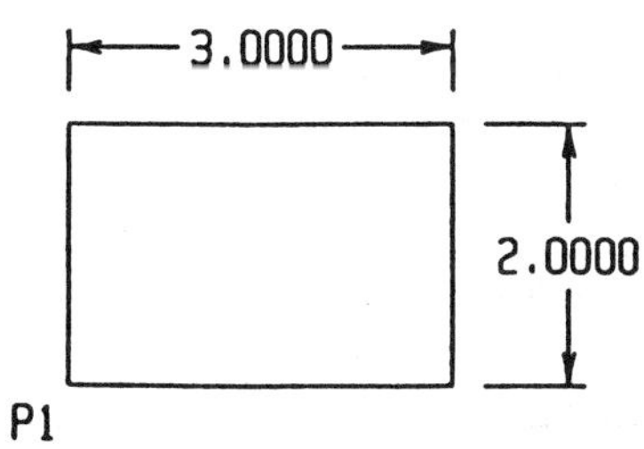

Figure 5.56

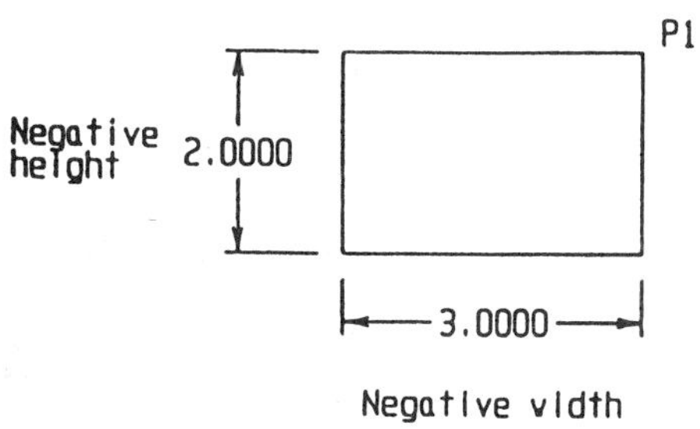

Figure 5.57

Create → Rectangle → **2 points**

Create a rectangle by giving its two corner points.

Procedure:

Enter the lower left corner <using position menu>: Pick **P1**
Enter the upper right corner <using position menu>: Pick **P2**

The selection sequence is not that important. For example, you can select the upper right corner first, then, the lower left corner.

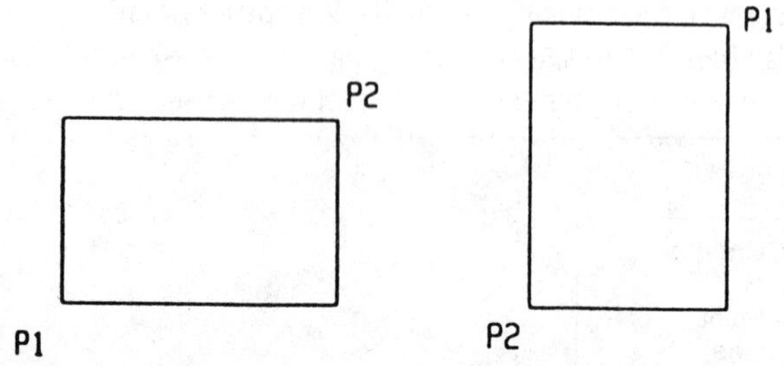

Figure 5.58

Create → Rectangle → **Options**

Brings you to the Rectangle Options dialog box where you can predefine the kind of rectangle to be made. There are five options:

Rectangular Shape:	creates a rectangle with a certain shape
Rotation:	creates the rectangle with a rotation angle you define
Corner Fillets:	creates a rectangle with fillets
Corner Center Point:	creates a rectangular with a center point
Surface Creation:	creates a rectangular surface in NURBS or Parametric

Procedure:

Make desired selection before creating the rectangle using the **1 point** or **2 points** method

Example:

Set the options in the Rectangle Options dialog as shown

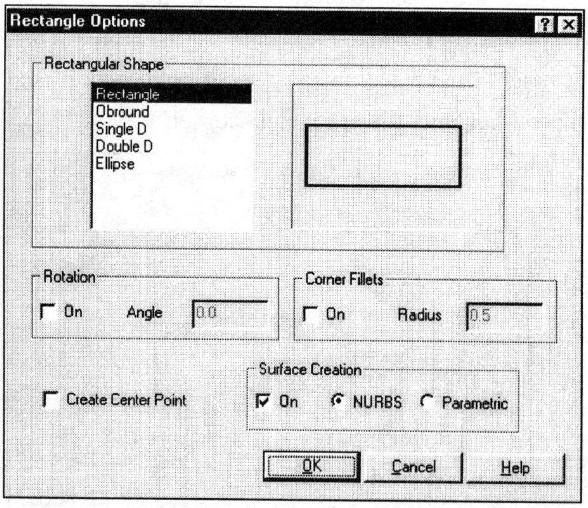

Figure 5.59

Select **2 points**
Enter the lower left corner <using position menu>: Pick **P1**
Enter the upper right corner <using position menu>:Pick **P2**

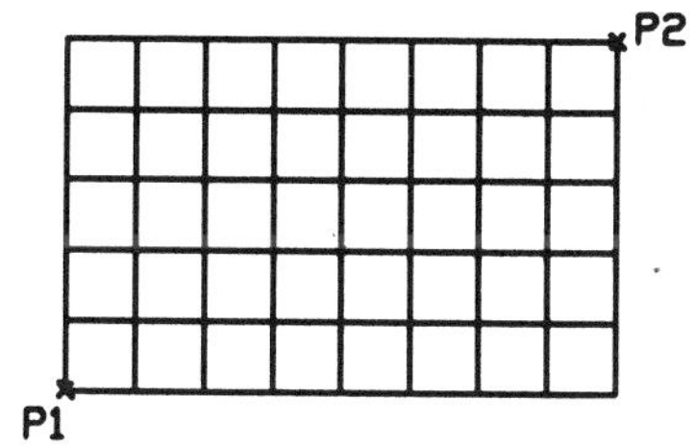

Figure 5.60

Note: To **turn off** the surface option for rectangle; toggle the **Surface Creation** option to **off**.

5.9 Chamfer and the Chamfer Submenu

The chamfer menu sequence is **Create → Next menu → Chamfer**. This command is used to create a chamfer between two non-parallel lines with two given distances. There is an option under the Chamfer command to change the chamfer distance:

Distances:	To change the default chamfer distance(s) of the chamfer. In general, there are two distances can be changed. The first distance related to the first picked point (**P1**), and the second distance related to the second picked point (**P2**).

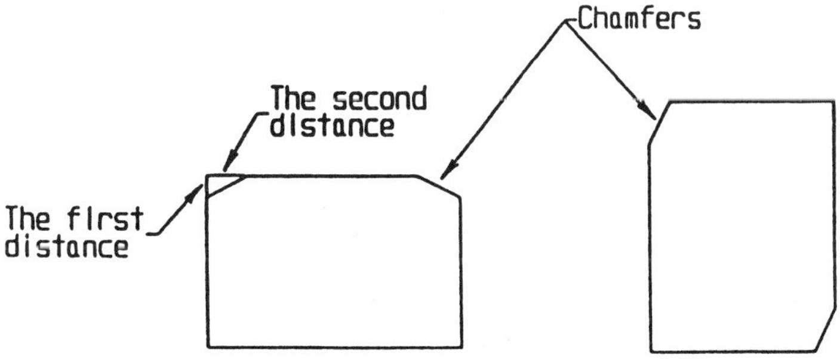

Figure 5.61

Tips 1. The chamfer command operates very similar to the Fillet command.

2. To change the distances, select Distances or enter D at the keyboard, and specify the first and second chamfer distance.

Note: The system prompts the following message for default values in the System Response Area:
first distance = (def value)
second distance = (def val)
(Make sure the first distance = 0.25 and the second distance = 0.50)

Procedure:
Create a rectangle.
Select the first line: Pick **P1**
Select the second line: Pick **P2**
(If you can't see the chamfer, increase the distance value.)

Figure 5.62

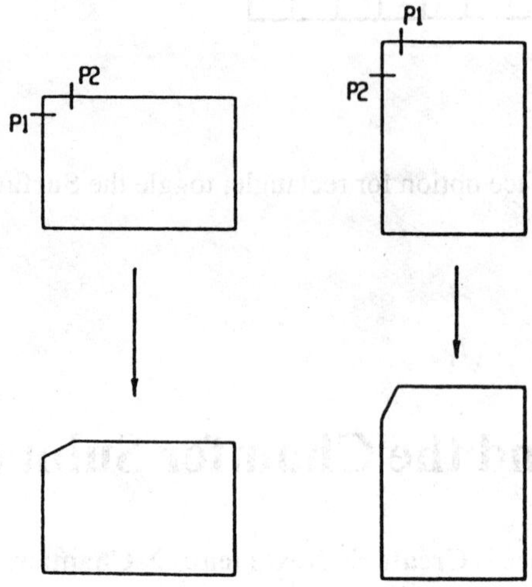

5.10 Letters and the Letter Submenu

Letter geometries can be useful for cutting letters on plaques. In Mastercam, there are two methods to create these letter geometries. The first method creates the geometry using Mastercam's **Letters** command. This command lets you use Windows standard Truetype fonts as geometry and create geometry from the current Mastercam drafting fonts.

With the second method you create a "**Note**" in Drafting, and then change its attributes and reposition it. The details of these two methods are described in this section.

Method 1: Using the Letters Command

The letters command sequence is **Create → Next menu → Letters.**

The sub menu for Lettering includes **three** options:

TrueType(R):	Use the Windows standard TrueType fonts and convert them to geometry.
Drafting:	Create geometry from the current Mastercam drafting font.
File:	Use Mastercam's pre-defined letter files.

Create → Next menu → Letters → **True Type**

Create geometry from standard TrueType fonts. Review Windows documentation for more information about TrueType fonts.

Procedure:

After this item is selected, Mastercam displays the Standard Windows font dialog box.

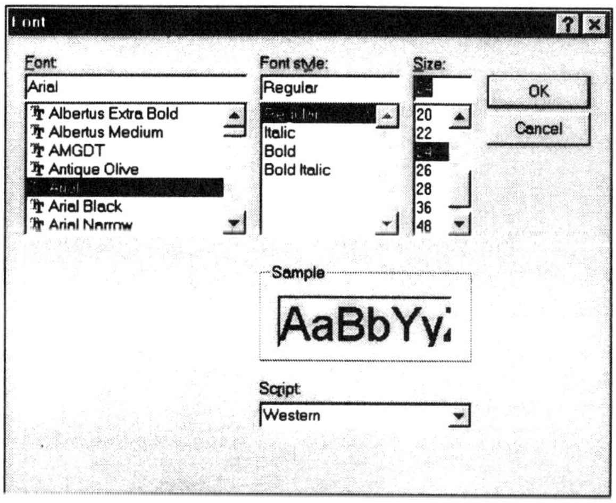

Figure 5.63 Standard Windows font dialog box

Select the **font** and the **font style.** Ignore the font size and select **OK.**
Enter letters: **Mastercam** ↵
Enter letter height (def val): **2.0** ↵
Selection a direction for the TrueType letters:
Note: The system will give you **four** options described in Figure 5.64.

Horizontal:	Write letters in the horizontal direction
Vertical:	Write the letters in the vertical direction
Top of arc:	Write letters on top of an arc
Btm of arc:	Write on the bottom of an arc.

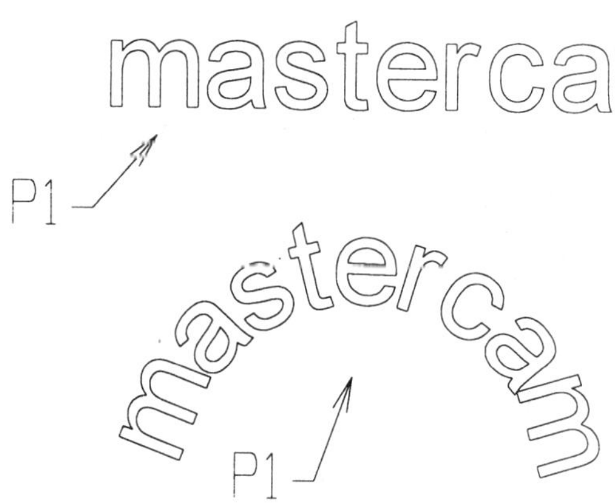

Figure 5.64 Letter orientations

Enter letter spacing (def val): **0.2** ↵

Note: The system will have different prompts after this step. There is one more step for horizontal and vertical letters, and two more steps for top arc and bottom arc letters.

For horizontal and vertical letters:
Enter starting location of letters: Pick **P1**

For top and bottom arc letters:
Enter coordinates of arc center: Pick **P1**
Enter arc radius: **4.0** ↵

Create → Next menu → Letters → **Drafting**

Create geometry from the current Mastercam drafting font.
Procedure:
Enter letters: **Mastercam** ↵
Enter letter height: **2.0** ↵
Enter starting location of letters: Pick **P1**

Figure 5.65

Note: The current Mastercam drafting font can be changed by picking Global from the Menu Area. Then select Dimension Text or Note Text to change the font. The available drafting fonts are Stick, Roman, European, Swiss, Hartford, Old English, Palatino and Dayville.

Create → Next menu → Letters → **File**

Create Mastercam letter geometry. As shown in Figure 5.66 below, there are **four** font styles available in Mastercam 8.0. Be sure these font styles are installed on your computer before you attempt to use them. For example, the box font can be installed in C:\Mcam8\Common\Fonts\Box directory. Note that these font files have no TrueType equivalent and create only upper case letter geometries. For more details, see your Mastercam version 8.0 documentation.

Box:	Box font
Block:	Block font
Roman:	Roman font
Slant:	Slant font
Other:	

Figure 5.66

<u>**Procedure:**</u>
Select Font directory: **Block**
Enter letter height (def val): **1.0** ↵
Enter letter spacing (def val): **0.2** ↵
Write letters on an arc (Y/N)?
Select **Yes** to accept an arc letter.
Select **No** to accept a line letter.

Note: The system will have different prompts after this step. There are **four** more steps for arc letters and **two** more steps for line letters.

For arc letters
Enter coordinates of arc center: Pick **P1**
Enter arc radius (def val): **5.0** ↵
Write on top or bottom of the arc: Select **Top** or **Bottom** ↵

Note: Refer to Figure 5.67 for the type of arc.
Enter letters: **ARC LETTERS** ↵

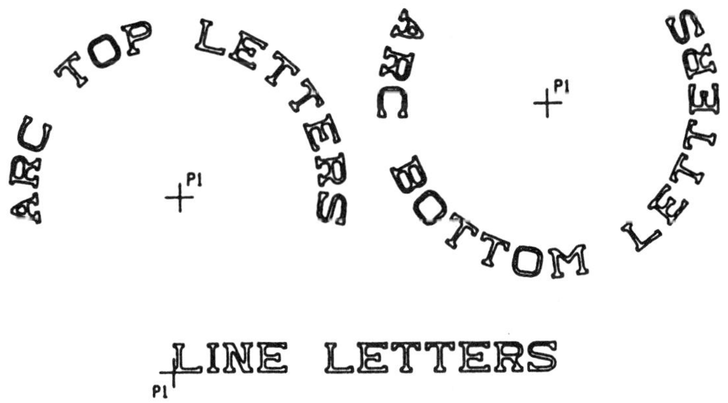

Figure 5.67 Arc and line letters

For line letters
Enter starting location of letters: Pick **P1**
Enter letters: **LINE LETTERS** ↵

Method 2: Using Note and Modify Commands

In this method, you will create a string of letters using the "Note" command in Drafting.

Procedure:
Create a string of letters using the "Note" command in the drafting section.
Change the attributes including the height, aspect ratio, font type and spacing.
Convert the Note into chains of geometry entities by using
Modify → Break → Draft/line commands.
Reposition the letters string to a new position, if necessary.

In the following example, we are creating a letter geometry (Mastercam) using a European font with a height = 0.5, aspect = 0.6 and spacing = 0.25.

The sequence is **Create → Drafting**
Note Dialog Appears

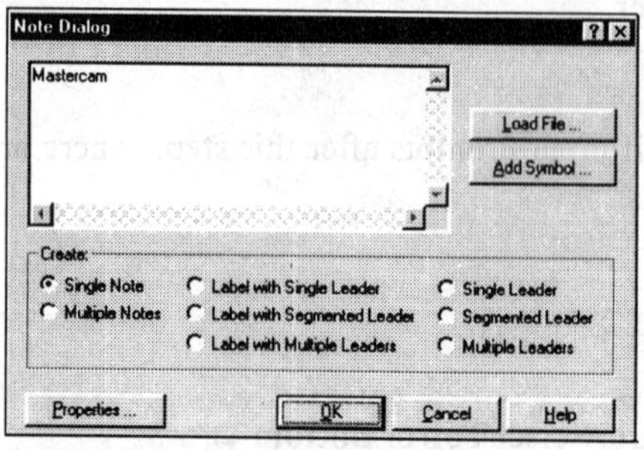

Text: **Mastercam** ↵
Enter line 2 (press Enter when done): ↵
Select a Point: Pick **P1**
Text: Press **<ESC>** when done

Figure 5.68

Select **BACKUP → Multi edit**
Select the note just created **→ Done**

In the Drafting Global Parameters pop-up:
Select Note Text Height: **0.5**
Select down arrow symbol, scroll to **European font**

Select Character Width: **0.6**
Select Extra Char Spacing: **0.25**
Select **OK**
(Notice the changes in System Response Area: Attribute style: **European**)

Figure 5.69

Select **MAIN MENU → Modify → Break → Draft/line**
Select note: Pick at **the note**
Select **Done**
After this step, the note is turned into geometry.
Note: You may use the **Analyze** (F4) key to see if the original note has changed geometries.

5.11 Ellipse and Ellipse Submenu

The ellipse menu sequence is **Create → Next menu → Ellipse.**

An ellipse or an elliptical arc can be created by specifying the following **five parameters** in addition to the center point:

A radius:	Set the ellipse's X-axis radius.
B radius:	Set the ellipse's Y-axis radius.
Start angle:	Set the starting angle.
End angle:	Set the ending angle.
Rot angle:	Set the angle of rotation about the X-axis direction.
Do it:	Set the center of the ellipse. Mastercam displays the ellipse after you set the center point.

⌛**Tips** 1. Mastercam displays information about the ellipse in the System Response Area.

2. All the angles are measured in degrees in the counterclockwise direction.

Procedure: Example 1
Adjust the ellipse with these following specifications:

A (X-axis radius) = **3.0**
B (Y-axis radius) = **1.5**
Start anglc = **30.0**
End angle = **300.0**
Rotation angle = **0.0**

Select **Do it**
Enter the center point: Pick **P1**

Procedure: Example 2
Adjust the ellipse with these following specifications:

A (X-axis radius) = **3.0**
B (Y-axis radius) = **1.5**
Start anglc = **0.0**
End angle = **360.0**
Rotation angle = **15.0**

Select **Do it**
Enter the center point: Pick **P1**

Figure 5.70

5.12 Polygon and Polygon Submenu

The polygon sequence is **Create → Next menu → Polygon**

To create a polygon in Mastercam, you need to specify the following **five parameters** with a given center point.

No. sides:	Set the number of sides for the polygon.
Radius:	Set the distance from the center of the polygon to its edge. See Meas crnr for more information.
Start Angle:	Set the starting angle of the polygon about the X-axis direction.
Meas crnr Y:	A toggle switch to measure the radius distance. Y: Radius distance is measured from the center to the apex of a corner. N: Radius distance is measured from the center to the midpoint of a flat side
Make NURBS N:	A toggle switch to make the polygon to be a single NURBS curve or multi-line entities. Y: Create the polygon as a single NURBS curve. N: Create the polygon as multi-line segments.
Do it:	Set the center of the polygon. Mastercam displays the polygon after you set the centerpoint.

Tips 1. Mastercam displays information about your polygon in the System Response Area.

2. The starting angle is measured in degrees in the counterclockwise direction.

Procedure: Example 1

Adjust the polygon #1 with the following specifications:

Polygon number of sides = **5**
Polygon radius = **1.0**
Polygon starting angle = **0.0**
Measure Radius to **Corner**
Create **Lines**

Select **Do it**
Enter the center point Pick **P1**

Procedure: Example 2

Adjust the polygon#2 with the following specifications:

Polygon number of sides = **5**
Polygon radius = **1.0**
Polygon starting angle = **30.0**
Measure Radius to **Flat**
Create **NURBS spline**

Select **Do it**
Enter the center point Pick **P1**

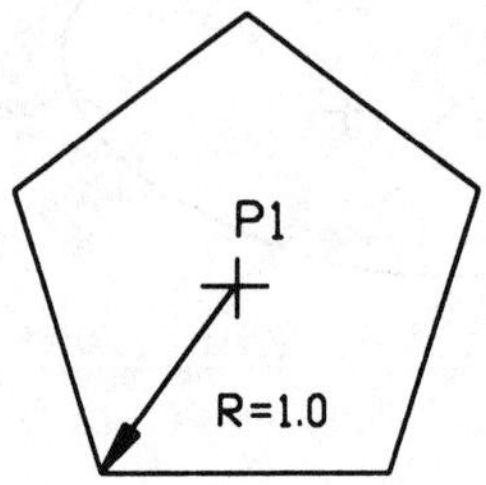

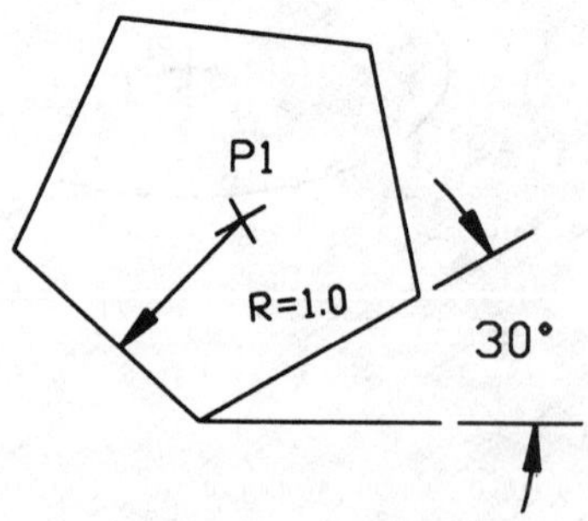

Figure 5.71

5.13 2-D Geometry Construction Project

In the following five projects, you will practice a combination of commands introduced in this chapter. A step by step procedure is provided. Save each project under the file name specified. You will retrieve these files to generate the toolpaths for producing the part in chapters 7 and 8.

Project 1.

Create a part geometry as shown in Figure 5.72. Save the file as **contour1.** This file will be used in project 1 of chapter 7.

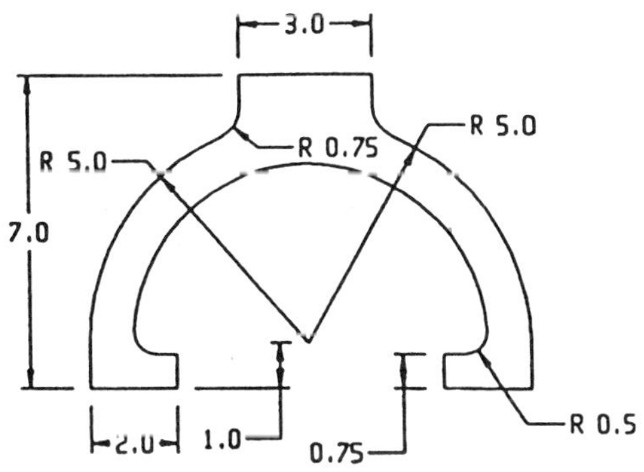

Figure 5.72

Tips 1. The geometry is symmetrical about the Y-axis. Create one-half of the geometry and then use the Mirror command (see section 6.3.1) to create the other half.
2. The basic geometry consists of two rectangles, two arcs and two fillets.

Step 1. Create two rectangles.

Select **MAIN MENU → Create → Rectangle → 2 points**
Enter the lower left corner: **3,-1** ↵
Enter the upper right corner: **5,-.25** ↵ for the first rectangle
Enter the lower left corner: **0,6** ↵
Enter the upper right corner: **1.5,5** ↵ for the second rectangle

Press **Alt** and **F1** simultaneously, then **F2** to fit the geometry on the screen
The two rectangles should appear as Figure 5.73.

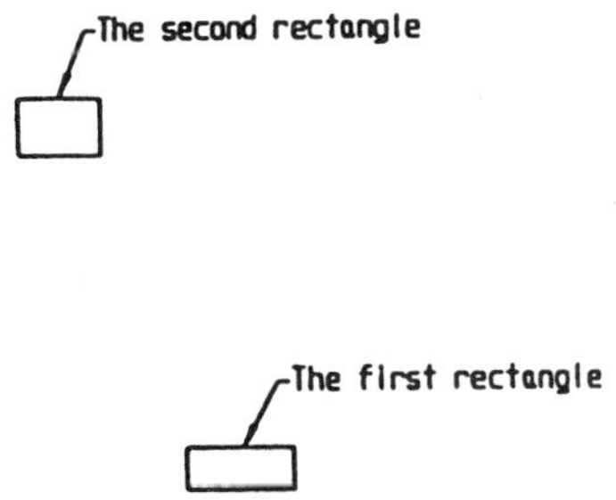

Figure 5.73

Step 2. Create two arcs.

Select **MAIN MENU → Create → Arc → Polar → Center pt**
Enter the center point: **0,0** ↵
Enter the radius: **5** ↵
Enter the initial angle: **0** ↵
Enter the final angle: **90** ↵ for the first arc
Enter the center point: **0,0** ↵
Enter the radius: **4** ↵
Enter the initial angle: **0** ↵
Enter the final angle: **90** ↵ for the second arc

The new drawing becomes Figure 5.74

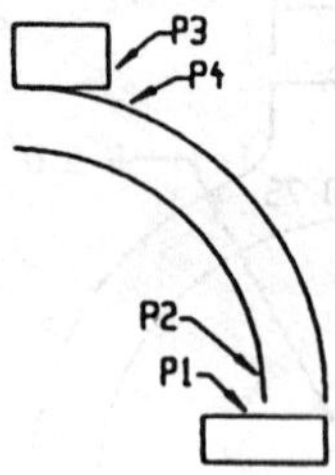

Figure 5.74

Step 3. Create two fillets using the pick points in Figure 5.74.

Select **MAIN MENU → Create → Fillet → Radius**
Enter the fillet radius: **0.5**

Note: Make certain the other two options are correct. If the fillet angle is less than 180; trim to fillet.

Select an entity: Pick **P1**
Select another entity: Pick **P2**
Select **Radius**
Enter the radius: **0.75** ↵
Select an entity: Pick **P3**
Select another entity: Pick **P4**

The two fillets are added as shown in Figure 5.75.

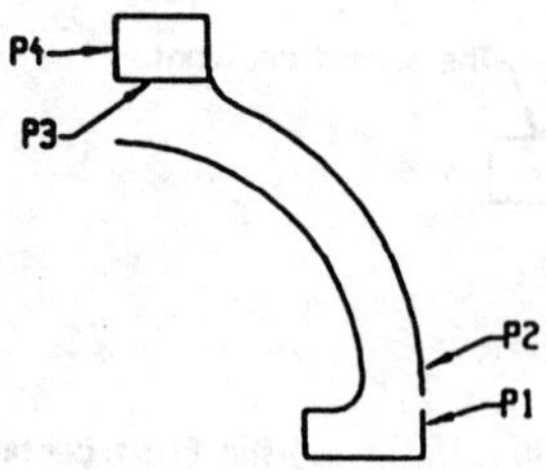

Figure 5.75

Step 4. Trim and delete the unnecessary lines using the pick points in Figure 5.75 on the last page.

Select **MAIN MENU → Modify → Trim → 1 entity**
Select the entity to trim: Pick **P1**
Select the entity to trim to: Pick **P2**
Select **MAIN MENU → Delete**
Select an entity or: Pick **P3**
Select an entity or: Pick **P4**
The half geometry should look like Figure 5.76.

Figure 5.76

Step 5. Mirror about the Y axis.

Select **MAIN MENU→Xform→ Mirror→ All→Entities→Done→Y axis→Copy →OK**
The complete geometry appears as Figure 5.77.

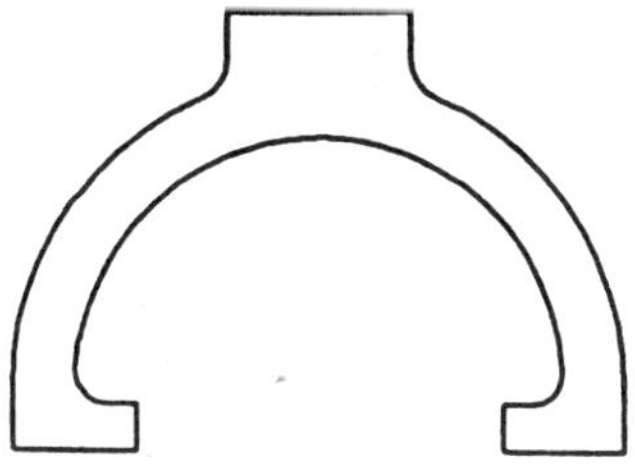

Figure 5.77

Step 6. Save to a file.

Select **MAIN MENU → File → Save**
Enter file name: **contour1**

2 Project 2.

Create a part geometry as shown in Figure 5.78. Save the file as **contour3**. This file will be used to generate the toolpaths for contouring in project 3 of chapter 7.

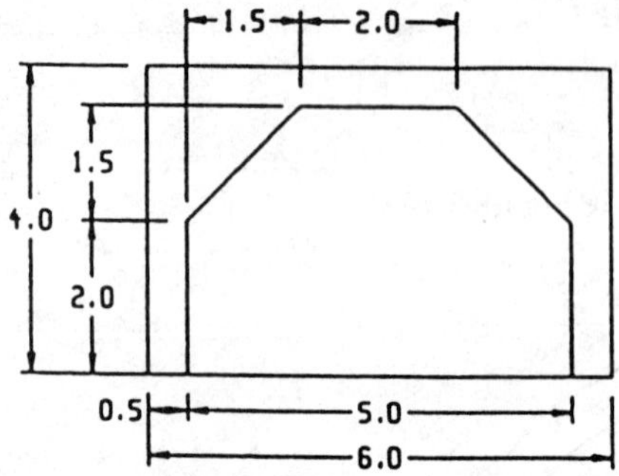

Figure 5.78

> **Tips** 1. This geometry can be created using a rectangle and several lines.
>
> 2. The coordinates of keypoints are shown in Figure 5.79.

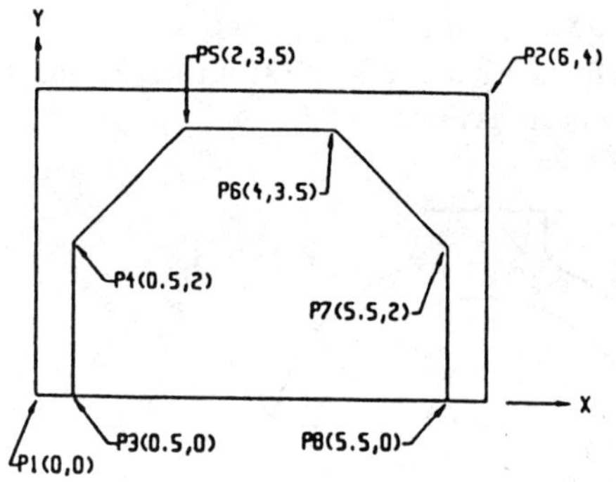

Figure 5.79

Step 1. Create a rectangle.

Select **MAIN MENU →Create → Rectangle → 2 points**
Enter the lower left corner: **0,0** ↵
Enter the upper right corner: **6,4** ↵

Step 2. Create five lines.

Select **MAIN MENU → Create → Line → Multi**
Specify endpoint 1: Enter **0.5,0** ↵
Specify endpoint 2: Enter **0.5,2** ↵
Specify endpoint 3: Enter **2,3.5** ↵
Specify endpoint 4: Enter **4,3.5** ↵
Specify endpoint 5: Enter **5.5,2** ↵
Specify endpoint 6: Enter **5.5,0** ↵

Step 3. Save to a file.

Select **MAIN MENU → File → Save**
Enter file name: **contour3**

Project 3.

Construct a geometry as shown in Figure 5.80. Save the file as **pocket1**. This file will be used to generate the toolpaths for pocketing in project 5 of chapter 7.

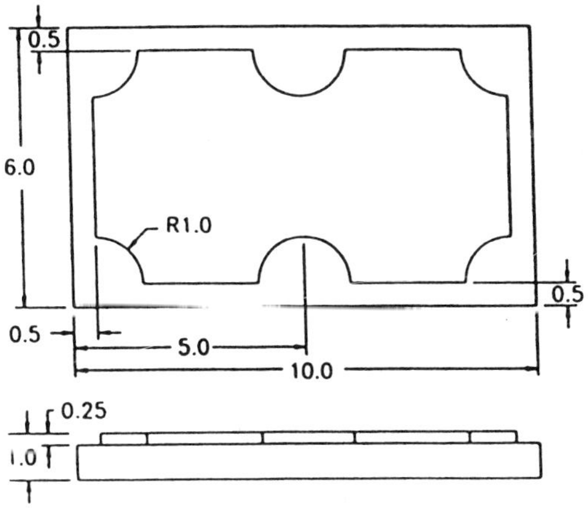

Figure 5.80

Tips 1. Create two rectangles and six circles.

2. Break the two horizontal lines of the inside rectangle into two pieces to allow for the trimming of the two circles in the middle.
3. Trim the six circles and four lines using 3 entities command.

Step 1. Create two rectangles.

Select **MAIN MENU → Create → Rectangle → 2 points**
Enter the lower left corner: **0,0** ↵
Enter the upper right corner: **10,6** ↵ for the first rectangle
Enter the lower left corner: **0.5,0.5** ↵
Enter the upper right corner: **9.5,5.5** ↵ for the second rectangle
Press **Alt + F1** simultaneously and then **F2** to fit the drawing in the screen
The two rectangles should look like Figure 5.81.

Figure 5.81

Step 2. Create six circles.

Select **MAIN MENU → Create → Arc → Circ pt+rad**
Enter the radius: **1** ↵
Enter the center point: **0.5,0.5** ↵
Enter the center point: **5,0.5** ↵
Enter the center point: **9.5,0.5** ↵
Enter the center point: **0.5,5.5** ↵
Enter the center point: **5,5.5** ↵
Enter the center point: **9.5,5.5** ↵

The six circles are added as shown in Figure 5.82.

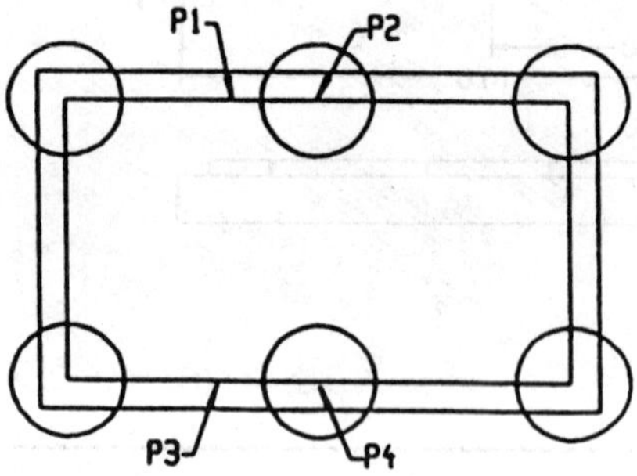

Figure 5.82

Step 3. Break two horizontal lines of the inside rectangle into two pieces.

Use the pick points in Figure 5.82.
Select **MAIN MENU → Modify → Break → 2 pieces**
Select an entity: pick **P1**
Enter the break point: pick **P2** to break the first line
Select an entity: pick **P3**
Enter the break point: pick **P4** to break the second line
After breaking two lines the drawing still looks the same as before breaking.
This drawing is redrawn in Figure 5.83.

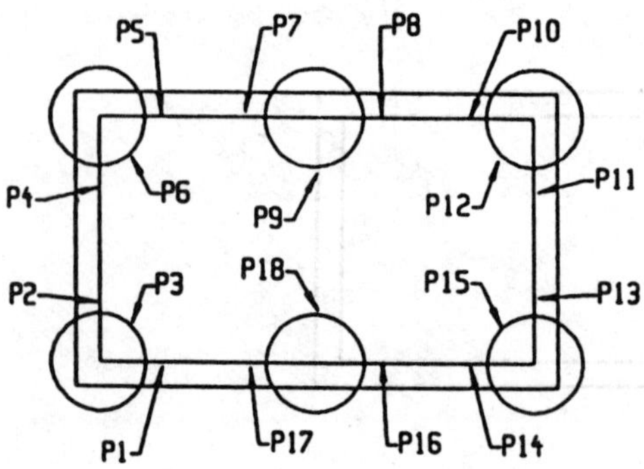

Figure 5.83

Step 4. Trim the six circles using the pick points in Figure 5.83.

Select **MAIN MENU** → **Modify** → **Trim** → **3 entities**
Select the first entity to trim: pick **P1**
Select the second entity to trim: pick **P2**
Select the entity to trim to: pick **P3** to complete the trimming of first circle

Sequentially pick **P4 - P18** to complete the trimming of the remaining five circles

The final geometry should look like Figure 5.84.

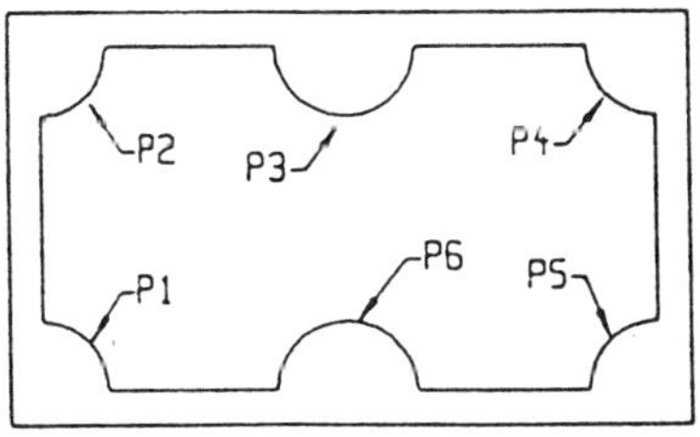

Figure 5.84

Step 5. Save the file (pocket1).

Select **MAIN MENU** → **File** → **Save**
Enter file name: **pocket1**

Note: Continue steps 6 and 7 to add six points for another project.

Step 6. Create six points at the center of each arc.

Use the pick points labeled in Figure 5.84 above.
Select **MAIN MENU** → **Create** → **Point** → **Position** → **Center**
Specify a point: pick **P1** to create the first point
Select **Center**
Sequentially pick **P2 - P6** to create the remaining five points
The six points are added as shown in Figure 5.85.

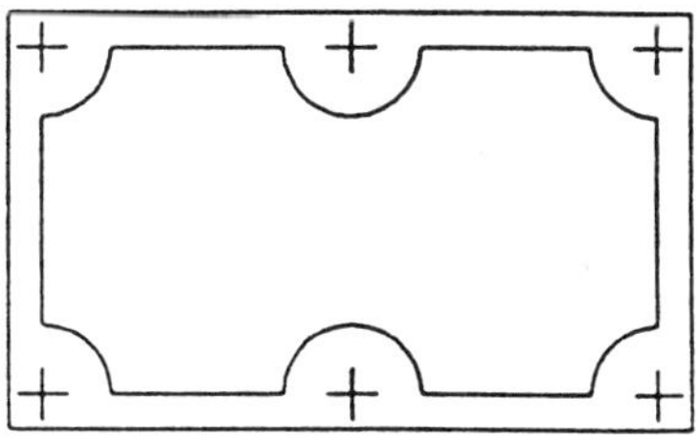

Figure 5.85

Step 7. Save to another file (drill2).

Select **MAIN MENU** → **File** → **Save**
Enter file name: **drill2**

Note: The geometry file **drill2** is used to drilling and tapping six holes in project 8 of chapter 7.

4 Project 4.

Create a rectangle and four points as shown in Figure 5.86.
Save this file as **drill3**. This file will be used in project 8 of chapter 7.

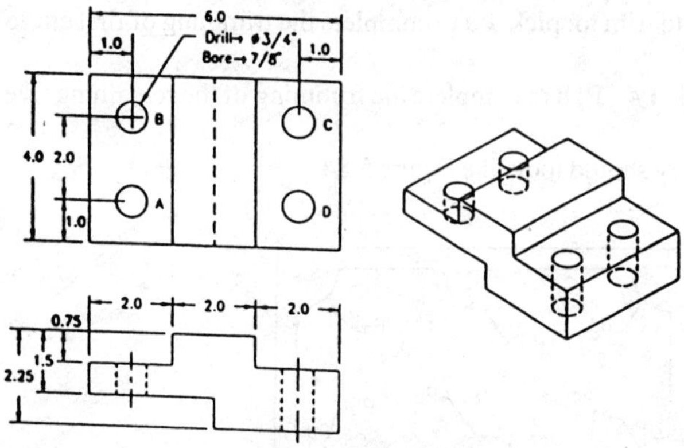

Figure 5.86

This geometry consists of a rectangle and four points. The coordinates of keypoints are shown in Figure 5.87.

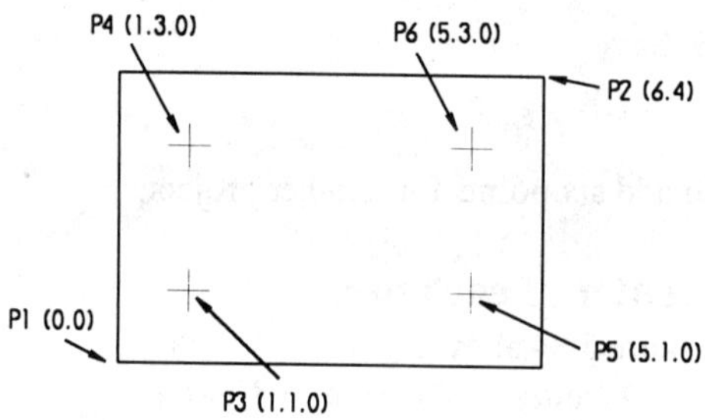

Figure 5.87

Step 1. Create a rectangle.

Select **MAIN MENU → Create → Rectangle → 2 points**
Enter the lower left corner: **0,0** ↵
Enter the upper right corner: **6,4** ↵

Step 2. Create four points.

Select **MAIN MENU → Create → Point → Position**
Enter coordinates: **1,1, 0** ↵
Enter coordinates: **1,3, 0** ↵
Enter coordinates: **5,1, 0** ↵
Enter coordinates: **5,3, 0** ↵

Step 3. Save to a file.

Select **MAIN MENU → File → Save**
Enter file name: **drill3**

Project 5.

Use the Letters command to create a geometry as shown in Figure 5.88. This geometry consists of two circles and five strings of letters in **three** true type fonts; News Gothic MT, Arial, and TimesNew Roman. Use these three fonts to create letters as follows:

1. EASTERN MICHIGAN UNIVERSITY
   Font = News Gothic MT (Regular)
   Height = 0.3
   Spacing = 0.05
   Arc Radius=2.3
2. INDUSTRIAL TECHNOLOGY
   Font = News Gothic MT (Regular)
   Height = 0.3
   Spacing = 0.05
   Arc Radius=2.5
3. CAD CAM
   Font=Arial (Regular)
   Height=0.4
   Spacing=0.1
   Arc Radius=1.4
4. CNC
   Font=Arial (Bold Italic)
   Height=0.6
   Spacing=0.15
   Starting point= (-1,-.3)
5. YES
   Font=Times New Roman
   Height=0.6
   Spacing=0.2
   Arc Radius=1.4

Figure 5.88

Tips 1. Use different levels and colors for different groups of geometry and letters.

2. The letter strings EASTERN MICHIGAN UNIVERSITY and INDUSTRIAL TECHNOLOGY can be changed to your school name and department name.

Step 1. Create two circles

Select **MAIN MENU → Create → Arc → Circ pt+dia**
Enter the diameter: **6**↵
Enter the center point: **0,0** ↵
Select **BACKUP → Circ pt + dia**
Enter the diameter: **4.5** ↵
Enter the center point: **0,0** ↵

The two circles appear as Figure 5.89.

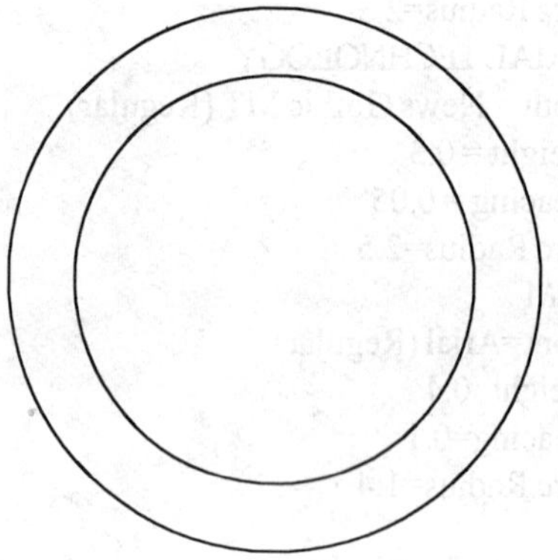

Figure 5.89

Step 2. Create a string of News Gothic MT letters using level 2 and color 12.

Select **Level** then enter **2 →OK**
Select **Color** then enter **12 →OK**
Select **MAIN MENU → Create → Next menu → Letters → TrueType(R)**
Select **News Gothic MT → Regular → OK**
Enter letters: **EASTERN MICHIGAN UNIVERSITY** (or your school name) ↵
Enter letter height: **0.3** ↵
Select **Top of arc**
Enter letter spacing: **0.05** ↵
Enter coordinates of arc center: **0,0** ↵
Enter arc radius: **2.45** ↵

Step 3. Create a string of News Gothic MT letters in the bottom arc.

Select **TrueType(R) → News Gothic MT → Regular → OK**
Enter letters: **INDUSTRIAL TECHNOLOGY** (or your department name) ↵
Enter letter height: **0.3** ↵
Select **Btm of arc**
Enter letter spacing: **0.05** ↵
Enter coordinates of arc center: **0,0** ↵
Enter arc radius: **2.5** ↵

Two strings of News Gothic MT letters should look like Figure 5.90.

Figure 5.90

Step 4. Change level to 3 and color to 13.

Select **Level** then enter **3 → OK**
Select **Color** then enter **13 → OK**

Step 5. Create a string of Arial letters on an arc.

Select **TrueType(R)→ Arial → Regular → OK**
Enter letters: **CAD CAM** ↵
Enter letter height: **0.4** ↵
Select **Top of arc**
Enter letter spacing: **0.1** ↵
Enter coordinates of arc center: **0,0** ↵
Enter arc radius: **1.4** ↵

The letter string of Arial font appears as Figure 5.91.

Figure 5.91

Step 6. Create the letters string CNC along a line.

Select **TrueType(R) →Arial → Bold Italic → OK**
Enter letters: **CNC** ↵
Enter letter height: **0.6** ↵
Select **Horizontal**
Enter letter spacing: **0.15** ↵
Enter starting location of letters: **-1,-0.3** ↵

The CNC letters are added as in Figure 5.92.

Figure 5.92

Step 7. Create the letters string YES along a bottom arc.

Select **TrueType(R) → Times New Roman → Regular → OK**
Enter letters: **YES ↵**
Enter letter height: **0.6** ↵
Select **Btm of arc**
Enter letter spacing: **0.2** ↵
Enter coordinates of arc center: **0,0** ↵
Enter arc radius: **1.4** ↵

The final drawing should look like Figure 5.93.

Figure 5.93

Step 8. Save to a file.

Select **MAIN MENU → File → Save**
Enter file name: **letter2**

Project 6. 6

Change the letters CNC from level 3 and color 13 to level 4 and color 14.

Step 1. Retrieve the file Letter2.MC8 saved in Project 5.

Select **MAIN MENU → File → Get**
Specify File name to Read: **Letter2.mc8**

Step 2. Change the current settings to color 14.

Select **Level**, then enter **4 → OK**
Select **Color**, then enter **14 → OK**
Select **MAIN MENU → Screen → Chg colors**
Select entity to change: Select **Window**
Enter the first window corner: Pick **P1** (Figure 5.94)
Enter the second window corner: Pick **P2** (Figure 5.94)

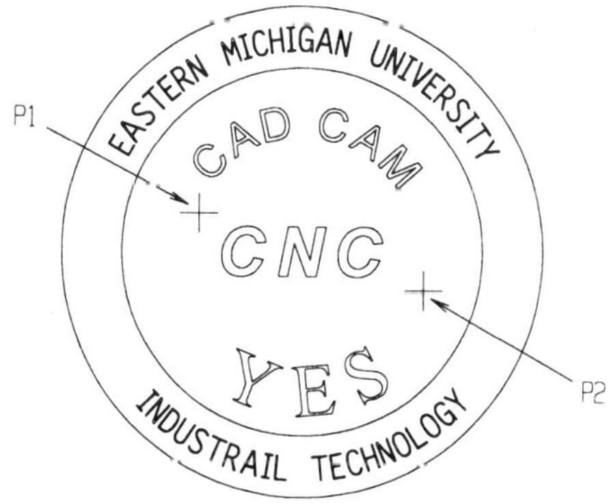

Figure 5.94

The letter CNC should be changed to color 14.

Step 3. Change the current settings to level 4.

Select **MAIN MENU → Screen → Chg levels**
Make the selections in the Change Levels dialog as shown at right

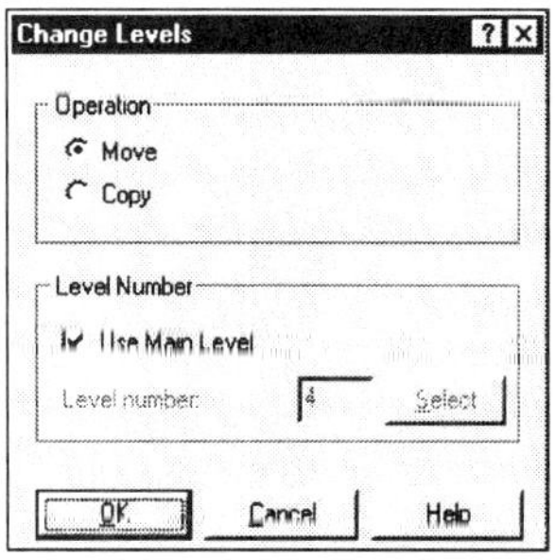

Select **OK**
Select entity to change: Select **Window**
Enter the first window corner: Pick **P1** (Figure 5.94)
Enter the second window corner: Pick **P2** (Figure 5.94)

The letters CNC should now be changed to level 4. You can verify the change using the Analyze (F4) command. You do not need to save this project to a file for future use.

Ex Exercises

1. Use a drawing to show how Mastercam uses cascaded menus for creating geometry entities.

2. A point can be defined in Mastercam with how many options ?

3. How many options can be used to create a line in Mastercam?

4. Describe how the feature of the Multi command creates lines.

5. Describe the difference between arcs and circles.

6. How many options can define an arc in Mastercam?

7. How many options can define a circle in Mastercam?

8. What are the three fillet parameters? Describe, with drawings, how these three parameters change the fillets.

9. What is a spline?

10. What is the minimum number of points required to define a spline?

11. What are two common types of curves for 2-D geometry in Mastercam?

12. What is the full name of NURBS?

13. Describe the major difference between splines and NURBS curves.

14. Use a drawing to show how Mastercam creates a rectangle with (a)one point and (b)two points options.

15. Describe the procedure used in Mastercam for creating a Windows Truetype font letter geometry.

Problems

16. Create the geometry shown in Figure 5.95. Save the file as **contour8.** This file is used in problem 39 of chapter 7.

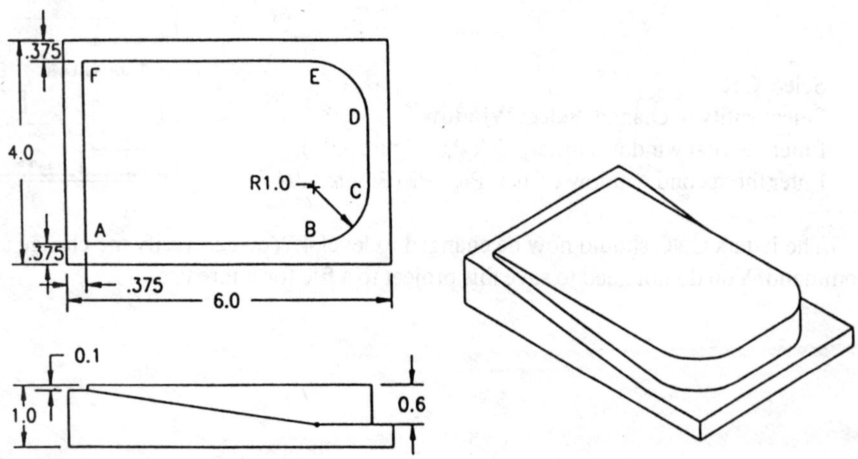

Figure 5.95

17. Create the geometry shown in Figure 5.96. Save the file as contour9. This file is used in problem 40 of chapter 7.

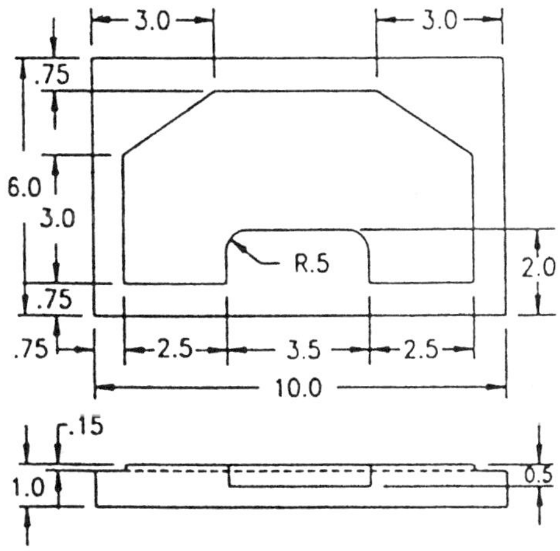

Figure 5.96

18. Create the geometry shown in Figure 5.97. Save the file as **drill4.** This file is used in problem 44 of chapter 7.

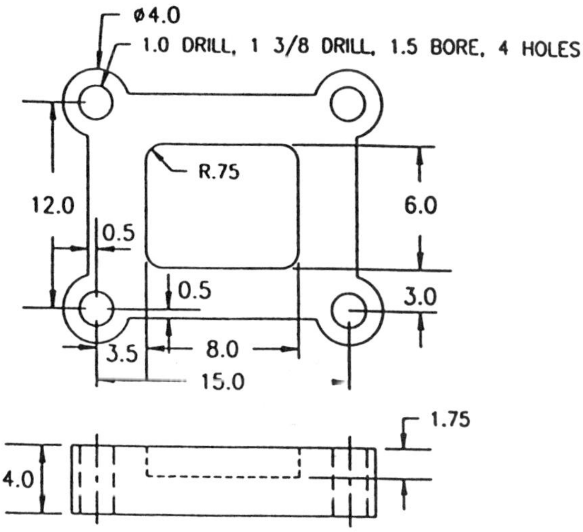

Figure 5.97

19. Create the geometry shown in Figure 5.98. Save the file as **comb2**. This file is used in problem 46 of chapter 7.

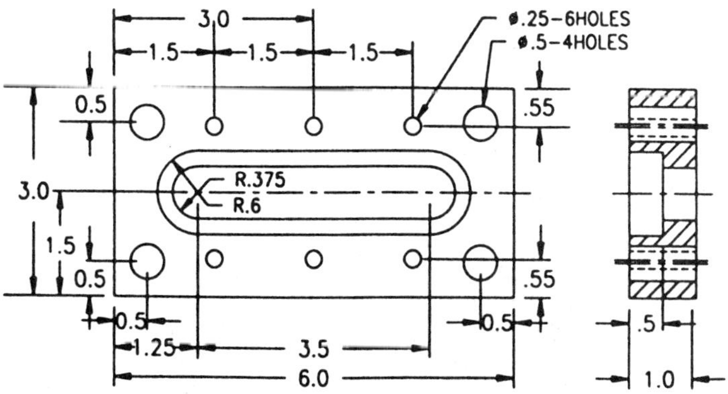

Figure 5.98

20. Create the part geometry shown in Figure 5.99. and save the files as **trans2.** This file is used later in problem 18 of chapter 9.

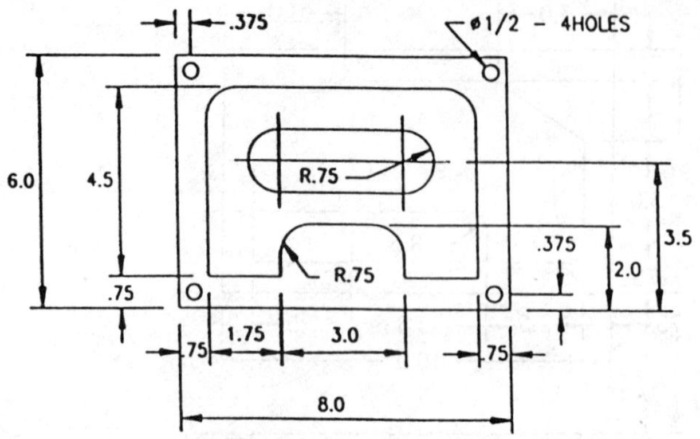

Figure 5.99

21. Create the geometry and letter strings as shown in Figure 5.100. Save the file as letters4 which will be used in problem 49 in chapter 7. Replace the string EMU IT with your school name and department name. Some helpful tips are listed.

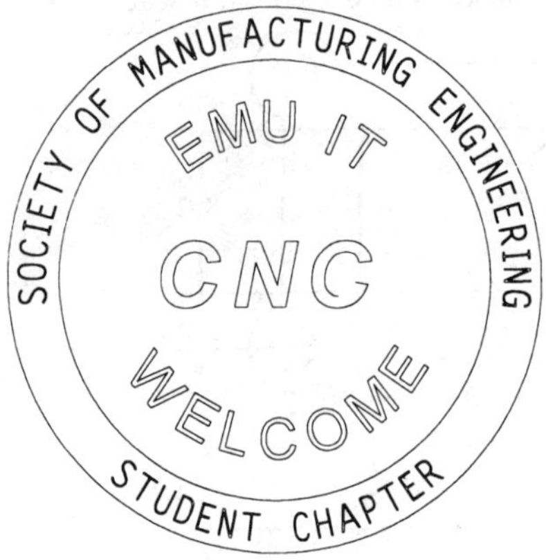

Figure 5.100

1. The geometry file is organized by level and color as below:

Two circles:	level 1 and color 10
Box font:	level 2 and color 12
Roman font:	level 3 and color 13
Block font:	level 4 and color 14

2. Box font: SOCIETY OF MANUFACTURING ENGINEERING and STUDENT CHAPTER

Roman font:	EMU IT and WELCOME
Block font:	CNC

3. Height,spacing, radius, and starting point:

Box font:	height = 0.5" Spacing = 0.15" Radius = 4.25"
Roman font:	height = 0.75" Spacing = 0.2" Radius = 2.5"
Block font:	height = 1.0" Spacing = 0.25" Starting point is (-2.1,-0.3)

Chapter 6

Modify Existing Geometry

Objectives:

1. Understand the features of geometry modification functions and know when to apply them.
2. Apply geometry modification functions, Delete, Modify, and Xform, to simplify the geometric creation process.

Overview

The geometry creation functions presented in chapter 5 are used to produce simple part geometries. It will be very time consuming, if not impossible, to use those basic functions to create complex part geometries. Like most CAD software, Mastercam provides a variety of functions to modify existing geometric entities. All of these modifying functions make geometric construction easier and faster. Three groups of modifying functions are covered in this chapter including delete, modify, and Xform.

6.1 Delete Function

The delete function is used for removing a single entity or a group of entities from the screen and the system's database. Select **Delete** from the main menu (or press **F5** on the keyboard), and you will have an option to select an entity or use its submenu options shown in Figure 6.1.

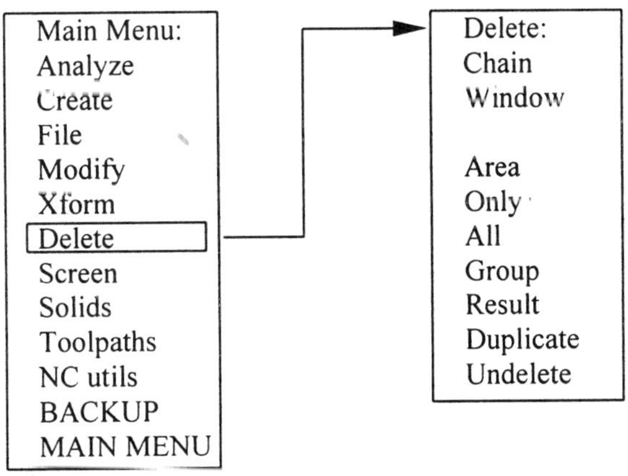

Figure 6.1 Submenu for Delete

The submenu options for **Delete** can be described as follows:

Chain:	deletes a chain of connected entities.
Window:	deletes all the entities either inside or outside a defined rectangular Window **Alt-F5** is a shortcut key for this operation.
Area:	deletes all Color mask, Level mask, Plane mask, Ignore mask, Set start of chain from point entities, and Entity mask.
Only:	deletes only a certain type of entities such as points, lines, splines, etc. User selection is required.
All:	deletes all entities of a certain type. User selection is not required.
Group:	deletes the current group defined by the Xform→ Group function.
Result:	deletes the result of the transformed entities.
Duplicate:	deletes duplicate entities occupying the same space.
Undelete:	undeletes previously deleted entities.

Undelete

Undelete recreates the deleted entities in the order they were deleted. This function is under the submenu of Delete, and it includes **three** options: **Single, Number** and **All**.

Single:	restores the single entity that was most recently deleted.
Number:	restores a number of entities that were most recently deleted.
All:	restores all the previously deleted entities of a certain type. You may choose to undelete all arcs, all points, all splines, all surfaces, etc.

6.2 Modify Functions

A group of modifying functions are grouped under the **Modify** menu. They are used to change existing entities. Select Modify from the main menu and you will have the submenu options shown in Figure 6.2.

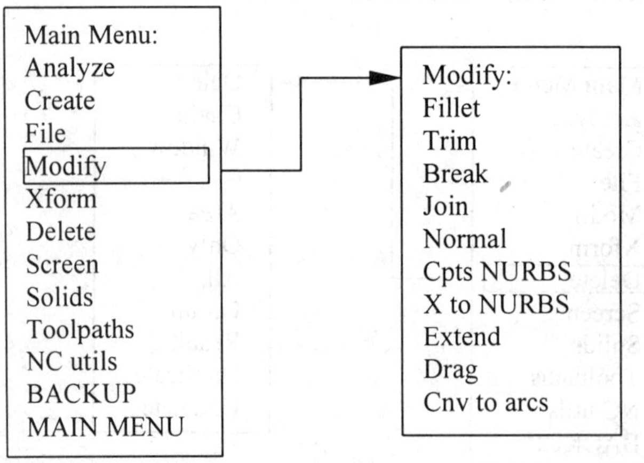

Figure 6.2: Submenu for Modify

The submenu options for **Modify** can be described as follows:

Fillet:	creates a fillet between two intersected entities.
Trim:	trims up to three entities to specified boundaries.
Break:	divides entities (lines, arcs, or splines) into two or more segments.
Join:	joins two segments into one entity. It undoes what break does.
Normal:	modifies the normal directions of a 3-D surface.
Cpts NURBS:	modifies the control points of a NURBS curve.
X to NURBS:	transforms arcs or lines into NURBS format.
Extend:	extend a line or arc by a desired length
Drag:	dynamically drags (moves or copies) entities on screen.
Cnv to Arcs:	convert circular spline or NURBS to an arc.

Fillet Function

This function is used to create a fillet between two entities. The procedures for filleting are the same as shown in section 5.5. Figure 6.3 shows two filleting examples.

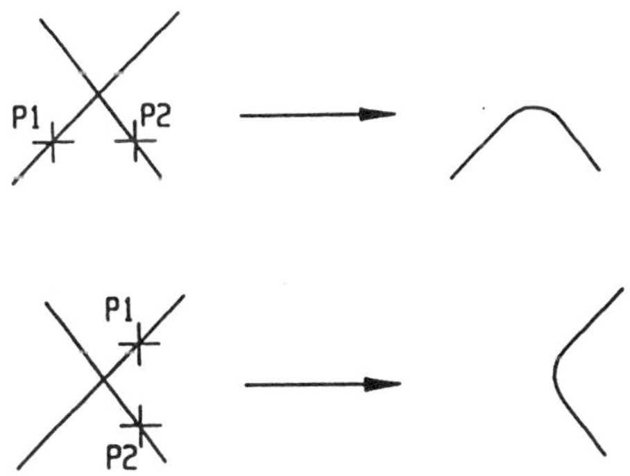

Figure 6.3

Trim Function

The Trim function is used to trim up to three entities to a specified boundaries. The trimming can trim or extend entities to their intersection points. **Eight** options are available:

1 entity:	trims an entity by selecting the entity and an entity to trim to.
2 entities:	trims two entities at the same time at their intersection point.
3 entities:	trims three entities in the same time at their intersection point(s).
To point:	trims or extends the selected entity to a point selected.
Many:	trims several entities at once.
Close arc:	converts any arc to a full circle.
Divide:	trims a line or curve between two other lines or curves.
Surface:	trims surfaces. This topic will not be discussed in this chapter.

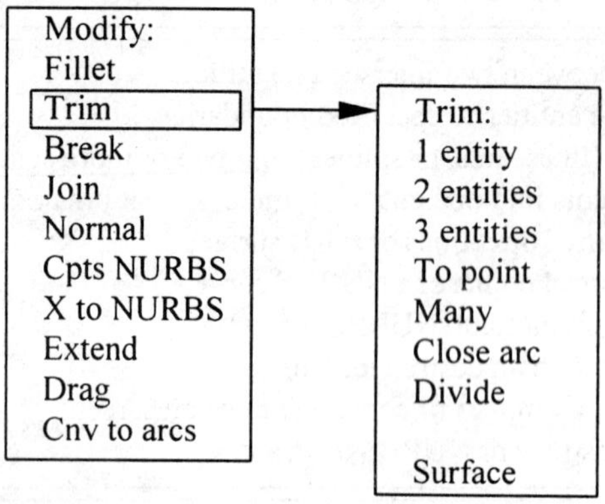

Figure 6.4

1 Entity Trimming

Menu selection sequence is **Modify → Trim → 1 entity**.

This function trims an entity by selecting the segment of the object you wish to retain first, then pick the entity you wish to trim to.

Procedure: (Figure 6.5)

1. Select the entity to trim: Pick **P1**
2. Select the entity to trim to: Pick **P2**

> **Tip** On step 1, pick the segment of the entity you wish to retain first.

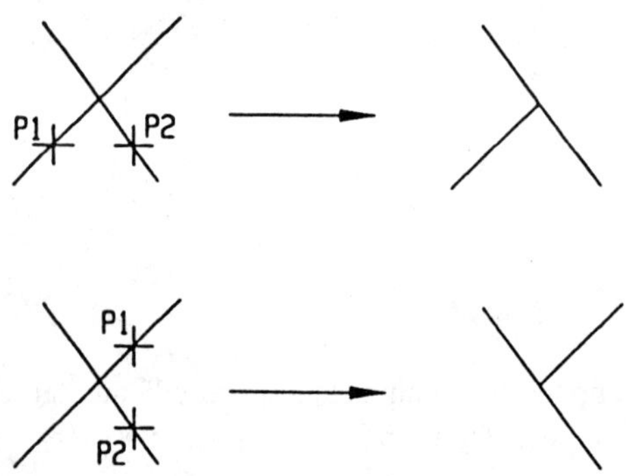

Figure 6.5

2 Entities Trimming

Menu selection sequence is **Modify → Trim → 2 entities.**

This function trims two entities simultaneously to their intersection point.

Procedure: (Figure 6.6)

1. Select the entity to trim: Pick **P1**
2. Select the entity to trim to: Pick **P2**

Tips 1. These two entities need to have an intersection point.

2. Pick the segments to be kept on both entities.

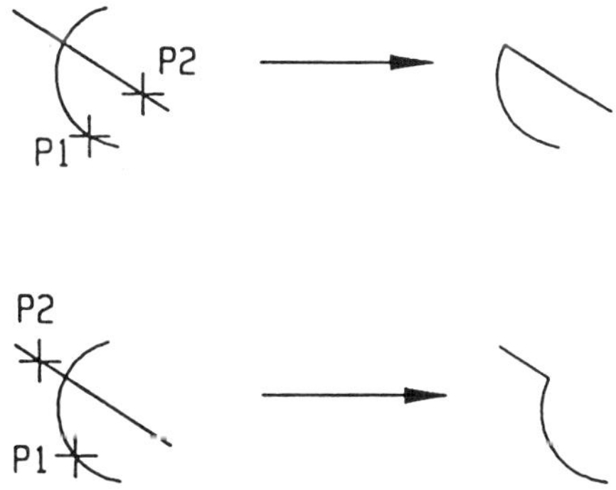

Figure 6.6

3 Entities Trimming

Menu selection sequence is **Modify → Trim → 3 entities.**

This function trims three entities simultaneously to their intersection points.

Procedure: (Figure 6.7)

1. Select the first entity to trim: Pick **P1**
2. Select the second entity to trim: Pick **P2**
3. Select the third entity to trim: Pick **P3**

Tips 1. These three entities need to intersect with one another at three different points.

2. The first two entities will become the boundaries of the third entity.

3. Pick the segments to be kept on these three entities.

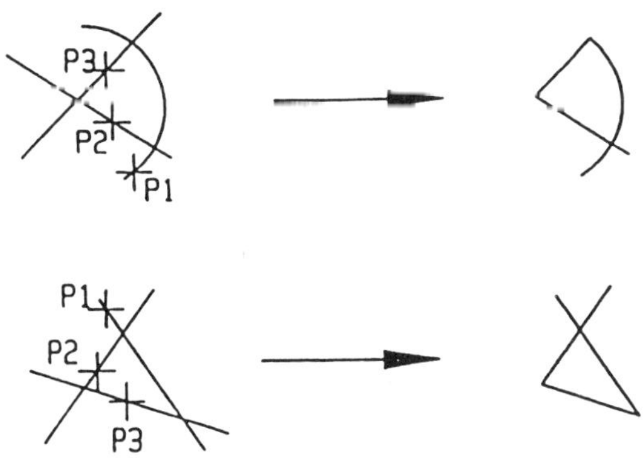

Figure 6.7

Trimming An Entity To a Point

Menu selection is **Modify → Trim → To point.**

This command trims or extends the selected line or arc entity to a point selected. The selected entity will be trimmed at or extended to the point where the perpendicular relationship occurs.

Procedure: (Figure 6.8)
1. Select Line or Arc entity to TRIM/EXTEND: Pick **P1**
2. Indicate TRIM/EXTEND location <position option>: Pick **P2**

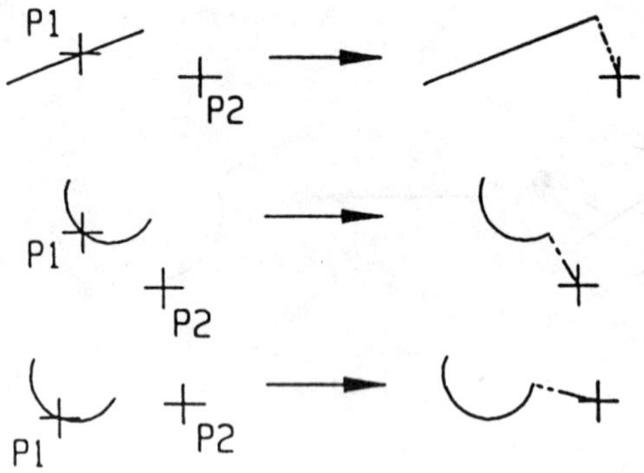

Figure 6.8

Trimming Many Entities at a Time

Menu select is **Modify → Trim → Many**

This command trims several entities at once.

Procedure: (Figure 6.9)
1. Select Curves to trim <entity selection options>: Sequentially pick **P1 - P6.**
2. Select Done
3. Select Trimming Curve: Pick **P7**
4. Indicate Side of Trimming Curve: Pick **P8**

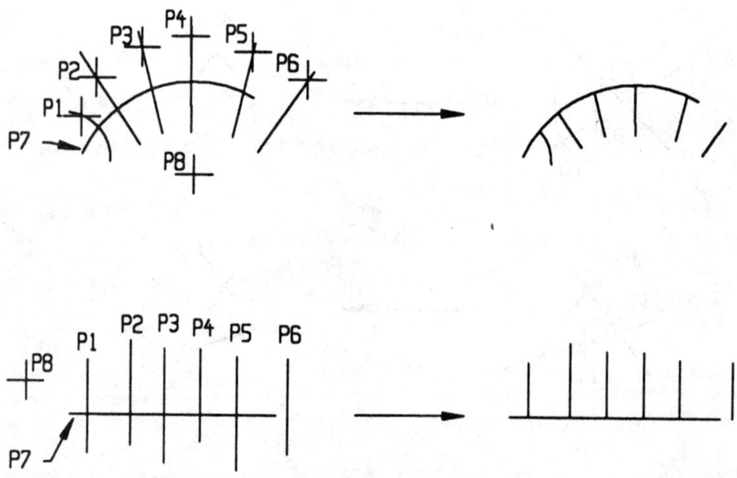

Figure 6.9

Convert an Arc to a Full Circle

Menu select is **Modify → Trim → Close arc**

This command converts an arc to a full circle.

Procedure: (Figure 6.10)

1. Select an Arc to convert to a full circle: Pick **P1**

Figure 6.10

Trimming a Curve Between Two Other Curves

Menu select is **Modify → Trim → Divide**

This command trims a line or curve between two other lines or curves.

Procedure: (Figure 6.11)

1. Select curve to divide: Pick **P1**
2. Select first dividing curve: Pick **P2**
3. Select second dividing curve: Pick **P3**

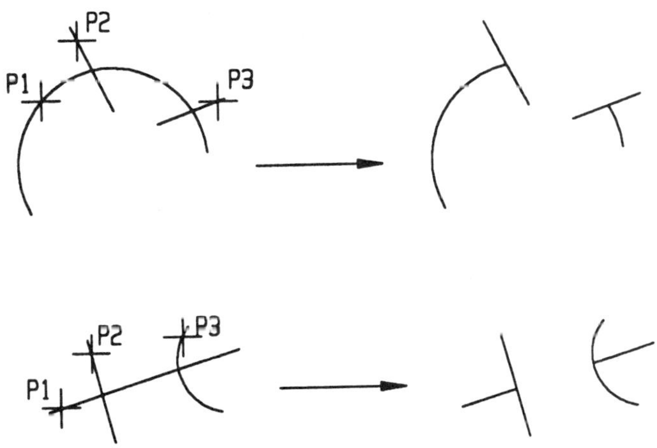

Figure 6.11

Project 1. Filleting and Trimming

Create the geometry shown in Figure 6.12a. Save the file as **array1**. This file is used in project 6 of chapter 8 to generate a set of toolpaths to produce three pockets as shown in Figure 6.12b.

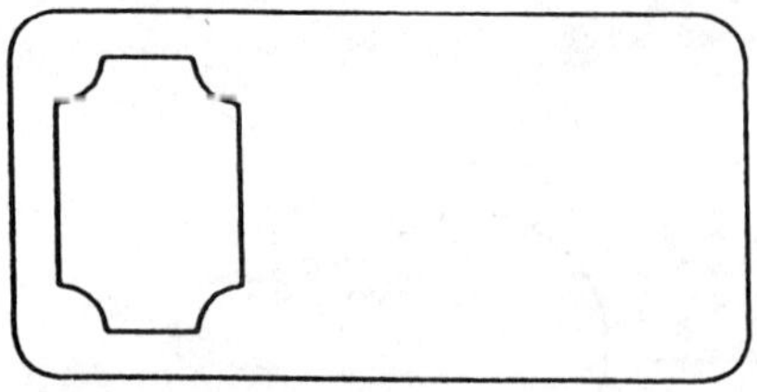

Figure 6.12a

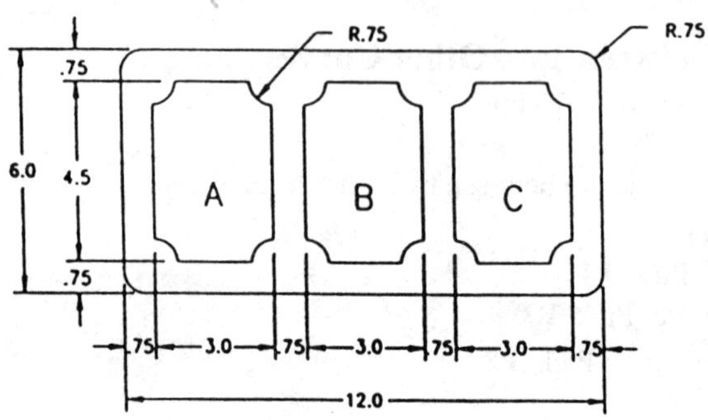

Figure 6.12.b

Tips: 1. Create two rectangles.
2. Add four fillets at the corners of the outer rectangle.
3. Create four circles at the corners of the inside rectangle.
4. Use Trim → 3 entities commands to trim the four circles to their desired arcs.

Step 1. Create two rectangles.

Select **MAIN MENU → Create → Rectangle → 2 points**
Enter the lower left corner: **0,0** ↵
Enter the upper right corner: **12,6** ↵ for the outer rectangle
Enter the lower left corner: **0.75,0.75** ↵
Enter the upper right corner: **3.75,5.25** ↵ for the inside rectangle

Press **Alt** and **F1** simultaneously to fit the drawing.

The two rectangles appear as Figure 6.13.

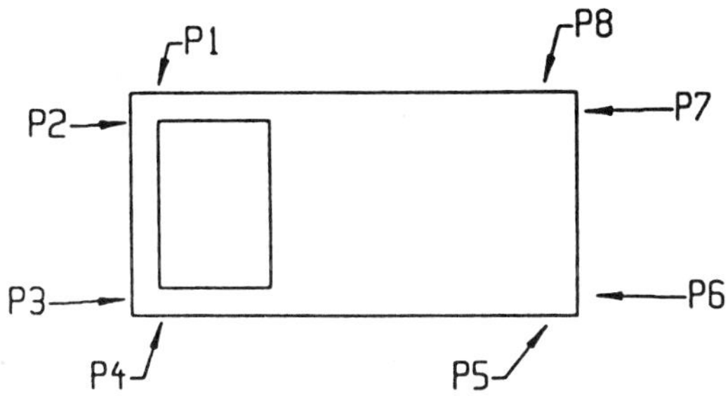

Figure 6.13

Step 2. Create four fillets at corners of outer rectangle. Use the pick points in Figure 6.13.
Select **MAIN MENU → Create → Fillet → Radius**
Enter the first radius: **0.75** ↵

Note: Make sure the other two parameters' settings are correct. The fillet angle is less than 180; trim to fillet.

Select an entity: pick **P1**
Select another entity: pick **P2** to complete the first fillet
Sequentially pick **P3 - P8** to complete the remaining three fillets

The four fillets are added as in Figure 6.14.

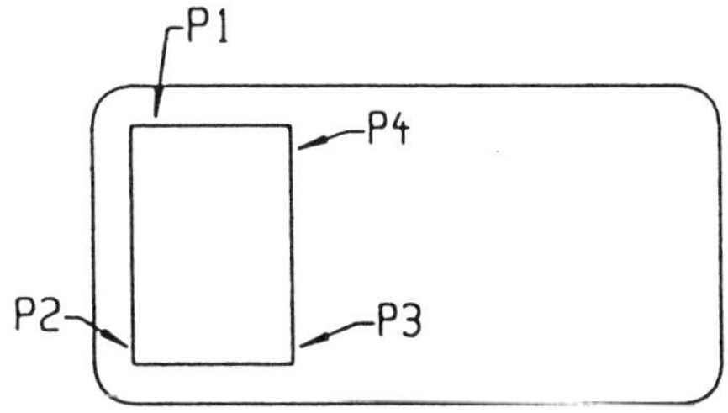

Figure 6.14

Step 3. Create four circles at corners of the inner rectangle.
Use the pick points from the Figure 6.14 above.
Select **MAIN MENU → Create → Arc → Cir pt+rad**
Enter the radius: **0.75** ↵
Select **Endpoint**
Select line, arc or spline:
Pick **P1** to complete the first circle
Pick **P2** for the second circle
Pick **P3** for the third circle
Pick **P4** for the fourth circle

Four circles are added as in Figure 6.15.

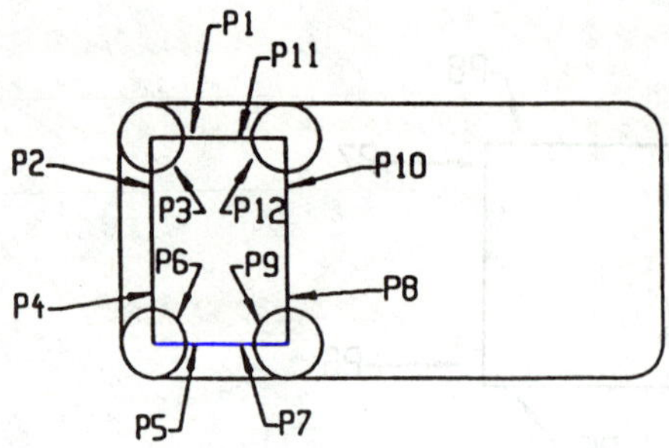

Figure 6.15

Step 4. Trim four circles to become arcs. Use the pick points in Figure 6.15.

Select **MAIN MENU → Modify → Trim → 3 entities**
Select the first entity to trim: pick **P1**
Select the second entity to trim: pick **P2**
Select the entity to trim to: pick **P3** to complete the trimming of the first corner
Sequentially pick **P4 - P12** to trim the remaining three corners

The final drawing should look like Figure 6.16.

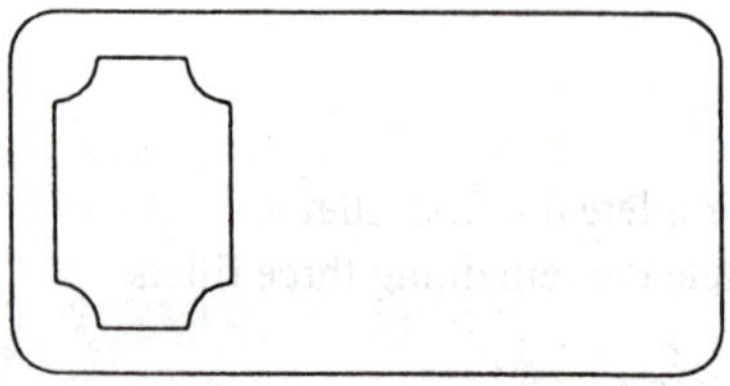

Figure 6.16

Step 5. Save to a file (array1).

Select **MAIN MENU → File → Save**
Enter file name: **array1**

Break Function

This function separates an entity into two or more entities. The new entities can be different from the original entity type. The options under Break are:

2 pieces:	breaks lines, arcs, splines and NURBS curve into two pieces.
At length:	breaks a line, arc or spline at a distance along the entity.
Mny pieces:	breaks lines, arcs, splines and NURBS curve into more than two pieces.
At inters:	breaks lines, arcs, splines and NURBS curve into two pieces.
Spl to arcs:	breaks spline into many pieces.
Draft/line:	breaks notes, lables, witness lines, and leader lines into geometry.
Hatch/line:	breaks a crosshatch entity into line segments.
Cdata/line:	breaks a copious data entity into points or line segments.
Breakcir:	not available.

Tip These new line and arc segments are difficult to distinguish on screen. Use **Analyze** (F4) command to examine these segments.

Join Function

Join combines two separated entities together to become a new entity.

Tips 1. NURBS or parametric curves can not be joined unless they were originally created as the same entity.

2. Note that these two entities have to be compatible. The system checks the database for each entity and tries to join them together. An error message displays if the two entities selected are not compatible. For example:
"Cannot join the lines - they are not collinear."
"Cannot join the arcs - they do not have the same center and radius."

Normal Function

This function is used to change the normal direction of surfaces.

Cpts NURBS Function

This function modifies the control points of NURBS curves and surfaces, and creates a new NURBS curve and surface.

<u>**Procedure:**</u> (Figure 6.17)

1. Select a NURBS curve or surface: Pick **P1**
   The yellow control points and red control lines will appear on screen.
2. Select a control point: Pick **P2**
3. Modify NURBS Cpts: Select **Dynamic**

Dynamic -dynamically drag the control point and see the new curve in blue. **Point entry** - input, or select, a new XYZ coordinates for the control points.

4. Enter the starting point: Pick **P2** again.
5. Move to **P3** and press the mouse button.

Tip **F3** key to repaint the drawing.

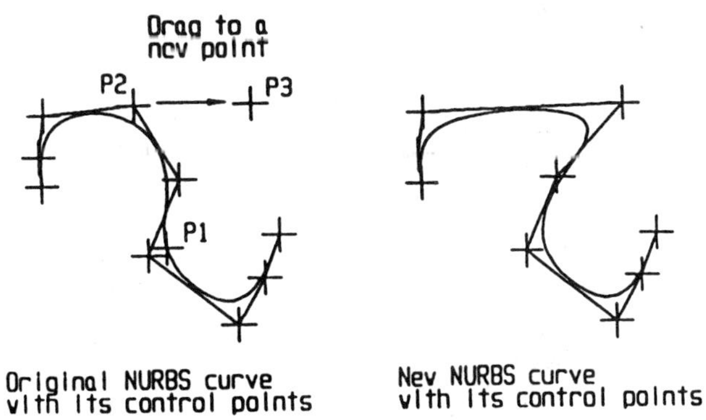

Figure 6.17.

X to NURBS Function

This function converts lines, arcs, splines and surfaces to the NURBS format. The new entities are saved to the drawing database as NURBS curves.

Procedure:

1. Select line arc, spline, or surface to convert to NURBS.
2. Select **Done**

Tip	Use **Analyze** (F4) to confirm the changes.

Extend Function

This function allows the user to extend a line or arc by a desired length. The user types in the desired length and selects a line or arc near the endpoint to direct the extension.

Drag Function

This function dynamically moves or copies drawing entities when given the new location. Drag helps you see the results of the command before it is finished.

Cnv to arcs

This function converts a circular spline or NURBS to an arc.

Procedure:

1. Select splines
2. Select **Done**
3. Select **Do it**

6.3 Xform Functions

Mastercam provides nine very useful editing functions to change the position, orientation, and size of exiting geometries. These **nine** functions are mirror, rotate, scale, scalexyz, translate, offset, ofs ctour stretch and roll. They are grouped under the Xform command. The submenu of Xform is shown in Figure 6.18.

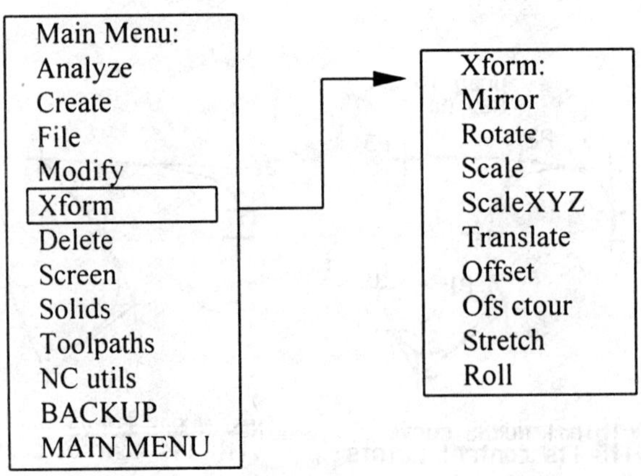

Figure 6.18

The nine editing functions are described below:

Mirror: produces a mirror image of a drawing, detail, or part.
Rotate: rotates the selected entities about any point.
Scale: scales the selected entities to increase or decrease their sizes.
Scale XYZ: scales the selected entities by the given x, y and z values.
Translate: moves or copies objects to new location(s).
Offset: moves or copies a line or arc away from itself in a perpendicular direction with an offset distance to the line or arc.
Ofs ctour: offsets several connected lines or arcs by chaining their entities.
Stretch: translates entities and stretch lines relative to a selection windows.
Roll: rolls and wraps entities as though around a cylinder or unwraps rolled entities.

Entity Selection Option and Its Procedures

When Mirror, Rotate, Scale, Translate or Offset is selected, the following **entity selection option** will appear on the Main Menu Area. You can select an entity one after another, use chain, window, or combine different options in the menu. The selected entity will be highlighted in white. You can select **Done** to finish the selection process and proceed to the next step, or select **Unselected** to abort the selected entities.

Unselect: clears the current selected group.
Chain: selects a group of entities that are chained together.
Window: selects all the entities that are inside or outside the window.
Area: has two options; mode and Options.
Only: selects a group of entities with a specific entity type, i.e., lines, arcs, etc. Select the specific kind of entity one after another to add into the database.
All: selects a group of entities of a specific entity type, i.e., lines, arcs, splines, etc. The options automatically selects all the entities in th **P**articular entity type.
Group: retrieves and selects the current group from the database.
Result: shows the current result.
Done: sets this switch to Y to ungroup entities or N to group them.

Transformation Parameters

Mastercam uses different dialog boxes with different parameters to perform a transformation. An example for rotate is shown in the following figure.

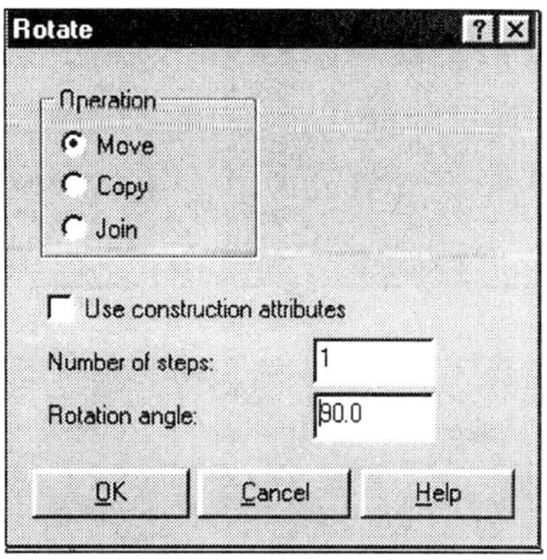

Figure 6.19

Move:	moves the original entities.
Copy:	copies the original entities.
Join:	joins the new transformed entities to original entities at their end points.
Number of Steps:	specifies the number of steps to be performed by the transformation function.
Rotation Angle:	specifies the angle of rotation.

Mirror Function

This function produces a **mirror** image of selected entities about the X axis, Y axis, an existing line, or 2 points. It is best suited for those parts that have identical features being symmetrical about an axis or a line.

Procedure: (Figure 6.20)

1. Entity selection option: Pick **P1**
2. Entity selection option: Select **Done**
3. Mirror about: Select **Line**

X axis:	mirrors with respect to X axis.
Y axis:	mirrors with respect to Y axis.
Line:	mirrors with respect to an existing line. The system will prompt after this selection.
2 Points:	mirrors with respect to two selected points.

4. Select line to mirror across: Pick **P2**
5. Select **Copy → OK** from the pop-up dialog box.

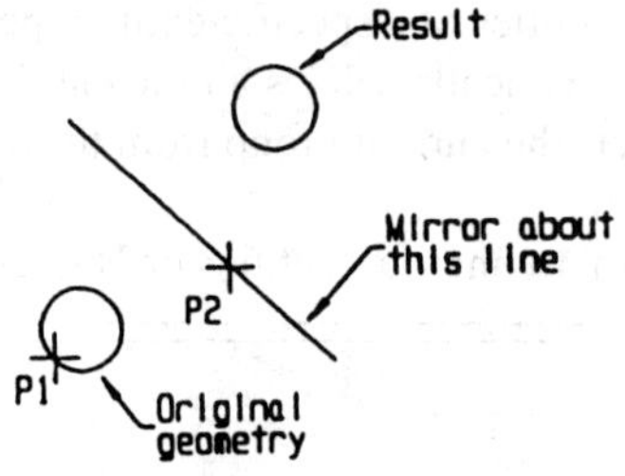

Figure 6.20: Mirroring an entity about an existing line

Tips 1. Select **Move → OK** or **Copy → OK** in step 5 to delete or retain the original entities.
2. Use the **Repaint** (F3) command to see the complete drawing after modification.

Project 2. Mirroring

Create a hexagon and a rectangle as shown in Figure 6.21. Save the file as **scale1**. This file is used in project 4 of chapter 8 to generate a set of toolpaths for pocketing three hexagons at different depths.

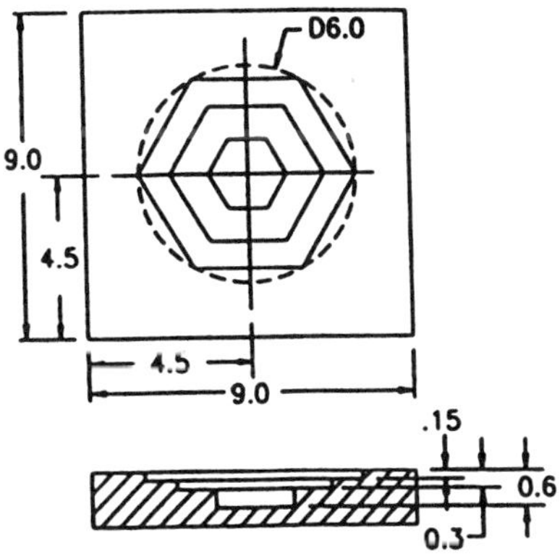

Figure 6.21

Tips: 1. Create three sides of upper half of hexagon.
2. Mirror the three sides of hexagon about the X-axis to form the hexagon.

Step 1. Create two lines.

Select **MAIN MENU → Create → Line → Polar**
Specify an endpoint: **3,0** ↵
Enter the angle in degree: **120** ↵
Enter the length: **3** ↵
Specify an endpoint: **-3,0** ↵
Enter the angle in degree: **60** ↵
Enter the length: **3** ↵

The drawing appears as Figure 6.22.

Figure 6.22

Step 2. Create another line using the pick points in Figure 6.22.

Select **BACKUP → Endpoints → Endpoint**
Specify the first endpoint: Pick **P1**
Specify the second endpoint: Pick **P2**

The new drawing becomes Figure 6.23.

Figure 6.23

Step 3. Mirror about X axis.

Select **MAIN MENU → Xform → Mirror → All → Entities → Done**
Select **X axis → Copy → OK**

The hexagon appears as in Figure 6.24.

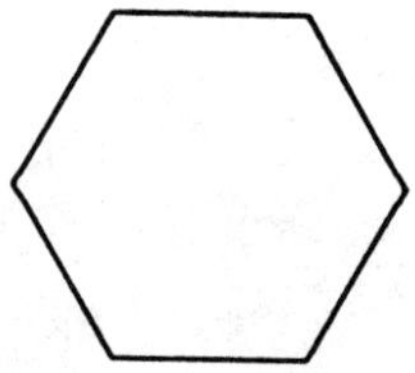

Figure 6.24

Step 4. Create a rectangle.

Select **MAIN MENU → Create → Rectangle → 2 points**
Enter the lower left corner: **-4.5,-4.5** ↵
Enter the upper right corner: **4.5,4.5** ↵

The final drawing should look like Figure 6.25.

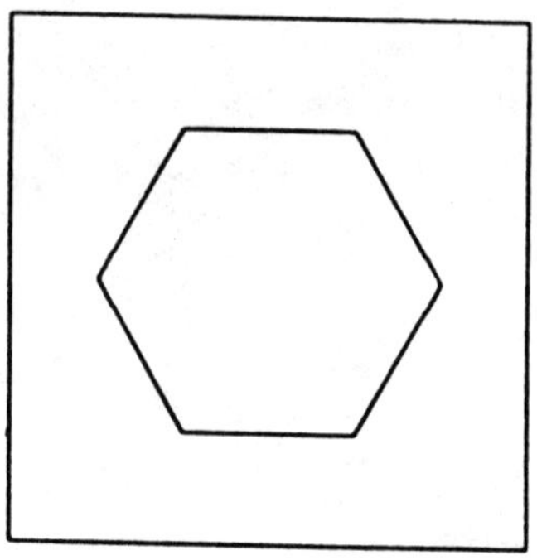

Figure 6.25

Step 5. Save to a file (scale1).

Select **MAIN MENU → File → Save**
Enter file name: **Scale1**

Project 3. Mirroring

Create a geometry as shown in Figure 6.26. Save the file as **contour2.** This file is used in project 2 of chapter 7 to generate the toolpaths to cut the internal profile.

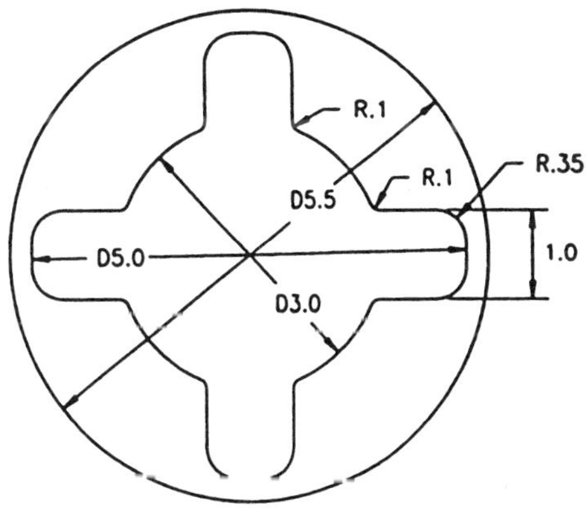

Figure 6.26

> **Tips:** 1. Create three 45° construction arcs and one construction line at 45° with the X axis.
> 2. Add two fillets to form the basic profile.
> 3. Mirror the basic profile about the 45° line to form a quarter of the part profile.
> 4. The quarter profile is then mirrored twice to complete the final part profile. The first time mirror about the Y axis. The second time mirror about the X axis.

Step 1. Create three 45° arcs.

Select **MAIN MENU → Create → Arc → Polar → Center pt**
Enter the center point: **0,0** ↵
Enter the radius: **2.75** ↵
Enter the initial angle: **0** ↵
Enter the final angle: **45** ↵
Enter the center point: **0,0** ↵
Enter the radius: **2.5** ↵
Enter the initial angle: **0** ↵
Enter the final angle: **45** ↵
Enter the center point: **0,0** ↵
Enter the radius: **1.5** ↵
Enter the initial angle: **0** ↵
Enter the final angle: **45** ↵

The three 45° arcs are shown in Figure 6.27.

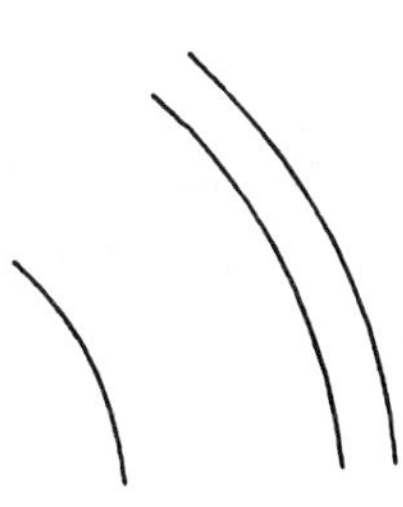

Figure 6.27

Step 2. Create a horizontal line at y = 0.5 and a 45° line.

Select **MAIN MENU** → **Create** → **Line** → **Endpoints**
Specify the first endpoint: Enter **0,0.5** ↵
Specify the second endpoint: Enter **2.5,0.5** ↵
Specify the first endpoint: Enter **0,0** ↵
Specify the second endpoint: Enter **3,3** ↵

Two lines are added as in Figure 6.28.

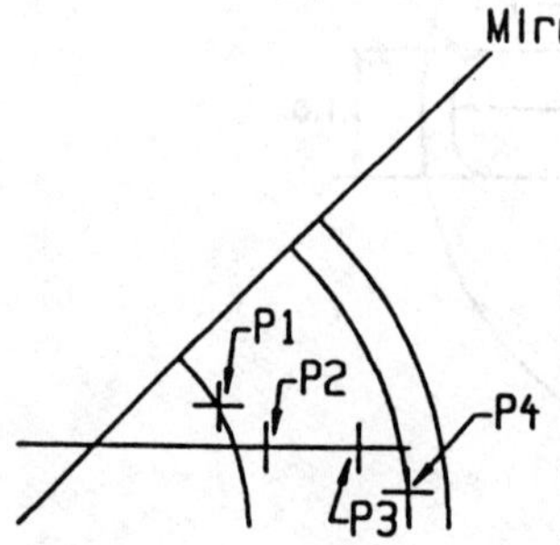

Figure 6.28

Step 3. Create two fillets using the pick points in Figure 6.28.

Select **MAIN MENU** → **Create** → **Fillet** → **Radius**
Enter the fillet radius: **0.1** ↵

Note: Be sure the other two options are correct. The fillet angle is less than 180; trim to the fillet.

Select an entity: pick **P1**
Select another entity: pick **P2**
Select **Radius**
Enter the radius: **0.35** ↵
Select an entity: pick **P3**
Select another entity: pick **P4**

Two fillets are added as in Figure 6.29.

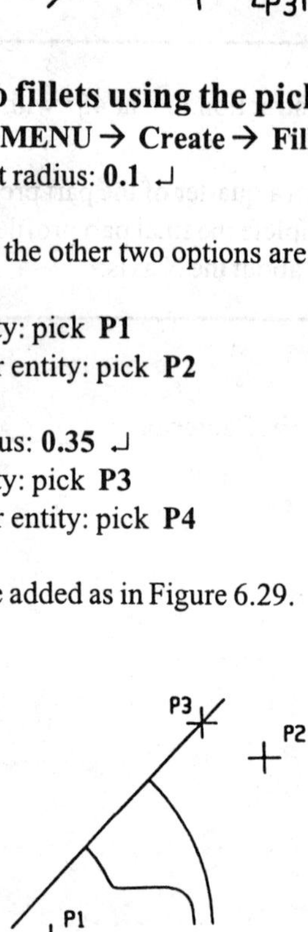

Figure 6.29

Step 4. Mirror the basic profile about the 45° line using the pick points in Figure 6.29.

Select **MAIN MENU** → **Xform** → **Mirror** → **Window** → **Inside**
Select the first corner: pick **P1**
Select the second corner: pick **P2**
Select **Done** → **Line**
Select line about which to mirror: pick **P3**
Select **Copy** → **OK**

The mirrored profile should look like Figure 6.30.

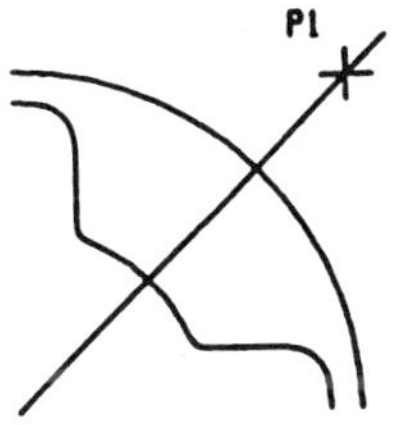

Figure 6.30

Step 5. Delete the mirror line using the pick point in Figure 6.30.

Select **MAIN MENU → Delete**
Select an entity or: pick **P1**

The new drawing appears as Figure 6.31.

Figure 6.31

Step 6. Complete the geometry by using the Mirror command twice.

Select **MAIN MENU → Xform → Mirror → All → Entities → Done → Y axis**
Select **Copy → OK→ All → Entities → Done → X axis→Copy → OK**

The final drawing should resemble Figure 6.32.

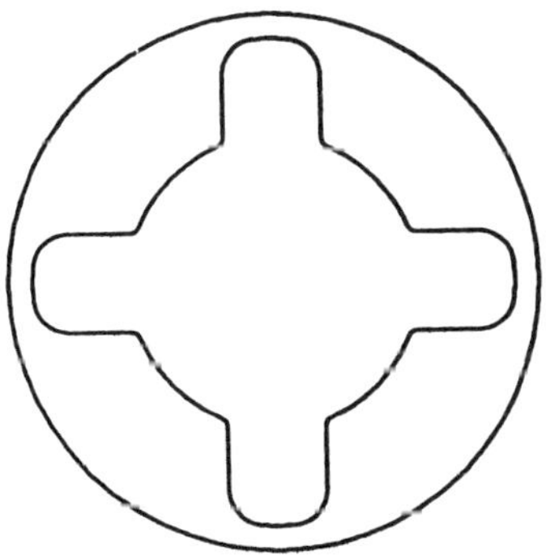

Figure 6.32

Step 7. Save to a file.

Select **MAIN MENU → File → Save**
Enter file name: **contour2**

Project 4. Mirroring

Create a geometry as shown in Figure 6.33. Save the file as **rotate1.** This file is used in project 3 of chapter 8 to generate toolpaths.

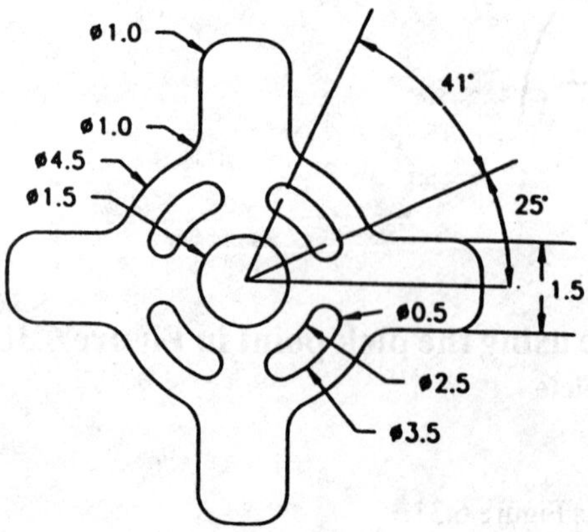

Figure 6.33

Tips: 1. Create a basic profile that encompasses 45° of the profile.

2. Mirror the basic profile about the 45° line to complete a profile of 90°.
3. Mirror the profile of 90° about the Y axis to generate another profile of 180°.
4. Mirror the 180° profile about the X axis to complete the geometry.

Step 1. Create five circles.

Select **MAIN MENU → Create → Arc → Circ pt + rad**
Enter the radius: **4.0** ↵
Enter the coordinates: **0,0** ↵

Enter **BACKUP → Circ pt + rad**
Enter the radius: **2.25** ↵
Enter the coordinates: **0,0** ↵

Enter **BACKUP → Circ pt + rad**
Enter the radius: **1.75** ↵
Enter the coordinates: **0,0** ↵

Enter **BACKUP → Circ pt + rad**
Enter the radius: **1.25** ↵
Enter the coordinates: **0,0** ↵

Enter **BACKUP → Circ pt + rad**
Enter the radius: **0.75** ↵
Enter the coordinates: **0,0** ↵

Step 2. Create a 45° line.

Select **MAIN MENU → Create → Line → Polar**
Specify an endpoint: Enter **0,0** ↵
Enter angle in degrees: **45** ↵
Enter the line length: **4.5** ↵
The drawing should look like Figure 6.34.

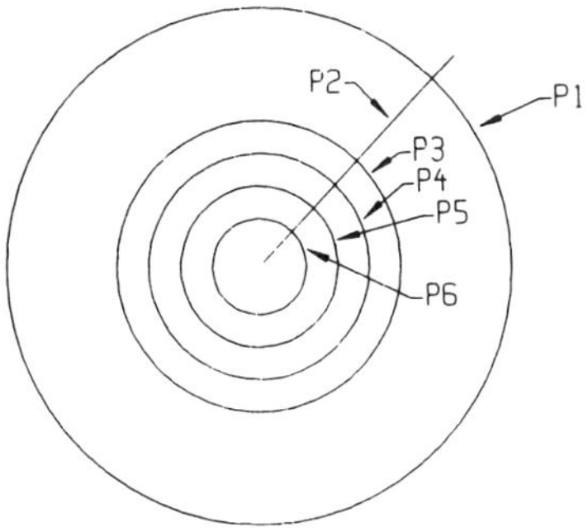

Figure 6.34

Step 3. Trim the circles to the line. Use pick points in Figure 6.34.

Select **MAIN MENU → Modify → Trim → 1 entity**
Select the entity to trim: pick **P1**
Select the entity to trim to: pick **P2**
Select the entity to trim: pick **P3**
Select the entity to trim to: pick **P2**
Select the entity to trim: pick **P4**
Select the entity to trim to: pick **P2**
Select the entity to trim: pick **P5**
Select the entity to trim to: pick **P2**
Select the entity to trim: pick **P6**
Select the entity to trim to: pick **P2**

These trimmed arcs should appear as Figure 6.35.

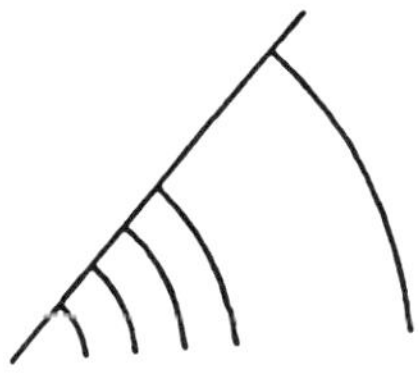

Figure 6.35

Tip Step 3 can be done by the following procedures:

Select **MAIN MENU → Modify → Trim → Many → All →Arcs →Done**
Select trimming curve: pick **P2**
Indicate side of the trimming curve: pick **P2**

Step 4. Create two lines for fillets.

Select **MAIN MENU → Create → Line → Polar**
Specify an endpoint: Enter **0,0** ↵
Enter angle in degrees: **25** ↵
Enter the line length: **2.5** ↵
Select **BACKUP → Endpoints**
Specify the first endpoint: Enter **2.25, .75** ↵
Specify the second endpoint: Enter **4, .75** ↵

The two lines are added as in Figure 6.36.

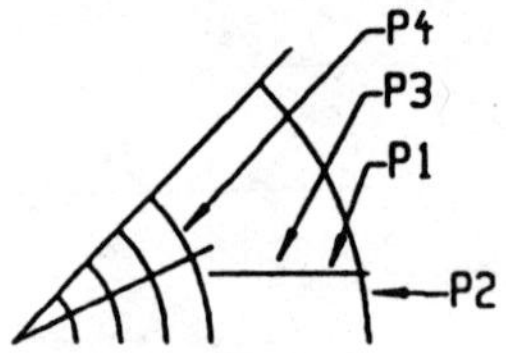

Figure 6.36

Step 5. Create two fillets using the pick points in Figure 6.36.

Select **MAIN MENU → Create → Fillet → Radius**
Enter the fillet radius: **0.5** ↵

Note: Make sure the other two options are correct. The fillet angle is less than 180; trim to fillet.

Select an entity: pick **P1**
Select another entity: pick **P2**
Select an entity: pick **P3**
Select another entity: pick **P4**

The new drawing becomes Figure 6.37.

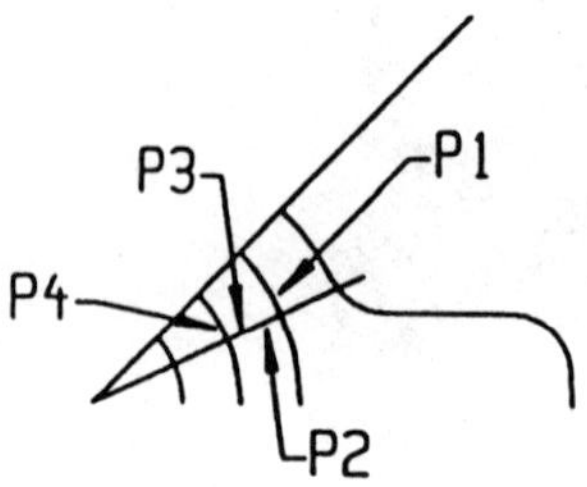

Figure 6.37

Step 6. Trim entities using the pick points in Figure 6.37.

Select **MAIN MENU → Modify → Trim → 2 entities**
Select the entity to trim: pick **P1**
Select the entity to trim to: pick **P2**
Select the entity to trim: pick **P3**
Select the entity to trim to: pick **P4**

The drawing should look like Figure 6.38.

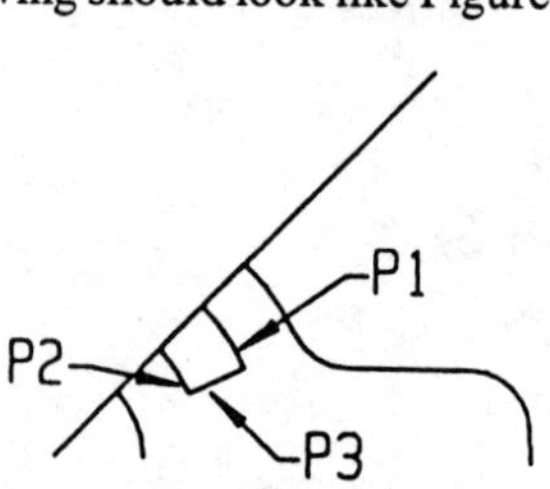

Figure 6.38

Step 7. Create an arc and delete a line using the pick points in Figure 6.38.

Select **MAIN MENU → Create → Arc → Endpoints → Endpoint**
Enter the first point: pick **P1**
Enter the second point: pick **P2**
Enter the radius: **0.25** ↵
Select an arc: pick at the bottom arc
Select **MAIN MENU → Delete**
Select an entity or: pick **P3**

The arc should appear in Figure 6.39.

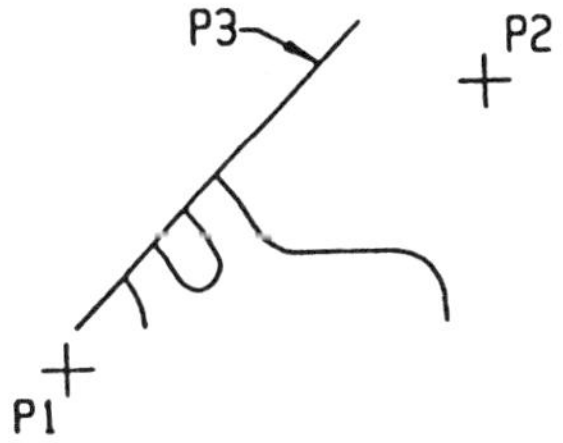

Figure 6.39

Step 8. Mirror about the 45° line. Use the pick points in Figure 6.39.

Select **MAIN MENU → Xform → Mirror → Window →Inside**
Select the first corner: pick **P1**
Select the second corner: pick **P2**
Select **Done → Line**
Select line about which to mirror: pick **P3**
Select **Copy → OK**

The mirrored drawing should look like Figure 6.40.

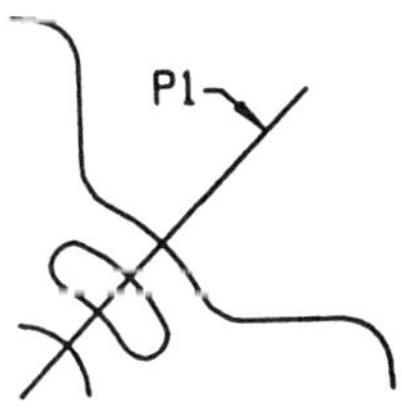

Figure 6.40

Step 9. Delete the 45° line using the pick point in Figure 6.40.

Select **MAIN MENU → Delete**
Select an **entity** or pick **P1**
The new drawing becomes Figure 6.41.

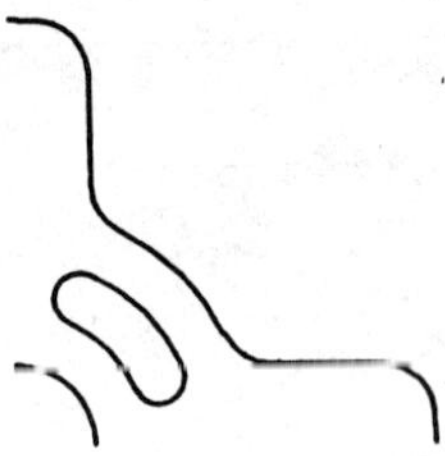

Figure 6.41

Step 10. Mirror all entities twice.

Mirror the first time about the Y axis and second time about the X axis.
Select **MAIN MENU → Xform → Mirror → All → Entities →Done → Y axis → Copy → OK**
Select **All → Entities → Done → X axis → Copy → OK**

The final drawing should resemble Figure 6.42.

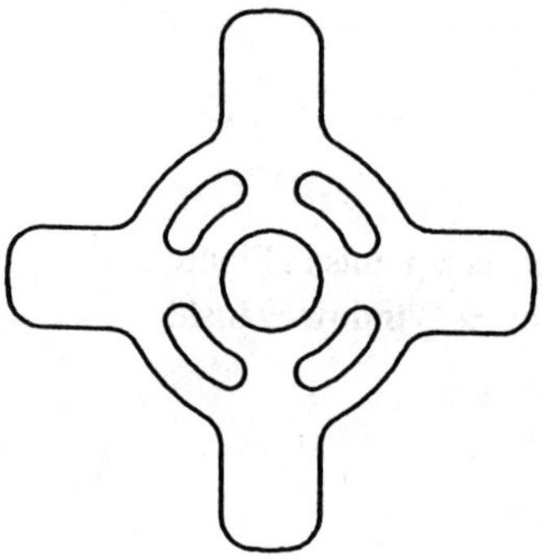

Figure 6.42

Step 11. Save to a file.

Select **MAIN MENU → File → Save**
Enter file name: **rotate1**

💻 Project 5. Mirroring

Create a part geometry as shown in Figure 6.43. Save the file as **pocket2**. This file is used in project 6 of chapter 7 to generate a set of toolpaths for pocketing the internal profile with an island.

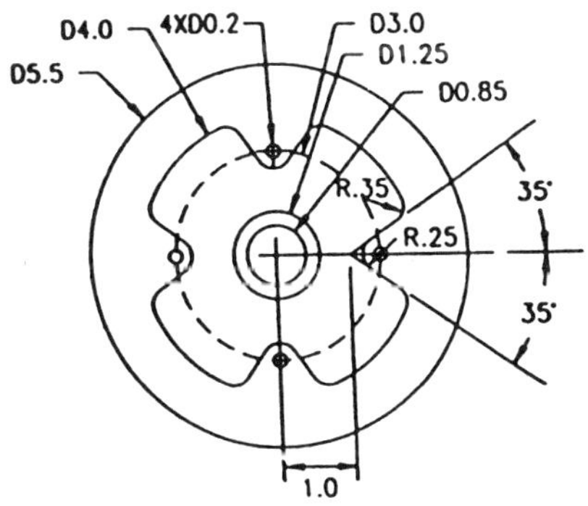

Figure 6.43

⏳**Tips:** 1. Create a basic (partial) profile. This basic profile is then mirrored about a 45° line from the +X axis to form a quarter profile.
2. Mirror the quarter profile twice, first with the Y axis and then with the X axis.
3. Create the remaining seven circles.

Step 1. Create a circle.

Select **MAIN MENU → Create → Arc → Circ pt + dia**
Enter the diameter: **4** ↵
Enter coordinates: **0,0** ↵

Step 2. Create two lines for fillets and two lines for trimming and mirroring.

Select **MAIN MENU → Create → Line → Polar**
Specify an endpoint: **1.0, 0** ↵
Enter angle in degrees: **35** ↵
Enter the line length: **1.5** ↵
Specify an endpoint: **1.0, 0** ↵
Enter angle in degrees: **-35** ↵
Enter the line length: **1.5** ↵
Specify an endpoint: **0,0** ↵
Enter angle in degrees: **45** ↵
Enter the line length: **3** ↵
Specify an endpoint: **0,0** ↵
Enter angle in degrees: **0** ↵
Enter the line length: **3** ↵

The drawing should look like Figure 6.44 on the next page.

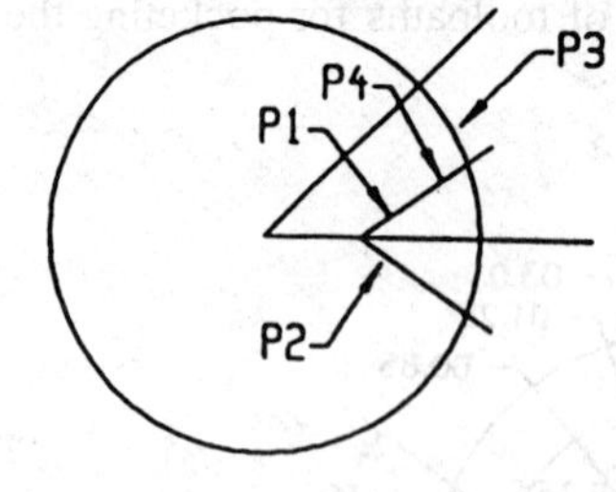

Figure 6.44

Step 3. Create two fillets. Use the pick points in Figure 6.44.

Select **MAIN MENU → Create → Fillet → Radius**
Enter the fillet radius: **0.25** ↵
Select an entity: pick **P1**
Select another entity: pick **P2**
Select **Radius**
Enter the fillet radius: **0.35** ↵
Select an entity: pick **P3**
Select another entity: pick **P4**

The new drawing appears as Figure 6.45.

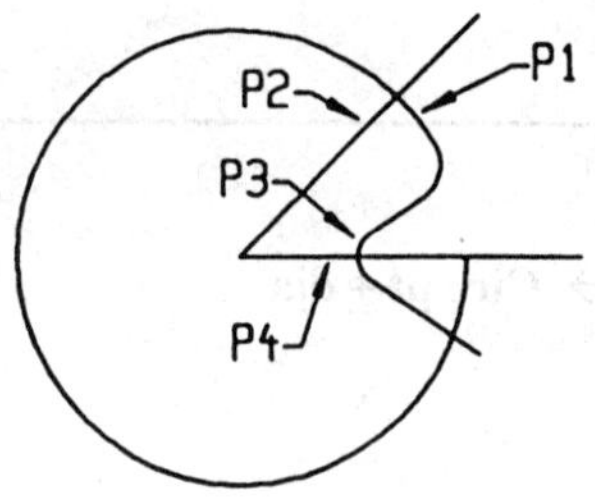

Figure 6.45

Step 4. Trim entities using the pick points in Figure 6.45 above.

Select **MAIN MENU → Modify → Trim → 1 entity**
Select the entity to trim: pick **P1**
Select the entity to trim to: pick **P2**
Select the entity to trim: pick **P3**
Select the entity to trim to: pick **P4**

The trimmed geometry appears as Figure 6.46.

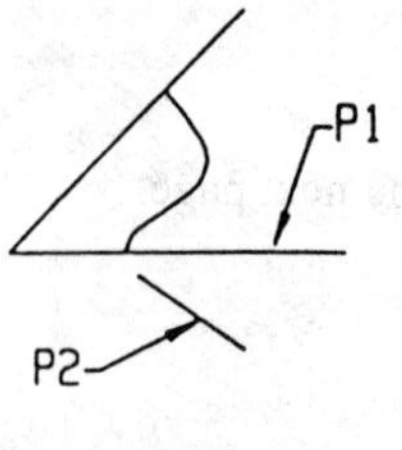

Figure 6.46

Step 5. Delete two construction entities using the pick points in Figure 6.46.

Select **MAIN MENU → Delete**
Select an entity: pick **P1**
Select an entity: pick **P2**

New drawing with the basic profile should resemble Figure 6.47.

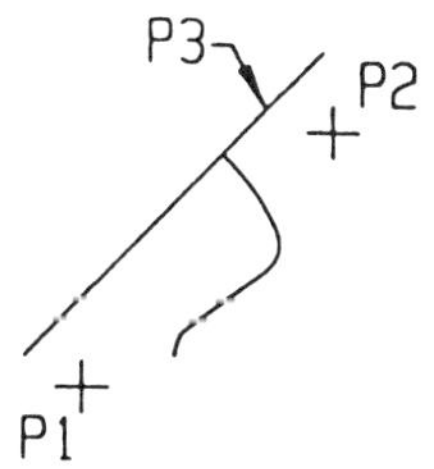

Figure 6.47

Step 6. Mirror the basic profile about the 45° line.

Use the pick points marked in Figure 6.47.
Select **MAIN MENU → Xform → Mirror → Window → Inside**
Select the first corner: pick **P1**
Select the second corner: pick **P2**
Select **Done → Line**
Select line about which to mirror: pick **P3**
Select **Copy → OK**

The new profile becomes as shown in Figure 6.48.

Figure 6.48

Step 7. Delete the 45° construction line using the pick point in Figure 6.48.

Select **MAIN MENU → Delete**
Select an entity or: pick **P1**

The profile should resemble Figure 6.49.

Figure 6.49

Step 8. Mirror the profile twice.

Select **MAIN MENU → Xform → Mirror → All → Entities → Done→ Y axis→ Copy → OK**
Select **All → Entities → Done → X axis→Copy → OK**

The complete profile should look like Figure 6.50.

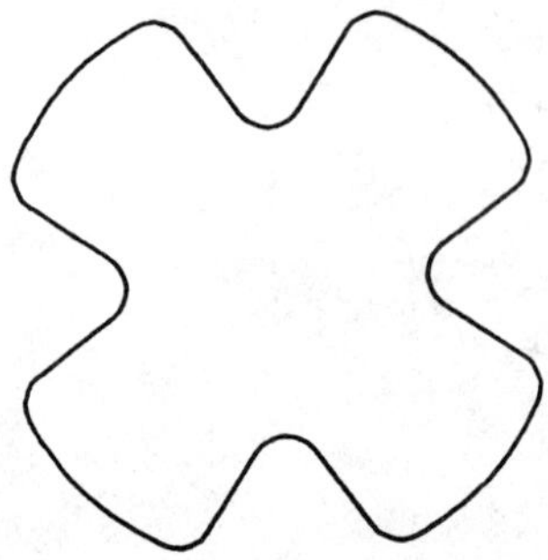

Figure 6.50

Step 9. Create the remaining seven circles.

Select **MAIN MENU → Create → Arc → Circ pt + dia**

Enter the diameter: **5.5** ↵
Enter the coordinates: **0,0** ↵

Enter **BACKUP → Circ pt + rad**
Enter the diameter: **1.25** ↵
Enter the coordinates: **0,0** ↵

Enter **BACKUP → Circ pt + rad**
Enter the diameter: **0.85** ↵
Enter the coordinates: **0,0** ↵

Enter **BACKUP → Circ pt + rad**
Enter the diameter: **0.2** ↵
Enter the coordinates: **1.5, 0** ↵

Enter **BACKUP → Circ pt + rad**
Enter the diameter: **0.2** ↵
Enter the coordinates; **0, 1.5** ↵

Enter **BACKUP → Circ pt + rad**
Enter the diameter: **0.2** ↵
Enter the coordinates: **-1.5, 0** ↵

Enter **BACKUP → Circ pt + rad**
Enter the diameter: **0.2** ↵
Enter the coordinates: **0, -1.5** ↵

The seven circles are added as in Figure 6.51.

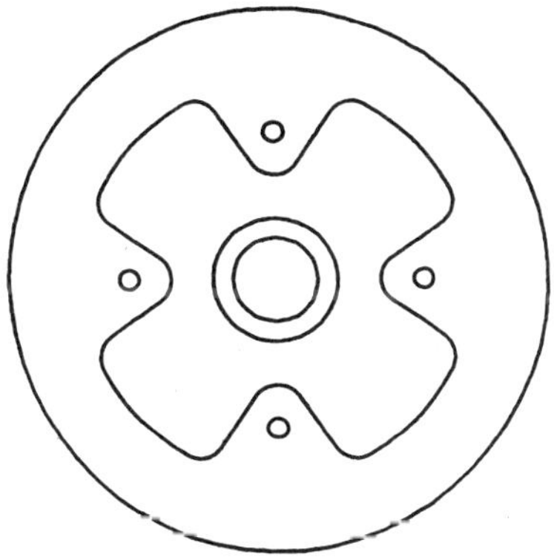

Figure 6.51

Step 10. Save to a file.

Select **MAIN MENU → File → Save**

Enter file name: **pocket2**

Rotate Function

The rotate function moves or copies existing entities by rotating about the origin or any given point. It is best suited to generating geometries for identical patterns or features that are symmetrical about a point.

Procedure: (Figure 6.52)

1. Select an entity to rotate: Pick at **P1**
2. Select **Done**
3. Point Entry <position options>:Select **Point**
4. Select a point: Pick **P2**
5. Select **Rotation angle** option in the dialogue box = **90** ↵
   (Make sure the Number of steps =1.)
6. Select **Copy → OK**

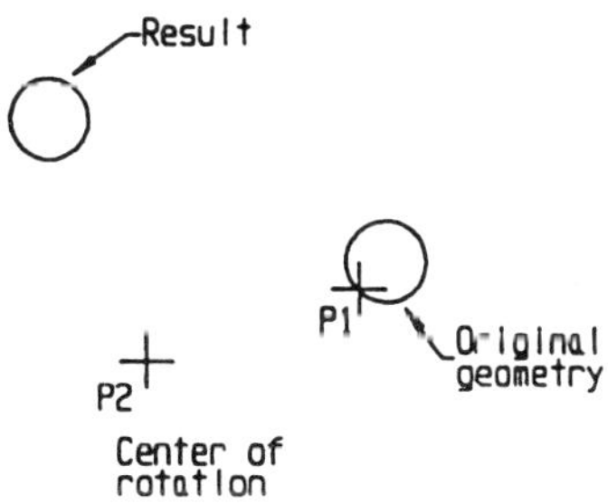

Figure 6.52: Rotating an entity about an existing point for 90-degree

Project 6. Rotating

Create the geometry as shown in Figure 6.53a. Save the file as **mirror1**. This geometry file is used in project 2 of chapter 8 to generate the toolpaths to cut the four pockets shown in Figure 6.53b.

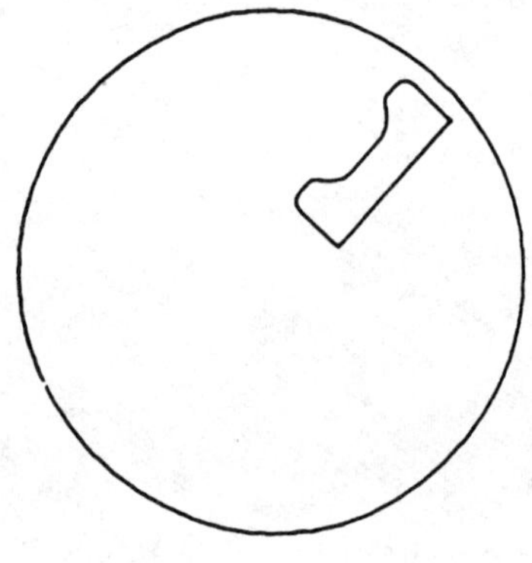

Figure 6.53a

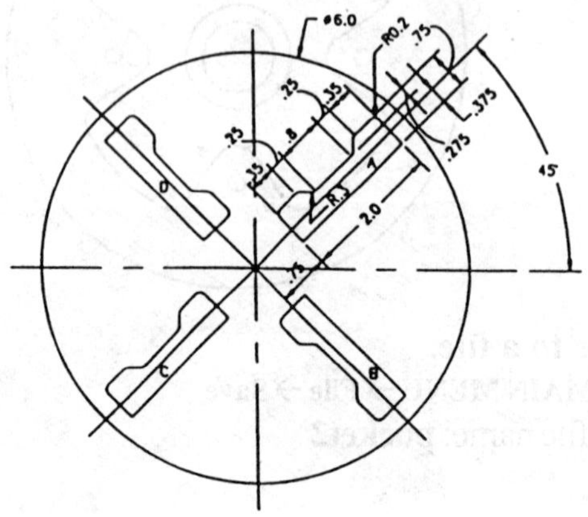

Figure 6.53b

Tips: 1. Create the entities of the pocket profile in the +X direction. Then rotate them 45° in the counterclockwise direction.
2. Use the Multi line command to create the basic pocket profile consisting of eight lines. Their end coordinates are illustrated in Figure 6.54 on the next page.

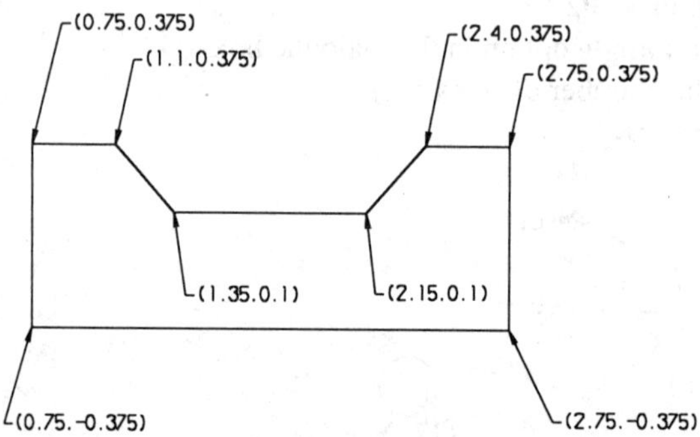

Figure 6.54

Step 1. Create eight lines

Select **MAIN MENU → Create → Line → Multi**
Specify endpoint 1: Enter **.75,-.375** ↵
Specify endpoint 2: Enter **2.75,-.375** ↵
Specify endpoint 3: Enter **2.75,.375** ↵
Specify endpoint 4: Enter **2.4,.375** ↵
Specify endpoint 5: Enter **2.15,.1** ↵
Specify endpoint 6: Enter **1.35,.1** ↵
Specify endpoint 7: Enter **1.1,.375** ↵
Specify endpoint 8: Enter **.75,.375** ↵
Specify endpoint 9: Enter **.75,-.375** ↵
The basic pocket profile appears as Figure 6.55.

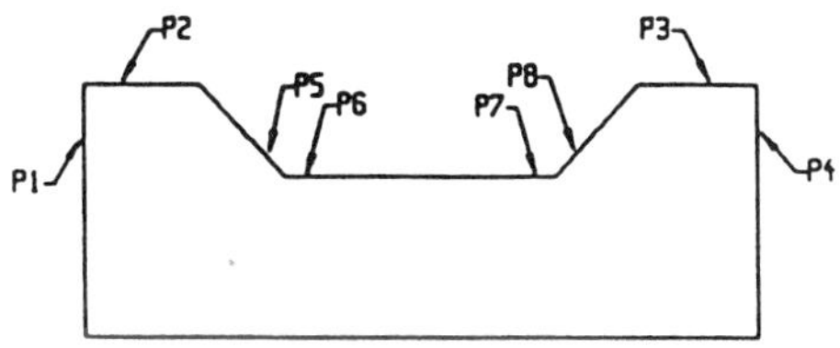

Figure 6.55

Step 2. Create four fillets using the pick points in Figure 6.55.

Select **MAIN MENU → Create → Fillet → Radius**
Enter the fillet radius: **0.15** ↵

Note: Make sure the other two options are correct. The fillet angle is less than 180; trim to fillet.
Select an entity: Pick **P1**
Select another entity: Pick **P2**
Select an entity: Pick **P3**
Select another entity: Pick **P4**
Select **Radius**
Enter the fillet radius: **0.3** ↵
Select an entity: Pick **P5**
Select another entity: Pick **P6**
Select an entity: Pick **P7**
Select another entity: Pick **P8**
The four fillets are added to the drawing as shown in Figure 6.56 below.

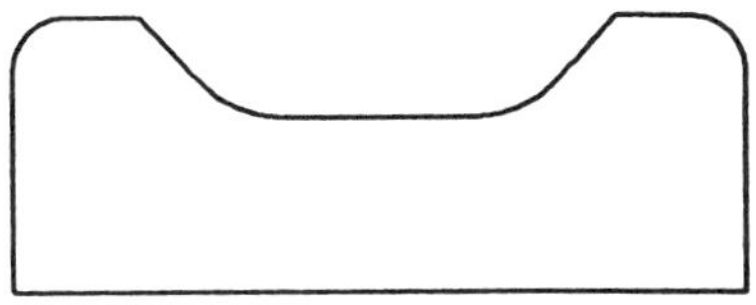

Figure 6.56

Step 3. Rotate the geometry for 45° in counterclockwise direction about the origin.

Select **MAIN MENU → Xform → Rotate → All → Entities → Done → Origin**
Select Rotation angle option in the dialog box: **45** ↵
(Make sure the Number of steps = 1)
Select **Move →OK**

The rotated geometry entities are shown in Figure 6.57.

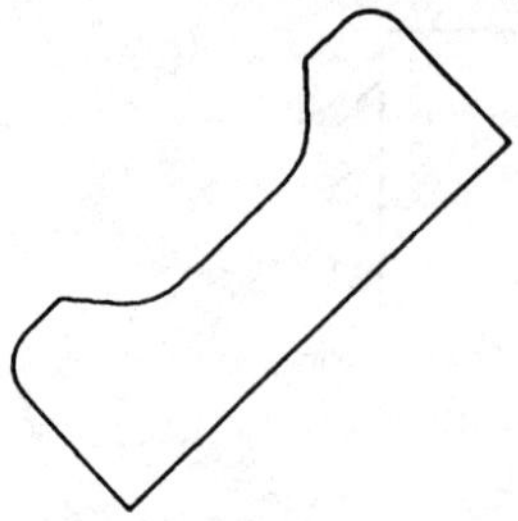

Figure 6.57

Step 4. Create an outside circle.

Select **MAIN MENU → Create → Arc → Circ pt+dia**
Enter the diameter: **6** ↵
Enter the coordinates: **0, 0** ↵
The complete drawing should resemble Figure 6.58.

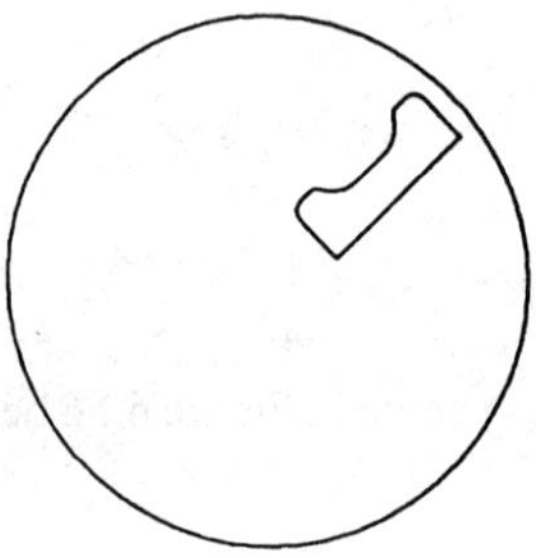

Figure 6.58

Step 5. Save to a file.

Select **MAIN MENU → File → Save**
Enter file name: **mirror1**

Project 7. Rotating

Use the basic create commands and the rotate function to create a geometry as shown in Figure 6.59a. The file is saved as **trans1**. This file is used in project 5 of chapter 8 to generate a set of toolpaths for producing three pockets as shown in figure 6.59b.

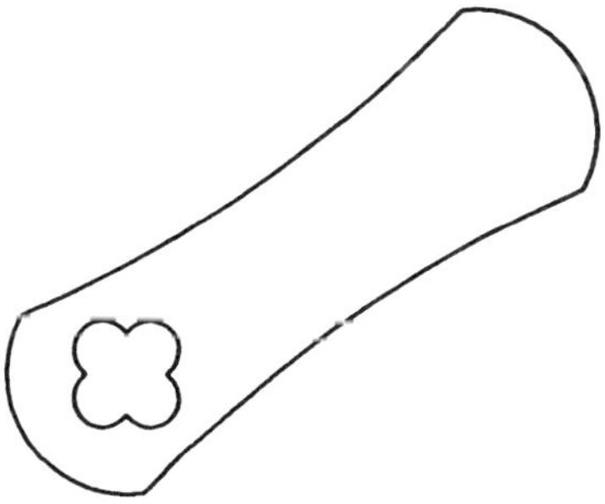

Figure 6.59a

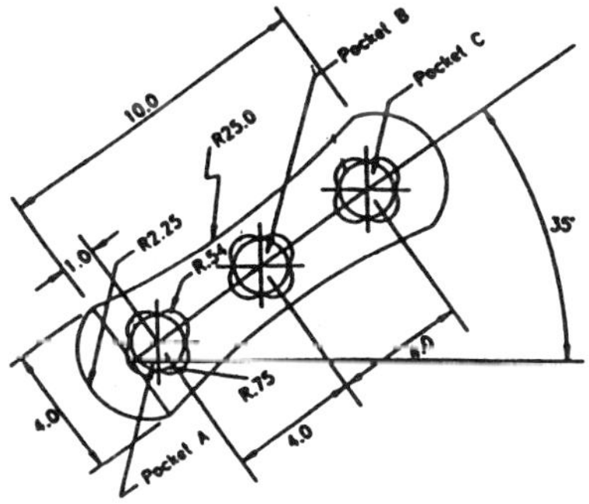

Figure 6.59b

> **Tips:** 1. Create the outer curved profile in the X direction. This profile is then rotated 35° in the counterclockwise direction to its desired location.
> 2. Create a construction circle and two construction lines to create an arc. This arc is then rotated by 90° to three other locations.

Step 1. Create a construction rectangle.

Select **MAIN MENU → Create → Rectangle → 2 points**
Enter the lower left corner: **0,-2** ↵
Enter the upper right corner: **10,2** ↵

Note: Press **Alt-F1** (Fit) to see the whole geometry

The rectangle should appear as Figure 6.60.

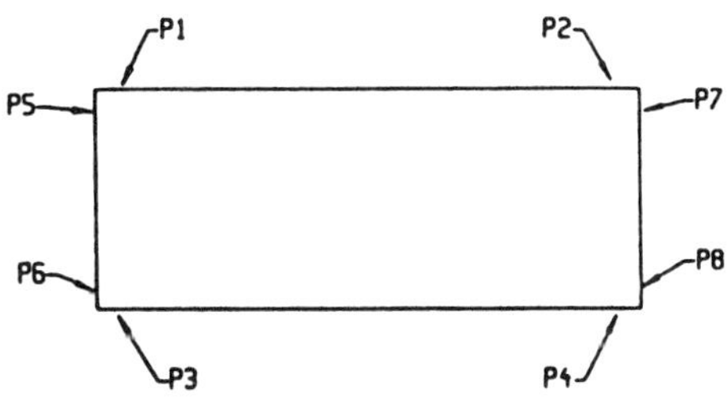

Figure 6.60

Step 2. Create four arcs using the pick points in Figure 6.60.

Select **MAIN MENU → Create → Arc → Endpoints → Endpoint**
Enter the first point: Pick **P1**
Enter the second point: Pick **P2**
Enter the radius: **25** ↵
Select an arc: Pick at the correct arc *Note:* there are four choices

Step 2, continued.

Enter the first point: Pick **P3**
Enter the second point: Pick **P4**
Enter the radius: **25** ↵
Select an arc: Pick at the correct arc
Enter the first point: Pick **P5**
Enter the second point: Pick **P6**
Enter the radius: **2.25** ↵
Select an arc: Pick at the correct arc
Enter the first point: Pick **P7**
Enter the second point: Pick **P8**
Enter the radius: **2.25** ↵
Select an arc: Pick at the correct arc

The four arcs are added as in Figure 6.61.

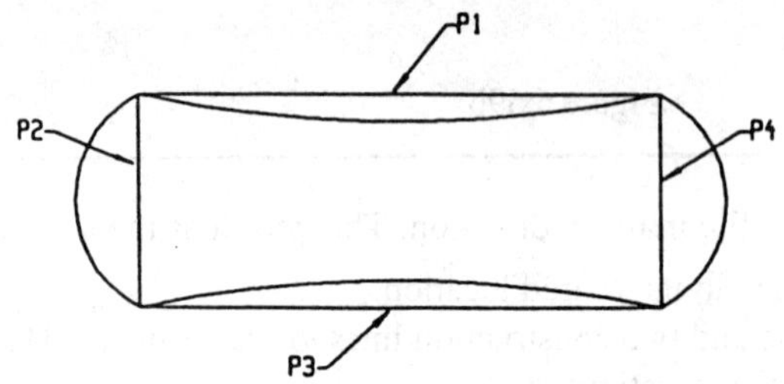

Figure 6.61

Step 3. Delete the rectangle using the pick points in Figure 6.61.

Select **MAIN MENU → Delete**
Select an entity or: pick **P1**
Select an entity or: pick **P2**
Select an entity or: pick **P3**
Select an entity or: pick **P4**

The outer profile should look like Figure 6.62.

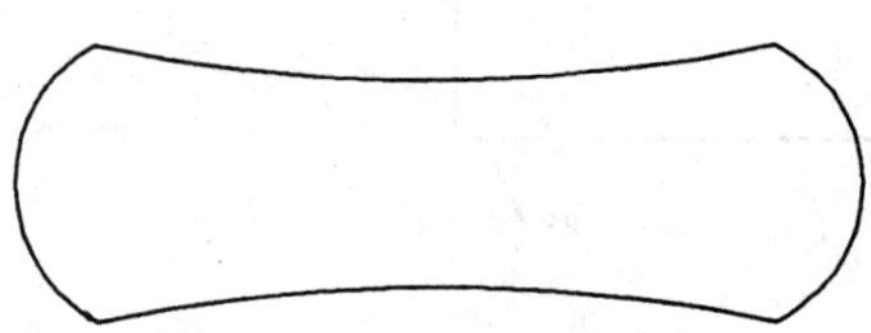

Figure 6.62

Step 4. Create a construction circle.

Select **MAIN MENU → Create → Arc → Circ pt +rad**
Enter the radius: **.75** ↵
Enter the coordinates: **1,0** ↵

The circle is added as in Figure 6.63.

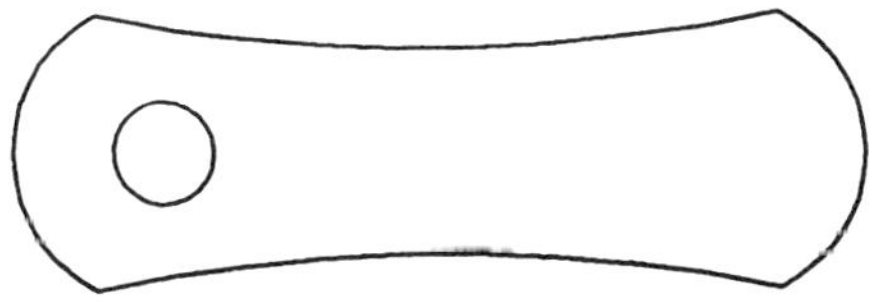

Figure 6.63

Step 5. Rotate all entities for 35° in the counterclockwise direction.

Select **MAIN MENU → Xform → Rotate → All → Entities → Done → Center**
Pick the circle
Select the Rotation angle option in the dialog box= **35** ↵
(Make sure the Number of steps = 1)
Select **Move →OK**

The rotated geometry becomes Figure 6.64.

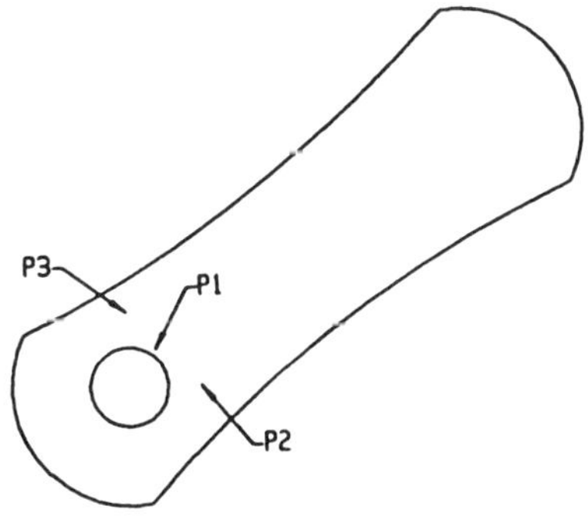

Figure 6.64

Step 6. Create two construction lines. Use the pick points in Figure 6.64.

Select **MAIN MENU → Create → Line → Horizontal → Center**
Specify the first endpoint: pick **P1**
Specify the second endpoint: pick **P2**
Enter the **Y** coordinate: **0** ↵
Select **BACKUP → Vertical → Center**
Specify the first endpoint: Pick **P1**
Specify the second endpoint: Pick **P3**
Enter the **X** coordinate: **1** ↵

The two lines are added as in Figure 6.65.

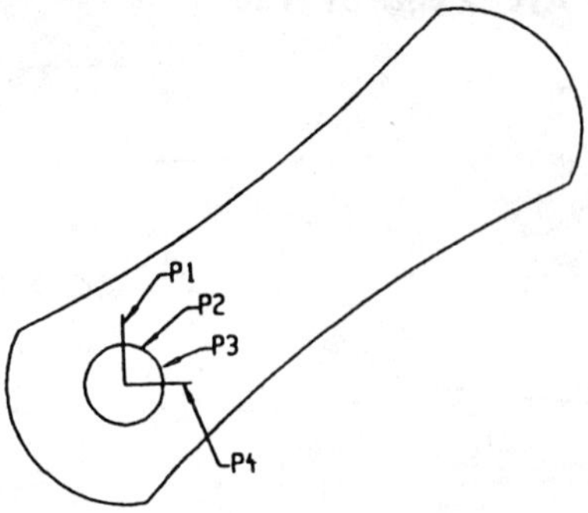

Figure 6.65

Step 7. Create an arc using the pick points in Figure 6.65 on the previous page.

Select **MAIN MENU → Create → Arc → Endpoints → Intersec**
Enter the first point: pick **P1**
Enter the first point: pick **P2**
Enter the second point: pick **P3**
Enter the second point: pick **P4**
Enter the radius: **.54** ↵
Select an arc: Pick at the outside one on the upper-right corner
Note: there are four choices

The arc is added as in Figure 6.66.

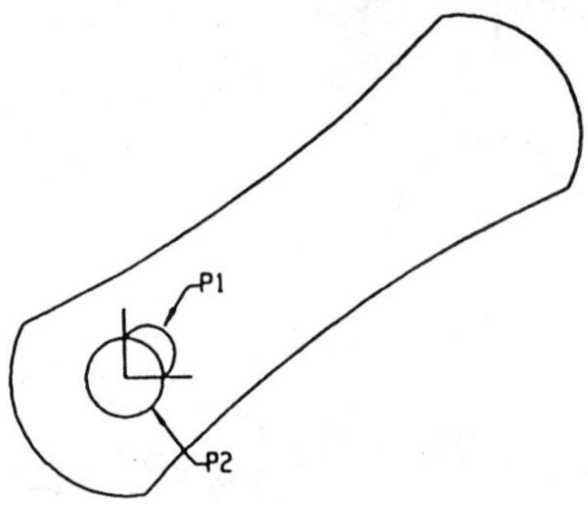

Figure 6.66

Step 8. Rotate the arc by 90° to other three locations.

Use the pick points in Figure 6.66.
Select **MAIN MENU → Xform → Rotate**
Pick **P1** to select the arc to be rotated
Select **Done → Center**
Pick **P2**
Select Rotation angle option in the dialog box = **90** ↵
Select the Number of steps option in the dialog box = **3** ↵
Select **Copy → OK**

Three arcs are added as shown in Figure 6.67.

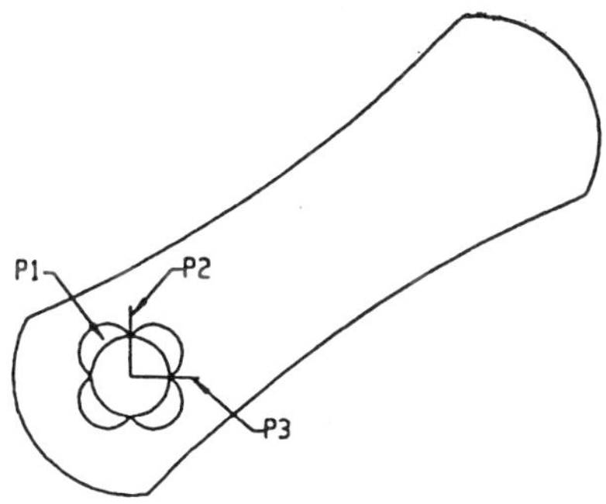

Figure 6.67

Step 9. Delete a construction circle and two construction lines.

Use the pick points in Figure 6.67.
Select **MAIN MENU → Delete**
Select an entity or: pick **P1**
Select an entity or: pick **P2**
Select an entity or: pick **P3**
The final drawing should look like Figure 6.68.

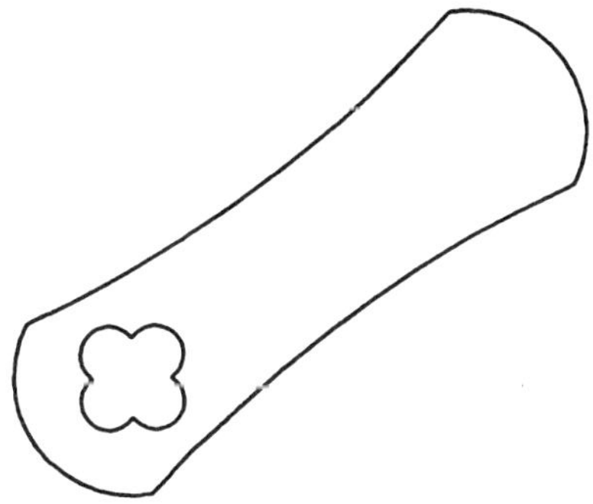

Figure 6.68

Step 10. Save to a file.

Select **MAIN MENU → File → Save**
Enter file name: **trans1**

Project 8. Rotating

Create 24 circles and 24 points at their centers (Figure 6.69). Three construction circles are added to show their positions. Save the file as **drill1**. This file will be used to generate the drilling toolpaths in project 7 of chapter 7.

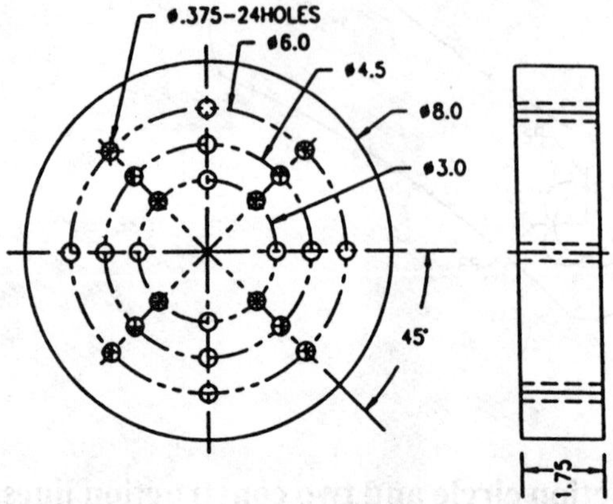

Figure 6.69

Tips: 1. Create 3 circles and three points at their centers in the X axis.
2. Rotate these 3 circles and 3 points by 45° to the other 7 locations.
3. Construct three construction circles. Set the line type to hidden.

Step 1. Create three circles.

Select **MAIN MENU → Create → Arc → Circ pt + dia**
Enter the diameter: **0.375** ↵
Enter the coordinates: **1.5,0** ↵

Enter the coordinates: **2.25,0** ↵
Enter the coordinates: **3,0** ↵
Three arcs appear as in figure 6.70.

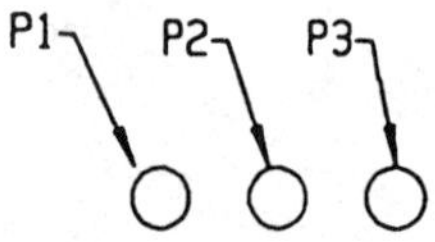

Figure 6.70

Step 2. Create points at the center of the circles using the pick points in Figure 6.70.

Select **MAIN MENU → Create → Point → Position → Center**
Define the three points: Pick **P1**
Select Center again, then pick **P2**
Select Center again, then pick **P3**

Three points are added as in Figure 6.71.

Figure 6.71

Step 3. Rotate these six entities 45° about the origin, seven times. 8

Select **MAIN MENU → Xform → Rotate → All → Entities → Done → Origin**

In the pop-up dialog box:

Number of steps: **7**

Rotation angle: **45**

Select **Copy → OK**

Twenty-four circles are created as shown in Figure 6.72.

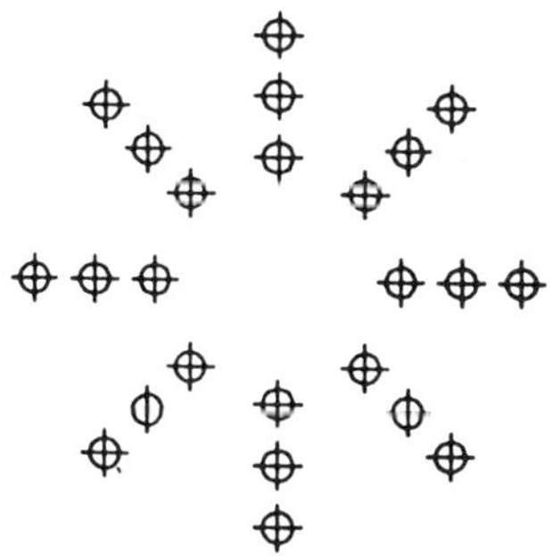

Figure 6.72

Step 4. Create three construction circles.

Double-click to select **-Style/Width-** from the left Menu

Select the line style parameter to **hidden**

Select **OK** to complete the setting

Select **MAIN MENU →Create → Arc → Circ pt +dia**

Enter the diameter: **3** ↵

Enter the coordinatest: **0,0** ↵

Enter **BACKUP → Circ pt + rad**

Enter the diameter: **4.5** ↵

Enter the coordinates: **0,0** ↵

Enter **BACKUP → Circ pt + rad**

Enter the diameter: **6.0** ↵

Enter the coordinates: **0,0** ↵

The final drawing should resemble Figure 6.73.

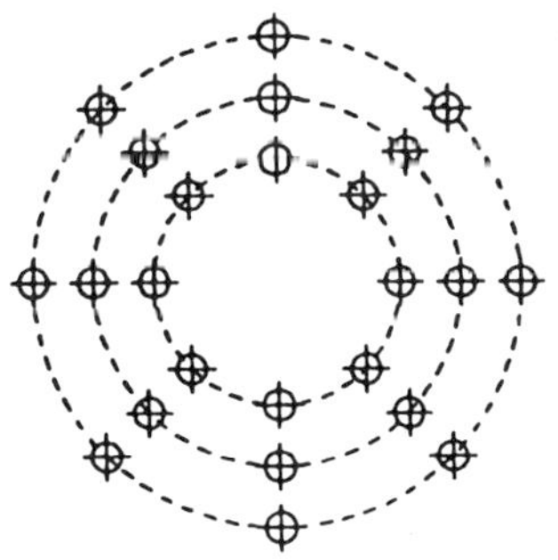

Figure 6.73

Step 5. Save to a file.

Select **MAIN MENU → File → Save**

Enter file name: **drill1**

Scale Function

The scale function increases or decreases the sizes of geometry entities by a specified scale factor. Two important factors to be determined in scaling are the scaling center and the scaling factor. The scaling center is the point from which the scaling of the geometric entity starts. The scaling factor determines the size.

Scaling factor > 1	enlarges the entity size
Scaling factor = 1	sizes do not change
Scaling factor < 1	reduces the entity size

Procedure: (Figure 6.74)
1. Select entity to scale: Pick **P1**
2. Select **Done**
3. Point Entry <position options>: Select **Point**
4. Select a point: Pick **P2**
5. Adjust the parameters in the pop-up dialog box:
   Number of steps = 1
   Scale factor = 2.0
6. Select **Copy → OK**

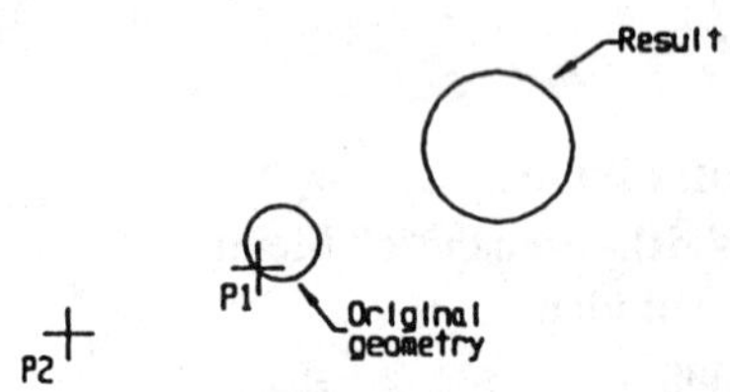

Figure 6.74 Scaling an entity about an existing point for a factor of 2

ScaleXYZ Function

The scaleXyz is the other scale function and is similar to the Scale discussed in section 6.3.3. It gives the user an opportunity to specify the x, y and z scale factors individually. By adjusting the scale factors properly, it is possible to transform a circle into an ellipse.

Procedure: (Figure 6.75)
1. Select entities to scale <entity selection options>: Pick **P1**
2. Select **Done → Center**
3. Enter the point to scale about: Pick **P1**
4. In the dialog box: Number of steps: **1**
   X scale factor: **0.5**
   Y scale factor: **2.0**
   Z scale factor: **1.0**
5. Select **Move → OK**
6. Press <Enter> to continue: ↵

Note: The original circle was converted to a NURBS curve.

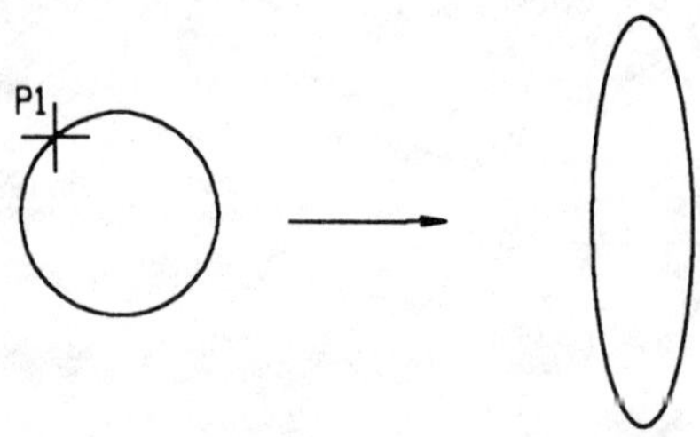

Figure 6.75

Translate Function

The translate function moves or copies the selected geometric entities to new locations.

Procedure: (Figure 6.76)

1. Entity selection option (see section 6.3): Pick **P1**
2. Entity selection option: Select **Done**
3. Translate: Refer to Figure 6.76 to select **an appropriate method**

Rectang: enters a rectangular (Cartesian) coordinate vector for the X and Y translation.

4. Enter the translation vector: **1,0.5** ↵

Polar: enters a polar coordinate vector for the translation.

4a. Enter the translation distance: **1.5** ↵
4b. Enter the translation angle: **30** ↵

Between pts: selects the beginning and ending points for the translation.

4a. Enter the point to translate from <position option>: Pick **P2**
4b. Enter the point to translate to <position option>: Pick **P3**

Between vws: translates the entities between viewport.

5. In the pop-up dialog box:

Number of steps = **1**
Select **Copy →OK**

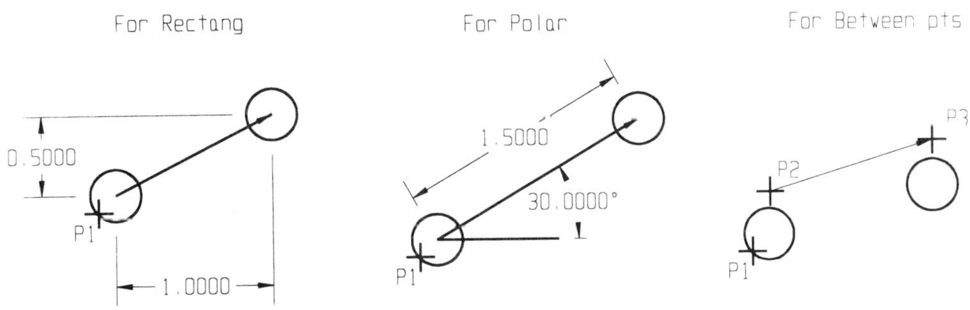

Figure 6.76: Translating using different methods

Project 9. Translating

Copy the inside pocket contour of the drawing shown in Figure 6.77a to two locations by using the **Translate → Rectang** commands. The file for Figure 6.77a is **array1** which is created in project 1 of this chapter. The complete part geometry is shown in Figure 6.77b.

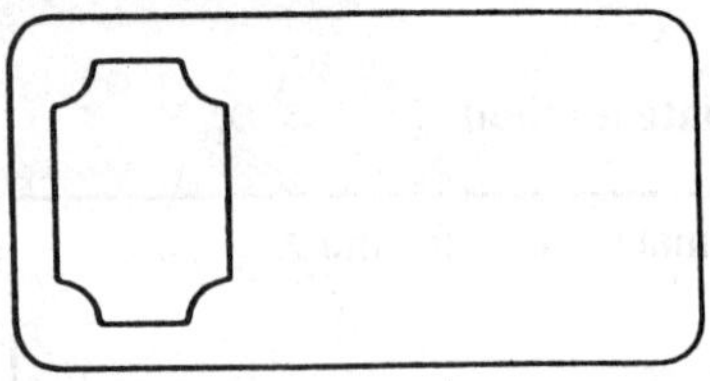

Figure 6.77a

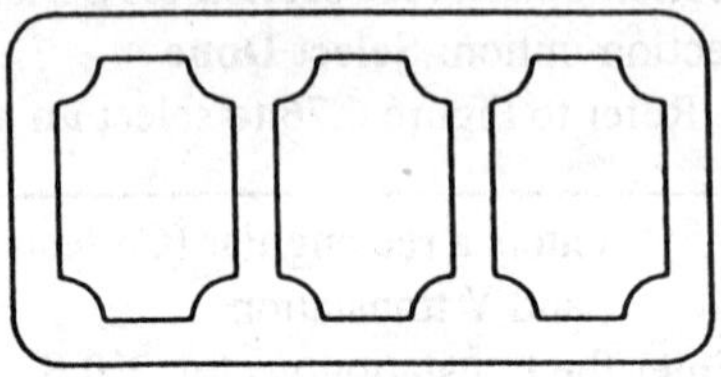

Figure 6.77b

Tips: 1. Use the file array1 which is created in project 1 of this chapter.
2. Use Xform → Translate → Rectang commands to copy the pocket profile.
3. Set the number of steps to 2.

Step 1. Load the geometry file array1.

Select **MAIN MENU → File → Get**
Enter file name: **array1**
The part geometry should appear as Figure 6.78.

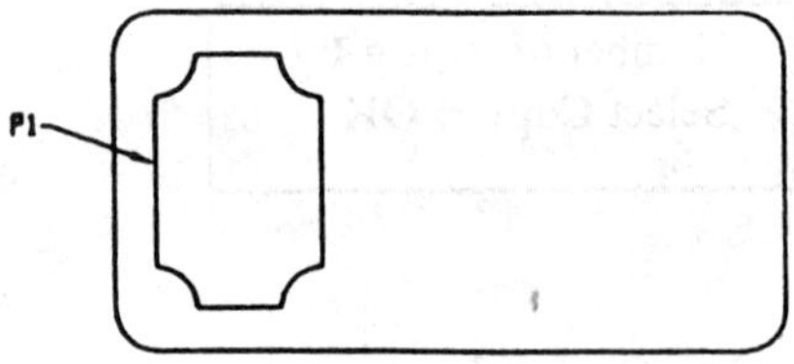

Figure 6.78

Step 2. Initiate the Translate command.

Select **MAIN MENU → Xform →Translate → Chain**

Step 3. Define the contour using the pick point in Figure 6.78.

Pick **P1**
Select **Done → Done** (again)

Step 4. Define Translate parameters.

Select **Rectang**
Enter the translation vector: **X3.75 ←**
In the pop-up dialog box: Set the Number of steps = **2**
Select **Copy →OK**
The two translated profiles are shown in Figure 6.79.

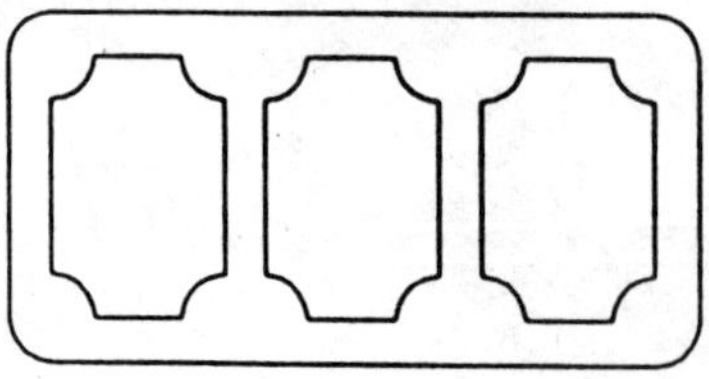

Figure 6.79

Offset Function

The offset function moves or copies a line, arc, spline, or curve away from itself in a perpendicular direction with an offset distance to the selected entity. *Note:* this function only works for a single entity.

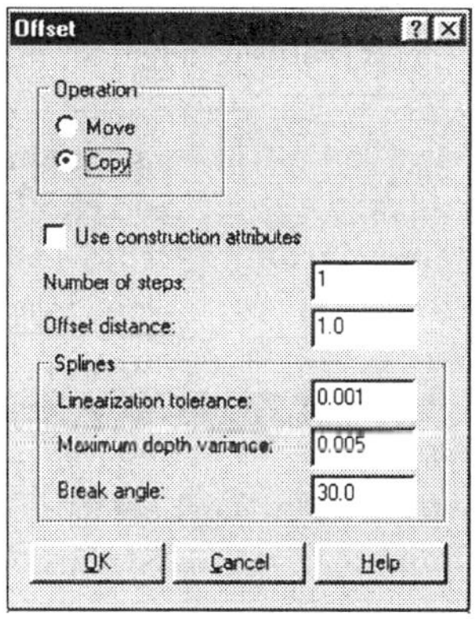

Procedure: (Figure 6.80)

1. In the pop-up dialog box:
2. Select **OK**
3. Select the line, arc, spline, or curve to offset: Pick **P1**
4. Indicate the offset direction: Pick **P2**

Note: In general, there are two perpendicular directions. Indicate the appropriate direction using the mouse.

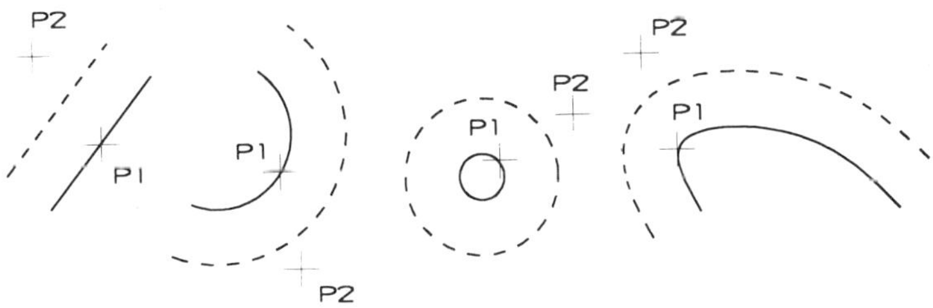

Figure 6.80

Ofs ctour Function

This option allows the user to offset several connected lines or arcs by chaining the entities. The process is similar to the toolpath contour function. This function will offset only lines and arcs.

Procedure: (Figure 6.81)

1. Chaining method: Select **Chain**
2. Select chain1: Pick **P1**
3. Select → **Done**
4. Add the parameters as in the Offset Contour dialog box shown here.
5. Select **OK**

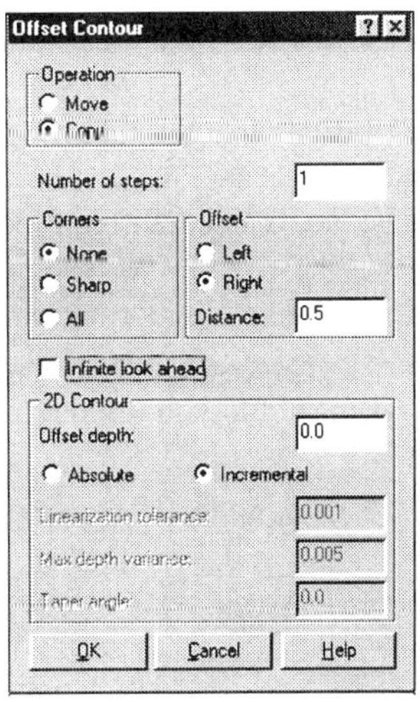

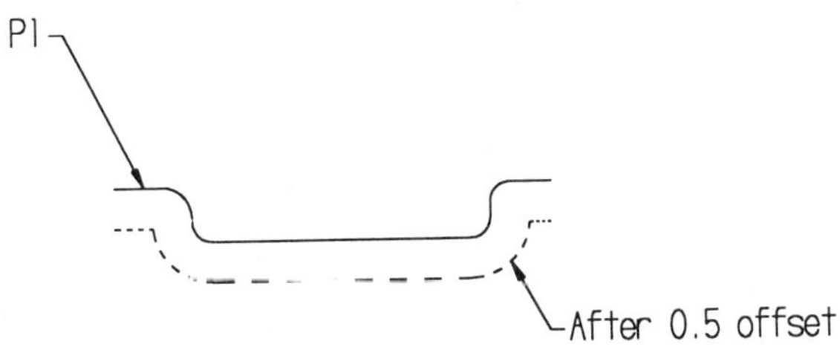

Figure 6.81

Groups Parameter

Group selects and defines a collection of entities to be used in Xform. The last Group is saved in the database and can be used in other Xform functions such as Mirror, Rotate, Scale, ScaleXYZ and Translate. The Entity Selection menu provides the Group selection method for this purpose. Note that Offset can not take advantage of Group since it only works with a single entity.

When **Group** is selected, these Group selection options appear on the Groups dialog box:

New:	Gather entities into a single unit for selection.
Add to:	Add entities from a group.
Remove from:	Remove entities from a group.
View:	View grouped entities.
Delete:	Ungroup entities.
Subgroup:	Create a subgroup.
Undo sub:	Remove a subgroup.
Select:	Selects a group by an entity.
Colors:	Assign a color to a group.

You can use different method to select the entities for the group, then select **OK** to exit the groups dialog box and save the database.

Ex Exercises

1. What does the delete function do?

2. What does the undelete function do?

3. What does the trim function do?

4. Describe the difference between the following three trim commands:
   1 entity
   2 entities
   3 entities

5. Describe what the break function does?

6. Describe what the join function does?

7. List the first six editing functions under the Xform command.

8. List the five transformation parameters and describe what they are.

9. When should you use the mirror function?

10. When should you use rotate function?

11. Explain how to use the scale function to increase or decrease the size of geometry entities.

12. When should you use the translate function.

13. When should you use the offset function.

14. Create the geometry shown in Figure 6.82. Save the file as **contour5**. This file is used in problem 36 of chapter 7.

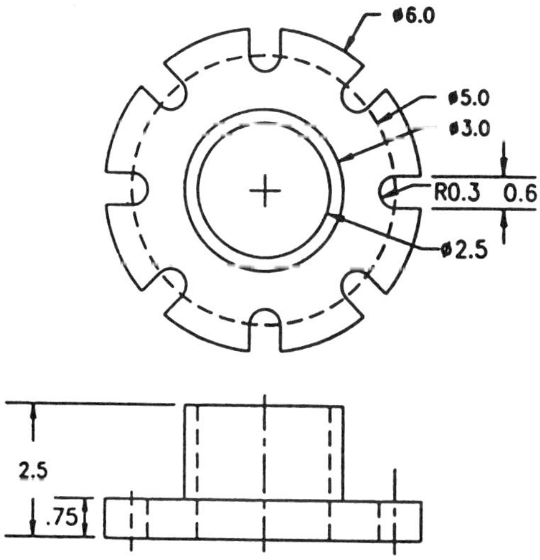

Figure 6.82

15. Create the geometry shown in Figure 6.83 and save the file as **contour6**. This file is used to generate the toolpath in problem 37 of chapter 7.

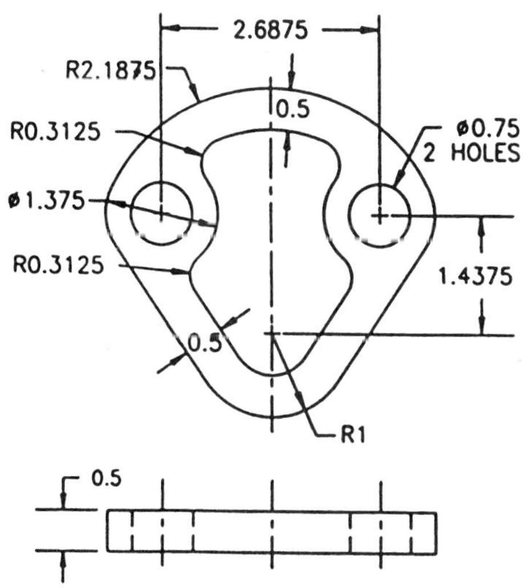

Figure 6.83

16. Create the part geometry as shown in Figure 6.84. Save the file as **contour7**. This part geometry is used to generate the toolpath for problem 38 in chapter 7.

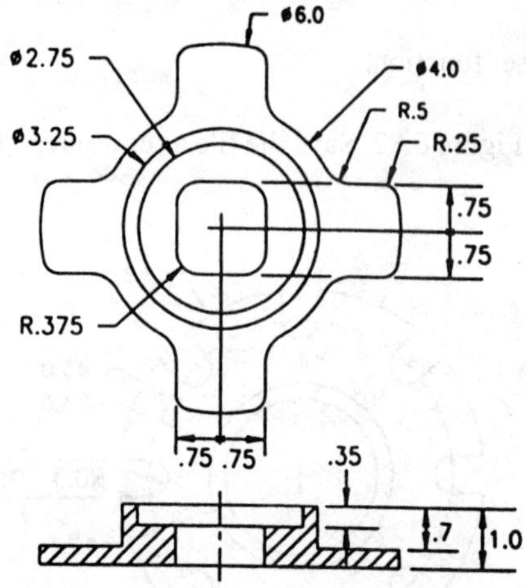

Figure 6.84

17. Create the part geometry for Figure 6.85. Save the geometry file as **pocket3**. This geometry file is used to generate the pocketing toolpath for problem 41 in chapter 7.

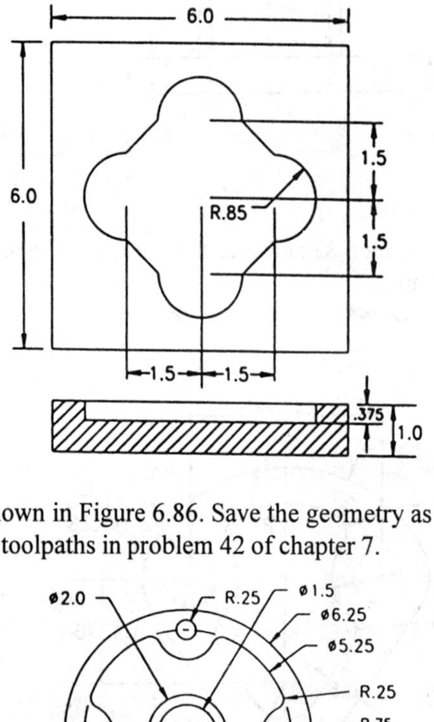

Figure 6.85

18. Create the geometry shown in Figure 6.86. Save the geometry as **pocket4**. This file is used to generate the pocketing toolpaths in problem 42 of chapter 7.

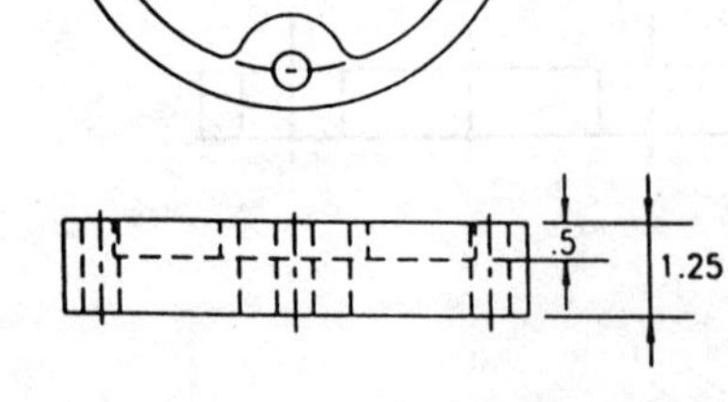

Figure 6.86

19. Create the part geometry as shown in Figure 6.87 and save the file as **pocket5**. This geometry will be used to generate the toolpath for pocketing with an island in problem 43 of chapter 7.

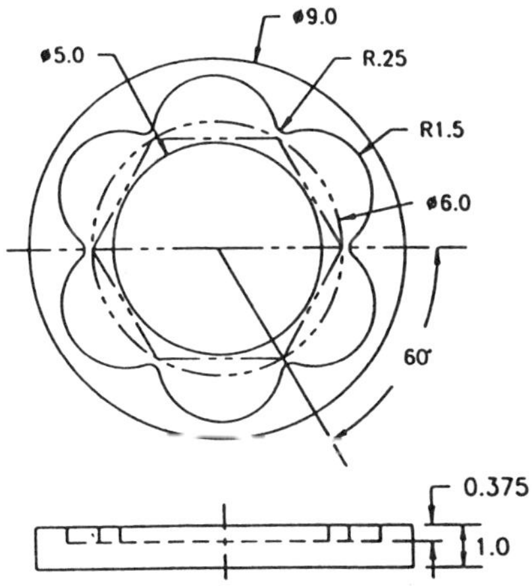

Figure 6.87

20. Create the part geometry shown in Figure 6.88. Save the file as **comb1**. This geometry will be used to generate the toolpaths for contouring, pocketing, and drilling in problem 45 of chapter 7.

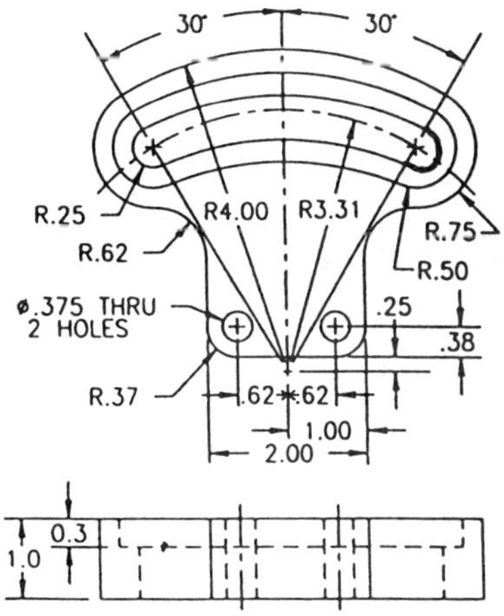

Figure 6.88

21. Create the part geometry shown in Figure 6.89 and save the file as **comb3**. The file is used to generate the toolpaths in problem 47 of chapter 7.

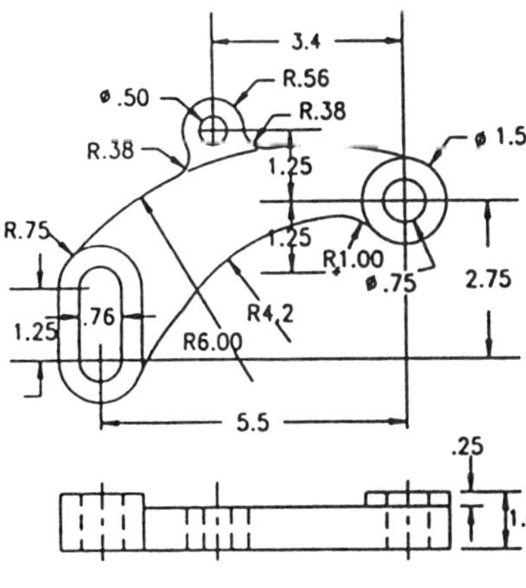

Figure 6.89

22. Create the geometry as shown in Figure 6.90 and save this file as **comb4**. This geometry is used to generate the toolpaths in problem 48 of chapter 7.

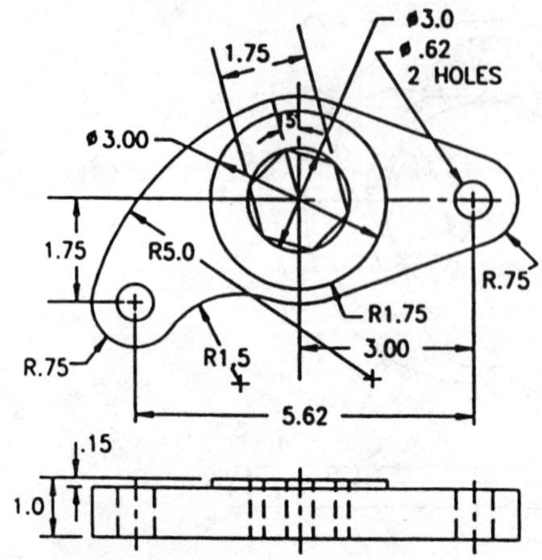

Figure 6.90

23. Create the part geometry shown in Figure 6.91 and save the file as **rotate2**. This geometry is used to generate the toolpaths in problem 15 of chapter 9.

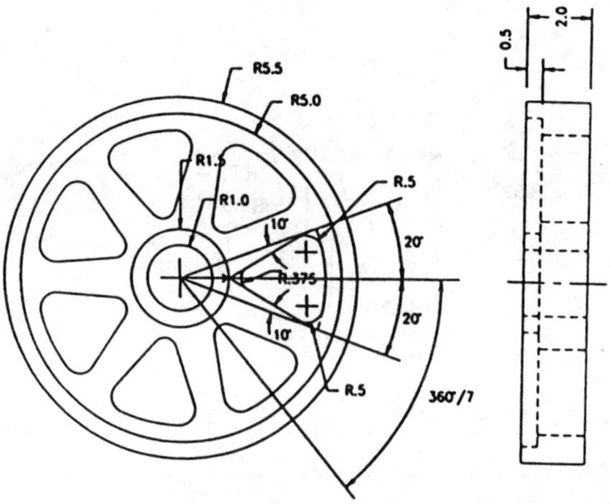

Figure 6.91

24. Create the part geometry shown in Figure 6.92 and save the file as **mirror2**. The file is used to generate a set of toolpaths to machine one part and then copy to machine another part by using the mirror function in problem 16 of chapter 9.

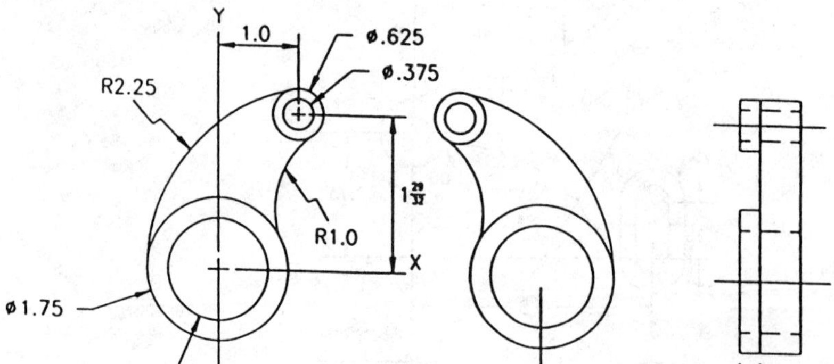

Figure 6.92

Chapter 7

2D Toolpath Generation: From Print to Part

Objectives:

1. Identify five types of 2D toolpath modules and know when to use them.
2. Define common tool parameters used in 2D toolpath modules.
3. Apply five 2D toolpath modules to generate NC programs for producing parts.

7.1 2D Toolpath Modules

Mastercam provides three groups of toolpath modules for generating toolpaths: **2D modules**, **3D modules**, and **multiple-axis modules**. Use 2D modules to generate toolpaths for machining workpieces in a 2D plane, 3D toolpath modules for machining various forms of 3D surfaces, and multiple-axis for machining complex parts. This chapter presents 2D toolpath modules. Mastercam has five 2D toolpath modules: **contour, pocket, drill, circmill**, and **point**. Table 7.1 summaries the features and applications of these 2D toolpath modules.

Table 7.2 2D Toolpath Module

Module	Description	Application	Illustration
Contour	Generate the toolpaths along a series of geometric entities chained as a contour. Required geometry: lines, arcs, or splines.	Cutting external and internal part profiles.	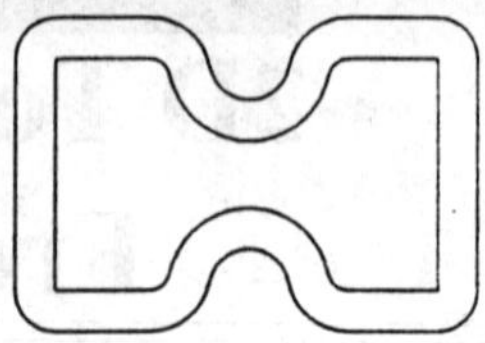
Drill	Generate the toolpaths to perform drilling, boring, or tapping holes. Required geometry: points	Drilling Boring Tapping	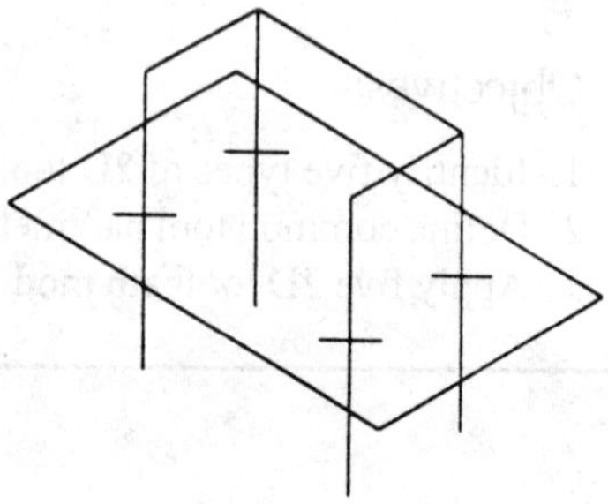
Pocket	Generate the toolpaths to remove the material by a closed contour. Required geometry: closed boundary	Cutting pockets Facing large flat Surfaces.	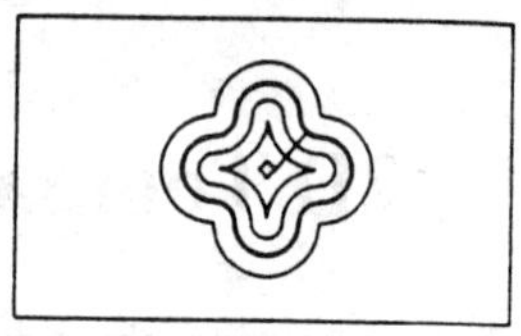
Face	Generate toolpaths to face flat surfaces on the selected closed boundaries. Required geometry: closed boundary.	Facing large flat surfaces	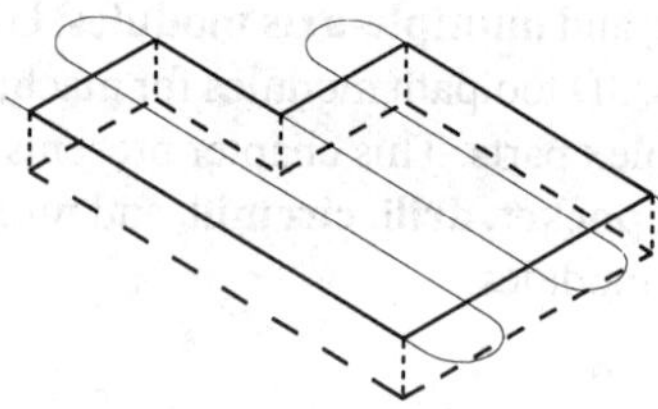
Circ tlpths			
Circle mill	Generate the toolpaths to cut a complete circle with an entry arc, two 180-degrees arcs, and an exit arc.	Cut the internal shape of a circle.	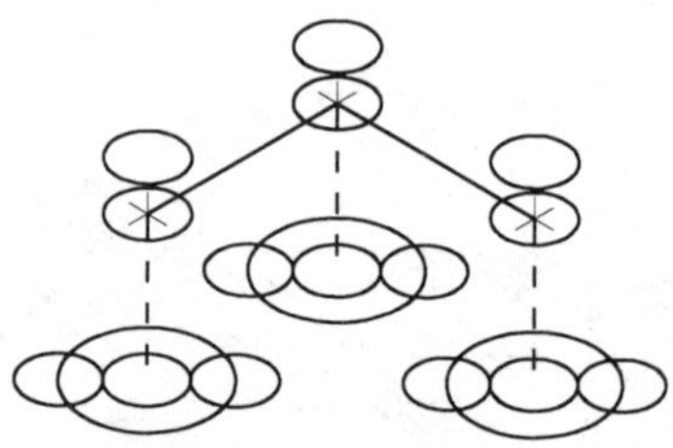
Thread mill	Generate a series of helical toolpaths for machining a thread with a thread mill.	Cut internal or external threads	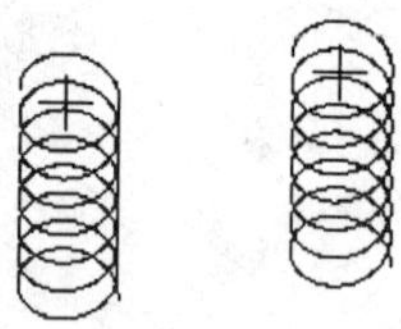
Point	Generate the toolpaths that jump over a clamp or fixture on the machine tool.	Jump the tools over clamps or fixtures	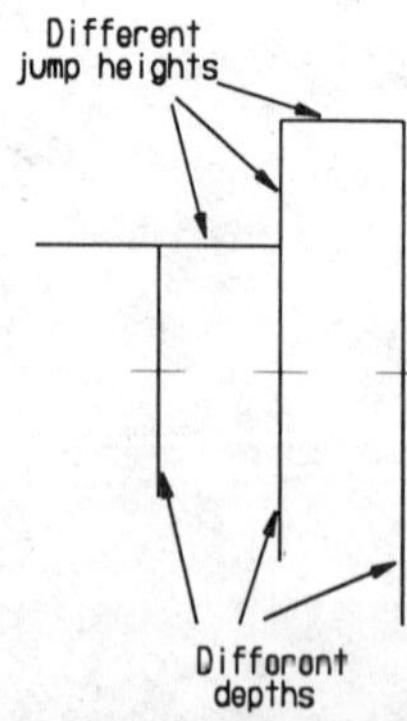

7.2 Tool Definition

Mastercam uses various types of parameters to define the information required to generate toolpaths. These parameters can be classified into three groups: **tool definition, tool parameters** and **module specific parameters**. Tool definition allows the user to define a new tool, select an existing tool from the tool library, or edit an existing tool. Tool parameters are also referred to as common parameters because they are commonly used in all toolpath modules, while module specific parameters are unique to the particular module and are not applicable to any other modules. This section focuses on how to define a new tool, select a tool from tool library, and edit an existing tool.

Tools Manager

Mastercam uses Tools Manager dialog box to define, select, or edit a tool. The empty Tools Manager dialog box appears below.

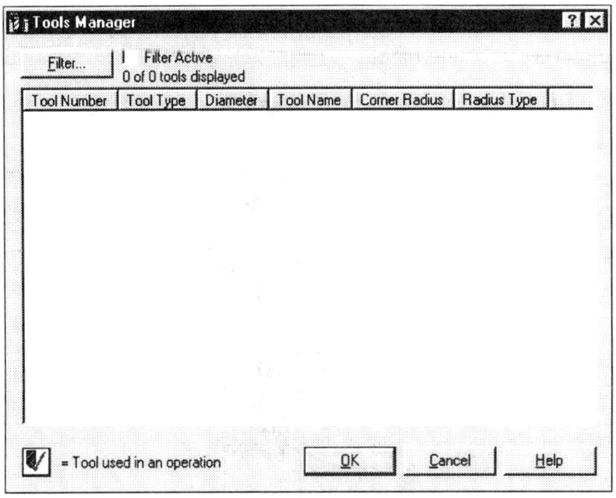

There are two ways to open the Tool Manager dialog box:

- **Toolpaths → Job setup → Tools**

  or
- **UC utils→ Def. tools → Current**

Click the right mouse button to bring up the tools manager option as below. The top three options will be dimmed out if no existing tools in the active file.

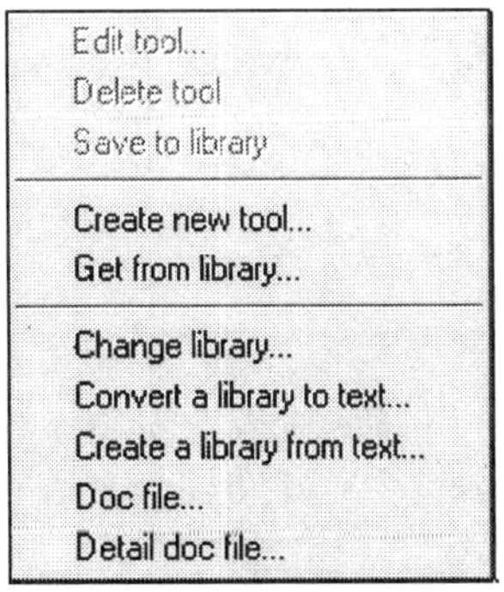

The tools manager options are described below:

Edit tool:	edit an existing tool used in the project.
Delete tool:	delete an existing tool used in the project.
Save to library:	save the tool you create or modify to the tool library.
Create new tool:	define a new tool.
Get from library:	retrieve an existing tool from the tool library.
Change library:	select a new tool library.
Convert a library to text:	export the current tool library from a TL7 file to a TXT file.
Create a library from text:	import a new tool library from a TXT file to a TL7 file.
Doc file:	create a document listing all tools in the current job or the current tool library.
Detail doc file:	create a document listing detail information of all tools in the current job or the current tool library.

Creating A New Tool

Creating a new tool involves using three sets of dialog box: **tool type, tool/holder definition**, and **tool parameters**. Their dialog boxes are shown below.

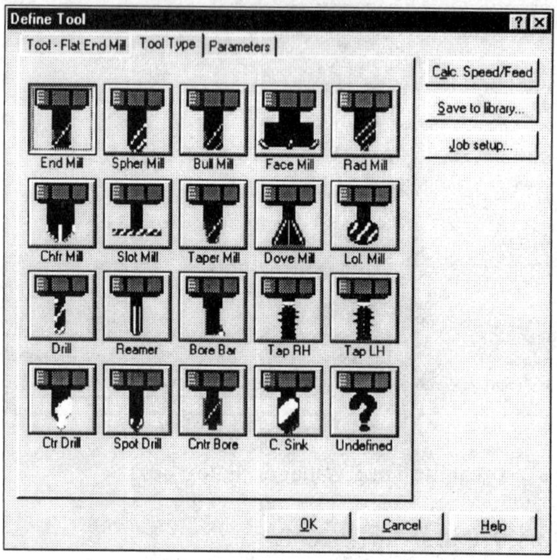

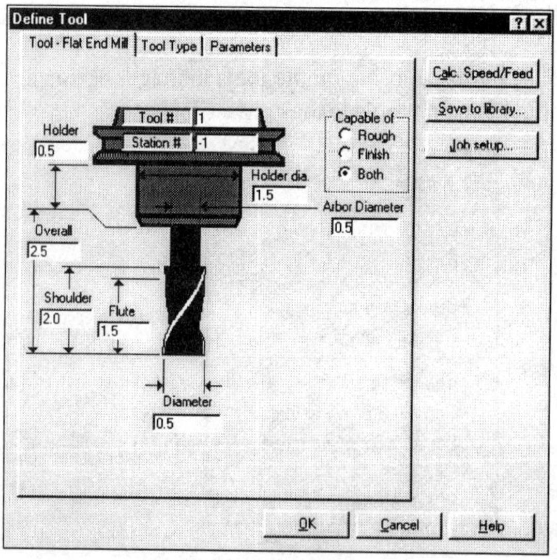

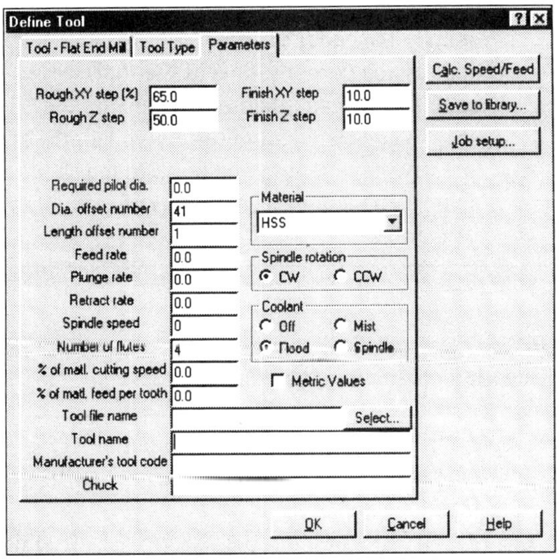

Tool type

Click the "Tool Type" tag in the Define Tool menu to open the tool type dialog box. Mastercam provides twenty tool types to choose from. The "Tool Type" selection menu appears.

Tool/Holder definition

Click "Tool-tool type" tag on the top of the Define Tool menu to open the Tool/Holder dialog box. Different tool/holder dialog boxes may appear for different tool types. Three sets of data are defined in this dialog box: **tool size, holder size**, and **machining type**. We use a spherical end mill as an example. The tool/holder dialog box of a spherical end mill should appear as below.

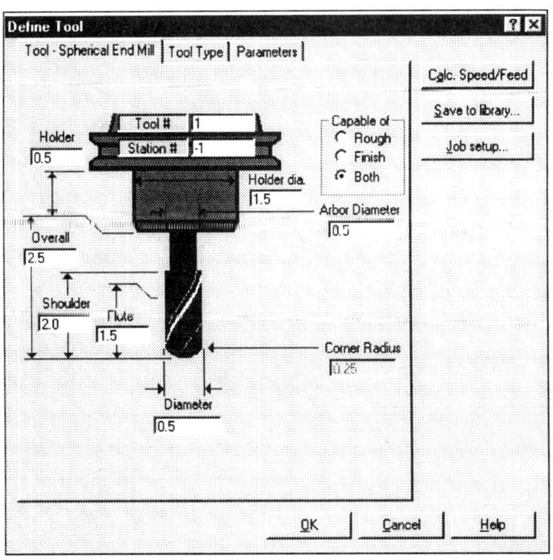

Tool size parameters

Mastercam uses the following parameters to fully define a tool:

Diameter: specify the cutter diameter.
Corner radius: specify the corner radius of the tool.
Arbor diameter: specify the shank diameter of the tool.
Flute: specify the flute length (effective length) of the tool.
Shoulder: specify the length from the tip to the shoulder of the tool.
Overall: specify the length from the tip of the tool to the end face of the holder.

Holder size parameters

Mastercam uses the following parameters to define a holder:

Holder diameter: specify the diameter of the holder.
Holder: specify the length measured from the flange face to the holder end face.
Tool number: specify the tool number used to identify this tool.

Machining type

In some tool types Mastercam provides a "Capable of" parameter to indicate the machining type a particular tool is capable of performing. It has the following three options:

Rough: the tool is capable of roughing cut only.
Finish: the tool is capable of finish cut only.
Both: the tool is capable of both roughing and finishing cuts.

Tool Parameters

Mastercam uses a set of parameters in "Parameters" dialog box to define machining data and other related information for a tool. The "Parameters" dialog box is shown below.

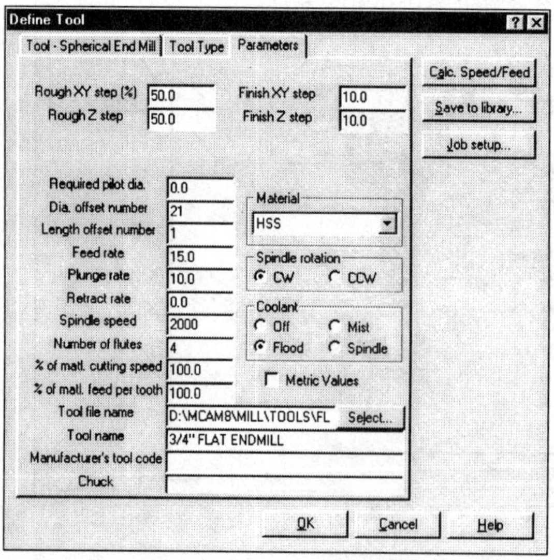

The parameters for **defining machining data and tooling information** are described below.

Rough XY step(%) This parameter specifies the percentage of tool's diameter engagement with the workpiece in roughing cuts. In other words, it specifies the stepover value of roughing passes. A 1-inch flat end mill with 60% of rough step XY value, for example, will have 0.6" stepover distance for roughing passes.

Finish XY step This parameter specifies the percentage of tool's diameter engagement with the workpiece in finishing cuts. It indicates the stepover value of finishing passes. A 1-inch flat end mill with 10% of finish step XY value, for example, will have 0.1" stepover distance for finishing passes.

Rough Z step This parameter specifies the depth of cut in Z-direction for roughing passes. It is expressed as the percent of tool's diameter. A 1-inch flat end mill with 50% of rough step Z value will have 0.5" depth of cut for roughing passes.

Finish Z step This parameter specifies the depth of cut in Z-direction for finishing passes. It is expressed as the percent of tool's diameter. A 1-inch flat end mill with 10% of finish step Z value will have 0.1" depth of cut for finishing passes.

Required pilot dia. This parameter is used to specify the diameter of pilot hole required for this particular tool. Pilot holes are normally needed for tapping, boring, drilling large holes, or milling a pocket.

Material This parameter is used to select the tool material. It has these **six** options:

HSS:	high speed steel tool
Carbide:	carbide tool
C Carbide:	coated carbide tool
Ceramic:	ceramic tool
Borzon:	borzon tool
Unknown:	tool material to be defined

% of matl. cutting speed This parameter indicates the default cutting speed in the percentage of suggested surface speed from the database. The surface speed is mainly determined by the tool material and the type of material to be cut.

% of matl. feed per tooth This parameter specifies the default feed rate in the percentage of suggested feed rate from the database. The feed rate is mainly determined by the tool material, type of material to be cut, depth of cut, tool diameter, etc.

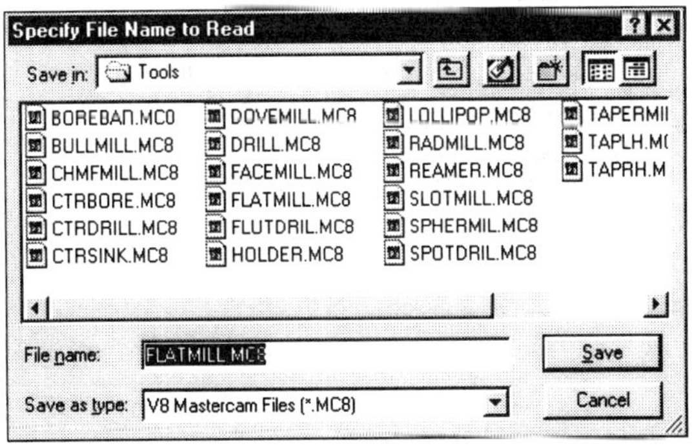

Tool file name This parameter selects the tool geometry file to be displayed. Mastercam provides a list of tool geometry files for you as shown on the previous page.

Tool name This parameter is used to enter a name for the tool. You can enter any descriptive comment for the tool.

Spindle rotation This parameter is used to specify the spindle rotation either in clockwise (CW) direction or counterclockwise (CCW) direction.

Coolant This parameter specifies the coolant control mode to be one the following four modes:

> **Off:** turn coolant off.
> **Mist:** turn coolant on in mist mode.
> **Flood:** turn coolant on in flood mode.
> **Spindle:** turn coolant on through the tool.

Creating a new tool

There are two ways to access the utility for creating a new tool. One way is to use the Tools command under the Toolpaths function. The other way is to access on the fly. The Tool Type dialog box should appear as below.

The procedure for creating a new tool using Tools command is:

1. Select **Toolpaths → Job setup → Tools** to open the Tools Manager dialog box
2. Click the right mouse button to open the tools manager menu, then select Create new tool
3. Select Tool Type from Define Tool dialog box

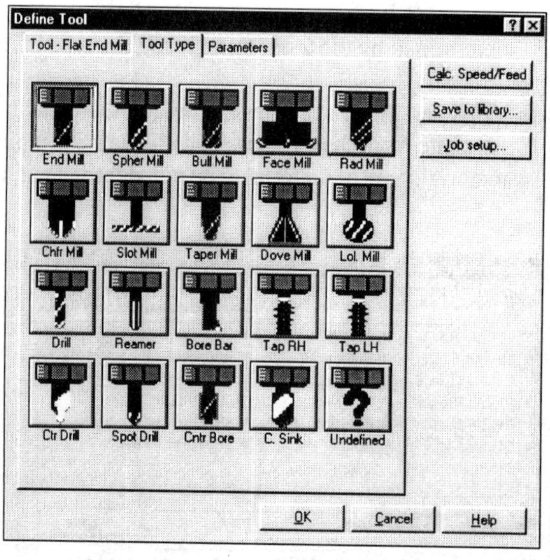

Select End Mill from the dialog box. The flat end mill definition dialog box should appear. Define the tooling information for tool and tool holder as below.

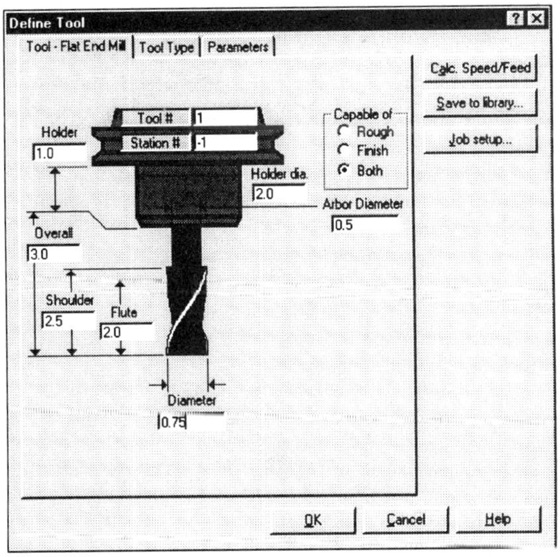

Click the Parameters tag to open the parameters dialog box. Define the parameters as below.

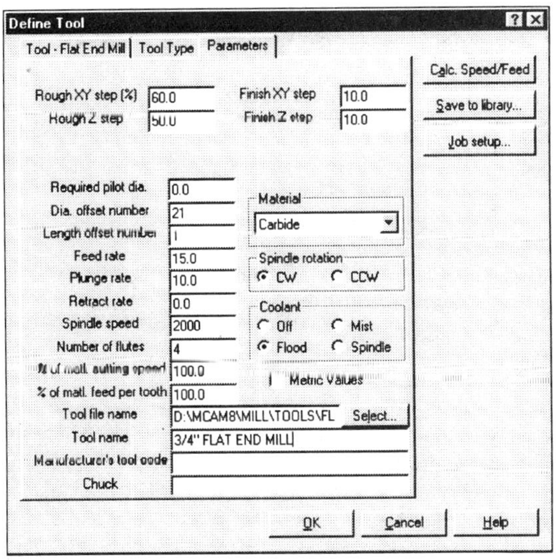

Select the OK button from the Define tool dialog box. The system will return back to Tools Manager dialog box as below.

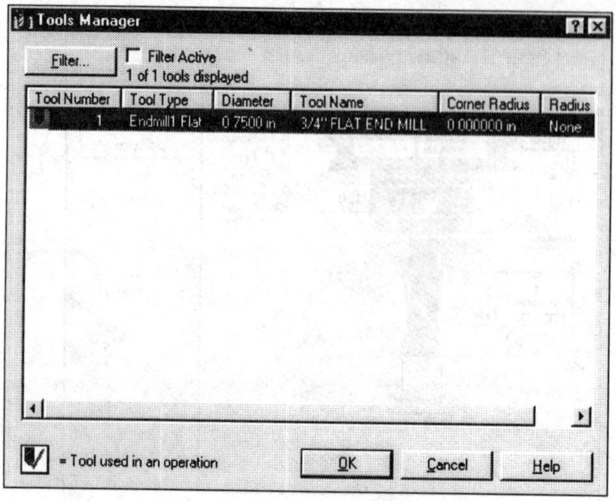

The procedure for creating a new tool using on the fly method is:

1. Select **Toolpaths → Contour** (or one of toolpath module)
2. Chain the contour profile.

   A contour properties dialog box will appear. It may contain exiting tools as shown below or may be empty depending on whether tools have been added.

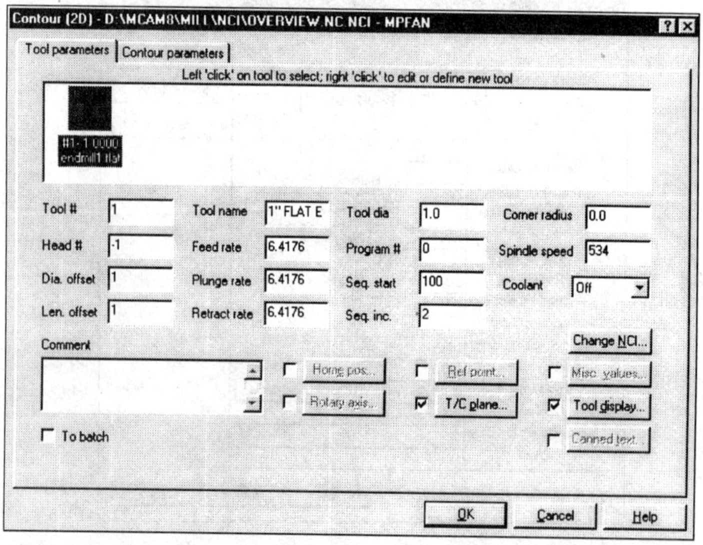

3. Click the right mouse button to open the tools manager menu. Select "Create new tool" to open the Define Tool dialog box.
4. Repeat the steps 4 – 6 in the previous section to define a new tool.

The procedure for selecting a tool from tool library

Follow these steps to retrieve an existing tool from tool library:

1. Select **Toolpaths → Job setup → Tools** to open the Tools Manager dialog box.
2. Click right mouse button to bring up the Tools Manager menu.
3. Select "Get from library" to open the tool list as below.

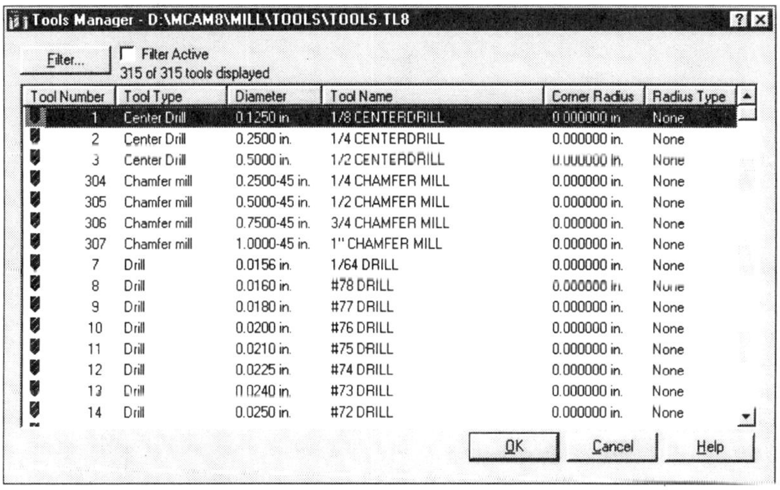

4. Scroll the tool list to find the one you want "1-in flat end mill", then select OK.
   The tool is retrieved to the Tool Manager dialog box as below.

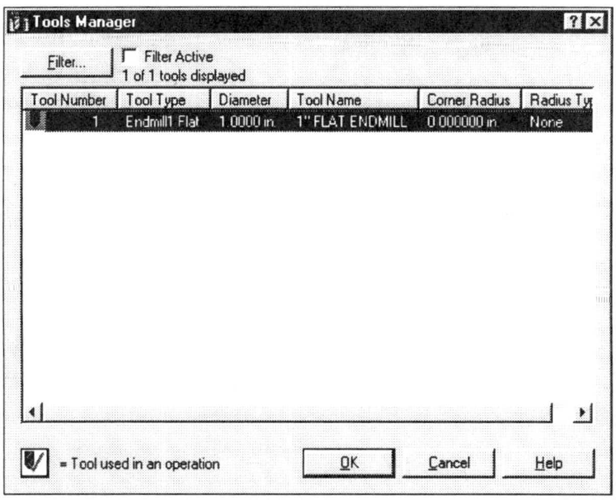

5. Repeat steps 2 – 4 to retrieve another tool (1/2" drill).
   Two tools are now shown in Tools Manager dialog box as below.

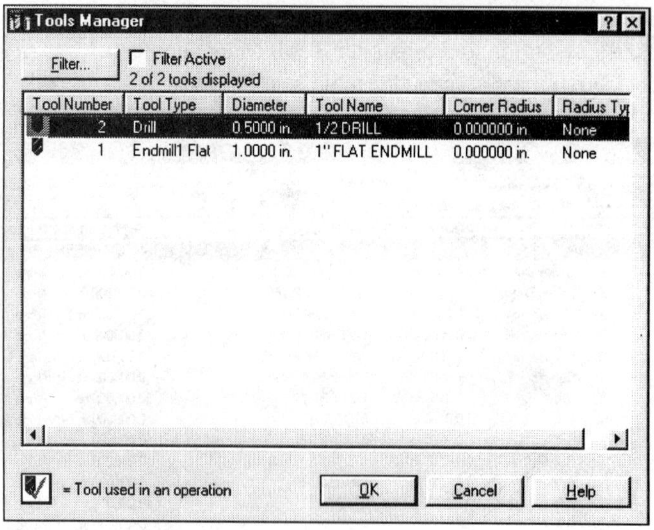

The procedure for editing an existing tool

Tools in Tools Manager dialog box can be modified.

1. Place the mouse on the tool to be modified in "Tools Manager" dialog box (1" flat end mill in this example), then click the right mouse button.
2. Select "Edit Tool" from Tools Manager menu. The Define Tool menu should appear as below.

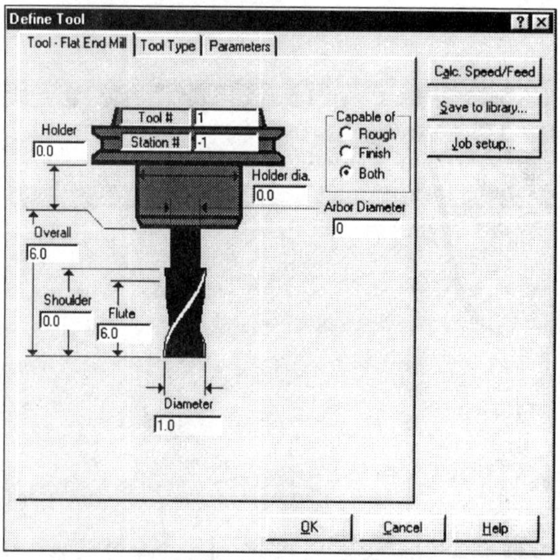

3. Redefine the tool and holder parameters as below.

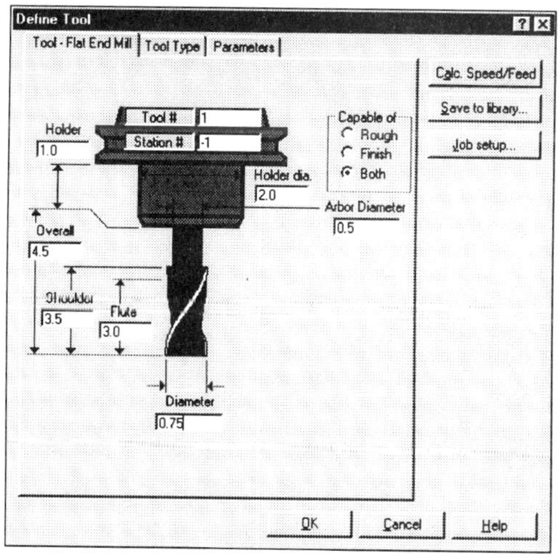

4. Select "Parameters" tag to open the Parameters dialog box as below.

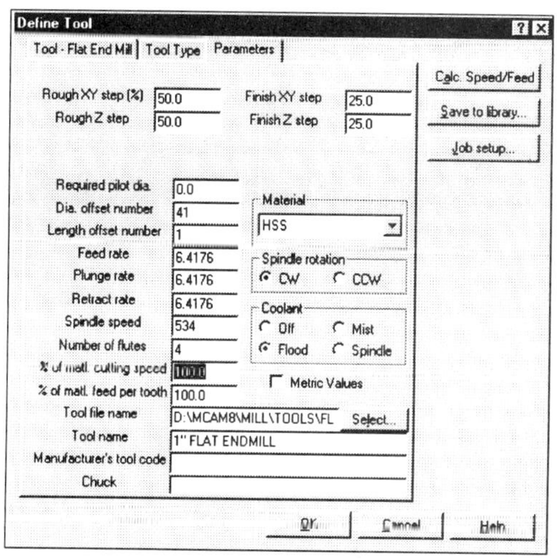

5. Redefine the machining data and tooling information as below.

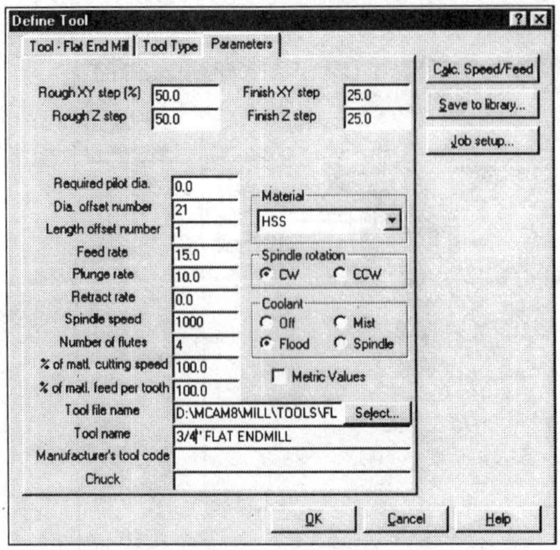

6. Select OK to complete the tool editing and return to Tools Manager dialog box. The old "1-in flat end mill now has been changed to ¾" flat end mill as below.

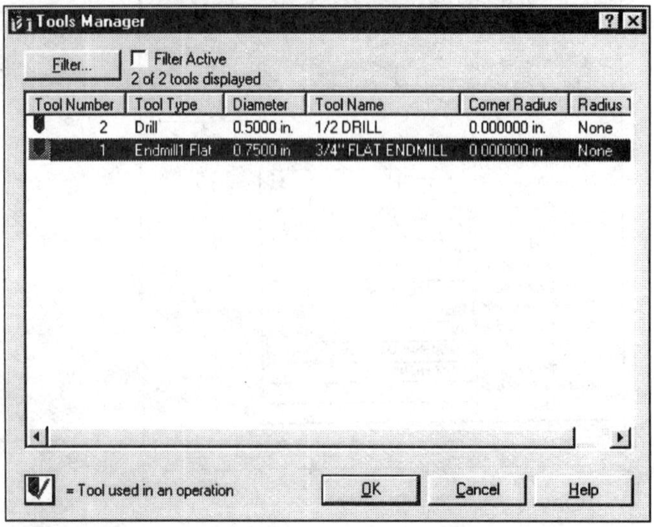

7.3 Operations Manager

After toolpaths have been generated, they can be graphically verified, post-processed to generate NC codes, and regenerated based on new machining data and tooling information. Mastercam groups these operation functions under the "Operations Manager" dialog box. The four functions included in the Operations Manager dialog box are:

Regen Path:	regenerating the toolpath based on the new parameters.
Backplot:	generating backplot of selected toolpaths on the screen.
Verify:	executing toolpath verification
Post:	converting toolpath location data to NC program.
Highfeed:	computing feed rates that reduce machining time without sacrificing accuracy.

<u>The procedure to open the Operations Manager dialog box:</u>

1.Select Toolpaths → Operations

2. The Operations Manager dialog box with existing toolpaths data should appear as below.

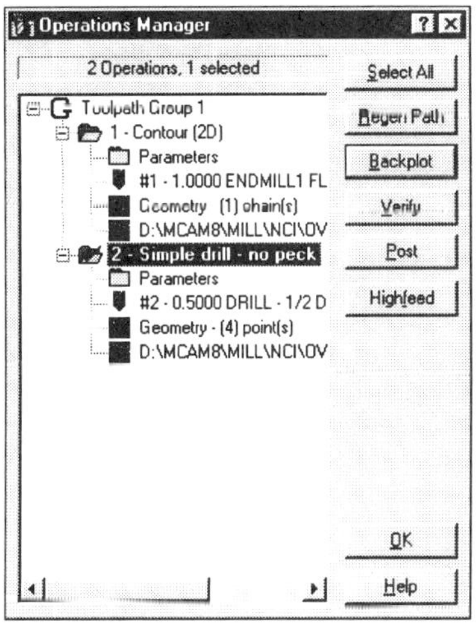

7.4 Backplot Function

The backplot function redisplays the toolpaths in a given mode. The backplot menu appears as shown here.

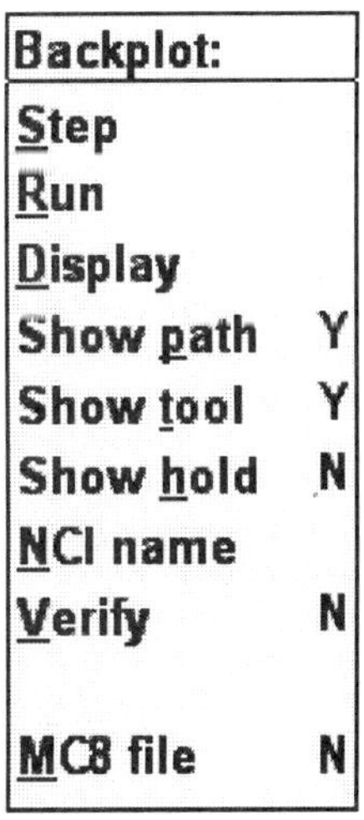

Execution mode

The backplot can be implemented in the following two modes:

Step:	tool moves one increment when the Step command is selected once. You need to continually select the Step command to complete the backplot of toolpaths.
Run:	tool continues to run until the end of the entire toolpaths.

Other backplot options are explained here:

Show path:	leave a trace of tool center along the toolpaths after backplotting (Figure 7.1).
Show tool:	show the cutting tool during backplotting (Figure 7.2).
Show hold:	show the tool holder during backplotting (Figure 7.3).
Verify:	leave a trace of shade for showing the material to be removed (Figure 7.4).
MC8 file:	backplot different MC8 files in order to view the tool's path on the existing drawing or compare to a new drawing.

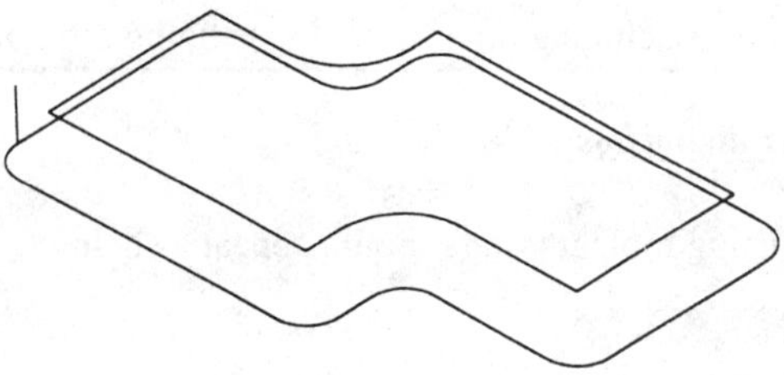

Figure 7.1

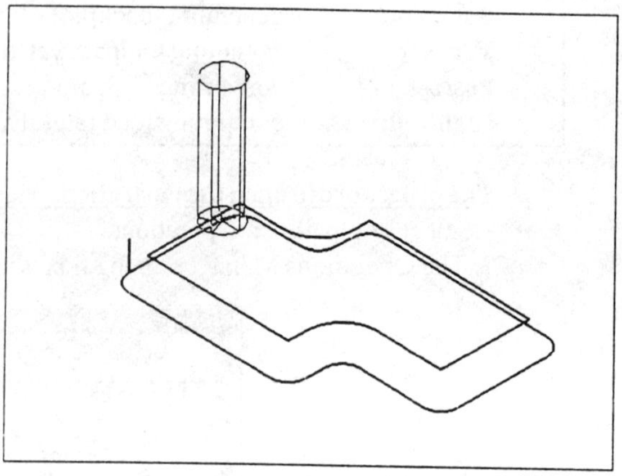

Figure 7.2

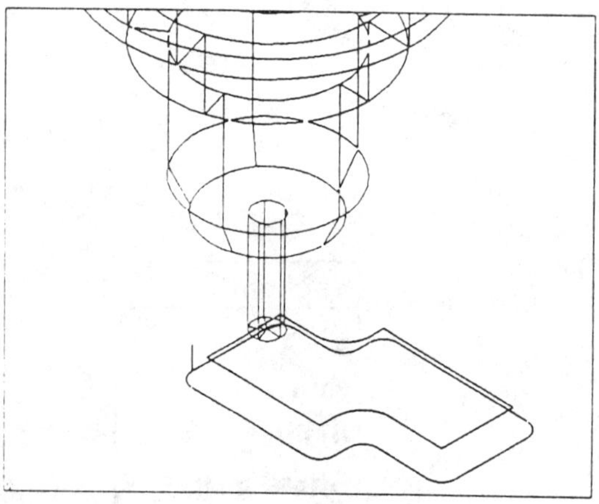

Figure 7.3

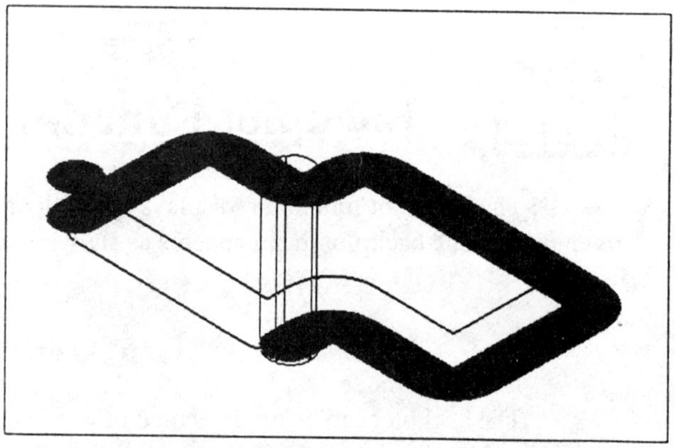

Figure 7.4

Display mode

Mastercam provides various parameters to display the tool and toolpaths. The backplot display parameters menu is shown below.

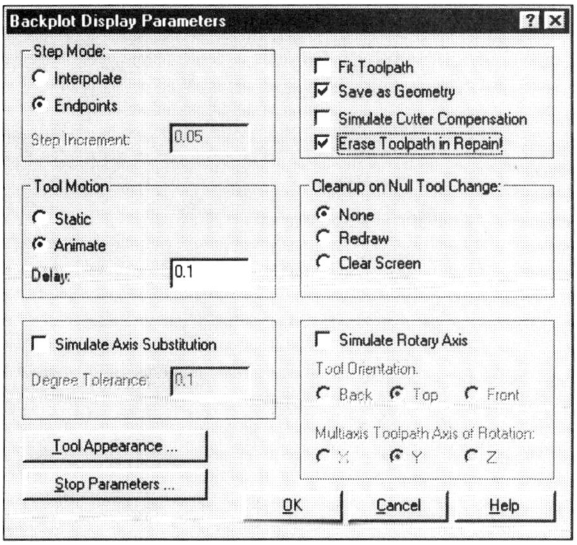

Step mode

Tool display can be set to one of the following two modes (Figure 7.5):

Interpolate:	tool is shown at increments of specified step size (Figure 7.5a).
Endpoints:	tool is shown at each endpoint of the toolpath (Figure 7.5b).

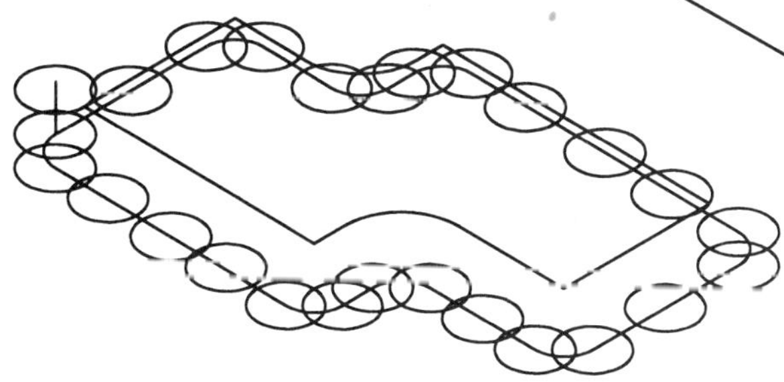

Figure 7.5a

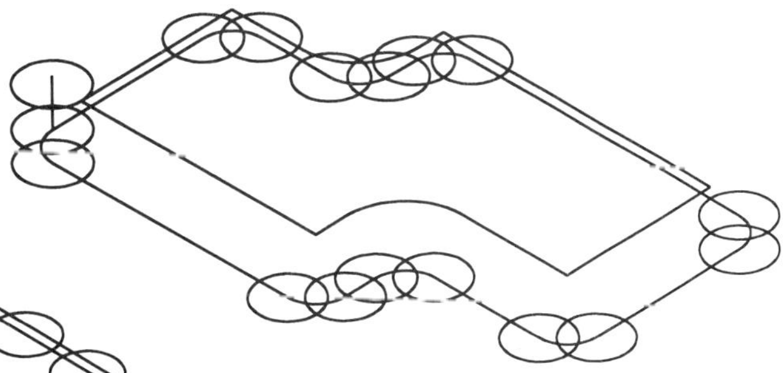

Figure 7.5b

The Step Increment option allows you to specify the step distance for the tool display.

Tool motion

The display parameters allow us to select the display mode for tool and toolpath. The tool motion can be shown in animated mode or static mode. In animated mode, the tool will appear and disappear at each point along the toolpath and as if it were moving. In static mode, the tool will appear at every point along the toolpaths and will not be erased.

The system uses the Delay function to allow for specifying how long the tool will be displayed each time it appears on the screen. Use delay of 0.0 for large files.

The remaining backplot display parameters are briefly described as below:

Simulate Axis Substitution:	wrap geometry on a cylinder for rotary axis toolpaths.
Erase Toolpath in Repaint:	remove the displayed backplot from the graphics window when the screen refreshes.
Fit Toolpath:	display the entire toolpath on the screen.
Save as Geometry:	create geometry from the backplot toolpath moves.
Cleanup on Null Tool Change:	select the operation mode for refreshing the screen during each null tool change.
Simulate Rotary Axis:	Simulate the motion of a C axis for a rotary axis toolpath.

Tool Appearance

Click the Tool Appearance button near the bottom of the Backplot Display Parameters dialog box to bring up the Tool Appearance Parameters dialog box as here.

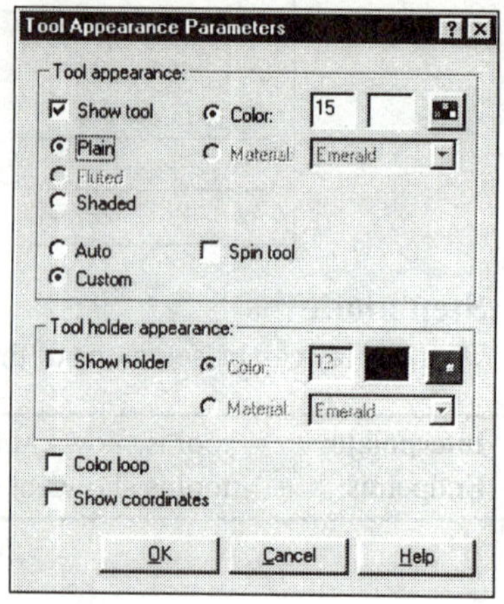

Tool appearance

This parameter is used to define how a cutting appears during backplotting.

Show tool:	show the cutting tool during the backplot. It has **three modes:** **Plain:** the cutting tool is shown in plain straight shape (Figure 7.6a) **Fluted:**the flutes of the cutting tool are shown (figure 7.6b) **Shaded:** the cuttingtool is shown shaded (Figure 7.6c)
Spin tool:	spin the tool during backplotting.

Tool holder appearance

Show holder: show the toolholder during the backpolot.

Stop parameters

You may stop the backplot function at specific points in the toolpath by making settings in the Stop parameters. Click the Stop Parameters button at the bottom of the Backplot Display Parameters dialog box to bring up the Stop parameters dialog box as here.

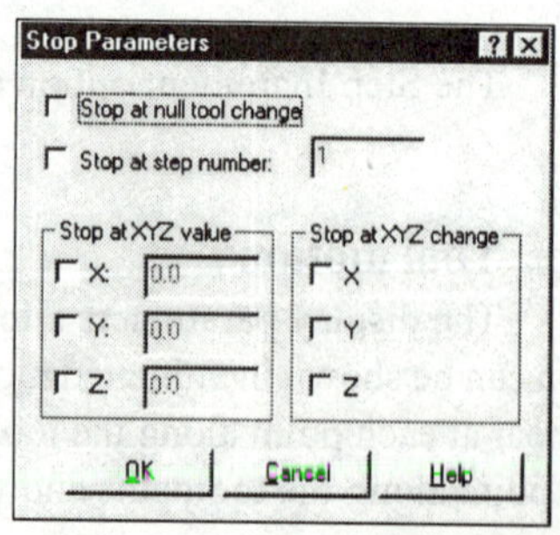

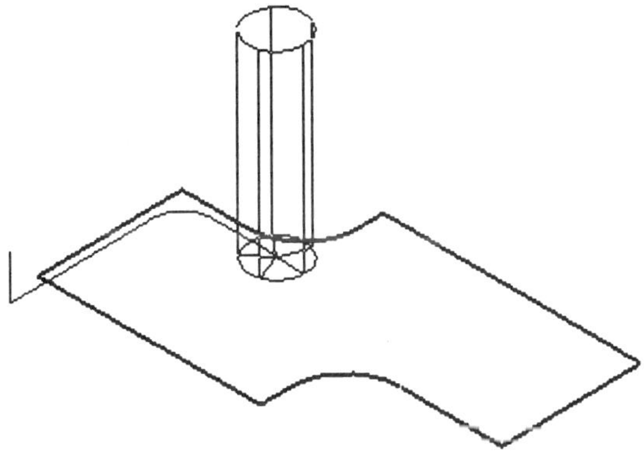

Figure 7.6a Plain

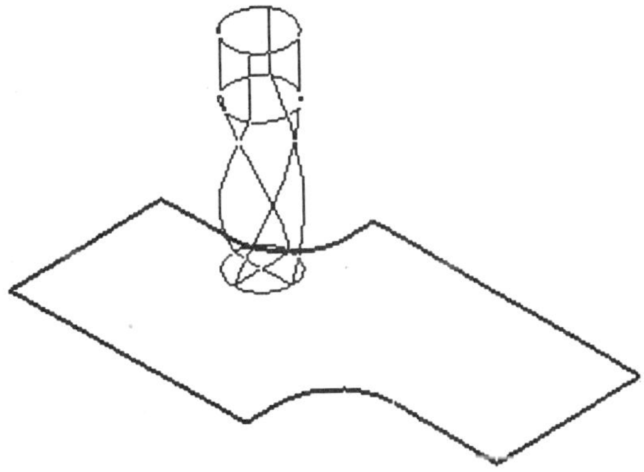

Figure 7.6b Fluted

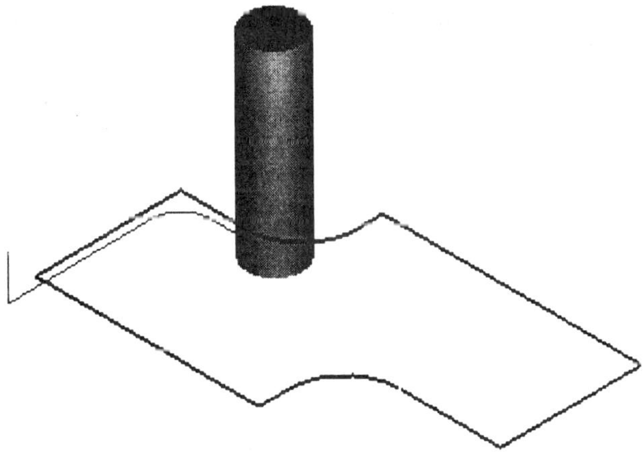

Figure 7..6c Shaded

Colors and Material for tool and holder

The display color for tool and tool holder can be selected by either the color type or material type both in the tool appearance and tool holder apperance parameter. The two options for tool and holder each are briefly described below:

Here are some frequently used parameters:

Stop at null tool change:	instruct the system to stop at each tool change and null tool change while implementing the backplot.
Stop at step number:	instruct the system to stop at a certain step.

Other parameters related to tool appearance:

Color loop:	display the backplot path in color.
Show coord:	display the coordinate values of the backplot path.

7.5 Verify

The Verify function is a powerful solid-model NC verification tool for Mastercam. This function uses the NCI file as the input to show the toolpath and the finished part in solid model form. Toolpath verification is very important in NC programming for the following reasons:

- Detect potential errors in part programs before they are used in tryout run.
- Simulate graphically the machining of the part programs.
- Eliminate the need for tryout run.
- Reduce the production lead time from design to part.
- Reduce costs.

Standard Turbo dialog box

The Turbo dialog box appears as below:

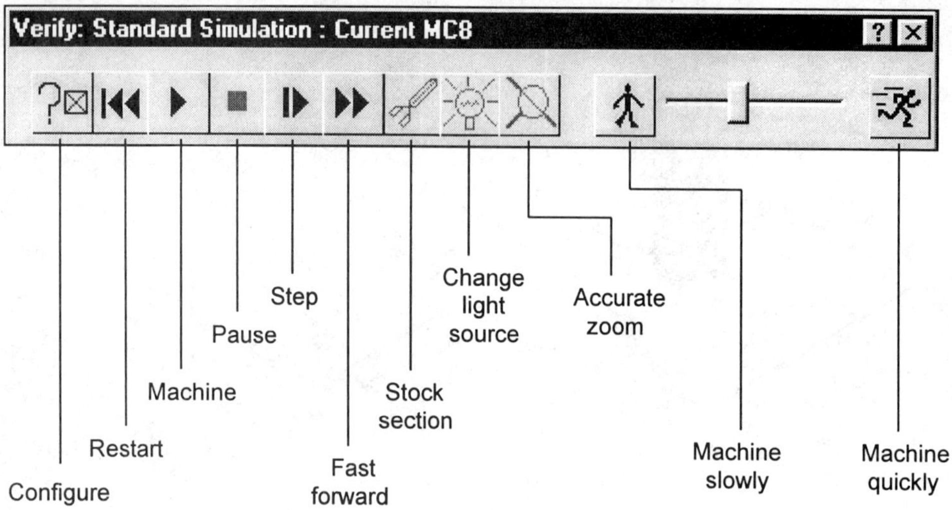

Verify Configuration

Click the "Configure" to open the verify configuration menu as shown below. There are five groups of parameters: **stock shape, tool display, display control, miscellaneous,** and **NCI file selection.**

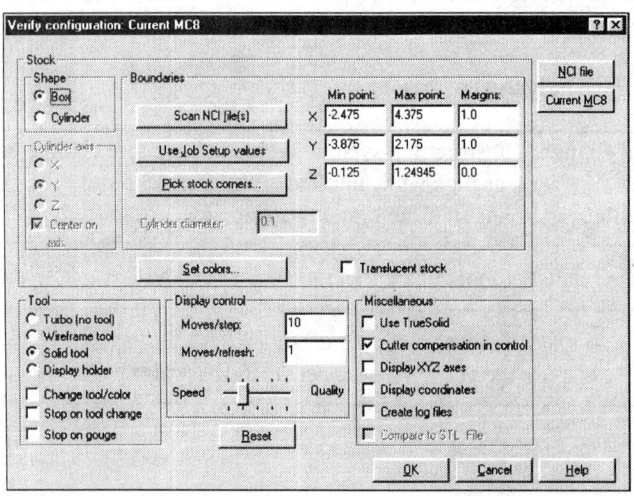

Stock shape

The boundary of stock can be defined in **box** and **cylinder**.

Box boundary Box boundary uses two points: **min point** and **max point** to define the length, eidth, and height of the box. Margins can be added to three directions.

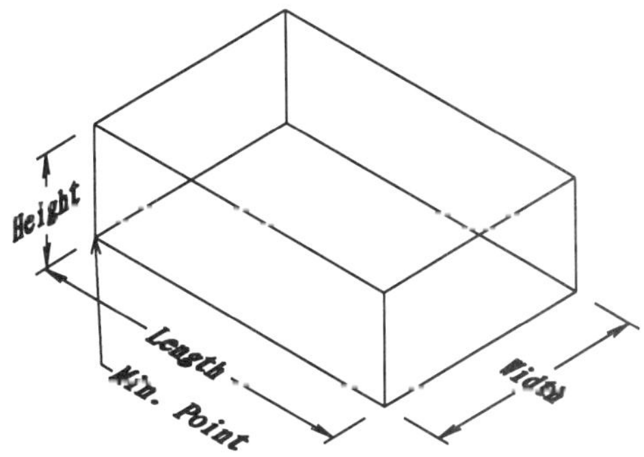

Figure 7.7

The box boundaries can be defined by one of the following three ways:

Scan NCI fiel(s):	use the coordinate values of the selected toolpath files as the stock boundaries.
UseJob Setup values:	use the stock boundaries defined in the job setup.
Pick stock corners:	pick two points from the graphic window to define the box boundaries.

Cylinder boundary Cylinder boundary uses the cylinder axis, cylinder diameter, min. Z and max Z to define the cylinder stock.

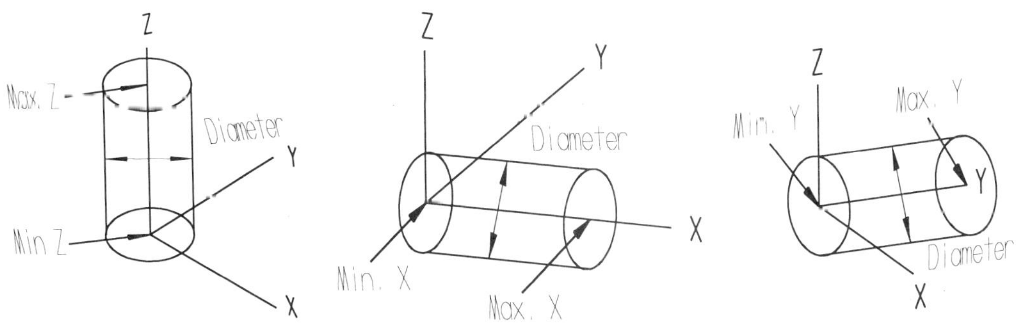

a. Center on Z-axis b. Center on X-axis c. Center on Y-axis

Figure 7.8

Tool display

The cutting tools can be displayed in three modes: turbo, wireframe, and solid. Three parameters are used to temporarily stop the tool movement in verification.

Turbo (no tool): no tool can be seen during verification.
Wireframe tool: tools are shown in wireframe mode.
Solid tool: tools are shown in solid mode.
Display holder: toolholder is added to the tool during verification.
Chanage tool/color: display different colors (in set colors parameter) in stock cutting area.
Stop on tool change: temporarily stop the verification when the tool change command is encountered.
Stop on gouge: temporarily stop the verification when a gouge is detected.

Display control

The display of verification are controlled by these parameters:

Moves/step: define number of moves per step. Select the verification mode to be automatic (machine) or step-by-step. In the Machine mode, the system verifies the toolpath continuously. The system verifies the cut for one step at a time. Click on the "step" button to continue to the next step.
Moves/refresh: the tool moves along the toolpath and refreshes at each move.
Speed--Quality: this parameter sets the speed of verification. Fast speed takes less time for verifying the cut, while sacrificing the quality of the model displayed.

Miscellaneous

Miscellaneous parameters consist of these five items:

Use TrueSolid: use the advanced solid modeling technology to create and manipulate complete and accurate solid models for toolpath simulation.
Cutter compensation in control: display whether the cutter compensation in control is used.
Display XYZ axes: display XYZ axes of the verification model.
Display coordinates: display the coordinate values while verifying.
Create log files: create a log file for futhre use.

File selection

There are two ways to select the NCI file for verification: NCI file and Current MC8.

NCI File: select an NCI file stored on the disk for verification.
Current MC8: use the active NCI file of the current MC8 file.

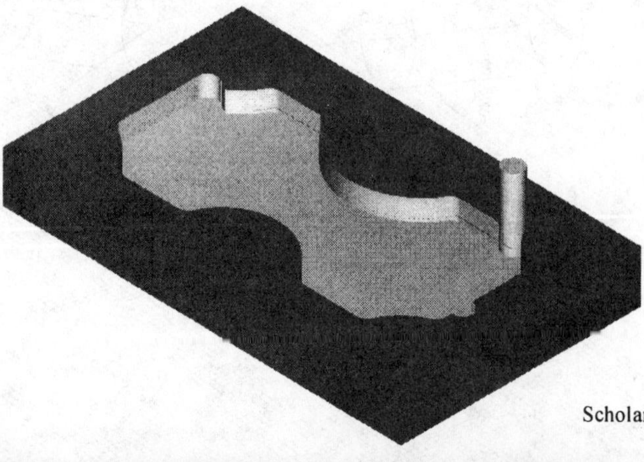

Figure 7.9

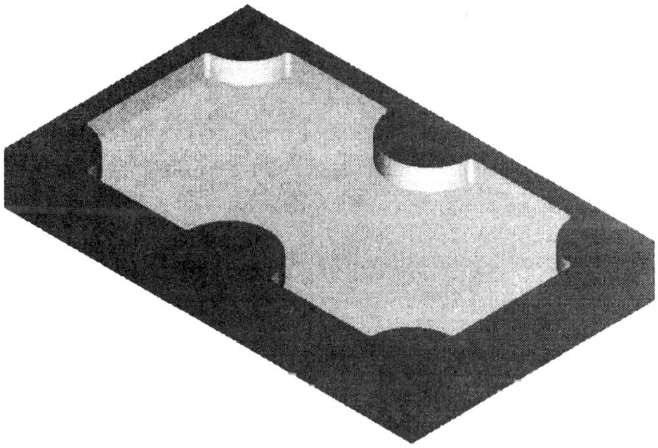

Figure 7.10

The Verify function can be initiated in two ways: from **Operations Manager mode** or from **NC utilities mode**.

<u>The procedure Initiated from Operations Manager mode:</u>

1. Select "Operations" to open Operations Manager menu
2. Select Verify button to open the Verify function
3. The raw material block model should appear on the screen.
4. Select "Machine" to verify the toolpath.

<u>The procedure Initiated from NC Utilities mode:</u>

1. Select NC utils → Verify
2. The raw material block model should appear on the screen.
3. Select "Machine" to verify the toolpath.

7.6 Job Setup

The job setup function is used to define the workpiece setup information. Its dialog box is given below.

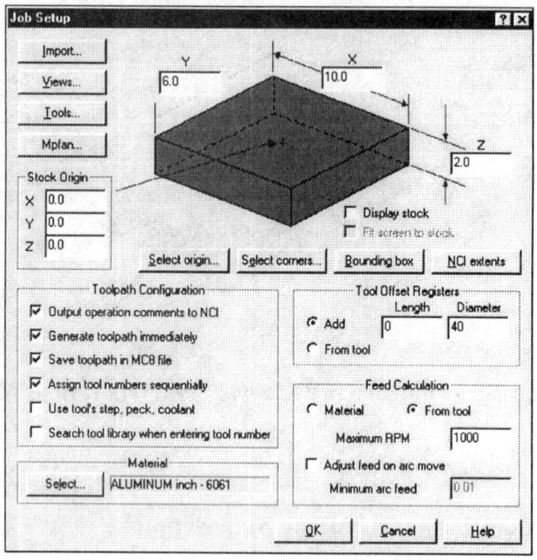

Stock Origin and Size

You can define the stock origin in two ways; pick a corner or center and pick at any location. There are ten possible locations that can be selected as the stock origin including eight locations at corners and two at the center of top and bottom surfaces. A small cross-mark with an arrow is used to indicate the corner or center you pick as the stock origin.

There are four buttons can be used to define the stock:

Select Origin:	use one of point entry methods to define the stock origin.
Select Corners:	use one of point entry methods to define the stock corners.
Bounding box:	find the extents of the selected geometry to define the stock limits.
NCI extents:	automatically calculates the stock boundaries based on the tool movements in the NCI file.

The stock size are fully defined by its X, Y, and z dimensions as shown below.

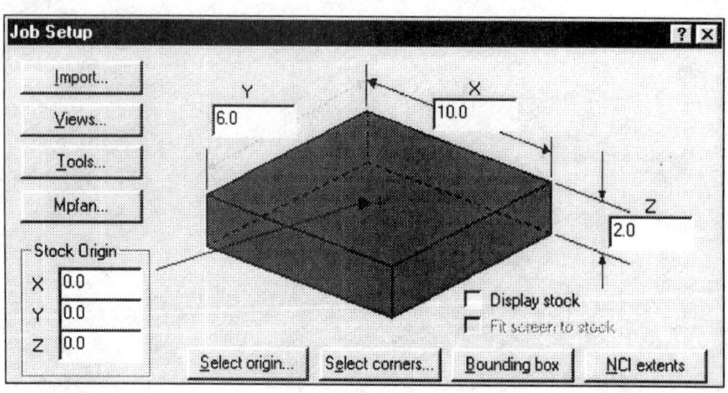

Material selection

The job setup also includes material type. Click the Select button in the Material section to bring up a material list as below.

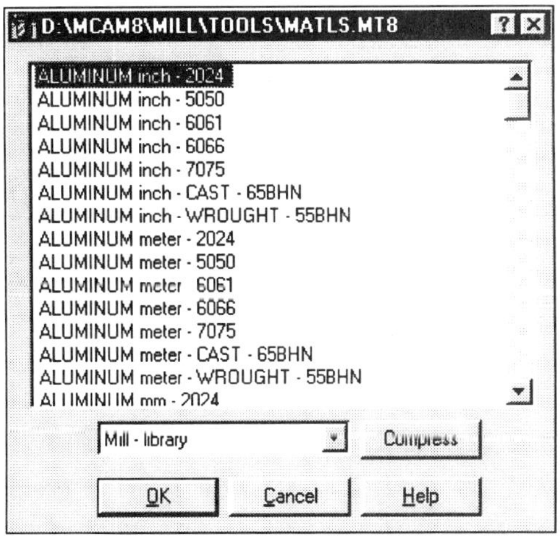

Tool Offset Registers

The register numbers for tool length offset and diameter compensation can be specified either in the job setup dialog box or directly taken from tooling information as shown below.

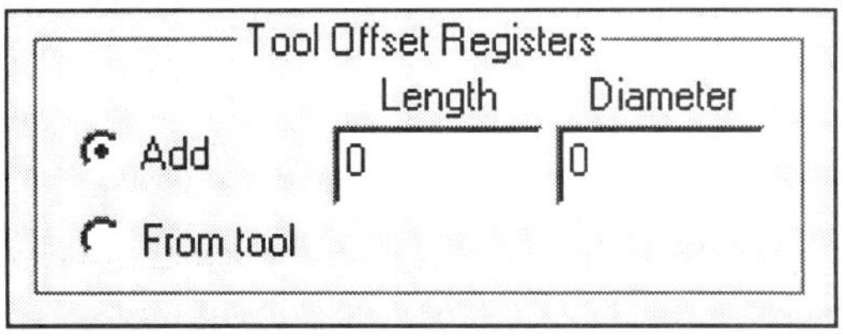

Toolpath Configuration Parameters

The following six parameters that can be selected for configuring the toolpaths format:

1. Output operation comments to NCI
2. Generate toolpath immediately
3. Save toolpath in MC8 file
4. Assign tool numbers sequentially
5. Use tool's step, peck, coolant
6. Search tool library when entering tool number

Feed Calculation Parameters

Mastercam provides two modes to calculate feed: **material** and **from tool**. Feed can be assigned either using the material data table or machining data from tooling data. Maximum RPM can be assigned also. The dialog box of this category is shown below.

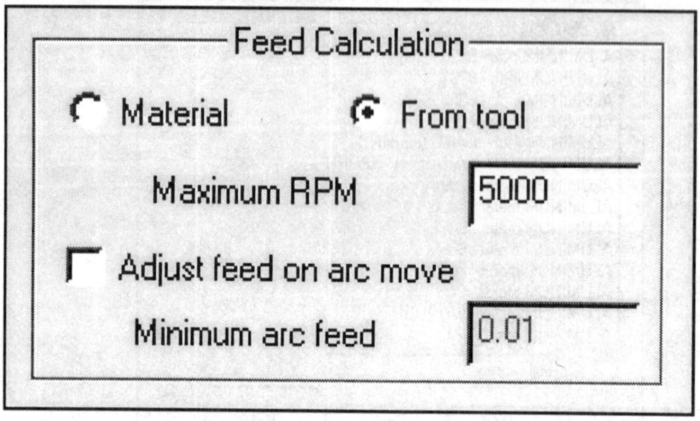

7.7 Contour definition

A contour consists of a number of connected geometric entities to form a part profile for machining. The benefit of defining a contour is to allow multiple entities of a part shape to be formed as a single entity. This facilitates profile or pocket cutting in one tool motion command.

Chaining direction

The pick point of the first entity of the contour determines the starting position of the contour and the chaining direction of the contour. The chaining direction is also the contour direction. The chaining direction starts at one entity end point, traps the end point that is closer to the picked position, and points to the other end point (Figure 7.11).

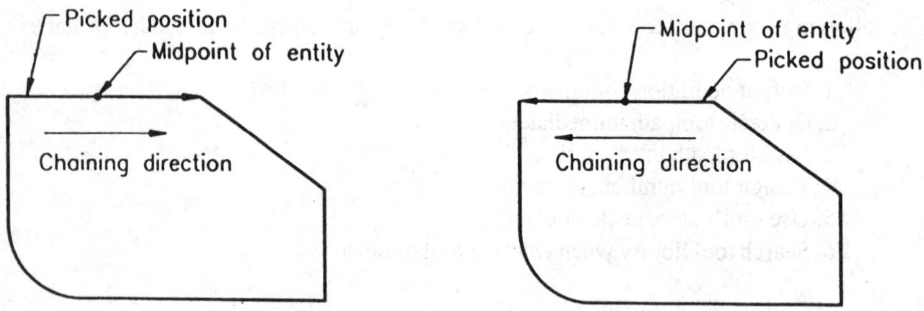

Figure 7.11

There are two types of contours: **closed** and **open**. In a closed contour, the first and last entities are connected (Figure 7.12a). In an open contour, the first and last entities are not connected (Figure 7.12b). The contours used in pocketing must be the closed type.

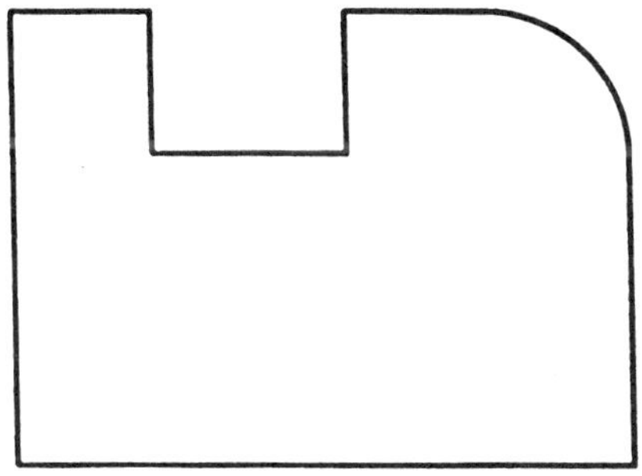

Figure 7.12a

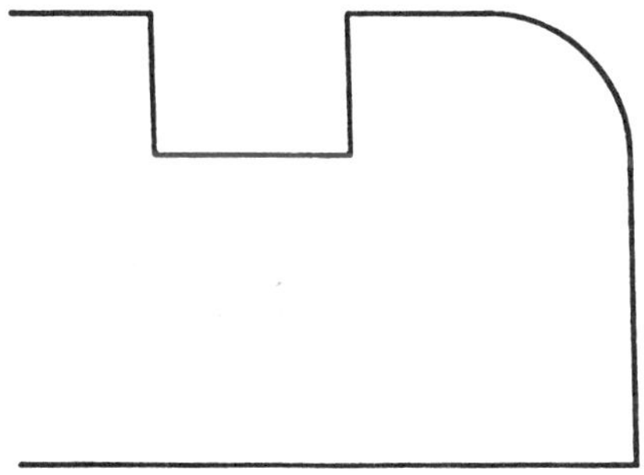

Figure 7.12b

Chaining methods

Mastercam provides various methods for chaining entities into contours. Table 7.2 describes these chaining methods.

Table 7.2 Contour chaining methods

Method	Description	Illustration
Chain	defining a contour consisting of one or more connected entities.	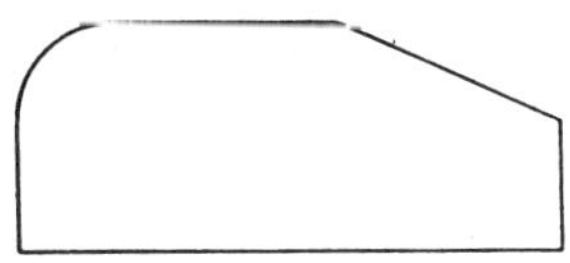
Window	defining one or more contours from those entities completely within a window.	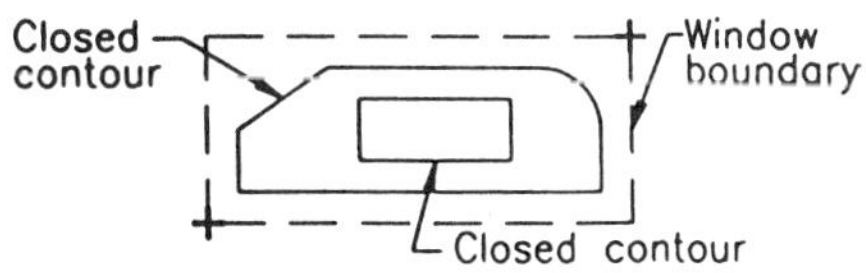
Area	defining a contour from a group of contours.	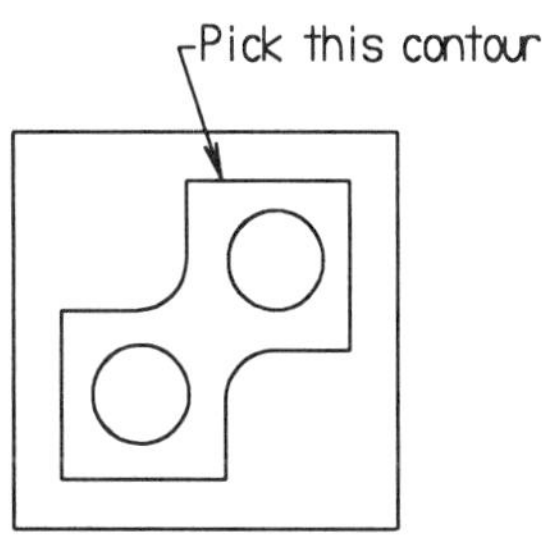

Table 7.2 continued.

Single	defining a contour consisting of only a single entity.	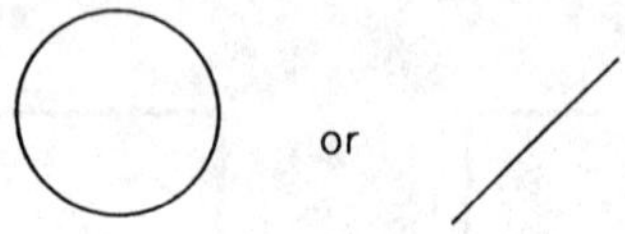
Section	defining a contour with a section of connected entities.	
Point	defining a clear point to rapid to.	
Last	recalling the last group of chained contours for new operations.	
Unselect	undoing the contour selection just made.	

Chain option

The chain option is used to automatically chain a series of connected entities as a chained contour. The picked entity becomes the first entity of the chained contour (Figure 7.13).

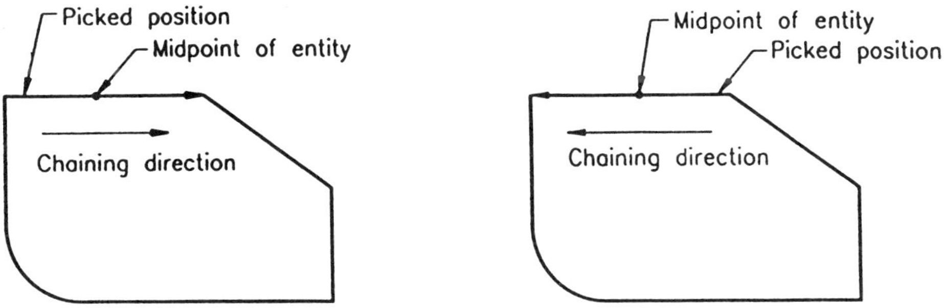

Figure 7.13

After picking the starting entity of the chained contour, Mastercam provides the following functions to modify the chaining direction and starting entity of the contour:

Reverse:	reverse the chaining direction to its opposite direction (Figure 7.14).
Move fwd:	change the starting entity to next entity in the chain (Figure 7.15).
Move back:	change the starting entity back one preceding entity in the chain (Figure 7.16).
Select str:	select an entity as the new starting entity of the chained contour (Figure 7.17).

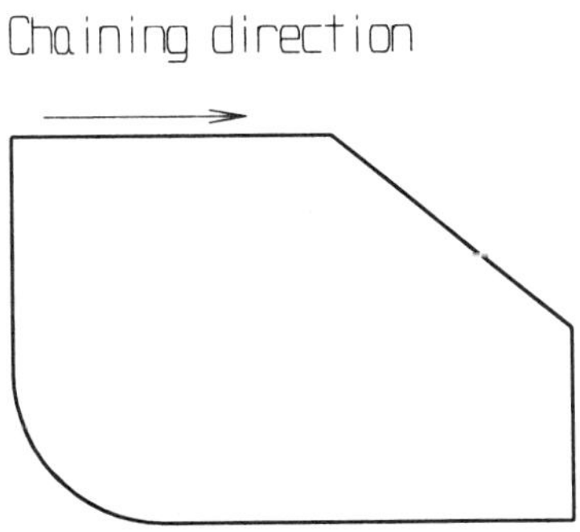

Figure 7.14a Original direction

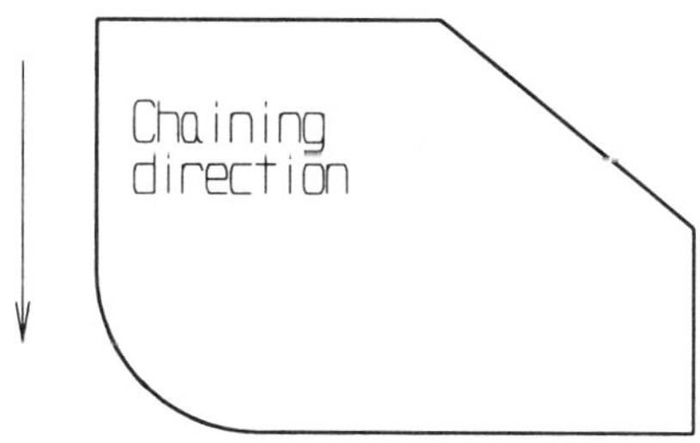

Figure 7.14b After reverse

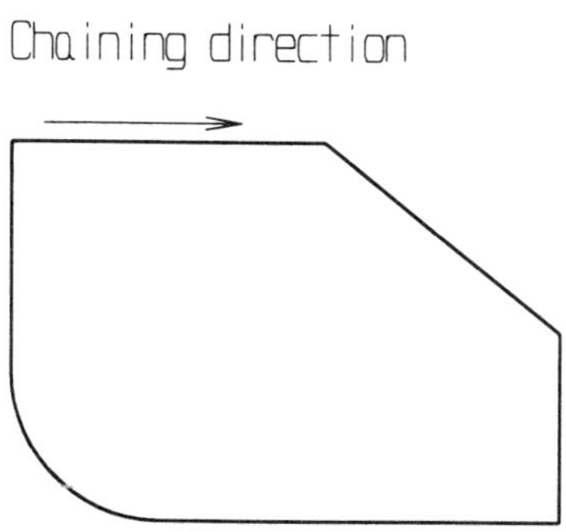

Figure 7.15a Original direction

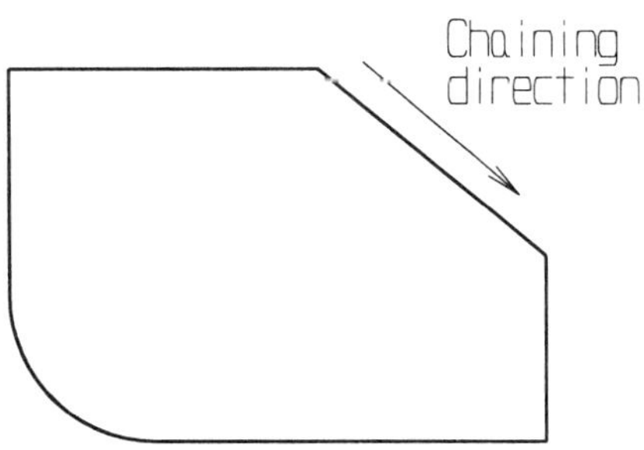

Figure 7.15b After move forward

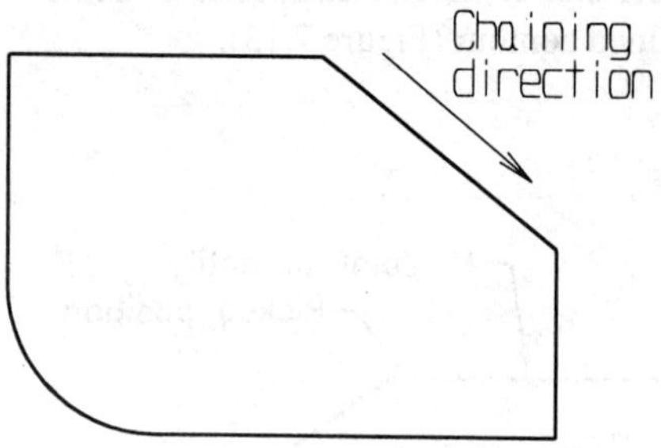

Figure 7.16a Original direction

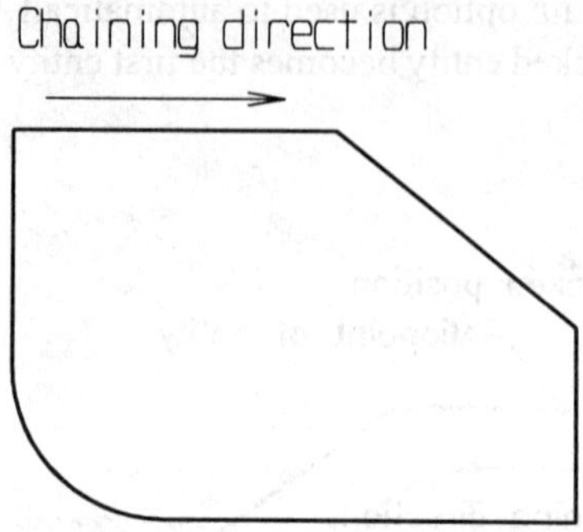

Figure 7.16b After move back

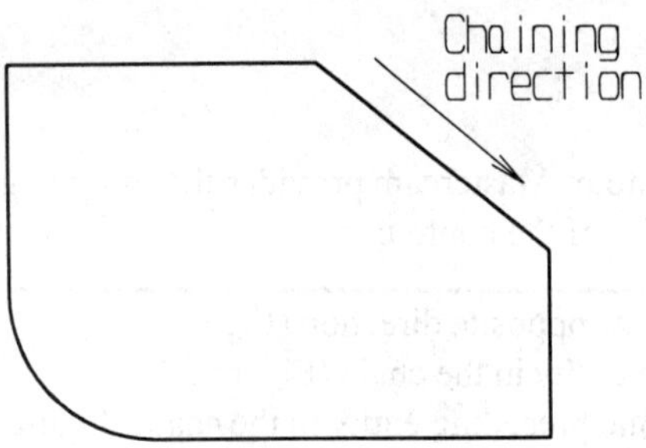

Figure 7.17a Original direction

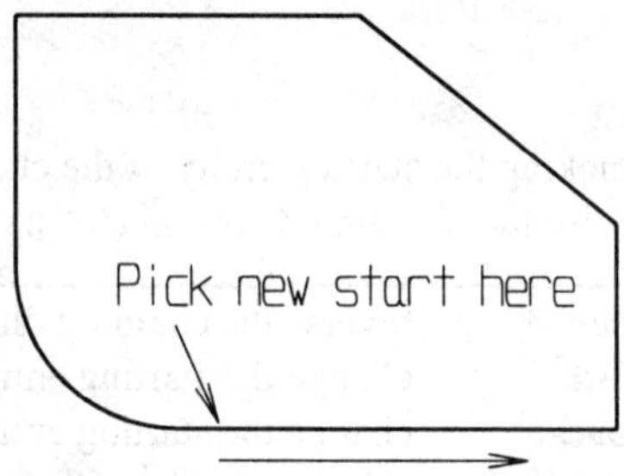

Figure 7.17b After select new start

Options

Mastercam provides various ways to mask entities to be included in the chain and other parameters to make chaining preferences. These options are grouped under Chaining Options menu as shown below.

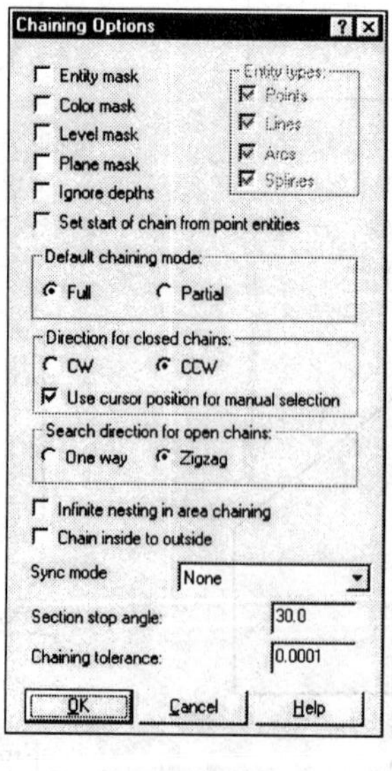

Rectangle and Polygon options (under Window options)

This option allows picking a series of points for defining a polygon as the searching boundary for defining the contour. It has the following five options:

Inside:	include all entities completely inside the polygon (Figure 7.18).
In + intr:	include all entities inside or on the polygon boundary (Figure 7.19).
Intersect:	include only those entities on the polygon boundary (Figure 7.20).
Out + intr:	include all entities outside or on the polygon boundary (Figure 7.21).
Outside:	include all entities completely outside the polygon (Figure 7.22).

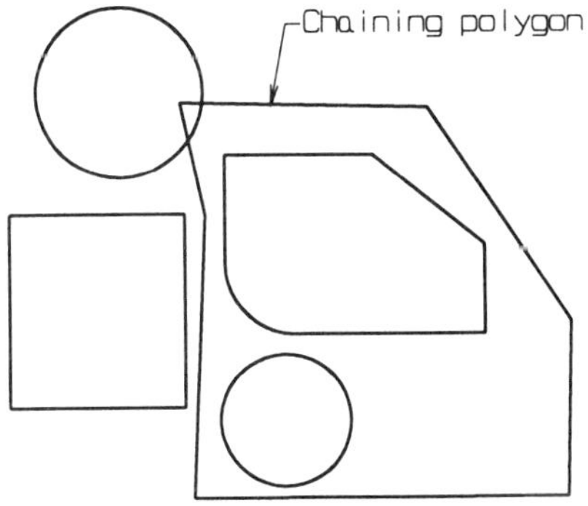

Figure 7.18a

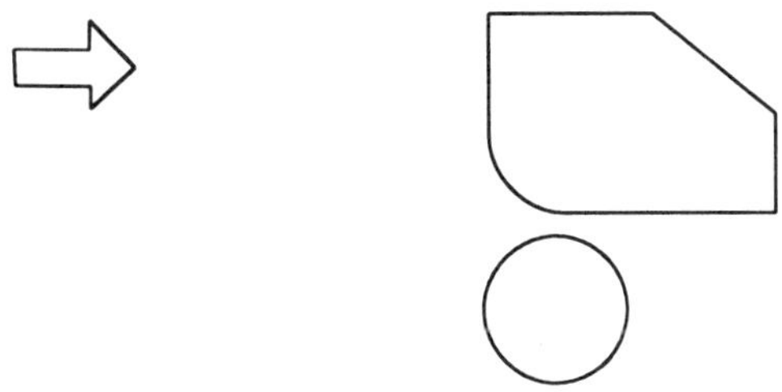

Figure 7.18b Inside polygon

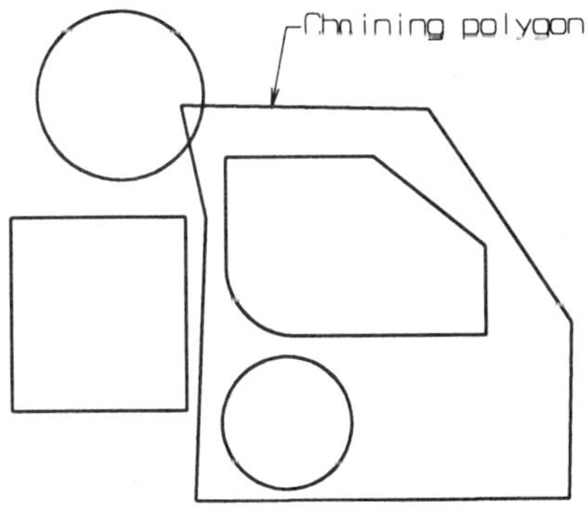

Figure 7.19a

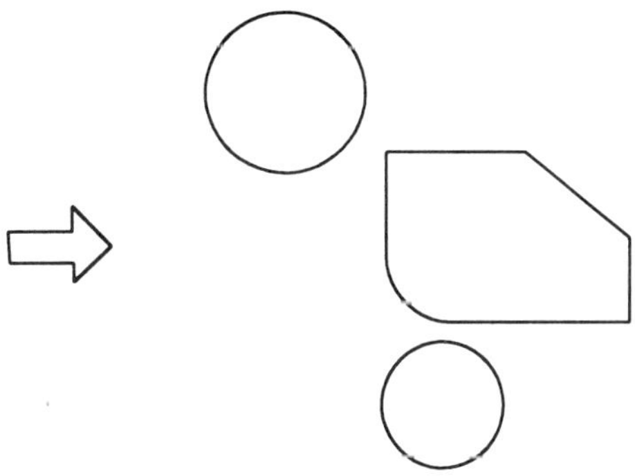

Figure 7.19b Inside and on the polygon

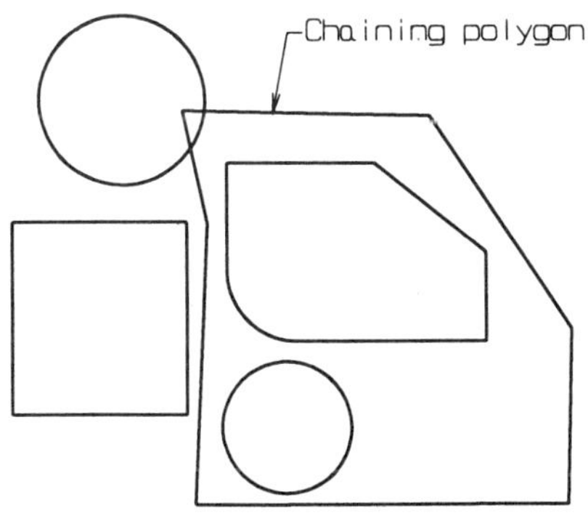

Figure 7.20a

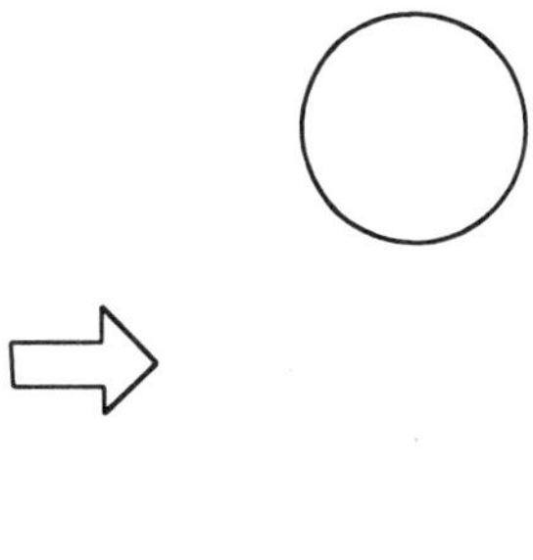

Figure 7.20b On the polygon boundary

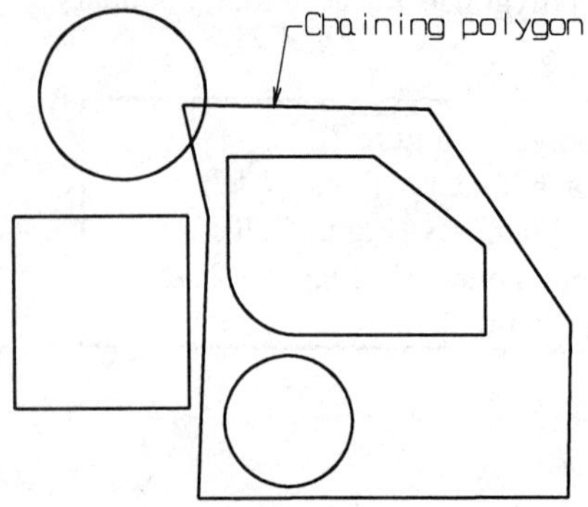

Figure 7.21a

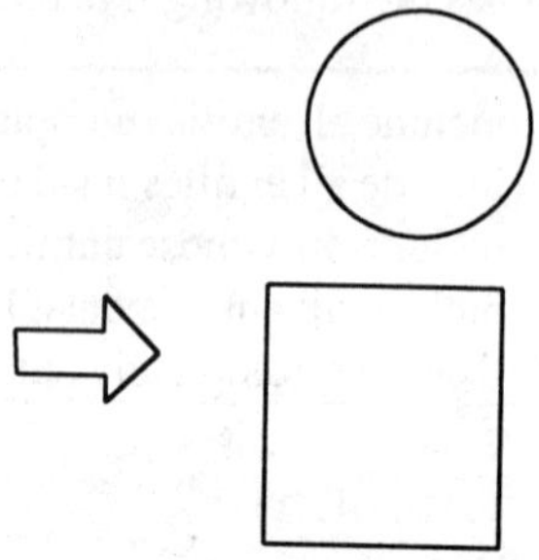

Figure 7.21b Outside and on the polygon boundary

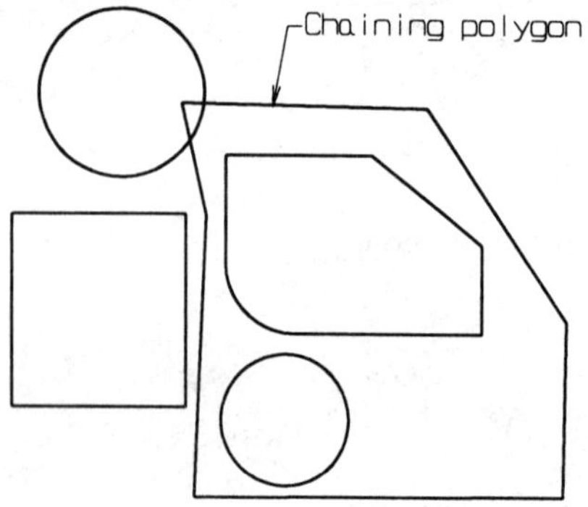

Figure 7.22a

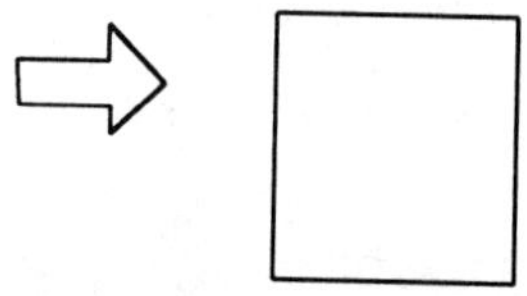

Figure 7.22b Outside the polygon

Area option This option allows picking a contour from a groups of contours. The connected entities will be included in the area (Figure 7.23).

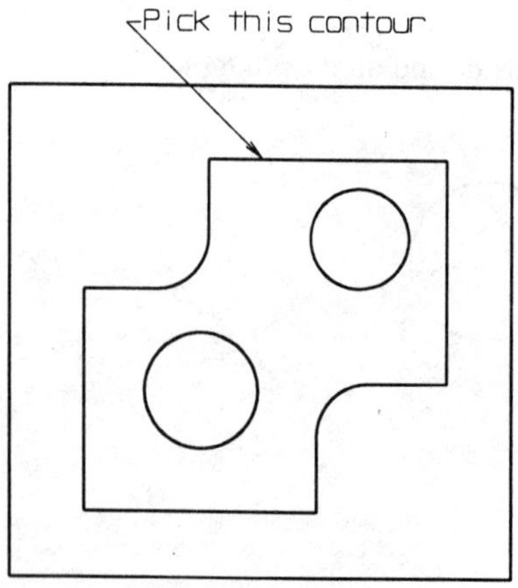

Figure 7.23a

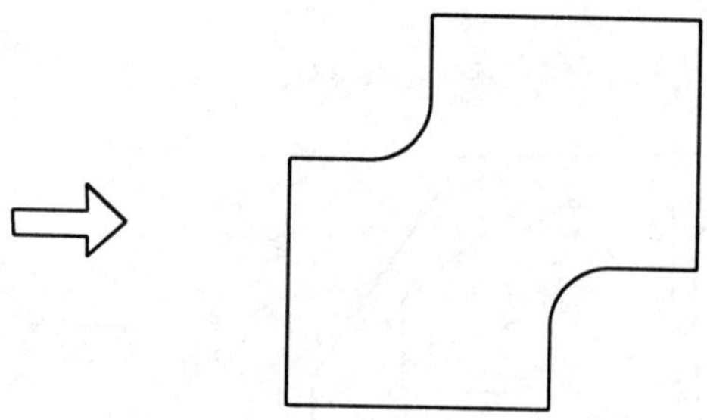

Figure 7.23b After picking an area

Single option: This option selects a single entity as a contour.
Section option: The section option is used to select a section of entities as a chained contour.

The range of section is determined by where you pick the entity. The section is terminated by two consecutive line entities. When a line that has an adjacent line in both ends is selected, only the selected line is included in the chained contour (Figure 7.24). Figure 7.25 shows an example that a section of entities is chained as a contour.

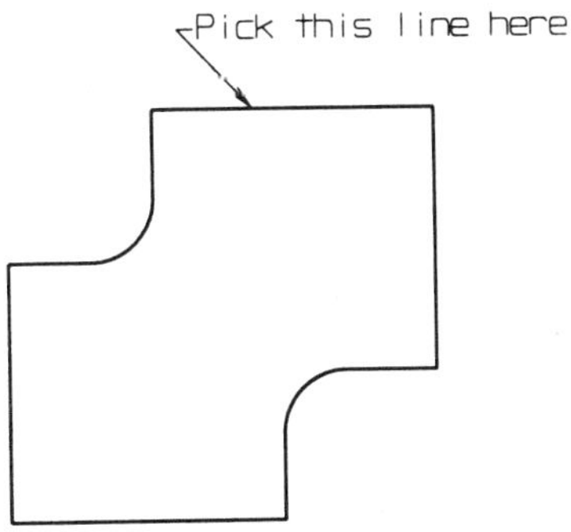

Figure 7.24a

Figure 7.24b Result of section selection

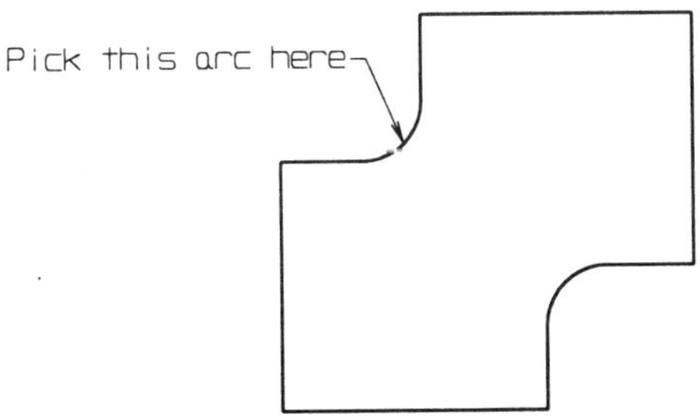

Figure 7.25a

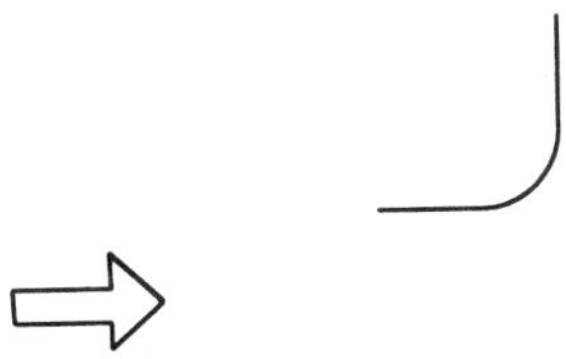

Figure 7.25b Result of selection

Point option: The point option is to specify a single point as the contour.

Last option: This option selects the last chained contour for the new operation.

Unselect option: This option undo the contour selection just made.

7.8 Coordinate Setting

Mastercam uses four functions to define the work coordinates of the part program. They are **home position, reference point, rotary axis**, and **tool/construction plane**. They are described below.

Home Position

This function specifies the intermediate position for reference point return. Most CNC controls use reference return commands to generate paths for the spindle and worktable to return to machine origin. Home position dialog box appears as shown here:

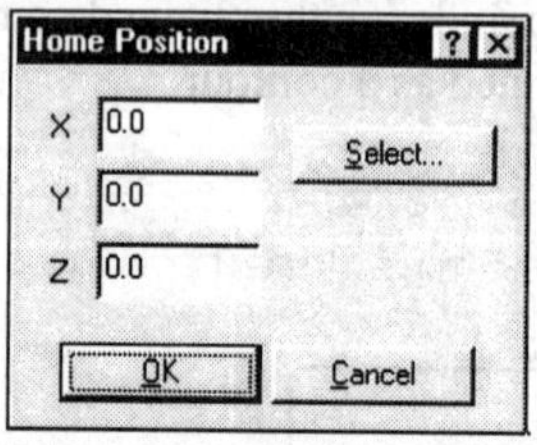

Reference point return commands have the following formats:

	G90 G28 Xx Yy Zz	(absolute positioning mode)
Or	**G91 G28 Xx Yy Zz**	(incremental positioning mode)

where G90: absolute positioning mode
G91: incremental positioning mode
G28: reference point return command
x, y, and z are the coordinate values of the intermediate point

The toolpath pattern of the reference point return G28 is shown in Figure 7.26. In fact, we arrange the reference return point command into two block statements as below:

G91 G28 Z0.0
G91 G28 X0.0 Y0.0

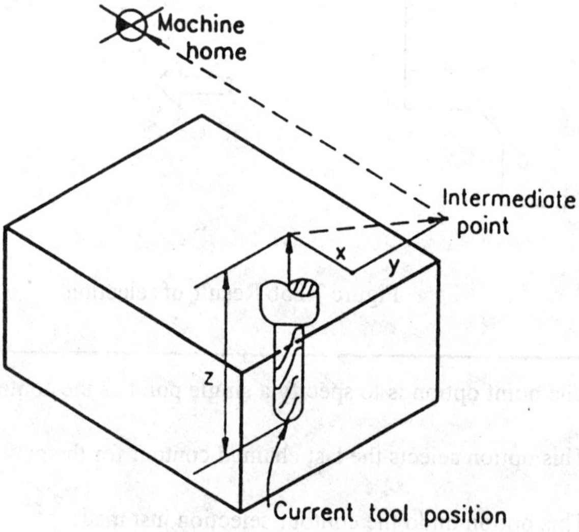

Figure 7.26

This arrangement allows the cutter to be retracted in the Z direction before the worktable moves in the X and Y plane, and avoids interference.

In Mastercam the coordinate values of the Home Position are used as the x, y, and z values of the reference return point. With the default value (X0 Y0 Z0) of home position, the reference return point commands become:

G91 G28 Z0.0
G91 G28 X0.0 Y0.0

With the coordinate value of (X1.0 Y1.0 Z2.0), the reference return point commands becomes:

G91 G28 Z2.0
G91 G28 X1.0 Y1.0

The reference point return commands are used in the following two conditions:

1. Execution of tool change. Tool change has to be implemented at the machine origin in most CNC machines.
2. At the end of the part program. The spindle and worktable should be moved to machine origin to (1) make the control ready for the next operation, and (2) load and unload the workpieces.

Tip Always use (X0 Y0 Z0) for Home Position and set the positioning system command to incremental mode in the postprocessor. This setting can be used in any workpiece machining. Care must be exercised when other coordinate values are given to this parameter, otherwise an undesirable toolpath may result.

Reference Point

This function is used to define additional reference return point beside the home position for the tool to return. Its dialog box appears as below.

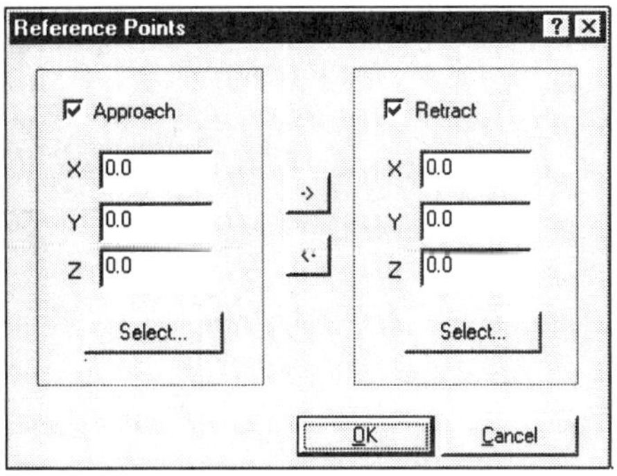

Tool Origin and Tool Plane

Mastercam allows to define three possible origins: **system origin, construction plane origin**, and **tool plane origin**. The system origin is the fixed coordinate system automatically setup by the system. The construction origin is used to redefine the origin for geometry construction. The tool plane origin redefines the tool path origin. All three origins are located at the system origin unless they are redefined.

The principle of redefining tool plane origin is the same as programming the work coordinate setting command G92. The coordinate values given in this parameter indicate the coordinate values of the system origin in the tool plane coordinate system. Figure 7.27 shows three cases of tool plane origin setup.

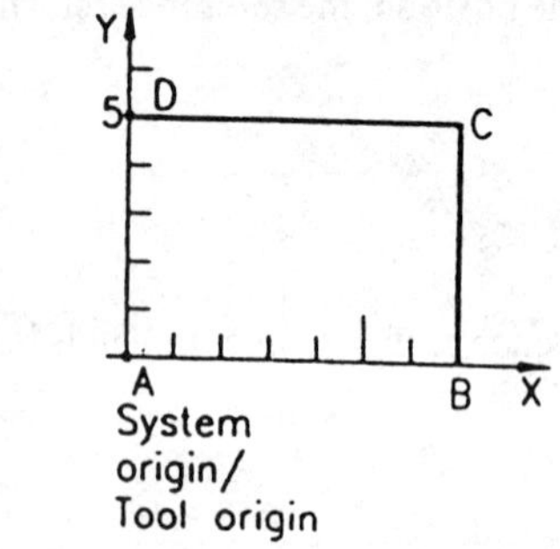

	Toolpath Coord.	
	X-Coord.	Y-Coord.
A	0	0
B	7.0	0.0
C	7.0	5.0
D	0	5.0

a. Tool origin: X0 Y0

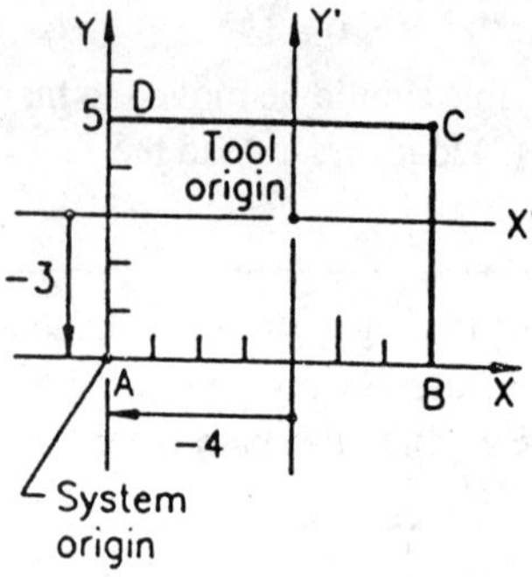

	Toolpath Coord.	
	X-Coord.	Y-Coord.
A	-4.0	-3.0
B	3.0	-3.0
C	3.0	2.0
D	-4.0	2.0

b. Tool origin: X-4.0 Y-3.0

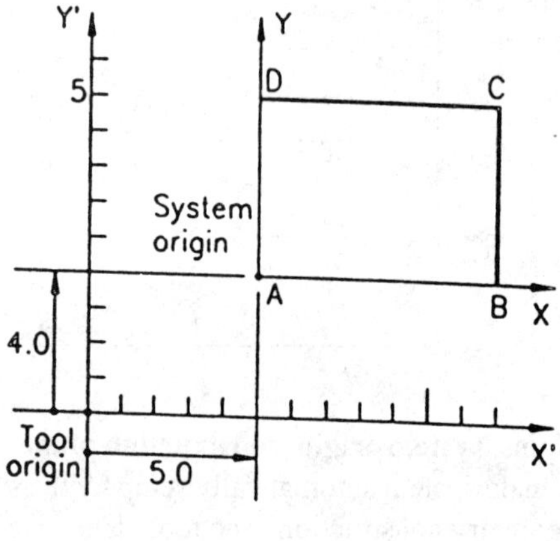

	Toolpath Coord.	
	X-Coord.	Y-Coord.
A	5.0	4.0
B	12.0	4.0
C	12.0	9.0
D	5.0	9.0

c. Tool origin: X5.0 Y4.0

Figure 7.27

The tool plane parameter is used to select the tool plane for the current operation. There are three principal tool planes: XY-plane, ZX-plane, and YZ-plane. The system will issue a plane selection command code to the part program as shown below. Figure 7.28 shows a number of examples of selecting a proper tool plane.

Plane selection	Command code
XY-plane	G17
ZX-plane	G18
YZ-plane	G19

Tool plane parameters can be toggled to these options:

Off	Tool plane defaulted to top view.
Top	Top view
Front	Front view
Side	Side view
Number	View identified by its number
2 Lines	View defined by two mutually perpendicular lines
Arc	View contained an arc
Rotate	View defined by rotating a construction plane about an axis
Normal	View which is perpendicular to a normal vector

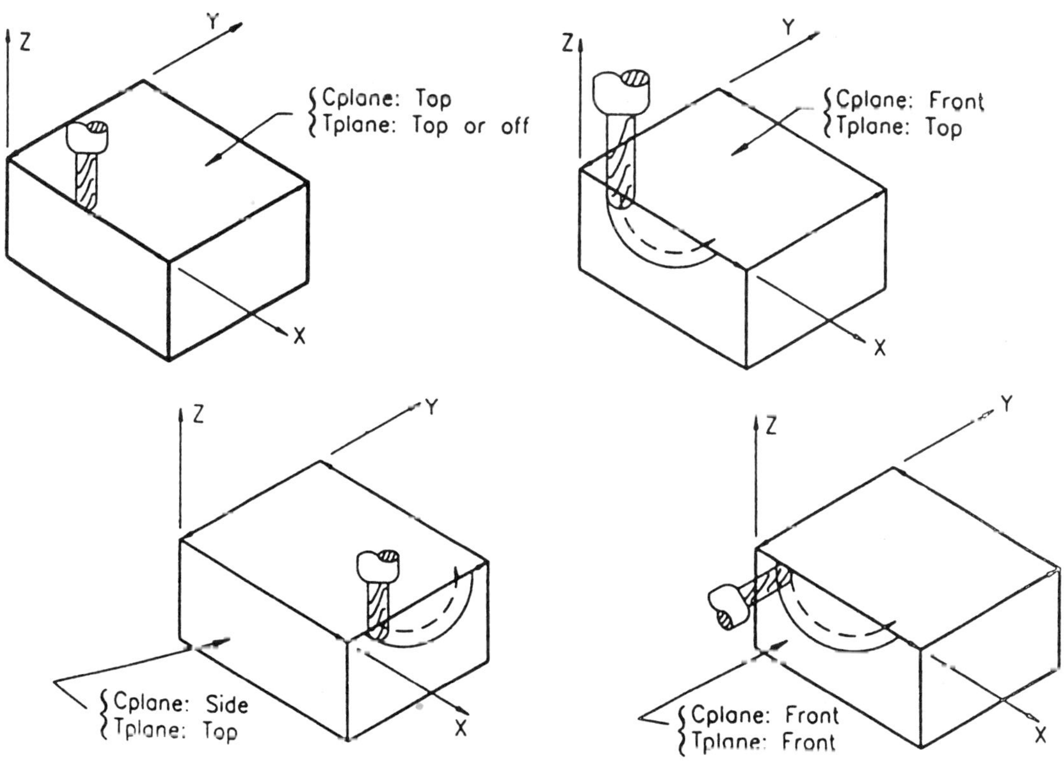

Figure 7.28

Click the "T/C planes" button at the bottom of the Tool Parameters menu to open the Tool Plane/ Construction Plane dialog box as below.

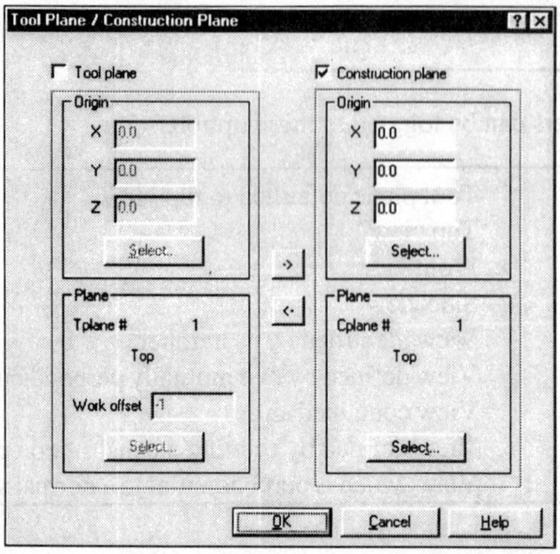

Rotary Axis

The rotary axis function is used to indicate which axis, X or Y, the rotary axis is to replace. The dialog box of rotary axis function is shown below.

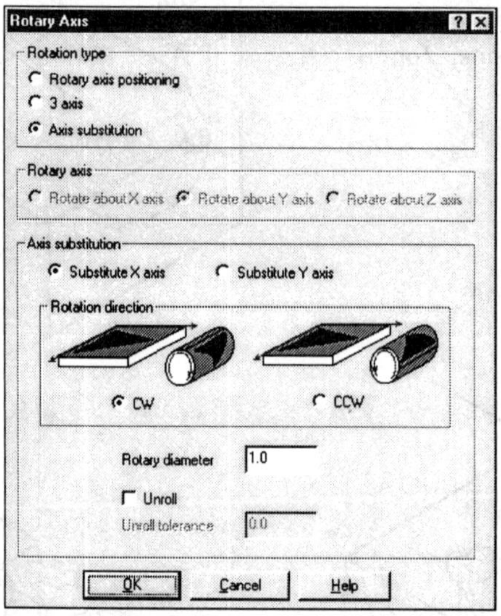

7.9 Contour Module

The contour module is used to generate cutter paths along a series of lines and arcs that form the profile of a part. Contouring is normally implemented on 2D profiles, in which the depth of cut remains constant (Figure 7.29).

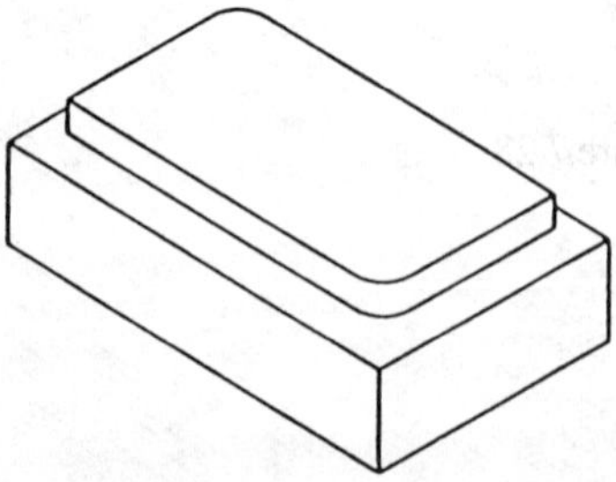

Figure 7.29

Contour Parameters

In addition to the tool parameters presented in previous sections, the contour module uses a set of contour specific parameters to define how the contouring toolpaths are generated. The contour parameters menu is shown below.

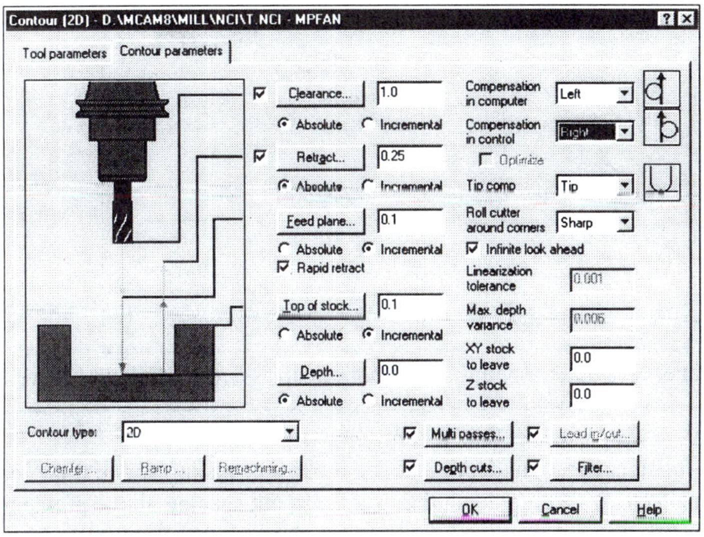

The contour parameters can be grouped into the following six categories; **Z-depth parameters, Depth cuts, Stock to leave, Multi passes, Compensations,** and **Lead in/out**.

Z-depth parameters Mastercam uses the following five parameters to define the Z-depths for generating contouring toolpaths:

Clearance:	define the clearance level at which the tool is traveled between operations.
Retract:	define the retraction level to which the tool is retracted after the end of operations.
Feed plane:	specify the distance above the top of stock from which the tool start to change its motion from rapid mode to feed mode.
Top of stock:	specify the Z-coordinate value of the top of stock.
Depth:	Specify the final depth of contouring toolpaths.

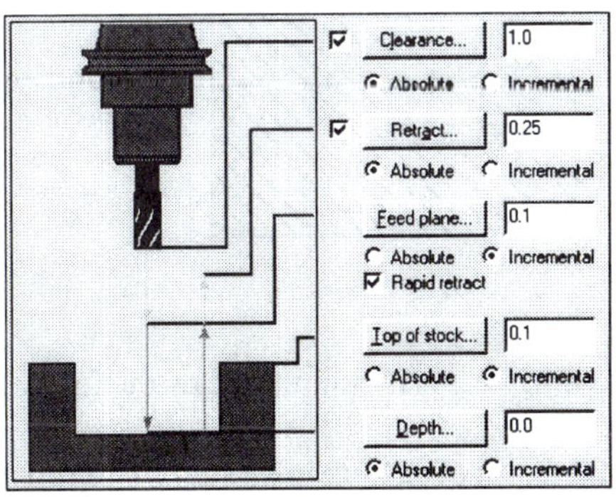

The total depth of material to be removed is determined by the two parameters; **top of stock** and **depth**. The total cutting depth is the sum of top of stock and depth.

Depth cuts The depth cuts parameters specify the number of roughing and finish cuts to be taken in the Z direction. It allows us to set the maximum roughing depth of each roughing pass and the number of finish cuts with the specified depth of each finish cut. The total number of cutting passes is the sum of the roughing cuts and finish cuts. The four parameters in depth cuts dialog box appear as here.

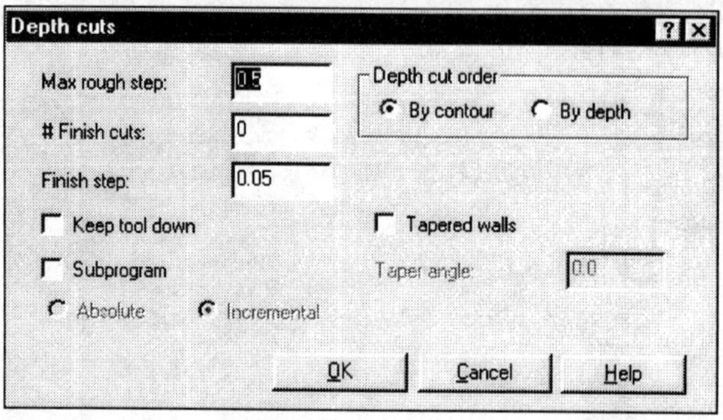

The cutting sequence is determined from the bottom up as defined below (Figure 7.30):

Last finish cut: cut at final depth.
Second to last finish cut: cut at depth that is a finish cut spacing above final depth.
Subsequent finish cut: cut at depth that is a finish cut spacing above previous finish cut.
Last roughing cut: cut at depth that is a roughing cut spacing above first finish cut.
Next to last roughing cut: cut at depth that is a roughing cut spacing above the last roughing cut.
Subsequent roughing cuts: cut at depth that is a roughing cut spacing above previous roughing cut.

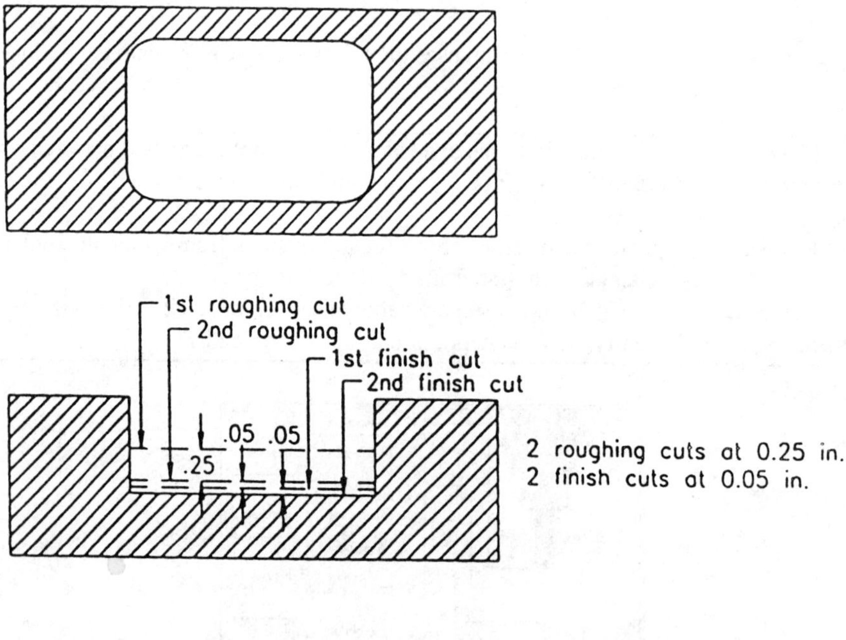

Figure 7.30

The required number of roughing passes is determined by the following formula:

$$\text{\#of roughing passes} = \frac{[\text{Total depth of cut} - (\text{Finish step x \# of finish passes})]}{\text{Max rough step}}$$

The result will be rounded to next integer number. The actual roughing step will be automatically recalculate based on the formula below:

$$\textbf{Roughing step} = \frac{\textbf{[Total depth of cut} - \textbf{(Finish step x \# of finish passes)]}}{\textbf{\# of roughing passes}}$$

Keep tool down The "Keep tool down" parameter is used to specify whether the tool will be retracted to "Feed" level after each roughing or finish pass. Click the check box with a (mark to keep tool down and plunge the tool from the current Z-level to the next cutting Z-level directly. Remove the (mark will retract the tool up to the "Feed" level at the end of each cutting pass. The tool plunges to the Z-depth of next cutting pass.

Stock to leave in XY-direction The "stock to leave" parameter specifies a certain amount of material to be left on the workpiece for further machining. The stock is allowed in both the XY-direction and Z direction. The stock in Z direction is specified in the "Depth cuts" dialog box. This parameter in the contour parameters dialog box is only applied to the stock in XY-direction. Leaving stock in XY-direction is shown in Figure 7.31. When a non-zero value is given to "Stock to leave" parameter, the final tool pass will leave the given amount of material on the part. The direction of stock to leave is determined by the offset side parameter. The stock is left on the left side when the compensation side is set to left, likewise, when it is set to right the stock is on the right. If the compensation side is set to Off, the stock to leave is ignored.

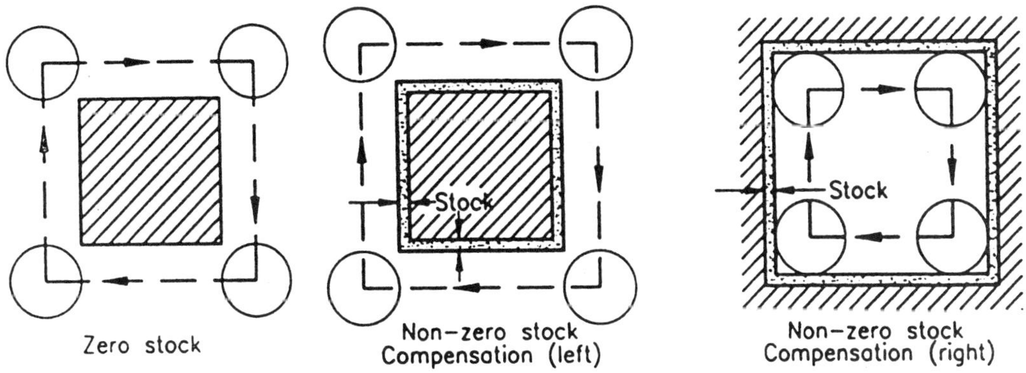

Figure 7.31

Multi passes Mastercam uses four parameters in "Multi Passes" dialog box to specify the number of roughing and finish cuts to be taken and their stepover distance in the selected cutting plane. The Multi Passes dialog box is shown here.

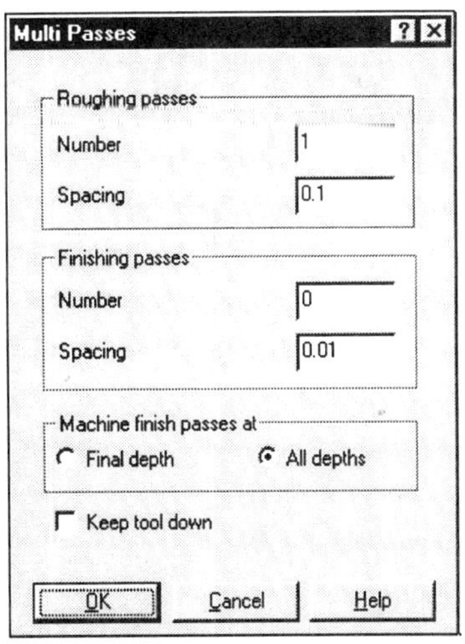

The total number of contouring passes to be taken is the sum of the number of roughing cuts and the number of finish passes. The spacing for roughing cuts is determined by the size of cutter diameter. Normally, the roughing spacing is about 60 to 75 percent of the cutter diameter. The required number of roughing cuts is determined by dividing the amount of material to be removed by the roughing spacing. If the amount of material to be removed is 1.25 in. and the roughing cut spacing is 0.7 in. (assuming 1-in. flat end mill is used), 2 (or 1.25/.7) roughing cuts should be used.

Figure 7.32 shows the toolpath pattern for the toolpath parameters having the following setting:

Number of roughing passes = 2 Spacing of roughing passes = 0.25 Number of finishing passes = 2 Spacing of finishing passes = 0.05

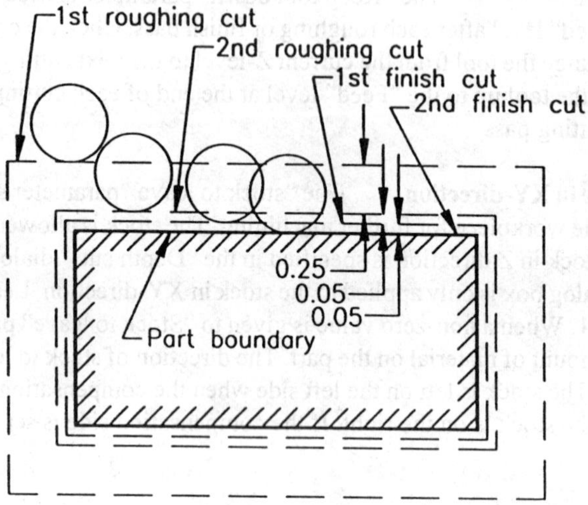

Figure 7.32

Machine finish passes at The "Machine finish passes at" parameter is used to specify whether finish passes to be implemented in final depth only or in all depths. When the "Final depth" option is selected, the finish passes are generated only at the final Z-depth passes. When the "All depths" option is selected, the finish passes are generated at each Z-depth passes. Figure 7.33 shows the contrast of these two options using the same toolpath parameters.

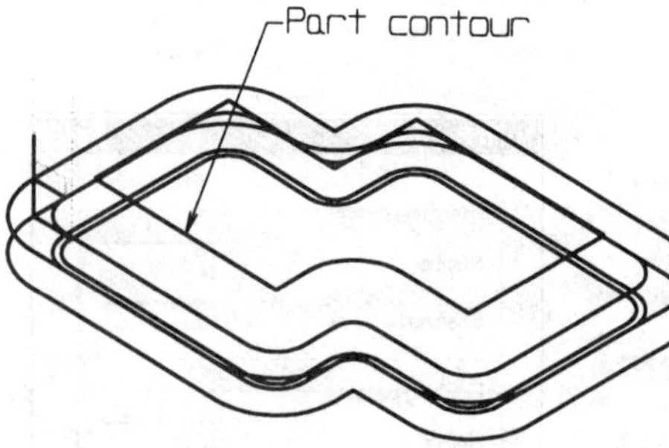

Figure 7.33a At final depth

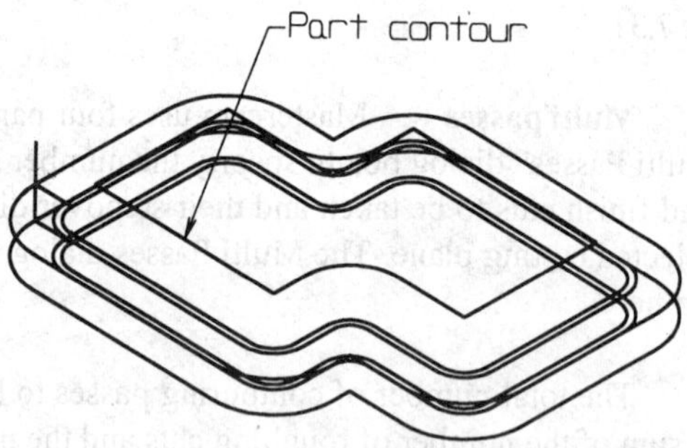

Figure 7.33b At all depths

Compensations Cutter compensation displaces the cutter center by a distance from the specified side of the programmed path. It is often referred to as cutter diameter compensation (CDC) or cutter radius compensation. It can be used in the following applications:

1. Allow the programmer to prepare the required tool path with reference to part coordinates directly.
2. Allow to use a cutter whose diameter differs from that specified by the part programmer without rewriting the program.
3. Compensate the variation in tool size due to wear, regrinding, etc.
4. Allow roughing and finishing cuts to be done with the same part program. Clearance or stock for the finishing cuts has to be set aside during the roughing cuts.

Cutter compensation parameters in Mastercam can be toggled to one of three options: tool left (CDC left), tool right (CAD right), and tool on (CDC off).

Tool left:	The cutting edge of the tool is offset to the left of the programmed path.
Tool right:	The cutting edge of the tool is offset to the right of the programmed path.
Tool on:	The cutter center is on the programmed path.

Figure 7.34 shows the effect of these three commands on the tool paths. To determine the cutter compensation option, look in the chaining direction. Use *tool left* if the cutter is offset to the left of the contour. Use *tool right* when the cutter is displaced to the right of the contour path. Use *tool on* when the cutter coincides with the contour.

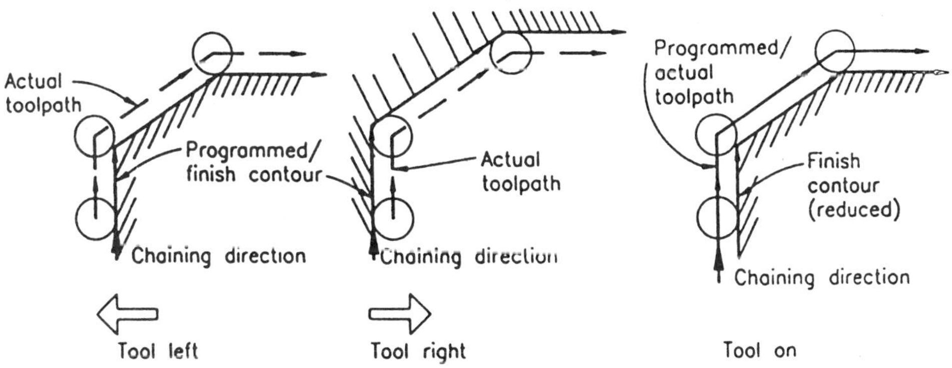

Figure 7.34

These three cutter compensation commands are converted into the following three G-codes during post processing stage:

CDC left:	**G41**
CDC right:	**G42**
CDC off:	**G40**

Mastercam uses three cutter compensation parameters to specify cutter compensation: compensation in computer, compensation in control, and tip compensation. The dialog box for these three compensations is shown here.

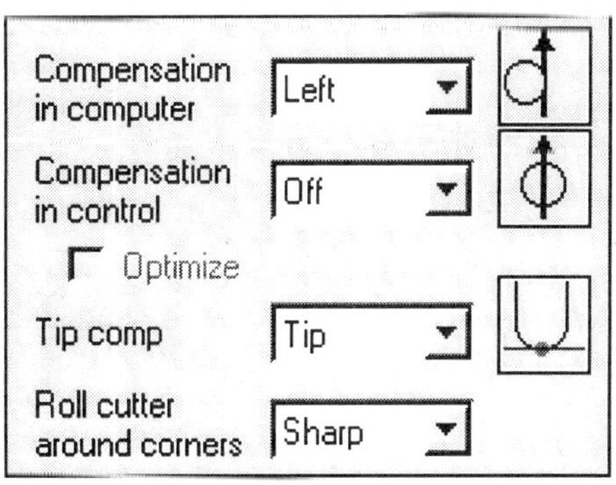

Compensation in Control This parameter generates a cutter compensation command (G40, G41, or G42) for the part program according to the selection. You can set this parameter to ""Off", "Left", or "Right". A compensation register number (Dia.ofst. n.) is assigned to the compensation in control. The compensation value is stored in the specified register. The compensation value can be (1) the actual tool diameter, or (2) the variation value between the designated tool diameter and the actual tool diameter.

Cutter compensation in control	**Command in part program**
Left	G41 Dd
Right	G42 Dd
Off	G40

where d is the diameter offset number (Dia. Ofst. n.).

The offset value is stored in this register in the CNC control. Figure 7.35 shows the effect of an offset value on the programmed tool paths.

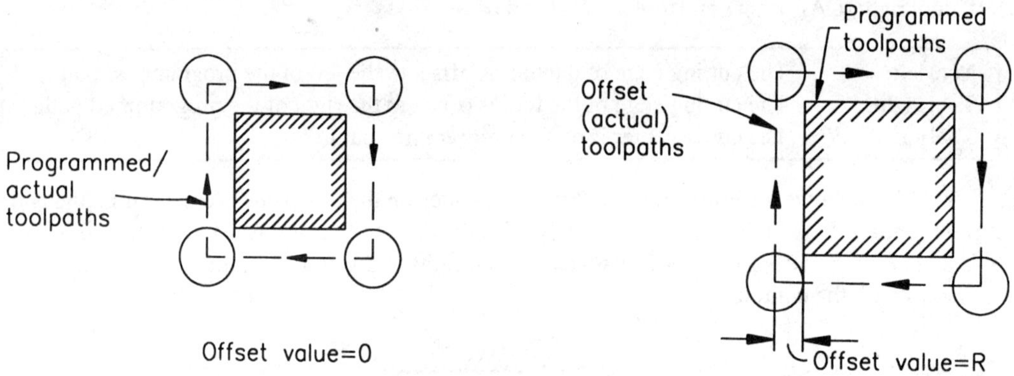

Figure 7.35

Note: On the computer screen, the cutter center does not offset even through the cutter compensation in the control is set to the right or left.

Compensation in Computer This parameter causes the cutter center to be displaced in the specified direction by the designated cutter radius distance. This parameter can be selected to left, right, or off. No cutter diameter compensation code will be inserted into the part program even though the compensation in the system parameter is toggled to the left or right. Note that this parameter changes the coordinate values of the cutter center paths. Figure 7.36 shows the effect of compensation in computer on the tool path.

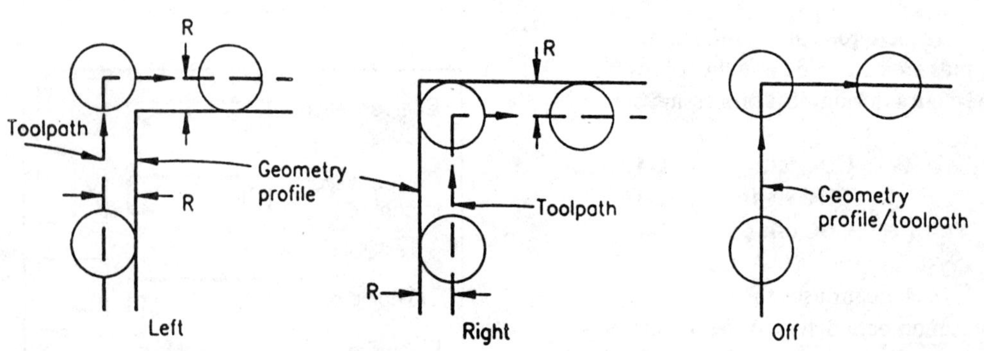

Figure 7.36

Note: Selecting the proper setting of cutter compensation parameters for a particular application is often very confusing. Two factors to be considered in selecting cutter compensation are:

(1) Is the actual cutter diameter identical to the programmed diameter?

(2) Is tool wear present?

Table 7.3 shows combinations in which two cutter compensation parameters can be applied.

Table 7.3 The use of cutter compensation in control and in system

Compensation in control	Compensation in system	CDC command	Remark	Illustration
Off	Off	None	Produces an inaccurate part profile. The dimensional error in all sides is equal to the value of the tool radius.	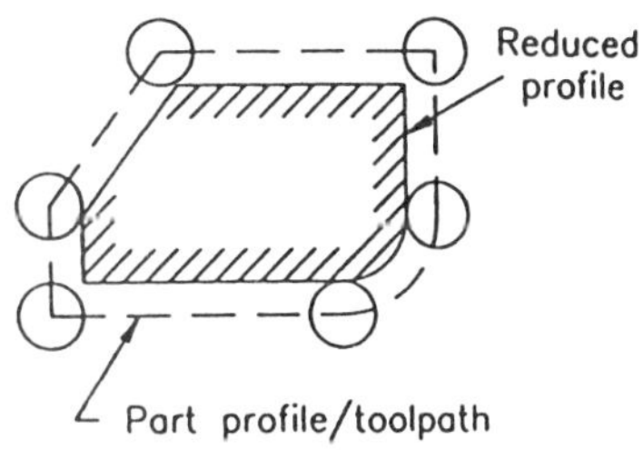
Off	On (Right or Left)	None	Actual tool diameter must be the same as designated diameter, otherwise a positional error will be encountered. The positional error is equal to one-half of the difference between the designated diameter and actual diameter.	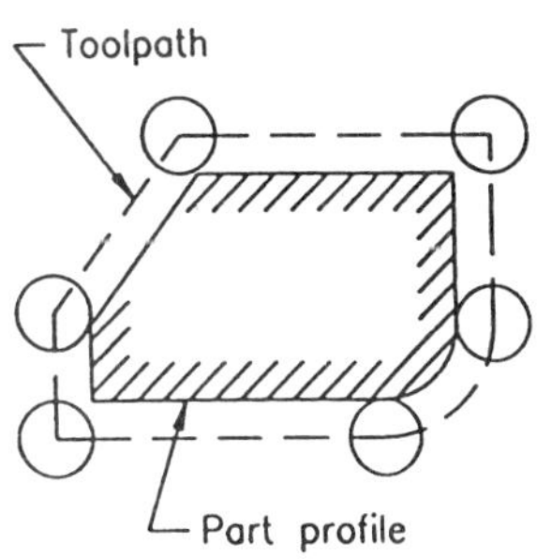
On (Right or Left)	Off	G41 Dxx or G42 Dxx	The actual cutter diameter must be input to the specified register (Dxx) to produce an accurate part profile.	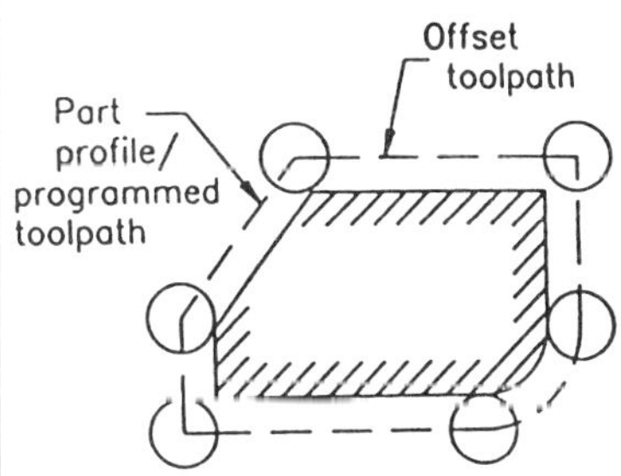
On (Right or Left)	On (Right or Left)	G41 Dxx or G42 Dxx	The difference between the actual and designated tool diameter should be input to the selected register.	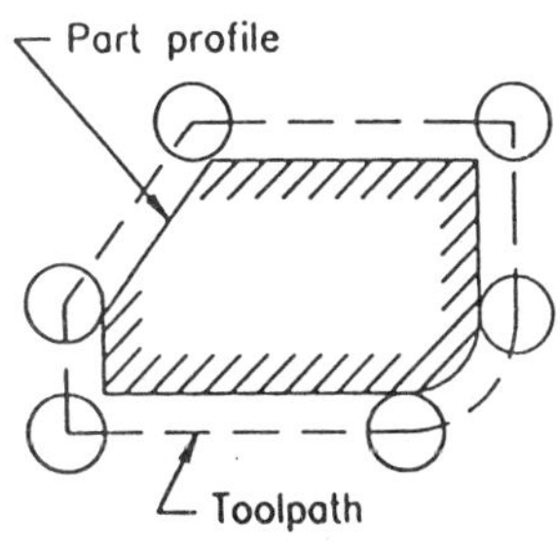

⌛Tip Set both compensation in computer and compensation in control to On (Right or Left). This allows the tool to be offset to the proper locations by the compensation in computer, and also permits the variation between the actual and designated cutter diameter to be compensated by using the compensation in control. The compensation value given in the register should be zero when no diameter variation exists, otherwise, the compensation value is the difference between the two diameters.

Tip Compensation This parameter allows you to select cutter compensation to the cutter's center or tip. Figure 7.37 shows the definition of cutter center and tip for three common cutter types: flat end, ball end (spherical), and bull nose. Figure 7.38 illustrates the effect of selection of cutter center and tip on 3D toolpaths.

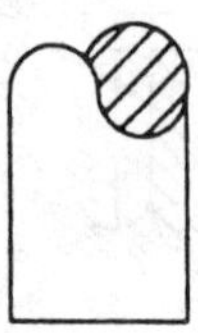

Figure 7.37a Flat end

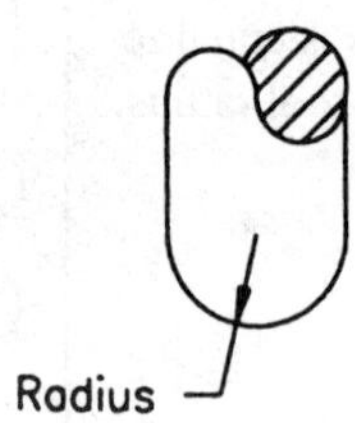

Figure 7.37b Ball end

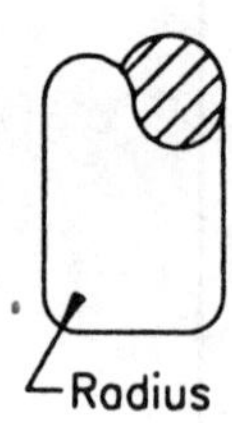

Figure 7.37c Bull nose

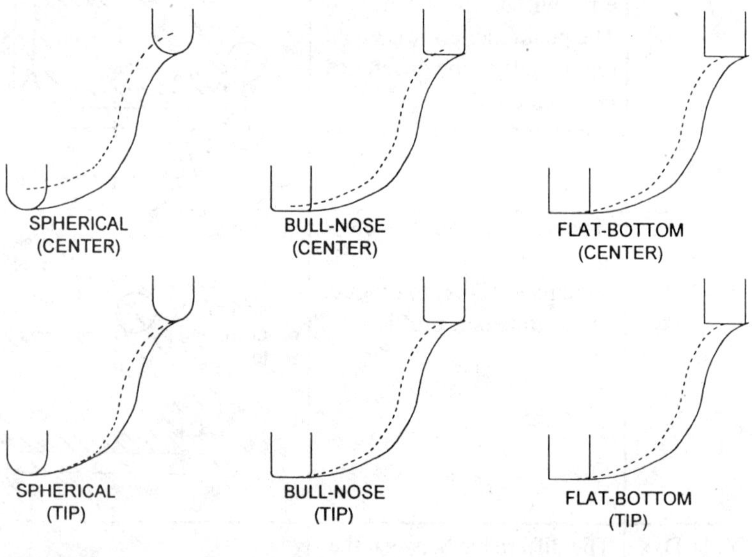

Figure 7.38 The effect of selecting the cutter center and tip on 3D toolpaths.

Roll Cutter Around Corners This parameter determines the toolpath at the corners which are formed by two joined lines. An arc move may be inserted around the corners depending on which mode is selected. The parameter can be toggled to (1) sharp corners (Sharp), (2) no corners (None), and (3) all corners (All). A sharp corner is defined as an included angle which is less than 180 (in the material side (Figure 7.39). Table 7.4 gives typical toolpaths around corners for the three modes.

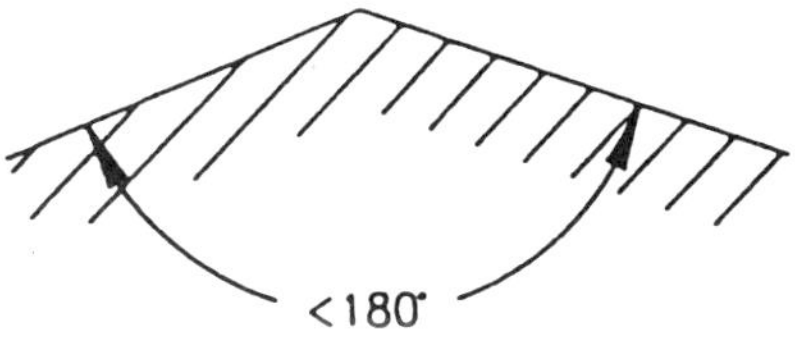

Figure 7.39a Sharp corner

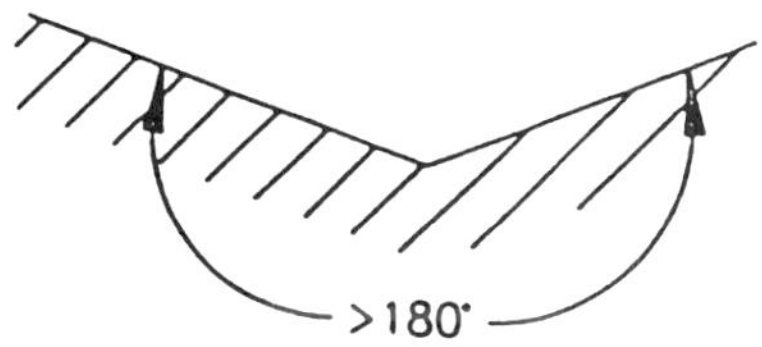

Figure 7.39b Not a sharp corner

Table 7.4 Toolpath around corners

Mode	Toolpath
Sharp corners	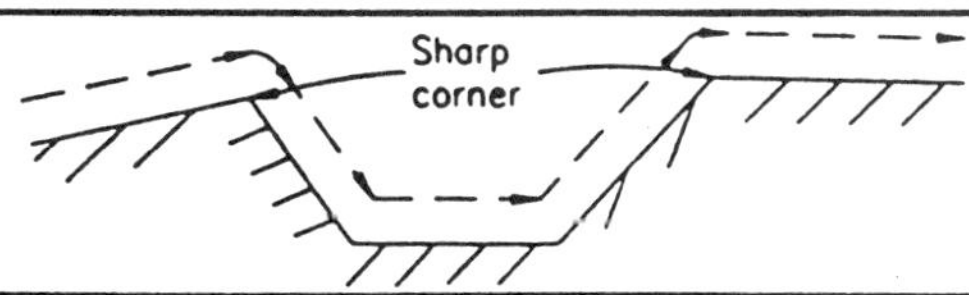
All corners	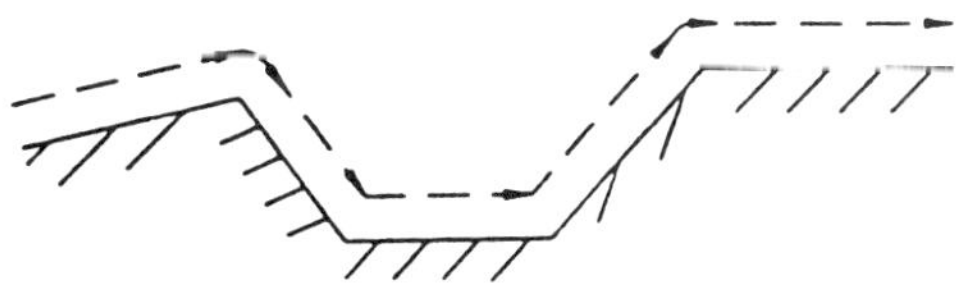
No corner	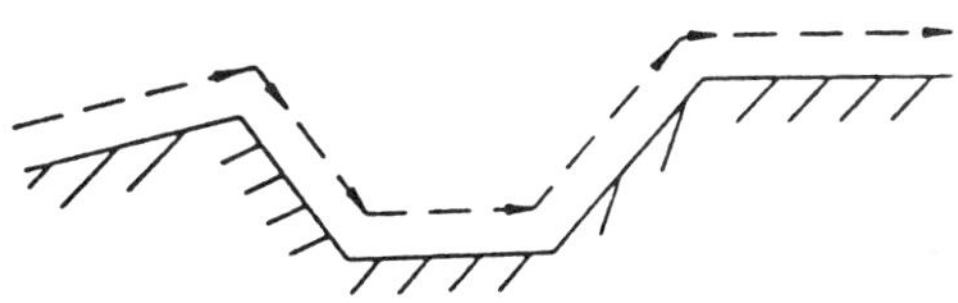

Lead in/out Mastercam allows adding a line move and/or an arc move to the beginning and/or the end of the toolpaths to smoothly engage the tool with the workpiece (Figure 7.40). The move added to the beginning of the toolpath is referred to as the lead in (or entry) move. The move added to the end of the toolpaths is called lead out (or exit) move.

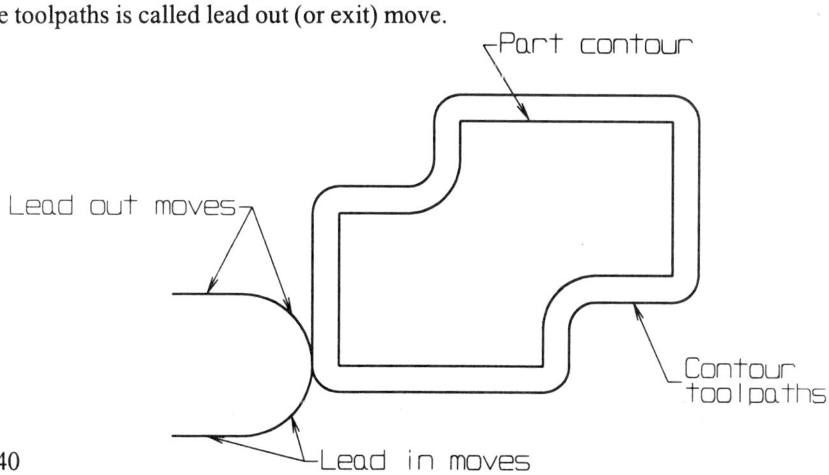

Figure 7.40

The Lead In/Out dialog box is shown below.

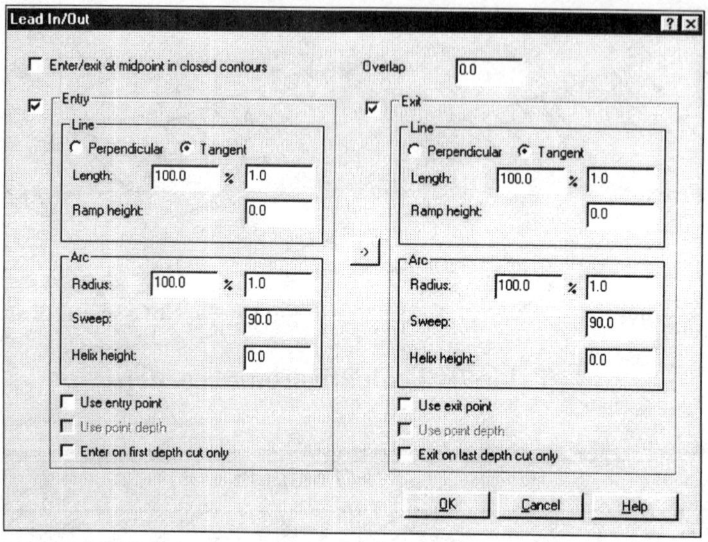

Entry/Exit line A line move can be added in two modes; perpendicular and tangent (Figure 7.41). The perpendicular mode adds the line that has its orientation perpendicular to the adjacent toolpath segment, while the tangent mode adds the line that is tangent to the adjacent toolpath segment.

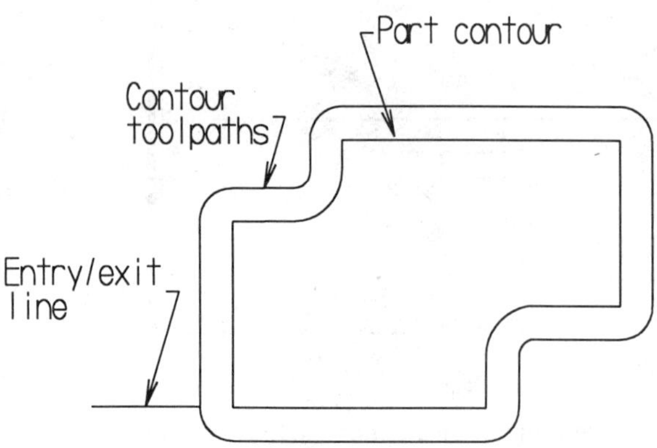

Figure 7.41a Perpendicular mode

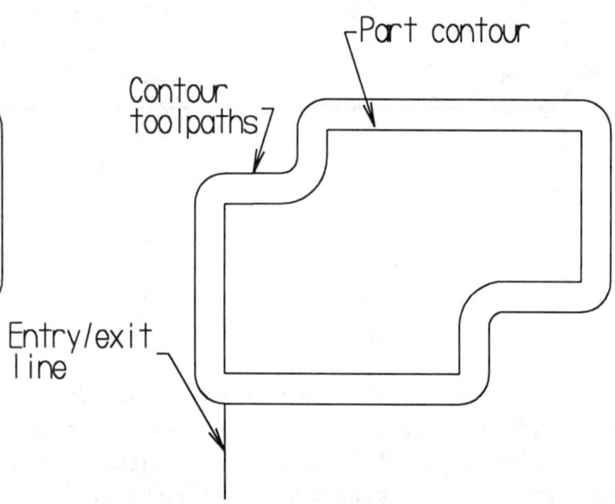

Figure 7.41b Tangent mode

The parameter "Ramp height" specifies Z-depth for the entry move to plunge from the start of the line move to end of the move (Figure 7.42), or the Z-depth for the exit move to retract from the start of the line move to end of the move.

Entry/Exit arc An arc move added to the entry and/or exit of toolpaths are defined by the following three parameters (Figure 7.43):

Radius:	specify the radius value of the entry or exit arc.
Sweep:	specify the angle of the entry or exit arc.
Helix height:	specify the Z-depth change of helix spline (added arc).

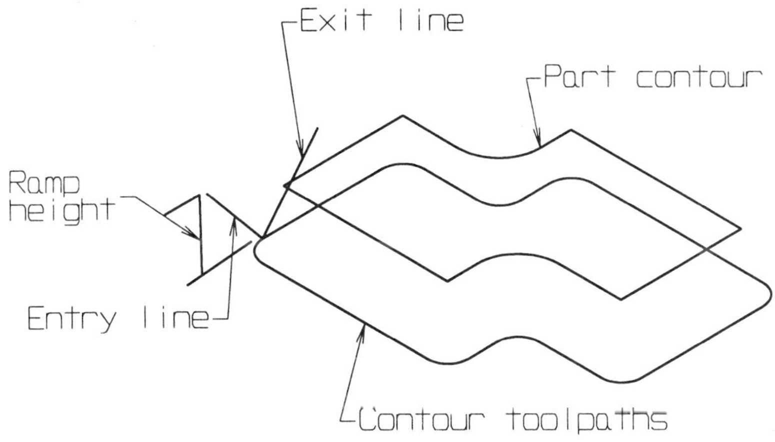

Figure 7.42

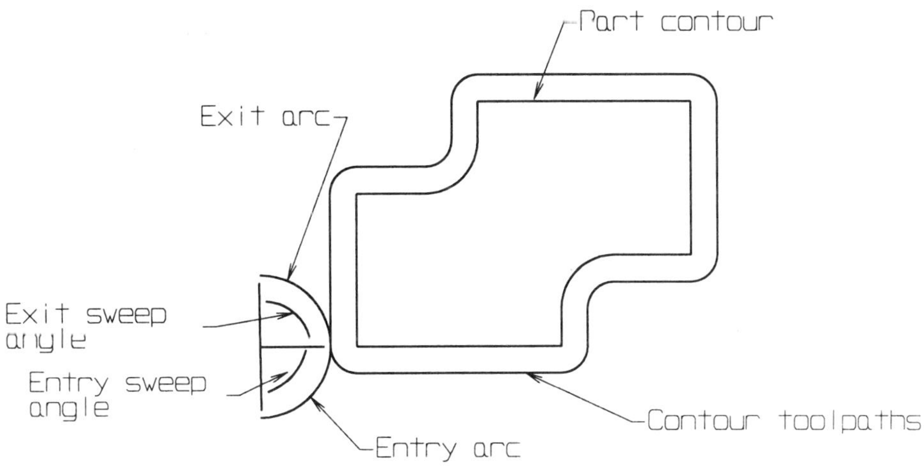

Figure 7.43

Figure 7.44 shows the effect of helix height on the entry/exit arc moves.

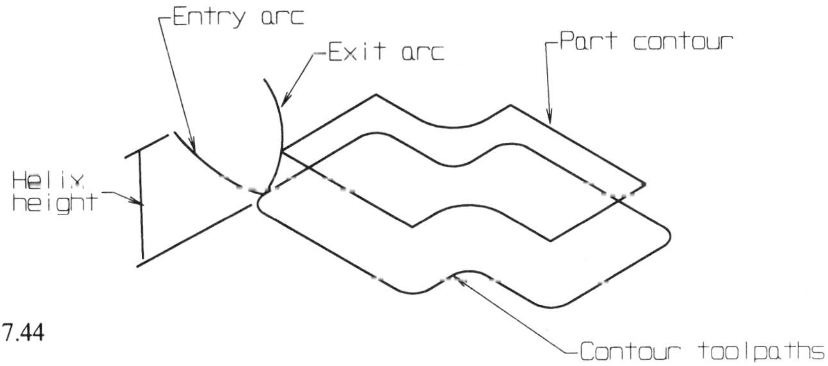

Figure 7.44

The remaining parameters in Lead In/Out dialog box are briefly described below:

Enter/exit at midpoint in closed contours:	add entry/exit at the midpoint of closed contour.
Use entry point:	specify the entry point.
Use point depth:	use the depth of selected point.
Enter on first depth cut only:	add entry moves only to the first depth cut.
Exit on last depth cut only:	add exit moves only to the last depth cut.

Project 1. Contouring external profile

Use the contour module to generate toolpaths to cut an external profile shown in Figure 7.45. The total depth of cut is 1-in. The raw material is the casted workpiece which is about ¼-in. larger than the finished dimensions in all directions.

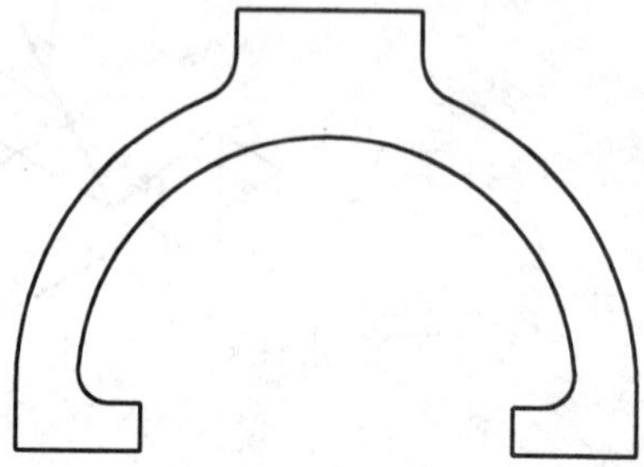

Figure 7.45a

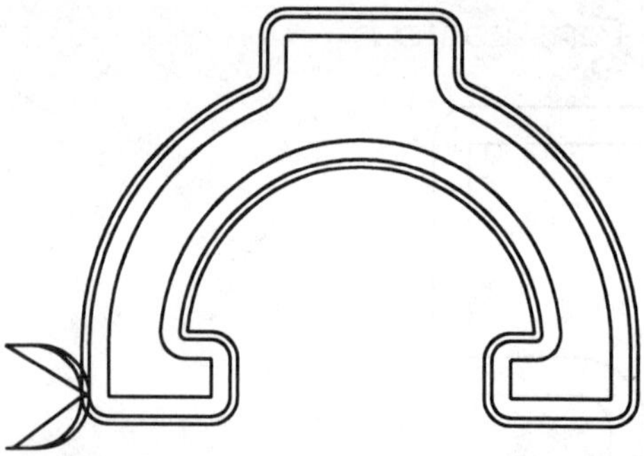

Figure 7.45b

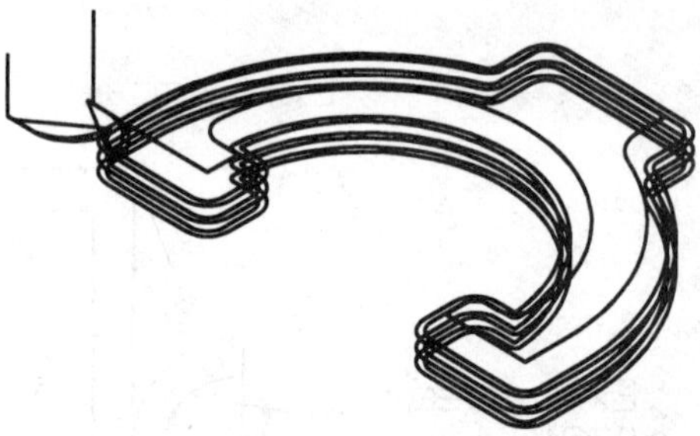

Figure 7.45c

Tips 1. Use a ¾" end mill.

2. Use one roughing cut and one finish cut for the machining taking place in the XY-plane. The stock for the finish pass is 0.1-in.

3. Use three passes (two roughing cuts and one finish pass) in the depth cut (Z) direction. The two roughing cuts take 0.35" each and the finish pass takes 0.3".

4. Set the entry/exit length to 0.5", the entry/exit arc has a radius of 1" and an angle of 90°.

5. Set cutter compensation in control to off and cutter compensation in computer to left center.

Step 1. Load the geometry file contour1.mc8.

(or create the geometric model by following the procedure given in project 1 of chapter 5.)
Select **MAIN MENU → File → Get**
File name: **contour1**

1

The drawing should appear as Figure 7.46.

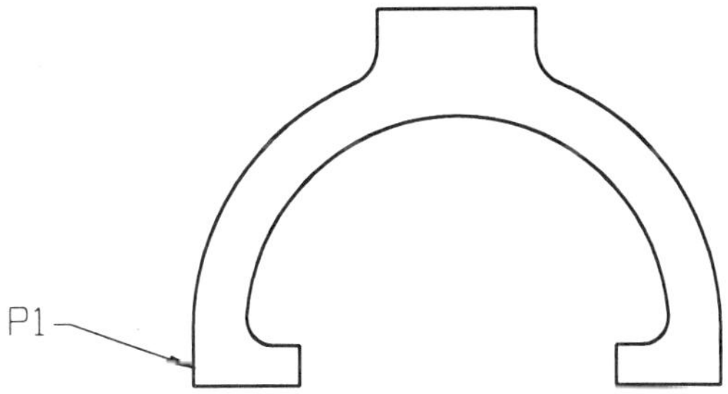

Figure 7.46

Step 2. Set both the construction plane and graphics view to Top.

Select **Cplane** → **Top**
Select **Gview** → **Top**

Step 3. Initiate the contour module.

Select **MAIN MENU** → **Toolpaths** → **Contour**

Step 4. Define the contour using the pick point in Figure 7.46.

Select **Chain** from the chaining method menu
Pick **P1** to select the first entity of the contour
Select **Done**

Step 5. Select a tool from the tool library.

The Contour Properties dialog box should appear as below.

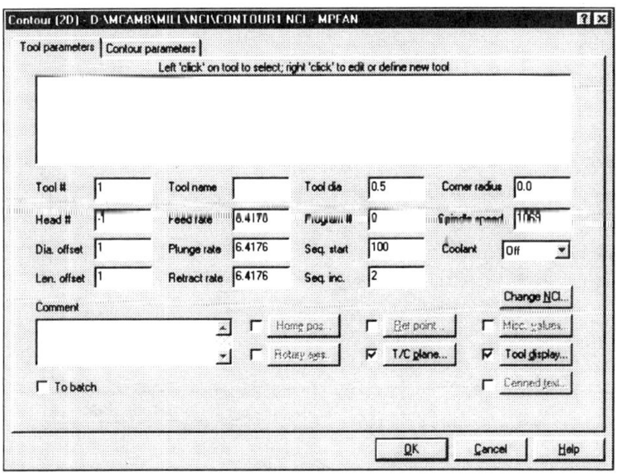

Place the mouse on the larger blank space within the dialog box, then click the right mouse button to open the selection menu as below.

Select **Get tool from library**
The Tool Manager menu appears as below.

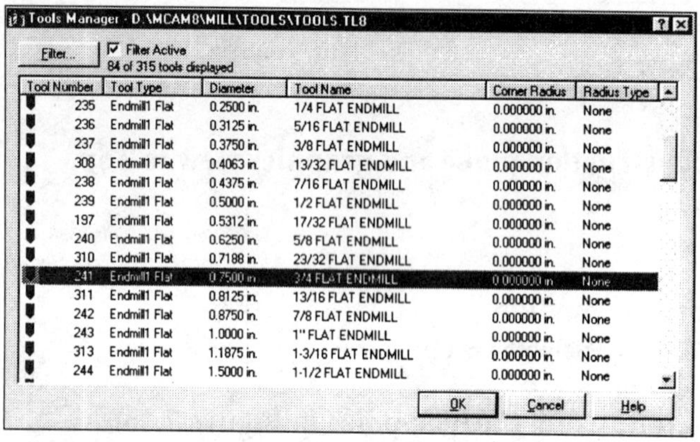

Select **3/4" end mill** from the list
Select **OK**
The 0.75" end mill has been added to the Contour Properties menu as shown below.

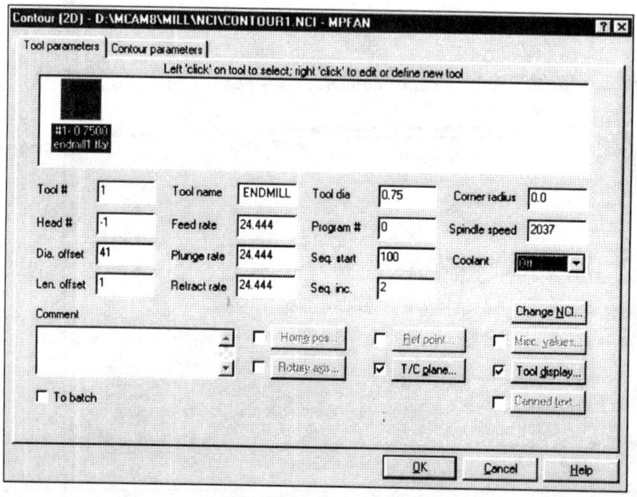

Step 6. Define tool and toolholder parameters.

Place the mouse on the tool icon (#1-0.7500 endmill flat), then click the right mouse button to open the Define tool dialog box.
Set their parameters as shown next.

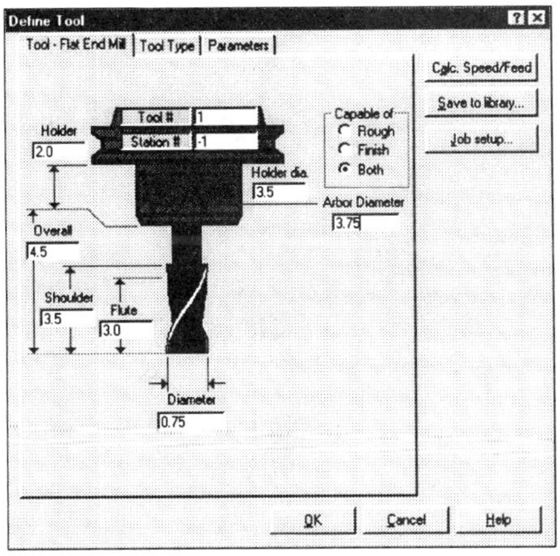

Select the Parameters button to set the tool parameters as shown below.

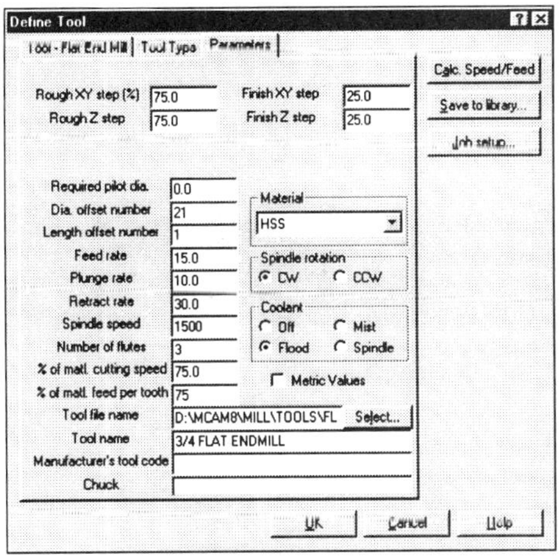

Select **OK**
Set the tool parameters as below.

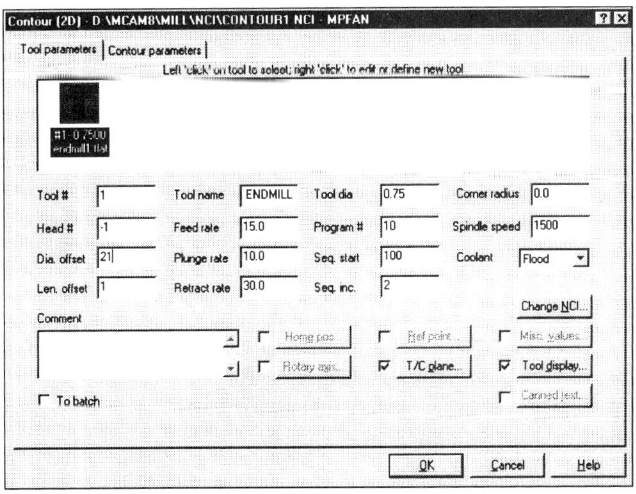

Step 7. Define the Contour parameters.

Select the **Contour parameters button**

Set the NC parameters as below.

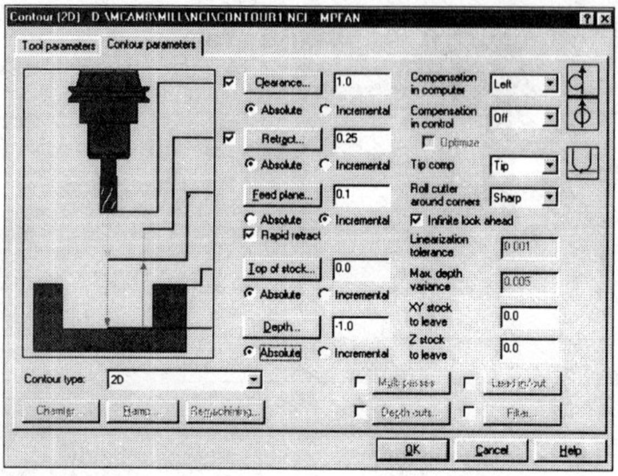

Step 8. Define the depth cuts parameters.

Click the check box of Depth Cuts, then click the **Depth Cuts** button to open its dialog box

Set depth cuts parameters as here.

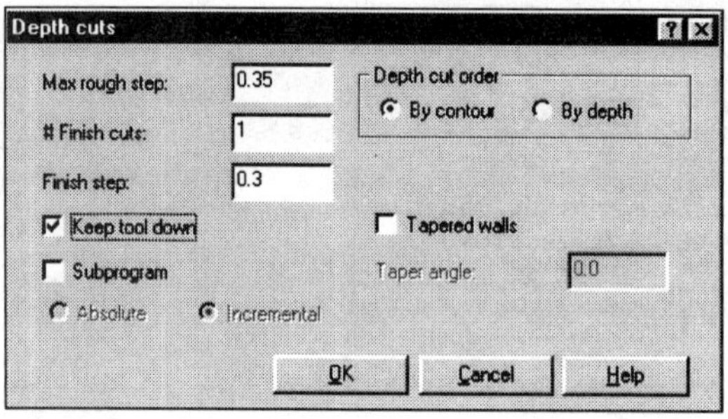

Select **OK**

Step 9. Define the multiple-passes parameters.

Click the check box of Multi passes, then click the **Multi passes** button to open its dialog box

Set the multiple passes parameters as here.

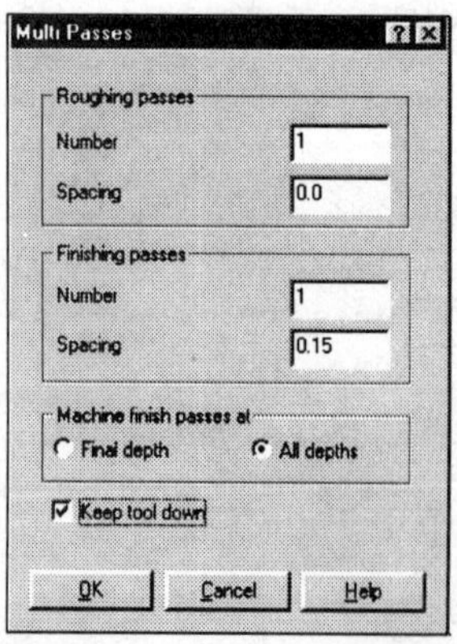

Select **OK**

Step 10. Define the lead in/out parameters.

Click the Lead in/out check box, then click **Lead in/out** button to open its dialog box
Set lead in/out parameters as below.

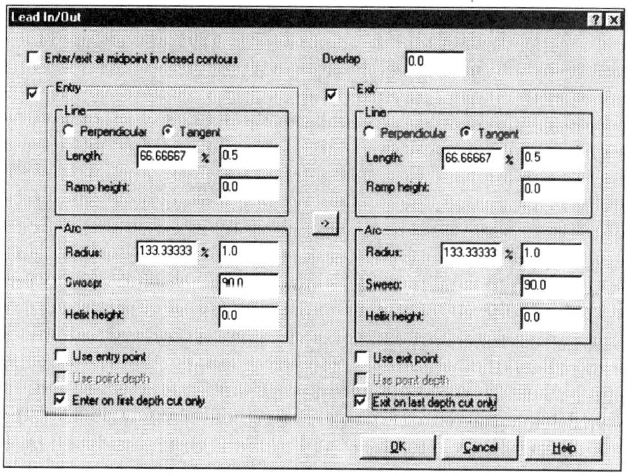

Select **OK** to return to tool parameters menu
Select **OK** to generate toolpaths
The toolpaths should appear as in Figure 7.47.

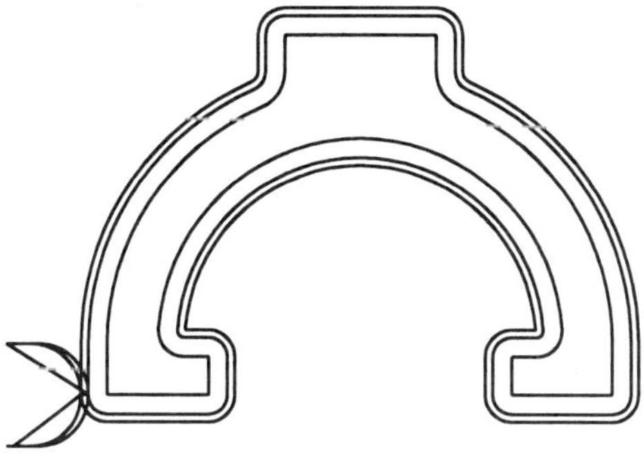

Figure 7.47

Step 11. Change Gview to Isometric

Select **Gview → Isometric**
The toolpath shown in isometric view appears as Figure 7.48.

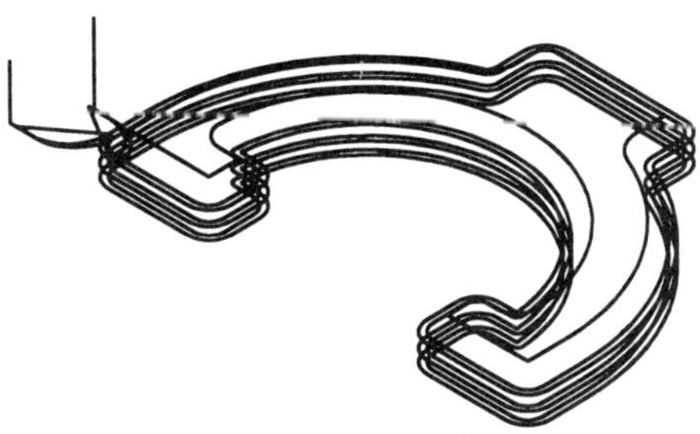

Figure 7.48

Step 12. Run the post processor.

Select **Operations**

The Operations Manager menu appears below.

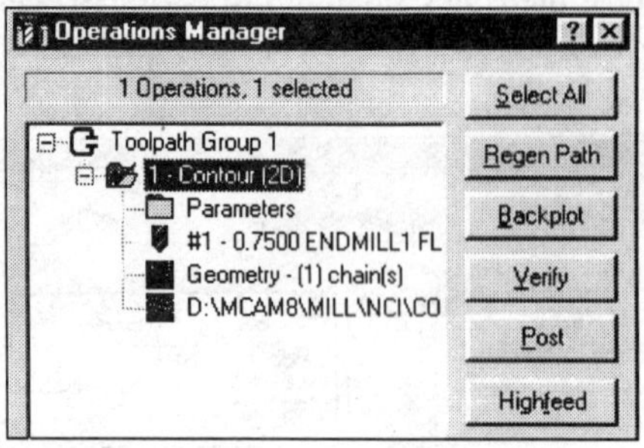

Select **Post**
Select **Save NC file → OK**
File name for NC: **Contour1.NC**
Select **Save → OK**

Step 13. View the NC file

Select **MAIN MENU → File → Edit → NC**
File name for NC:**Contour1.NC**
Select **Open**

The partial program is listed below. (Your program may look somewhat different from the one listed here because your version may be using a different post processor).

```
%
O0010
(PROGRAM NAME - CONTOUR1)
(DATE=DD-MM-YY - 21-06-00 TIME=HH:MM - 17:41)
N100G20
N102G0G17G40G49G80G90
(3/4 FLAT ENDMILL TOOL - 1 DIA. OFF. - 21 LEN. - 1 DIA. - .75)
N104T1M6
N106G0G90G54X-7.025Y-
2.A0.S1500M3
N108G43H1Z1.M8
N110Z.1
N112G1Z-.35F10.
N114X-6.525F15.
N116G3X-5.525Y-1.R1.
N118G1Y0.
   -
   -
   -
N442G1X3.4911
N444G3X3.6161Y.25R.125
N446X3.6157Y.2589R.125
N448X0.Y3.625R3.625
N450X-3.6157Y.2589R3.625
N452X-3.6161Y.25R.125
```

continued in next column

```
N454X-3.4911Y.125R.125
N456G1X-3.
N458G2X-2.625Y-.25R.375
N460G1Y-1.
N462G2X-3.Y-1.375R.375
N464G1X-5.
N466G2X-5.375Y-1.R.375
N468G3X-6.375Y0.R1.
N470G1X-6.875
N472G0Z1.
N474M5
N476G91G28Z0.M9
N478G28X0.Y0.A0.
N480M30
%
```

Step 14. Exit file edit mode.

Click the **File list** button at the upper left corner
Select **Close** to return to the Operations Manager mode

Step 15. Backplot the toolpaths.

Click the **Backplot** button in the Operations Manager dialog box
Select **Display**
Set the display parameters as below.

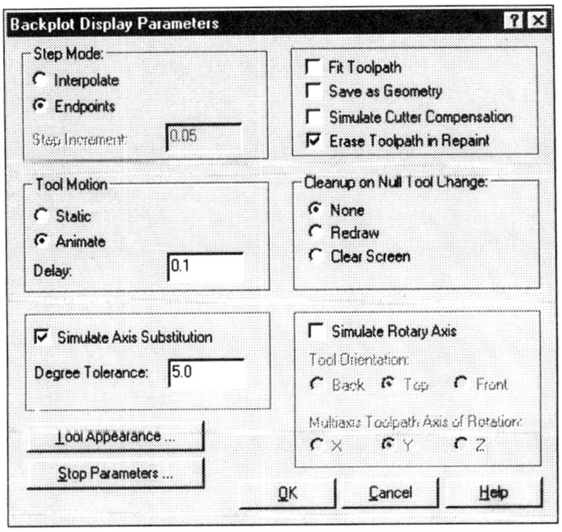

Select **OK**
Set backplot parameters as here.
Select **Run** to animate the toolpath on the screen as shown in Figure 7.49.

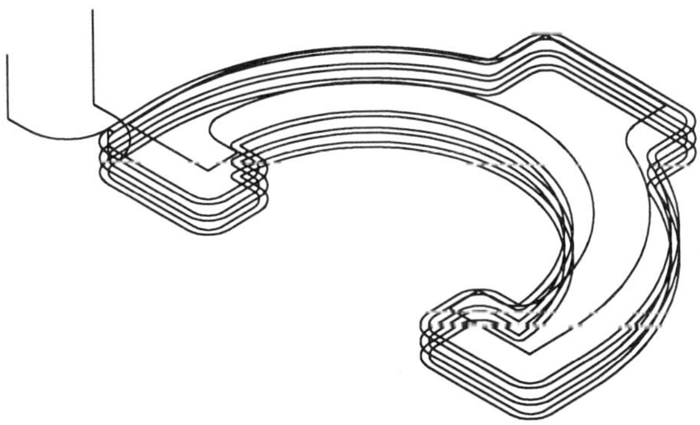

Figure 7.49

Select **MAIN MENU** to return to Operations Manager menu
Select **OK** to return back to graphic mode

Step 16. Save the project file.

Select **MAIN MENU → File → Save**
File name: **contour1t**

💻 Project 2. Contouring internal profile

Use the contour module to generate toolpaths to take the cutter along the internal profile of the part shown in Figure 7.50. The workpiece has been casted to its rough size. Therefore, it requires only one finish pass to cut to the desired profile. The depth of cut in the Z direction is 0.5-in.

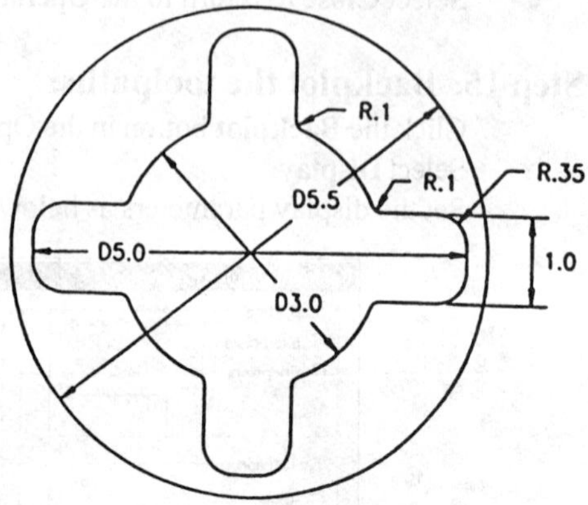

Figure 7.50a

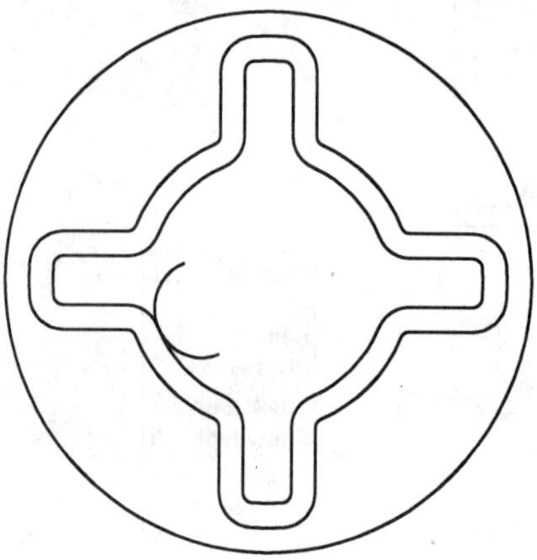

Figure 7.50b

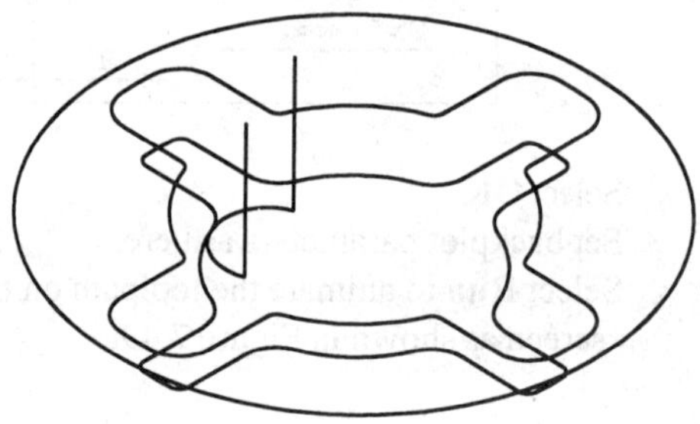

Figure 7.50c

⌛**Tips** 1. Use a ½" end mill.

2. Define the contour direction to be in the counterclockwise direction to obtain climb milling for a better surface finish.
3. Set entry/exit length to 0 and arc radius to 0.5 and angle to 90(.

4. Set cutter compensation in control to left and cutter compensation in computer to left center.

5. Set rapid depth to 0.3 and contour depth to –0.5.

Step 1. Load the geometry file contour2.mc8.

(or create the geometry by following the procedure given in project 3 of chapter 6.)
Select **MAIN MENU → File → Get**
Enter file name: **contour2**

The drawing should appear as Figure 7.51.

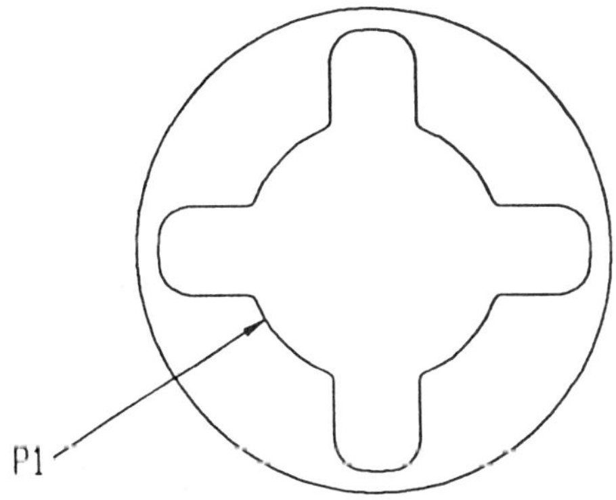

Figure 7.51

Step 2. Set both Cplane and Gview to Top view if necessary.

Select **Cplane → Top**
Select **Gview → Top**

Step 3. Initiate the contour module.

Select **MAIN MENU → Toolpaths → Contour**

Step 4. Define the Contour using the pick point in Figure 7.51.

Select **Chain**
Pick **P1** to select the starting entity of the contour
Select **Done**

Step 5. Select ½" end mill from tool library and set tool parameters.

The Contour Properties dialog box should appear on screen.
Click the right mouse button, then select **Get tool from library**
Select **tool number 239** (1/2 flat end mill)
Select **OK**
Set the tool parameters as below.

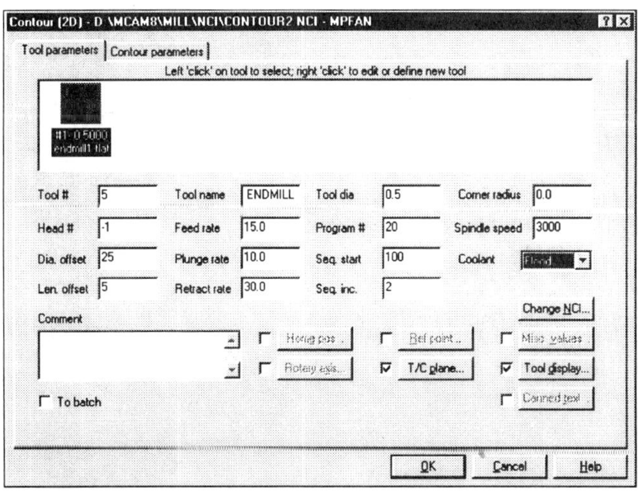

Step 6. Define the contour parameters.

Click the Contour parameters button

Set the contour parameters as below.

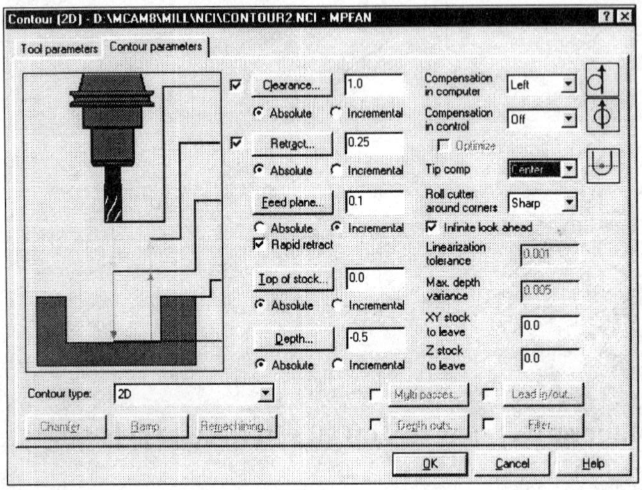

Step 7. Define lead in/out parameters.

Toggle the check box of Lead in/out to on, then click **Lead in/out** button

Set the lead in/out parameters as below.

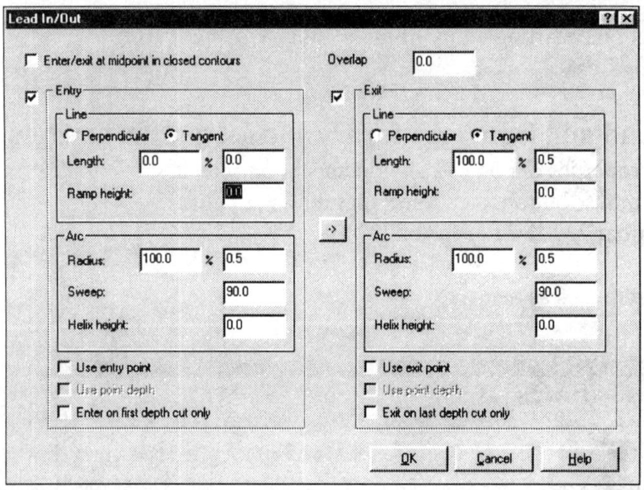

Select **OK** to return to contour parameters menu

Select **OK** to generate toolpaths

The toolpaths should appear as Figure 7.52.

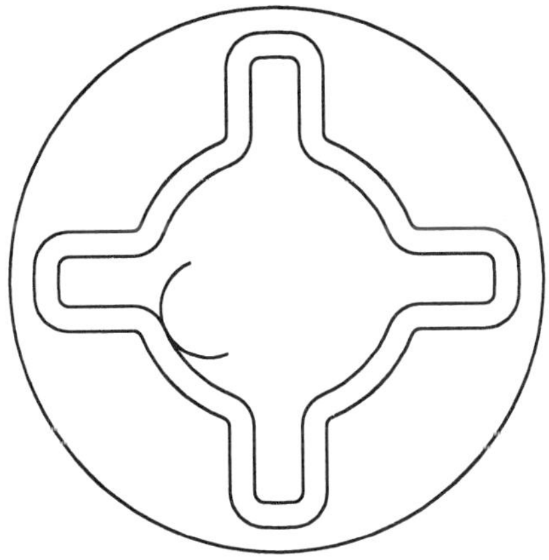

Figure 7.52

Step 8. Show the toolpaths in isometric view.

Select **Gview → Isometric**
The toolpaths shown in isometric view appear as in Figure 7.53.

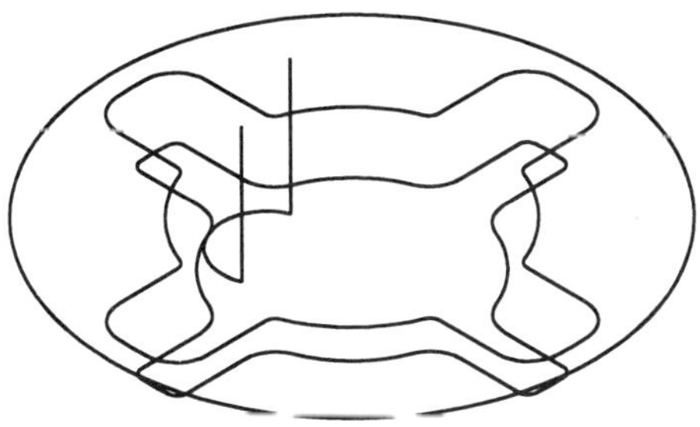

Figure 7.53

Step 9. Run the post processor.

Select **Operations** to open Operations Manager dialog box
Select **Post**
Select **Save NC file → OK**
File name for NC program: **contour2**
Select **Save**
Select **OK** to exit Operations Manager dialog box

Step 10. Edit the part program file.

Select **MAIN MENU → File → Edit → NC**
File name: **contour2** ↵

The NC Editor with the part program should appear as below.

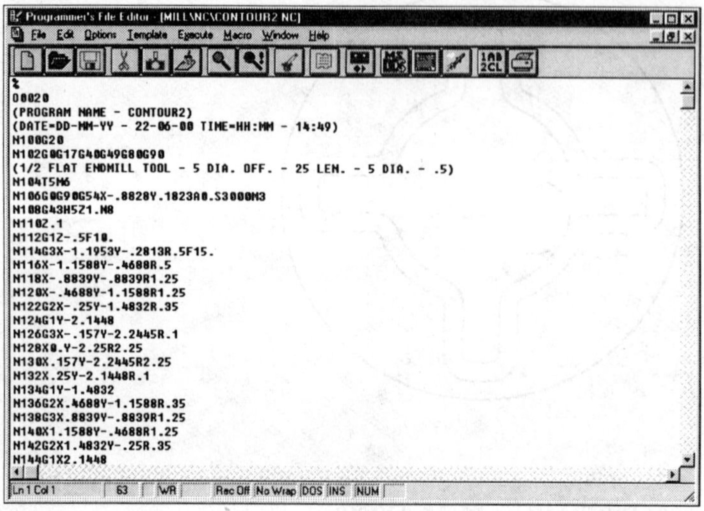

Do all necessary editing and save the file as **Contour2t**

Step 11. Exit the NC Editor.

Select **File → Exit**

Project 3. Contouring along an open profile

This project uses the contour module to generate toolpaths for cutting an open profile. Multiple passes are used along the profile to ensure the two angle corners are removed. Figure 7.54 shows geometry and toolpaths.

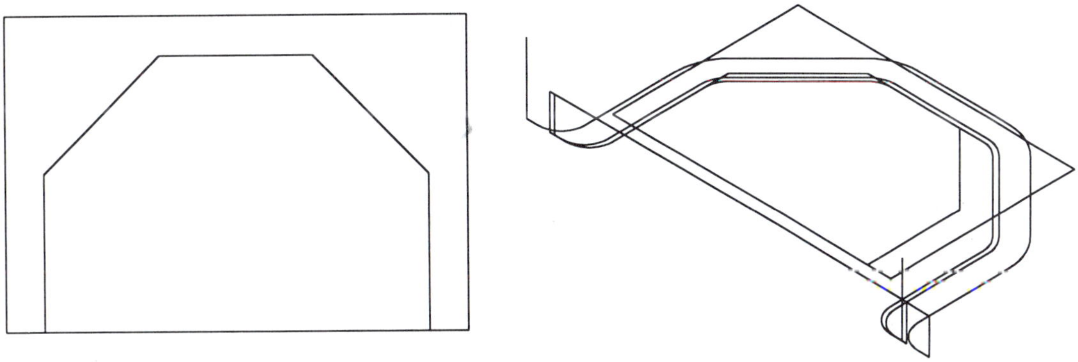

Figure 7.54

> **Tips** 1. Use the geometry file contour3.
>
> 2. Use thc contour module to generate toolpaths.

Step 1. Open the part geometry file contour3.mc7.

Select **MAIN MENU → File → Get**
Enter file name: **contour3** ↵
The part geometry appears as in Figure 7.55.

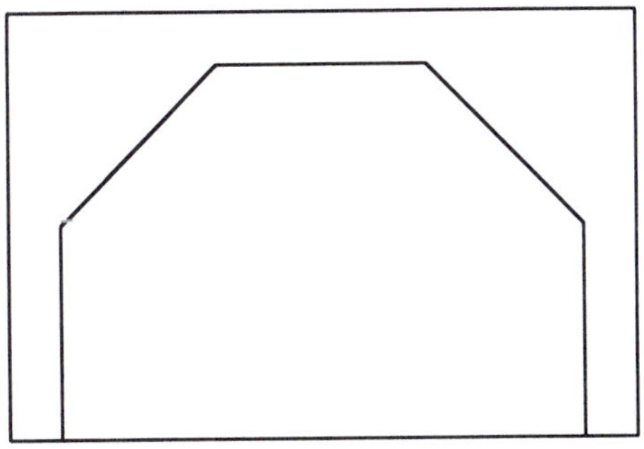

Figure 7.55

Stcp 2. Set Gview to isometric and Cplane to top.

Select **Gview → Isometric**
The isometric view of the part geometry appears as in Figure 7.56.

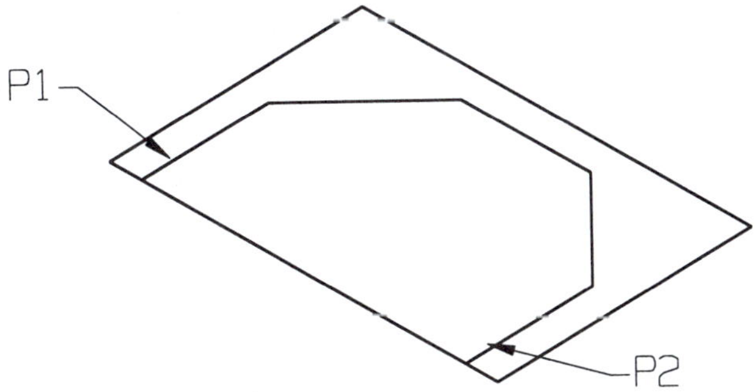

Figure 7.56

Step 3. Initiate the contour module using the pick point in Figure 7.56.

Select **MAIN MENU → Toolpaths → Contour**
Select **Chain → Partial**
Pick **P1** and **P2** to select in the contour
Select **Done**

Step 4. Define the tool parameters.

Click the right mouse button, then select **Get tool from library**
Select **tool #243** (1-in. end mill) **→ OK**
Set the tool parameters as below.

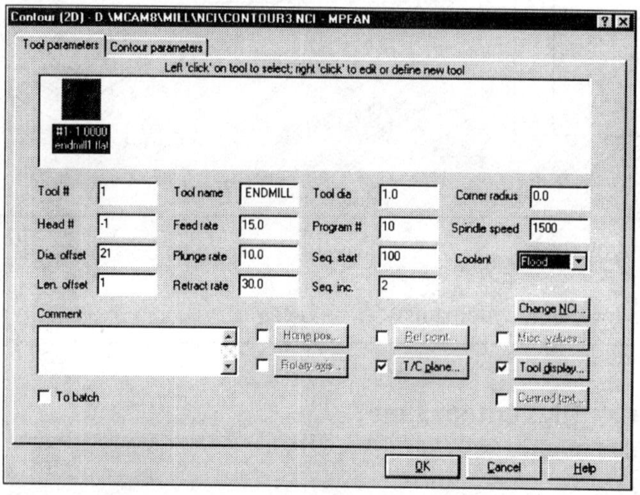

Step 5. Define the contour parameters.

Click the "**Contour parameters**" button and set the contour parameters as below.

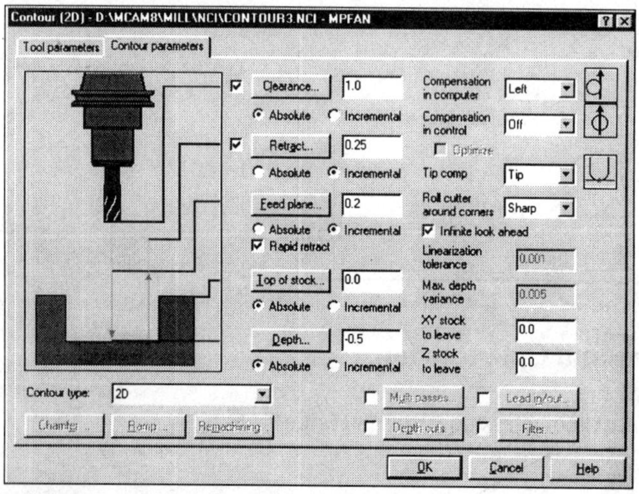

Step 6. Define the multi-pass parameters.

Click the check box of the "**Multi passes**" button
Click the **Multi passes** button
Set the multi passes parameters as here.

Select **OK** to exit Multi passes menu

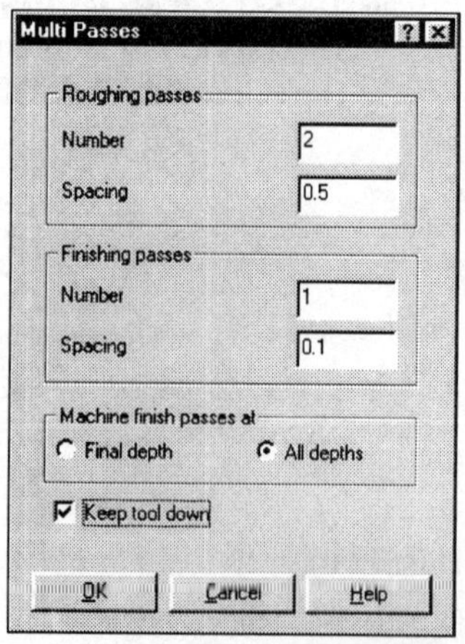

Step 7. Define lead in/out parameters.

Click the check box of the **Lead in/out** button
Click the **Lead in/out** button
Set the lead in/out parameters as below.

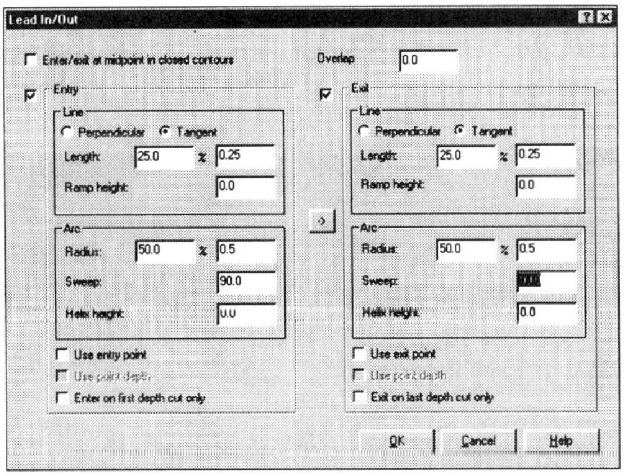

Select **OK** to exit lead in/out menu
Select **OK** to generate toolpaths as in Figure 7.57.

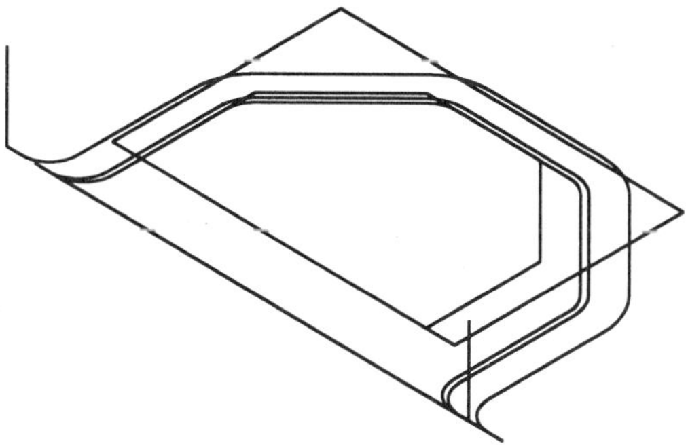

Figure 7.57

Step 8. Change to top view.

Select **Gview → Top view**
The toolpaths shown in top view appear as in Figure 7.58.

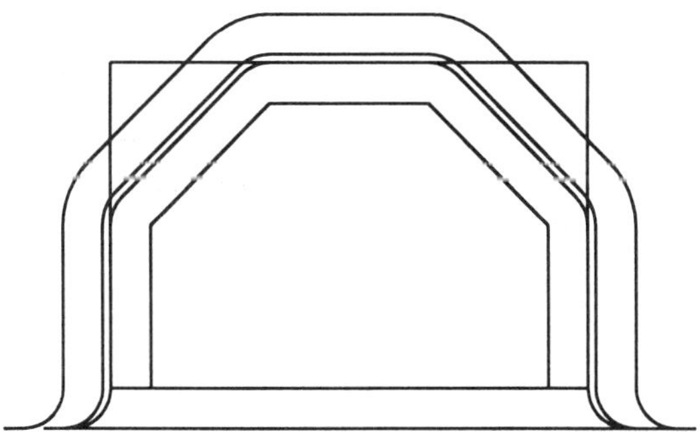

Figure 7.58

Step 9. Save the toolpaths.

Select **MAIN MENU → File → Save**
File name: **contour3t** ↵

7.10 Pocket Module

The pocket module is used to generate a set of toolpaths to (1) remove the material enclosed by a closed contour, (2) face a flat surface, and (3) rough cut a local pocket. The pocket module has two major dialog boxes used to define pocketing and machining parameters. They are entitled as pocketing parameters and roughing/finishing parameters as below.

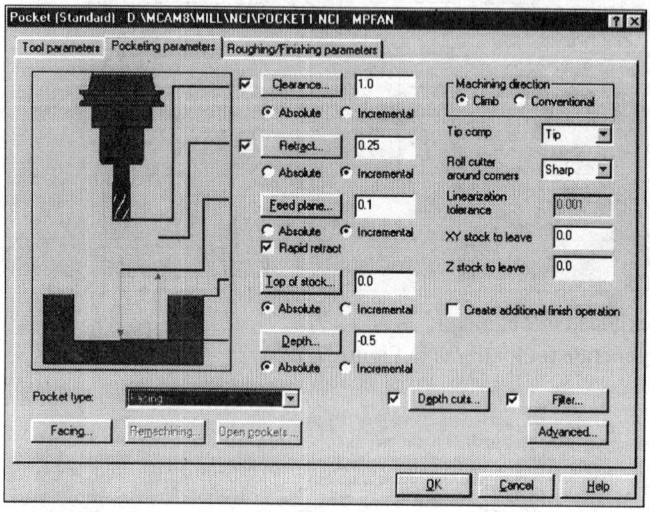

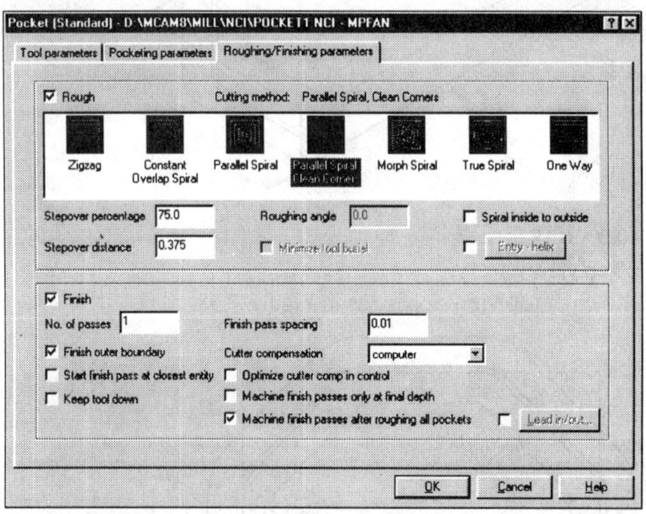

Pocketing parameters

The pocketing parameters dialog box has been shown above. It consists of the following six groups of parameters: **Z-depth parameters, Depth cuts parameters, Facing parameters, Advanced parameters, Machining direction**, and **Others**.

Z-depth parameters This group of parameters is used to define the Z-depth of pocketing toolpaths. They are identical to those used in the contour module. Here we only show their definition without detailed discussion (Figure 7.59).

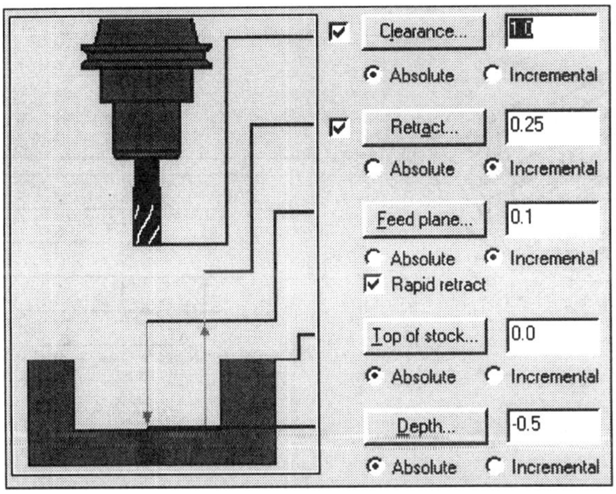

Figure 7.59

Depth cuts parameters The ten parameters in the depth cuts dialog box is shown below. These parameters are identical to those used in the contour module except for the adding "Use island depths" parameter. The "Use island depths" parameter specifies the pocketing depth to be set to the island depths. The "Tapered walls" parameter enables the generation of a set of toolpaths to cut a pocket with a tapered wall as shown in Figure 7.60 in the next page. Toggle the "Tapered walls" parameter to make its selections active.

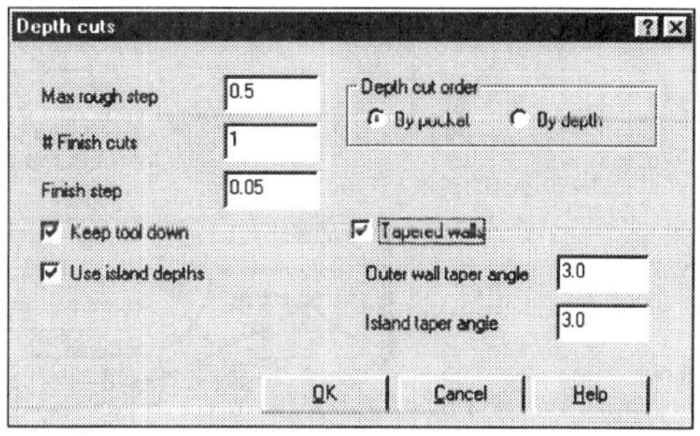

Facing parameters The four facing parameters are used to extend the pocketing toolpaths to the pocketing boundary. Figure 7.61 shows the contrast between the toolpaths using facing function and without using facing function.

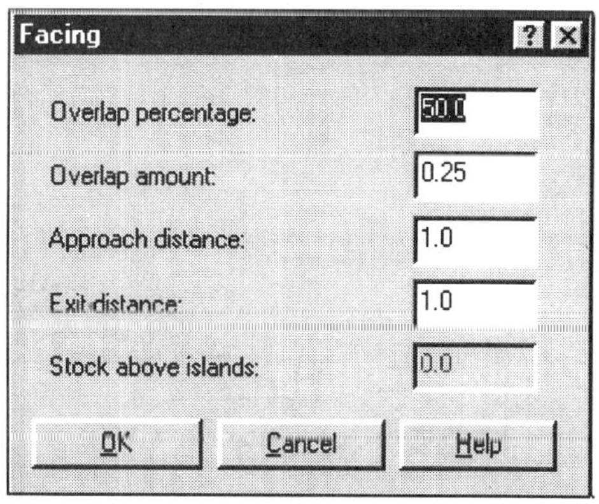

The amount of extending toolpaths over the pocket boundary is specified by using either one of these two parameters:

Overlap percentage:	the overlap amount is specified by the percentage of cutter diameter.
Overlap amount:	the overlap amount is directly specified by the value given in this parameter.

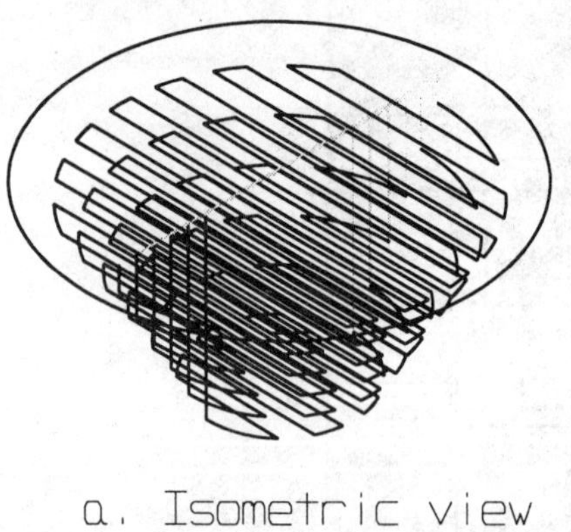

Figure 7.60a Isometric

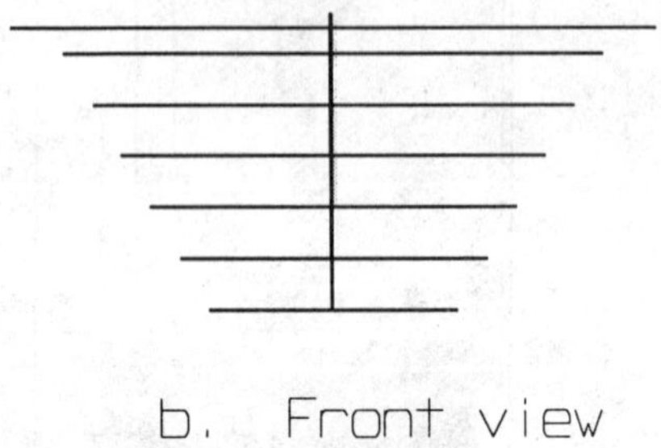

Figure 7.60b Front view

Figure 7.61 shows the result of using different overlap value on the pocketing toolpaths.

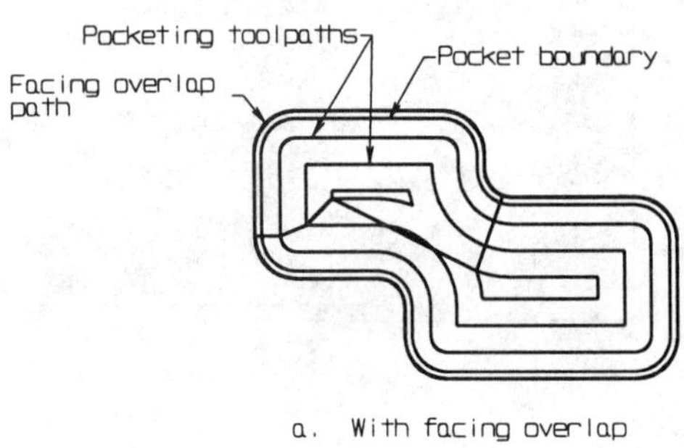

Figure 7.61a With facing overlap

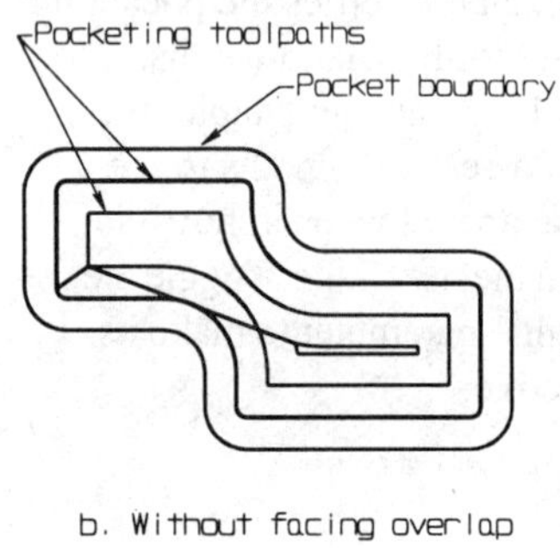

Figure 7.60b Without facing overlap

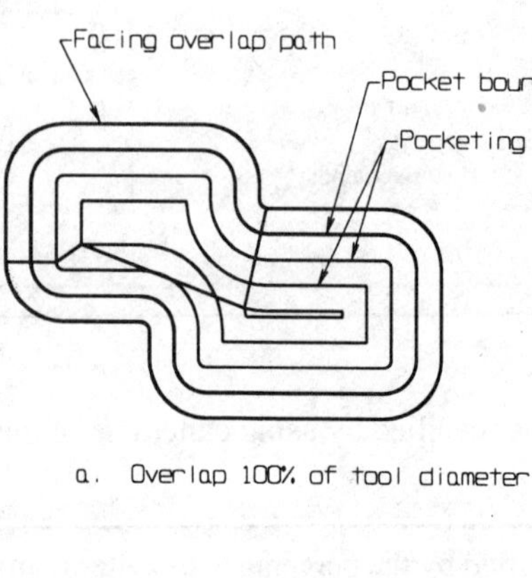

Figure 7.62a Overlap 100% of tool diameter

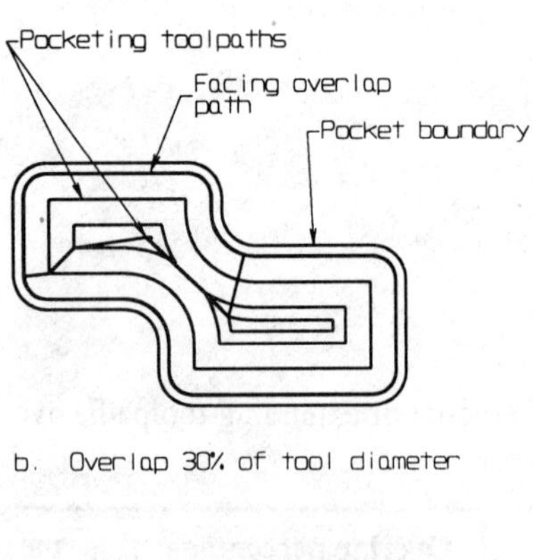

Figure 7.62bOverlap 30% of tool diameter

Machining direction This parameter specifies the milling type to be implemented in pocketing. It has the following two options:

Climb:	generate the pocketing toolpaths following the climb milling direction.
Conventional:	generate the pocketing toolpaths following the conventional milling direction.

In climb milling, the direction of feed is the same as the direction of tool rotation (Figure 7.63). In conventional milling, the direction of feed is opposed to the direction of cutter rotation (Figure 7.64).

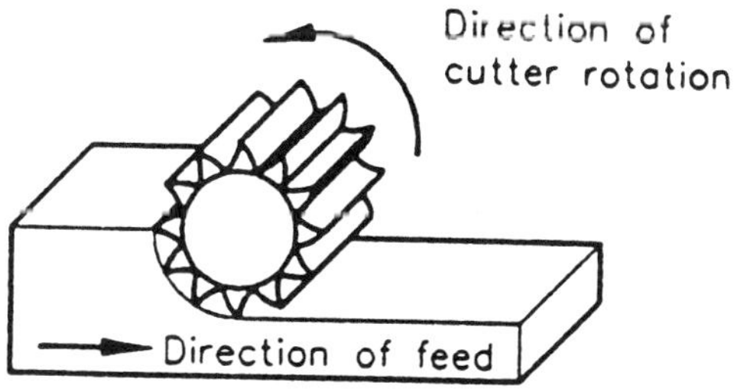

Figure 7.63a Climb milling plain milling cutter

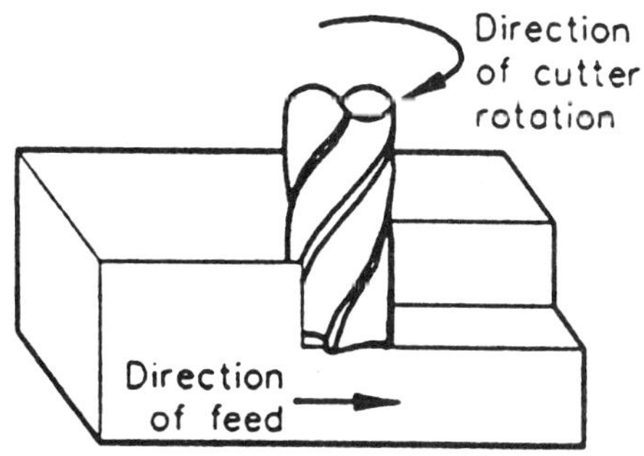

Figure 7.63b Climb milling with end mill

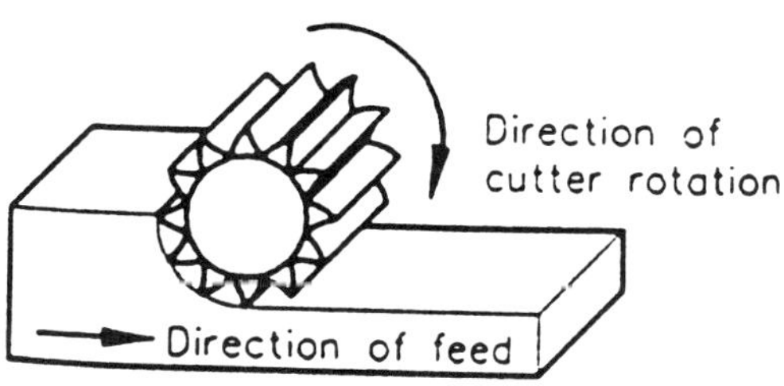

Figure 7.64a Conventional milling plain milling cutter

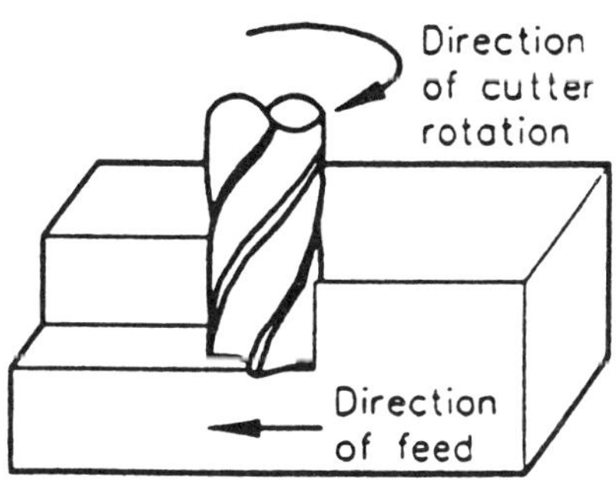

Figure 7.64b With end mill

Advanced parameters The advanced parameters are used to specify the tolerance for remachining and constant overlap spiral. Its dialog box is shown below.

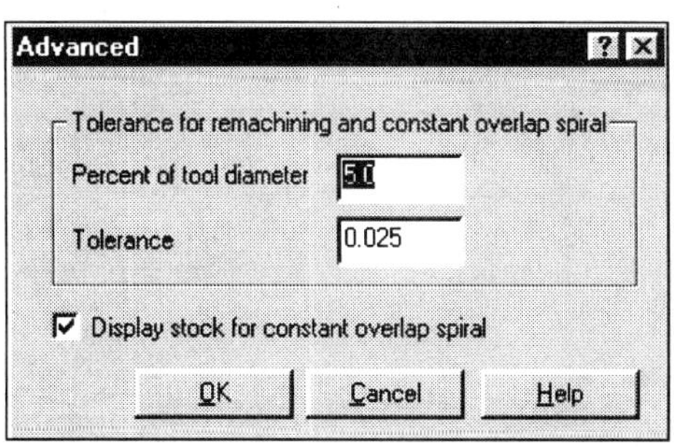

Other parameters The remaining pocketing parameters are listed below:

Tip comp: specify the tool compensation either to Tip or Center.
Roll cutter around corners: specify the roll corners type (sharp, all, or none)
Linearization tolerance: specify the tolerance value for linearization of curves.
XY stock to leave: specify the XYstock amount to be left for further machining.
Z stock to leave: specify the Z stock amount to be left forturther machining.

Roughing/Finishing parameters

The roughing/finishing parameters dialog box appears as below.

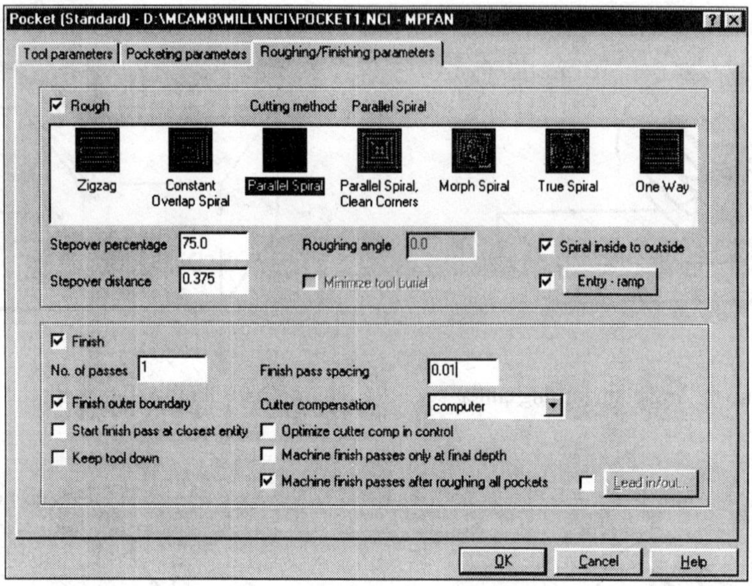

Cutting method Mastercam provides seven cutting methods for pocketing: zigzag, constant overlap spiral, constant overlap spiral, parallel spiral, parallel spiral/clean corners, morph spiral, true spiral, and one way. These seven cutting methods can be grouped under two categories: zigzag and spiral. The zigzag group has two options; zigzag and one way. The spiral group has the remaining five options.

Zigzag method This method generates a set of back and forth linear toolpaths to rough the pocket (Figure 7.65). The orientation of the toolpath is specified by the roughing angle parameter. The roughing angle also decides the start point of the pocketing toolpaths.

The cutting angle is measured from the positive X-axis and has a positive angle in the counter-clockwise direction and a negative angle in the clockwise direction (Figure 7.66).

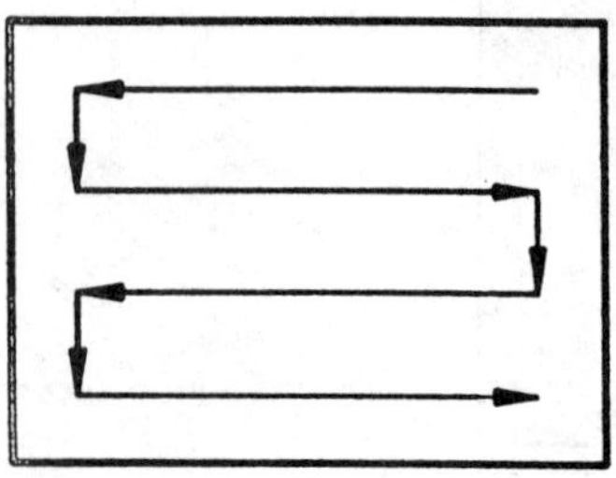

Figure 7.65

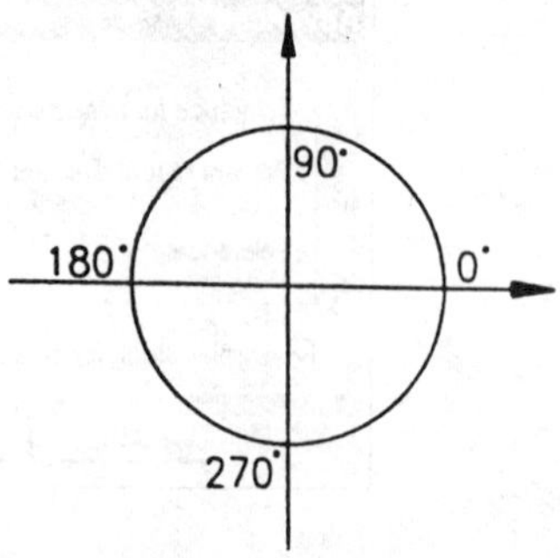

Figure 7.66

Figure 7.67 shows a number of common roughing angles and their toolpaths starting points.

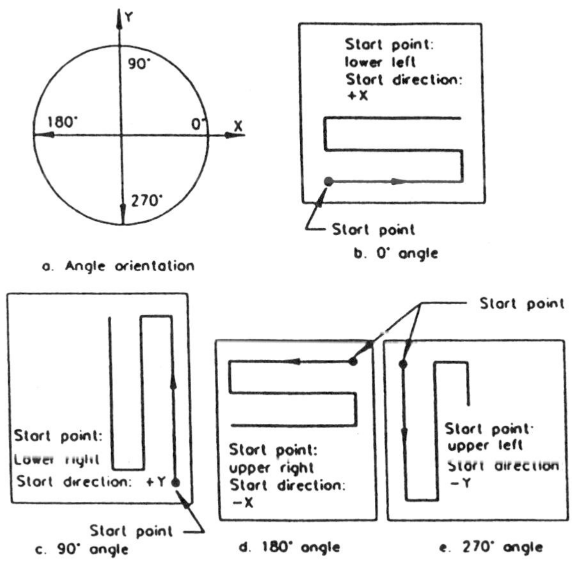

Figure 7.67

The "One Way" cutting method generates a similar set of toolpaths as the zigzag method. The difference is that one way method generates toolpaths that cut in the same direction. They make a pass, then retract in the Z direction, rapid to another starting point, and take another pass in the specified direction. The toolpath pattern is repeated until the pocket cutting is completed (Figure 7.68). The direction of the cutting paths is determined whether the climb milling or conventional milling is specified.

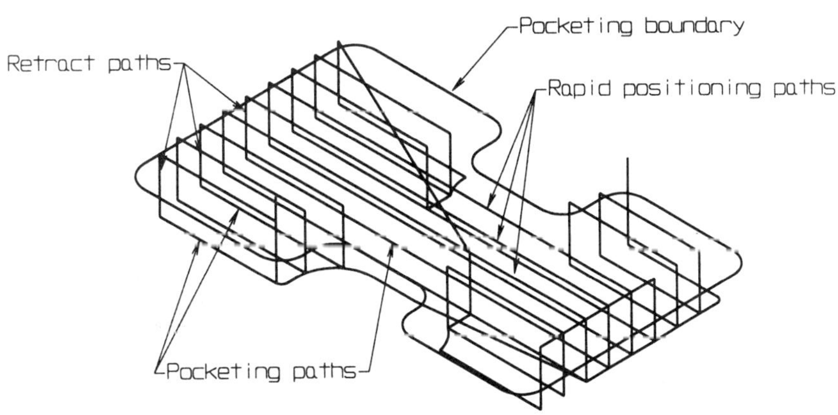

Figure 7.68

Spiral method The spiral method starts the cutter at the pocket center or specified pocket start point and spiral it to the wall of the pocket. It has the following five modes:

Constant overlap spiral:	generate pocketing toolpaths in spiral pattern with constant overlap (Figure 7.69).
Parallel spiral:	generate pocketing toolpaths in parallel-spiral pattern (Figure 7.70).
Parallel spiral, clean corners:	generate pocketing toolpaths in parallel-spiral pattern with clean corners (Figure 7.71).
Morph spiral:	generate pocketing toolpaths in morph-spiral pattern (Figure 7.72). This mode requires at least one island. It generates much more toolpath segments than other modes.
True spiral:	generate pocketing toolpaths in circular-spiral pattern (Figure 7.73).

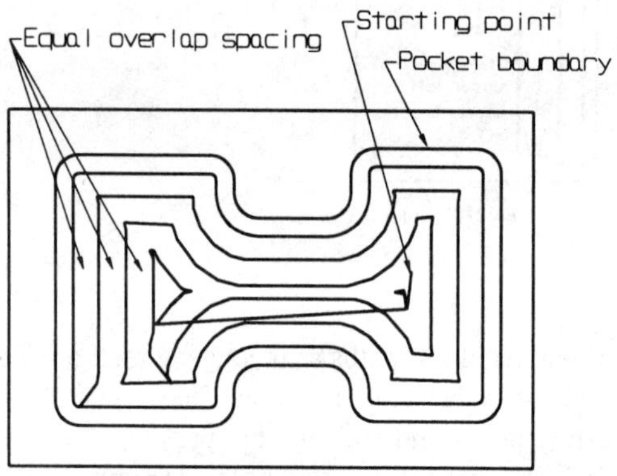

Figure 7.69

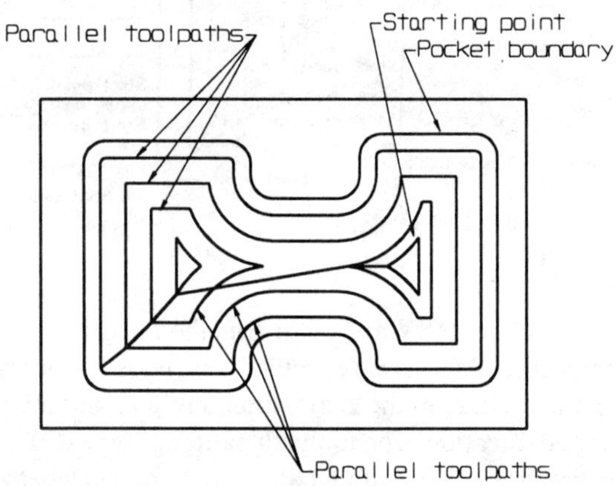

Figure 7.70

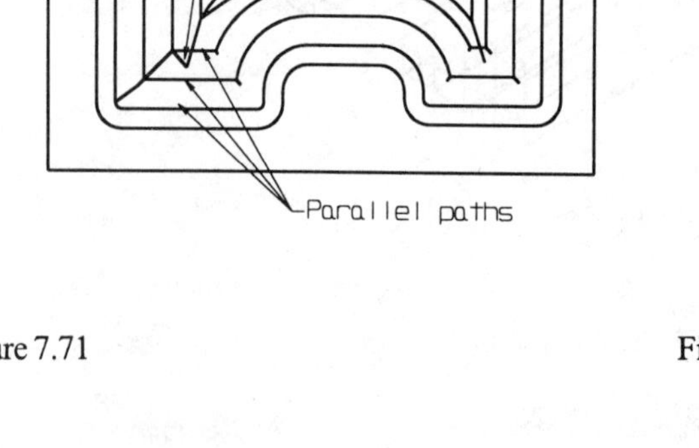

Figure 7.71

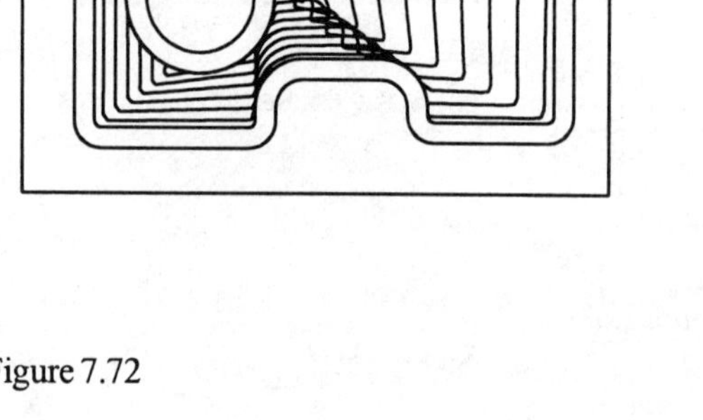

Figure 7.72

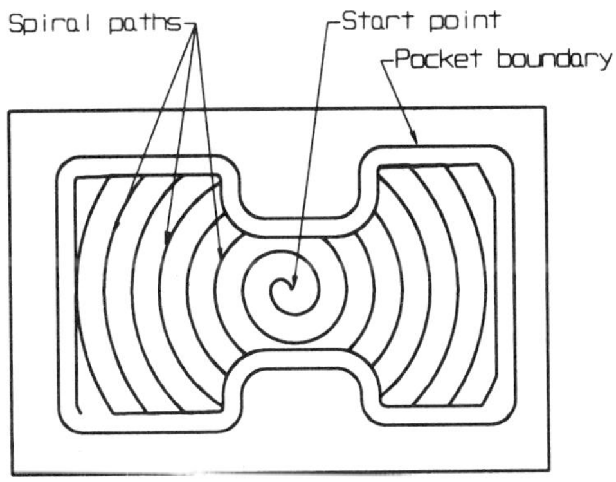

Figure 7.73

Each spiral pocketing mode has two ways to determine where to start pocketing; spiral out and spiral-in. Mastercam uses the "Spiral inside to outside" parameter to indicate which method to use. The spiral-out method starts the cutter at the pocket center or specified pocket start point and spirals it to the wall of the pocket (Figure 7.74). The spiral-in method spirals the cutter from the outside wall of the pocket to the pocket center (Figure 7.75).

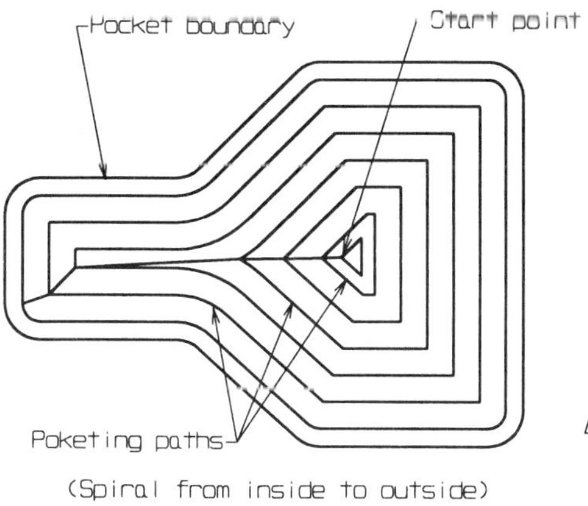

Figure 7.74

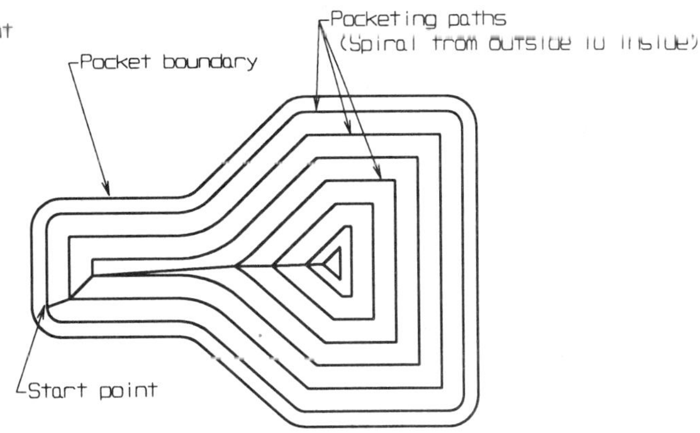

Figure 7.75

Stepover The stepover value is the distance between two adjacent pocketing paths. This value can be determined by the following two parameters:

Stepover percentage:	specify the stepover distance in the percentage of cutter diameter.
Stepover distance:	specify the stepover distance by a constant value.

The system will automatically adjust the value in the other parameter when a value is given to one parameter.

Islands and Pocket Loops

Islands are areas inside the pocket boundary that are not intended to be machined during pocketing (Figure 7.76). The islands must be closed contours. Mastercam is capable of handling multiple profiles with multiple loops that are commonly found in workpieces. A wide variety of profile looping combinations can be formed. Some examples are shown below in Figure 7.77 through 7.82.

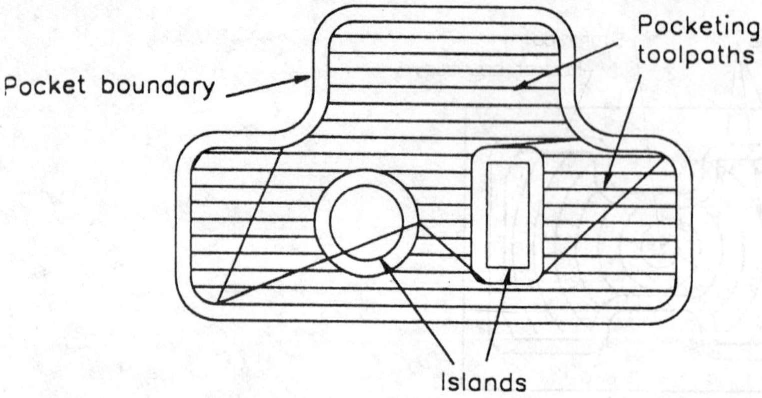

Figure 7.76

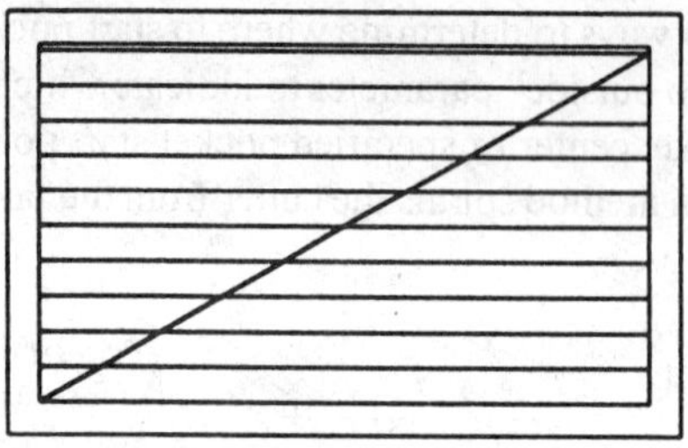

Figure 7.77

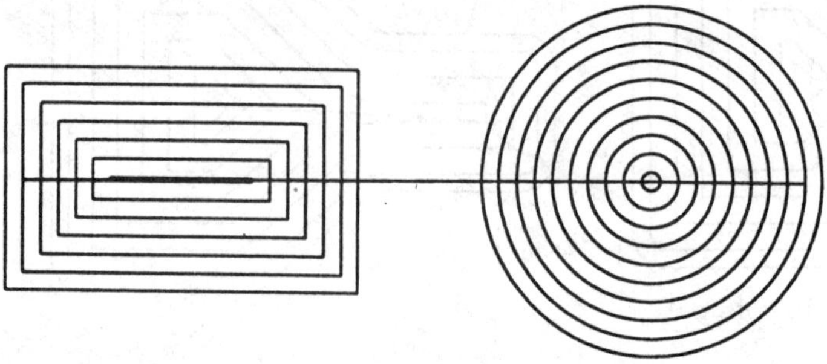

Figure 7.78

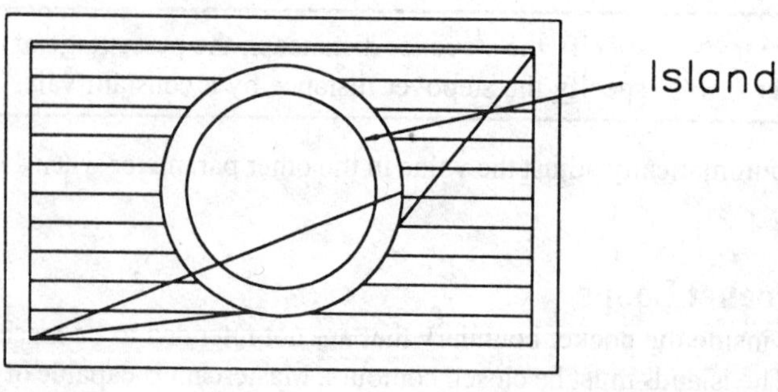

Figure 7.79

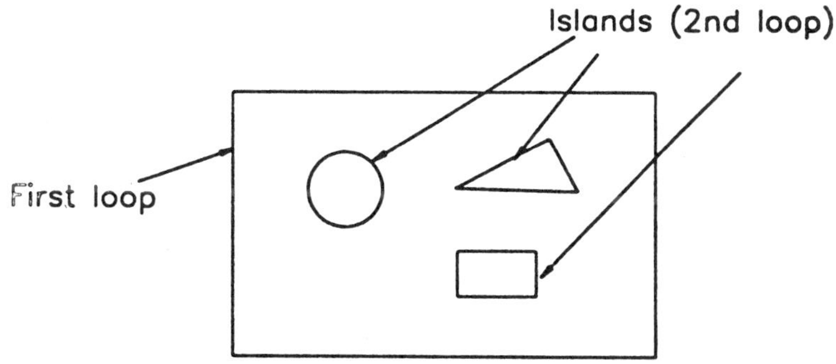

Figure 7.80

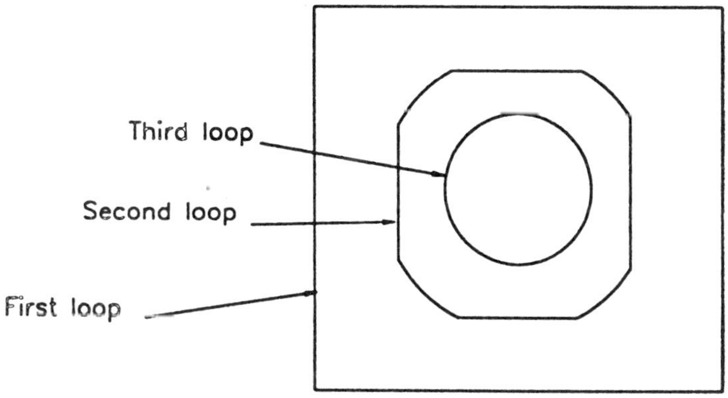

Figure 7.81

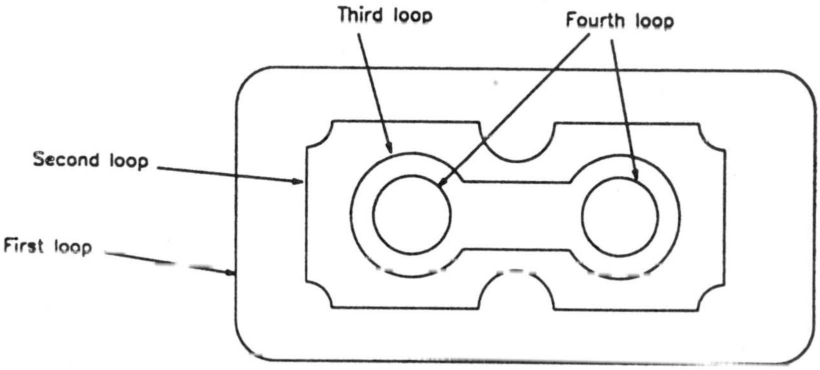

Figure 7.82

Pocketing with multiple loops can generate different sets of pocketing toolpaths depending on the pocket in which the loop is chosen. In a two-loop case, the system will prompt "click inside a pocket". If the pocket in the first loop is chosen, the pocketing is performed in the first loop, the contours in the second loop become islands (Figure 7.83). If a contour in the second loop is chosen, the pocketing is performed in all contours in the second loop (Figure 7.84).

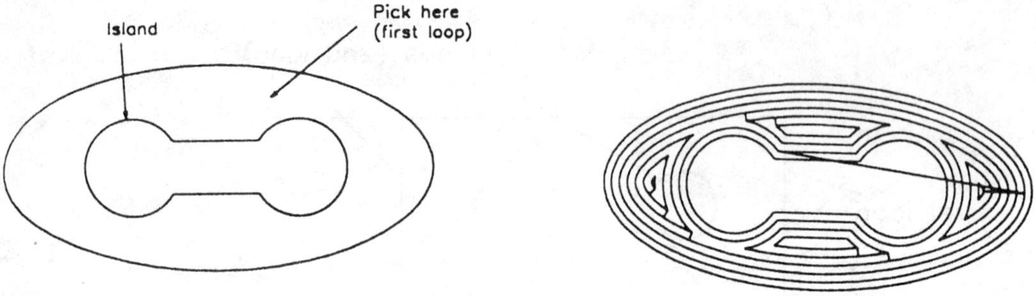

Figure 7.83

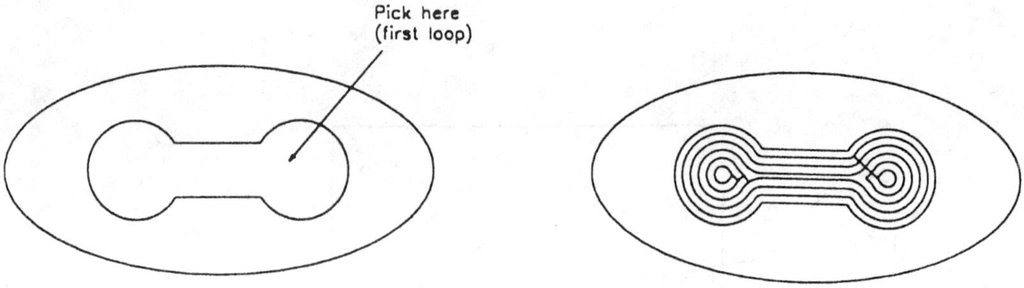

Figure 7.84

In a three-loop case, the pocketing toolpaths can be one of the three possibilities:

Click inside a pocket	**Pocketing toolpaths**
1. Selecting first loop	The pocketing is performed in the first and third loop, the second loop becomes the island (Figure 7.85).
2. Selecting second loop	The pocketing is performed in the second loop, the First and third loop become islands (Figure 7.86).
3. Selecting third loop	The pocketing is performed only in the third loop (Figure 7.87).

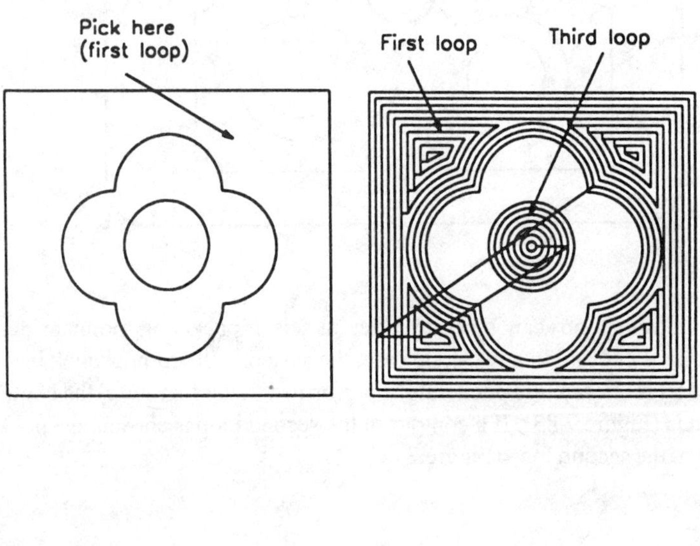

Figure 7.85

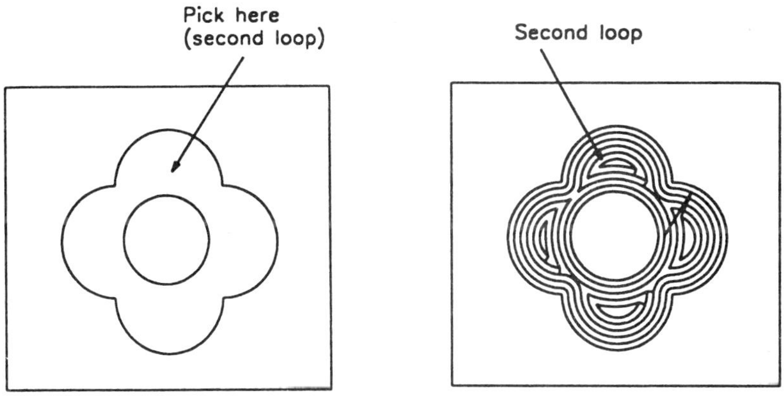

Figure 7.86

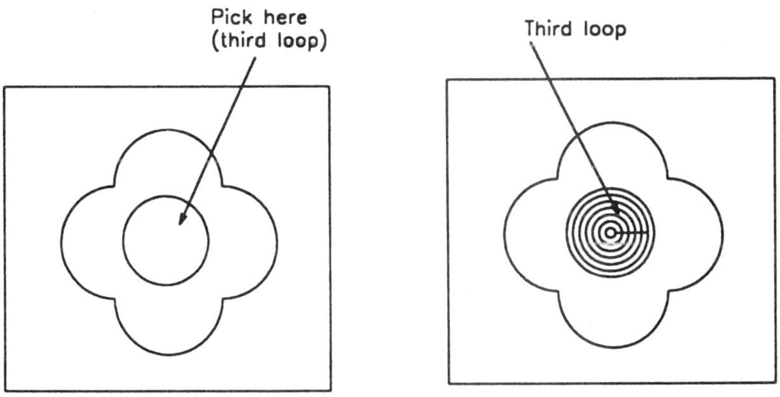

Figure 7.87

In a four-loop case, the pocketing toolpaths can be one of the following four possibilities:

Click inside a pocket	Pocketing toolpaths
1. Selecting first loop	The pocketing is performed in the first and third loop, the Second and fourth loop become islands (Figure 7.88).
2. Selecting second loop	The pocketing is performed in the second and fourth loops, and the first and third loops become islands (Figure 7.89).
3. Selecting third loop	The pocketing is performed only in the third loop, the second And fourth loops become islands (Figure 7.90).
4. Selecting fourth loop	The pocketing is performed only in the fourth loop (Figure 7.91)

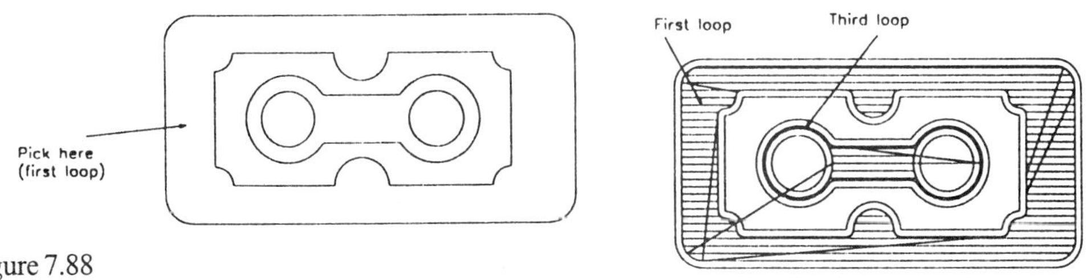

Figure 7.88

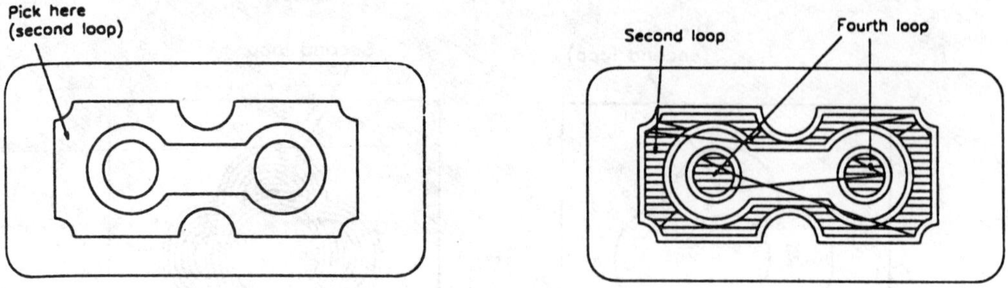

Figure 7.89

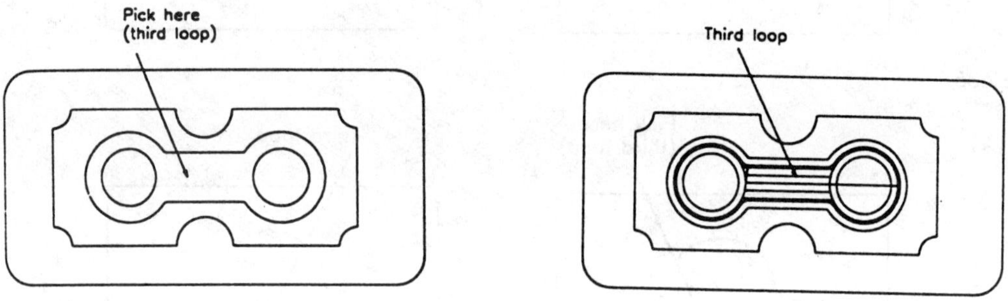

Figure 7.90

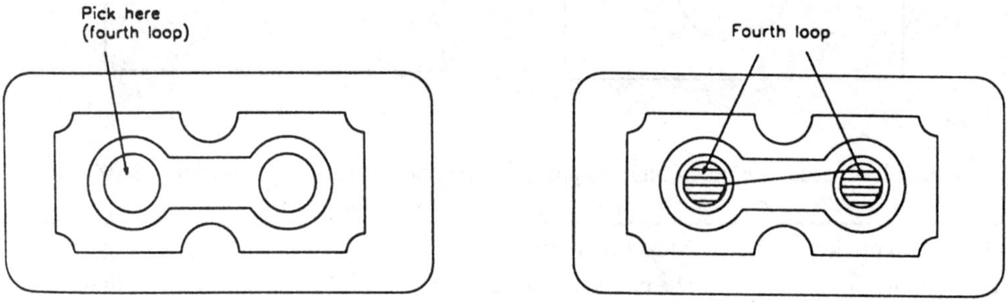

Figure 7.91

Entry - helix/ramp

The rough entry function specifies the pattern of how the cutter enters the parts. Click the "Rough Entry" button in the middle of the "Roughing/Finishing parameters" menu to open the Rough Entry dialog box. There are two forms of Rough Entry dialog box; one for helix and the other for ramp as shown next.

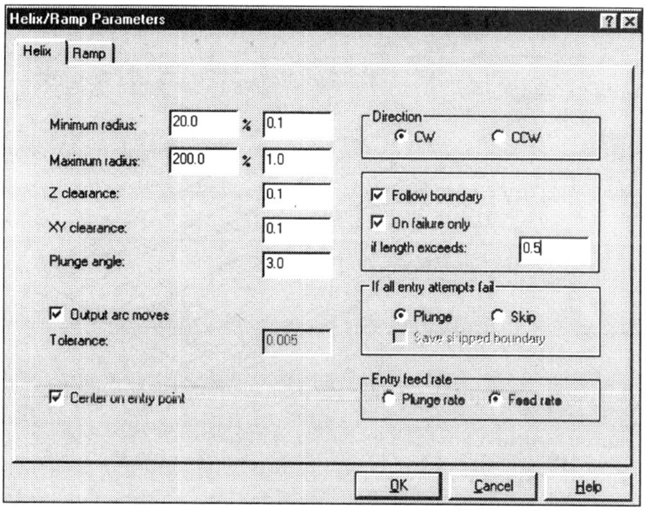

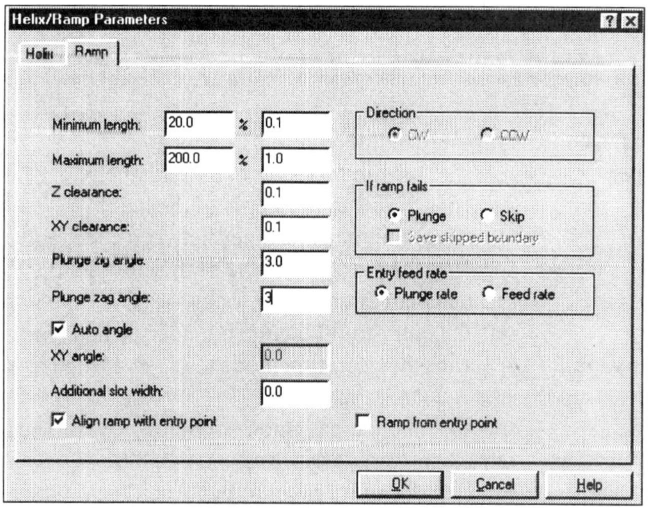

There are **three rough entry patterns**: **off, helix,** and **ramp**.

Off pattern In the off pattern, the tool plunges straight into the workpiece from the initial level to the desired depth (Figure 7.92). If the check box for "Rough Entry" button in "Roughing/Finishing parameters" menu is not activated (without √), the tool entry pattern is set to off mode.

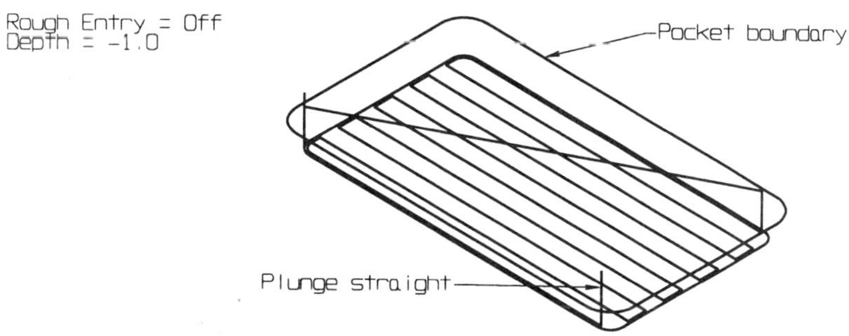

Figure 7.92

Helix mode With the helix mode, the cutter first plunges down to the starting level, then engages the workpiece in a spiral-down pattern until reaching the desired depth (Figure 7.93).

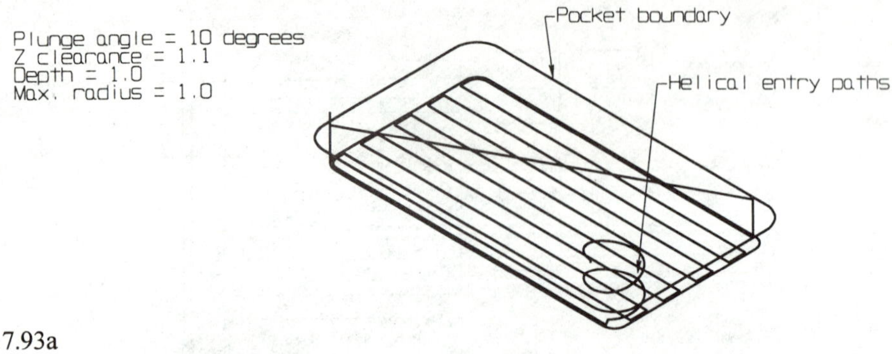

Figure 7.93a

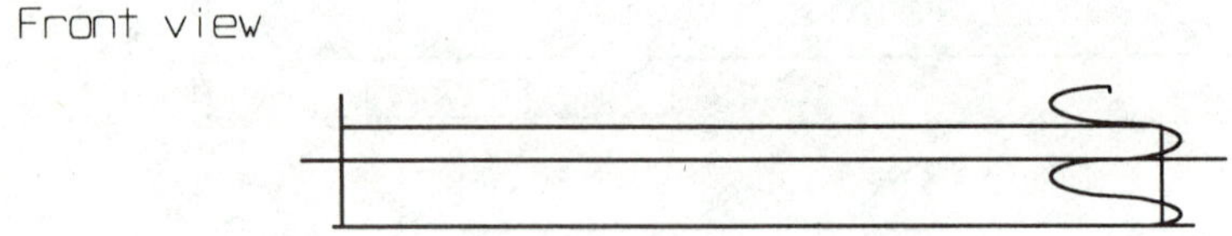

Figure 7.93b Front view

The parameters associated with the helical entry mode are described below:

Minimum radius:	specifies minimum radius of the entry helix.
Maximum radius:	specifies maximum radius of the entry helix.
Z clearance:	specifies the clearance depth of the helix.
XY clearance:	specifies minimum clearance between cutter and finished pocket wall.
Plunge angle:	specifies the engaging angle of the entry helix.
Direction:	sets helix cut direction to clockwise (CW) or counterclockwise CCW).
Follow boundary:	sets the entry to follow the boundary when entry fails.
If all entryattemps fail:	specifies the operation mode to either plunge or skip when all entry attempts fail.
Output arc moves:	specifies the toolpath mode of helix moves to be arc moves or linear approximated moves.
Center on entry point:	specifies the entry point to be located near the center of the pocket.

Using helix entry mode, the plunge angle parameter determines the length of the entry toolpath. The smaller the entry angle, the longer the entry toolpath (Figure 17.94).

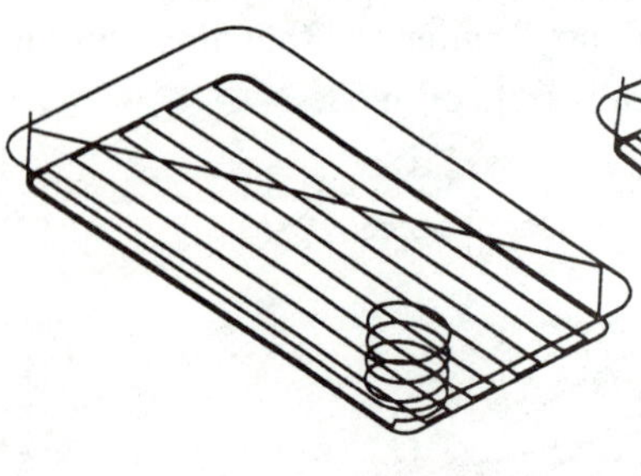

Figure 7.94a Plunge angle = 5^{0}

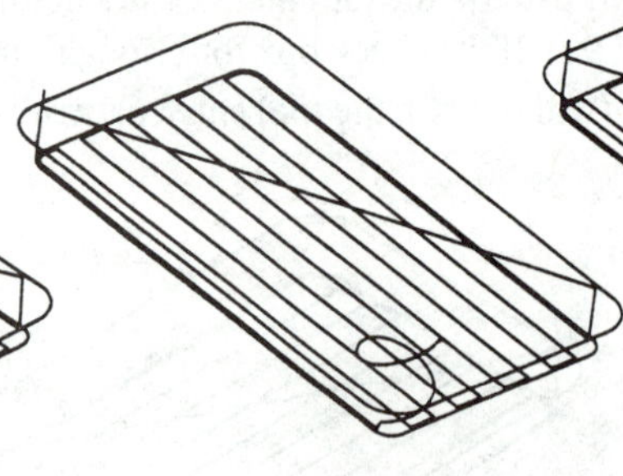

Figure 7.94b Plunge angle = 15^{0}

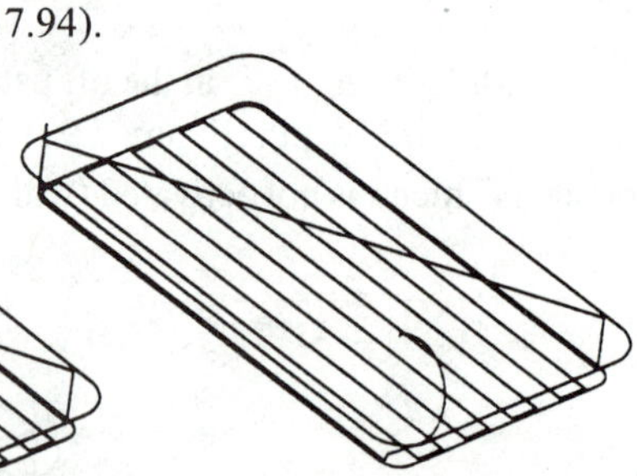

Figure 7.94c Plunge angle=30^{0}

Tolerance parameter The tolerance parameter dictates the number of entry path segments. The helix entry path is approximated by a series of straight lines when the "Output arc moves" parameter is not toggled to On (with (mark). The smaller tolerance value results in a larger number of line segments. It is recommended that you use a larger tolerance value.

With the **ramp mode**, the cutter engages the workpiece in a straight ramp downward path as in Figure 7.95.

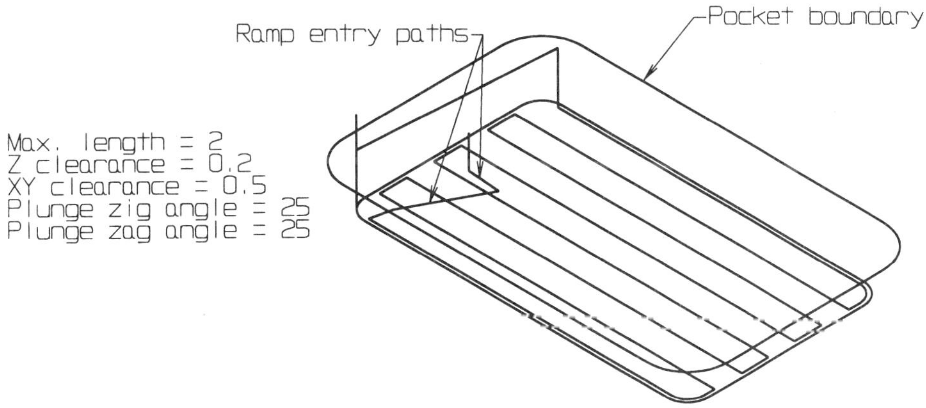

Figure 7.95a

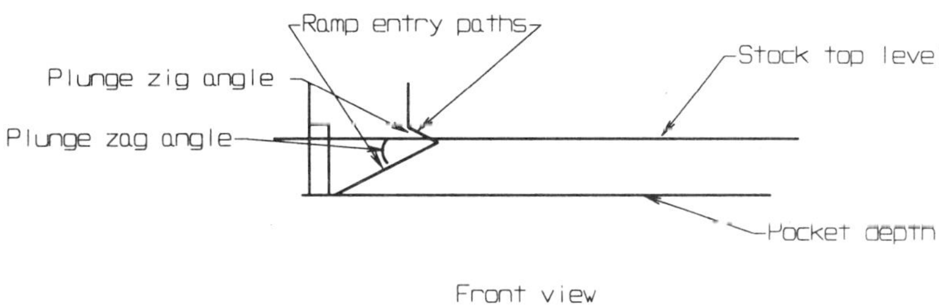

Figure 7.95b Front view

The parameters associated with the ramp entry mode are described below:

Minimum length:	specifies minimum distance of the segment of entry path.
Maximum length:	specifies maximum distance of the segment of entry path.
Z clearance:	specifies the clearance depth of the entry path. It is the distance above the top of stock.
XY clearance:	specifies the minimum clearance between the cutter the finished pocket wall.
Plunge zig angle:	specifies the plunge angle for zig path.
Plunge zag angle:	specifies the plunge angle for zag path.
Auto/XY angle:	specifies the ramping angle in XY-direction either by the system automatically or by a given value.
Additional slot width:	adds an additional amount of toolpath segment to the end of each plunge path.
Align ramp with Entry point:	aligns the entry ramp path with the entry point.
Ramp from entry point:	has the entry ramp path starting from the entry point.
If ramp fails:	specifies the operation mode to as either plunge or skip when the entry fails.

There are three parameters that dictate the number of zig-zag ramp-down segments; **maximum length, plunge zig angle** and **plunge zag angle**. Figure 7.96 shows how maximum length effects the ramp-down segments. The segments increase from 2 to 4 when the maximum length changes from 1.0 to 0.5. Figure 7.97 shows the effect of plunge zig angle and plunge zag angle on the entry path. As the angle increases, the number of ramp segments reduces.

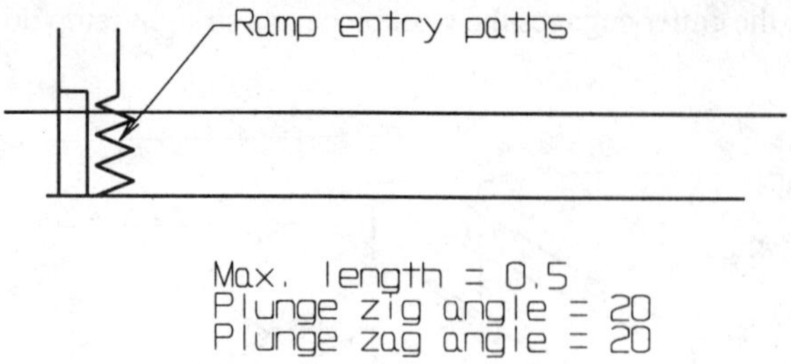

Figure 7.96a

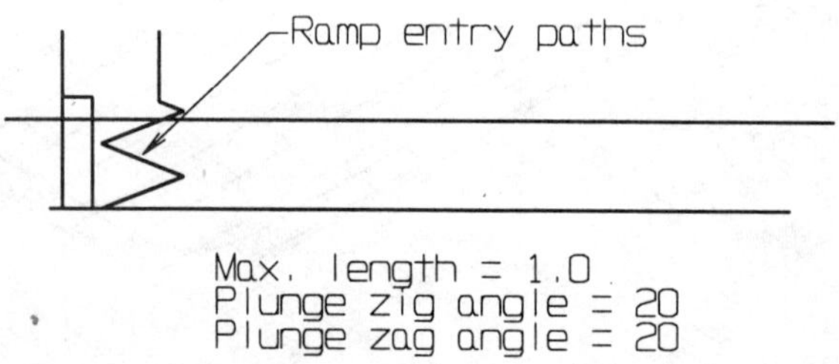

Figure 7.96b

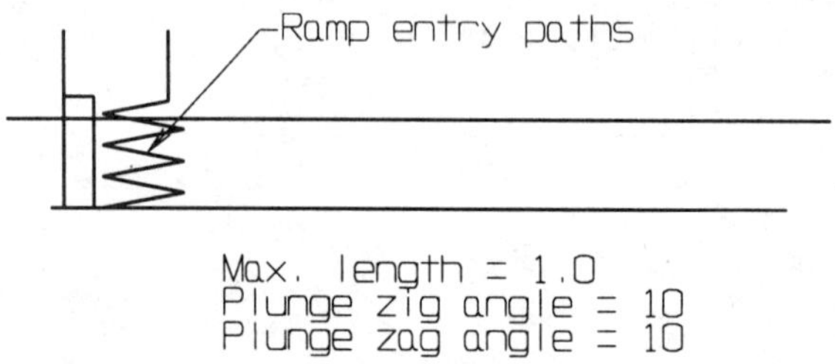

Figure 7.97a

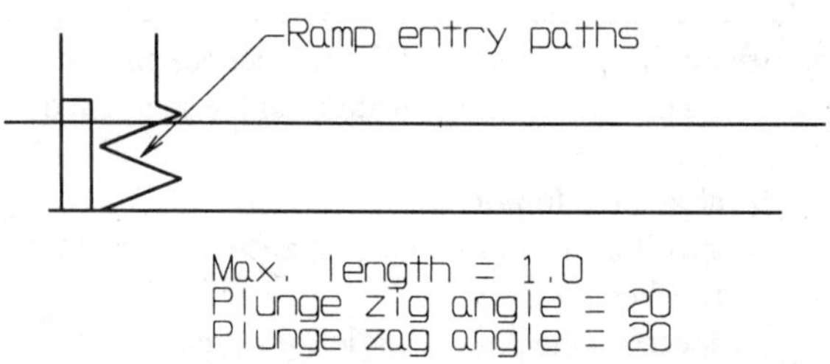

Figure 7.97b

The procedure for Selecting the Proper Rough Entry Mode

Straight end mills are often used to perform pocketing operations. Two common types of end mills are center-hole and center-cutting types. Cutting blades extend beyond the cutter in center-cutting end mills. As a result, they can be used to perform both plunging, cutting and side cutting. Center-hole type end mills are designed only for side cutting. They cannot be used for plunging operations. The following are some technical tips to help the selection of cutting engaging modes and their parameters.

⌛Tips

1. Always use helix or ramp mode. The Off (straight plunge) mode should be used only when there is a limited space in the pocket for the cutter to ramp down, and the cutter should be the center-cutting type.
2. It is recommended that you use a 30-degree helix or ramp angle. A small angle will takes a longer time to engage the cutter to the workpiece, while a large angle produces undesired scrapping on the cutter end.
3. The maximum radius width should be in a range between 1/3 to ½ of the pocket width.

Project 4. Pocketing an internal pocket

Use the pocket module to generate the toolpaths to cut the internal pocket for the part. Figure 7.98 shows the part geometry, toolpath and verification model.

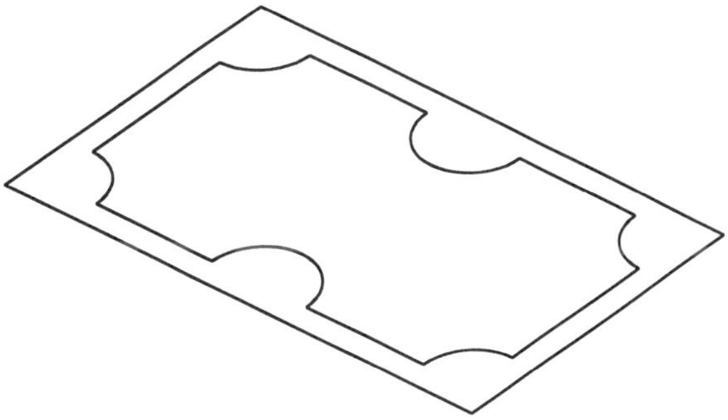

Figure 7.98a

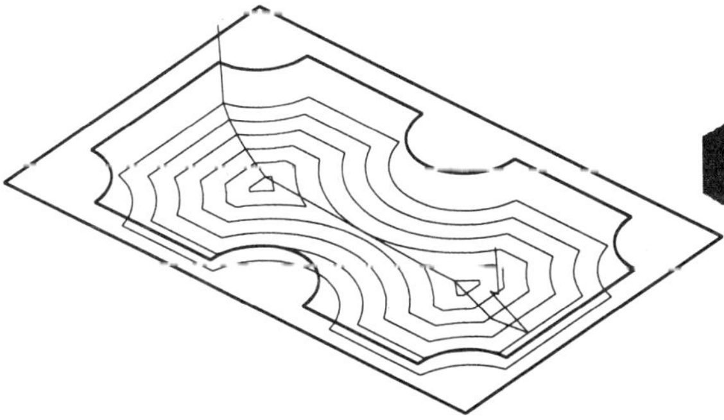

Figure 7.98b

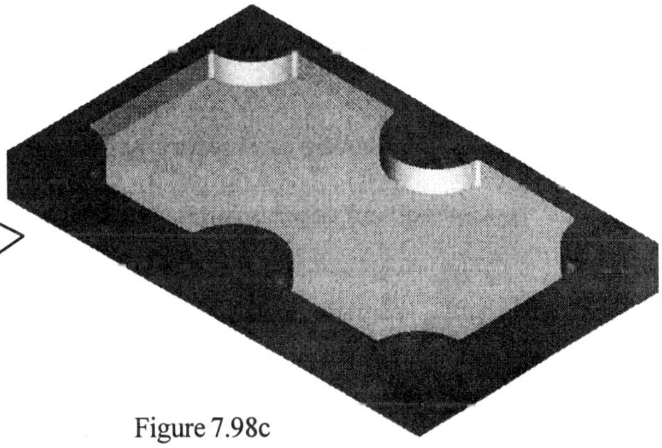

Figure 7.98c

Tips

1. Define the contour in the counterclockwise direction to obtain the climb milling operations.
2. Use a spiral inside out cutting method because there is no island involved.
3. Use two cutters, 0.5" end mill for roughing cuts and 0.25" end mill for the finish pass.
4. The roughing cut spacing is 0.35" (or 0.7D).
5. The number of finish pass is 1 and finishing pass spacing is 0.1".

Step 1. Open the part geometry file pocket1.

Select **MAIN MENU → File → Get**

File name: **pocket1** ↵

The part geometry should appear on the screen as Figure 7.99

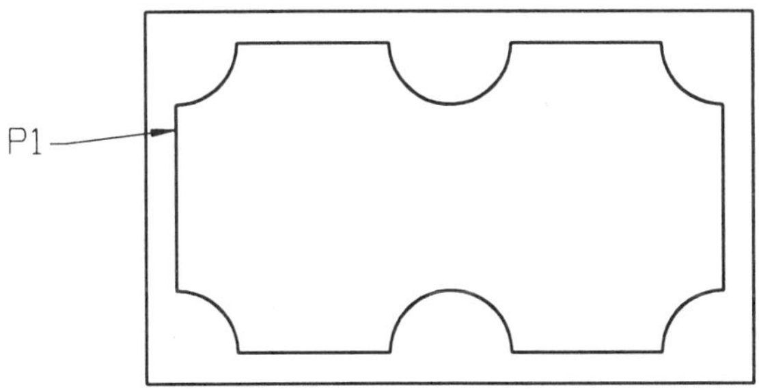

Figure 7.99

Step 2. Initiate the pocket module.

Use the pick point in Figure 7.99.
Select **MAIN MENU → Toolpaths → Pocket**
Select **Chain**, then pick **P1** to automatically select the chained profile
Select **Done**

Step 3. Select a ½" end mill.

Click the right mouse button, then select **Get tool from library**
Select **tool #239** (1/2 flat end mill)
Select **OK**

Step 4. Define the tool parameters as below.

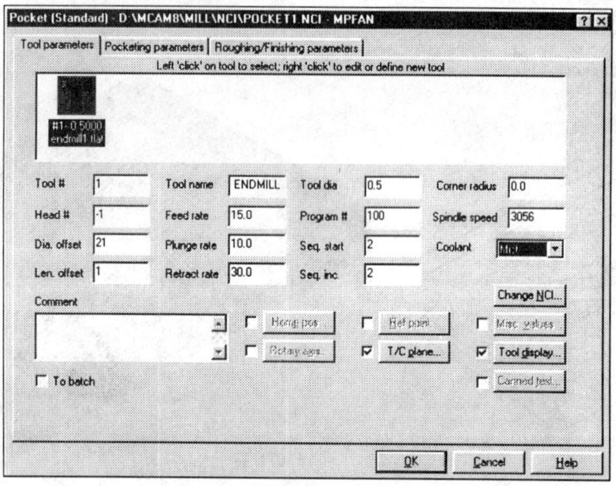

Step 5. Define the pocketing parameters.

Click the **Pocketing parameters** button
Set the pocketing parameters as below.

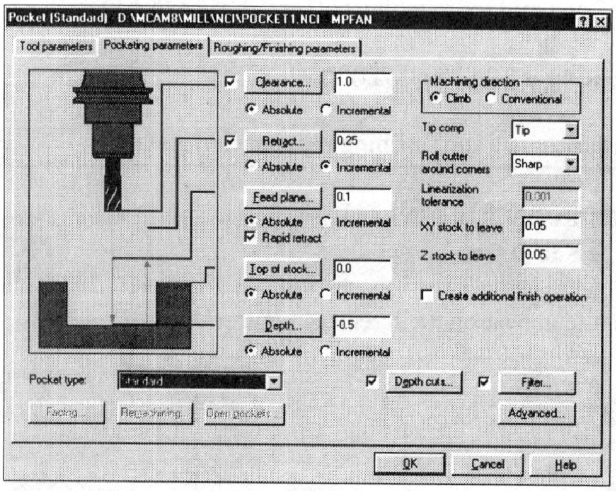

Step 6. Define the roughing/finishing parameters.

Click the **Roughing/Finishing parameters** button

Set the roughing and finishing parameters as below.

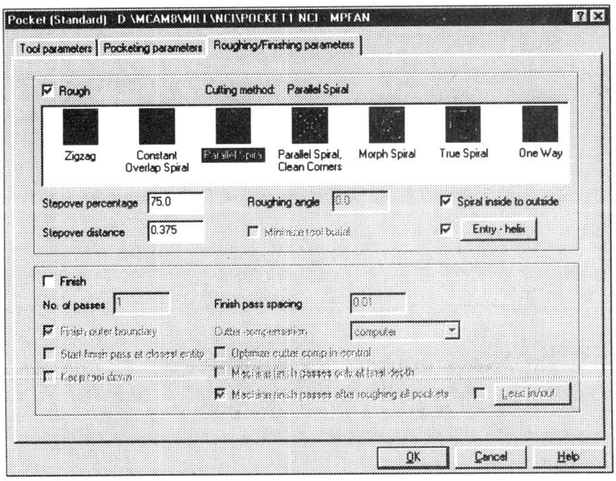

Step 7. Define the helix/ramp parameters.

Click the **Entry-helix (ramp)** button

Select the **Ramp** tab

Set the rough entry parameters as below.

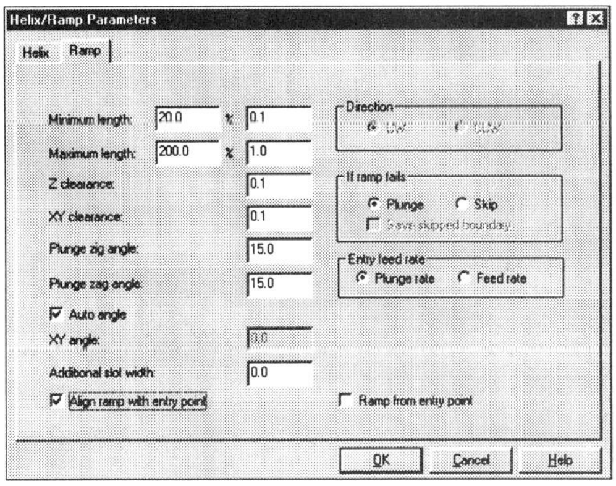

Select **OK** from Helix/Ramp Parameters

Select **OK** from Pocket menu

The pocketing toolpaths are generated as shown in Figure 7.100.

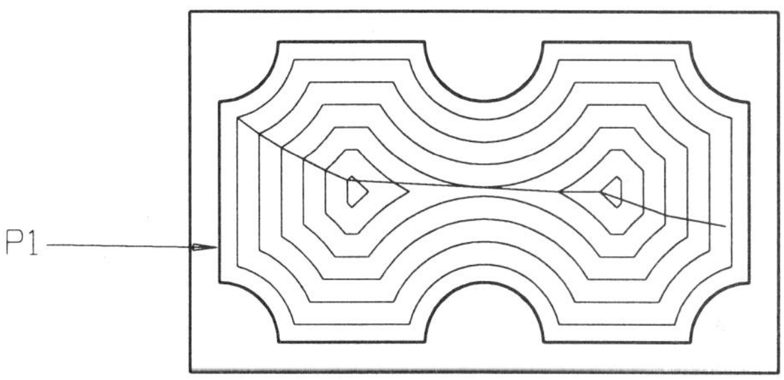

Figure 7.100

Step 8. Initiate the contour module.

Use the pick point in Figure 7.100.
Select **Contour → Chain**
Pick **P1** to select the contour
Select **Done**

Step 9. Select the finish tool.

Click the right mouse button, then select **Get tool from library**
Select **tool #234** (3/16 flat end mill)
Select **OK**
Set the tool parameters as below.

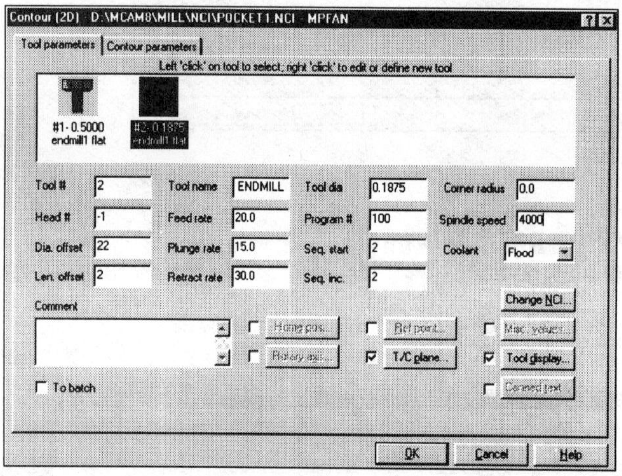

Step 10. Define the contour parameters.

Click the **Contour parameters** button
Set the contour parameters as below.

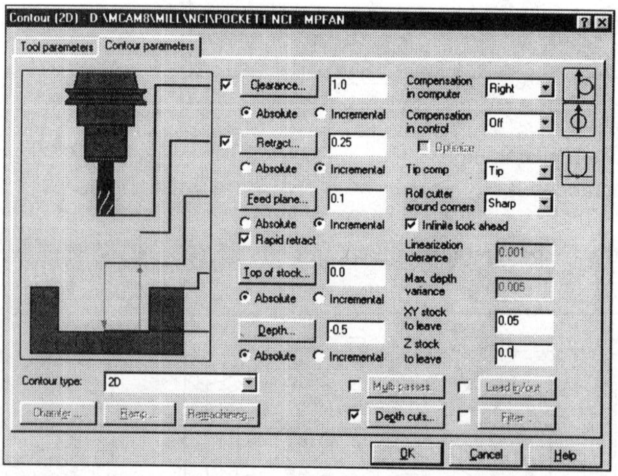

Step 11. Define the depth cuts parameters.

Click the **Depth cuts** button

Set the depth cuts parameters as here.

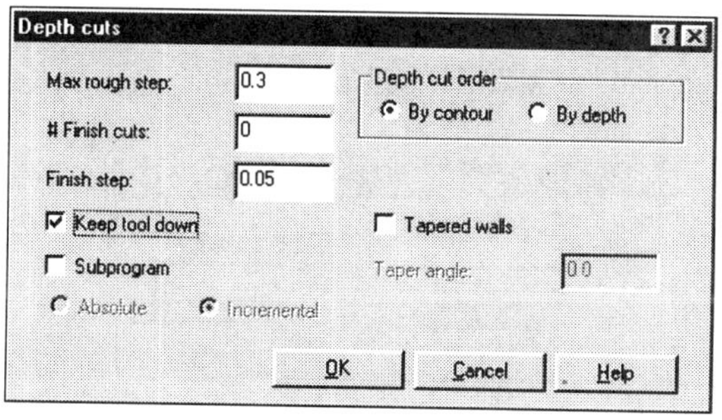

Select **OK** → **OK** to generate contouring toolpath

Step 12. Change to isometric view.

Select **Gview** → **Isometric**

The geometry model with toolpaths are shown in Figure 7.101.

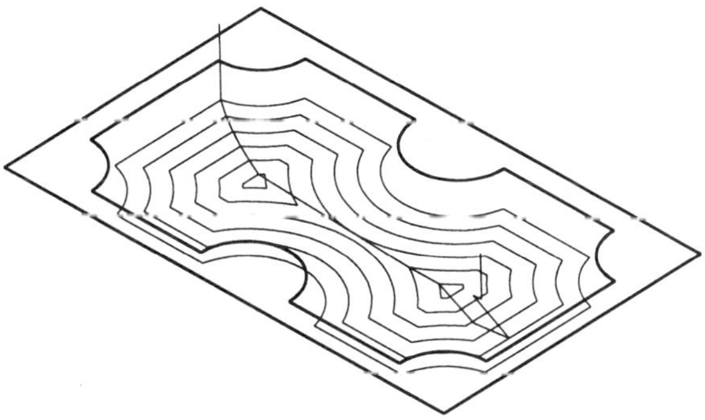

Figure 7.101

Stcp 13. Dcfinc the job setup.

Select **Job setup**

Set the job setup parameters as below.

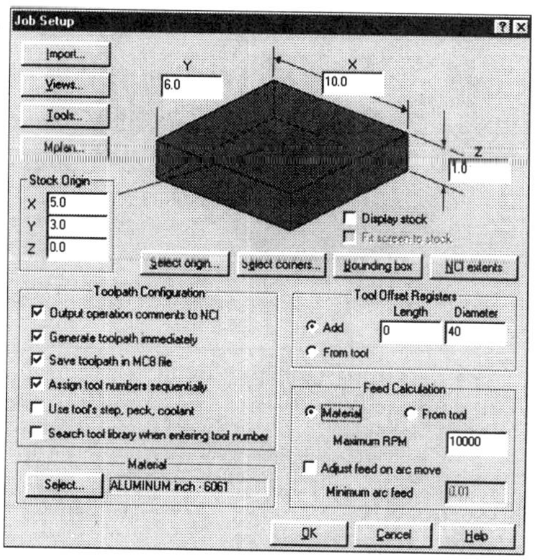

Select **OK** to exit the job setup menu

Select **OK** to exit the job setup menu

Step 14. Verify the toolpaths.

Select **Operations**

The Operations Manager menu with two sets of toolpaths should appear as below.

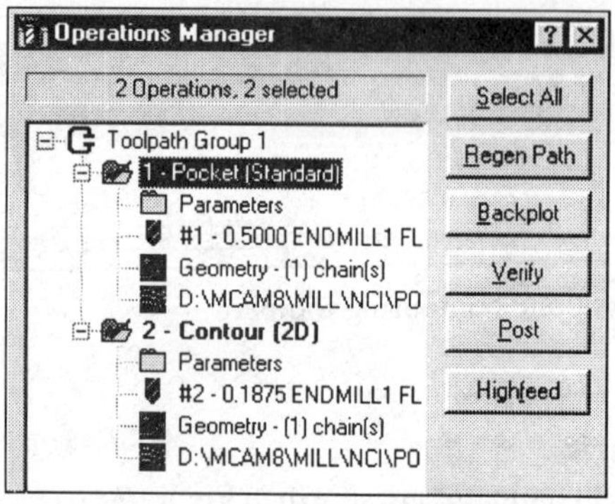

Select **Select All** to include both toolpath operations

Select **Verify**

A raw material block should appear on the screen.

Select **Machine** in the verify window.

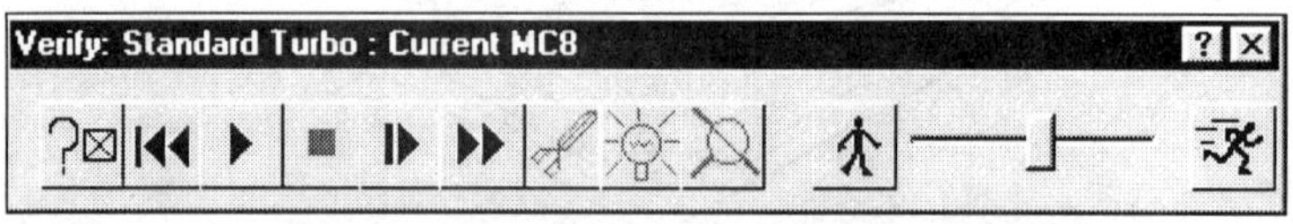

Toolpaths with two cutters are animated on screen. Figure 7.102 shows the final verified model.

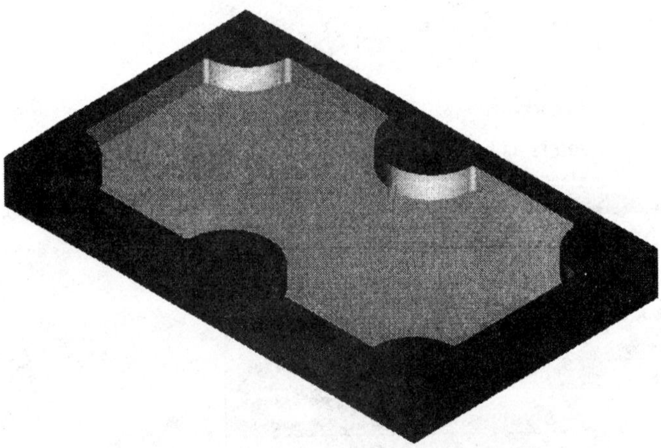

Figure 7.102

Select **BACKUP** to return back to Operations Manager menu

Select **OK** to return back to graphic mode

Step 15. Save the toolpaths.

Select **MAIN MENU → File → Save**

File name: **pocket1t** ↵

Project 5. Facing top flat surface and pocketing with an island 5

In the part shown in Figure 7.103a, the pocket module is used three times to generate the toolpaths to (1) face the top flat surface, (2) pocket the internal profile with a circle island at the center, and (3) pocket a circular profile. The raw material is a solid circular block. The outer circular profile of the block has been premachined to the desired dimensions. One face of the block has also been faced. The thickness of the block is about 1.03". Figure 7.103b shows the three sets of pocketing toolpaths.

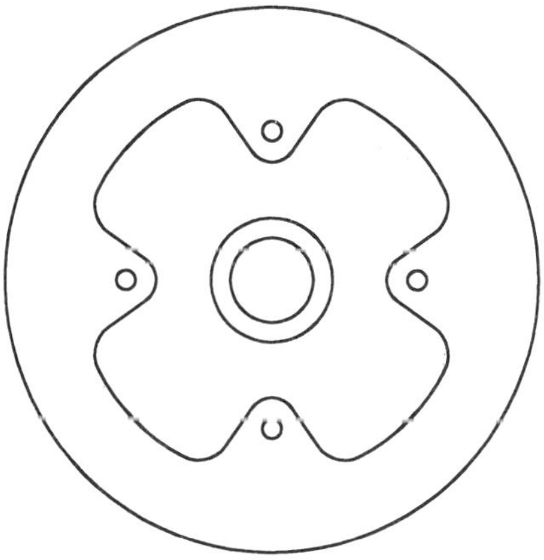

Figure 7.103a

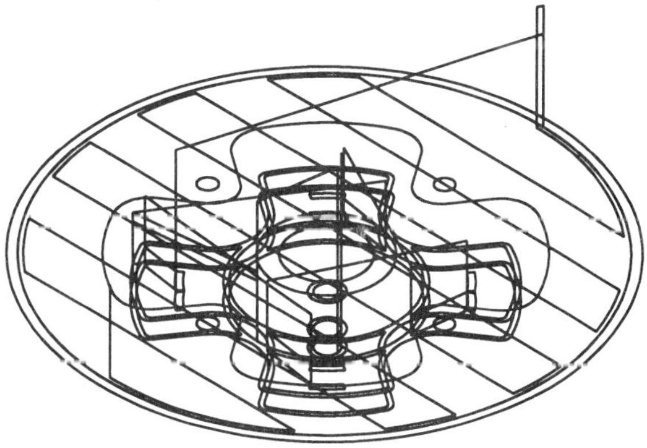

Figure 7.103b

Figure 7.103c

Tips

1. Start the operation sequence with facing the top flat surface followed by pocketing the larger internal profile, and finally pocketing the circular profile.
2. Two cutters are used including:
   1-in end mill for facing the top flat surface.
   ½-in end mill for two pocketing operations.
3. A construction circle which has a larger diameter than the outer circle should be added to serve as the outside pocket boundary for facing the top flat surface. If the original outer circle is used as the outside pocketing boundary, several pieces of uncut material may be left around the perimeter of the boundary. The diameter of this construction circle is suggested as 5.7-in.

Tips continued.

4. Main pocketing parameters for the facing are:
    1 roughing cut and 1 finish cut
    Roughing cut spacing = 0.6"
    Cutting method = Zig zag
5. Main pocketing parameters for pocketing the larger profile are:
    Cutting method: Spiral inside out
    Roughing cut spacing = 0.35"
    Pocket depth = -0.5"
    Number of finish passes = 1
    Finishing pass spacing = 0.05"
    No entry/exit length and arc
    Machine finish passes at final depth
    Two passes of depth cut: Rough: 1 cut at 0.0 Finish: 1 cut at 0.2"
6. Main pocketing parameters for pocketing the circular profile include:
    Cutting method: spiral inside out
    Rough cut spacing = 0.35"
    Pocket depth = -1.0"
    Number of finish passes = 1
    Finishing pass spacing = 0.05"
    No entry/exit length and arc
    Machine finish passes at all depths
    Three passes of depth cut: Rough: 2 cuts at 0.4"
    Finish: 1 cut at 0.2"

Step 1. Open the part geometry file pocket2.

Select **MAIN MENU → File → Get**
File name: **pocket2** ↵
The part geometry appears as Figure 7.104.

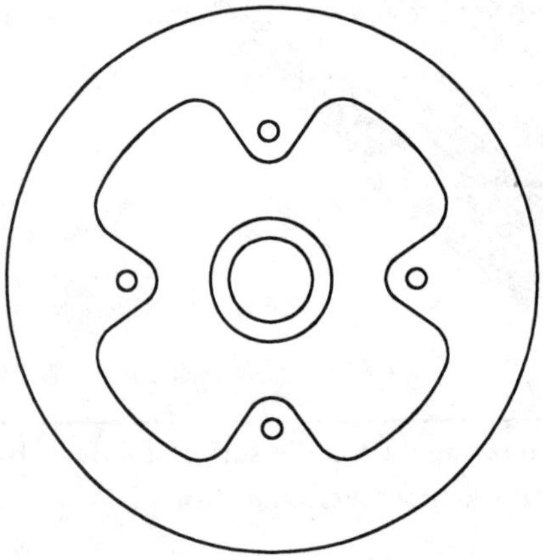

Figure 7.104

Step 2. Create a construction circle.

Select **MAIN MENU → Create → Arc → Circ pt+dia**
Enter the diameter: **5.7** ↵
Enter the center point: **0,0** ↵

The circle is added as in Figure 7.105.

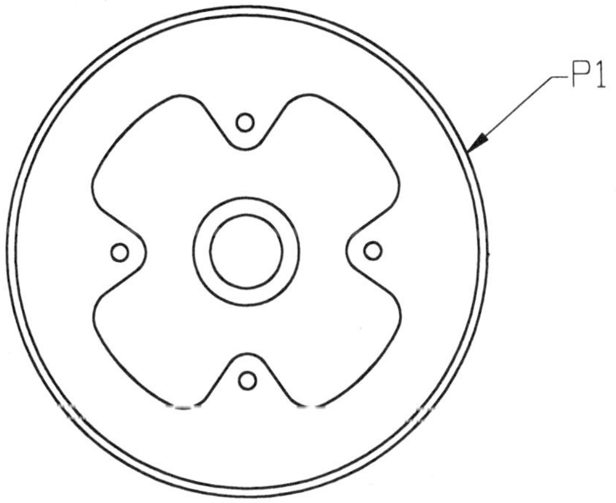

Figure 7.105

Step 3. Initiate the pocket module.

Use the pick point in Figure 7.105.
Select **MAIN MENU → Toolpaths → Pocket**
Select **Single** then pick **P1** to select the circle
Select **Done**

Step 4. Select a 1-in end mill and set tool parameters.

Click the right mouse button, then select **Get tool from library**
Select **tool #243** (1-in end mill)
Select **OK**
Set the tool parameters as below.

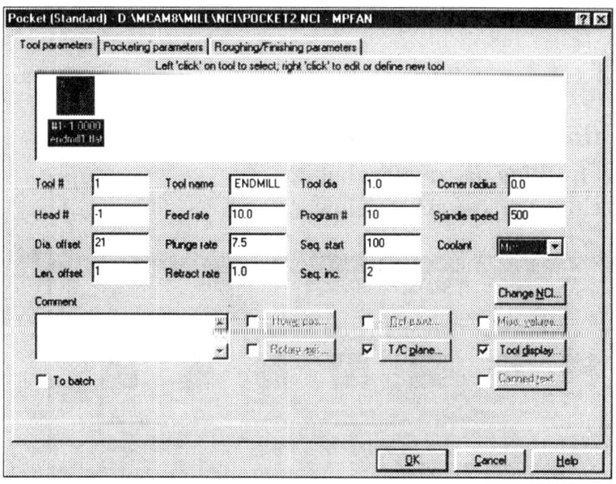

Step 5. Define the pocketing parameters.

Click the **Pocketing parameters** button

Set the pocketing parameters as below.

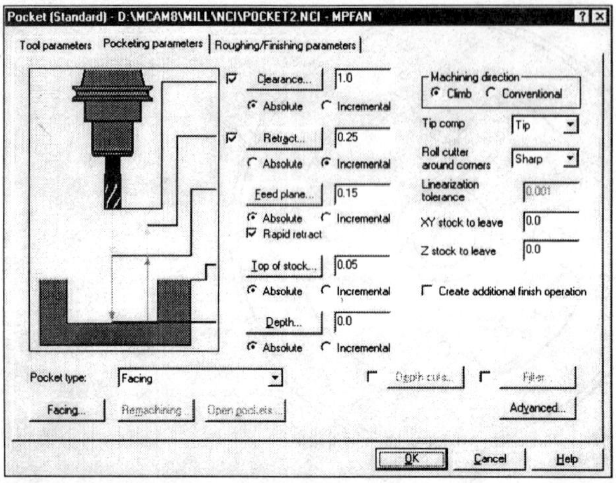

Step 6. Define the facing parameters.

Click the **Facing** button at the bottom of the menu
Set the facing parameters as here.

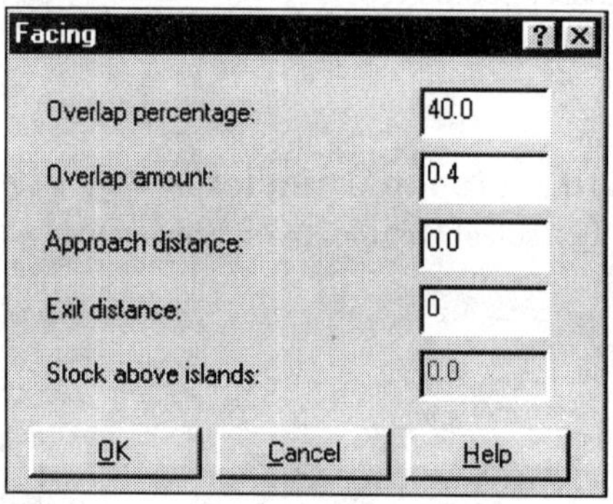

Select **OK**

Step 7. Define the roughing/finishing parameters.

Click the **Roughing/Finishing parameters** button
Set the roughing/finishing parameters as below.

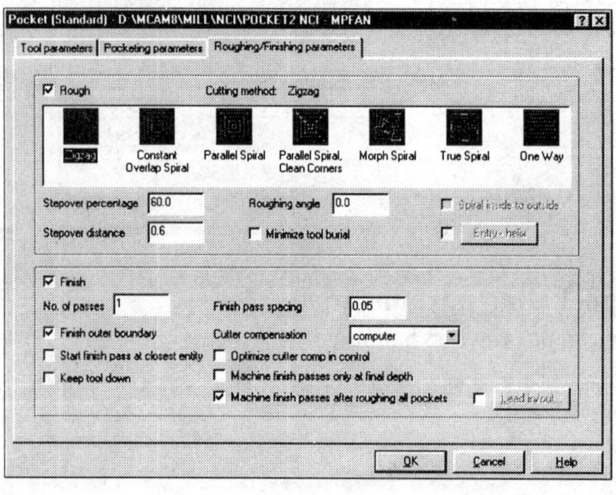

Select **OK** to generate toolpaths as shown in Figure 7.106.

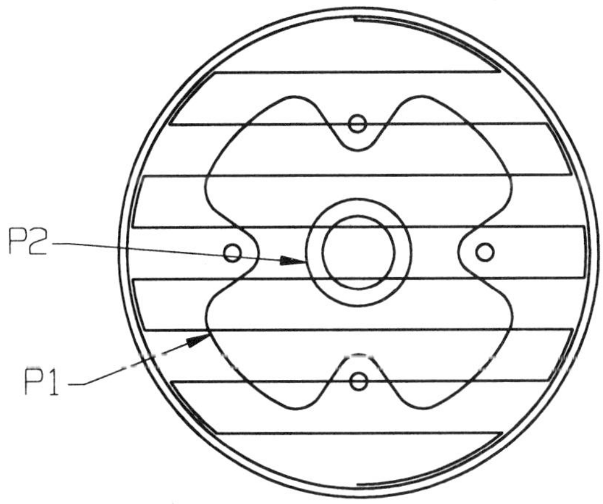

Figure 7.106

Step 8. Initiate pocket module for pocketing the larger internal profile.

Use the pick points in Figure 7.106.
Select **Pocket → Chain**
Pick **P1** to chain the contour
Select **Mode → Single**, then pick **P2** to select the circle as an island
Select **Done**

Step 9. Select a ½-in end mill and define the tool parameters.

Click the right mouse button, then select **Get tool from library**
Select **tool #239** (1/2-in flat end mill)
Select **OK**
Set the tool parameters as below.

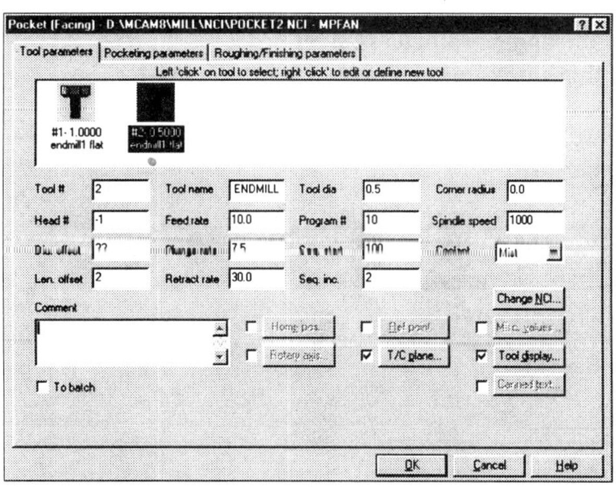

Step 10. Define the pocketing parameters.

Click the **Pocketing parameters** button

Define the pocketing parameters as below.

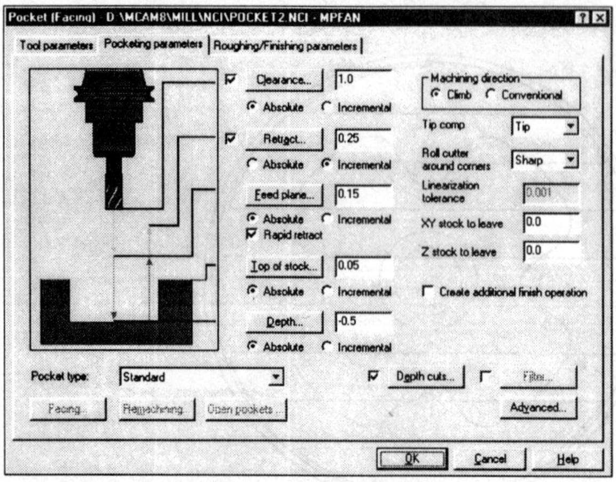

Step 11. Define the depth cuts parameters.

Click the **Depth cuts** button at the bottom of the menu
Set the depth cuts parameters as below.

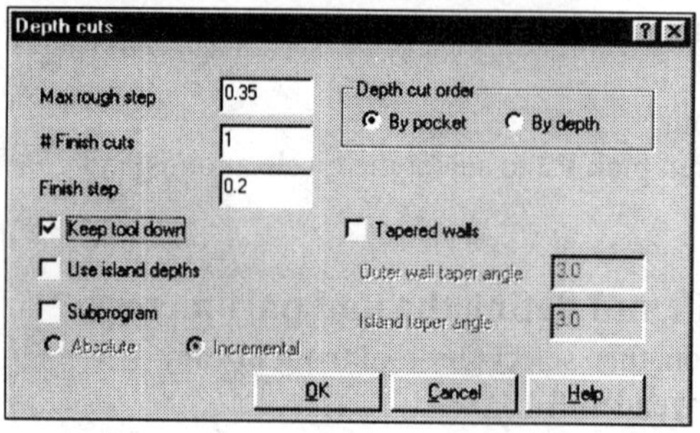

Select **OK**

Step 12. Define the roughing/Finishing parameters.

Click the **Roughing/Finishing parameters** button
Set the roughing and finishing parameters as below.

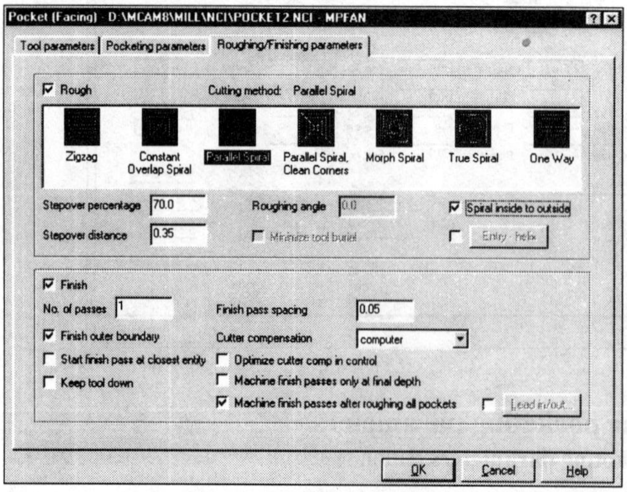

Select **OK** to generate the pocketing toolpaths as shown in Figure 7.107.

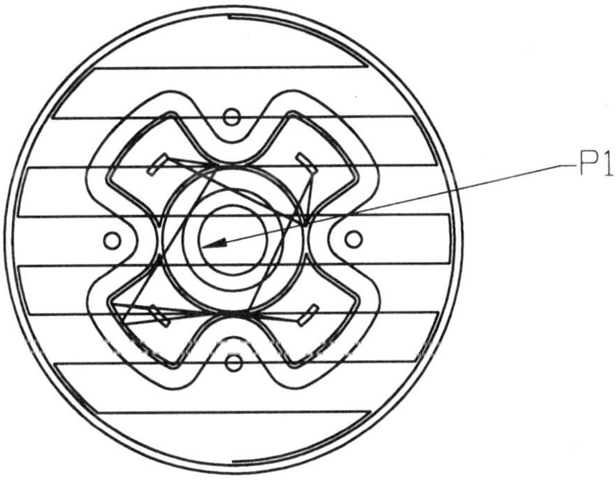

Figure 7.107

Step 13. Initiate the pocket module again.

Use the pick point in Figure 7.107.
Select **Pocket → Single**
Pick **P1** to select the inner circle, then select **Done**
Define the tool parameters as below.

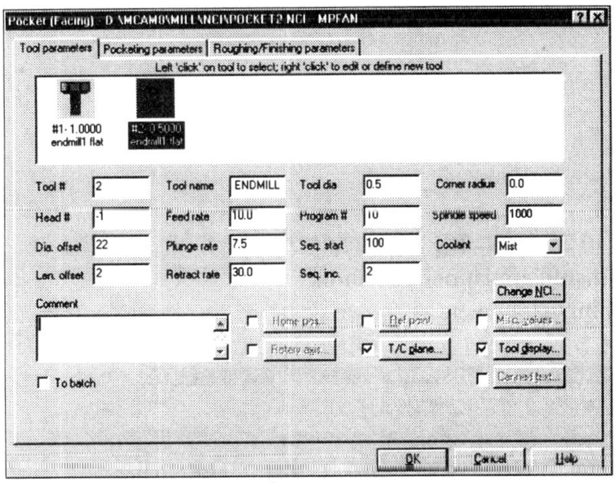

Step 14. Define the pocketing parameters.

Click the **Pocketing parameters** button

Set the pocketing parameters as below.

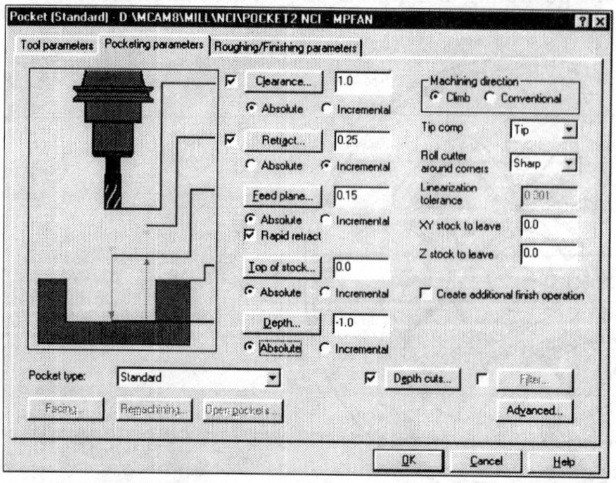

Step 15. Define the depth cuts parameters.

Select the **Depth cuts** button

Set the depth cuts parameters as below.

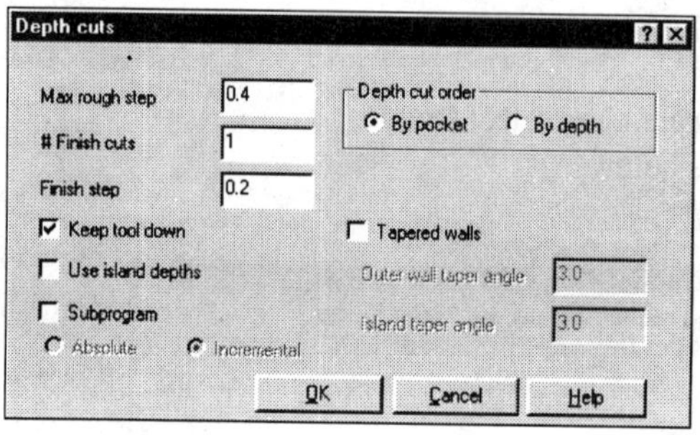

Select **OK**

Step 16. Define the roughing/finishing parameters.

Click the **Roughing/Finishing parameters** button

Set roughing and finishing parameters as shown next.

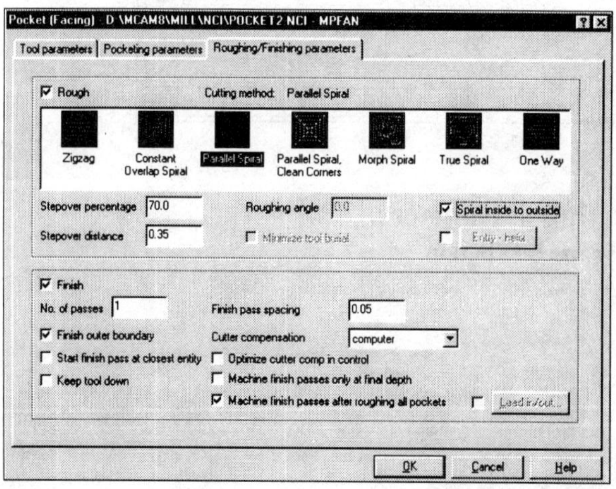

Select **OK** to generate pocketing toolpaths

Select **Gview → Isometric**

The three sets of toolpaths are displayed in Figure 7.108.

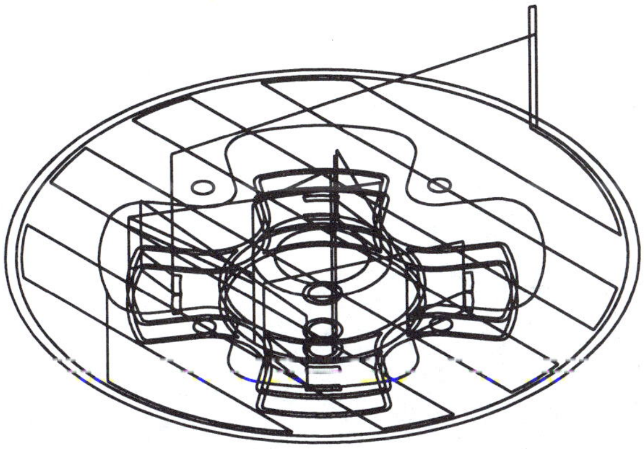

Figure 7.108

Step 17. Define the job setup parameters.

Select **Job setup**

Set the job setup parameters as below.

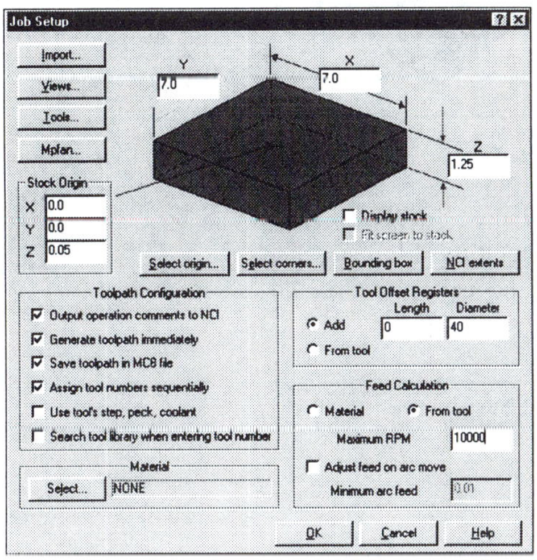

Select **OK**

Step 18. Verify the toolpaths.

Select **Operations**

The three sets of toolpaths are included in the Operations Manager menu as below.

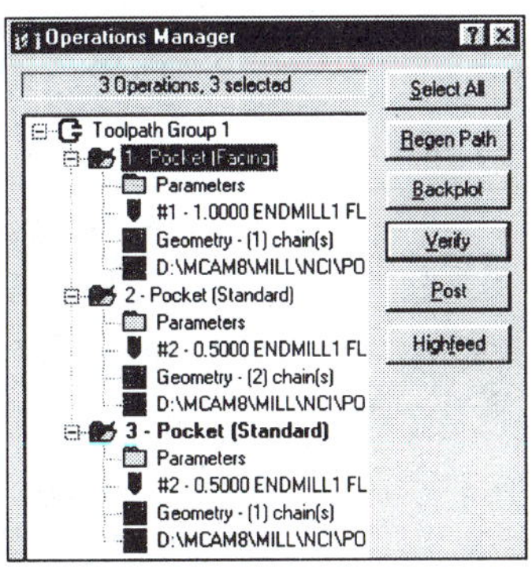

Select **Select All**
Select **Verify**

A rectangular block should appear on the screen.
Select **Machine** to verify the toolpaths

Figure 7.109 shows the verify model of this project.

Figure 7.109

Select **BACKUP** to return to Operations Manager menu
Select **OK** to exit Operations Manager menu

Step 19. Save the toolpath file.

Select **MAIN MENU → File → Save**
File name to save: **pocket2t**

7.11 Drill Module

Mastercam's drill module is used to generate toolpaths for drilling, boring, and tapping. Setting drill parameters to proper operating modes and values, and selecting points for the operation to be implemented, are very crucial to the successful execution of the drill module.

Drill Parameters

The drill parameters dialog box is shown below.

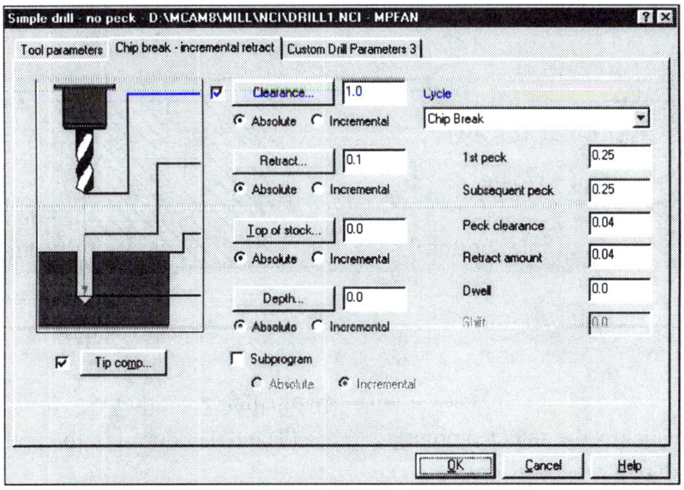

Those drilling parameters can be divided into four groups: **Z-depth, cycle mode, pecking parameters**, and **tip compensation**.

Z-depth Four Z value parameters are involved in cycle operations (Figure 7.110):

Clearance:	The cutter travels at this Z value to the specified hole center.
Retract:	The cutter moves down in rapid mode to this Z value.
Top of stock:	This level specifies the Z value for the top of stock.
Depth:	The cutter feeds down to this Z value which is the Z value of hole bottom.

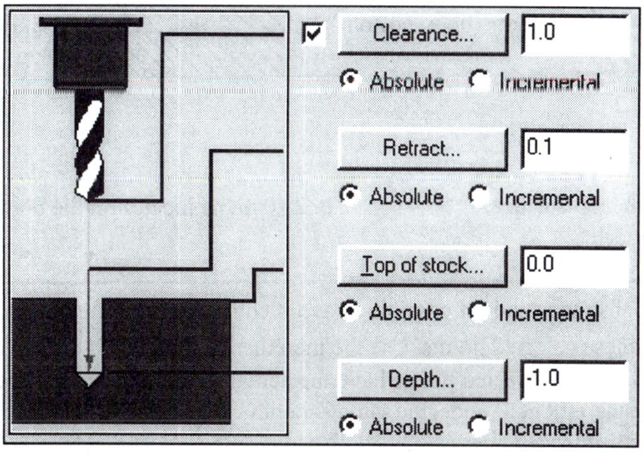

Figure 7.110

Mastercam allows Z values to be specified in either absolute or incremental mode. The depth is the distance between the selected point position to the bottom of the hole. The sign is determined as negative (-) if the hole bottom is below the selected point (Figure 7.111a) and positive (+) if the hole bottom is above the selected point (Figure 7.111b).

How the specified Z-value is measured depends on whether Incremental or Absolute mode is chosen. When it is set to Incremental mode, the Z-value is measured from the Z-coordinate of the selected point to the hole bottom as shown in Figure 7.111. If the selected point has the coordinate of (3,5,1), the following two commands define the Z-depth being at Z=-1.0: **Depth = -2.0 (Incremental)**

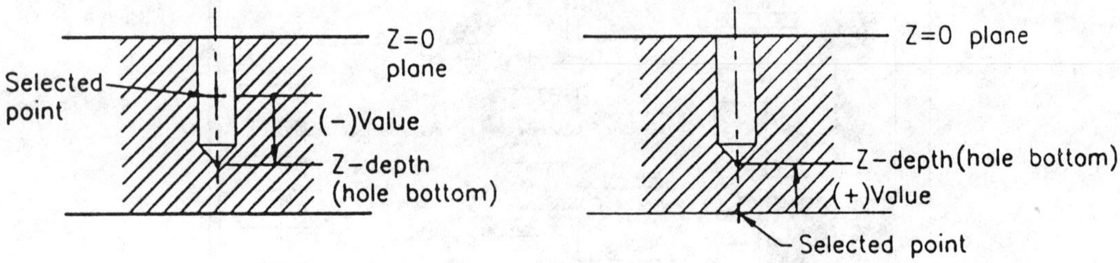

a. Negative Z value (The hole bottom is below the selected point)

b. Positive Z value (The hole bottom is above the selected point)

Figure 7.111 Incremental mode

In absolute mode, the Z-value is measured always from the Z-zero plane to the hole bottom (Figure 7.112). When this mode is used, the system ignores the Z-coordinate of the selected point and uses the Z-zero plane as the reference to measure the Z-depth.

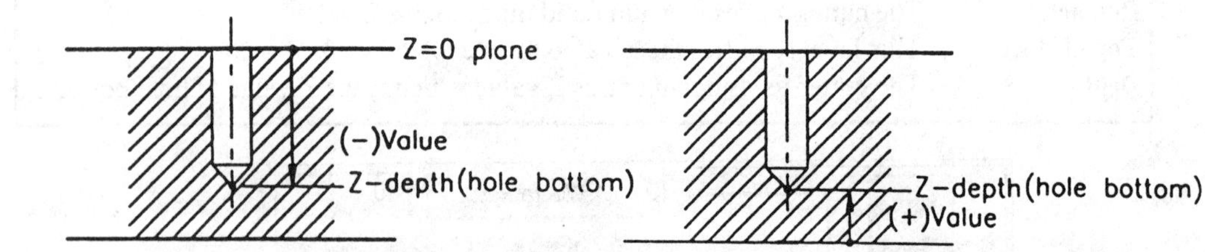

a. Z=0 plane locates on the top surface

b. Z=0 plane locates on the bottom surface

Figure 7.112 Absolute mode

> **Tip** Always use the absolute mode if possible to avoid confusion because you may not know the exact Z-vale of those selected points. Use the incremental mode only when the holes having different depths and the selected points have the actual Z-value of the hole bottoms (Figure 7.113). With the incremental mode, the same Z-depth value can be used for all holes although holes may have different depths.

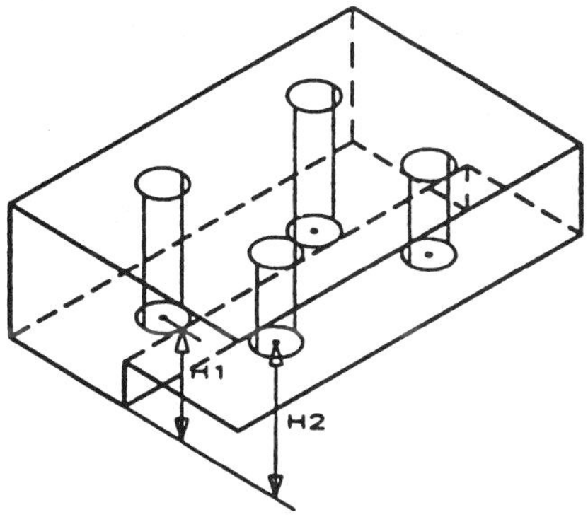

Figure 7.113

Cycle mode Mastercam provides a total of eight cycle commands with six standard types and two optional types. The two optional commands Misc. #1 and Misc. #2 are user defined cycles. They are unique and therefore are not discussed here. The six standard cycles are described in Table 7.3.

Table 7.3 Six standard cycles

Cycle Type	NC Command	Example	Typical Applications
Drill/Cbore 1. Dwell=0 2. Dwell≠0	 G81 G82	 G81 X1.0 Y1.0 Z-1.0 R0.2 F15.0 G82 X1.0 Y1.0 Z-1.0 R0.2 P0.5 F15.0	Drilling or counterboring holes whose depths are shorter than three times of cutter diameter.
Peck drill	G83	G83 X1.0 Y1.0 Z-3.0 Q0.7 R.2 F15.0	Drilling deep holes whose depths are longer than three times cutter diameter. Especially suited for applications where chips are difficult to remove.
Chip break	G73	G73 X1.0 Y1.0 Z-3.0 Q0.7 R.2 F15.0	Drilling deep holes whose depths are longer than three times cutter diameter.
Tap	G84	G84 X1.0 Y1.0 Z-1.0 R0.2 P0.25 F50.0	Tapping right-hand internal threads.
Bore #1 1. Dwell=0 G85 2. Dwell≠0 G89	 G85	 X1.0 Y1.0 Z-1.0 R0.2 F15.0 G89 X1.0 Y1.0 Z-1.0 R0.2 P0.25 F15.0	Boring holes with feed-in and feed-out paths.
Bore #2	G86	G86 X1.0 Y1.0 Z-1.0 R0.2 P0.25 F15.0	Boring holes with feed-in, spindle stop, rapid-out paths.

The operation sequence of the common drilling or boring operation is listed below. See Figure 7.114.

1. Rapid to the hole center with Z at the clearance level. 2. Rapid Z to the retract level. 3. Feed Z to the Z-depth of the hole bottom. 4. Dwell at the hole bottom for a period of time (if specified) 5. Retract Z to the retract level or clearance level.

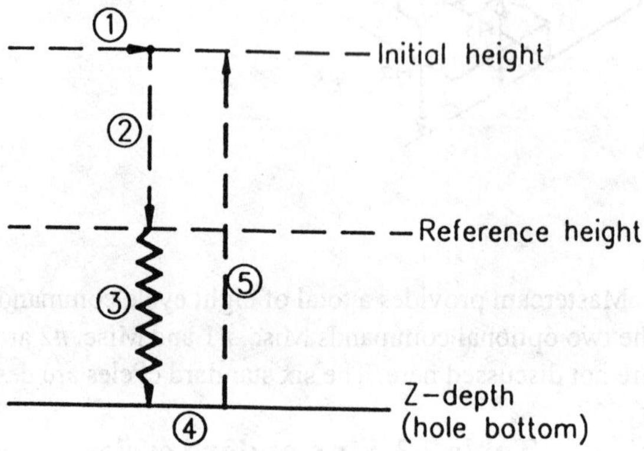

Figure 7.114

Pecking parameters Drilling deep holes are normally performed by two methods: peck drilling and chip break drilling. They are used when the depth of holes is larger than three times of the cutter diameter. Figure 7.115 illustrates the difference of these two deep hole drilling cycles.

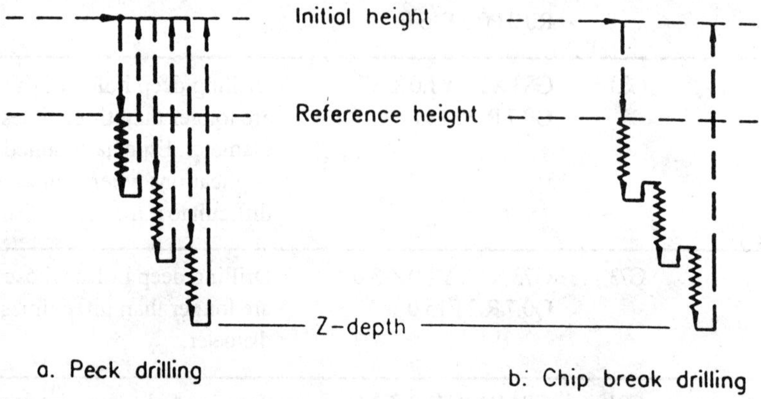

Figure 7.115

The operation sequence of the peck drilling cycle is listed below:

1. Rapid to the hole center with Z at clearance level. 2. Rapid Z to the retract level. 3. Feed Z down with one peck distance. 4. Rapidly retract Z with the retraction amount. 5. Rapid Z down to one peck clearance up form the previous drilled depth. 6. Feed Z down with one peck distance. 7. Repeat steps 4-6 until the hole bottom is reached.

Tip compensation Mastercam allows the user to compensate the drill tip which is about 118 degrees. Click "Tip comp" button at the right bottom of the drill menu to open the tip compensation dialog box as below.

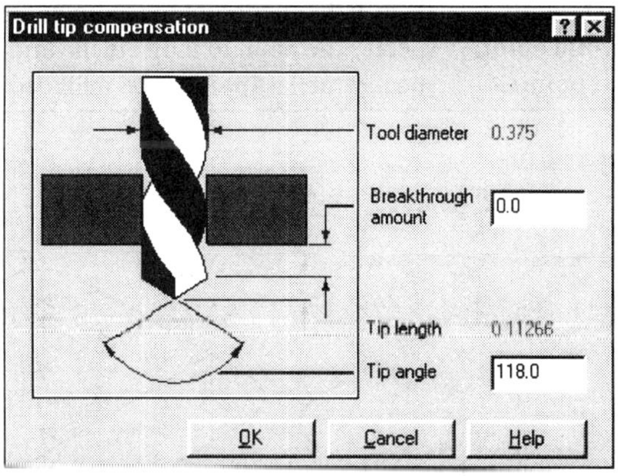

The four parameters included in tip compensation dialog box are:

Tool diameter:	specify the diameter of cutter.
Breakthrough:	specify the penetration distance of the tool.
Tip length:	specify the length of drill lip.
Tip angle:	specify the included angle of the drill lip.

Point Selection for (Drill module)

Mastercam provides a variety of methods for selecting points as the drilling center coordinates. They are briefly described below:

Add points	Description
Manual	manually defines the drilling center points.
Automatic	system automatically selects a series of existing points as the drilling center locations.
Entities	defines the endpoints of selected entities as the drilling center locations.
Window pts	selects all existing points within a window as the drilling center locations.
Last	uses the point set used in the last operation as the drilling center locations.
Mask on arc	selects the arc centers in the mask group as the drilling center locations.
Patterns	creates a rectangular point grid or circular pattern as the drilling center locations.

Manual method These are the options for the user to define the drilling center locations:

Values:	define drilling center locations by entering their X and Y coordinate value.
Center:	define drilling center locations by selecting existing arcs or circles.
Endpoint:	define drilling center locations by selecting the endpoints of existing entities.
Intersec:	define drilling center locations at the intersecting point of two intersecting entities.
Midpoint:	define drilling center locations at the midpoint of selecting entities.
Point:	define drilling center locations at existing points.
Last:	use the last set of points that is used in drilling operation as the center locations for new drilling operation.
Relative:	define drilling center locations by referencing to a known point.
Quadrant:	define drilling center locations at one of the four quadrants of existing arcs or circle.
Sketch:	define drilling center locations at mouse picked locations.

Automatic method The automatic method allows the system to automatically select an array of existing points as the drilling center locations. It uses the following three selection points to define the points to be included (Figure 7.116):

Select the first point:	specify the first point in the point array.
Select the second point:	specify the point to indicate the array direction.
Select the last point:	specify the last point to be included.

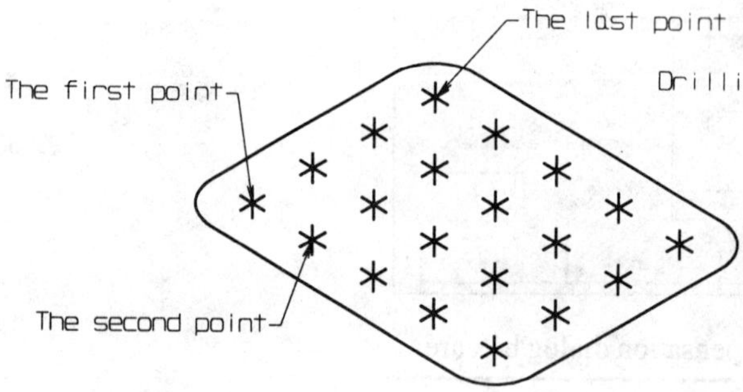

Figure 7.116a

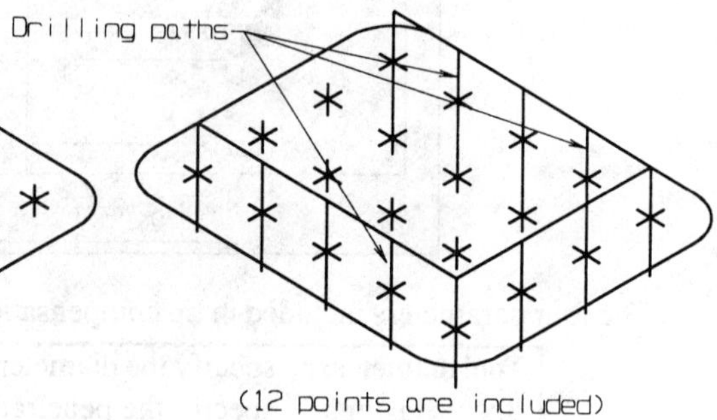

Figure 7.116b

Entities This option allows to select the end points of a group of entities as the drilling center locations. The entities can be selected using the chain, window polygon, and area option. Figure 7.117 shows an example of using entities option to select the drilling locations.

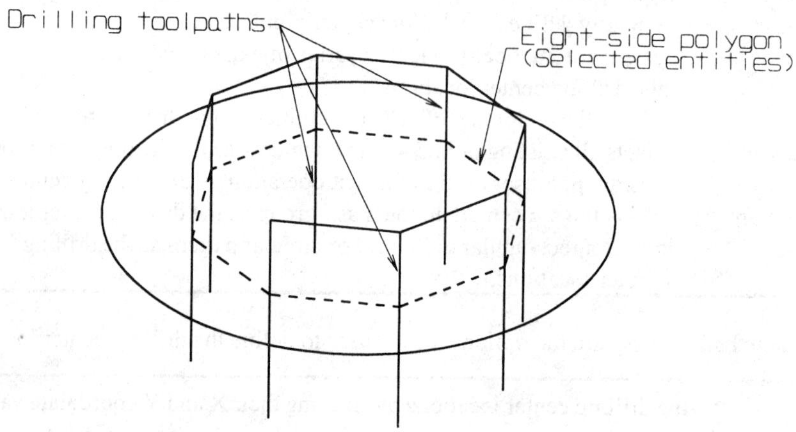

Figure 7.117

Window pts This option picks two locations to form a window for including all point entities as the drilling locations. The system will pick all points within the window and arrange the drilling sequence according to the given "Point Sorting Option". Figure 7.118 shows a drilling example in which the twenty drilling points are selected by using the "Window pts" option.

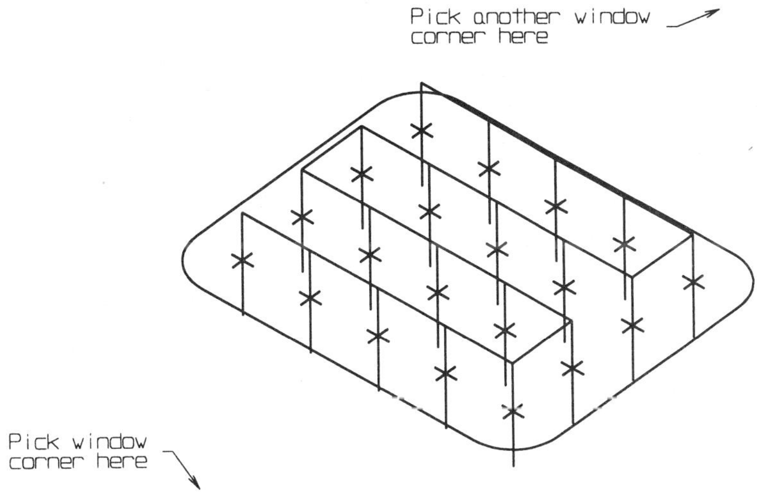

Figure 7.118

Option The option function is used to define the point sorting method for arranging the drilling sequence. Mastercam provides seventeen sorting methods to arrange the point pattern for drilling. The "Point Sorting" dialog box is shown here.

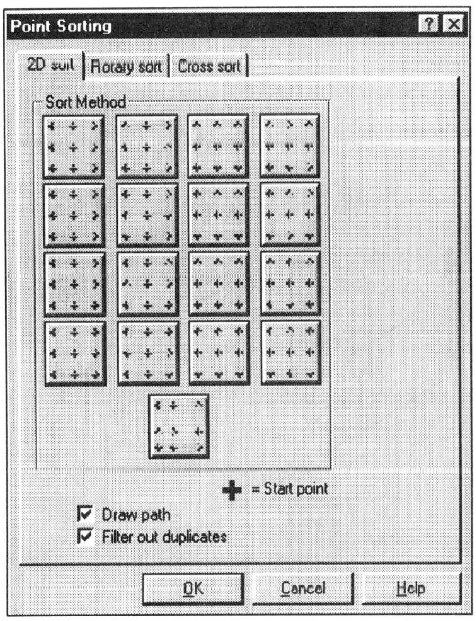

Patterns This point defining method is used to define an array of points that are arranged in either rectangular grid or circular grid pattern. It has two options; **grid pattern** and **bolt circle pattern**.

Grid pattern Mastercam uses the following parameters to define a point grid pattern (Figure 7.119):

Specify the grid origin: 0,0
Enter amount of point in X: 5
Enter X grid spacing: 1
Enter amount of point in Y: 4
Enter Y grid spacing: 1
Enter amount to shift X points: 0
Enter amount to shift Y points: 0

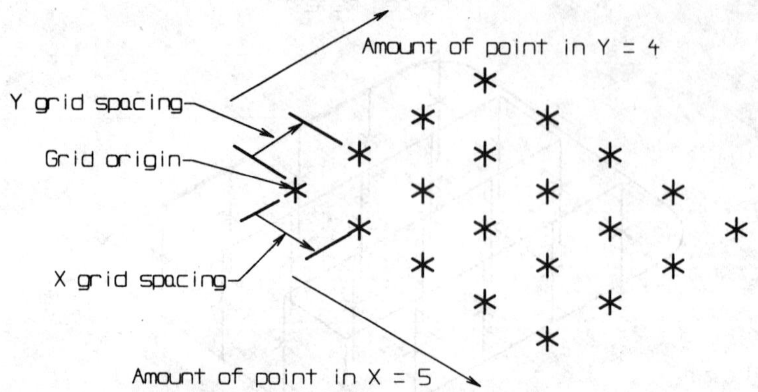

Figure 7.119

Bolt circle pattern Mastercam uses the following parameters to define a point bolt circle pattern (Figure 7.120):

Specify the bolt circle origin: 0,0
Enter bolt circle radius: 2
Enter start angle (0 = 3 o'clock): 0
Enter angle between points: 30
Enter number of points: 12

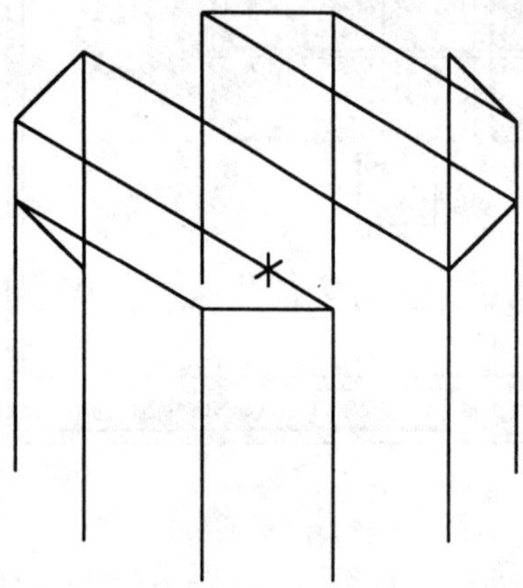

Figure 7.120a

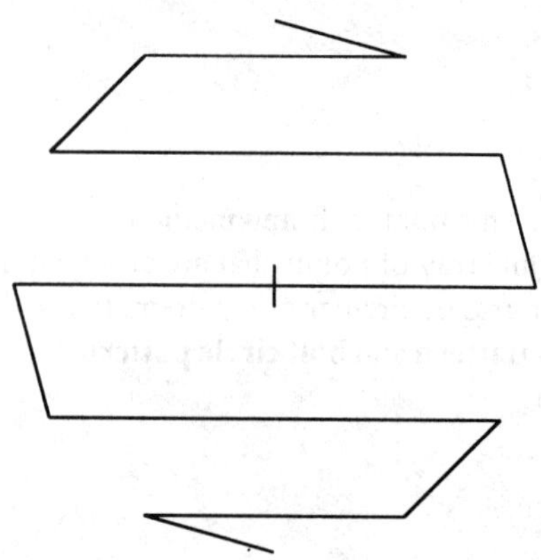

Figure 7.120b

Figure 7.121 shows how the sorting option affects the drilling sequence.

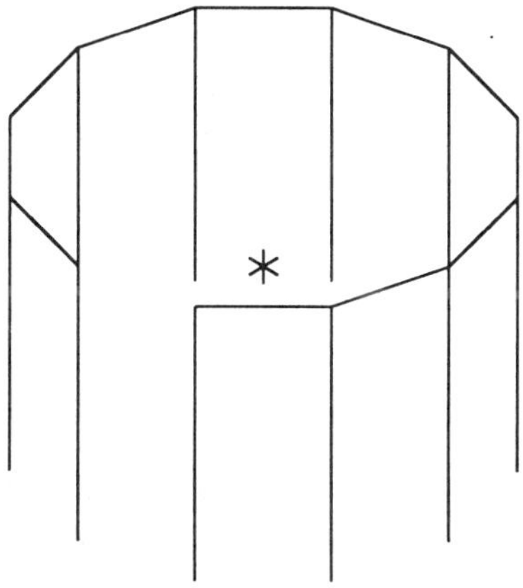

Figure 7.121a

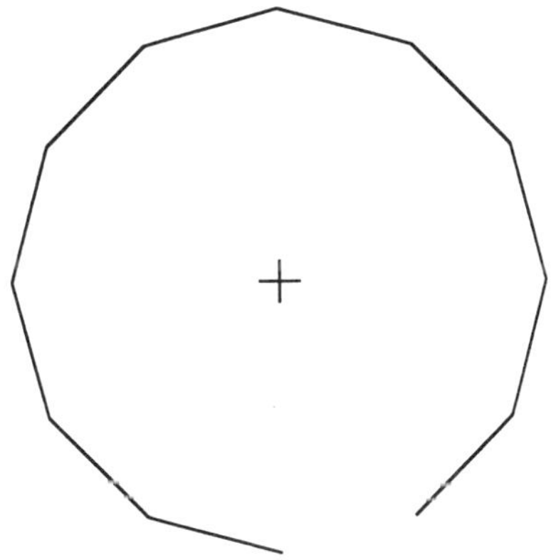

Figure 7.121b

Tips for drilling operations

1. Suggestions for selecting clearance level, retract level, and Z depth.
   The clearance level must be high enough to clear any interference such as steps, clamping devices, etc.

   Retract level = 0.15" above the part surface to be drilled (for smooth surfaces)
   = 0.3" above the part surface to be drilled (for rough surfaces)

   Z depth: (a) Blind holes: (Figure 7.122a)
   Z depth = full-diameter depth + 0.3 D
   where D = drill diameter
   (b) through holes: (Figure 7.122b)
   Z depth = hole depth + 0.3 D + 0.1
   where 0.1 is the penetration (breakthrough) distance

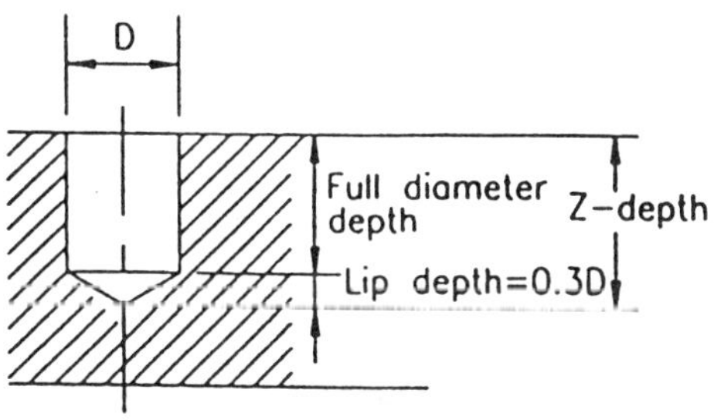

Figure 7.122a Blind hole

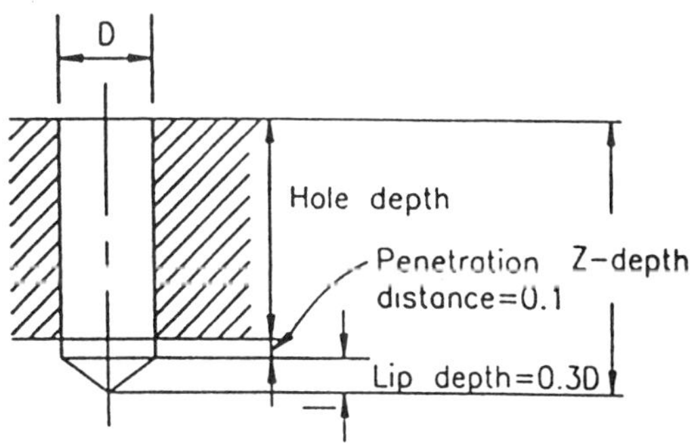

Figure 7.122b Through hole

2. Always use absolute mode to specify the Z depth (hole bottom) of the holes. The incremental mode is only recommended for drilling holes with different depths with two conditions:
   (1) the Z-value of selected points for drilling is specified and must be the exact Z-coordinate of the hole bottom and
   (2) the top surfaces are in the same horizontal plane.

Tips continued.

3. When the Z coordinate of selected points is zero, the Z depth has the same value for both incremental and absolute mode.

4. Use peck or chip break cycle when the depth of hole is longer than three times the cutter diameter. The peck drilling cycle is recommended when the chips are hard to remove from the holes. Using the chip break cycle can shorten the operation time because the drill does not retract back to clearance level or retract level. However, its chip removing ability is not as good as the peck cycle.

5. The drilling distance for each peck is about 1.5 times the drill diameter.

6. In the tapping operation, the feedrate and spindle speed must be synchronized to obtain the required thread accuracy. The following formulas can be used to obtain the proper feedrate and spindle speed:

Feedrate (inch per minute) = Pitch x RPM
Feedrate (inch per revolution) = Pitch
Where Pitch = 1/number of threads per inch
RPM = spindle speed

7. When multiple operations such as drilling, boring, and tapping, must be performed in the same set of holes, use the "Last" option to eliminate the need for repeatedly selecting points of subsequent operations.

8. Mastercam allows to define different drilling depths in one operation. Use the following commands to change the drilling depth of selected points:

Select Edit → Edit depth
Pick a point
The system prompts to enter depth (absolute relative to toolplane): -0.5

Figure 7.123 shows an example of drilling holes with different depths in one operation.

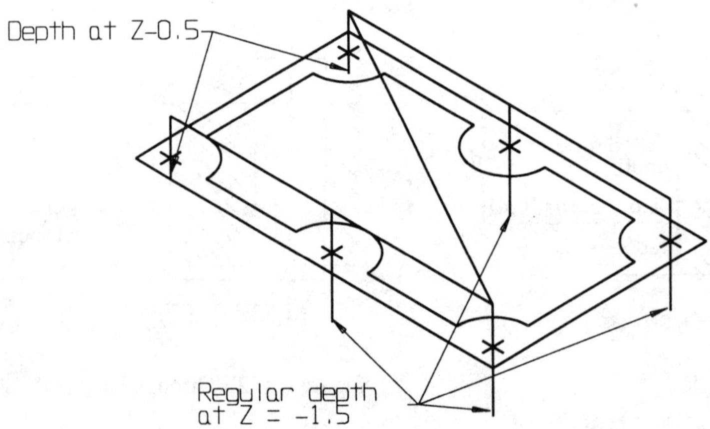

Figure 7.123

9. Use the "Edit jump" command to allow the cutter to be moved between holes at a height higher than the reference plane height. This is especially useful in avoiding interference with clamps or steps as shown in Figure 7.124.

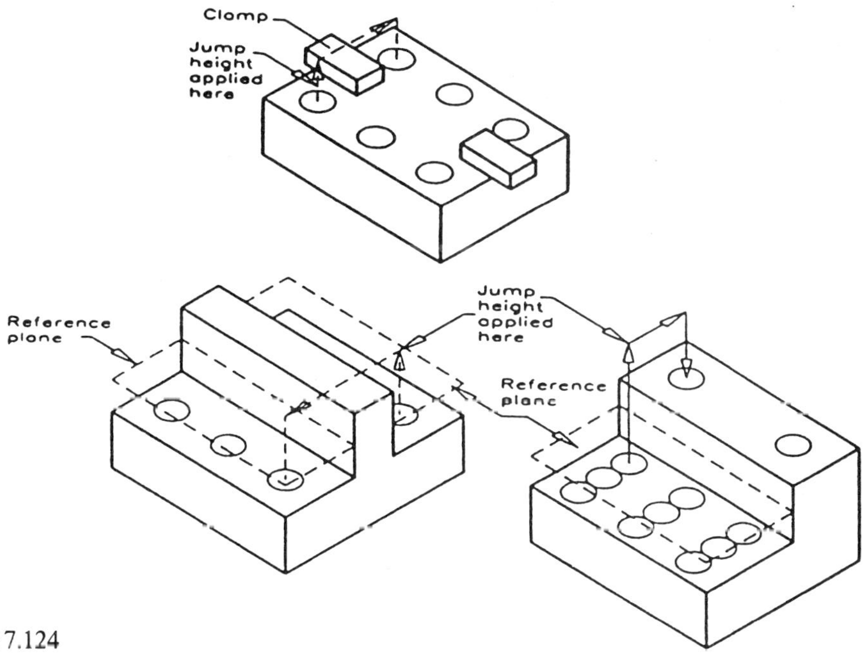

Figure 7.124

When a point is selected to apply "Edit jump" function, the system will prompt "Apply change to subsequent planar points." Select "Yes" to this prompt to cause the new jump height being applied to all subsequent points (Figure 7.125). Select "No" to keep the jump to only the selected point.

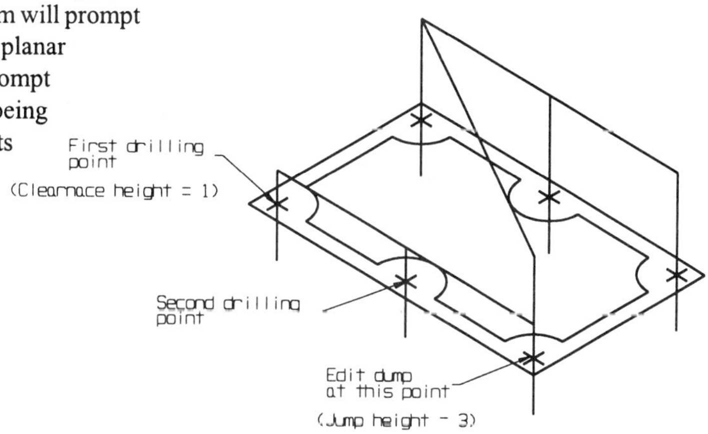

Figure 7.125

The "Rstr jump" command delete jumps in the selected points (Figure 7.126). This command often works together with the Edit jump command to control the retracting height of the drilling operations.

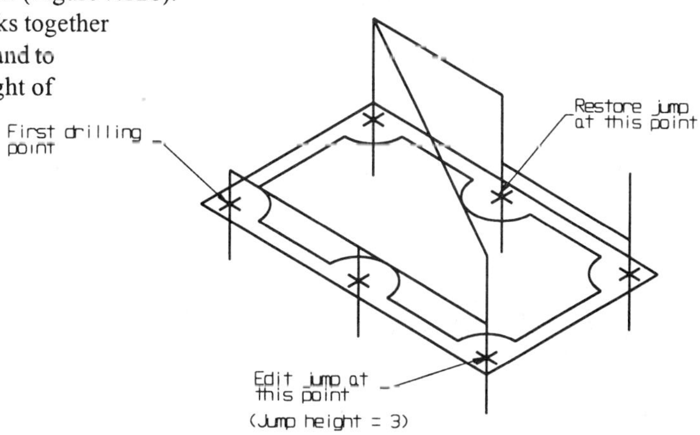

Figure 7.126

Project 6. Using the peck cycle to drill 24 deep holes

The peck drill cycle is used to drill 24 holes around three circles as shown in 7.127. The depth of the holes is 1.75-in. which is longer than 3 times hole diameter.

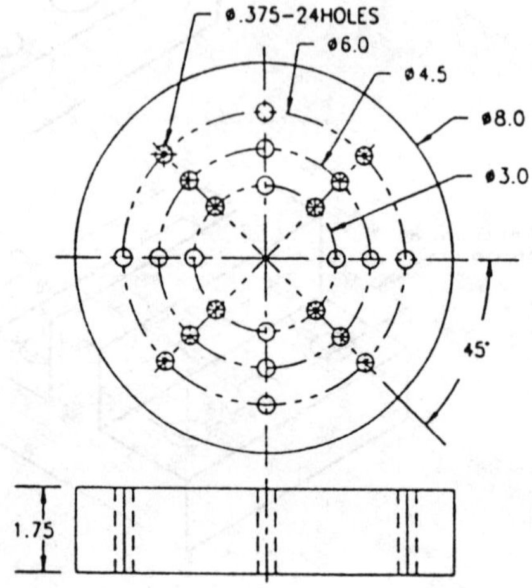

Figure 7.127a

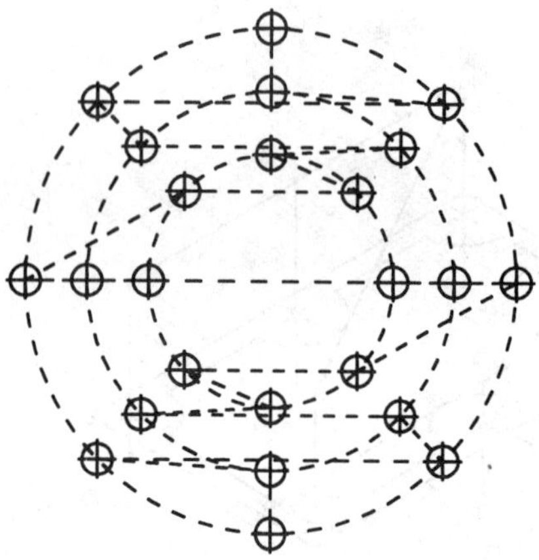

Figure 7.127b

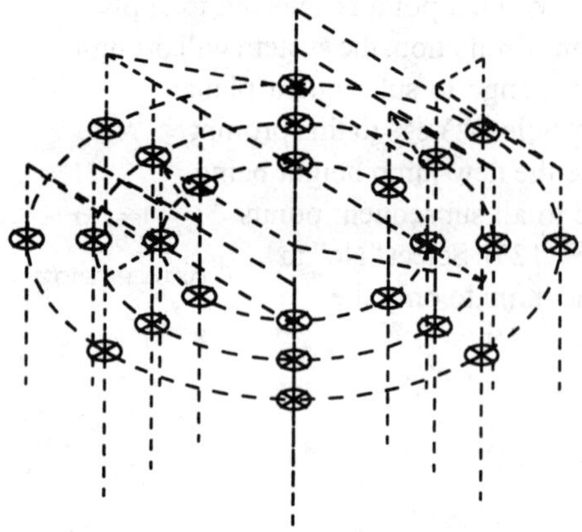

Figure 7.127c

Tips 1. Use the peck drill cycle. The main drill parameters are set as below:

Initial height = 1.0
Reference height = 0.2
Depth = Absolute
Depth = -1.8625 (or 1.75 + 0.3 x 3/8)
First peck increment = 0.7

2. Use Window command to select points to be drilled.

Step 1. Open the part geometry file drill1.

Select **MAIN MENU → File → Get**
File name: **drill1**

The part drawing should appear as Figure 7.128.

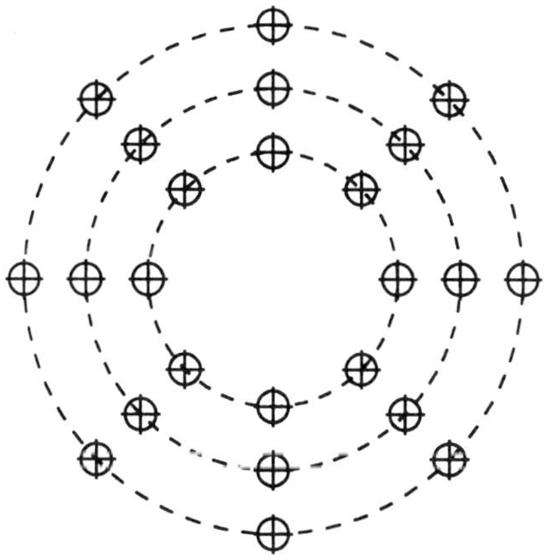

Figure 7.128

Step 2. Initiate the drill module.

Select **MAIN MENU → Toolpaths → Drill**
Select **Options**
The point sorting menu should appear as here.

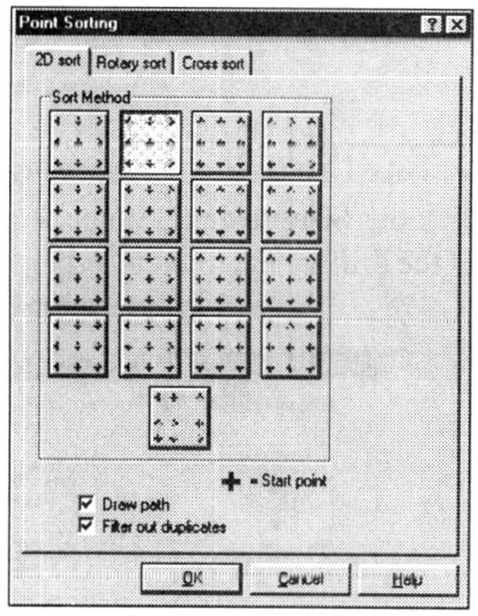

Select the **X ZIG+ Y+** option which is located at second left of the top row
Select **OK**
Select **Window pts**
Pick two points to form a window including all points

The drilling paths should appear as in Figure 7.129.

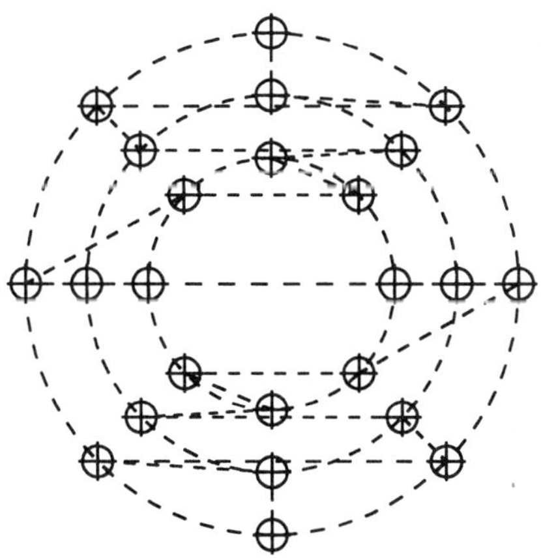

Figure 7.129

Select **Done**

Step 3. Select a 3/8" drill and define the tool parameters.

Click the right mouse button, then select **Get tool from library**
Select **tool #128** (3/8 drill)
Select **OK**
Set the tool parameters as below.

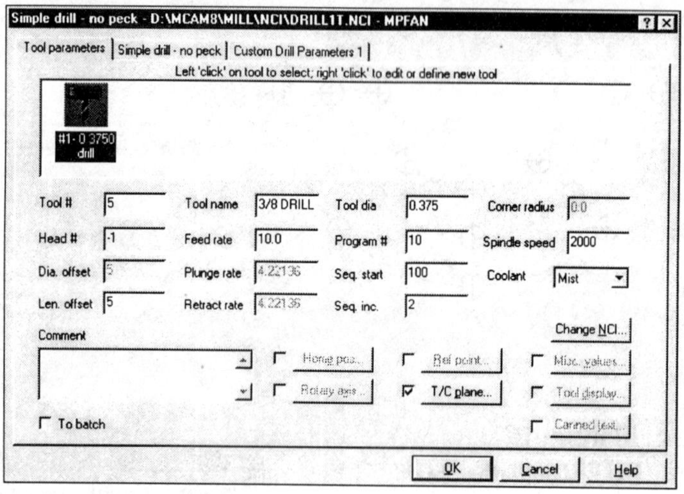

Step 4. Define the drill parameters.

Click the **Simple drill - no peck** button
Set the drilling parameters as below.

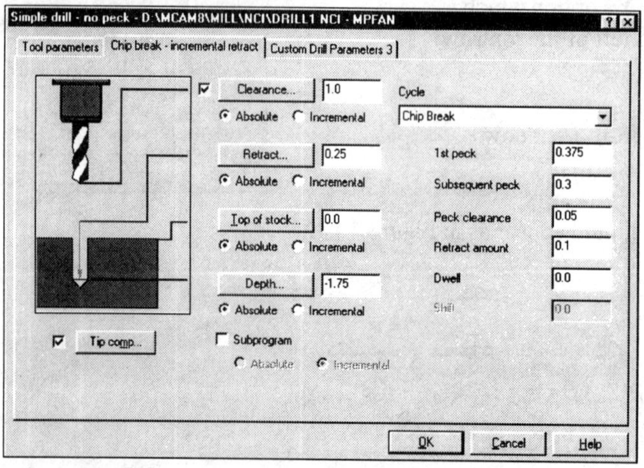

Step 5. Define the tip compensation parameters.

Click the **Tip comp** button

Set the tip compensation parameters as below.

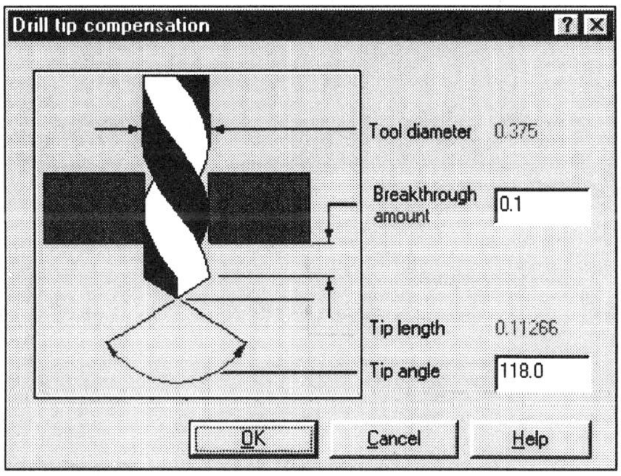

Select **OK → OK**
Select **Gview → Isometric**
The drilling toolpaths are shown in Figure 7.130.

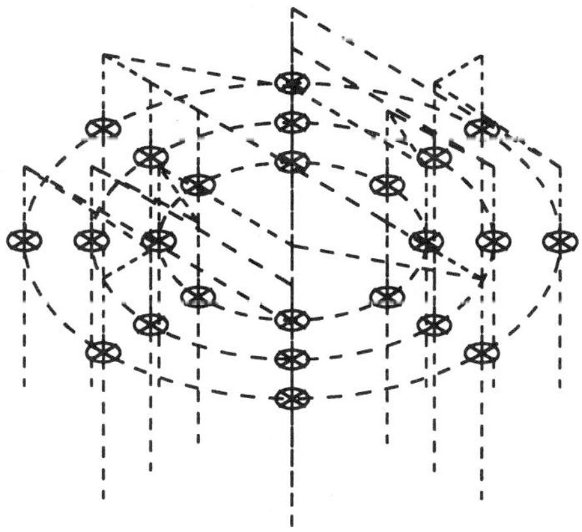

Figure 7.130

Step 6. Backplot the toolpaths.

Select **Operations**
The Operations Manager menu appears on the screen as below.

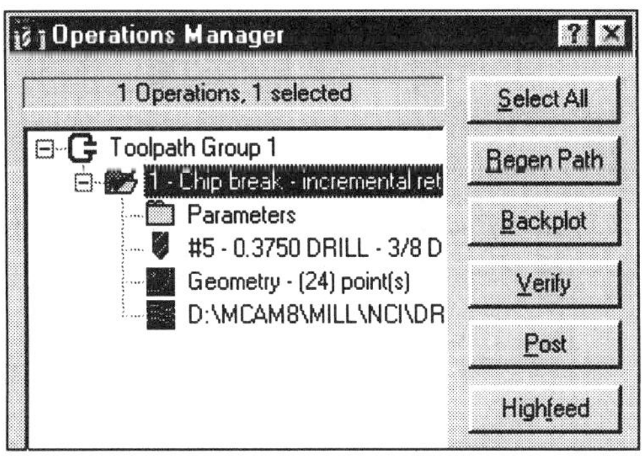

Select **Backplot → Display**
Set the display parameters as shown next.

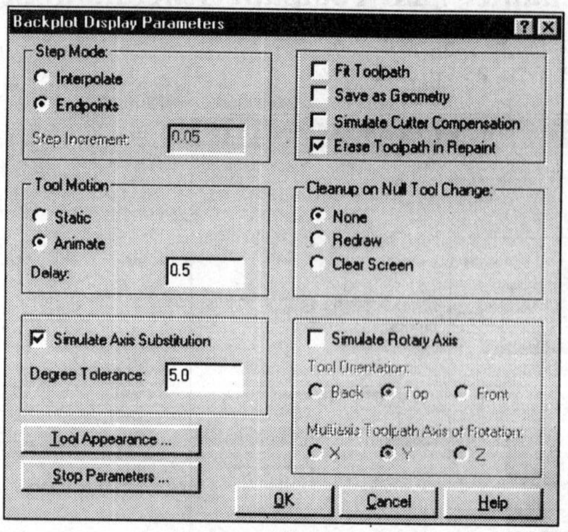

Select **OK**
Select **Run**
The drilling toolpaths will be plotted on the screen.
You will see the sequence of drilling holes.
Select **BACKUP**

Step 7. Run the post processor.

Select **Post** from the Operations Manager menu
Select **Save NC file → OK**
File name for NC: **drill1→ Save**

Step 8. Edit the part program.

Select **OK** from the Operations Manager menu
Select **MAIN MENU → File → Edit → NC**
File name: **drill1**
The NC Editor menu appears as below.

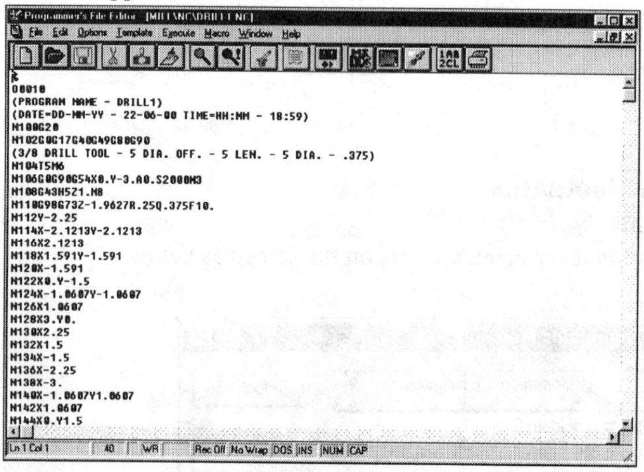

Note: Your part program may be somewhat different from the one listed here if you use a different post processor. Do all necessary changes to the program.

Step 9. Exit the NC editor.

Select **File → Exit**

Step 10. Save the toolpaths.

Select **MAIN MENU → File → Save**
File name: **drill1t**

Project 7. Drilling and tapping six holes

The part shown in Figure 7.131a has six 9/16-12 internal threads. Producing these six internal threads requires two operations, drilling and tapping. The tap drill size is 31/64 in. Figure 7.131b shows the drilling and tapping toolpaths.

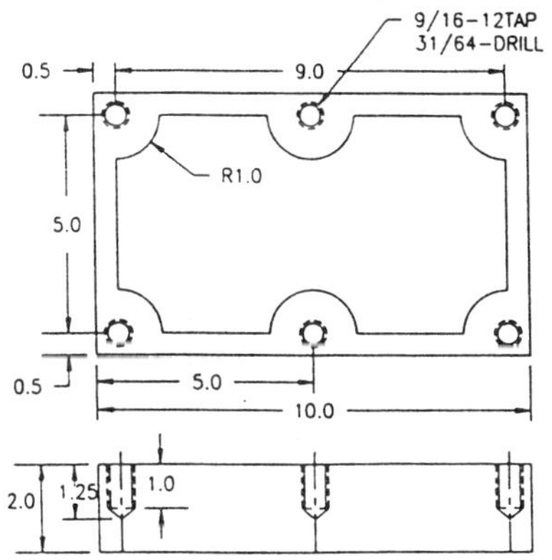

Figure 7.131a

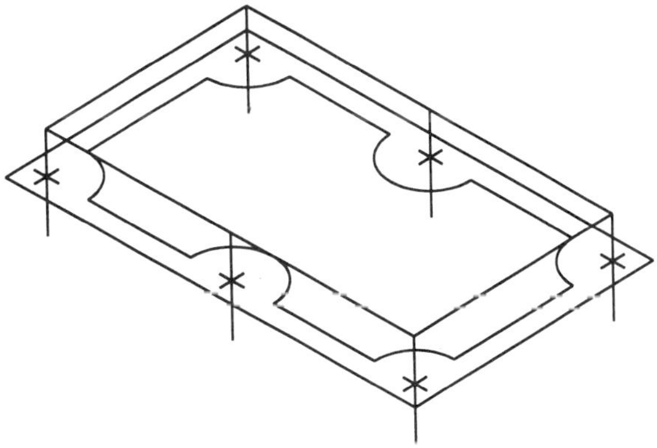

Figure 7.131b

Tips
1. The operation sequence starts with drilling all six holes and then is following by tapping.

2. Use the "Automatic" option to select the points to be drilled, then use "Repeat the points" option to select the drilled points for tapping.
3. The drilling depth is calculated as follows:

4. Drilling depth = Thread depth + 0.3 D + 0.1
   or = $-(1.0 + 0.3 \times (31/64) + 0.1) = -1.25$
   where D is drill diameter
   0.1 is the buffer distance for tapping

Step 1. Open the part geometry file drill2.

Select **MAIN MENU → File → Get**

File name: **drill2**

The part geometry appears as in Figure 7.132.

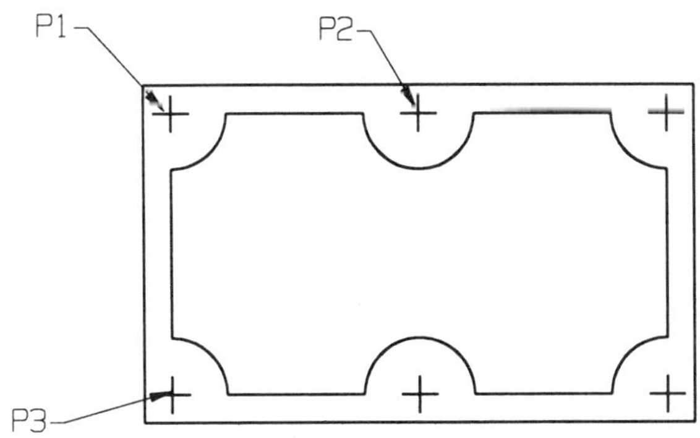

Figure 7.132

Step 2. Initiate the drill module.

Select **MAIN MENU → Toolpaths → Drill**
Select **Options**
Select the **X ZIG+ Y-** option from the point sorting menu as here.

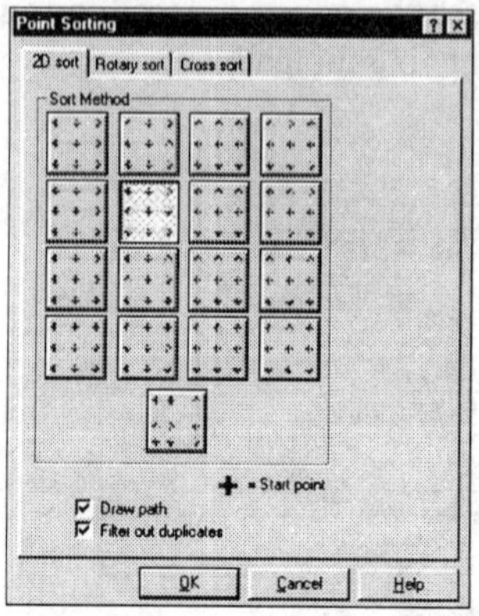

Select **OK**
Select **Automatic**
Pick **P1** as the first point
Pick **P2** as the second point
Pick **P3** as the last point
Select **Done**
Select **Gview → Isometric**

Six points are included in this selection and their path sequence is shown in Figure 7.133.

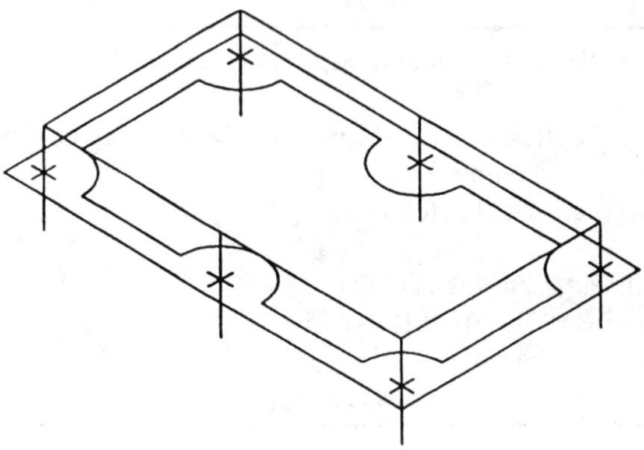

Figure 7.133

Step 3. Select a 31/64" drill.

Click the right mouse button, then select **Get tool from library**
Select **tool #140** (31/64 drill)
Select **OK**
Set the tool parameters as below.

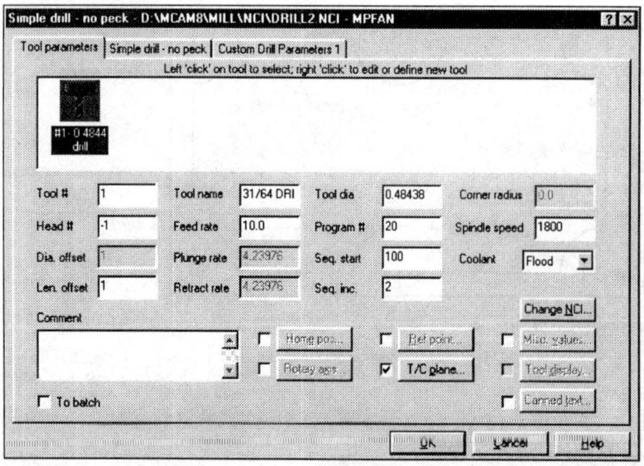

Step 4. Define drilling parameters.

Click the **Simple drill – no peck** button
Set the drilling parameters as below.

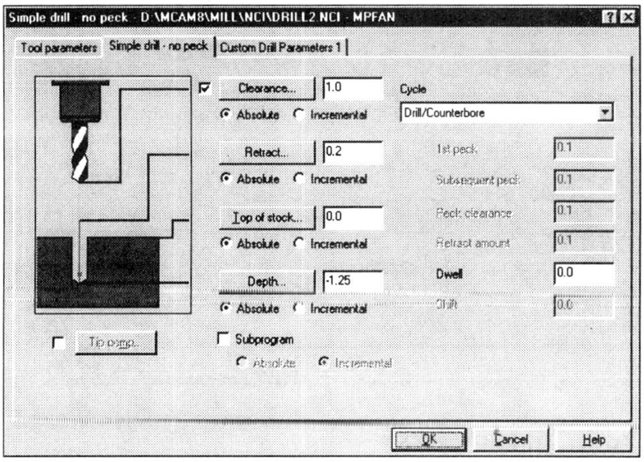

Select **OK** to generate drilling toolpaths

The drilling toolpaths are shown in figure 7.133.

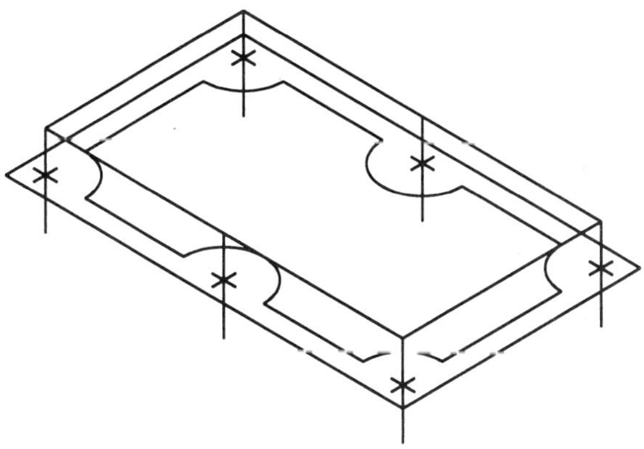

Figure 7.133

Step 5. Initiate the drill module again.

Select **Drill**
Select **Last** to use the previous point set
Select **Done**

Step 6. Select a 9/16 – 12 tap and set the tool parameters.

Click the right mouse button, then select **Get tool from library**
Select **tool #209** (9/16 – 12 right hand tap)
Select **OK**

Set the tool parameters as below.

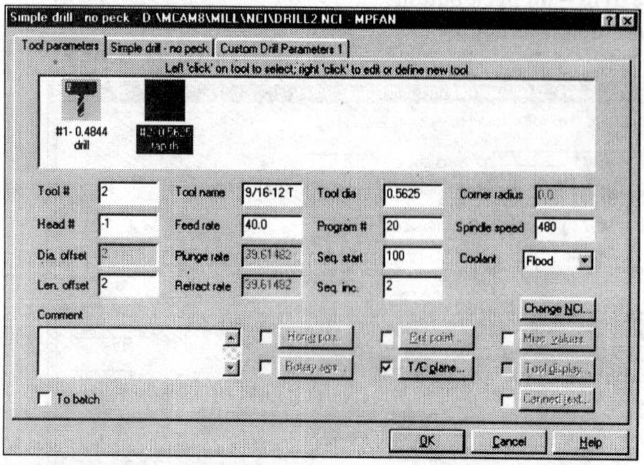

Step 7. Define the tapping parameters.

Click the **Simple drill - no peck** button

Set the tapping parameters as below.

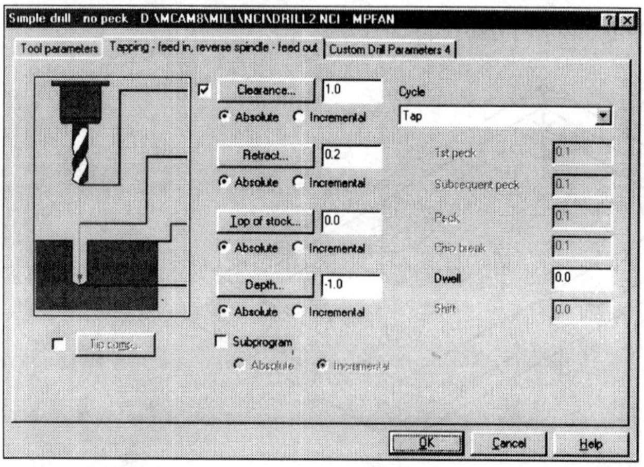

Select **OK** to generate the tapping toolpaths

Step 8. Backplot the toolpaths.

Select **Operations**

Two sets of toolpaths are included in the Operations Manager menu as below.

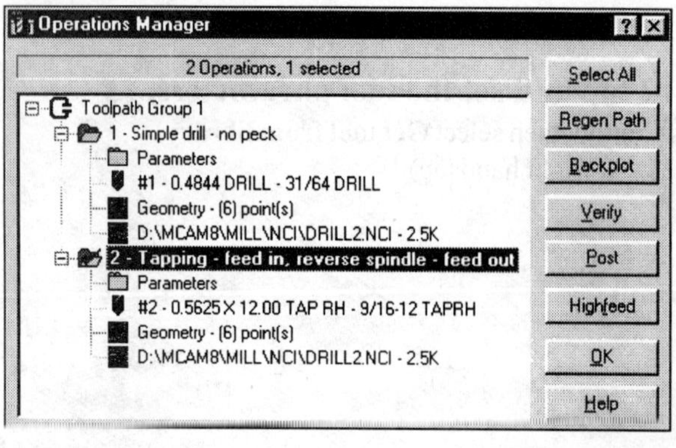

Select **Select All** to include both sets of toolpaths
Select **Backplot**
Select **Run** to backplot the two sets of toolpaths on the screen
Select **BACKUP** to return to Operations Manager menu

Step 9. Run the post processor.

Select **Post**
Toggle **Save NC file** and **Edit (NC)**
Select **OK**
File name for part program: **drill2**
Select **Save**
The file list for the part program appears on the screen. The NC program is listed below.

```
%
O0020
(PROGRAM NAME - DRILL2)
(DATE=DD-MM-YY - 05-07-00 TIME=HH:MM - 14:56)
N100G20
N102G0G17G40G49G80G90
(31/64 DRILL TOOL - 1 DIA. OFF. - 1 LEN. - 1 DIA. - .48438)
N104T1M6
N106G0G90G54X.5Y5.5A0.S1800M3
N108G43H1Z1.M8
N110G98G81Z-1.25R.2F10.
N112X5.
N114X9.5
N116Y.5
N118X5.
N120X.5
N122G80
N124M5
N126G91G28Z0.M9
N128G28X0.Y0.A0.
N130M01
(9/16-12 TAPRH TOOL - 2 DIA. OFF. - 2 LEN. - 2 DIA. - .5625)
N132T2M6
N134G0G90G54X.5Y5.5A0.S480M3
N136G43H2Z1.M8
N138G98G84Z-1.R.2F40.
N140X5.
N142X9.5
N144Y.5
N146X5.
N148X.5
N150G80
N152M5
N154G91G28Z0.M9
N156G28X0.Y0.A0.
N158M30
%
```

Click the **Close** button to exit the file list program
Select **OK** to leave the Operations Manager

Step 10. Save the toolpaths.

Select **MAIN MENU → File → Save**
File name: **drill2t**

Project 8. Drilling and boring four holes

This project generates toolpaths for drilling four holes with two different depths and two different retraction heights as shown in Figure 7.134. The drill has a diameter of ¾ in All four holes have the same top surface level (Z = -0.75). The Z-value of the bottom depth for holes A and B is –1.5 in. and for holes C and D is –2.25 in. This is an ideal case to use the edit depth command for defining different depths. As can be seen, there is a step between the two rows of holes. The edit jump command can be readily used to define the retract height for two Z-levels.

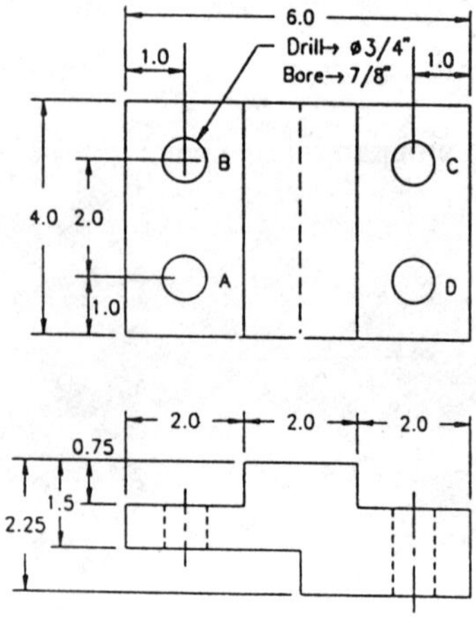

Figure 7.134a

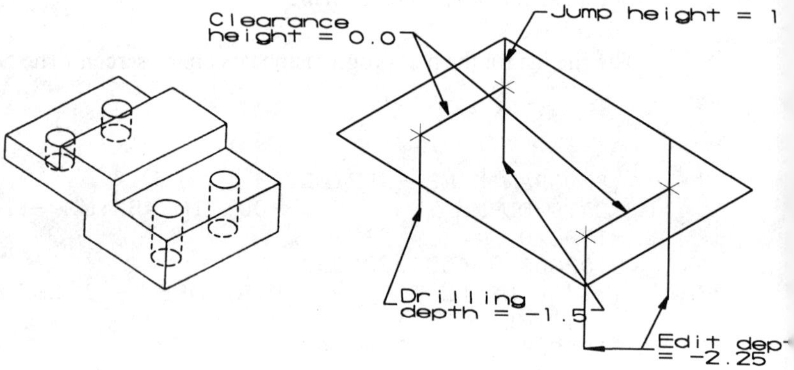

Figure 7.134b

> **Tips** 1. Use edit depth command to change the drilling depth to Z = –2.25 at points C and D.
>
> 2. Use edit jump command to change the retract level at point B to retract the cutter higher than the step for moving to point C.

Step 1. Open the part geometry file drill3.

Select **MAIN MENU → File → Get**

File name: **drill3**

The part drawing should appear as in Figure 7.135.

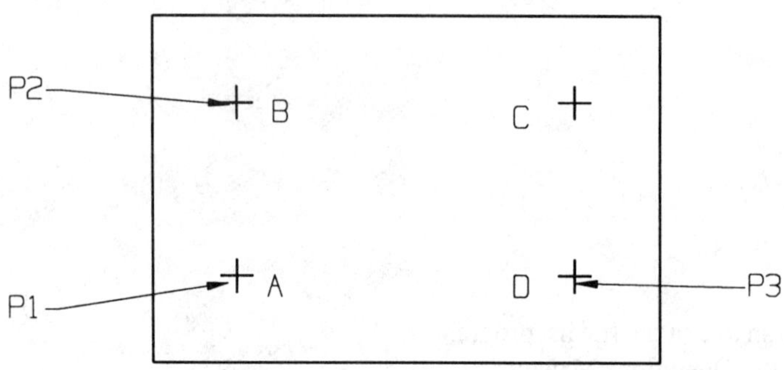

Figure 7.135

Step 2. Initiate the drill module.

Use the pick points in Figure 7.135.
Select **MAIN MENU → Toolpaths → Drill**
Select **Options**
Select the **Y ZIG+ X+** option as shown here.

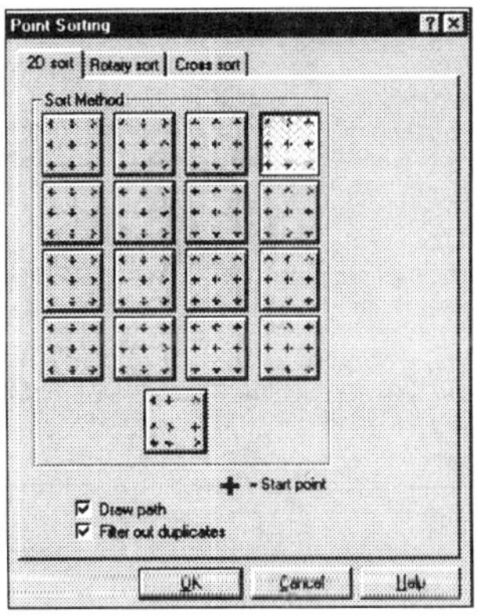

Select **OK**
Select **Automatic**
Pick **P1** as the first point
Pick **P2** as the second point
Pick **P3** as the last point
Select **Gview → Isometric**
The drilling paths are shown in Figure 7.136.

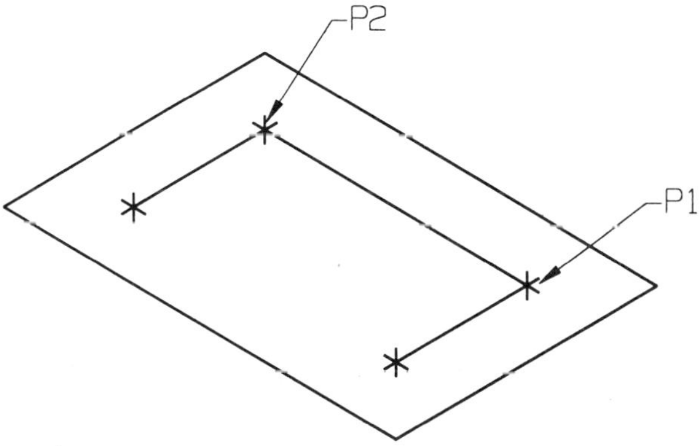

Figure 7.136

Step 3. Change the drilling depth for holes C and D.

Use the pick points in Figure 7.136.
Select **Edit → Edit depth**
Pick **P1** to select hole C
Enter depth (absolute relative to toolplane): **-2.25** ↵
Select **Yes** to "Apply change to subsequent planar points?"
Select **BACKUP**

Step 4. Change the retract height for hole B.

Select **Edit jump**
Pick **P2** to select hole B
Enter jump height (absolute relative to toolplane): **1.0**↵
Select **No** to "Apply change to subsequent planar points?"
Select **BACKUP**
Select **Done → Done**

Step 5. Define the tool parameters.

Click the right mouse button, then select **Get tool from library**
Select tool # **214** (3/4 drill)
Select **OK**

Define the tool parameters as below.

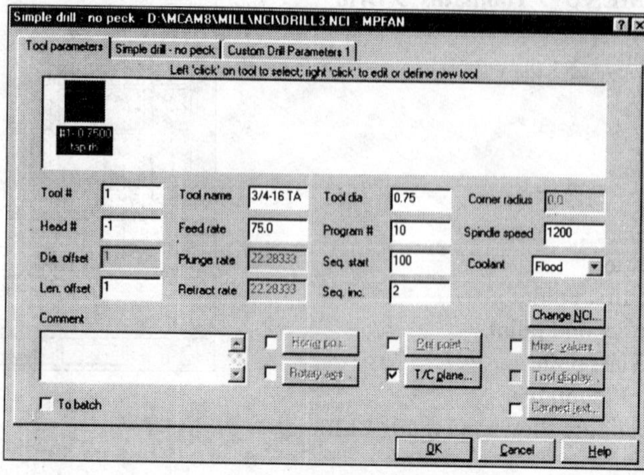

Step 6. Define the drilling parameters.

Click the **Simple drill – no peck** button

Set the drilling parameters as below.

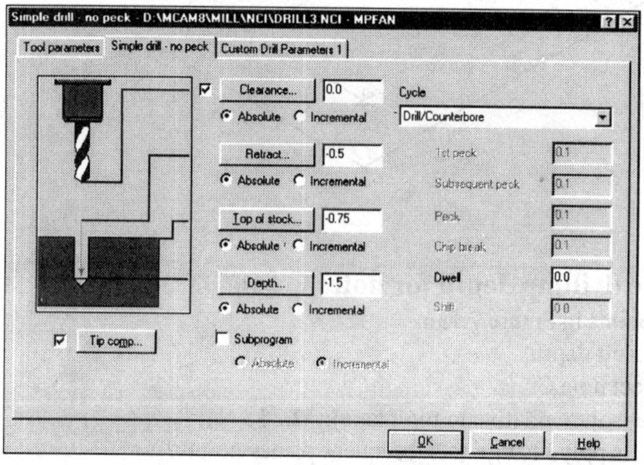

Select **OK** to generate drilling toolpaths

Drilling toolpaths with different depths and retraction levels are shown in Figure 7.137.

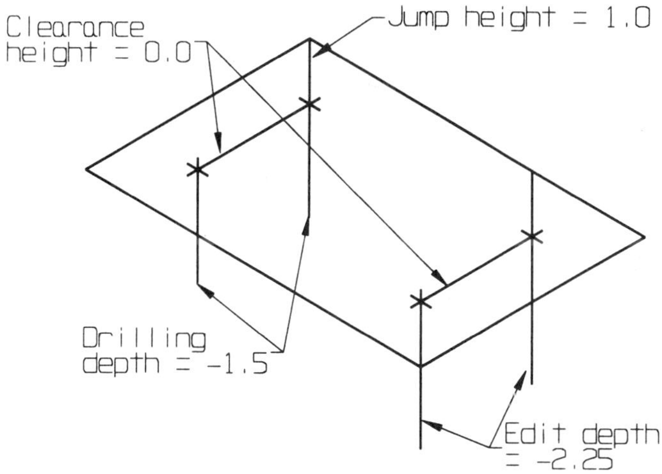

Figure 7.137

Step 7. Backplot the drilling toolpaths.

Select **Operations** to open the Operations Manager menu
Select **Backplot**
Select **Step** to plot the first toolpath
Note: The coordinate value of each toolpath end point will be displayed. Check to verify the various Z-depths.
Continue to select **Step** until the end of toolpaths
Select **OK** to "Backplot complete"
Select **BACKUP** to return to the Operations Manager menu
Select **OK** to exit the Operations Manager

Step 8. Save the toolpaths.

Select **MAIN MENU → File → Save**
File name: **drill3t**

7.12 Circle mill Module

This toolpath module is used to generate a toolpath pattern for cutting a circle. Its toolpath pattern is listed below (Figure 7.138):

1. Plunge to the circle center
2. Add an entry line move
3. Add an entry arc move
4. Cut the circle
5. Add an exit arc move
6. Add an exit line move

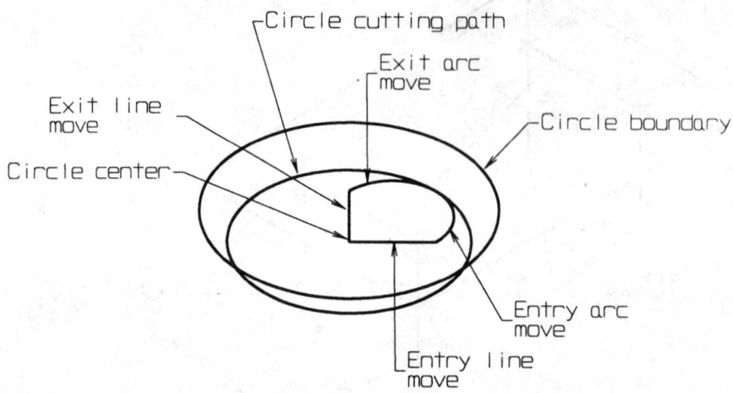

Figure 7.138a

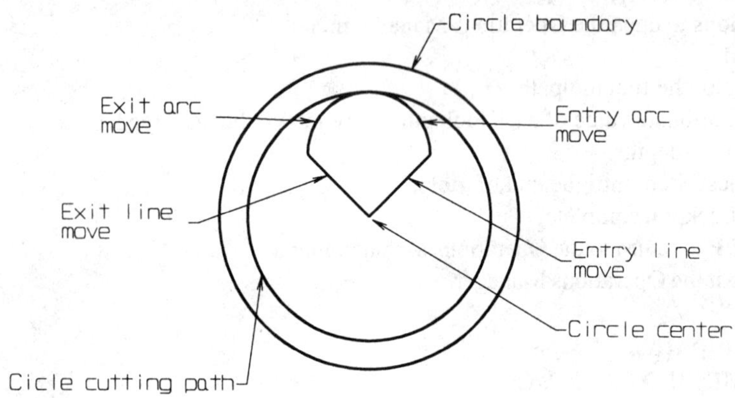

Figure 7.138b

The Circmill parameter dialog box appears as below.

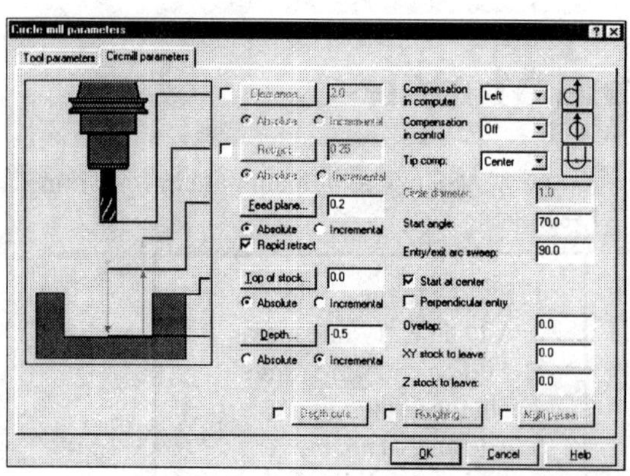

Project 9. Using circmill function to cut internal circle

This is a very simple project to show how to use the circmill function to generate toolpaths to cut a circle. Figure 7.139 shows the circle geometry and toolpaths.

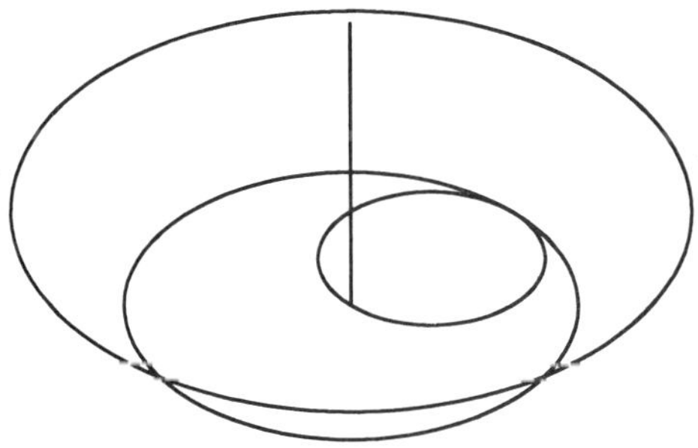

Figure 7.139

Step 1. Create a circle with its center at (0,0) and a diameter of 3-in.

Select **MAIN MENU → Create → Arc → Circ pt+dia**
Enter the diameter: **3** ↵
Enter the center point: **0,0** ↵
Select **Gview → Isometric**
The circle appears as in Figure 7.140.

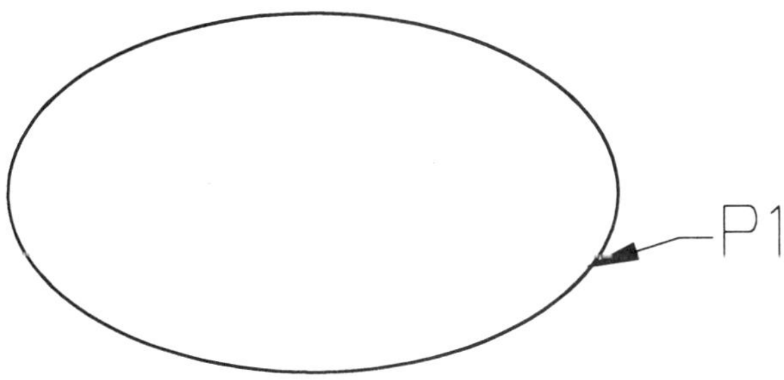

Figure 7.140

Step 2. Initiate the circmill module.

Select **MAIN MENU → Toolpaths → Next menu → Circ tlpths → Circle mill → Entities**
Pick **P1** to select the circle
Select **Done**

Step 3. Select a .5 flatend mill and set the tool parameters

Click on the right mouse button
Select **Get tool from library**
Select **tool #239** (0.500 flatend mill) → **OK**

Set the tool parameters as below.

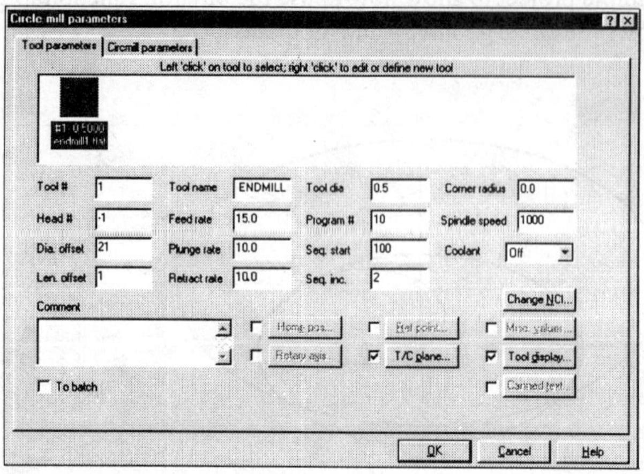

Step 4. Define the Circmill parameters.

Click the **Circmill parameters tab**

Set the parameters as below.

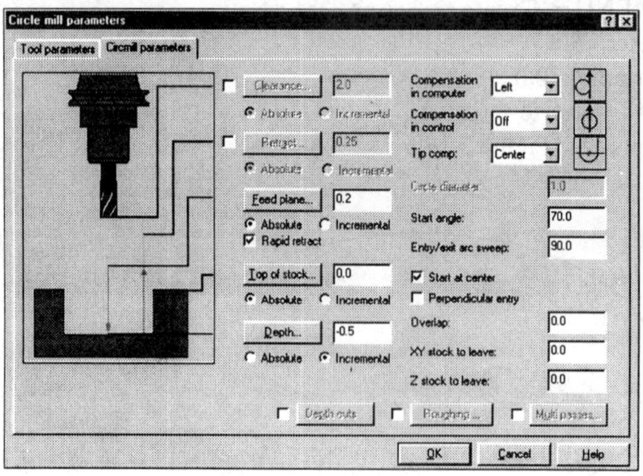

Select **OK**

The toolpaths are generated as in Figure 7.141.

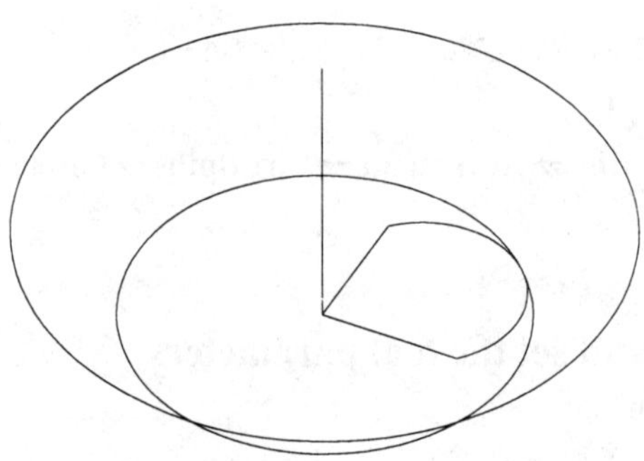

Figure 7.141

Step 5. Save the toolpath file.

Select **MAIN MENU → File → Save**

File name: **circmillt**

7.13 Point Module

This toolpath module is used to generate a set of linear toolpaths that position the tool at specified locations. Its menu appears as below.

Goto XY:	specify the point locations using X and Y.
Goto XYZ:	specify the point locations using X, Y and Z.
Tool up:	move the tool down.
Tool down:	move the tool up.
Backup:	removes last point in toolpath and moves back to previous point.
Feed rate:	sets feed rate between points.
Jump ht:	sets Z height.
Depth:	sets Z depth.

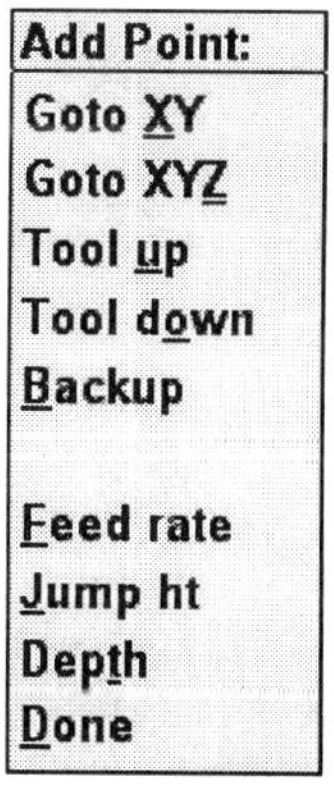

The point parameters menu appears as below.

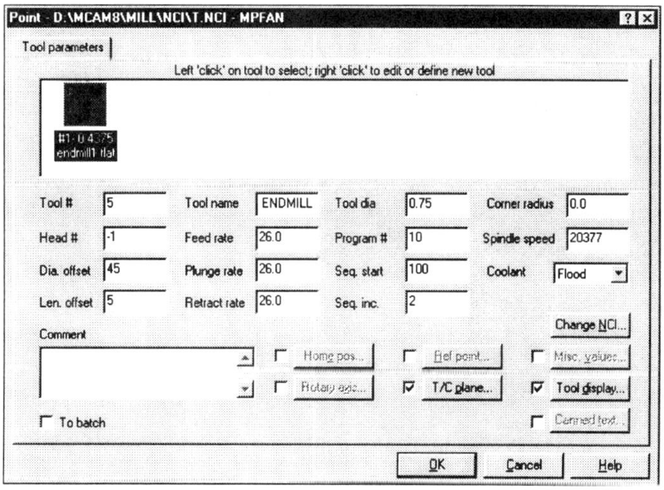

7.14 Engraving Letters

Engraving letters on part surfaces is a common machining application. Letters of various types and sizes can be created by using the Letters function. The contour or pocket toolpath module is then used to generate toolpaths from the existing lettering geometry. Lettering geometries can be created in two ways: **letters function** and the **edit note method**. These two methods are presented in chapter 5.

This section presents two lettering projects. The first project uses the contour and pocket modules to generate toolpaths for letters in which their geometries have been defined by using the Create → Letters commands. The second project involves using the Edit note method to create lettering geometries. These notes are modified to various fonts, sizes, and orientation. Finally the contour toolpath module is used to generate toolpaths for cutting letters.

Project 10. Using the contour and pocket module to generate toolpaths for cutting existing lettering geometries

Figure 7.142a

Figure 7.142b

Figure 7.142c

Figure 7.142d

Tips 1. Use the geometry file (letter2).

2. Use the contour module to generate toolpaths for engraving letters in the outside circle.

3. Use the pocket module to generate toolpaths for letters in the inner circle. The inner circle is used as the outside contour and profiles of these letters as islands.

4. Verify the toolpaths.

Step 1. Open the geometry file letter2.

Select **MAIN MENU → File → Open**
File name: **letter2**
The part drawing appears as Figure 7.143.

Figure 7.143

Step 2. Make levels 1 and 3 invisible.

Select **Level**
Toggle levels **1** and **3** to invisible (check unmarked)
Select **OK → OK** to return to graphic mode
The new drawing becomes Figure 7.144.

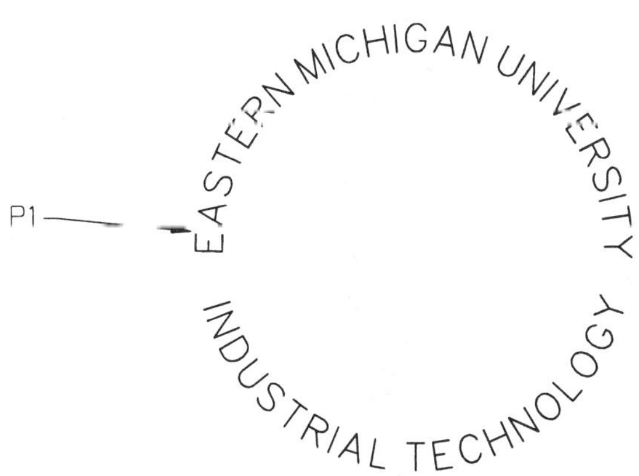

Figure 7.144

Step 3. Initiate the contour toolpath module.

Use the pick point in Figure 7.144.

Select **MAIN MENU → Toolpaths → Contour**

Select **Window**

Pick two points to include all entities

Select **Endpoint**, then pick **P1** to select a search point

Select **Done**

Step 4. Select a tool and define the tool parameters.

Click the right mouse button, then select **Get tool from library**

Select **tool #248** (3/32 sphere end mill)

Select **OK**

Set the tool parameters as below.

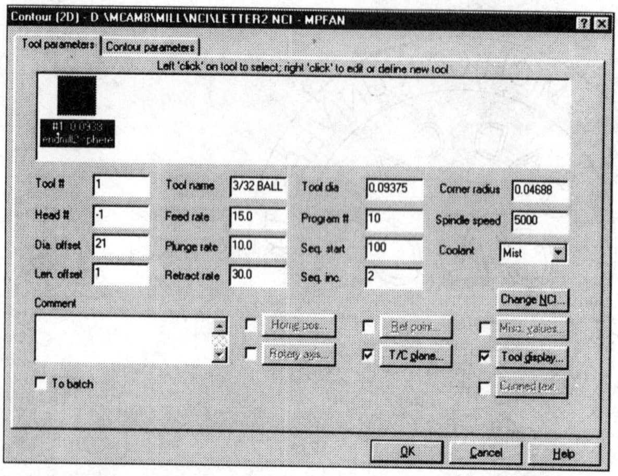

Step 5. Define the contour parameters.

Click the **Contour parameters** button

Set the contour parameters as below.

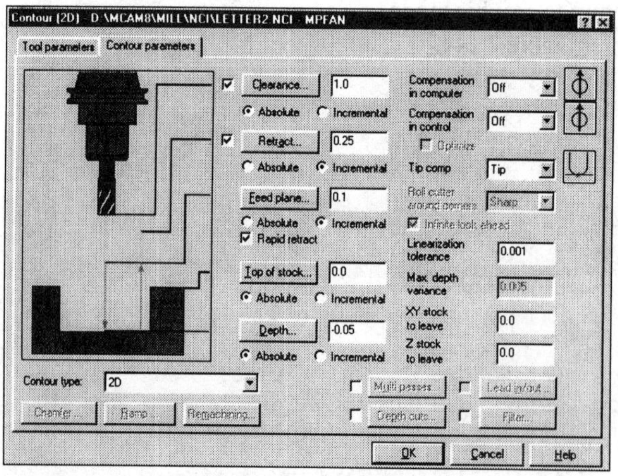

Select **OK**

The toolpaths should appear onscreen as Figure 7.145.

Figure 7.145

Step 6. Make level 2 invisible and levels 1 and 3 visible.

Select **Level**
Toggle levels **1** and **3** to visible (check marked) and level **2** to invisible (check unmarked)
Select OK to return to graphic mode
The new drawings should look like Figure 7.146.
Note: the toolpaths are still visible on the screen.

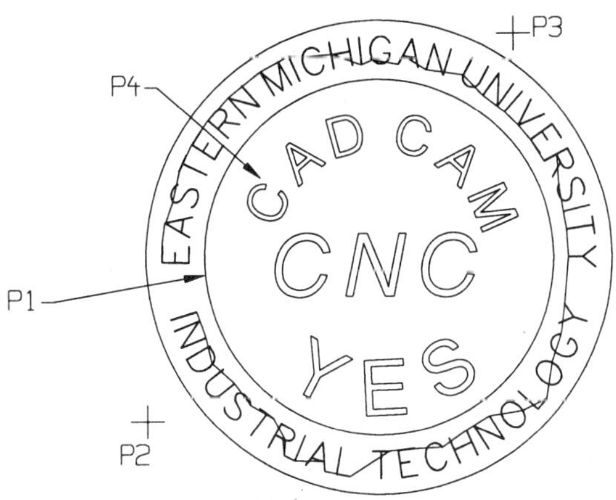

Figure 7.146

Step 7. Initiate the pocket module.

Select **MAIN MENU → Toolpaths → Pocket**
Pick **P1** to select the first contour
Select **Mode → Window**
Pick **P2** and **P3** to include all letter strings yet the inside circle is not fully included
Select **Endpoint**, then pick **P4**
Select **Done**

Set the tool parameters as below.

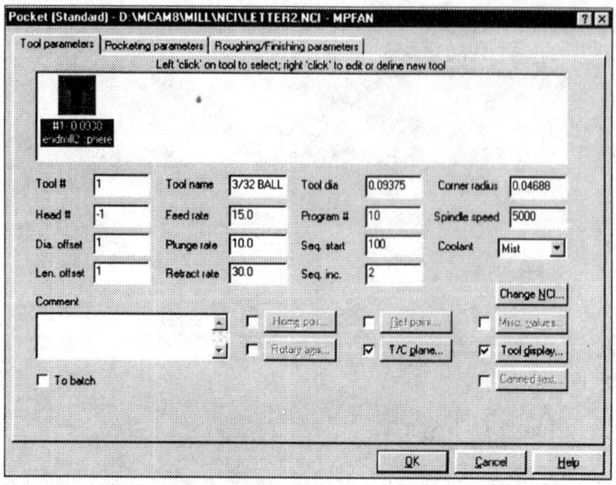

Step 8. Define the pocketing parameters.

Click the **Pocketing parameters** button
Set the pocketing parameters as below.

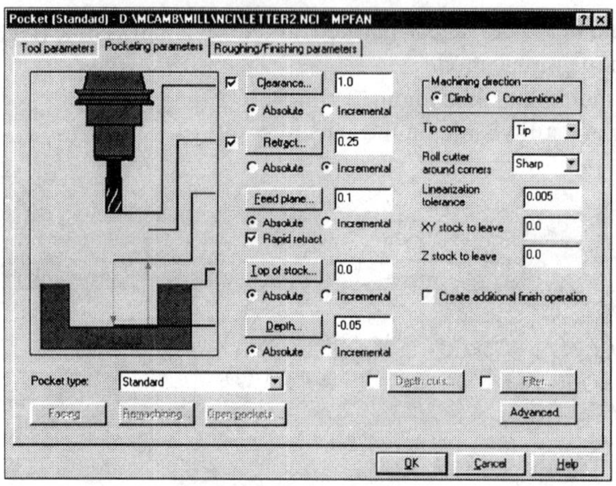

Step 9. Define the roughing/finishing parameters.

Click the **Roughing/Finishing parameters** button
Set the roughing and finishing parameters as below.

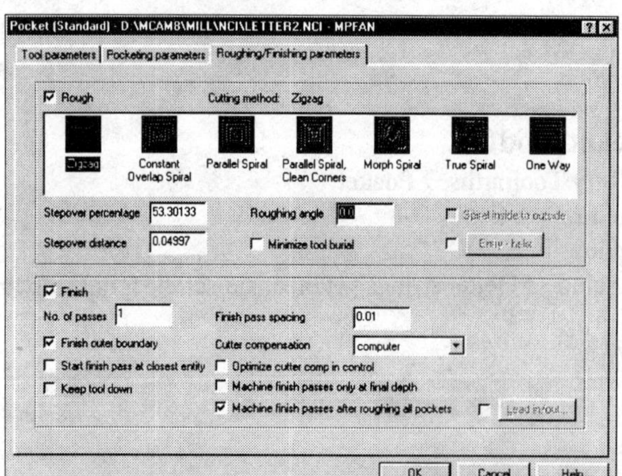

Select **OK** to generate the toolpaths as shown in Figure 7.147.

Figure 7.147

Step 10. Change to isometric view.

Select **Gview → Isometric**

The model with toolpaths shown in isometric view appear as Figure 7.148.

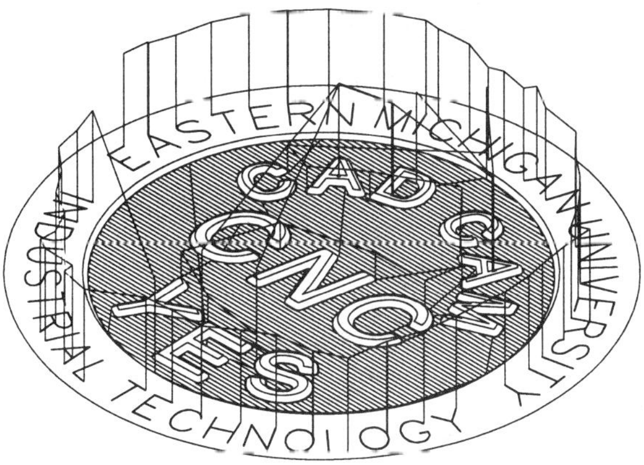

Figure 7.148

Step 11. Define the job setup parameters.

Select **Job setup**

Set the job setup parameters as below.

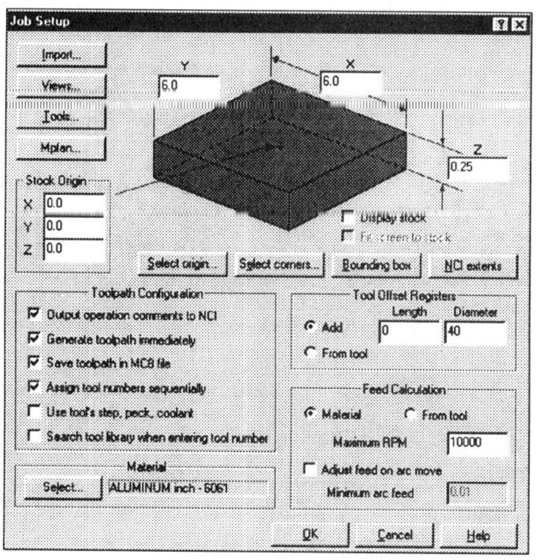

Select **OK**

Step 12. Verify the toolpaths.

Select **Operations** to open Operations Manager menu
Select **Select All**
Select **Verify**
Select **Configure**
Select **Turbo (no tool) in Tool parameter → OK**
Select **Machine**
The model shown in isometric view should look like Figure 7.149.

Figure 7.149

Step 13. Show the model in the top view.

Select **Gview → Top**
The model shown in the top view appears as in Figure 7.150.

Figure 7.150

Step 14. Save the model.

Select **BACKUP** to return to Operations Manager menu
Select **OK** to return to graphic mode
Select **MAIN MENU → File → Save**
File name: **letter2t**

Project 12. Using the contour module to generate toolpaths for cutting lettering geometires that are converted from notes 12

This project generates toolpaths to cut three strings of letters that are in different fonts and a combination of upper and lower cases. The lettering geometries must be created by the edit note method because lower case letters are involved. The specifications of these lettering strings are shown in Figure 7.151.

Modern

Font: Old English
Height = 0.4"
Aspect = 0.5
Location = (0.3,1.45)

CNC

Font: Swiss
Height = 0.6"
Aspect = 0.6
Location = (2.25,0.25)

Technology

Font: European
Height = 0.45"
Aspect = 0.5
Location = (0.5,0.1) then rotate 26.565 degrees

Figure 7.151a

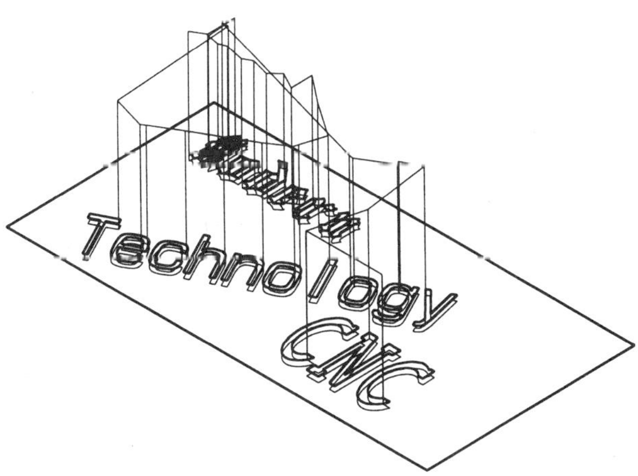

Figure 7.151b

Figure 7.151c

> ⌛**Tips** 1. Use the edit note method to create lettering geometries. The procedures are:
>
> a. Create three notes using the following commands:
> **Create → Drafting → Note**
>
> b. Edit these three notes to their desired size, font, and orientation using commands:
> **Create → Drafting → Multi edit → Note**
>
> c. Convert these three notes to geometries by using the following commands:
> **Modify → Break → Craft/line**
>
> 2. Use the contour toolpath module to generate toolpaths.
>
> 3. The cutter is a 1/16" end mill.

Step 1. Create a rectangle 4" x 2".

Select **MAIN MENU → Create → Rectangle → 2 points**
Enter the lower left corner: **0,0** ↵
Enter the upper right corner: **4,2** ↵
Press **Alt** + **F1** then **F2** to fit the drawing.
The rectangle should appear as in Figure 7.152.

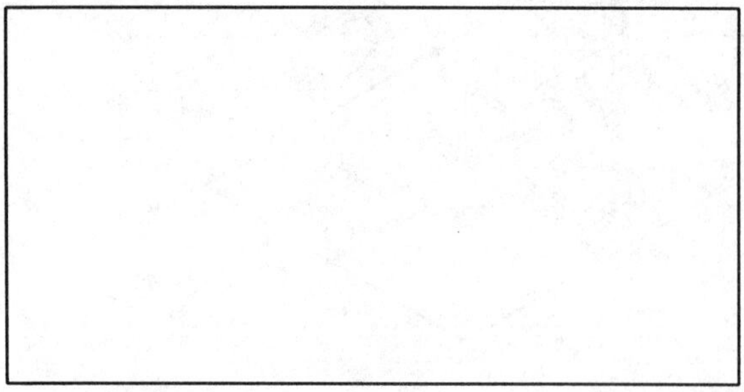

Figure 7.152

Step 2. Set the character height to 0.12" and character aspect to 0.5.

Select **MAIN MENU → Create → Drafting → Globals**
Select **Note Text** Tab
Set **Text Height** at 0.12 as shown here:

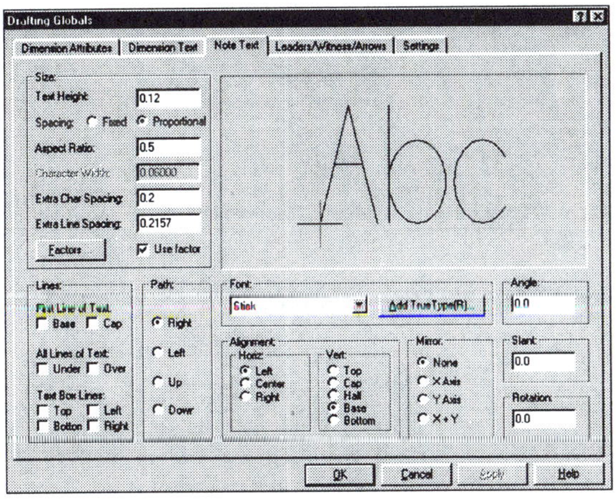

Select **OK** to return to graphic mode

Step 3. Create three notes.

Select **MAIN MENU → Create → Drafting → Note**
Key in text: **Modern**
Select **Multiple Notes → OK**
Press **P** for point entry
Enter coordinate values **(0.3, 1.45)** ↵
Press **T** for Text entry
Text: **Technology → OK**
Press **P** for point entry
Enter coordinate values **(0.5, 0.1)** for the second note ↵
Press **T** for Text entry
Text: **CNC → OK**
Press **P** for point entry
Enter coordinate values **(2.25, 0.25)** for the third note ↵
Press the **Esc key** to exit the note creation function
The three notes are added as shown in Figure 7.153.

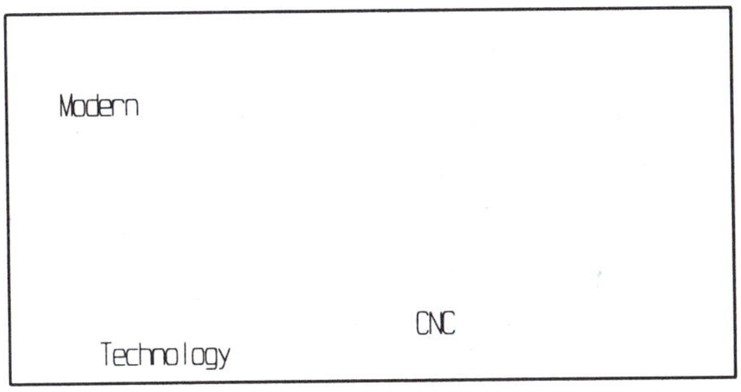

Figure 7.153

Step 4. Edit the first note "Modern".

Select **MAIN MENU → Create → Drafting → Multi edit**

Select Drafting Entities: pick the note **Modern**, then select **Done**

Change the Note Text Height and Font type as below.

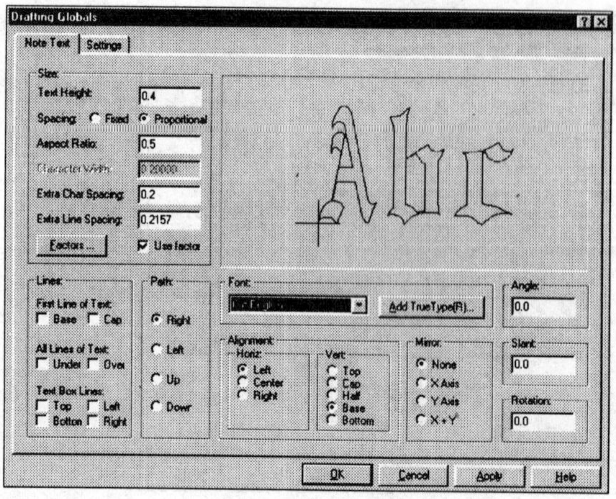

Select **OK**

The note "Modern" has been changed as shown in Figure 7.154.

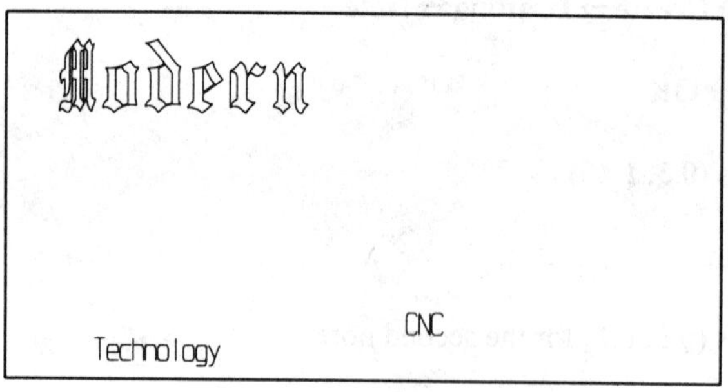

Figure 7.154

Step 5. Edit the second note "Technology".

Select **Multi edit**

Pick the note **Technology**, then select **Done**

Change the Note height and font type as below.

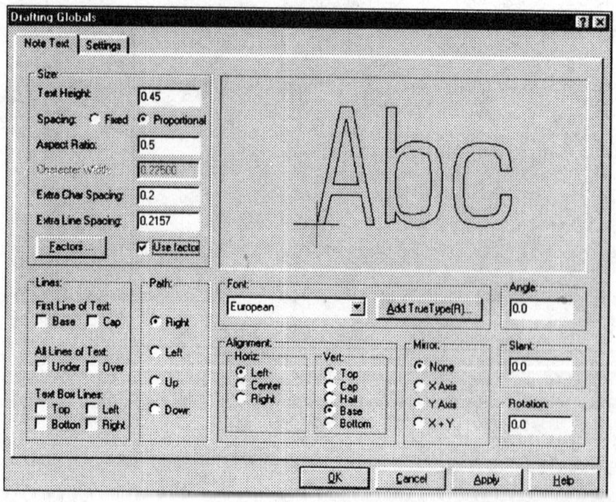

Select **OK**

The note "Technology" has been changed as shown in Figure 7.155.

Figure 7.155

Step 6. Rotate the note "Technology" by an angle of 26.565 degrees.

Select **MAIN MENU → Xform → Rotate**

Select entities to rotate: pick the note **Technology**

Select **Done**

Enter the point to rotate about: **0.5, 0.1**

Set the rotate parameters as below.

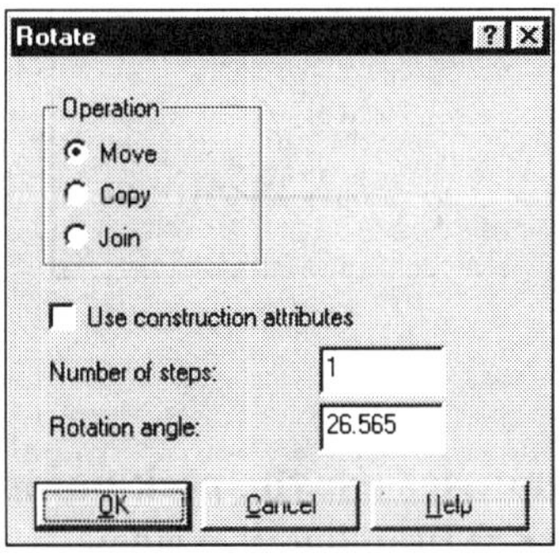

Select **OK**

The note "Technology" has been rotated to a new position as shown in Figure 7.156.

Figure 7.156

Step 7. Edit the third note "CNC".

Select **MAIN MENU → Create → Drafting → Multi edit**

Select drafting entities: pick the note **CNC**, then select **Done**

Change note height and font type as below.

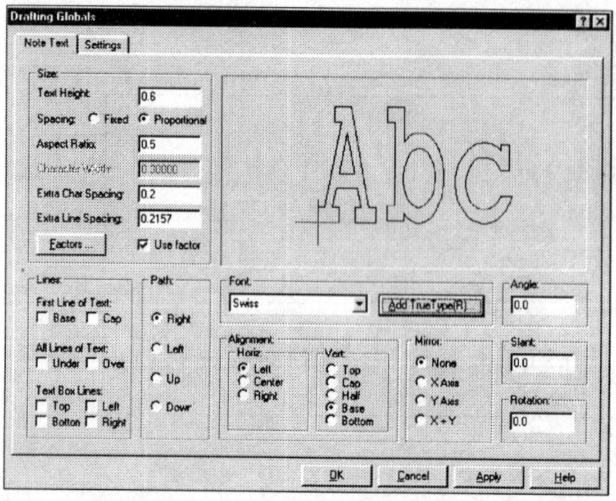

Select **OK**

The new drawing becomes Figure 7.157.

Figure 7.157

Step 8. Convert the three notes to geometries use the pick points in Figure 7.157.

Select **MAIN MENU → Modify → Break → Draft/line → Window**

Pck at **P1** and **P2** to select all three notes

Select **Done**

Note: These three notes have been converted to geometries. You may not see the difference graphically. The drawing is redrawn in Figure 7.158.

Figure 7.158

Step 9. Save the geometry file as letter3.

Select **MAIN MENU → File → Save**
File name: **letter3**

Step 10. Initiate the contour toolpath module.

Use the pick points in Figure 7.158.
Select **MAIN MENU → Toolpaths → Contour**
Select **Window**
Pick **P1** and **P2** to include all lettering geometries
Select **Endpoint**, then pick **P3** to select the search point
Select **Done**

Step 11. Select a cutter and define the tool parameters.

Click the right mouse button, then select **Get tool from library**
Select **tool #229** (1/32 flat endmill)
Select **OK**
Set the tool parameters as below.

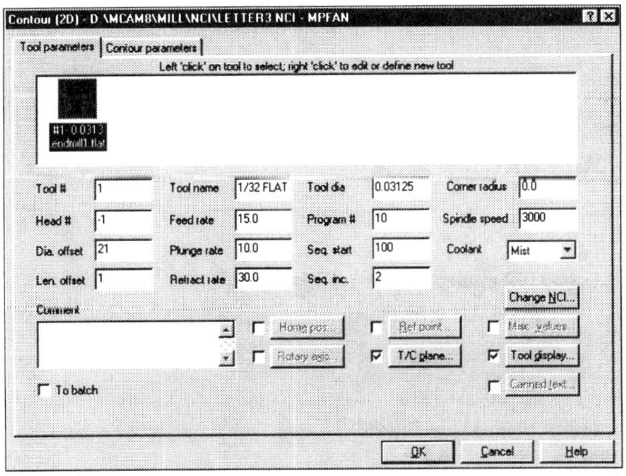

Step 12. Define the contour parameters.

Click the **Contour parameters** button
Set the contour parameters as below.

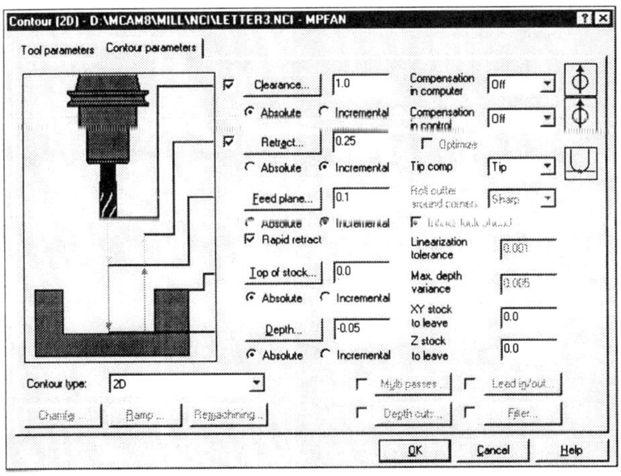

Select **OK** to generate the lettering toolpaths

Step 13. Change to isometric view.

Select **Gview → Isometric**

The geometries and toolpaths are shown in Figure 7.159.

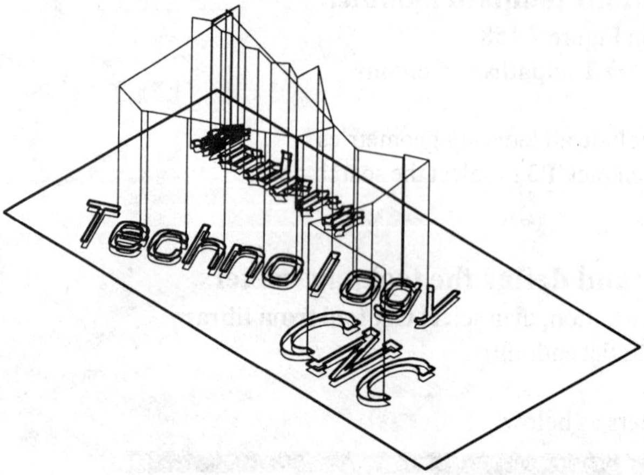

Figure 7.159

Step 14. Define the job setup parameters.

Select **Job setup**

Set the job setup parameters as below.

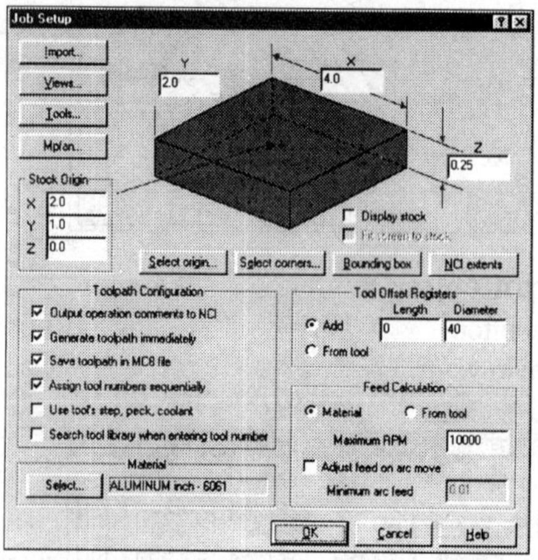

Select **OK**

Step 15. Verify the toolpaths.

Select **Operations → Verify**

Select **Machine**

Figure 7.160

Step 16. Exit the Verify utility.

Select **BACKUP** to return to Operations Manager menu
Select **OK** to return to graphic mode
Select **MAIN MENU → File → Save**
File name: **letter3t**

Ex Exercises

1. List the five 2D toolpath modules in Mastercam and briefly describe what they are.
2. What are three groups of parameters used to generate toolpaths?
3. What are the tool parameters?
4. List the commands to access the Tool Manager.
5. What is the operations manager?
6. List the four functions included in theoperations manager.
7. List the advantages of using the Verify utility.
8. What is job setup?
9. What is a contour?
10. Use drawings to describe how the picked entity affects the chaining direction of the contour.
11. What are the two types of contours?

12. List the four functions Mastercam uses to define the work coordinates of the part program.

13. Explain when you should use the contour module.

14. Use a drawing to describe these five Z-depth parameters.
    Clearance Retract Feed Top of stock Depth

15. Use a drawing to illustrate how the depth cut parameters affect the toolpaths in the Z-direction.

16. Use a drawing to illustrate how the multi-passes parameters affect toolpaths in the XY-direction.

17. Use drawings to illustrate the effect of stock to leave in toolpaths.

18. Describe the purposes of cutter compensation.

19. Describe the difference between the cutter compensation in control and cutter compensation in computer.

20. Explain how the selection of cutter compensation in computer (left, right or off) affects the toolpaths.

21. Write the proper command codes for three options (right, left and off) of cutter compensation in control with the assigned register number for diameter offset.

22. What are the purposes of using lead in and lead out moves?

23. Describe when to use the pocket module.

24. What are the seven cutting methods available in the pocket module?

25. What are islands?

26. Use a drawing to explain how to determine pocket loops and how the pocket loops affect toolpaths.

27. What are the two forms of rought entry?

28. Explain when the drill module should be used.

29. Use a drawing to define the following four Z-depth parameters used in the drill module:
    Clearance Retract Top of stock Depth

30. List the six standard cycle modes of the drill module.

31. Use a drawing to show how to create a point bolt circle pattern.

32. Use a drawing to show how to create a point grid pattern.

33. Explain how to use the Circle mill module.

34. Use a drawing to illustrate the toolpath pattern of the circle mill operation.

35. When to use NC point module?

Problems

36. Use the contour module to generate toolpaths for machining the part shown in Figure 7.161. The raw material is a hollow plate with an outside diameter of 6.1" and an inside diameter of 2.5". The part geometry file is **contour5** which is constructed in problem 14 of chapter 6.

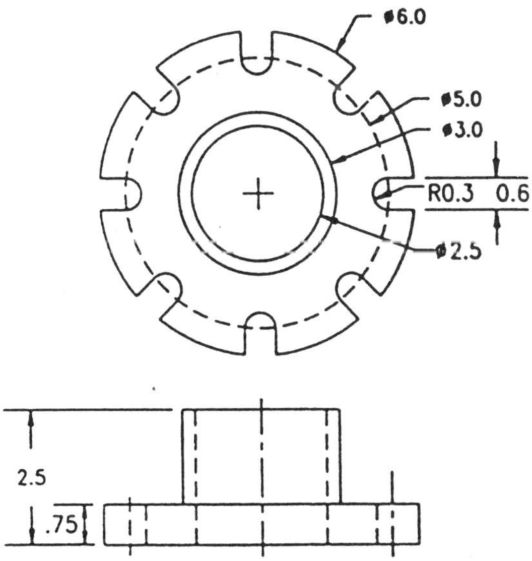

Figure 7.161

37. The raw material for the part shown in Figure 7.162 has been casted to its rough shape and size. Cut the internal profile using a 1/2" end mill to produce the profile. Only one finish pass is suggested because the material has been casted to its rough shape. The part geometry file is **contour6** which is constructed in problem 15 of chapter 6.

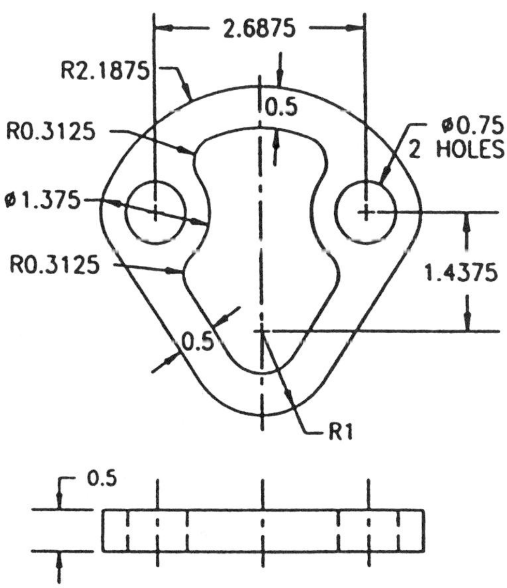

Figure 7.162

38. The raw material for the part shown in Figure 7.163 has been casted to its rough shape. There are four features to be produced, two external profiles and two internal profiles. The contour module is used four times to generate toopaths for cutting these four features. The part geometry file is **contour7** which is created in problem 16 of chapter 6.

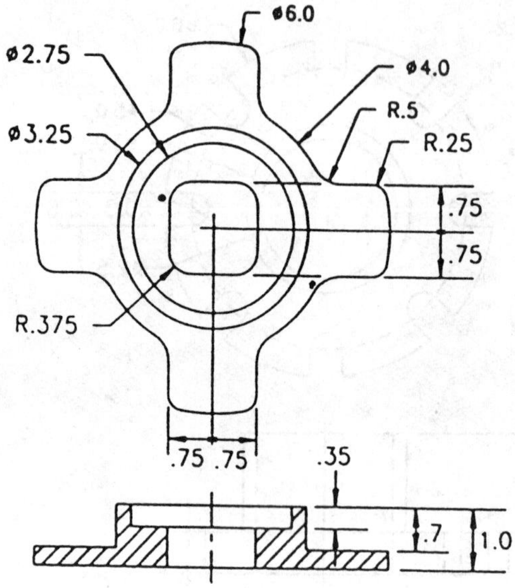

Figure 7.163

39. The part shown in Figure 7.164 has two depth changes in profile. The depth of line profile AB linearly changes from Z-0.1" at point A to Z-0.6" at point B. The depth remains at Z-0.6 from B to E. The depth linearly changes from E(Z-0.6) to F(Z-0.1). The part geometry file name is **contour8** which is constructed in problem 16 of chapter 5.

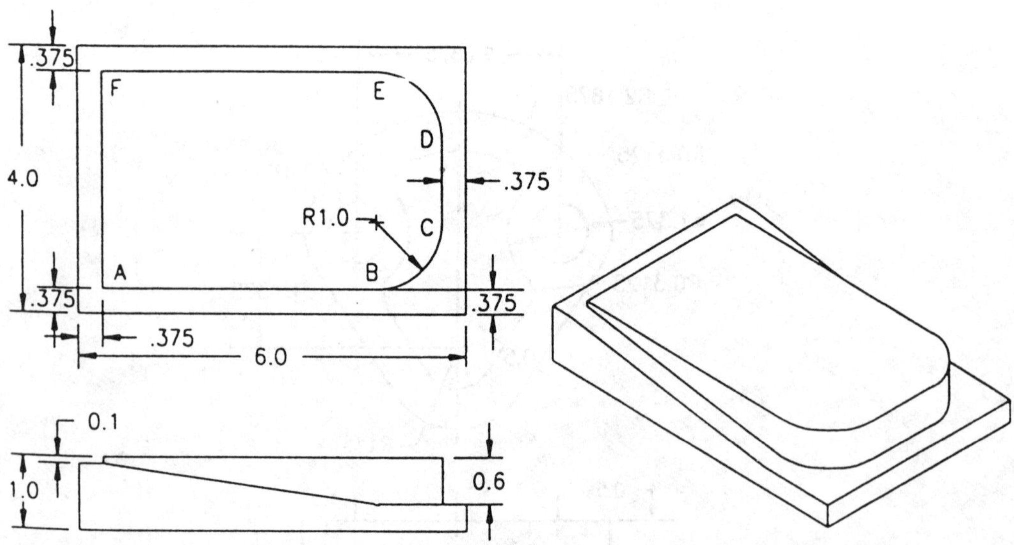

Figure 7.164

40. The profile of the part shown in Figure 7.165 has a depth change between A and B. The profile has a depth of Z-0.5" and between A and B it is Z-0.5". The part geometry file is **contour9** which is created in problem 17of chapter 5.

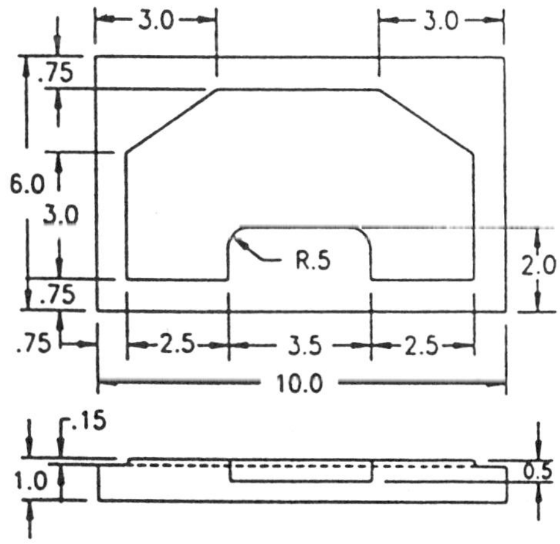

Figure 7.165

41. There are two features, top flat surface and internal pocket, to be produced for the part shown in Figure 7.166. The pocket module can be used to produce both features. The part geometry file name is **pocket3** which is created in problem 17 of chapter 6.

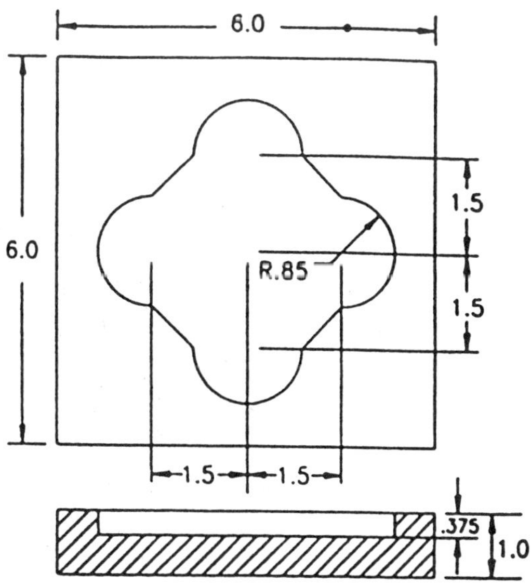

Figure 7.166

42. The part shown in Figure 7.167 consists of two internal pockets, one circular pocket in the center and one contour pocket with an island. The part geometry file name is **pocket4** which is created in problem 18 of chapter 6.

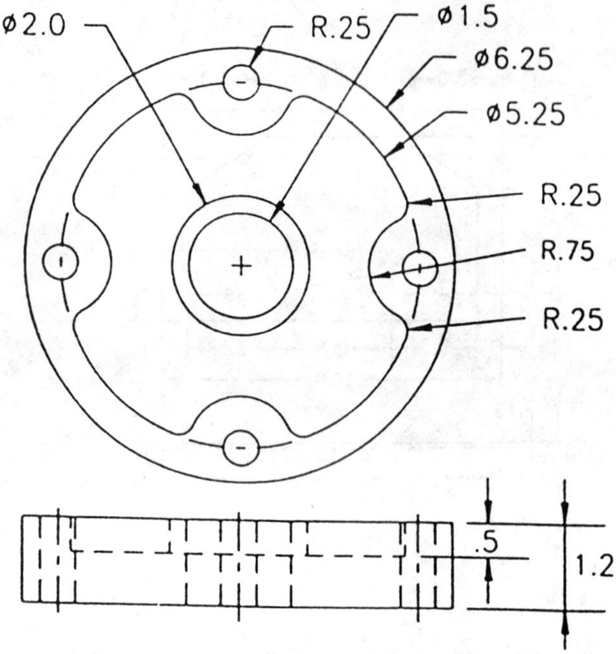

Figure 7.167

43. The part shown in Figure 7.168 consists of one internal pocket with an island. The island and the pocket profile are so close that six pocket regions are formed when a larger roughing cutter is used. The part geometry file name is **pocket5** which is constructed in problem 19 of chapter 16.

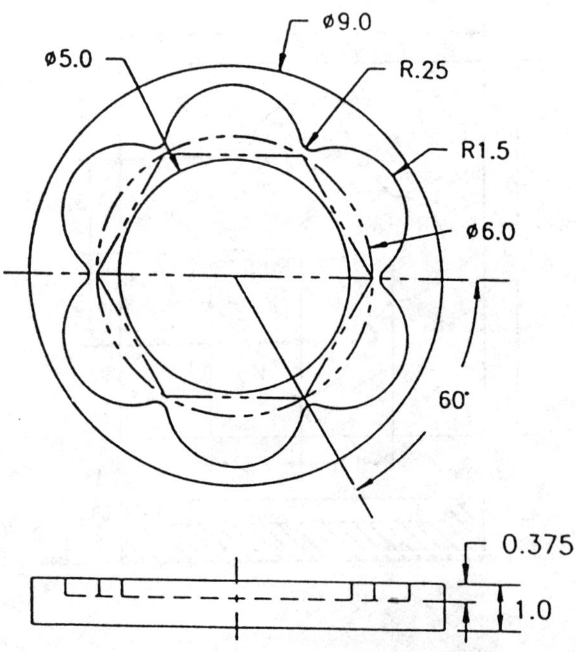

Figure 7.168

44. Four fine finish holes are required in the part shown in Figure 7.169. The holes are produced from the solid stock. Various cycle modes of the drill module should be used to produce these holes. The part geometry file name is **drill4** which is constructed in problem 18 of chapter 5.

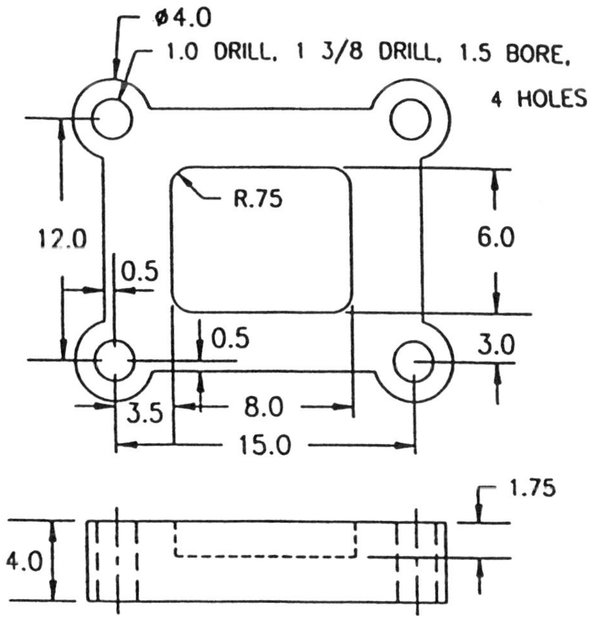

Figure 7.169

45. Three modules are used to generate toolpaths for machining the part shown in Figure 7.170. The part geometry file name is **comb1** which is created in problem 20 of chapter 6.

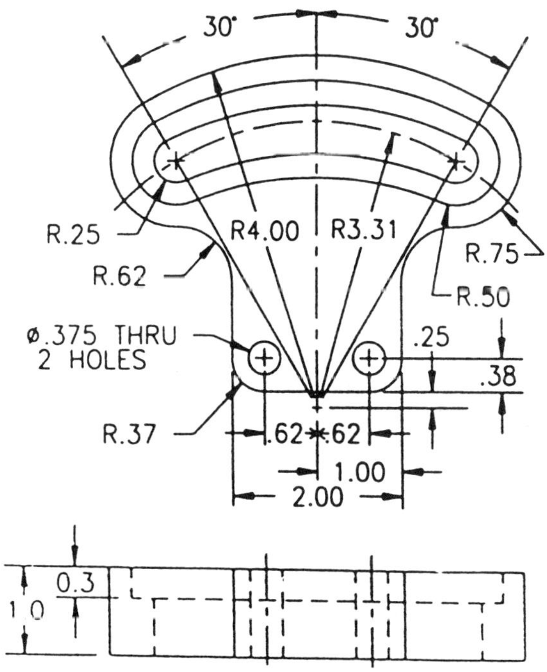

Figure 7.170

46. Five features are produced for the part shown in Figure 7.171. They include the top flat surface, two pockets, four 1/2'" holes, and six 1/4" holes. Two toolpath modules, pocket and drill, are involved in the project. The part geometry file name is **comb2** which is created in problem 19 of chapter 5.

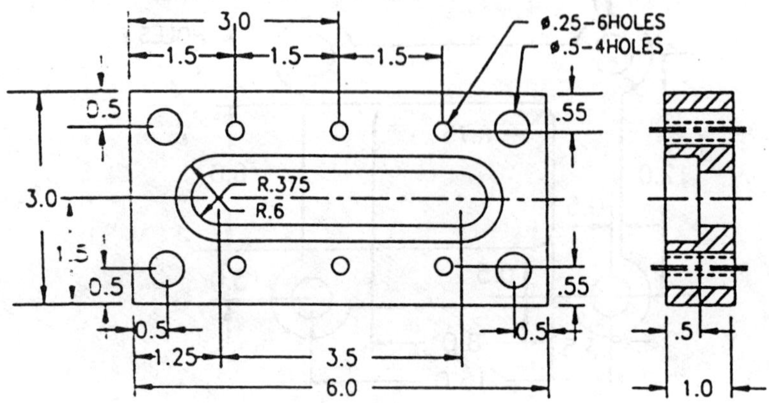

Figure 7.171

47. Six features are to be produced for the part shown in Figure 7.172. They include the external profile, two small local profiles, a slot pocket, and two holes of different size. The raw material has been casted into its rough shape. The part geometry file name is **comb3** which is created in problem 21of chapter 6.

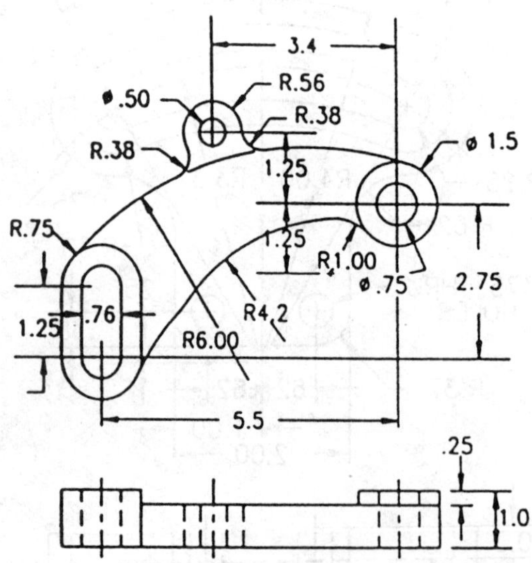

Figure 7.172

48. The part shown in Figure 7.173 consists of five features including the external profile, top flat surface, circular flange, hexagonal pocket and two holes. The part geometry file name is **comb4** which is constructed in problem 22 of chapter 6.

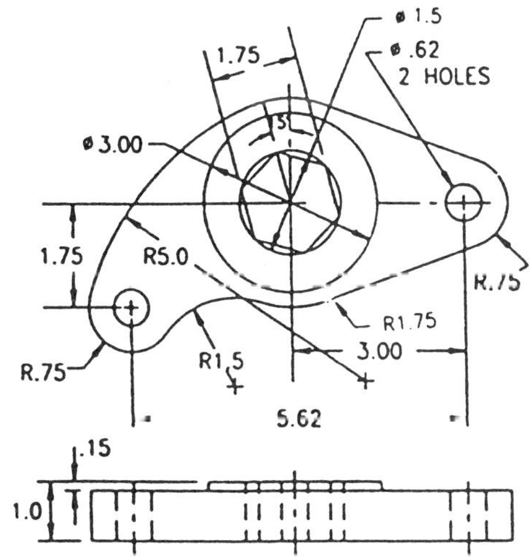

Figure 7.173

49. Five strings of letters are engraving in a circular plate as shown in Figure 7.174. The part geometry file name is **letters4** which is created in problem 21 of chapter 5. Replace the string "EMU IT" with your school name and department name.

Figure 7.174

Chapter 8
Associativity and its Applications

Objectives:

1. Principles of associativity.
2. Associativity features.
3. Modifying toolpaths using asociative features
4. Modifying tool, holder, and machining parameters of an existing toolpath.
5. Using the chain manager to edit the chained geometries of an associative toolpath.

Overview

Often times the toolpaths must be modified or edited for some reasons after they have been generated. Mastercam provides a variety of editing functions to modify toolpaths to meet your needs. Mastercam version 7 provides a new feature "Associativity" which links geometry with toolpath, tool, material, and machining parameters to form a complete operation. We can regenerate the operation to reflect any change in parameters to other related pieces without having to recreate the whole operation. This is a very useful tool to edit an existing toolpath.

This chapter also covers file structure of toolpaths, two ways for deleting toolpaths, four toolpath editing functions, and linear array function. These editing functions can be used to significantly simplify the toolpath generation process especially for those parts having several identical features arranging in symmetrical or linear patterns.

8.1 Associativity

Associativity links geometry with toolpath, tool, material, and parameter information to form a complete operation. When any part of operation changes, the other related pieces can be regenerated to reflect the change without having to recreate the whole operation. Typical information under the associativity in a project includes the following:

• Tools manager	• Define tool
• Tool parameters	• Operation manager
• Chain manager	• Job setup

All the above associativity information for a project are stored in an MC7 file. Job setup, tool manager, define tool, and tool parameter utilities are presented in chapter 7. They are briefly reviewed here in section 8.2. The Operations manager and the Chain manager are presented in detail in the following sections.

8.2 Job Setup, Tool Manager, Define Tool, and Tool Parameters

The Job Setup is the utility for **defining stock setup, NCI configuration**, and **tool offset parameters** for the current job. The job setup function has been presented in section 6 of chapter 7.

The Tool Manager provides a list of tools stored in the current MC8 file. It allows you to **select tools** from a tool library, **edit tools, delete tools,** and **open** the "Define Tool" utility to define new tools.

Define Tool is the utility used for defining a new tool including **selecting tool type, defining tool** and **holder geometry**, as well as **tooling and machining parameters**.

The Tool Parameters menu contains NC common parameters that are commonly used in various operations. Typical tool parameters include **tool number, diameter offset number, tool length offset number, feedrates, spindle speed, tool display**, etc.

8.3 Operations Manager

An operation in Mastercam is referred to as a complete machining process which includes chained geometry entities, tool, machining parameters, and toolpaths. The toolpath with its associated information generated by using a toolpath module is treated as an operation. The Operations Manager is used for managing tools to sort, edit, regenerate, and post any selected operations. It lists all operations in the current job. Follow these commands to open the "Operations Manager" menu:

Select MAIN MENU → Toolpaths → Operations

If **no operation** exists in the current job, an empty Operations Manager menu should appear as below.

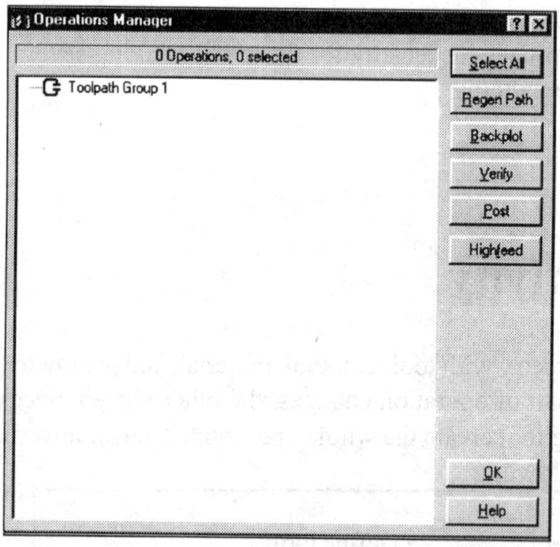

The operations will be listed in the Operations Manager menu as shown below when the current job contains any operations.

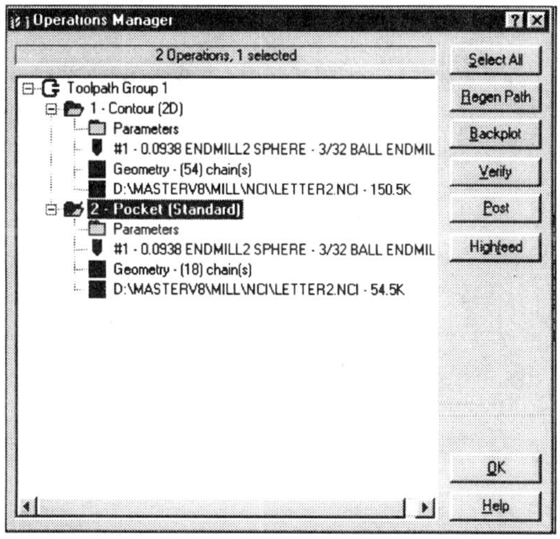

The seven function buttons of the Operations Manager menu are briefly described below:

Select All:	Select all operations listed in the Operations Manager.
Regen Path:	Recreate the selected operations to reflect the changes made to the operations.
Backplot:	Display the NCI file and catch any errors in the program before machining the part.
Verify:	Verifies the toolpaths.
Post:	(1) Create an ASCII NCI file for the selected Operations; and (2) Generates an NC part program from the NCI file.
Highspeed:	Optimize feed rates for 2.5-axis and 3-axis mill toolpath and compute feed rates that reduce machining time without sacrificing accuracy.
OK:	Select this button to exit the Operations Manager menu.

Moving Operations

The Operations Manager allows you to readily move and copy operations. Moving an operation to change the operation sequence in the current job. There are two ways to move an operation. **pick-and-place method** and **option command method.**

The procedure for using the pick-and-place method for moving an operation is:

1. Click on the yellow file folder of the operation to move.

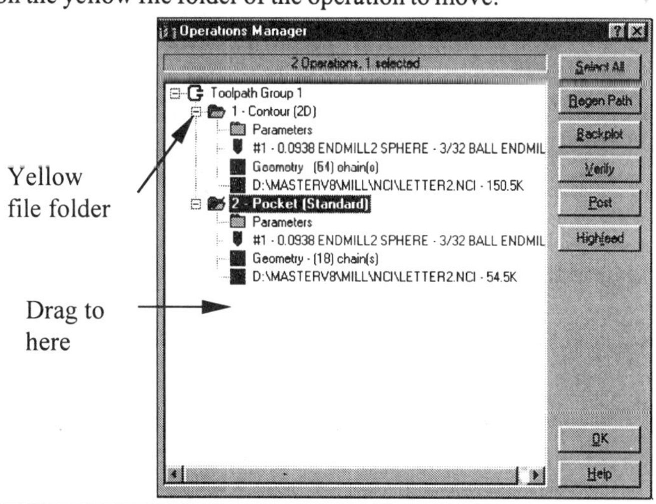

Procedure continued:

2. Drag the folder to the new position in the operation list.

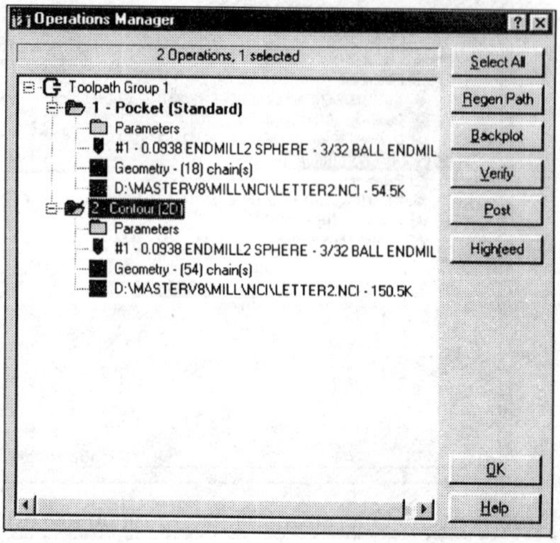

Option command method The option command menu provides the following two functions to move a selected operation to a specified location:

Move before:	moves the selected operation before the highlighted operation.
Move after:	moves the selected operation after the highlighted operation.

<u>The procedure of using the option command method for moving an operation is:</u>

1. Right-click on the yellow file folder of the operation to move.

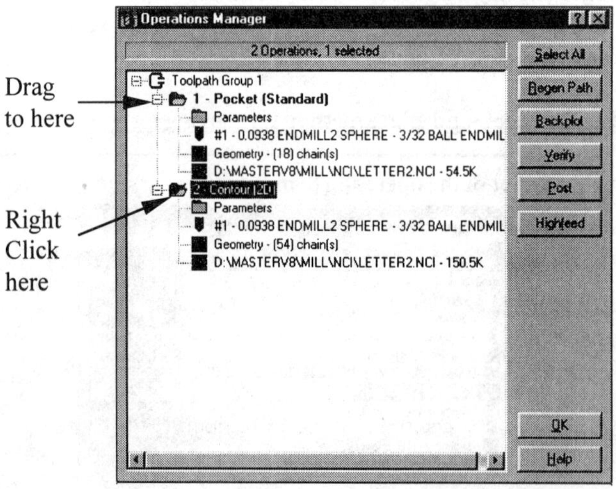

Procedure continued:

2. Drag the folder over another operation in the list, an option command menu will appear when you release the right mouse button as below.

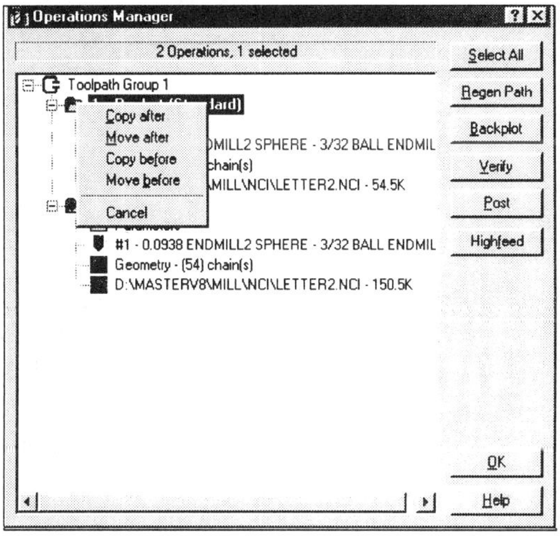

3. Select "Move before" from the list to place the selected operation as below.

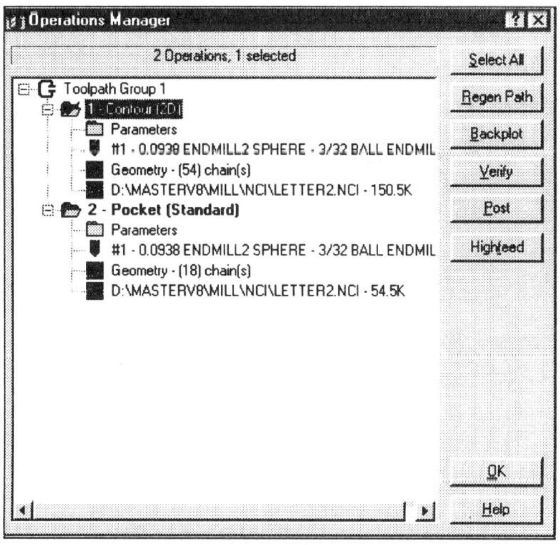

Copying Operations

The option command menu provides the following two functions to copy a selected operation to a specified location:

Copy after:	places a copy of the selected operation after the highlighted operation.
Copy before:	places a copy of the selected operation before the highlighted operation.

The procedure to copy an operation is:

1. Right-click on the yellow file folder of the operation to copy.

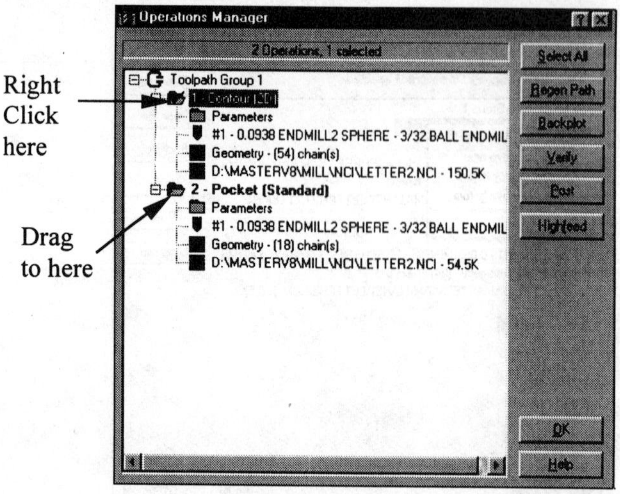

2. Drag the folder over another operation in the list, an option command menu will appear when you release the right mouse button as below.

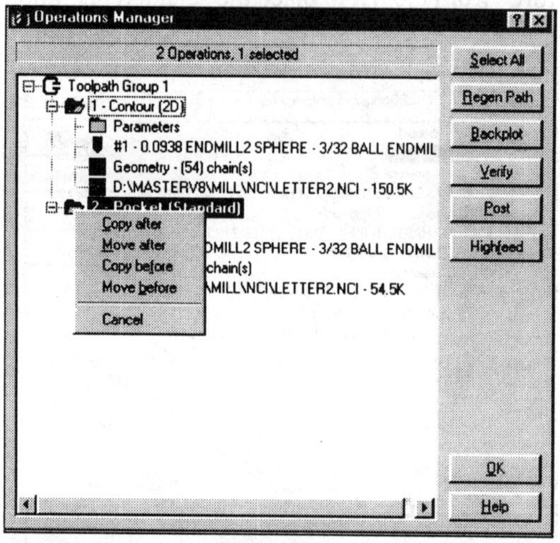

3. Select "Copy after" from the list to copy the selected operation as below.

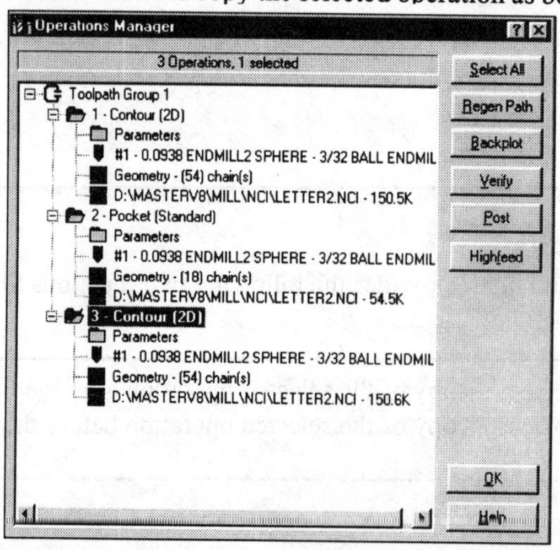

Copying Parameters

It is possible to copy parameters in one operation to another operation of the same type. Click on the gray Parameters icon for the operation to copy it and drag it on top of the Parameters icon to be replaced. The system will prompt "Copying parameters to another operation. Are you sure?". Select "Yes" to allow the system to automatically update the toolpath parameters of the second operation to match those in the first operation.

You can only copy parameters between the same operation types (ex: contour parameters to contour parameters, pocket parameters to pocket parameters). A warning message "Copy not successfully. Operations must be of a similar type." will be issued when you attempt to copy parameters to different type of operation.

Copying Tools

The way to copy a tool from one operation to another operation is similar to those for copying parameters. Click on the Tool Definition icon for the operation to copy and drag it on top of the Tool Definition icon for the operation to replace. The system will prompt "Copying tool parameters to another operation. Are you sure?". Select "Yes" to update the tool parameters of the second operation to match those in the first operation.

Copying Geometry

To copy chains or drill points from one operation to another operation of a similar type, click on the Geometry icon for one operation and drag it on top of the Geometry icon for another operation. The system will prompt "Copying toolpath geometry to another operation. Are you sure?". Select "Yes" to complete the geometry copy. Note that you can only copy chains between contour operations, pocket operations, or drill operations.

Right Click Menu

Mastercam provides a list of very useful functions for you to use to edit operations. To open this group of functions, click the right mouse button on a selected operation to open the menu as here.

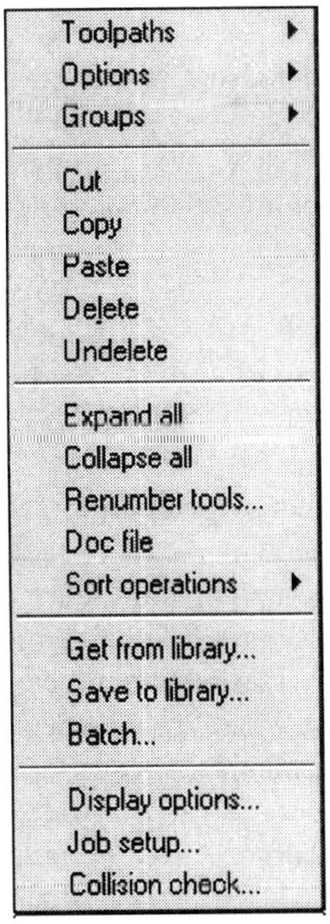

The **nineteen functions** in the right click menu are briefly summarized in groups below:

Toolpaths:

The toolpaths parameters add toolpath operations to the existing file and are shown in the menu here:

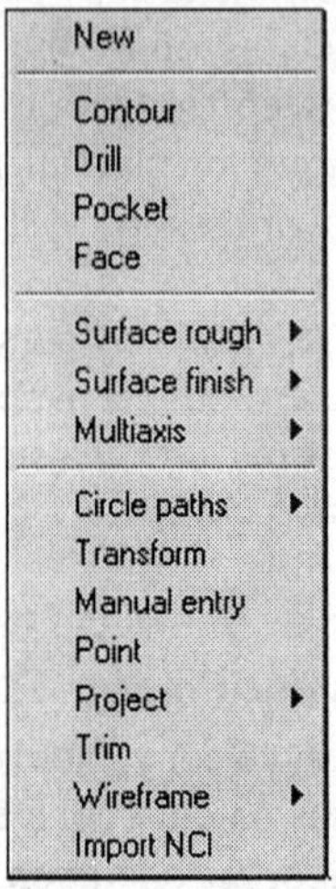

New: Use this to delete all operations and tools or add toolpath operations to the existing file.

Options: The options menu is listed here:

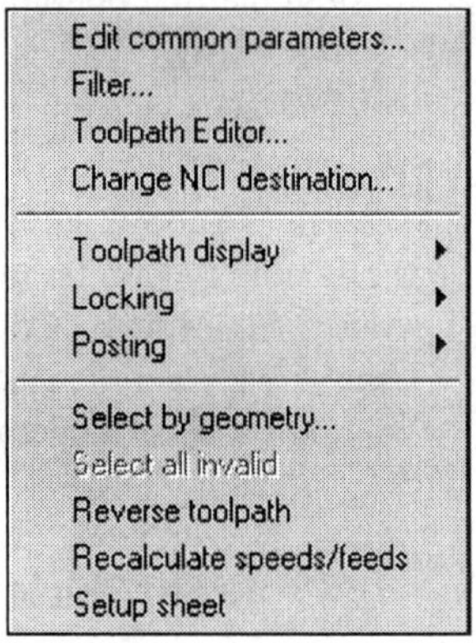

Edit common parameters: open "Common parameters" dialog box for changing parameter settings.

Filter: open "Filter settings" dialog box for changing parameter values.

Toolpath Editor: open "Toolpath Editor" dialog box for editing the selected toolpath operation.

Change NCI destination: change the file storage location for the selected NCI file.

Toolpath display: toggle the toolpath display to ON or OFF for the selected toolpath operation.

Locking: toggle the selected toolpath operations to locked or unlocked. The locked NCI file prevents from regenerating the toolpaths.

Posting: toggle the toolpath files to be posted.

Select by geometry: select the toolpath operations by selecting entities used in a toolpath.

Select all invalid: select all invalid or "dirty" operations that require regeneration.

Reverse toolpath: reverse the toolpath cutting direction of the selected toolpath operations.

Recalculate speeds/feeds: adjust the feed rate, plunge rate, retract rate, and spindle speed for multiple toolpaths based on a new stock material.

Setup sheet: open the setup sheet for modification.

Groups: Provides a series of group operations which are displayed in the menu here:

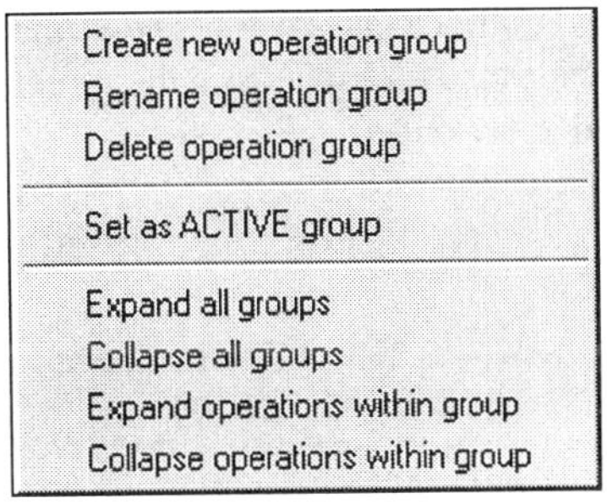

Cut: cut the selected toolpath operations from the file. The cut operation can be pasted in the selected location.

Copy: copy thc selected toolpath operations to the selected location

Paste: place the cut toolpath operations to the selected location.

Delete: delete the selected toolpath operation(s).

Undelete: restore the deleted toolpath operations.

Expand all: expand all groups from the menu.

Collapse all: collapse all groups from the menu.

Renumber tools: renumber tools relative to the current order of operations.

Doc file: specify the file name to write for operation list.

Sort operations: sort in ascending or descending order by tool number, tool plane, NCI destination, work offset, or creation order.

Get from library: import those operations in operations libraries into an MC8 file.

Save to library: create operations libraries (*.OP8) that are collections of toolpath operations.

Batch: open the "Batch Manager" to set up batch operations for processing.

Display options: open "Operation Manager Display Options" dialog box to select the display modes.

Job setup: open "Job Setup" dialog box to define job setup parameters.

Collision check: open "Collision/gouge check" dialog box to setup stock definition and collision check parameters.

Toolpath display on/off

Two parameters are used to control whether the toolpath is to be displayed on the screen. "**Toolpath display on**" shows the toolpath on the screen as shown in Figure 8.1a. "**Toolpath display off**" hides the toolpath from the screen (Figure 8.1b). Use the following commands to select the Toolpath display on/off.

The procedure for setting the display on or off:

1. Select "**Options**" from the right-click menu
2. Select **Toolpath display → On** or **Off**

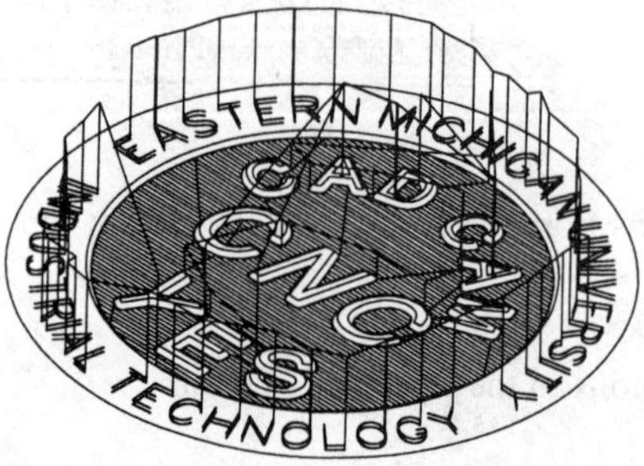

Figure 8.1a Show toolpath

Figure 8.1b Hide toolpath

Setup sheet

This function exports the setup sheet for the operation to a document (DOC) file. Follow these instructions to generate the setup sheet of the current job:

The procedure for generating a setup sheet:

1. Select **Options** from the right-click menu.
2. Select **Setup sheet**
3. Select **Yes** to "File already exists, overwrite?" if necessary
4. The setup sheet dialog box open

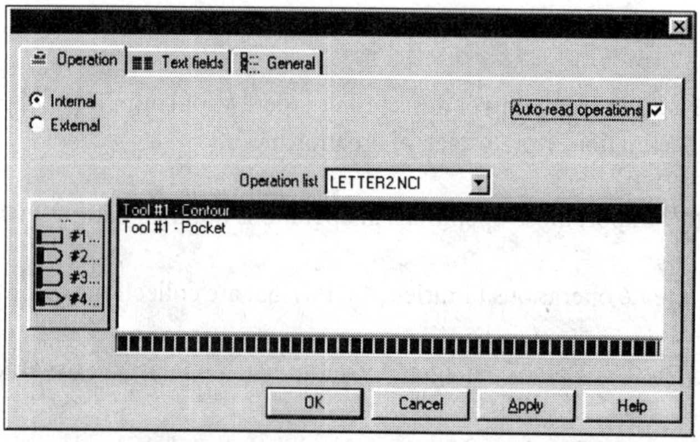

5. Select the source of operations:
   Select **Internal** (the current MC8 file as a source of operations)
   or select **External** then select the NCI file
6. Check **Auto-read operations** to have Mastercam automatically scan the operations for setup sheet or clear it to enter all values manually
7. Select **Text fields** tab to define the text to be displayed at the bottom of the setup sheet

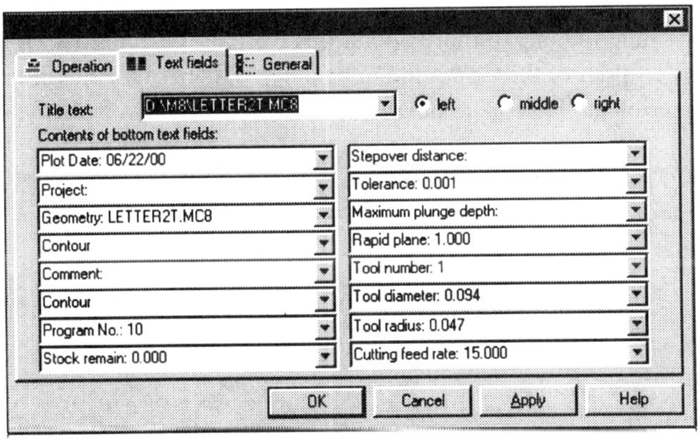

8. Select **General** tab to set the grid parameters

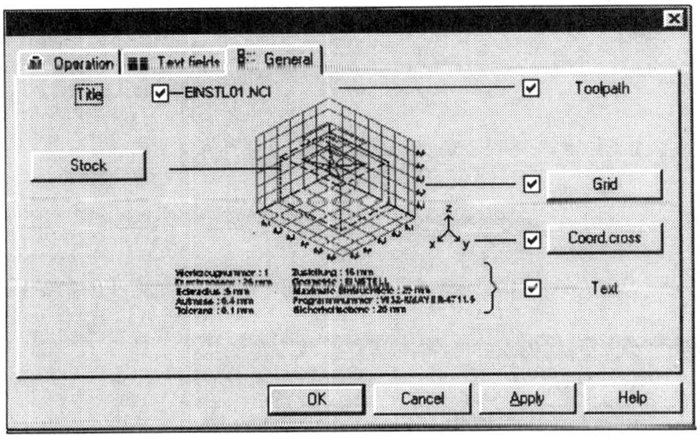

9. Click on the tool list icon
   to display the tool or operations list
   or select **OK** to create the setup sheet.

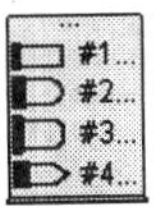

The setup sheet for the current project will appear as below.

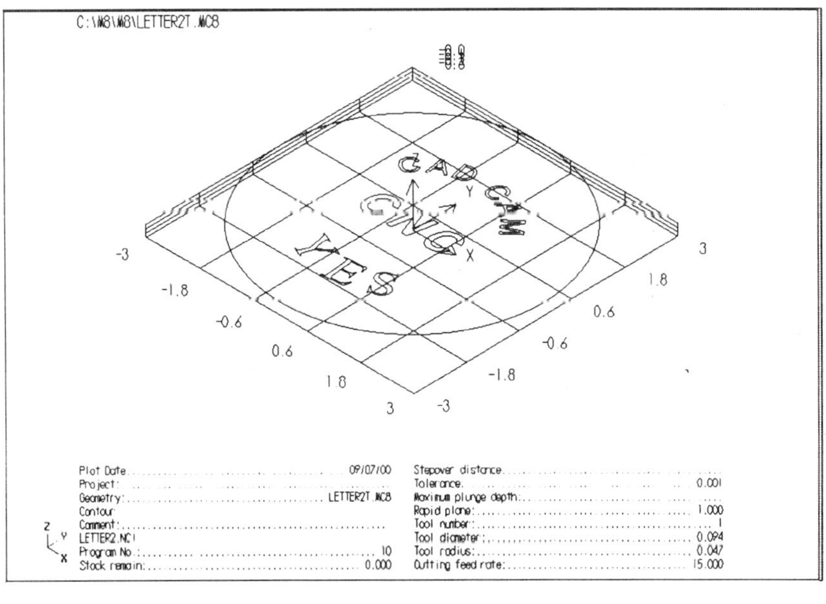

Deleting operations

The Delete function allows deleting one or more operations from the current job. To delete a single operation, click the yellow file folder of the Operation to be deleted, then click the right mouse button to open the right-click menu. Select "Delete" to delete the selected operation from the current job.

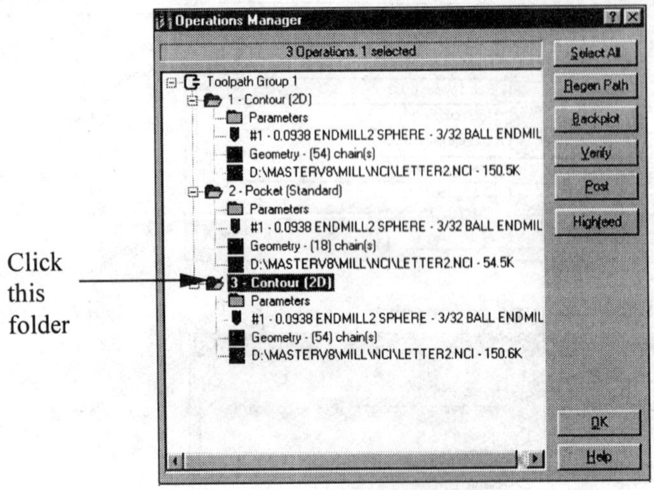

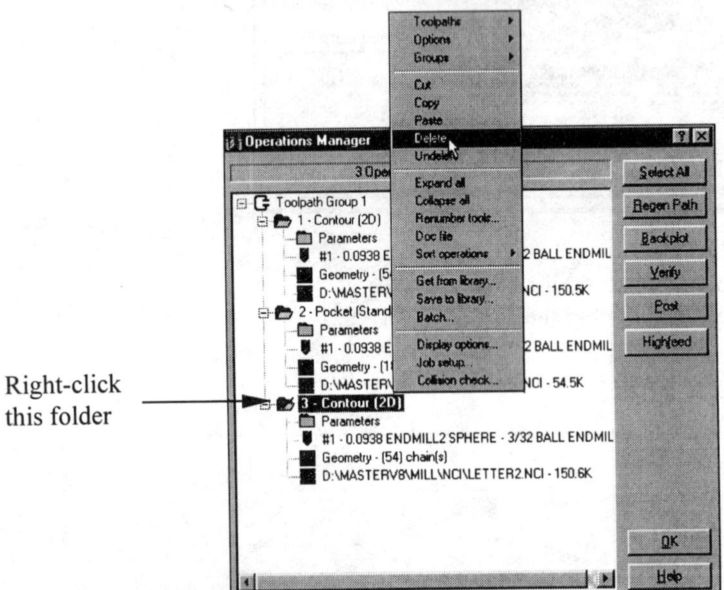

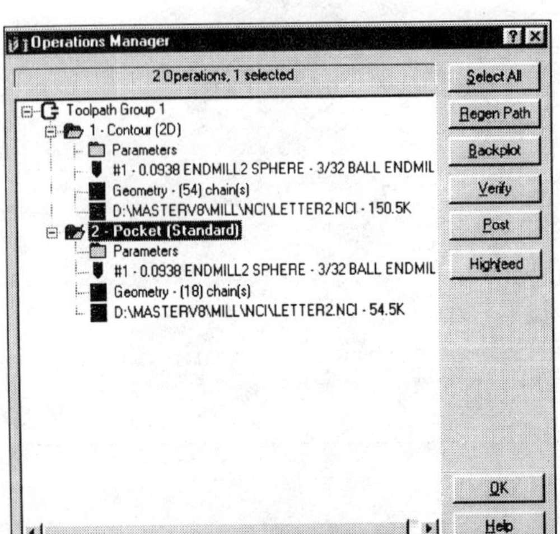

To delete all operations in the current job, select the "**Select All**" button then click the right mouse button to open the right-click menu. Select "**Delete**" to delete all operations from the current job.

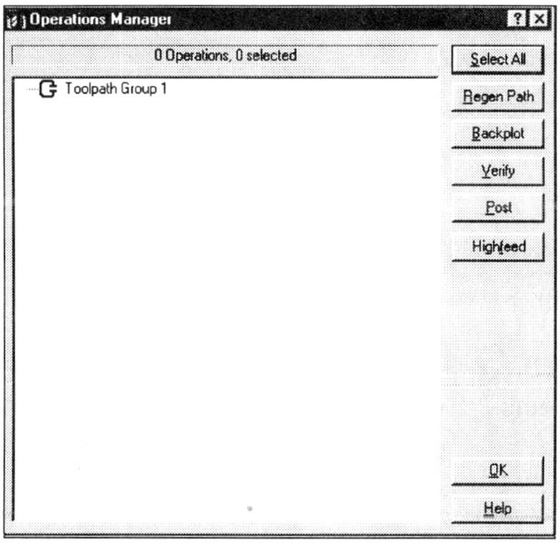

Tree directory control

Mastercam uses two commands in the right-click menu to control how the elements of operations are to be shown in the operations list area.

Expand all:	shows all elements of the operations
Collapse all:	condenses the tree directory to show only the file folder for operations.

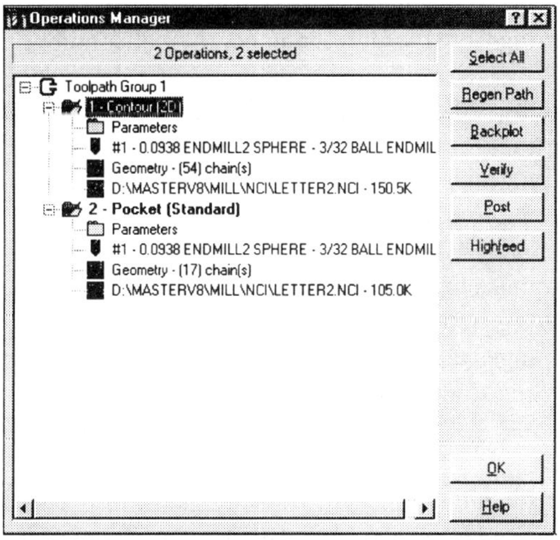

a. Expand all

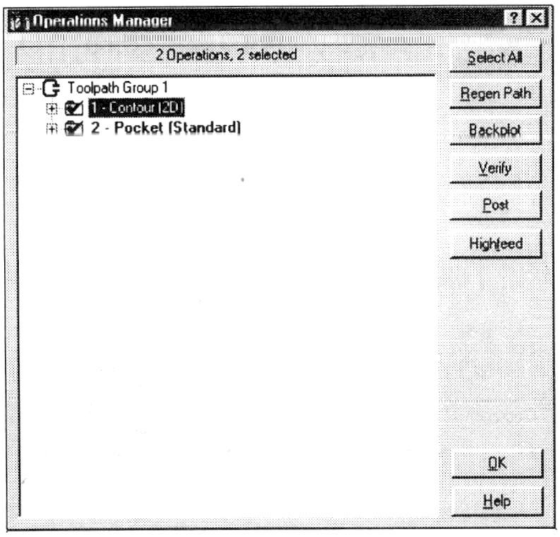

b. Collapse all

Sort operations: This function resequences the operations according to specified criteria. Click this function to open its option menu as shown below.

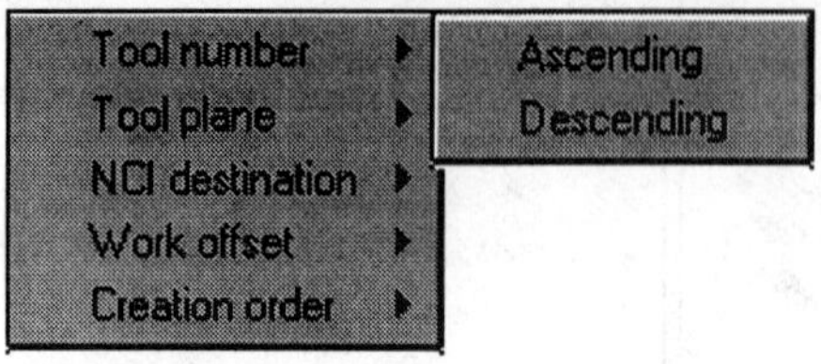

Tool number

ascending: rearranges the operations in the order of tool numbers starting from smallest number to larger number.

descending: rearranges the operations in the order of tool numbers starting from largest number to smaller number.

Tool plane

ascending: rearranges the operations in the order of tool plane view number starting from smallest number to larger number.

descending: rearranges the operations in the order of tool plane view number starting from largest number to smaller number.

NCI destination

ascending: rearranges the operations in the order of NCI destination starting from smallest number to larger number.

descending: rearranges the operations in the order of NCI destination starting from the largest number to smaller number.

Work offset

ascending: rearranges the operations in the order of work offset number starting from the smallest number to larger number.

descending: rearranges the operations in the order of work offset number starting from largest number to smaller number.

Creation order

ascending: rearranges the operations in the order of creating sequence starting from the first to last.

descending: rearranges the operations in the order of creating sequence starting from the last to first.

DOC file This function outputs the operations list of the current job to a document (DOC) file. Click "DOC file" function to open the "Specify File Name to Write" menu as below.

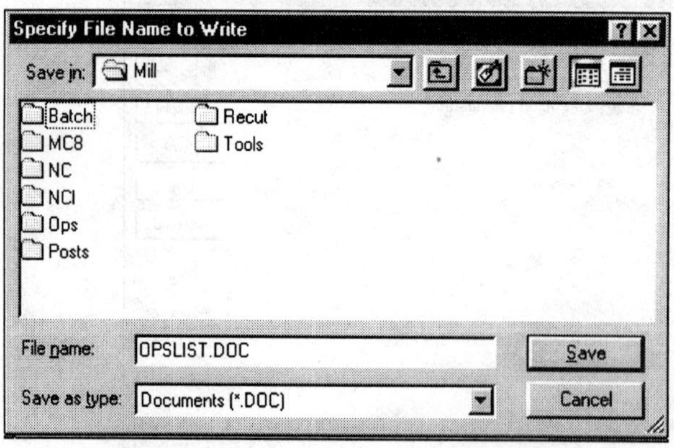

Select "Save" to save the DOC file to the specified file name and directory.

Use this procedure to open the DOC file:

1. Select MAIN MENU → File → Edit → DOC
2. File name to read: opslist

The DOC file for the operation list appears as below.

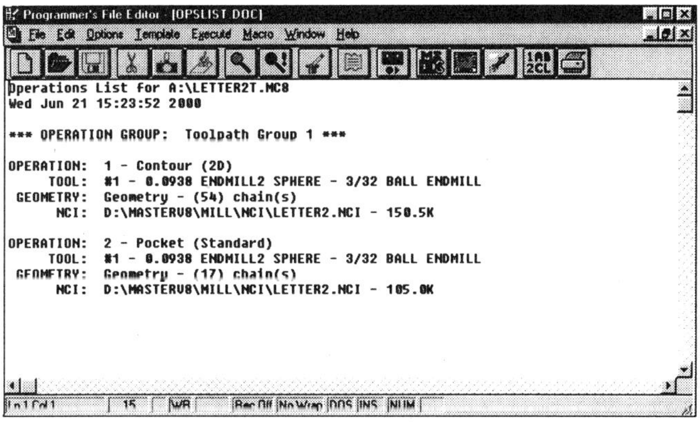

Job setup

This function opens the job setup utility as below for you to define job setup parameters.

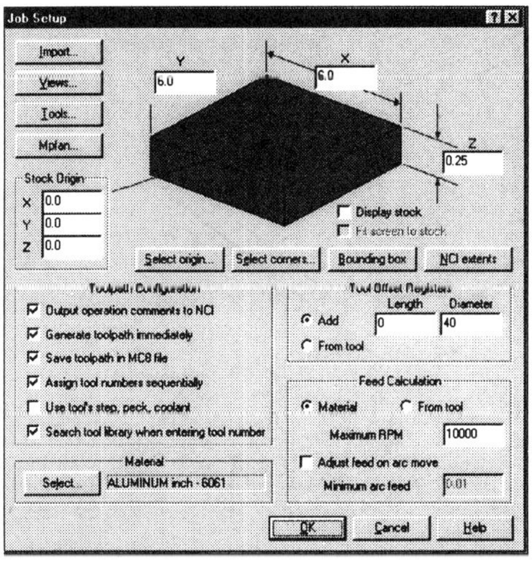

Two projects are presented in this section to show how to use various associative features to modify the existing toolpaths.

Project 1. Modifying toolpaths using associativity features

This project modifies the cutter size and machining parameters of an existing toolpath file (pocket1). Figure 8.2 shows the two sets of toolpaths before and after modification. The ½" end mill for rough pocketing is replaced by a ¾" end mill. The depth and stepover distance of the roughing pocketing are also changed.

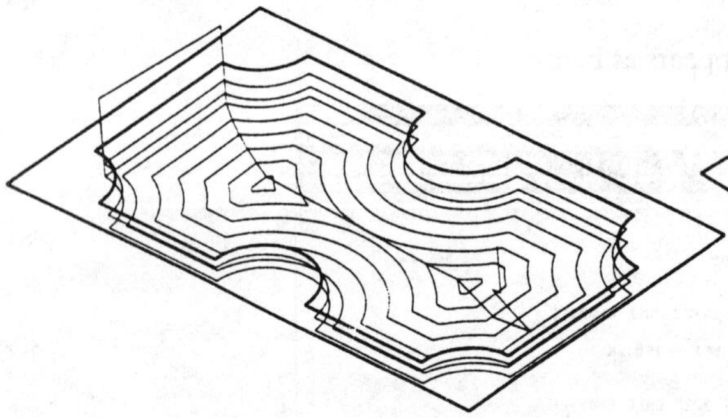

Figure 8.2a

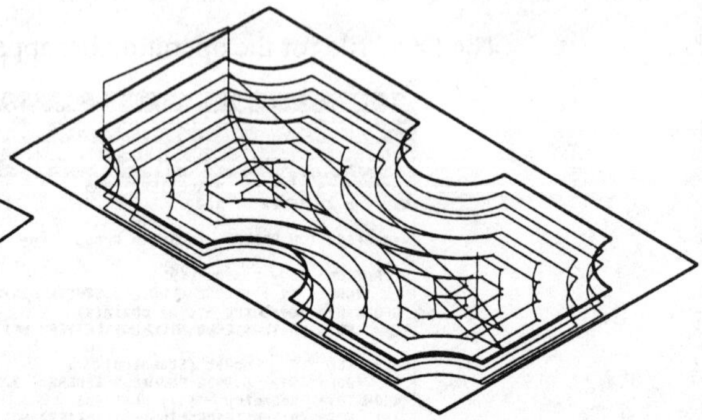

Figure 8.2b

Step 1. Open a part file with toolpath pocket1.

Select **File → Get**

File name: **pocket1t** ↲

The part geometry should appear as in Figure 8.3.

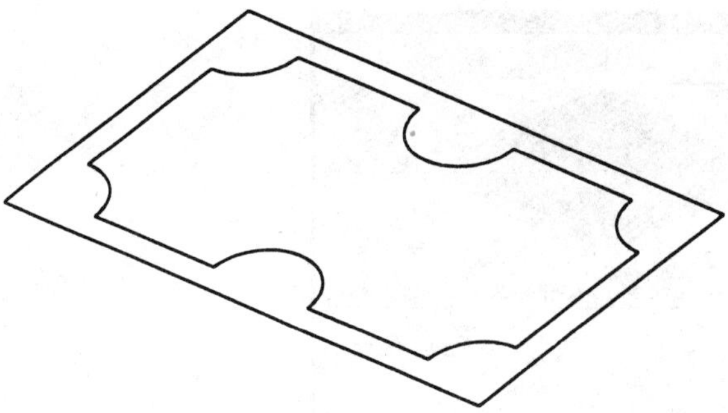

Figure 8.3

Step 2. Open the toolpaths.

Select **MAIN MENU → Toolpaths**

The existing toolpaths appear as in Figure 8.4.

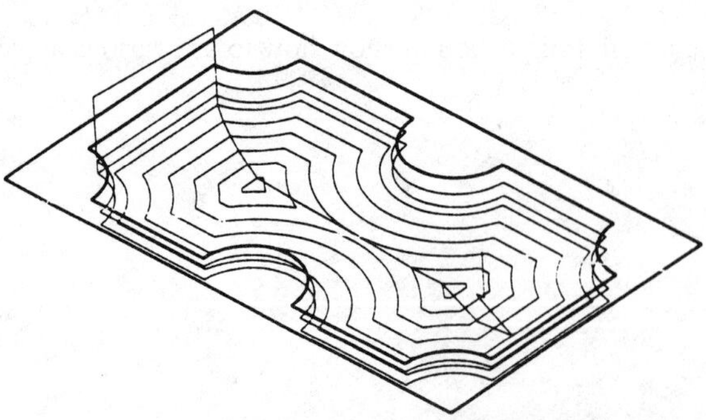

Figure 8.4

ep 3. Open the Operations Manager menu.

Select **Operations**

The Operations Manager menu with two sets of toolpaths appears as here.

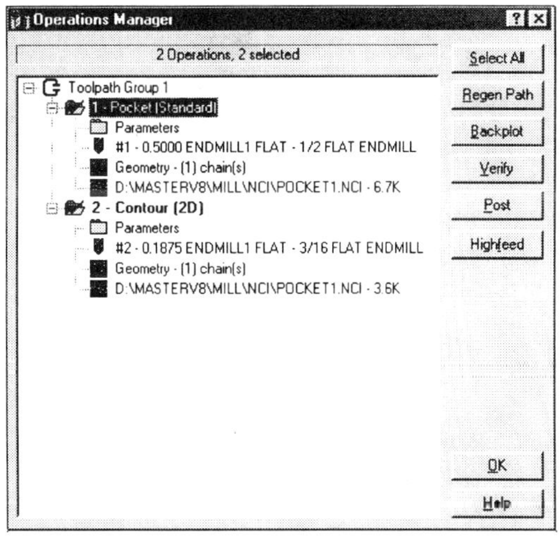

tep 4. Change the machining parameters for the pocket operation.

Click the "Parameters" icon in the Pocket operation

The existing tool parameters are shown below.

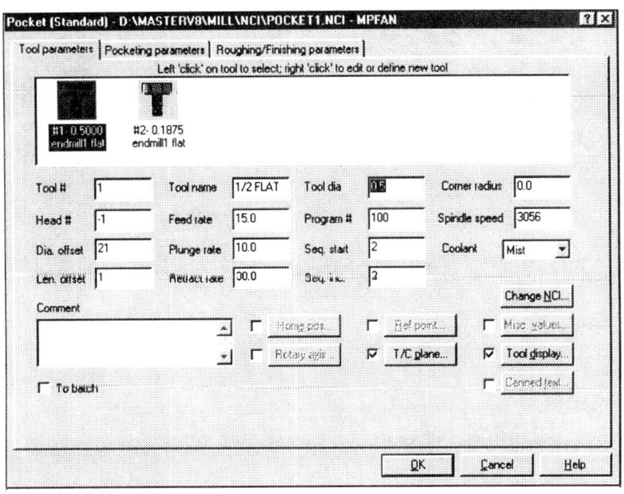

Click the right mouse button, then select "Get tool from library"

Select **tool #241** (3/4 flat endmill)

Select **OK**

Modify the tool parameters as below.

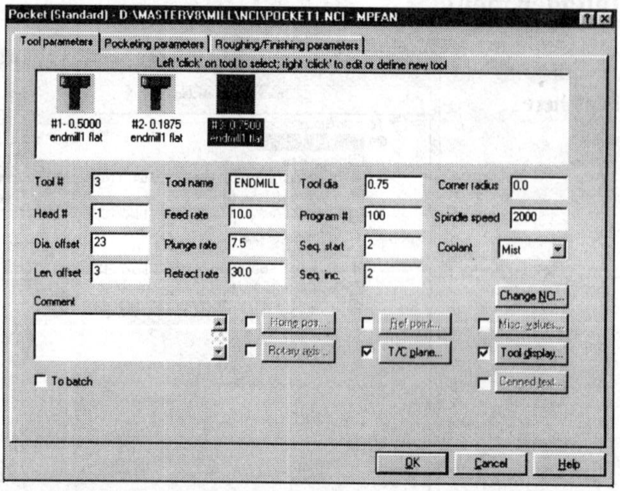

Step 5. Modify the pocketing parameters.

Click on the "Pocketing parameters" button

Set the pocketing parameters as below.

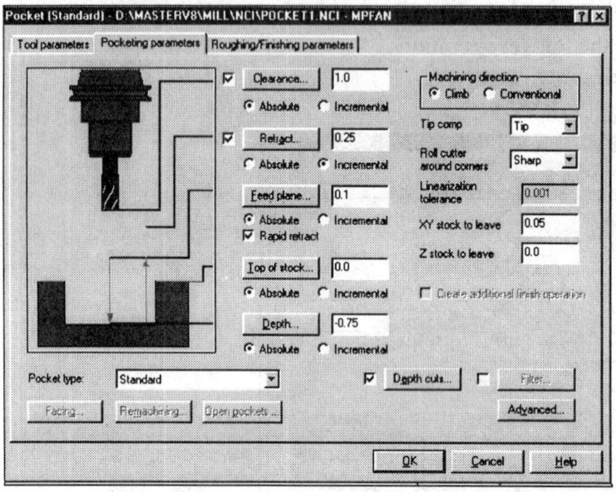

Step 6. Modify the depth cuts parameters.

Click the "Depth cuts" button. Set the depth cuts parameters as shown here.

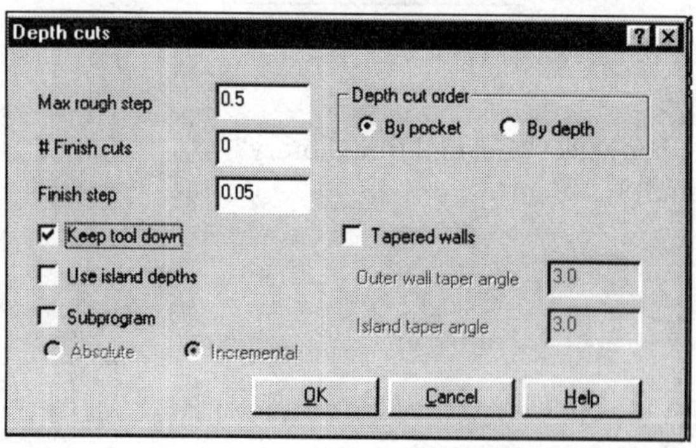

Select **OK**

Step 7. Modify roughing and finishing parameters.

Click the "Roughing/Finishing parameters" button

Set the roughing and finishing parameters as below.

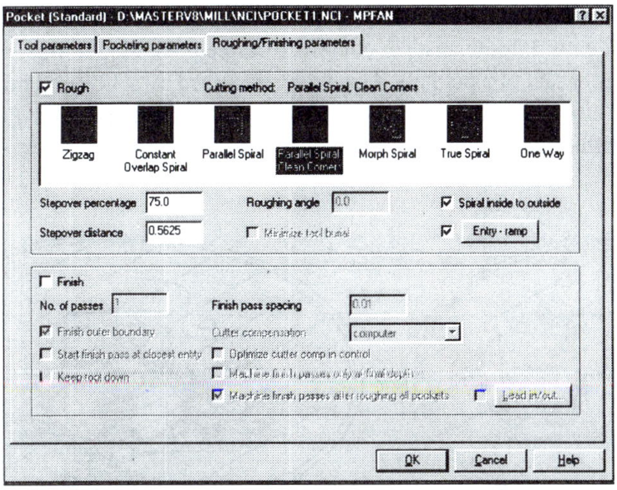

Select **OK**

Step 8. Regenerate the toolpaths.

Select **Regen Path** to regenerate the pocketing toolpaths
Select **OK** to exit the Opeations Manager menu
The new set of toolpaths should resemble Figure 8.5.

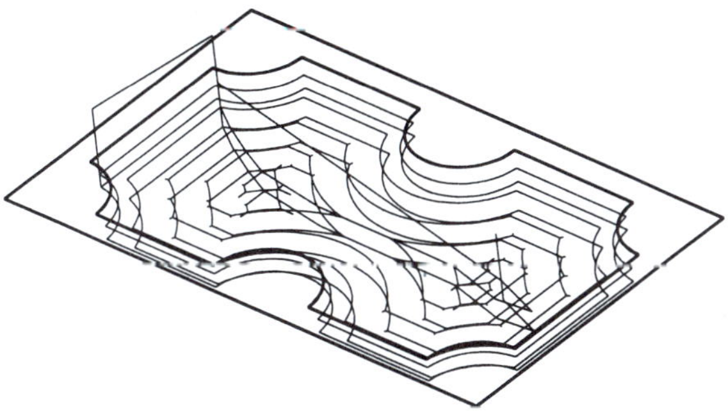

Figure 8.5

Step 9. Save the new toolpaths as pocket1n.

Select **MAIN MENU → File → Save**
File name: **pocket1n**

Project 2. Modifying tool, holder, and machining parameters of an existing toolpath

The existing toolpath file used in this project consists of three pocketing toolpaths. A ½" end mill is originally used for cutting the last two pockets. This tool is replaced by a 3/8" end mill. In addition, holder parameters and some machining parameters associated with this tool are modified. Figure 8.6 shows the toolpaths before and after modification.

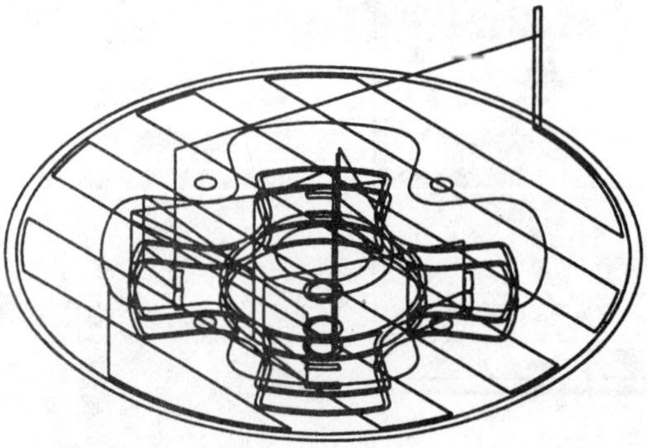

Figure 8.6a

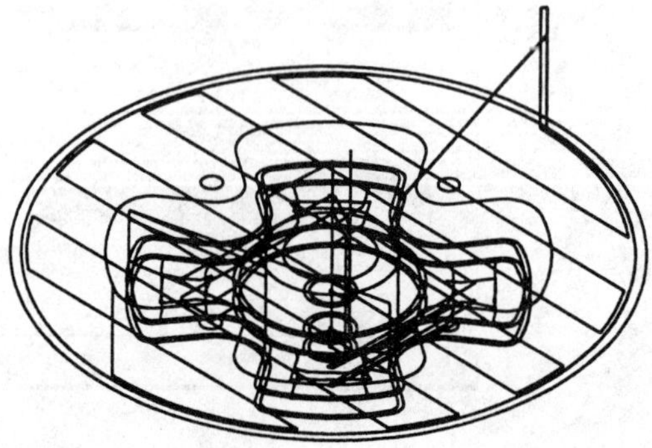

Figure 8.6b

Step 1. Open a file pocket2.

Select **MAIN MENU → File**

File name: **pocket2 ↵**

The part geometry of pocket2 should appear as Figure 8.7.

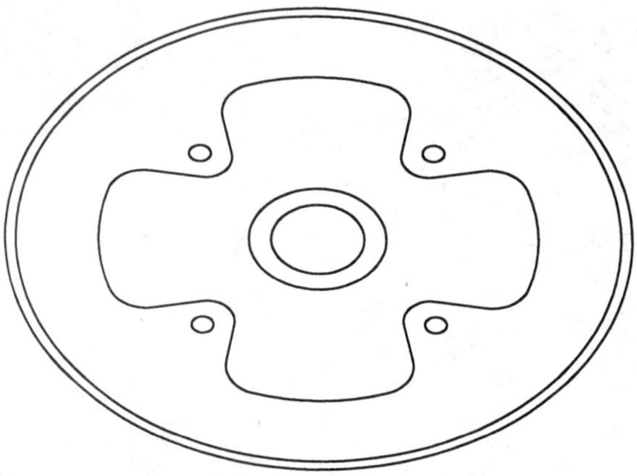

Figure 8.7

Step 2. Open the existing toolpath in the file.

Select **MAIN MENU → Toolpaths**

The existing toolpaths appear as in Figure 8.8.

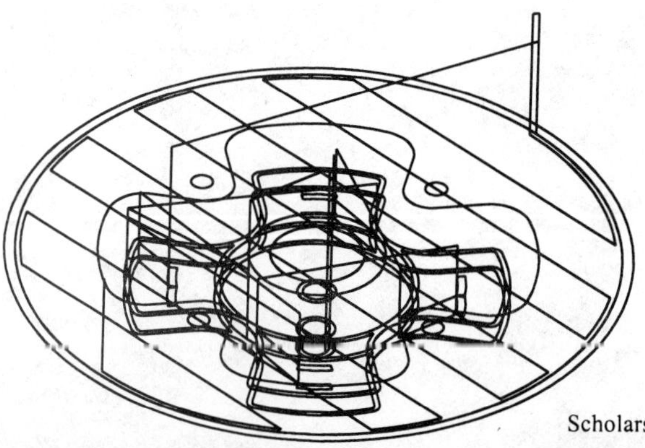

Figure 8.8

Step 3. Redefine a tool and its holder. 2

Select **Operations**

The toolpaths for three operations are listed in the Operations Manager menu as shown here.

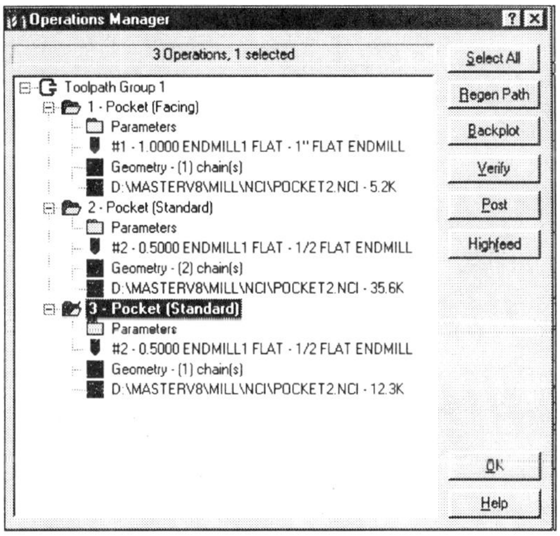

Click the tool icon for the third pocket operation

The "Define Tool" menu should appear as below.

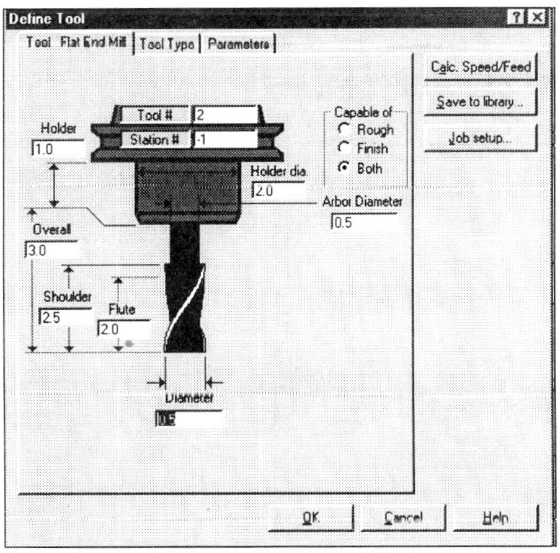

Set the tool and holder dimensions as below.

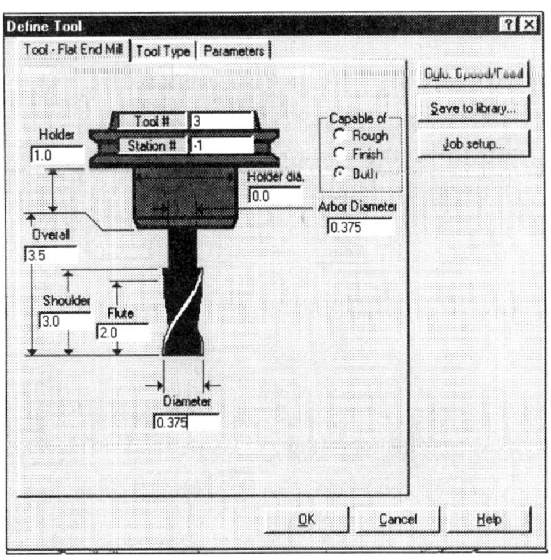

Step 4. Define the parameters.

Select the "**Parameters**" tab
Set the parameters as below.

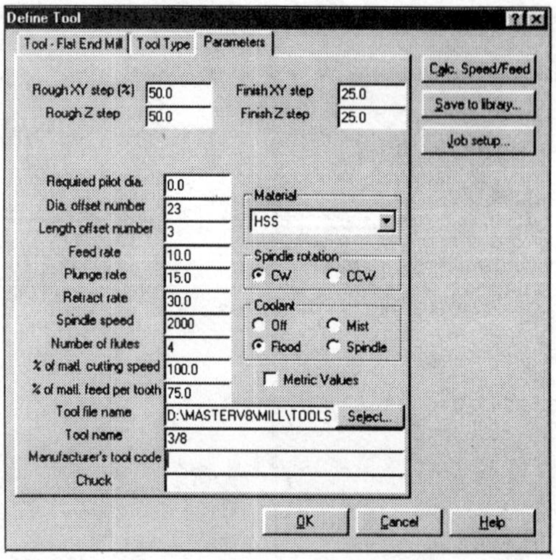

Select **OK**
Select **Yes** to "changing this tool will update your operations. Continue?"
The tool for second and third pocket operations changes to the new one as shown here.

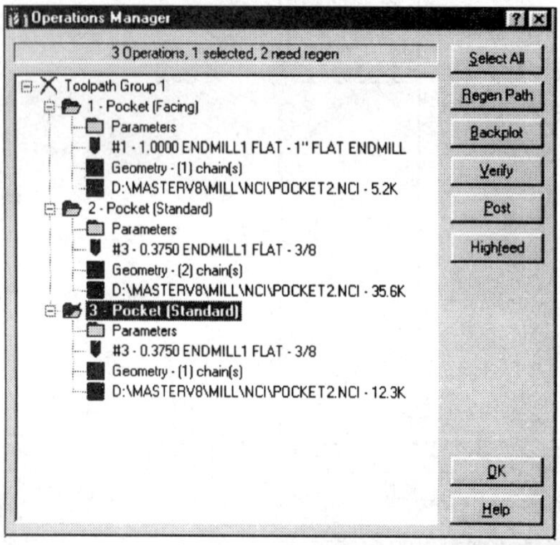

Step 5. Modify the parameters for the second pocket operation.

Click the "**Parameters**" icon in the second pocket operation
The tool parameters menu should appear on the screen
Select the "**Roughing/Finishing parameters**" button

Set the roughing and finishing parameters as below.

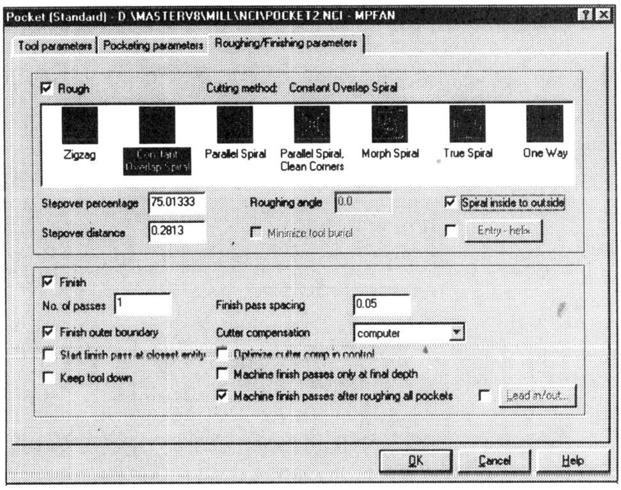

Select **OK** to return to Operations Manager menu

Step 6. Regenerate the toolpaths.

Select **All** to include all three operations
Select the "**Regen Path**" button to generate the toolpaths
Select **OK** from Operations Manager menu
The new toolpaths for second and third pocketing operations appear as in Figure 8.9.

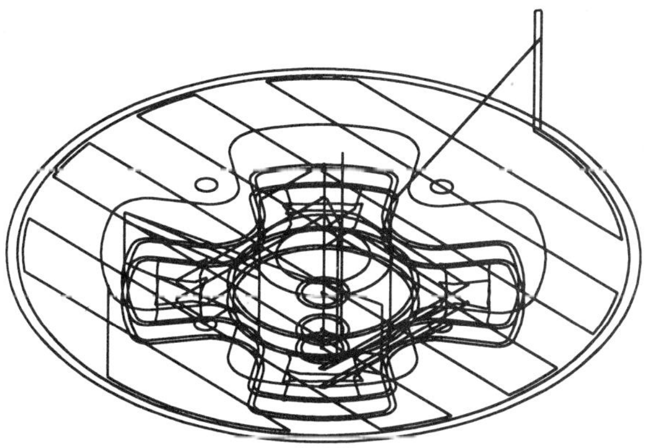

Figure 8.9

8.4 Chain Manager

The Chain Manager utility allows you to edit the chained geometry to change toolpaths.

The commands to access the Chain Manager menu are:

1. Select MAIN MENU → Toolpaths → Operations to open the Operations Manager menu
2. Select the Geometry icon for a selected operation to open the Chain Manager menu as above.

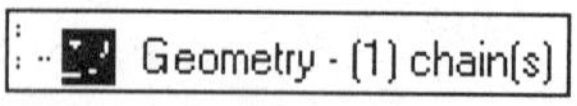

The editing functions related to Chain Manager menu are grouped in a right click menu. Click the right mouse button to open the option menu as below:

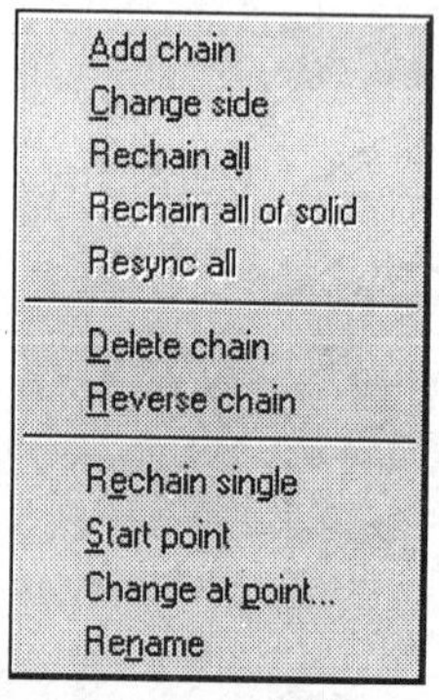

The **eleven** functions in the option menu are briefly summarized as below. Four of them are explained in more detail after the chart.

Add chain: add a chain to the operation.

Change side: reverse the side of cutter compensation.

Rechain all: delete all existing chains and displays the chaining method menu to reselect all chains.

Rechain all of solid: allow editing of solid chains used in toolpaths.

Chain manager functions, continued.

Resync all:	resynchronize chains for ruled toolpaths.
Delete chain:	delete the selected chain(s).
Reverse chain:	change the selected chain(s) to the opposite direction.
Rechain single:	reselect the chain in the graphics window using the chaining method menu.
Start point:	return to the graphics window to select a new start point for the chain.
Change at point:	specify a parameter change for a specific point on the geometry.
Rename:	rename the selected chain.

Add chain

This function allows you to add more chains to the existing operation. The toolpaths are automatically generated for the added chains without repeating the process of defining the tool and parameters. The chaining method menu will appear to define new chains when this function is selected. Figure 8.10 shows the toolpaths before and after a new chain is added.

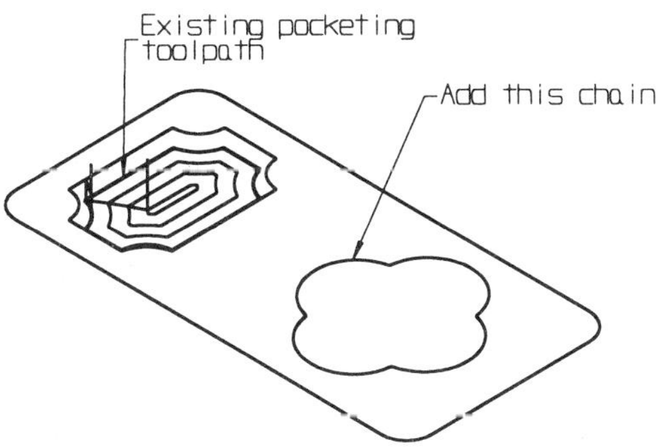

Figure 8.10a

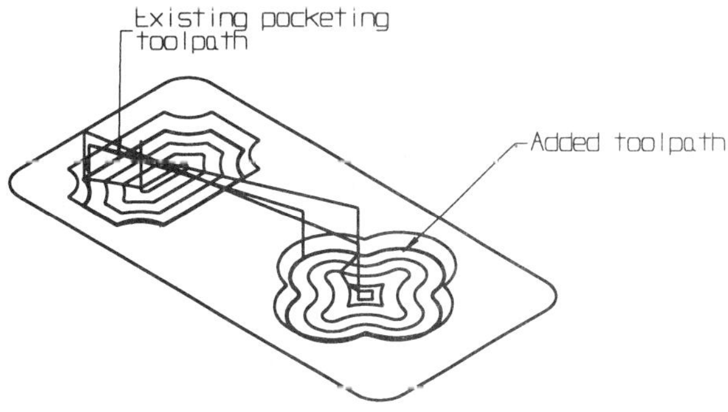

Figure 8.10b

Change side

The Change Side function reverses the side of the cutter compensation. This function is only applicable to the contour module, and is not used for the pocket module. It has a significant effect on the toolpaths due to the change in the side of cutter compensation. Figure 8.11 shows the effect of changing the side on the toolpaths.

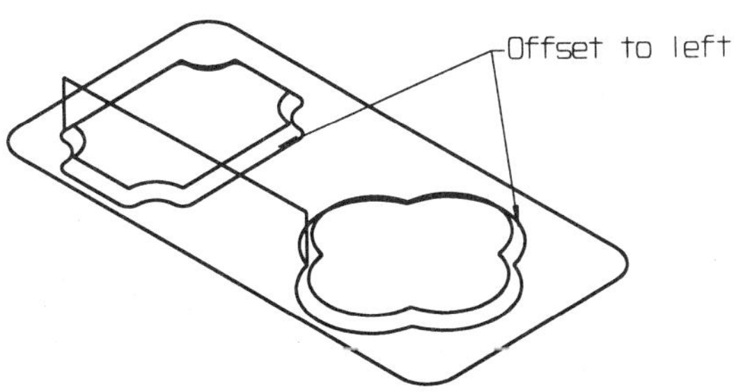

Figure 8.11a

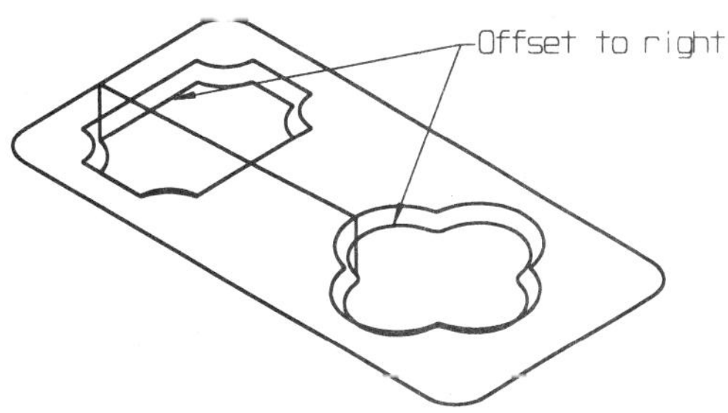

Figure 8.11b

Reverse chain

This function reverses the chaining direction of the selected chain. When the chain direction is reversed, the toolpath side along the geometry is changed as shown in Figure 8.12.

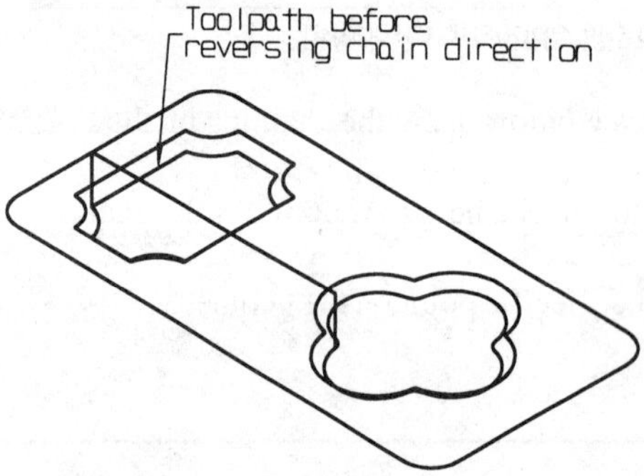

Figure 8.12a

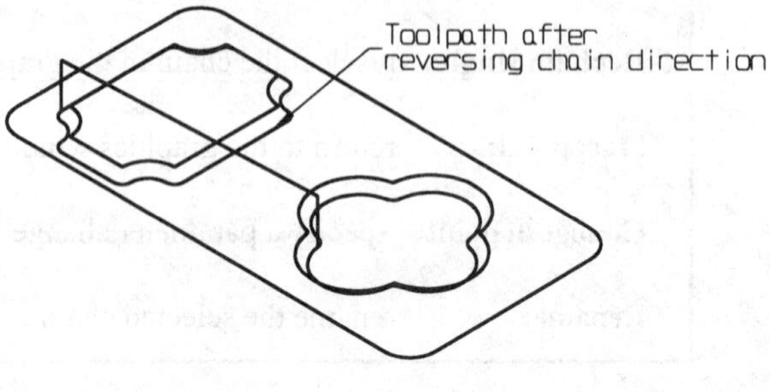

Figure 8.12b

Change at point

This function allows you to change such parameters as cutter compensation, depth, feed rate, spindle speed, etc. at the selected point in the geometry. This function applies only to contour operations. Its menu appears as shown here.

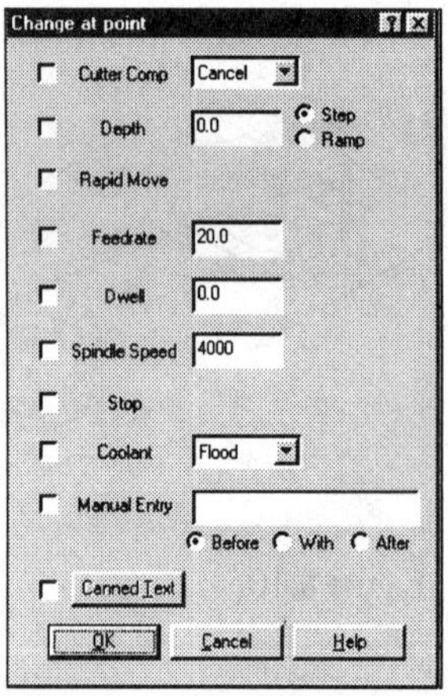

Project 3. Editing toolpaths using chain manager functions

The intent of this project is to show how to effectively use the functions of chain manager for modifying toolpaths. The part geometry file array1 is used in this project. A four-arc profile is added to the model. The contour function is used to generate a toolpath for the rectangular profile first. Use the "Add chain" function to add the four-arc chain to the contour operation. The effect of "Change side" and "Reverse chain" functions is then demonstrated. The contour operation is copied and placed after the original operation. Parameter changes are made to the second operation including tool size and stock amount for producing finishing toolpaths. Figure 8.13 shows the initial contour toolpath and edited toolpaths using chain manager functions.

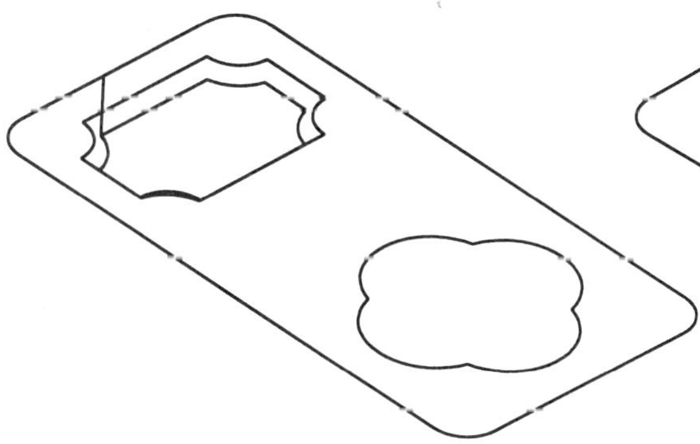

Figure 8.13a

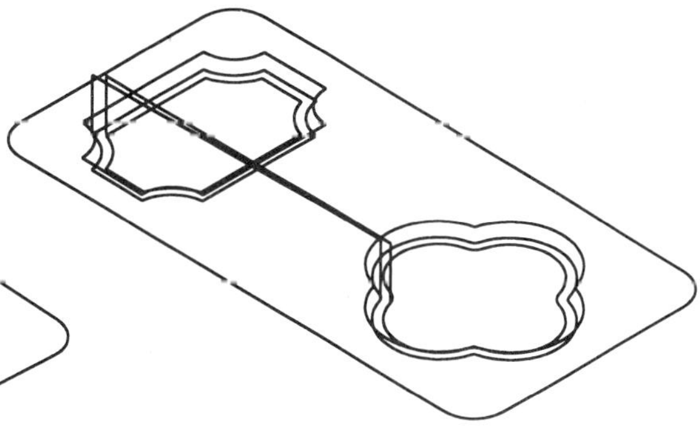

Figure 8.13b

Step 1. Open the geometry file array1.

Select **MAIN MENU → File → Get**

File name: **array1**

The part geometry appears as in Figure 8.14.

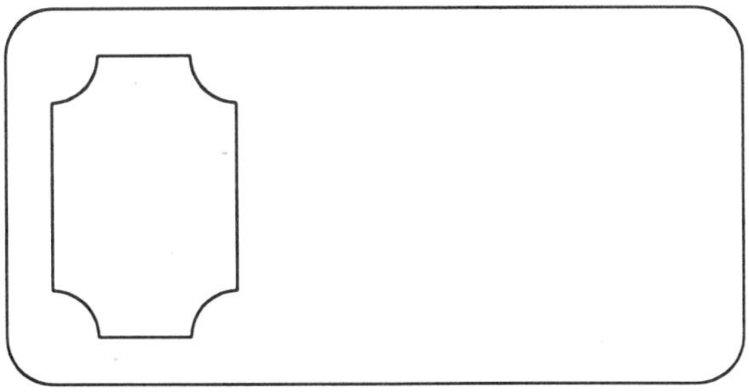

Figure 8.14

Step 2. Add four connected arcs.

Select **Level**, then enter **2**

Select **MAIN MENU → Create → Arc → Endpoints → Values**

Enter the following four sets of endpoint coordinates with the radius of 1.3:
(Note: select the second arc from outside out of the four possible arcs.)

First end point	Second end point	Radius
7.75, 4.25	7.75, 1.75	1.3
7.75, 1.75	10.25, 1.75	1.3
10.25, 1.75	10.25, 4.25	1.3
10.25, 4.25	7.75, 4.25	1.3

The four arcs are added as in Figure 8.15.

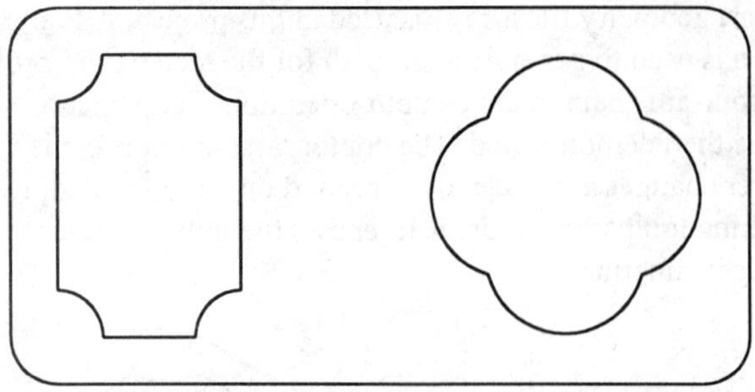

Figure 8.15

Step 3. Change to isometric view.

Select **Gview → Isometric**
The new drawing should resemble Figure 8.16.

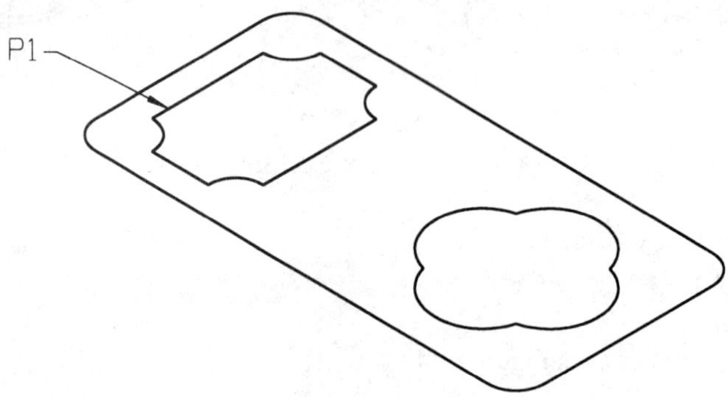

Figure 8.16

Step 4. Save the new drawing as chain.

Select **MAIN MENU → File → Save**
File name to save: **chain** ↵

Step 5. Generate contouring toolpath for the rectangular profile.

Use the pick point in Figure 8.16.
Select **MAIN MENU → Toolpaths → Contour**
File name for NCI: **chain** ↵
Select **Chain**, then pick **P1**
Select **Done**
Click the right mouse button, then select **"Get tool from library"**

Select **tool #239** (1/2" flat endmill)
Select **OK**

Step 6. Define the tool parameters as below.

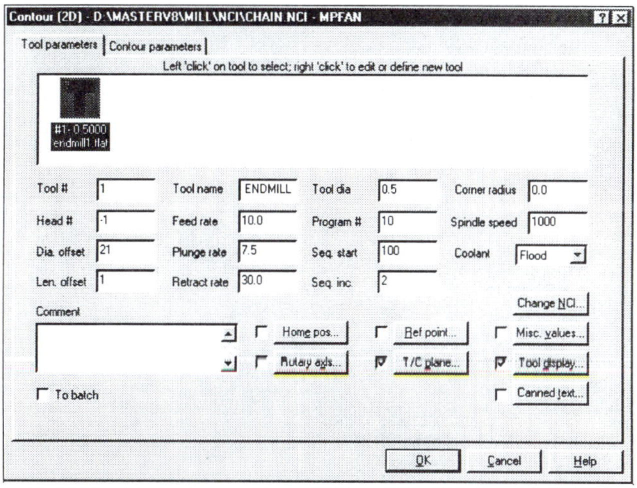

Step 7. Define the contour parameters.

Click the "**Contour parameters**" button

Set the contour parameters as below.

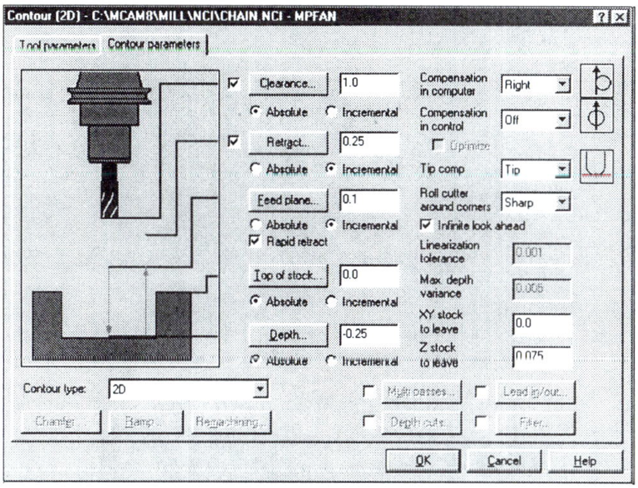

Select **OK**

The toolpath is generated as in Figure 8.17.

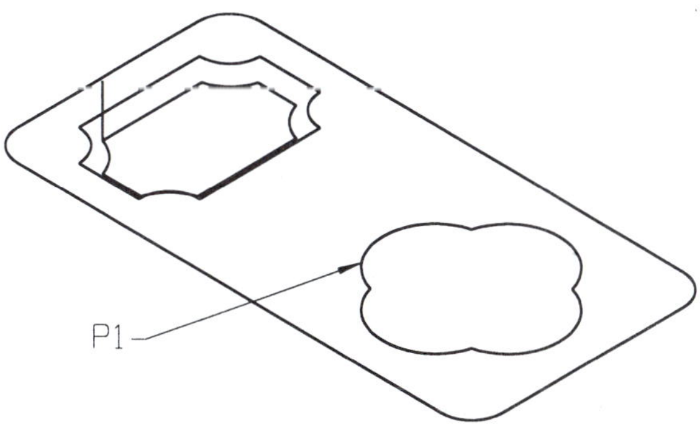

Figure 8.17

Step 8. Add a chain to the contour operation.

Use the pick point in Figure 8.17.
Select **Operations**
The Operations Manager menu appears as below.

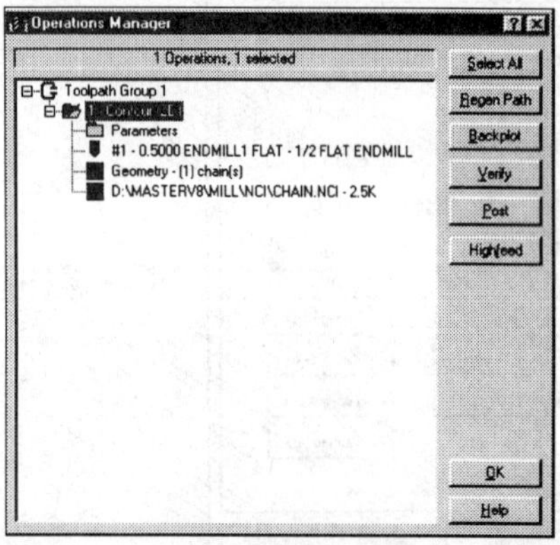

Click the green geometry icon to open the Chain Manager menu as here.

Click the right mouse button to select **Chain 1**
Select **Add chain** from the option menu
Select **Chain**, then pick **P1**
Select **Done**
The "Chain 2" is added to the Chain Manager menu as shown here.

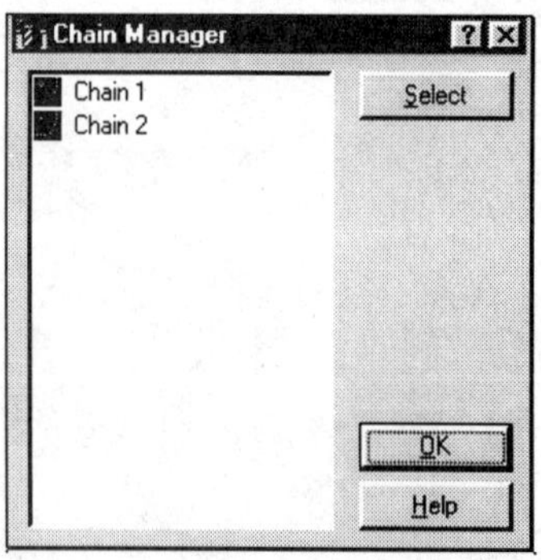

Select **OK** to return to Operations Manager menu

Step 9. Regenerate the toolpaths.

Select **Regen Path** to regenerate the toolpaths

The new toolpath is added for the second chain as shown in Figure 8.18.

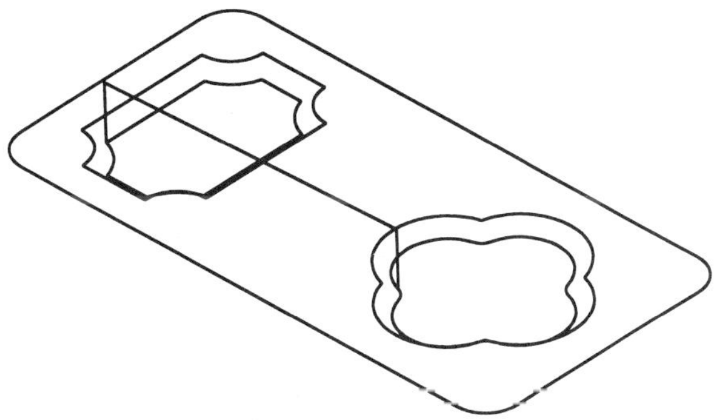

Figure 8.18

Step 10. Change side of cutter compensation.

Click the green geometry icon to open the Chain Manager menu
Click the right mouse button to select **Chain 1** to open the option menu
Select **Change side**
Select **OK** from Chain Manager menu

Step 11. Regenerate the toolpaths to reflect the side change.

Select **Regen Path** to regenerate the toolpaths
Select **OK** to "1 associative operations regenerated successfully."
The new toolpaths with new cutter compensation side are shown in Figure 8.19.

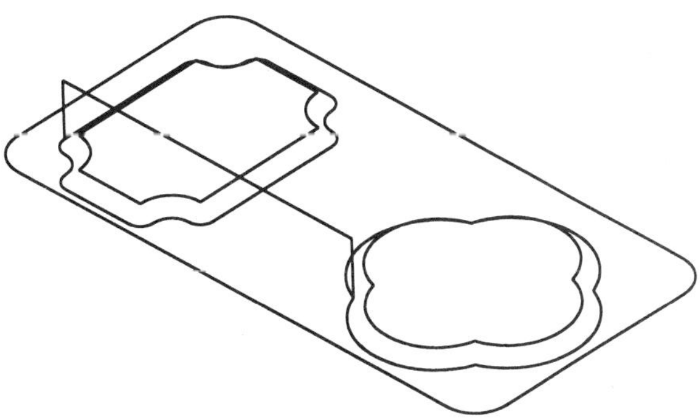

Figure 8.19

Step 12. Reverse the chain direction.

Click the green geometry icon to open the Chain Manager menu
Select **Chain 1**, then press the **Ctrl** key and select **Chain 2** to select both chains
Click the right mouse button to select **Chain 2** to open the option menu
Select **Reverse chain**
Select **OK** to return to Operations Manager menu

Step 13. Regenerate the toolpaths to reflect the reversing of chain direction.

Select **Regen Path** to regenerate the toolpaths
Select **OK** to "1 associative operations regenerated successfully."

The new toolpaths appear as in Figure 8.20.

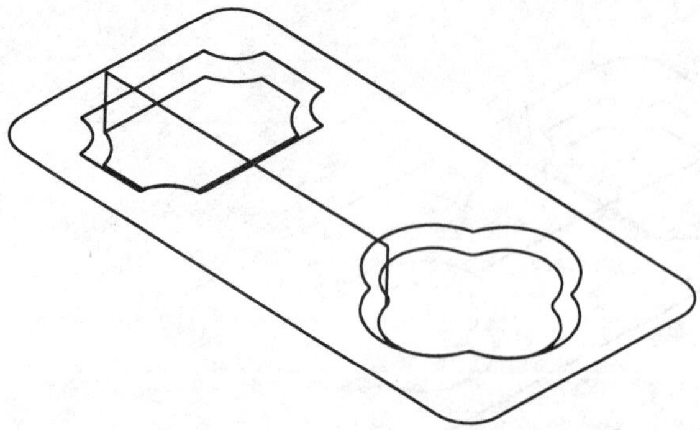

Figure 8.20

Step 14. Copy the toolpaths.

Click the right mouse button on the yellow "Contour" icon, then drag it down to the bottom of the operation list

The five-option menu should appear as here.

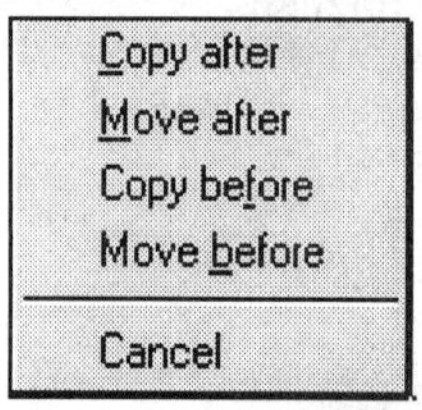

Select **Copy after** from the list

The operation has been copied as shown here.

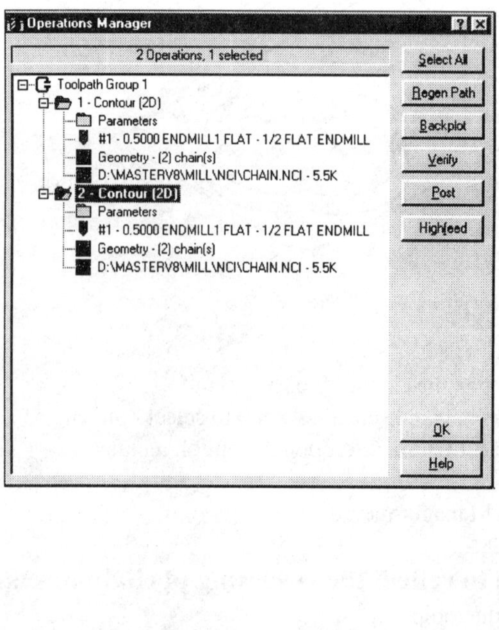

Step 15. Change the parameters for the second operation.

Click the gray parameters icon to open the parameters menu

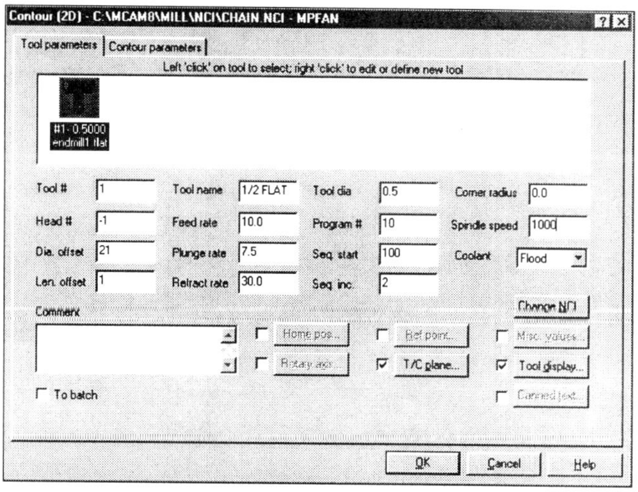

Click the right mouse button, then select "Get tool from library"
Select **tool #235** for (1/4" flat end mill)
Select **OK** to return to parameters menu
Set the tool parameters as below.

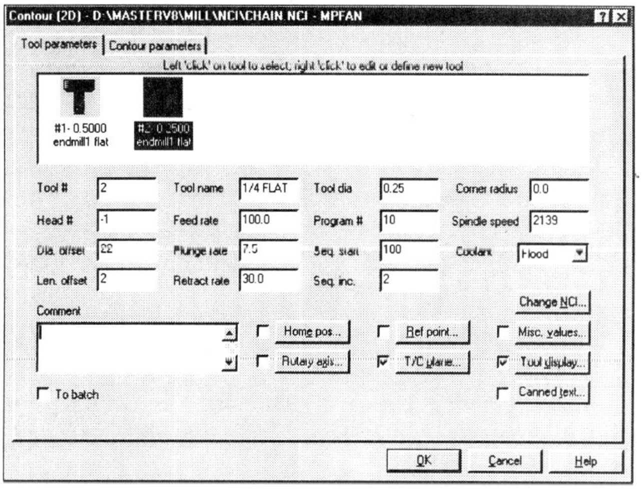

Step 16. Define the Contour parameters.

Click the "**Contour parameters**" button

Set the contour parameters as below.
(*Note:* only change "Stock to leave = 0.0")

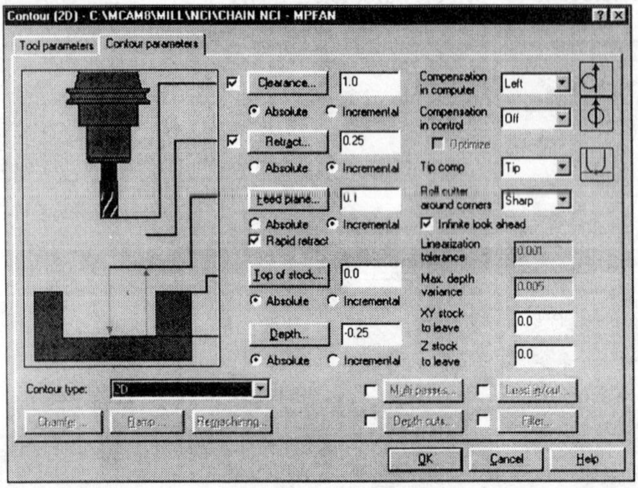

Select **OK**

Step 17. Regenerate the toolpaths to reflect the change in tool and stock.

Select **Regen Path**
Select **OK**

The new toolpaths becomes Figure 8.21.

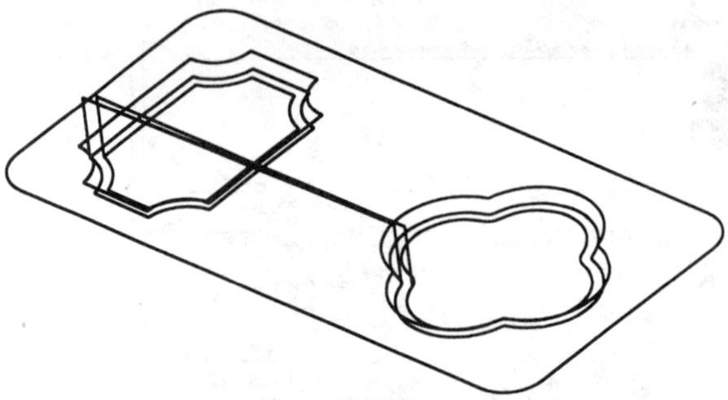

Figure 8.21

Step 18. Backplot two operations.

Select **Select All**
Select **Backplot**
Set display and backplot parameters to desired setting
Select **Run** to animate toolpaths on the screen
Note: the ½" end mill should rough cut the two chains first, followed by the ¼" end mill for finish cut.

Select **BACKUP** to return to Operations Manager menu
Select **OK** to exit Operations Manager menu

Step 19. Save the toolpath file as chain.

Select **MAIN MENU → File → Save**
File name to write: **chain**

Ex Exercises

1. What is "Associativity" in Mastercam?
2. What are the six types of associative information included in a project?
3. Define an operation in Mastercam.
4. What is the Operations Manager?
5. List the two methods of moving an operation.
6. Explain the procedure for moving an operation using the pick-and-place method.
7. Explain the procedure for moving an operation using the option command method.
8. Describe these two copy operation commands; Copy after and Copy before
9. Explain how to copy parameters between the same operation types.
10. Describe how to delete a single operation.
11. Describe how to delete all operations.
12. Explain the two tree directory control modes; Expand all and Collapse all.
13. Describe the main functions of the Chain Manager.
14. Explain the procedure to open the Chain Manager.
15. Describe the advantage of using "Add chain" function.
16. Use a drawing to show the effect of "Change side" to the toolpaths.
17. Use a drawing to show the effect of "Reverse chain" to the toolpaths.

Chapter 9
2D Toolpath Editing

Objectives:

1. Know the toolpath file structure and determine the number of toolpaths sections for various operations.
2. Delete the toolpath sections from an existing toolpath file.
3. Know three toolpath editing functions; translate, rotate, and mirror.
4. Understand the features of these toolpath editing functions and know when to apply them.
5. Apply toolpath editing functions to simplify toolpath generation process.

Overview

Previously generated toolpaths can be edited in Mastercam. There are three ways to edit toolpaths; the Operations Manager method and the Edit NCI C-Hook method and the transform toolpath method. Using the Operations Manager method to modify toolpaths was largely presented in chapter 8. Edit NCI C-Hook functions include: parameters, cut, copy, plot, merge and transform. Some of these functions can be performed with the Operations Manager method. Some functions such as scale and merge are still unique to the Edit NCI C-Hook method. This chapter covers using the transform toolpath method to modify toolpaths. Transformation has three functions; translate, rotate, and mirror.

This chapter starts with the toolpath file structure, deleting toolpaths and editing toolpaths using the three transform functions. The examples given in this chapter are not necessarily the best way to generate or edit toolpaths for a particular project. Our intent is to show how to use the transform toolpath method rather than present the best way to complete the project.

9.1 File Structure of Toolpaths

After toolpaths have been generated by using various toolpath modules, we may need to manipulate these toolpaths. Mastercam provides a variety of ways to modify toolpaths including **deleting, merging,** and **editing**. Understanding the file structure of Mastercam toolpaths is very crucial to successfully implementing these editing features.

Mastercam organizes the toolpaths into sections so that they can be edited. The toolpath sections are assigned according to their generation sequence. The toolpath generated by one operation is normally identified as one operation or section. Therefore, a section of toolpaths is generated by using the contour, pocket, drill, or surface module. Three operations, for example, are used to machine the part shown in Figure 9.1. The operation sequence starts with using the contour module to machine the outer profile, followed by using the pocket module for pocketing the rectangular pocket and using the drill module to drill the four holes. The toolpaths in this example contain three sections and are organized as:

Section No.	**Toolpaths**
Section 1	Contour module
	-
	-
Section 2	Pocket module
	-
	-
Section 3	Drill module
	-
	-
End of file	EOF

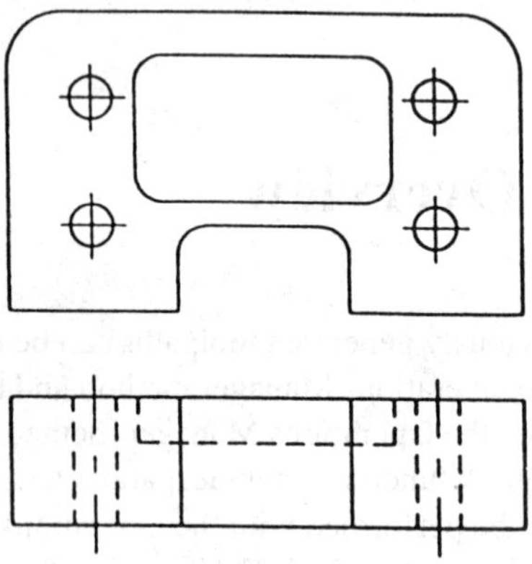

Figure 9.1

Often, more than one section is assigned to the toolpaths generated by one operation. This occurs when the contour module is used when

(1) the sum of roughing passes and finish passes is more than one or
(2) the sum of rough cuts and finish cuts in depth cut is more than one.

The number of toolpath sections for using the contour module can be calculated as:

$$NC = (NR + NF) \times (NRD + NFD)$$

where NC = total number of toolpath sections for contouring
NR = number of rough cuts
NF = number of finish passes
NRD = number of rough passes in depth cut
NFD = number of finish passes in depth cut

Example 9.1 Number of toolpath sections in contouring

The contour module is used to cut an external profile with these cutting parameters:

Number of rough cuts (NR) = **1**
Number of finish passes (NF) = **1**
Number of rough passes in depth cut (NRD) = **0**
Number of finish passes In depth cut (NFD) = **1**

The total number of toolpath sections for this particular operation is:

$$\begin{aligned} NC &= (NR + NF) \times (NRD + NFD) \\ &= (1 + 1) \text{ X } (1 + 0) \\ &= 2 \text{ toolpath sections} \end{aligned}$$

Example 9.2 Number of toolpath sections in contouring

Find the total number of toolpath sections for contouring a profile with these cutting parameters:

Number of rough cuts (NR) = **2**
Number of finish passes (NF) = **1**
Number of rough passes in depth cut (NRD) = **2**
Number of finish passes In depth cut (NFD) = **1**

The total number of toolpath sections for this particular operation is:

$$\begin{aligned} NC &= (NR + NF) \times (NRD + NFD) \\ &= (2 + 1) \text{ X } (2 + 1) \\ &= 9 \text{ toolpath sections} \end{aligned}$$

In pocketing, the number of toolpath sections is the sum of rough cuts and finish cuts in depth cut parameters. The number of finish passes in the XY-plane does not affect the number of toolpath sections. The formula listed below can be used to find the total number of toolpath sections in pocketing:

$$\mathbf{NP = NRD + NFD}$$

where NP = total number of toolpath sections for pocketing

Example 9.3 Number of toolpath sections in pocketing

Calculate the total number of toolpath sections in pocketing a rectangular pocket under the following cutting parameters:

Number of finish passes (NF) = **2**
Number of rough passes in depth cut (NRD) = **0**
Number of finish passes in depth cut (NFD) =**1**

The total number of toolpath sections in this pocketing operation is:

$$\begin{aligned} NP &= NRD + NFD \\ &= 0 + 1 \\ &= 1 \text{ toolpath section} \end{aligned}$$

Example 9.4 Number of toolpath sections in pocketing

Calculate the number of toolpath sections in pocketing an enclosed profile under the following cutting parameters:

Number of finish passes (NF) = **2**
Number of rough passes in depth cut (NRD) = **2**
Number of finish passes in depth cut (NFD) =**1**

The total number of toolpath sections in this pocketing operation is:

$$
\begin{aligned}
NP &= NRD + NFD \\
&= 2 + 1 \\
&= 3 \text{ toolpath sections}
\end{aligned}
$$

The number of toolpath segments is always **1** when the drill module is used. When a part program contains the toolpaths generated by using more than one operation (contour, pocket, drill, or surface module), the total number of toolpath sections is the sum of toolpath sections of each operation.

Example 9.5 Number of toolpath sections for multiple operations

A part program consists of the toolpaths generated by three operations (contour, pocket, and drill). Find the number of toolpath sections for the following two sets of cutting parameters:

Case 1:

Contour: Number of roughing cuts = 0
Number of finish passes = 1
Depth cut: Rough: 0 cut at 0.0 Finish: 1 cut at 0.0

Pocket: Number of finish passes = 1
Depth cut: Rough: 0 cut at 0.0 Finish: 1 cut at 0.0

Drill: Drilling operation always has one toolpath section

The total number of toolpath section is the sum of these three operations which is:

$$
\begin{aligned}
N &= 1 + 1 + 1 \\
&= 3 \text{ toolpath sections}
\end{aligned}
$$

The total number of toolpath sections for the operation conditions listed above is 3 (one for contouring, one for pocketing, and one for drilling).

Case 2:

Contour: Number of roughing cuts = 2
Number of finish passes = 1
Depth cut: Rough: 1 cut at 0.0 Finish: 1 cut at 0.2

Pocket: Number of finish passes = 1
Depth cut: Rough: 0 cut at 0.0 Finish: 1 cut at 0.0

Drill: Drilling operation always has one toolpath section

The contouring operation has 6 toolpath sections. The pocketing has 1 section and drilling 1 section. Therefore, the total number of toolpath sections is 8.

The Procedure to Find the List of Toolpath Sections:

Use the following commands to list the toolpath sections of a toolpath file:

1. Press [**Alt +C**], select **Editnci.dll**, and choose **Open.**
2. The Edit NCI menu should appear as below.

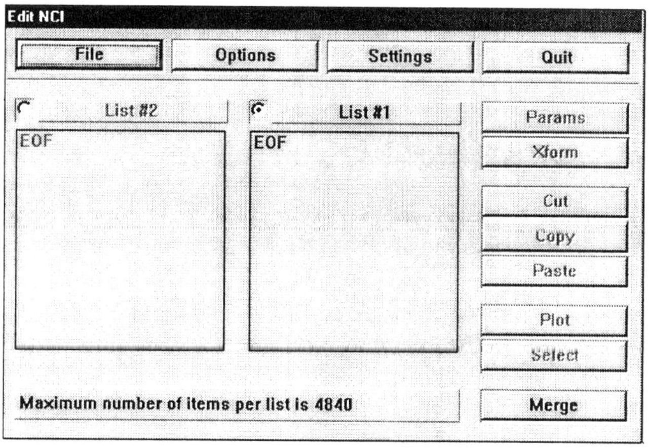

3. Select **File** → **Open**
4. Enter file name: **POCKET1.NCI** (specify your own file's name)
5. Select **Open**

The toolpath sections should appear under POCKET1.NCI as shown below.

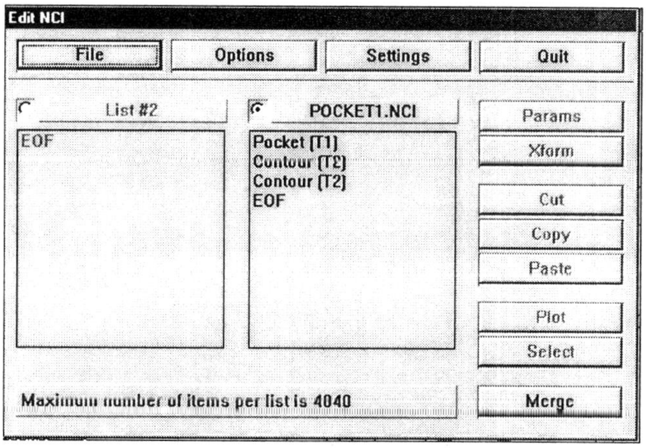

9.2 Deleting Toolpaths using Operations Manager

Often we need to delete the toolpaths that have become a part of the toolpath file. Mastercam uses two ways to delete the selected toolpath sections: the **Operation Managers** method and the **Edit NCI** method.

The operations manager method allows deleting toolpaths for one operation or all operations. Follow the following procedure to delete the toolpaths.

The Procedure for Deleting a Single Operation Toolpath:

1. Select Toolpaths → Operations to open the Operations Manager menu.

2. Click the toolpath to be deleted, then click the right mouse button to open the option menu as shown here:

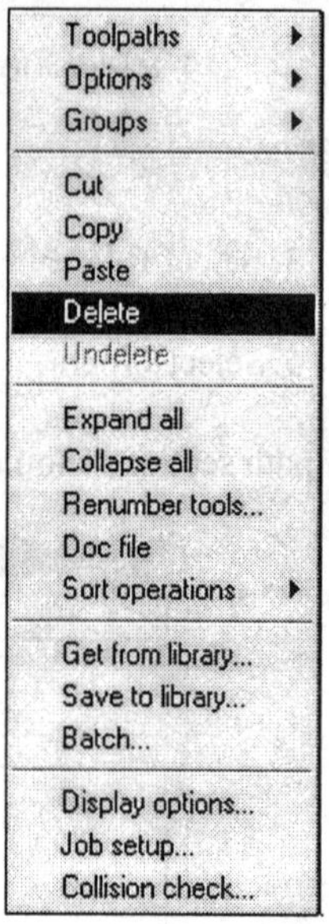

3. Select Delete

4. Repeat steps 2 – 3 to delete toolpaths for other operations one by one.

The Procedure for Deleting the Entire Toolpath File:

1. Select Toolpaths → Operations to open the Operations Manager menu

2. Select "Select All" from the Operations Manager menu

3. Click the right mouse button to open the option menu

4. Select Delete

Project 1. Delete toolpaths using the operations manager method

This project uses the pocket2t project to show how to delete toolpaths for a selected operation. The toolpaths in this project consist of three pocketing operations. We delete the first pocket operation by using the single operation option, then delete the remaining two pocket operations using the entire toolpath file option. The part geometry and its existing toolpaths are shown in Figure 9.2.

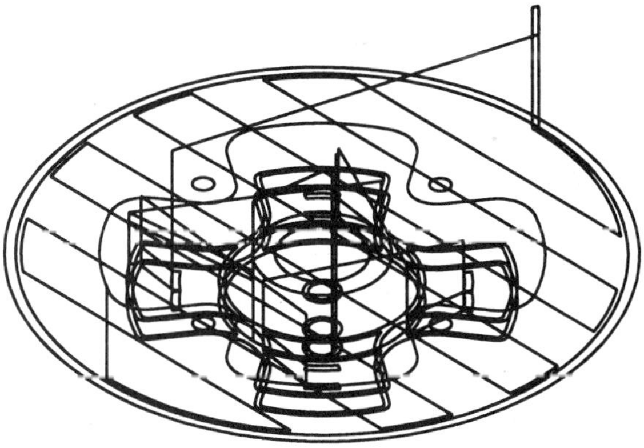

Figure 9.2

Step 1. Open the pocket2t file.

Select **MAIN MENU → File → Get**
File name: **pocket2t** ↵
The part geometry should appear on the screen.

Step 2. Open the toolpaths.

Select **MAIN MENU → Toolpaths**
The toolpaths for three pocketing operations are displayed as in Figure 9.3.

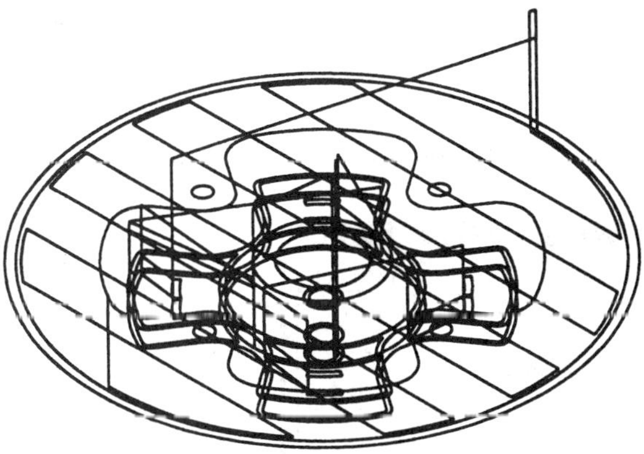

Figure 9.3

Step 3. Open the Operations Manager menu.

Select **Operations** to open the Operations Manager menu

The Operations Manager menu appears as below.

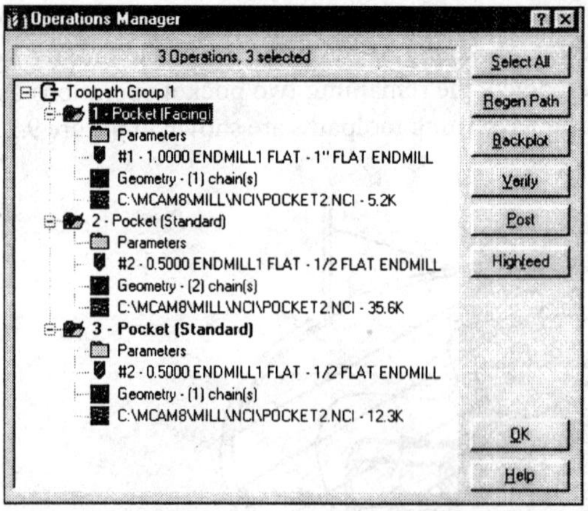

Step 4. Delete the first pocketing operation.

Click the "**Pocket**" icon of the first pocket operation
Click the right mouse button to open
the option menu as here.

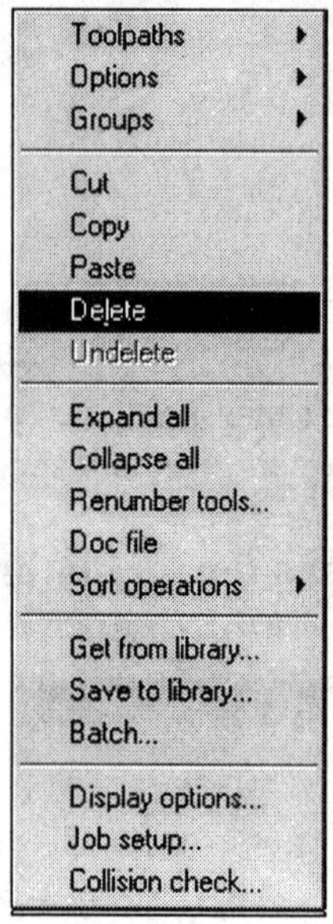

Select **Delete**

The toolpath of the first pocket operation has been removed as shown below.

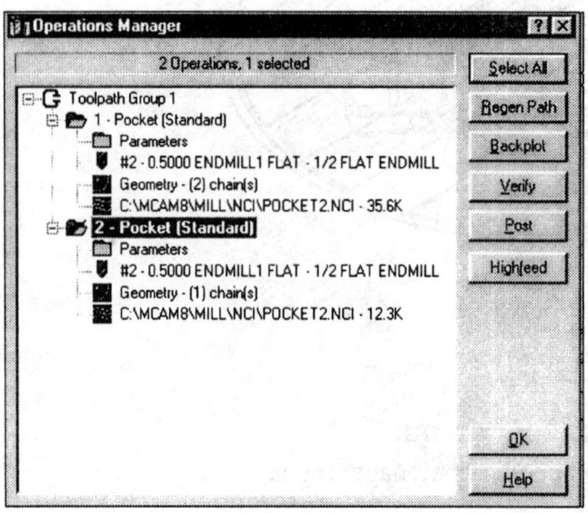

Step 5. Delete the remaining two pocketing operations.

Select the "**Select All**" button from the Operations Manager menu
Click the right mouse button, then select **Delete**

The remaining two pocketing operations have been removed from the Operations Manager as shown below.

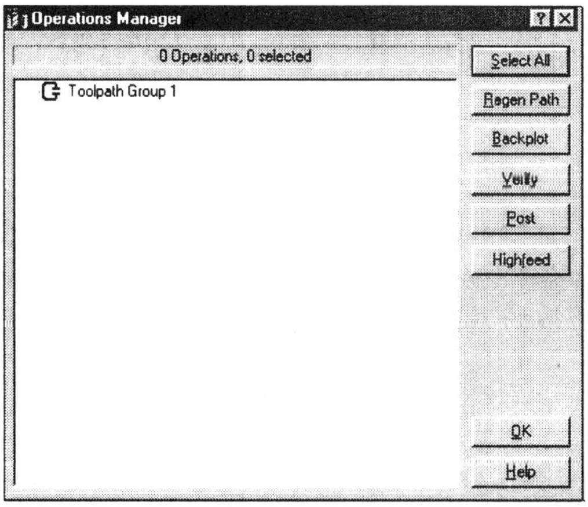

Select **OK** from the Operations Manager menu

9.3 Transform Toolpaths

Mastercam provides a very useful toolpath editing function, **transform toolpaths**, to change the position, orientation, and size of existing toolpaths. This function allows you to **translate, rotate** or **mirror** operations.

The toolpaths to be transformed must exist before the transform function can be used. The transform toolpath is associative. If the transform function is used on any operation and the original toolpath is changed, the transformed operation that is linked to the toolpath is also updated.

Note: You can also translate, rotate, mirror, or scale operations using the Edit NCI C-Hook, but the resulting toolpaths are not associative.

The Transform Operation Parameters are given below:

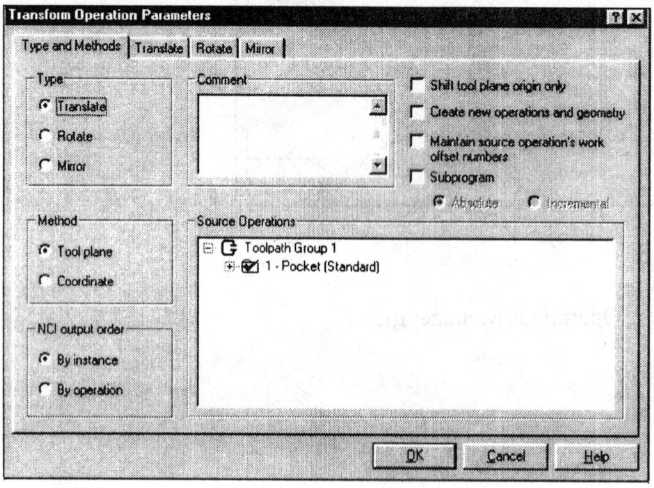

Transform types

There are three transform types which are grouped under the Transform Operation Parameters; translate, rotate, and mirror.

Translate: moves or copies the toolpaths to the specified new locations.

Rotate: rotates the toolpaths about the origin or any other point relative to the current construction plane.

Mirror: mirrors the toolpaths about the X axis, Y axis or any given line.

Subprogram

Subprogram is an option within the Transform toolpath parameters. This function falls into two categories: transform subprograms and non-transform subprograms. Both categories support motion with absolute positioning or incremental positioning in the subprogram.

The major advantages of using toolpath editing functions are (1) eliminating the need to create the identical or similar feature geometries, and (2) eliminating the need to repeatedly use the NC modules to generate toolpaths for machining identical or similar part features.

The procedure for toolpath editing functions is:

1. Create a toolpath.

2. Select MAIN MENU → Toolpaths → Next menu → Transform.

3. Select Translate from the Type area (for example, use Translate function).

4. Enter the Transform Operation parameters.

5. Select the Translate tab. The Translate parameters should appear as below.

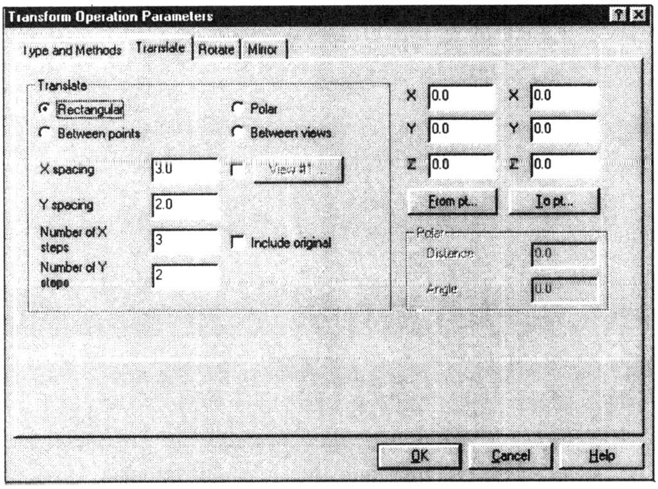

6. Define the Translate parameters.

7. Select OK to implement the editing.

9.4 Translating Toolpaths

The translate function moves or copies the toolpath of selected operations to new locations. The translate parameters are shown as below:

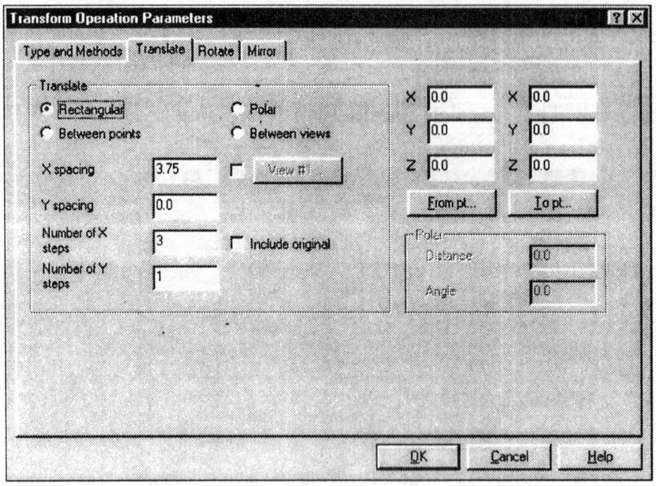

The movement method can be defined by one of the following four options:

Rectang:	specifies the incremental distance to be translated in the X, Y, and Z directions.
Polar:	specifies the incremental distance and the desired angle to define the translation position. (Figure 9.4a)
Between points:	specifies the translation distance between two points. (Figure 9.4b)
Between views:	translates the toolpaths from one view to another. (Figure 9.4c)

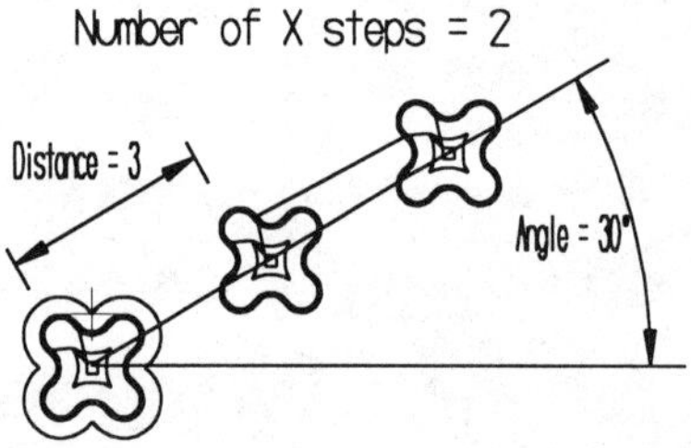

Figure 9.4a For polar

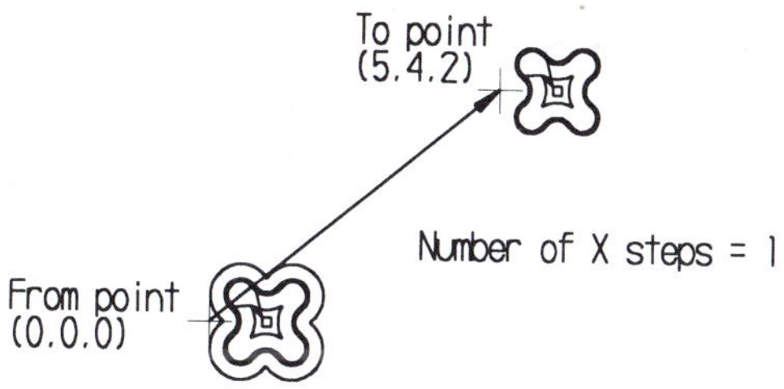

Figure 9.4b For Between points

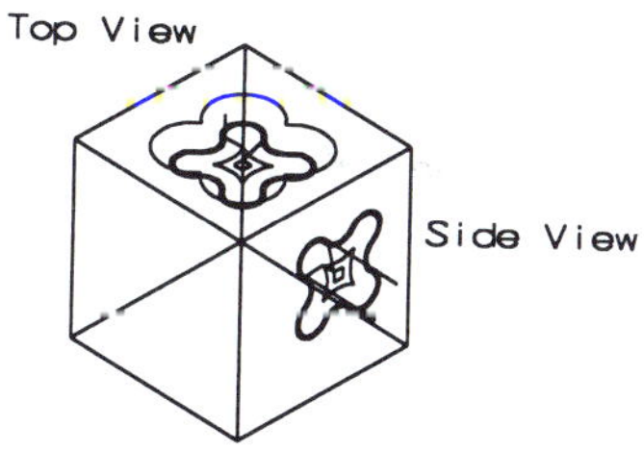

Figure 9.4c For Between views

Rectang:

The rectang function allows us to generate a set of duplicated toolpaths. These toolpaths can be located at a specified distance along the X and/or Y direction (Figure 9.5). It is defined by the following four parameters:

Number of X steps:	number of times to step and repeat the toolpath along the X axis.
Number of Y steps:	number of times to step and repeat the toolpath along the Y axis.
X spacing:	spacing distance of each step in X direction.
Y spacing:	spacing distance of each step in Y direction.

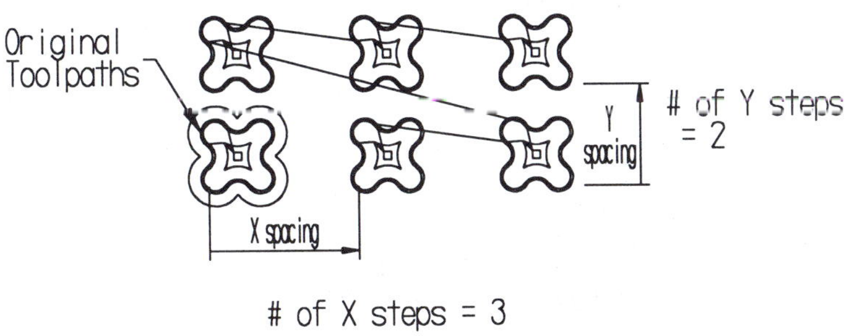

Figure 9.5

Table 9.1 on the following page illustrates how to define the number of steps in X and number of steps in Y to generate the duplicate toolpaths.

Table 9.1 Defining number of X steps and number of Y steps parameters

Number of X steps	Number of Y steps	Description	Illustration
1	1	No duplicated toolpath is generated.	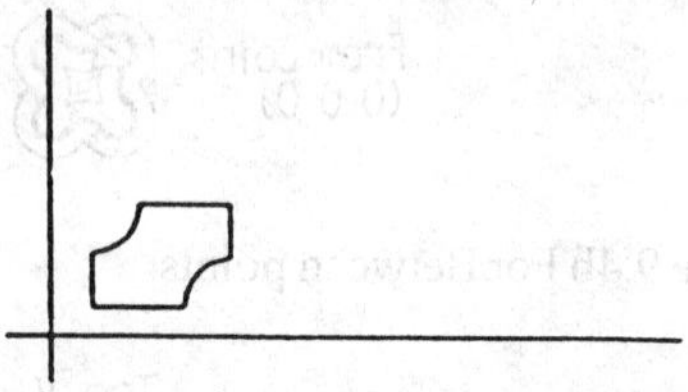
2	1	One duplicated toolpath is generated in X direction.	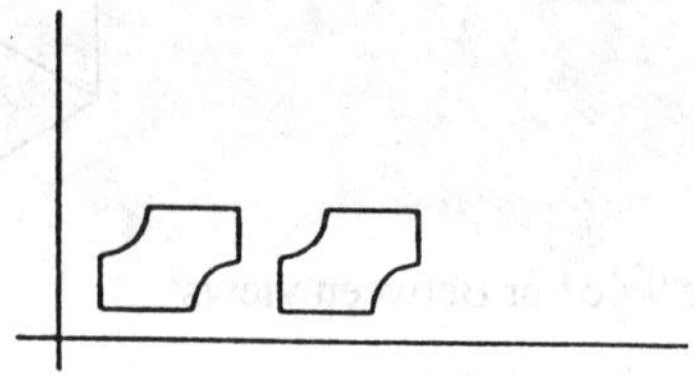
3	1	Two duplicated toolpaths are generated in the X direction.	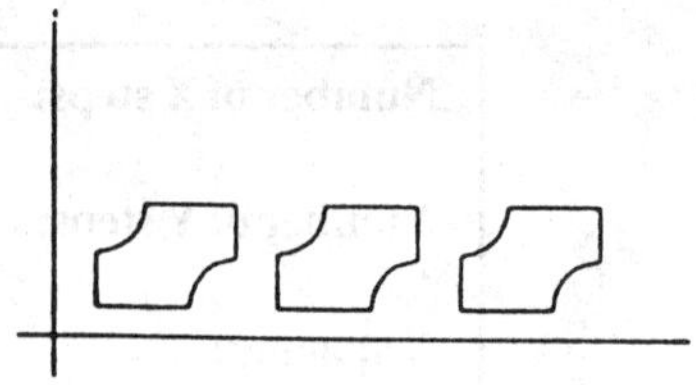
2	2	Three duplicated toolpaths are generated (one in the X-direction and two in the Y-direction).	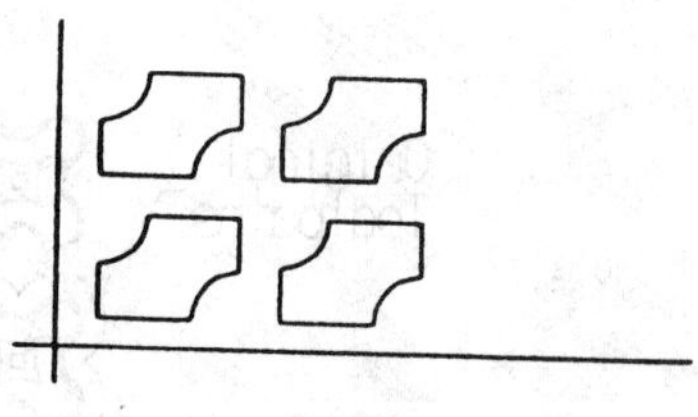
3	2	Five duplicated toolpaths are generated (two in the X-direction and three in the Y-direction).	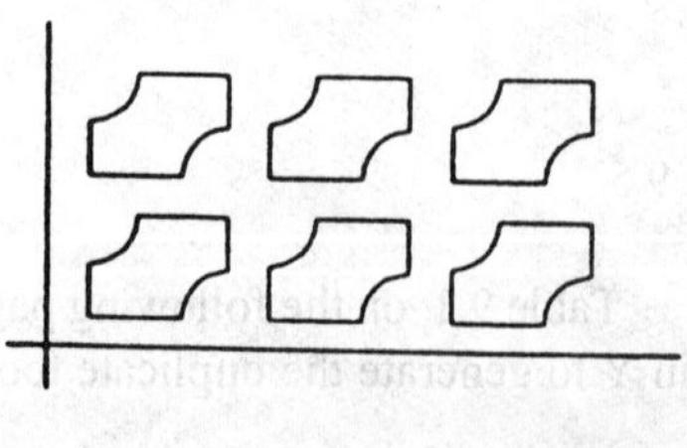

The translation function can be readily applied in the following **three applications:**

1. **Change coordinate system** (Figure 9.6). When the toolpaths are translated, this can be regarded as an altered coordinate system.

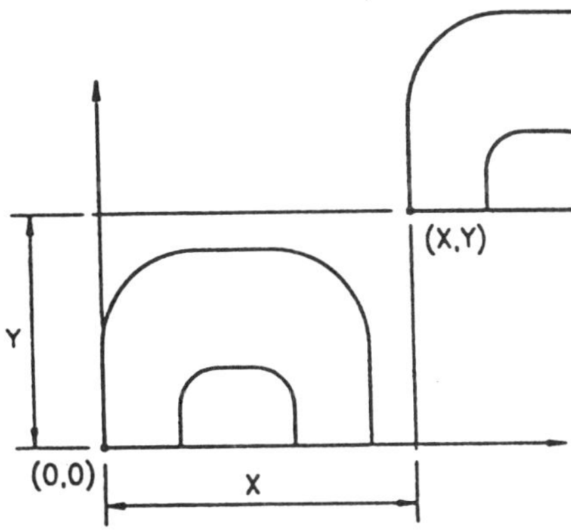

Figure 9.6

2. Generate toolpaths for identical part features **located at different locations** on the same workpiece (Figure 9.7).

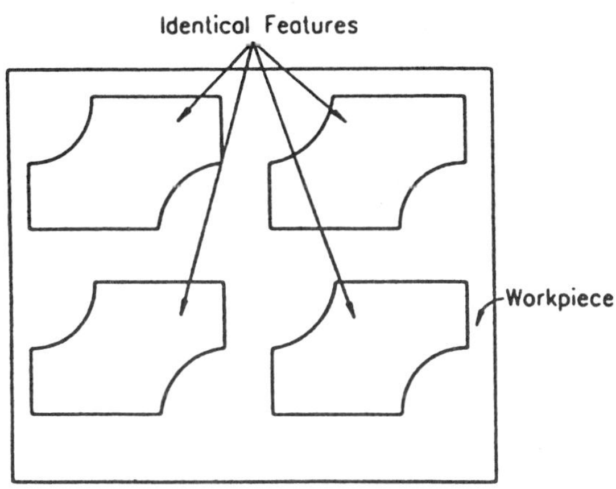

Figure 9.7

3. Generate toolpaths for producing **multiple identical workpieces** in one part program (Figure 9.8). This facilitates the machining of multiple workpieces in one machine setup.

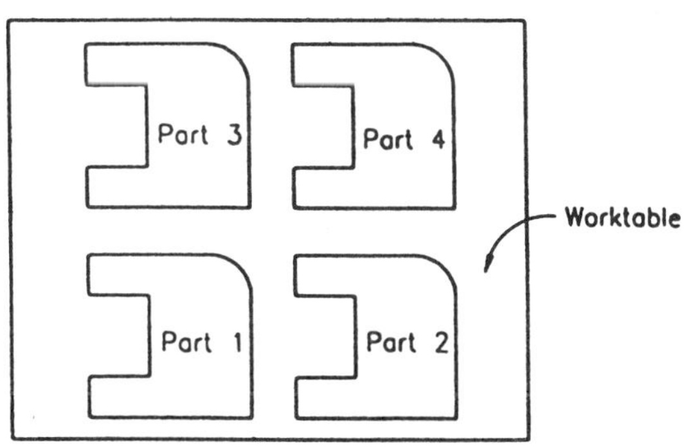

Figure 9.8

💻 Project 2. Translating project

The part shown in Figure 9.9 has three identical features. We can generate the toolpaths for one feature and then use the Transform → Translate function to copy the toolpaths to the other two locations.

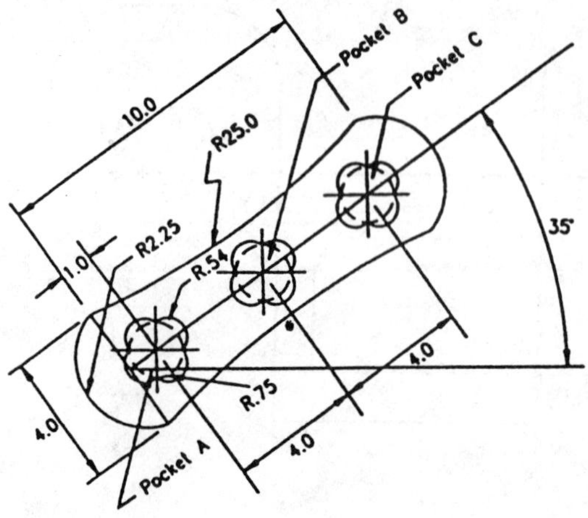

Figure 9.9a

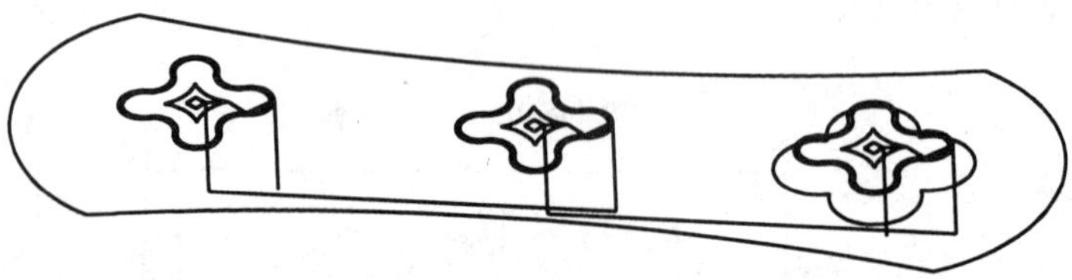

Figure 9.9b

⌛**Tips**	1. Cutter diameter = 0.5".
	2. Use the pocket module to generate the toolpaths for cutting the pocket A.
	3. Use Toolpaths → Next menu → Transform → Translate function to copy the pocketing toolpaths to the other two locations.

Step 1. Open the part geometry file trans1.

Select **MAIN MENU → File → Get**

File name: **trans1**↵

The part geometry appears as in Figure 9.10.

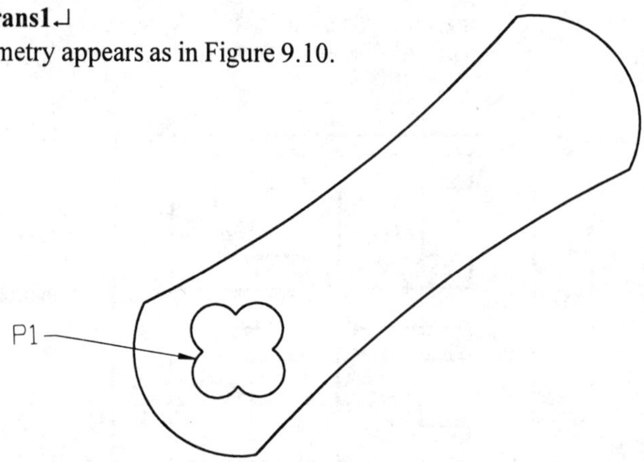

Figure 9.10

Step 2. Initiate the pocket module using the pick point in Figure 9.10. 2

Select **MAIN MENU → Toolpaths → Pocket**
Select **Chain**
Pick **P1**, then select **Done**
Click the right mouse button, then select "**Get tool from library**"
Select **tool #239** (1/2 flat end mill)
Select **OK**
Set the tool parameters as below.

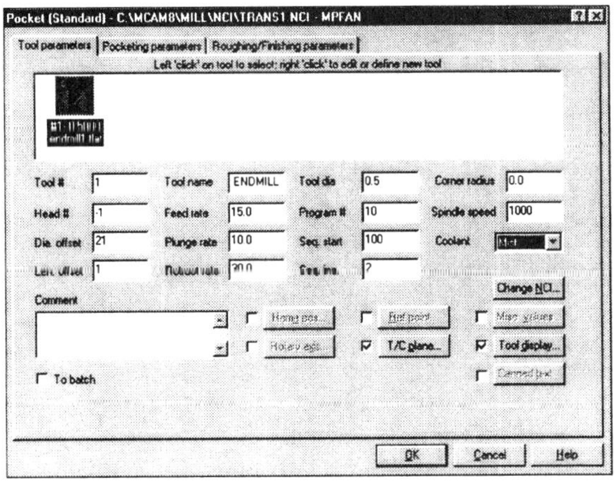

Step 3. Define the pocketing parameters.

Click on the "**Pocketing parameters**" button
Define the pocketing parameters as below.

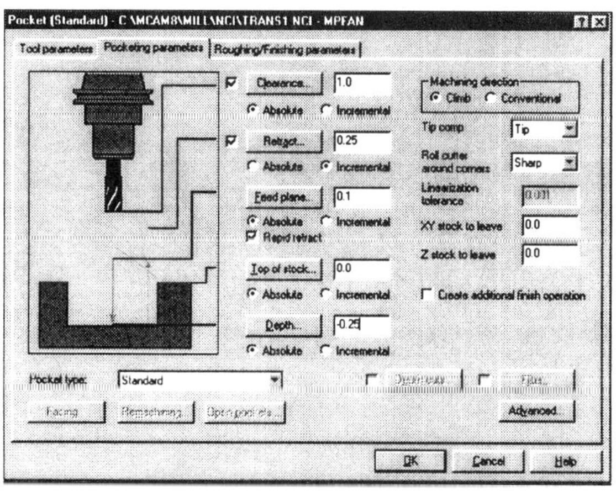

Step 4. Define the roughing and finishing parameters.

Click on the "**Roughing/Finishing parameters**" button

Set the roughing and finishing parameters as below.

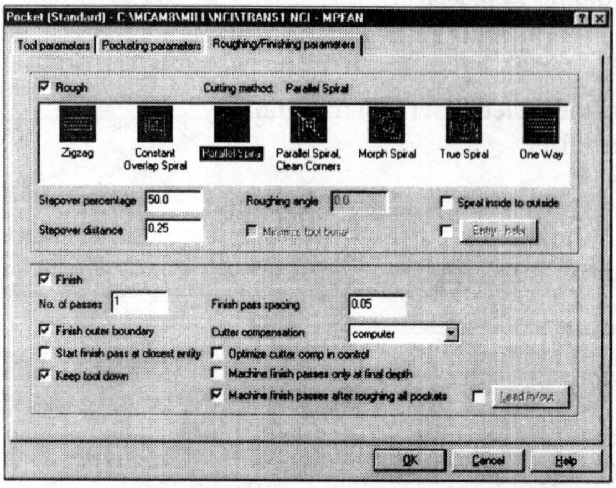

Select **OK** to generate the pocketing toolpaths as in Figure 9.11.

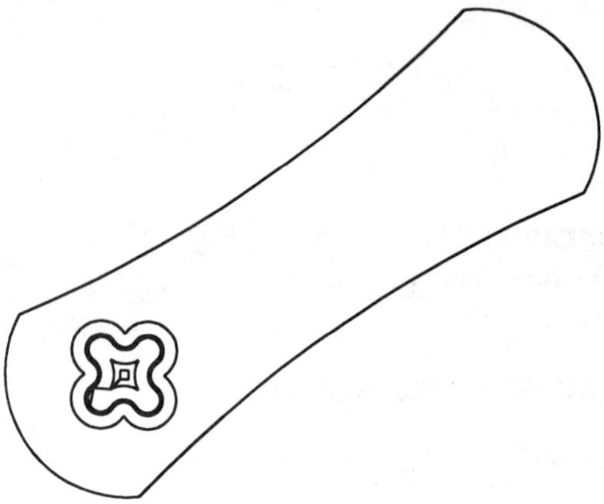

Figure 9.11

Step 5. Translate the toolpaths to two locations.

Select **Next menu → Transform**

The Transform Operation Parameters menu should appear.

Set the Types and Methods parameters to the following settings.

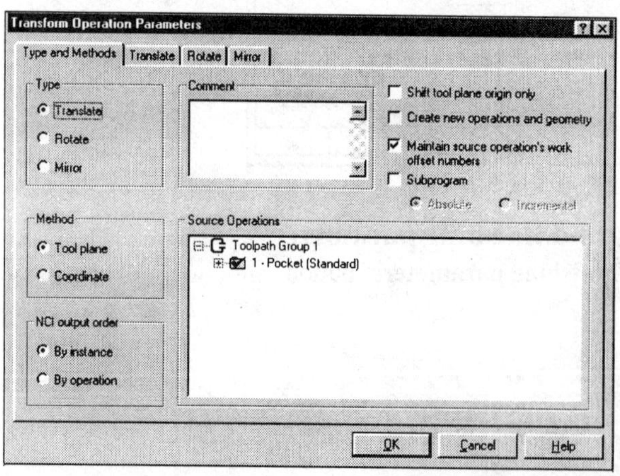

Select the **Translate** tab
Set the translation parameters as shown below.

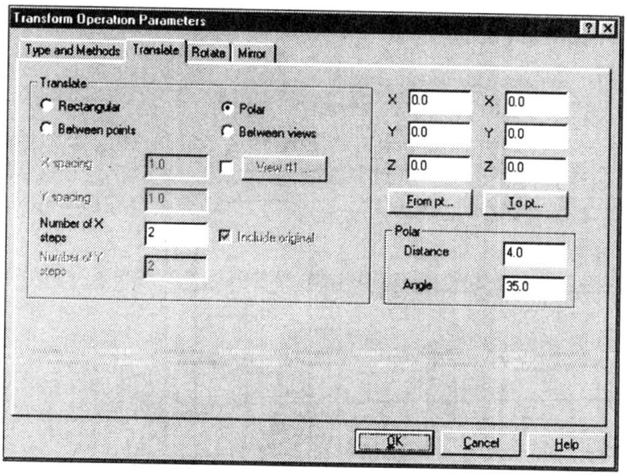

The two sets of toolpaths are added as in Figure 9.12.

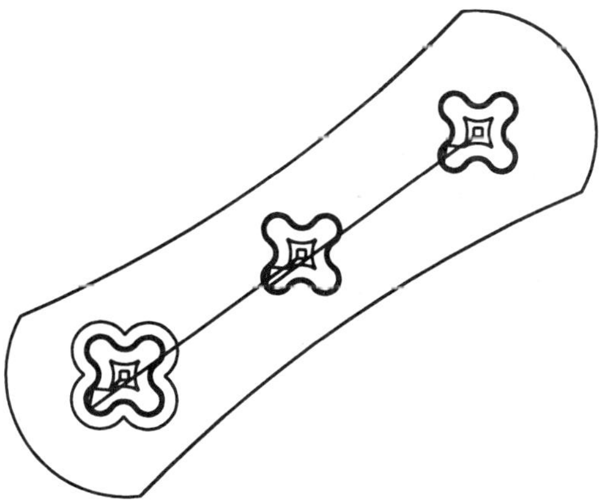

Figure 9.12

Step 6. Verify the toolpaths.

Select **Gview → Isometric**
Select **MAIN MENU → Toolpaths → Operations → Backplot**
Select **Run**
The toolpaths in isometric view should look like Figure 9.13.

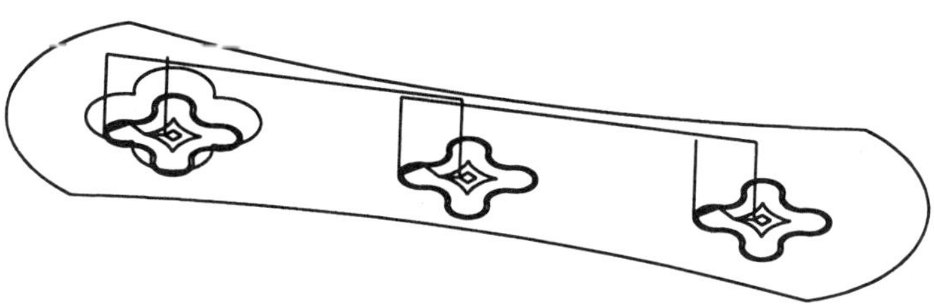

Figure 9.13

Project 3. Translating toolpaths

The part shown in Figure 9.14 consists of three identical pockets that are equally spaced in the X direction. This is the ideal project for using the translate function. The pocketing toolpaths for pocket A can be copied to the other two locations.

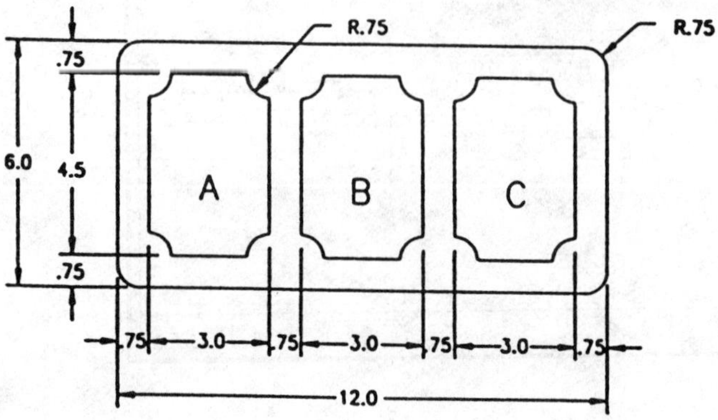

Figure 9.14a

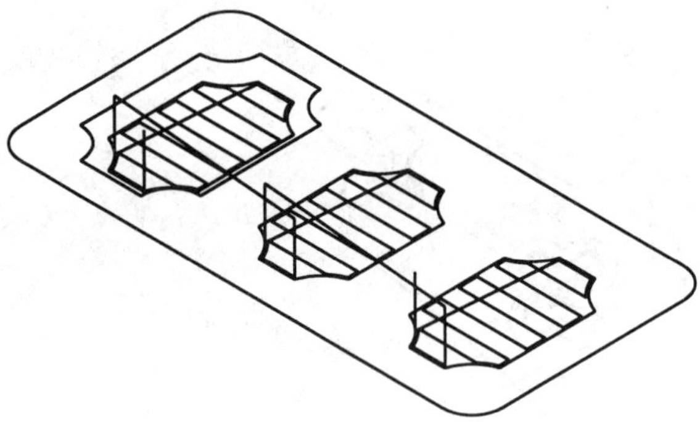

Figure 9.14b

> **Tips** The translate parameters should be set as:
>
> Number of X steps = **3**
> Number of Y steps = **1**
> X spacing = **3.75**
> Y spacing = **0.0**
>
> The system will generate the roughing toolpaths for three pockets first, then will be followed by the finish toolpaths.

Step 1. Open the part geometry file array1.

Select **MAIN MENU → File → Get**
File name: **array1↵**

The part geometry drawing should appear as Figure 9.15.

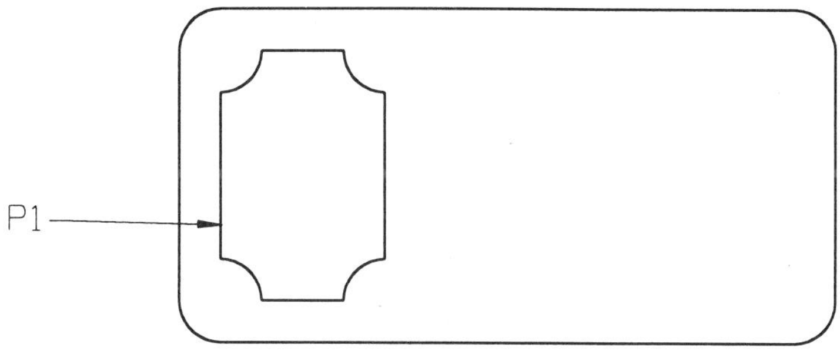

Figure 9.15

Step 2. Initiate the pocket module.

Use the pick point in Figure 9.15.
Select **MAIN MENU → Toolpaths → Pocket**
Select **Chain**, then pick **P1**
Select **Done**
Click the right mouse button, then select "**Get tool from library**"
Select **tool #241** (3/4 flat end mill)
Select **OK**
Set the tool parameters as below.

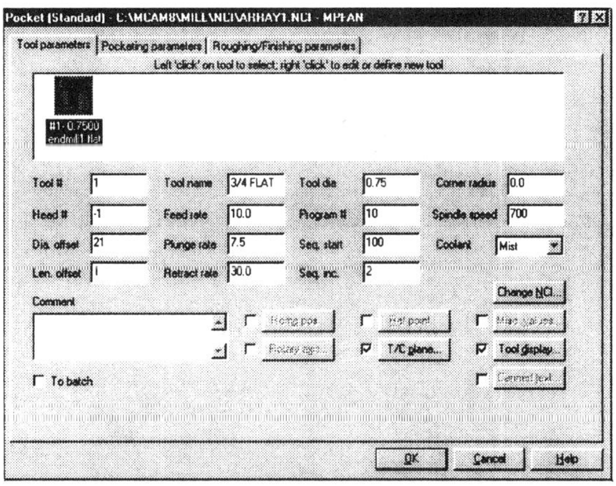

Step 3. Define the pocketing parameters.

Click "**Pocketing parameters**" button

Set the pocketing parameters as below.

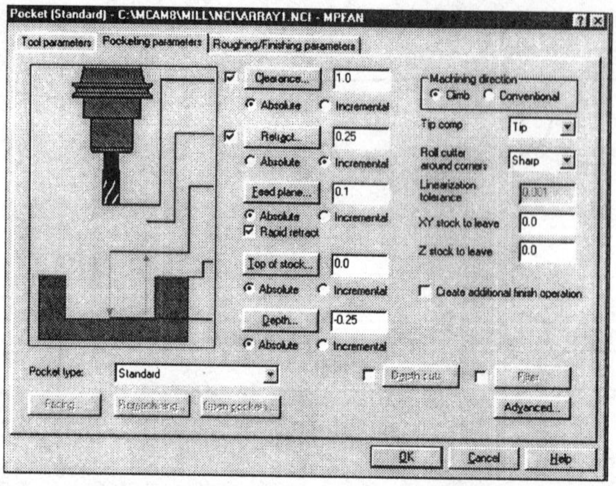

Step 4. Define the roughing and finishing parameters.

Click on the "**Roughing/Finishing parameters**" tab

Set the roughing and finishing parameters as below.

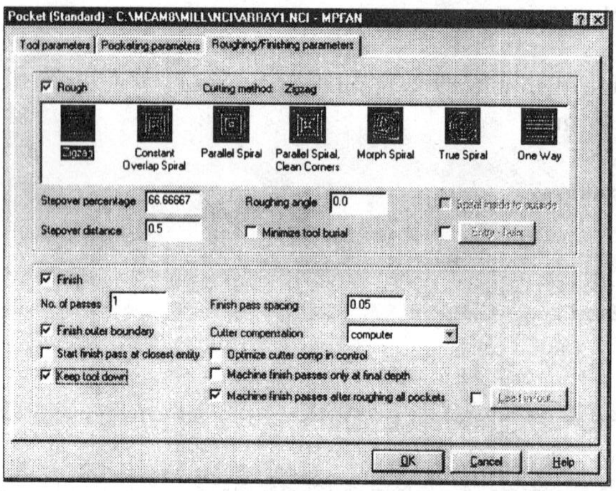

Select **OK** to generate pocketing toolpaths

The pocketing toolpaths are shown in Figure 9.16.

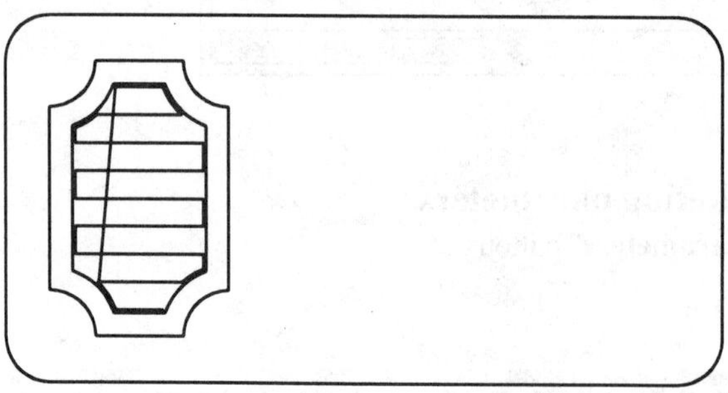

Figure 9.16

Step 5. Initiate the Transform toolpath function.

Select **Next menu → Transform**

Set the Type and Methods parameters as below.

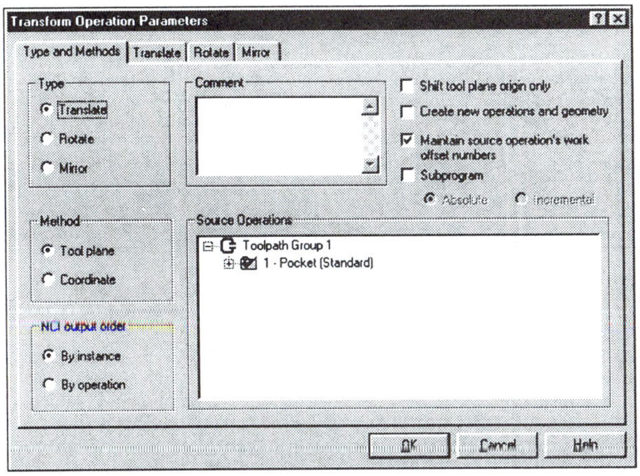

Select the **Translate** tab from the Transform Operation Parameters

Define the translation parameters as below.

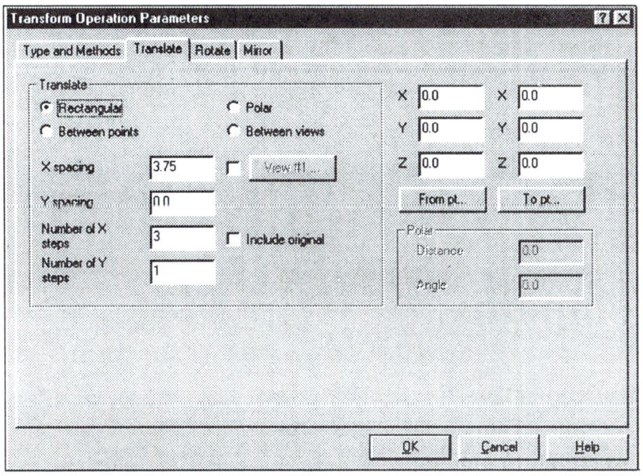

Select **OK** to execute the translate function

The pocketing toolpaths have been copied to two locations as shown in Figure 9.17.

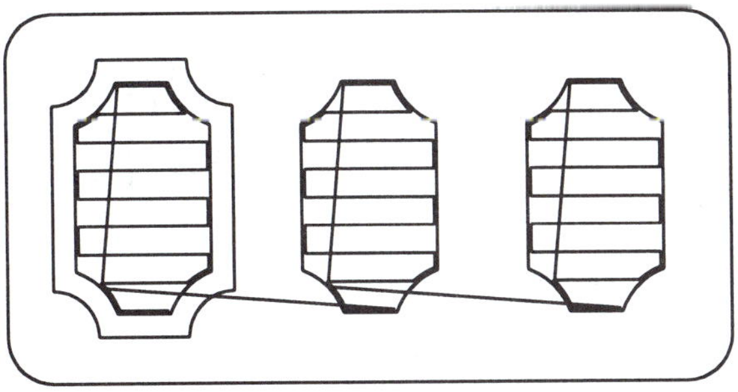

Figure 9.17

Step 6. Change to isometric view.

Select **Gview → Isometric**

The model shown in isometric view appears as in Figure 9.18.

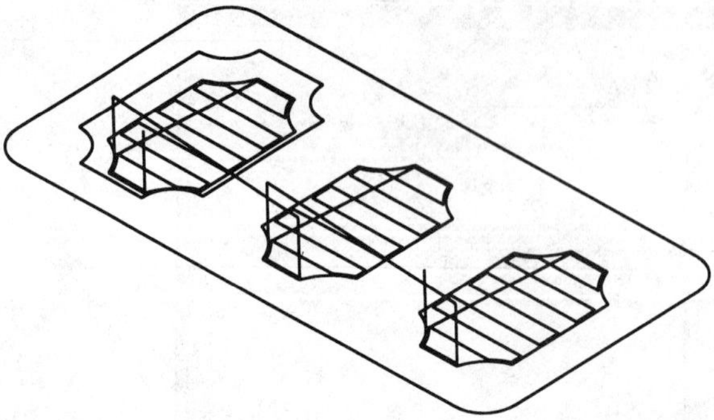

Figure 9.18

Step 7. Save the project.

Select **MAIN MENU → File → Save**

File name: **array1t** ↵

9.5 Rotating Toolpaths

The Rotate function moves (or copies) existing toolpaths of selected operations by rotating them about the origin or any given point. It is best suited to generate the toolpaths for identical patterns or features that are symmetrical about a point. (Figure 9.19).

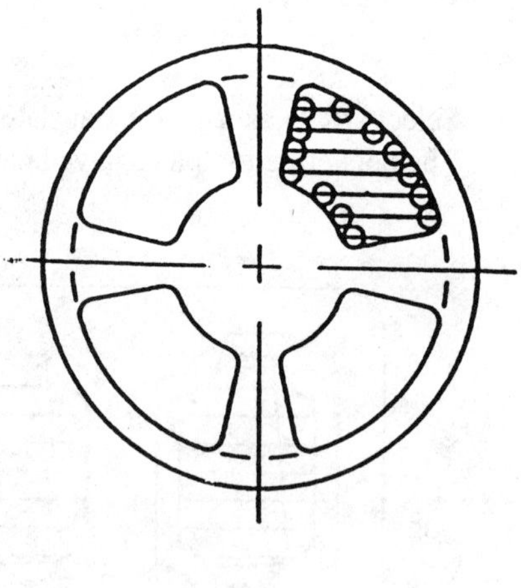

Figure 9.19

Figure 9.20 illustrates the definition of a rotation angle. In the Top and Front Cplanes, the angle is measured from the +X direction and is positive in the counterclockwise direction. In Side Cplane, the angle is measured from +Y axis.

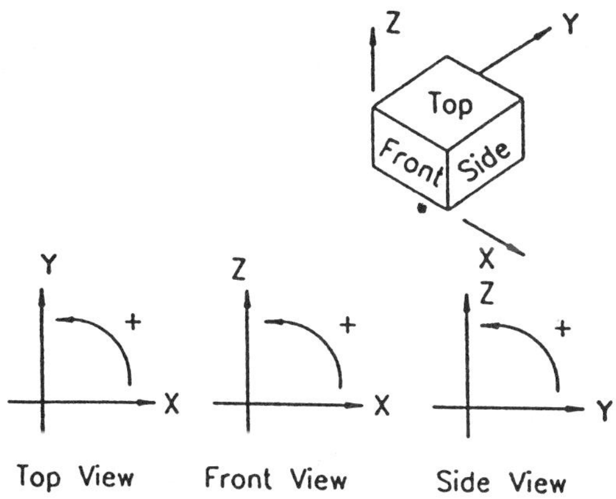

Figure 9.20

Procedure for using the rotate function:

1. Generate the toolpaths for the features to be rotated.

2. Select MAIN MENU → Toolpaths → Next menu → Transform to open the Transform Operation Parameters.

3. Select Rotate in the Type area and define other "Type and Methods" parameters.

4. Click the Rotate tab and enter the rotation parameters.

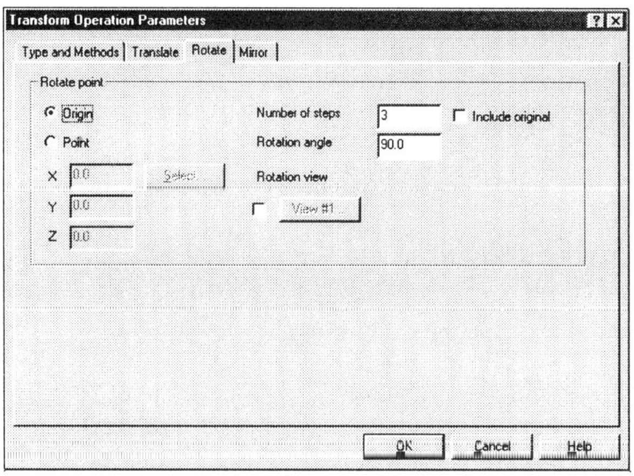

5. Define the rotation parameters.

6. Select OK to show the rotated toolpaths.

Project 4. Rotating toolpaths about the origin

The process of generating toolpaths for cutting the part shown in Figure 9.21 can be significantly simplified by using the Transform → Rotate function. The raw material is a solid circular plate.

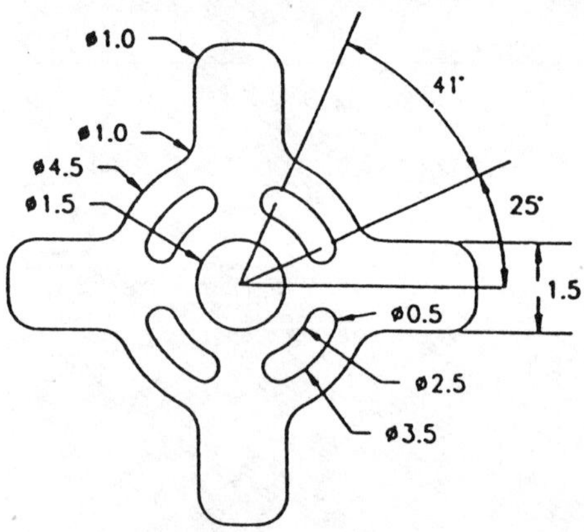

Figure 9.21a

Figure 9.21b

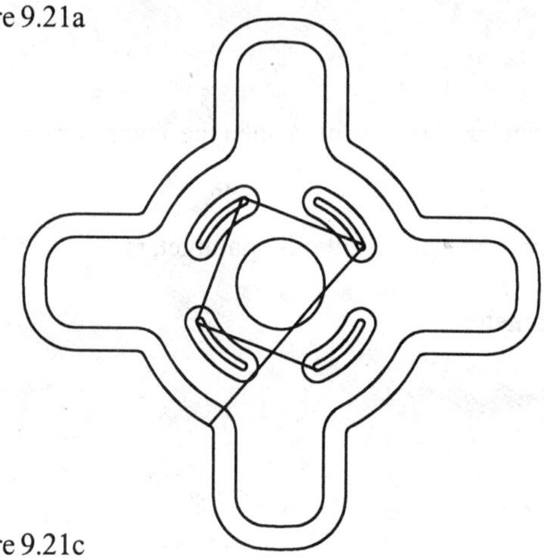

Figure 9.21c

Tips

1. Use the pocket module to rough cut one of the four pockets. The roughing toolpaths are then copied to the other three locations by the rotate command. This allows the final external profile to be produced by using the contour module in one pass.
2. Open the geometry file (rotate1) again. Use the contour module to cut the external profile.
3. Use the contour module to cut one of four circular grooves. Cutter diameter for grooving is 3/8". The rotate command is used again to copy the toolpaths to the other three positions.

Step 1. Open the part geometry file rotate1.

Select **MAIN MENU → File → Get**

File name: **rotate1**↵

The part geometry should appear as Figure 9.22.

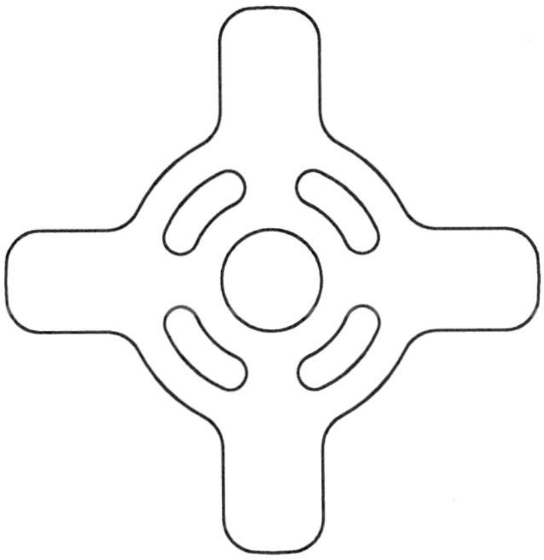

Figure 9.22

Step 2. Create a construction circle.

Select **MAIN MENU → Create → Arc → Cir pt+dia**
Enter the diameter: **8.4** ↵
Enter the coordinate: **0, 0** ↵
The new drawing becomes Figure 9.23.

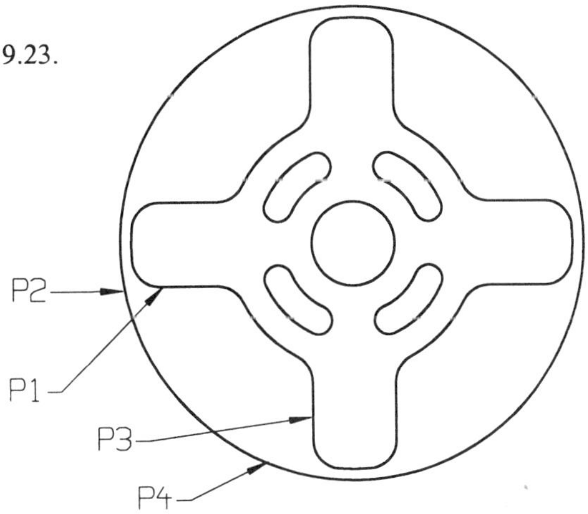

Figure 9.23

Step 3. Extend two lines to form a closed contour for pocketing.

Use the pick points in Figure 9.23.
Select **MAIN MENU → Modify → Trim → 1 entity**
Pick **P1** to select the entity to trim
Pick **P2** to select the entity to trim to
Pick **P3** to select the entity to trim
Pick **P4** to select the entity to trim to
The two extended lines are shown in Figure 9.24.

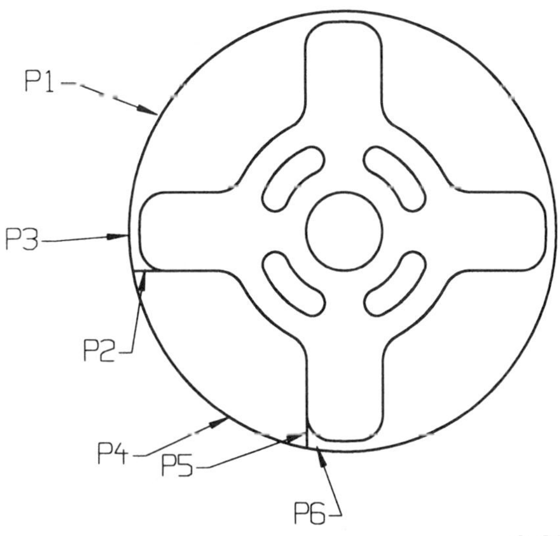

Figure 9.24

Step 4. Break the construction circle into three segments at the intersection points with the two extended lines.

Use the pick points in Figure 9.24.
Select **MAIN MENU → Modify → Break → 2 pieces**
Pick **P1** to select the entity to break
Select **Intersec** from the Point menu
Pick **P2** and **P3** to determine the breaking point
Pick **P4** to select the entity to break
Select **Intersec**
Pick **P5** and **P6** to determine the breaking point
The drawing appearing on the screen does not change even though the outer circle has been broken into 3 pieces. The drawing is redrawn in Figure 9.25.

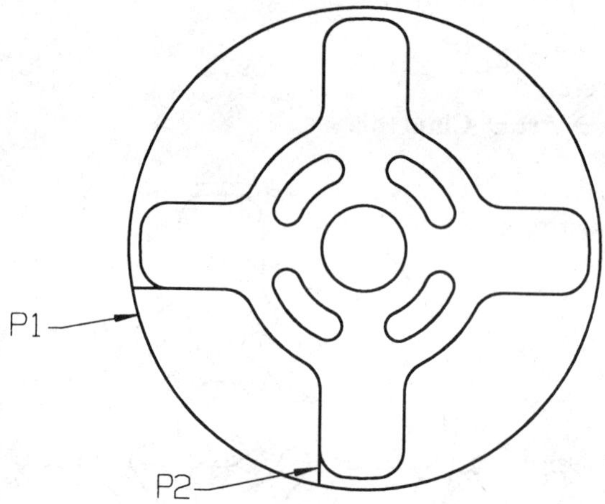

Figure 9.25

Step 5. Initiate the pocket module using pick points in Figure 9.25.

Select **MAIN MENU → Toolpaths → Pocket**
Enter file name for NCI file: **part1**
Select **Chain**, then pick **P1** and **P2**
Select **End here → Done**
Click the right mouse button, then select "**Get tool from library**"
Select **tool #241** (3/4 flat end mill)
Select **OK**
Set the tool parameters as below.

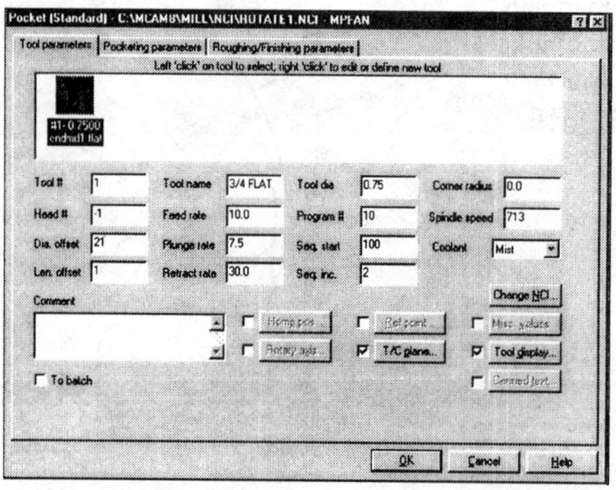

Step 6. Define the pocketing parameters.

Click the "**Pocketing parameters**" tab
Set the pocketing parameters as below.

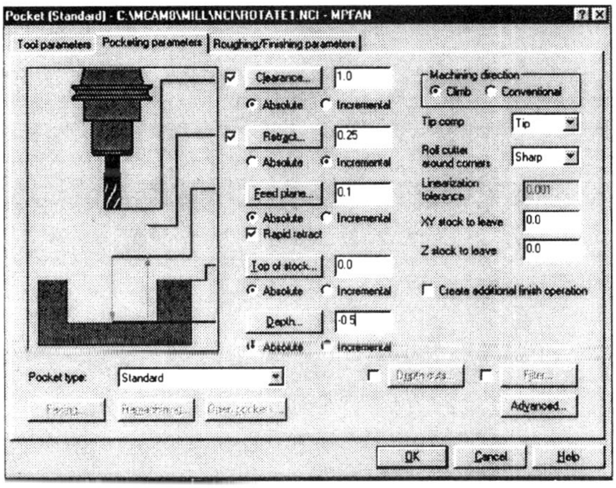

Step 7. Define the roughing and finishing parameters.

Click the "**Roughing/Finishing parameters**" tab
Set the roughing and finishing parameters as below.

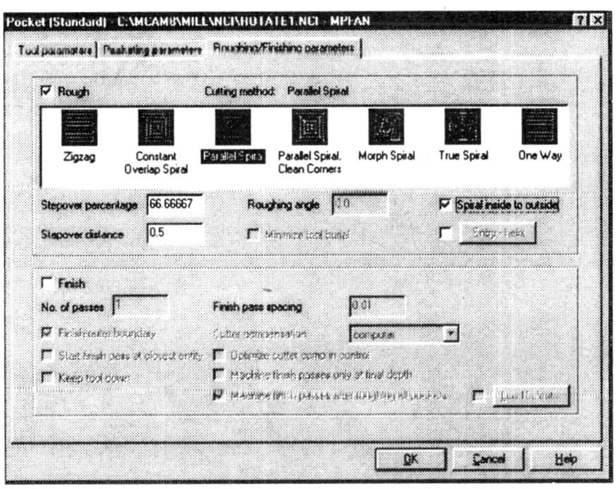

Select **OK** to generate the pocketing toolpaths as shown in Figure 9.26.

Figure 9.26

Step 8. Copy the pocketing toolpaths to three locations.

Select **Next menu → Transform** to enter the Transform Operation Parameters
Set The Type and Methods parameters as below.

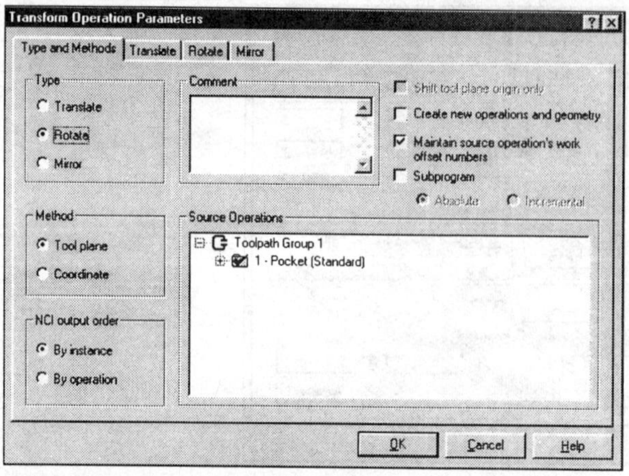

Select the **Rotate** tab to open the rotation parameters
Define the rotation parameters as below.

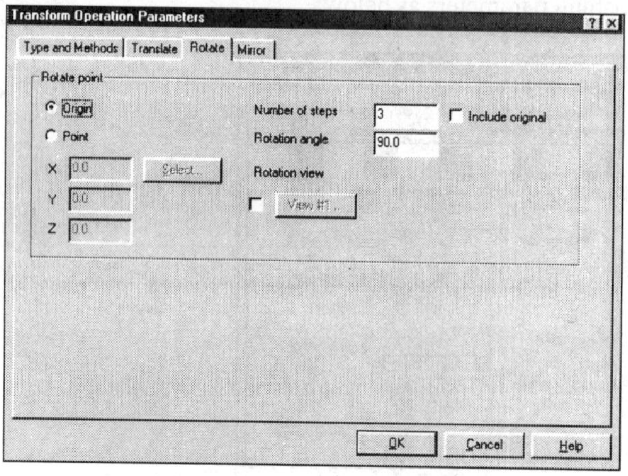

Select **OK** to copy the toolpaths to three locations
The four sets of toolpaths appear as in Figure 9.27.

Figure 9.27

Step 9. Open the geometry file rotate1 again.

Select **MAIN MENU → File → Get**
File name: **rotate1**↵
Select **No** to "MC8 file has changed. Save it?"
The part geometry should appear as in Figure 9.28.

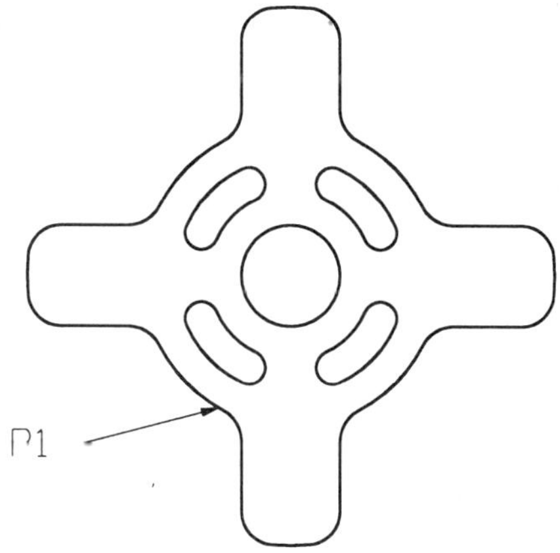

Figure 9.28

Step 10. Initiate the contour module using the pick point in Figure 9.28.

Select **MAIN MENU → Toolpaths → Contour**
Enter file name for NCI file: **part2** ↵
Select **Chain**
Pick **P1**, then select **Done**
Choose **#241 Tool**
Set the tool parameters as below.

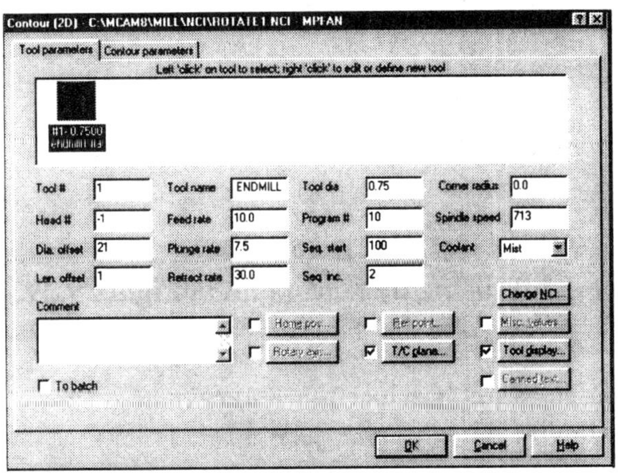

Step 11. Define the contour parameters.

Click the "**Contour parameters**" tab
Set the contour parameters as shown next .

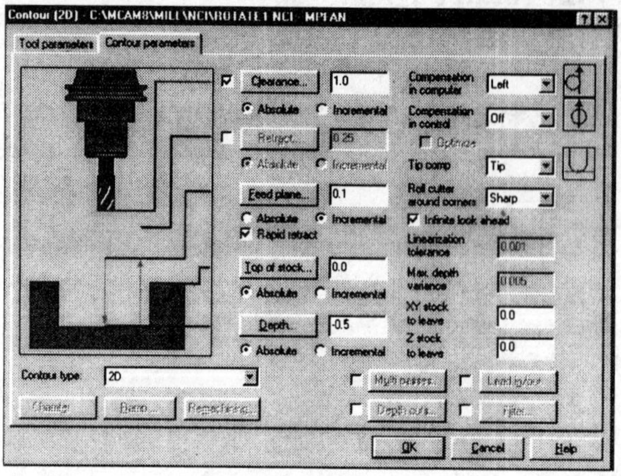

Select **OK** to generate the contouring toolpaths as shown in Figure 9.29.

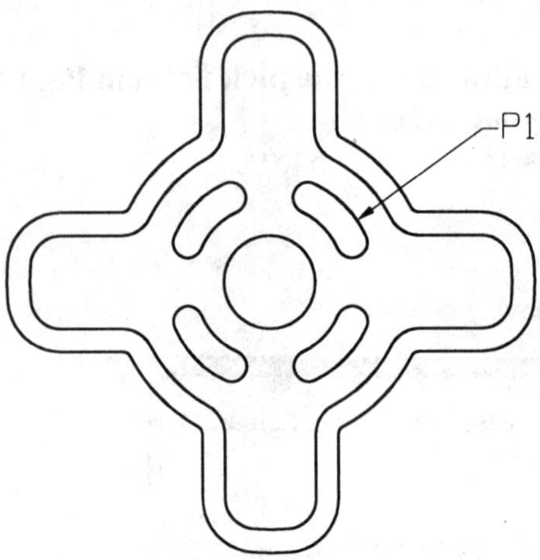

Figure 9.29

Step 12. Initiate the contour module using the pick point in Figure 9.29.

Select **Contour → Chain**
Pick **P1**, then select **Done**
Click the right mouse button, then select "**Get tool from library**"
Select **tool #237** (3/8 flat end mill)
Select **OK**
Set the tool parameters as shown next.

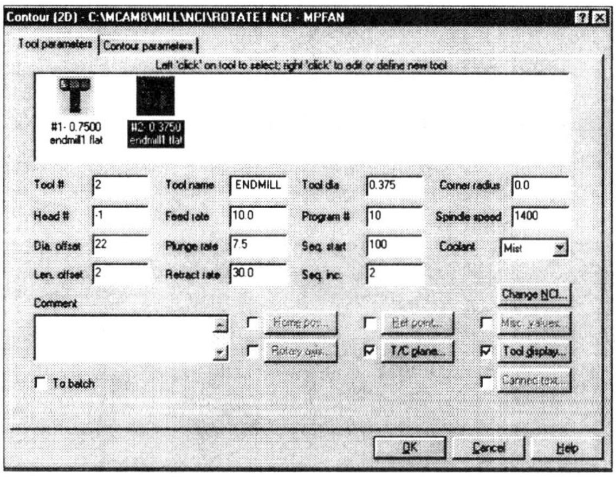

Step 13. Define the contour parameters.

Click on the "**Contour parameters**" tab

Set the contour parameters as below.

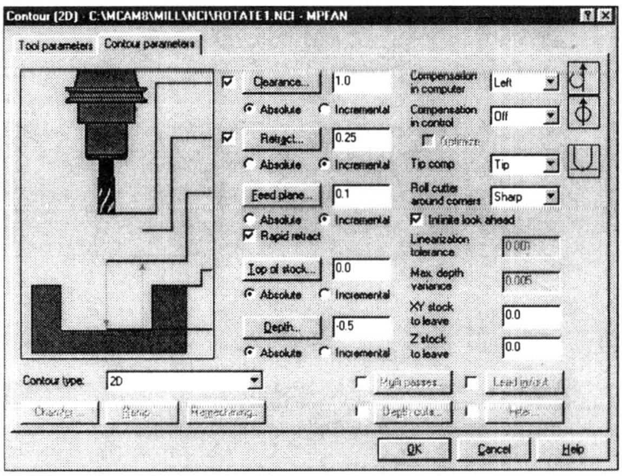

Select **OK** to generate contouring toolpaths as shown in Figure 9.30.

Figure 9.30

Step 14. Copy the sets of toolpaths to their other locations.

Select **Next menu** → **Transform** to open the Transform Operation Parameters
Set the "Type and Methods" menu options as shown below.

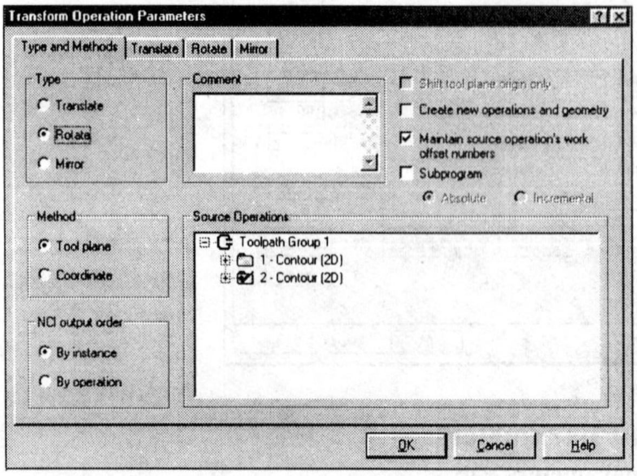

Select the **Rotate** tab to open the rotation parameters
Define the rotation parameters as below.

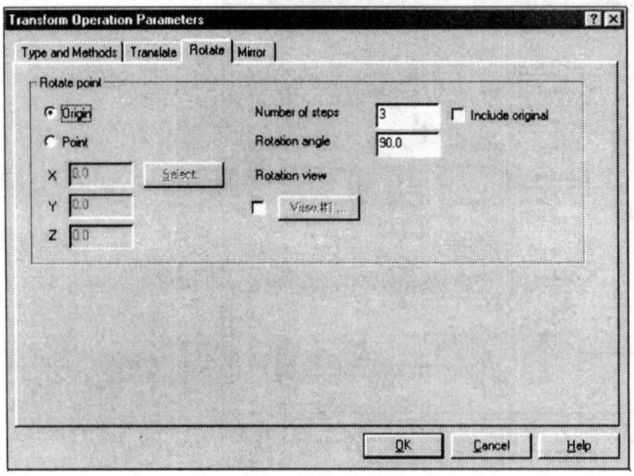

Select **OK**
The groove contouring toolpath is copied to three locations as shown in Figure 9.31.

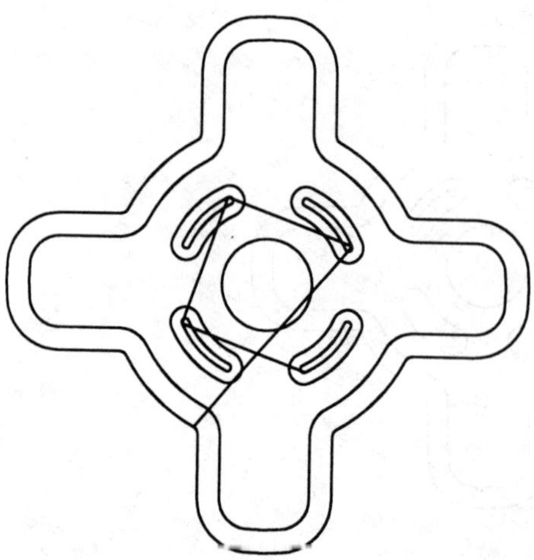

Figure 9.31

9.6 Mirroring Toolpaths

This function mirrors the existing toolpaths about an axis or a line. It is best suited for (1) those parts that have identical features that are symmetrical about an axis or a line (Figure 9.32a), and for (2) generating toolpaths to machine multiple workpieces that are symmetrically placed about an axis or a line (Figure 9.32b).

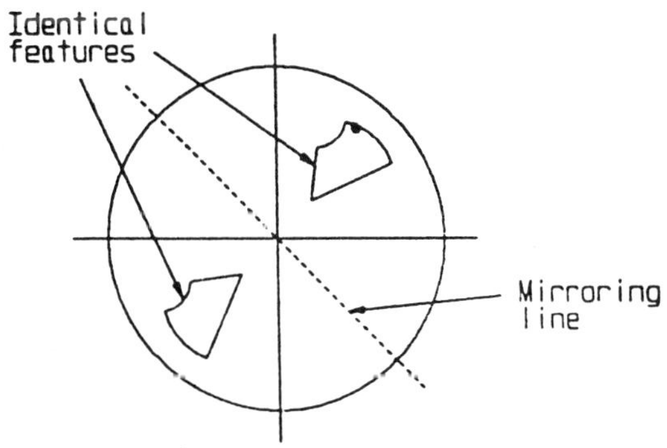

Figure 9.32a

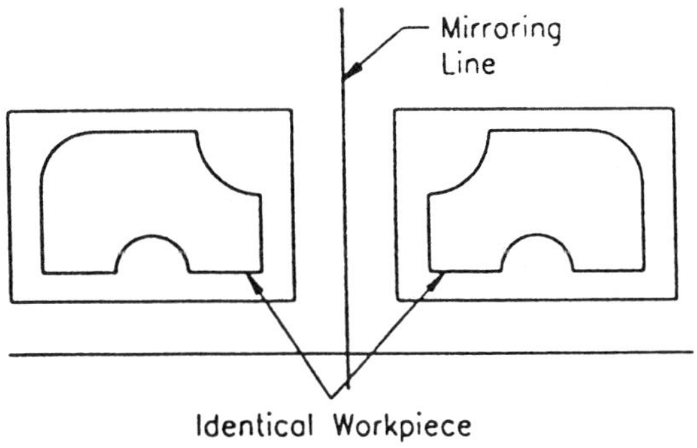

Figure 9.32b

When you click on the Mirror tab in the Transform Operation Parameters, the mirroring parameters should appear as below:

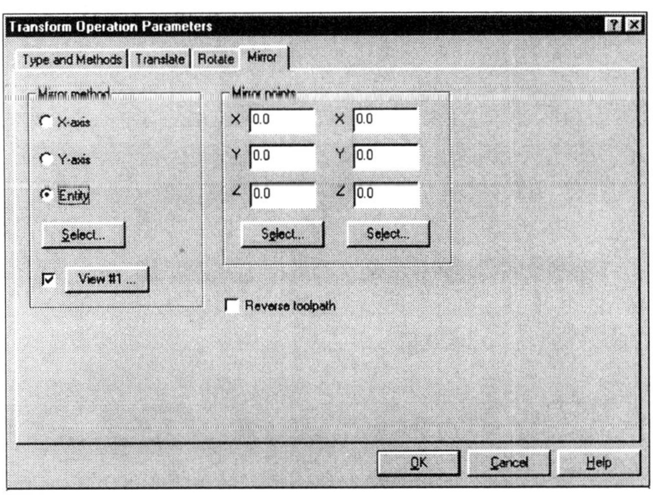

The mirroring parameters includes one of more of the following:

Mirror method

X axis: mirrors the selected operation about the Cplane's X axis.
Y axis: mirrors the selected operation about the Cplane's Y axis.
Entity: mirrors the selected operation about a selected entity.

Mirror points: displays the X, Y, Z coordinates of the mirror points. You can choose these points using the Select option or enter values in the text boxes.

View #: changes the Cplane.

Select: returns to the graphics window to select the point about which you would like to mirror the selected operation.

Reverse toolpath: reverses the cutter toolpath on the selected NCI operations.

Procedure for using the mirror function:

1. Generate the toolpaths to be mirrored. An existing toolpath should be available before using this function.

2. Select MAIN MENU → Toolpaths → Next menu → Transform to open the Transform Operation Parameters.

3. Select Mirror in the Type area and define the transform operation parameters.

4. Click the Mirror tab to open the mirror parameters.

5. Define the mirror parameters.

6. Select OK to show the mirrored toolpaths.

Project 5. Mirroring the toolpaths of a feature about X and Y axes to generate the toolpaths for three other locations

The part shown in Figure 9.33 has four features that are symmetrical about the X, Y axes and a point. The Transform - Mirror function is best suited for this project. We only need to create the geometry of one feature. Use the pocket module to generate the toolpaths for cutting this feature. This set of toolpaths is then copied to one adjacent side using the mirror function about the X axis. The toolpaths are again copied to the other two locations by mirroring them about the Y axis and about an entity.

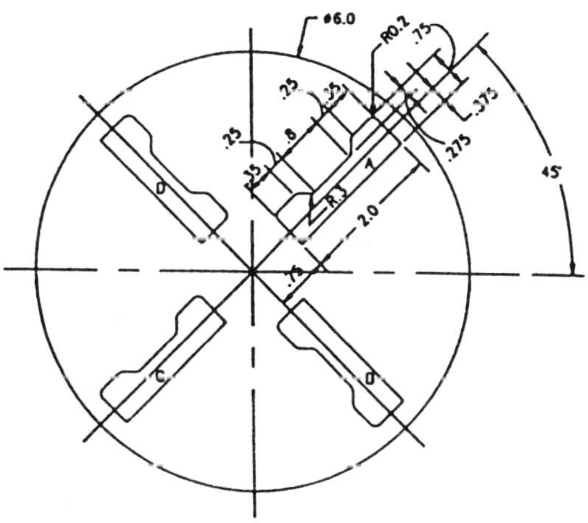

Figure 9.33a

Figure 9.33b

Tips

1. Cutter diameter is 0.25".
2. Cutting parameters are:
3. Roughing cut spacing = 0.2"
4. One finish cut with spacing of 0.05"
5. Use the pocket module to generate toolpaths for feature A.
6. Use Transform → Mirror function to copy the toolpaths to feature B. Mirror about X axis.
7. Mirror the toolpaths of features A about the Y axis and about an entity to produce the other two features.

Step 1. Open the geometry file mirror1.

Select **MAIN MENU → File → Get**

File name: **mirror1**↵

The part drawing should appear as Figure 9.34.

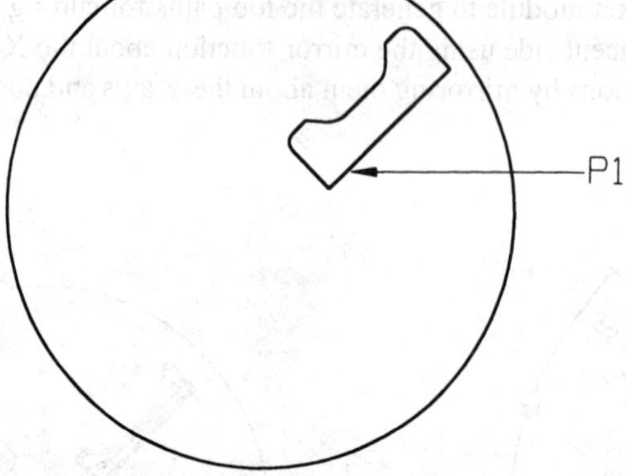

Figure 9.34

Step 2. Initiate the pocket module.

Select **MAIN MENU → Toolpaths → Pocket**
Select **Chain**, then pick **P1**
Select **Done**
Click the right mouse button, then select "**Get tool from library**"
Select **tool #235** (1/4 flat end mill)
Select **OK**
Set the tool parameters as below.

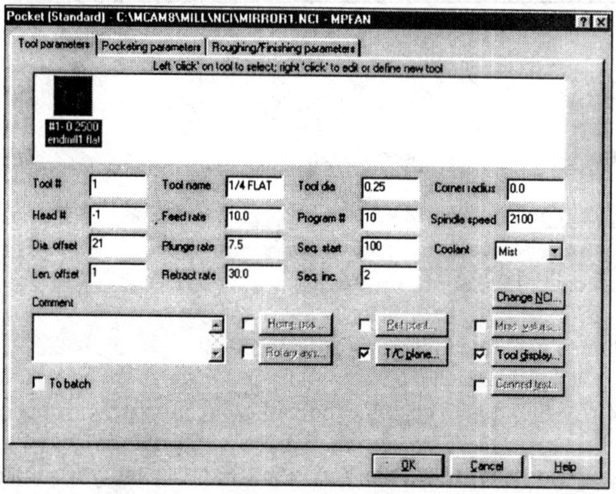

Step 3. Define the pocketing parameters.

Click the "**Pocketing parameters**" tab

Set the pocketing parameters as below.

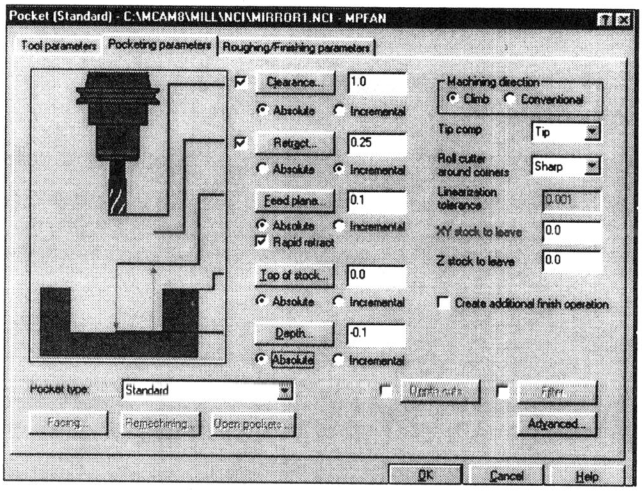

Step 4. Define the roughing and finishing parameters.

Click the "**Roughing/Finishing parameters**" tab

Set the roughing and finishing parameters as below.

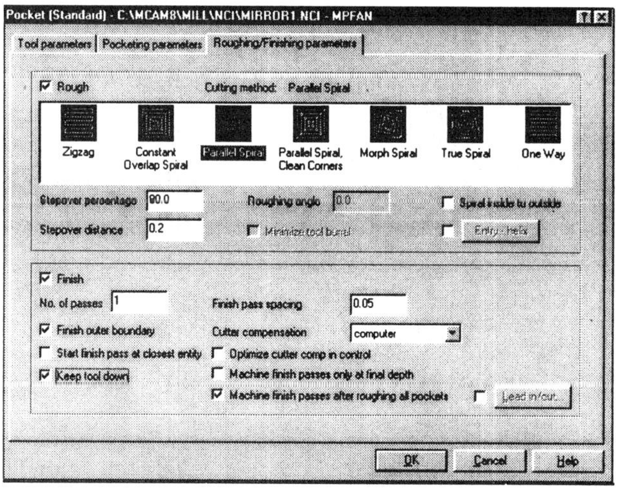

Select **OK** to generate pocketing toolpaths

The pocketing toolpaths are shown in Figure 9.35.

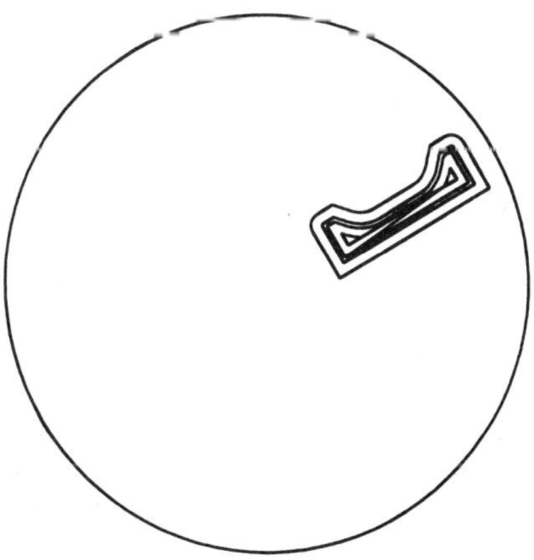

Figure 9.35

Step 5. Mirror the toolpaths about the X-axis.

Select **Next menu → Transform** and set the Transform Operation Parameters as below.

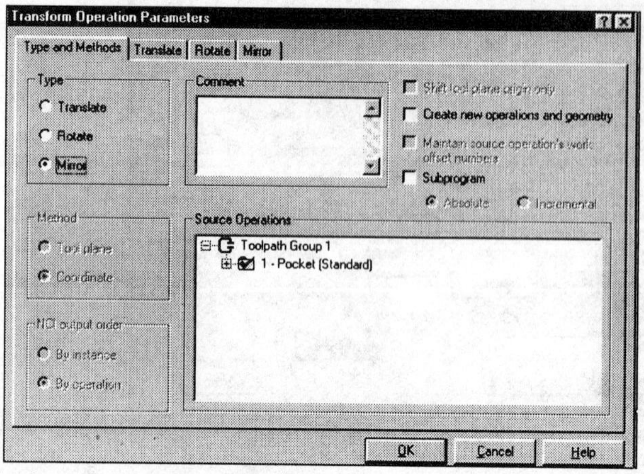

Click **Mirror** tab and open the mirroring parameters
Set the mirroring parameters as below.

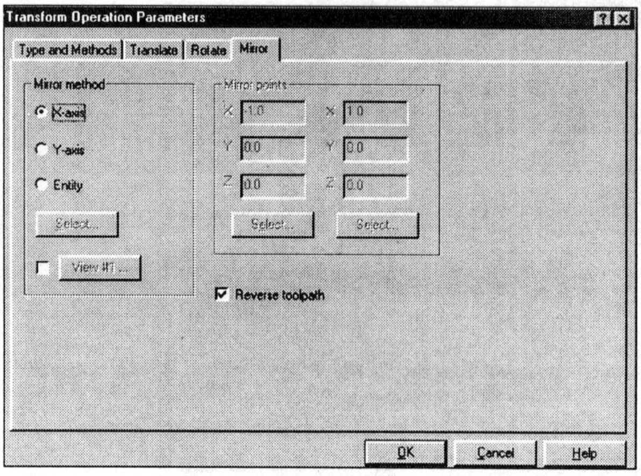

Select **OK**
The mirrored toolpaths are added as in Figure 9.36.

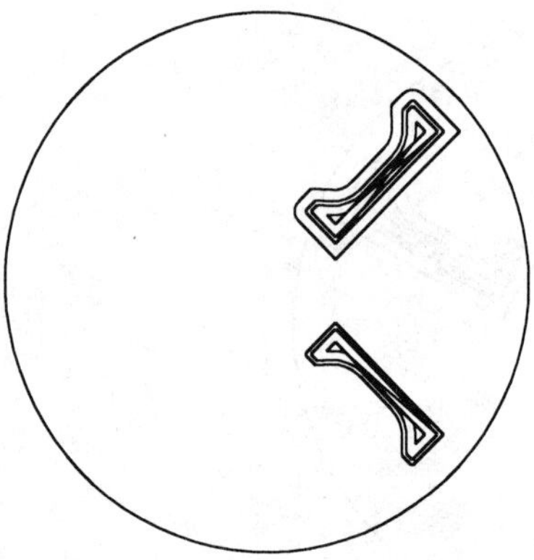

Figure 9.36

Step 6. Mirror the toolpaths for two pockets about the Y axis.

Select **Transform** to open the Transform Operation Parameters.
Select **Mirror** in the Type area and click the **Mirror** tab to open the "Mirror" parameters
Define the mirroring parameters as below.

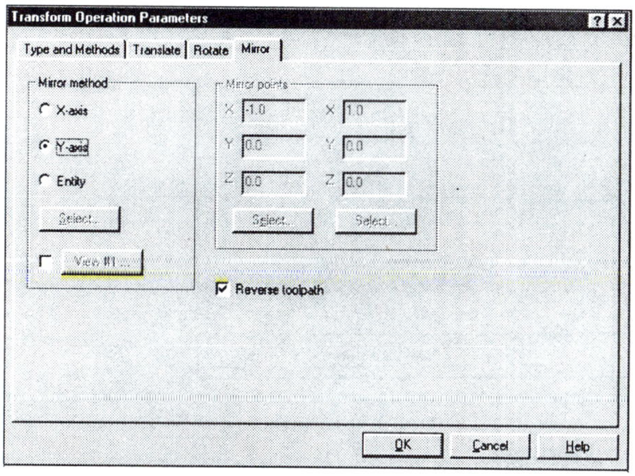

Select **OK** to complete the mirroring
The final toolpaths should resemble Figure 9.37.

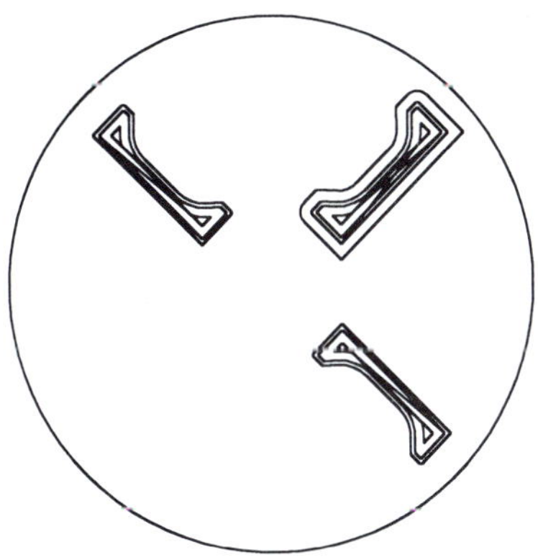

Figure 9.37

Step 7. Mirror the toolpaths for two pockets about an entity.

Select **Transform** to open the Transform Operation Parameters.
Select **MIrror** in the Type area and click the **MIrror** tab to open the "Mirror" parameters

Define the mirroring parameters as below.

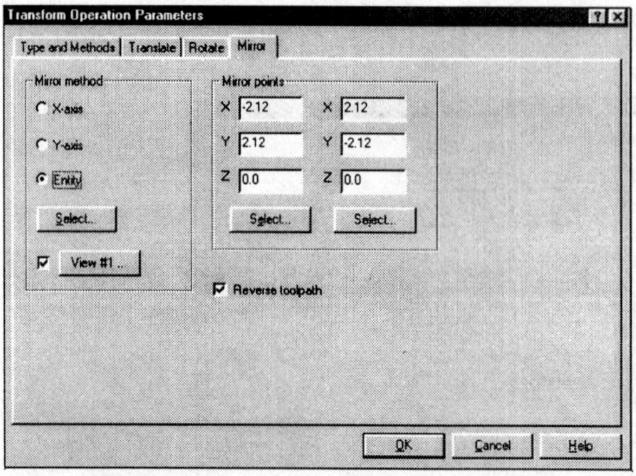

Select **OK** to complete the mirroring
The final toolpaths should resemble Figure 9.38.

Figure 9.38

Ex Exercises

1. Describe how Mastercam organizes its toolpath file structure.

2. Explain how the following four parameters affect the number of toolpath sections generated in using the contour module:
   Number of roughing passes
   Number of finish passes
   Number of rough cuts in depth
   Number of finish cuts in depth

3. Determine the number of toolpath sections for using the contour module to cut an internal profile under the following conditions:
   Number of roughing passes =2
   Number of finish passes =1
   Number of rough cuts in depth =2
   Number of finish cuts in depth =1

4. What are the two main factors determining the number of toolpath sections in using the pocket module?

5. Determine the number of toolpath sections for pocketing under the following conditions:
   Number of finish passes =1
   Number of rough passes in depth =2
   Number of finish passes in depth =1

6. Explain how an existing toolpath section can be deleted in Mastercam.

7. List the three toolpath editing functions in Mastercam and briefly describe what they are.

8. Describe the advantages of using toolpath editing functions.

9. Explain when to use the mirror function.

10. Explain when to use the rotate function.

11. Under what conditions should you use the translate function?

12. Use the pocket module twice to generate toolpaths for pocketing the larger circular pocket and pocketing one of seven small pockets as shown in Figure 9.39. The toolpaths for the small pocket are then copied to six locations by using the rotate command. The part geometry file name is **rotate2** which is created in chapter 6.

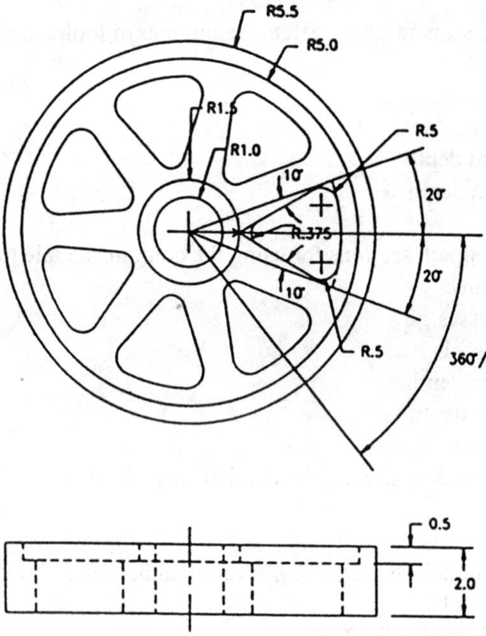

Figure 9.39

13. As illustrated in Figure 9.40, two identical parts are machined in one machine setup. These two parts are located symmetrically about a vertical line. This is the ideal case to use the mirror function. Toolpaths for producing one part are generated first, then they are duplicated for the other part by using the Toolpaths → Next menu → Mirror commands. The part geometry file name is **mirror2**.

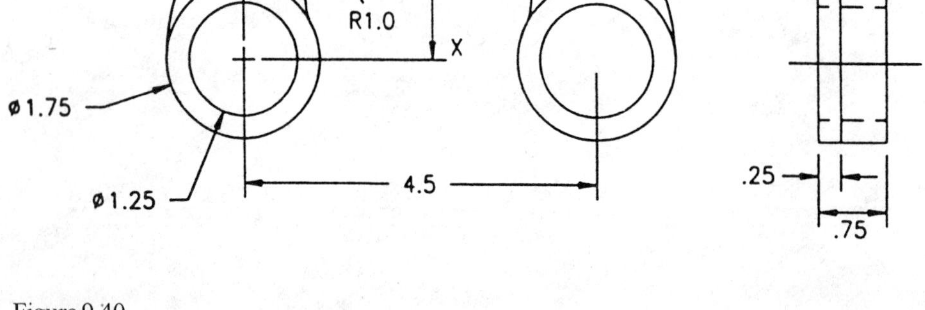

Figure 9.40

14. Two identical workpieces are to be produced in one machine setup as shown in Figure 9.41. The set of toolpaths for cutting one part is copied to another location as specified by using the translation function. The part geometry file name is **trans2** which is created in chapter 5. The generation of toolpaths for machining the part includes using the contour, pocket and drill modules.

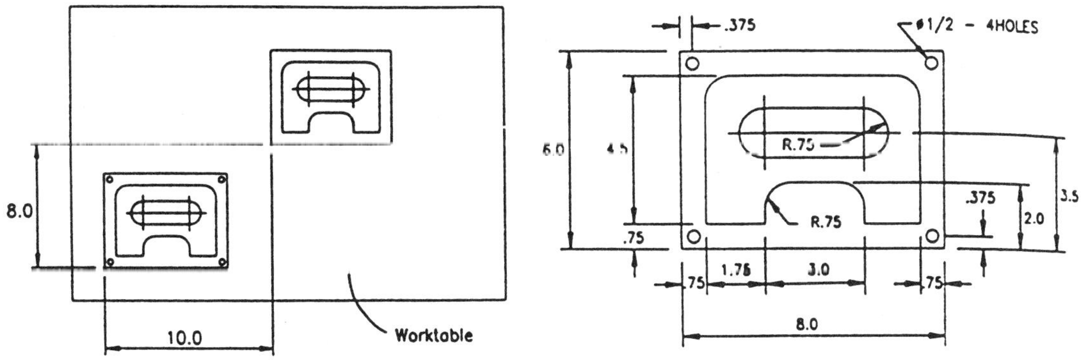

Figure 9.41

15. Use the translate function to generate the toolpaths for cutting four identical parts in one part program. This allows four parts to be machined in one machine setup. The workholding layout of these four parts is shown in Figure 9.42. The part geometry file name is **trans2** which is identical to the file used in problem 15.

Translate parameters: Nx, Ny = 2 2
Dx, Dy = 10.0 8.0

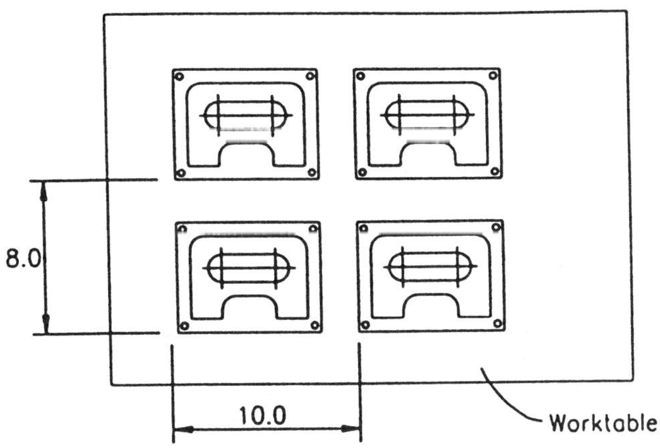

Figure 9.42

Chapter 10

Mastercam Process and Toolpath Planning

Objectives:

1. Understand toolpath generation procedure using Mastercam.
2. Identify part features to be machined from the given part and raw material drawings.
3. Select proper processes and processing sequence to machine features of the part.
4. Select proper toolpath module for the selected process to produce a particular feature.
5. Select proper cutting tools and their machining data.
6. Prepare process plan sheets.

Overview

Mastercam is a very powerful software that can be used to generate toolpaths for machining almost any parts, simple or complex. To effectively use Mastercam's power, the user must have the following knowledge:

- Be familiar with a CAD system to create part geometry
- Know basic CNC programming principles and commands
- Have a good knowledge of machining practices
- Know the CAM system (NC toolpath modules)
- Select proper tooling and machining parameters

In addition, the user must also follow a certain procedure to generate the NC part programs. Process and toolpath planning is the road map for the successful completion of the project. The **benefits** of good planning include: (1) avoiding errors, (2) eliminating the need for toolpaht editing, and (3) serving as a record, reference guide and communication medium. Process and toolpath planning is very useful for the beginners who need to follow a logical sequence in completing any project. Planning also is important for experienced users who generate toolpaths for machining complex parts.

Figure 10.1 on the following page is a flow chart that shows the procedure for using the Mastercam system to generate a toolpath to machine a part. This flow chart indicates the input and output relationships of the major tasks in CAD/CAM NC programming.

10.1 Part and Raw Material Drawings

A part drawing describes the shape and size of a part. It provides the following useful information to the part programmer in generating the toolpath:

- Part features to be produced
- Dimensions, tolerances and surface roughnesses
- Material to be machined
- Initial shape and size of the material to be machined
- Amount of material to be removed

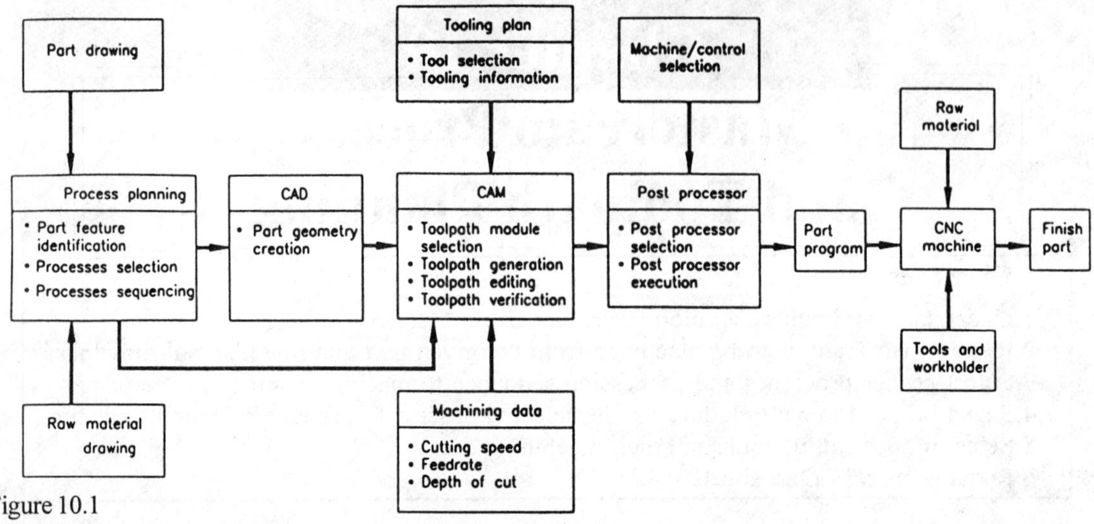

Figure 10.1

Part features

A part feature is the distinctive shape and size to be produced in a part. Typical part features include:

For milling operations:	For turning operations:
1. Flat surfaces	1. End faces
2. Slots	2. External profiles
3. Shoulders or steps	3. Internal profiles
4. Holes	4. Internal threads
5. Internal threads	5. External threads
6. Profiles (or contours)	6. Grooves
7. Letters	7. Holes
8. Spline curves	8. Spline curves
9. 3-D surfaces	9. Cut-offs

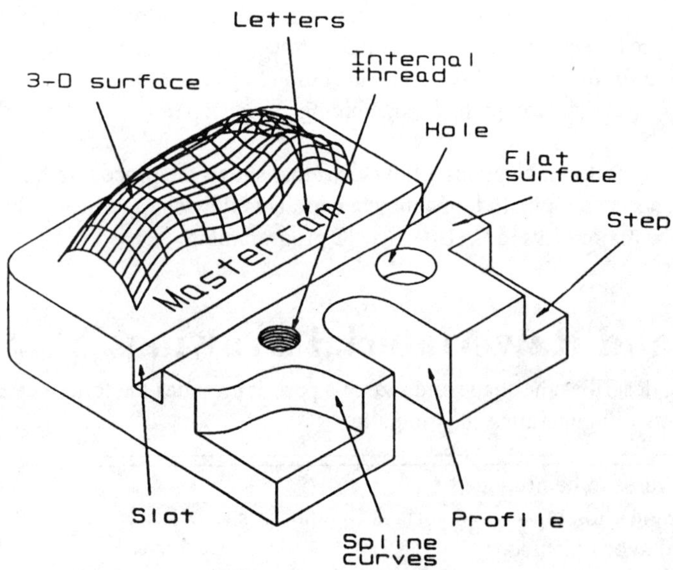

Figure 10.2

Typical part features in turning operations are:
1. End faces
2. External profiles
3. Internal profiles
4. Internal threads
5. External threads
6. Grooves
7. Holes
8. Spline curves
9. Cut-offs

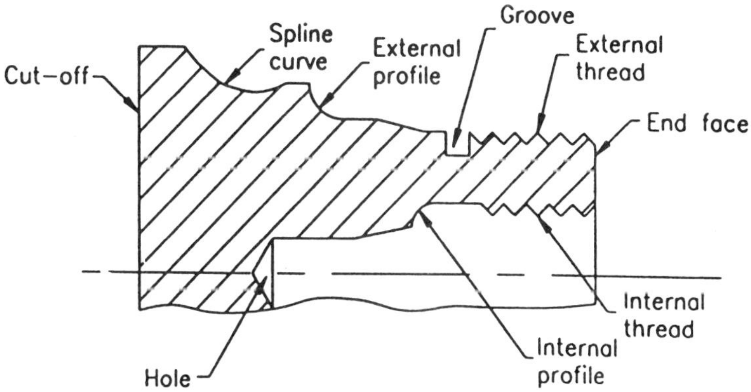

Figure 10.3

Dimensions, Tolerances, and Surface Roughnesses

Selecting a proper process to produce a part feature is dictated by the process capability. Process capability refers to positional accuracy, surface roughness and amount of material to be removed during a particular machining process. A part drawing should provide the detailed information about dimensions, tolerances and surface roughness of a part feature.

Raw Material Drawing

A raw material drawing depicts the initial shape and size of the workpiece before it is processed. It can be an intermediate form of the part. A comparison of a part drawing and a raw material drawing should reveal the amount of material to be removed to produce a part feature. The information in material removal can be further used to determine (1) the required cutter type and size, and (2) the required number of cutting passes including roughing and finishing.

Processes Selection

After part features have been identified, we need to select the proper processes to produce each feature. Commonly used processes for producing part features in milling are listed below:

Milling Operations	
Process	Feature to be produced
Facing	produce flat surfaces
Profiling	produce external and internal contours
Pocketing	produce internal pockets enclosed by a closed contour
Slot cutting	produce blind and through slots
Shoulder	cutting produce shoulders or steps
Drilling	produce and/or enlarge holes
Boring	enlarge holes
Tapping	produce internal threads
Surface cutting	produce various forms of 3-D surfaces
Lettering	engrave a string of letters

Commonly used processes for producing part features in turning operations are listed below:

Turning Operations	
Process	Feature to be produced
Roughing	produce a rough shape of finished part
Facing	produce a flat end face
Turning	produce external and internal profiles
Grooving	produce grooves
Threading	produce external and internal threads
Drilling	produce and/or enlarge hole
Boring	enlarge holes
Tapping	produce internal threads

Process Sequencing

The processes required to produce the part features of a piece should be arranged in a proper sequence. Some features must be produced prior to other features. The **criteria in sequencing** machining processes include:

1. Datum surfaces have precedence. Datum surfaces should be machined first if multiple workholding setups are required.
2. Machine larger surfaces first. Larger surfaces are more adaptable to disturbances resulting from subsequent machining operations.
3. Avoid feature interference. Feature interference happens when the machining of one feature destroys a requirement for the production of other features.
4. Pre-process must be performed first. For example, drilling must be performed before tapping threads in a hole.

Example 1:

Identify the part features to be produced and the machining process(es) to produce each feature for the part shown in Figure 10.4. Also provide the process sequence.

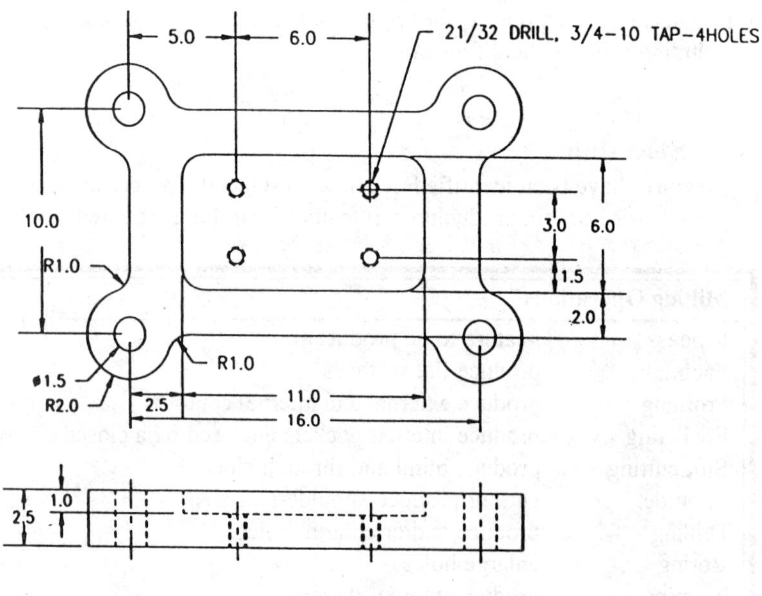

Figure 10.4

Part features:

Flat top surface External profile Rectangular pocket Four holes Internal threads in four holes]

Process selection:

Feature	Process(es)
Flat top surface	Facing
External profile	Profiling
Rectangular pocket	Pocketing
Four holes	Drilling and boring
Internal threads in four holes	Drilling and tapping

Processes sequence:

Based on the criteria given above, the suggested process sequence for this part is:

1. Facing the top surface
2. Profiling the external profile
3. Pocketing the internal pocket
4. Drilling four holes
5. Boring four holes
6. Drilling the four holes for the threading
7. Tapping threads in four holes

10.2 Part Features Geometry creation

The geometric entities that describe each part feature should be created. There are two types of geometric entities: **true entities** and **construction entities**. True entities are used to directly define the part features to be produced. They have the true shapes and sizes of the part features. Construction entities are used to help generate toolpaths in machining a part feature. A large rectangle, for example, is used to define the boundary for generating the toolpaths to face a flat surface that has a similar size to the rectangle as in Figure 10.5. The geometric entities of this rectangle are construction entities.

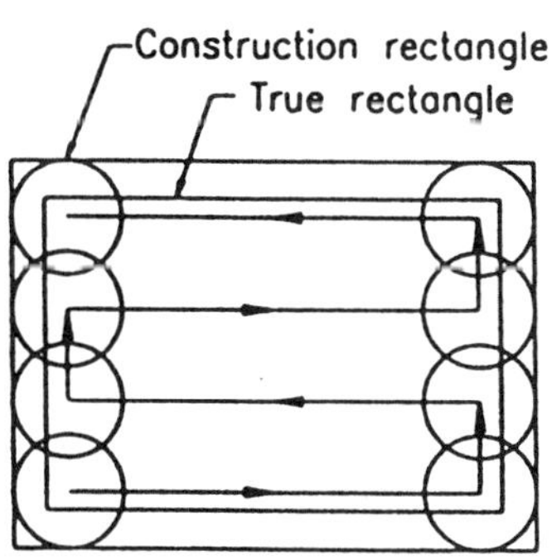

Figure 10.5

10.3 Toolpath Modules Selection

Mastercam provides a variety of toolpath modules for generating the toolpaths to produce part features. The selection of toolpath modules depends on the part feature and the process type. Table 10.3 lists the possible use of toolpath modules for various part features and processes.

Table 10.3 Toolpath Modules

Part Feature	Process	Module	Illustration	Remark
Flat surface	Facing	Pocket	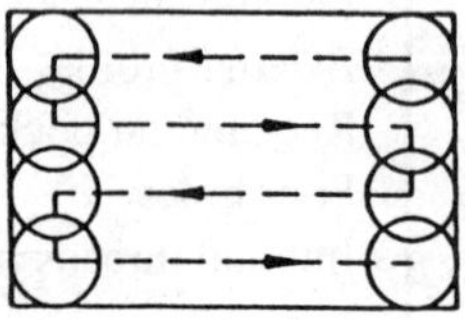	1. Use the larger face mill or end mill to shorten machining time. 2. Create a large pocket boundary to ensure all areas are cut.
Profile/contour	Profiling	Contour	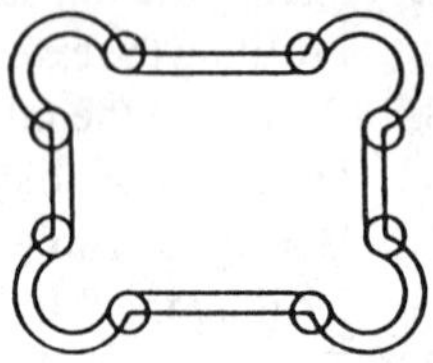	1. Use end mill to move along the part profile. 2. Select proper contour direction to obtain climb or conventional milling type.
Pocket	Pocketing	Pocket	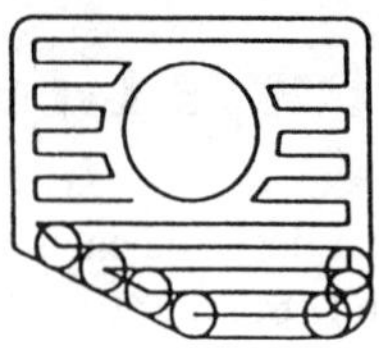	Use end mill to remove the material enclosed by a closed boundary.
Slot	Slot cutting	Contour or pocket	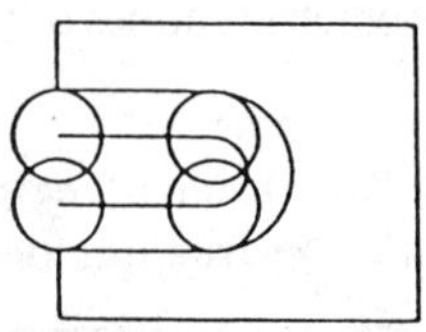	Use end mill to cut open or blind slots
Shoulder	Shoulder cutting	Contour or pocket	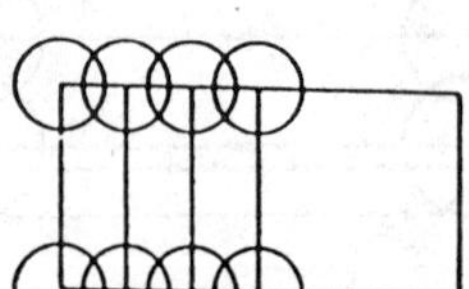	Use end mill to produce steps or shoulders.

Table 10.3 (Continued)

Part Feature	Process	Module	Illustration	Remark
Hole	Drilling and/or boring	Drill/Bore	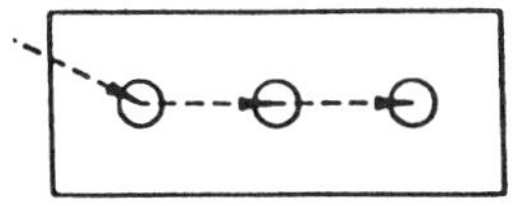	Use drill and/or boring to produce holes.
Internal thread	Drilling and tapping	Drill/Tap	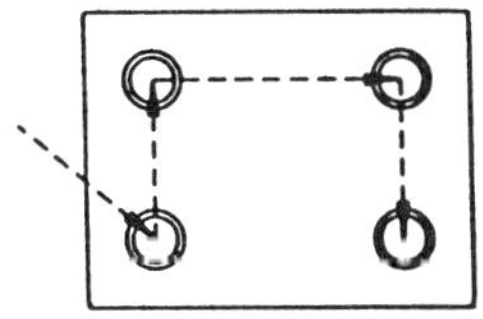	Use tap to produce internal threads of holes.
Letters	Lettering	Letters		Use end mill to engrave letters on part surfaces
Spline curves	Curve cutting	Profile or pocket		Use end mill to cut along spline curves.
Single 3-D surface	Surface cutting	3-D toolpaths modules such as ruled, loft, swept, coons, and flowline	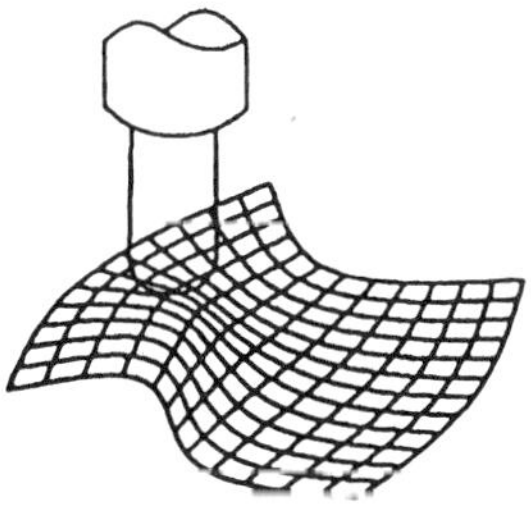	Use ball-end mill to cut 3-D surfaces.
Composite surface	Surface cutting	Multisurf	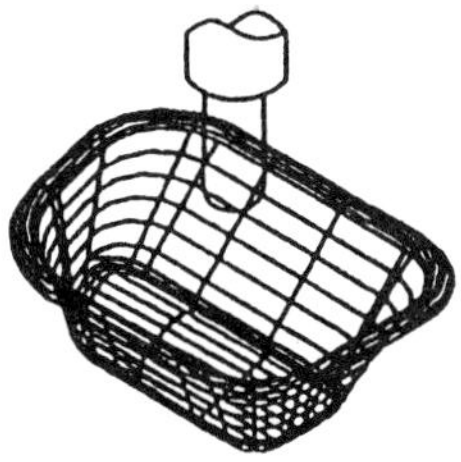	Use ball-end mill to cut multiple surfaces

10.4 Tooling Data and Machining Data

There are **two** types of information that determine the efficiency of CNC machining: **tooling data** and **machining data**. Tooling data includes information related to **defining the size of the cutter**, the **assignment of tool number**, **tool length offset**, and **CDC offset**. Machining data basically consists of three components: **cutting speed**, **feedrate**, and **depth of cut**.

Cutting speed, expressed in fpm, normally is not used directly in the milling operations, instead, it is used to calculate the required spindle speed (RPM) using this formula:

$$N = \frac{12 \cdot CS}{\pi \cdot D}$$

CS = Cutting speed
N = Spindle speed
D = Cutter diameter

Feedrate refers to the speed of the cutter moving along the workpiece. In milling, the feedrate is often expressed in the units of inches/minute.

The proper selection of tooling data and machining data is provided in chapter 2 of this book.

10.5 Process Plan Sheet Preparation

The blank sheet shown in Figure 10.6 can be used to plan the activities for machining a part. This process plan sheet includes the following important information:

- Part identification and material
- Machining to be used and post processor
- Processes and sequencing
- Process illustration
- Toolpath module used in each machining process
- Tools
- Machining data

Example 2: Process planning

Use the sheet given in Figure 10.6 on the next page to develop a process plan for the part shown in Figure 10.7 on the following page. The raw material is a steel circular plate of D8.1" X 1.55"

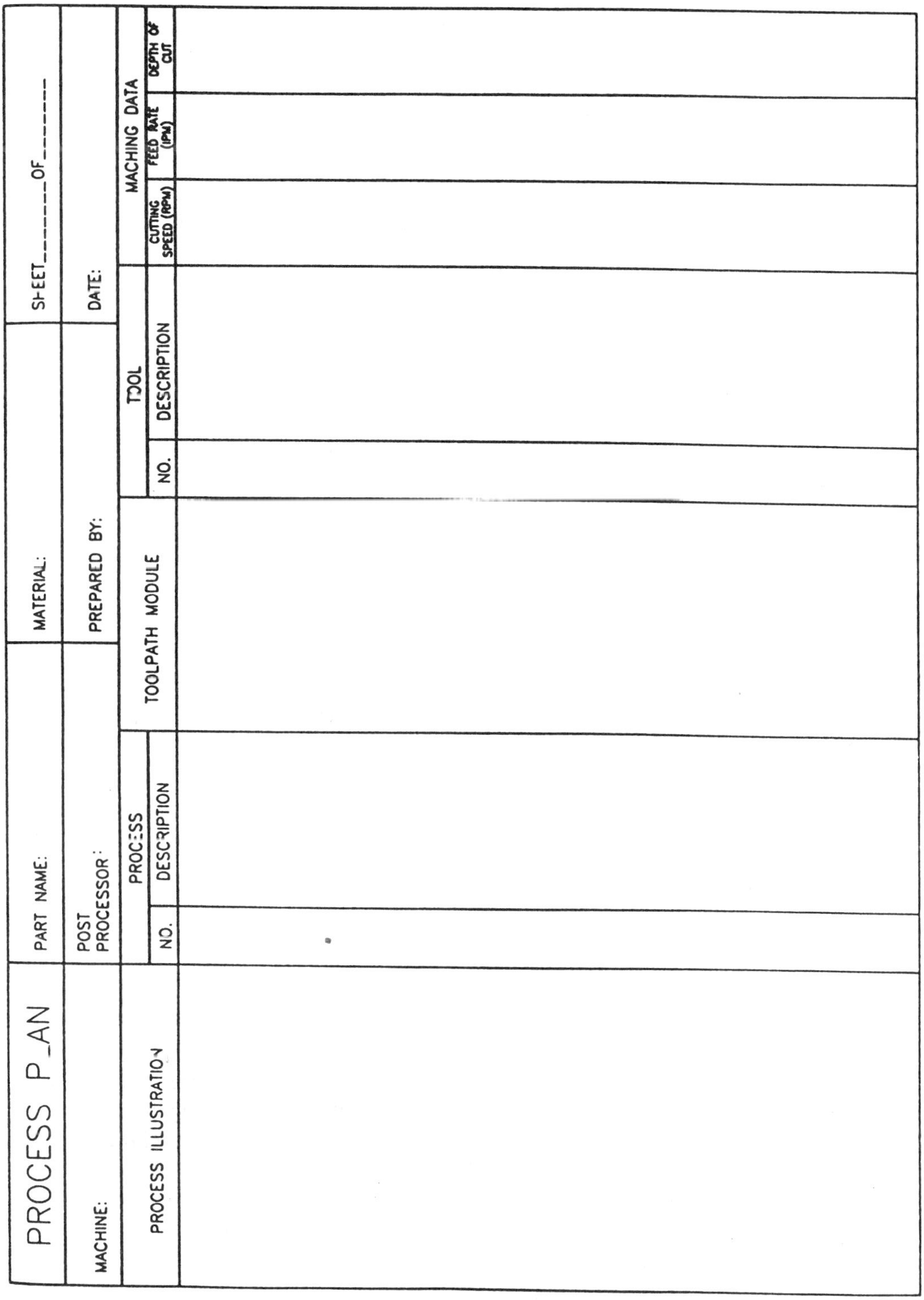

Figure 10.6 Blank process plan sheet

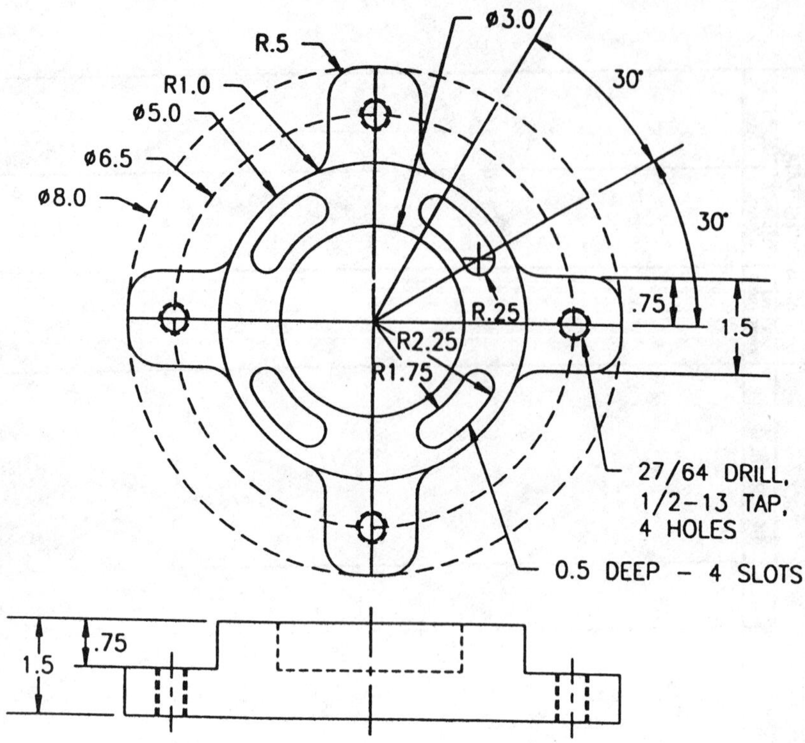

Figure 10.7

Part Features:

The study of theabove part drawing reveals that there are seven part features to be produced in this piece:

1. Bottom flat surface
2. Top flat surface
3. Upper circular profile
4. External profile
5. Circular pocket
6. Four circular slots
7. Four holes with internal threads

Process Sequencing:

This project involves two workpiece setups. The first setup is to cut the bottom flat surface which is used as the datum for the second setup for the remaining machining operations. Thus, the machining of the bottom fat surface must be the first process. Using the sequencing criteria given in the previous section, we can arrange the process sequence as below:

1. Facing the bottom flat surface
2. Facing the top flat surface
3. Cutting the upper circular profile
4. Cutting the external profile
5. Cutting the circular pocket
6. Cutting four circular slots
7. Drilling four holes for the threading
8. Tapping internal threads in four holes

Module Selection

The pocket module is used for facing the bottom and top flat surfaces, circular pocket, and four circular slots. The drill module is used to drill four holes and the drill/tap option is used for tapping four holes. A careful consideration must be given to the upper circular profile and the external profile.

We have two ways to generate the toolpaths for cutting the upper circular profile. One way is to use the contour module and select the circle as the contour boundary. Since the material to be removed is relatively large, it requires the use of several roughing passes and one finish pass. Another way is to use the pocket module with the circle as the island. A construction circle must be created to serve as the outer pocketing boundary as shown in Figure 10.8. Finally we choose to use the contour module for cutting the upper circular profile.

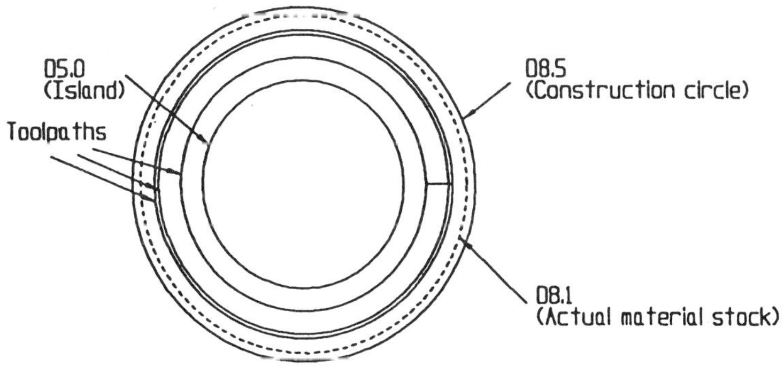

Figure 10.8

There are four local pockets formed between the four "ears" of the external profile. A more direct way to cut the external profile is to use the contour module with several roughing passes and one finish pass. An alternate way is to use the pocket module to cut one local pocket, then copy the toolpaths onto the other three pockets (Figure 10.9), and finally use the contour module to perform the finish cut as in Figure 10.10. In this project, we use the latter approach for cutting the external profile.

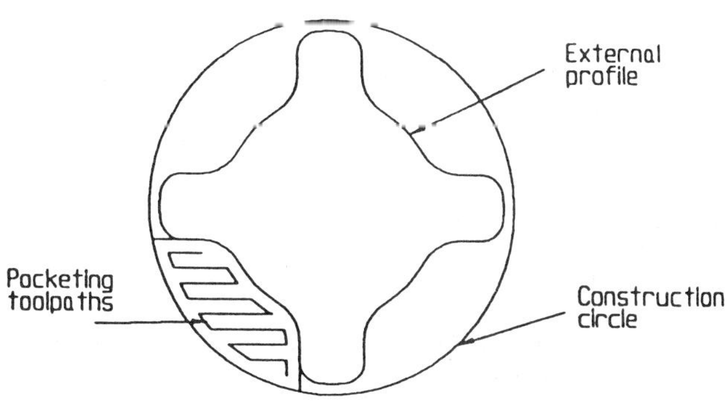

Figure 10.9

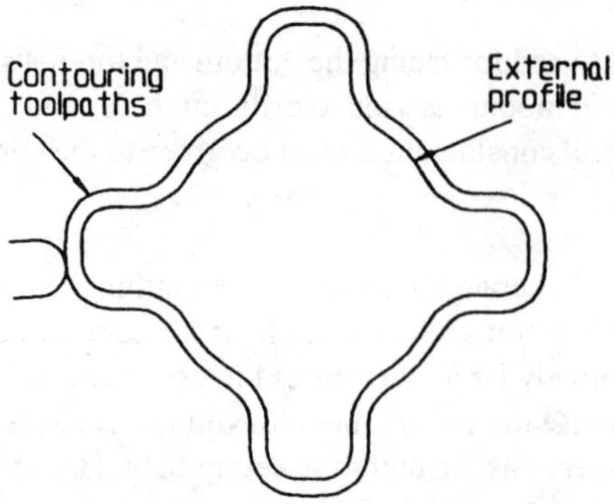

Figure 10.10

Tool and Machining Data

Six cutting tools are used in this project. They are:

4' face mill for facing bottom and top flat surface
1" end mill for cutting upper circular profile
½" end mill for cutting pockets and finish profile of the external profile, and to cut the internal circular pocket
¼" end mill to cut the four circular slots
17/32" drill to drill four thread holes
5/8-11 tap to tap four holes

The machining data for each cutting tool and process is given in Figure 10.11. The completed process plan sheet for this project is given in Figure 10.11 on the next two pages.

10.6 Post Processor Selection

The toolpath file generated from the CAM system is a generic type called an NCI file in Mastercam. This file must be further processed by a software program called a post processor. The main task of a post processor is to convert the NCI file into the NC part program. The output from the post processor is the part program that is readable by a CNC controller. Since the CNC controllers of different vendors require different codes and they are used by different machines, there is no one universal post processor that can be used for all machines. In common practice, one controller/machine combination requires a dedicated post processor. The required post processor will be determined automatically once a CNC machine is chosen to machine a particular project.

Note: It is best to select the post processor you will be using **before** you begin your tool paths.

PROCESS PLAN	PART NAME: Project 5		MATERIAL: Steel			SHEET 2 OF 2		
MACHINE: LEAD-M1	POST PROCESSOR: LMC-1		PREPARED BY: J. L.			DATE: 10-8-4		
PROCESS ILLUSTRATION	PROCESS		TOOLPATH MODULE	TOOL		MACHING DATA		
	NO.	DESCRIPTION		NO.	DESCRIPTION	CUTTING SPEED (RPM)	FEED RATE (IPM)	DEPTH OF CUT
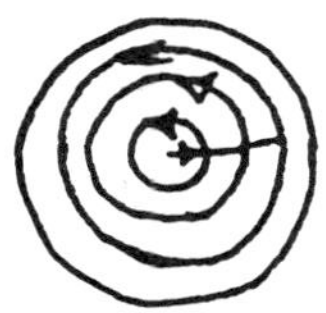	5	Cutting circular pocket	Pocket	3	1/2" end mill	600	12.5	0.2
	6	Cutting four circular slots	Pocket	4	1/4" end mill	1200	10	0.1
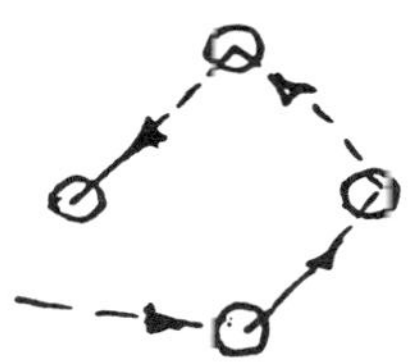	7	Drilling four holes	Drill	5	17/32 drill	500	10	—
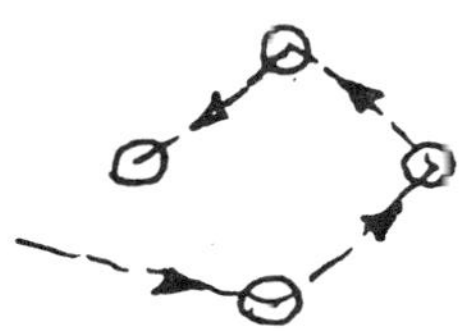	8	Tapping for internal threads	Drill	6	5/8-11 tap	200	18.18	—

Figure 10.11

PROCESS PLAN	PART NAME: Projeit 5			MATERIAL: Steal			SHEET 1 OF 2	
MACHINE: LEAD-MI	POST PROCESSOR: LMC-1			PREPARED BY: J Lin			DATE: 10-8-94	
PROCESS ILLUSTRATION	PROCESS		TOOLPATH MODULE	TOOL		MACHING DATA		
	NO.	DESCRIPTION		NO.	DESCRIPTION	CUTTING SPEED (RPM)	FEED RATE (IPM)	DEPTH OF CUT
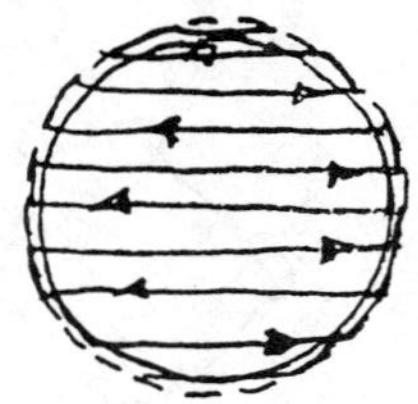	1	Facing bottom flat surface	Pocket	1	2" face mill	150	10	0.15
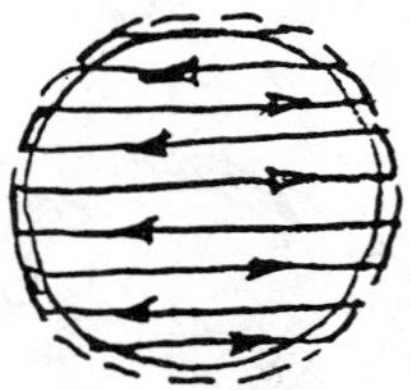	2	Facing the top surface	Pocket	1	2" fale mill	150	10	0.15
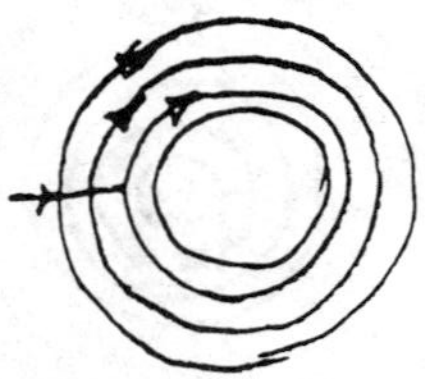	3	Cutting upper circular profile	Contour	2	1" end mill	300	12.5	0.2
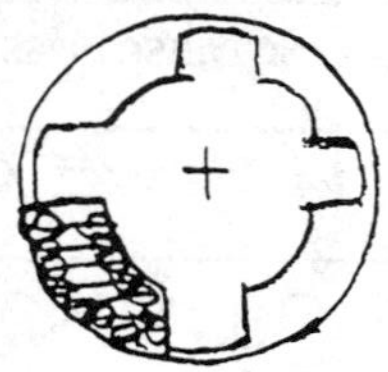	4	Cutting external profile	Pocket and Contour	3	1/2" end mill	600	12.5	0.2

Figure 10.11, continued

Ex Exercises

1. What types of knowledge must a user have in order to effectively use a CAD/CAM system?
2. List the three benefits of good process and toolpath planning.
3. What is a part feature?
4. List at least seven common part features in milling operations.
5. List at least seven common part features in turning operations.
6. Describe how to determine the amount of material removed in producing a part feature.
7. What are the four basic criteria for sequencing machining processes?
8. What are the two types of geometric entities used to describe part features?
9. What is tooling data?
10. What is machining data?
11. Describe the reasons for using a post processor.
12. Explain the main purpose of a post processor.
13. Use the blank process planning sheet given in Figure 10.6 to develop a process plan for the part shown in figure 10.12.

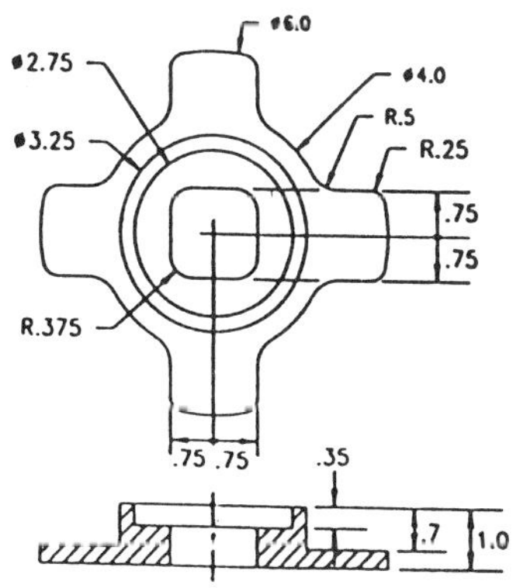

Figure 10.12

14. Use the blank process planning sheet given in Figure 10.6 to develop a process plan for the part shown in Figure 10.13.

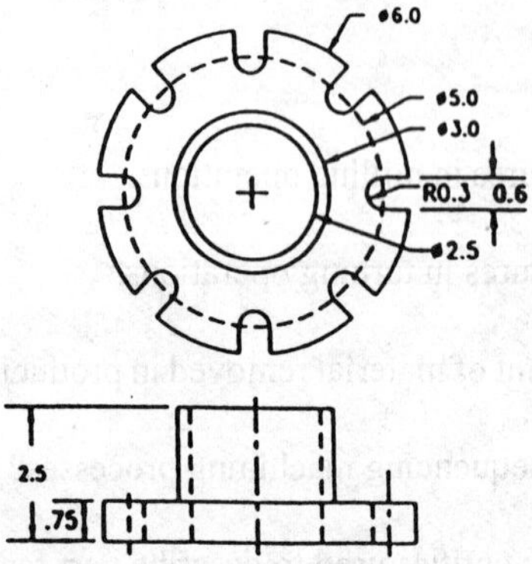

Figure 10.13

Chapter 11
Constructing 3D Wireframe Models

Objectives:

1. Understand the features of wireframe models and surface models.
2. Know the basic elements of the surface edge profiles.
3. Select proper construction planes.
4. Use proper Z depth control.
5. Construct wireframe models.

Overview

This chapter presents important concepts and techniques in constructing wireframe models for 3D surfaces. Features of different wireframe models and surface models are included. The success in constructing a wireframe model depends on the user's ability to create profile elements, use construction planes and Z-depth control. In some cases only a partial wireframe model is needed to generate surfaces.

Sixteen examples are presented to show how the edge profiles of the surfaces are constructed. These examples are arranged in an increasing order of difficulty. They are so designed that new techniques are added in each succeeding example. These examples are used in the later chapters for creating various types of surfaces and the toolpaths to produce the surfaces.

11.1 Wireframe Modeling Fundamentals

Wireframe Models

A wireframe model is normally required to create a surface. Wireframe models represent an object by defining its edges (Figure 11.1). It is impossible to completely define surfaces with wireframe models except for simple flat surfaces. Wireframe models cannot be directly used in generating 3D surface tool paths, however, they are used as surface boundaries and cross-sectional features for developing surface models.

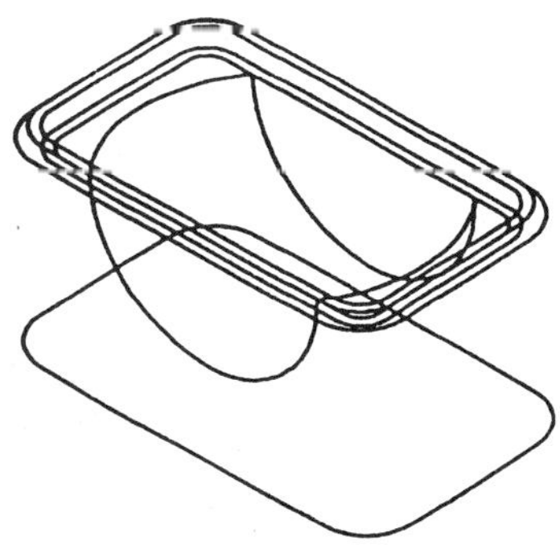

Figure 11.1

Surface Models

Surface models define surfaces, including the edges of each surface. They take the modeling of an object one step further than wireframe models. They show not only the edges of surfaces, but also the shapes. Surface models can be directly used to create a toolpath for machining surfaces. They provide more information, and can be edited and shaded. However, surface models provide no information about the weight of the workpiece. Figure 11.2 shows the surface model of its wireframe counterpart shown in Figure 11.1.

Figure 11.2

Profile Elements of Surfaces

Primitive geometric elements are normally used to form the surface edge profiles or boundaries. They include lines, arcs, splines, and ellipses (Figure 11.3). Figure 11.4 is an example in which wireframe boundaries and cross-sectional features of surfaces are defined by smooth profiles created by using these basic profile elements.

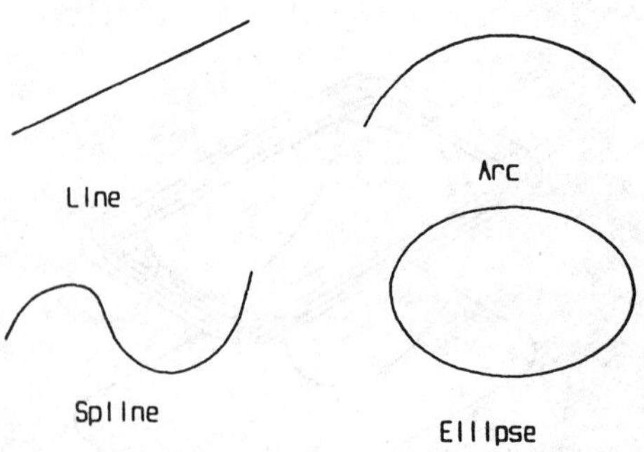

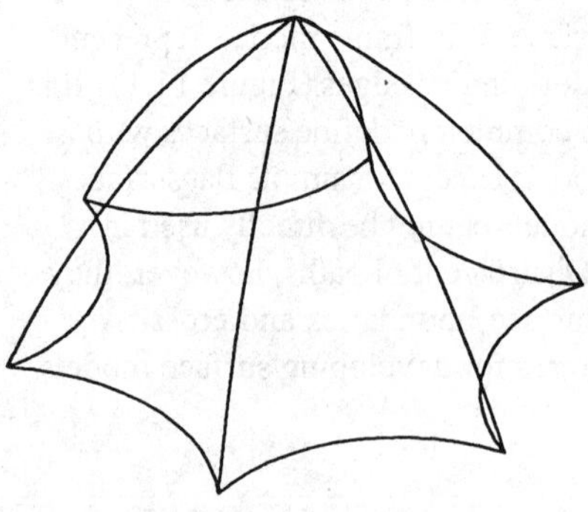

Figure 11.3

Figure 11.4

Construction Plane

A construction plane determines a plane orientation in which a geometric entity is to be placed. An arc, for example, can be constructed on a plane either parallel to the principal XY-, ZX-, or YZ-plane depending on which construction plane is chosen. A construction plane must be specified **before** any geometric entity can be created in a CAD system. Mastercam provides the following **nine standard construction planes**:

• Top Cplane	• Front Cplane	•Last
• Side Cplane	• 3D Cplane	•Entry
• Number	• Normal Cplane	•Rotate

Figure 11.5 shows the axis orientations of the **three** principal construction planes: top, front, and side. The axis orientations for the Top construction plane are the most familiar. Note that the axis assignments are changed when the construction plane is changed to the front or side. The keys to determine the axis orientation for each plane are as follows:

- The X axis is always in the horizontal direction when viewed from the direction normal to the selected plane.
- The Y axis is in the vertical direction on the selected plane.
- The Z axis is perpendicular to both the X and Y axes.

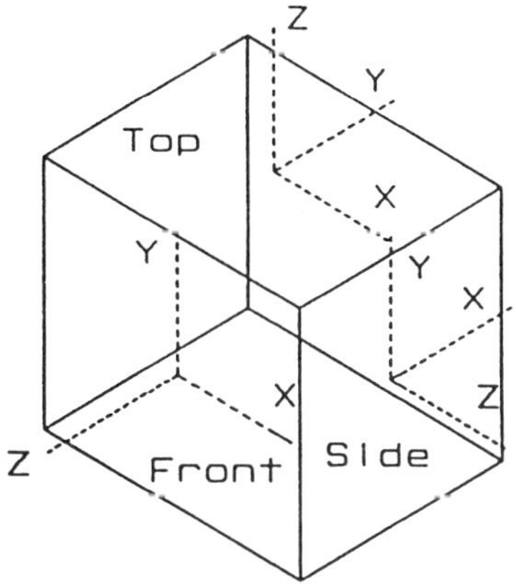

Figure 11.5

The 3D Cplane has similar axis designations to that of the Top plane. The only difference is that it allows lines to be constructed at any two specified endpoints which do not necessarily lie parallel to any one of three principal planes (Figure 11.6).

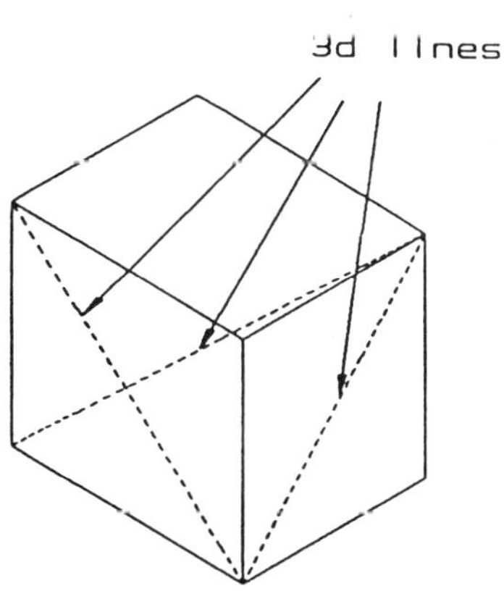

Figure 11.6

2-line Plane

Any two perpendicular lines in the space can be used to define a construction plane. The first line you pick is designated as the X axis and the second picked line becomes the Y axis. The Z axis is perpendicular to both X and Y axes (Figure 11.7).

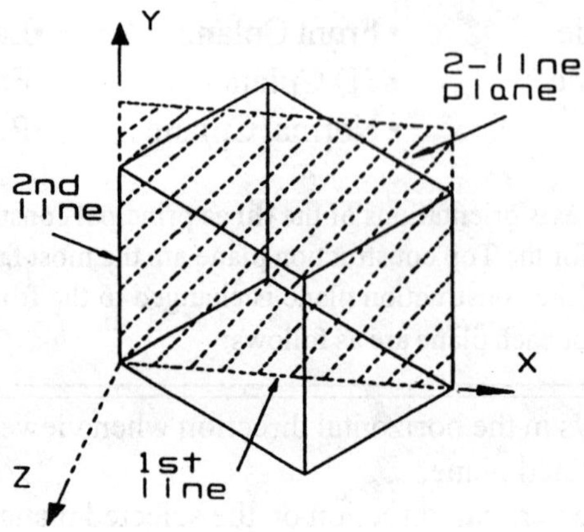

Figure 11.7

Normal Plane

A normal plane is defined by being normal (or perpendicular) to a given line at the selected point (Figure 11.8). An example of using a normal plane is illustrated in Figure 11.9. Two arcs are created using the normal plane which is perpendicular to the given line. These two arcs are located at both ends of the line.

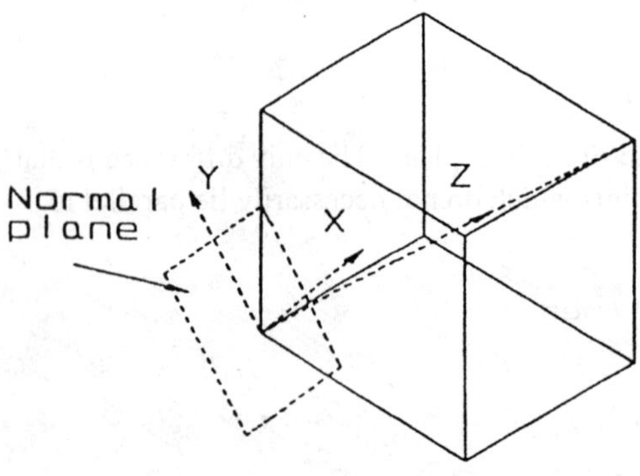

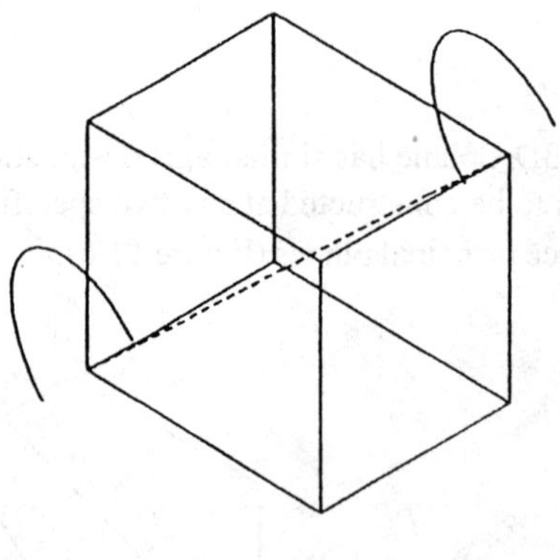

Figure 11.8

Figure 11.9

Z-Depth Control

The Mastercam system uses the Z command in the Secondary Menu to specify the Z value of the geometric entities. Figure 11.10 illustrates how to specify the Z value to properly place the construction plane in a location.

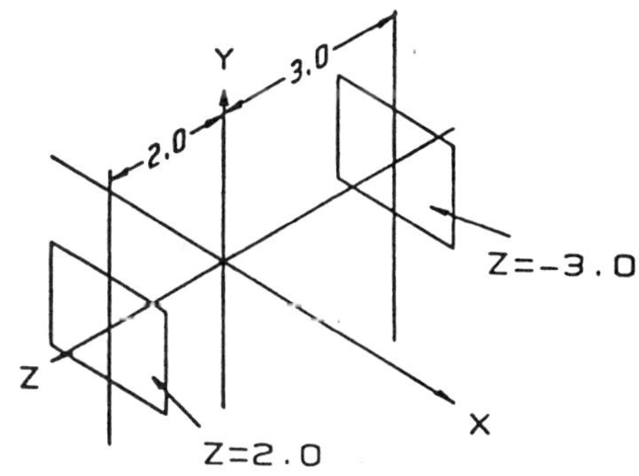

a. Front Cplane

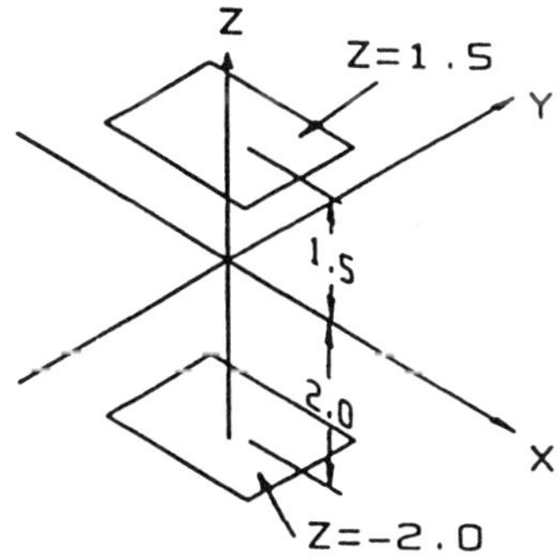

b. Top Cplane

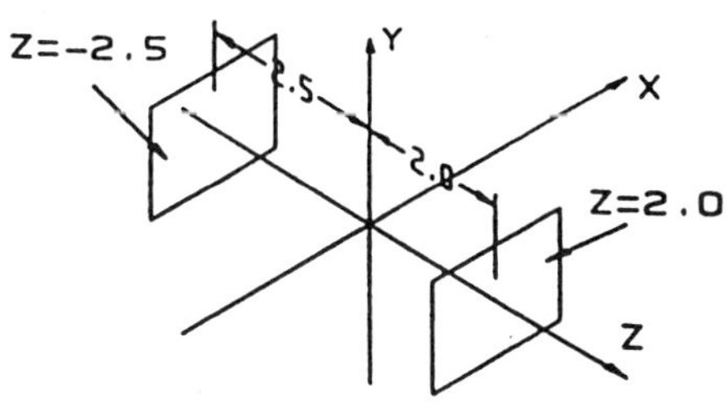

c. Side Cplane

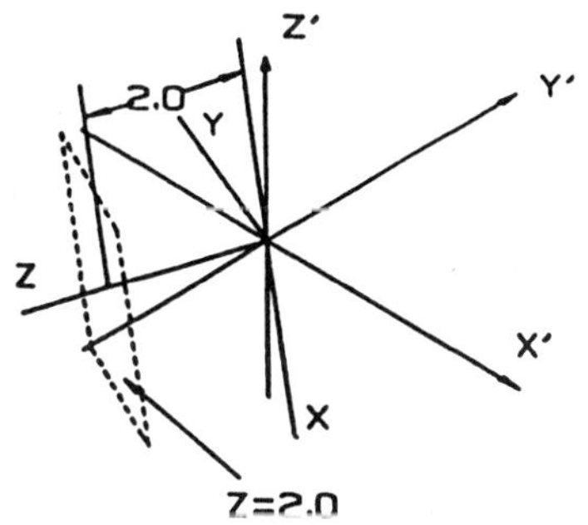

d. Normal Cplane

Figure 11.10

11.2 Wireframe Model Construction Examples

There are sixteen projects presented in this chapter. Each project gives a step-by-step procedure to complete the wireframe model. Only a partial wireframe profile is given in some projects. Useful tips for the edge profiles are provided for most projects. Each wireframe model is used to create the surface model and the toolpath to machine the surface in the following chapters.

Project 1

In this project, you will learn to use **Front, Side, and 3D** construction planes to create 4 arcs and 2 lines as shown in Figure 11.11. These surface profile entities are then used to create two ruled surfaces and two fillet surfaces in chapters 12 and 13, respectively.

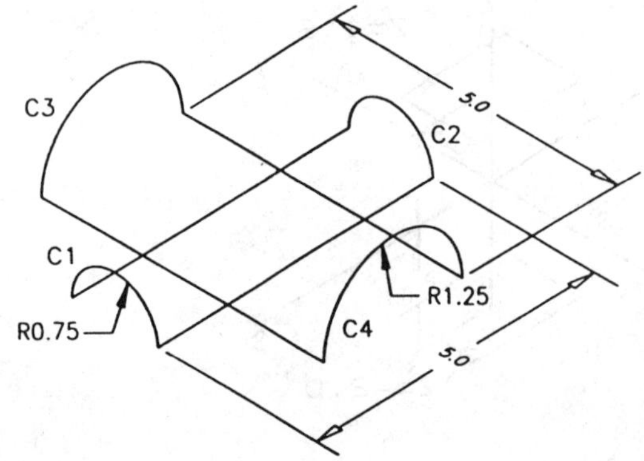

Figure 11.11a. Wireframe model

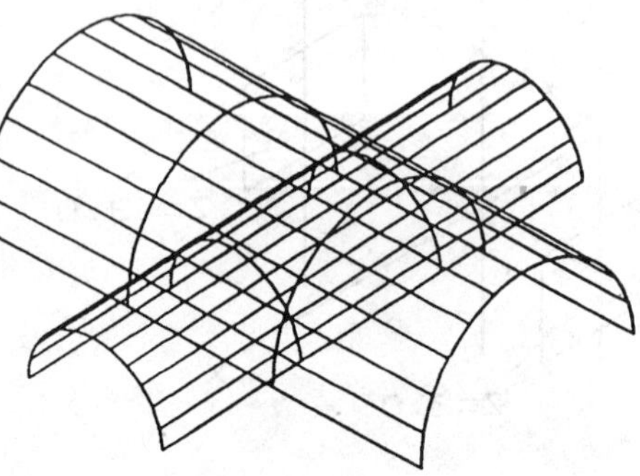

Figure 11.11b. Surface model

Tips 1. Use the Front Cplane to construct the two arcs of .75-in. radius. The front arc has a Z value of 2.5 and the rear arc has the same Z value of 2.5.
2. Use the Side Cplane to create the two arcs of 1.25-in. radius. The right and left arcs have Z values of 2.5.
3. Use the 3D Cplane to construct the four lines connecting the endpoints of the four arcs.

Step 1. Enter the Mastercam Mill.

Follow the procedure in chapter 3 to enter the Mastercam Mill 8.
Press **F9** to show the coordinate axes on the screen

The screen should look like Figure 11.12, with the MAIN MENU on the left side.

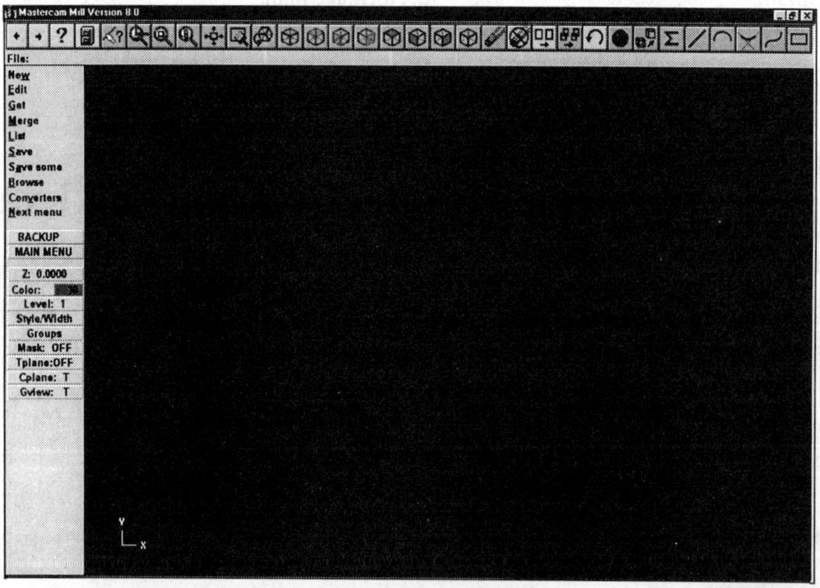

Figure 11.12

Step 2. Select front construction plane and isometric graphics view. 1

Select **Gview** from the Secondary Menu,
then pick **Isometric** from the Gview Menu
Select **Cplane** from the Secondary Menu,
then pick **Front** from the Cplane Menu

Step 3. Create the circle C1.

Select **Z** from the Secondary Menu, and then enter **2.5**
Select **MAIN MENU → Create → Arc → Polar → Center pt**
Enter the center point: **0,0** ↵
Enter the radius (1.0): **0.75** ↵
Enter the initial angle (0.0): ↵ to accept the default .
Enter the final angle (0.0): **180** ↵

Step 4. Create the circle C2.

Select **Z** from the Secondary Menu, and then enter **-2.5** ↵
Enter the center point: **0,0** ↵
Enter the radius (0.75): ↵ to accept the default
Enter the initial angle (0.0): ↵
Enter the final angle (180.0): ↵

Your drawing should currently look like Figure 11.13.

Figure 11.13

Step 5. Create the circle C3 using the side construction plane.

Select **Cplane** from the Secondary Menu,
then pick **Side** from the Cplane Menu
Enter the center point: **0,0** ↵
Enter the radius (0.75): **1.25** ↵
Enter the initial angle (0.0): ↵ to accept the default
Enter the final angle (180.0): ↵ to accept the default

Step 6. Create the circle C4.

Select **Z** from the Secondary Menu, and then enter **2.5** ↵
Enter the center point: **0,0** ↵
Enter the radius (1.25): ↵
Enter the initial angle (0.0): ↵ to accept the default
Enter the final angle (180.0): ↵ to accept the default

The drawing appears as in Figure 11.14.

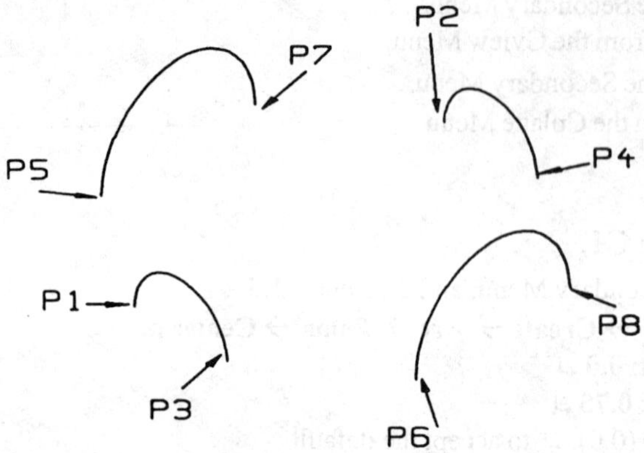

Figure 11.14

Step 7. Create four lines to connect those arcs using a 3D construction plane.

Use the pick points in Figure 11.14.
Select **Cplane → 3D**
Select **MAIN MENU → Create → Line → Endpoints → Endpoint**
Specify the first endpoint: pick **P1**
Specify the second endpoint: pick **P2** to complete the first line
Sequentially pick **P3, P4, P5, P6, P7,** and **P8** to complete the remaining three lines.

The complete drawing would look like Figure 11.15.

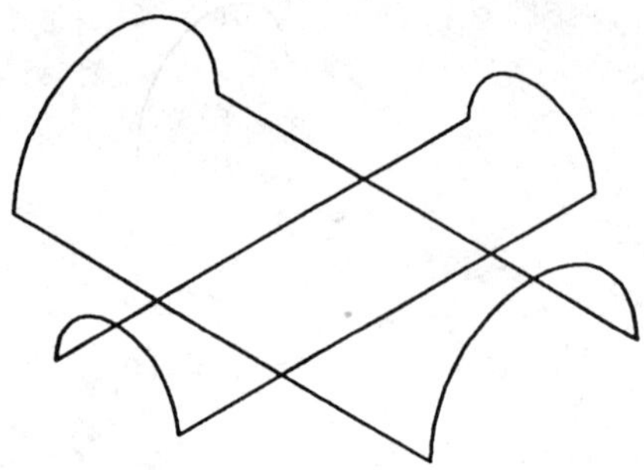

Figure 11.15

Step 8. Save the drawing (ruled1).

Select **MAIN MENU → File → Save**
Enter file name: **ruled1** ↵

Note: This drawing will be used in the following places:
1. For creating two ruled surfaces and two fillet surfaces in chapter 12.
2. For generating intersecting curves and trimming surfaces in chapter 13.

Project 2

In this project, a normal construction plane is used to create two arcs that are perpendicular to a line. The drawing to be constructed is shown in Figure 11.16.

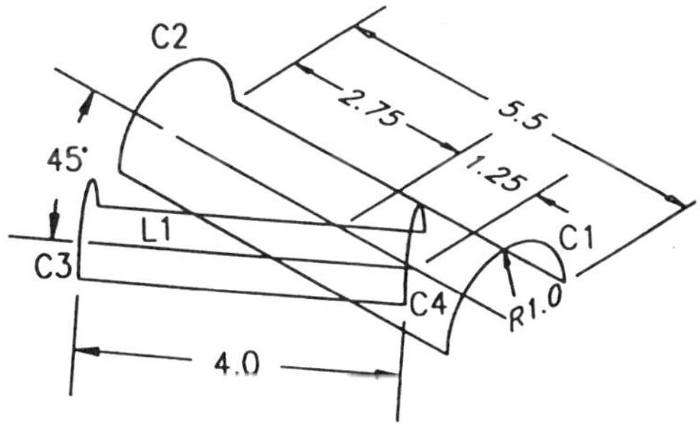

Figure 11.16a. Wireframe model

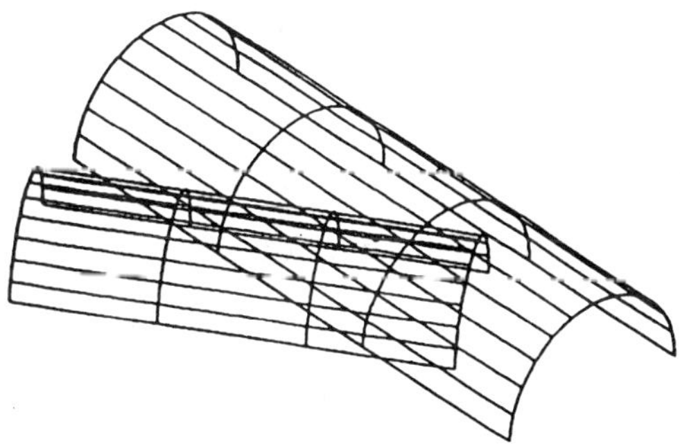

Figure 11.16b. Surface model

Tips

1. Use the Side Cplane to construct two arcs of 1-in. radius. The right arc has a Z value of 2.75 and the left arc is located at Z-2.75.
2. Use the Top Cplane to create a line L1 which has a 45 degree angle with the X axis.
3. Define a normal plane which is perpendicular to line L1.
4. Use the Normal Cplane to create the two arcs that are perpendicular to the line L1. Use **Z → Endpoint** commands and pick at the front end of the angle line to obtain the Z value for the center of the arc.
5. Use 3d Cplane to generate four lines connecting the endpoints of the four arcs.

Step 1. Create the arc C1 using the side construction plane.

First initialize the screen to begin a new start.

Select **MAIN MENU → File → New → Yes** to initialize Mastercam
Select **Gview → Isometric**
Select **Cplane → Side**
Select **Z** and then enter **2.75** ↵
Select **MAIN MENU → Create → Arc → Polar → Center pt**
Enter the center point: **0,0** ↵
Enter the radius (1.0): **1.0** ↵
Enter the initial angle (0.0): ↵ to accept the default
Enter the final angle (360.0): **180** ↵

Step 2. Create the arc C2.

Select **Z** and then enter **-2.75** ↵
Select **BACKUP → Center pt**
Enter the center point: **0,0** ↵
Enter the radius (1.0): ↵
Enter the initial angle (0.0): ↵
Enter the final angle (180.0): ↵
The drawing of two arcs should appear as in Figure 11.17

Figure 11.17

Step 3. Create line L1 using the top construction plane.

Select **Cplane → Top**
Select **Z**, and then enter **0** ↵
Select **MAIN MENU → Create → Line → Polar**
Specify an endpoint: **1.25,0** ↵
Enter the angle in degrees (0.0): **215** ↵
Enter the line length (1.0): **4** ↵
The drawing now should look like Figure 11.18.

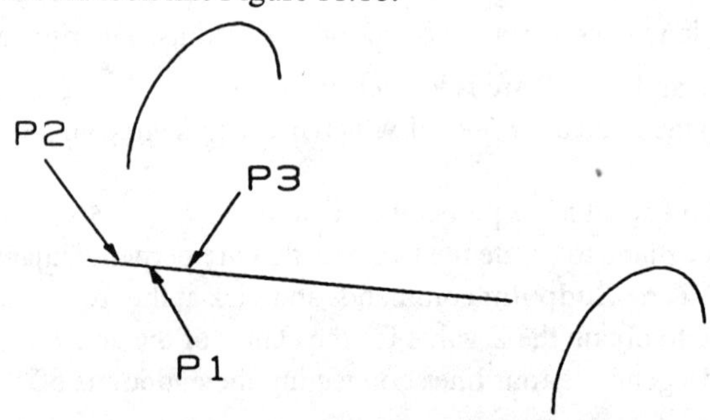

Figure 11.18

Step 4. Create arc C3 using the normal construction plane.

Use the pick points labeled in Figure 11.18.
Select **Cplane → Normal**
Select the normal line: pick **P1**
Select plane: pick **Save**
Select **Z**, and then select **Endpoint** from the point menu
Pick **P2** to trap the endpoint
Select **MAIN MENU → Create → Arc → Polar → Center pt → Endpoint**
Enter the center point: **P3**
Enter the radius (1.0): **0.75** ↵
Enter the initial angle (0.0): **180** ↵
Enter the final angle (0.0): **0** ↵

Your drawing should appear as in Figure 11.19.

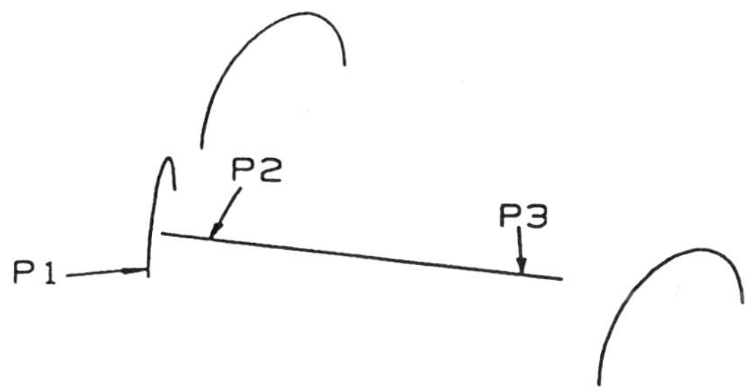

Figure 11.19

Step 5. Create the arc C4 using the transformation command.

Use the pick points in Figure 11.19 on the previous page.
Select **Cplane → 3D**
Select **MAIN MENU → Xform → Translate → Only → Arcs**
Select an entity: pick **P1**
Select **BACKUP → Done → Between pts →Endpoint**
Enter the point to translate from: pick **P2**
Enter the point to translate to : pick **P3**
Set the parameters as shown
in the translate window:

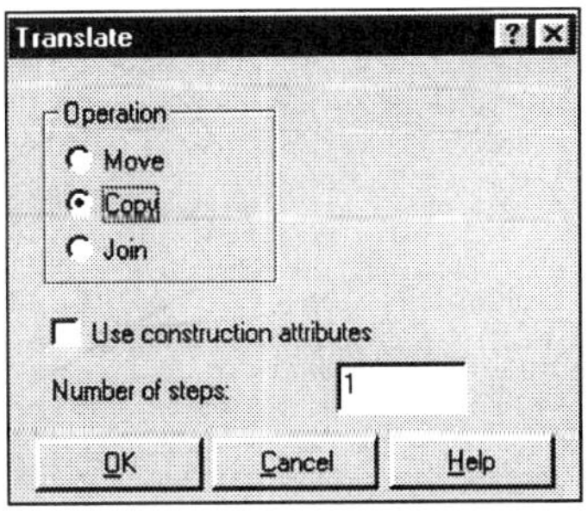

Select **OK**

The drawing with four arcs should look like Figure 11.20.

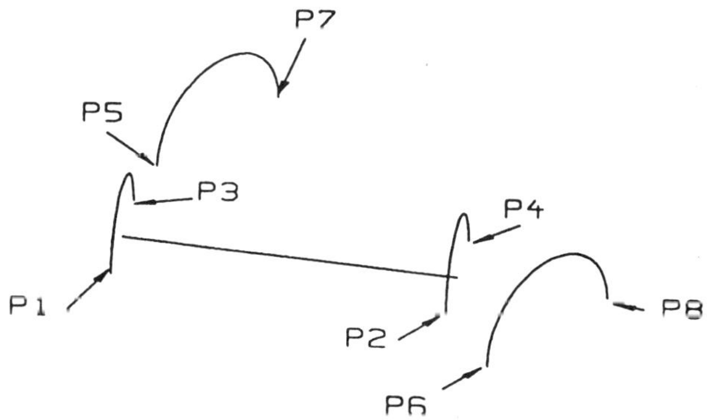

Figure 11.20

Step 6. Construct four lines.

Use the pick points in Figure 11.20.
Select **MAIN MENU → Create → Line → Endpoints**
Specify the first end point: pick **P1**
Specify the second endpoint: pick **P2** to complete the first line.
Sequentially pick the entities **P3 - P8** to complete the remaining three lines.

The complete drawing appears in Figure 11.21a.

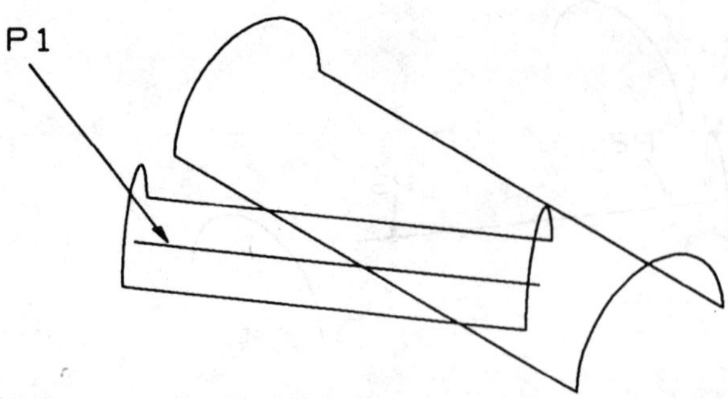

Figure 11.21a

Step 7. Delete the construction line using the pick point in Figure 11.21a.

Select **MAIN MENU → Delete**
Pick **P1** to delete the construction line.
The complete drawing should look like Figure 11.21b.

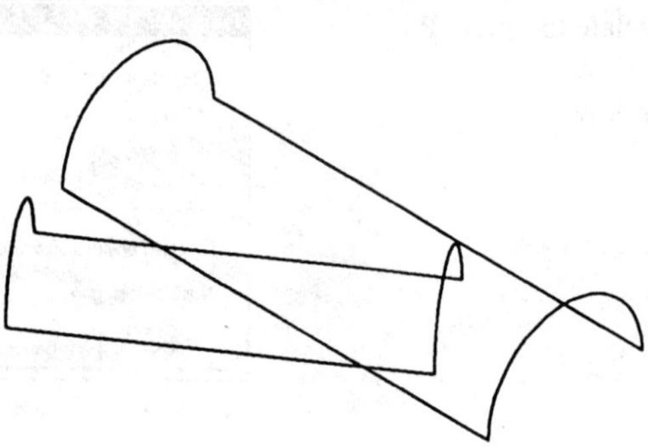

Figure 11.21b

Step 8. Save the drawing ruled2.

Select **MAIN MENU → File → Save**
Enter file name: **ruled2** ↵

Note: This drawing is used to generate ruled surfaces, and fillet surfaces with a 2-variable radius in chapter 11.

Project 3

In this project three entities are constructed at three different Z levels as shown in Figure 11.22. These three entities will be used to create a ruled surface and a loft surface, respectively, in chapter 12.

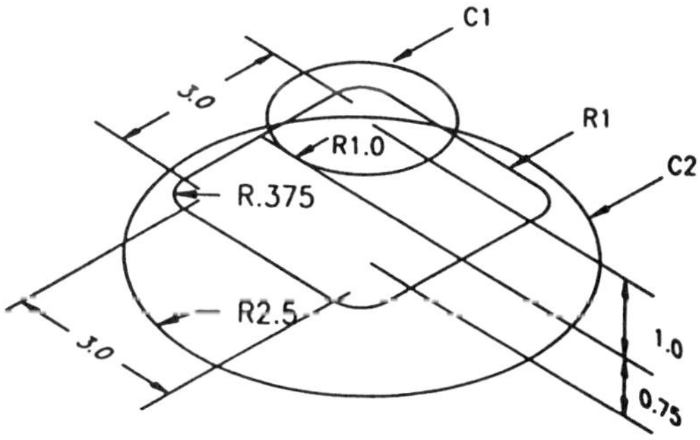

Figure 11.22a. Wireframe model

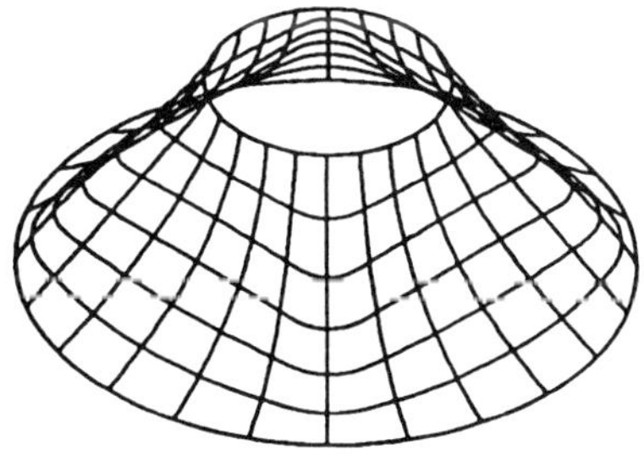

Figure 11.22b. Surface model

Step 1. Create the circle C1 using the Top construction plane.

Initialize the screen if necessary
Select **Gview** → **Isometric** to select the isometric graphics view
Select **Cplane** → **Top** to select the top construction plane
Select **Z**, and then enter **0** ↵ if necessary
Select **MAIN MENU** → **Create** → **Arc** → **Circ pt+rad**
Enter the radius (0.0): **1.0** ↵
Enter the center point: **0,0** ↵

Step 2. Create the rectangle R1.

Select **Z**, and then enter **-1.0** ↵
Select **MAIN MENU** → **Create** → **Rectangle** → **1 point**
Enter the width (2.0): **3** ↵
Enter the height (1.0): **3** ↵
Select the lower left corner
Select **OK**
Enter coordinates: **-1.5,-1.5** ↵

Your drawing should appear as Figure 11.23.

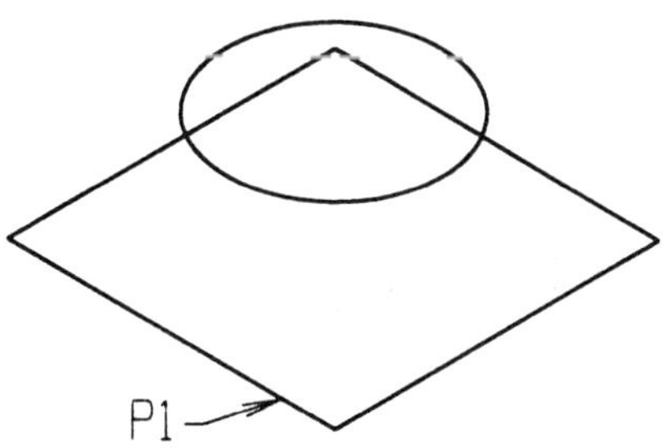

Figure 11.23

Step 3. Add fillets to the four corners of the rectangle.

Use the pick point in Figure 11.23.
Select **MAIN MENU → Modify → Fillet**
Pick **Radius** from the parameter menu
Enter the fillet radius: **0.375** ↵
Select **Chain**
Pick **P1**
Select **Done**
The four fillets are shown in Figure 11.24.

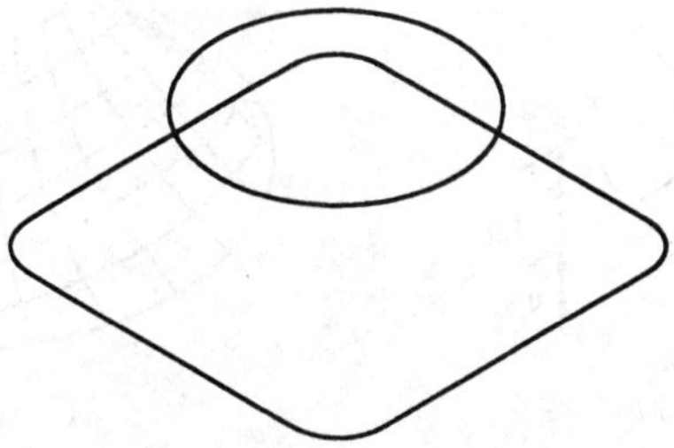

Figure 11.24

Step 4. Create the arc C2.

Select **Z**, and then enter **-1.75** ↵
Select **MAIN MENU → Create → Arc → Circ pt+ rad**
Enter the radius (1.0): **2.5** ↵
Enter the center point: **0,0** ↵

Your drawing would appear as Figure 11.25.

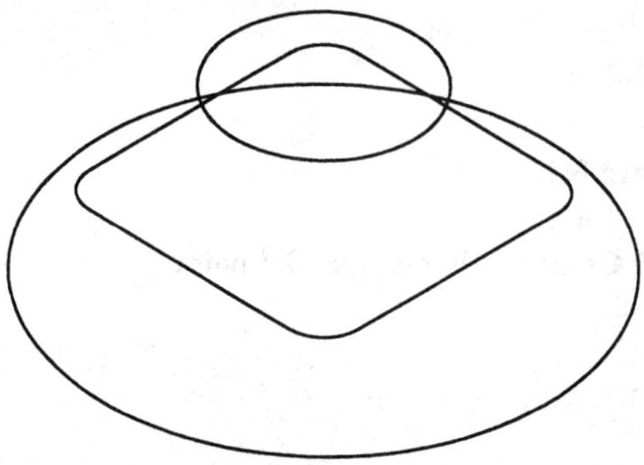

Figure 11.25

Step 5. Save the drawing using the name: 3contour.

Select **MAIN MENU → File → Save**
Enter the file name: **3contour**

Note: This drawing is used to create a ruled surface with three defining contours. It is also used to generate a loft surface in chapter 12.

Project 4

Nineteen elliptical contours are created in the side construction plane (Figure 11.26) in this example. The first and the last contours are rotated by 90° and -90°, respectively, about their end points. The rotation of these two contours must be made by using the front construction plane. These cross-sectional contours are the ideal case for creating a **loft surface.**

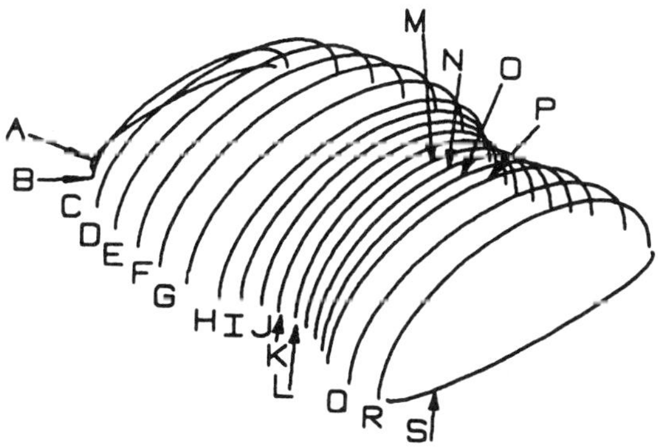

Figure 11.26a. Wireframe model

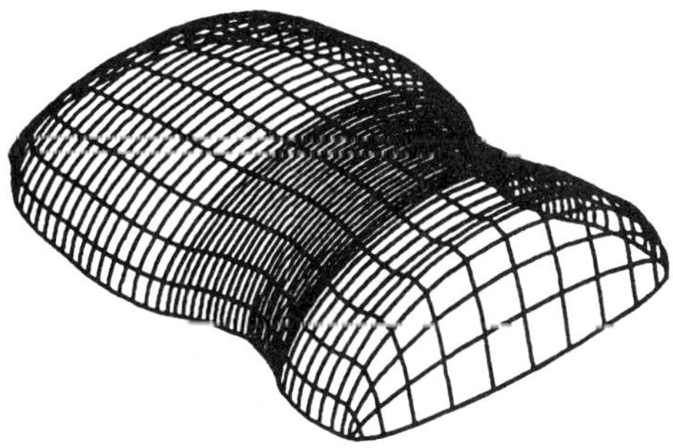

Figure 11.26b. Surface model

The section position (Z coordinate in the side construction plane) and the axis radii of these elliptical contours at each section are tabulated below.

Section	Z-value	Major axis radius (a)	Minor axis radius (b)
A	0.2	0.8	0.2
B	0.25	0.875	0.375
C	0.5	1.083	0.563
D	0.75	1.167	0.638
E	1.0	1.2	0.7
F	1.25	1.25	0.75
G	1.5	1.25	0.75
H	1.75	1.2	0.75
I	1.875	1.125	0.75
J	2.0	1.063	0.75
K	2.125	1.03	0.75
L	2.25	1.0	0.75
M	2.375	1.03	0.75
N	2.5	1.06	0.75
O	2.625	1.125	0.75
P	2.75	1.2	0.75
Q	3.0	1.25	0.75
R	3.25	1.25	0.75
S	3.3	1.2	0.2

Tips 1. Use Side Cplane to construct all ninteen contours.

2. Contours A and S are rotated 90° and -90°, respectively, using the Front Cplane.

Step 1. Enter Mastercam. Set the Secondary Menu to the following settings:

Initialize the screen if necessary
Select **Z**, and then enter **0.2** ↵
Select **Cplane → Side**
Select **Gview → Isometric**

Step 2. Construct the first contour A.

Select **MAIN MENU → Create → Next menu → Ellipse**
Select **A radius**, enter a (X axis radius) (2.00): **0.8** ↵
Select **B radius**, enter b (Y axis radius) (1.00): **0.2** ↵
Select **Start angle**, enter the starting angle (0.00): ↵ to accept the default
Select **End angle**, enter the final angle (360.00): **180** ↵
Select **Rot angle**, enter the rotation angle (0.00): ↵ to accept the default
Select **Do it**, enter the center: **0,0** ↵
The drawing with the contour A should appear as in Figure 11.27.

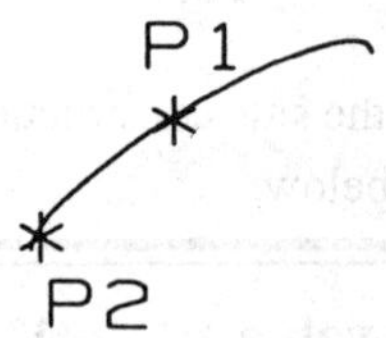

Figure 11.27

Step 3. Rotate the contour A by 90° using the Front construction plane.

Use the pick points of Figure 11.27.
Select **Cplane → Front**
Select **MAIN MENU → Xform → Rotate → Only → Splines**
Pick **P1** to select the entity
Select **BACKUP → Done → Endpoint**
Pick **P2** to select the endpoint of the ellipse
Enter the rotation parameters as below:

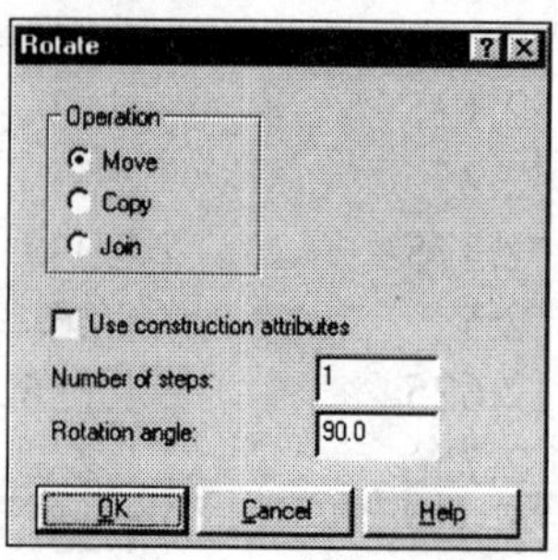

Select **OK**

The rotated ellipse contour should resemble Figure 11.28.

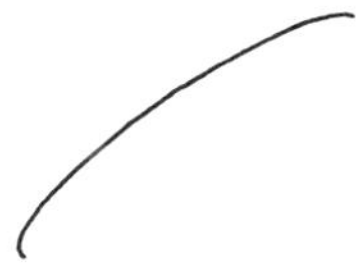

Figure 11.28

Step 4. Construct the second contour B using the side construction plane.

Select **Cplane → Side**
Select **Z**, and then enter **0.25** ↵
Select **MAIN MENU → Create → Next menu → Ellipse**
Enter **A radius: 0.875** ↵
Enter **B radius: 0.375** ↵
Enter **Starting angle** (0.00): ↵ to accept the default
Enter **Final angle** (180.00): ↵ to accept the default
Enter **Rotation angle** (0.00); ↵ to accept the default
Select **Do it**
Enter the center: **0,0** ↵

Step 5. Construct the remaining seventeen contours.

Repeat step 4 by using the Z value, X axis radius (a), and Y axis radius (b) given in the table on page 11-15 to complete the remaining contours.

The nineteen contours should appear as Figure 11.29.

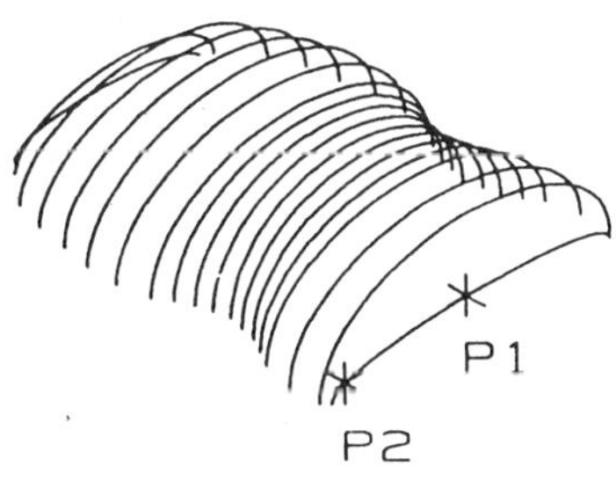

Figure 11.29

Step 6. Rotate the last contour S by -90° using the front construction plane.

Use the pick points in Figure 11.29.
Select **Cplane → Front**
Select **MAIN MENU → Xform → Rotate → Only → Splines**
Pick **P1** to select the last contour S for rotation

Select **BACKUP** → **Done** → **Endpoint**
Pick **P2** to select the end point of the contour
Set the Rotate parameters as below:

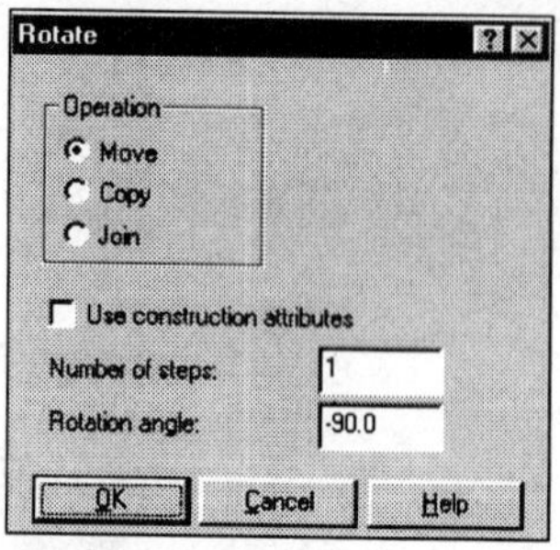

Select **OK** to complete the rotation.

Your final drawing should appear as Figure 11.30.

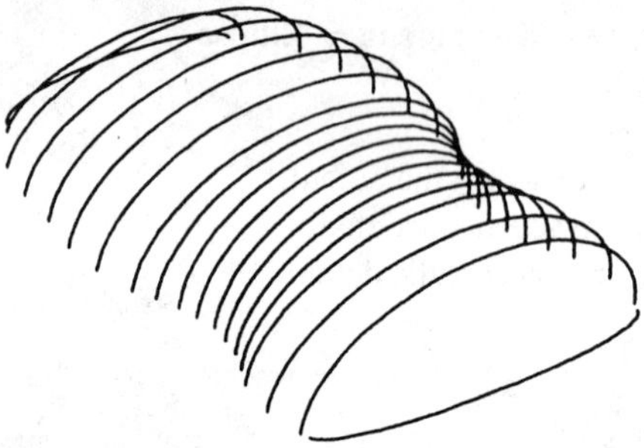

Figure 11.30

Step 7. Save the drawing using the filename loft2.

Select **MAIN MENU** → **File** → **Save**
Enter the file name: **loft2** ↵
Note: This drawing will be used to generate a loft surface in chapter 12.

Project 5

A wireframe model consisting of four contours as shown in Figure 11.31 are created in this example. A rectangular box is constructed first in the top plane. Arcs C1 and C2 are created using the front plane, and the other two contours are generated using the side plane.

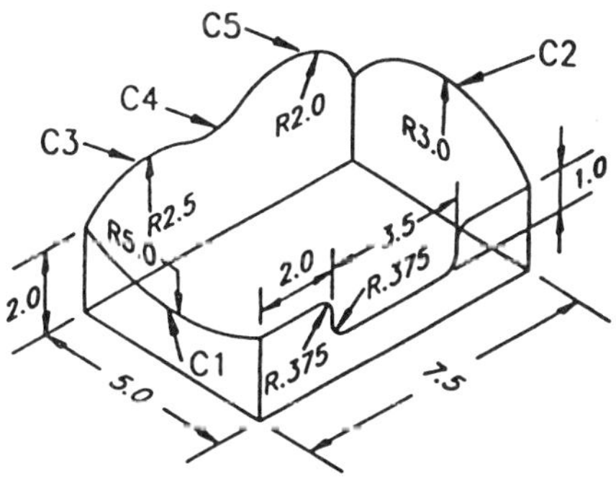

Figure 11.31a. Wireframe model

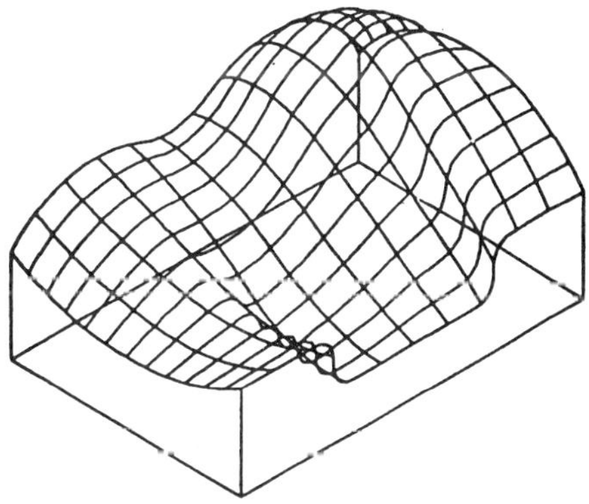

Figure 11.31b. Surface model

Tips 1. Create a rectangular box using Top Cplane.

2. Use Front Cplane to create arcs C1 and C2. Both arcs are defined by endpoints and radius.

3. Use Side Cplane to create the other two contours.

4. Generate three construction lines for creating the right contour.

5. Create a vertical construction line to help determine the endpoints of the two base arcs in the left contour.

Step 1. Enter Mastercam Mill and set the Secondary Menu to the proper settings.

Initialize the screen if necessary.
Select **Z**, and then enter **0** ↵ if necessary
Select **Cplane** → **Top** if necessary
Select **Gview** → **Isometric**

Step 2. Create a rectangular box.

Select **MAIN MENU** → **Create** → **Rectangle** → **2 points**
Enter **0,0** ↵ for the lower left corner
Enter **5,7.5** ↵ for the upper right corner
Press **Alt** + **F1** then **F2** to fit the drawing.
Select **MAIN MENU** → **Xform**
Select **Translate** → **All** → **Lines** → **Done** → **Rectangang**
Enter the translation vector: **Z-2** ↵

Set the parameters as here:

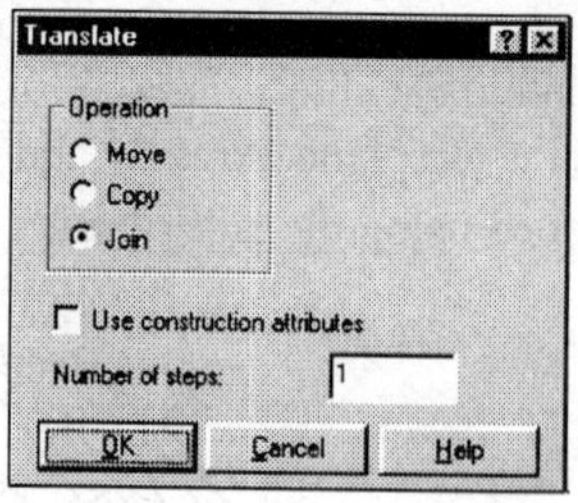

Select **OK**

The rectangular box should appear as Figure 11.32.

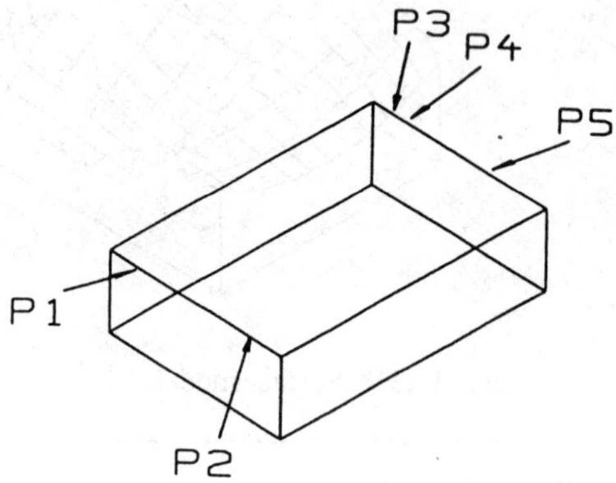

Figure 11.32

Step 3. Create the two arcs C1 and C2 using the front construction plane.

Use the pick points in Figure 11.32.
Select **Cplane → Front**
Select **MAIN MENU →Create → Arc → Endpoints → Endpoint**
Pick **P1** and **P2**
Enter the radius (1.00): **5** ↵
Four arc segments should appear on the screen.
Use the mouse to pick the desired arc for C1 (3rd arc from the top).
Select **Z → Endpoint**
Pick **P3** to trap to the endpoint of the selected line
Pick **P4** and **P5** to trap the end points for the second arc
Enter the radius (5.00): **3** ↵
Pick the desired arc (2nd arc from the top) to complete the arc C2

The drawing should look like Figure 11.33.

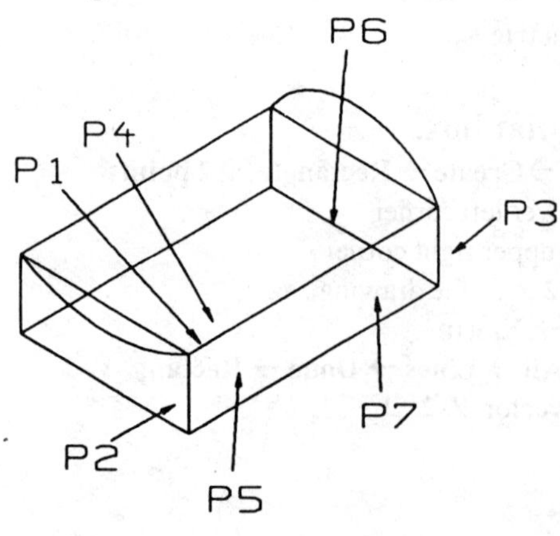

Figure 11.33

Step 4. Create three construction lines using pick points in Figure 11.33.

Select **Cplane** → **Side**
Select **Z** → **Endpoint**
Pick **P1** to obtain the Z value of the picked line (Z5.00 should appear)

Select **MAIN MENU** → **Create** → **Line** → **Horizontal**
Pick **P2** and **P3**, then enter **-1.0** for the Y coordinate
Select **BACKUP** → **Vertical**
Pick **P4** and **P5**, then enter **2.0** for the X coordinate
Pick **P6** and **P7**, then enter **5.5** for the X coordinate

The drawing should resemble Figure 11.34.

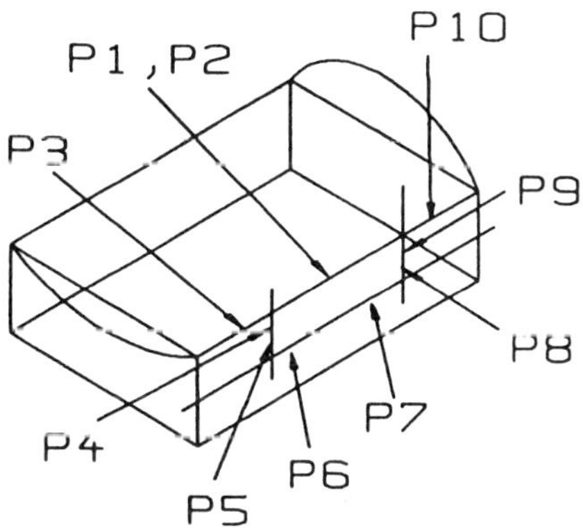

Figure 11.34

Step 5. Add four fillets. Use the pick points in Figure 11.34.

Select **MAIN MENU** → **Modify** → **Break** → **2 pieces**
Pick **P1** to select the entity to break
Select the **Midpoint**
Pick **P2** to enter the breakpoint
Select **MAIN MENU** → **Modify** → **Fillet** → **Radius**
Enter the fillet radius (0.25): **0.375** ↵
Sequentially pick **P3, P4, P5, P6, P7, P8, P9,** and **P10** to complete the four fillets.

The drawing should appear as Figure 11.35.

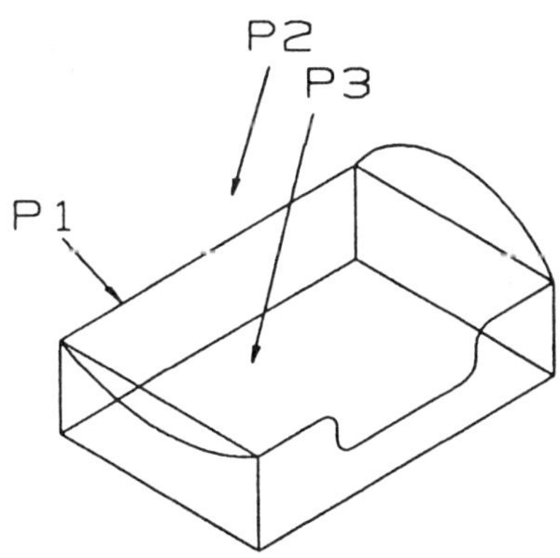

Figure 11.35

Step 6. Create a vertical construction line for creating the three arcs, (C3, C4,& C5).

Use the pick points in Figure 11.35.
Select **Z → Endpoint**
Pick **P1** to set the Z value (Z=0 should appear)
Select **MAIN MENU → Create → Line → Vertical**
Pick **P2** and **P3**
Enter **3.75** ↵ for the X coordinate
The vertical construction line should appear as Figure 11.36.

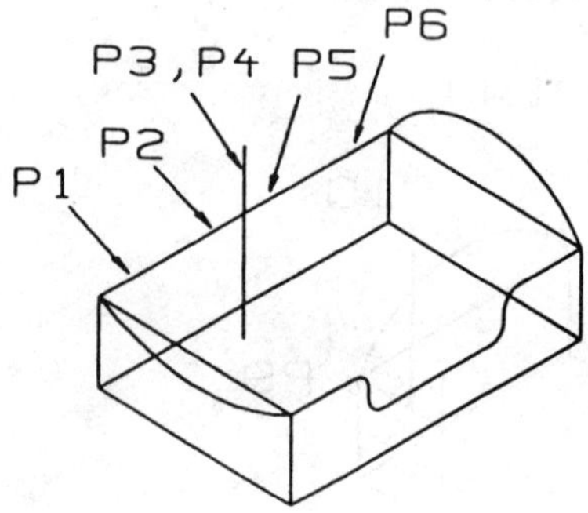

Figure 11.36

Step 7. Create two arcs C3 and C4. Use the pick points from Figure 11.36 .

Select **MAIN MENU → Create → Arc →Endpoints → Endpoint**
Pick **P1** for the first point
Select **Intersec** from the point menu
Pick **P2** and **P3** to determine the second point
Enter **2.5** ↵ for the radius (Four arc segments will appear.)
Use the mouse to pick the desired arc (2nd from the top) for C3
Select **Intersec**
Pick **P4** and **P5** for the first point of arc C4
Select **Endpoint** from the point menu, than pick **P6** for the second point
Enter **2.0** ↵ for the radius
Pick the desired arc (2nd arc from the top) from the given four arc segments

The two arcs C3 and C4 should appear as in Figure 11.37.

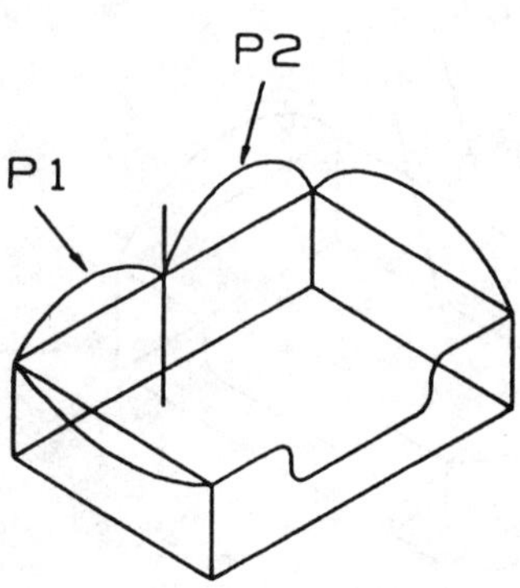

Figure 11.37

Step 8. Create a fillet C5 that is tangent to two arcs C3 and C4.

Use the pick points in Figure 11.37.

Select **MAIN MENU → Modify → Fillet → Radius**

Enter **1.5** ↵ for the radius

Pick **P1** and **P2** to complete the fillet

The drawing should look like Figure 11.38.

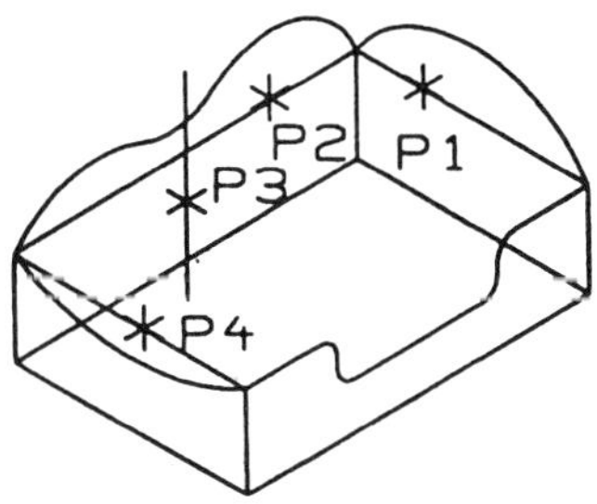

Figure 11.38

Step 9. Delete construction lines.

Use the pick points in Figure 11.38.

Select **MAIN MENU → Delete**

Pick **P1, P2, P3,** and **P4** to delect four lines

The final drawing should appear as Figure 11.39.

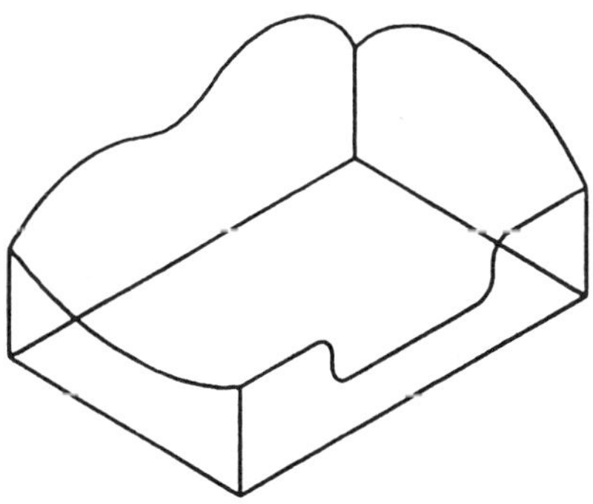

Figure 11.39

Step 10. Save the drawing in the filename coons1.

Select **MAIN MENU → File → Save**

Enter **coons1** for the file name

Project 6

A wireframe model as shown in Figure 11.40a is constructed in this example. It is used to generate a surface shown in Figure 11.40b.

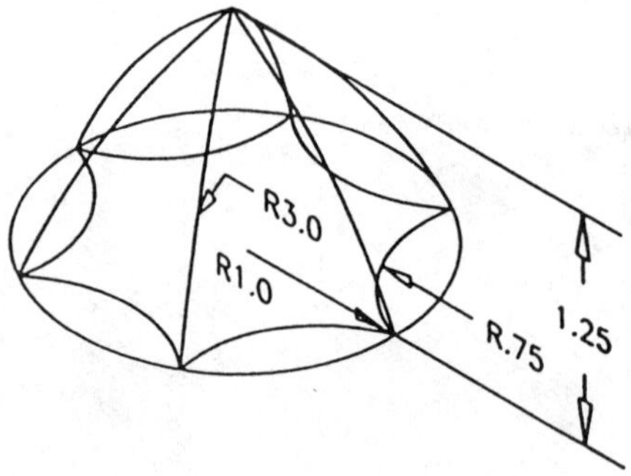

Figure 11.40a. Wireframe model

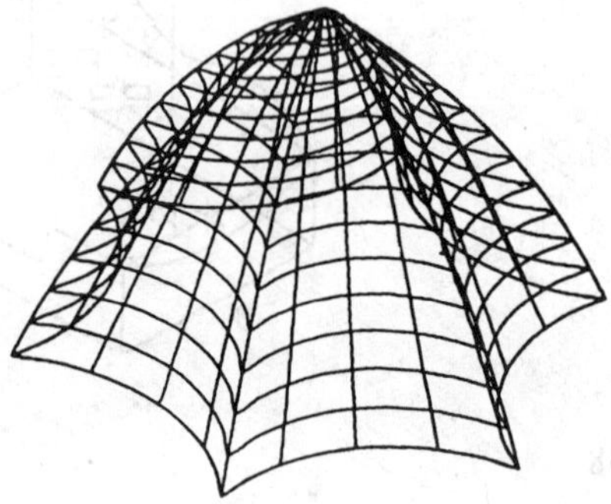

Figure 11.40b. Surface model

Tips 1. Create a base circle and a line that starts from the origin and is parallel to the X axis in the Top Cplane. Copy this line 5 times by rotating about the origin.
2. Use the intersection points between the base circle and the six lines as the endpoints to create six arcs.
3. Use Front Cplane to create a profile arc. This profile arc is then copied 5 times by rotating about the origin in Top Cplane.

Step 1. Enter the Mastercam Mill and set the Secondary Menu to the following settings if necessary:

Z=0
Cplane: Top
Gview: Top

Step 2. Create one circle and two lines.

Select **MAIN MENU → Create → Arc → Circ pt+rad**
Enter the radius (1.00): **1.0** ↵
Enter the center point: **0,0** ↵ (A circle will appear on the screen.)
Select **MAIN MENU → Create → Line → Polar**
Specify an endpoint: **0,0** ↵
Enter the angle in degrees (0.00): **0** ↵
Enter the line length (1.00): **1.5** ↵
Specify an endpoint: **0,0** ↵
Enter the angle in degrees: **60** ↵
Enter the line length: **1.5** ↵

The drawing should appear as Figure 11.41.

6

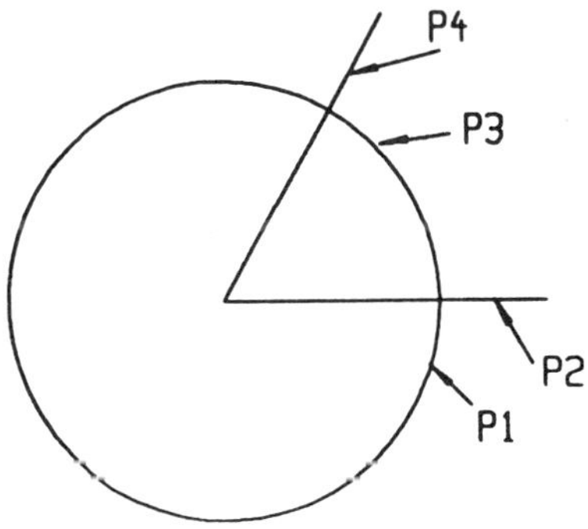

Figure 11.41

Step 3. Create an arc. Use the pick points in Figure 11.41 on the previous page.

Select **MAIN MENU → Create → Arc → Endpoints → Intersec**
Enter the first point: pick **P1** and **P2**
Select **Intersec** again
Enter the second point: pick **P3** and **P4**
Enter the radius (1.00): **0.75** ↵ (Four arc segments should appear.)
Pick at the desired arc (3rd arc from the right) to complete the selection.
The arc is added as shown in Figure 11.42 as shown at the top of the next page.

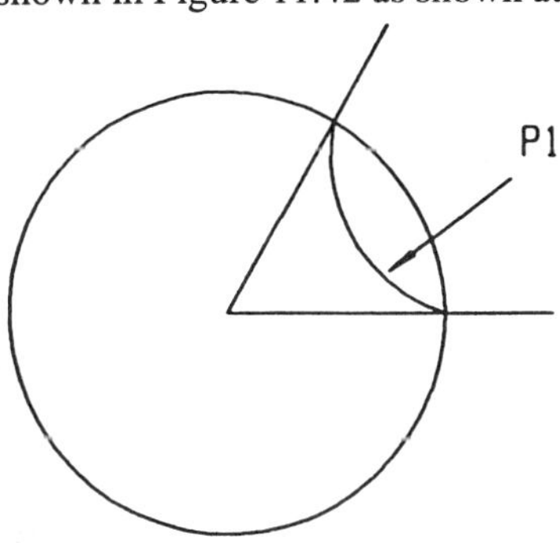

Figure 11.42

Step 4. Create the remaining five arcs.

Rotate the arc five times, at 60° intervals each.
Use the pick point in Figure 11.42.
Select **MAIN MENU → Xform → Rotate → Only → Arcs**
Pick **P1** to select the arc to rotate
Select **BACKUP → Done → Origin**
Set the Rotate parameters as below:

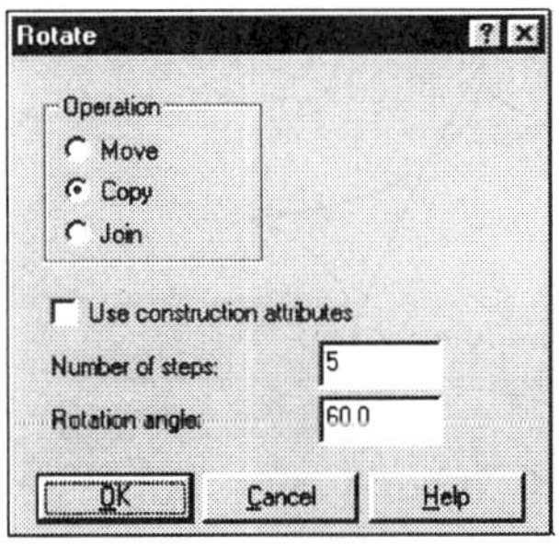

Select **OK**

Your drawing should look like Figure 11.43.

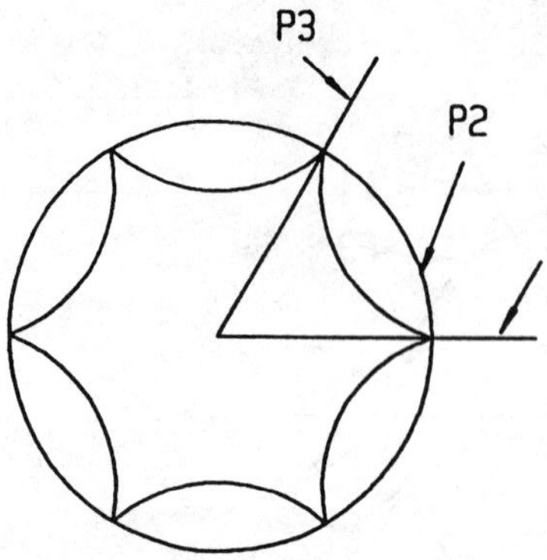

Figure 11.43

Step 5. Delete the construction lines and arc. Use the pick points in Figure 11.43.

Select **MAIN MENU → Delete**
Sequentially pick **P1 - P3** to erase 2 lines and 1 arc
Select **Gview → Isometric**

The drawing should resemble Figure 11.44.

Figure 11.44

Step 6. Create the profile arc using the Front construction plane.

Use the pick points in Figure 11.44.
Select **Cplane → Front**
Select **MAIN MENU → Create → Arc → Endpoints → Endpoint**
Enter the first point: pick **P1**
Enter the second point: enter **0,1.25** ↵
Enter the radius (.75): **3** ↵
Select an arc: pick at the desired arc (the small convex arc)

The drawing should look like Figure 11.45.

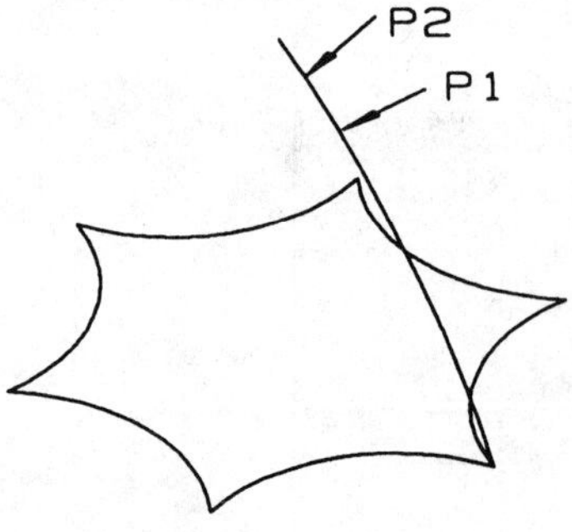

Figure 11.45

Step 7. Copy the arc profile to the other five locations using the Top construction plane. Use the pick points in Figure 11.45.

Select **Cplane → Top**
Select **MAIN MENU → Xform → Rotate**
Select an entity: pick **P1**
Select **Done → Endpoint**
Pick **P2** to select the point to rotate about
Set the rotate parameters as shown here:

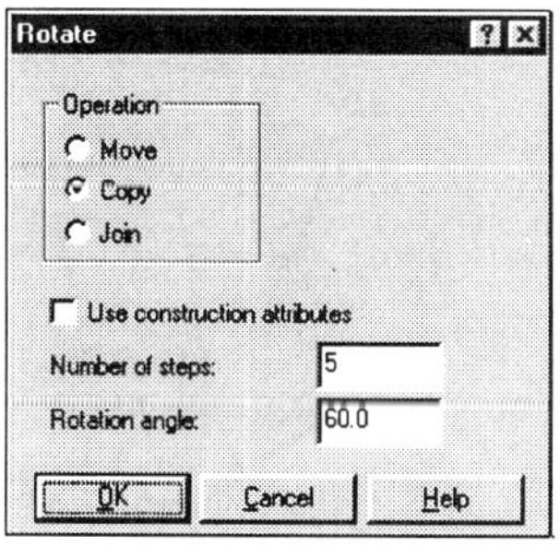

Select **OK**
The final drawing should resemble Figure 11.46.

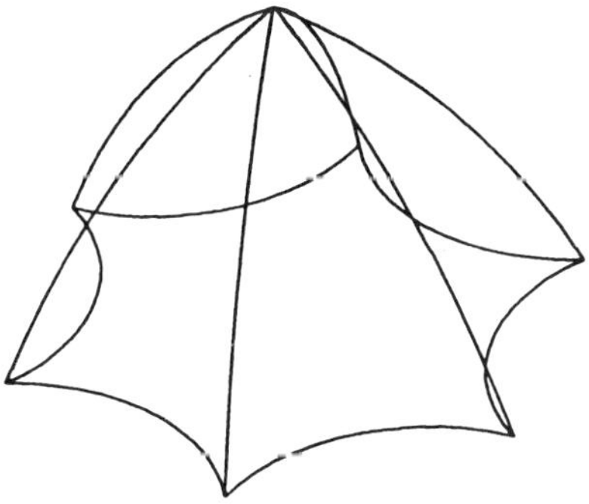

Figure 11.46

Step 8. Save the drawing (coons3).

Select **MAIN MENU → File → Save**
Enter file name: **coons3** ↵

Note: This drawing is an ideal case for creating a coons surface.

Project 7

The wireframe model of an object with 26 faces, Figure 11.47, is presented in this example.

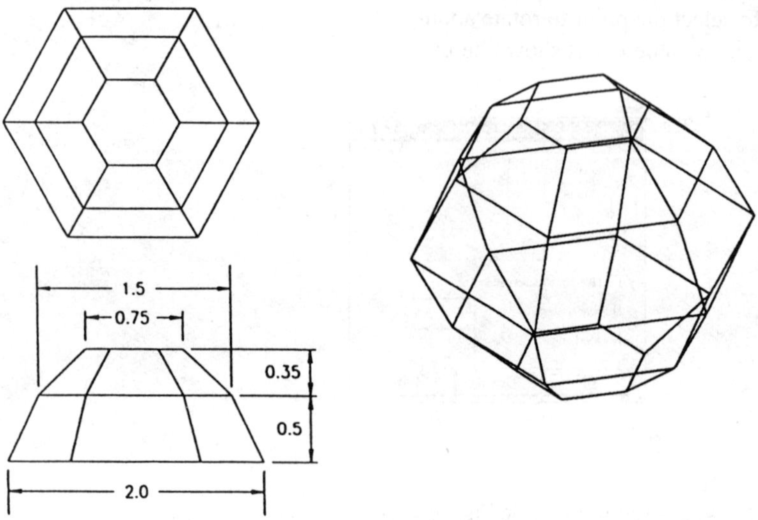

Figure 11.47

Tips 1. Create 3 construction circles and six lines to find the vertices of the three hexagons.

2. The two smaller hexagons are then translated to the proper Z positions, Z0.5 and Z0.85, respectively.
3. Use the Top Gview and the 3-d construction plane to connect the lines between the vertices. The use of the Top Gview helps in picking the right vertices which are not so easily seen in the isometric view.
4. Rotate the upper half model by 180° about the origin using the Front construction plane.

Step 1. Create three construction arcs using the Top construction plane.

Select **MAIN MENU →Create→ Arc→ Circ pt + rad**
Enter **0.375** ↵ for the radius for the center circle
Select **Origin → BACKUP → Circ pt + rad**
Enter **0.75** ↵ for the radius of the middle circle
Select **Origin → BACKUP → Circ pt + rad**
Enter **1** ↵ for the radius of the outer circle
Select **Origin** to place the outer circle
Press **Alt + F1**, and then **F2** to fit the drawing.
The drawing with three arcs should resemble Figure 11.48.

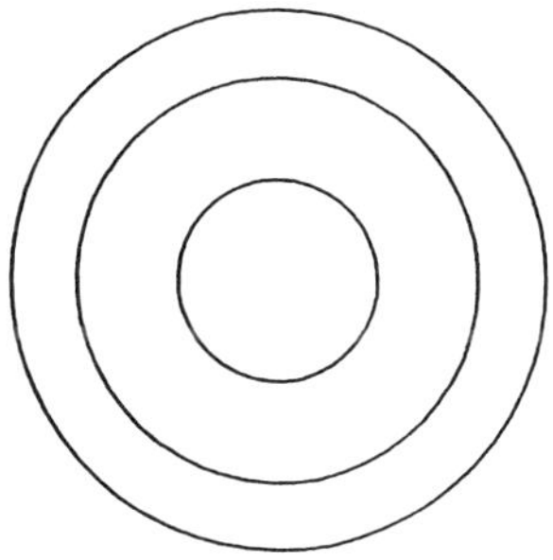

Figure 11.48

Step 2. Create six construction lines. Use the pick point in Figure 11.48.

Select **MAIN MENU → Create → Line → Polar**
Enter **0,0** ↵ for an endpoint
Enter **0** ↵ for the angle
Enter **1.25** ↵ for the line length to complete the first line
The new drawing should look like Figure 11.49.

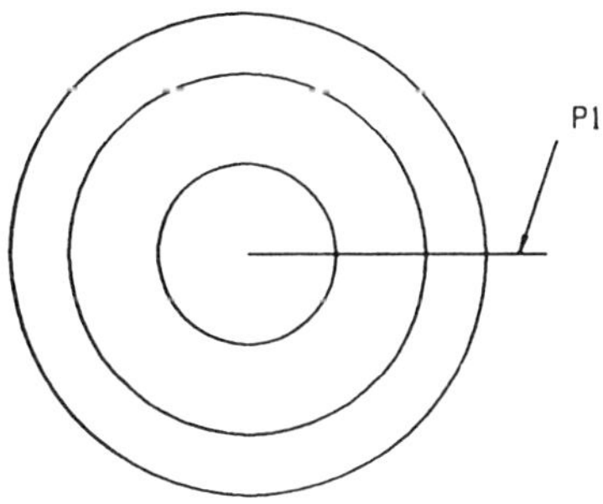

Figure 11.49

Select **MAIN MENU → Xform → Rotate → Only → Lines**
Pick **P1** to select the line to rotate from Figure 11.49
Select **BACKUP → Done → Origin**
Set the Rotate parameters as shown:

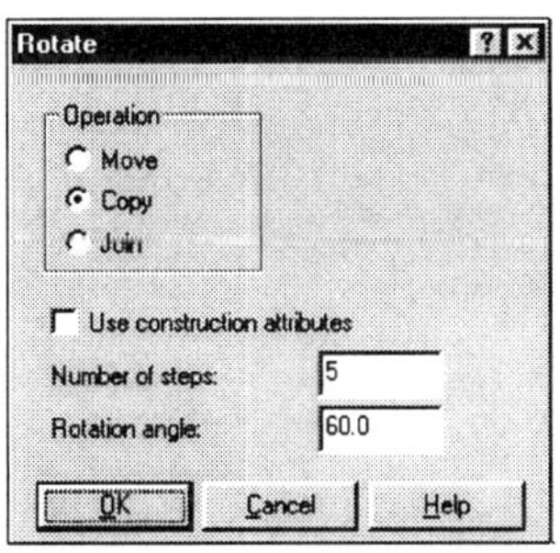

Select **OK**

The drawing should appear as Figure 11.50.

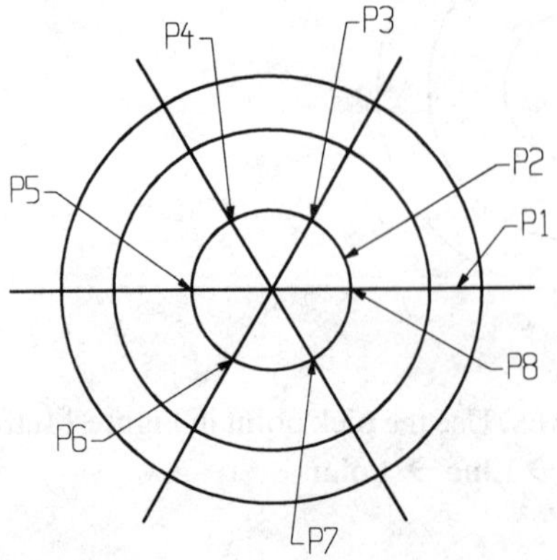

Figure 11.50

Step 3. Construct the first polygon around the smallest circle.

Use the pick points in Figure 11.50 above.
Select **MAIN MENU → Create → Line → Multi → Intersec**
Sequentially pick **P1 - P8** to complete the polygon around the smallest circle.

The first polygon should resemble Figure 11.51.

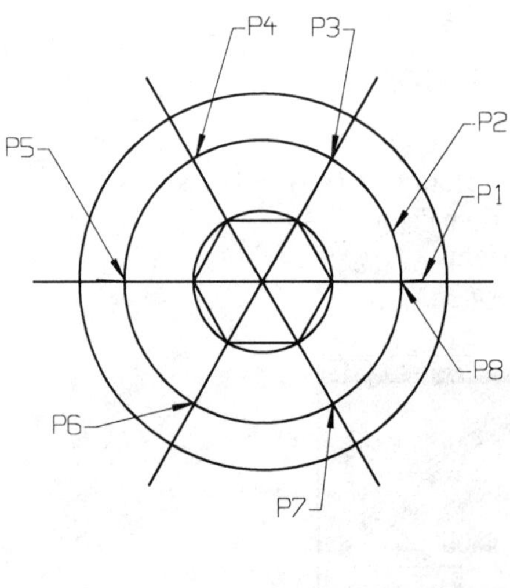

Figure 11.51

Step 4. Construct the second polygon around the mid-sized circle.

Use the pick points in Figure 11.51 on the prevoius page.
Select **BACKUP → Multi → Intersec**
Sequentially pick **P1 - P8** to complete the polygon

The new drawing should appear as Figure 11.52.

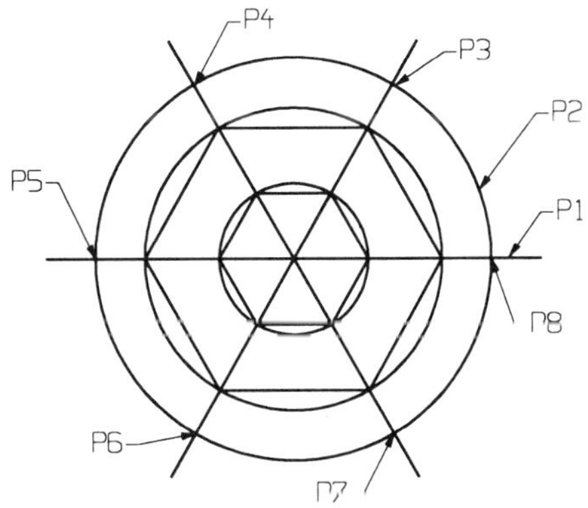

Figure 11.52

Step 5. Create a third polygon around the largest circle. Use pick points in Figure 11.52.

Select **BACKUP → Multi → Intersec**

Sequentially pick **P1 - P8** to complete the polygon

The drawing now should look like Figure 11.53.

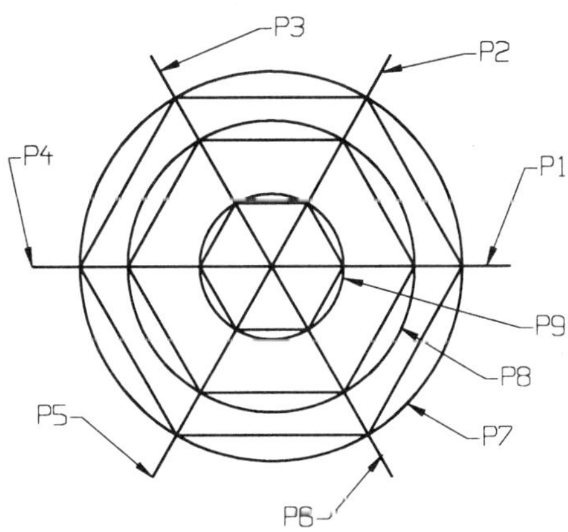

Figure 11.53

Step 6. Delete construction lines and arcs.

Use the pick points in Figure 11. 53.

Select **MAIN MENU → Delete**

Pick **P1 - P9** to delete the six construction lines and three construction circles

The new drawing appears as in Figure 11.54.

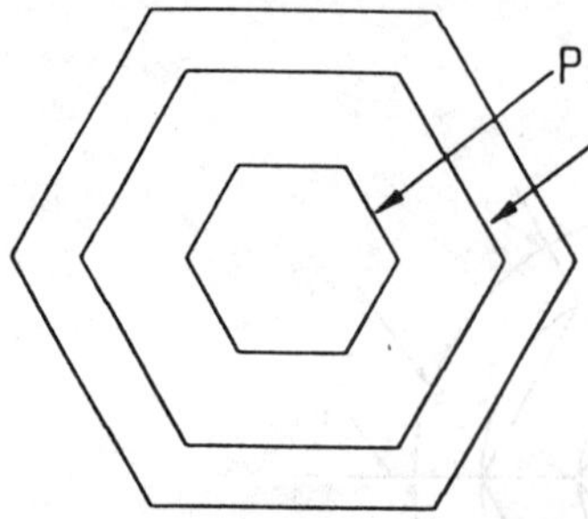

Figure 11.54

Step 7. Translate the smallest polygon to Z.85.

Use the pick points in above Figure 11.54.
Select **MAIN MENU → Xform → Translate → Chain**
Pick **P1**, then select **Done → Done → Rectang**
Enter the translation vector: **Z.85** ↵ to complete the translation
Set the Translate parameters as below:

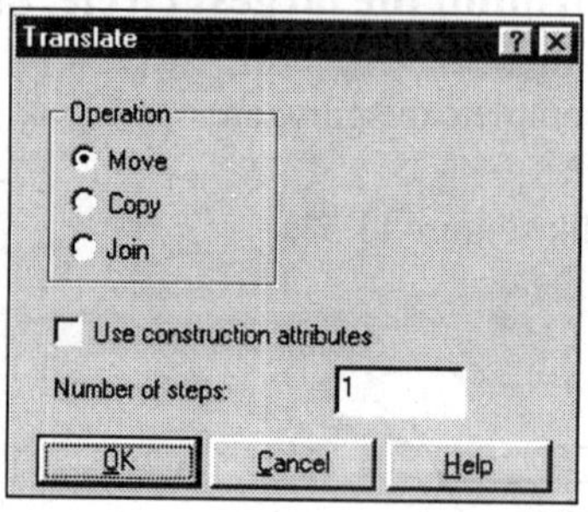

Select **OK**

Note: Your translated polygon may disappear from the screen. It will come back when you change the Gview to isometric.

Step 8. Translate the mid-sized polygon to Z.5.

Use the pick point in previous Figure 11.54.
Select **Chain**, and then pick **P2**
Select **Done → Done → Rectang**
Enter the translation vector: **Z.5** ↵
Set the Translate parameters as below:

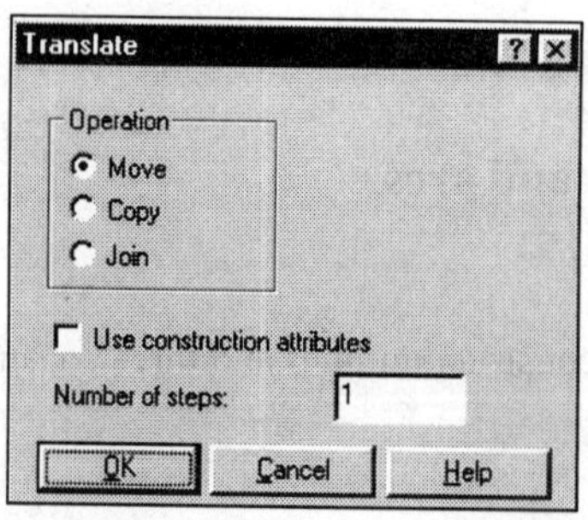

Select **OK**

Select **Gview → Isometric**
The three polygons should appear as Figure 11.55.

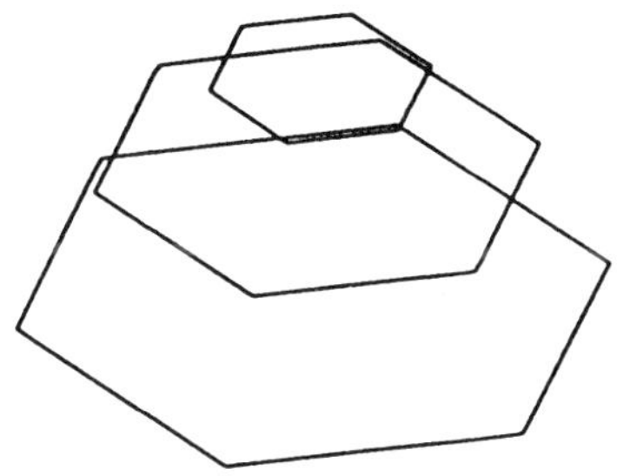

Figure 11.55

Step 9. Return the drawing to Top view to make it easier to connect the lines between the vertices.
Select **Gview → Top**

The drawing displayed in the top view should look like Figure 11.56.

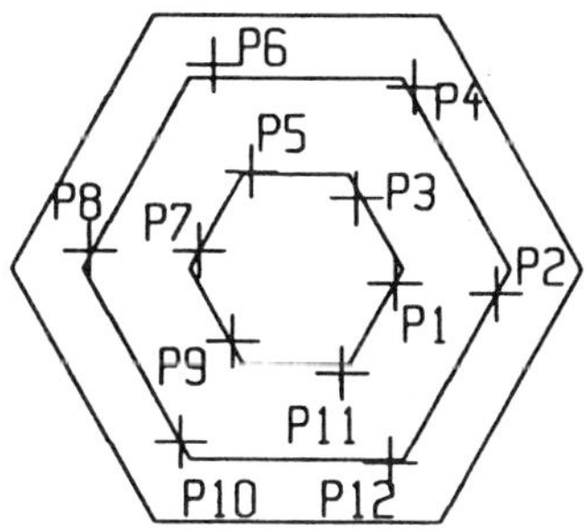

Figure 11.56

Step 10. Connect two inner polygons with lines using the 3D construction plane.
Use the pick points in Figure 11.56.
Select **Cplane → 3D**
Select **MAIN MENU → Create → Line → Endpoints → Endpoint**
Sequentially pick **P1 - P12** to complete the connecting lines
Select **Gview → Isometric**

The drawing now should look like Figure 11.57.

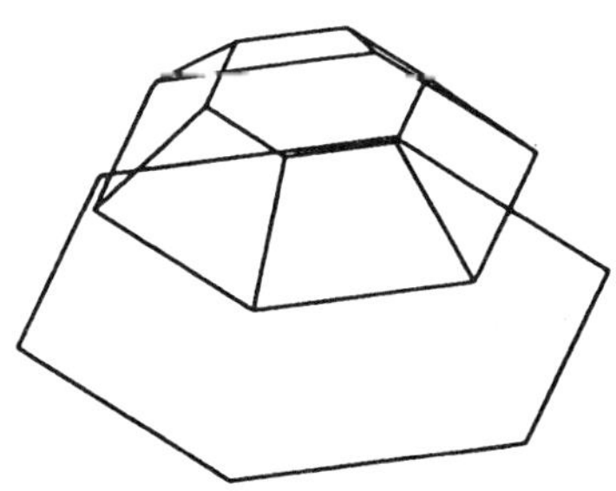

Figure 11.57

Again, change the Gview back to Top view to make picking the points easy for connecting the lines between the two outer polygons.
Select **Gview → Top**

The top view of the drawing should resemble Figure 11.58.

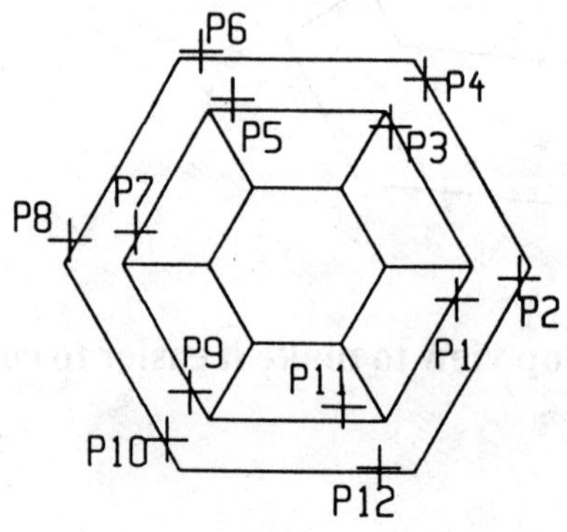

Figure 11.58

Step 11. Connect two outer polygons with lines.

Use the pick points in above Figure 11.58.
Select **BACKUP → Endpoints → Endpoint**
Sequentially pick **P1 - P12** to complete the connecting lines
Select **Gview → Isometric**

The upper half of the wireframe is done and shall look like Figure 11.59. Actually, for modeling purposes, the upper half of the model is all we need since the object is symmetrical. For visualization purposes, the entire model can be obtained by rotating the upper half of the model by 180° about the origin using the Front construction plane.

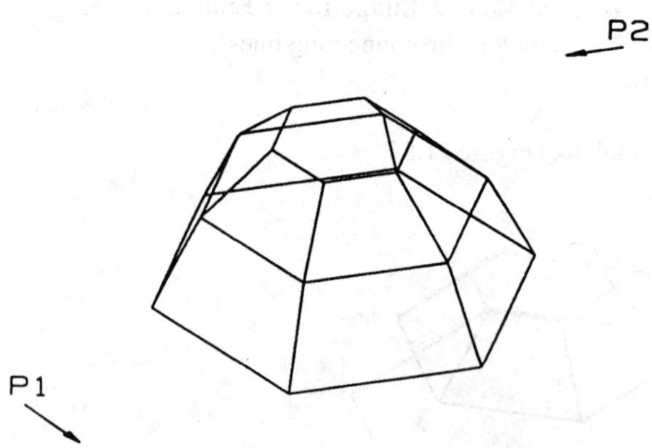

Figure 11.59

Step 12. Save the drawing coons4.

Select **MAIN MENU → File → Save**
Enter **coons4** for the file name

Step 13. Copy the upper half model to the lower half using the Front construction plane. Use the pick points in Figure 11.59.

Select **Cplane → Front**
Select **MAIN MENU → Xform → Rotate → Window**
Pick **P1** and **P2** to completely include the entire drawing
Select **Done → Origin**
Set the Rotate parameters as below:

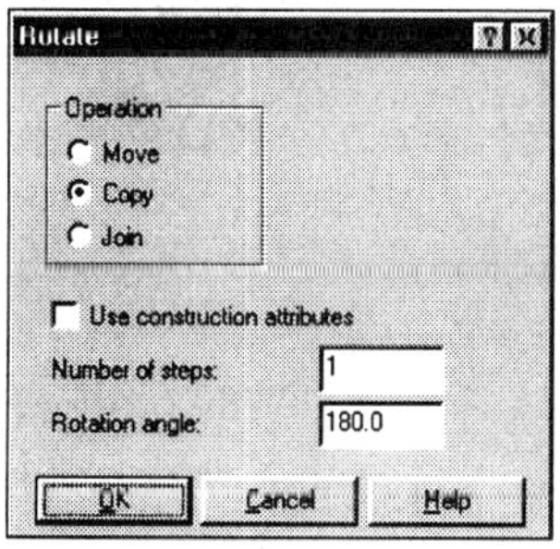

Select **OK**

The complete wireframe model is shown in Figure 11.60.

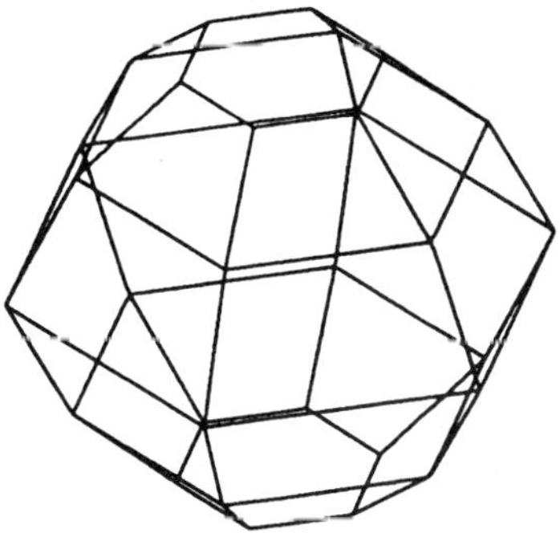

Figure 11.60

Note: This wireframe model will be used to generate two coons surfaces in the next chapter.

Project 8

This example illustrates how to construct the wireframe surface profile for a cup shown in Figure 11.61.

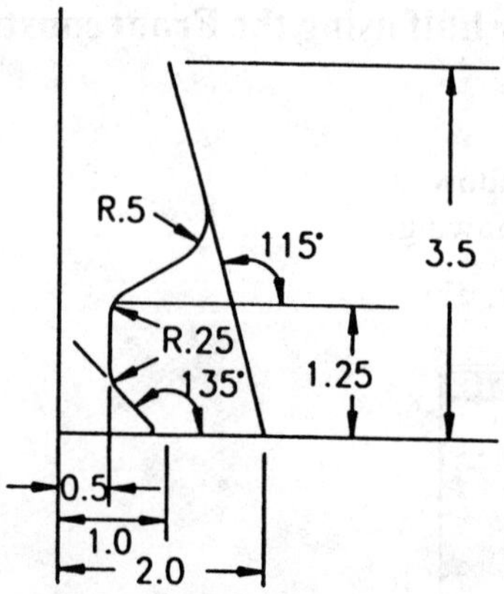

Figure 11.61a. Wireframe profile

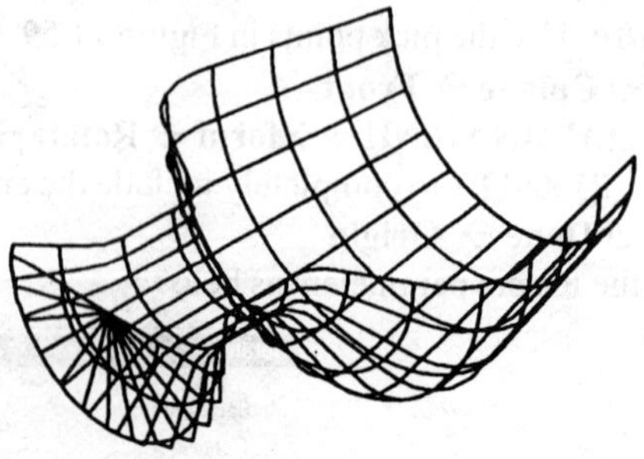

Figure 11.61b. Surface model

Tips 1. Create two slope lines using the polar method in the top construction view.

2. Create three horizontal lines and two vertical lines.

3. Create another slope line using the polar method with one intersection point as the end poin

4. Create four fillets.

5. Delete the construction entities.

Step 1. Enter the Mastercam Mill.

Set the Secondary Menu to the following settings if necessary:

Z: **0**
Cplane: **Top**
Gview: **Top**

Step 2. Create two slope lines.

Select **MAIN MENU →Create → Line → Polar**
Enter **1.0,0** ↵ for an endpoint
Enter **135** ↵ for the angle
Enter **1.5** ↵ for the line length to complete the first line
Enter **2.0,0** ↵ for an endpoint
Enter **105** ↵ for the angle
Enter **5** ↵ for the line length

Press **Alt + F1**, and then **F2** to fit the drawing

The drawing appears as in Figure 11.62.

Figure 11.62

Step 3. Create three horizontal lines and two vertical lines.

Select **BACKUP → Endpoints**

Sequentially enter the following five pairs of point data to complete the five lines:

First end point	Second end point
0,0	**1,0**
0,1.25	**2,1.25**
0,3.5	**2.5,3.5**
0,-0.5	**0,4**
0.5,0.2	**0.5,2**

The drawing now should look like Figure 11.63.

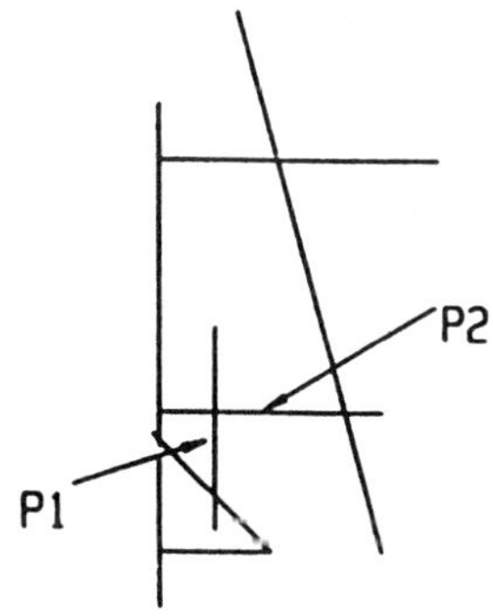

Figure 11.63

Step 4. Create a slope line that passes through the intersection point of two lines.

Use the pick points in Figure 11.63.

Select **BACKUP → Polar → Intersec**

Pick **P1** and **P2** to trap at the intersection point

Enter **30** ↵ for the angle

Enter **1.5** ↵ for the line length

The drawing now should resemble Figure 11.64.

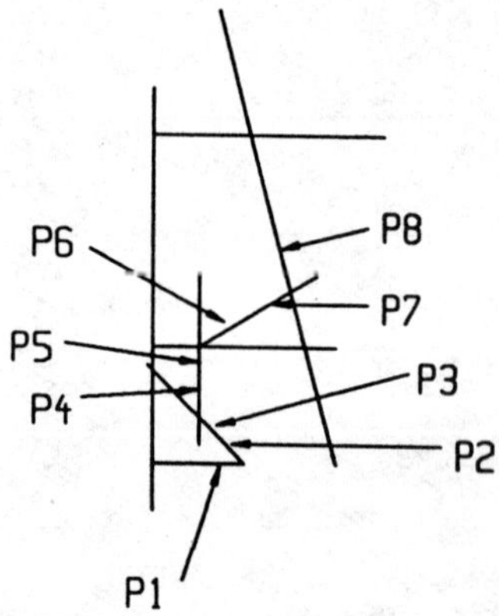

Figure 11.64

Step 5. Add four fillets. Use the pick points in Figure 11.64.

Select **MAIN MENU → Modify → Fillet → Radius**
Enter **0.05** ↵ for the fillet radius
Pick **P1** and **P2** to complete the first fillet
Select **Radius**
Enter **.25** ↵ for the fillet radius
Pick **P3, P4, P5,** and **P6** to complete the two fillets having .25 radius
Select **Radius**
Enter **0.5** ↵ for the fillet radius
Pick **P7** and **P8** to complete the fillet of **.5** radius

The drawing should appear as Figure 11.65.

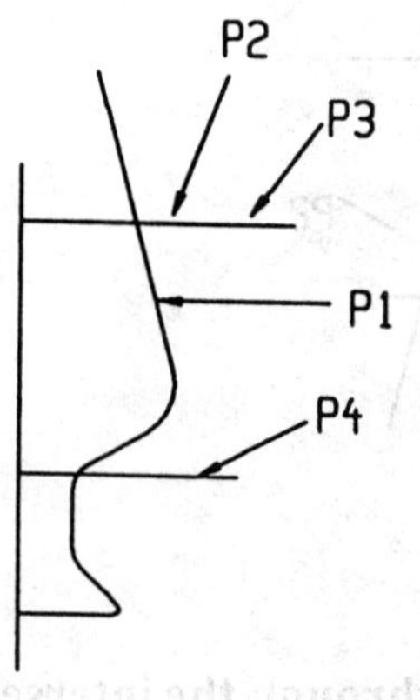

Figure 11.65

Step 6. Trim the slope line and delete two construction lines.

Use the pick points in Figure 11.65.

Select **MAIN MENU → Modify → Trim → 1 entity**

Pick **P1** and **P2** to trim the slope line

Select **MAIN MENU → Delete**

Pick **P3** and **P4** to delete the two construction lines

The final drawing should appear as Figure 11.66.

Figure 11.66

Step 7. Save the drawing. Use the file name: **cup**.

Select **MAIN MENU → File → Save**

Enter the file name: **cup**

Note: This wireframe model can be used to create the surface by using the revolved or swept command.

Project 9

In this example, the surface profiles for a channel surface model are constructed. The cross section of the channel varies from a rectangular shape down to a circle as shown in Figure 11.67.

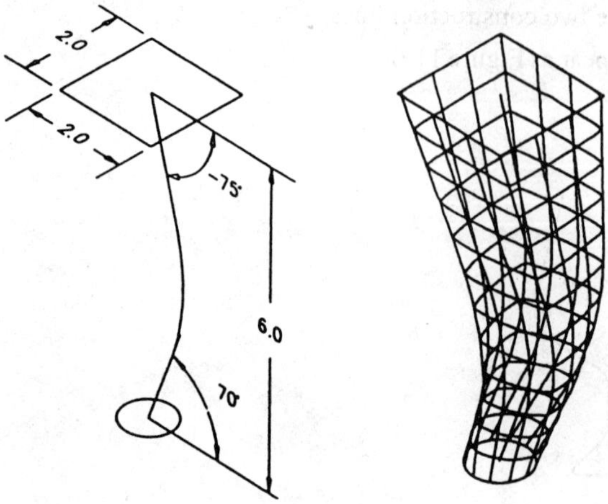

Figure 11.67

> **Tips** 1. Use Front Cplane to construct the profile consisting of two lines and a fillet.
>
> 2. Use Top Cplane to create the rectangle and the circle.

Step 1. Construct two slope lines using Front Cplane.

Select **Gview** → **Isometric**
Select **Cplane** → **Front**
Select **Z** then enter **0** ↵ if necessary
Select **MAIN MENU** ↵ **Create** → **Line** → **Polar**
Specify and endpoint: **0,0** ↵
Enter the angle in degrees: **-75** ↵
Enter the line length: **5** ↵ to complete the first line
Specify an endpoint: **0,-6** ↵
Enter the angle in degrees: **70** ↵
Enter the line length: **5** ↵ for the second line
The drawing of the two lines should appear as in Figure 11.68.

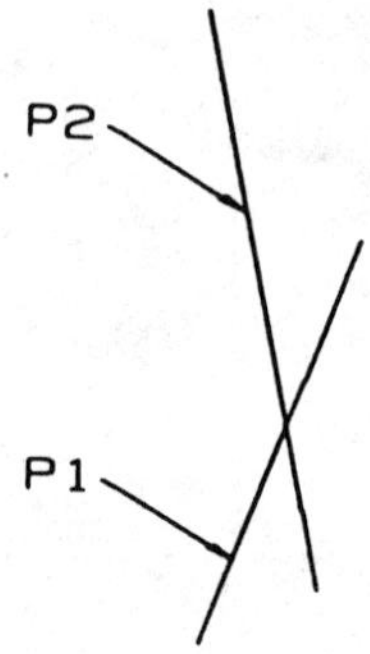

Figure 11.68

Step 2. Add a fillet using the pick points in Figure 11.68. 9

Select **MAIN MENU → Modify → Fillet → Radius**
Enter the fillet radius: **4** ↵
Pick **P1** and **P2** to complete the fillet

The new drawing becomes Figure 11.69.

Figure 11.69

Step 3. Create a rectangle using Top Cplane.

Select **Cplane → Top**
Select **MAIN MENU → Create → Rectangle → 1 point**
Enter the width: **2** ↵
Enter the height: **2** ↵
Select the **lower left corner → OK**
Enter coordinates: **-1, -1** ↵
The drawing should look like Figure 11.70.

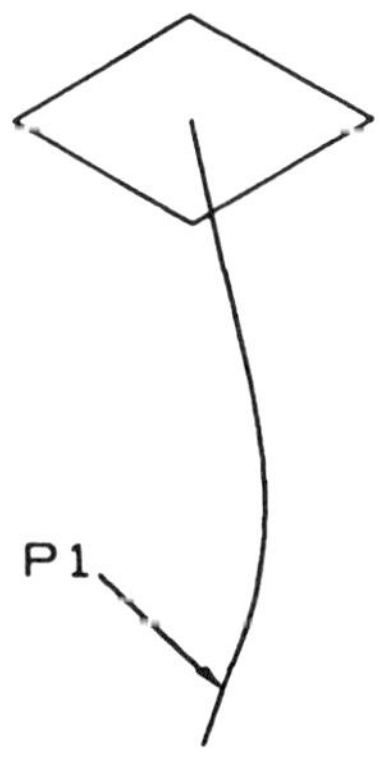

Figure 11.70

Step 4. Create a circle using the pick point in Figure 11.70.

Select **Z → Endpoint**
Pick **P1** to trap the Z value (Z-6.0 should appear in the Secondary Menu)
Select **MAIN MENU → Create → Arc → Circ pt + dia**
Enter the diameter: **1** ↵
Enter the center point: **0,0** ↵

The complete wireframe model appears in Figure 11.71.

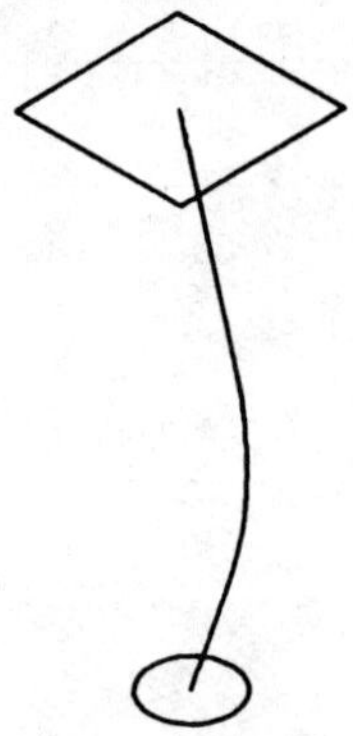

Figure 11.71

Step 5. Save the drawing. Use the file name: **Swept2**.

Select **MAIN MENU → File → Save**

Enter the file name **Swept2**

Note: This wireframe model will be used to generate a surface model using swept modeling technique in chapter 12.

Project 10

This example creates a wireframe model, Figure 11.72a, of the swept surface (Figure 11.72b).

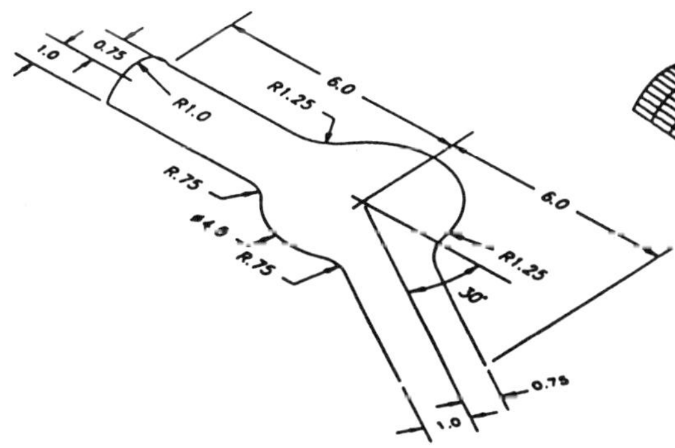

Figure 11.72a. Wireframe model

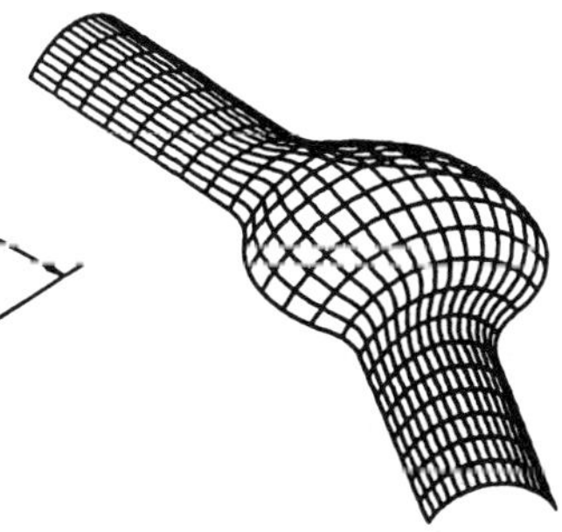

Figure 11.72b. Surface model

> **Tips** 1. Create two construction lines that start from the center of the circle. These two lines are then offset to the two sides by 0.75-in. and 1-in., respectively.
> 2. The circle must be broken into four pieces in order to add four fillets with proper trimming.
> 3. Create the across arc using the Side Cplane.

Step 1. Create an arc using Top Cplane.

Select **Cplane → Top**
Select **Z** then enter **0** ↵ if necessary
Select **Gview → Top**
Select **MAIN MENU → Create → Arc → Circ pt + dia**
Enter the diameter: **4** ↵
Enter the center point: **0,0** ↵

Step 2. Create two construction lines.

Select **MAIN MENU → Create → Line → Polar**
Specify an endpoint: **0,0** ↵
Enter the angle in degrees: **-30** ↵
Enter the line length: **6** ↵ to complete the first line
Specify an endpoint: **0,0** ↵
Enter the angle in degrees: **180** ↵
Enter the line length: **6** ↵

The drawing should look like Figure 11.73.

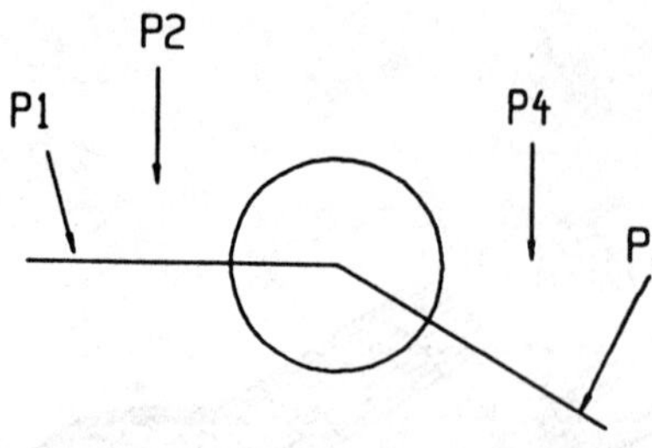

Figure 11.73

Step 3. Offset the two construction lines to the specified side by 0.75-in. using the pick points in Figure 11.73.

Select **MAIN MENU → Xform →Offset**

Set the parameters for Offset as below:

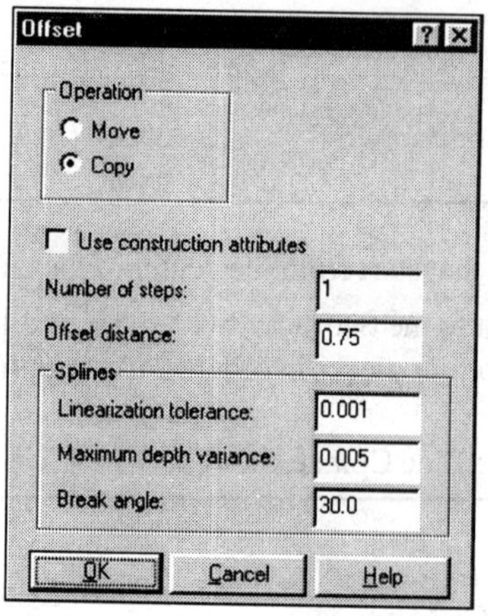

Select **OK**

Select the line or arc to offset: pick **P1**

Indicate the offset direction: pick **P2**

Select the line or arc to offset: pick **P3**

Indicate the offset direction: pick **P4**

Two offset lines will be added to the drawing as in Figure 11.74.

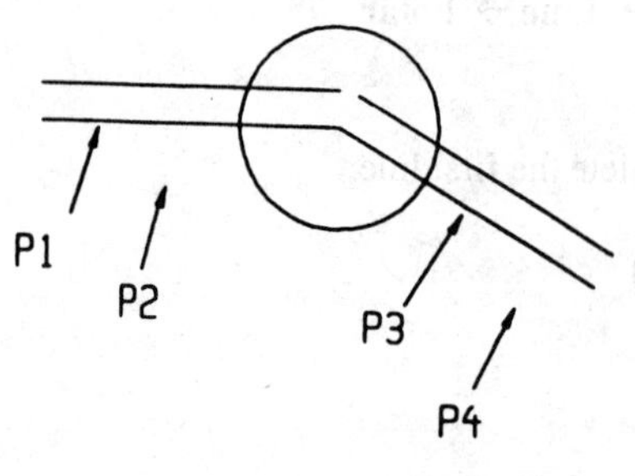

Figure 11.74

Step 4. Offset the two construction lines to the other side by 1-in.

Use the pick points in Figure 11.74.
Select **BACKUP → Offset**
Set the Offset parameters as here:

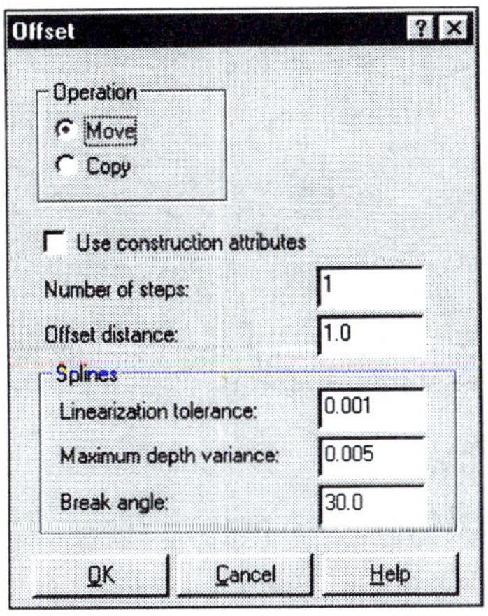

Select **OK**

Select the line or arc to offset: pick **P1** ↵
Indicate the offset direction: pick **P2** ↵
Select the line or arc to offset: pick **P3** ↵
Indicate the offset direction: pick **P4** ↵

The four offset lines should resemble Figure 11.75.

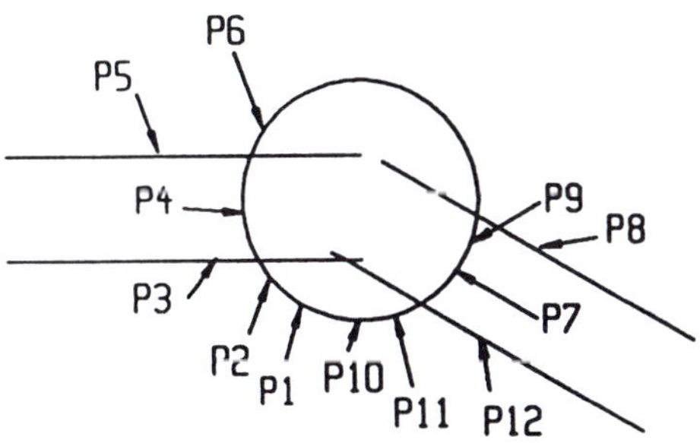

Figure 11.75

Step 5. Break the arc into four pieces using the pick points in above Figure 11.75.

Select **MAIN MENU → Modify → Break → 2 pieces**
Select an entity: pick **P1**
Select **Intersec** from the Point menu and then pick **P2** and **P3** to break the arc

Note: Select Intersec before picking two intersecting elements.

Sequentially pick **P4 - P6** to break the second time
Sequentially pick **P7 - P9** to break the third time
Sequentially pick **P10 - P12** to break the fourth time

Note: The broken arc does not look different before breaking. The drawing reappears in Figure 11.76 to show the pick points for next step.

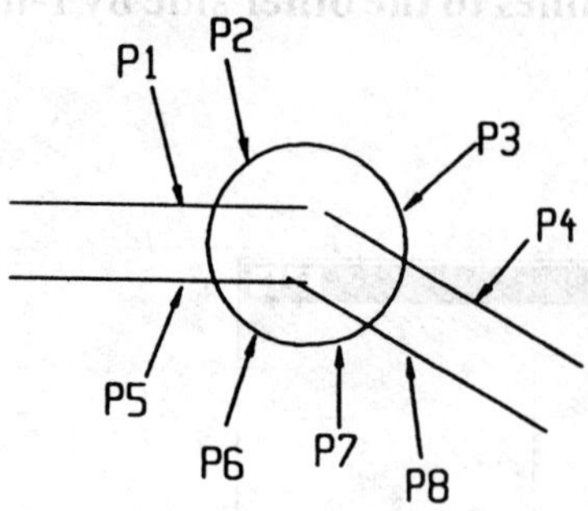

Figure 11.76

Step 6. Add four fillets using the pick points in Figure 11.76.

Select **MAIN MENU → Modify → Fillet → Radius**
Enter the fillet radius: **1.25**
Pick **P1** and **P2** to complete the 1st fillet
Pick **P3** and **P4** to complete the 2nd fillet
Select **Radius** from the Fillet menu
Enter the fillet radius: **.75** ↵
Pick **P5** and **P6** for the 3rd fillet
Pick **P7** and **P8** for the 4th fillet

The new drawing should resemble Figure 11.77.

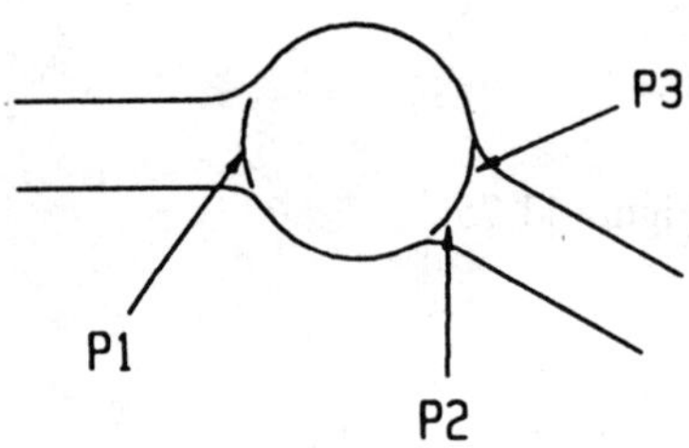

Figure 11.77

Step 7. Delete three unwanted arc segments using the pick points in Figure 11.77.

Select **MAIN MENU → Delete**
Pick **P1**, **P2** and **P3** to complete the deletion

The drawing becomes Figure 11.78.

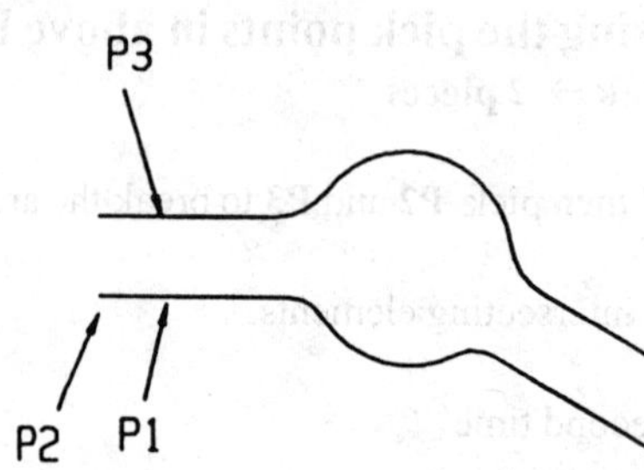

Figure 11.78

Step 8. Create an across arc using Side Cplane.

Use the pick points in Figure 11.78
Select **Gview → Isometric**
Select **Cplane → Side**
Select **Z → Endpoint**, then pick **P1**

Z-6.0 should appear in the Secondary Menu.

Select **MAIN MENU → Create → Arc → Endpoints**
Pick **P2** and **P3** to select two endpoints
Enter the radius: **1**
Select an arc: pick the desired arc (2nd from the top)
The wireframe model should resemble Figure 11.79.

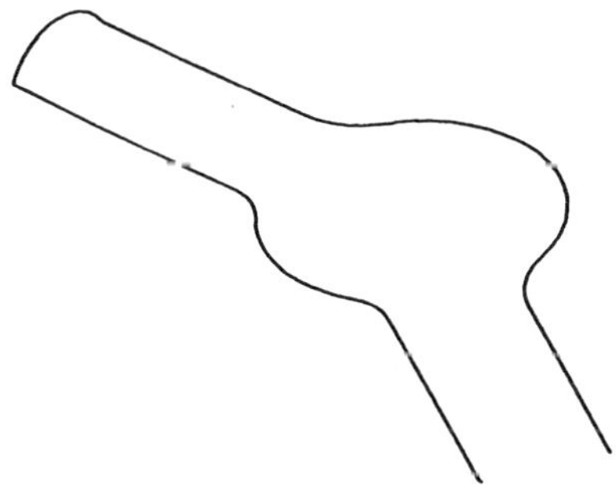

Figure 11.79

Step 9. Save the drawing. Use the file name: Swept3.

Select **MAIN MENU → File → Save**
Enter the file name: **Swept3**

Project 11

The part shown in Figure 11.80 consists of **four** surfaces: a flat surface at the bottom, a wall surface, a fillet surface between the wall and the bottom, and a rim surface. The required wireframe model for these four surfaces is given in Figure 11.80a.

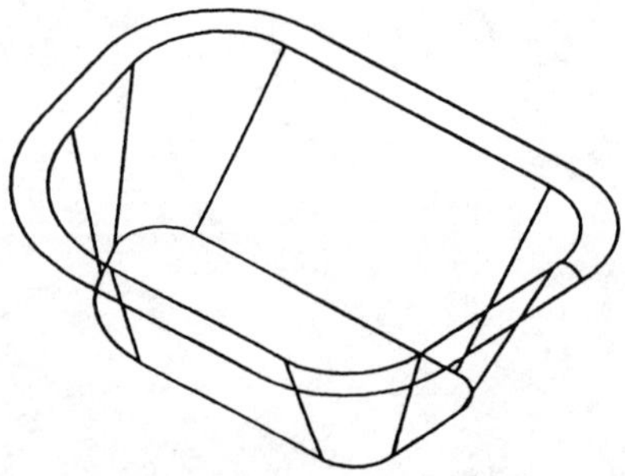

Figure 11.80a. Wireframe model

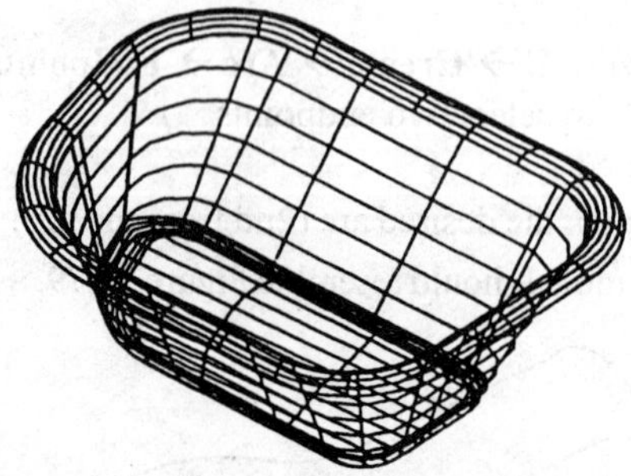

Figure 11.80b. Surface model

Tips 1. Use the Top construction plane to construct the top and the bottom frames of the part.

2. Use the 3d construction plane to create the connecting lines between the top and the bottom frame. The connecting points of these lines are trapped at the end points of each arc.
3. Use the side construction plane to create the sweeping arc of the rim.

Step 1. Enter the Mastercam Mill.

Set the Secondary Menu to the proper settings if necessary.
Select **Cplane → Top**
Select **Gview → Top**
Select **Z** and then enter **0** ↵

Step 2. Construct a rectangle.

Select **MAIN MENU → Create → Rectangle → 1 point**
Enter the width: **6** ↵
Enter the height **4** ↵
Select the **lower left corner → OK**
Enter coordinates: **0,0** ↵
Press **Alt + F1** then **F2** to fit the drawing.
A rectangle should appear as Figure 11.81.

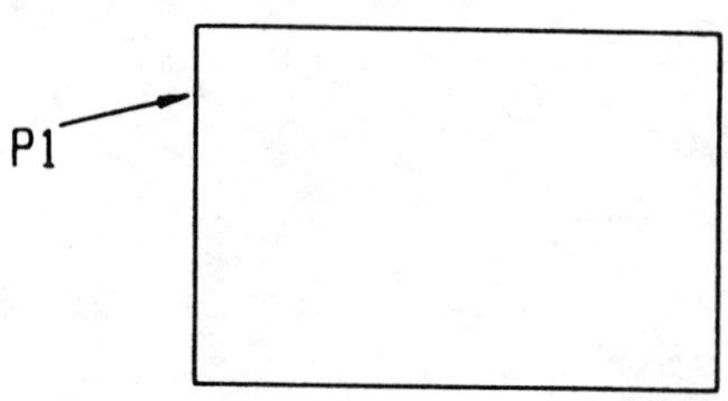

Figure 11.81

Step 3. Construct a slope line to the rectangle.

Use the pick point in Figure 11.81.

Select **MAIN MENU → Create → Line → Endpoints → Endpoint**

Pick **P1** for the first point

Enter **1,0** ↵ for the second point

The drawing should look like Figure 11.82.

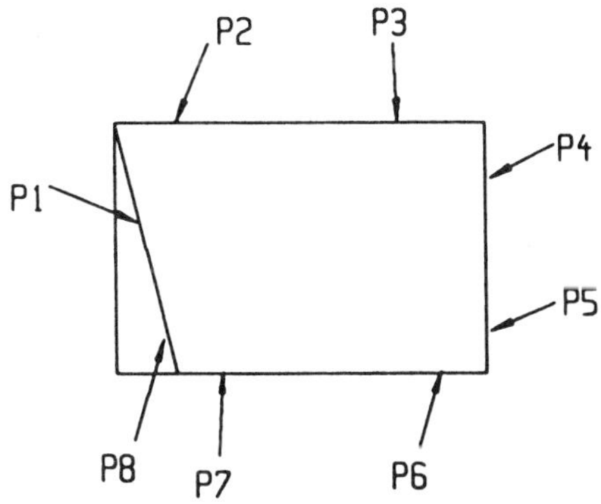

Figure 11.82

Step 4. Add four arcs at corners.

Use the pick points in Figure 11.82.

Select **MAIN MENU → Modify → Fillet → Radius**

Enter **1.0** ↵ for the radius value

Sequentially pick **P1 - P6** to complete the three fillets

Select **Radius**, and then enter **2.0** ↵ for the radius value

Pick **P7** and **P8** to complete the larger fillet

The drawing now should resemble Figure 11.83.

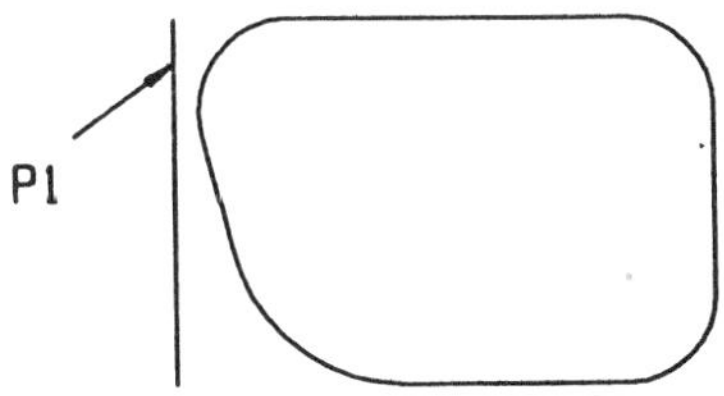

Figure 11.83

Step 5. Delete a line. Use the pick point in Figure 11.83.

Select **MAIN MENU → Delete**

Pick **P1**

The top frame appears as in Figure 11.84.

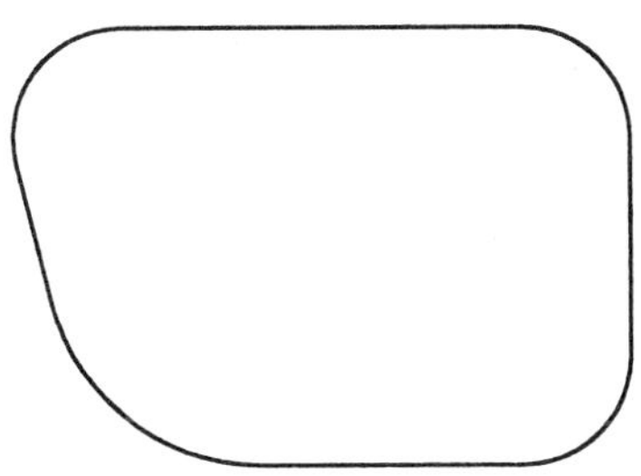

Figure 11.84

Step 6. Create the outer contour by offseting the top frame just created.

Use the pick points in Figure 11.84.
Select **MAIN MENU → Xform → Ofs ctour → Chain**
Pick any element on the contour (Be sure the contour direction runs in the clockwise direction.)
Select **Done**
Set the Offset parameters as below:

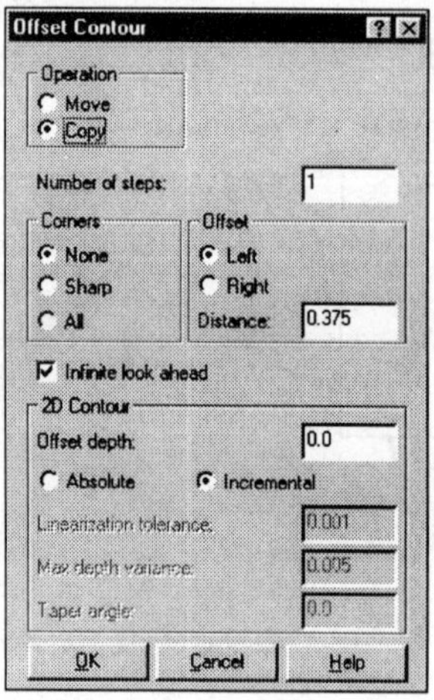

Select **OK**
The drawing now should look like Figure 11.85.

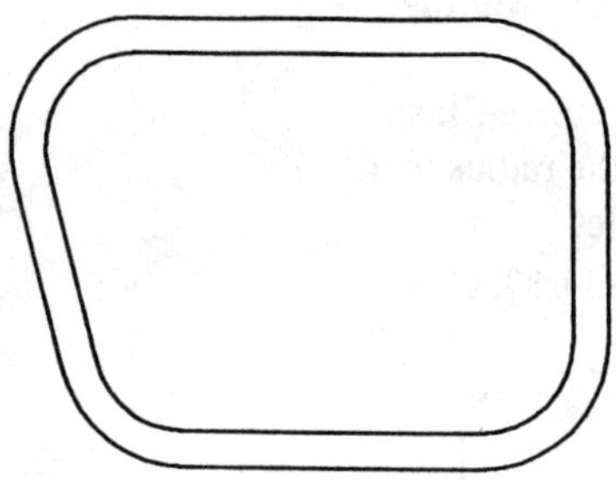

Figure 11.85

Step 7. Create the rectangle for the bottom frame.

Select **Z** and then enter **-1.5** ↵
Select **MAIN MENU → Create → Rectangle → 1 point**
Enter the width: **5** ↵
Enter the height: **2** ↵
Select the **lower left corner → OK**
Enter coordinates: **0.5,0.5** ↵
The drawing appears as Figure 11.86.

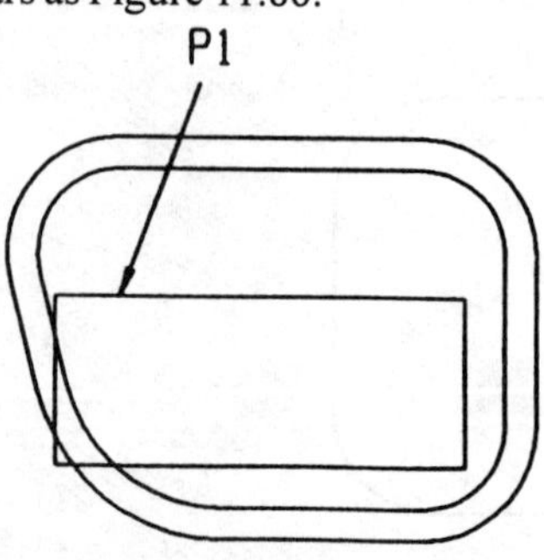

Figure 11.86

Step 8. Create a slope line to the rectangle. Use the pick point In Figure 11.86.

Select **MAIN MENU → Create → Line → Endpoints → Endpoint**
Pick **P1** to define the first point
Enter **1.5,0.5** ↵ for the second point
Now the drawing should look like Figure 11.87.

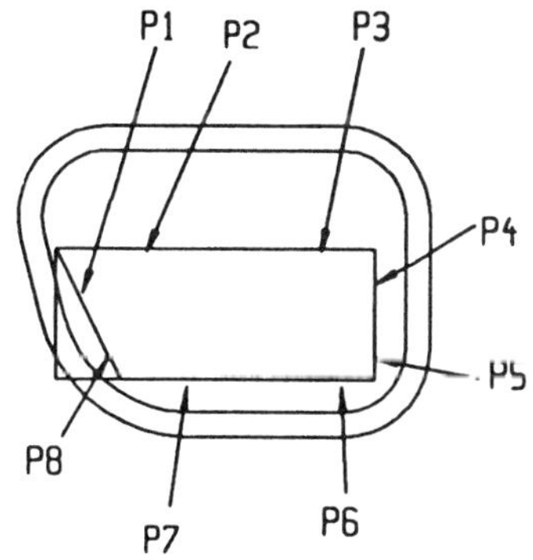

Figure 11.87

Step 9. Add fillets to four corners. Use the pick points in Figure 11.87.

Select **MAIN MENU → Modify → Fillet → Radius**
Enter **0.5** ↵ for the fillet radius
Sequentially pick **P1 - P6** to complete three three fillets
Select **Radius**, and then enter **1.5** ↵
Pick **P7** and **P8** to complete the fourth fillet
The drawing should resemble Figure 11.88.

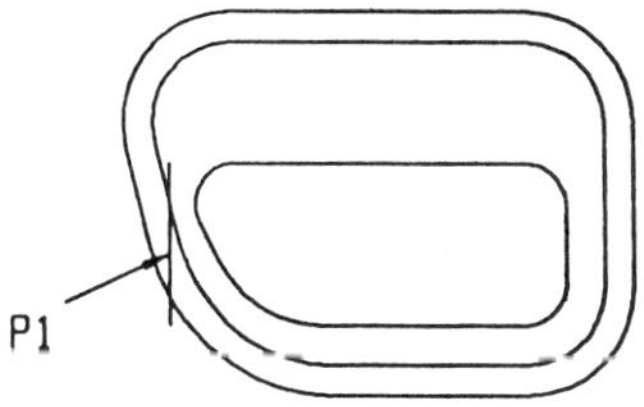

Figure 11.88

Step 10. Delete one line. Use the pick point in Figure 11.88.

Select **MAIN MENU → Delete**
Pick **P1** to delete the line
The new drawing appears as Figure 11.89.

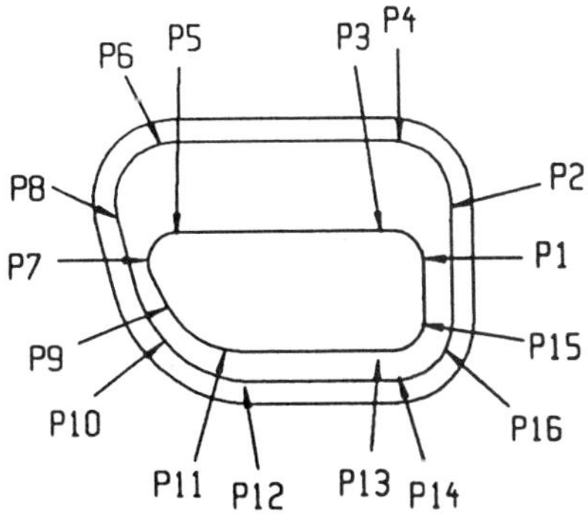

Figure 11.89

Step 11. Connect the top and bottom frames with straight lines using the 3D construction plane. Use the pick points in Figure 11.89.

Select **Cplane → 3D**
Select **MAIN MENU → Create → Line → Endpoints**
Sequentially pick **P1 - P16**
Select **Gview → Isometric**
Press **Alt + F1** and then **F2** to fit the drawing.
The new drawing should resemble Figure 11.90.

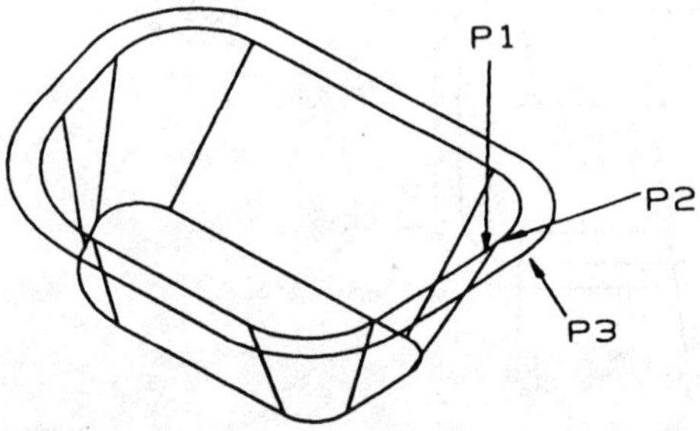

Figure 11.90

Step 12. Create the sweeping arc of the rim using the front construction plane.

Use the pick points in Figure 11.90.
Select **Cplane → Front**
Select **Z → Endpoint**
Pick **P1** to find the Z depth of the entity endpoint

Z-3.0 should appear in the Secondary Menu.
Select **Create → Arc → Endpoints**
Pick **P2** and **P3** to define the two endpoints
Enter **0.2** ↵ for the rac radius
Pick at the desired arc (the second from the top)
The final drawing should resemble Figure 11.91.

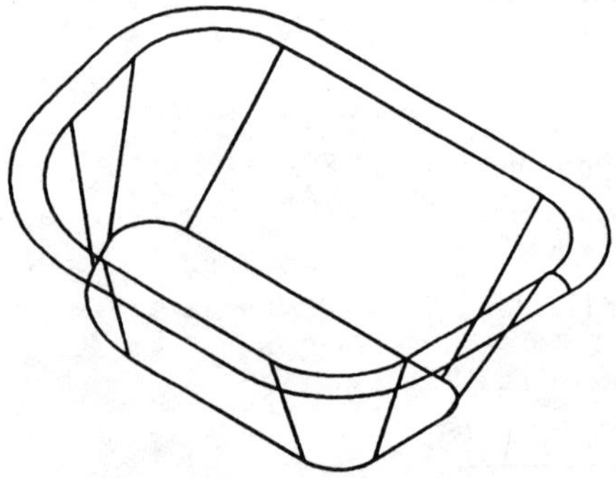

Figure 11.91

Step 13. Save the drawing. Use the file name: **basket**.

Select **MAIN MENU → File → Save**
Enter the file name: **basket**

Project 12 Flashlight

12

Construct the wireframe model of the flash light shown in Figure 11.92. The surface model consists of six surfaces: an outer frame surface, a top rim surface, a vertical wall surface, an inner top flat surface, a curved surface, and a fillet surface between the vertical wall surface and the inner top flat surface.

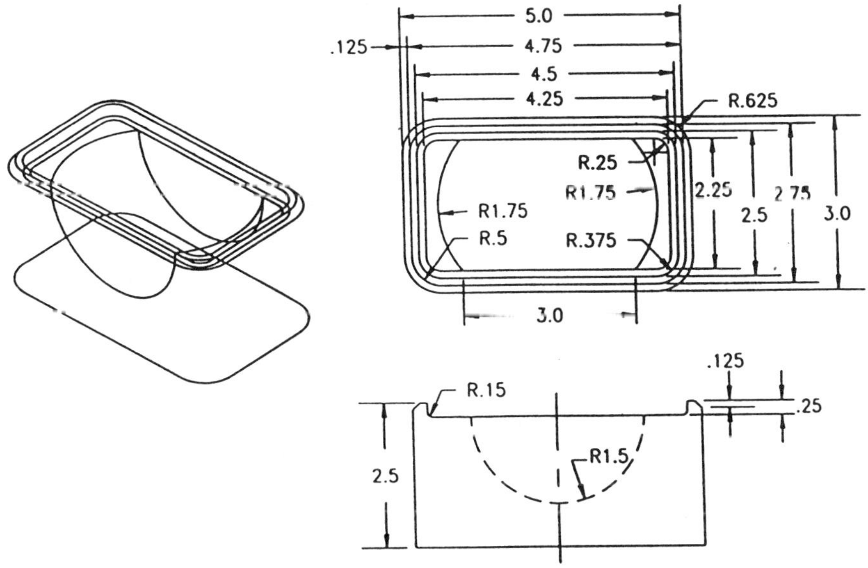

a. Wireframe model

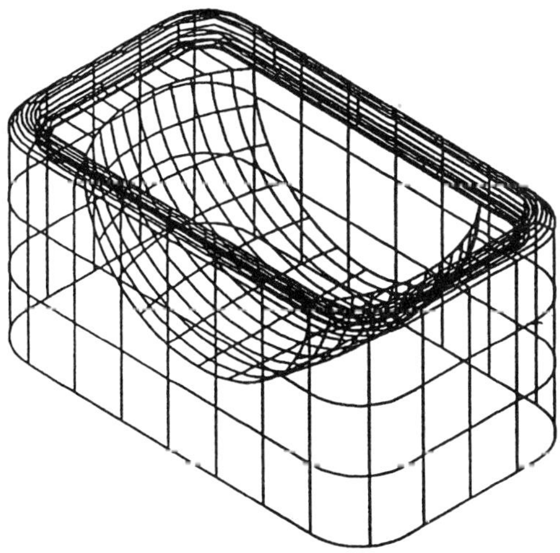

b. Surface model
Figure 11.92

Tips 1. Create four rectangles with corner arcs at the specified Z depth in the top view.

2. Translate the outer profile in the negative Z direction to form the bottom profile of the outer frame surface.
3. Construct two arcs in the top view and another two arcs in the front view to define the edge profile for the recessed surface.

Step 1. Enter the Mastercam Mill.

Set the Secondary Menu to these settings:

Cplane:	**Top**
Gview:	**Top**
Z:	**-0.125**

Step 2. Create the first rectangle.

Select **MAIN MENU →Create → Rectangle → 1 Point**

Enter the width: **5** ↵

Enter the height: **3** ↵

Select the **lower left corner → OK**

Enter coordinates: **-2.5, -1.5** ↵

The rectangle will appear on the screen like Figure 11.93.

Figure 11.93

Step 3. Add four filletts using the pick points from Figure 11.93.

Select **MAIN MENU → Modify → Fillet → Radius**

Enter the fillet radius: **0.625** ↵

Select **Chain**

Select the first entity in the contour: pick **P1**

Select **Done** to complete the four fillets.

Now the drawing should look like Figure 11.94

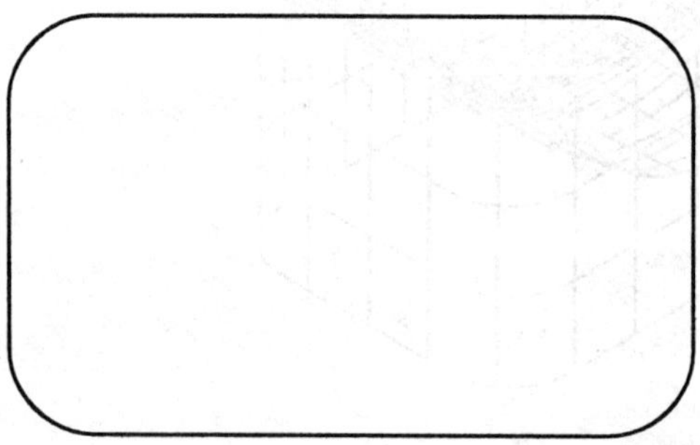

Figure 11.94

Step 4. Create the second rectangle.

Select **Z** from the Secondary Menu and then enter **0**

Select **MAIN MENU → Create → Rectangle → 1 point**

Enter the width: **4.75** ↵

Enter the height: **2.75** ↵

Select the **lower left corner → OK**

Enter the coordinates: **-2.375,-1.375** ↵

The drawing should resemble Figure 11.95.

Figure 11.95

Step 5. Add four fillets to the second rectangle.

Use the pick points from Figure 11.95 on the previous page.
Select **MAIN MENU → Modify → Fillet → Radius**
Enter the fillet radius: **0.5** ↵
Select **Chain**
Pick **P1**
Select **Done** to complete the four fillets.
The drawing should look like Figure 11.96.

Figure 11.96

Step 6. Create the third rectangle.

Select **MAIN MENU → Create → Rectangle → 1 point**
Enter the width: **4.5** ↵
Enter the height: **2.5** ↵
Select **lower left corner → OK**
Enter coordinates: **-2.25,-1.25** ↵
The drawing now should appear as in Figure 11.97.

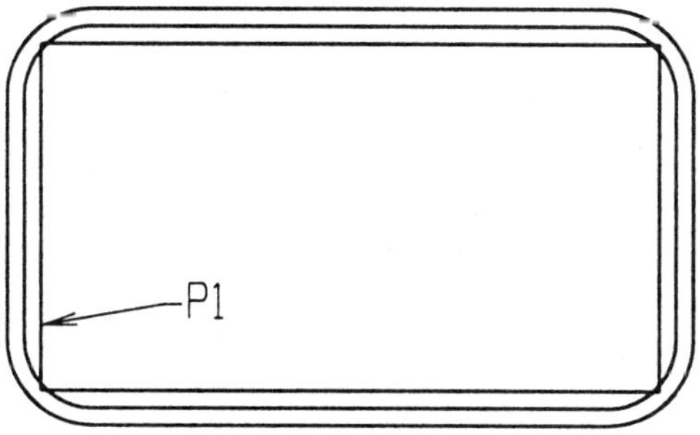

Figure 11.97

Step 7. Add four fillets to the third rectangle. Use the pick points in Figure 11.97.

Select **MAIN MENU → Modify → Fillet → Radius**
Enter the fillet radius: **0.375** ↵
Select **Chain,** pick **P1**
Select **Done** to complete the four fillets.
Now the drawing should look like Figure 11.98.

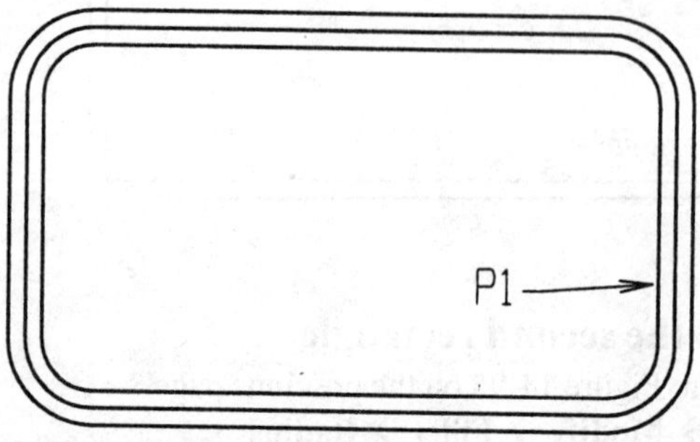

Figure 11.98

Step 8. Translate the third rectangle with fillets to Z-0.25.

Use the pick points in Figure 11.98.
Select **MAIN MENU → Xform → Translate → Chain**
Pick **P1**
Select **Done → Done → Rectang**
Enter the translation vector: **Z-0.25** ↵
Set the Translate parameters as below:

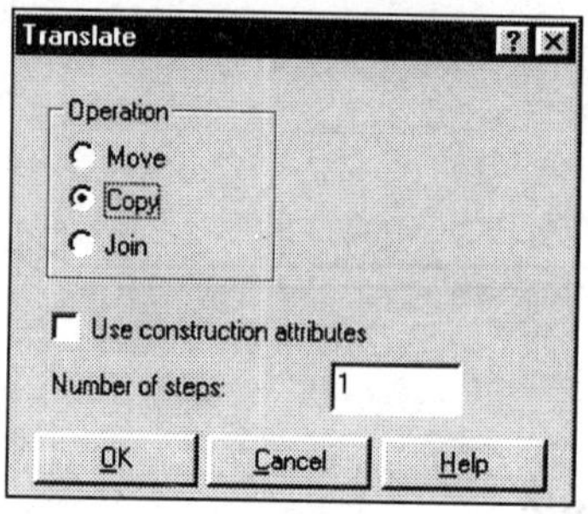

Select **OK**
Select **Gview → Isometric**

The drawing should resemble Figure 11.99.

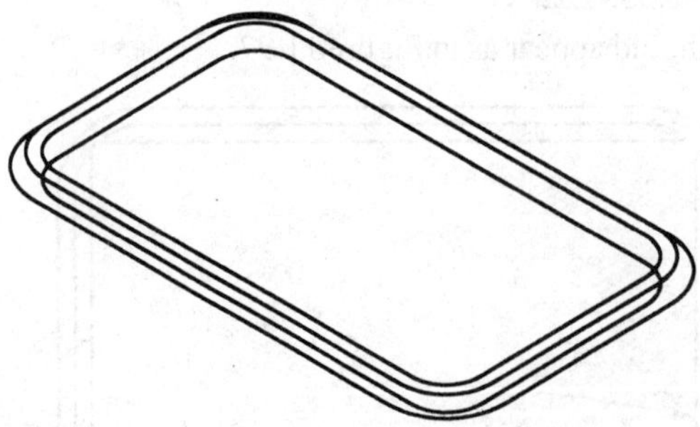

Figure 11.99

Select **Gview** → **Top**

Now the drawing in the top view should look like Figure 11.100.

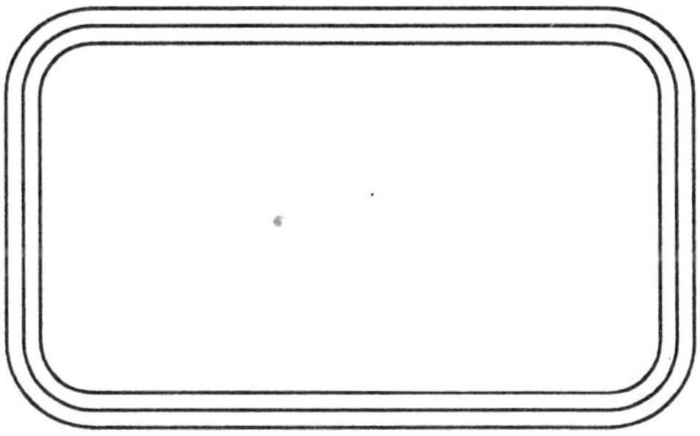

Figure 11.100

Step 9. Create the fourth rectangle.

Select **Z** and then enter **-0.25** ↵

Select **MAIN MENU** → **Create** → **Rectangle** → **1 point**

Enter the width: **4.25** ↵

Enter the height: **2.25** ↵

Select the **lower left corner** → **OK**

Enter coordinates: **2.125,-1.125** ↵

The drawing now appears as in Figure 11.101.

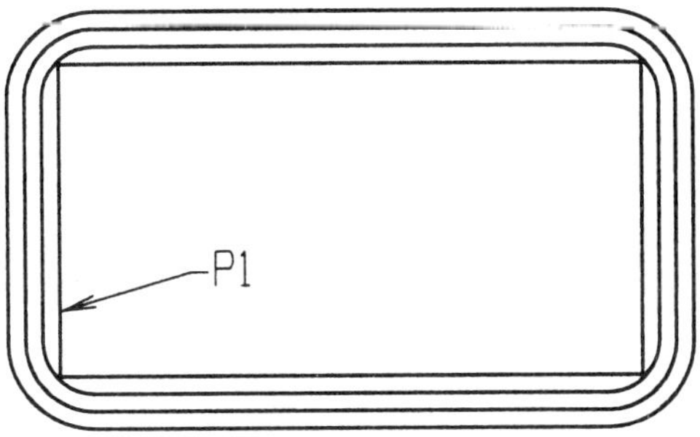

Figure 11.101

Step 10. Add four fillets to the fourth rectangle.

Use the pick points shown in Figure 11.101.

Select **MAIN MENU** ← **Modify** ← **Fillet** ← **Radius**

Enter the fillet radius: **0.25** ↵

Select **Chain**

Pick **P1**

Select **Done** to complete the four fillets.

The drawing should look like Figure 11.102.

Figure 11.102

Step 11. Create two arcs on the top construction plane.

Select **MAIN MENU → Create → Arc → Endpoints**
Enter the first point: **-1.5, -1.125** ↵
Enter the second point: **-1.5, 1.125** ↵
Enter the radius: **1.75** ↵
Select an arc: pick the desired arc (3rd arc from the right)
Enter the first point: **1.5, -1.125** ↵
Enter the second point: **1.5, 1.125** ↵
Enter the radius: **1.75** ↵
Select an arc: pick the desired arc (2nd arc from the right)
Select **Gview → Isometric**
The drawing should resemble Figure 11.103.

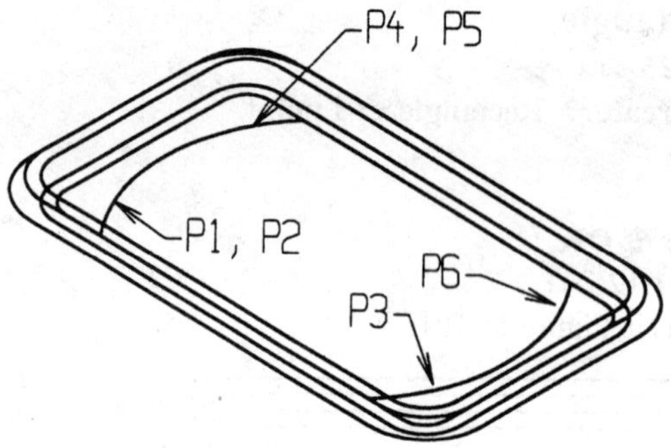

Figure 11.103

Step 12. Create the other two arcs using the front construction plane.

Use the pick points in Figure 11.103.
Select **Cplane → Front**
Select **Z → Endpoint**
Pick **P1** to obtain the Z value of the picked endpoint

Z1.125 should appear in the Secondary Menu.

Select **MAIN MENU → Create → Arc → Endpoints → Endpoint**
Pick **P2,** select endpoint **P3** for the first and second point, respectively
Enter the radius: **1.5** ↵
Select an arc: pick the lower half of the arc to complete the first arc
Select **Z → Endpoint**
Pick **P4** to obtain the Z value of the picked endpoint

Z-1.125 should appear in the Secondary Menu.
Select **Endpoint**

Pick **P5**, select endpoint **P6** for the first and second point, respectively
Enter the radius: **1.5** ↵
Select an arc: pick the desired arc (lower half)

The drawing will appear as in Figure 11.104 .

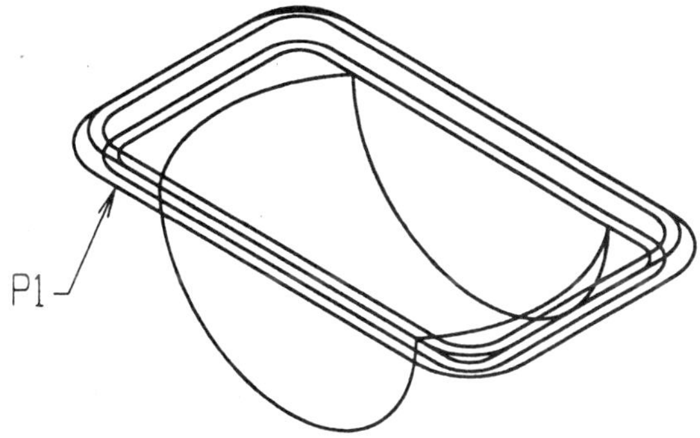

Figure 11.104

Step 13. Translate the outer rectangle to form a rectangular box.

Use the pick points in Figure 11.104.
Select **Cplane → Top**
Sclcct **MAIN MENU → Xform → Translate → Chain**
Selete the first entity in the contour: pick **P1** ↵
Select **Done → Done → Rectang**
Enter the translation vector: **Z-2.375** ↵
Set the Translate parameters as below:

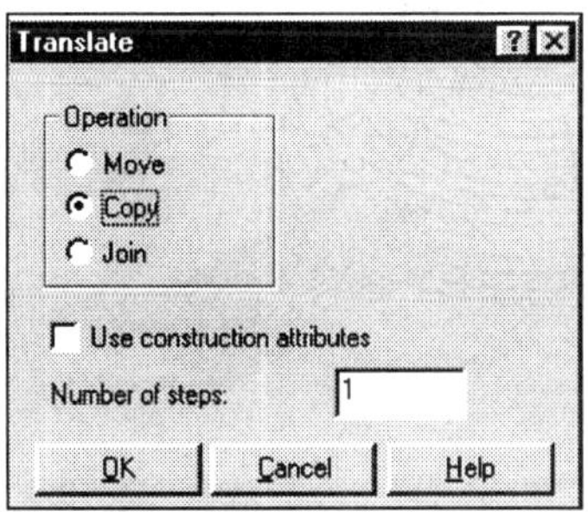

Select **OK**
The final drawing should look like Figure 11.105.

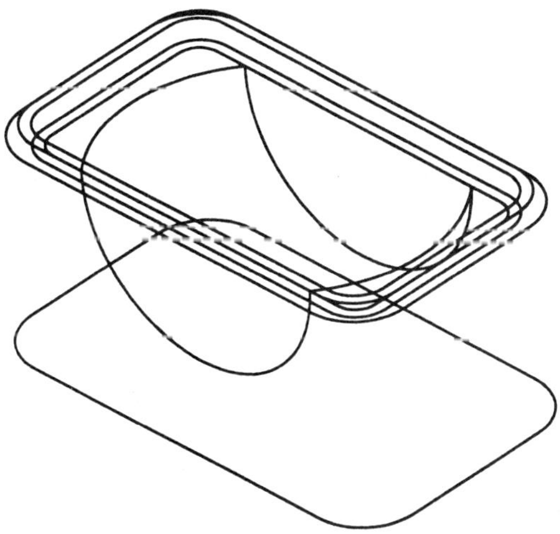

Figure 11.105

Step 14. Save the drawing. Usc the file name flash.

Select **MAIN MENU → File → Save**
Enter the file name: **flash**

Project 13 Hair dryer

The hair dryer consists of three segments: handle, frame, and tube. The wireframe model is shown in Figure 11.106.

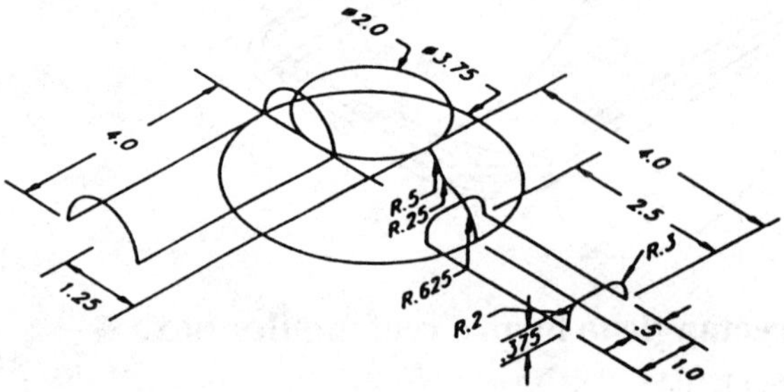

a. Wireframe model

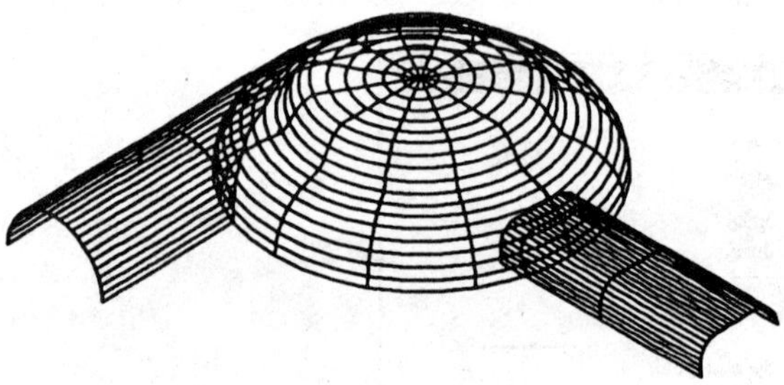

b. Surface model
Figure 11.106

Tips 1. Create three circles in the top construction plane.

2. Construct the edge profile of the frame which is formed by three tangent arcs in the front construction view.
3. Create two semi-circles for making the tube in the front construction view.

4. Construct the handle profile using the top construction view.

5. The edge profiles for the tube and the handle are made longer than needed to ensure that the surfaces intersect.

Step 1. Enter the Mastercam Mill.

Set the Secondary Menu to the following settings:

Z:	**1.0**
Cplane:	**Top**
Gview:	**Top**

Step 2. Create three construction circles using the top construction plane. 13

Select **MAIN MENU →Create → Arc→ Circ pt+rad**
Enter the radius: **1** ↵
Enter the center point: **0,0** ↵
Select **Z**, and then enter **0.625** ↵
Select **BACKUP → Circ pt+rad**
Enter the radius: **1.25 → Origin**
Select **Z**, and then enter **0** ↵
Select **BACKUP → Circ pt+rad**
Enter the radius: **1.875 → Origin**
Select **Gview → Isometric**
The drawing of these three circles should look like Figure 11.107.

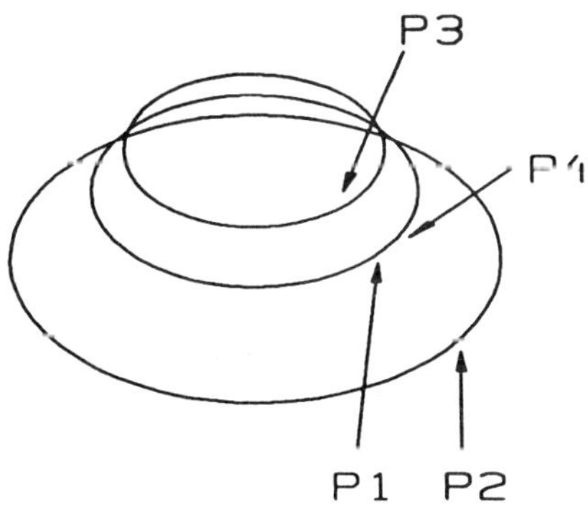

Figure 11.107

Step 3. Create the edge profile of the frame using the front consturction plane.

Use the pick points in Figure 11.107.
Select **Cplane → Front**
Select **Z** and then enter **0** ↵ if necessary
Select **MAIN MENU → Create → Arc → Endpoints → Endpoint**
Pick **P1**, select endpoint **P2**
Enter the radius: **0.625** ↵
Select an arc: pick the desired arc segment (2nd from the right)
Select endpoint: **P3**
Select endpoint: **P4**
Enter the radius: **0.5** ↵
Select an arc: pick the desired arc segment (2nd from the right)

The drawing should look like Figure 11.108.

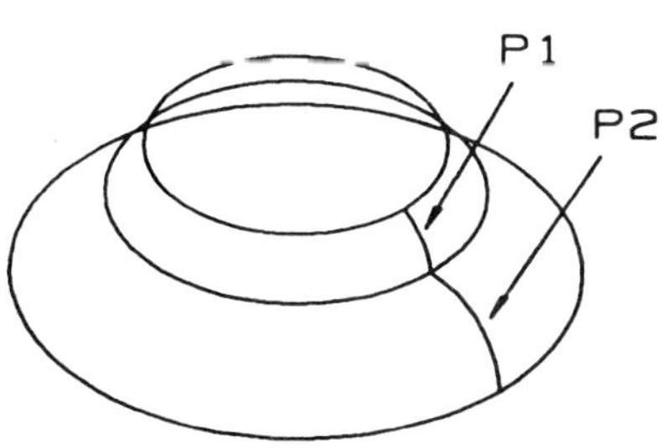

Figure 11.108

Step 4. Create an arc tangent to the two arcs.

Use the pick points from Figure 11.108.
Select **MAIN MENU → Modify → Fillet → Radius**
Enter the fillet radius: **0.25** ↵
Select an entity: pick **P1**
Select another entity: pick **P2**

Now the drawing should appear as in Figure 11.109.

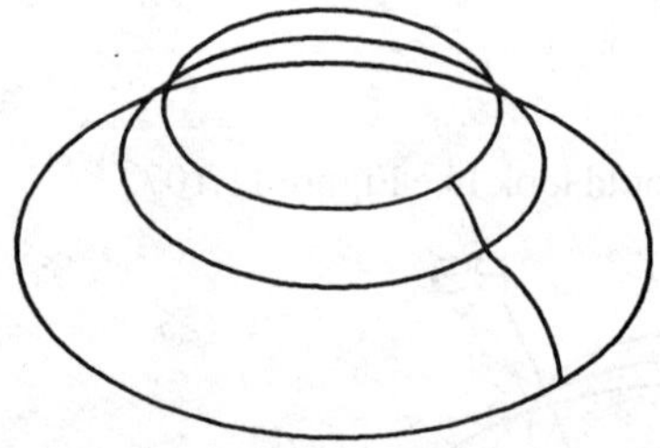

Figure 11.109

Step 5. Create two arcs for the tube.

Select **MAIN MENU → Create → Arc → Polar → Center pt**
Enter the center point: **-1.25,0** ↵
Enter the radius: **0.625** ↵
Enter the initial angle: **0** ↵
Enter the final angle: **180** ↵
Select **Z** and then enter **3.5** ↵
Enter the center point: **-1.25,0** ↵
Enter the radius: **0.625** ↵
Enter the initial angle: **0** ↵
Enter the final angle: **180** ↵

The drawing should appear as in Figure 11.110.

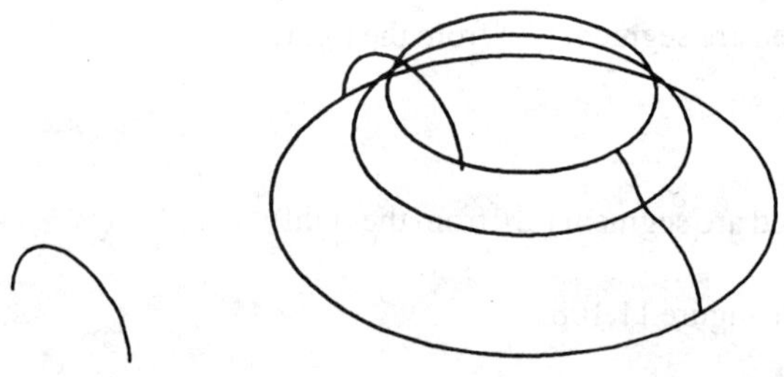

Figure 11.110

Step 6. Create the edge profile of the handle using the side construction view.

Select **Cplane → Side**
Select **Z** and then enter **4.0** ↵
Select **MAIN MENU → Create → Rectangle → 2 points**
Enter the lower left corner: **-0.5, 0** ↵
Enter the upper right corner: **0.5, 0.375** ↵

The drawing should resemble Figure 11.111.

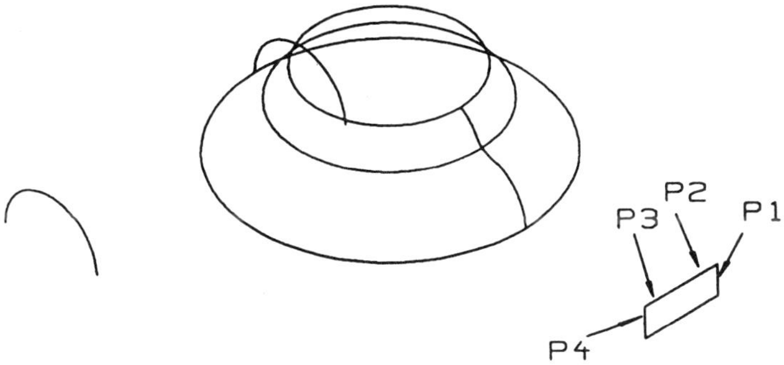

Figure 11.111

Step 7. Add two arcs. Use the pick points in Figure 11.111.

Select **MAIN MENU → Modify → Fillet → Radius**
Enter the fillet radius: **0.3** ↵
Select an entity: pick **P1** ↵
Select another entity: pick **P2** ↵
Select **Radius**
Enter the fillet radius: **0.2** ↵
Select an entity: pick **P3**
Select another entity: pick **P4**
The drawing should appear as Figure 11.112.

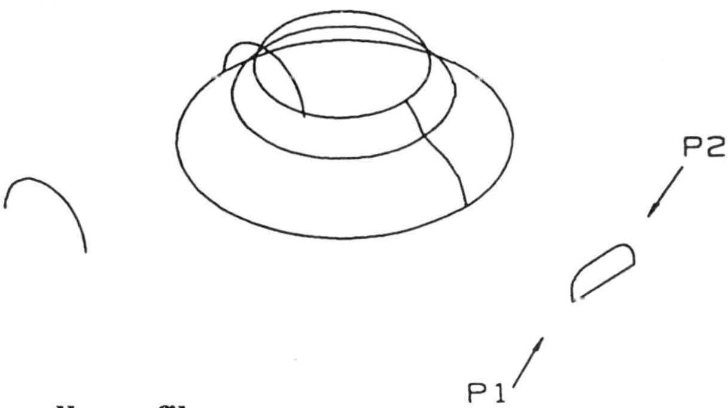

Figure 11.112

Step 8. Translate the handle profile.

Use the pick points in Figure 11.112.
Select **MAIN MENU → Xform → Translate → Window**
Enter the first corner: pick **P1**
Enter the second corner: pick **P2**
Select **Done → Rectang**
Enter the translation vector: **Z-2.5** ↵
Set the Translate paramenters as here:

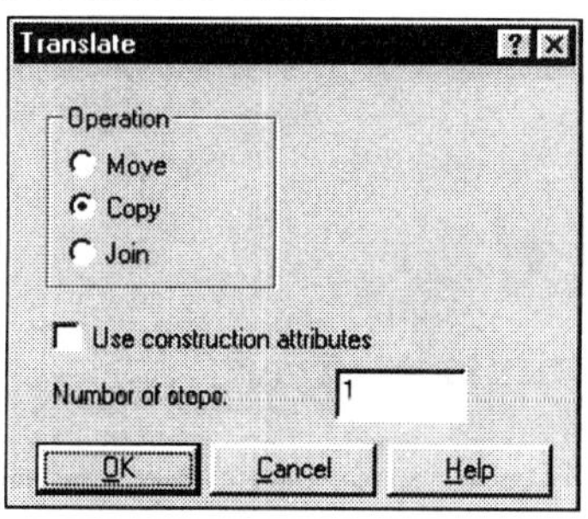

Select **OK**

The drawing should resemble Figure 11.113.

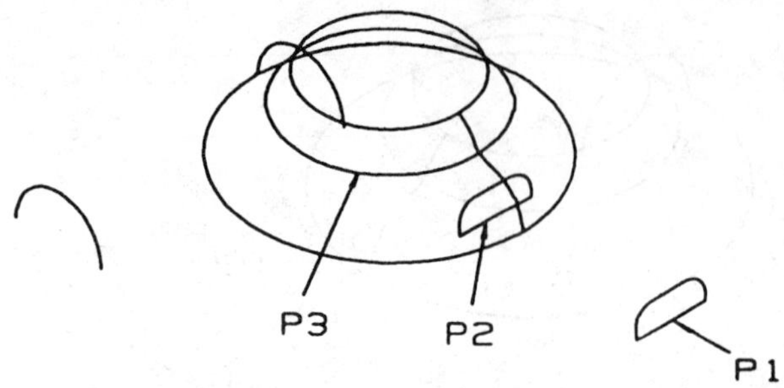

Figure 11.113

Step 9. Delete construction lines. Use the pick points in Figure 11.113.

Select **MAIN MENU** → **Delete**

Pick **P1, P2,** and **P3**

The new drawing appears as Figure 11.114.

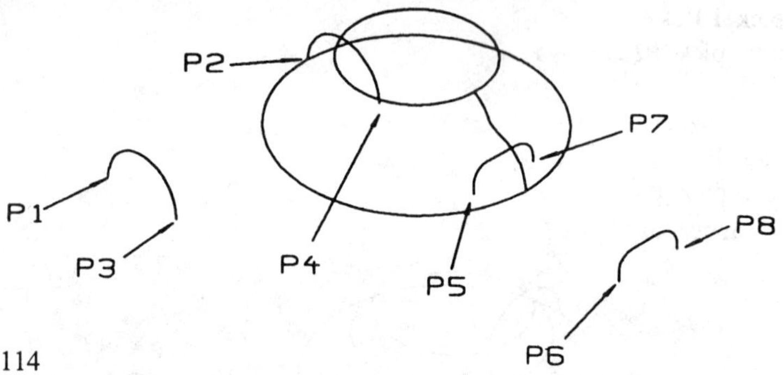

Figure 11.114

Step 10. Construct four lines to join two arcs and two handle profiles using the 3D construction plane. Use the pick points in Figure 11.114.

Select **Cplane** → **3D**

Select **MAIN MENU** → **Create** → **Line** → **Endpoints**

Sequentially pick **P1 - P8** to complete the four lines

The final drawing should resemble Figure 11.115.

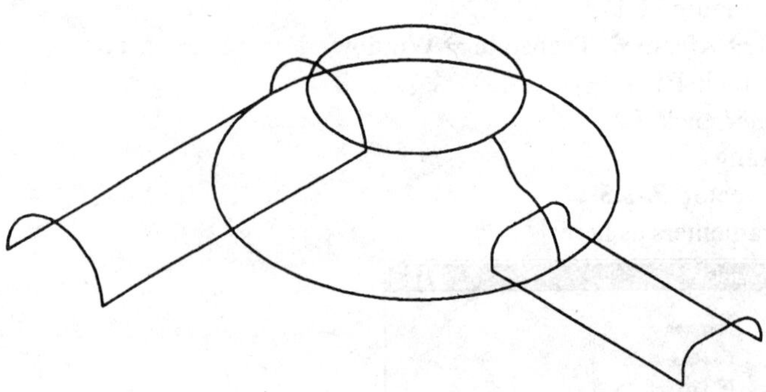

Figure 11.115

Step 11. Save the drawing using the filename: dryer.

Select **MAIN MENU** → **File** → **Save**

Enter the file name: **dryer**

Project 14

The surface shown in Figure 11.116 is defined by **five** contours including one circle at one end, one line-profile at the other end, and three ellipses. These three ellipses are obtained by rotating a circle at a specified angle and then projecting it onto a vertical plannar surface as shown in Figure 11.117. Since the part is symmetrical about the axis, only one half of the part profile contours is required. The other half is obtained by mirroring the profile contours about the X axis. The plannar surface used for the curves to be projected onto in obtaining a surface curve can be generated as a ruled surface. Ruled surfaces are covered in chapter 12.

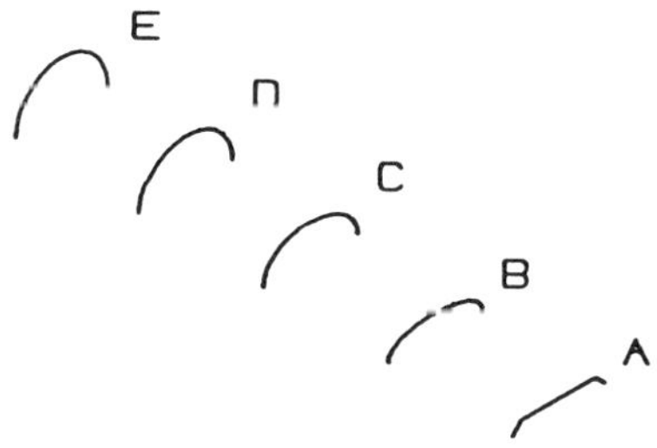

Figure 11.116a. Wireframe model

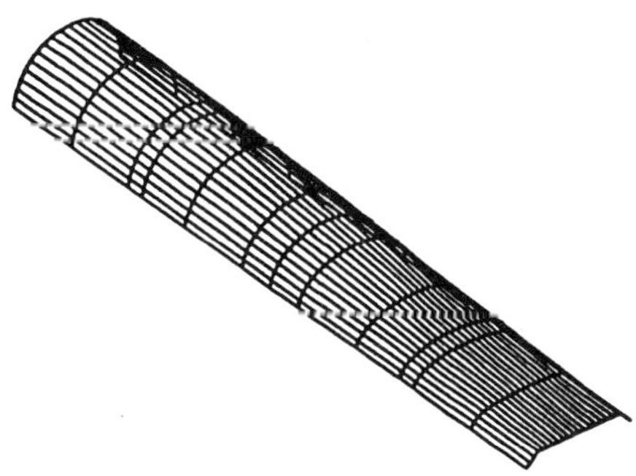

Figure 11.116b. Surface model

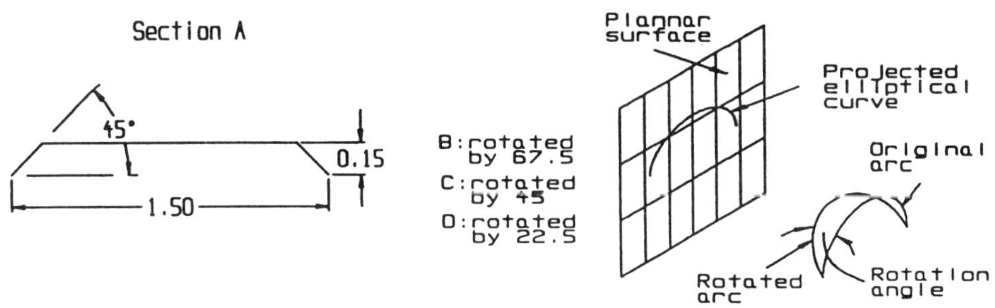

Figure 11.117

Step 1. Enter the Mastercam Mill.

Set these values: Gview to Isometric, Cplane to side plane, and Z value to 3.0.

Select **Gview → Isometric**

Select **Cplane → Side**

Select **Z** and then enter **3.0** ↵

Step 2. Create a semi-circle.

Select **MAIN MENU →Create → Arc → Polar → Center pt**

Enter the center point: **0,0** ↵

Enter the radius: **0.75** ↵

Enter the initial angle: **0** ↵

Enter the final angle: **180** ↵

The drawing should resemble Figure 11.118.

The drawing should resemble Figure 11.118.

Figure 11.118

Step 3. Create two horizontal lines for generating a ruled surface.

Select **Z** and then enter **0.5** ↵

Select **MAIN MENU → Create → Line → Endpoints**

Enter the first endpoint: **-1.5, 1.5** ↵

Enter the second endpoint: **1.5, 1.5** ↵

Enter the first endpoint: **-1.5, -1.5** ↵

Enter the second endpoint: **1.5, -1.5** ↵

These two lines now appear as in Figure 11.119.

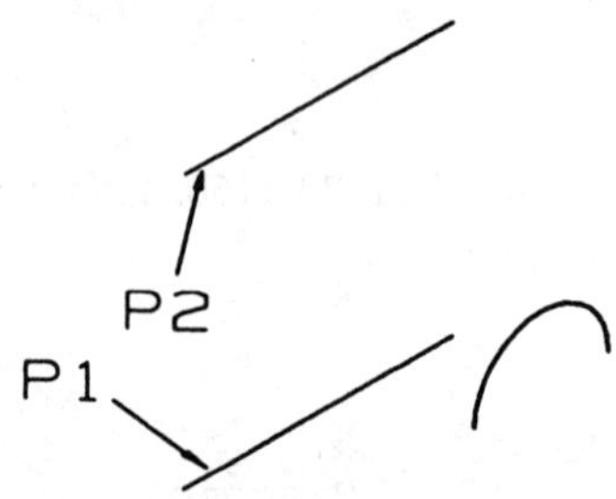

Figure 11.119

Step 4. Create a ruled surface.

Use the pick points in Figure 11.119.

Select **MAIN MENU → Create → Surface → Ruled**

Select **Single** from the chaining method menu, then pick **P1** for contour 1

Pick **P2** for contour 2

Select **Done** to complete the selection

Toggle Surface type to **N** (for NURBS)

Select **Do it** from the ruled surface parameters menu

The ruled surface should appear as in Figure 11.120.

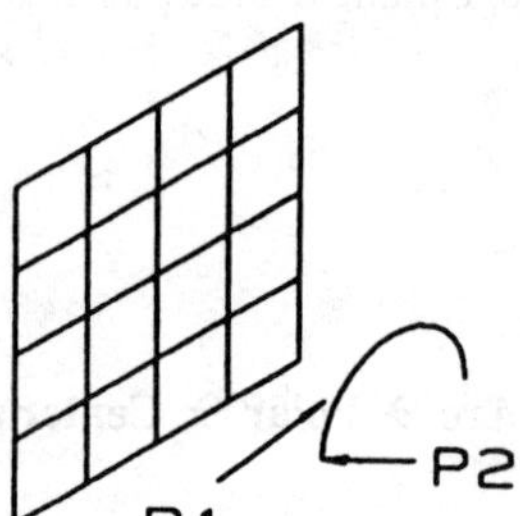

Figure 11.120

Step 5. Copy the arc twice by 22.5°, use 3 as the number of steps.

Use the pick points in Figure 11.120.
Select **Cplane → Front**
Select **MAIN MENU → Xform → Rotate → Only → Arcs**
Pick **P1** to select the entity
Select **BACKUP → Done → Endpoint**
Pick **P2** to trap the endpoint of the entity
Set the Rotate parameters as here:

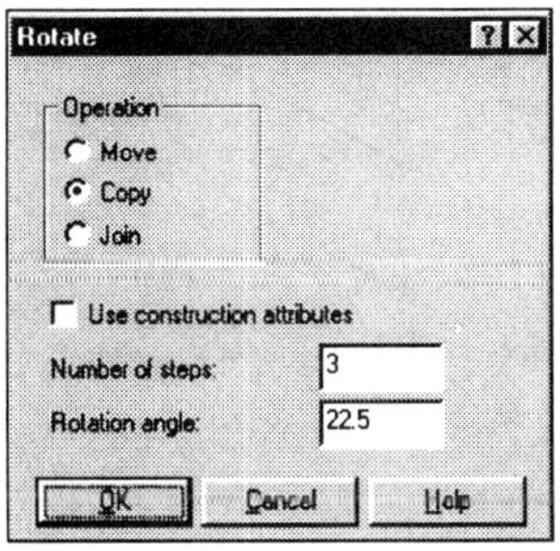

Select **OK**
The drawing is shown in Figure 11.121.

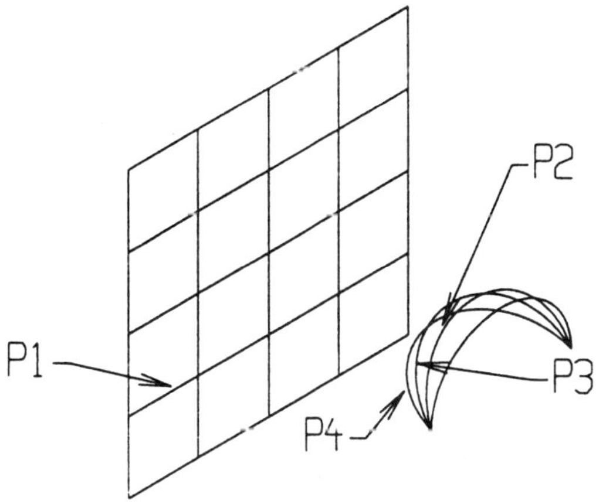

Figure 11.121

Step 6. Project the three arcs onto the plannar plane. Use the Side construction plane.

Usc the pick points in Figure 11.121.
Select **Cplane → Side**
Select **MAIN MENU → Create → Curve → Project**

Pick **P1** to select the ruled surface
Select **Done**
Select **Single** from the chaining method menu
Pick **P2** to **P4** to select three arcs
Select **Done → Do it**

The new drawing becomes Figure 11.122.

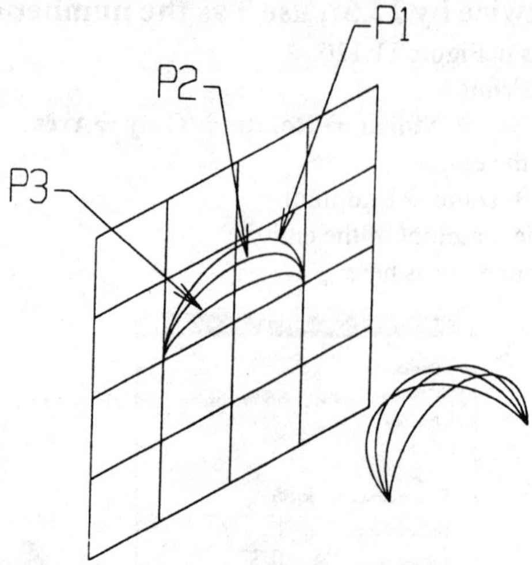

Figure 11.122

Step 7. Translate the 3 curves to their proper positions.

Use the pick points labeled above in Figure 11.122.
Select **MAIN MENU → Xform → Translate → Only → Splines**
Pick **P1** to select the entity
Select **BACKUP → Done → Rectang**
Enter the translation vector: **Z-6.5**
Set the Translate parameters as shown here:

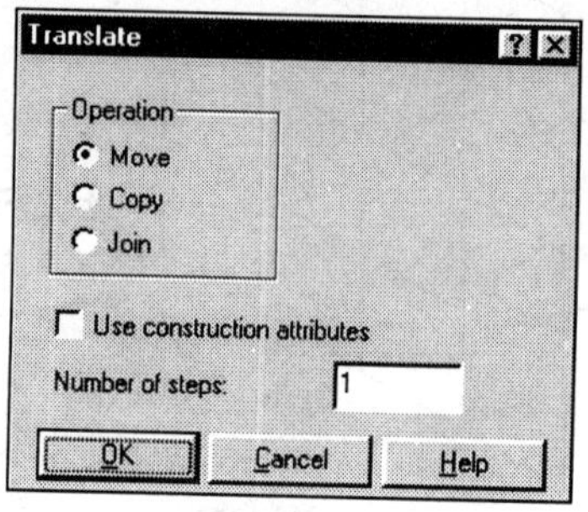

Select **OK** to move the first curve

Pick **P2** to select the second curve
Select **Done → Rectang**
Enter the translation vector: **Z-4.5**

Select **OK** from the Translation dialog box
Pick **P3** to select the third curve
Select **Done → Rectang**
Enter the translation vector: **Z-2.5**

Select **OK** from the Translate dialog box

The new drawing becomes Figure 11.123.

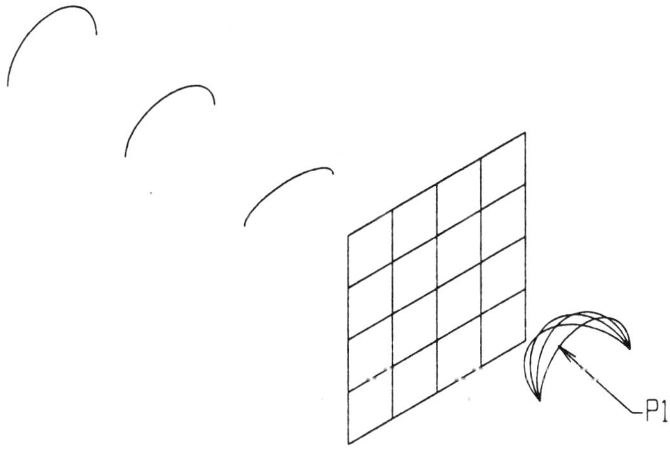

Figure 11.123

Step 8. Translate the original arc.

Use the Pick points in Figure 11.123.
Pick **P1** to select the original arc
Select **Done → Rectang**
Enter the translation vector: **Z-11**
Select **OK** from the Translate dialog box

The new drawing becomes Figure 11.124.

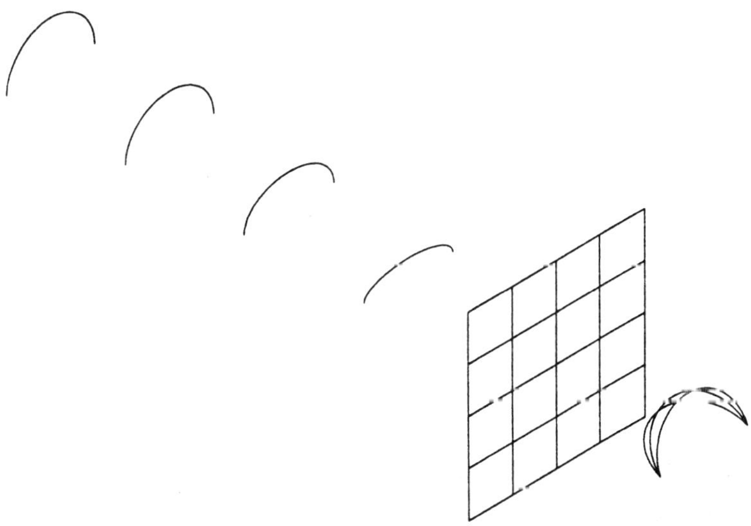

Figure 11.124

Step 9. Delete three curves, two lines and one surface.

Select **MAIN MENU → Delete**
Pick three curves, ruled surface, and two lines to delete from the model.

The drawing should resemble Figure 11.125.

Figure 11.125

Step 10. Construct the sectional profile at A.

Select **Z** and then enter **0** ↵
Select **MAIN MENU → Create → Line → Multi**
Specify point 1: **-0.75, 0** ↵
Specify point 2: **-0.6, 0.15** ↵
Specify point 3: **0.6, 0.15** ↵
Specify point 4: **0.75, 0** ↵

The final drawing should resemble Figure 11.126.

Figure 11.126

Step 11. Save the drawing. Use the Filename: loft3.

Select **MAIN MENU → File → Save**
Enter the file name: **loft3**

Project 15

A fan, shown in Figure 11.127, consists of seven blades that are evenly spaced around the hub. The two ends of each blade have the same cross section profile (Figure 11.128). The inside end is rotated 15° with the horizontal line and the outside end is rotated 40° with respect to the line. The end profile is curved along the hub profile.

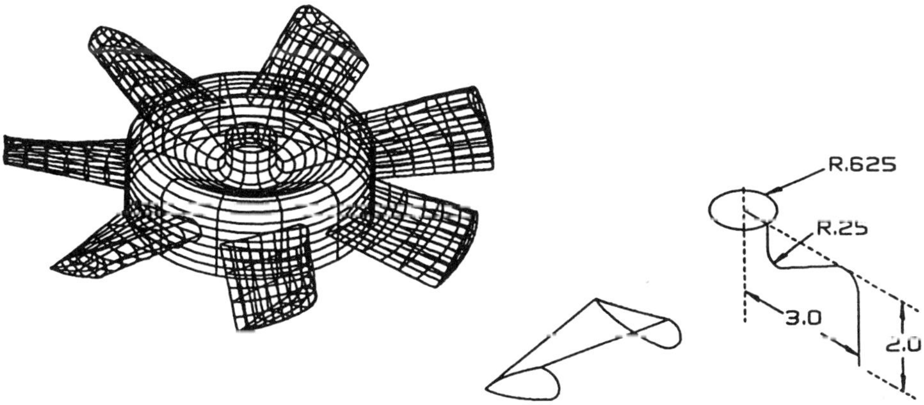

Figure 11.127

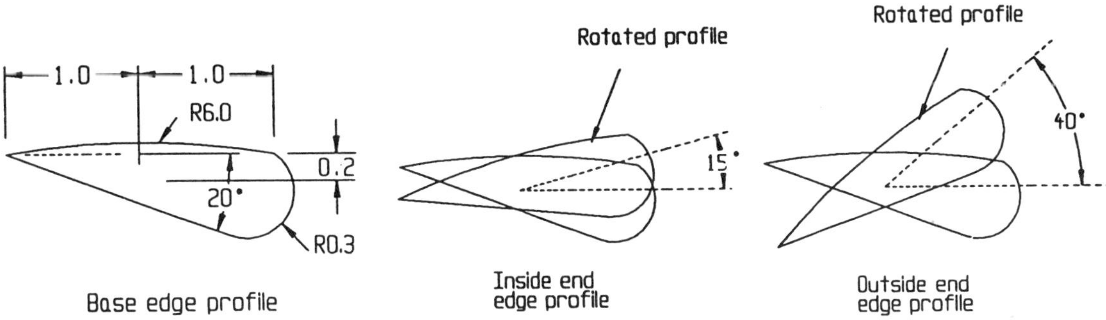

Figure 11.128

Tips 1. Create the edge profile for the hub using the Front Cplane.

2. Construct the cross section profile of the blade in the Front Cplane.

3. Create a swept surface for the outer rim which is a cylinder. This surface is used to obtain the surface curves by projecting the cross section profile onto this surface.
4. Rotate the blade edge profile by 15° with the horizontal axis, and then project it onto the outer rim surface to obtain a curved edge profile for the inside end.
5. Rotate the blade profile by 40° with the horizontal axis and then project it onto the outer rim surface to obtain the outside edge profile of the blade. This edge profile is then translated to the specified position.
6. Use different levels and colors to facilitate the creation of the wireframe model.

Select **Cplane → Front**
Select **Gview → Front**
Select **MAIN MENU → Create → Line → Multi**
Specify endpoint 1: **0,1** ↵
Specify endpoint 2: **0.625,1** ↵
Specify endpoint 3: **0.625,0** ↵
Specify endpoint 4: **2.5,1** ↵

The drawing with three lines should appears as Figure 11.129.

Figure 11.129

Step 2. Create a horizontal line and a vertical line.

Select **BACKUP → Endpoints**
Specify the first endpoint: **1,1** ↵
Specify the second endpoint: **4,1** ↵
Specify the first endpoint: **3,1.5** ↵
Specify the second endpoint: **3, -1** ↵

The new drawing should look like Figure 11.130.

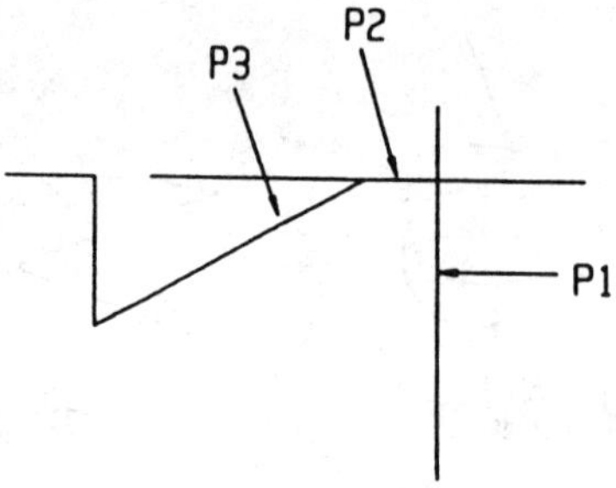

Figure 11.130

Step 3. Create an arc using the pick points in Figure 11.130.

Select **MAIN MENU → Create → Arc → Tangent → 3 ents/pts**
Pick **P1, P2,** and **P3** to select the three entities

The arc added to the drawing now appears as Figure 11.131.

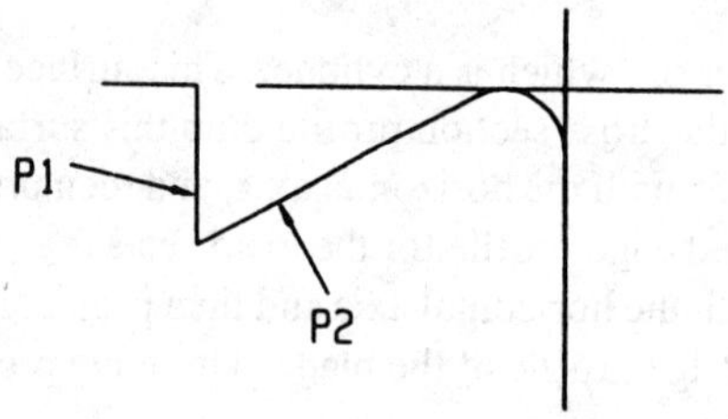

Figure 11.131

Step 4. Create a fillet using the pick points in Figure 11.131.

Select **MAIN MENU → Modify → Fillet → Radius**
Enter the fillet radius: **0.25** ↵
Pick **P1** and **P2**

The fillet is added to the drawing as shown in Figure 11.132.

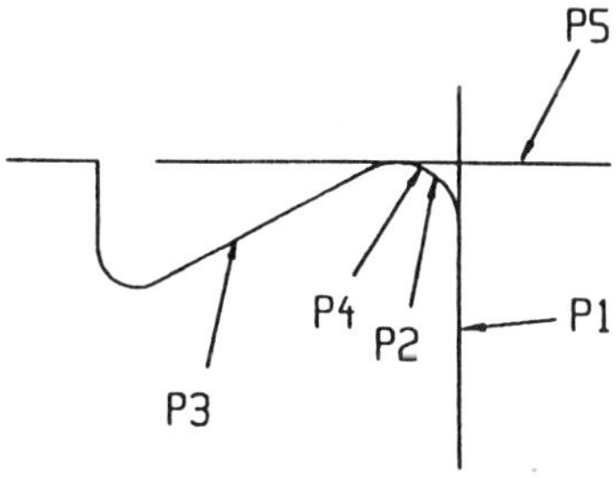

Figure 11.132

Step 5. Trim the vertical line and the slope line.

Then delete the horizontal line using the pick points in Figure 11.132 .
Select **BACKUP → Trim → 1 entity**
Pick **P1** and **P2** to trim the vertical line
Pick **P3** and **P4** to trim the slope line
Select **MAIN MENU → Delete**
Pick **P5** to delete the horizontal line

The hub profile should look like Figure 11.133.

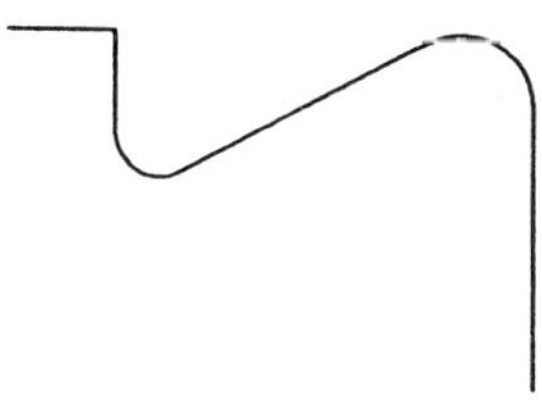

Figure 11.133

Step 6. Create a circle using Top Cplane. Change Gview to Isometric.

Select **Cplane → Top**
Select **Gview → Isometric**
Select **Z** then enter **1** ↵
Select **MAIN MENU → Create → Arc → Circ pt + rad**
Enter the radius: **0.625** ↵
Enter the center point: **0,0** ↵

The hub profile should resemble Figure 11.134.

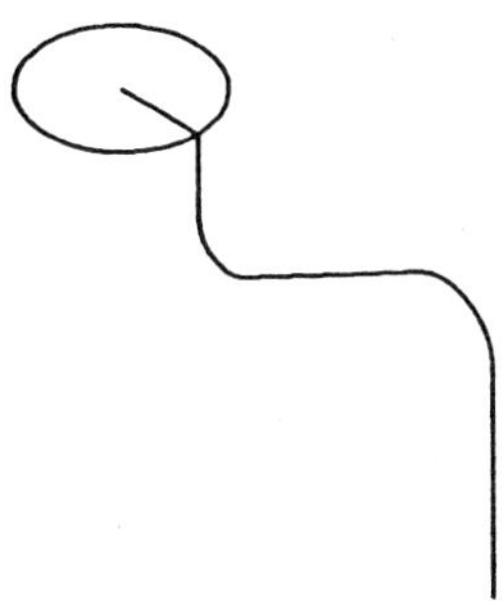

Figure 11.134

Step 7. Create the blade edge profile using Front Cplane.

Change the level to 2 and the color to 11.
Select **Level**, then enter **2** ↵
Select **Color** then **11** ↵
Select **Cplane** → **Front**
Select **Z** then enter **6** ↵
Select **MAIN MENU** → **Create** → **Arc** → **Endpoints**
Enter the first point: **-1,0.2** ↵
Enter the second point: **1,0.2** ↵
Enter the radius: **6** ↵
Select an arc: pick at the desired arc segment (smaller concave arc)

The arc appears on the screen as Figure 11.135.

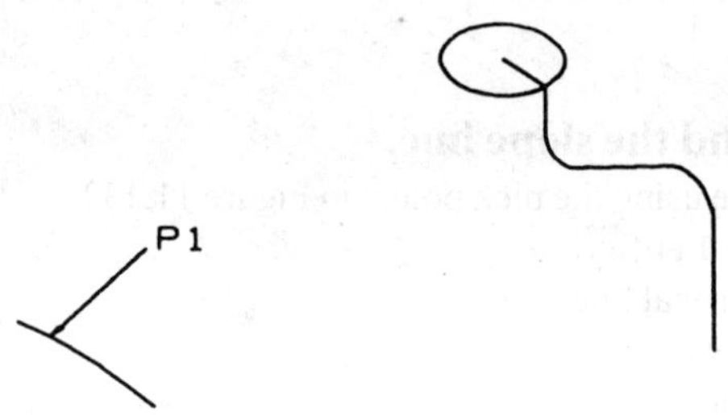

Figure 11.135

Step 8. Create a slope line using the pick points in Figure 11.135.

Select **MAIN MENU** → **Create** → **Line** → **Polar** → **Endpoint**
Pick **P1**
Enter the angle in degrees: **-20** ↵
Enter the line length: **3** ↵

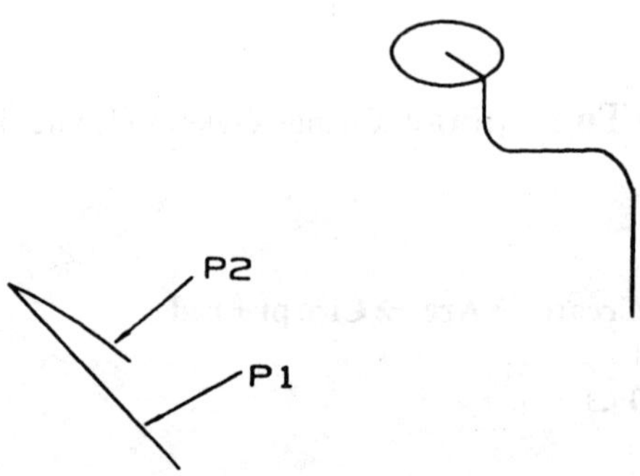

Figure 11.136

Step 9. Create an arc tangent to the slope line.

Use pick points from Figure 11.136.
Select **MAIN MENU** → **Create** → **Arc** → **Tangent** → **Point**
Pick **P1** for the arc to be tangent to
Enter the thru point: select **Endpoint** from the Point Menu
Pick **P2**
Enter the radius: **.35** ↵
Select an arc: pick at the desired arc segment (2nd arc from right)

The new drawing should look like Figure 11.137.

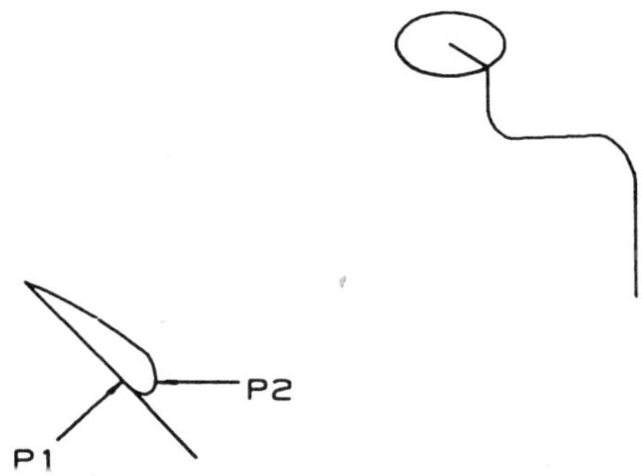

Figure 11.137

Step 10. Trim the slope line using the pick points in Figure 11.137.

Select **MAIN MENU → Modify → Trim → 1 entity**

Sequentially pick **P1** and **P2** to complete the trimming

The trimmed profile should appear as Figure 11.138.

Figure 11.138

Step 11. Extend the vertical line.

Use the pick point in Figure 11.138.

Select **MAIN MENU →Modify → Extend → Length**

Enter the length to extend: **2**

Pick **P1** to extend the line

The line is extended as in Figure 11.139.

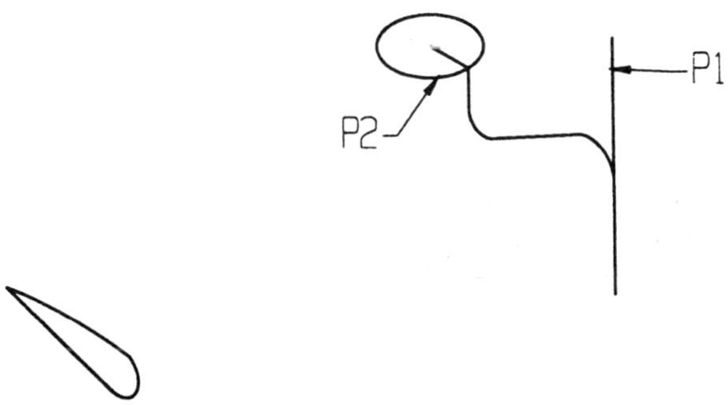

Figure 11.139

Step 12. Create a swept surface using the pick points in Figure 11.139.

Change level to 3 and color to 12.
Select **Level** then enter **3 →OK**
Select **Color** then enter **12 →OK**
Select **MAIN MENU → Create → Surface → Sweep**
Define the across contour: select **Single**, then pick **P1→Done**
Define the along contour 1: pick **P2→ Done**
Set the Sweep surface parameters to the following settings:

Surface error tolerance = **0.002** Surface type = **NURBS** **Rotate** the across contour

Select **Do it** to complete the surface

The swept surface appears as Figure 11.140.

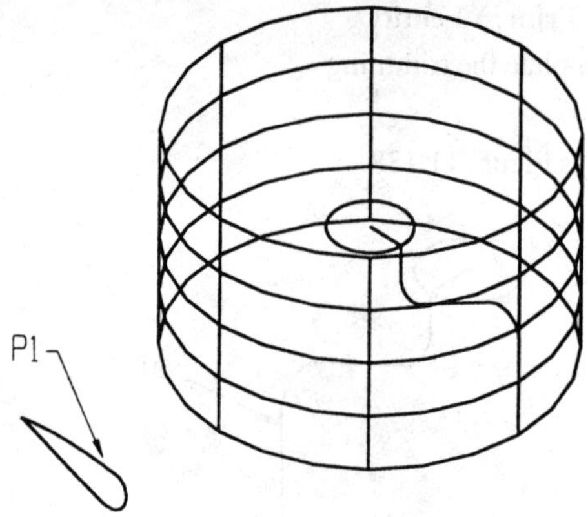

Figure 11.140

Step 13. Rotate the blade edge profile by 15°, use the pick points in Figure11.140.

Change level to 4 and color to 13.
Select **Level** then enter **4 →OK**
Select **Color** then enter **13 →OK**
Select **MAIN MENU → Xform → Rotate → Chain**
Pick **P1**
Select **Done → Done → Origin**
Set the Rotate parameters here:

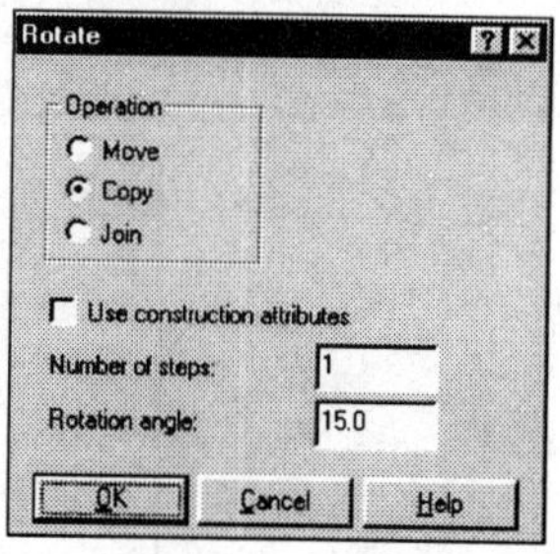

Select **OK**

The rotated profile is shown in Figure 11.141

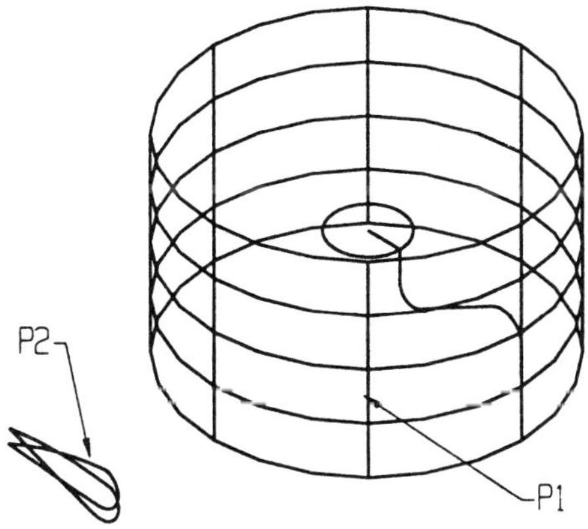

Figure 11.141

Step 14. Projcct the rotated profile onto the swept surface using the pick points in Figure 11.141.

Select **MAIN MENU → Create → Curve → Project**
Pick **P1** to select a surface **→Done**
Select **Chain** then pick **P2**
Select **Done**
Sclcct **Options**
Set the projection Curve parameters as shown in this menu:

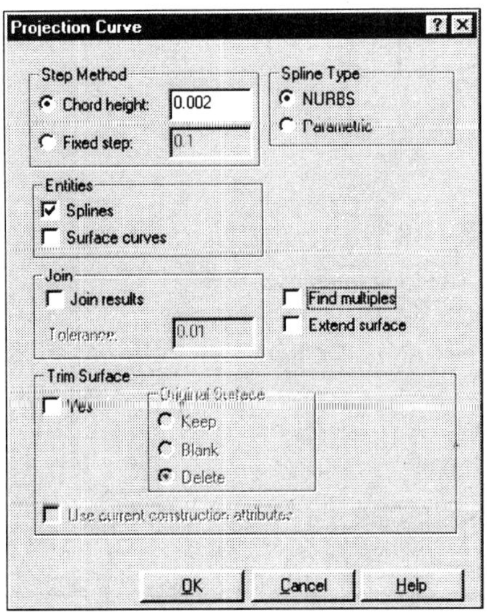

Select **OK**
Set view/norm to **V** (for view)
Set Trim to **N** (for No)
Select **Do It**

The surface curve on the Swept surface is shown in Figure 11.142.

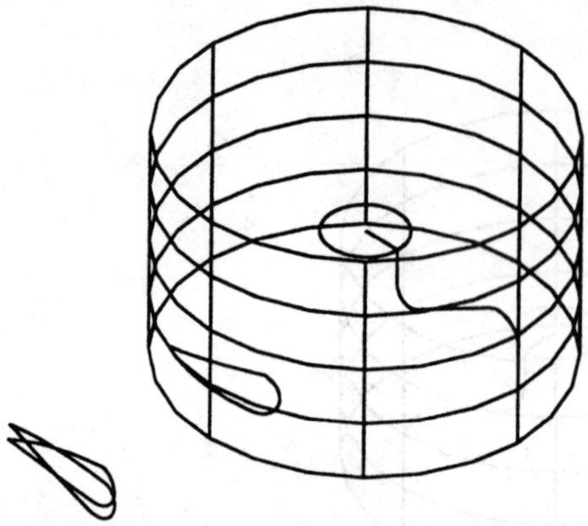

Figure 11.142

Step 15. Make level 4 invisible.

Select **Level**, then uncheck **Visible** for level 4,
then **OK** → **OK** to return back to graphic mode
The drawing becomes Figure 11.143.

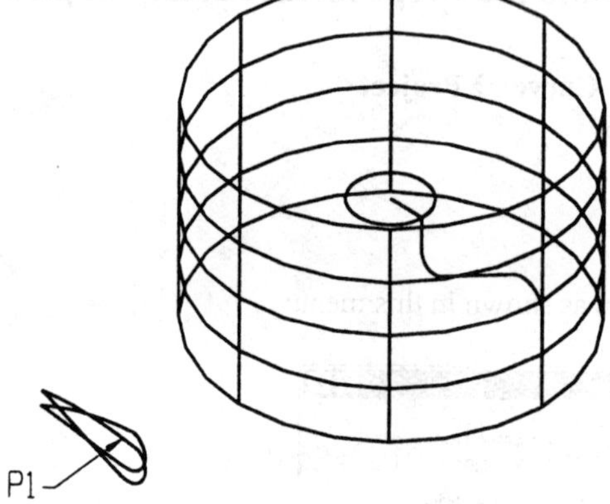

Figure 11.143

Step 16. Rotate the edge profile by 40°.

Use the pick points in Figure 11.143. Change level to 5.
Select **Level,** then enter **5** →**OK**
Select **MAIN MENU** → **Xform** → **Rotate** → **Chain**
Pick **P1**
Select **Done** → **Done** → **Origin**
Set the Rotate parameters as below:

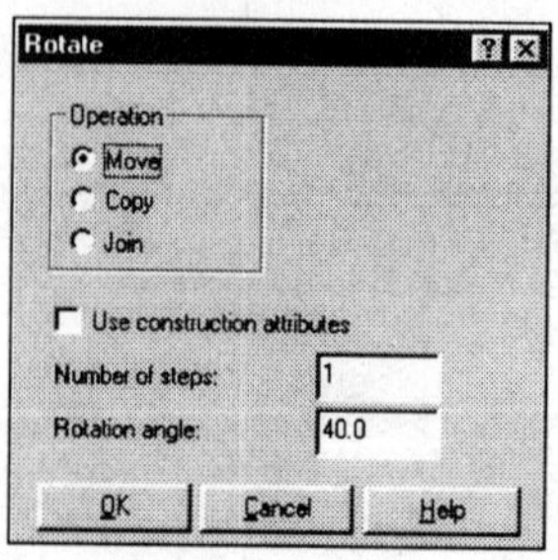

Select **OK**

The rotated profile is shown in Figure 11.144.

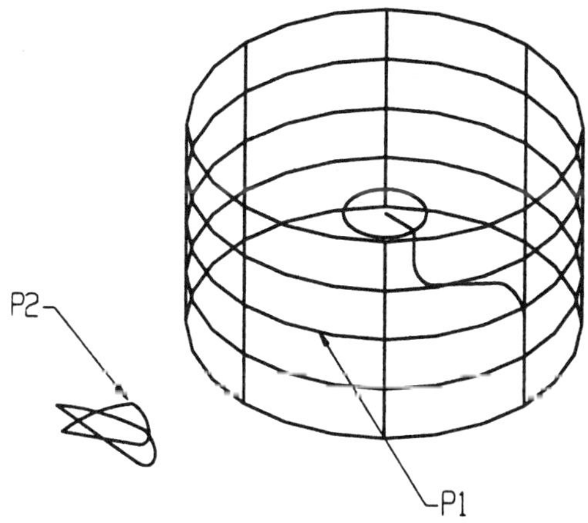

Figure 11.144

Step 17. Project the profile onto the surface using the pick points in Figure 11.144.

Select **MAIN MENU → Create → Curve → Project**
Pick **P1** to select the surface
Select **Done**
Select **Chain** then pick **P2**
Select **Done → Do it**

The drawing should resemble Figure 11.145.

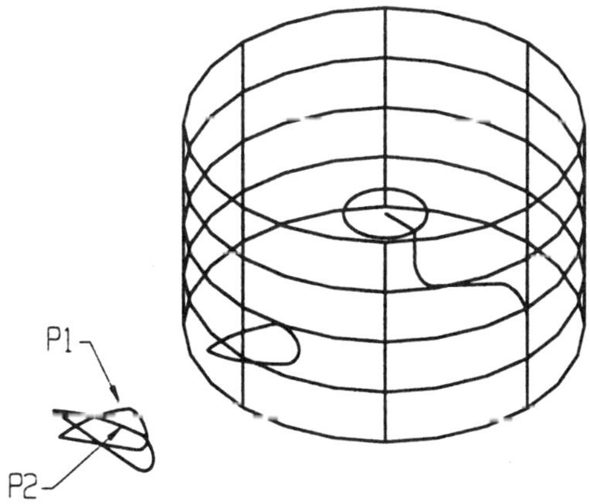

Figure 11.145

Step 18. Delete the rotated profile using the pick points in Figure 11.145.

Select **MAIN MENU → Delete →Chain**
Pick **P1** and **P2**
Select **Done** to delete the two contours

The new drawing should look like Figure 11.146.

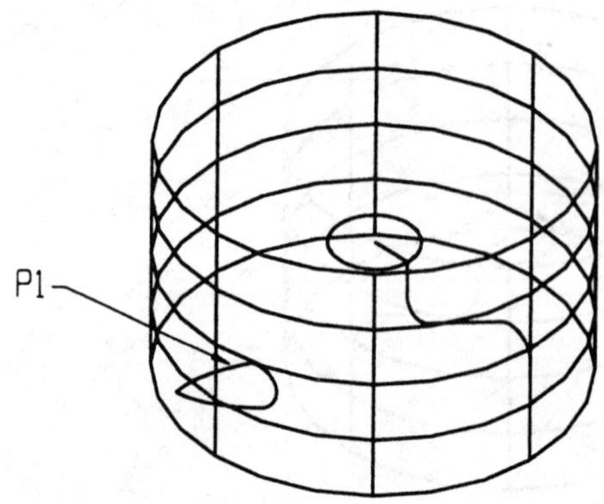

Figure 11.146

Step 19. Translate the projected curve back to the desired position using the pick points in Figure 11.146.

Select **MAIN MENU → Xform → Translate → Chain**
Pick **P1**
Select **Done → Done → Rectang**
Enter the translation vector: **Z3** ↵
Set the Translate parameters as below:

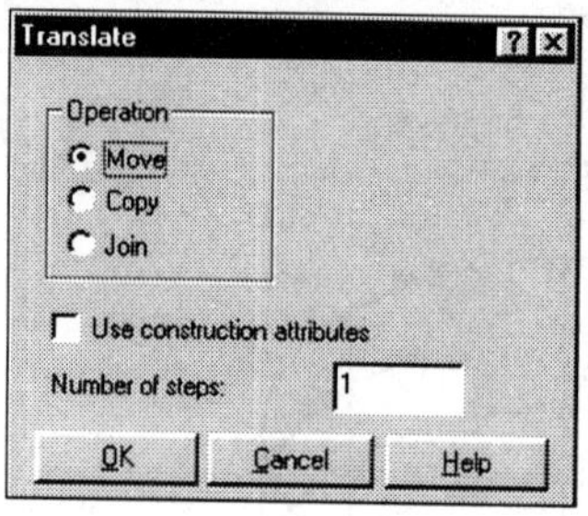

Select **OK**

The drawing becomes Figure 11.147.

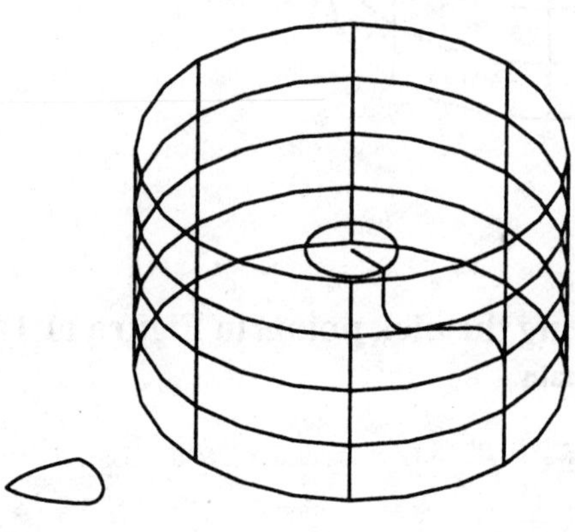

Figure 11.147

Step 20. Make level 4 visible.

Select **Level**, then check **Visible** on the level 4

Click on the **OK** to return back to graphic mode

The new drawing should resemble Figure 11.148.

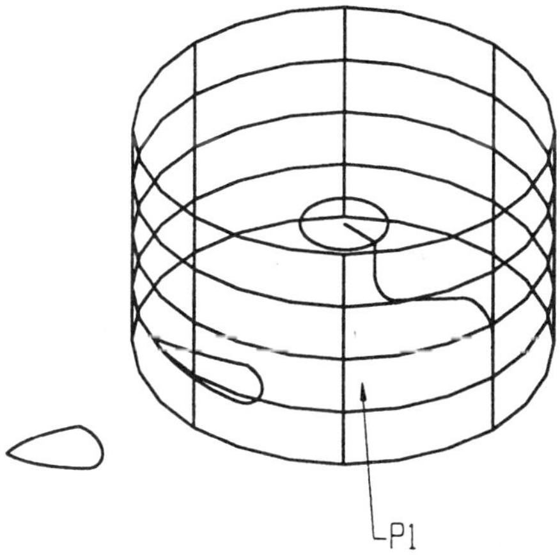

Figure 11.148

Step 21. Delete the surface curve and the swept surface using the pick points in Figure 11.148.

Select **MAIN MENU → Delete**

Pick **P1** to delete the swept surface

The drawing should look like Figure 11.149.

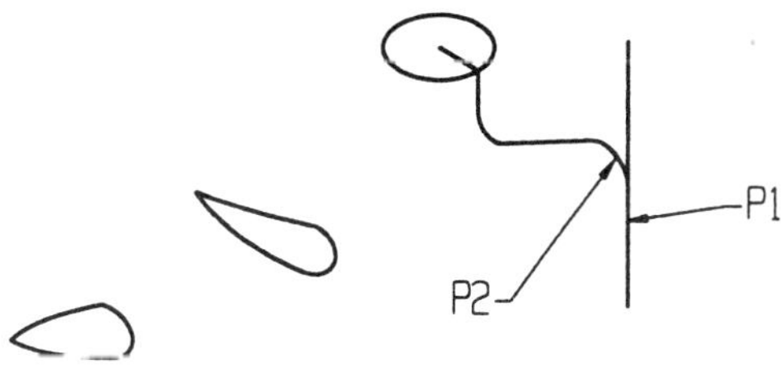

Figure 11.149

Step 22. Trim the vertical line.

Use the pick points in Figure 11.149.

Select **MAIN MENU → Modify → Trim → 1 entity**

Pick **P1** and **P2** sequentially to trim the line

The new drawing becomes Figure 11.150.

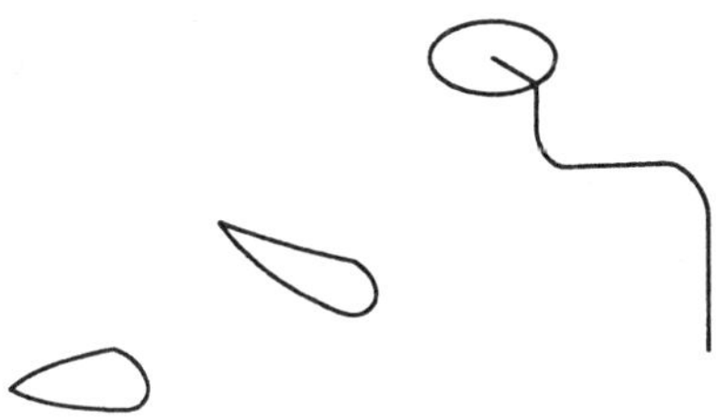

Figure 11.150

Step 23. Make level 1 invisible.

Select **Level,** then uncheck Visible on **level 1**

Select **OK** to return back to graphic mode

The drawing becomes Figure 11.151.

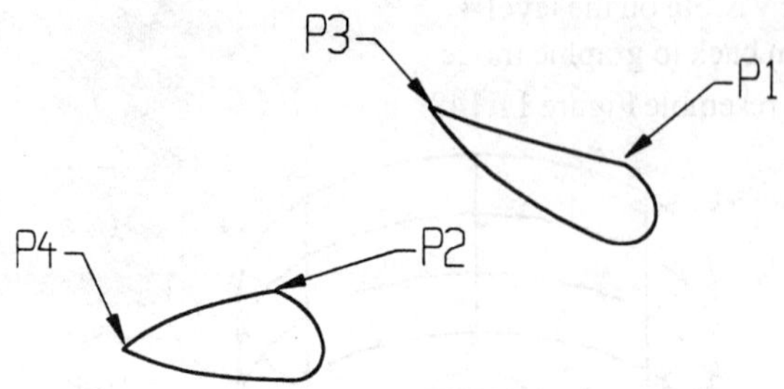

Figure 11.151

Step 24. Create two lines connecting the two profiles using the pick points in Figure 11.151. Use the 3D Cplane.

Select **Cplane → 3D**
Select **MAIN MENU → Create → Line → Endpoints**
Pick **P1** and **P2** for the first line
Pick **P3** and **P4** for the second line
The wireframe model needed of the blade should resemble Figure 11.152.

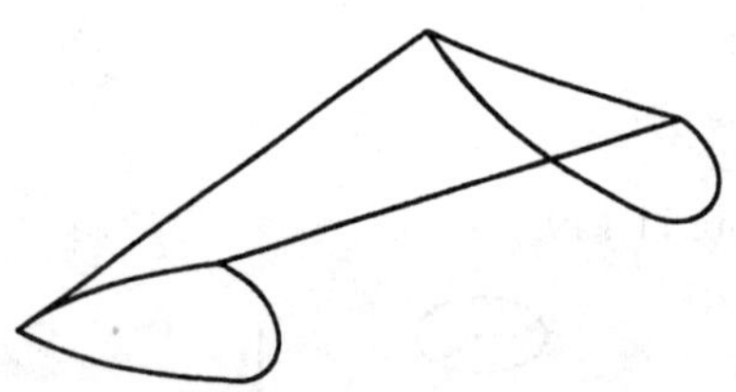

Figure 11.152

Step 25. Toggle level 1 back to visible.

Select **Level**, check **Visible** on **level 1**
Select **OK** to return back to graphic mode
The final wireframe model should look like Figure 11.153.

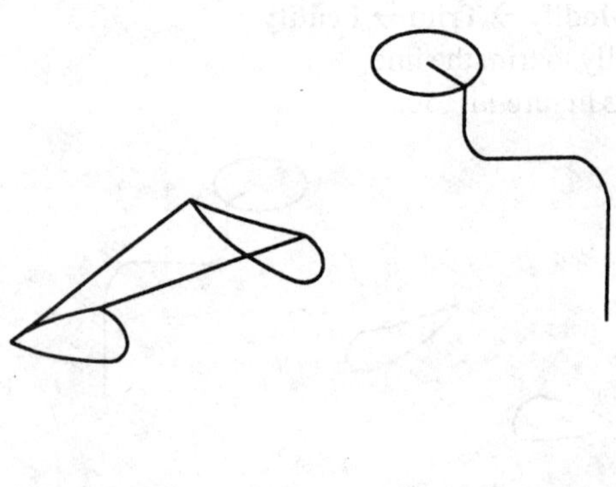

Figure 11.153

Step 26. Save the drawing file as fan.

Select **MAIN MENU → File → Save**
Enter file name: **fan**

Project 16

Construct a wireframe model for the surface model of a car wheel (Figure 11.154b & c). The model consists of a hub, a rim, and six pockets. The two edge curves of the pockets are shown in Figure 11.154a. The coordinate values of critical points for hub and rim edge profiles are tabulated below:

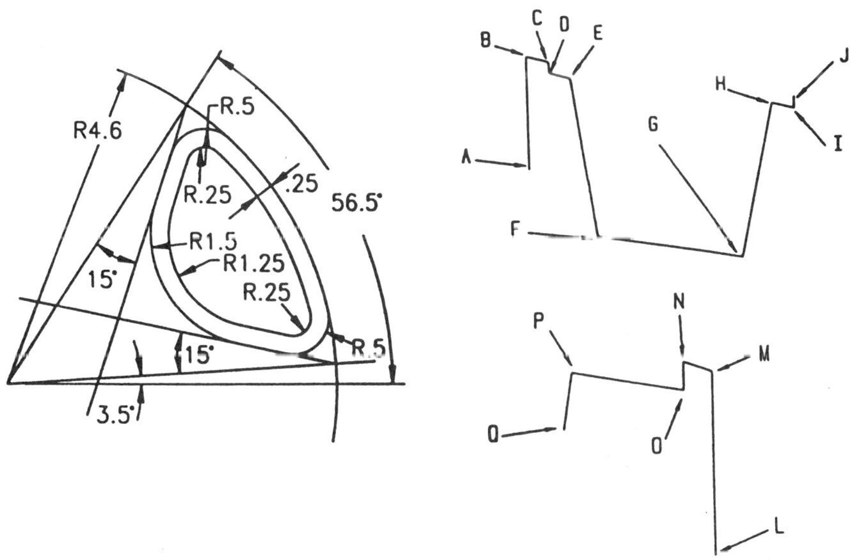

Figure 11.154a. Project profile

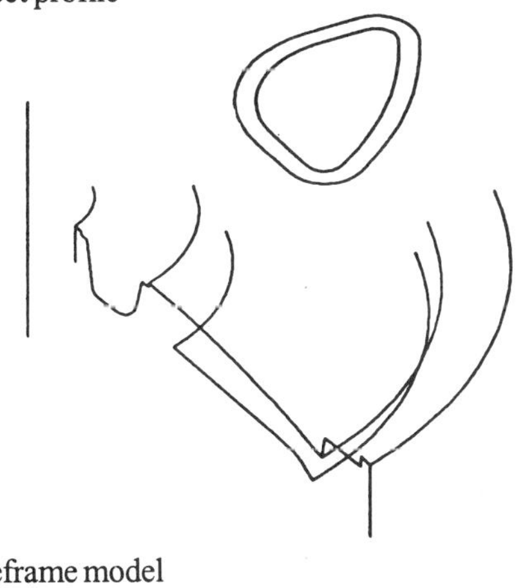

Figure 11.154b. Wireframe model

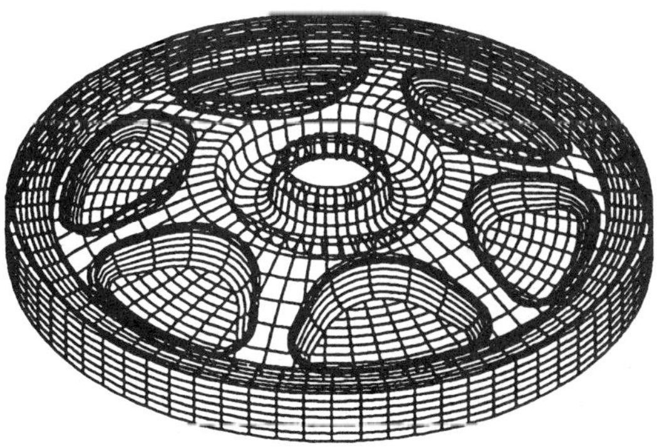

Figure 11.154c. Surface model

Tips 1. Use Front Cplane to construct the edge profiles of the hub, rim, and frame, as well as two upper and lower surfaces.
2. Use Top Cplane to create two of the contours for the pocket surface. The outer contour is created first. The six entities in the outer contour are then offset by a distance of 0.25-in. to obtain the inner contour. Note that these two contours are projected onto the two surfaces to obtain two surface curves for defining the pocket surface in chapter 13.

Step 1. Construct a series of lines for the hub profile using the Front construction plane.

Select **Cplane → Front**
Select **Gview → Front**
Select **MAIN MENU → Create → Line → Multi**
Specify endpoint 1: **0.8,1.4** ↵
Specify endpoint 2: **0.8,1.9** ↵
Specify endpoint 3: **0.9,1.875** ↵
Specify endpoint 4: **0.9,1.825** ↵
Specify endpoint 5: **1,1.8** ↵
Specify endpoint 6: **1.1,1.1** ↵
Specify endpoint 7: **1.75,1.0** ↵
Specify endpoint 8: **1.9,1.675** ↵
Specify endpoint 9: **2,1.65** ↵
Specify endpoint 10: **2,1.7** ↵

Your drawing will appear as Figure 11.155.

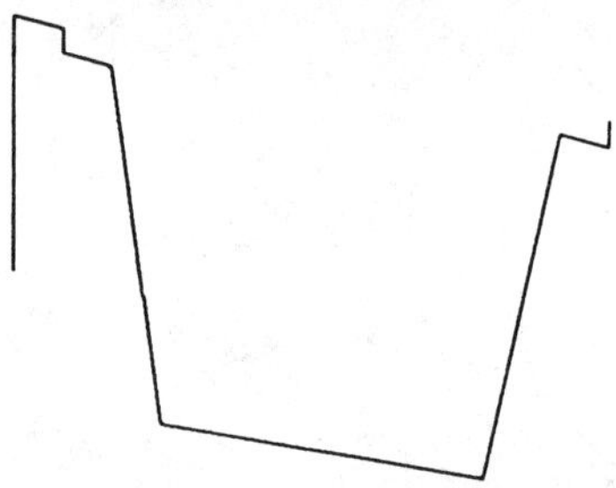

Figure 11.155

Step 2. Create another set of lines for the outer rim.

Select **BACKUP → Multi**
Specify endpoint 1: **5.65,0** ↵
Specify endpoint 2: **5.65,1** ↵

Press **Alt** + **F1** and then **F2** to fit the drawing in the screen

Specify endpoint 3: **5.5,1.05** ↵
Specify endpoint 4: **5.5,0.9** ↵
Specify endpoint 5: **4.9,1.0** ↵
Specify endpoint 6: **4.85,0.7** ↵

The drawing should look like Figure 11.156.

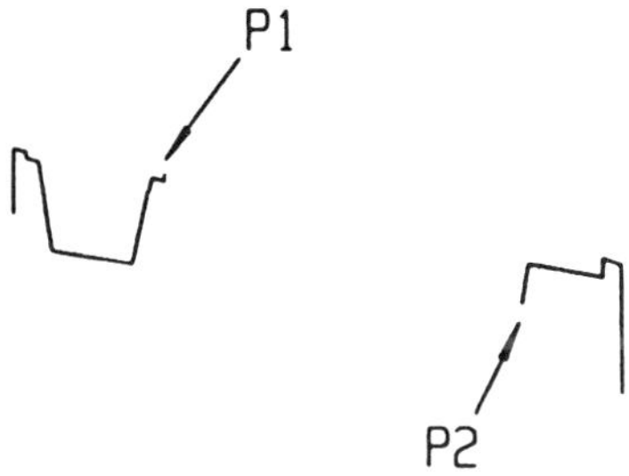

Figure 11.156

Step 3. Construct the arc for creating the top surface.

Use the pick points in Figure 11.156.
Select **MAIN MENU → Create → Arc → Endpoints → Endpoint**
Enter the first point: Pick **P1,** then select **Endpoint**
Enter the second point: Pick **P2**
Enter the radius: **10** ↵
Select an arc: Pick the upper arc to complete the arc selection.

Your drawing should appear as Figure 11.157.

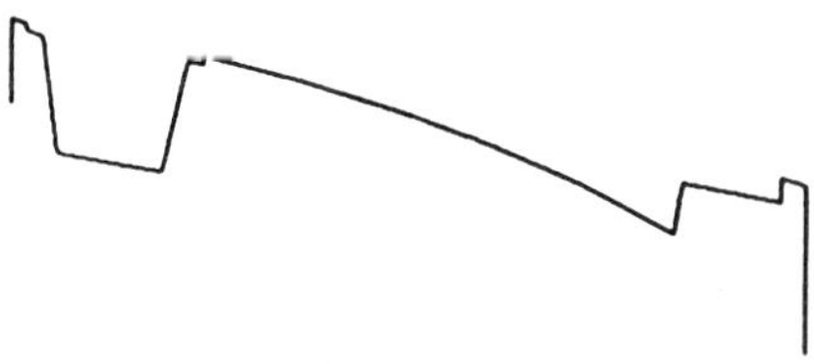

Figure 11.157

Step 4. Construct the edge profile for the lower surface.

Select **MAIN MENU → Create → Line → Polar**
Specify an endpoint: **2.4,1** ↵
Enter the angle in degrees (0.00): **-12.5** ↵
Enter the line length (1.00): **3** ↵

The drawing should look like Figure 11.158.

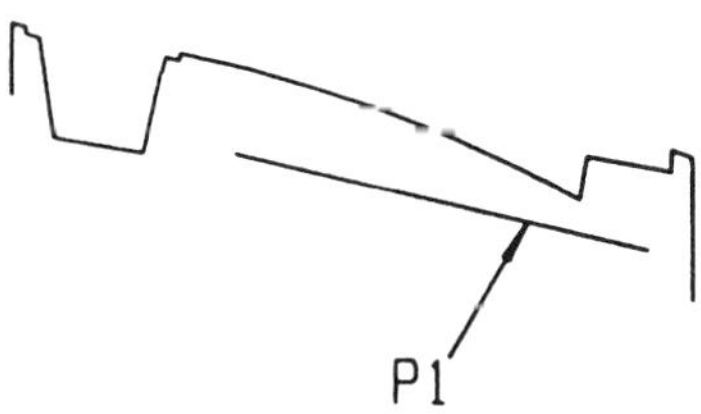

Figure 11.158

Step 5. Create the arc tangent to the line.

Use the pick points in Figure 11.158.
Select **MAIN MENU → Create → Arc → Tangent → Point**
Pick **P1** to select the entity that the arc is to be tangent to
Enter the thru point: **4.7,0.3** ↵
Enter the radius: **0.8** ↵
Select the right arc to complete the arc

The drawing will appear as Figure 11.159.

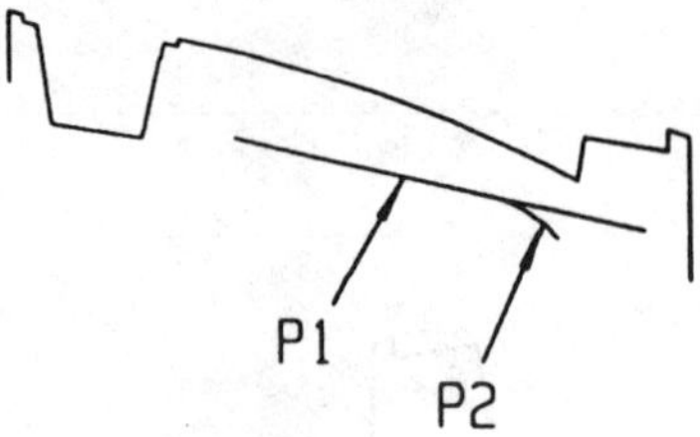

Figure 11.159

Step 6. Trim the line to the tangent point.

Use the pick points in Figure 11.159.
Select **MAIN MENU → Modify → Trim → 1 entity**
Select the entity to trim: pick **P1**
Select the entity to trim to: pick **P2**

The resulted drawing is shown in Figure 11.160.

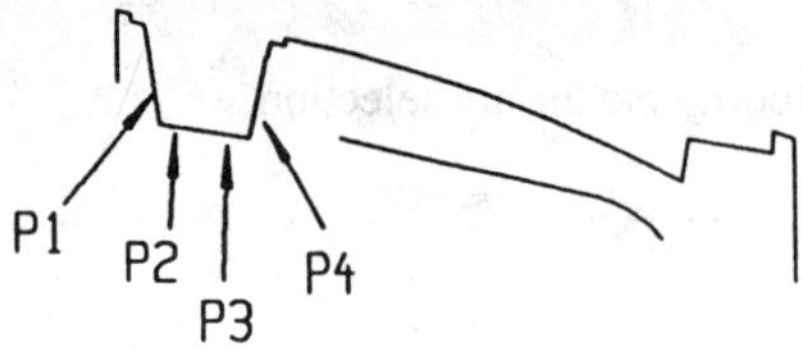

Figure 11.160

Step 7. Add two fillets. Use the pick points in Figure 11.160.

Select **MAIN MENU → Modify → Fillet**
Pick **Radius**, and then enter **0.1** ↵
Pick **P1** to select an entity
Pick **P2** to select another entity to complete the first fillet
Pick **Radius**, and then enter **0.3** ↵
Pick **P3** to select an entity
Pick **P4** to select another entity to complete the second fillet

The drawing will appear as Figure 11.161.

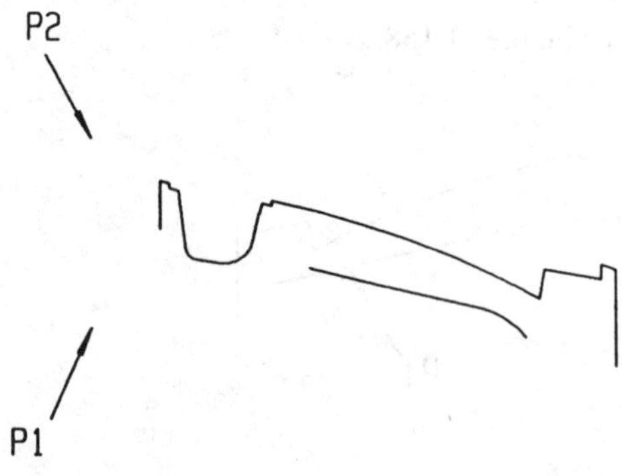

Figure 11.161

Step 8. Create a vertical line.

Use the pick points in Figure 11.161.
Select **MAIN MENU → Create → Line → Vertical → Sketch**
Pick **P1** and **P2**, and then enter **0** ↵ for X coordinate
Press **Alt** + **F1** to fit the drawing if necessary.

The drawing should appear as Figure 11.162.

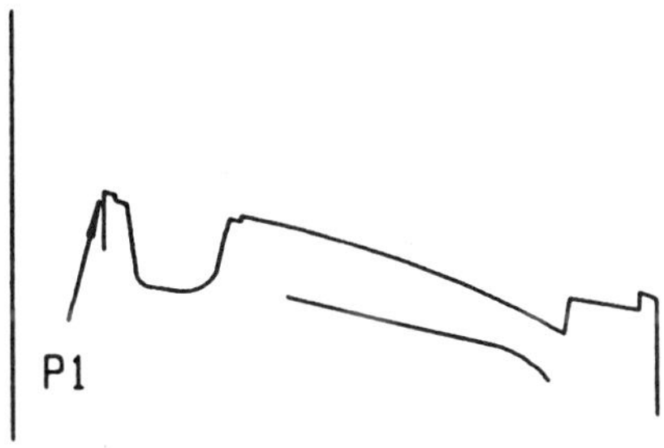

Figure 11.162

Step 9. Create six arcs using the top construction plane.

Use the pick points labeled in Figure 11.162.
Select **Cplane → Top**
Select **Gview → Isometric**
Select **Z → Endpoint** and then pick **P1** to set the Z value

Z1.9 should appear in the secondary menu

Select **MAIN MENU → Create → Arc → Polar → Center pt**
Enter the center point: **0, 0** ↵
Enter the radius (1.00): **0.8** ↵
Enter the initial angle (0.0): press ↵ to accept the default value
Enter the final angle (360.0): **60** ↵

The drawing now becomes Figure 11.163.

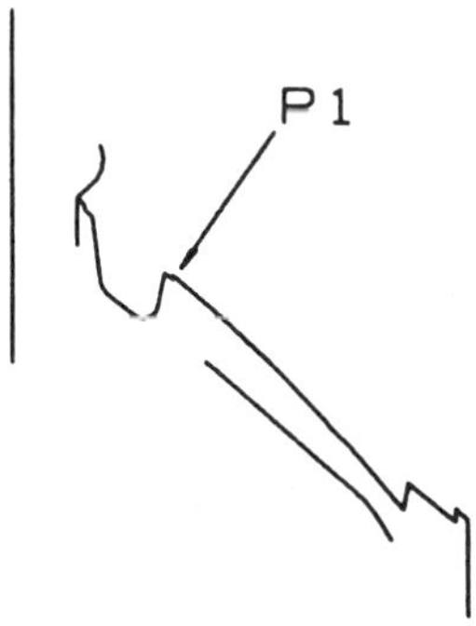

Figure 11.163

Step 10. Create the second arc using the pick points in Figure 11.163.

Pick **Z → Endpoint** and then pick **P1**
Z1.7 should appear in the Secondary menu

Select **MAIN MENU → Create → Arc → Polar → Center pt**
Enter the center point: **0,0** ↵
Enter the radius (0.8): **2** ↵
Enter the initial angle (0.0): ↵
Enter the final angle (60.0): ↵

The drawing will appear as Figure 11.164.

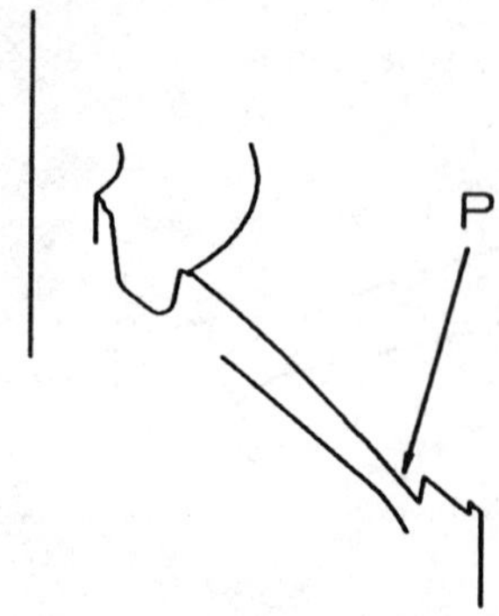

Figure 11.164

Step 11. Create the third arc.

Use the pick point in Figure 11.164.
Select **Z → Endpoint** and then pick **P1**

Z0.7 should appear in the Secondary menu

Select **MAIN MENU → Create → Arc → Polar → Center pt**
Enter the center point: **0,0** ↵
Enter the radius: **4.85** ↵
Enter the initial angle (0.0): ↵
Enter the final angle (60.0): ↵

The drawing should resemble Figure 11.165.

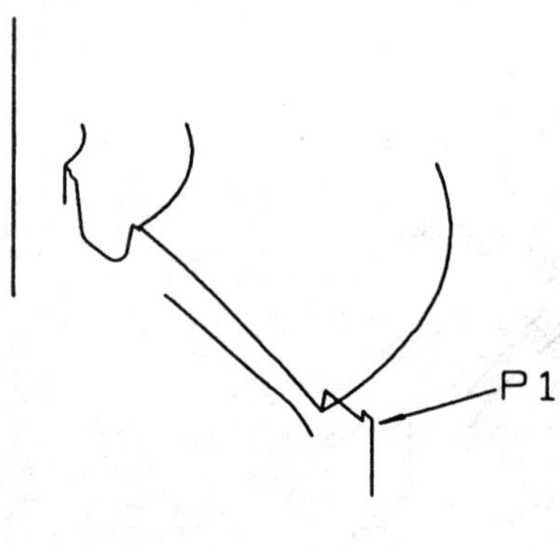

Figure 11.165

Step 12. Create the fourth arc using the pick point in Figure 11.165.

Pick **Z → Endpoint** and then pick **P1**
Z1.0 should appear in the Secondary menu

Enter the center point: **0,0** ↵
Enter the radius: **5.65** ↵
Enter the initial angle (0.0): ↵
Enter the final angle (60.0): ↵

Your drawing should appear as Figure 11.166.

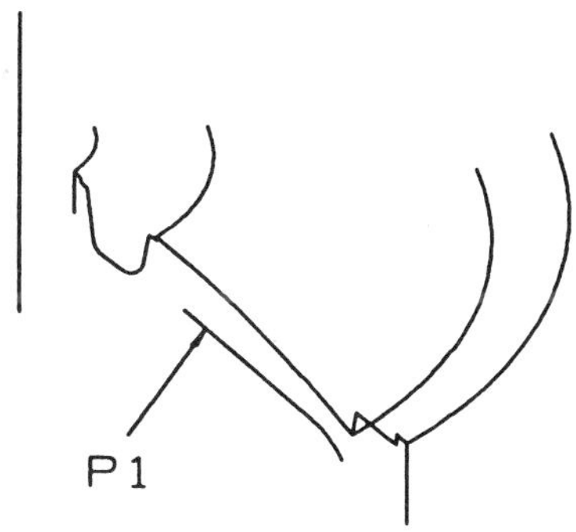

Figure 11.166

Step 13. Create the fifth arc.

Use the pick point in Figure 11.166.
Pick **Z → Endpoint** and then pick **P1**
Z1.0 should appear in the Secondary menu

Enter the center point: **0,0** ↵
Enter the radius: **2.4** ↵
Enter the initial angle (0.0): ↵
Enter the final angle (60.0): ↵

The drawing should resemble Figure 11.167.

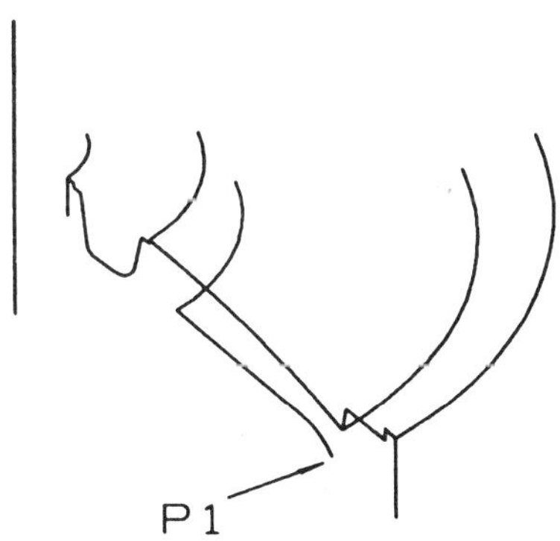

Figure 11.167

Step 14. Create the sixth arc using the pick point in Figure 11.167.

Pick **Z → Endpoint** and then pick **P1**
Z0.3 should appear in the Secondary menu

Enter the center point: **0,0** ↵
Enter the radius: **4.7** ↵
Enter the initial angle (0.0): ↵
Enter the final angle (60.0): ↵

The drawing now should look like Figure 11.168.

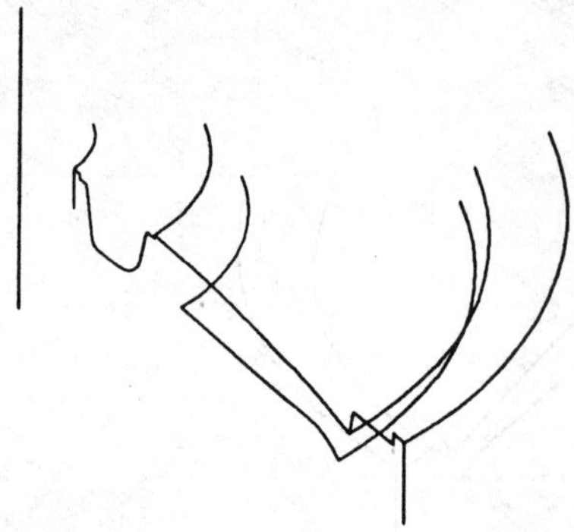

Figure 11.168

Step 15. Make level 1 invisible.

Set the Secondary menu parameters to the following settings:
Select **Level**, then uncheck **Visible** on **level 1**
Select **OK → OK** to return back to graphic mode
Select **Level** and then enter **2** ↵
Select **Color** and then enter **12** ↵
Select **Z** and then enter **4** ↵
Select **Gview → Top**

Step 16. Create an arc.

Select **MAIN MENU → Create → Arc → Polar → Center pt**
Enter the center point: **0,0** ↵
Enter the radius: **4.6** ↵
Enter the initial angle: **-10** ↵
Enter the final angle: **70** ↵

Step 17. Create two construction lines.

Select **MAIN MENU → Create → Line → Polar**
Enter coordinates: **0,0** ↵
Enter the angle in degrees (0.0): **3.5** ↵
Enter the line length (3.0): **5.5** ↵
Enter coordinates: **0,0** ↵
Enter the angle in degrees (0.0): **56.5** ↵
Enter the line length (5.5): ↵ to accept the default value
The drawing now will look like Figure 11.169.

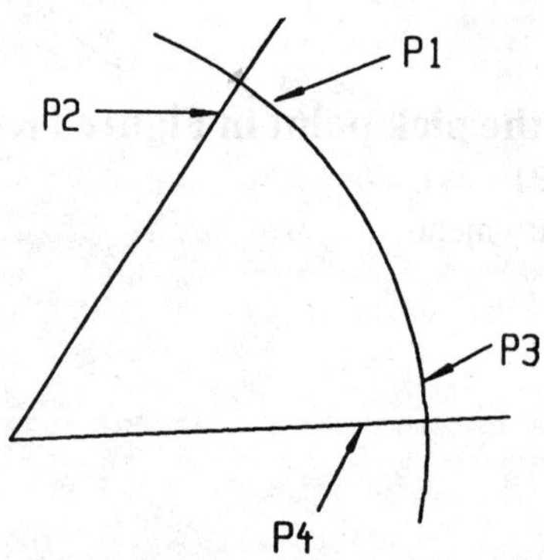

Figure 11.169

Step 18. Create another two construction lines.

Use the pick points in Figure 11.169.
Select **Intersec** then pick **P1** and **P2**
Enter the angle in degrees: **-108.5 (or 180 - 56.5 - 15)** ↵
Enter the line length: **4.5** ↵ for the first line
Select **Intersec**
Pick **P3** and **P4**
Enter the angle in degrees: **168.5 (or 180 - 15 + 3.5)** ↵
Enter the line length: **4.5** ↵ to complete the second line

The drawing now should resemble Figure 11.170.

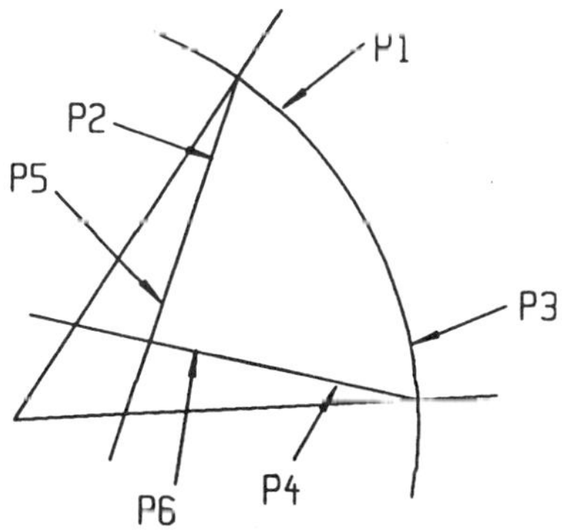

Figure 11.170

Step 19. Add three fillets.

Use the pick points in Figure 11.170.
Select **MAIN MENU → Modify → Fillet**
Select **Radius** from the parameter menu, and then enter **0.5** ← for fillet radius
Select an entity: pick **P1**
Select another entity: pick **P2** for the first fillet
Select an entity: pick **P3**
Select another entity: pick **P4** for the second fillet
Select **Radius** then enter **1.5** ↵
Pick **P5** and **P6** to complete the third fillet

The new drawing will appear as Figure 11.171.

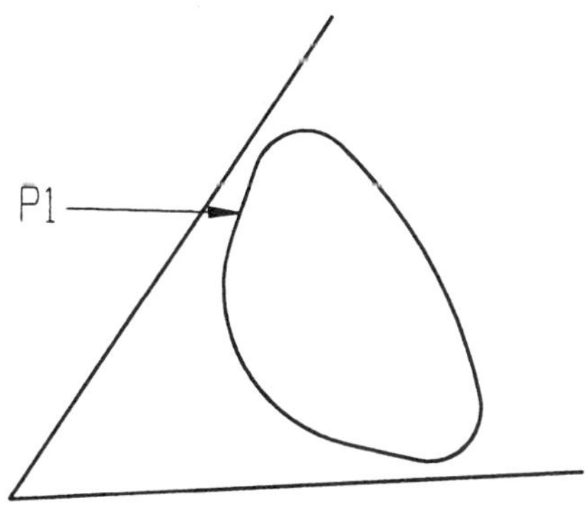

Figure 11.171

Step 20. Create the inner pocket using the offset command.

Use the pick points in Figure 11.171.
Select **MAIN MENU → Xform → Ofs ctour → Chain**
Pick **P1** to select the contour (make sure the chain direction is counterclockwise)
Select **Done**
Set the Offset Contour Parameters as shown in this menu:

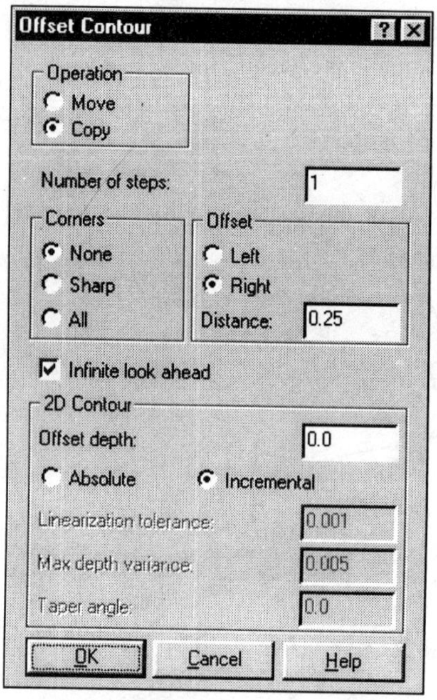

Select **OK** from the Offset Contour dialog box
The resultant inner pocket shows in Figure 11.172.

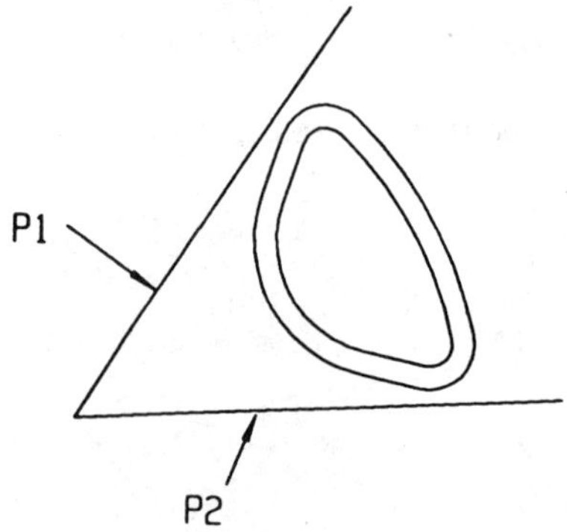

Figure 11.172

Step 21. Delete two construction lines using the pick points in Figure 11.172.

Select **MAIN MENU → Delete**
Pick **P1** and **P2**

The final drawing in Top Gview should resemble Figure 11.173.

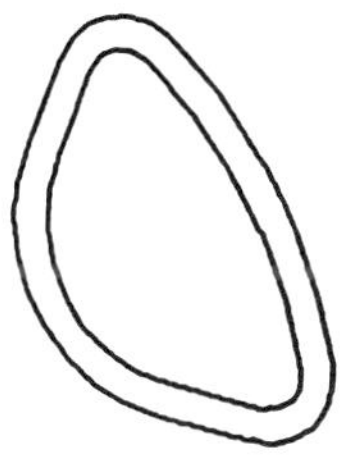

Figure 11.173

Step 22. Make level 1 visible and change Gview to isometric.

Select **Level**, then check **Visible** on **level 1**
Select **OK** to return back to graphic mode
Select **Gview → Isometric**

The final drawing should look like Figure 11.174.

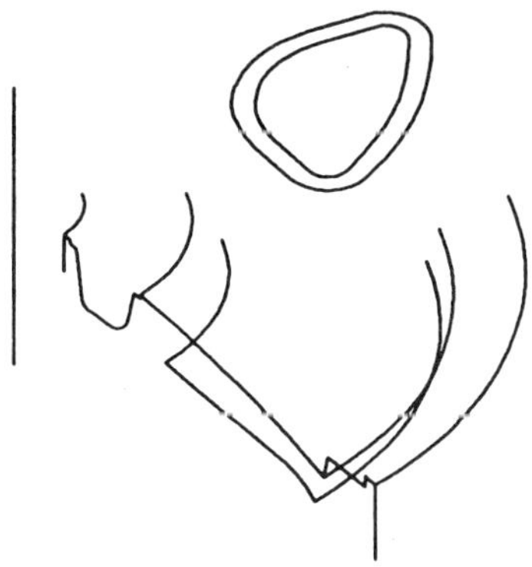

Figure 11.174

Step 23. Save the wireframe model file using the filename: wheel.

Select **MAIN MENU → File → Save**

Enter file name: **wheel** ↵

Ex Exercises

1. Explain how a wireframe model describes an object.

2. What additional information does a surface model provide over a wireframe model?

3. What is construction plane?

4. What are the three principal construction planes? Use a drawing to illustrate the definition of these three principal planes.

5. What are the six Mastercam construction planes?

6. Give the reasons we use a 3D construction plane.

7. Use a drawing to show how to define a 2-line construction plane. Explain when to use a 2-line construction plane.

8. Use a drawing to show how to define a normal construction plane; and explain when to use a normal construction plane.

9. Use drawings to show how to specify Z-depth in various construction planes.

10. Construct a wireframe model as shown in Figure 11.175. The model consists of two semi-circles, two profiles, and four lines. Save the drawing in the file name **E1**. This model can be used to generate two ruled surfaces and two fillet surfaces in chapter 12. Some helpful hints are given below.

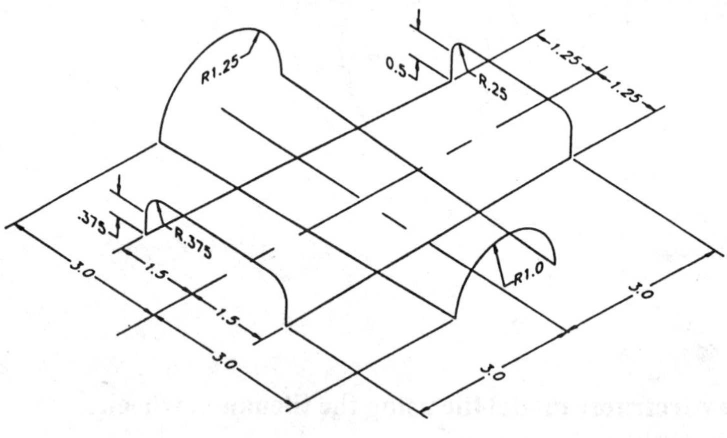

Figure 11.175

Tips 1. Follow the instructions in project 1.

2. Create two semi-circles using the side construction plane. The Z-depth is 3.0 and -3.0 for the two semi-circles, respectively.
3. Create two profiles using the front construction plane. The Z-depth is 3.0 and -3.0 for the two profiles, respectively.
4. Create four lines connecting the end points of the entities. Use the 3d construction plane.

11. Construct the wireframe model shown in Figure 11.176. This model consists of four arcs and one rectangular box. It can be used to create two ruled surfaces, generate a fillet surface, and trim the smaller ruled surface to the fillet surface. Save the file name as **E2**. Tips are suggested below.

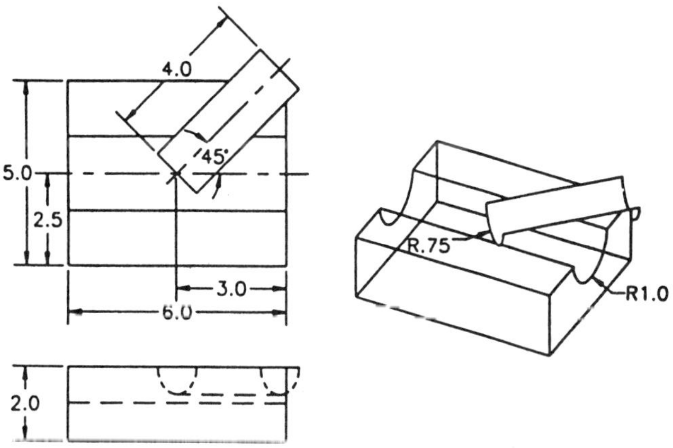

Figure 11.176

Tips 1. Study the instructions from Project 2.

2. Construct a rectangular box using the top Cplane.
3. Create the two arcs of 1.0" radius using the side Cplane.
4. Create a slope line that has a 45° with the X axis.
5. Define a normal Cplane which is perpendicular to the slope line.
6. Create two arcs of 0.75" radius using the normal Cplane.
7. Break the two upper side lines of the rectangular box into two pieces. This allows these two lines to be trimmed to the two arcs.
8. Connect four lines using 3D Cplane.

12. Construct the wireframe model consisting three cross-section profiles and four lines as shown in Figure 11.177. This model can be used to create a ruled surface, a loft surface, or a Coons surface. Save the file name as **E3**.

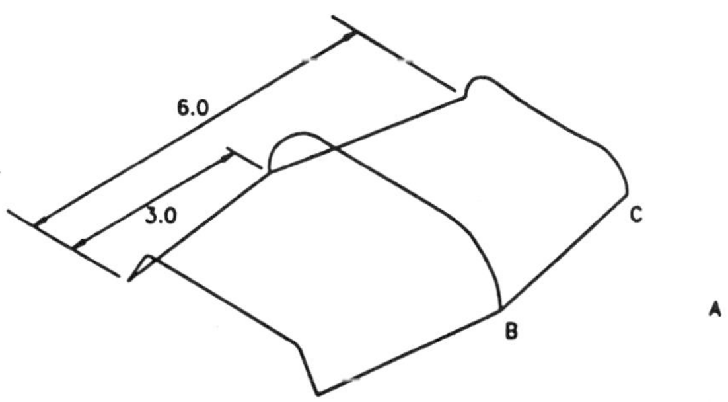

Figure 11.177a

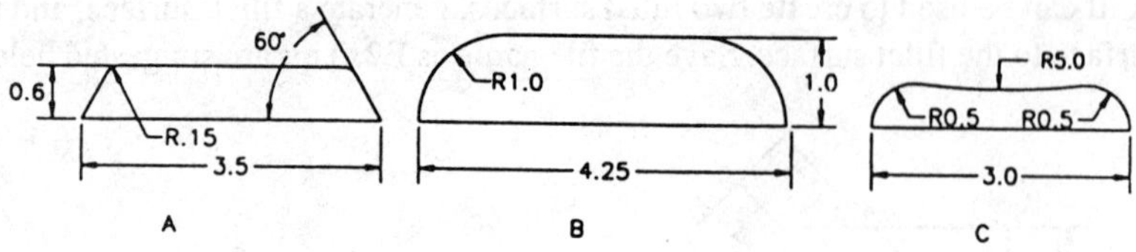

Figure 11.177b

Tips 1. Construct three profiles using Front Cplane.

2. Use the Endpoints command to create the two 0.5" radius arcs. Then use Modify → Fillet commands to create the tangent arc of 8" radius.
3. There are two ways you can place profiles B and C in the proper Z loaction. One is set Z-3.0 for profile B and Z-6.0 for profile C. The other method is to create the profile at Z0.0, then use Xform → Translate commands to move the profile to correct position.
4. Connect the four lines using the 3D Cplane.

13. Construct a wireframe model consisting of four arcs as shown in Figure 11.178. This model is used to create a Coons surface. Save the file name as **E4**. Some helpful tips are listed below.

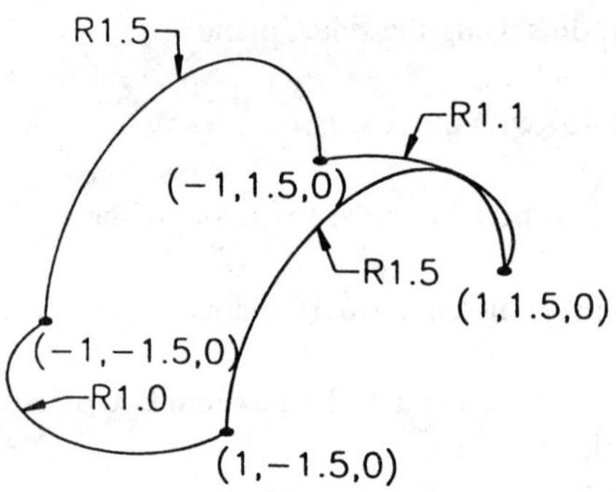

Figure 11.178

Tips 1. Create two arcs of 1.5" radius using the Side Cplane and the other two arcs in Top Cplane.

2. Use Arc → Endpoints command to construct these four arcs.

14. Construct the wireframe model shown in Figure 11.179. The model consists of four profiles set in four sides of a rectangular box. This model is used to create a Coons surface. Save the file as **E5**. Hints are provided on the next page.

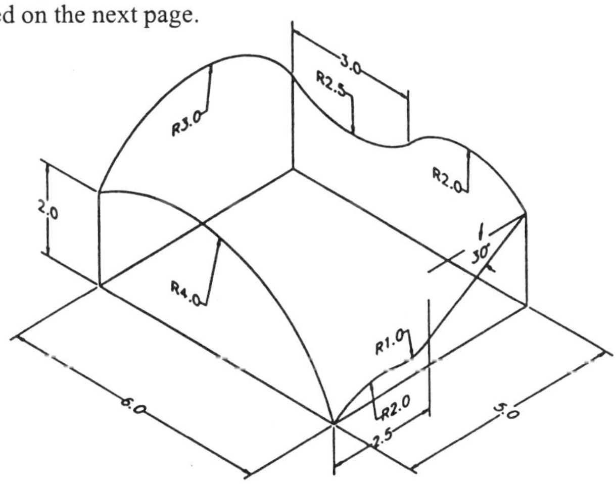

Figure 11.179

Tips 1. Study the instructions given in project 5.

2. Use Arc → Endpoints commands to construct four arcs C1, C3, C5, and C6.

3. Use Arc → Tangent commands to with Point option to create arc C2.

4. Use Modify → Fillet commands to construct arc C4.

5. Construct arcs C1, C2, and C5 using Front Cplane, and Arcs C3, C4, and C6 in Side Cplane.

15. Construct a wireframe model as shown in Figure 11.180. The model consists of eight triangular slope surfaces whose vertices joined at one point. The model can be used to create a Coons surface connecting the eight lines and the eight-sided polygon and a ruled surface on the top flat surface. Save the file as **E6**. Hints are given on below.

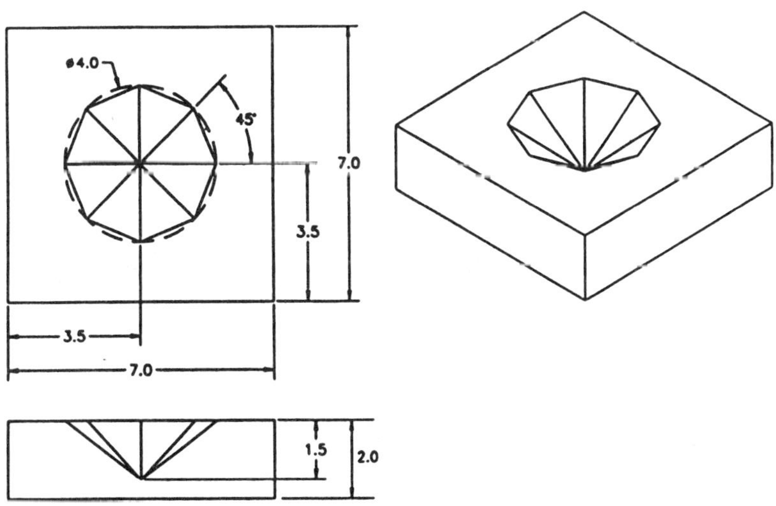

Figure 11.180

Tips 1. Study the instructions given in projects 6 and 7.

2. Create a rectangle and an octagon using Top Cplane.

3. Create eight lines connecting the eight vertices of the octagon and the common joined point using 3d Cplane.

16. Create the wireframe model for a multiple-faced part shown in Figure 11.181. The model has two octagons at different Z levels. A total of 16 faces are formed in the upper half of the part. The bottom half also has 16 faces that can be created from the upper half by using the mirror function. Save the file as **E7**. Useful tips are given below.

Tips 1. Study the instructions given in project 7.

2. Create two construction circles and eight lines to find the vertices of the two octagons.

3. Use Top Gview and 3d Cplane to connect the lines between vertices, and between the vertices and the common join point.

4. Save the drawing of the upper half of the model.

5. Rotate the upper half model by 180° about the origin using Front Cplane to complete the entire wireframe model.

Note: Do not use the complete wireframe model for surfacing. This makes picking correct entities more difficult in surfacing because the one entity appearing in Top Gview may represent two or more entities in the model.

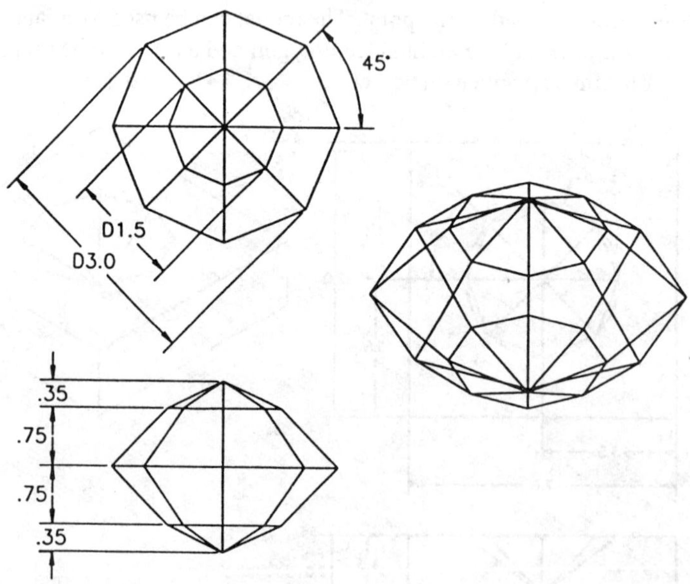

Figure 11.181

17. Construct the wireframe profile for a cup shown in Figure 11.182. The model can be used to generate a revolved surface or a swept surface. Save the file as **E8**. Tips are listed below.

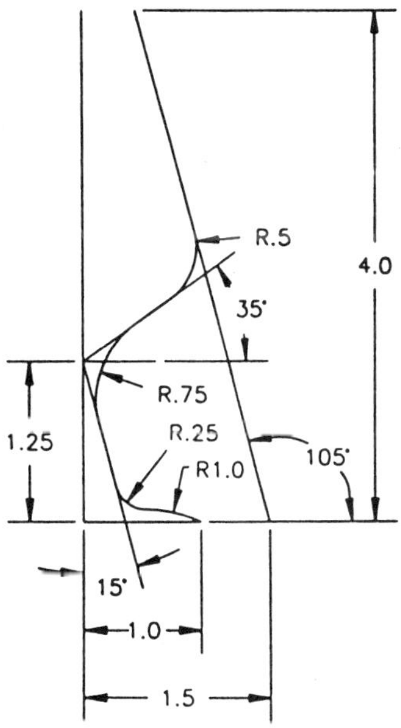

Figure 11.182

Tips 1. Study the instructions given in project 8.

2. Construct five lines, one vertical, one horizontal, and three sloped.

3. Add three fillets.

4. Use Arc → Tangent → Point commands to create the arc near the base.

18. Construct the wireframe profile for a cup shown in Figure 11.183. The model can be used to generate a revolved surface or a swept surface. Save the file as **E9**. Tips are listed below.

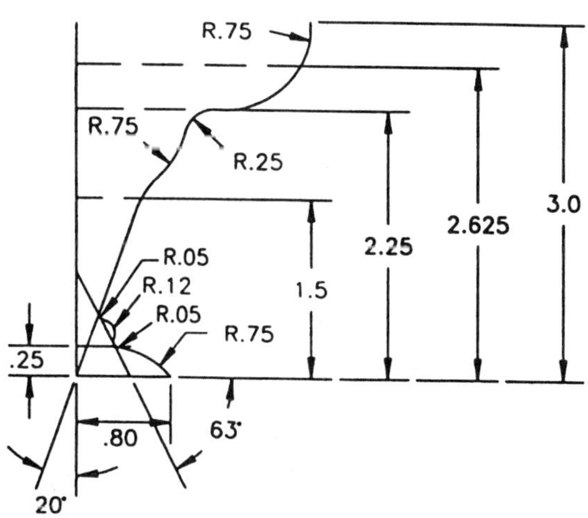

Figure 11.183

Tips 1. Study the instructions given in project 8.

2. Create necessary construction lines to help determining the end points of arcs.

3. Use Arc → Endpoints to create most of the arcs.

19. Create a wireframe model for the fly disk as shown in Figure 11.184. This model can be used to create a revolved surface or a swept surface. Save the file as **E10**. Hints are listed below.

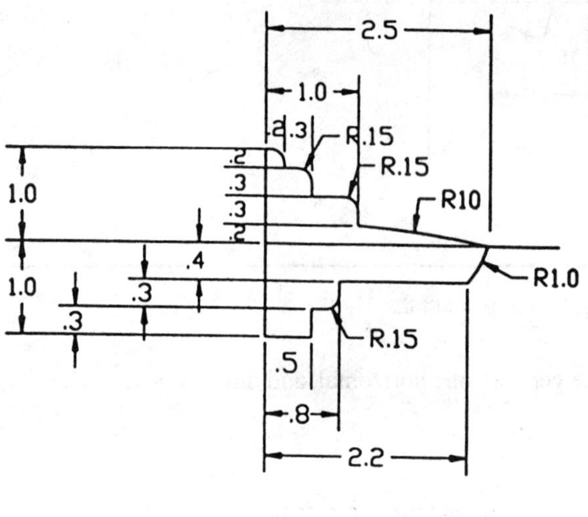

Figure 11.184

Tips 1. Create necessary construction lines to help determining the end points of arcs.

2. Use Arc → Endpoints commands to create arcs.

20. Construct the wireframe model for the part shown in Figure 11.185. The model consists of two rectangles with fillets at four corners and a section profile. One larger rectangle is located on the top to define the outer boundary of the top rim, and the smaller rectangle defines the shape of the part bottom. The section profile defines the wall and the top rim. This model is used to create a composite surface model in which multiple surfaces are blended together. Save the file as **E11**. Some hints are given below.

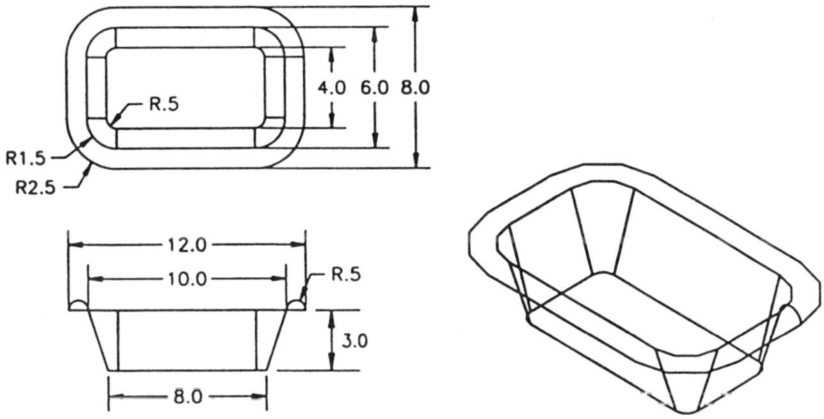

Figure 11.185

Tips 1. Use Top Cplane to construct the two rectangles with fillets. Note that the two rectangles have different Z depths.

2. Create the section profile in Front Cplane.

21. Create the wireframe model for the part shown in Figure 11.186. The model consists of two circles, one profile arc, eight identical edge profiles, and eight lines connecting end points of eight edge profiles. This model is used to create a composite surface model. Save the file as **E12**. Hints are given on the next page.

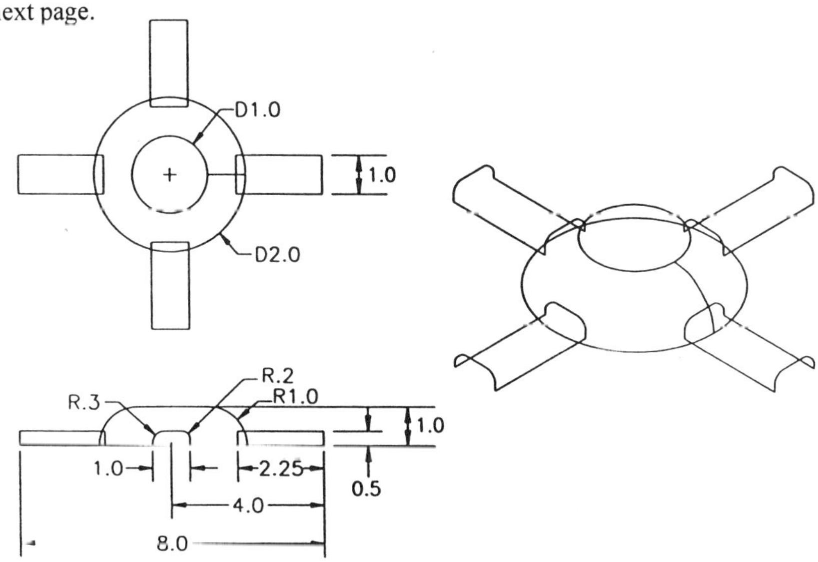

Figure 11.186

Tips 1. Construct two circles in the Top Cplane with different depths.

2. Create four edge profiles and an arc profile which connects two circles in Front Cplane.

3. Construct the other four edge profiles in Side Cplane.

4. Create eight connecting lines between eight profiles in 3d Cplane.

Chapter 12

Surfaces Modeling I: Fundamentals and Creation

Objectives:

1. Know surfaces and their applications.
2. Understand surface mathematics.
3. Identify surface types.
4. Use Mastercam surface modules to create surfaces.
5. Know what works, and what doesn't, in creating surfaces.

Overview

This chapter covers important surfacing mathematics and techniques. Four surface mathematics styles and a comparison of their features are described. Sixteen projects are presented to show how to create primitive surfaces and free-form surfaces from the wireframe models in Mastercam. Useful tips are provided to help in your understanding of the principles and procedures of each surfacing technique. Derived surfacing techniques and their examples as well as several composite surface models are presented in chapter 13.

12.1 Surfaces

A surface is the shape representation of a part's skin defined by mathematical equations. A surface normally consists of many sections or patches that are smoothly blended together to form an entity. Due to the increased computer power and the new surface modeling techniques, today's surface modeling in CAD/CAM systems can accurately and completely describe a complex part shape. In addition the multiple surfaces found in many complex parts, can be blended together to form a single surface model for design analysis and NC tool path generation. This kind of multi-surfaces model is often called the **composite surface.**

Surface modeling is widely used to describe complex objects such as a car, ship, and airplane body, as well as their dies and molds. The information of surface models can be used to perform the following engineering, design, and manufacturing functions:

- Part geometric design and representation
- Mass properties calculation
- Interference checking between mating parts
- Cross-sectioned views generation
- Finite element meshes generation
- NC tool paths generation

12.2 Surface Mathematics

All surfaces are created by using one of the following four mathematical methods: Coons surface, Bezier surface, B-spline surface, and NURBS surface. They are briefly described in this section.

Coons Surface

A Coons surface is often referred to as the **Coons patch**. A single Coons patch is a surface patch constructed by blending four boundary curves (Figure 12.1). The multiple-patches Coons surface is generated from several individual patches smoothly blended together (Figure 12.2). The blending functions used in Coons surfaces could be either bi-linear or bi-cubic.

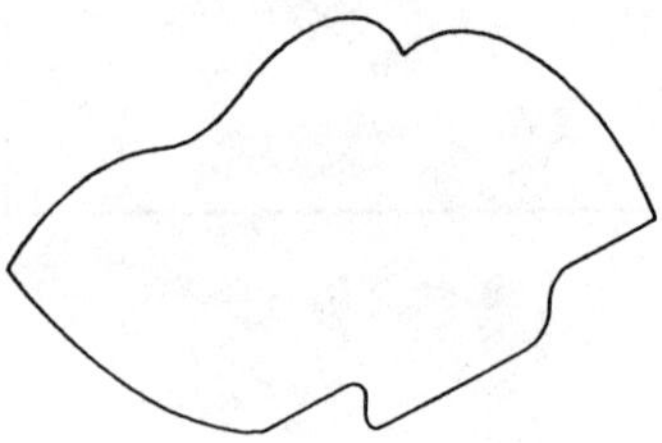

a. Wireframe model

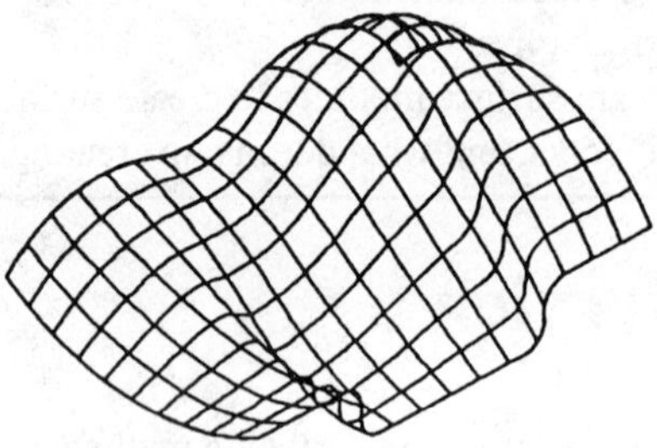

b. Surface model

Figure 12.1

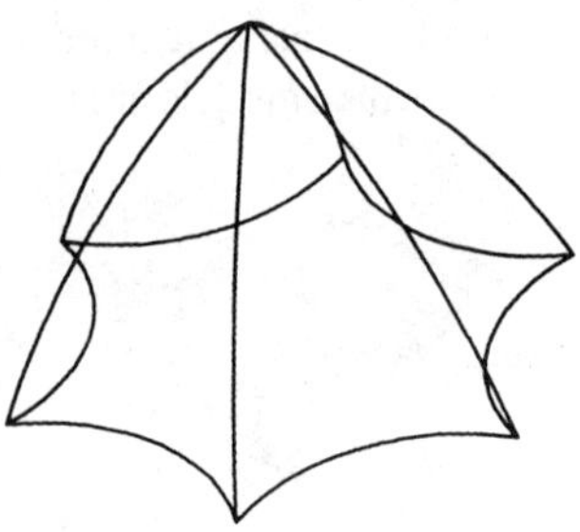

a. Wireframe model

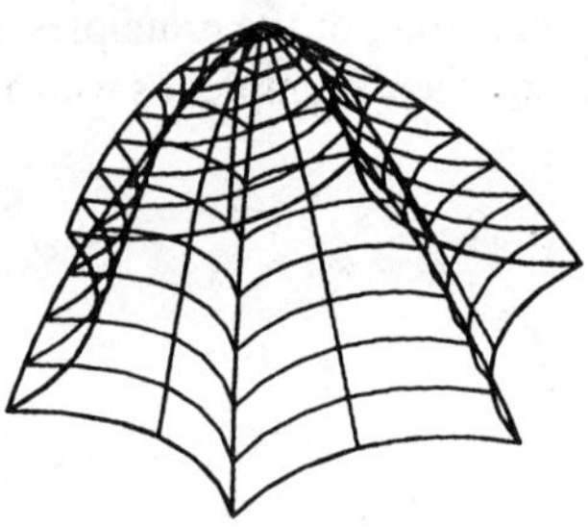

b. Surface model

Figure 12.2

The strength of the Coons surfaces is their ability to fit a smooth surface precisely throughout the wireframe curves or digitized point data. In other words, the surface must pass through all control points. The weakness is that a change of a shape of a surface requires that the control curves be altered.

Bezier Surface

A Bezier surface is created by blending all the connecting lines or facets formed by a grid of control points (Figure 12.3). Multiple-patches Bezier surfaces are formed in a way similar to Coons surfaces that smoothly blend individual Bezier patches together.

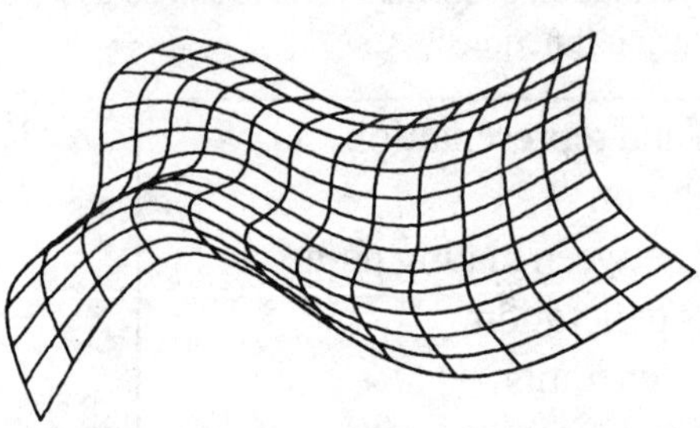

Figure 12.3

The advantage of using Bezier surfaces lies in their ability to reshape the surface by manipulating the control points. Control points can be pulled to create a new design. The weakness of Bezier surfaces is that the entire surface shape is affected simply by moving any one of the control points. They produce approximated surfaces in which specific cross-sectional shapes in particular positions are hard to obtain (if not impossible to obtain.)

B-Spline Surface

A B-spline surface possesses the combined strong features of both Coons and Bezier surfaces. Similar to the Coons patch, B-spline surfaces can be formed from a set of cross-sectional curves, and like the Bezier patch, it also has control points which can be manipulated to alter the surface texture.

A multiple-patches B-spline surface is possible and the continuity between adjacent patches can be guaranteed regardless of how the control points are moved.

The weakness of using B-spline surfaces is that primitive surfaces such as cylinders, spheres, and cones cannot be represented precisely. These surfaces can only be approximated, therefore, unacceptable dimensional errors may occur when machining these simple surfaces.

NURBS Surface

The term NURBS is an acronym for **Non-Uniform Rational B-Spline**. A rational surface is a surface in which each point described has a weight associated with it. A non-rational surface is a surface whose mathematical equations are not a rational number. NURBS surfaces are rational. They have all of B-spline surface abilities. In addition, they provide a weighting function to change the effect of the control points on the surface texture. When the weight function has a constant value of one, the NURBS surface is equivalent to a B-spline surface.

NURBS surfaces overcome the problem of the B-spline in modeling primitive surfaces. Surfaces based on conics, arcs, or spheres can be precisely represented by a NURBS surface. NURBS surface modeling is the most advanced technique of surface mathematics.

12.3 Surface Types

Surfaces can be classified into the following **three** categories: geometrical surfaces, free-form surfaces, and derived surfaces.

Geometrical Surfaces

Geometrical surfaces have constant geometrical shapes such as spheres, cones, and cyliners as well as draft surfaces and surfaces of revolution. They are generated with entities like lines, arcs, splines, and cones. Thus, there is little ambiguity in the definitions of these surfaces. Mastercam provides **two** surfacing techniques to create geometrical surfaces: draft surface modeling and revolved surface modeling. Table 12.1 on the following page summarizes these two geometrical surfacing techniques.

Table 12.1 Geometrical Surfaces

Surface type	Description	Applications	Example
Draft surface (Extruded)	A surface created by extruding a sectional shape straight along a line. The line is defined by a length and an angle.	Used to create cones, cylinders. Draft angles on molds, and tabulated cyllinders.	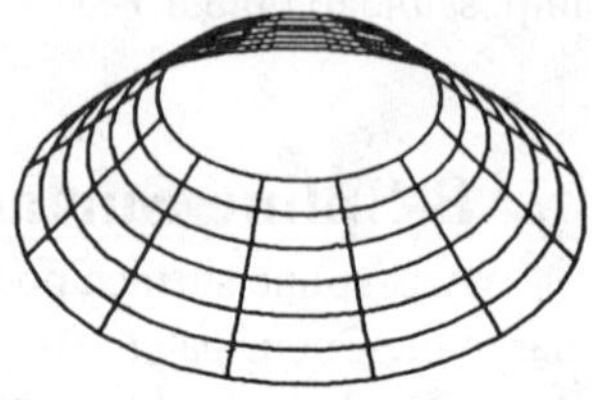
Revolved surface	A surface created by rotating a sectional shape around an axis or a line.	Used on any part that requires surfaces with arc or circular cross sections.	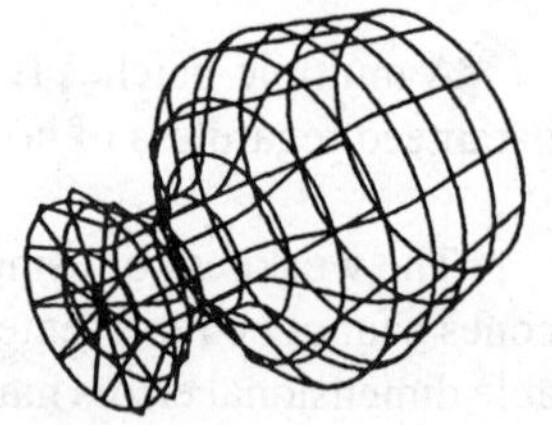

Free-Form Surfaces

Free-form surfaces follow no set geometric pattern and are normally generated from arbitrarily shaped lines and curves. These surfaces require more sophisticated surface mathematics such as Coons patches, Bezier patches, B-spline surfaces, and NURBS surfaces.

Free-form surfaces may be classified further into **two kinds** by their use: constrained surfaces and unconstrained surfaces. **Constrained surfaces** are restricted to existing data sets that may be in the form of sections or cross sections. In other words, the surfaces must pass through the given sections exactly. Coons patches is a typical constrained surface because of its direct relationship to the geometry.

Unconstrained surfaces are not restricted to pre-existing sets of data points or curves. They use control points to create the surface shape that is not necessarily passed through all pre-defined data points or curves. They are mainly used in conceptual designs. Bezier, B-spline, and NURBS surfaces are unconstrained surface types. Table 12.2 summarizes surface types, their desription, typical applications, and examples of free-form surfaces.

Derived Surfaces

Derived surfaces are surfaces that are generated from existing surfaces. They are also called edited surfaces. Table 12.3 on the next page shows **four** commonly used derived surfaces; offset, trimmed, fillet and blend.

Table 12.2 Free-form surfaces

Surface Type	Description	Applications	Example
Ruled surface	A surface created by connecting straight lines between two or more lines or curves.	Used any time a surface must be fit between two or more curves.	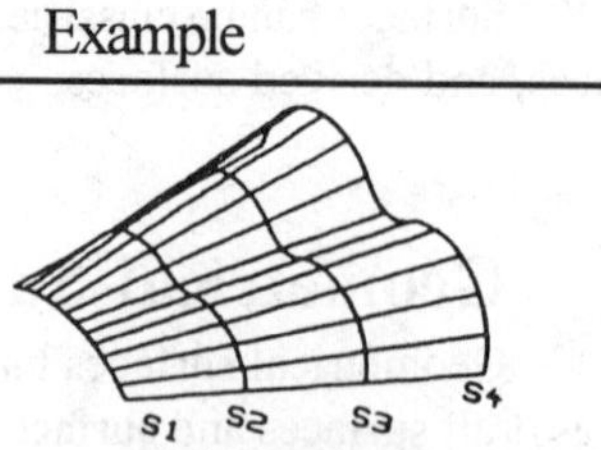
Lofted surface	A surface created by fitting through a set of cross sectional curves.	Used when a surface must be parabolically blended through more than two curves.	

Table 12.2 Continued

Drag surface (2-D swept)	A surface created by translating or rotating a sectional profile along a drive curve.	Used when the cross section of the surface at any point remain constant.	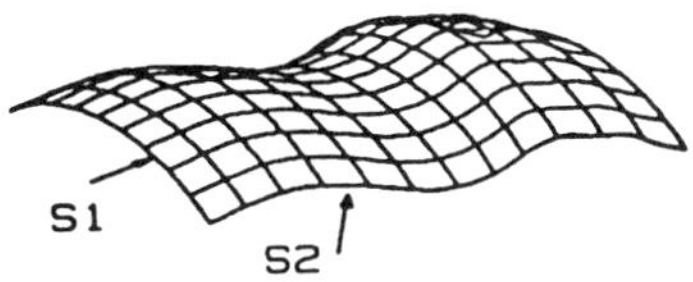
3-D swept surface (Drag with blending)	A surface created by (1) translating a sectional profile along two drive curves, (2) translating two sectional profiles along a drive curve	Used when the across sections at any section is not constant.	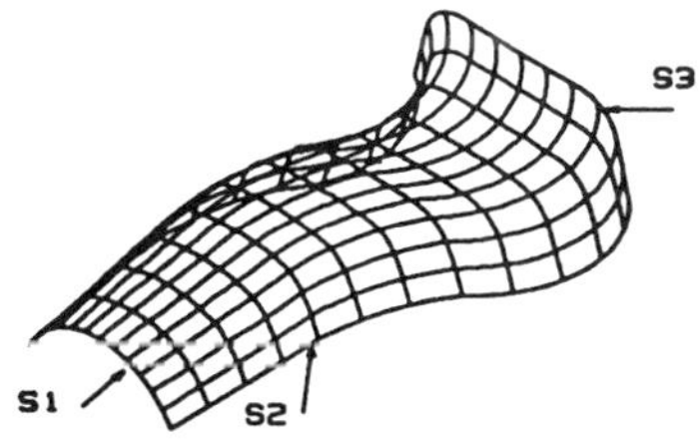
Coons surface	A surface created by blending a number of patches that have four prescribed intersecting curves which form a closed boundary.	Used when a surface is formed by a set of patches.	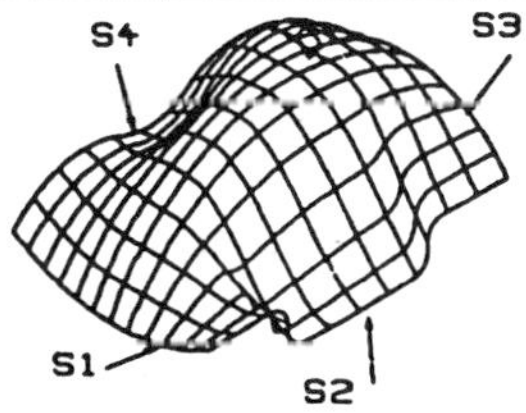

Table 12.3 Derived surfaces

Surface Type	Description	Applications	Example
Offset surface	A surface created by offsetting an existing surface by a distance. The offset is applied normal (perpendicular) to the original surface.	Used to create a new surface that is offset from the original surface.	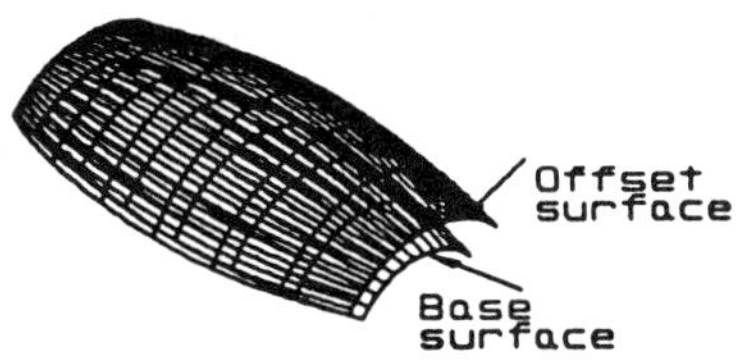
Trimmed surface	A surface created by trimming an existing surface to a specified boundary.	Used to redefine the borders of the existing surfaces.	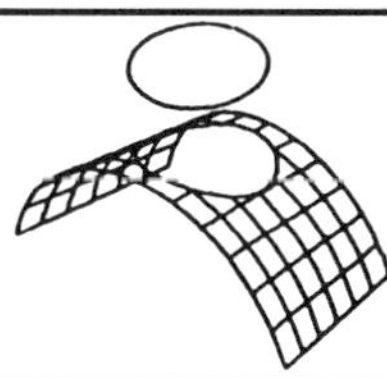
Fillet surface	A surface created by generating arc cross sections that are tangent to two surfaces.	Used to smooth sharp edges.	
Blend surface	A surface created by joining two existing surfaces, and is tangent to each parent surface.		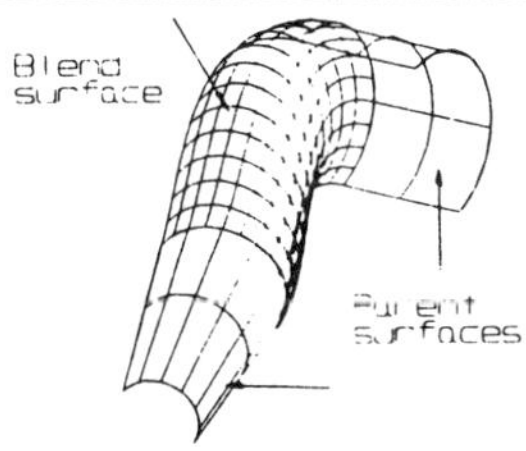

12.4 Mastercam Surfaces

The Mastercam software provides a series of very powerful surfacing techniques including:

two geometric surface models: revolved and draft
four free-form surface models: ruled, loft, Coons, and swept
three derived surface models: fillet, offset, and trimmed.

These free-form and derived surfaces are primarily based on three surfacing mathematics principles: blend, parametric, and NURBS. Table 12.4 gives the available surfacing methods for **four** types of free-form surfaces in Mastercam.

Blend: approximates a surface by blending between the boundaries of piecewise surface contours.

Parametric:uses bi-cubic approximation to create parametric splines along and across an array of points that lie on the surface. The parametric bi-cubic surface patch connects four corner data points and utilize a bi-cublic equation.

NURBS:interpolates a surface by weighting the effect of the control points on the surface skin.

Table 12.4 Surfacing methods of free-form surfaces in Mastercam

Surface Types	Surface Methods		
	Blend	Parametric	NURBS
Loft	Yes	Yes	Yes
Coons	No	Yes	Yes
Ruled	Yes	Yes	Yes
Sweep	No	Yes	Yes

Surfacing Projects

The examples given in this chapter use the wireframe models constructed in chapter 11. They are arranged in such a way that each surface modeling method begins with important tips which outline what to do for the sussessful completion of the surface model. Additional examples are used to re-enforce the use of each modeling method. The derived surfaces and composite surfaces are presented in chapter 13.

12.5 Ruled Surfaces Modeling

Mastercam's ruled surfaces modeling allows two or more contours to be linearly blended to form a surface. Follow these four tips to master this process.

> **Tip** 1. The first pick position of each contour affects the shape of the surface (Figure 12.4). Make each contour start from the same orientation.

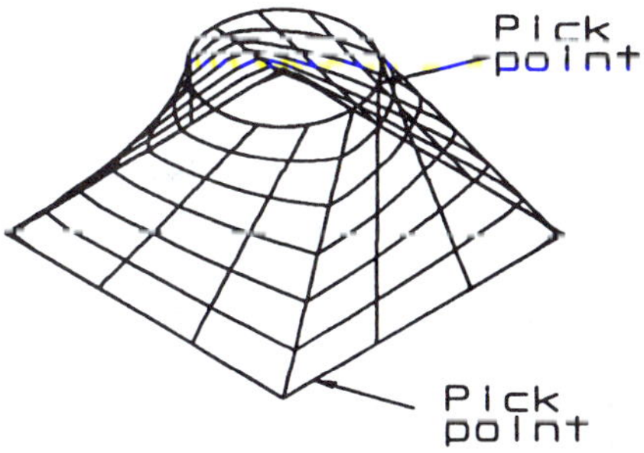

Figure 12.4a. Twisted surface shape

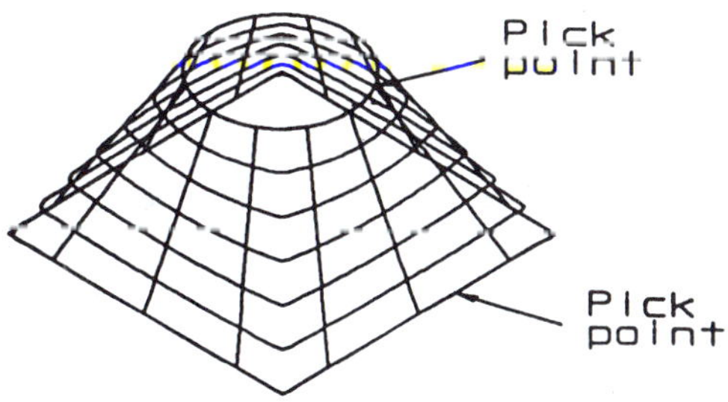

Figure 12.4b. Correct surface shape

> **Tip** 2. An entity sometimes has to be broken into two entities in order to allow the contours to start from the same orientation. The right vertical line in Figure 12.5, for example, is broken into two segments to permit the alignment of starting point.

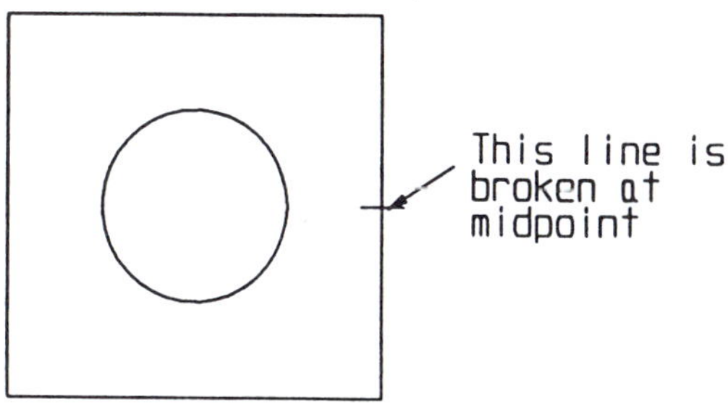

Figure 12.5a. Top view

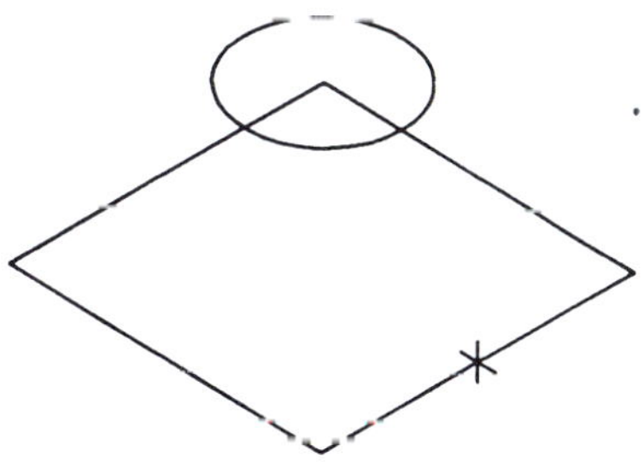

Figure 12.5b. Isometric view

> **Tip** 3. Contours must be orderly selected. Any alteration of the picking order may result in a unacceptable surface (Figure 12.6).

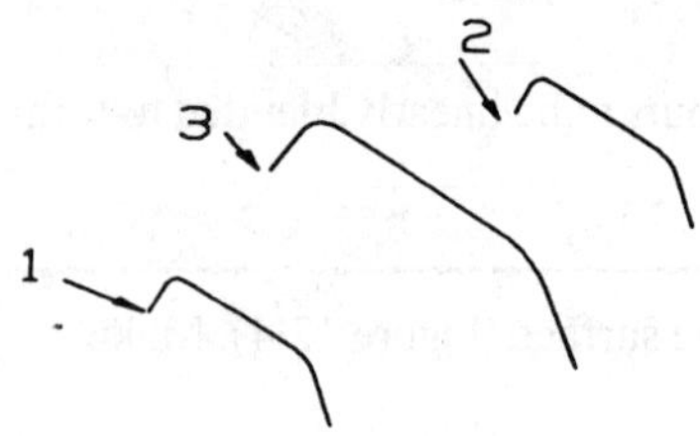

Figure 12.6a. Pick order

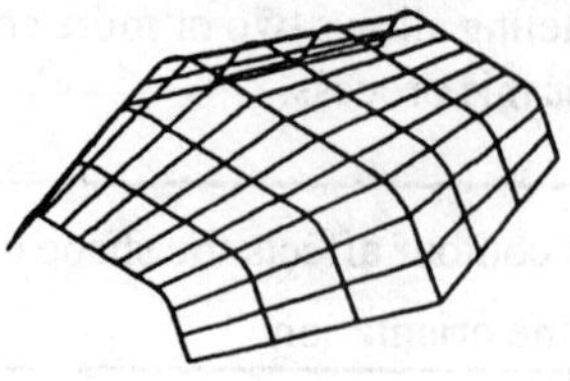

Figure 12.6b. Proper surface

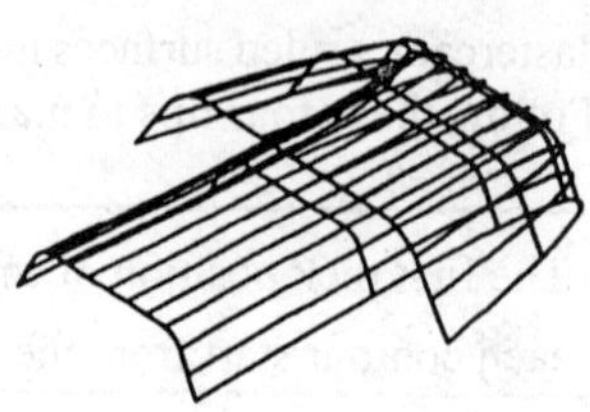

Figure 12.6c. Twisted surface

Tips continued.

4. Use the Top Gview to pick the contours as the number of contours increases. Isometric Gview tends to cause confusion when the wireframe model becomes complicated. Use the Window command to automatically define the order of contours.

5. Have the same chaining direction for all contours. Reversing the chaining direction of one entity results in an improper surface (Figure 12.7).

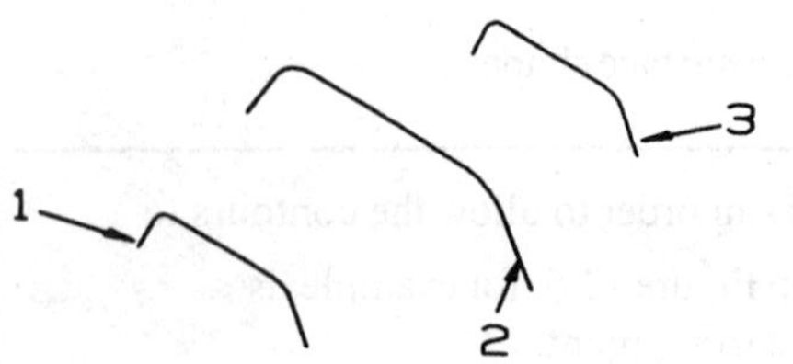

a. Contour directions

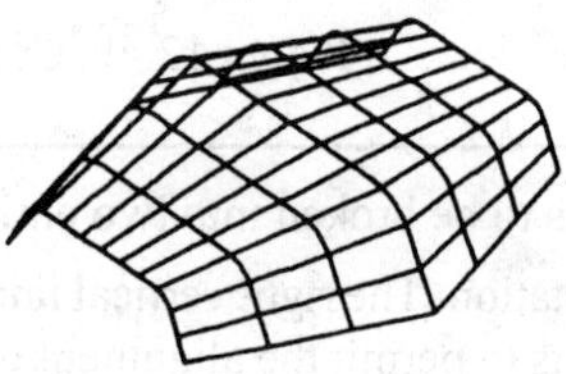

b. Proper surface

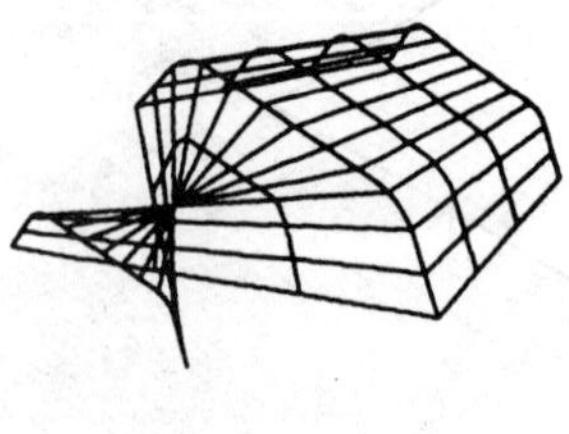

c. Twisted surface
Figure 12.7

Project 1. Creating two ruled surfaces, both formed by two contours 1

This example uses the wireframe model constructed in project 1 of chapter 11 to generate two ruled surfaces. The contour profiles is shown in Figure 12.8a and finished ruled surfaces in Figure 12.8b.

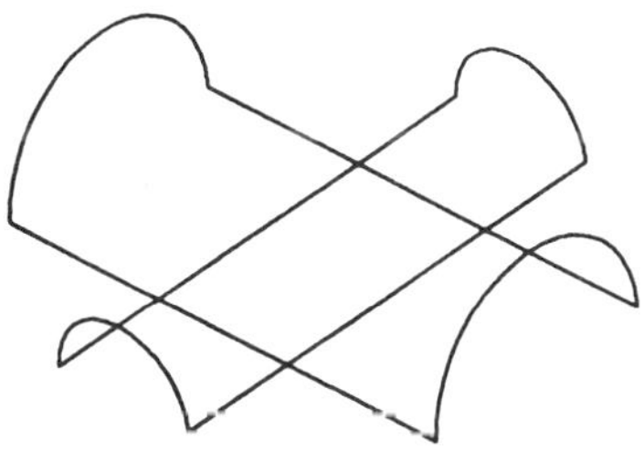

Figure 12.8a. Wireframe model

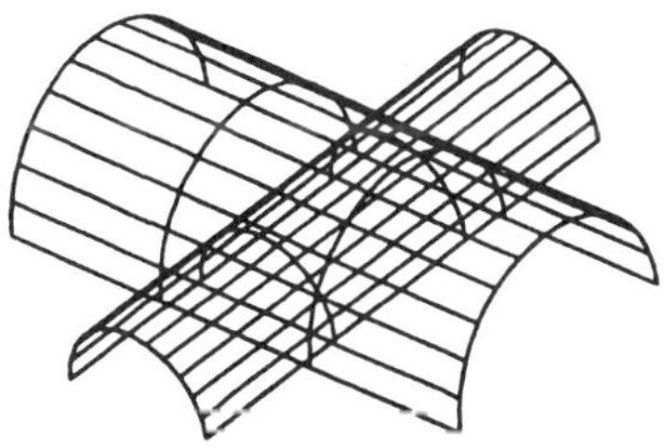

Figure 12.8b. Surface model

Step 1. Enter the Mastercam Mill and load the drawing file (ruled1).

If the wireframe model is not available, follow the step-by-step procedure given in the project 1 of chapter 11 to create the drawing.
Select **MAIN MENU → File → Get**
Enter file name: **ruled1** ↵
The drawing should appear as Figure 12.9.

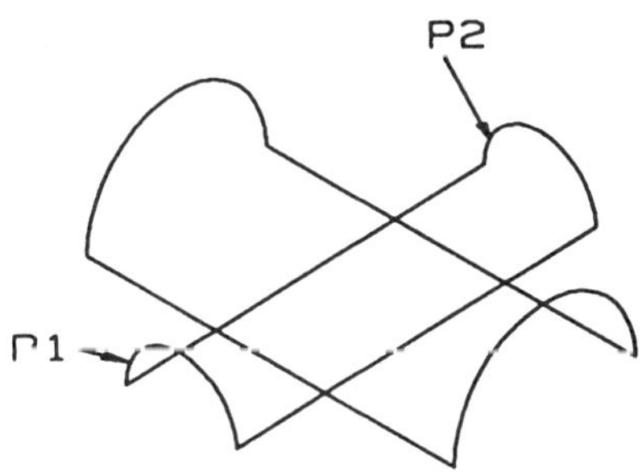

Figure 12.9

Step 2. Create the first ruled surface. Use the pick points in Figure 12.9.

Select **Level**
Double-click on **level #2** in the number column → **OK**
Select **MAIN MENU → Create → Surface → Ruled**
define contour 1: pick **Single** from the chaining method menu
Pick **P1** to select the first contour
Pick **P2** to select the second contour
define contour 3: pick **Done** from the chaining method menu to complete the first ruled surface
Toggle the type parameter to **N** to set the surface type = NURBS
Select **Do it** to generate the surface

The drawing with the first ruled surface should resemble Figure 12.10.

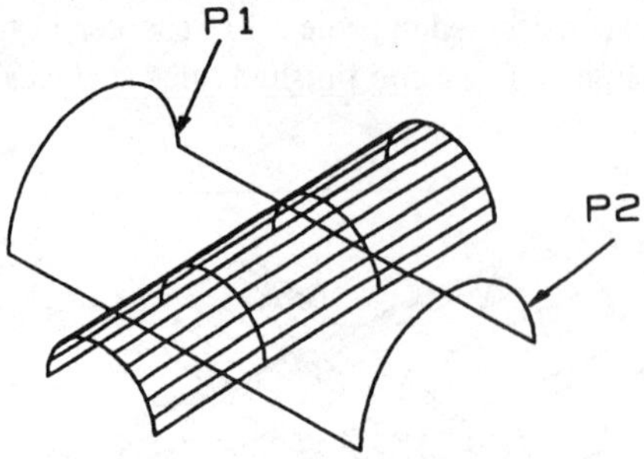

Figure 12.10

Step 3. Create the second ruled surface. Use the pick points in Figure 12.10.

Define contour 1: select **Single** and then pick **P1**
Define contour 2: pick **P2**
Define contour 3: select **Done** to complete the selection of the second ruled surface
Select **Do it** to generate the surface

The two ruled surfaces should look like Figure 12.11.

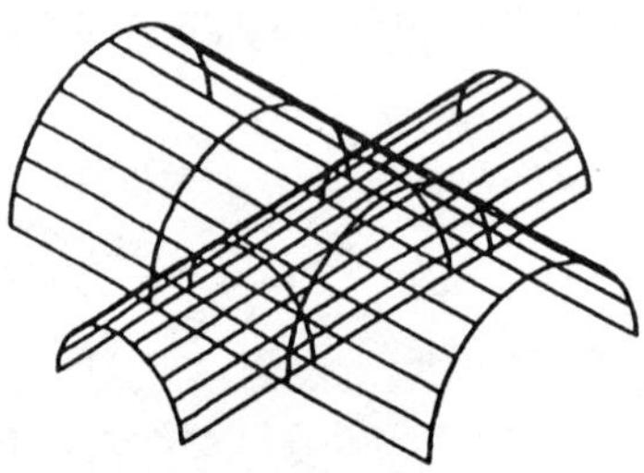

Figure 12.11

Step 4. Shade two surfaces

Select **MAIN MENU →Screen**
Select **Surf disp → Shading**
Set the Shading Setting dialog parameters to these settings:

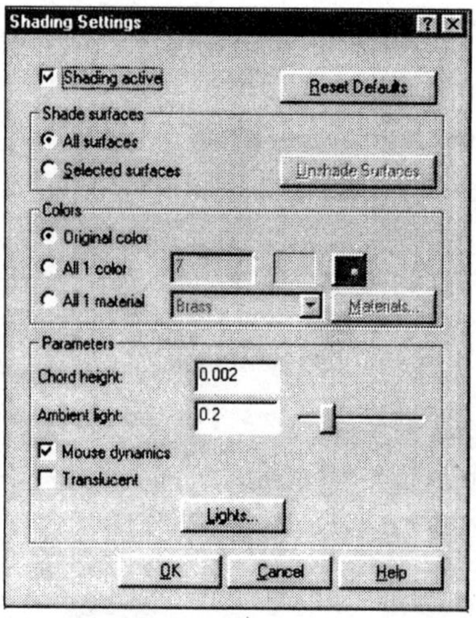

Select **OK**

Step 5. Change the Select Setting

Select **Shading**

Toggle the Shading active button to **Off** (no check mark) in the shading settings dailog box

Select **OK** to return back to the wireframe mode.

The shaded surfaces will appear on the screen as shown in Figure 12.11a.

Figure 12.11a

Step 6. Save the surfaces as ruleds1.

Select **MAIN MENU → File → Save**

Enter file name: **ruleds1**

Note: This surface is used to generate intersecting curves, fillet surfaces and trimmed surfaces in the preceeding chapters.

Project 2. Creating two ruled surfaces

In this example, we use the wireframe model constructed in the project 2 of chapter 11 to create two ruled surfaces. These two surfaces intersect forming an angle. The wireframe model is redrawn in Figure 12.12a, and the completed surface model is in Figure 12.12b.

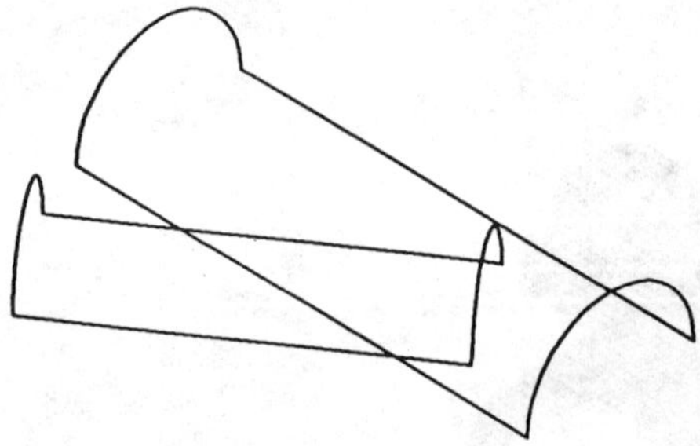

Figure 12.12a. Wireframe model

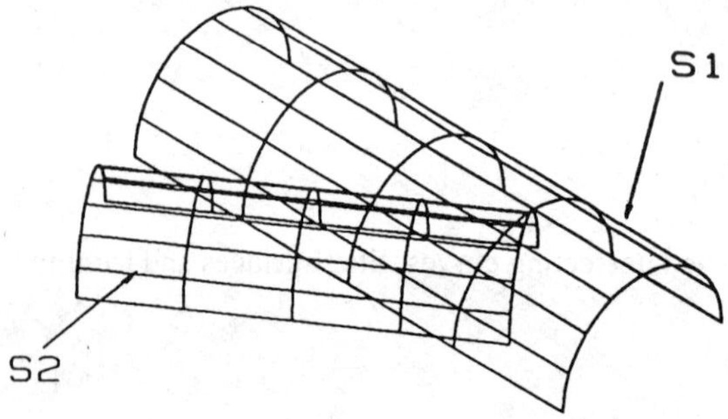

Figure 12.12b. Surface model

Step 1. Load the drawing file, or create the contour profiles by following the instructions in project 2 of chapter 11.

Select **MAIN MENU → File → Get**

Enter file name: **ruled2** ↵

The drawing on the screen should look like Figure 12.13.

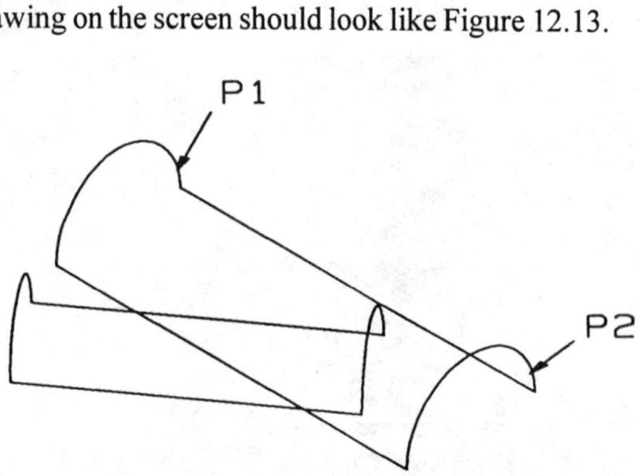

Figure 12.13

Step 2. Create the first ruled surface S1. 2

Use the pick points in Figure 12.13.
Select **Level**
Enter new level number: **2** → **OK**
Select **MAIN MENU** → **Create** → **Surface** → **Ruled**
Define contour 1: select **Single** and then pick **P1**
Define contour 2: pick **P2**
Define contour 3: select **Done** to complete the contour selection
Toggle the type parameter to **P** for parametric surface type
Select **Tolerance**
Set the Surface Error Tolerance = **0.001**
Select **Do it**

The first ruled surface should appear as Figure 12.14.

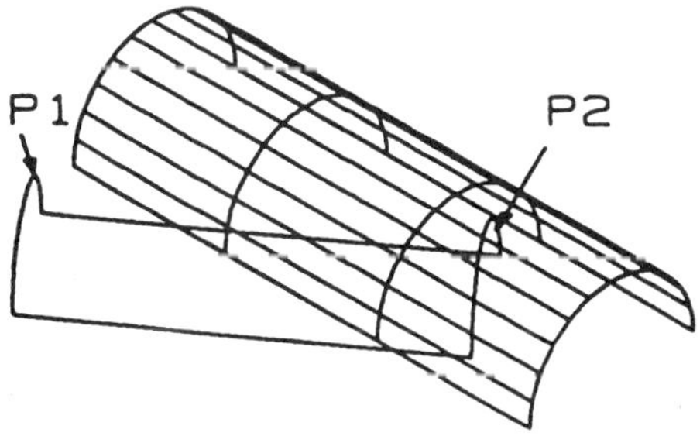

Figure 12.14

Step 3. Create the second ruled surface S2. Use the pick points in Figure 12.14.

Define contour 1: select **Single** and then pick **P1**
Define contour 2: pick **P2**
Define contour 3: select **Done** to complete the contour selection
Select **Do it**
The two ruled surfaces appear as Figure 12.15.

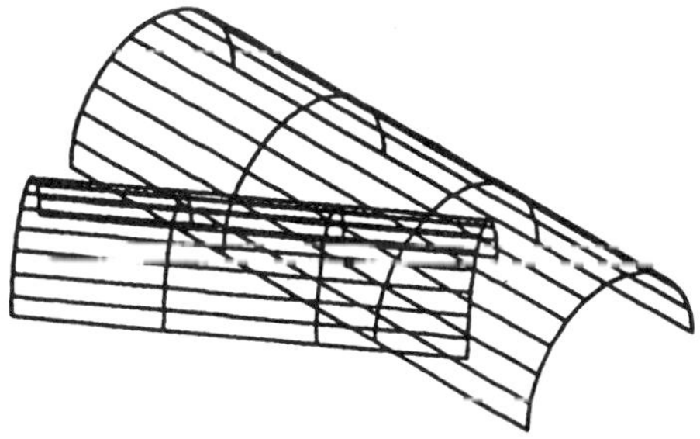

Figure 12.15

Step 4. Save the surfaces (ruleds2).

Select **MAIN MENU** → **File** → **Save**
Enter file name: **ruleds2**

Note: These two ruled surfaces are used to create two fillet surfaces with a variable radius in chapter 13.

Project 3. Creating a ruled surface formed by three contours

In this project, three contours are used to construct a ruled surface. The wireframe profiles are constructed in project 3 of chapter 11 which is redrawn in Figure 12.16a. The completed ruled surface is shown in Figure 12.16b.

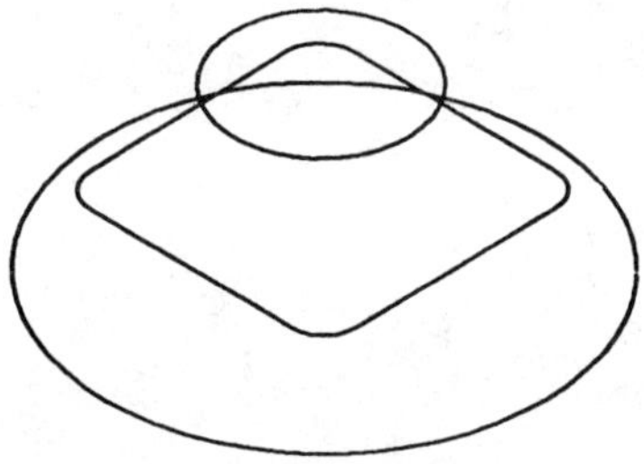

Figure 12.16a. Wireframe model

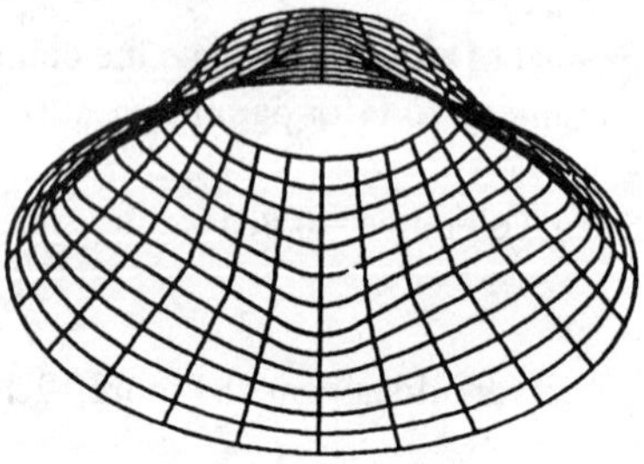

Figure 12.16b. Surface model

The keys to successfully create a ruled surface based on these three contours are:

> **Tips** 1. Use the Top Gview to give a better view of picking at entities.
>
> 2. Break the right vertical line of the rectangular contour into two pieces. This allows each contour to start at the same orientation.
>
> 3. The pick points at each contour should be placed on the position that make contours going the same direction.

Step 1. Load the wireframe model file (3contour) or create one according to the instructions given in project 3 of chapter 11.

Select **MAIN MENU → File → Get**

Enter file name: **3contour** ↵

The wireframe drawing should appear as Figure 12.17.

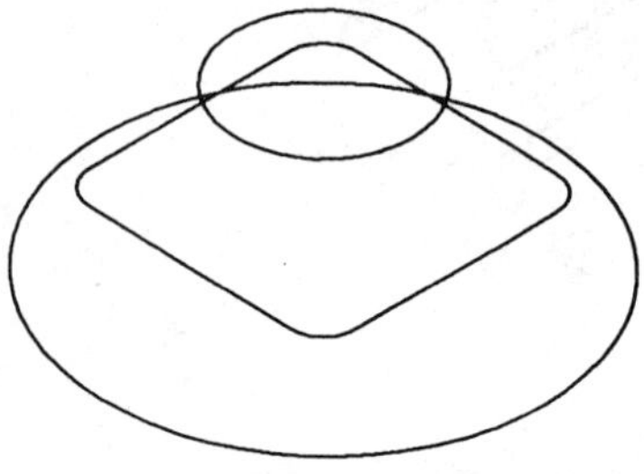

Figure 12.17

Step 2. Change to Top Gview. 3

Select **Gview → Top**

The drawing in Top Gview should resemble Figure 12.18.

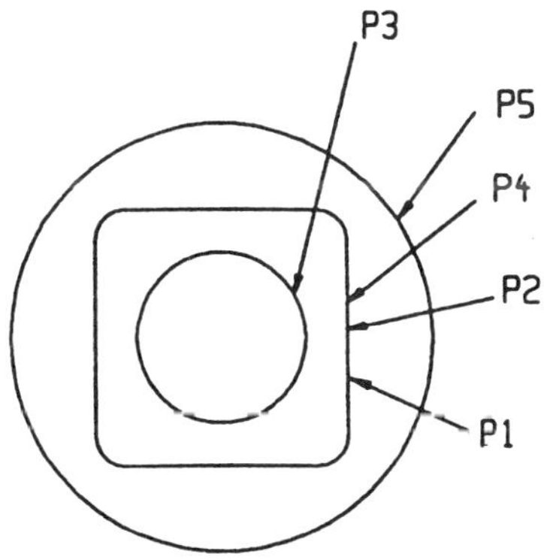

Figure 12.18

Step 3. Break the right vertical line of the rectangular contour into two pieces.

Use the pick points of Figure 12.18.
Select **MAIN MENU → Modify → Break → 2 pieces**
Pick **P1** to select the entity to break
Select **Midpoint** from the Point Menu
Pick **P2** to complete the breaking of the line

Step 4. Create a ruled surface. Continue to use the pick points in Figure 12.18.

Select **Level** (or use the short cut [Alt + Z])
Enter **2** in the Main level text box **→ OK**
Select **MAIN MENU → Create → Surface → Ruled**
Define contour 1: Select **Single** and then pick **P3** on the inside circle
Define contour 2: Select **Mode → Chain**
Select the rectangle: pick **P4**
Define contour 3: Select **Mode → Single** and then pick **P5** on the outside circle
Select **Done** to complete the contour selection
Toggle the surface type to **N**. Select **Do it**
Select **Gview → Isometric** to change drawing to isometric view

The surface drawing should resemble Figure 12.19 .

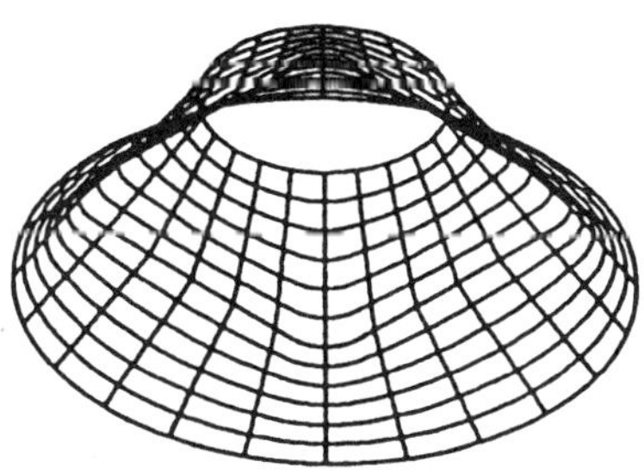

Figure 12.19

Step 5. Save the surface drawing as ruleds3.

Select **MAIN MENU → File → Save**
Enter file name: **ruleds3**

12.6 Loft Surfaces Modeling

Mastercam's loft surfaces modeling permits three or more sectional contours to be parabolically blended to form a smooth surface.

Keys to the successful completion of loft surfaces include:

Tips 1. The number of sectional contours must be more than two. When the number of contours is equal to two, the resulted surface is a ruled surface.

2. Break an entity into two pieces to allow the alignment of starting points for all contours when a contour has more than one entity. See the example in Figure 12.5.

3. Contours must be orderly selected.

4. Have the same chaining direction for all contours.

5. When the number of contours is relatively large and no contours are connected, use **Window → one way** commands to select the contours. This drastically reduces the time and the number of picking at entities and reduces the errors.

Project 4. Creating a loft surface formed by three contours 4

The three-contour wireframe model (3contour) is used again in this example to generate a loft surface. The contour profiles and the finished loft surface are shown in Figure 12.20.

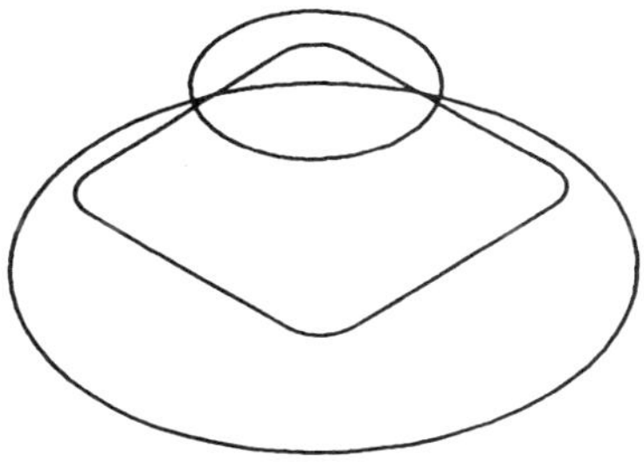

Figure 12.20a. Wireframe model

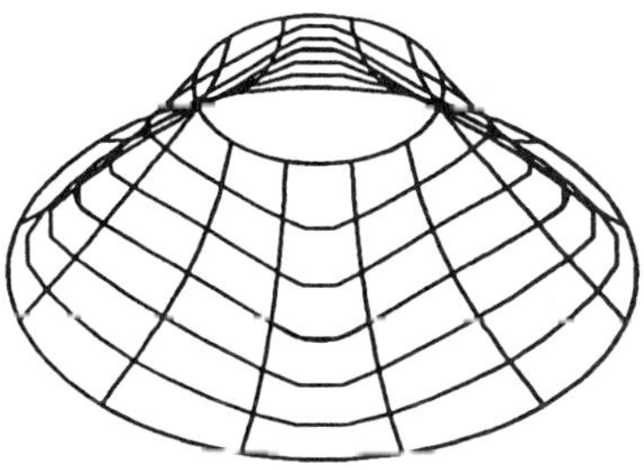

Figure 12.20b. Surface model

> **Tip** The right vertical edge of the rectangular contour must be broken into two pieces at the midpoint.

Step 1. Load the wireframe model file (3contour)

(or follow the instructions given in project 3 of chapter 11 to create one)
Select **MAIN MANU → File → Get**
Enter file name: **3contour** ↵
Select **Gview → Top** to change the Gview to Top view

The wireframe model on the screen appears as Figure 12.21.

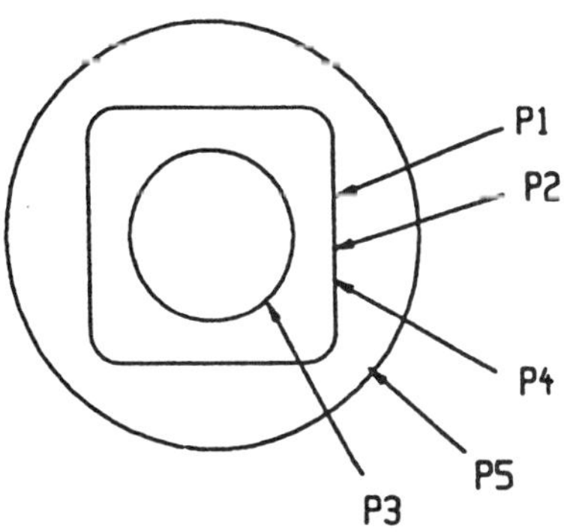

Figure 12.21

Step 2. Break the right vertical line of the rectangular contour into two pieces at the midpoint. Use the pick points in Figure 12.21.

Select **MAIN MENU → Modify → Break → 2 pieces**
Select an entity: pick **P1**
Enter the breakpoint: select **Midpoint** from the point menu and then pick **P2**

Step 3. Create the loft surface. Continue to use the pick points in Figure 12.21.

Select **Level**
Double-click on **level #2** in the Number column **→ OK**
Select **MAIN MENU → Create → Surface → Loft**
Define contour 1: select **Single** and then pick **P3** on the inside circle
Define contour 2: select **Mode → Chain** and then pick **P4**
Define contour 3: select **Mode → Single** and then pick **P5**
Select **Done** to complete the contour selection
Toggle the surface type to **N (Nurbs)**
Select **Do it** to complete the surface

The drawing in the Top Gview should appear on the screen as Figure 12.22.

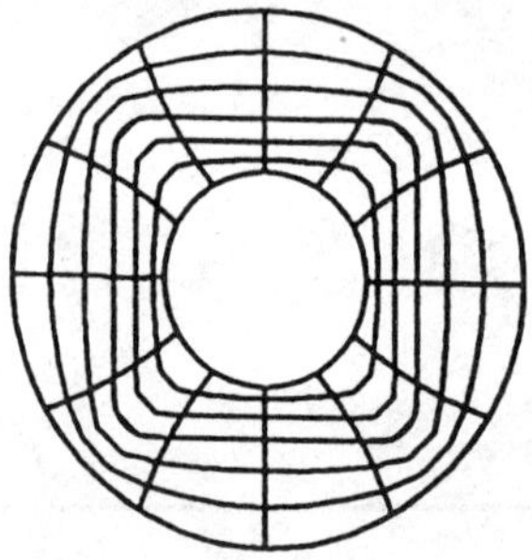

Figure 12.22

Step 4. Change the Gview to isometric.

Select **Gview → Isometric**

The final surface drawing should resemble Figure 12.23.

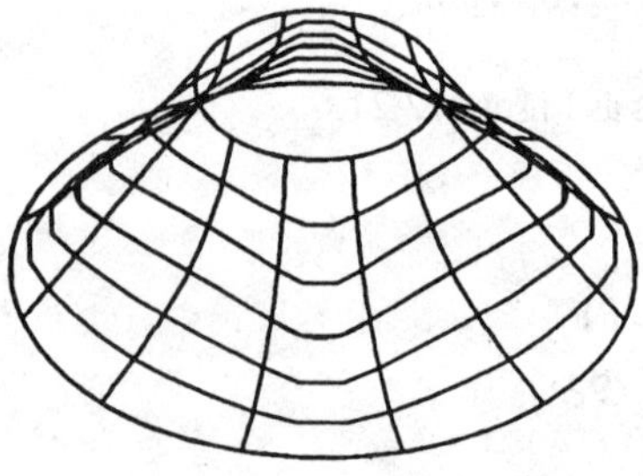

Figure 12.23

Step 5. Save the drawing file (lofts1).

Select **MAIN MENU → File → Save**
Enter file name: **lofts1**

Project 5. Creating a loft surface of ninteen sectional contours　5

The nineteen sectional contours created in the project 4 of chapter 11 are used to generate a loft surface. The wireframe model and the finished surface model are shown in Figure 12.24.

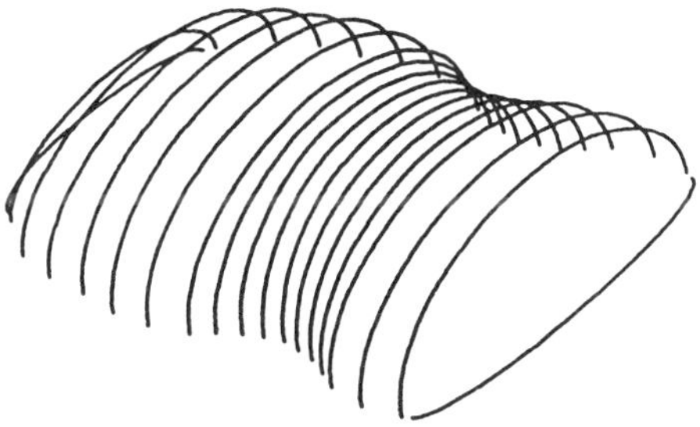

Figure 12.24a. Wireframe model

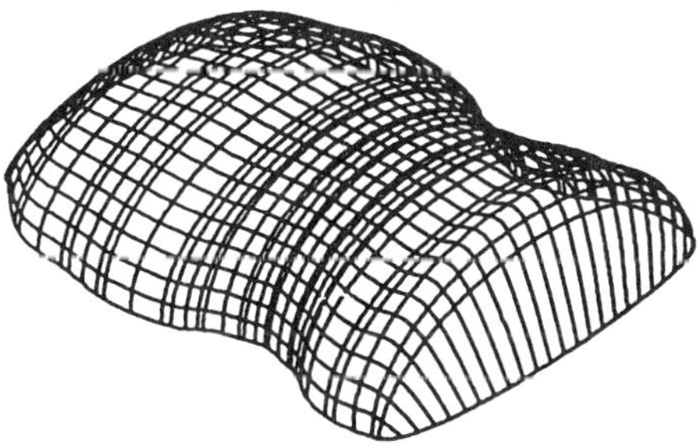

Figure 12.24b. Surface model

Tip: The Window chaining menu is used in this example to reduce the picking of contours.

Step 1. Load the wireframe model file (loft2)

(or follow the instructions in project 4 of chapter 11 to create one)
Select **MAIN MENU** → **File** → **Get**
Enter file name: **loft2** ↵
The wireframe model should appear as Figure 12.25.

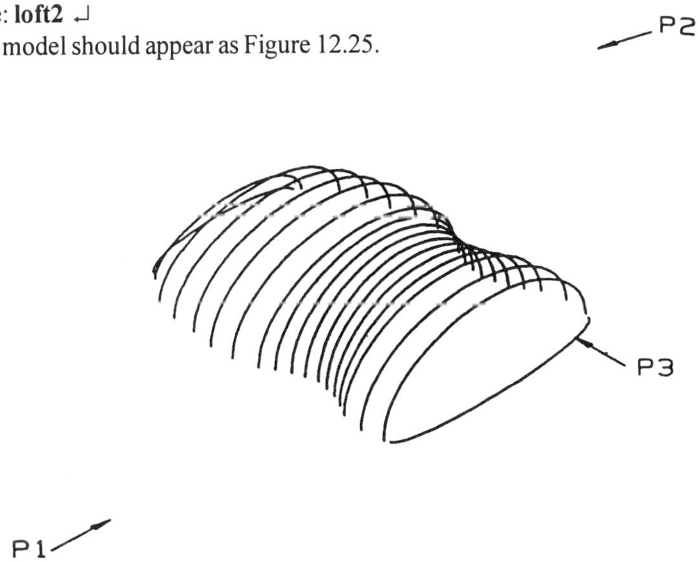

Figure 12.25

Step 2. Create the loft surface. Use the pick points in Figure 12.25.

Select **Level**
Enter **2** in the Main level text box → **OK**
Select **MAIN MENU** → **Create** → **Surface** → **Loft**
Select **Window** → **Options**
Set the Chaining Options as in the dialog box shown here:

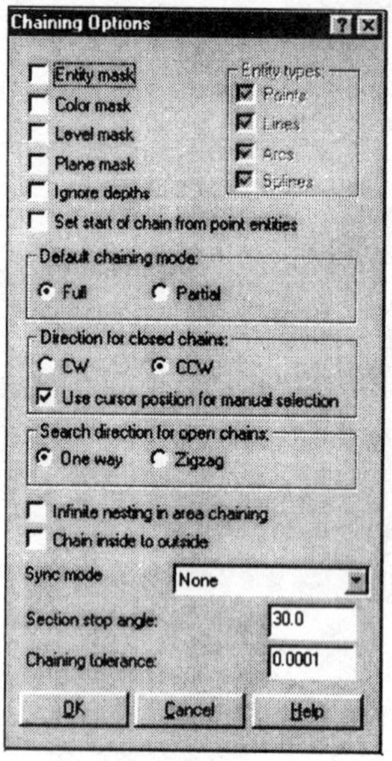

Select **OK**

Enter the first corner: pick **P1**
Enter the second corner: Pick **P2** to ensure all contours are included in the window
Enter search point: select **Endpoint** from the Point Menu and then pick **P3**
Select **Done** from the Chaining method Menu
Toggle surface type to **N (Nurbs)**
Select **Do it** to complete the surface

The loft surface should resemble Figure 12.26.

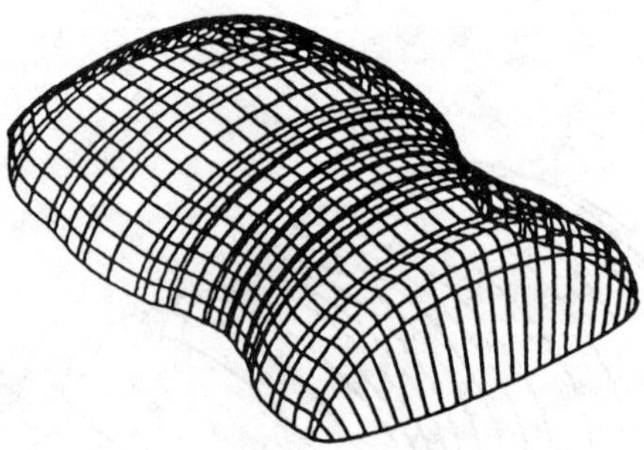

Figure 12.26

Step 3. Save the surface model file (lofts2).

Select **MAIN MENU** → **File** → **Save**
Enter file name: **lofts2**

Note: This surface model is used to create a trimmed surface in chapter 13.

Project 6. Creating a loft surface using five sectional contours 6

The five sectional contours constructed in the project 14 of chapter 11 are used to create a loft surface. The contours are redrawn in Figure 12.27a and the finished loft surface is in Figure 12.27b.

Figure 12.27a. Wireframe model

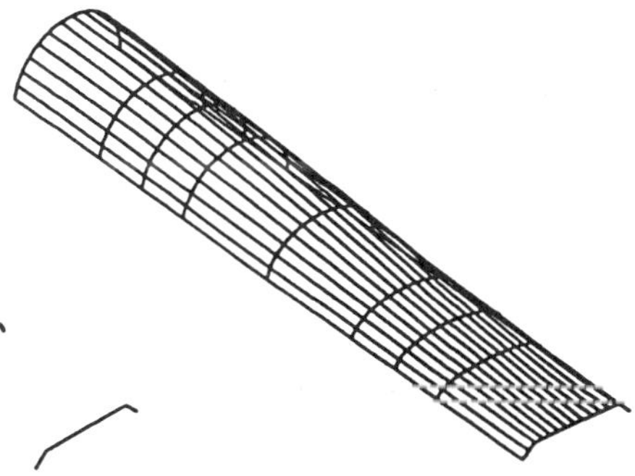

Figure 12.27b. Surface model

Tips 1. Create a loft surface based on the five sectional profiles.

2. Mirror the loft surface about the X axis to create the lower surface section. Note that the Cplane needs to be either Front or Side view.

Step 1. Load the wireframe model profiles (loft3)

(or create one by following instructions in project 14 of chapter 11.)
Select **MAIN MENU → File → Get**
Enter file name: **loft3** ↵
The five contours should look like Figure 12.28.

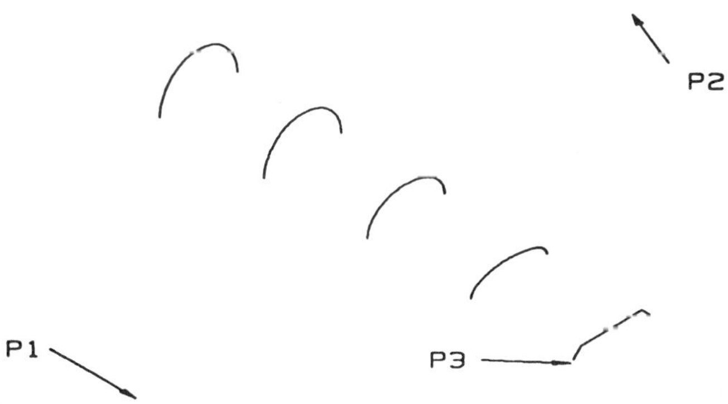

Figure 12.28

Step 2. Create a loft surface.

Use the pick points in Figure 12.28.
Select **Level**
Enter **2** in the Main Level text box → **OK**
Select **MAIN MENU → Create**
Select **Surface → Loft → Window**
Select **Options**

Set the Chaining Options dialog box as here:

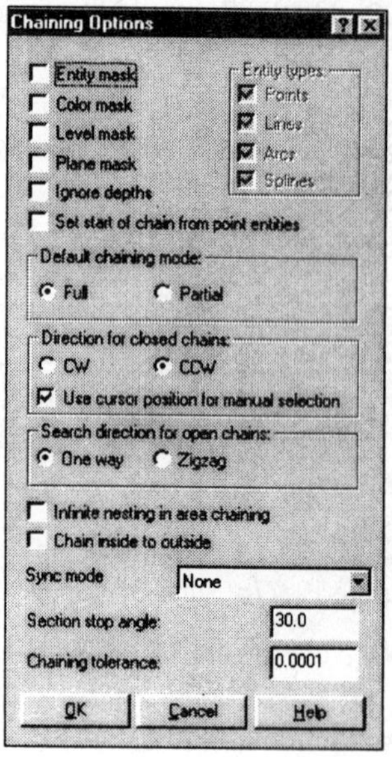

Select **OK**

Pick **P1** and **P2** to specify the window range
Select **Endpoint**
Pick **P3** to trap the endpoint for the search point
Select **Done**
Toggle surface type to **N (Nurbs)**
Set the surface error tolerance to **0.01**
Select **Do it** to complete the surface

Note: The system will display the message "Sharp corners in the Curve geometry will be ignored unless sync-ed"
Press **Enter** to generate the surface.

The loft surface should appear as Figure 12.29.

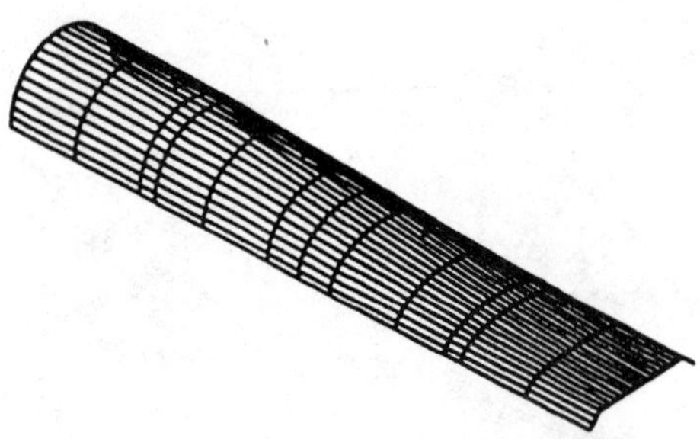

Figure 12.29

Step 3. Save the surface model file (lofts3).

Select **MAIN MENU → File → Save**

Enter file name: **lofts3**

Step 4. Mirror the surface about the X axis to create the lower surface section.

Use either Front or Side Cplane. Use the pick points in Figure 12.29.
Select **Cplane → Front**
Select **MAIN MENU → Xform → Mirror → All → Entities**
Select **Done → X axis**
Select **Copy → OK** from the Mirror parameters menu

The entire surface model now should appear as Figure 12.30.

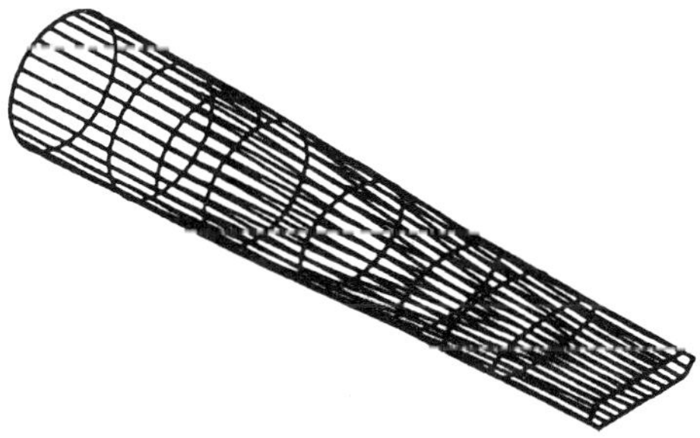

Figure 12.30

12.7 Coons Surfaces Modeling

A Coons surface is created by blending a set of surface patches, each formed by four edge curves. There are two chaining methods which are used to define surface patches; **automatic** chaining and **manual** chaining. The automatic chaining method defines the surface patch with three entities; the two curves that meet in the upper-left corner and one curve in the lower-right corner of the geometry (Figure 12.31.)

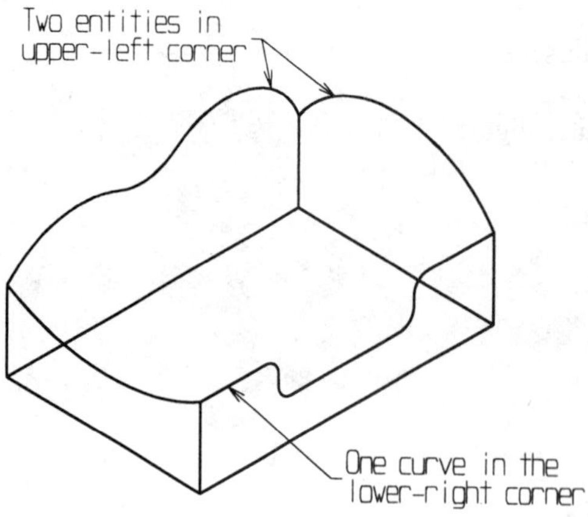

Figure 12.31a

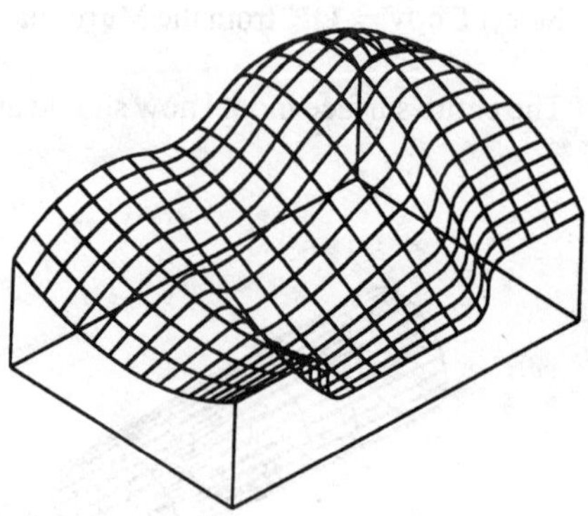

Figure 12.31b

The minimum branch angle is used to determine which of several intersecting entities to chain. Mastercam does not chain along any entity that intersects at an angle larger than the minimum branch angle.

Tips for **automatic** chaining:

1. Mastercam may not be able to determine the patch layout for a complex chaining which has many branch points. Use the manual chaining method for a complex patch layout. In this case, an error message "Automatic Chaining Failed - Cannot reach Last Point" will appear. Figure 12.32 shows a failed example of automatic chaining due to too many branches.

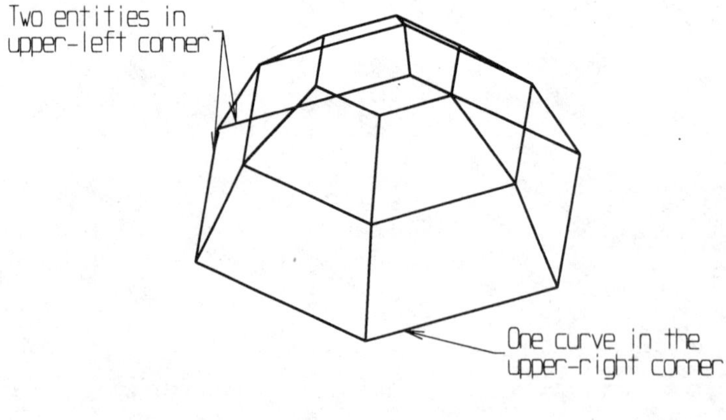

Figure 12.32

2. Automatic chaining will fail when the system cannot reach the last point. In this case, an error message "Automatic Chaining Failed - Cannot reach Last Point" appears. This error may be caused by one of these reasons:

   a. The upper-left corner was not selected (Figure 12.33.)
   b. The lower-right corner has not been selected (Figure 12.34.)
   c. The curves used for chaining are not intersecting properly.

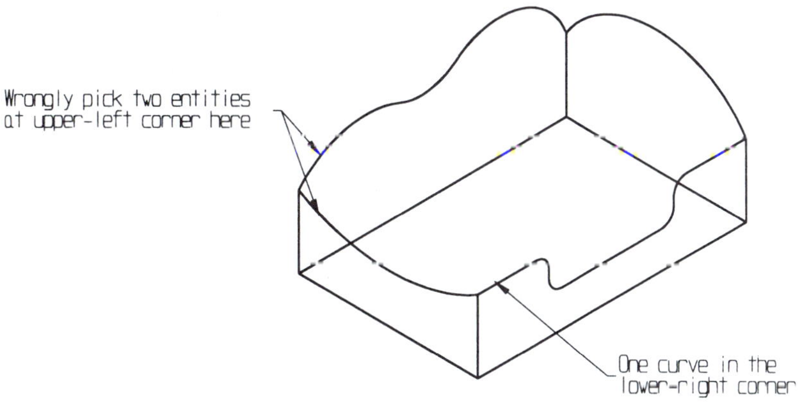

Figure 12.33

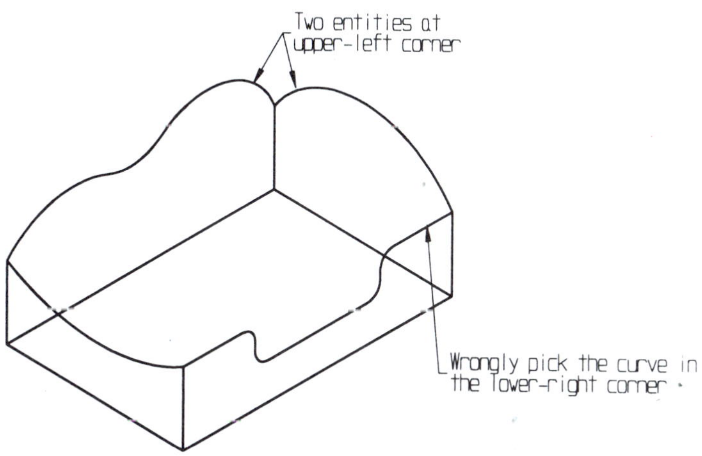

Figure 12.34

Try picking other intersecting curves to resolve the errors. If this does not work, use the manual chaining method.

The **manual** chaining method is a complicated process. These instructions should help in successfully completing a coons surface. Defining contours for Coons surfaces is a rather difficult process because they involve many more contours than other surface modeling techniques.

Tips 1. Select the start point. The start point is normally chosen at a join point of two contours. One of these two join contours becomes the first **along** contour, and the other is the first **across** contour. Figure 12.35 shows an example of selecting the start point of defining a Coons surface.

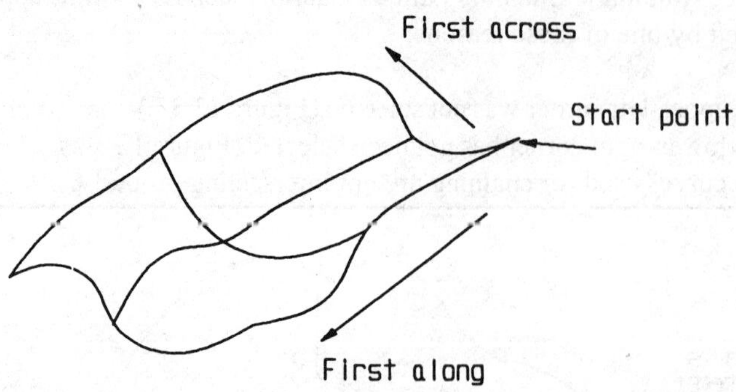

Figure 12.35

> 2. Determine the number of patches in the along direction and the number of patches in the across direction.

In the case of an open boundary where the first and the last contour are not connected as shown in Figure 12.36.

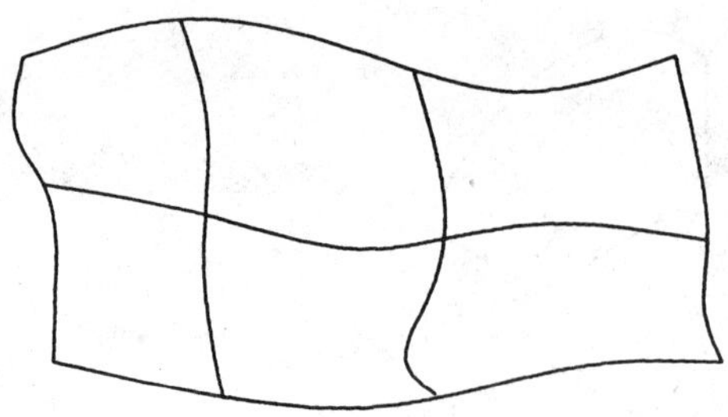

Figure 12.36

$$P_L = N_C - 1$$
$$P_C = N_L - 1$$
$$P_T = P_L \times P_C$$

where P_L = number of patches in along direction
P_C = number of patches in across direction
P_T = total number of patches
N_L = number of along contours
N_C = number of across contours

Example 12.1

Find the numbers of patches in along and across direction for the surface contours given in Figure 12.37.

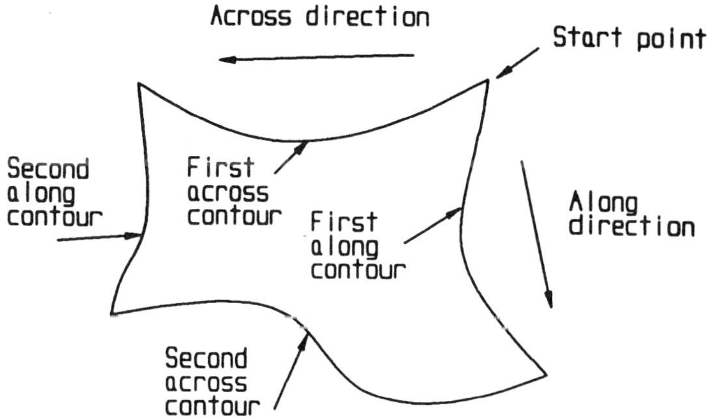

Figure 12.37

Solution:

Number of along contours $N_L = 2$
Number of across contours $N_C = 2$
Number of patches in along direction $P_L = N_C - 1 = 2 - 1 = 1$
Number of patches in across direction $P_C = N_L - 1 = 2 - 1 = 1$
Total number of patches $P_T = P_L \times P_C = 1 \times 1 = 1$

Example 12.2

Find the numbers of patches in along and across direction for the surface contours given in Figure 12.38.

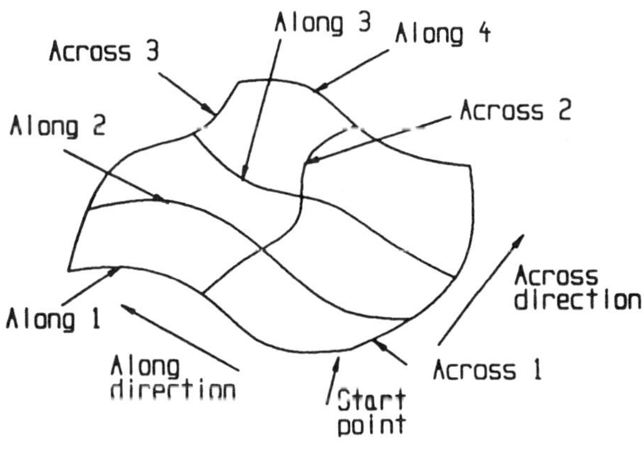

Figure 12.38

Solution:

$N_L = 4$
$N_C = 3$
$P_L = N_C - 1 \quad = 3 - 1 \quad = 2$
$P_C = N_L - 1 \quad = 4 - 1 \quad = 3$
$P_T = P_L \times P_C \quad = 2 \times 3 \quad = 6$

In the case of a close boundary where the first and the last contour are connected. Actually they are the identical contour (Figure 12.39).

The number of patches in along direction $P_L = N_C$
The number of patches in across direction $P_C = N_L - 1$

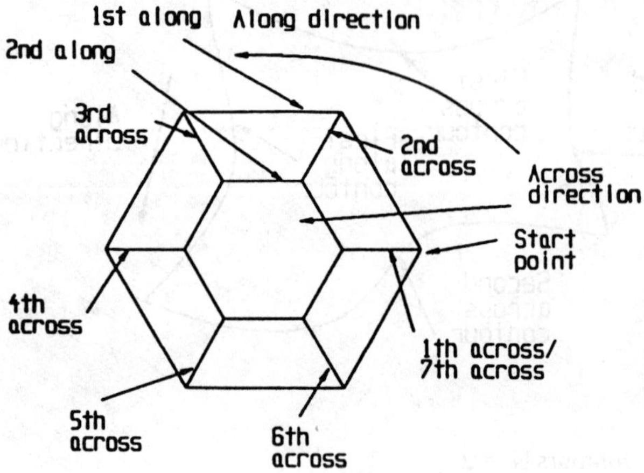

Figure 12.39

Example 12.3

Determine the number of patches in the along and across direction for the surface shown in Figure 12.40.

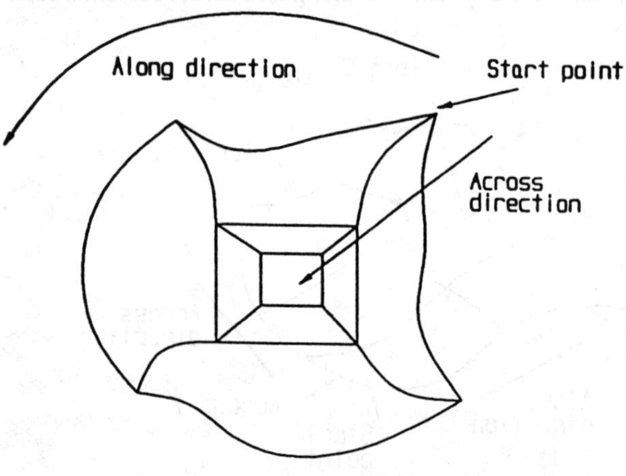

Figure 12.40

Solution

$N_L = 3$
$N_C = 4$
$P_L = N_C \quad = 4$
$P_C = N_L - 1 \quad = 3 - 1 \quad = 2$
$P_T = P_L \text{ X } P_C = 4 \text{ X } 2 = 8$

Tip 3. Assignment of along rows and across columns.

The surface patch boundaries are laid out in a grid. Along contours are assigned in rows and across contours in columns. Each contour in the grid is identified by an along row number and an across column number (Figure 12.41).

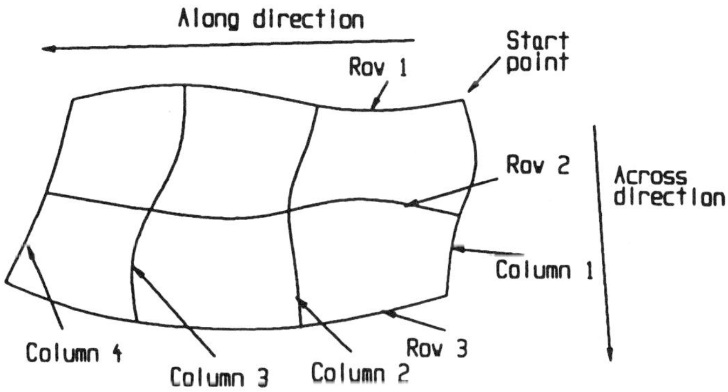

Figure 12.41

Tip 4. The order of contours selection.

The contours selection must follow a predetermined order that is along contours are sequentially selected first, followed by the across contours as follows:

Selection order	entity to be picked
1st selection	along row 1 - across column 1
2nd selection	along row 1 - across column 2
-	-
-	-
nth selection	along row 1 - across column n
n+1 selection	along row 2 - across column 1
n+2 selection	along row 2 - across column 2
-	-
-	-
2n selection	along row 2 - across column n
-	-
-	-
mn selection	along row m - across column n

Example 12.4

This example shows the contours selection sequence for the patches having an open boundary (Figure 12.42).

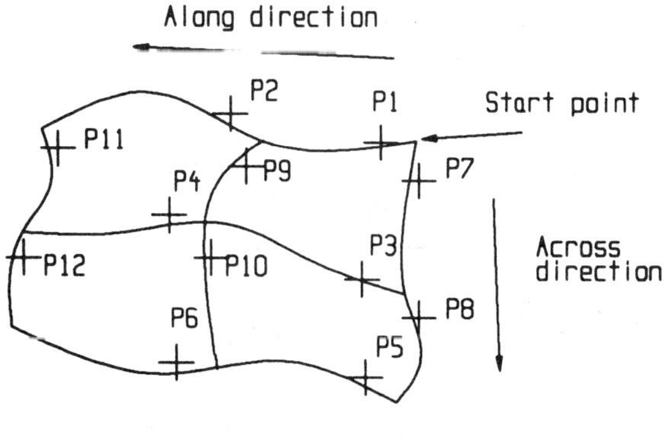

Figure 12.42

Example 12.5

In this example the contours selection sequence for the surface patches having a closed boundary is illustrated (Figure 12.43).

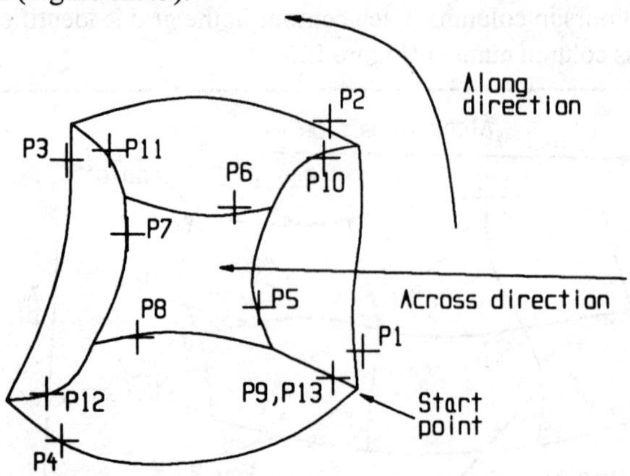

Figure 12.43

Example 12.6

Figure 12.44 shows an example where six lines are joined in one point. The patch grid layout requires two along contours and six across contours. The first along contour consists of the six sides of the hexagon. The second along contour is a point which is the common point the six lines joined.

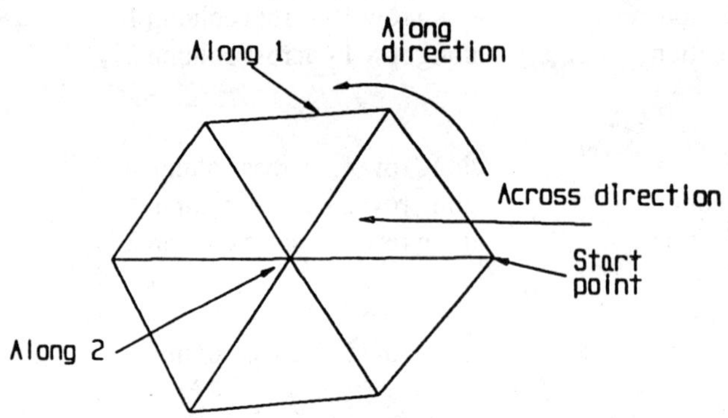

Figure 12.44

Tip 5. Selection of the blending method

There are four blending methods for generating a Coons surface:

Linear: used when surfaces are fairly flat
Parabolic: used when surfaces have greater curvatures
Cubic: used when surfaces have greater curvatures
Cubic with slope matching: used when parabolic or cubic produces flat spots on surfaces

Figure 12.45 compares the effect of these four blending methods on a surface.

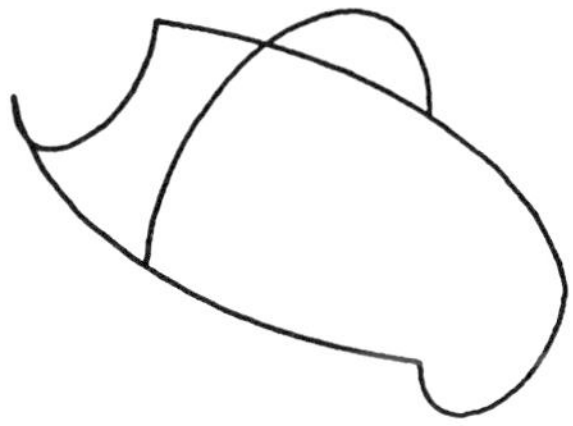

a. Wireframe model

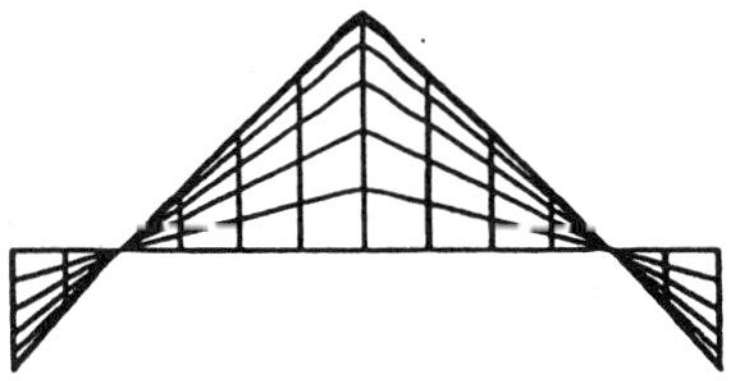

b. Linear

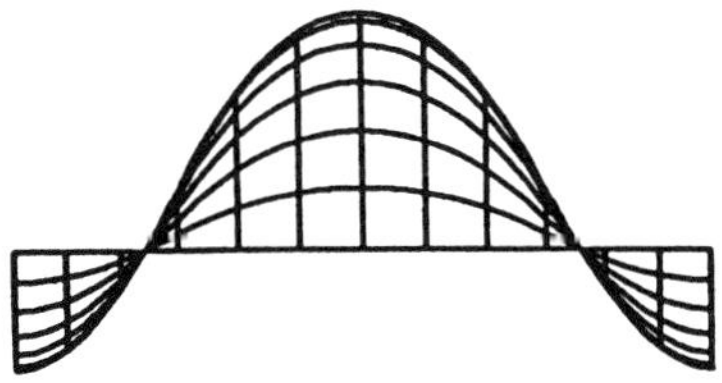

c. Parabolic

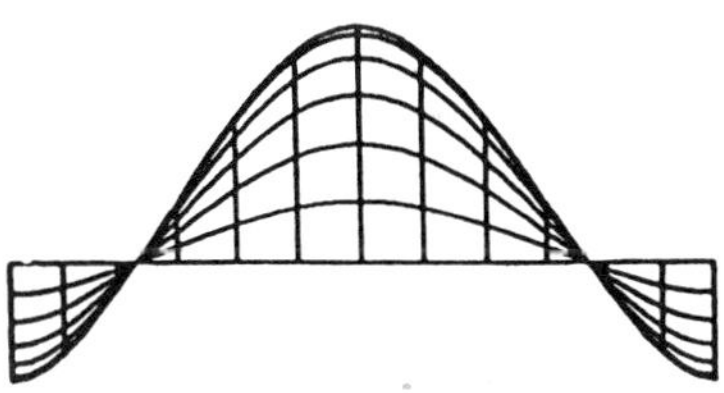

d. Cubic

e. Cubic with slope matching

Figure 12.45

Project 7. Creating a Coons surface of one patch

This example uses the wireframe model of project 5 in chapter 11 to generate a Coons surface. The wireframe model and the final surface model are shown in Figure 12.46.

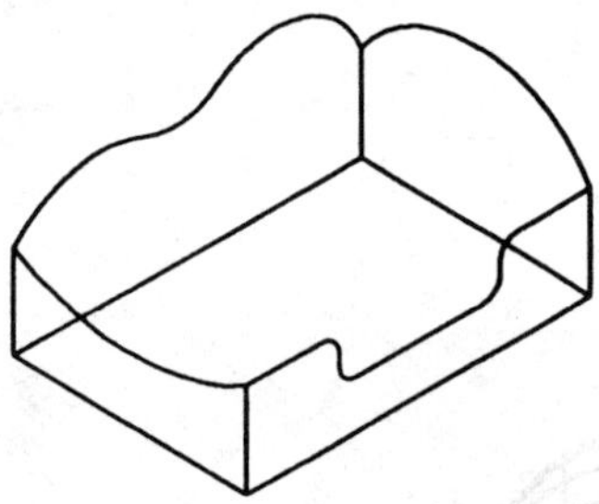

Figure 12.46a. Wireframe model

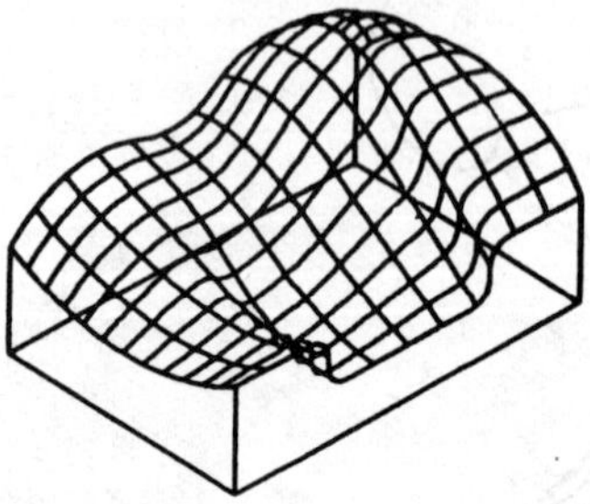

Figure 12.46b. Surface model

Tips 1. This is a single path surface.

2. Use the automatic chaining method to chain the contours.

Step 1. Load the wireframe model (coons1)

(or create one by following the instructions given in project 5 of chapter 11)
Select **MAIN MENU →File → Get**
Enter file name: **coons1** ↵

The wireframe model on the screen should resemble Figure 12.47.

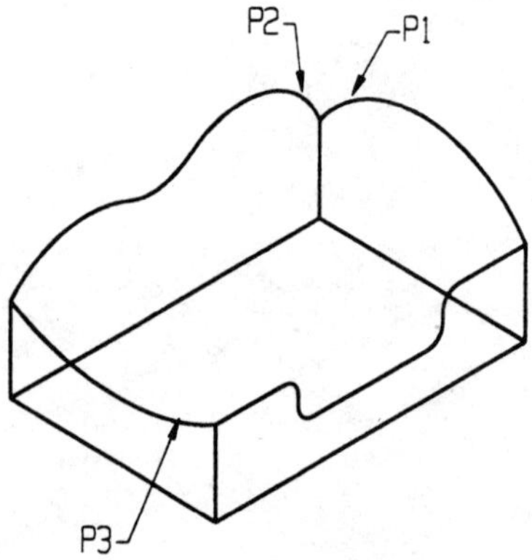

Figure 12.47

Step 2. Create the Coons surface. Use the pick points in Figure 12.47.

Select **Level**
Double-click on level #**2** in the Number Column → **OK**
Select **MAIN MENU** → **Create** → **Surface** → **Coons**
Select **Yes** to use automatic coons chaining
Pick **P1** and **P2** to select the curves which intersect at the upper-left corner.
Pick **P3** to select the end of one curve at the lower-right corner.
Toggle the surface to **N (Nurbs)**
Toggle **Blending** to **P (Parabolic)**
Select **Do it**

The newly created Coons surface should look like Figure 12.48.

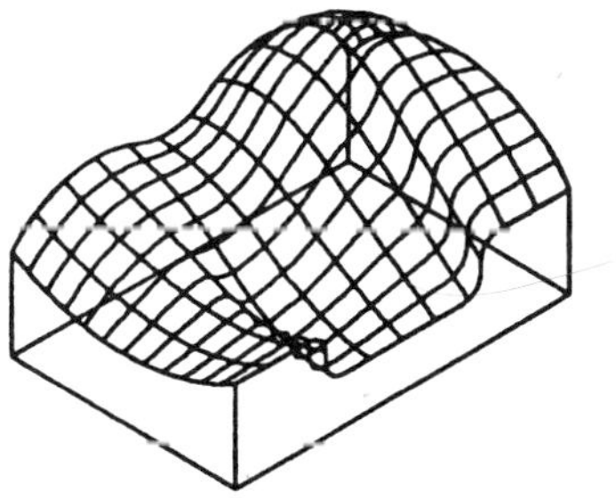

Figure 12.48

Step 3. Save the surface model file as coonss1.

Select **MAIN MENU** → **file** → **Save**
Entcr filc name: **coonss1**

Project 8. Creating a Coons surface of two patches

In this project, we still use the wireframe model of project 5 in chapter 11 except that we add an arc to form a three-along-contours surface. It is intended to show how the added contour changes the skin of the surface. The new wireframe model and the resulted surface are illustrated in Figure 12.49.

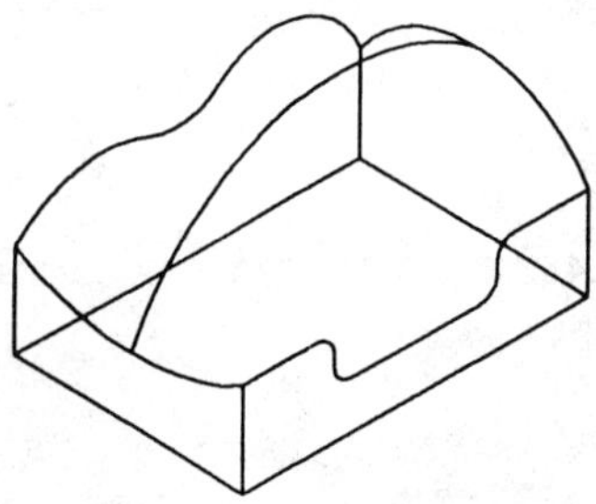

Figure 12.49a Wireframe model

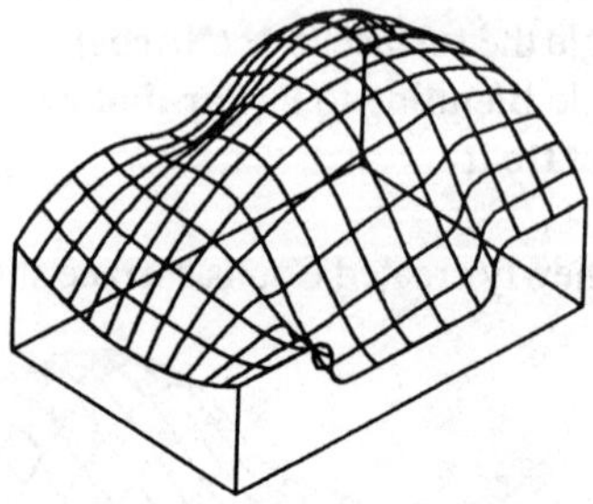

Figure 12.49b. Surface model

> **Tips** 1. Use the Side Cplane to add an arc between the midpoint of the two arcs in the across direction.
> 2. The number of patches is 2.
> 3. Each of two across arcs must be broken into two entities at the midpoints because an along contour is added to the profile.
> 4. Use the automatic coons chaining method to chaiun contours.

Step 1. Load the wireframe model file (coons1).

Select **MAIN MENU → File → Get**
Enter file name: **coons1** ↵

The wireframe model should appear as Figure 12.50.

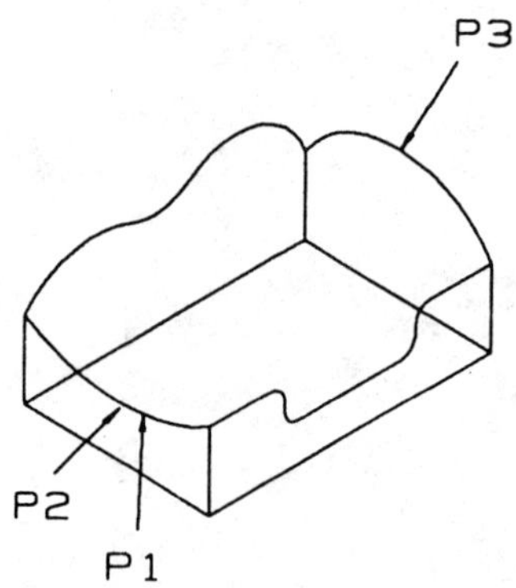

Figure 12.50

Step 2. Add an arc using the Side Cplane. 8

Use the pick points in Figure 12.50.
Select **Cplane → Side**
Select **Z → Midpoint** and then pick **P1**
Z2.5 should appear in the Secondary menu.
Select **MAIN MENU → Create → Arc → Endpoints → Midpoint**
Pick **P2**
Select **Midpoint,** then pick **P3**
Enter the radius: **5** ↵
Pick the second arc segment from the top to complete the arc
The new wireframe model should resemble Figure 12.51.

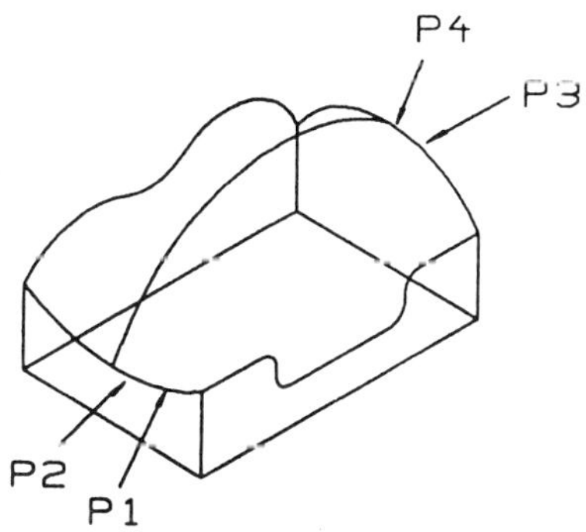

Figure 12.51

Step 3. Break the two arcs into two pieces each, using the Front Cplane.

Use the pick points in Figure 12.51.
Select **Cplane → Front**
Select **MAIN MENU → Modify → Break → 2 pieces**
Select an entity, pick **P1**
Enter the breakpoint: select **Midpoint** from the Point Menu
then pick **P2** to complete the breaking of the first arc
Select an entity: pick **P3**
Select **Midpoint**
Enter the breakpoint: pick **P4** for the breaking of the second arc

The new drawing looks identical to the one before breaking the two arcs. The drawing is redisplayed in Figure 12.52.

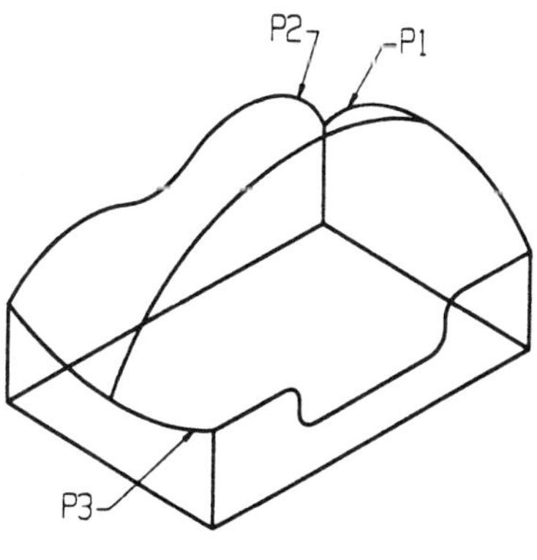

Figure 12.52

Step 4. Create the Coons surface using the pick points in Figure 12.52.

Select **Level,** then enter **2** in the Main Level text box → **OK**
Select **MAIN MENU** → **Create** → **Surface** → **Coons**
Select **Yes** to use automatic coons chaining
Pick **P1** and **P2** to select curves which intersect at the upper-left corner.
Pick **P3** to select the end of a curve at the lower-right corner.
Set the **Coons Surface** parameters as below:

Surface error tolerance = **0.01**

Surface type = **N (Nurbs)**
Blending = **C (Cubic)**

Select **Do it** to complete the chaining

The surface model should resemble Figure 12.53.

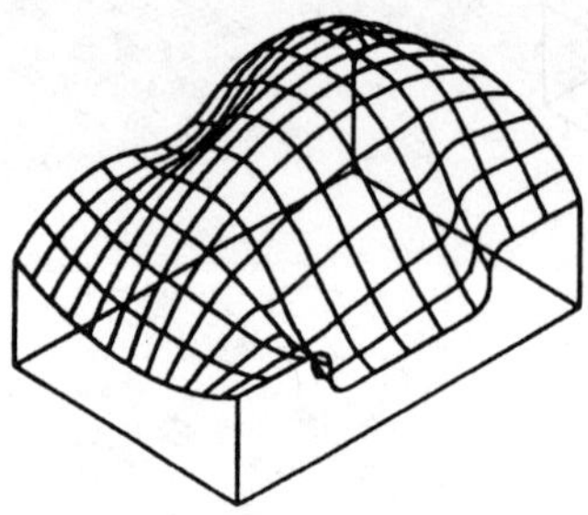

Figure 12.53

Step 5. Save the surface model file (coonss2).

Select **MAIN MENU** → **File** → **Save**
Enter file name: **coonss2**

Project 9. Creating a Coons surface with a joint point on along contours 9

This project uses a common join point as an along contour. The wireframe model is constructed in project 6 of chapter 11. The wireframe model and the final surface model are shown in Figure 12.54.

Figure 12.54a. Wireframe model

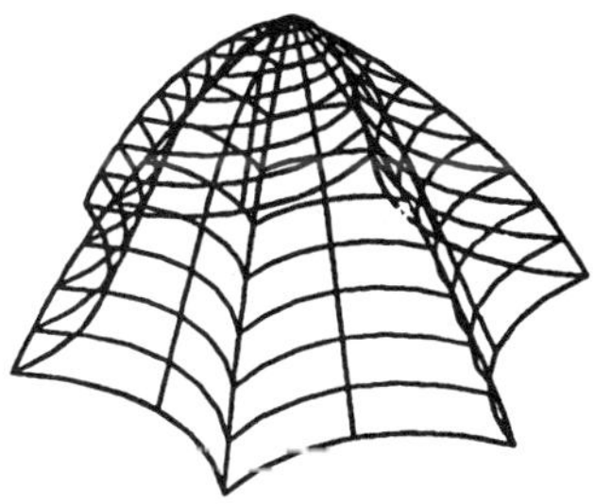

Figure 12.54b. Surface model

Tips 1. Use Top Gview to facilitate the picking at the contours.

2. Use the common join point as one of along contour.

3. Number of patches in the along direction is 6.

4. Number of patches in the across direction is 1.

Step 1. Load the wireframe model file coons3.

(or create one by following the instructions in project 6 of chapter 11.)
The drawing should appear as Figure 12.55.)
Select **MAIN MENU→ File → Get**
Enter file name: **coons3** ↵

Figure 12.55

Step 2. Change the Gview to Top.

Select **Gview → Top**

The drawing becomes Figure 12.56.

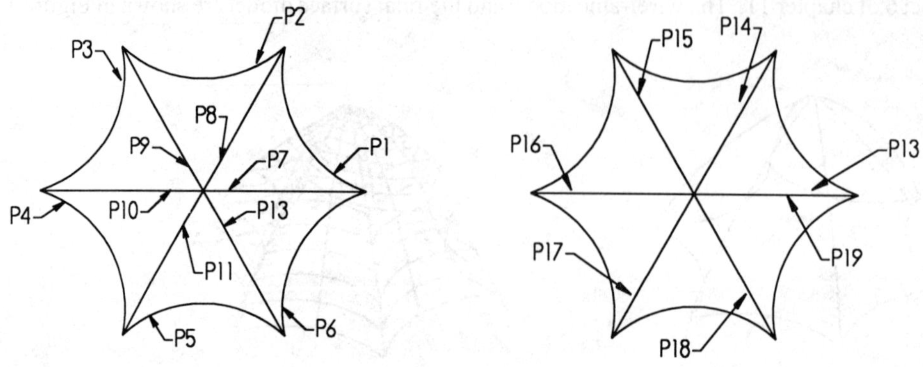

Figure 12.56

Step 3. Create the Coons surface using the pick points in Figure 12.56.

Select **Level,** then enter **2** in the Main Level text box → **OK**
Select **MAIN MENU** → **Create** → **Surface** → **Coons**
Select **No** to use automatic chaining.

Enter the number of patches in the along direction: **6** ↵
Enter the number of patches in the across direction: **1** ↵
Select **Single**
Sequentially pick **P1 - P6** to complete the along contour of row 1.
Select **Mode** → **Point** → **Endpoint**
Pick **P7**
Select **Point** → **Endpoint** → **P8** (repeat this step for remaining points **P9 - P12)**
Selecting **Mode** → **Single**
Sequentially pick **P13 - P19** to complete the across contour.

Select **Done** to complete the selection
Change the Coons surface parameters to the following settings:

Surface error tolerance = **0.05** Surface type = **N (Nurbs)** Blending = **C (Cubic)**

Select **Do it** to complete the surface
The surface model in Top Gview should appear as Figure 12.57

Figuro 12.57

Step 4. Change Gview to isometric.

Select **Gview → Isometric**

The surface model shown in isometric view should resemble Figure 12.58.

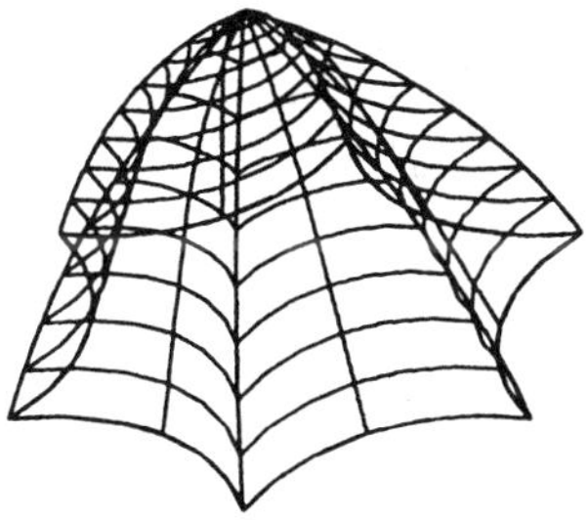

Figure 12.58

Step 5. Save the surface model file as coonss3.

Select **MAIN MENU → File → Save**

Enter file name:**coonss3**

Project 10. Creating a Coons surface of multiple faces

This project uses a wireframe model with thirteen faces to create a Coons surface. The wireframe model is shown in Figure 12.59a and the resultant Coons surface is illustrated in Figure 12.59b.

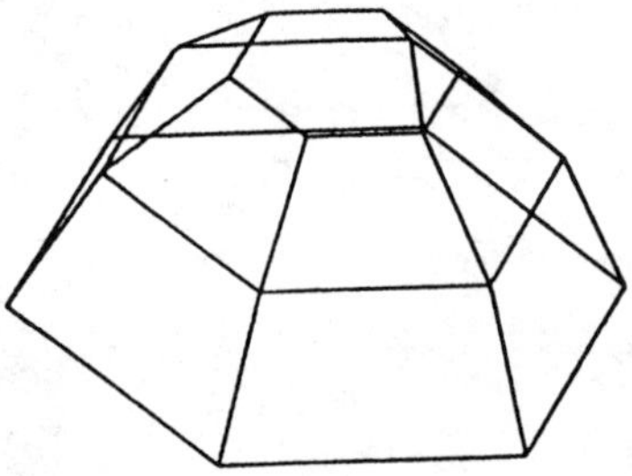

Figure 12.59a. Wireframe model

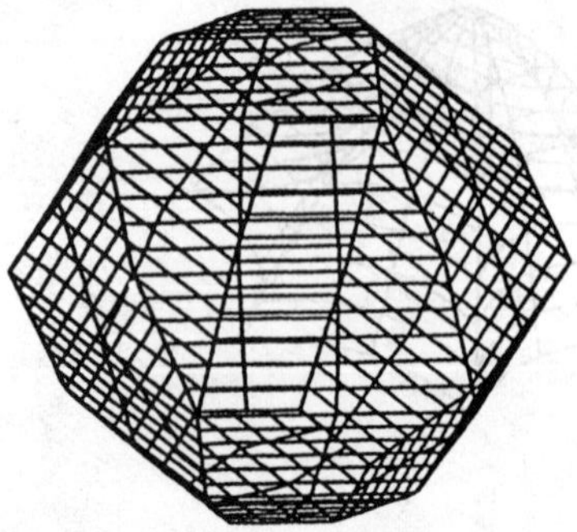

Figure 12.59b. Surface model

Tips 1. Use the Top Gview to facilitate the picking of contours.

2. Create a Coons surface based on the twelve faces.

3. The number of patches in the along direction is 6.

4. The number of patches in the across direction is 2.

5. Create a ruled surface for the top face.

6. Use separate levels and different colors for these two surfaces.

7. Mirror the two surfaces about the X axis using the Front Cplane to complete the surface model.

Step 1. Load the wireframe model file coons4.

(or create one by following the instructions in the project 7 of chapter 11.)
Select **MAIN MENU → File → Get**
Enter the file name: **coons4** ↵

The wireframe model drawing of thirteen faces should appear on your screen as it is shown in Figure 12.60.

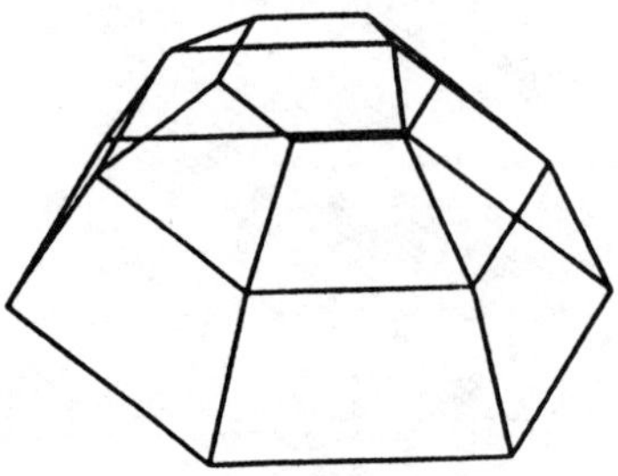

Figure 12.60

Step 2. Change the drawing to Top Gview.

10

Select **Gview → Top**

The drawing in the Top Gview appears as in Figure 12.61.

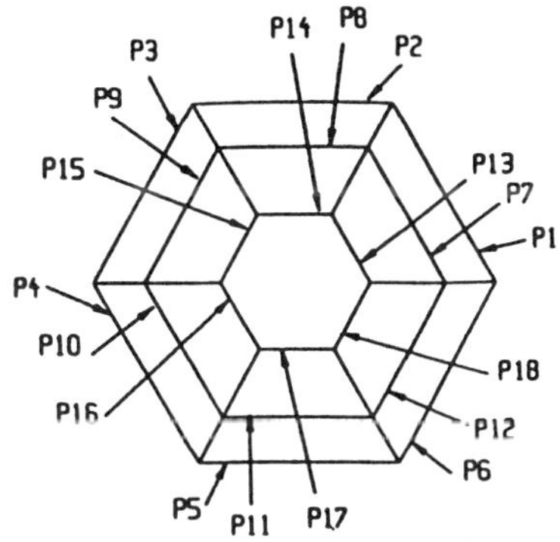

Figure 12.61a

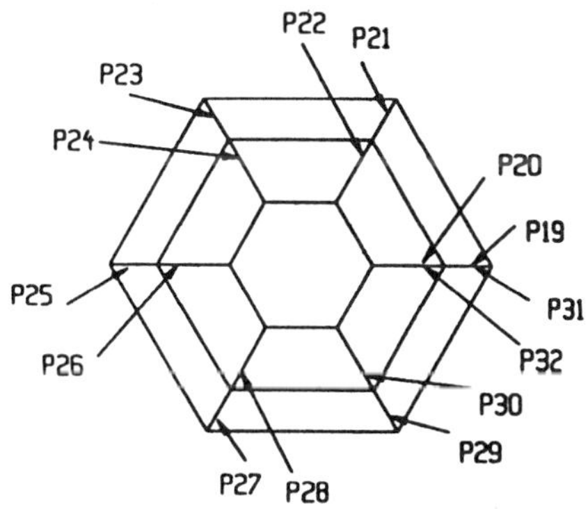

Figure 12.61b

Step 3. Create the Coons surface using the pick points in Figure 12.61.

Change the level to 2 and the color to 12.

Select **Level**, double-click at **2**, then select **OK**

Select **Color**, then enter **12**

Select **MAIN MENU → Create → Surface → Coons**

Select **No** to "Use automatice coons chaining?"

Enter the number of patches in the along direction: **6**↵

Enter the number of patches in the across direction: **2**↵

Select **Single**

Sequentially pick points **P1-P18** in Figure 12.61a

Pick **P19-P32** shown in Figure 12.61b to complete the selection of contours.

Select **Done**

Set the Coons surface parameters to the following settings:

Surface error tolerance = **0.005**
Surface type = **P** (Parametric)
Blending = **L** (Linear)

Select **Do it** to complete the surface

Select **Gview → Isometric** to display the surface in isometric view

The Coons surface should look like Figure 12.62.

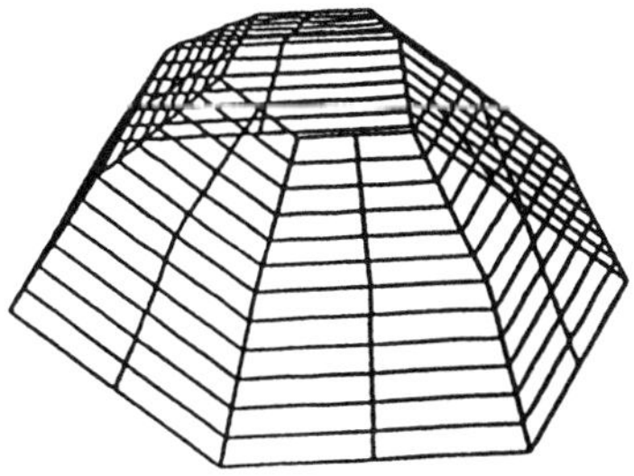

Figure 12.62

Step 4. Save the surface model file as coonss4.

Select **MAIN MENU → File → Save**
Enter file name: **coonss4.↵**

Step 5. Make the Coons surface in Level 2 invisible.

Select **Level**
Click the **#2** check mark in the Visible column to remove the check mark and hide the level
Select **OK → OK** to return to the graphic mode

Step 6. Change to Top Gview

Select **Gview → Top**

The drawing on the screen should resemble Figure 12.63.

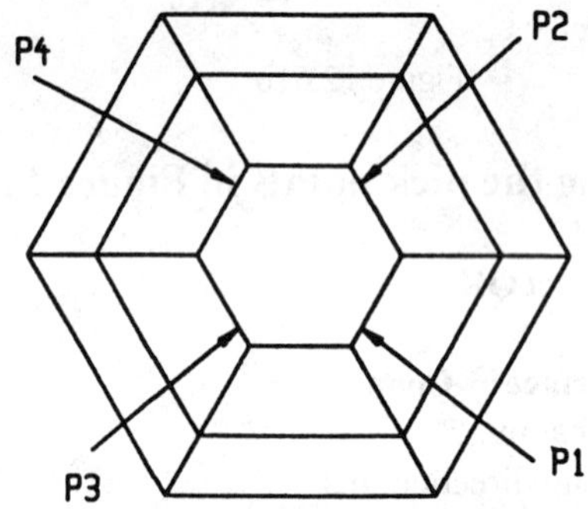

Figure 12.63

Step 7. Create a ruled surface for the top face using pick points in Figure 12.63.

Change to Level 3 and Color 13.
Select **Level**
Double-click the **#3** button, then select **OK**
Select **Color**, then enter **13**
Select **MAIN MENU → Create → Surface → Ruled → Sync**
The Syn Mode dialog box should appear as shown here:
Set the sync option to **by Entity**

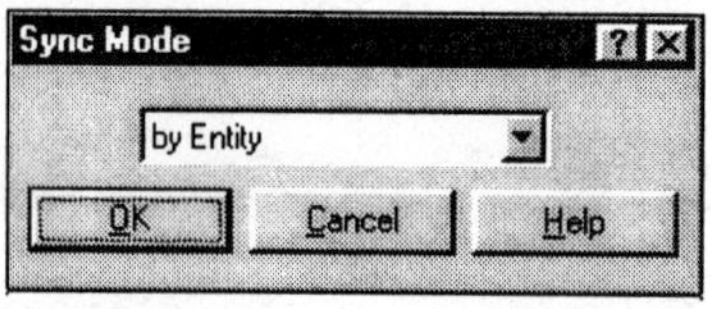

Select **OK**

Define contour 1: select **Chain** from the Chaining method menu,
Select **Partial**, then pick **P1→ P2**
Define contour 2: Select **Partial**, then pick **P3→ P4**
finally select **Done** to complete the contour selection.

Set the ruled surfaces parameters to these values:

Surface tolerance = **0.005**
Surface Type = **P (Parametric)**

Select **Do it** to create a ruled surface.

Step 8. Change Gview to Isometric and make Level 2 visible.

Select **Gview → Isometric**
Select **Level**
Click on theVisible column, **#2** to place a check mark in it
Select **OK** to return to the graphic mode.

The drawing with two surfaces should appear as in Figure 12.64.

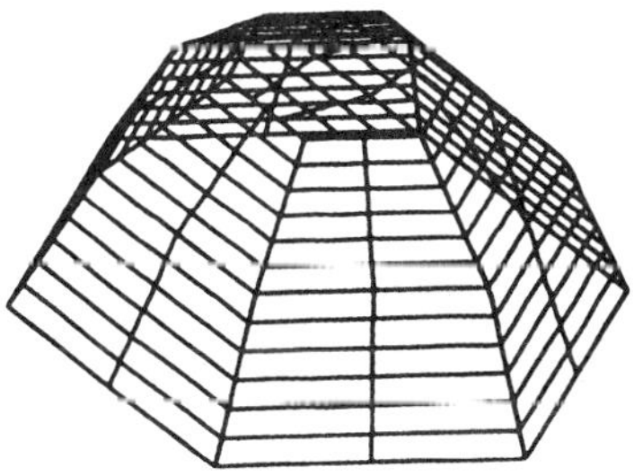

Figure 12.64

Step 9. Mirror the two surfaces about the X axis to generate the bottom half of the surface model.

Use Front or Side Cplane.
Select **Cplane → Front**
Select **MAIN MENU → Xform → Mirror → All → Surfaces → All → Lines → Done**
Select the **X axis**
Select **Copy → OK** from the Mirror Parameters menu to complete the Surface model.

The complete surface model should appear as in Figure 12.65.

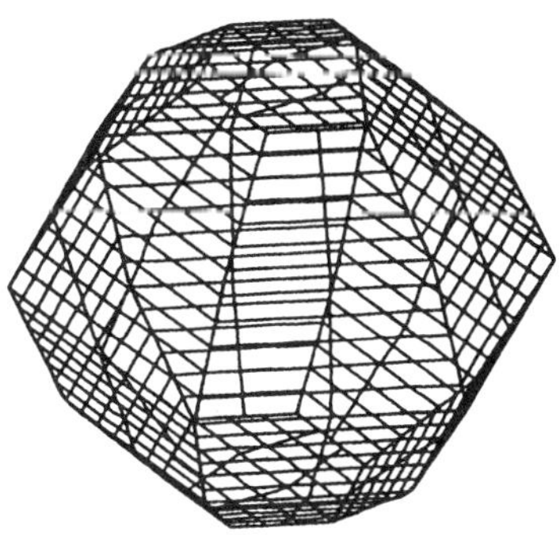

Figure 12.65

12.8 Revolved Surfaces Modeling

A revolved surface is created by revolving a geometric entity about an axis or a line. The geometric entity to be revolved is referred to as the generating curve, and the axis or line to be revolved about is called the revolving axis or line. The resulting surface is perpendicular to the revolving line.

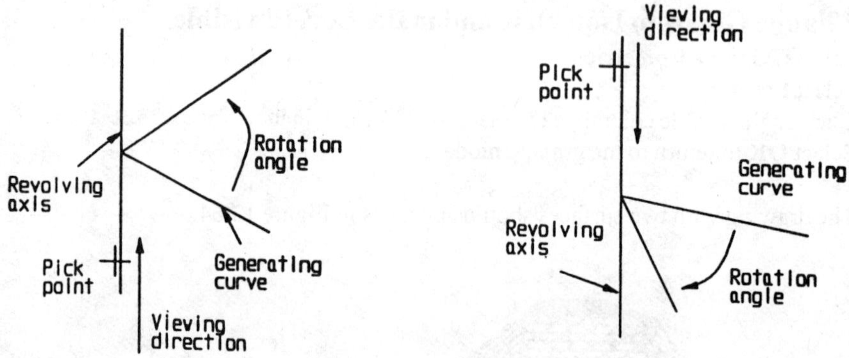

Figure 12.66

Tips 1. The revolved modeling technique generates a curve which can consist of more than one entity. You can use the Chain command to connect all entities together as a single generating curve. However, the number of resultant surfaces is eual to the number of entities included in the chained generating profile.

2. The rotation angle direction is determined by which end of the revolving axis is chosen when the user uses the mouse to pick the axis or line. A zero degree angle is assigned to the orientation of generating curve currently identified. Negative angles are invalid. The angle can rotate in either direction about the revolving axis. Figure 12.66 shows how the direction of the rotation angle is determined. The rotation direction is always in the clockwise direction when viewed from the selected end of the revolving axis toward the other end.

Project 11. Creating revolved surfaces to form a cup. 11

The revolved surface of a cup is created by using the wireframe model in project 8 of chapter 11. The wireframe model and the surface is shown in Figure 12.67.

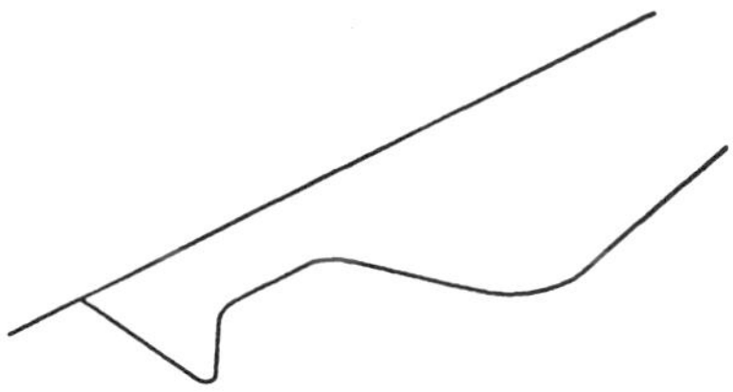

Figure 12.67a. Wireframe model

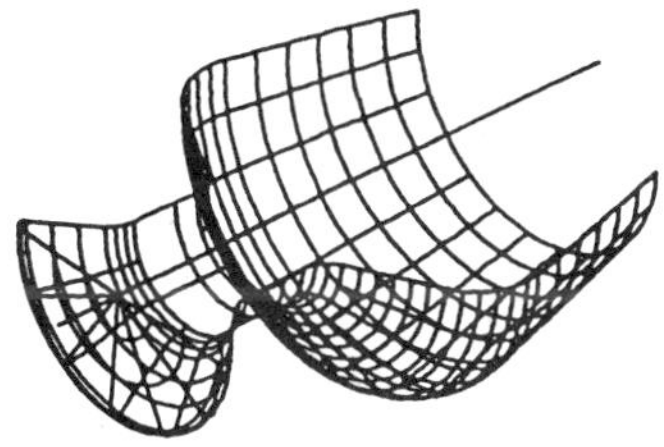

Figure 12.67b. Surface model

Tips

1. This surface model consists of nine revolved surfaces.
2. Each revolved surface is rotated 180° to form one-half of the surface model, or rotated 360° to form the complete surface model. In a manufacturing point of view, the cup mold requires one-half of the surface model.
3. The picking point on the revolving axis should be placed at the lower half segment of the line to create the correct revolving angle.

Step 1. Load the wireframe model file, cup.

(or create one by following instructions given in project 8 of chapter 11.)
Select **MAIN MENU → File → Get**
Enter file name: **cup** ↵
Select **Gview → Isometric**
The wireframe model drawing should resemble Figure 12.68.

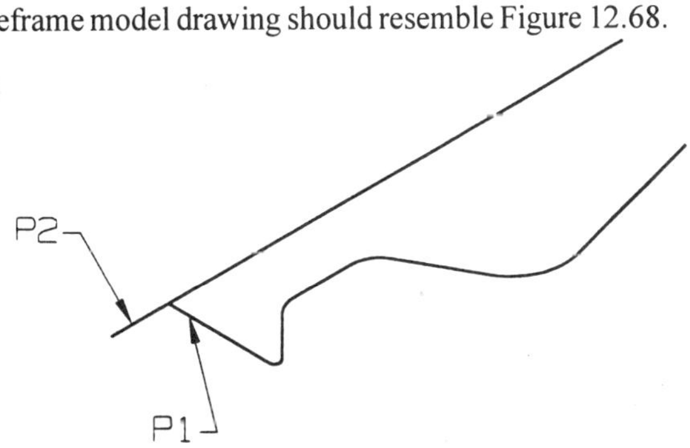

Figure 12.68

Step 2. Create the cup's first revolved surface using pick points from Figure 12.68.

Select **Level,** then enter **2** in the Main Level text box → **OK**
Select **MAIN MENU → Creat → Surface → Revolve**
Select the profile entities: select **Chain**, then pick **P1**
Select **Done**
Select the axis of rotation: pick **P2**
Select **Start angle**, enter **0**
Select **End angle**, enter **180**
Toggle Surface Type to **N** (NURBS)
Select **Do it**

The drawing with all nine revolved surfaces appears as Figure 12.69.

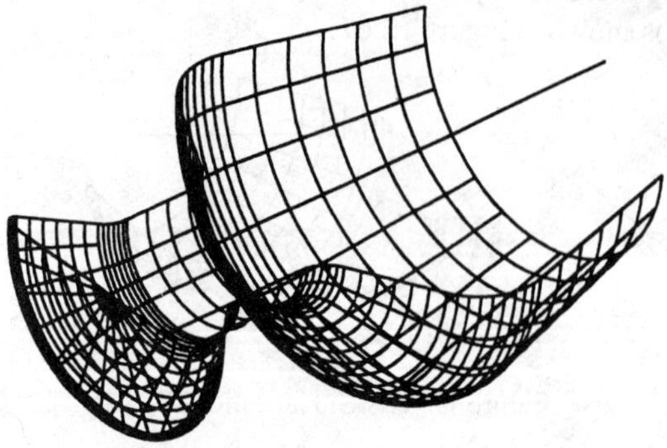

Figure 12.69

Step 3. Save the surface model file as cups.

Select **MAIN MENU → File → Save**

Enter the file name: **cups**

12.9 Draft Surfaces Modeling

A draft surface is created by extruding a sectional shape (or base curve) straight along a line (Figure 12.70). This line is defined by a length and an angle. The length is referred to as the draft length and the angle as the draft angle.

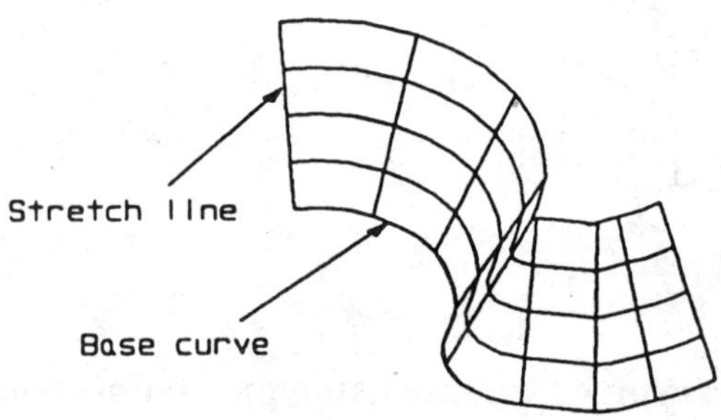

Figure 12.70

Tips 1. The base curve can be a line, an arc, a parametric spline, or a curve.

2. The draft modeling technique in Version 6 can chain more than one entity to create multiple draft surfaces. However, the number of draft surfaces is equal to the number of chained entities.
3. The draft length indicates how far the surface is to be stretched. It is measured in the direction perpendicular to the current Cplane. An arrow will appear to indicate the positive direction of the length (Figure 12.71). Entering a positive value will stretch the surface in the direction the arrow is pointing. Likewise, a negative value extends the surface in the opposite direction of the arrow.

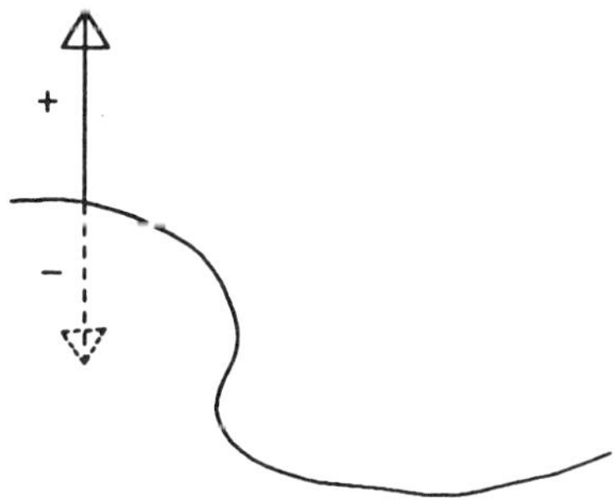

Figure 12.71

Tip 4. The draft angle specifies the orientation of the surface which in turn determines the shape of the surface. An arrow will appear to indicate the angle direction (Figure 12.72 on the next page). A positive angle will extend the surface in the direction of the angle arrow, while a negative angle value will extend the surface in the opposite direction of the indicator arrow.

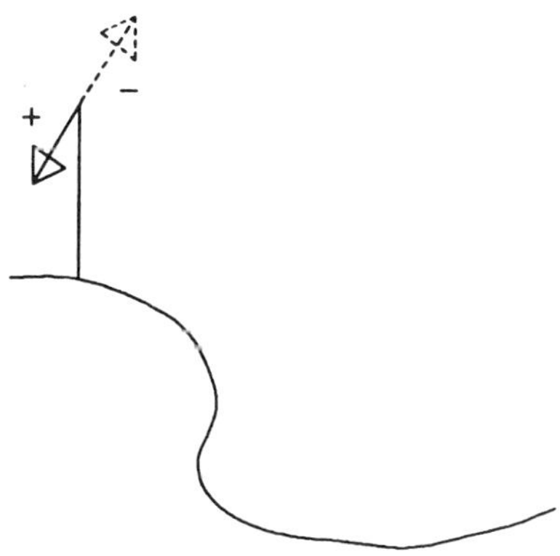

Figure 12.72

Project 12. Creating the draft surfaces to form a tabulated cylinder

This example creates a set of draft surfaces to form a tabulated cylinder based on a rectangle with a fillet at four corners as shown in Figure 12.73.

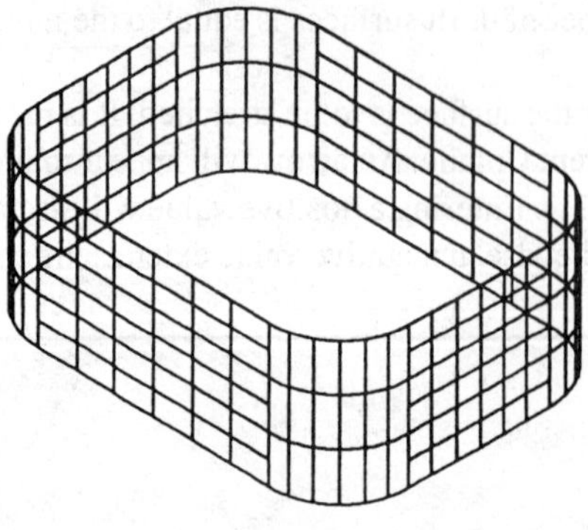

Figure 12.73

Tips 1. The base profile is a rectangle with a fillet at four corners. It is constructed in the Top Cplane.
2. The draft length is -1.5 in. and the draft angle is 0.
3. The surface model consists of eight draft surfaces.

Step 1. Create a rectangle using the Top Cplane.

Select **MAIN MENU → File → New → Yes** to initialize the screen
Select **Gview → Isometric**
Select **MAIN MENU → Create → Rectangle → 1 point**
Set the parameters in the Rectangle One Point dialog box as below:

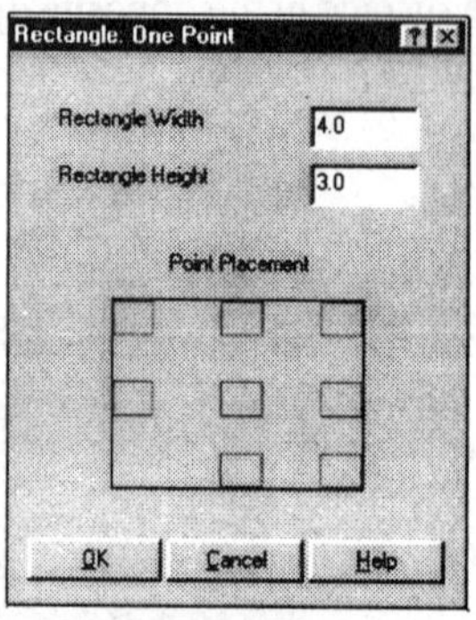

Select **OK**
Enter coordinates: **0,0** ↵ to position the rectangular shape in the graphics window
The rectangle should appear on the screen as Figure 12.74.

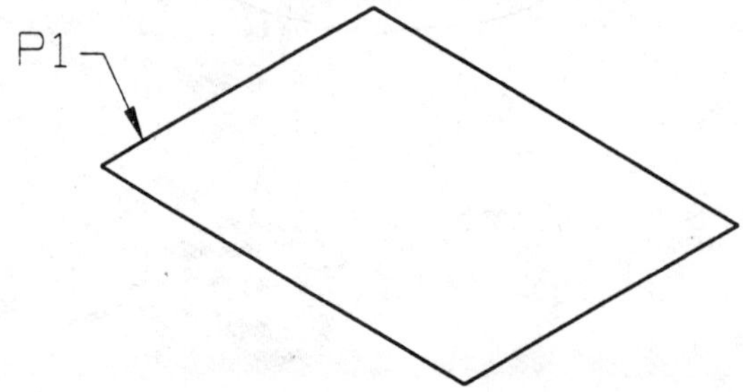

Figure 12.74

Step 2. Add four corner fillets using the pick points in Figure 12.74.

Select **MAIN MENU → Modify → Fillet → Radius**
Enter the fillet radius: **0.75** ↵
Select **Chain**
Pick **P1**
Select **Done** to complete the four fillets

The new drawing should look like Figure 12.75.

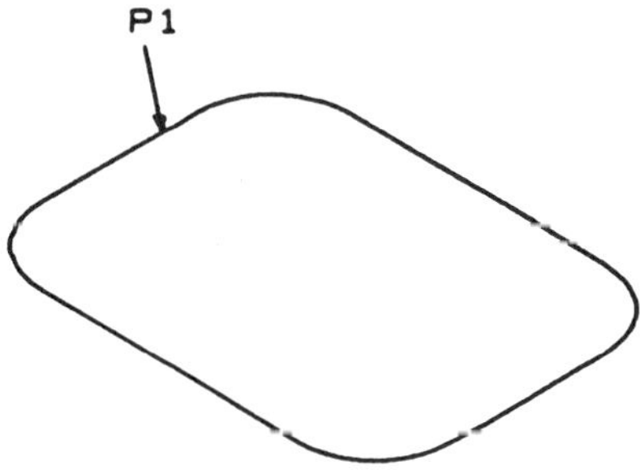

Figure 12.75

Step 3. Create eight draft surfaces using the pick points in Figure 12.71.

Select **MAIN MENU → Create → Surface → Draft**
Select the profile entities: Select **Chain** then pick **P1**
Select **Done**
Select **Length,** enter **-1.5** ↵
Select **Angle**, enter **0** ↵
Toggle Surface Type to **N** (NURBS)
Select **Do it**

The first draft surface should resemble Figure 12.76.

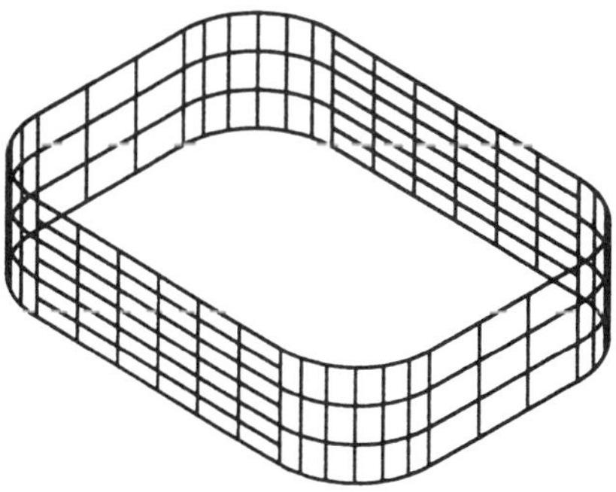

Figure 12.76

Step 4. Save the surface model as drafts1.

Select **MAIN MENU →File → Save**
Enter file name: **drafts1**

Project 13.

This example uses the draft surface modeling technique to create a cone surface,a spline surface, and a rectangular draft surface with four corner fillets as shown in these Figures 12.75a, b and c.

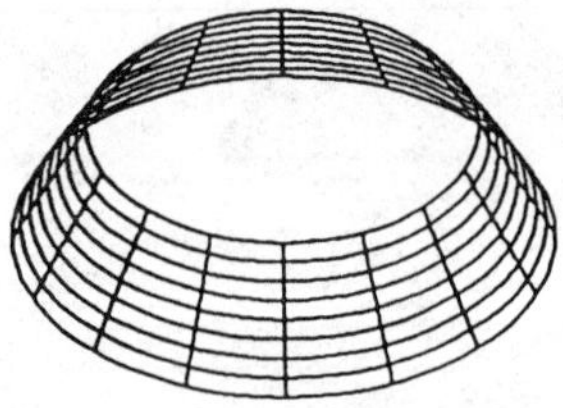

a. Cone surface

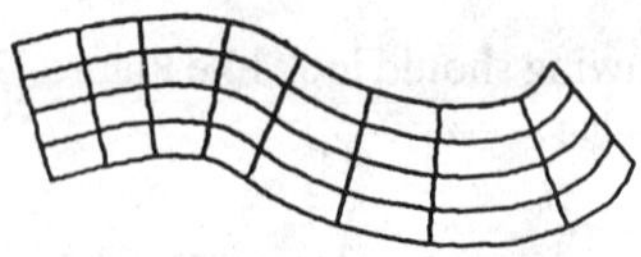

b. Spline surface

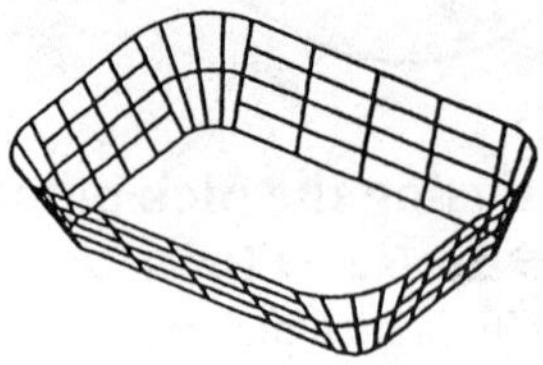

c. Rectangular draft surface

Figure 12.77

Cone Surface

The cone surface has a basic circle with a 3-in. diameter. The draft length is 1-in in the downward direction and the draft angle is 30° in the outward direction.

Step 1. Create the base circle. Initialize the system if necessary.

Select **Z** then enter **0** if necessary
Select **Cplane → Top** if necessary
Select **Gview → Isometric** if necessary
Select **MAIN MENU → Create → Arc → Circ pt+rad**
Enter the radius: **1.5** ↵
Enter the center point: **0,0** ↵

The circle should look like Figure 12.78

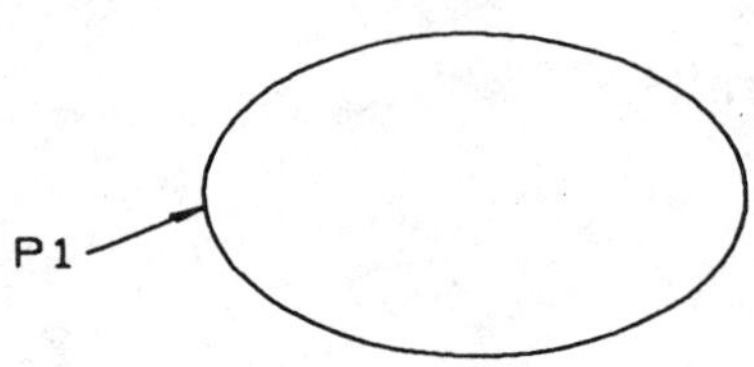

Figure 12.78

Step 2. Create the draft surface, use the pick point in Figure 12.78 on the last page. 13

Select **MAIN MENU → Create → Surface → Draft**
Select **Single,** then pick **P1,**
Select **Done**
Select **Length,** enter **-1** ↵
Select **Angle,** enter **-30** ↵
Select **Do it**

The cone surface should resemble Figure 12.79.

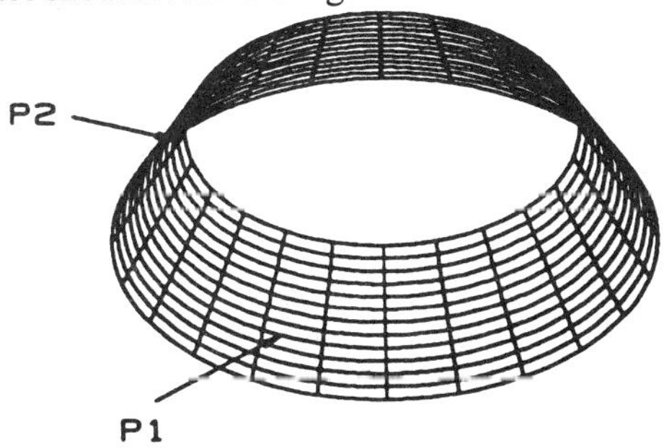

Figure 12.79

Step 3. Delete the circle and the surface using the pick points from Figure 12.79.

You may want to save the cone surface drawing for later use.
Select **MAIN MENU → Delete**
Pick **P1** and **P2**
This should give you a **clean screen** for your work.

Spline Surface

The base curve of the spline surface is a spline formed by nine points. The draft length is 1-in. in the downward direction and the draft angle is 35° in the inward direction.

Step 4. Create a spline using a set of point data.

Select **MAIN MENU → Create → Spline**
Toggle the spline Type to **N (NURBS)**
Select **Manual**
Sequentially enter the following sets of point data:

0,0 ↵
0.25, 0.48 ↵
0.5, 0.85 ↵
1, 1.32 ↵
1.75, 1.5 ↵
2.5, 1.4 ↵
3.25, 1.5 ↵
3.75, 1.72 ↵
4.15, 2.25 ↵
4,2.75 ↵

Press **Esc** to terminate the point data entry. The spline should resemble Figure 12.80.

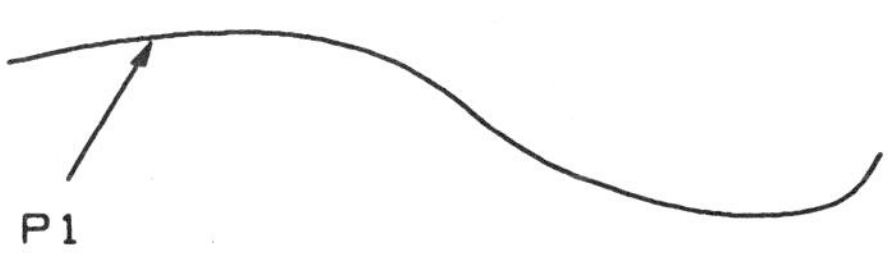

Figure 12.80

Step 5. Create a draft surface using the pick point in Figure 12.80.

Select **MAIN MENU → Create → Surface → Draft**
Select the base curve: pick **P1,** then select **Done**
Select **Length,** enter **-1** ↵
Select **Angle,** enter **-35** ↵
Select **Do it**

The draft surface should look like Figure 12.81.

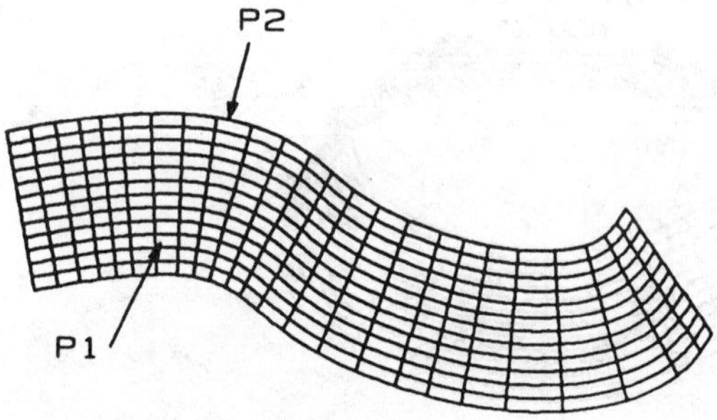

Figure 12.81

Step 6. Save the spline surface as drafts2.

Select **MAIN MENU → File → Save**
Enter file name: **drafts2**

Step 7. Delete the spline curve and surface using the pick points in Figure 12.81.

Select **MAIN MENU → Delete**
Pick **P1** and **P2**
This should give you a clean screen for your work.

Rectangular Draft Surfaces with four Corner Fillets

This surface model consists of eight draft surfaces which are extended in the downward direction by 1.25-in. and have a 25° draft angle in the inward direction.

Step 8. Create a rectangle.

Select **MAIN MENU →Create → Rectangle → 1 point**
Set the parameters in the Rectangle One Point dialog box as below:

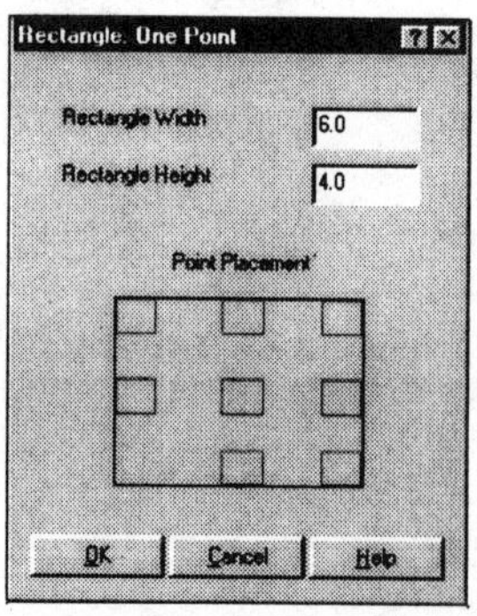

Select **OK**
Enter the lower left corner: **0,0** ↵ for the lower left corner

The rectangle should appear like Figure 12.82.

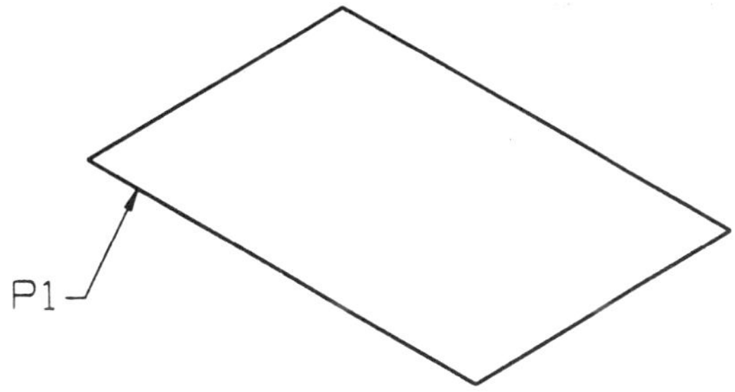

Figure 12.82

Step 9. Add four fillets using the points in Figure 12.82 on the previous page.

Select **MAIN MENU → Modify → Fillet → Radius**
Enter radius value: **1** ↵
Select **Chain**, then pick **P1**
Select **Done**

The new drawing should resemble Figure 12.83.

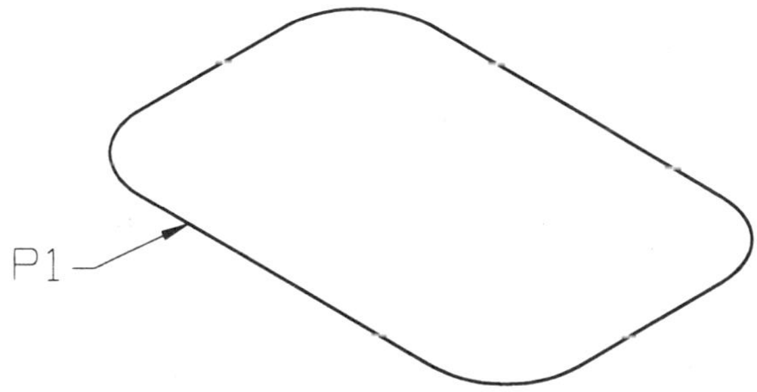

Figure 12.83

Step 10. Create eight draft surfaces. Use the pick point in Figure 12.83.

Select **MAIN MENU → Create → Surface → Draft**
Select the profile entities: Select **Chain,** then pick **P1**
Sclcct **Donc**
Select **Length,** enter **-1.25** ↵
Select **Angle,** enter **-25** ↵
Select **Do it**
The eight draft surfaces should appear as Figure 12.84.

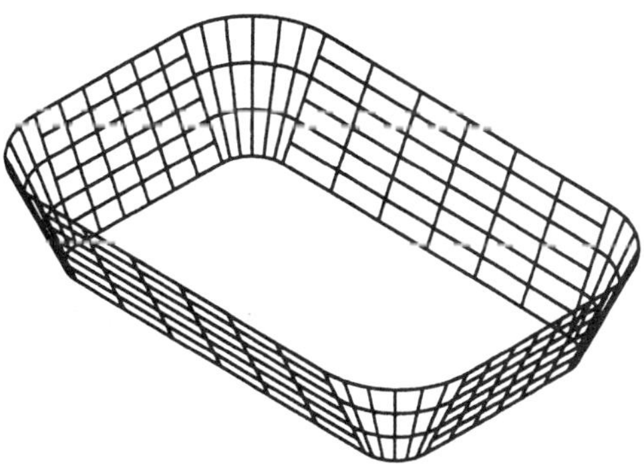

Figure 12.84

Step 11. Save the drawing as drafts3.

Select **MAIN MENU → File → Save**
Enter file name: **drafts3**

12.10 Swept Surfaces Modeling

A swept surface is created by either translating **a** sectional profile along one or two drive curves or translating **two** sectional profiles along a drive curve. Mastercam provides **three** types of swept surfaces: one across/one along, one across/two along, and two across/one along. Their descriptions and applications are given in Table 12.5.

Table 12.5 Swept surfaces modeling techniques

Surface type	Description	Application	Illustration
One across/ one along	Translate or rotate an across contour while following the along contour.	Used for a surface in which cross sections remain constant along a driving profile.	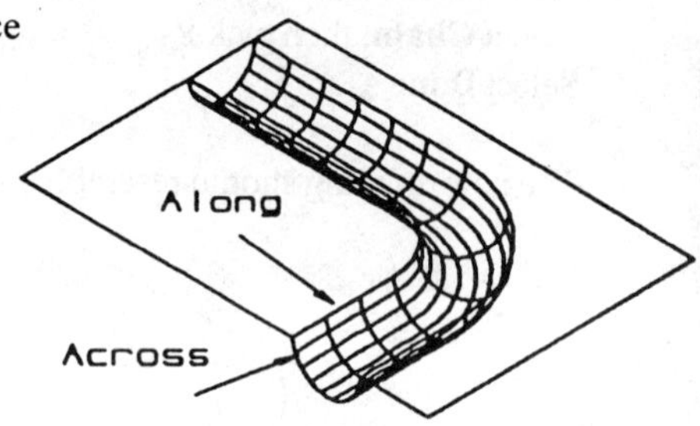
One across/ two along	Proportionally scale the across contour between the two along contours.	Used when cross sections are scaled along two driving profiles.	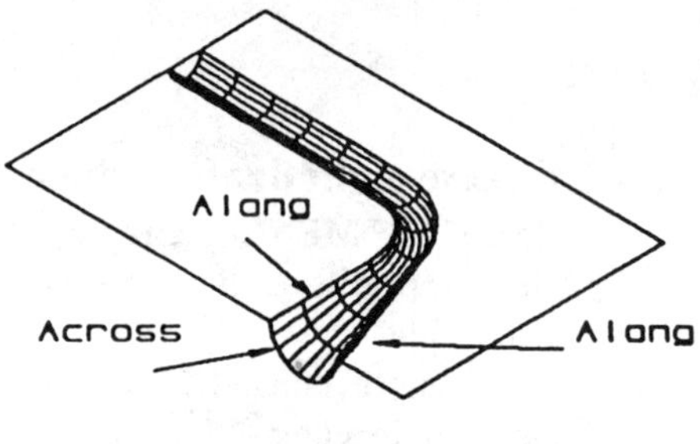
Two across/ one along	Perform a linear blend between the two across contours while following the along contour.	Used when two cross sections are linearly scaled along a driving profile.	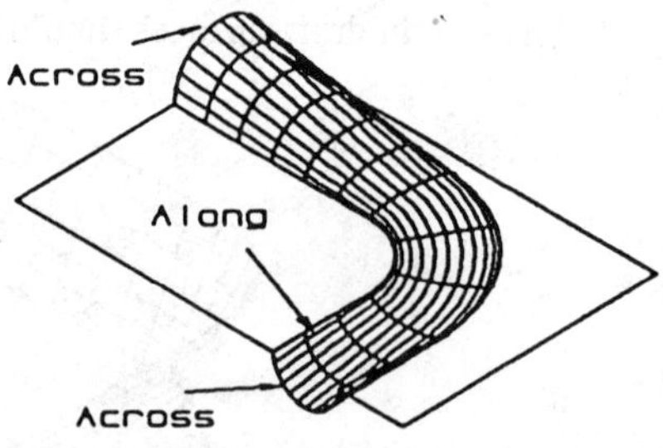

Project 14.

The swept surface modeling technique is used to create a surface model from the wireframe model of the cup given in project 8 of chapter 11. The advantage of modeling this cap with the swept method is that the entire surface profile can be chained as one entity to be swept along an arc which in turn generates all surfaces but is regarded only as a single surface entity. The wireframe model and the surface model of this cup are shown in Figure 12.85.

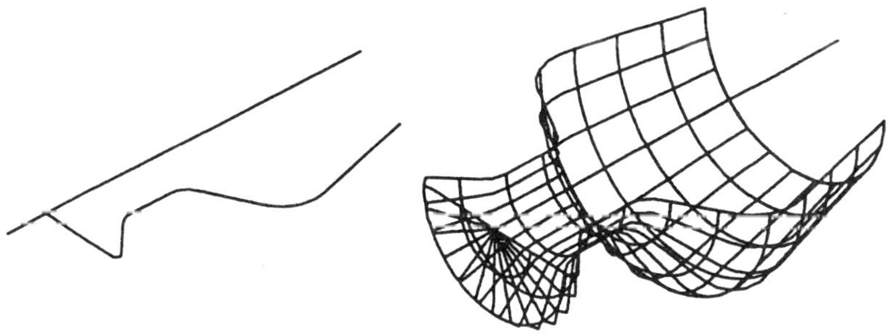

Figure 12.85

> **Tips** 1. A semi-circle has to be created in the Front Cplane to serve as the along contour in surface modeling.
> 2. Use one across/one along method using the edge profile of the cup as the across contour.

Step 1. Load the wireframe model file cup.

(or create one by following the instructions given in example 8 of chapter 11.)
Select **MAIN MENU → File → Get**
Enter file name: **cup** ↵
Select **Gview → Isometric**

The wireframe drawing appears on the screen as Figure 12.86.

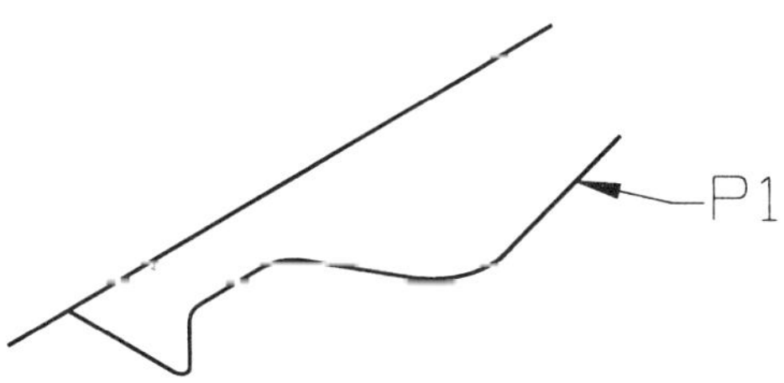

Figure 12.86

Step 2. Create an arc (semi-circle) using the Front Cplane.

Use the pick points in Figure 12.86 on the previous page.
Select **Cplane → Front**
Select **Z → Endpoint**,
then pick **P1** to obtain the Z coordinate of the trapped endpoint

Z-3.5 should appear in the Secondary Menu

Select **MAIN MENU → Create → Arc → Polar → Center pt**
Enter the center point: **0,0** ↵
Enter the radius: **1.062** ↵
Enter the initial angle: **180** ↵
Enter the final angle: **0** ↵

The added arc should appear on the screen as Figure 12.87.

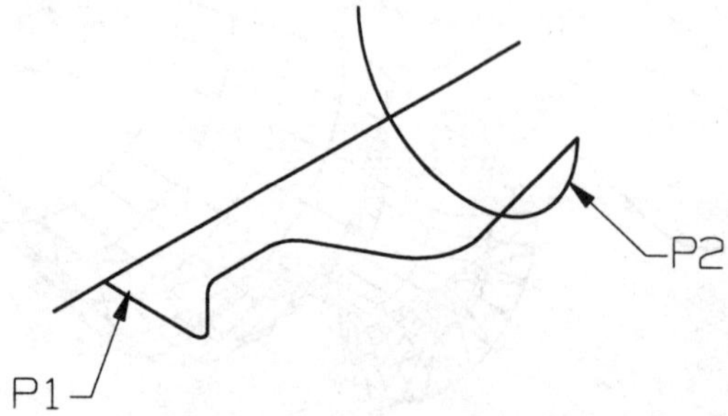

Figure 12.87

Step 3. Create a swept surface using the pick points in Figure 12.87 above.

Select **MAIN MENU → Create → Surface → Sweep**
Define the across contour: select **Chain** from the Chaining method menu,
Then pick **P1** to define the across contour 1
Select **Done**
Define the along contour 1: Select **Chain,** pick **P2**
Select **Done** to complete contours selection

Set the Swept surface parameters to the following settings:

Surface tolerance = **0.005** Surface type = **N (NURBS)** Rotate the across contour

Select **Do it** to compute the surface
Press Enter to display the surface model as shown here in Figure 12.88.

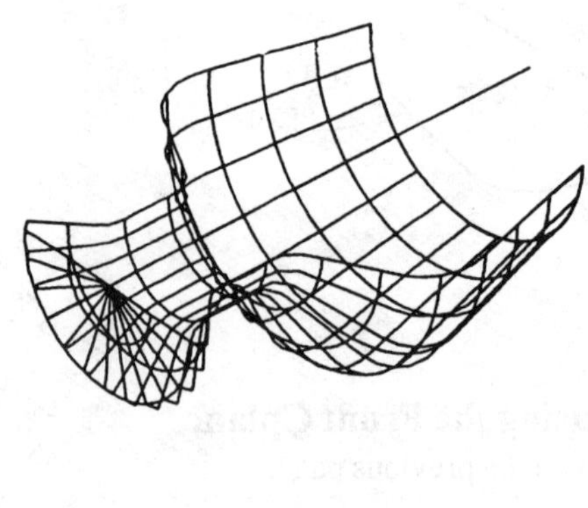

Figure 12.88

Step 4. Save the surface model swepts1.

Select **MAIN MENU → File → Save**
Enter file name: **swepts1** ↵

Project 15. 15

The wireframe model of project 9 in chapter 11 is used to create a swept surface. **Two** across contours are given, a rectangle on the top and a circle in the bottom. The along contour consists of two slope lines and a fillet in between. The wireframe model and surface model are illustrated in Figure 12.89.

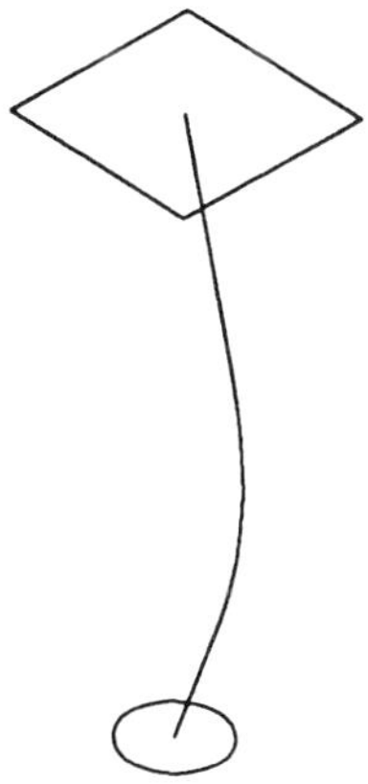

Figure 12.89a. Wireframe model

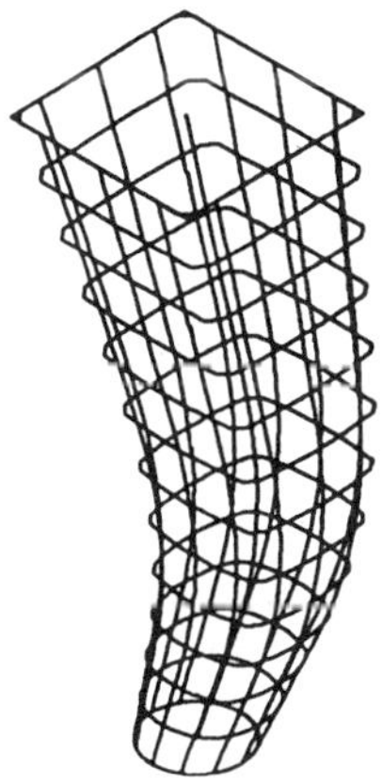

Figure 12.89b. Surface model

> **Tip** The right vertical line of the rectangle must be broken into two pieces to obtain the orientation alignment of the two across contours. In other words, these two contours start at the same orientation to prevent the surface from twisting.

Step 1. Load the wireframe model file

(or create one following the instructions given in project 9 of chapter 11.)
Select **MAIN MENU → File → Get**
Enter file name: **swept2** ↵

The wireframe model is shown in Figure 12.90.

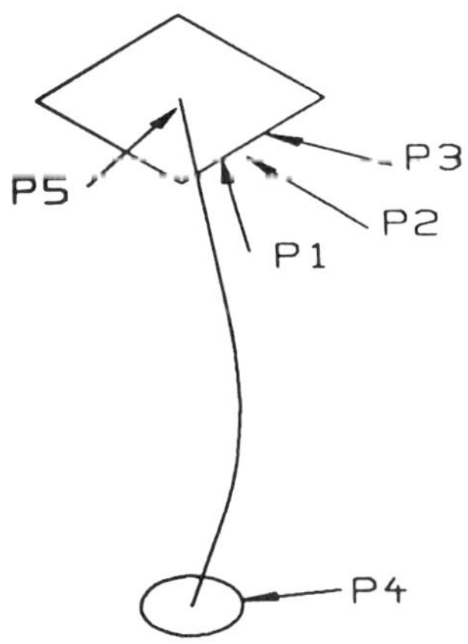

Figure 12.90

Step 2. Break the right vertical line of the rectangle into two segments using the pick points in Figure 12.90.

Select **MAIN MENU → Modify → Break → 2 pieces**
Select an entity: pick **P1**
Enter the breakpoint: select **Midpoint** from the Point Menu, and then pick **P2**

Step 3. Create the swept surface still use the pick points in Figure 12.90.

Select **MAIN MENU → Create → Surface → Sweep**
Define across contour: select **Chain** from the Chaining method menu, then pick **P3**
(Note: the **Chain Synchs** option must be in **"none"** mode by selecting **Syn → "none"**)
Define across contour 2: select **Mode → Single** from the Chaining method menu, then pick **P4,** select **Done**
Define the along contour: select **Chain** from the Chaining method menu, then pick **P5**
Select **Done** to complete the contours selection
Set the Swept surface parameters to the following settings:

Surface tolerance = **0.005** Surface type = **N (NURBS)**

Select **Do it** to complete the surface
Press **Enter** to ignore the sharp corners.

The surface model should look like Figure 12.91.

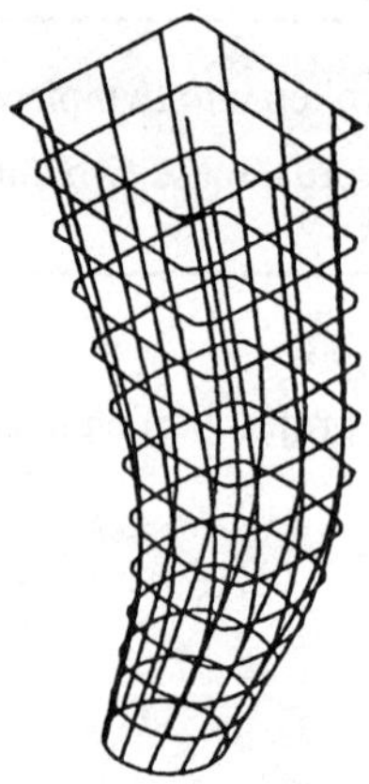

Figure 12.91

Step 4. Save the surface file as swepts2.

Select **MAIN MENU → File → Save**
Enter file name: **swepts2** ↵

Project 16.

This example uses the wireframe model of project 10 in chapter 11 to create a swept surface. The model consists of two along contours and one across contour. The wireframe and surface model are given in Figure 12.92.

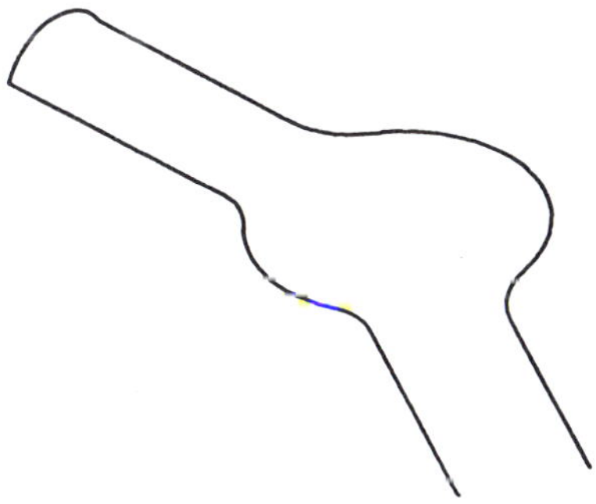

Figure 12.92a. Wireframe model

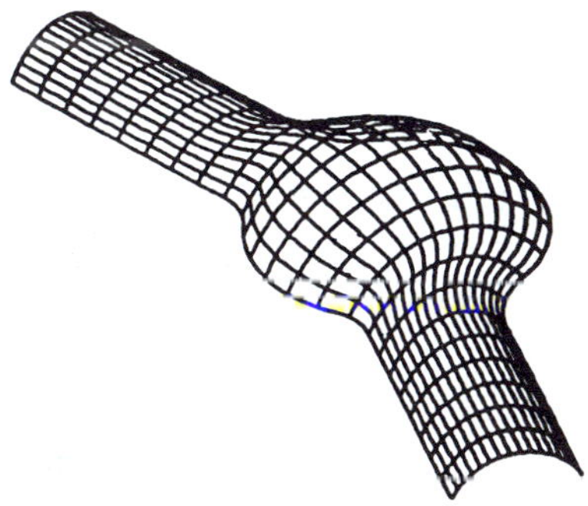

Figure 12.92b. Surface model

Step 1. Load the wireframe model file swept3.

(or create one by following the instructions of example in chapter 11.)
Select **MAIN MENU → File → Get**
Enter file name: **swept3** ↵

The wireframe model drawing should appear as Figure 12.93.

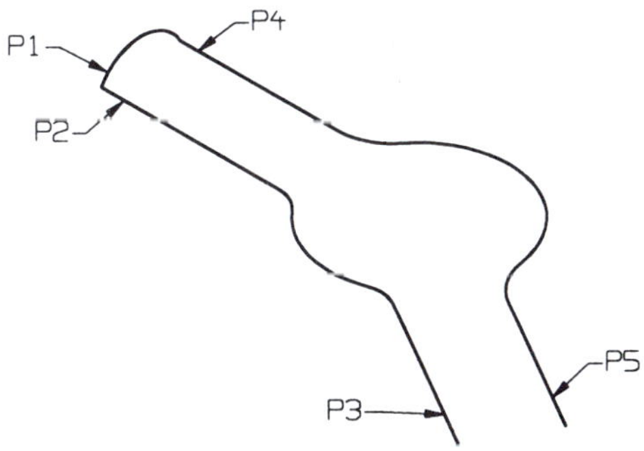

Figure 12.93

Step 2. Create a swept surface using the pick points in Figure 12.93.

Select **MAIN MENU → Create → Surface → Sweep**
Define the across contour: select **Single** from the Chaining method menu, then pick **P1**
Select **Done**
Define along contour: select **Chain → Partial**
Pick the first entity: **P2**
Pick the last entity: **P3**
Define along contour 2: select **Partial**
Pick the first entity: **P4**
Pick the last entity: **P5**

Define the Swept surface parameters to the following settings:

Surface error tolerance = **0.002**
Surface type = **N (NURBS)**

Select **Do it** from the parameters menu to complete the surface
The swept surface should resemble Figure 12.94.

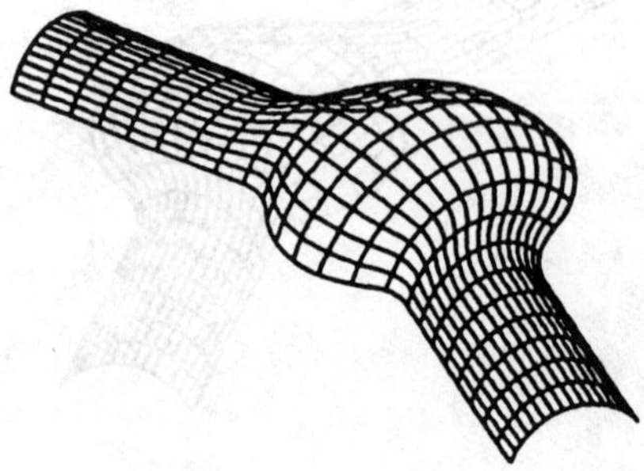

Figure 12.94

Step 3. Save the surface file as swepts3.

Select **MAIN MENU → File → Save**
Enter file name: **swepts3** ↵

Ex Exercises

1. Write a definition of a surface?

2. What is a composite surface model?

3. What are the four mathematical methods of modeling surfaces?

4. How is a Coons surface defined? Explain the strengths and weaknesses of a Coons surface.

5. Describe the strengths and weaknesses of Bezier surfaces.

6. Explain the strengths and weaknesses of B-spline surfaces.

7. What is NURBS surface?

8. Describe the major difference between the B-spline surface and NURBS surface.

9. List the three types of surfaces.

10. What are the two surface modeling techniques Mastercam provides to create geometrical surfaces?

11. What are free-form surfaces?

12. What are the two kinds of free-form surfaces? Describe their differences.

13. What are the four types of free-form surfaces that Mastercam provides?

14. What are derived surfaces?

15. List the three types of derived surfaces in Mastercam.

16. What are the three surfacing mathematics Mastercam uses to generate free-form and derived surfaces?

17. Use the wireframe model created in problem 11.10 to generate two ruled surfaces. The wireframe profile and the finished ruled surfaces are shown in Figure 12.95. The wireframe file is **E1**. Save the surface model file as **ES1**. Project 1 in this chapter is a similar example.

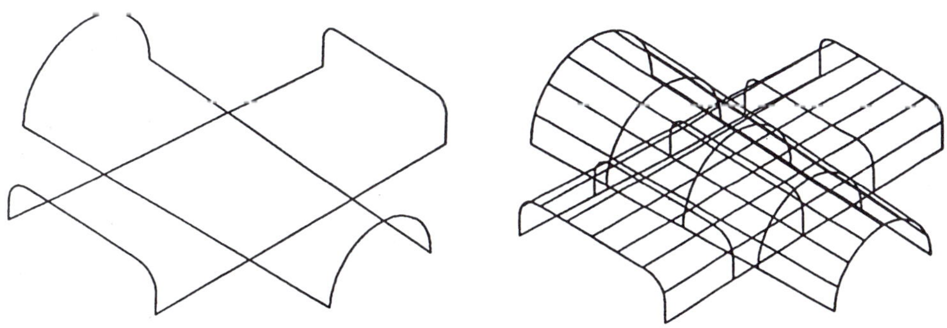

Figure 12.95

18. Use the wireframe model created in problem 11.11 to generate two ruled surfaces which intersect at an angle of 45°. The wireframe profile and the finished ruled surfaces look like Figure 12.96. The wireframe file is **E2**. Save the surface model file as **ES2**. A similar example is project 2 of this chapter.

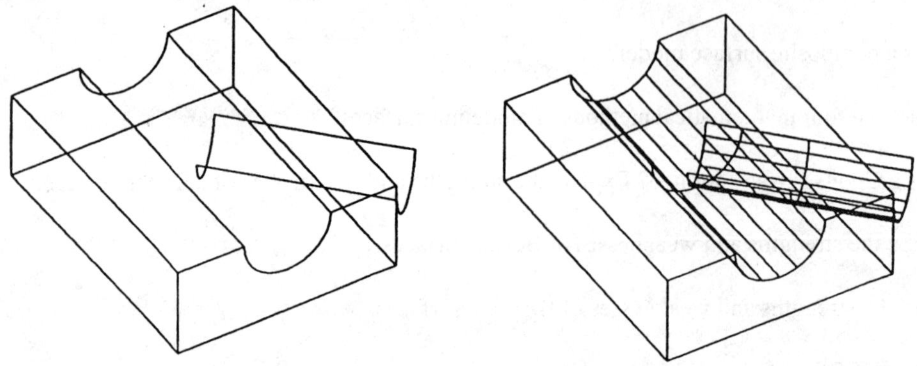

Figure 12.96

19. The three contours in problem 11.12 are used to create a ruled surface. The wireframe and finished surface model are shown in Figure 12.97. The wireframe model file is **E3**. Save the surface model file as **ES3**. A similar example in this chapter is project 3.

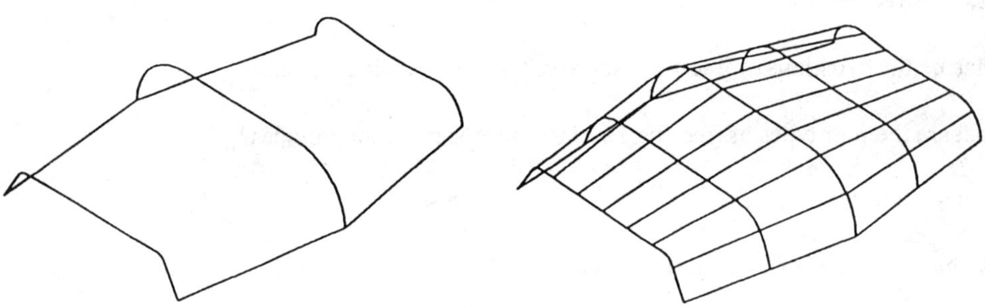

Figure 12.97

20. Use the three contours in problem 11.12 to create a loft surface. The wireframe and finished loft surface model resemble Figure 12.98. The wireframe model file is **E3**. Save the surface model file as **ES4**. A similar example is project 4 of this chapter.

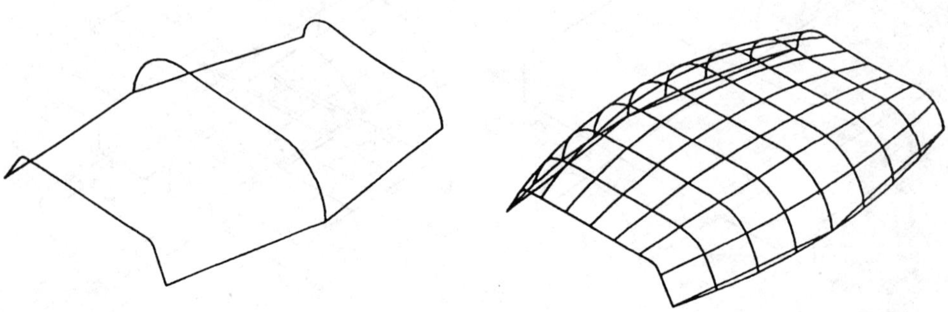

Figure 12.98

21. Use the four arcs in problem 11.13 to create a single-patch Coons surface. Both wireframe and surface models are illustrated in Figure 12.99. The wireframe model file is **E4**. Save the surface model file as **ES5**. A similar example is project 7 of this chapter.

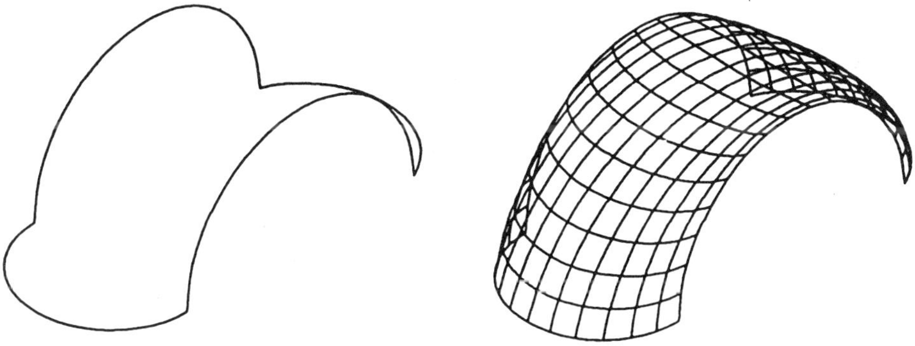

Figure 12.99

22. Create a single-patch Coons surface from the wireframe model of problem 11.14. The wireframe model filc is **E5**. Save the surface model file as **ES6**. Both wireframe and surface models are given in Figure 12.100. A similar example is project 7 in this chapter.

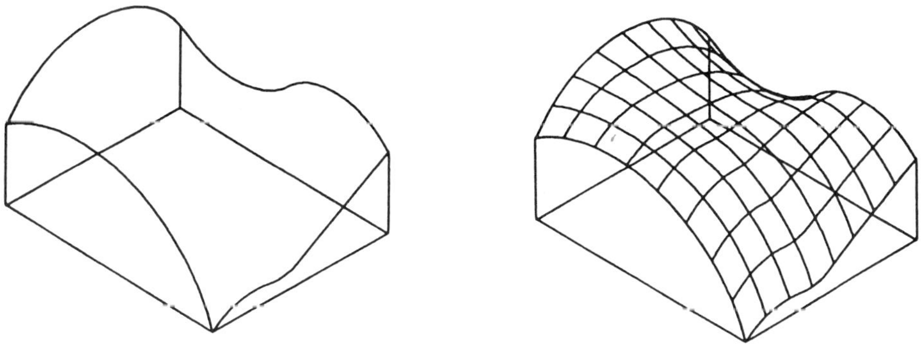

Figure 12.100

23. Use the wireframe model in problem 11.15 to create a multi-patch Coons surface. The wireframe model file is **E6**. Figure 12.101 shows both wireframe model and finished surface model. Save the surface model file as **ES7**. A similar example is project 9 of this chapter.

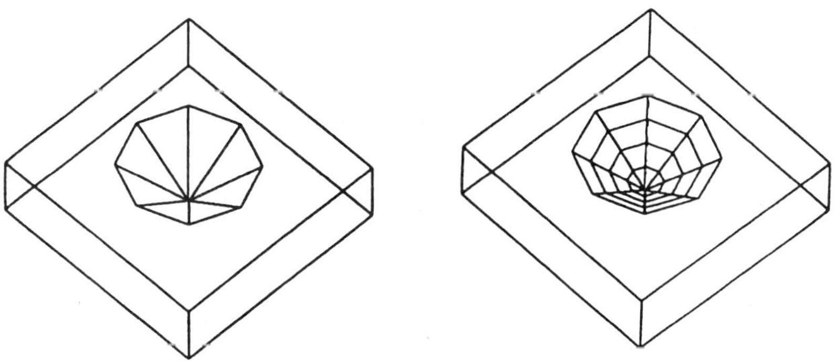

Figure 12.101

Mastercam Version 8
Scholars International Publishing Corp., 2001

24. Use the multi-faced wireframe model given in problem 11.16 to generate a Coons surface of multiple patches. The wireframe model file is **E7**. Save the surface model file as **ES8**. A similar example is project 10 in this chapter. Both wireframe and surface models should look like Figure 12.102.

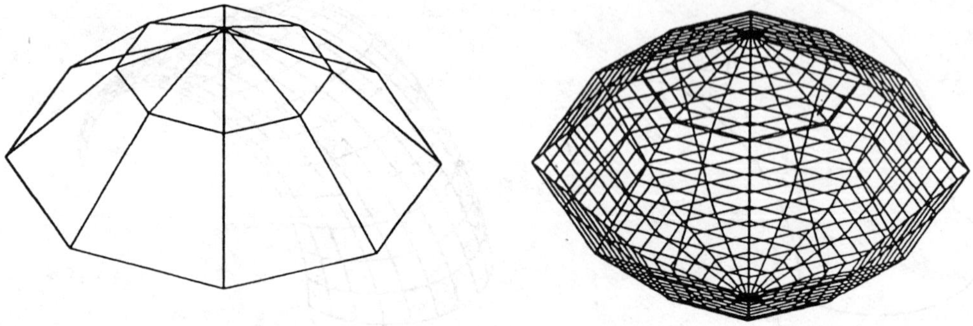

Figure 12.102

25. Use the revolved surfacing technique to creat a surface model from the wireframe model in problem 11.17. The wireframe model file is **E8**. Save the surface model file as **ES9**. Both models are illustrated in Figure 12.103. A similar example is project 11 of this chapter.

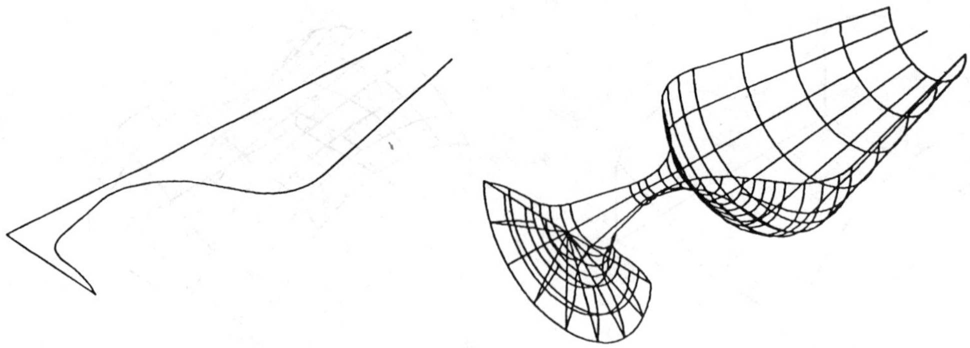

Figure 12.103

26. Use the revolved surfacing technique to create a surface model of a cup from the wireframe profiles in problem 11.18. The wireframe model file is **E9**. Save the surface model file as **ES10**. The wireframe and finished surface models are shown in Figure 12.104. A similar example is project 11 in this chapter.

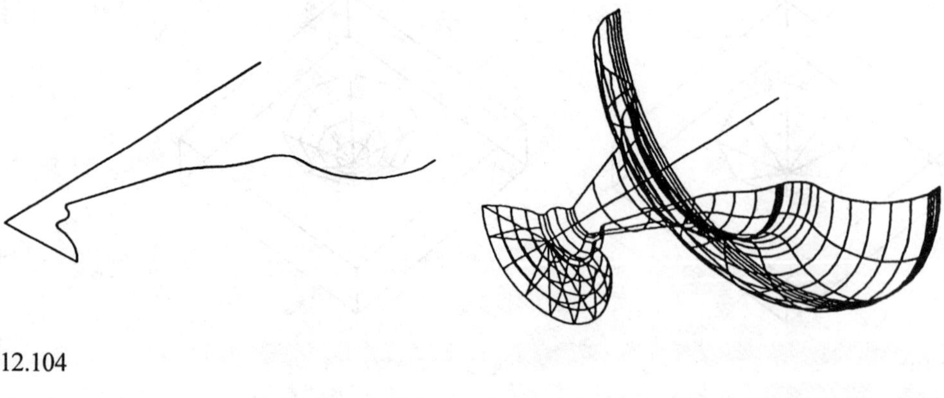

Figure 12.104

27. The wireframe model of a fly disk given in problem 11.19 is used to create a surface model by using the swept surfacing technique. The wireframe model file is **E10**. Both wireframe and surface models in front view are illustrated in Figure 12.105. Save the surface model file as **ES11**. A similar example is project 11 of this chapter.

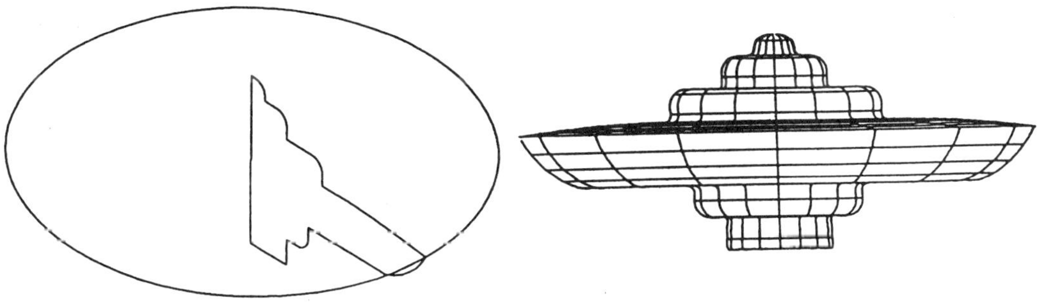

Figure 12.105

28. Create a draft surface using an 8" x 6" rectangle with a 1" fillet at four corners as the base profile. The draft length is -2" and the draft angle is 15° in the outward direction. The base profile and finished draft surfaces should resemble Figure 12.106.

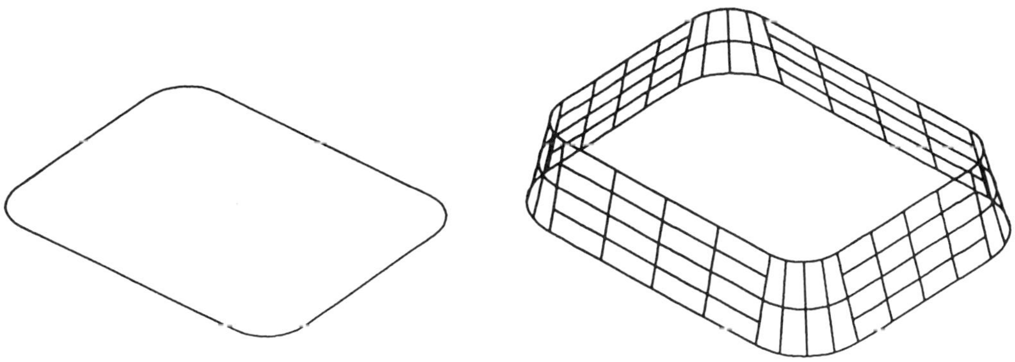

Figure 12.106

29. Create a draft surface from a spline which is defined by the the set of points given below. The draft length is 1.5" and the draft angle is 20° in the outward direction. The base spline and the finished draft surfaces are shown in Figure 12.107.

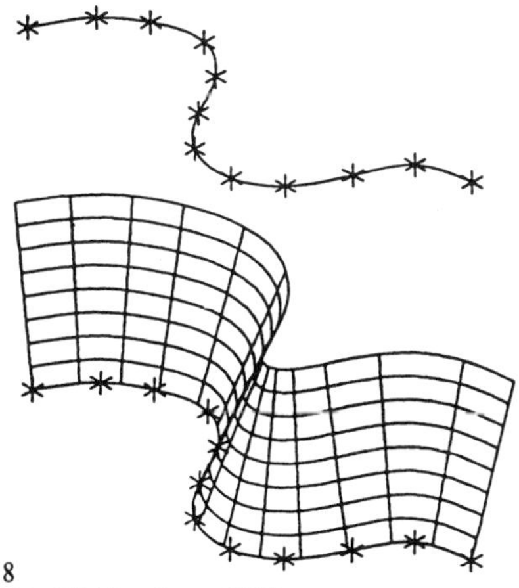

X	Y	Z
0.0	0.0	0.0
0.3	0.5	0.0
0.67	0.77	0.0
1.18	0.89	0.0
1.59	0.61	0.0
1.85	0.14	0.0
2.18	-0.24	0.0
2.69	-0.32	0.0
3.08	-0.08	0.0
3.36	0.42	0.0
3.62	0.89	0.0
4.11	1.05	0.0

Figure 12.107

Chapter 13

Surface Modeling II: Derived & Composite Surfaces

Objectives:

1. Use Mastercam to create derived surfaces from existing surfaces.
2. Create composite surface models.

Overview

Six basic surface modeling techniques and examples have been presented in chapter 12. In this chapter, four derived surfacing techniques are covered, followed by five composite surface modeling examples. Each of these five composite surface examples consists of several surfaces that are modeled by more than one surface modeling technique. They are arranged in increasing order of difficulty. Useful tips that lead to successful completion of the surface model are given in each example.

13.1 Derived surfaces Modeling

Derived surfaces are those surfaces that are generated from existing surfaces. They are used to modify or edit the existing surfaces, and because of this, they are also called **edited surfaces**. Mastercam provides **four derived surface modeling techniques**: fillet surface modeling, trimmed surface modeling, offset surface modeling, and blend surface modeling.

Fillet Surfaces Modeling

A fillet surface is created between two existing surfaces. Fillet surfaces are mainly used in two situations:

(1) adding a smooth fillet between two intersecting surface (Figure 13.1); and
(2) adding a fillet at the end of object (Figure 13.2).

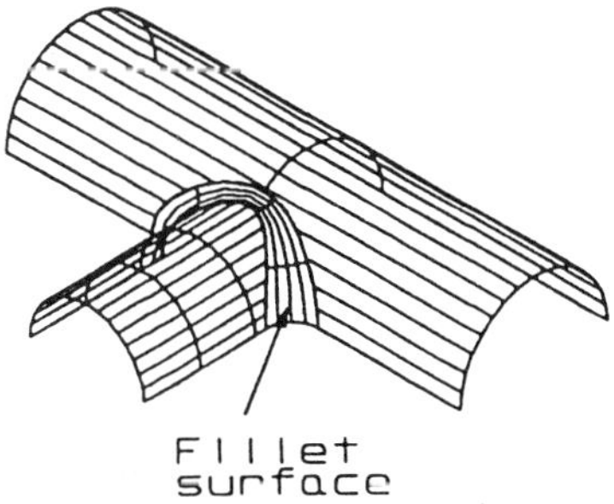

Figure 13.1

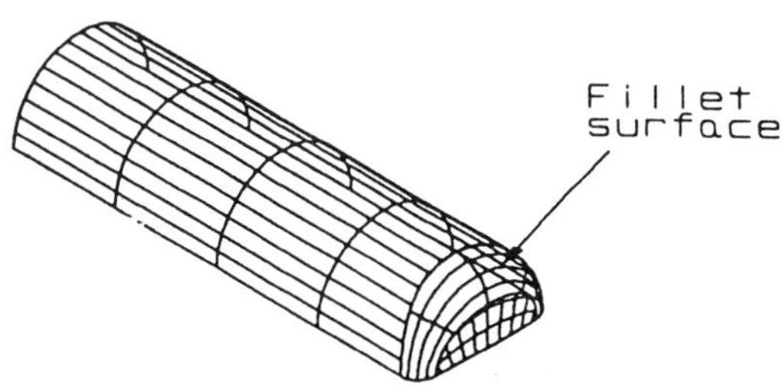

Figure 13.2

Fillet Surface Creating Methods

A fillet surface can be created between a surface and an element of one of three element types; plane, curve and surface. Table 13.1 summarizes the three methods of creating fillet surfaces.

Table 13.1 Fillet surface creating methods

<table>
<tr><th>Fillet Surface Method</th><th>Description</th><th>Illustration</th></tr>
<tr><td>Plane/Surf</td><td>Create a fillet surface between a plane and a surface.</td><td>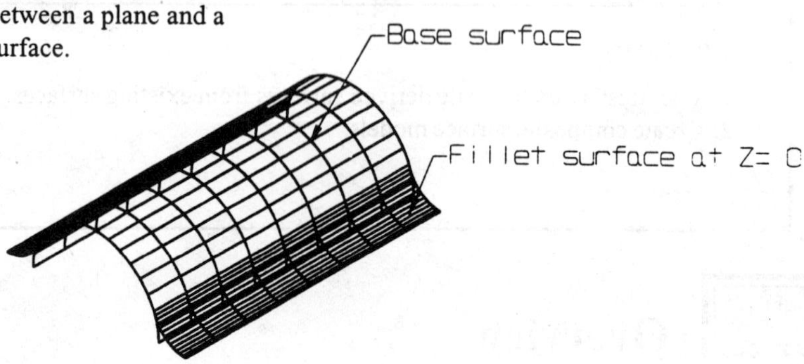
</td></tr>
<tr><td>Curve/Surf</td><td>Create a fillet surface between a curve and a surface.</td><td>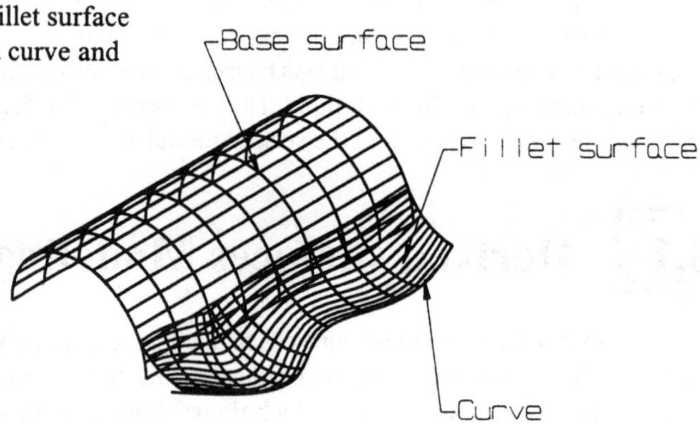
</td></tr>
<tr><td>Surf/Surf</td><td>Create a fillet surface between two or more surfaces.</td><td>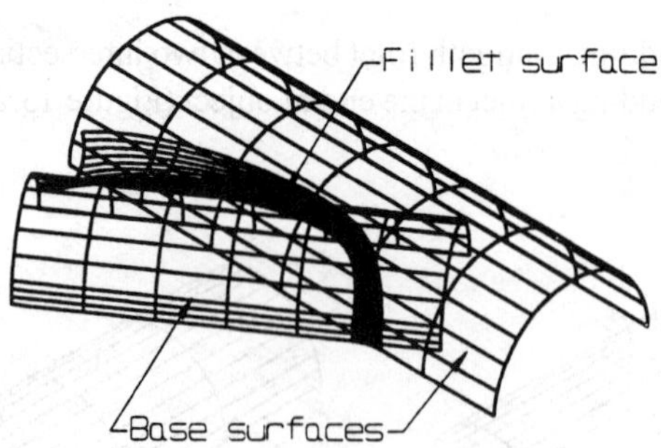
</td></tr>
</table>

Filleting parameters

The parameters used to define the fillet surfaces are placed in the options dialog box. The option dialog boxes for these three fillet surface creating methods are shown below. The main parameters in option dialog boxes are:

Step method	Entities to be created	Fillet Both Sides
Fillet type	Join results	Color
Find multiples	Trim surface	Join Tolerance
Extend Surfaces		

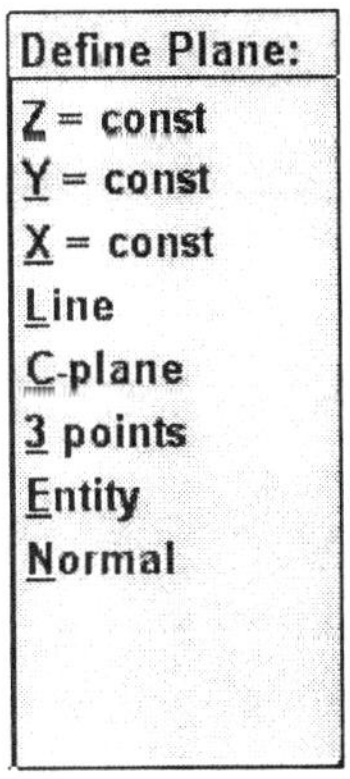

Plane-surface option

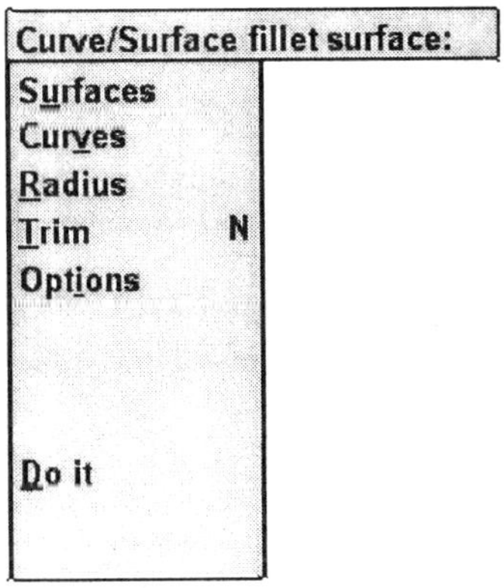

Curve-surface option

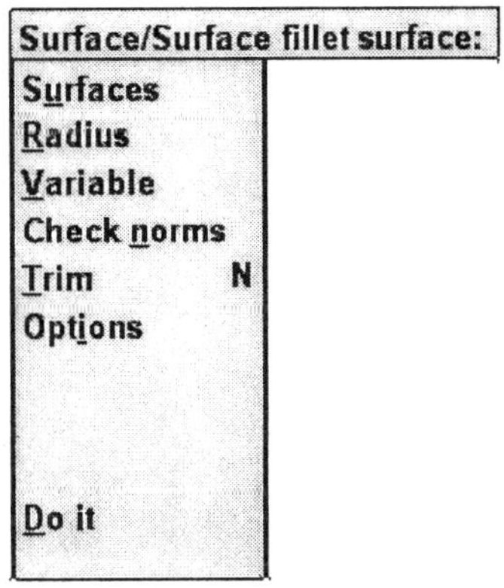

Surface-surface option

Step method

The stepping distance of the surface can be determined by two stepping methods: chord-height and fixed step. When using the chord deviation method, the given value of the stepping chord height is used to define the fillet surface. The fixed step method uses a constant stepping distance to define the fillet surface. Use fixed step method when the surface has relatively large curvature radii, has no sharp shapes, or does not require a close dimensional accuracy. Use chord-height method for those surfaces that have small curvature radii, have sharp shapes, or require a close dimensional tolerance. This method can accurately define the surface within the specified dimensional accuracy. Use smaller values for stepping parameters to tighten the accuracy of the surface. However, this will take the computer a longer amount of time to process the surface and will make the surface file bigger.

Entities to be generated

While creating a fillet surface, the system can generate the following four types of information. You can select to create any combination of the above four entity types during creating a fillet surface.

Fillet:	generating a fillet surface (NURBS, curve-generated, or parametric type) (Figure 13.3).
Rails:	generating two curve rails along the edges of the fillet surface (Figure 13.4).
Center:	generating a center curve of the fillet surface (Figure 13.5).
Surface curve:	generating a curve along the intersection between the existing surface and fillet surface (Figure 13.6).

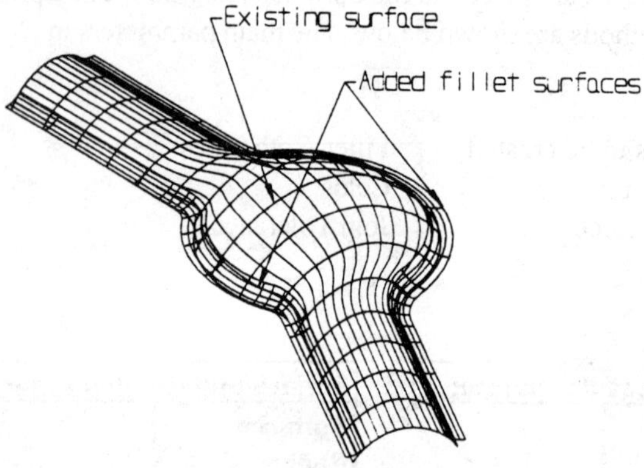

Figure 13.3

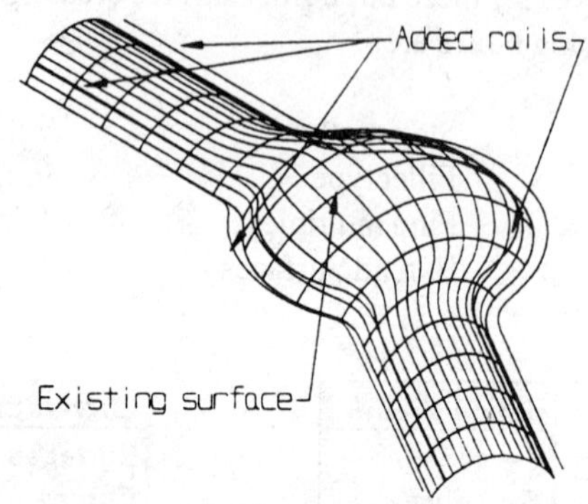

Figure 13.4

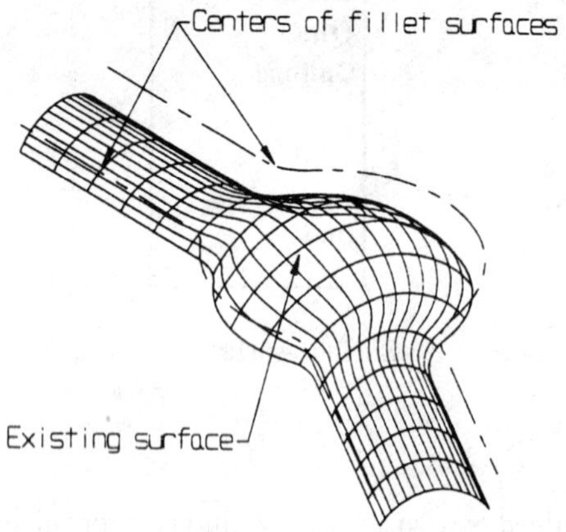

Figure 13.5

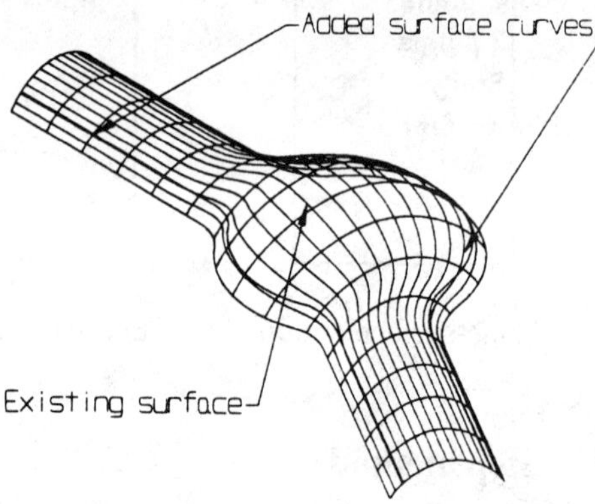

Figure 13.6

Fillet Type

The three fillet surface types you can select are: **Curve-generated**, **NURBS**, and **Parametric.**

Fillet Both Sides

Check this parameter "Yes" to create fillet surfaces on all sides of the surfaces, regardless of their surfaces or their surface normal directions. Clear this box to create fillet surfaces only where the positive surface normals point in the same direction.

Color

The Color parameter sets the color of each resulting fillet surface that is tangent to two surfaces whose positive surface normals do not point in the same direction. Enter a color number or choose the button to select a color from the Color dialog box.

Join Results

This parameter is used to join the resultant surfaces. Toggle this parameter to ON (with a check mark), the "Tolerance" parameter will become active for specifying the join tolerance.

Join Tolerance

This parameter is used to set the maximum distance that the ends of the fillet surfaces can be separated from one another and still be joined into one entity.

Find Multiples

It is possible to generate more than one fillet surface in one operation. Mastercam uses "Find multiples" parameter to indicate whether more than one fillet surface is to be generated if possible. Toggle this parameter to ON (with a check mark), the system will generate multiple fillet surfaces (Figure 13.7).

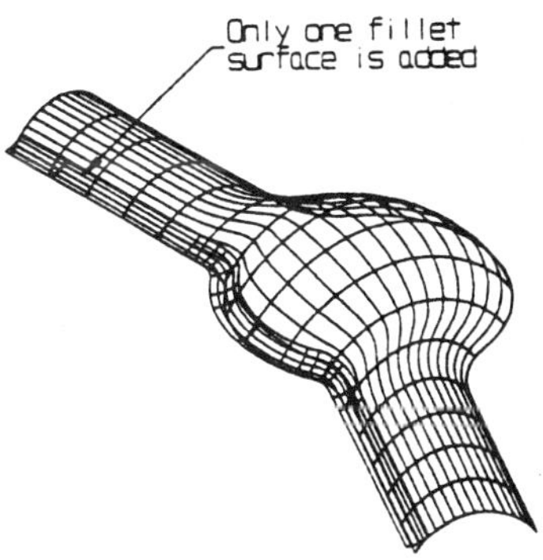

Figure 13.7a Find multiples = OFF

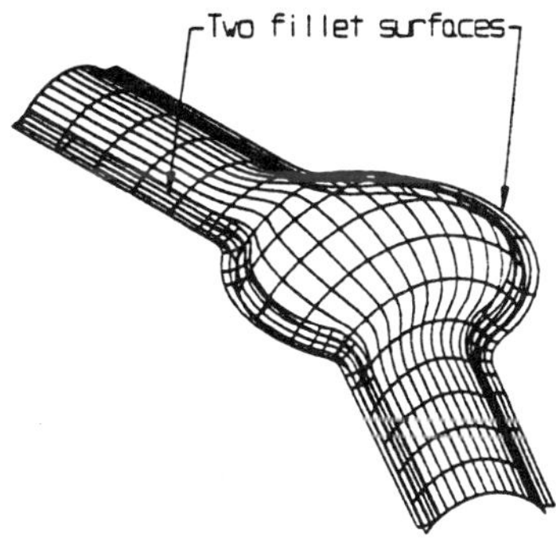

Figure 13.7b Find multiples = ON

Extend surfaces

This parameter is used to extend the resulting geometry the full length of the longer of the two tangent surfaces. When this option is not selected, the resulting geometry does not extend beyond the shorter of the two tangent surfaces

Trim Surface

Trim surface parameters appear somewhat different in three fillet surface creating methods. The **Surface to surface** method is the most commonly used method and its dialog menu appears below.

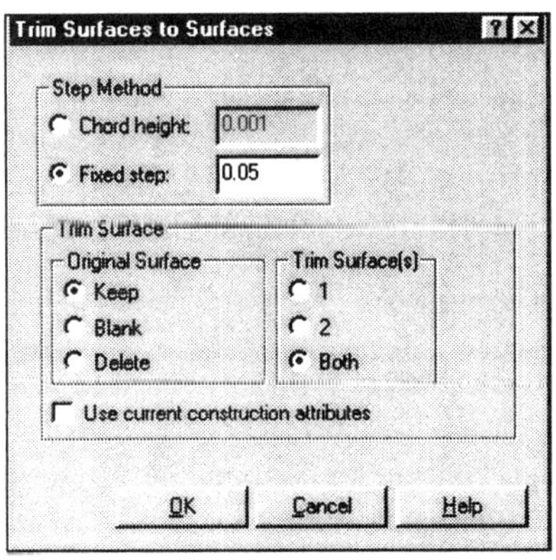

The "Yes" parameter is used to indicate whether the original surfaces are to be trimmed. Toggle this parameter to OFF (no check mark), no surface trimming will be implemented. Toggle this parameter to ON (with a check mark) to cause the original surfaces to be trimmed in the specified manner. Two sets of surfaces can be created from the fillet surfaces creating process: **fillet surfaces** and **trimmed surfaces** of the original surfaces. The original surfaces that are used to create fillet surfaces can be kept, or deleted from the model. It is somewhat confusing between "Surfaces" and "Original surfaces". The "Surfaces" are those surfaces created between the fillet surfaces and original surfaces. They are the surfaces created by trimming the original surfaces to the fillet surface boundaries. These surfaces are different from the original surfaces. Original surfaces can be handled in one of the following three ways:

Keep: keep the original surfaces after creating fillet surfaces and trimmed surfaces.

Blank: remove the original surfaces after creating fillet surfaces and trimmed surfaces.

Delete: delete the original surfaces after creating fillet surfaces and trimmed surfaces.

Select the "Delete" option unless you want to keep original surfaces for creating other surfaces.

Mastercam has these **three options** to select the surface trimming mode:

1: trim only the first set of surfaces (Figure 13.8).
2: trim only the second set of surfaces (Figure 13.9).
Both: trim both sets of surfaces (Figure 13.10).

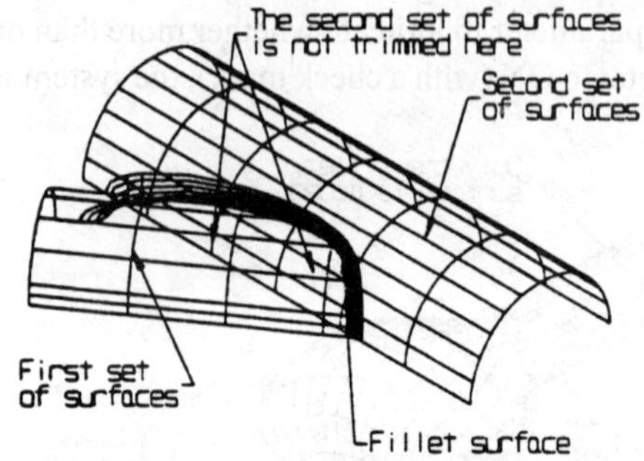

Figure 13.8

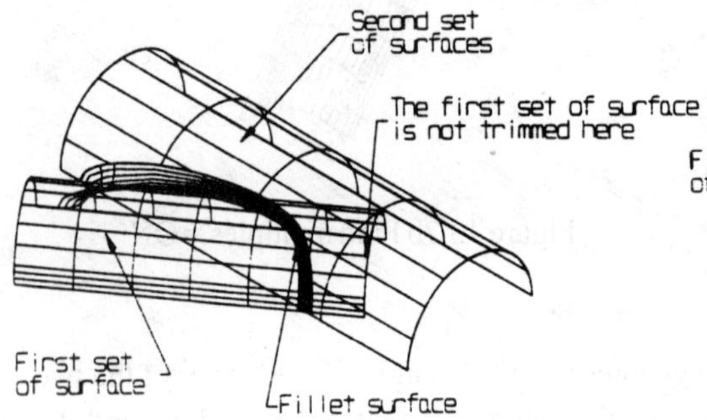

Figure 13.9

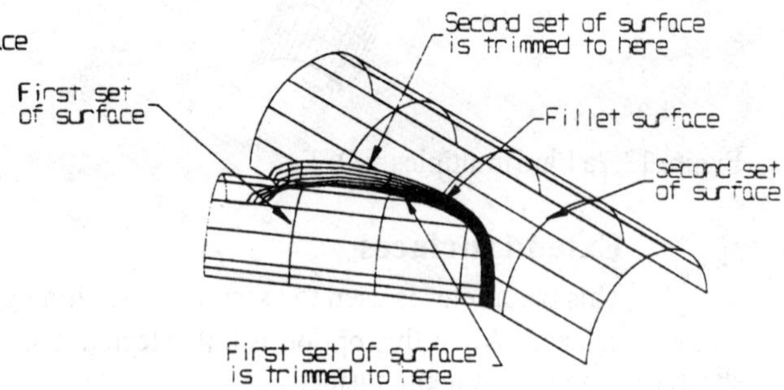

Figure 13.10

Use current construction attributes

Toggle this parameter to ON (with check mark) to create each trimmed surface using the current system attributes (color, level, line style/width). Toggle this parameter to OFF (no check mark), each trimmed surface using the attributes of the base (parent) surface.

Blank/delete surfaces on the other side of the plane

This parameter is used to blank or delete the selected surfaces that are not trimmed by the plane and that lie on the side of the plane that you choose to trim.

Variable Radius

There are two types of fillet surfaces: fillet surfaces with a constant radius and fillet surfaces with a variable radius. The fillet radius remains constant throughout the surface intersecting boundary for the constant radius type (Figure 13.11). The fillet radius varies along the center curve of the fillet surface in creating a fillet surface with a variable radius (Figure 13.12).

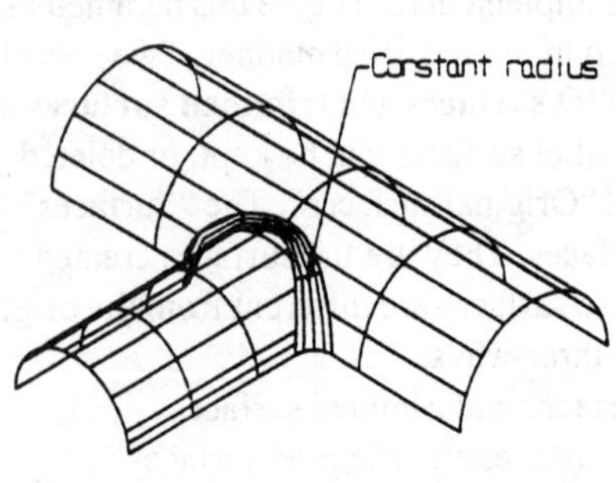

Figure 13.11a

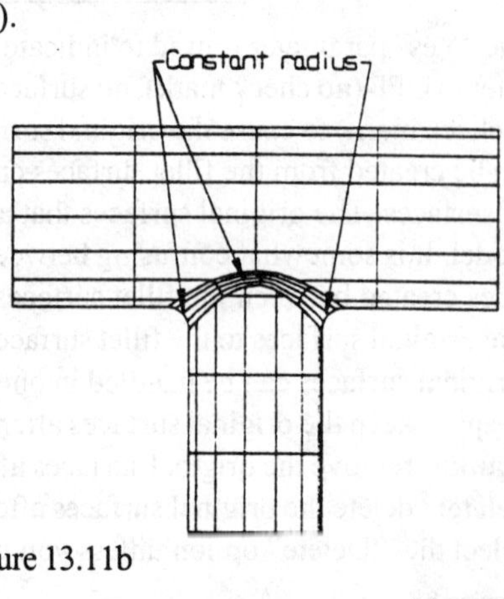

Figure 13.11b

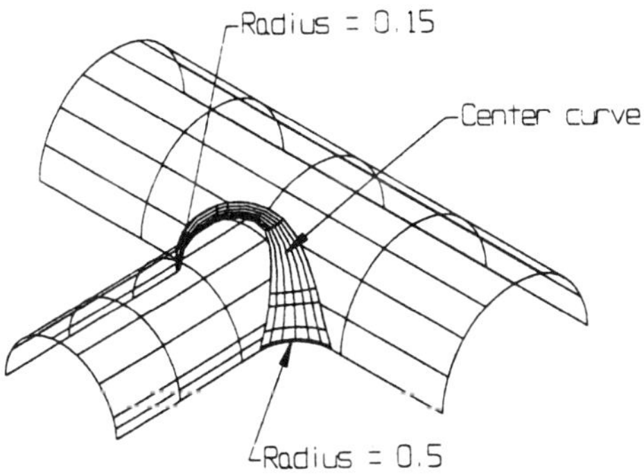

Figure 13.12a

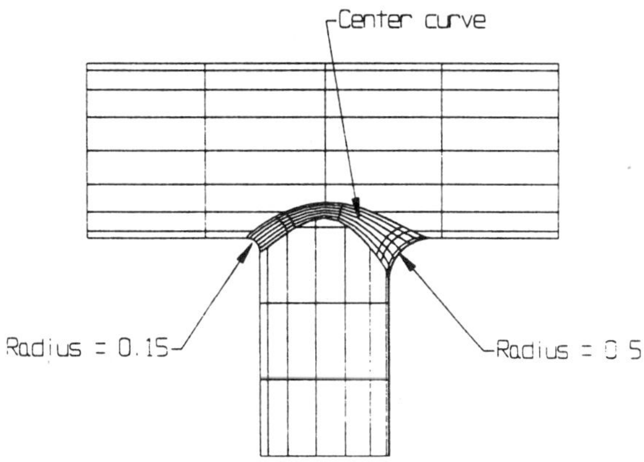

Figure 13.12b

Mastercam uses a set of control points along the center curve of the fillet surface to change the radius value of fillet curves. These control points are referred to as the radius markers in Mastercam. Each center curve of the fillet surface has two default radius markers that are located at both ends of the curve (Figure 13.13).

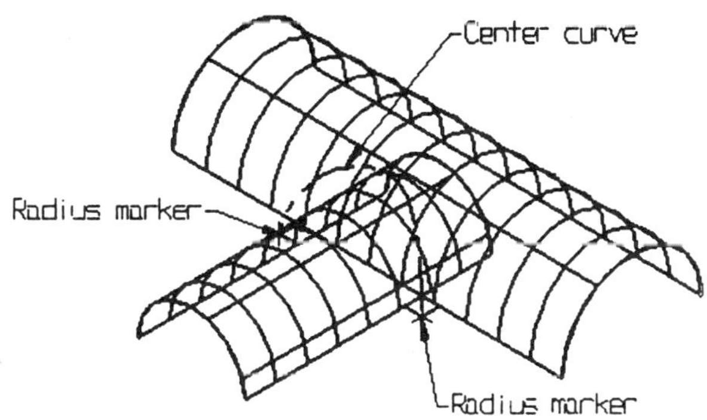

Figure 13.13

You can add more radius markers to the center curve for specifying a radius value for each radius marker. The two ways to add radius markers to the center curve are:

Insert dyn:	dynamically slide the arrow to desired location as a radius marker.
Insert mid:	add a radius marker to the midpoint between two selected radius markers.

Insert dyn mode

The procedure for inserting radius markers to the center curve is (Figures 13.14 – 13.16):

- Pick two filleting surfaces
- Enter the radius: 0.25
- Select Variable from the menu
- Select Insert dyn from the menu
- Pick a center curve
- Slide arrow to desired location and click as a radius marker
- Enter the radius: 0.5
- A new radius marker is added to the model

Repeat the above process to define as many radius markers as needed
Select **Done** → **Do it** to complete the fillet surface
The fillet surface with a variable radius is added as in Figure 13.16.

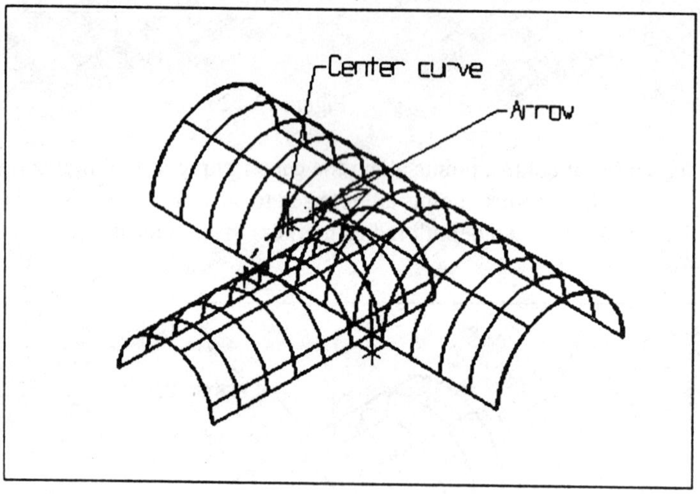

Figure 13.14

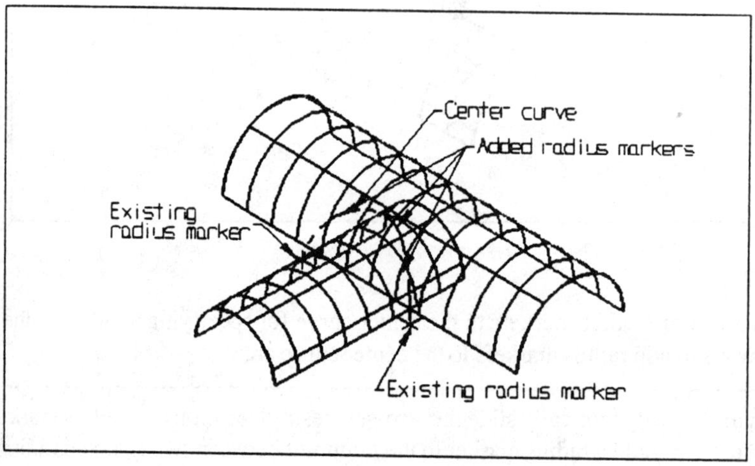

Figure 13.15

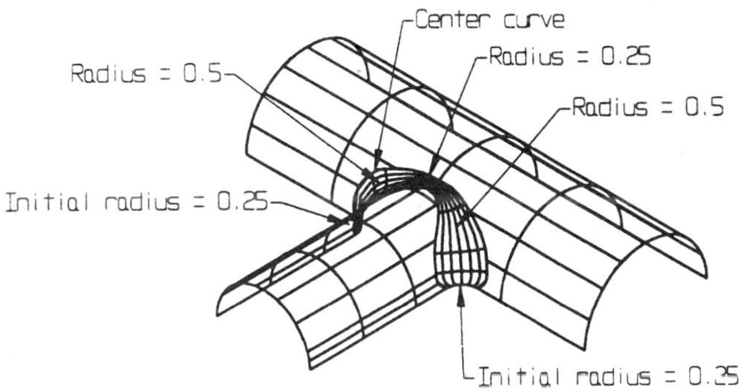

Figure 13.16

Insert mid mode

This mode adds a radius marker to the center curve at the midpoint between two selected radius markers. The second picked radius marker is referred to as "neighboring radius marker". This is a useful way to add a radius marker exactly at the midpoint of the center curve.

The procedure for adding a radius marker to the center curve is (Figures 13.17 – 13.18):

- Pick two filleting surfaces
- Enter the radius = 0.15
- Select Variable from the menu list
- Select Insert Mid from the menu
- Select a radius marker: pick the right end of center curve (Figure 13.17)
- Select a neighboring radius marker: pick the left end of center curve
- Enter the radius: 1
- Select Done
- Select Do it

The fillet surface is added to the model as in Figure 13.18.

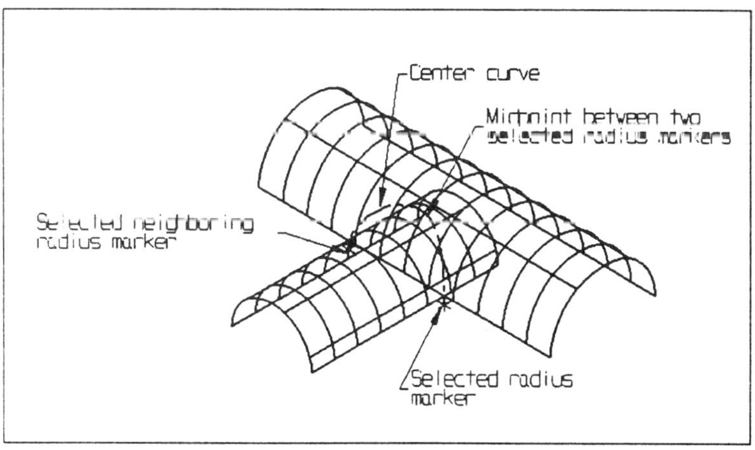

Figure 13.17

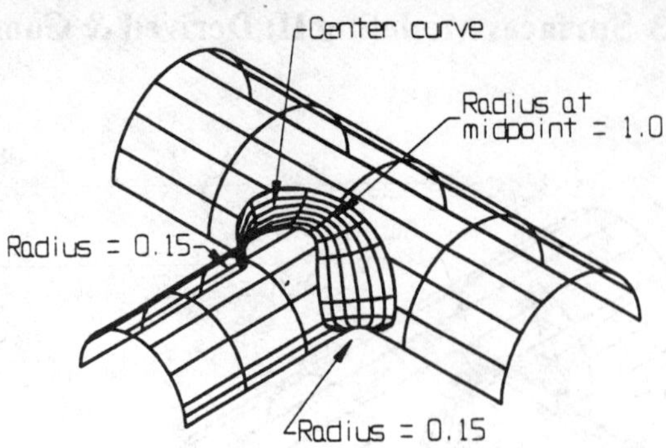

Figure 13.18

Modifying radius value at radius markers

Mastercam uses the Modify command to change the fillet radius value at radius markers. Figure 13.19 shows an example of modifying the fillet radius at a radius marker. The original radius at two existing radius markers is 0.15. The radius marker at the left end of the center curve is changed to 0.5.

The procedure:

- Select Modify from the list
- Select a radius marker: pick the radius marker at the left end
- Enter the radius = 0.5
- Select Done → Do it to complete the fillet surface

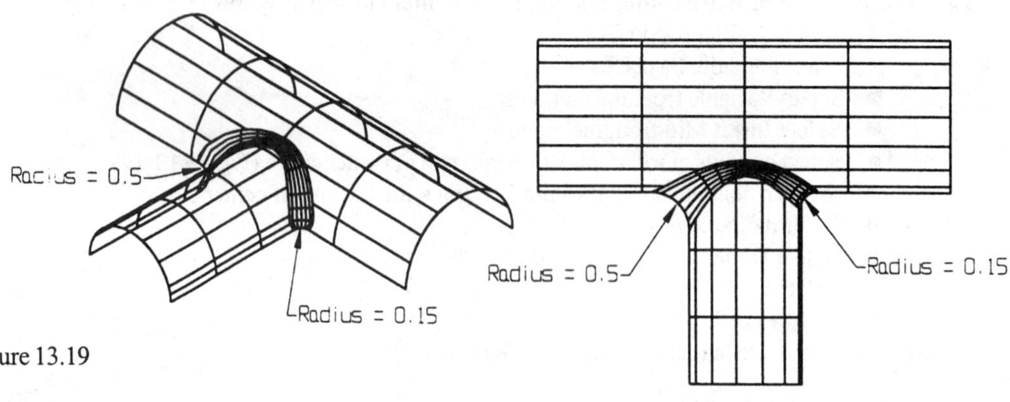

Figure 13.19

Creating a fillet surface between a plane and a surface

Mastercam allows to creating a fillet surface between an existing surface and a plane (Figure 13.20). The plane used to creating the fillet surface can be defined by one of eight methods. These eight plane defining methods are described in Table 13.2.

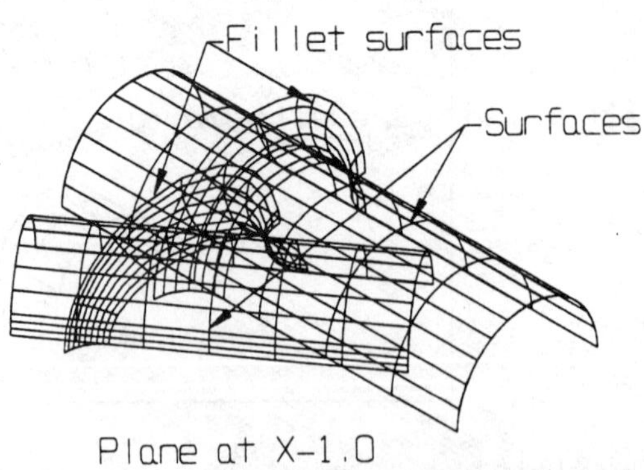

Figure 13.20

Table 13.2 Plane defining methods

Method	Description	Illustration
Z = const	A plane is defined as being parallel to the XY-plane and intersects Z axis at a given distance.	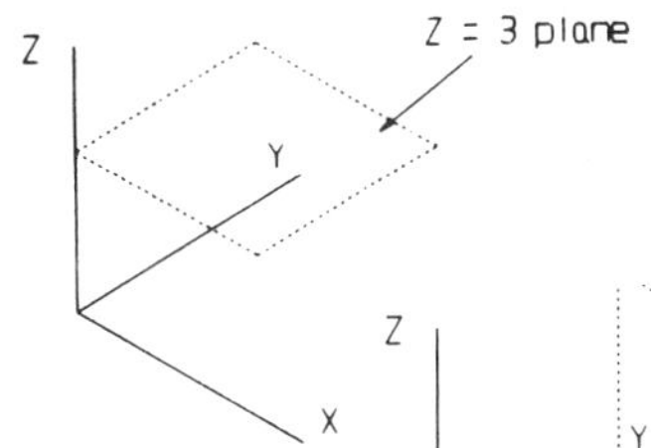
Y = const	A plane is defined as being parallel to the XZ-plane and intersects the Y axis at a given distance.	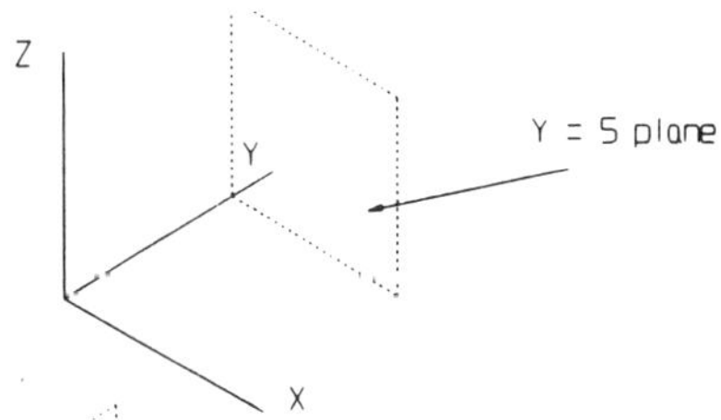
X = const	A plane is defined as being parallel to YZ plane and intersects the X axis at a given distance.	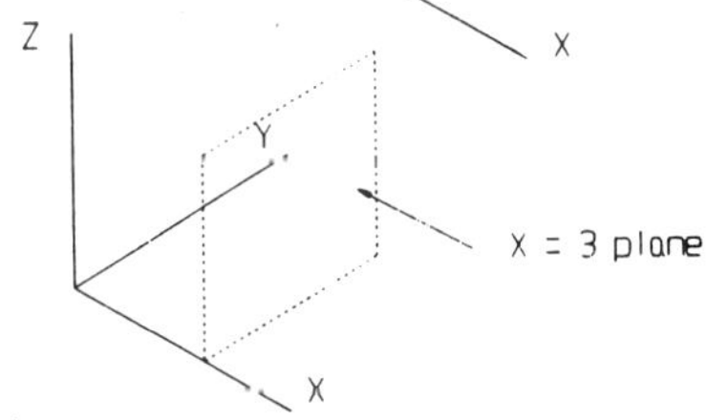
Line	A plane is defined as being co-planar with a line and perpendicular to the current Cplane.	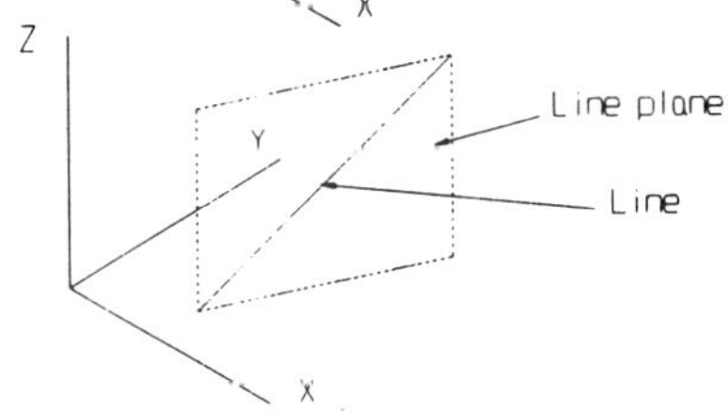
C-plane	A plane is defined as being parallel to the C-plane and intersects at a given Z-depth.	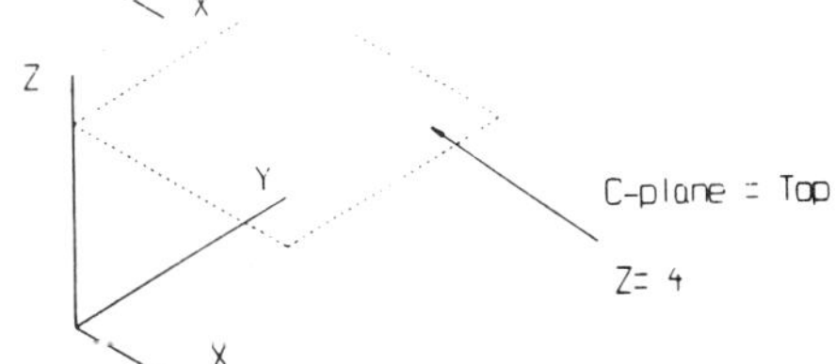
3-point	A plane is defined by three given non-collinear points.	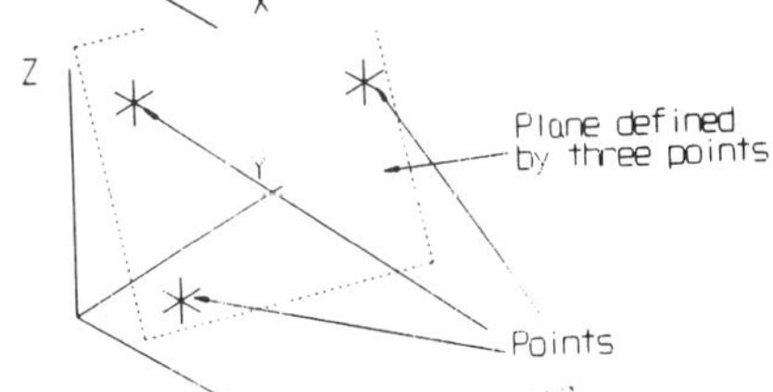
Entity	A plane is defined by: (1) an arc (2) a 2-D spline (3) two non-parallel lines (4) three non-collinear points	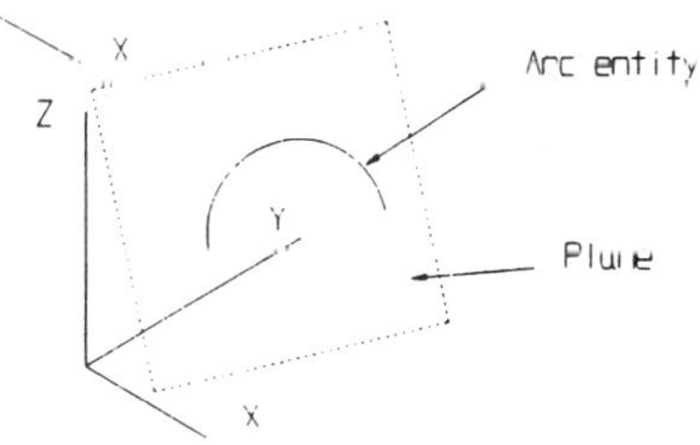
Normal	A plane is defined by being normal (perpendicular) to a given line.	

The option parameters dialog box for plane-surface method is shown here.

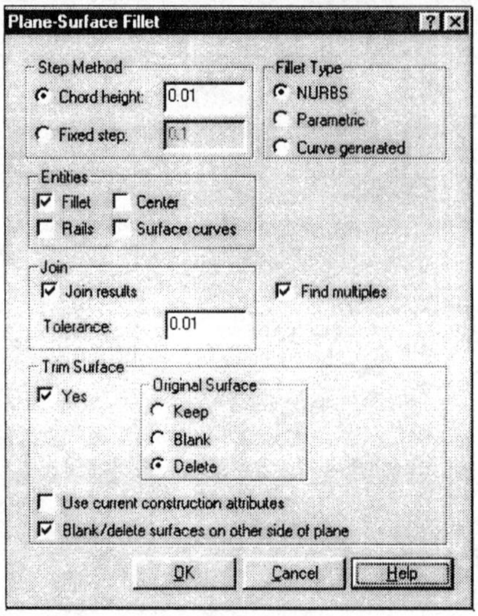

Procedure for creating a fillet surface between a plane and a surface (Figure 13.21):

- Select Create → Surface → Fillet → Plane/surf
- Pick a surface, then select Done
- Enter the radius: 0.25
- Select Plane: Select X = const
- Enter y-coordinate of plane: 0.0
- Side of Plane: select OK
- Select Do it

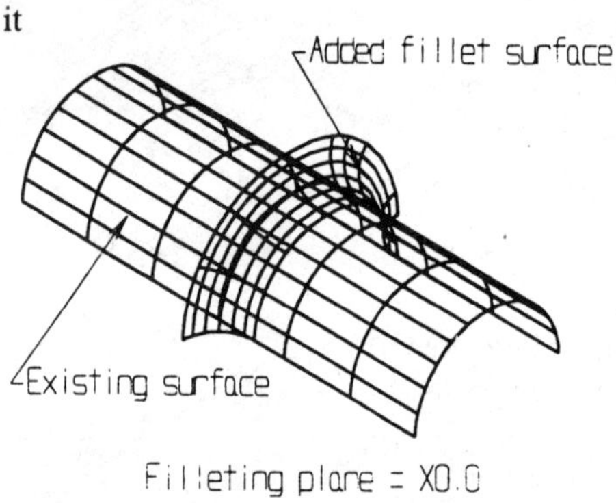

Figure 13.21

Creating a fillet surface between a curve and a surface

A fillet surface can be added between a curve and a surface (Figure 13.22). The fillet radius must be greater than the longest distance between the curve and the surface. Otherwise, it will produce partial fillet surfaces as shown in Figure 13.23. When the curve is selected, a direction arrow shall appear as in Figure 13.24. The system will prompt to select "Left" or "Right" to indicate to which side the fillet surface is added to the model (Figure 13.24).

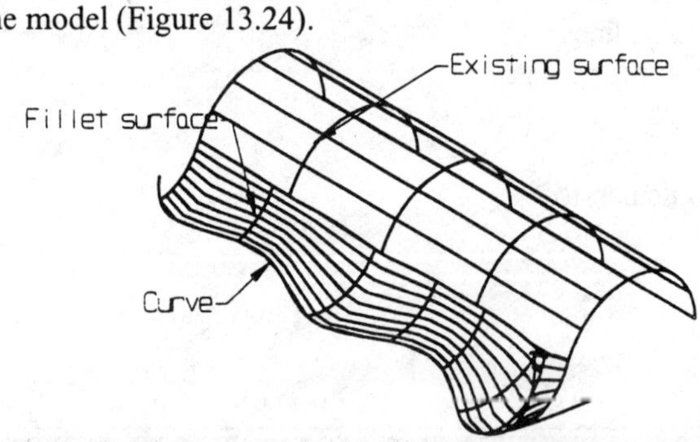

Figure 13.22

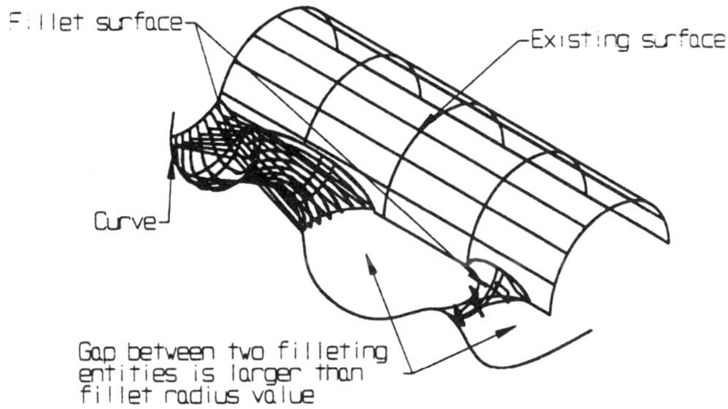

Figure 13.23

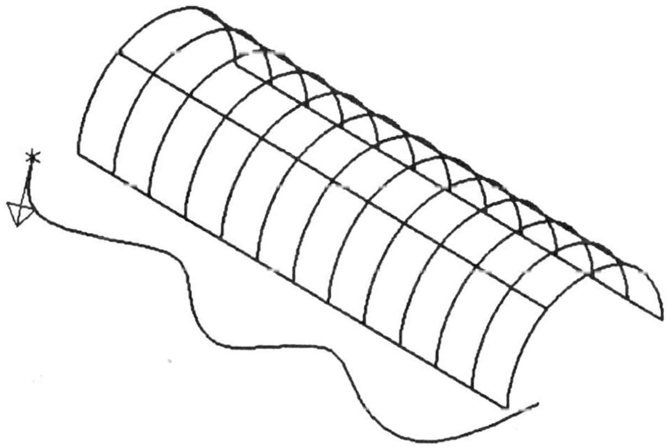

Figure 13.24

The procedure for creating a fillet surface between a curve and a surface is (Figure 13.25):

- Select Create → Surface → Fillet → Curve/surf
- Select surfaces: pick a surface, then select Done
- Enter the radius: 0.5
- Select chain 1: pick the curve, then select Done
- A direction arrow should appear as shown in Figure 13.24.
- Select side of curve: pick Left from the list
- Select Do it to complete the fillet surface

The fillet surface is added to the model as shown in Figure 13.25.

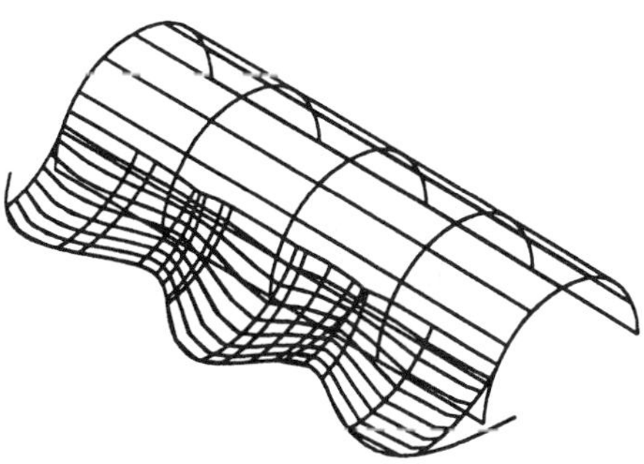

Figure 13.25

Creating a fillet surface between two surfaces

A fillet surface can be created between two existing surfaces (Figure 13.26). When two surfaces are intersected in two locations, it is possible to control whether to create only one fillet surface or two fillet surfaces (Figure 13.27). Mastercam uses "Find multiples" parameter in Options menu to control this option. With this parameter being set to Off (without a check mark), only one fillet surface is created (Figure 13.27a). With this parameter is set to On (with a check mark), two fillet surfaces are created (Figure 13.27b).

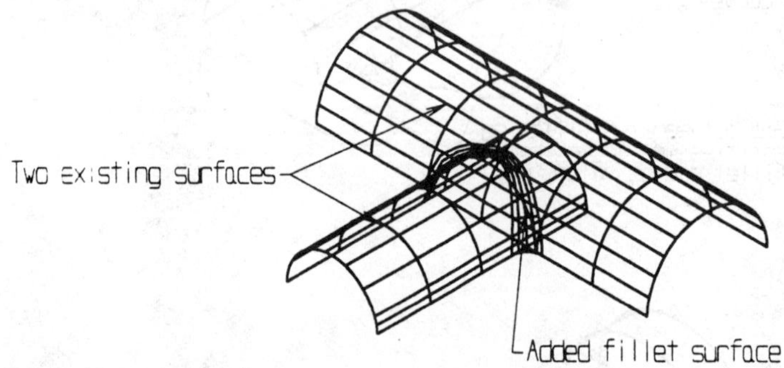

Figure 13.26

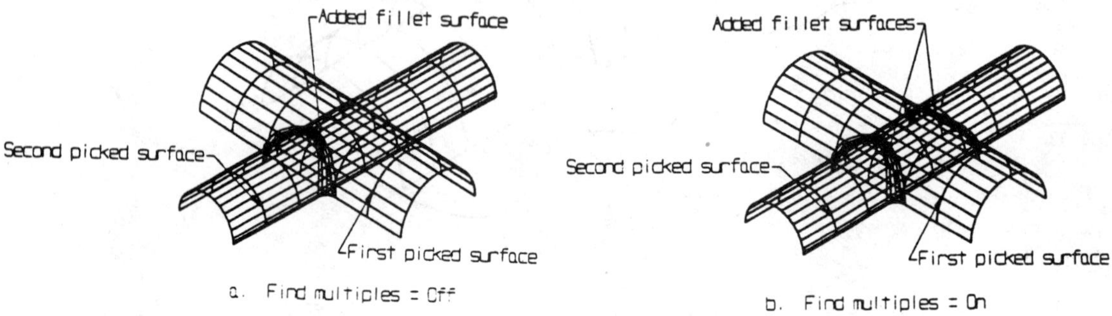

Figure 13.27a

Figure 13.27b

Actually Mastercam uses two sets of surfaces to create fillet surfaces. It is possible to have more than one surface in each set of surfaces. In this way, we can produce more than one fillet surface in one operation (Figure 13.28).

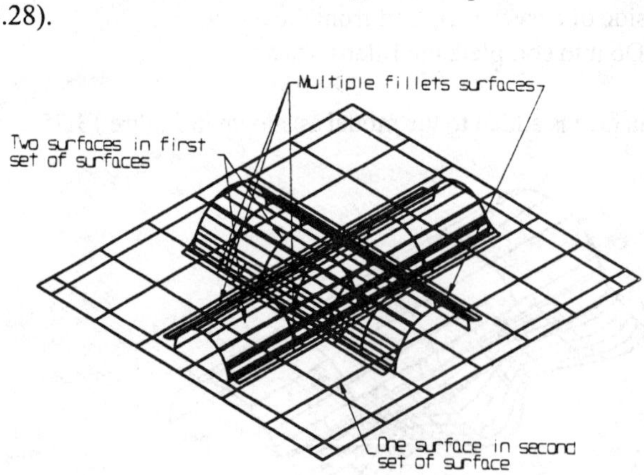

Figure 13.28

Creating a fillet surface between two existing surfaces requires the two surface normals pointing to the directions that intersect each other (Figure 13.29). If not, use Modify → Normal to set to the proper normal direction.

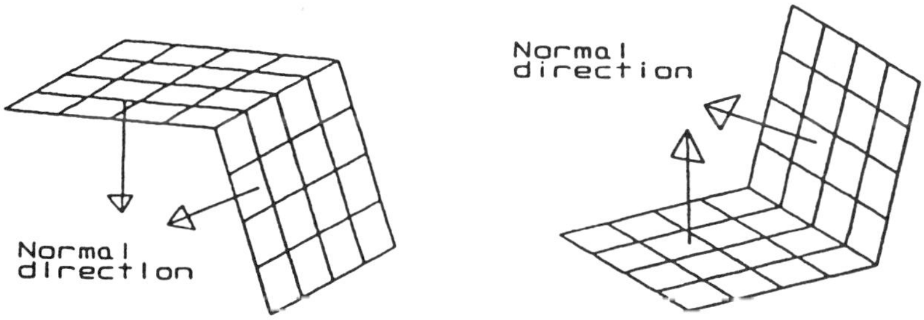

Figure 13.29

Two common problems in creating fillet surfaces are:

1. the surface normals are not in the proper direction,
2. the fillet radius may be too large to fit the two surfaces.

When a fillet surface can not be successfully generated, check the surface normals first. If the surface normals are correct and problem still exists, try to check if the fillet radius is too big to fit the surfaces.

Procedure for creating a fillet surface between two surfaces is (Figure 13.30):

- Select Create → Surface → Fillet → Surf/surf
- Pick the flat surface as the first set of surfaces, then select Done
- Pick the cone surface as the second set of surfaces, then select Done
- Enter the radius: 1
- Set the Options parameters if necessary
- Select Do it

The fillet surface is added to the model as in Figure 13.30.

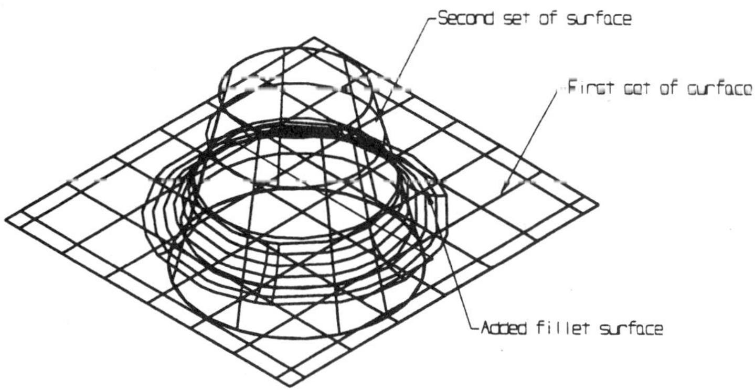

Figure 13.30

💻 Project 1. Two fillet surfaces with a constant radius

Two fillet surfaces are created at the intersection of two ruled surfaces (Figure 13.31). The two perpendicularly intersected ruled surfaces are created in project 1 of chapter 12. These two fillet surfaces have a constant radius of 0.25-in. Use the multi-surf function to create these two fillet surfaces simultaneously.

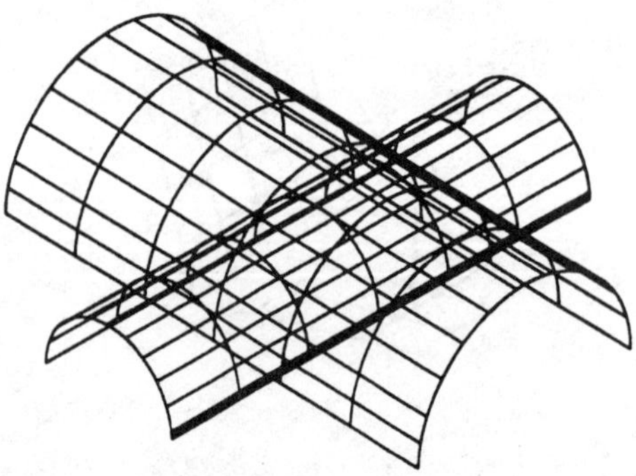

Figure 13.31a

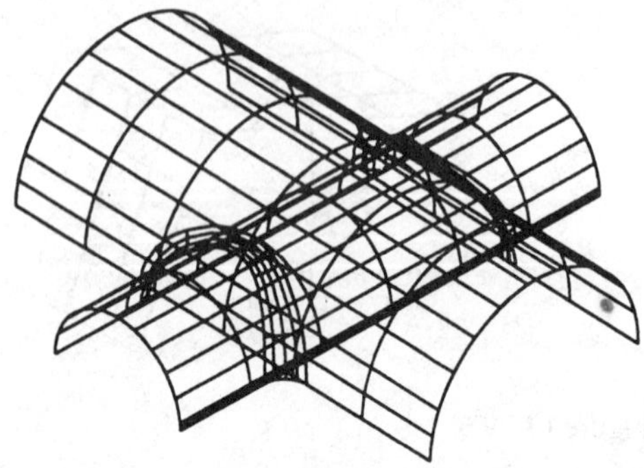

Figure 13.31b

Step 1. Load the surface model file ruleds1.

Select **MAIN MENU → File → Get**

Enter the filename: **ruleds1**

The drawing of two ruled surfaces should appear as Figure 13.32.

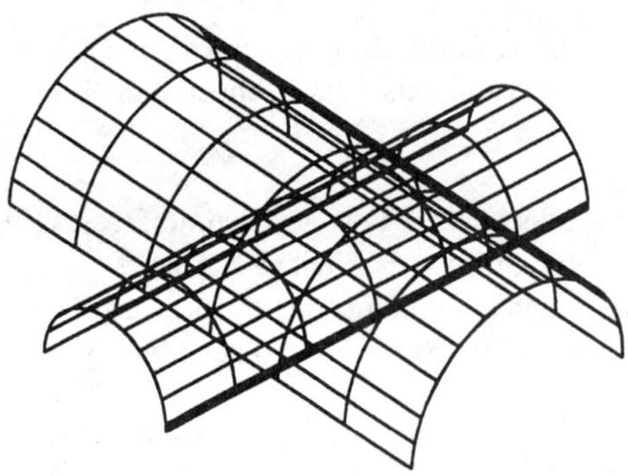

Figure 13.32

Step 2. Create the first fillet surface using the pick points in Figure 13.6.

Select **MAIN MENU → Create → Surface → Fillet → Surf/surf**

Pick the vertical surface as the first set of surface

Select **Done**

Pick the horizontal surface as the second set of surface

Select **Done**

Enter the radius: **0.25** ↵

Select **Options**

Set the surface-surface fillet parameters as shown here.

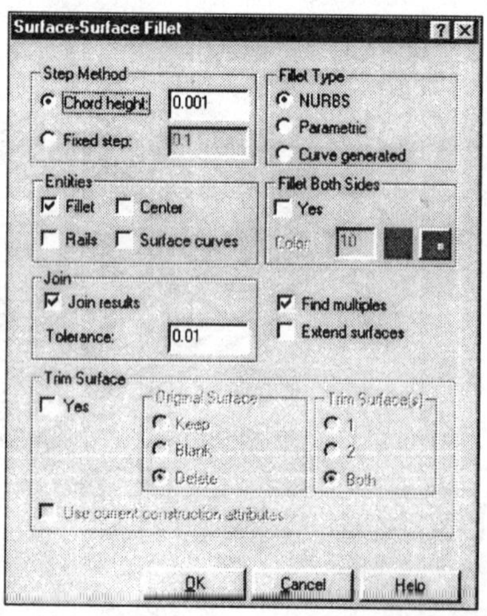

Select **OK → Do it**

The two fillet surfaces are created as shown in Figure 13.33. 1

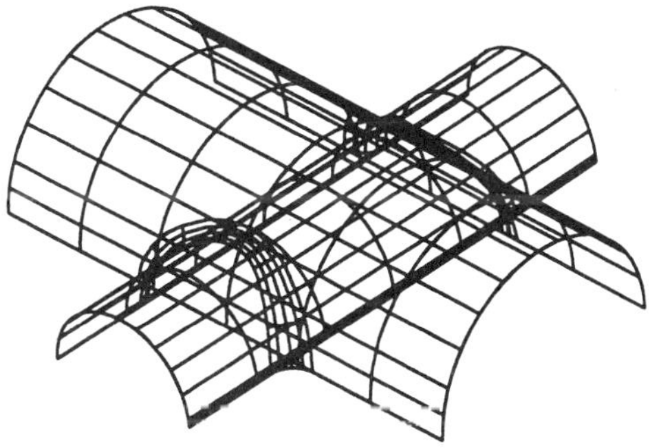

Figure 13.33

Step 3. Save the two fillet surfaces with two ruled surfaces.

Select **MAIN MENU → MAIN MENU → File → Save**

Enter file name: **fillets1**

Project 2. Two fillet surfaces with a variable radius

Create two fillet surfaces based on the two ruled surfaces generated in project 2 of chapter 12. Both two fillet surfaces have a variable radius. The radius of the fillet surface at the intersection of the two ruled surfaces varies in a linear pattern. The other fillet surface is added at the right end of the larger ruled surface. The radius of the second fillet surface changes in the Middle pattern. A ruled surface must be constructed at the right end before the fillet surface can be generated. Figure 13.34 shows both surface models before and after fillet surfaces are added.

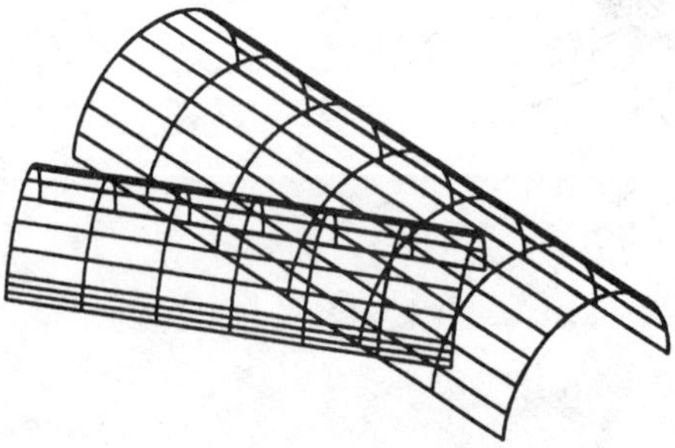

Figure 13.34a

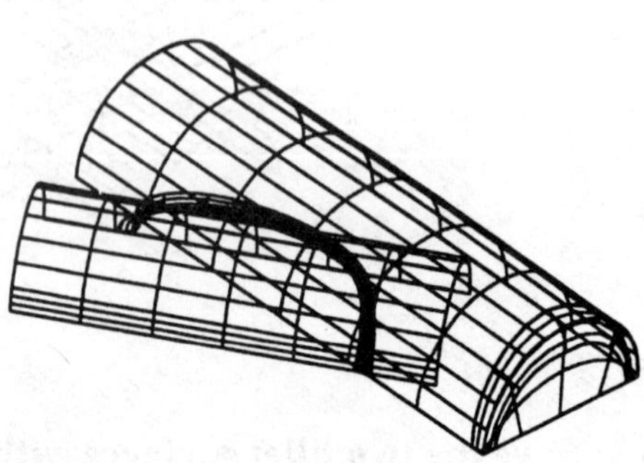

Figure 13.34b

Tips

1. Use different colors to display each surface.
2. The start fillet radius is 0.3-in and end fillet radius is 0.15-in for the fillet surface between two ruled surfaces.
3. Use the fixed step method to control the surface stepping pattern.
4. In the Surface-surface fillet dialog box, toggle the "Surf crvs" parameter to On. The two surface curves can be used to form the trimming boundary for trimming the surface in project 4 of this chapter.
5. A line should be added to the two endpoints at the right end of the larger ruled surface. This line is used with the arc to create a ruled surface.
6. The radius of the end fillet surface varies in a variable pattern. The radius starts with 0.15- in from one end and increases to 0.3-in in the middle and then decreases to 0.15-in at the other end.
7. The surface normals of both ruled surfaces for creating an end fillet surface must point toward the surfaces. Use Modify → Normal commands to change the surface normals if necessary.

Step 1. Load the surface model file ruleds2.

Select **MAIN MENU → File → Get**

Enter file name: **ruleds2**

The two ruled surfaces should appear as Figure 13.35.

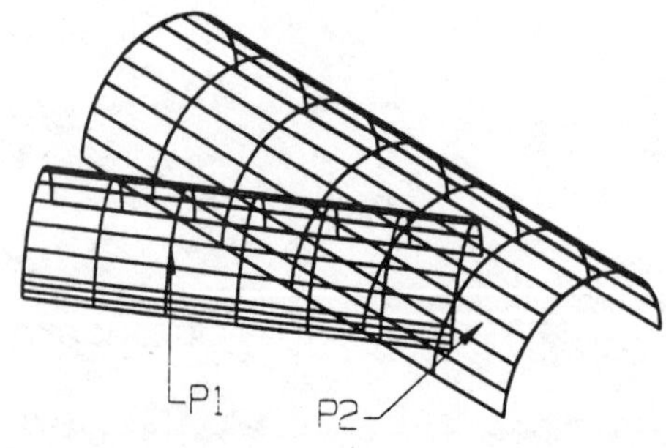

Figure 13.35

Step 2. Change color to 12.

2

From the Secondary menu select **Color** , then enter **12** ↵

Step 3. Create the first fillet surface between the two ruled surfaces.

Use the pick points in Figure 13.35.
Select **MAIN MENU → Create → Surface → Fillet → Surf/surf**
Pick **P1** as the first set of surface
Select **Done**
Pick **P2** as the second set of surfaces
Select **Done**
Enter the radius: **0.3** ↵
Select **Variable**
A center curve with two radius markers should appear as in Figure 13.36.

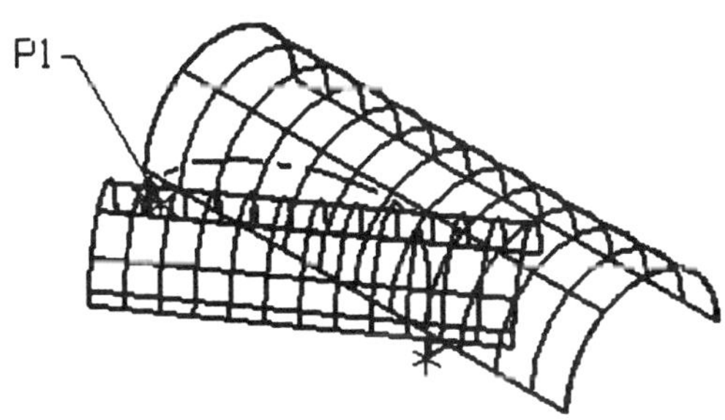

Figure 13.36

Select **Modify**
Select a Radius Marker: pick **P1** in Figure 13.36
Enter the radius: **0.15** ↵
Select **Done → Options**
Set the surface-surface fillet parameters as below.

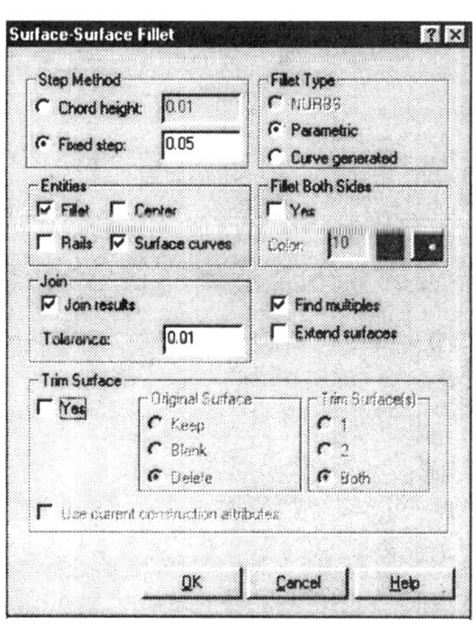

Select **OK → Do it**

The fillet surface is added as in Figure 13.37.

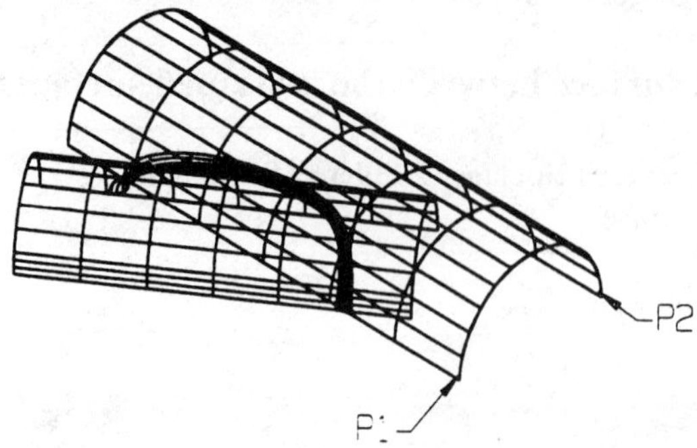

Figure 13.37

Step 4. Add a line to the right face of the larger ruled surface using 3D Cpalne.

Use the pick points in Figure 13.37.
Select **Cplane → 3D**
Select **MAIN MENU → Create → Line → Endpoints → Endpoint**
Pick **P1** and **P2** to complete the line
The line is added as shown in Figure 13.38.

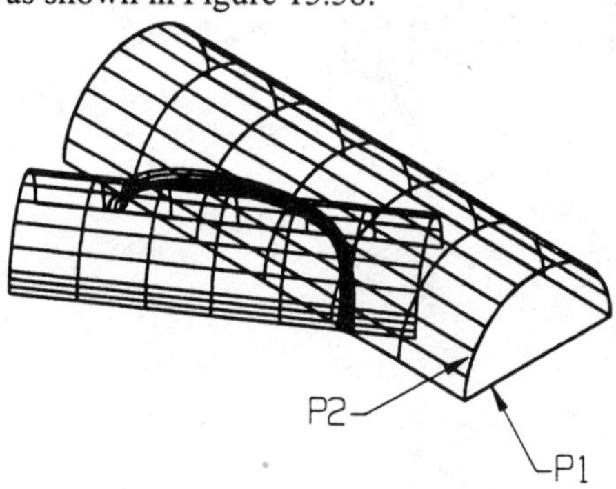

Figure 13.38

Step 5. Create a ruled surface at the right end of the semi-cone.

Use the pick points in Figure 13.38.
Select **MAIN MENU → Create → Surface → Ruled → Single**
Define contour 1: pick **P1**
Define contour 2: pick **P2**
Select **Done** to complete the contours selection
Set Surface type to **N** (NURBS)
Select **Do it** to generate the ruled surface.
The new ruled surface should appear on the screen as Figure 13.39.

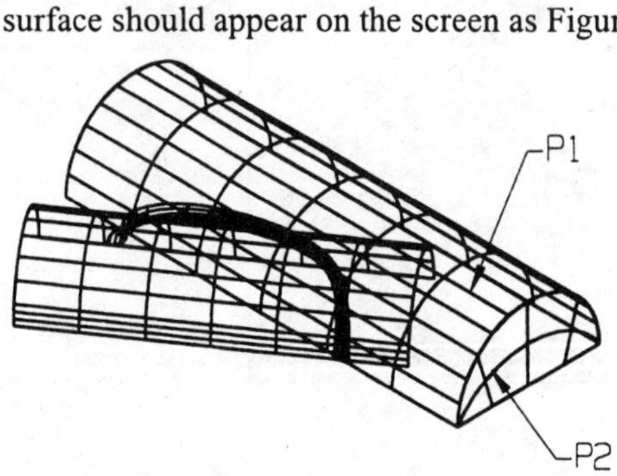

Figure 13.39

Step 6. Change the normal direction of the surfaces.

Use the pick points in Figure 13.39.
Select **MAIN MENU → Modify → Normal → Reverse**
Pick **P1** to select a surface

Note: Surface curves are dimmed when the surface normal direction is changed to point in the inward direction.

Pick **P2** to select the end surface to change the normal direction of the second surface
Note: Surface curves on both surfaces should appear dimmed.

The drawing on the screen should look like Figure 13.40.

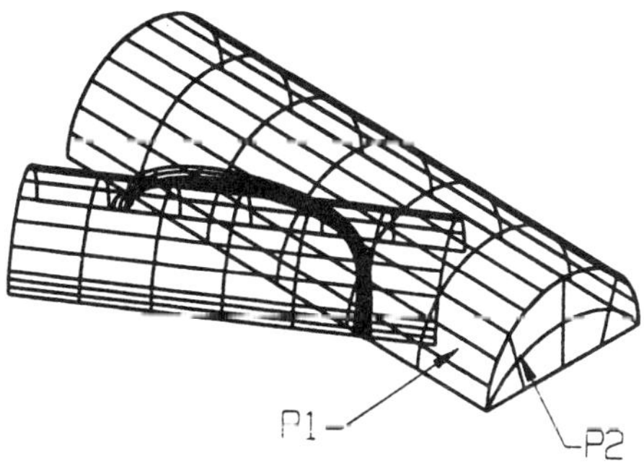

Figure 13.40

Step 7. Create a fillet with a variable radius.

Use the pick points in Figure 13.40.
From the Secondary menu select **Color**, and then enter **14** ↵
Select **MAIN MENU → Create → Surface → Fillet → Surf/surf**
Pick **P1** to select the first set of surfaces
Select **Done**
Pick **P2** to select the second set of surfaces
Select **Done**
Enter the Radius: **0.15** ↵
Select **Variable**

A center curve with two radius markers appear as in Figure 13.41.

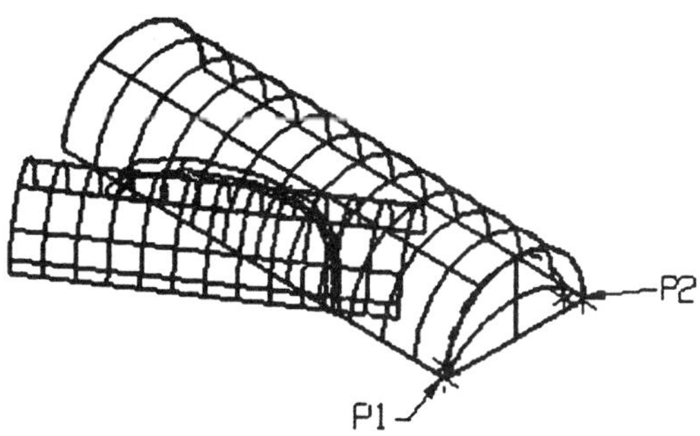

Figure 13.41

Select **Insert mid**
Select a Radius Marker: pick **P1**
Select a neighboring Radius Marker: pick **P2**
Enter the radius: **0.3** ↵
Select **Done → Do it**
The variable fillet surface is added to the model as in Figure 13.42.

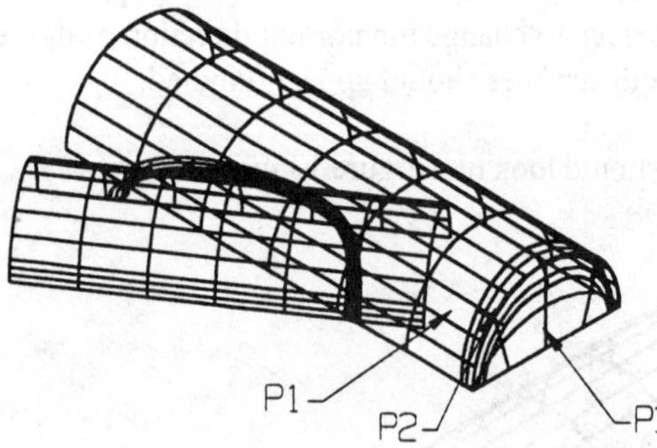

Figure 13.42

Step 8. Change three surface normals.

Use the pick points in Figure 13.42.
Select **MAIN MENU → Modify → Normal → Reverse**
Select three surfaces to change their normal direction to outward, pick **P1**, **P2**, and **P3**
The final drawing should resemble Figure 13.43.

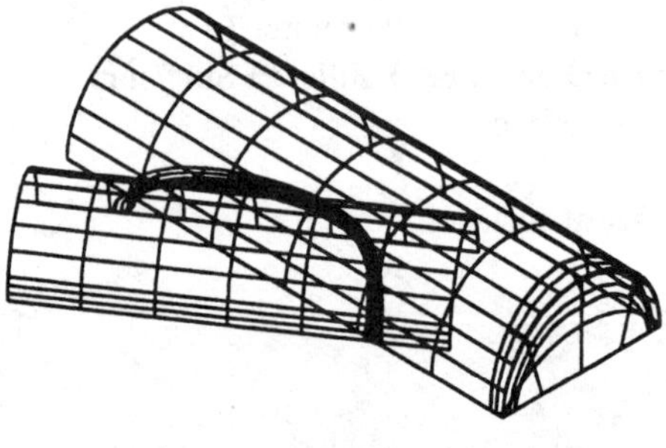

Figure 13.43

Step 9. Save the surface model file as fillets2.

Select **MAIN MENU → File → Save**
Enter file name: **fillets2**

13.2 Trim/Extend Surfaces Modeling

The Trim/Extend surface modeling technique is sued to create a trimmed surface from an existing surface (Figure 13.44). It requires an existing surface and at least one trim boundary. Table 13.4 summarizes the surface trimming methods.

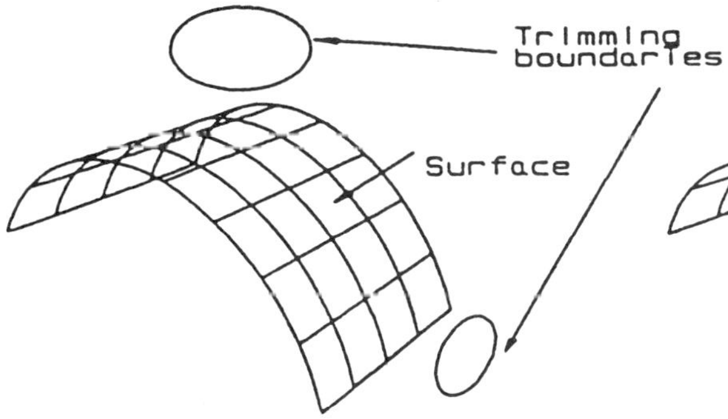

Figure 13.44a Before trimming

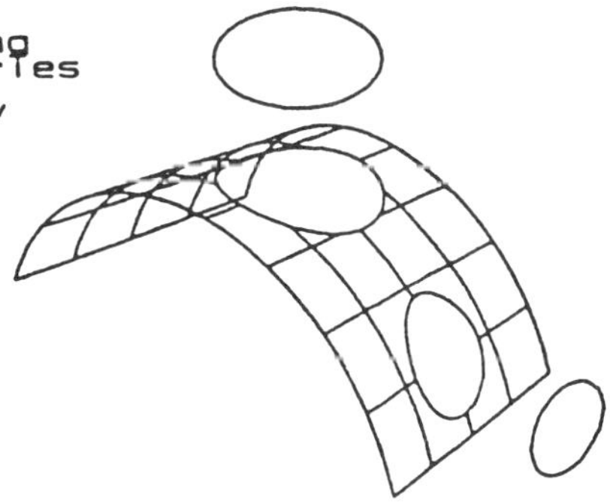

Figure 13.44b After trimming

The command chain for the Trim/Extend is:

MAIN MENU → Create → Surface → Trim/Extend

Table 13.4 Trim/Extend surfaces modeling methods

Method	Description	Illustration
To curves	Trim surface(s) to the given curves.	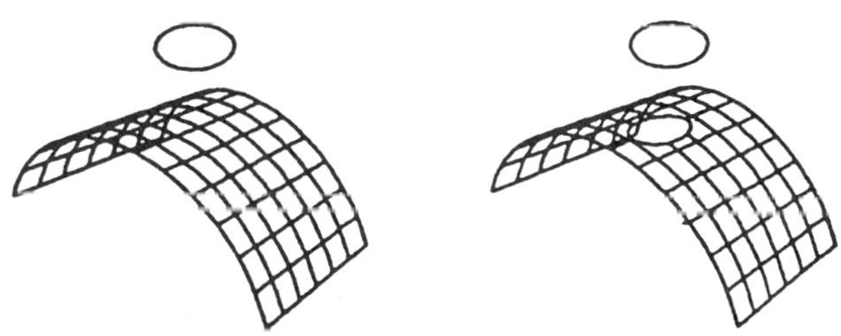
To plane	Trim surface(s) to a plane.	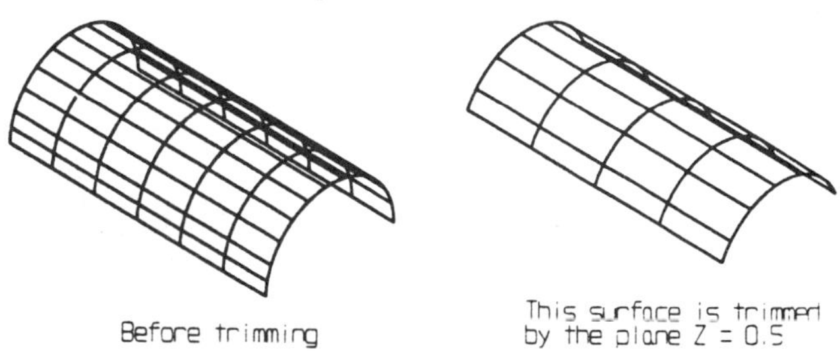

Trim/Extend surfaces modeling methods, continued.

To surfaces	Trim surface(s) to a surface.	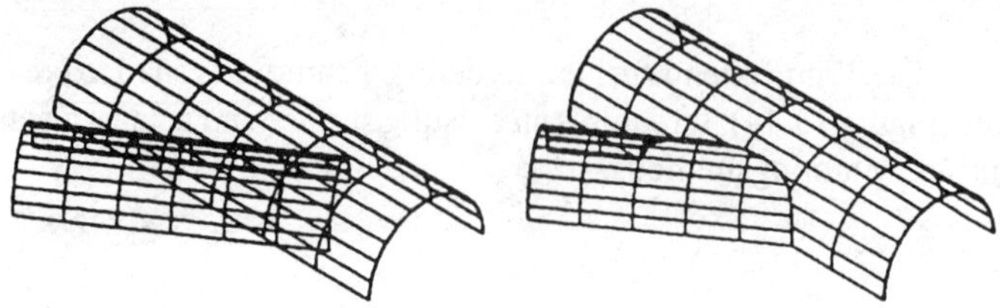
Flat bndy	Create a flat surface to the specified boundary.	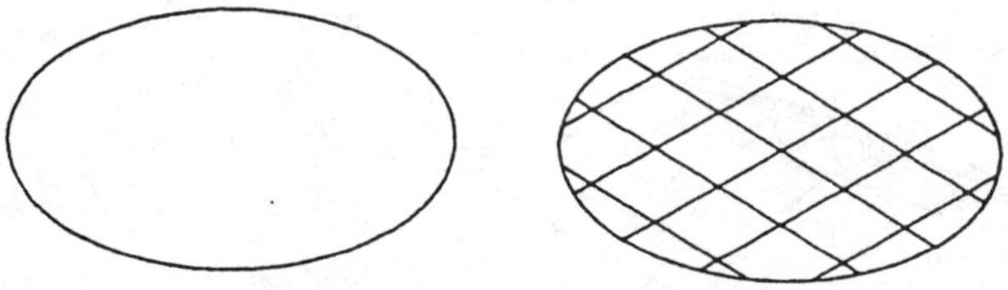
Split	Split a surface along a constant parameter into two separate surfaces.	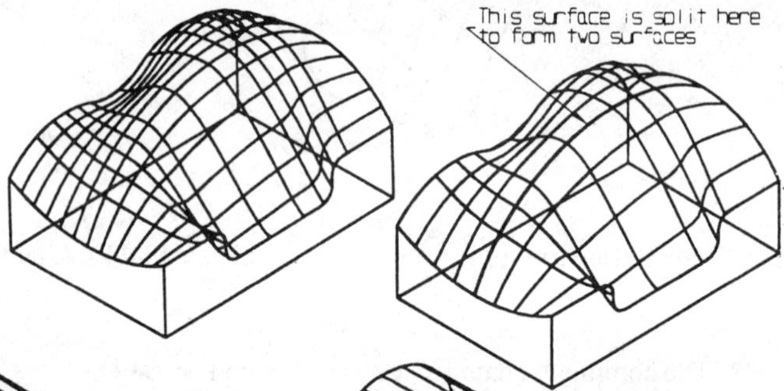
Untrim	Untrim trimmed surfaces.	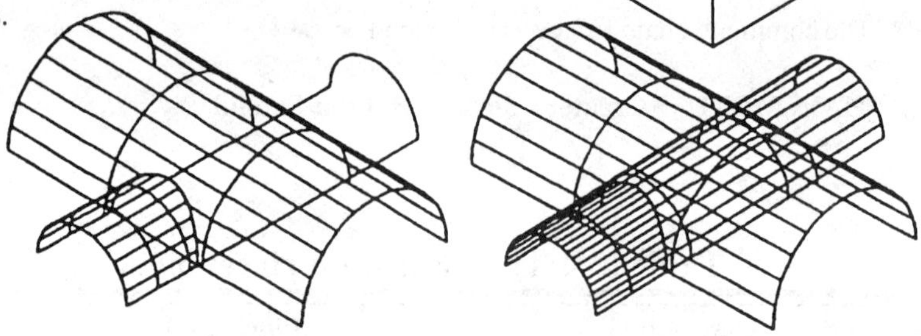
Remove bndy	Remove a boundary from a trimmed surface. The surface is extended beyond the surface.	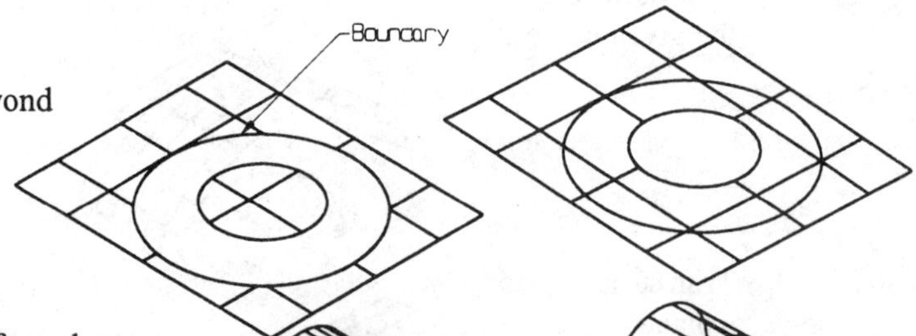
Extend	Extend a surface along one of its edges by a given distance or to a given plane.	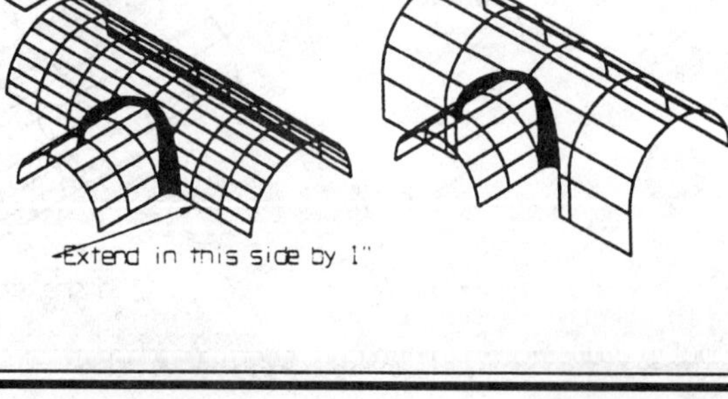

Project 3. Trimming two ruled surfaces to their intersection boundaries

Two intersecting ruled surfaces are trimmed to their intersecting boundaries. Both surface models before and after trimming are shown in Figure 13.45.

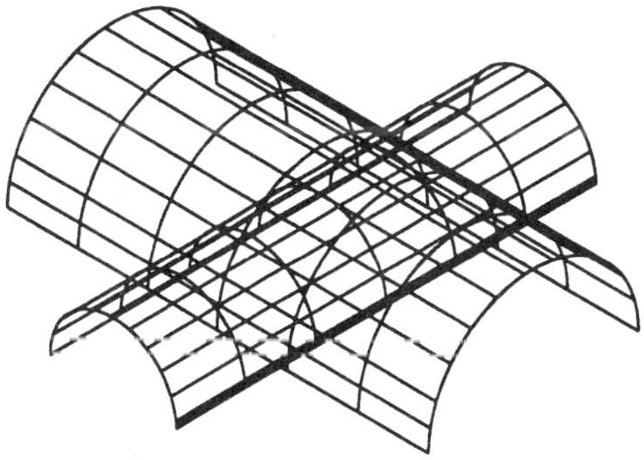

Figure 13.45a

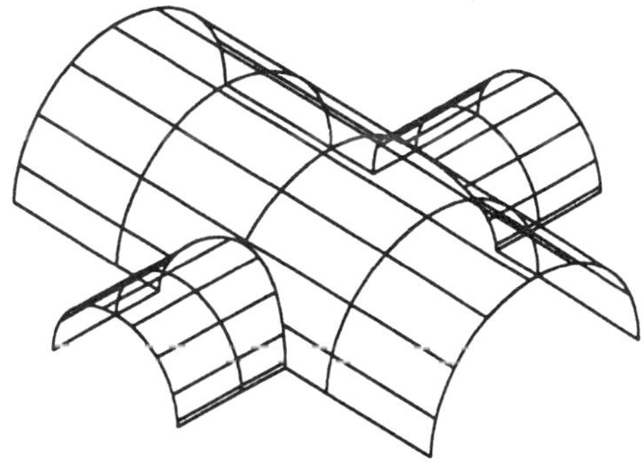

Figure 13.45b

Tips 1. The surface file to be trimmed is ruleds1.

2. Use the To surfaces method to trim both surfaces to their intersection boundaries.

3. These two ruled surfaces are intersected at two locations. Therefore, they need to be trimmed twice. After trimming at one end, the original surfaces must be kept to their original shape. The original surfaces are used again to be trimmed each other at the other end. Use the "Delete" option to delete two original surfaces in second trimming.

Step 1. Open the surface file ruleds1.

Select **MAIN MENU → File → Get**
Enter file name: **ruleds1** ↵
The two ruled surfaces should appear as in Figure 13.46.

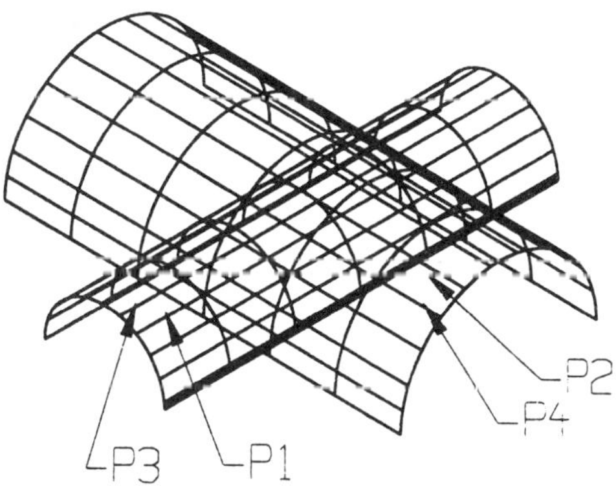

Figure 13.46

Step 2. Initiate the trimmed surface function.

Select **Level**, then enter **3** in the Main level number box → **OK**
Select **MAIN MENU → Create → Surface → Trim/extend → To surfaces**
To select first set of surfaces, pick **P1,** then **Done**
To select the second set of surfaces, pick **P2,** then **Done**
Select **Options**

Set Trim Surfaces to Surfaces parameters as shown here:

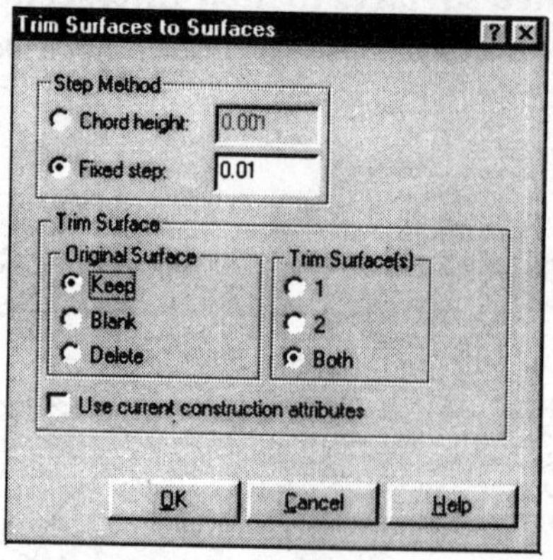

Select **OK → Do it**
Select a surface to be trimmed, pick **P1**
Indicate a location to keep after trimming, pick **P3**
Select a surface to be trimmed, pick **P2**
Indicate a location to keep after trimming, pick **P4**
The two surfaces are trimmed to their intersections as in Figure 13.47.

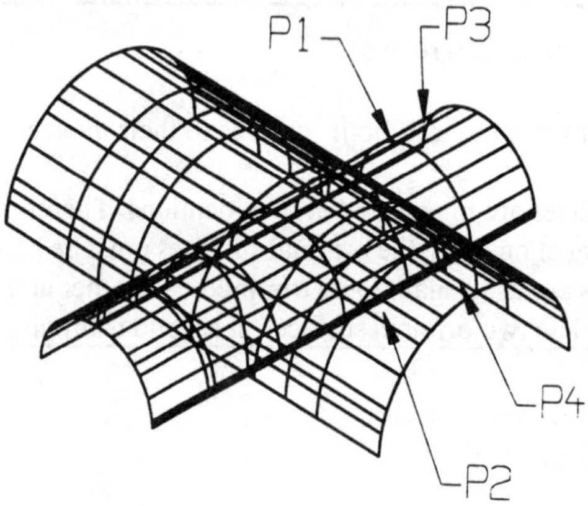

Figure 13.47

Step 3. Trim both surfaces to their intersection boundary at the other end.

Use the pick points in Figure 13.47.
Select **BACKUP → To Surfaces**
Select first set of surfaces, pick **P1** then **Done**
Select second set of surfaces, pick **P2** then **Done**
Select **Options**
Set trim surfaces to surfaces parameters as shown here.

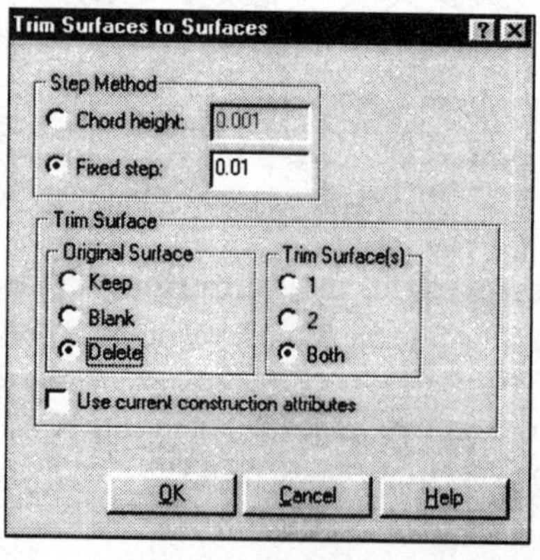

Select **OK → Do it**

Select a surface to be trimmed, pick **P1**
Indicate a location to keep after trimming, pick **P3**
Select a surface to be trimmed, pick **P2**
Indicate a location to keep after trimming, pick **P4**
New surface model becomes Figure 13.48.

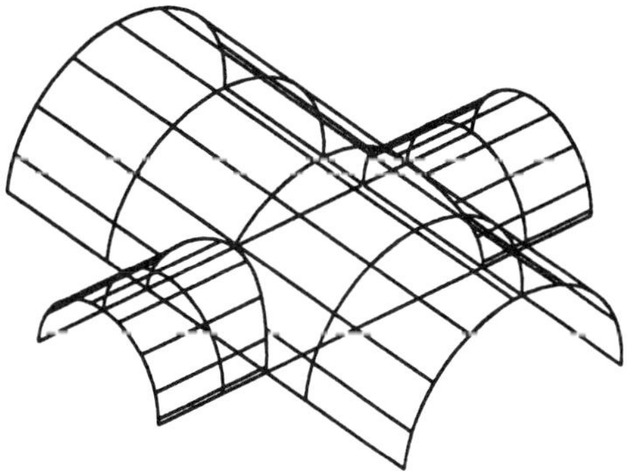

Figure 13.48

Step 4. Toggle level 1 to invisible.

Select **Level**
Click the check mark in the #1 Visible column to remove it and hide the level
Select **OK**
The final drawing appears as in Figure 13.49.

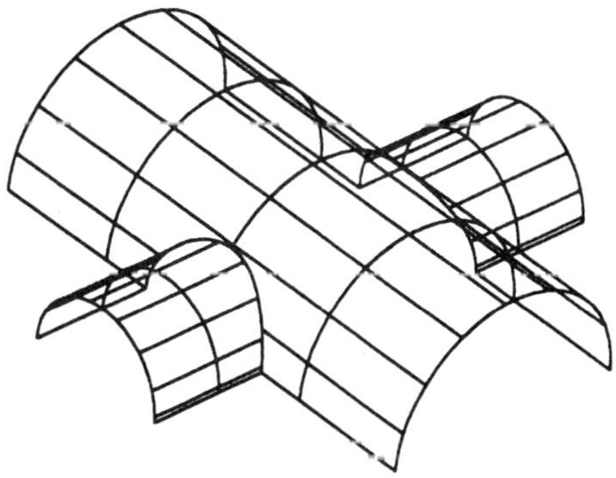

Figure 13.49

Step 5. Save the trimmed surfaces as trims1.

Select **MAIN MENU → File → Save**
Enter file name: **trims1**

Project 4. Trimming three surfaces to their surface boundaries

In this example, three trimmed surfaces are generated based on the surface model of project 2 in this chapter. These three ruled surfaces are trimmed to their surface boundary. The surface models before and after trimming are shown in Figure 13.50.

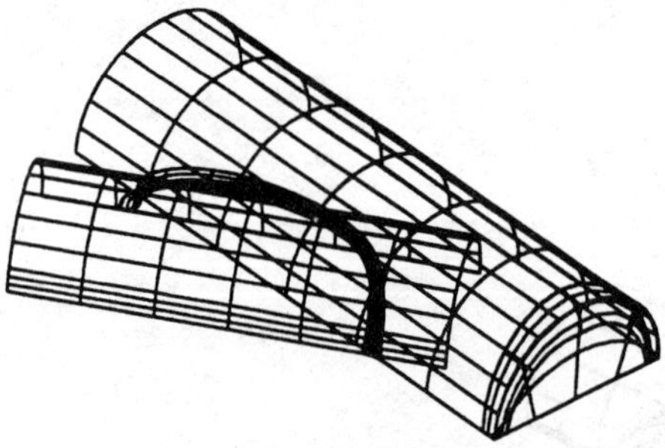

Figure 13.50a

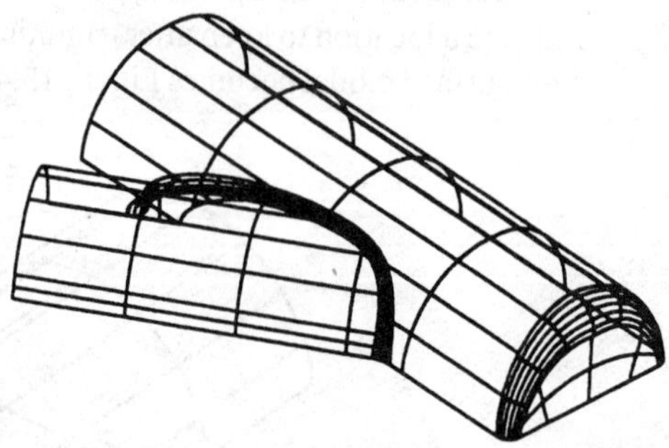

Figure 13.50b

Tips 1. Use the surface model file fillets2.

2. Use "To surfaces" option to trim two ruled surfaces to the fillet surface between them.

3. Use "To curves" option to trim the right end of the larger ruled surface and the right end surface to the surface curves of fillet surface.

Step 1. Open the surface model file fillets2.

Select **MAIN MENU → File → Get**
Enter file name: **fillets2**
The drawing should resemble Figure 13.51.

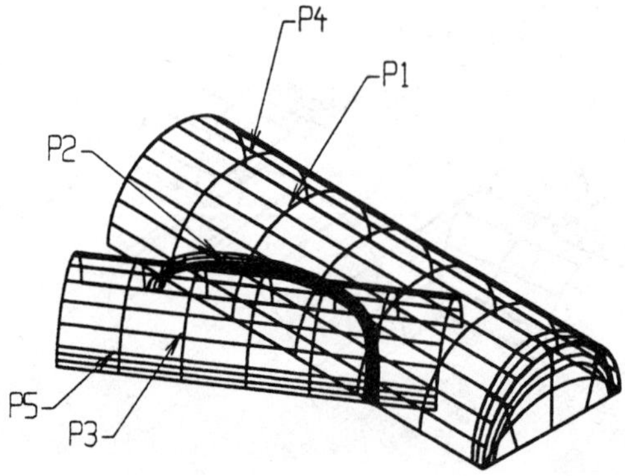

Figure 13.51

Step 2. Trim two ruled surfaces to the fillet surface.

Use the pick points in Figure 13.51.
Select **MAIN MENU → Create → Surface → Trim/extend → To surfaces**
Select first set of surfaces: pick **P1**, then select **Done**
Select second set of surfaces: pick **P2** and **P3**, then select **Done**
Select **Options**

Set trim surfaces to surfaces parameters as shown here. 4

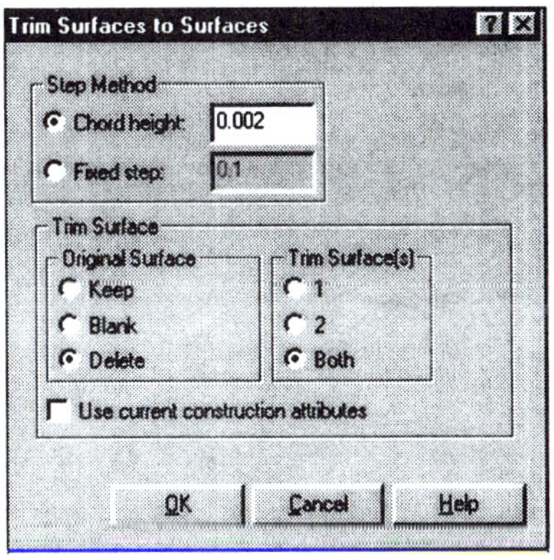

Select **OK → Do it**
Pick **P1** to select a surface, then select **P4**
Pick **P3** to select a surface, then select **P5**
The system trims two ruled surfaces to a fillet surface as shown in Figure 13.52.

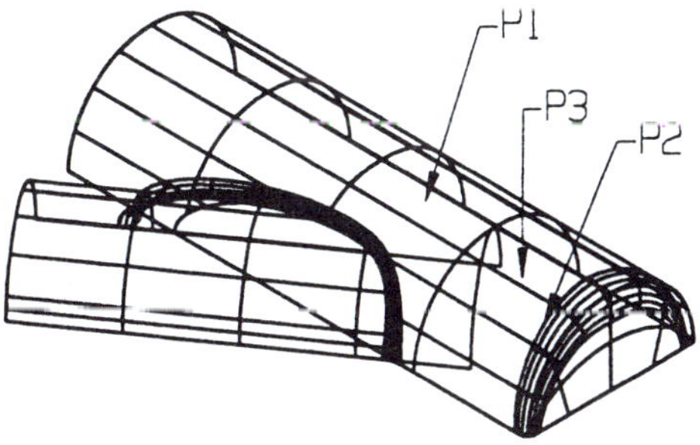

Figure 13.52

Step 3. Trim the larger ruled surface to a surface curve.

Use the pick points in Figure 13.52.
Select **BACKUP**
Select **to curves**
Pick **P1** to select a surface, then select **Done**
Select **BACKUP → Surface(s)**
Pick **P2** to select a surface curve
Select **Done → Options**
Set trim surfaces to curves parameters as shown here.

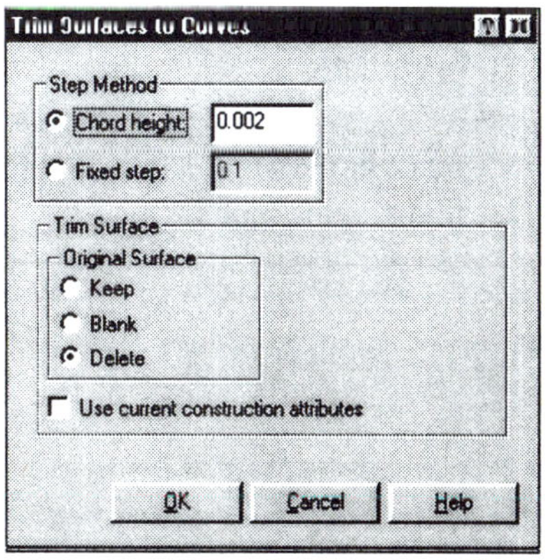

Select **OK → Do it**

Pick **P1** to select a surface to be trimmed
Pick **P3** to indicate a location to keep after trimming
The large ruled surface is trimmed as in Figure 13.53.

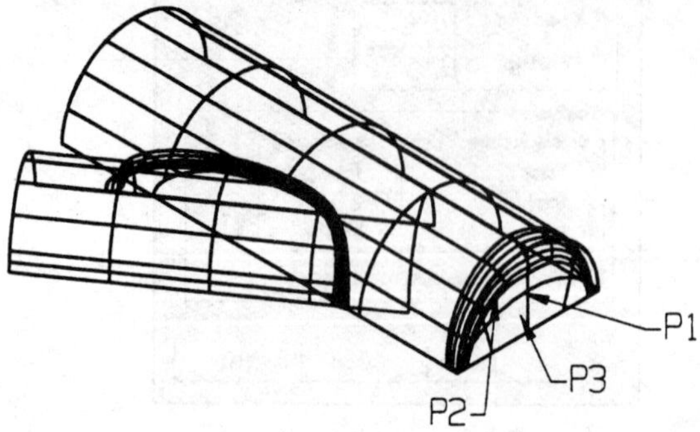

Figure 13.53

Step 4. Trim the ruled surface at the end face using the pick points in Figure 13.53.

Select **BACKUP → To curves**
Pick **P1** to select the end surface
Select **Done → BACKUP → Surface(s)**
Pick **P2** to select a surface curve
Select **Done → Do it**
Pick **P1** to select a surface to be trimmed
Pick **P3** to indicate a location to keep after trimming
The right end surface is trimmed as in Figure 13.54.

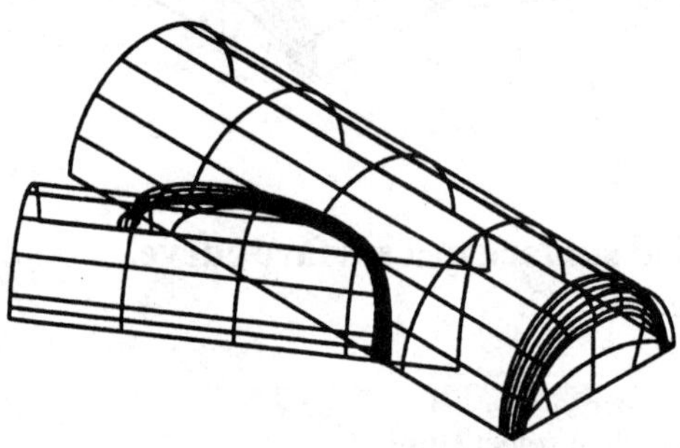

Figure 13.54

Step 5. Make level 1 invisible.

Select **Level**
Click at the check mark in the #1 Visible column to invisible
Select **OK** to return to graphic mode

The final drawing should resemble Figure 13.55.

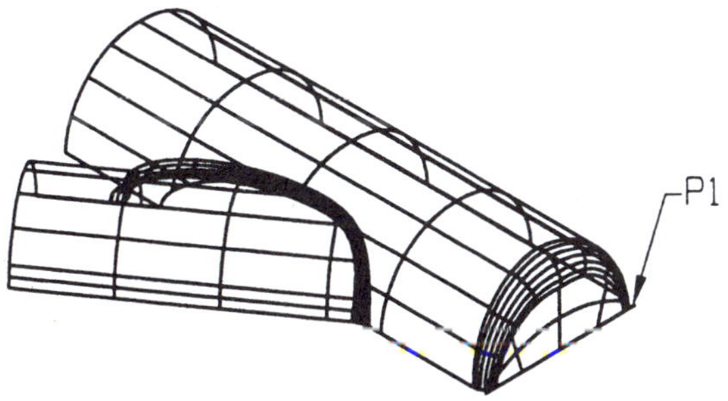

Figure 13.55

Step 6. Delete a line using the pick point in Figure 13.55.

Select **MAIN MENU → Delete**
Pick **P1** to delete a line
The final drawing appears as in Figure 13.56.

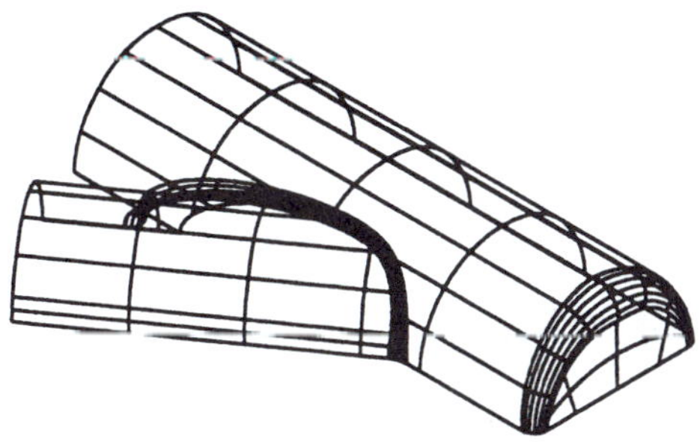

Figure 13.56

Step 7. Save the trimmed surfaces in the file trims2.

Select **MAIN MENU → File → Save**
Enter file name: **trims2**

🖳Project 5. Trimming a surface using a circle

This project trims a loft surface to a curve, which is a circle of 1.5" diameter. Its center is located at (1.6,0). The surface models before and after trimming are shown in Figure 13.57.

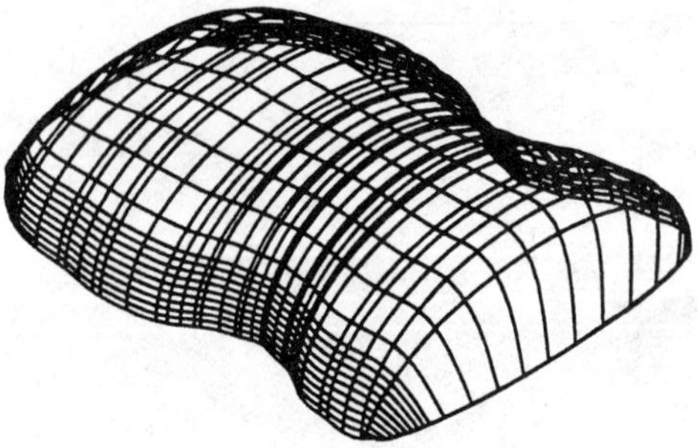

Figure 13.57a

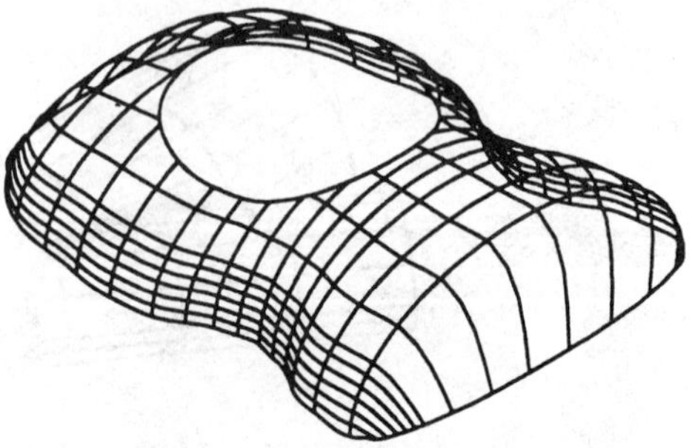

Figure 13.57b

⌛**Tips** 1. Create a circle to be used as the trimming curve. The curve does not necessary have to be on the surface to be trimmed.

2. Use the "To curves" method to trim the loft surface.

3. Select the "Project normal to the construction plane" mode. The construction plane should be in the Top Cplane. If "Project normal to the surface" mode is used, the trimmed area will be altered.

Step 1. Open the surface file lofts2.

Select **MAIN MENU → File → Get**
Enter file name: **lofts2**
The loft surface should appear as in Figure 13.58.

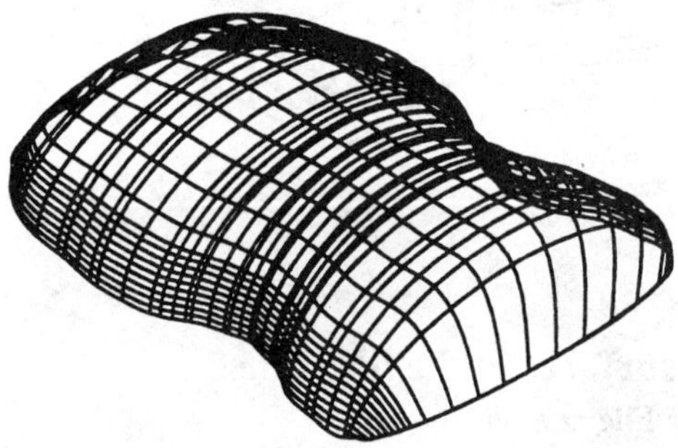

Figure 13.58

Step 2. Create a circle using Top Cplane; center located at (1.6,0), radius 0.75-in.

Select **Level**, then enter **3** ↵
Select **Color**, then enter **14** ↵
Select **Cplane → Top** if necessary
Select **Z**, then enter **2.5** ↵
Select **MAIN MENU → Create → Arc → Cir pt+rad**
Enter the radius: **0.75** ↵
Enter the center point: **1.6, 0** ↵

The circle is added to the drawing as shown in Figure 13.59. **5**

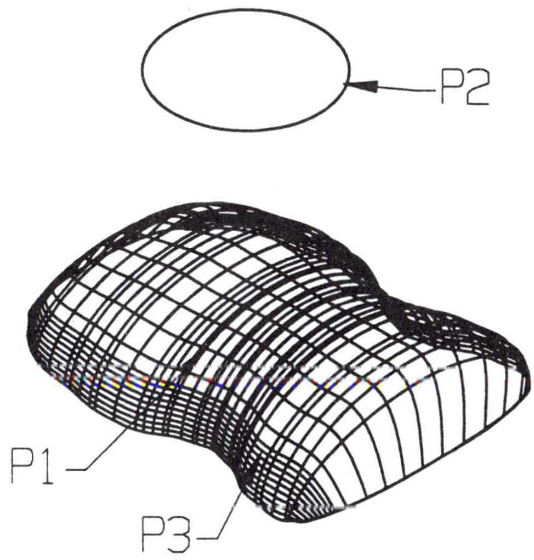

Figure 13.59

Step 3. Initiatc thc trim surface function.

Select **MAIN MENU → Create → Surface → Trim/extend → To curves**
Pick **P1** to select the loft surface
Select **Done**
Select **Single** then pick **P2** to select the circle
Select **Done**
Set View/Norm to **V** (for View)
Select **Options**
Set trim surfaces to curves parameters as shown here.

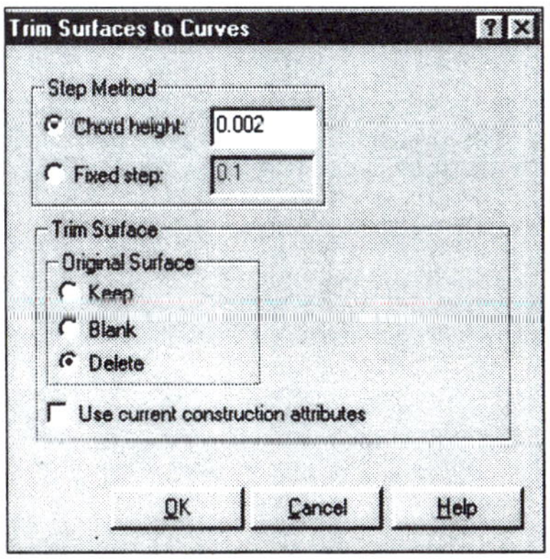

Select **OK → Do it**

Pick **P1** to select a surface to be trimmed
Pick **P3** to indicate a location to keep after trimming

The loft surface is trimmed to the circle as shown in Figure 13.60.

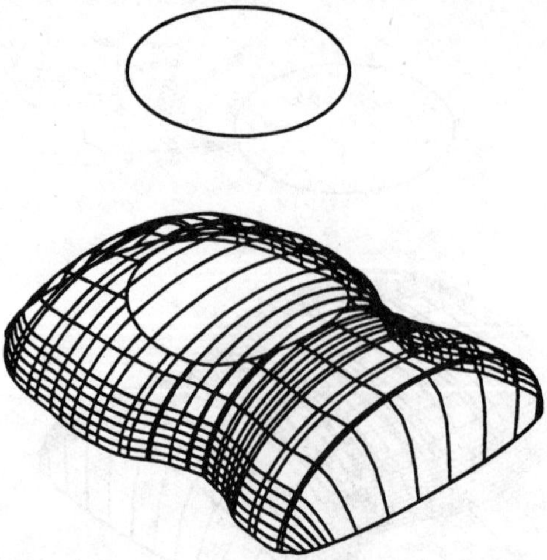

Figure 13.60

Step 4. Make levels 1 and 3 invisible.

Select **Level**
To hide levels #1 and #3, click the check mark in the #1 and #3 Visible column to invisible
Select **OK → OK** to return back to graphic mode
The trimmed surface is displayed as in Figure 13.61.

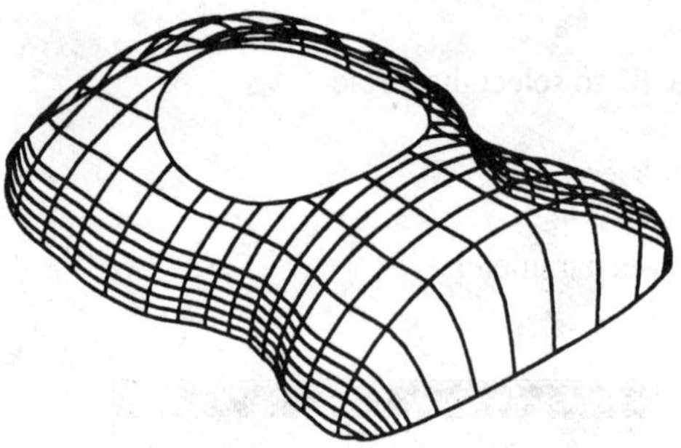

Figure 13.61

Step 5. Save the trimmed surface.

Select **MAIN MENU → File → Save**
Enter file name: **trims3**

Offset Surface Modeling

This technique creates a surface that is offset to a distance from an existing surface in the normal direction (Figure 13.62). It requires two inputs: an existing surface and an offset distance. The offset distance value can be either positive or negative. A positive offset distance value will offset the surface to the surface normal direction, while a negative value will offset to the opposite of the surface normal direction (Figure 13.63).

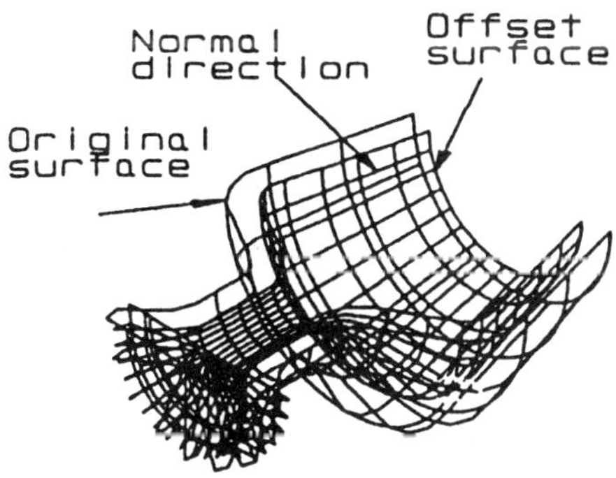

Figure 13.62

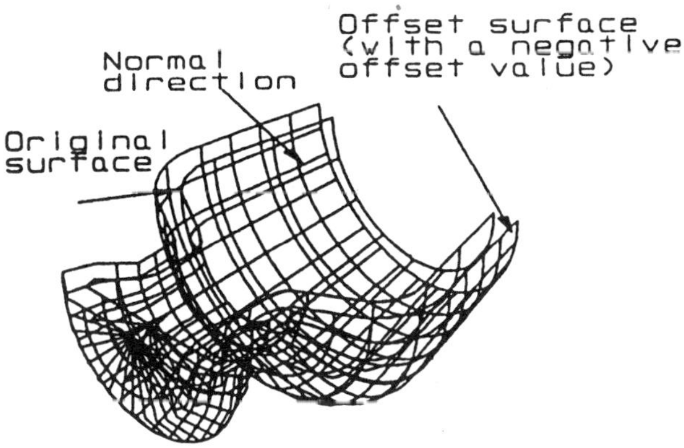

Figure 13.63

> ⌛**Tips for creating offset surfaces**
> 1. The trimmed surfaces can not be used to produce an offset surface. Only original surfaces can be used.
> 2. The surface normal direction and the sign of offset value determine the offset direction. You can use Modify → Normal commands to change the surface normal direction if necessary.

💻Project 6. Creating two offset surfaces.

Create two offset surfaces from the two ruled surfaces generated in project 1 of chapter 12. Both ruled surfaces are offset by 0.5-in in the outward direction. The offset surfaces are shown in Figure 13.64.

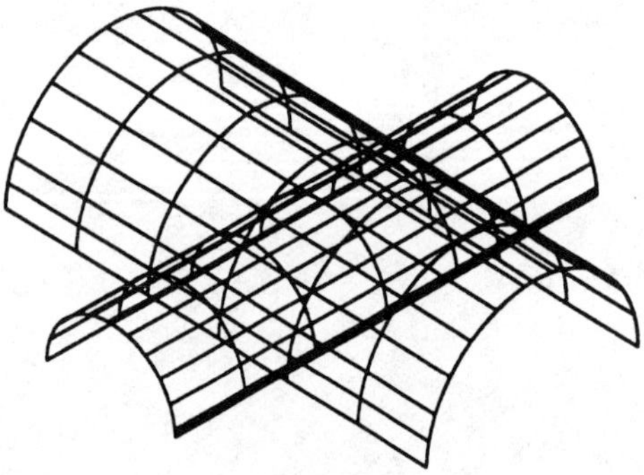

Figure 13.64a

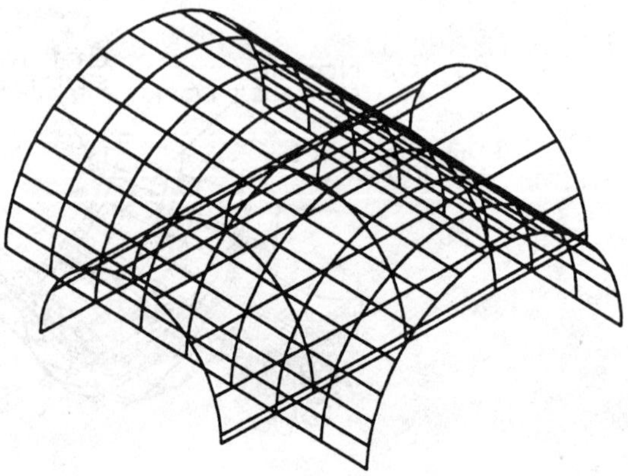

Figure 13.64b

Step 1. Open the existing surface model file ruleds1.

Select **MAIN MENU → File → Get**
Enter file name: **ruleds1↵**
The two ruled surfaces should appear on screen as Figure 13.65.

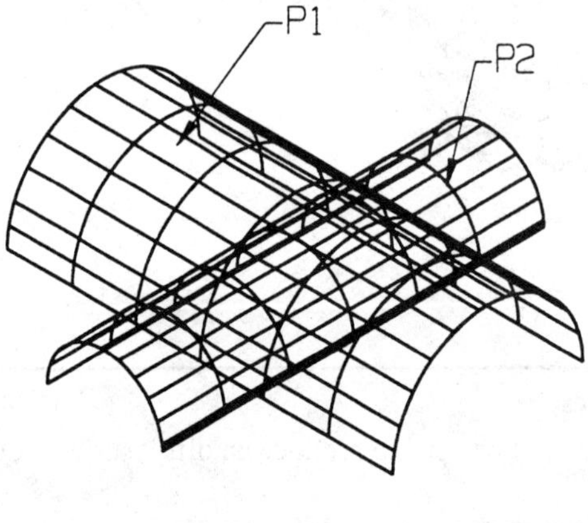

Figure 13.65

Step 2. Create two offset surfaces using the pick points in Figure 13.65.

Select **Level**, then enter **3** → OK
Select **MAIN MENU → Create → Surface → Offset**
Select surfaces: pick **P1** and **P2**
Select **Done**
Set **Dispose = K**
Select **Offset dist**
Enter offset distance: **0.5** ↵
Select **Do it**

The two offset surfaces are added as in Figure 13.66. 6

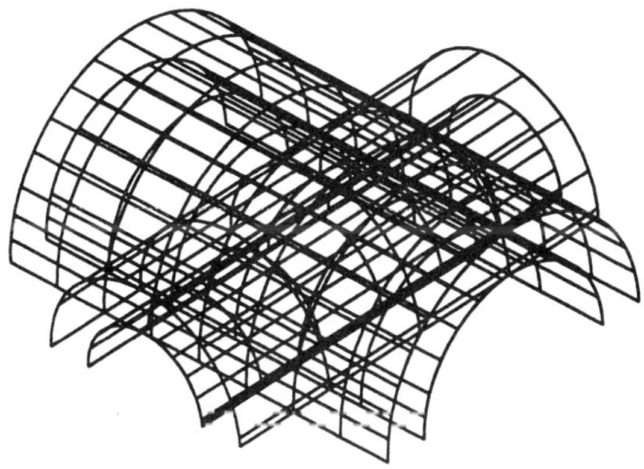

Figure 13.66

Step 3. Make levels 1 and 2 invisible.

Select **Level**
Click the check marks in the #1 and #2 visible column to remove them
Select **OK** to return to graphic mode

The two offset surfaces should look like Figure 13.67.

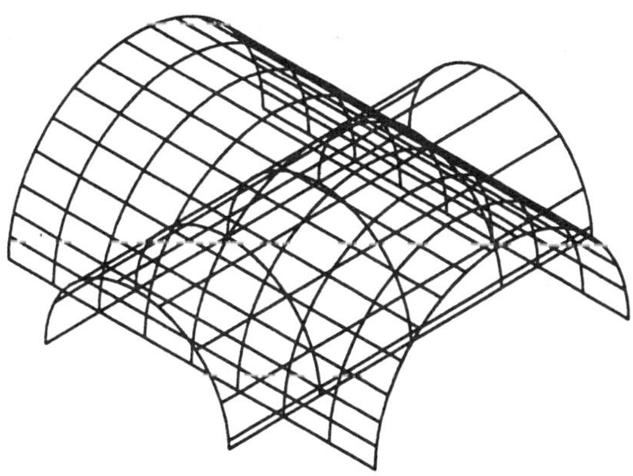

Figure 13.67

Step 4. Save the offset surface file offsets.

Select **MAIN MENU → File → Save**
Enter file name: **offsets**

Blend Surface Modeling

Blend surface modeling allows us to create a surface that smoothly joins two or three existing surfaces and is tangent to each parent surface. Figure 13.68 shows an example of adding a surface to join two intersected ruled surfaces. The two parent ruled surfaces are trimmed to the blending boundaries.

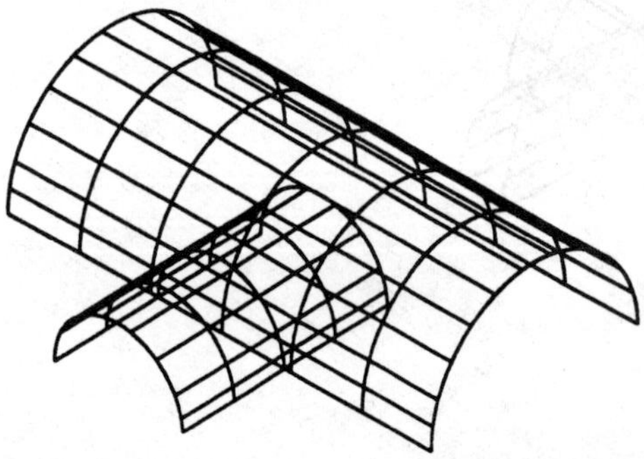

Figure 13.68a Before blending and trimming

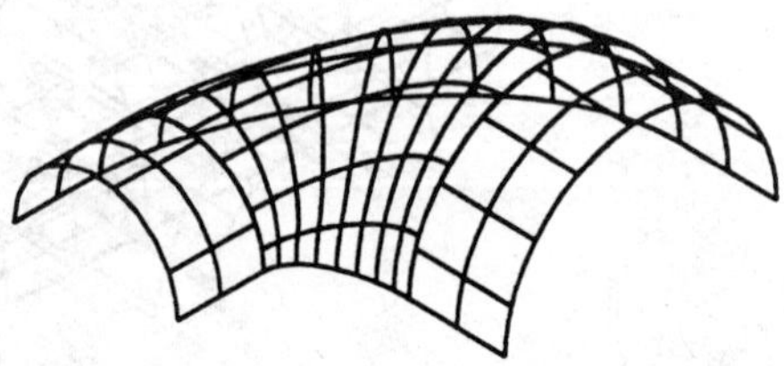

Figure 13.58b After blending and trimming

There are three surface blending methods: 2 surf blnd, 3 surf blnd, and Fillet blnd. They are briefly described here:

2 surf blnd:	creates a blend surface between two existing surfaces.
3 surf blnd:	create a blend surface between three existing surfaces.
Fillet blnd:	creates a blend surface of a three-sided blend or a six-sided blend between three existing fillet surfaces.

2 Surface Blending

The 2-surface blending method creates a blend surface between two existing surfaces. Use these commands to enter the surface blending menu:

Select **MAIN MENU → Create → Surface → Next menu → 2 Surf blnd**

The surface blending parameters are shown here:

Surf1:	The first picked surface to be blended onto.
Surf2:	the second picked surface to be blended onto.
Start mag:	Start blending magnitude on Surf1 and Surf2.
End mag:	End blending magnitude on Surf1 and Surf2.
End pts:	Indicate an end of one of blend location splines.
Reverse:	Manually reverse the blending curve direction.
Trim surfs:	Select the surface(s) to be trimmed to blending boundaries.
Keep crvs:	Select the blending curve(s) to be kept.
Surf type:	Specify the blending surface to be created being parametric or NURBS type.

⌛Tips for creating blend surfaces:

1. Theoretically, it requires two parent surfaces to create a blend surface. However, a single surface can be used to create a blend surface. This is done by carefully picking the surface twice and selecting the position to start blending. Figure 13.69 shows a blend surface created from a single ruled surface.
2. The position you pick to blend onto determines where the blend surface will be started. It also determines the size of the blend surface. Figure 13.70 and 13.71 illustrate the effect of picked locations on the blended surface.
3. The spline direction determines the orientation of the blend surface. The spline direction can be toggled to the along or across direction. The blend surface in normal (perpendicular) to the spline direction. Table 13.5 illustrates the effect of spline direction on blend surfaces.

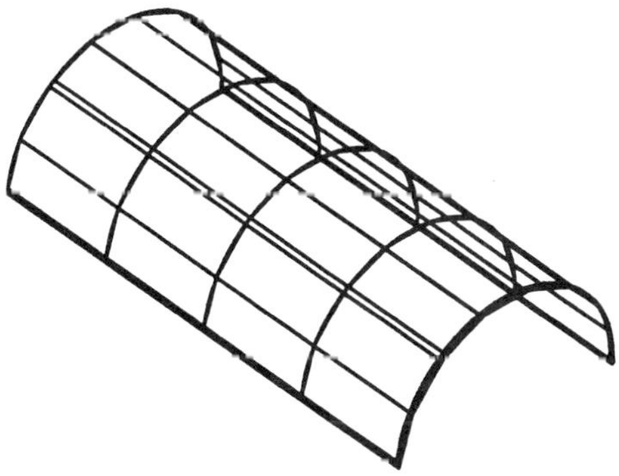

Figure 13.69a Ruled surface before blending

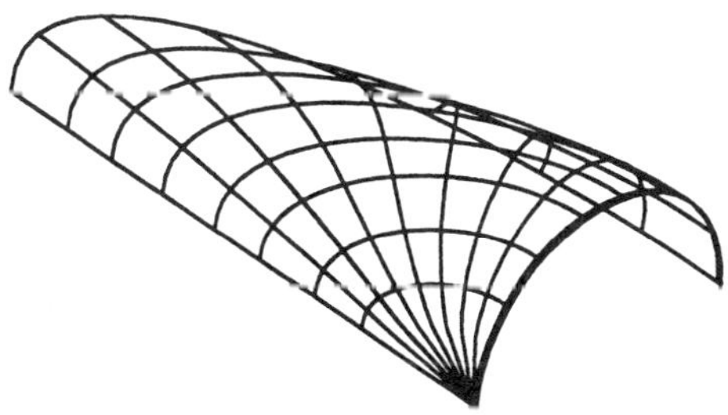

Figure 13.69b Blend surface

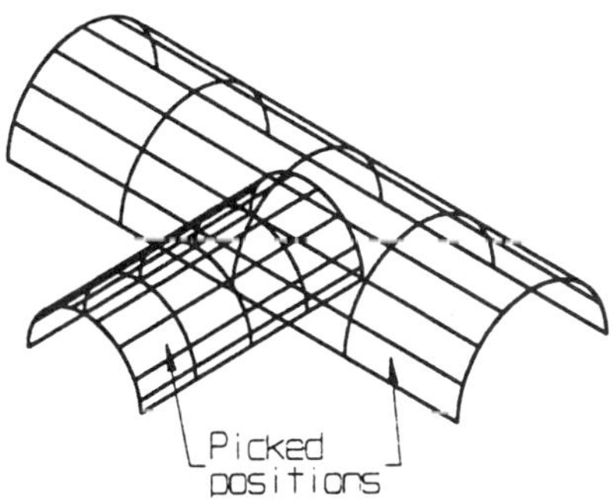

Figure 13.70a Picked positions

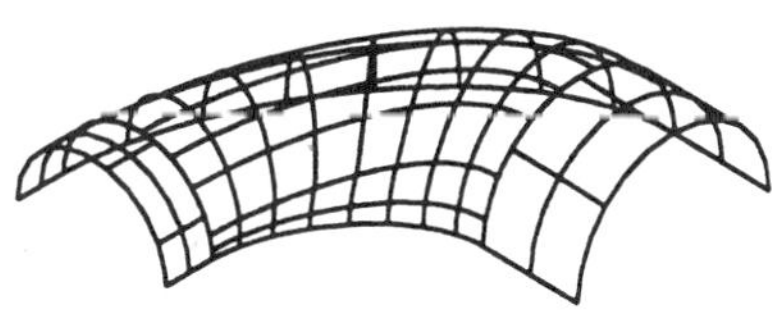

Figure 13.70b Blend surface

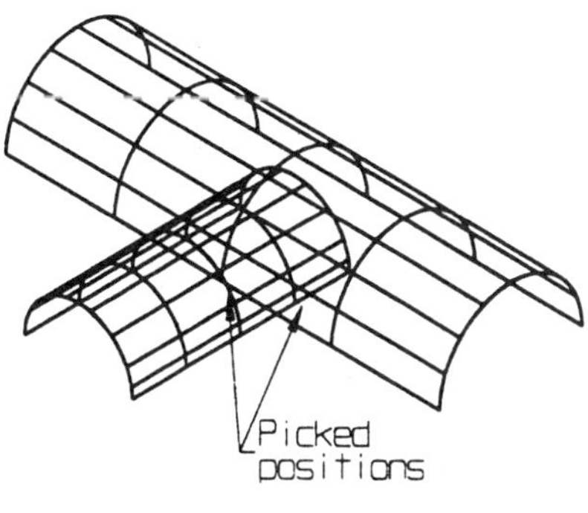

Figure 13.71a Picked positions

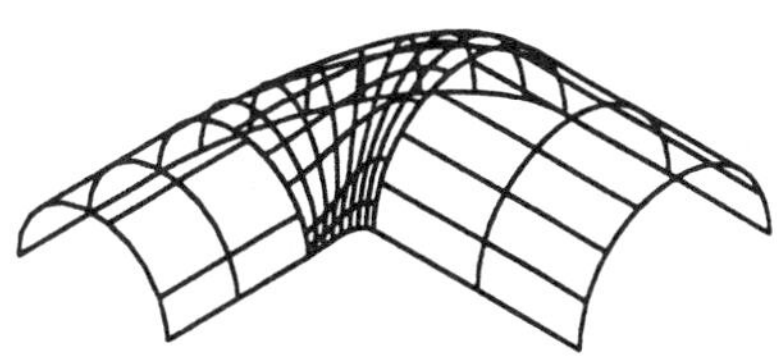

Figure 13.71b Blend surface

Table 13.5 Effects of spline direction on blend surface

Surf1	Surf2	Spline Direction	Resulted Blend Surface
Across	Across	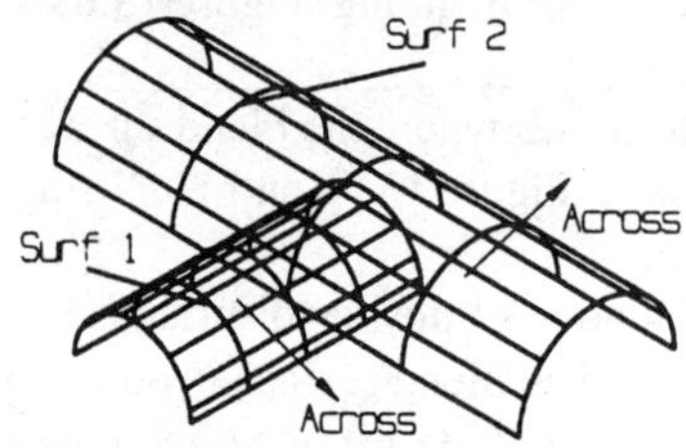	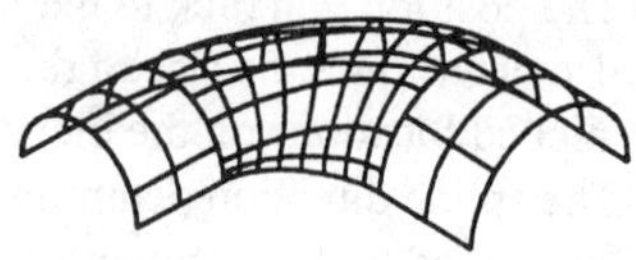
Across	Along	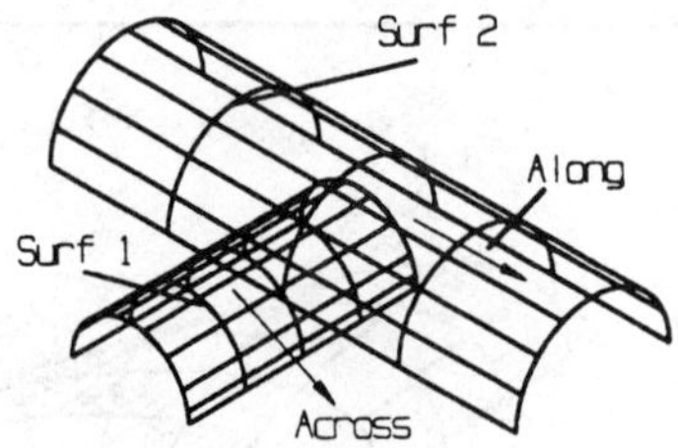	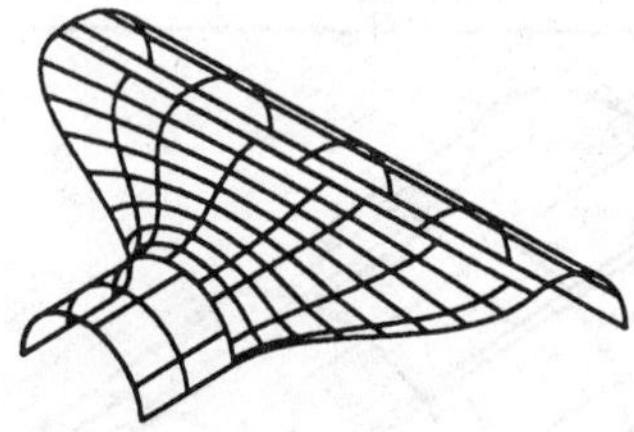
Along	Along	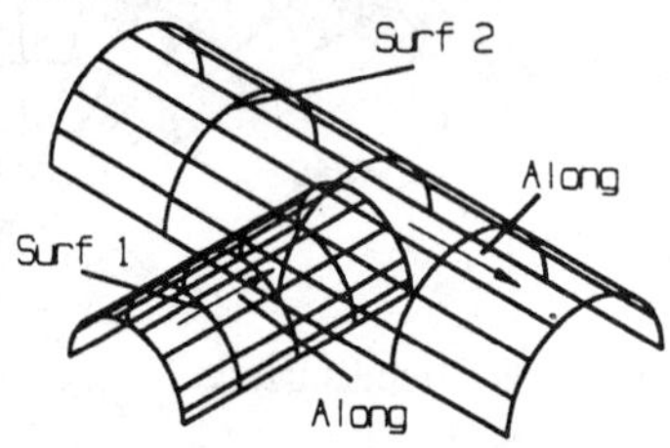	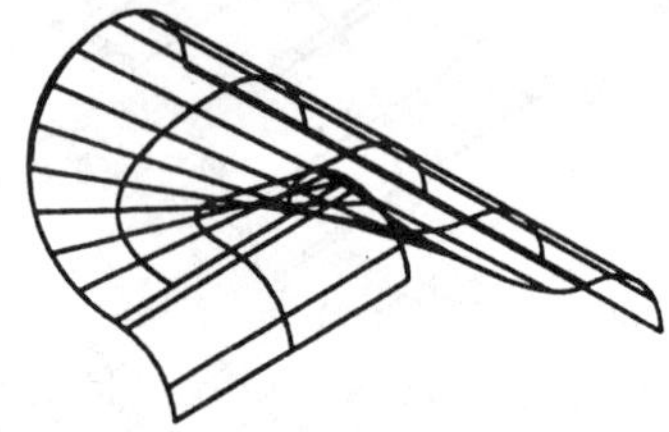

Tip 4. Blending magnitude values. There are two blending magnitude parameters for each surface to define the blend surface shape: start blending magnitude and end blending magnitude. The blending magnitude value can be regarded as the order of the curve that determines the skin form of the surface. Figure 13.72 shows how the magnitude value affects the blend surface.

Magnitude Value	Surface Order
0	a plane (1st order)
1	1st order
2	2nd order
3	3rd order

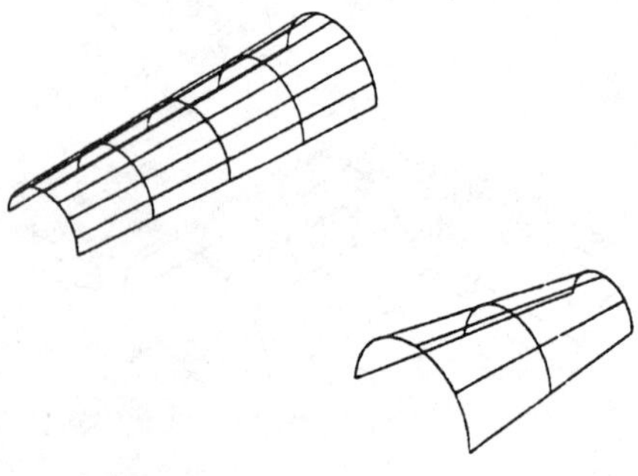

Figure 13.72a Two surfaces

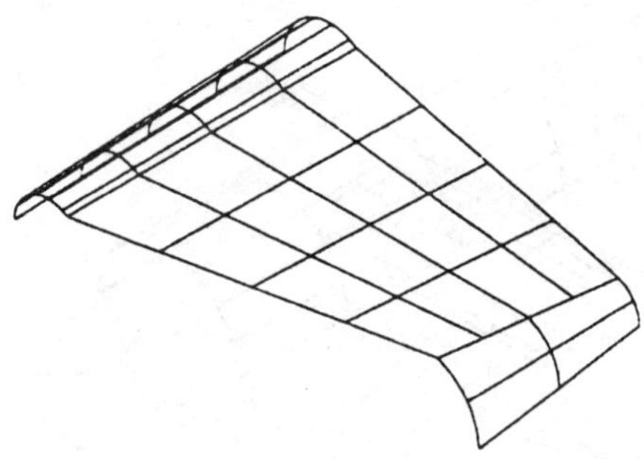

Figure 13.72b Start and end magnitudes are 0

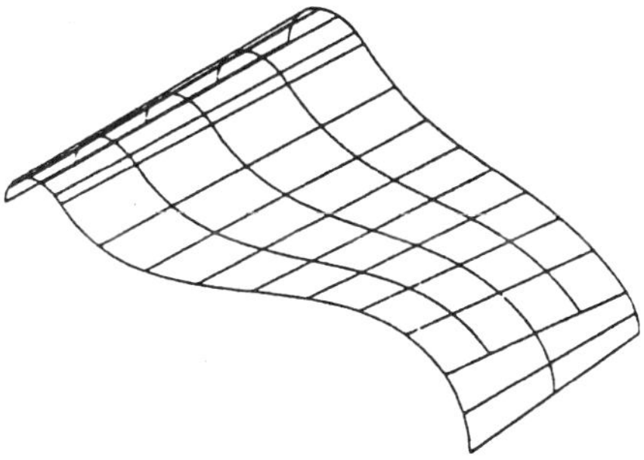

Figure 13.72c Start and end magnitudes are 1

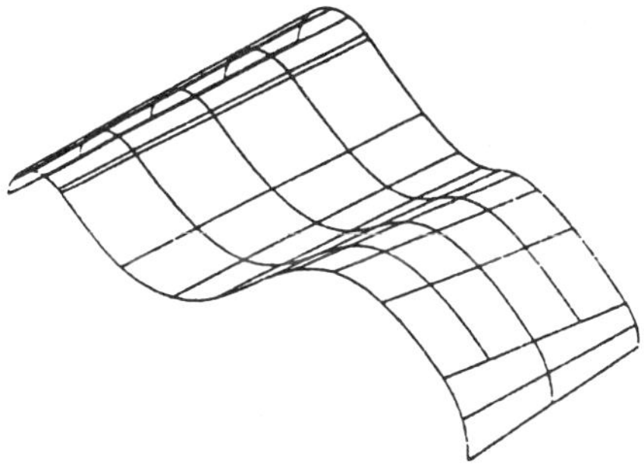

Figure 13.72d Start and end magnitudes are 2

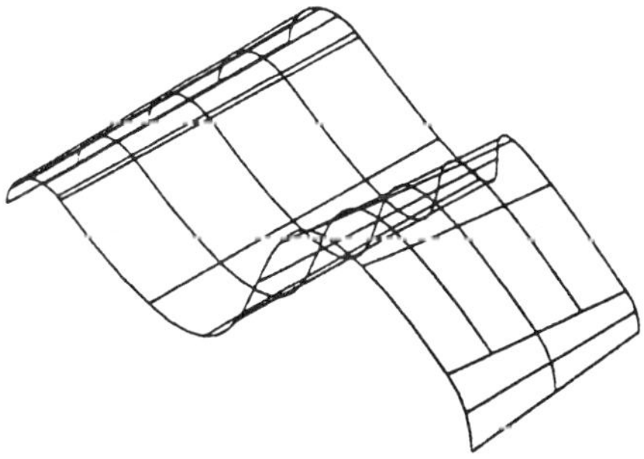

Figure 13.72e Start and end magnitudes are 3

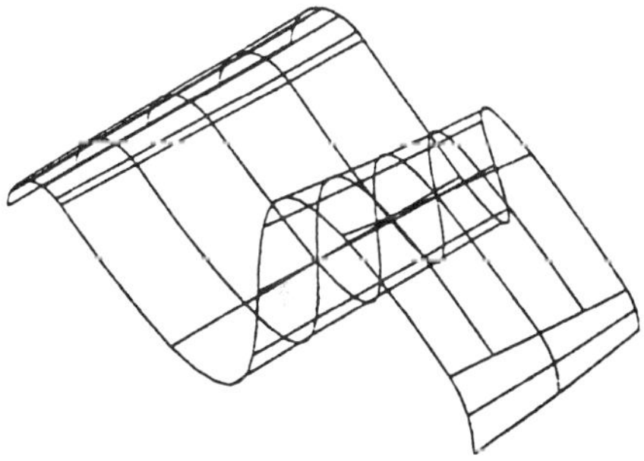

Figure 13.72f Start and end magnitudes are 4

It is possible to have different values for start and end magnitude as shown in Figure 13.73. The blend surface in Figure 13.73a has a value of 2 for the start magnitude and 1 for the end magnitude in both parent surfaces. In Figure 13.73b the start magnitude for surf1 is 3 and the remaining three magnitudes are 1.

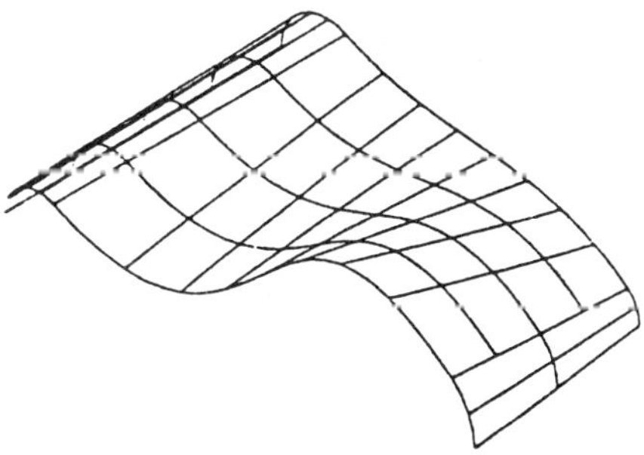

Figure 13.73a

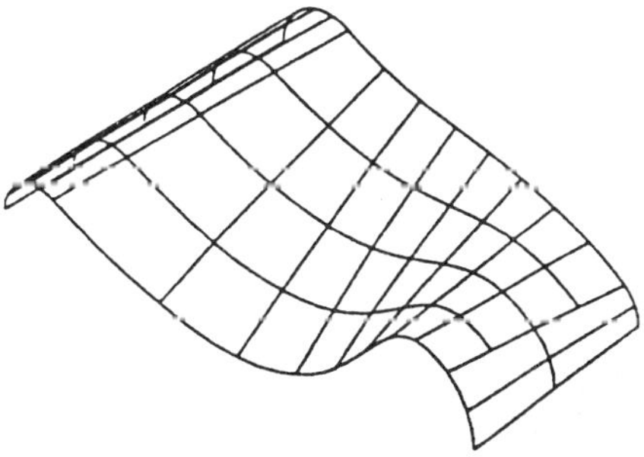

Figure 13.73b

⌛**Tip** 5. The selection of surface and the kept section

<u>Case 1:</u> Spline orientation is in a cross direction for both surfaces. The direction of the blend surface and the kept section of the two parent surfaces are decided by the relationship between the two picked points located on two surfaces. The blending directions on the two parent surfaces are always opposed to each other (Figure 13.74a & a', b & b'). If the trim parameter is set for one surface or both surfaces, the kept section is the one opposite to the blend surface direction.

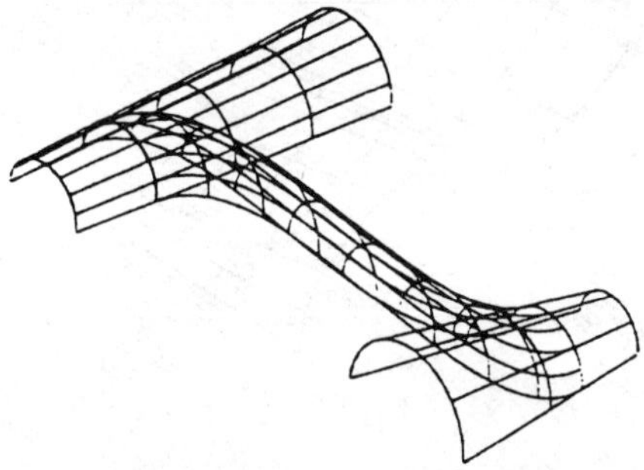

Figure 13.74a

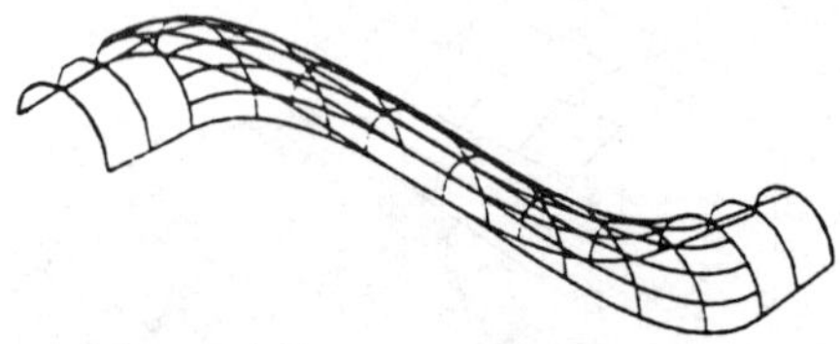

Figure 13.74a'

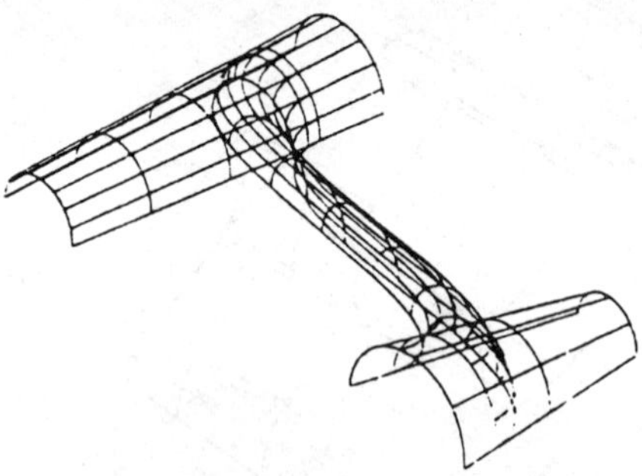

Figure 13.74b

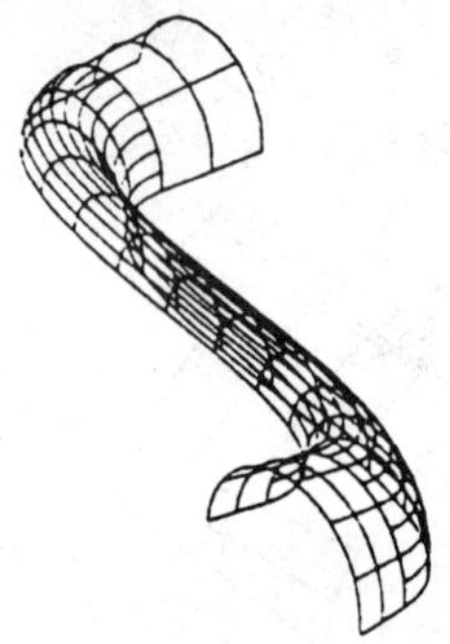

Figure 13.74b'

<u>Case 2:</u> Spline orientation of one surface is in along and the other in across.

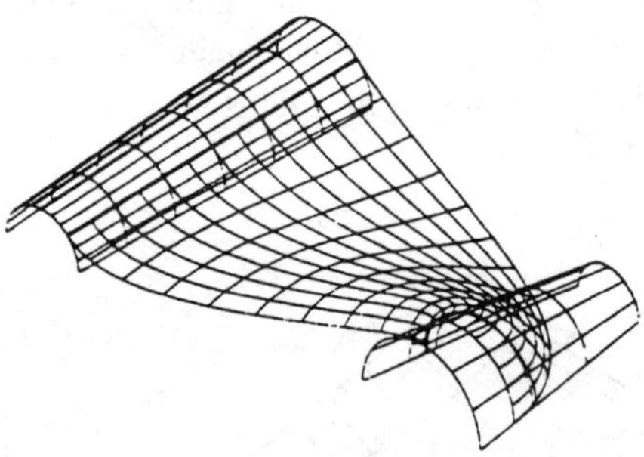

Figure 13.75a

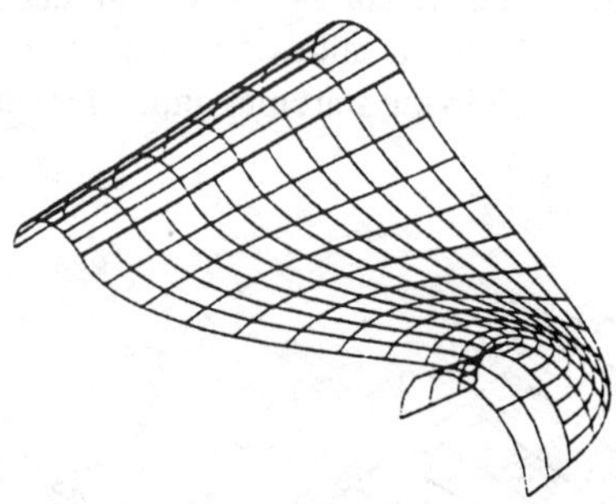

Figure 13.75a'

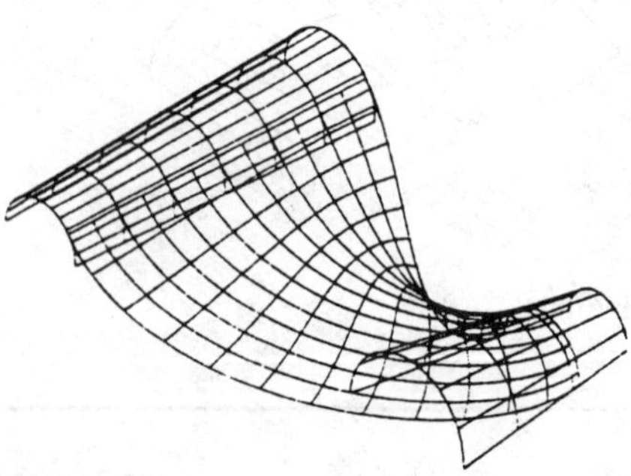

Figure 13.75b

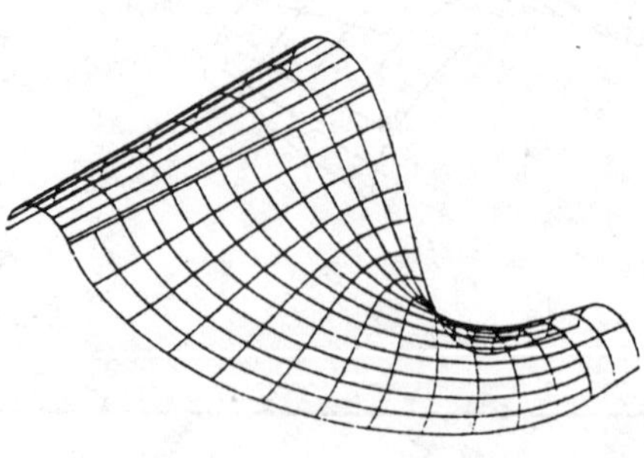

Figure 13.75b'

Case 3: Spline orientation in the along direction for both surfaces.

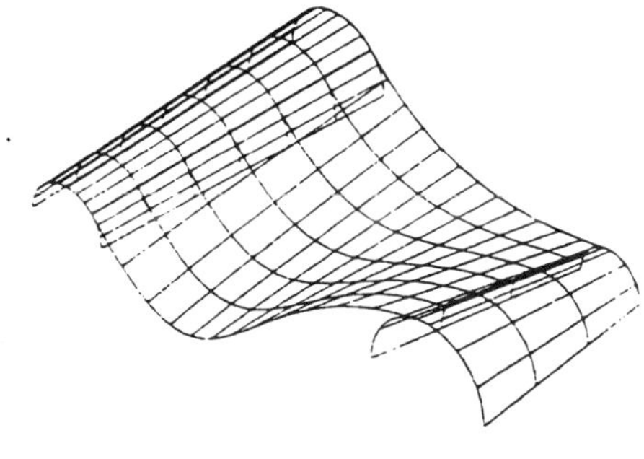

Figure 13.76a

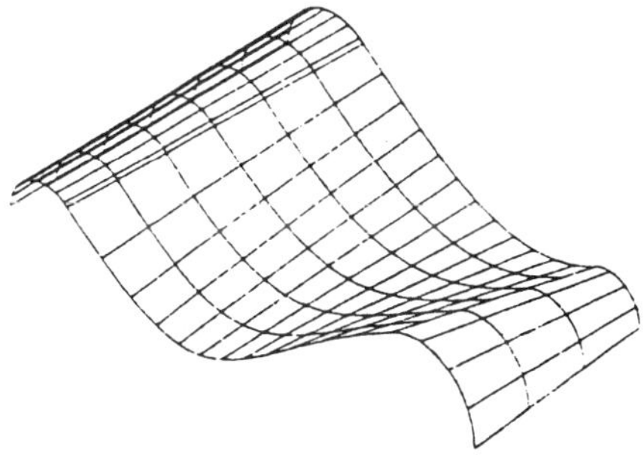

Figure 13.76b

⌛**Tip** 6. Use the Reverse function to change the mating ends of the blend surface on the two parent surfaces.

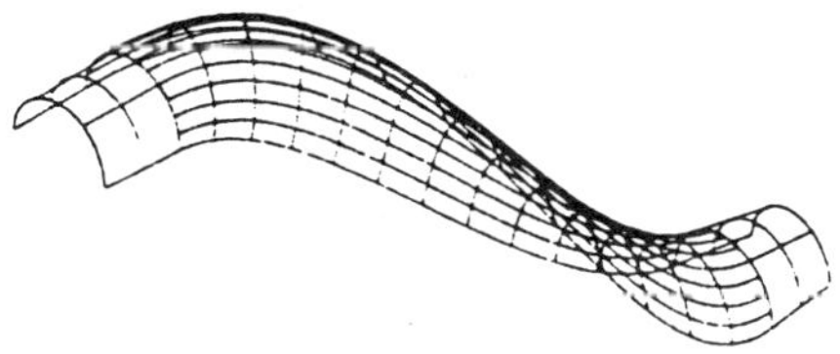

Figure 13.77a Before reverse

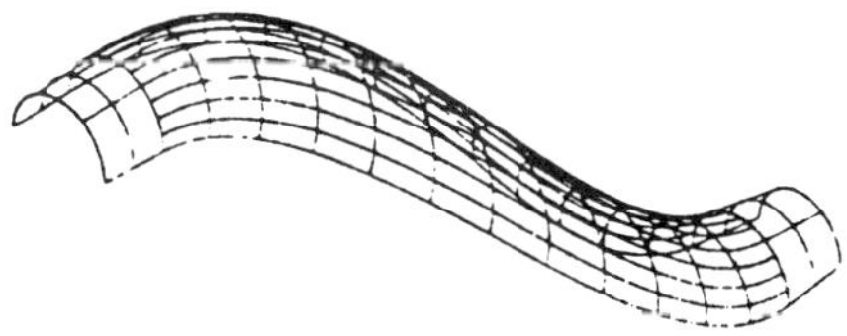

Figure 13.77a' After reverse

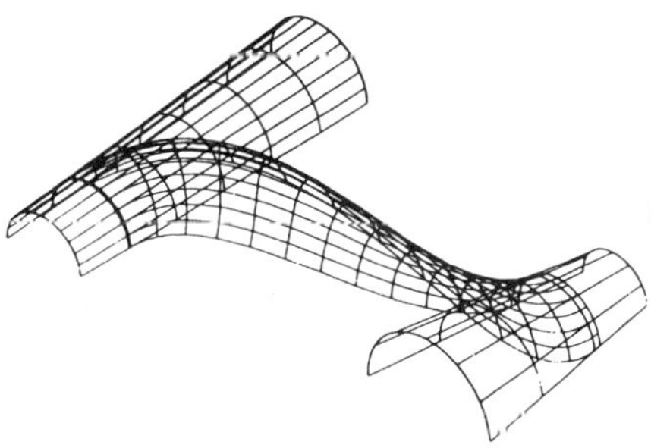

Figure 13.77b Before reverse

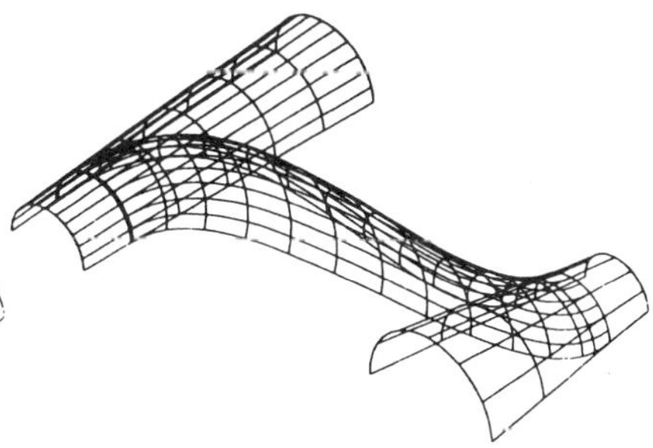

Figure 13.77b' After reverse

Project 7. Blend surfaces between two intersected surfaces

Create three blend surfaces based on the two intersected ruled surfaces generated in project 2 of chapter 12. Figure 13.78 shows original surface model and three blend surfaces.

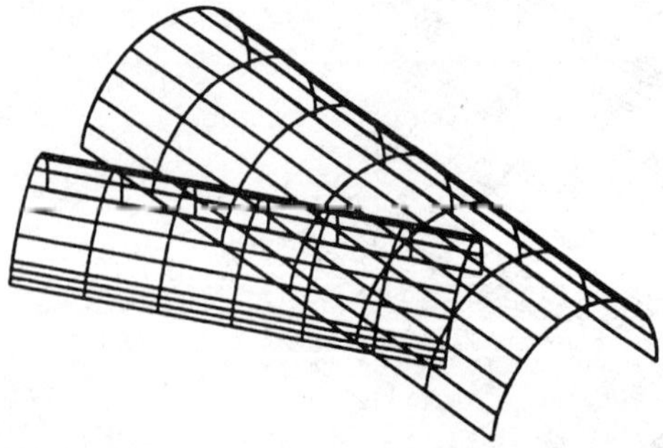

Figure 13.78a

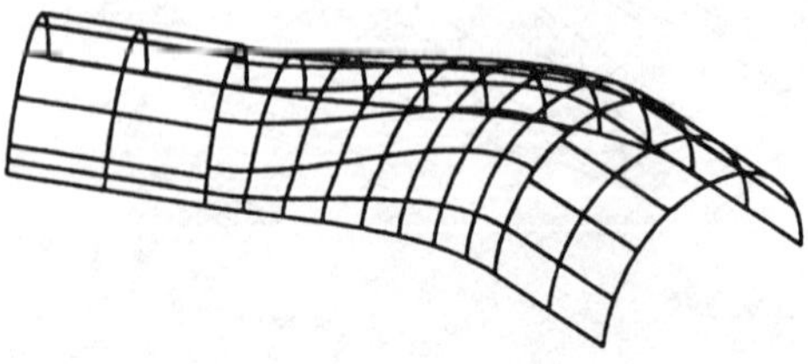

Figure 13.78b

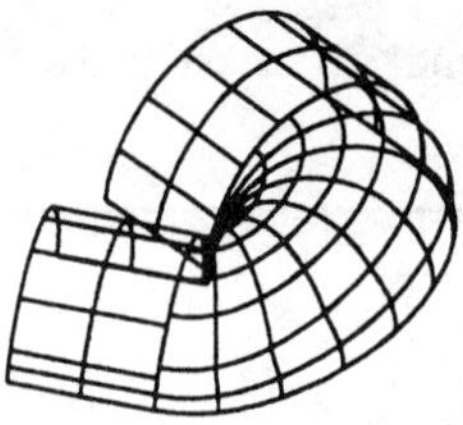

Figure 13.78c

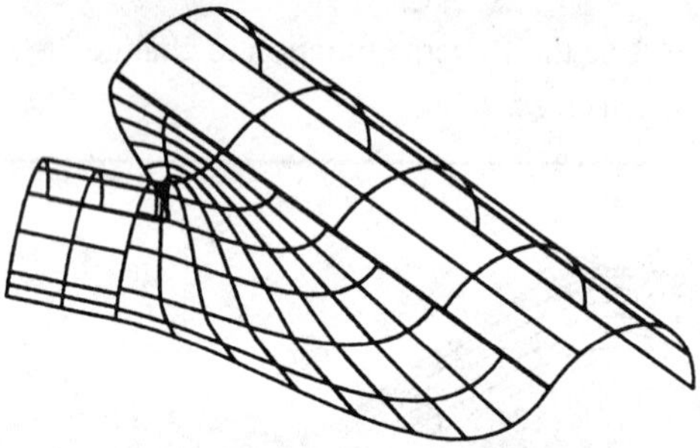

Figure 13.78d

Tips
1. The spline orientation of both parent surfaces should be set to the across direction for the first blend surface (Figure 13.78b) and second blend surface (Figure 13.78c). The third blend surface (Figure 13.78d) has the along direction in the main surface and the across direction in the other surface.
2. Set the Trim srfs parameter to B (both) to trim both parent surfaces to the spline curves.
3. Set surf type parameter to N (NURBS).

Case 1.

Step 1. Open the surface file ruleds2 and set level to 2.

Select **MAIN MENU → File → Get**
File name: **ruleds2** ↵
Select **Level**, then enter **3** in the Main Level box → **OK**
The two ruled surfaces should appear as Figure 13.79.

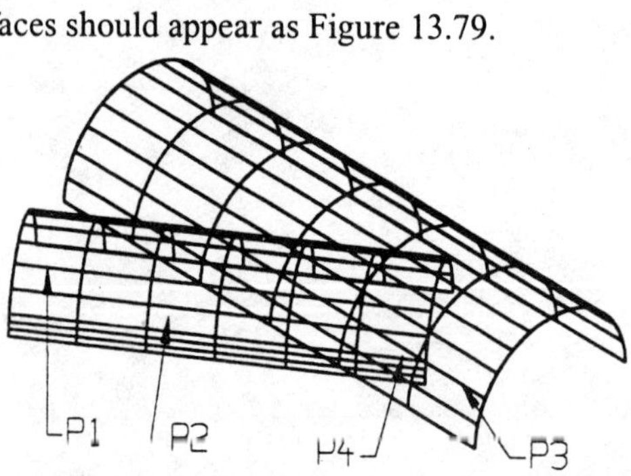

Mastercam Version 8,
Scholars International Publishing Corp., 2001

Step 2. Initiate the blend surface function. 7

Use pick points in Figure 13.79.
Select **MAIN MENU → Create → Surface → Next menu → 2 Surf blnd**
Pick **P1** to select a surface to blend onto
Indicate the position of the spline curve, pick **P2**
An arrow should appear to indicate the default spline orientation (in the along direction)
Select **Flip** to change the spline direction to the across direction if necessary
Select **OK** to accept the across direction
Pick **P3** to select the other surface to blend onto
Select the position of the spline curve, pick **P4**
Select **Flip** to change the spline direction to the across direction if necessary
Select **OK** to accept a spline orientation in the across direction
Set blending parameters as below:

Trim surfs:	= **B**
Keep crvs:	= **N**
Keep crvs:	= **N**

Select **Do it**
The blend surface mesh should appear as in Figure 13.80.

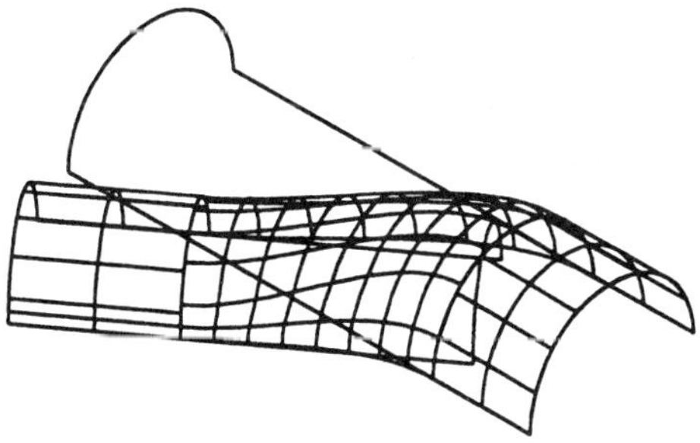

Figure 13.80

Step 3. Make level 1 to invisible.

Select **Level**
Toggle the check mark in the #1 Visible column to invisible
Select **OK** to return back to graphic mode
The blend surface with two kept surface sections of parent surfaces are shown in Figure 13.81.

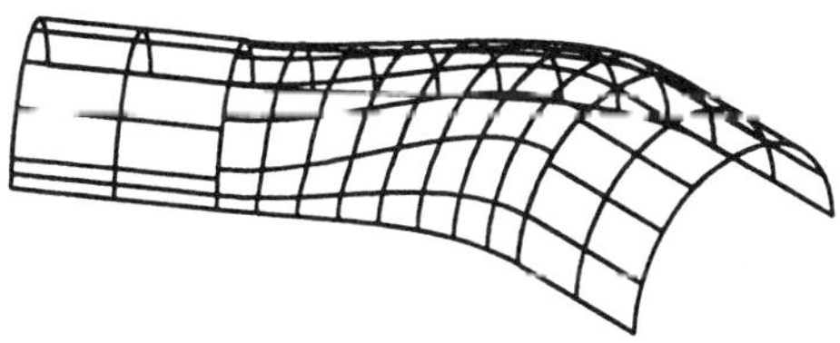

Figure 13.81

Step 4. Save the surface as blends1.

Select **MAIN MENU → File → Save**
Enter file name: **blends1**

Case 2:

Step 1. Load the surface file ruleds2.

Select **Get**
Enter file name: **ruleds2**
The surface model appears as Figure 13.82.

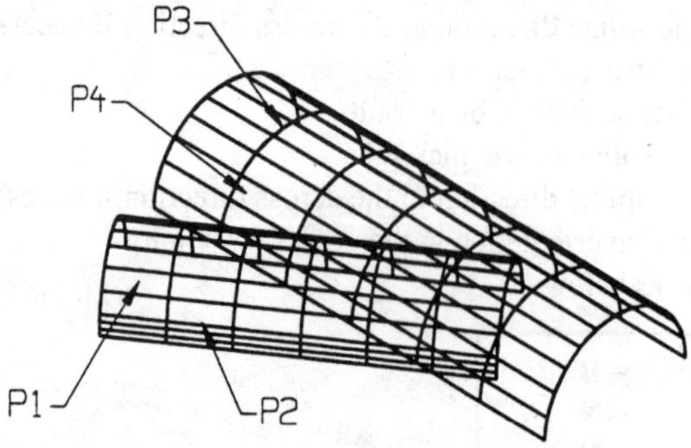

Figure 13.82

Step 2. Initiate the blend surface function.

Use the pick points in Figure 13.82.
Select **MAIN MENU → Create → Surface → Next menu → 2 surf blnd**
Pick **P1** to select a surface to blend onto
Decide the spline location, pick **P2**
Select **Flip** to change the spline direction to across if necessary
Select **OK** to accept the spline direction (across)
Pick **P3** to select another surface
Decide the spline location, pick **P4**
Select **Flip** to change the spline to the across direction if necessary
Select **OK** to accept the across spline direction

Step 3. Define the surface Blending parameters as below.

Trim srfs	= **B**
Keep crvs	= **N**
Surf type	= **N**

Select **Do it**
The blend surface should be added as in Figure 13.83.

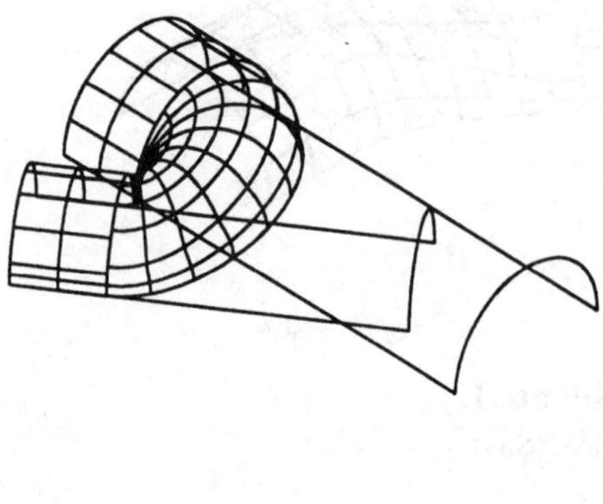

Figure 13.83

Step 4. Make level 1 invisible.

Select **Level**
Toggle level 1 check mark to invisible
Select **OK** to return to graphic mode.
The final blend surface should appear as in Figure 13.84.

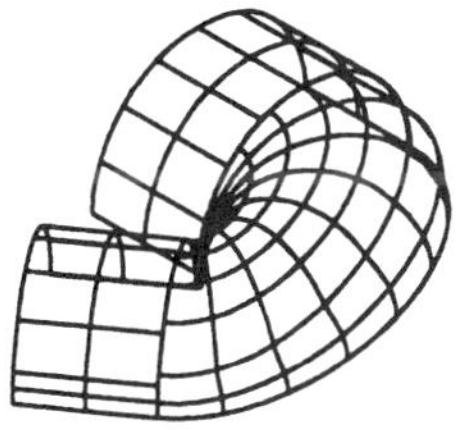

Figure 13.84

Step 5. Save the surface as blends2.

Select **MAIN MENU → File → Save**
File name: **blends2** ↵

Case 3:

Step 1. Load the surface file ruleds2.

Select **Get**
Enter file name: **ruleds2**
Select **Level**, then enter **3 →OK**
The surface model appears as Figure 13.85.

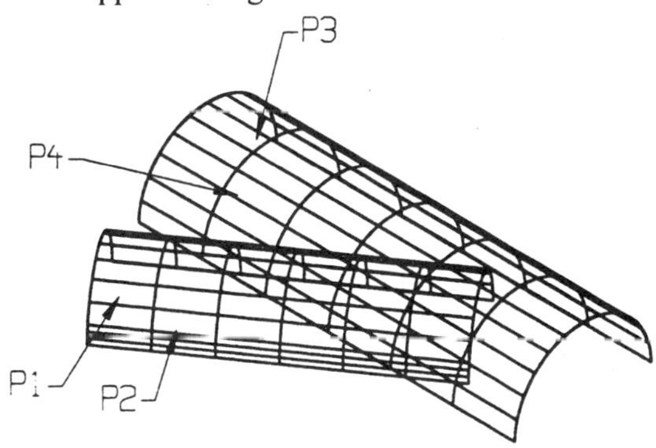

Figure 13.85

Step 2. Initiate the blend surface function and pick surfaces and spline locations.

Use the pick points in Figure 13.85
Select **MAIN MENU → Create → Surface → Next menu → 2 surf blnd**
Pick **P1** to select a surface to blend onto
Determine the spline location, pick **P2**
Select **Flip** to change the spline to the across direction if necessary
Select **OK** to accept the spline direction (across)
Pick **P3** to select another surface
Indicate the spline location, pick **P4**
Select **OK** to have the spline direction in along.

Step 3. Define the Surface Blending parameters as below.

Trim srfs	= **B**
Keep crvs	= **N**
Surf type	= **N**

Select **Do it**

The blend surface is added as in Figure 13.86.

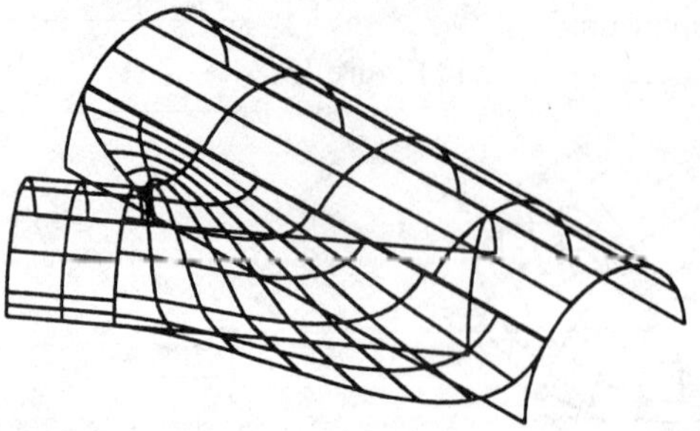

Figure 13.86

Step 4. Make level 1 invisible.

Select **Level**

Then toggle the level 1 check mark to invisible (dimmed)

Select **OK** to return to graphic mode

The final surface model should resemble Figure 13.87.

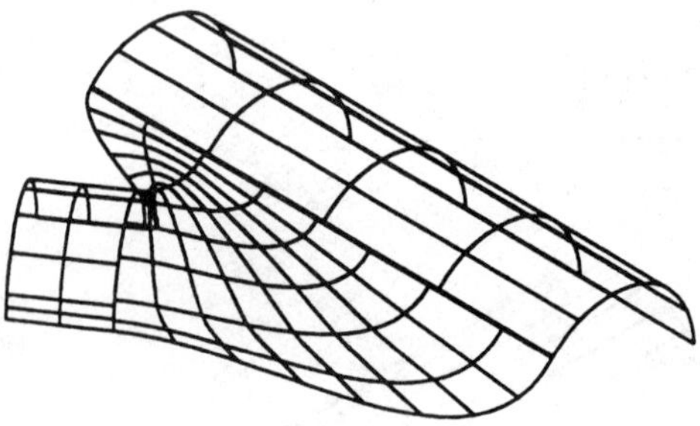

Figure 13.87

Step 5. Save the surface as blends3.

Select **MAIN MENU → File → Save**

Enter file name: **blends3**

3 Surface Blending

Mastercam provides two methods for creating a blend surface between three existing surfaces: 3-Surface and Fillet blnd. The 3 Surface method creates a blend surface from any three existing surfaces, while the Fillet blnd (three fillet blend) method creates a blend surface between three existing surface fillets.

Two examples are given in this section to show how to create a blend surface from three existing surfaces. The first example uses the 3 Surface method and the second one uses the fillet blend method.

This example is intended to practice creating blend surfaces between three surfaces. Figure 13.88 shows the three stages of the model; wireframe, 3 ruled surfaces and 3 blend surfaces, each between two surfaces, and complete model.

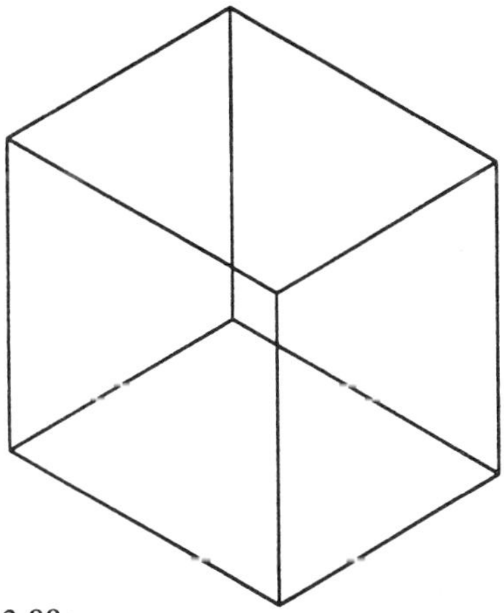

Figure 13.88a

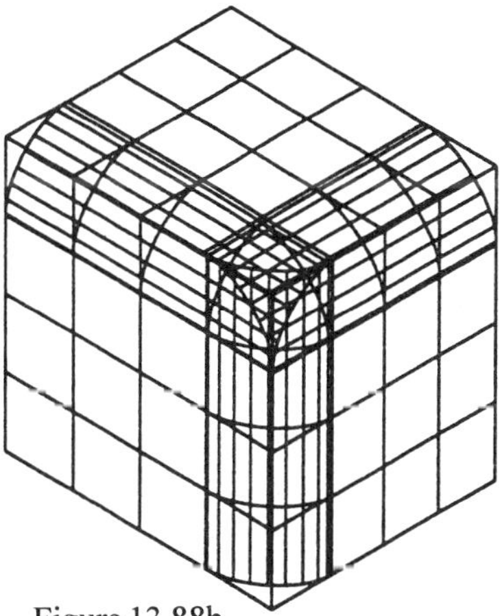

Figure 13.88b

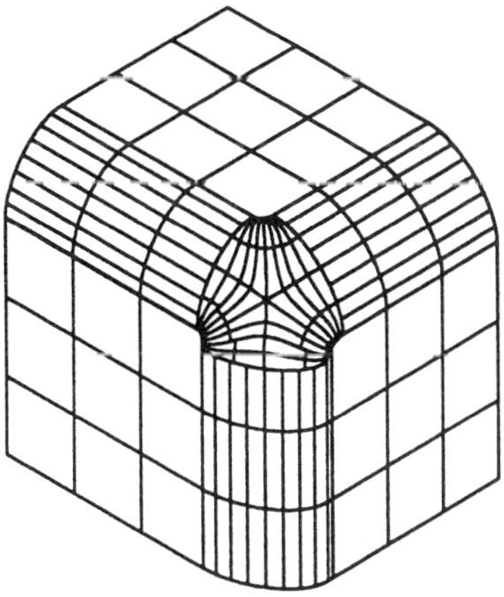

Figure 13.88c

Tips 1. Create a rectangular cube.

2. Create three flat ruled surfaces on three sides; top, front, and side.

3. Create three blend surfaces each between two ruled surfaces.

4. Trim three ruled surfaces to the surface curves of the blend surfaces.

5. Create a blend surface between three blend surfaces.

Step 1. Create a rectangle.

Select **Cplane → Top**
Select **Gview → Isometric**
Select **Create → Rectangle → 1 point**

Set the parameters in the Rectangle: OnePoint dialog box as below:

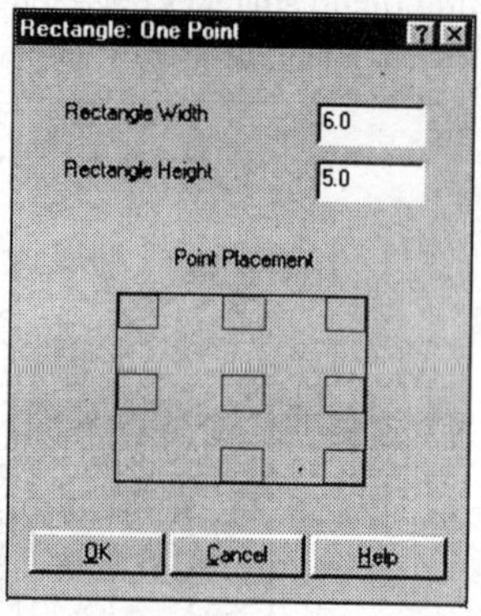

Enter coordinates: **0, 0** for the lower left corner.
Press **Alt+F1**, then **F2** to fit the drawing on the screen
The rectangle should appear on the screen as in Figure 13.89.

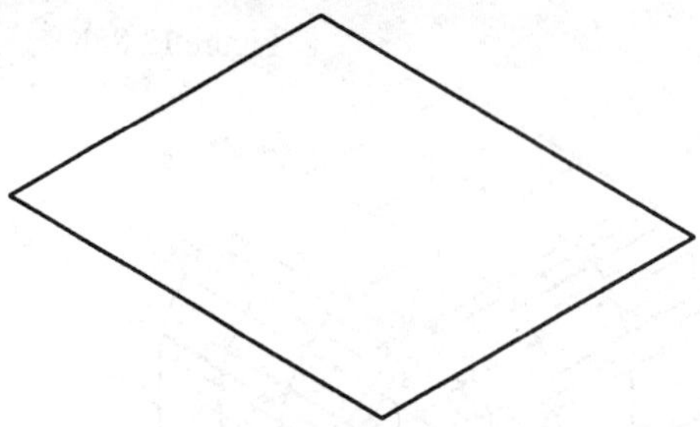

Figure 13.89

Step 2. Copy the rectangle to form a rectangular cube.

Select **MAIN MENU → Xfrom → Translate → Chain**
Pick any line on the rectangle
Select **Done → Done → Rectang**
Enter the translation vector: **z-6** ↵
Select **Join**
Number of Steps = **1**
Select **OK**
The rectangular cube is created as in Figure 13.90.

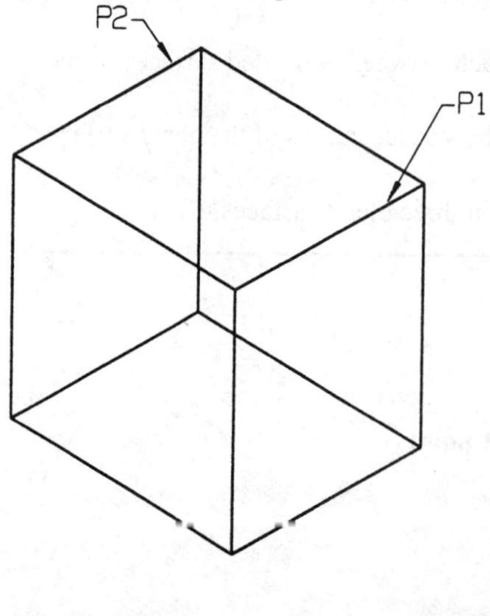

Figure 13.90

Step 3. Create a ruled surface on the top face.

Use the pick points in Figure 13.90
Select **Level**, then double-click **#2 → OK**
Select **Color**, then enter **10 → OK**
Select **MAIN MENU Create → Surface → Ruled → Single**
Pick **P1** and **P2** to define two contours
Select **Done**

Set the ruled surface parameters:

Surface error tolerance =**0.005**
Surface type = **N (NURBS)**

Select **Do it**

The ruled surface is added as in Figure 13.91.

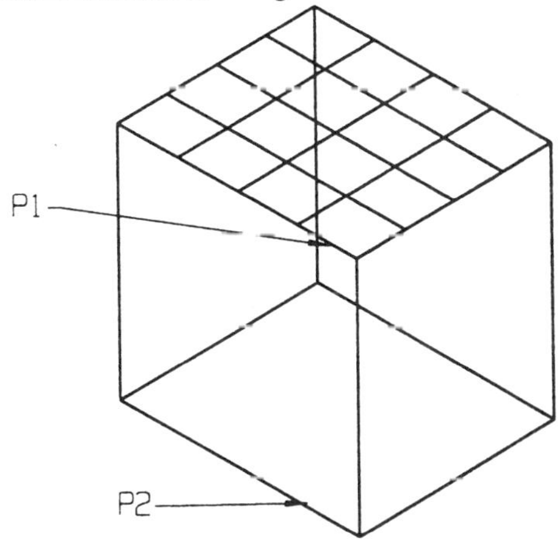

Figure 13.91

Step 4. Create a ruled surface on the front face.

Use the pick point in Figure 13.91
Select **Color**, then enter **11**↵
Select **Single**
Pick **P1** and **P2** to select two contours
Select **Done → Do it**
The second ruled surface is added as in Figure 13.92.

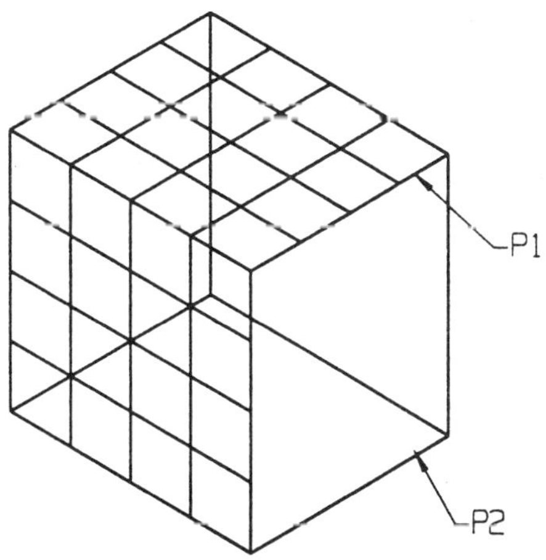

Figure 13.92

Step 5. Create a ruled surface on the side face.

Use the pick point in Figure 13.92
Select **Color**, then enter **12** ↵
Select **Single**
Pick **P1** and **P2**
Select **Done → Do it**
The third ruled surface appears as in Figure 13.93.

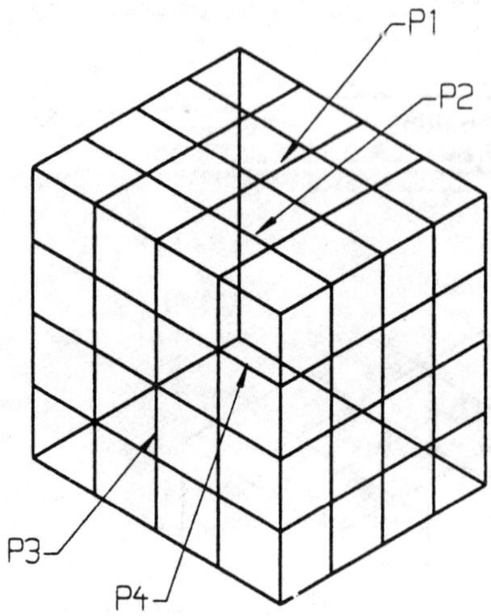

Figure 13.93

Step 6. Create a blend surface between top and front face.

Use the pick points in Figure 13.93
Select **Level**, then enter **3 →** OK
Select **Color**, then enter **13** ↵
Select **BACKUP → Next menu → 2 surf blnd**

Pick **P1** to select a surface to blend onto
Pick **P2** to position the blend surface

Set the Spline direction parallel to the X-axis
(click on the Flip command to change the direction if necessary)
Select **OK**

Pick **P3** to select another surface to blend onto
Pick **P4** to position the blend surface
Select **Flip** to set the spline direction parallel to the X-axis
Select **OK**
Set blending parameters as below

Trim surfs =	**N**
Keep crvs =	**B**
Surf type =	**N**

Select **Do it**

The blend surfaces is created as in Figure 13.94.

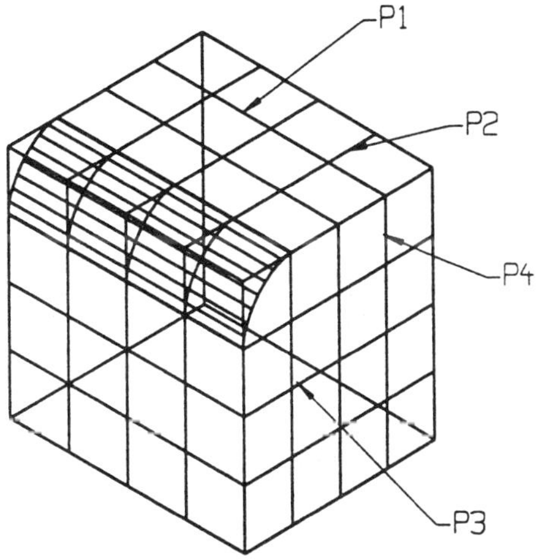

Figure 13.94

Step 7. Create a blend surface between top and side face.

Use the pick points in Figure 13.94
Select **Color**, then enter **14** ↵
Pick **P1** to select a surface to blend onto
Pick **P2** to position the blend surface
Set the spline direction **parallel to the Y-axis**, then select **OK**
Pick **P3** to select another surface to blend onto
Pick **P4** to position the blend surface
Set the spline direction **parallel to the Y-axis**, then select **OK**
Select **Do it**
The second blend surface is added as in Figure 13.95.

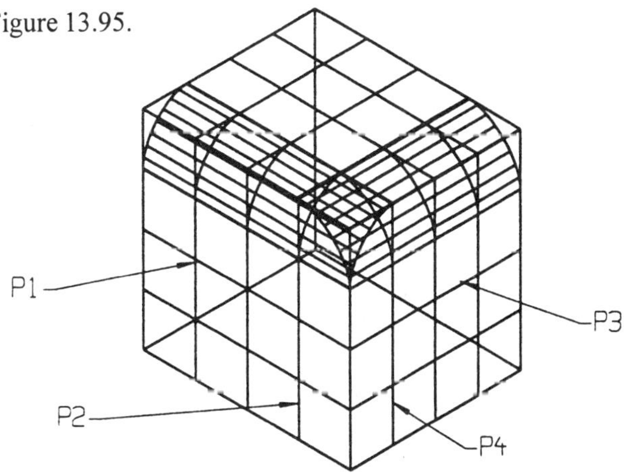

Figure 13.95

Step 8. Create a blend surface between the front and side face.

Use the pick points in Figure 13.95
Select **Color**, then enter **15** ↵
Pick **P1** to select a surface to blend onto
Pick **P2** to position the blend surface
Set the spline direction **parallel to the Z-axis**, then select **OK**
Pick **P3** to select a surface to blend onto
Pick **P4** to position the blend surface
Set the spline direction **parallel to the Z-axis**, then select **OK**

Select **Do it**

Select **Level,** then toggle the check mark in the Level 1 Visible column to **Off**

The third blend surface is added to the drawing which appears as in Figure 13.96.

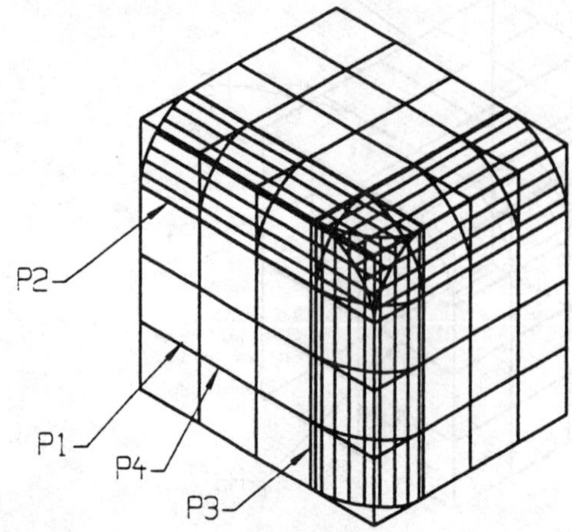

Figure 13.96

Select **MAIN MENU → File → Save**

Enter the file name: **3 blends**

Note: this file will be used in example 2.

Step 9. Trim the front face to two curves.

Use the pick points in Figure 13.96

Select **Level**, then enter **2 → OK**

Select **Color**, then enter **10 ↵**

Select **MAIN MENU → Create → Surface → Trim/extend**

Select **To curves**

Pick **P1** to select the surface to be trimmed

Select **Done**

Select **Single**, then pick **P2** and **P3** to select two curves

Select **Done**

Select **Option**

Set the Trim surfaces to curves parameters as here

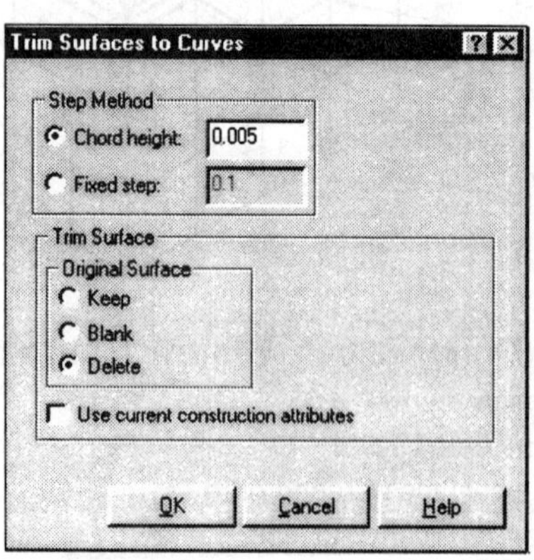

Select **OK**

Set **View/Norm** to **N**

Select **Do it**

Pick **P1** to select a surface to be trimmed

Pick **P4** to indicate a location to keep after trimming

The front surface is trimmed and the result is displayed in Figure 13.97.

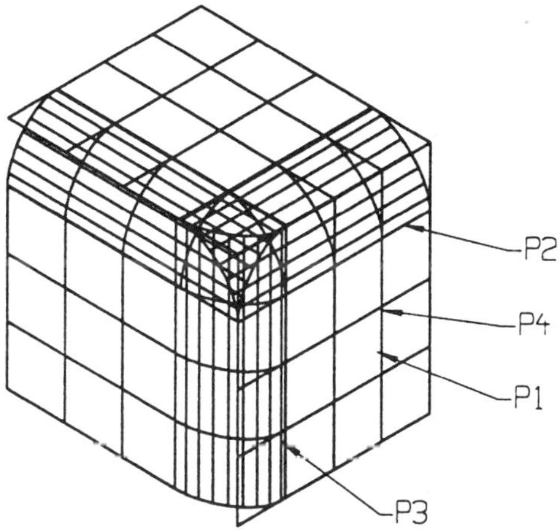

Figure 13.97

Step 10. Trim the side face to two curves.

Use the pick point in Figure 13.97
Select **BACKUP → To curves**
Pick **P1** to select the surface to trim
Select **Done**
Select **Single**, then pick **P2** and **P3** to select two curves
Select **Done → Do it**
Pick **P1** to select a surface to be trimmed
Pick **P4** to indicate the portion to keep after trimming
The side face is trimmed as shown in Figure 13.98.

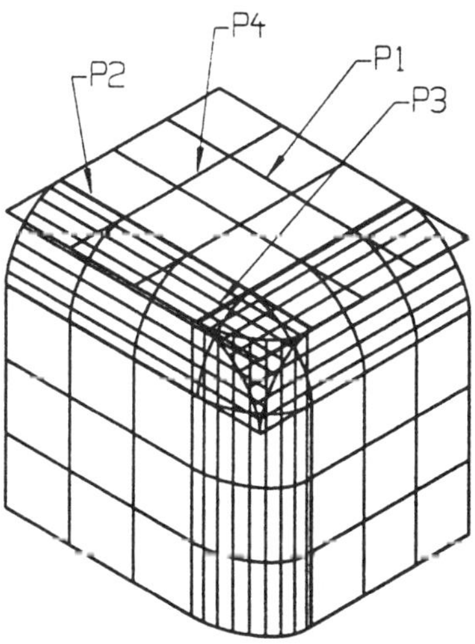

Figure 13.98

Step 11. Trim the top face to two curves.

Use the pick points in Figure 13.98
Select **BACKUP → To curves**
Pick **P1** to select the surface to trim
Select **Done**
Select **Single**, then pick **P2** and **P3** to select two curves
Select **Done → Do it**
Pick **P1** to select a surface to be trimmed
Pick **P4** to indicate the portion to keep after trimming

The top face is trimmed and the new drawing now becomes as Figure 13.99.

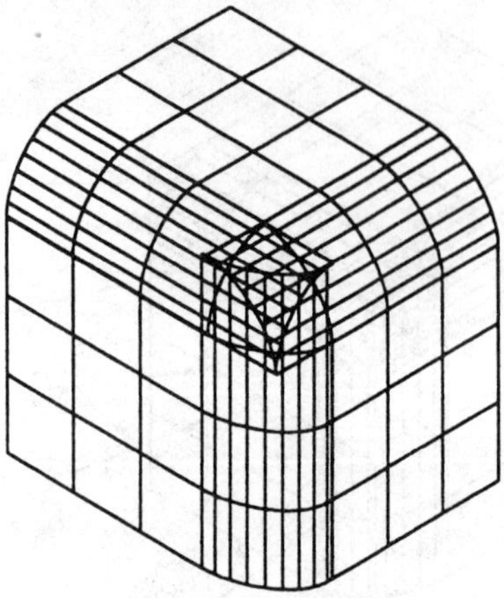

Figure 13.99

Step 12. Hide level 2.

Select **Level**, then toggle the check mark in the level 2 visible column to **off**
Select **OK → OK** to return to graphic mode
The new drawing becomes Figure 13.100.

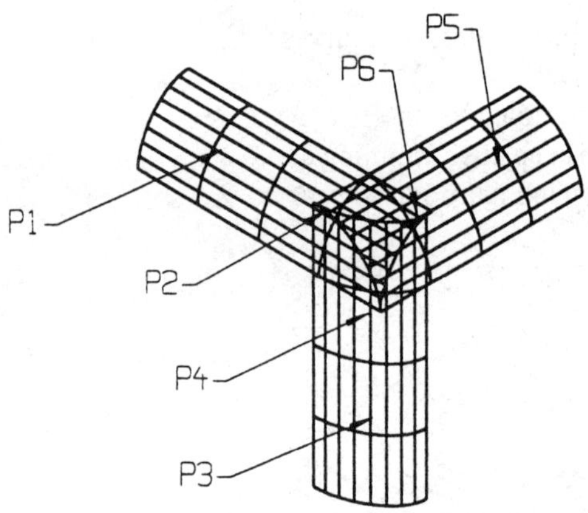

Figure 13.100

Step 13. Create a blend surface between three surfaces.

Use the pick points in Figure 13.100
Select **Level**, then enter **4** → OK
Select **Color**, then enter **10** ↵
Select **BACKUP → BACKUP → Next menu → 3 Surf blnd**
Pick **P1** to select the first surface
Pick **P2** to indicate a position to blend onto
Set the spline arrow in the **across direction**, then select **OK**
Pick **P3** to select the second surface
Pick **P4** to select a position to blend onto
Set the spline in the **across direction**, then select **OK**
Pick **P5** to select the third surface
Pick **P6** to select a position to blend onto

Set the spline in the **across direction**

Set blending parameters as below

Trim srfs =	**Y**
Keep crvs =	**N**
Surf type =	**N**

Select **Do it**

Note: It is very important to pick the proper position for the surface to blend onto. Pick slightly outside the intersection zone to create the proper trimming. Undo the results if they are not what you want. Try again until you obtain the desired result.

The blend surface is created as in Figure 13.101.

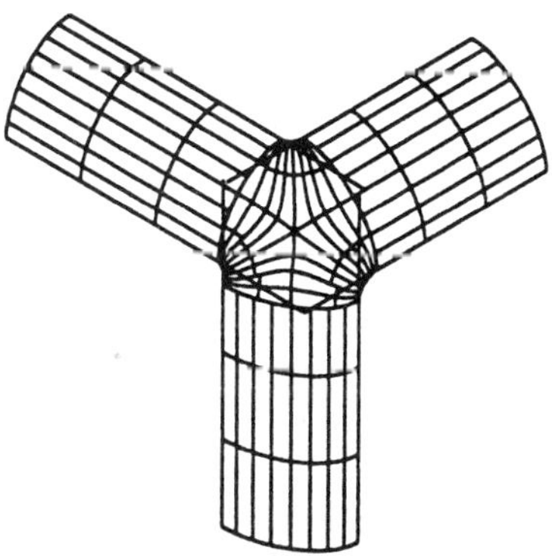

Figure 13.101

Step 14. Delete the unwanted surface curves.

Select **MAIN MENU → Delete → All → Splines**

The new drawing becomes Figure 13.102.

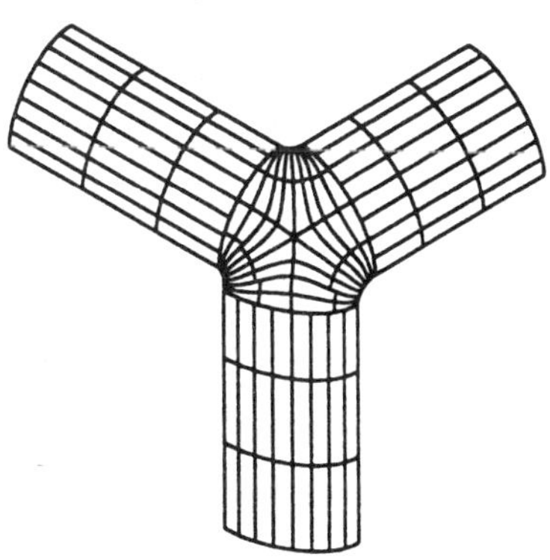

Figure 13.102

Step 15. Make level 2 visible.

Select **Level**

Click the check mark in the level 2 visible column, then select **OK**

The complete drawing is shown in Figure 13.103.

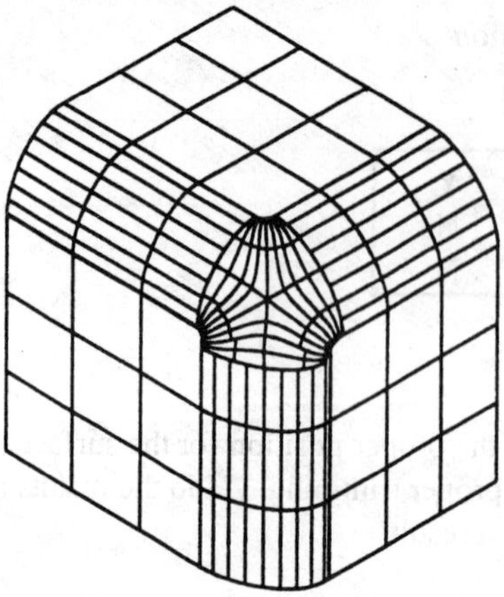

Figure 13.103

Step 16. Save the surface as blends4.

Select **MAIN MENU → File → Save**
Enter the file name: **Blends4**

Example 13.2 Creating a blend surface using three surface fillets

This example uses the three blend surfaces created in Example 1 to create a blend surface by using the Fillet blnd method. Figure 13.104 shows the surface model before and after creating a blend surface between three blend surfaces.

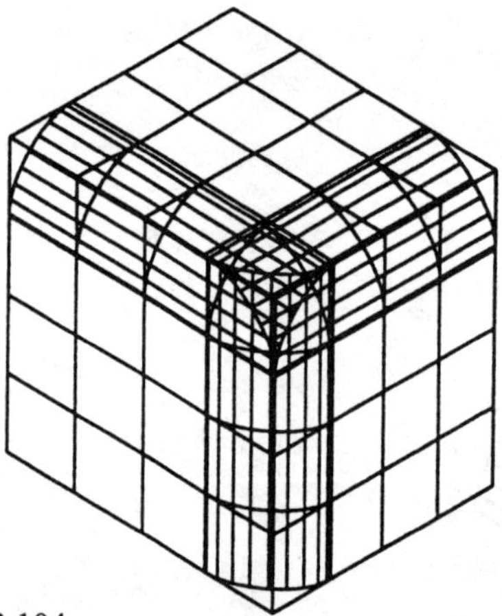

Figure 13.104a

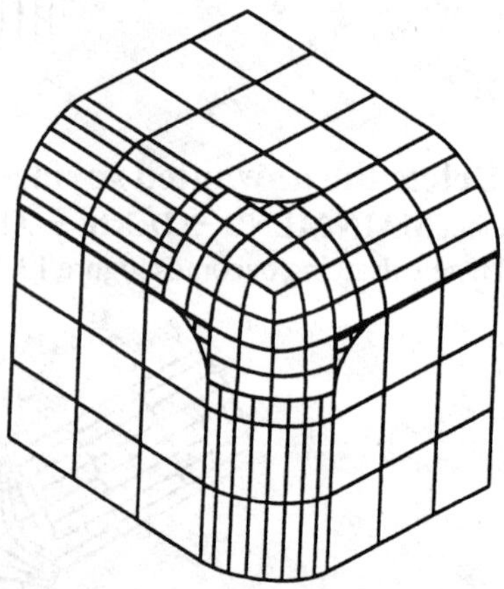

Figure 13.104b

> **Tips** 1. Use the surface model file 3blends created in Example 1 of this section.
>
> 2. Use the fillet blnd method to create a blend surface between 3 blend surfaces.
>
> 3. Trim three ruled surfaces to the surface curves of the blend surfaces.

Step 1. Load the file 3blends.

Select **MAIN MENU → File → Get**
Enter the file name: **3blends** ↵

If you do not have this file available, follow the instructions given in Step 1 to Step 8 of Example 1 in this section to create one.

The drawing should appear as Figure 13.105.

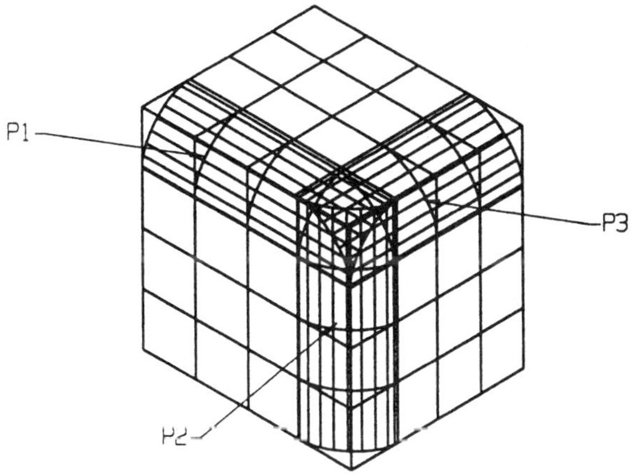

Figure 13.105

Step 2. Create a blend surface using three fillet surfaces.

Use the pick points in Figure 13.105

Select **MAIN MENU → Create → Surface → Next menu → Fillet blnd**

Select the first Fillet Surface; pick **P1**

Select the second Fillet Surface; pick **P2**

Select the third Fillet Surface; pick **P3**

Set the fillet blend parameters to the following settings:

Trim	=	**Y**
DisPose	=	**D**
Edge spl	=	**Y**
Sides	=	**6**
Surf Type	=	**N**

Select **Do it**

The blend surface is added as shown in Figure 13.106.

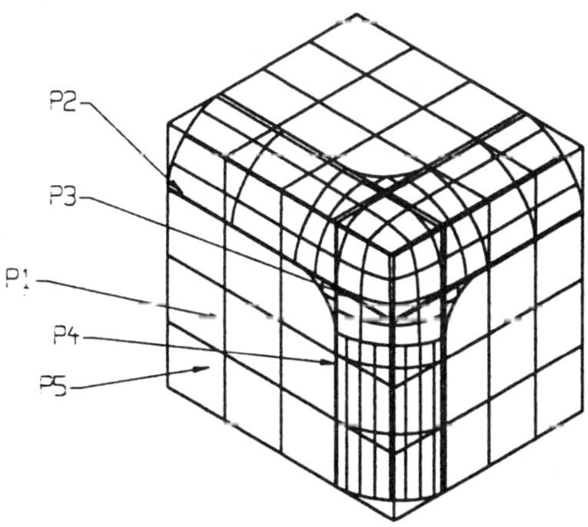

Figure 13.106

Step 3. Trim the front ruled surfaces.

Use the pick points in Figure 13.106

Select **MAIN MENU → Create → Surface → Trim/extend**

Select **to curves**

Pick **P1** to select the surface to trim
Select **Done**
Select **Single**, then pick **P2**, **P3** and **P4**
Select **Done**
Set View/Norm to **N**
Select **Options**
Set Trim Surfaces to Curves parameters as below

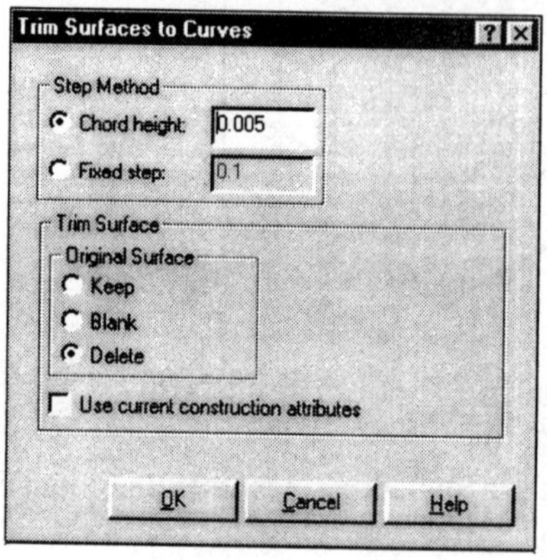

Select **OK**

Select **Do it**
Pick **P1** to select surface to trim
Pick **P5** to indicate a location to keep after trimming
The front surface is trimmed as in Figure 13.107.

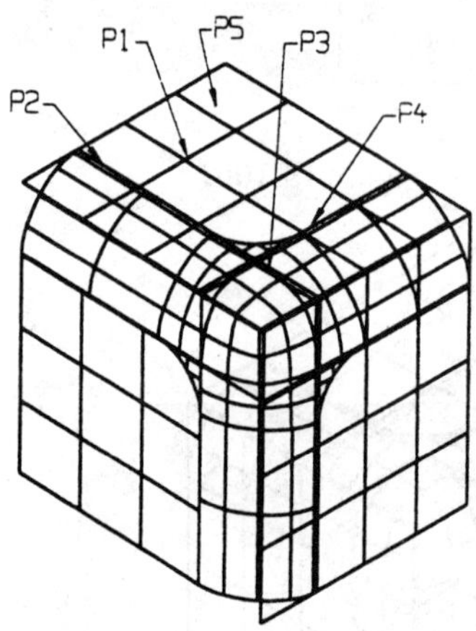

Figure 13.107

Step 4. Trim the top surface using the pick points in Figure 13.107.

Select **BACKUP → To curves**
Pick **P1** to select the surface to trim
Select **Done**
Select **Single**, then pick **P2**, **P3** and **P4**
Select **Done → Do it**
Pick **P1** to select the surface
Pick **P5** to indicate the surface area to keep

The new drawing should resemble Figure 13.108.

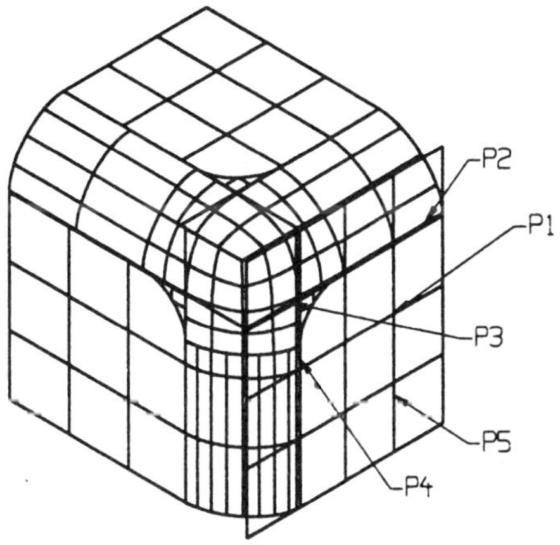

Figure 13.108

Step 5. Trim the side surface using the pick points in Figure 13.108.

Select **BACKUP → To curves**
Pick **P1** to select the surfaces
Select **Done**
Select **Single**, then pick **P2, P3** and **P4**
Select **Done → Do it**
Pick **P1** to select the surface
Pick **P5** to indicate a location to keep after trimming
The drawing becomes like Figure 13.109.

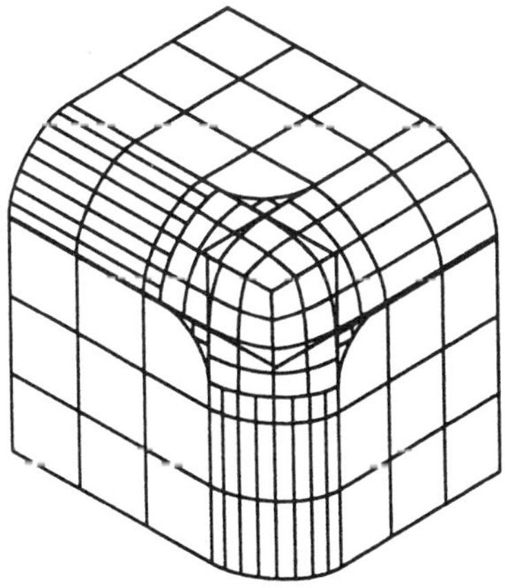

Figure 13.109

Step 6. Delete all splines.

Select **MAIN MENU → Delete → All → Splines**

The drawing should look like Figure 13.110.

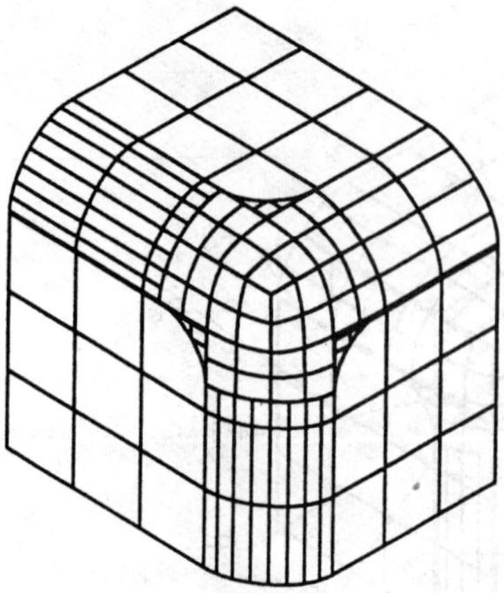

Figure 13.110

Step 7. Make level 2 invisible.

Select **Level**

Place a check mark in the level 2 visible column to set invisible

Select **OK** to return to graphic mode

The drawing changes to Figure 13.111.

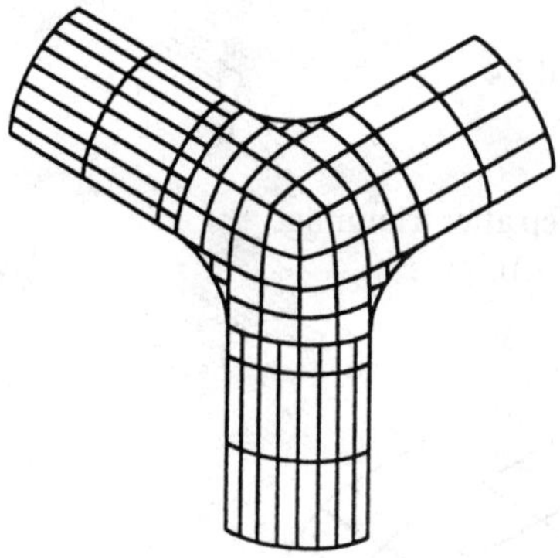

Figure 13.111

Step 8. Change to dynamic view.

Select **Gview → Dynamic**

Pick any point on the screen for drawing axes

Manipulate the mouse to dynamically view the model.

Figure 13.112 shows a dynamic view of the blend surfaces.

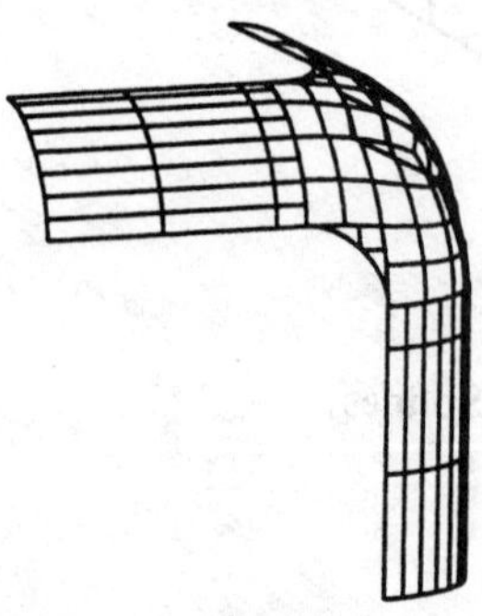

Figure 13.112

Step 9. Change to isometric view.

Select **Gview → Isometric**
Select **Level**
Click the level 2 Visible column to check mark it as visible
Select **OK**
The complete model is shown in Figure 13.113.

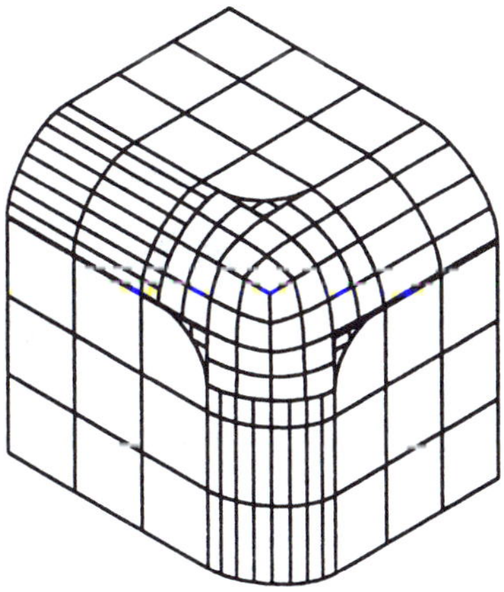

Figure 13.113

Step 10. Save the model as blends5.

Select **MAIN MENU → File → Save**
File name: **blends5**

13.3 Composite Surfaces Models

Composite surface models use more than one surfacing technique to create multiple surfaces in representing an object. In fact, most surface modeling of objects today are of the composite type. Five composite surface models are presenting in this section. They are arranged in increasing order of difficulty. Their wireframe models were presented in chapter 11.

Project 8. Basket surface model

The surface model of a basket shown in Figure 13.114 consists of four surfaces: top rim surface, wall surface surface, bottom flat surface, and fillet surface at the intersection between the wall surface and bottom flat surface.

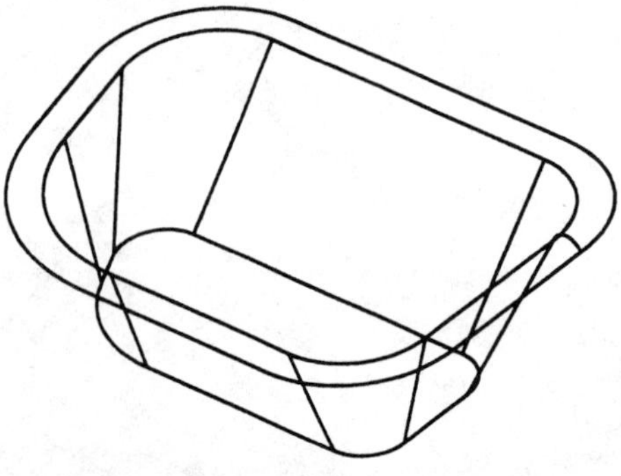

Figure 13.114a Wireframe model

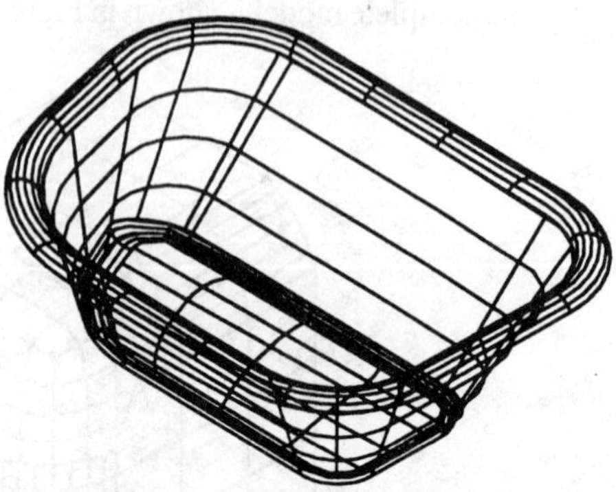

Figure 13.114b Surface model

Tips

1. Use two alone /one across swept surfacing technique to create the top rim surface. The two along contours are the two outer profiles. The across contour is the arc that encompasses these two profiles.
2. Use the Coons surfacing technique to generate the wall surface. The number of patches in the along direction is 8 and the number of patches in the across direction is 1.
3. The bottom flat surface can be modeled as a ruled surface.
4. Add a fillet surface between the wall surface and the bottom flat surface.
5. Use a different level and color for each surface.

Step 1. Load the wireframe model file basket.

Select **MAIN MENU → File → Get**
Enter file name: **basket ↵**
The wireframe model should appear as Figure 13.115.

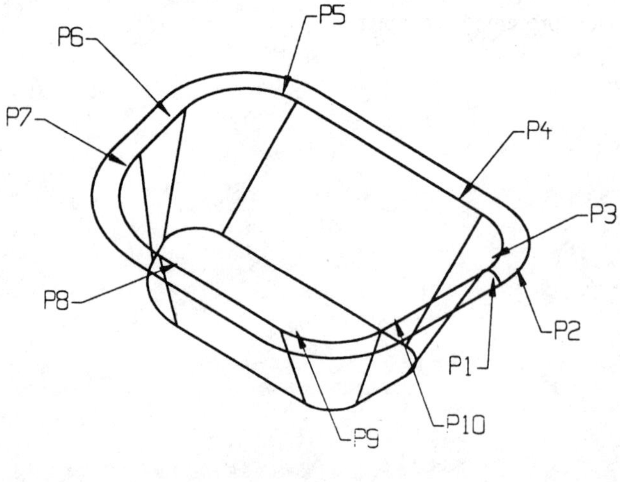

Figure 13.115

Step 2. Create the top rim surface using swept surfacing technique. 8

Use the pick points in Figure 13.91.
Change level 2 and color to **12**
Select **Cplane → Top**
Select **Level**, then enter **2** in the Main Level box → **OK**
Select **Color,** then enter **12** ↵
Select **MAIN MENU → Create → Surface → Sweep**
Define the across contour: select **Single**, then pick **P1→ Done**
Define along contour: Select **Chain**, then pick **P3 - P10**
Select **End here** to complete the along contour 1
Define along contour 2: select **Mode → Chain,** then pick **P2**

Set the Swept surface parameters to the following settings:

Surface error tolerance = **0.005**
Surface type = **NURBS**

Select **Do it** to complete the swept surface
The swept surface appearing on screen should look like Figure 13.116 on the next page.

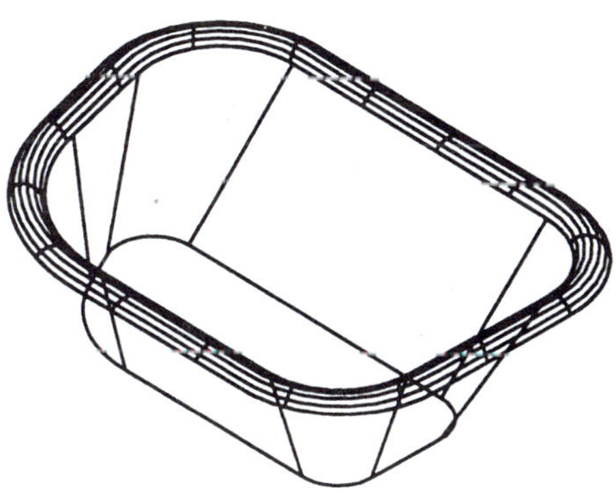

Figure 13.116

Step 3. Make level 2 invisible and change to Top Gview.

Select **Level → 3,** then click on button 2 to set invisible (without checkmark)
Select **OK** to return the screen back to graphic mode
Select **Gview → Top**
Press **Alt+F1**, then **F2** to fit the drawing, if necessary
The drawing becomes Figure 13.117

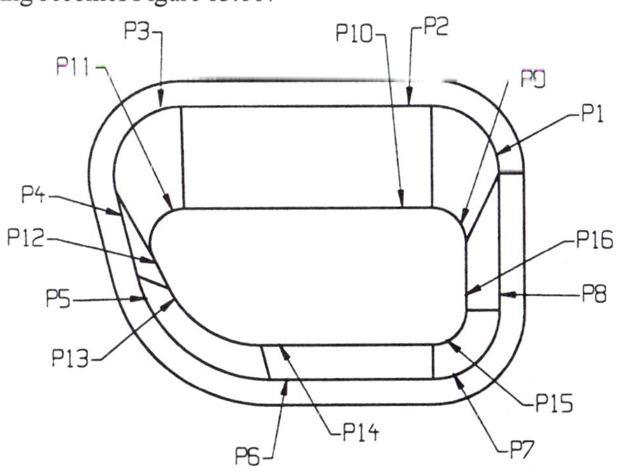

Figure 13.117a

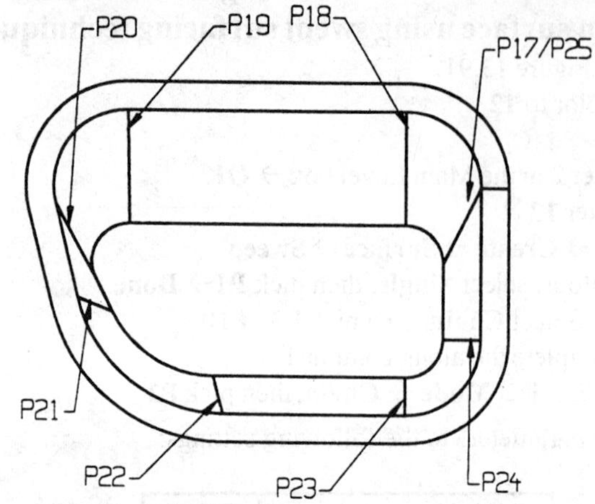

Figure 13.117b

Step 4. Create a Coons surface using the pick points in Figure 13.117.

Select **Color**, then enter **13** ↵
Select **MAIN MENU → Create → Surface → Coons**
Select **No** to "Use Automatic Coons surface chaining?"
Enter number of patches in the along direction: **8** ↵
Enter number of patches in the across direction: **1** ↵
Define along contour 1 of row: select **Single**, sequentially pick **P1 to P8** to complete the row 1.
Sequentially pick **P9 to P16** to complete the row 2
Sequentially pick **P17 to P25** to complete the across contour of column 1
Select **Done** to complete the chaining
Set the Coons surface parameters to the following settings:

Surface Error Tolerance = **0.005** Surface type = **NURBS** Blending = **Linear**

Select **Do it** to complete the Coons surface
The new Coons surface appears in Top Gview as in Figure 13.118.

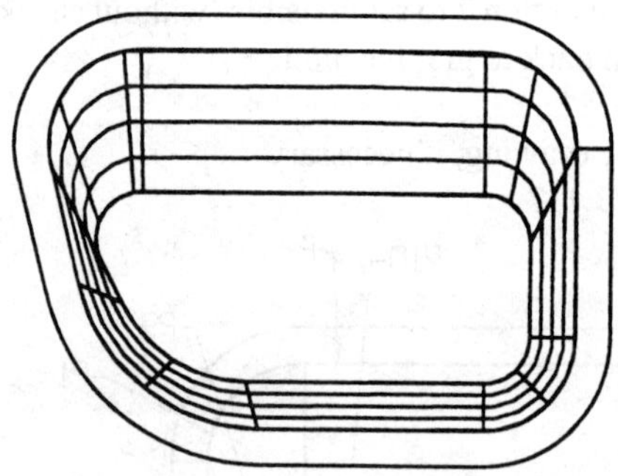

Figure 13.118

Step 5. Make level 3 invisible.

Select **Level**, then enter **4**
Click on button 3 to set invisible (without checkmark)
Select **OK** to return to graphic mode
The drawing now should look like Figure 13.119.

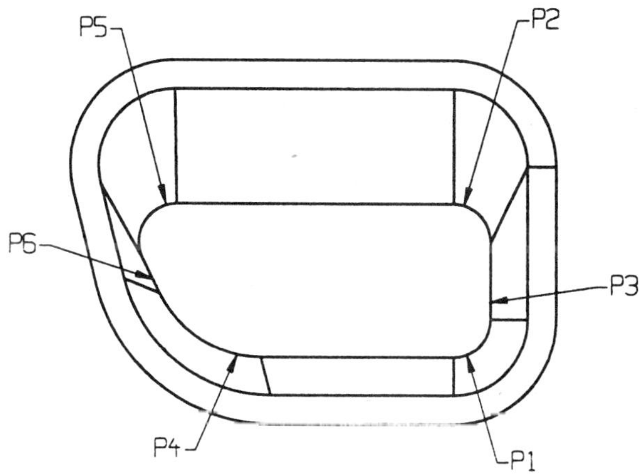

Figure 13.119

Step 6. Create a bottom ruled surface using pick points labeled in Figure 13.119.

Select **Color,** then enter **14** ↵
Select **MAIN MENU → Create → Surface → Ruled**
Define contour 1: select **Chain → Partial**
Pick **P1** as the first entity
Pick **P2** as the last entity
Pick **P3** to select new branch
Define contour 2: select **Partial,** then pick **P4** as the first entity
Pick **P5** as the last entity
Pick **P6** to select new branch
Select **Done** to complete contour selection
Select **Do it**
The ruled surface should resemble Figure 13.120.

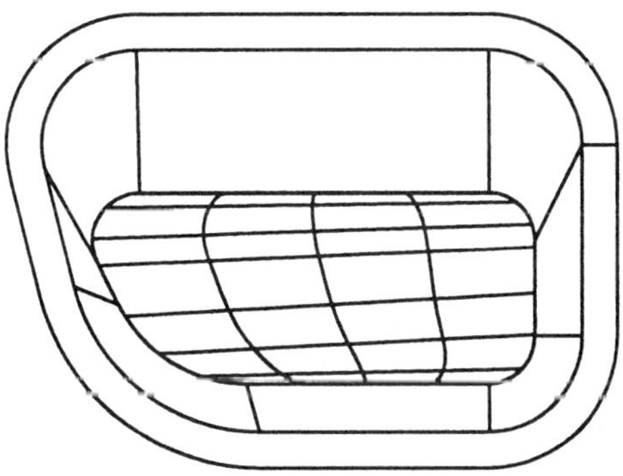

Figure 13.120

Step 7. Toggle level 3 to visible and change the level to 5.

Select **Level**
Click on button 3 to set visible (without checkmark)
In the **Main** level number box enter **5 → OK**
The drawing now should look like Figure 13.121.

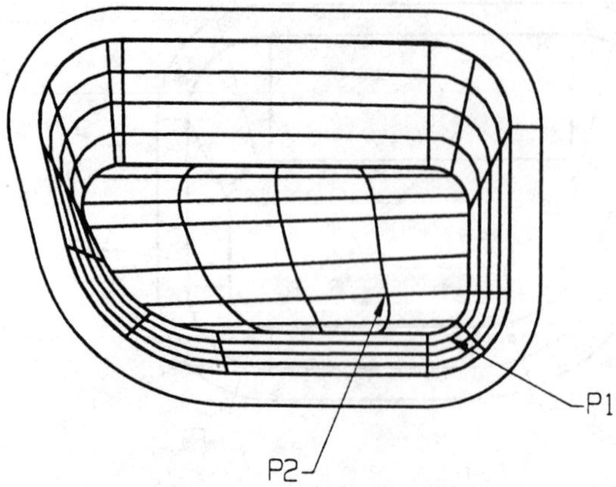

Figure 13.121

Step 8. Create a fillet surface at the intersection of the wall and bottom surfaces.

Use the pick points in Figure 13.121.
Select **Color**, then enter **15** ↵
Select **MAIN MENU → Create → Surface → Fillet → Surf/Surf**

Pick **P1**, then **Done** to select first set of surfaces
Pick **P2** then **Done** to select second set of surfaces
Enter the fillet radius: **0.25** ↵
Select **Options**

Set the surface fillet parameters
to the following settings:

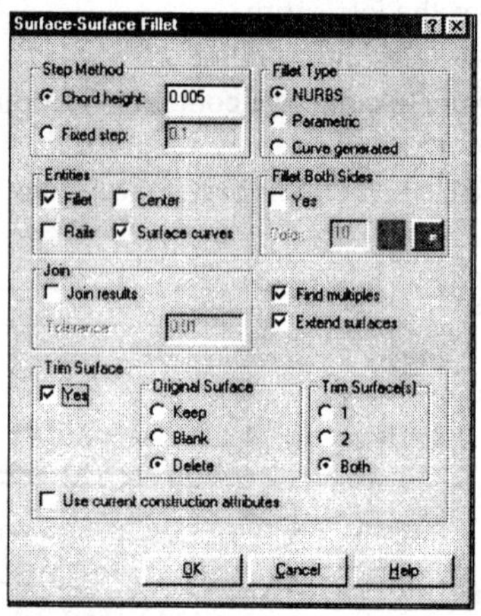

Select **OK → Do it**

The fillet surface is added to the model as in Figure 13.122.

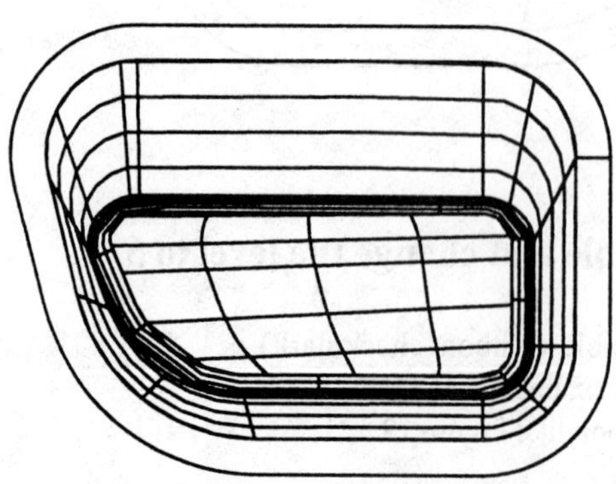

Figure 13.122

Step 9. Make all surface levels to visible and change to isometric Gview.

Select **Level**
Toggle level 2 to set visible (with check mark)
Then select **OK** to return to graphic mode
Select **Gview → Isometric**
The final surface model is shown in Figure 13.123.

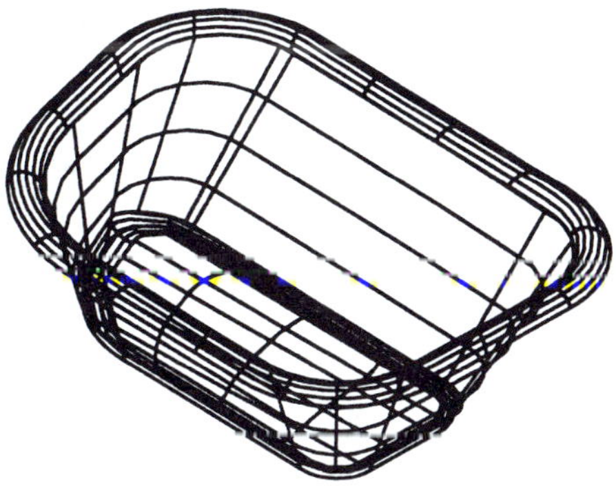

Figure 13.123

Step 10. Save the surface model (baskets).

Select **MAIN MENU → File → Save**
Enter file name: **baskets**

💻 Project 9. Flash light surface model

The flash light surface model (Figure 13.124b) consists of four ruled surfaces, one coons surface and one fillet surface. The wireframe model (Figure 13.124a) is presented in project 12 of chapter 11.

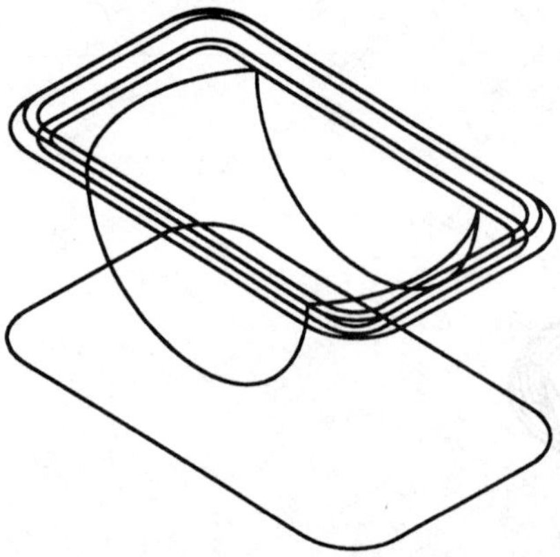

Figure 13.124a Wireframe model

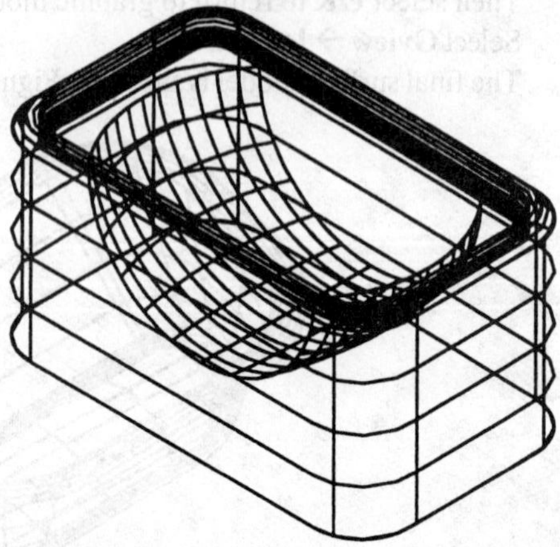

Figure 13.124b Surface model

Tips
1. Use two outer rectangular profiles to create a ruled surface for the outer frame.
2. Use three rectangular profiles to create a ruled surface for the top rim.
3. Create a vertical ruled surface for the inside wall.
4. The inner flat surface can be created as a ruled surface using the inner rectangular profile.
5. The curved surface is generated as a single-patch Coons surface.
6. The fillet surface is generated between the vertical ruled and the inner flat ruled surfaces.
7. The inner flat surface is trimmed by the surface curve created by projecting the Coons patch profile onto the inner flat ruled surface.
8. Use a different level and color for each surface.

Step 1. Load the wireframe model file "flash".

Select **MAIN MENU → File → Get**

Enter file name: **flash**

The wireframe model drawing should appear on screen as Figure 13.125.

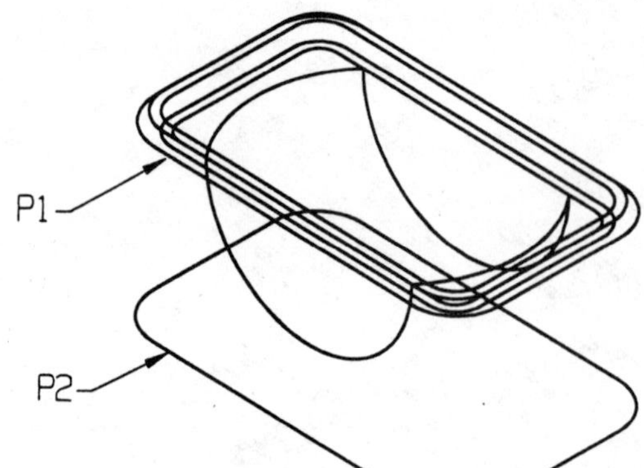

Figure 13.125

Step 2. Create a ruled surface for the outer frame. 9

Use the pick points labeled in Figure 13.125.
Select **Level**, then enter **2** → OK
Select **Color,** then enter **11** ↵
Select **MAIN MENU → Create → Surface → Ruled → Chain**
Pick **P1** to define contour 1
Pick **P2** to define contour 2
Select **Done**
Set the Ruled surface parameters as below:

Surface Error Tolerance = **0.005** Surface type = **NURBS**

Select **Do it** to complete the surface
The added ruled surface should look like Figure 13.126.

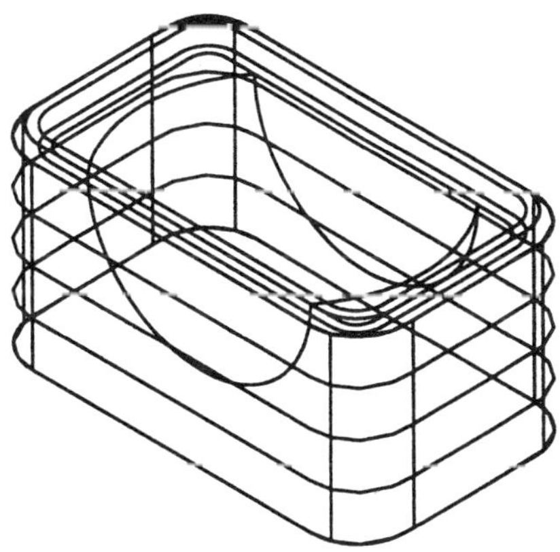

Figure 13.126

Step 3. Make level 2 invisible. Change to Top Gview.

Select **Level**, then enter **3**
Click on the check mark on the level 2 to set invisible
Select **OK** to return to graphic mode
The new drawing should resemble Figure 13.127.

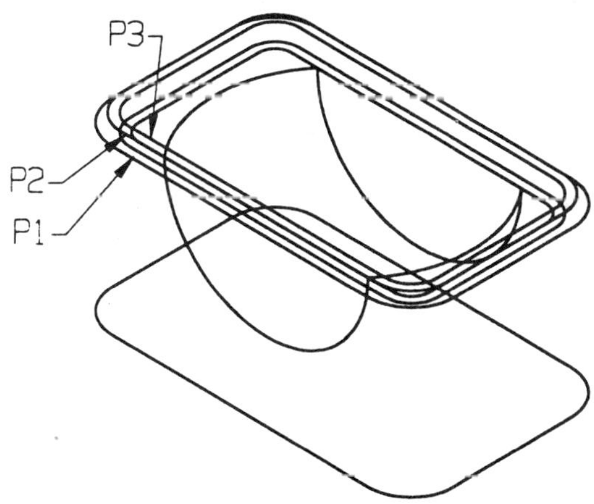

Figure 13.127

Step 4. Create a ruled surface on the top ring

Use the pick points labeled in Figure 13.127.
Select **Color,** then enter **12** ↵
Select **MAIN MENU → Create → Surface → Ruled → Chain**
Pick **P1** define contour 1
Pick **P2** to define contour 2
Pick **P3** to define contour 3
Select **Done → Do it** to complete the ruled surface
The new ruled surface is shown in Figure 13.128.

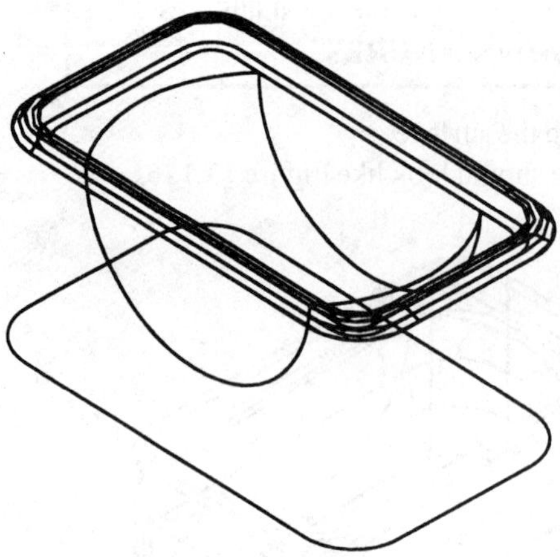

Figure 13.128

Step 5. Make level 3 invisible.

Select **Level**, then enter **4** in the Main Level box
Click on the check mark of the level 3 button to set to invisible (without checkmark)
Select **OK** to return to graphic mode
The drawing on the screen should resemble Figure 13.129.

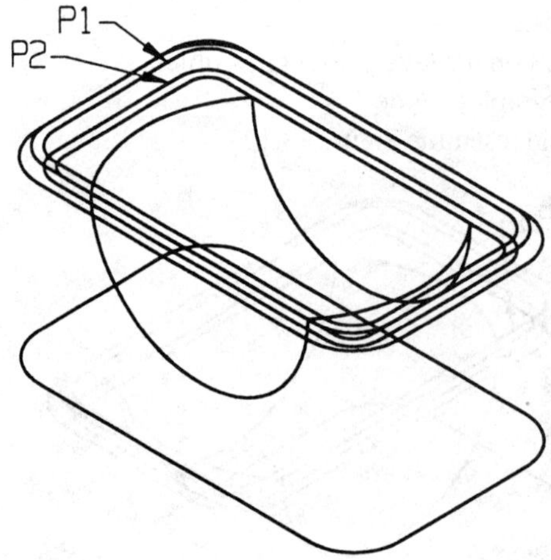

Figure 13.129

Step 6. Create a vertical ruled surface using the pick points in Figure 13.129.

Select **Color**, then enter **13** ↵
Select **MAIN MENU** → **Create** → **Surface** → **Ruled** → **Chain**
Pick **P1** to define contour 1
Pick **P2** to define contour 2
Select **Done** → **Do it** to complete the surface
The drawing should resemble Figure 13.130.

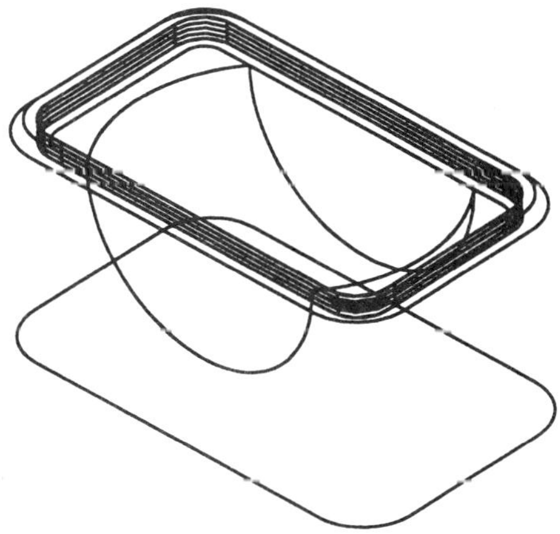

Figure 13.130

Step 7. Change to level 5 and make level 4 invisible.

Select **Level**, then enter **5** in the Main Level box
Click on the check mark of the level 4 button to set to invisible (without checkmark)
Select **OK** to return to graphic mode
The drawing now appears as Figure 13.131.

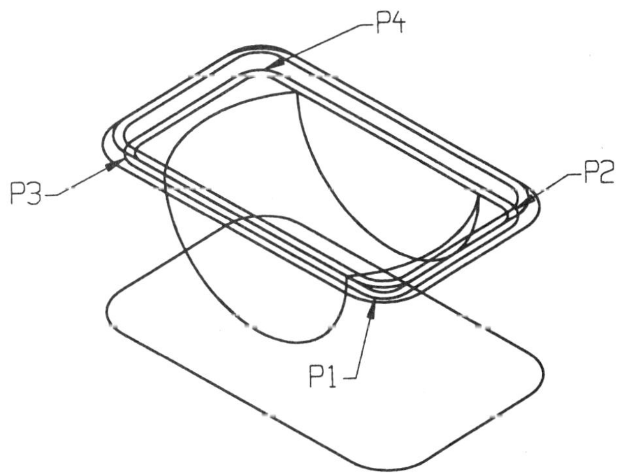

Figure 13.131

Step 8. Create a ruled surface for inner flat surface.

Use the pick points labeled in Figure 13.131.
Select **Color**, then enter **14** ↵
Select **BACKUP** → **Ruled** → **Chain** → **Partial**

Pick **P1** and **P2** to complete contour 1
Select **Partial**
Pick **P3** and **P4** to complete contour 2
Select **Done → Do it** to complete the surface
The surface model appears as Figure 13.132.

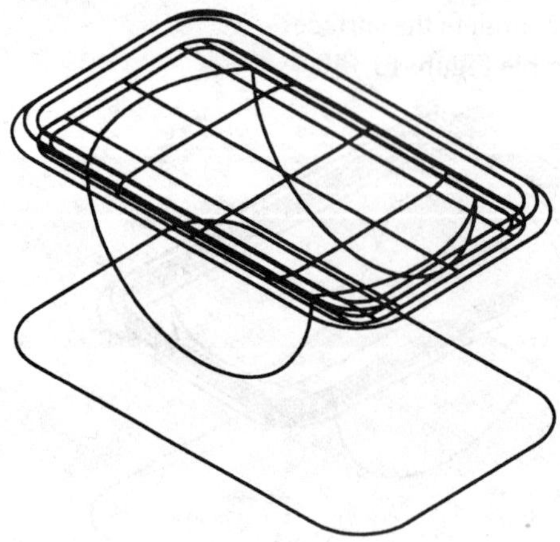

Figure 13.132

Step 9. Change to level 6 and make level 5 invisible.

Select **Level**, then enter **6** ↵
Click on the level 5 button to set to invisible (no checkmark)
Select **OK** to return to graphic mode
The drawing now should resemble Figure 13.133.

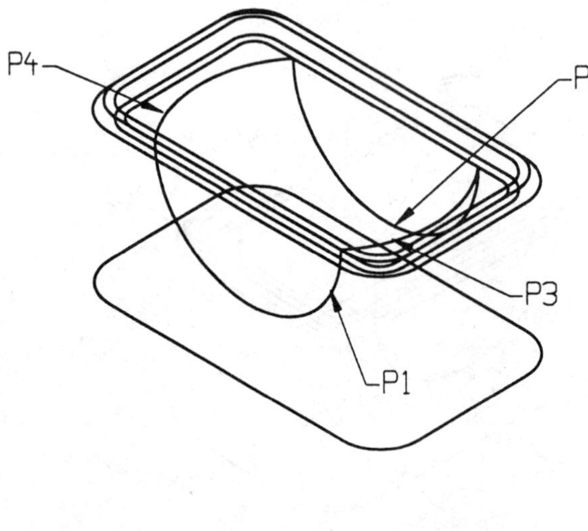

Figure 13.133

Step 10. Create a Coons surface using the pick points in Figure 13.133.

Select **Color**, then enter **15** ↵
Select **BACKUP → Coons**
Select **No** to "Use Automatic Coons surface chaining ?"
Enter number of patches in the along direction: **1** ↵
Enter number o patches in the across direction: **1** ↵

Select **Single**
Define along contour 1 of row 1: pick **P1**
Define along contour 1 of row 2: pick **P2**
Define across contour 1 of column 1: pick **P3**
Define across contour 1 of column 2: pick **P4**
Select **Done** to complete chaining
Set the Coons surface parameters to the following settings:

Surface Error Tolerance =	**0.005**
Surface Type =	**N (Nurbs)**
Blending =	**L (Linear)**

Select **Do it** to complete the surface
The Coons surface should appear as Figure 13.134.

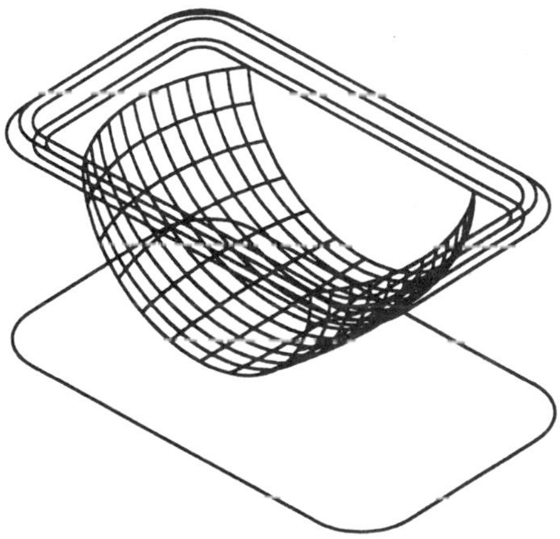

Figure 13.134

Step 11. Make level 6 invisible and level 4 and 5 visible.

Select **Level,** enter **7** in the Main Level box
Toggle the level 6 to invisible (without checkmark)
Toggle levels 4 and 5 to visible (with checkmark)
Select **OK** to return to graphic mode
The new drawing on the screen should resemble Figure 13.135.

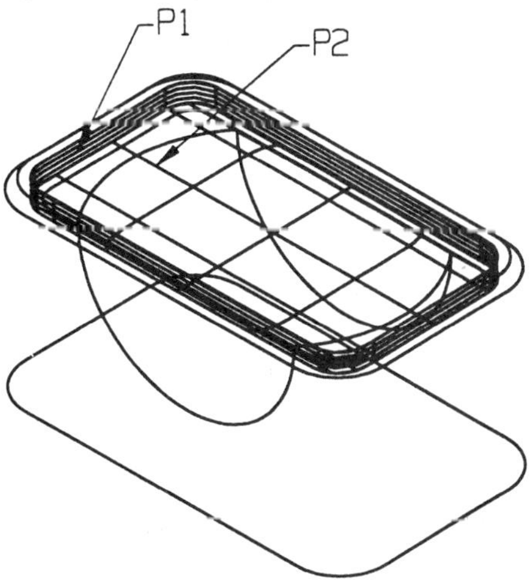

Figure 13.135

Step 12. Create a fillet surface at the intersection between the inner flat surface and the vertical wall surface.

Use the pick points in Figure 13.135.
Select **Color,** then enter **12** ↵
Select **BACKUP→ Fillet → Surf/surf**

Note: The normal direction of the vertical wall needs to be in the inward direction. Use **Modify → Normal** commands to check if necessary.

Pick **P1 → Done** to select first set of surfaces
Pick **P2 → Done** to select the second set of surfaces
Enter radius: **0.1** ↵
Select **Options**
Set Surface_Surface Fillet parameters as shown here

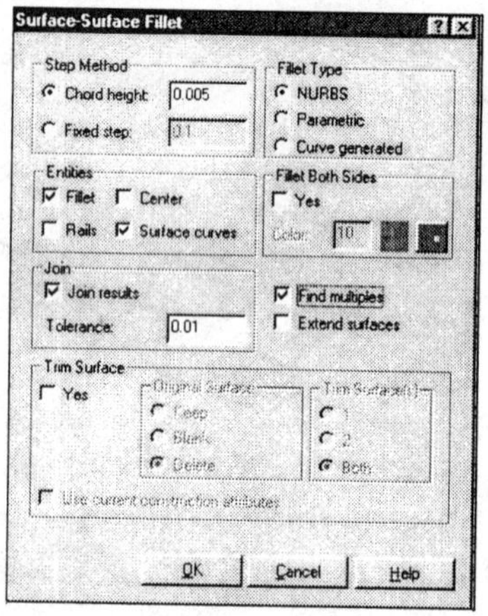

Select **OK → Do it**

The fillet surface should appear as Figure 13.136.

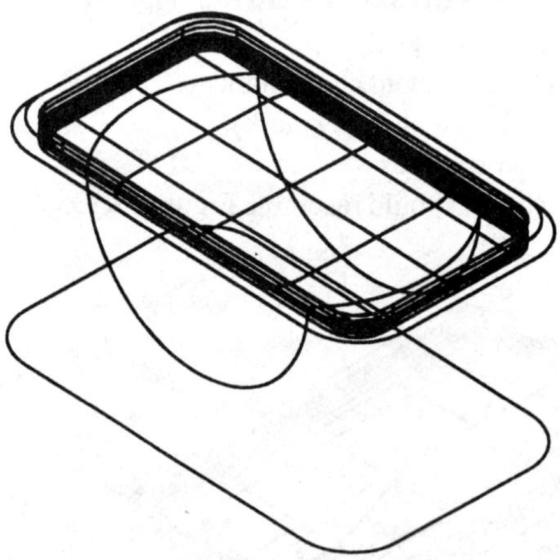

Figure 13.136

Step 13. Make levels 2, 3, 4, 6, and 7 invisible.

Select **Level,** enter **8**
Toggle only levels 1 and 5 to visible (with checkmarks) and level 7 to invisible
Select **OK** to return to graphic mode
The drawing should resemble Figure 13.137.

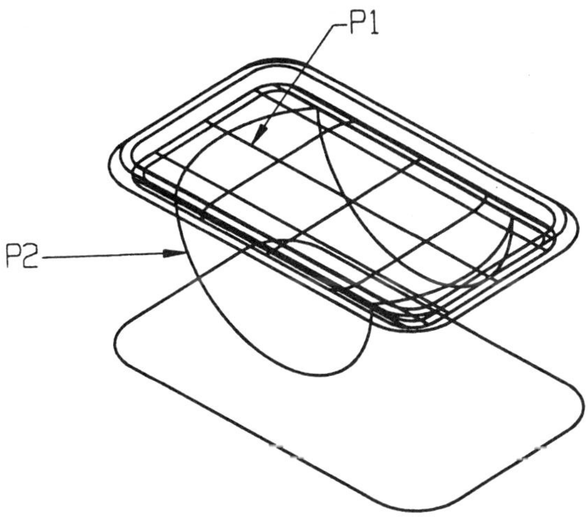

Figure 13.137

Step 14. Create the surface curve for trimming the inner flat ruled surface.

Use the pick points in Figure 13.137
Change color to **13**
Select **Color,** then enter **13** ↵
Select **MAIN MENU → Create → Curve → Project**
Pick **P1** to select the ruled surface
Select **Done**
Select **Chain**
Pick **P2** to select the first entity
Select **Done**
Toggle "View/norm" to **V**
Select **Options**
Set projection curve parameters as shown here:

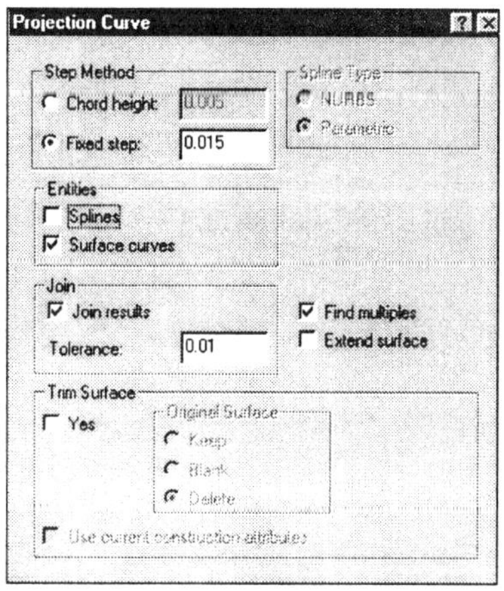

Select **OK → Do it**
The surface curve appearing on screen should look like Figure 13.138.

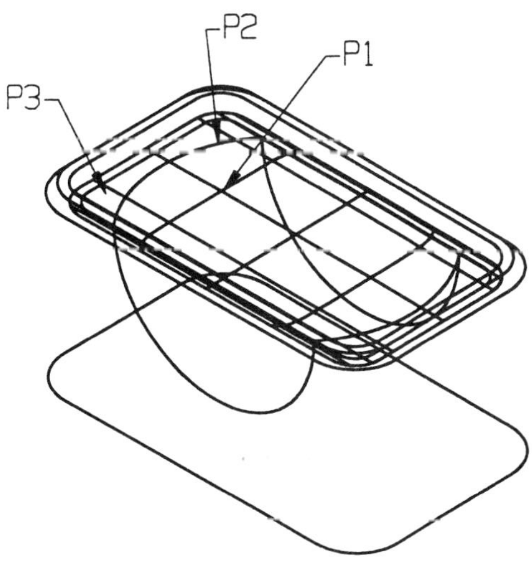

Figure 13.138

Step 15. Trim the inner flat ruled surface using the pick points in Figure 13.138.

Select **Level**, then enter **9 → OK**
Select **Color**, then enter **12** ↵
Select **MAIN MENU → Create → Surface → Trim/extend → To curves**
Pick **P1** to select the surface to be trimmed
Select **Done**
Select **Chain,** then pick **P2**
Select **Done → Options**
Set the Trim surface to Curve parameters
as shown here:

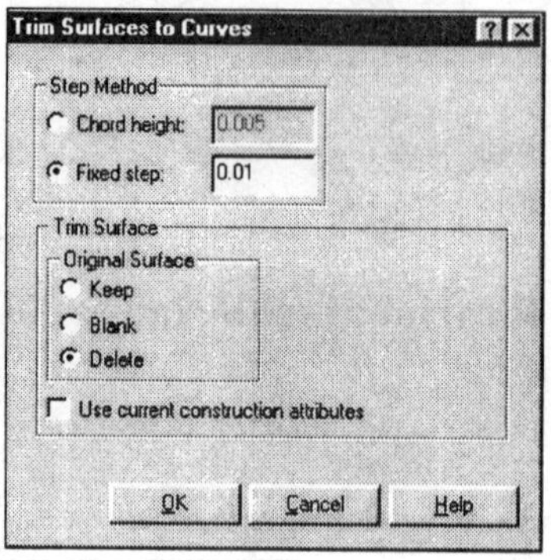

Select **OK → Do it**

Pick **P1** to select a surface to be trimmed
Pick **P3** to select a location to keep after trimming
The trimmed surface should look like Figure 13.139.

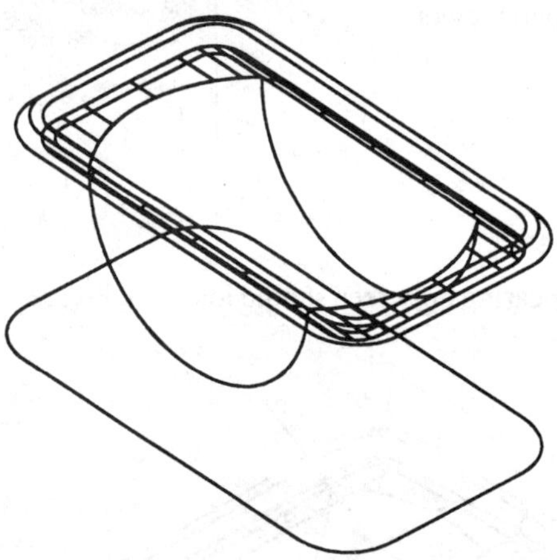

Figure 13.139

Step 16. Display all necessary surfaces.

Select **Level**
Toggle every level to visible except level 5
Press **OK** to return to graphic mode

The final surface model should look like Figure 13.140.

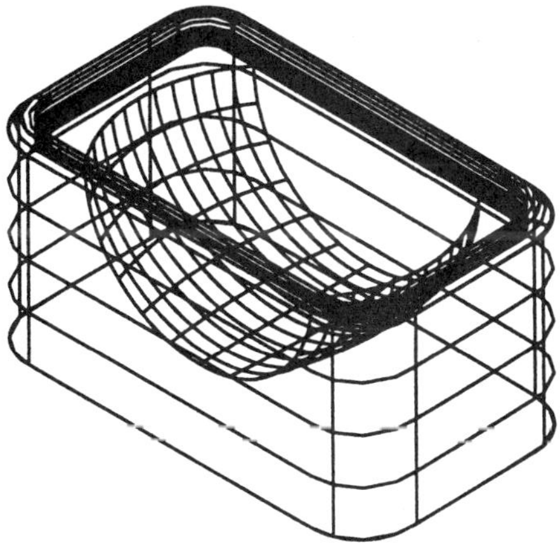

Figure 13.140

Step 17. Save the surface model as flashs.

Select **MAIN MENU → File → Save**
Enter file name: **flashs**

Project 10. Hair dryer surface model

The hair dryer surface model consists of four surfaces; two swept surfaces and two ruled surfaces (Figure 13.141). The two swept surfaces are the top surface and the frame surface. The two ruled surfaces include the tube surface and the handle surface. The two ruled surfaces are trimmed to the frame surface. These four surfaces are mirrored about the X axis in the Front Cplane to complete the surface model.

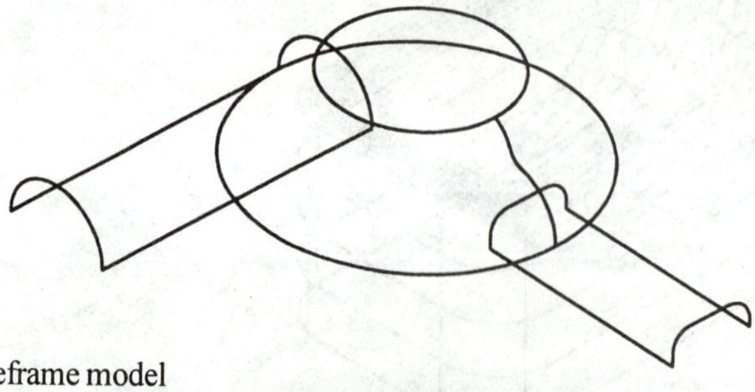

Figure 13.141a Wireframe model

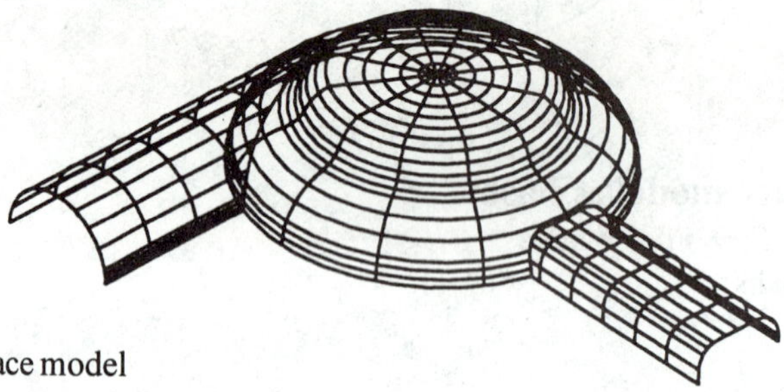

Figure 13.141b Surface model

Tips
1. The top flat face and the frame can be formed as a single swept surface. In this case we purposely create it as two separate swept surfaces because the top flat surface can be easily machined by using a flat end mill instead of a ball end cutter.
2. In this surface model, two ruled surfaces are constructed long enough to extrude into the frame surface. Therefore, they should be trimmed.
3. Two surface curves should be created at the intersection boundary between the frame surface and the tube surface, and between the frame surface and the handle surface. These two surface curves are then used to trim the two ruled surfaces.
4. Trimming both ruled surfaces requires us to redefine the outer boundary.
5. Use the Front Cplane to mirror the upper composite surface model about the X axis to complete the modeling of the object.

Step 1. Load the wireframe model file (dryer).

Select **MAIN MENU → File → Get**
Enter file name: **dryer ↵**
The wireframe model of hair dryer appears as Figure 13.142.

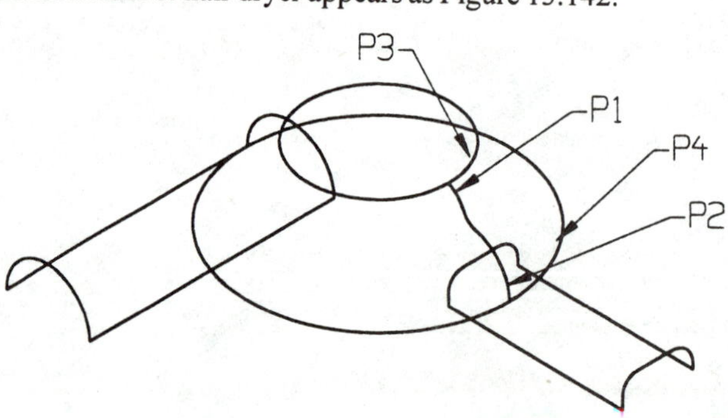

Figure 13.142

Mastercam Version 8,
Scholars International Publishing Corp., 2001

Step 2. Create a swept surface using the pick points in Figure 13.142. 10

Select **Level**, then enter **2** → **OK**
Select **Color**, then enter **11** ↵
Select **MAIN MENU** → **Create** → **Surface** → **Sweep**

Define the across contour: select **Chain** → **Partial** from the Changing method menu
Pick **P1** and **P2**
Select **Done**
Define along contour 1: select **Single**, then pick **P3**
Define along contour 2: pick **P4**
Select **Done** to complete contour selection
Set the Swept surface parameters to the following settings:

Surface Error Tolerance =	**0.005**
Surface Type =	**N (Nurbs)**

Select **Do it** to complete the swept surface
The swept surface should appear as Figure 13.143.

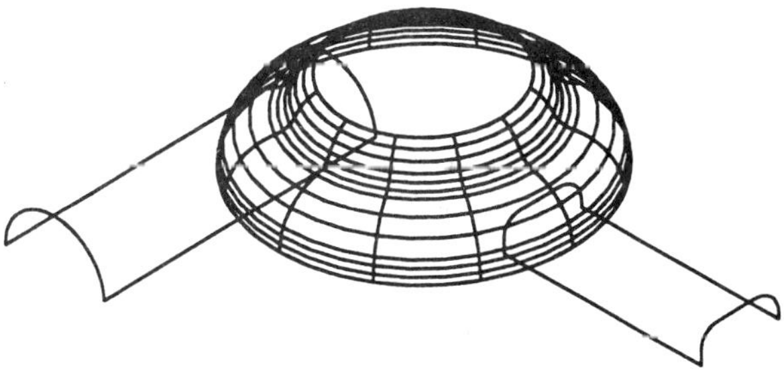

Figure 13.143

Step 3. Change to level 3 and make level 2 invisible.

Select **Level**, then enter **3** in the Main level box
Toggle the check mark in the level 2 Visible column to invisible
Select **OK** to return to graphic mode
The drawing becomes Figure 13.144.

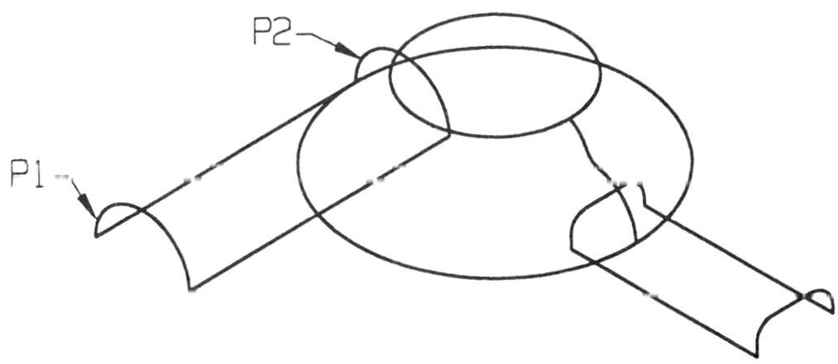

Figure 13.144

Step 4. Create a ruled surface for the tube using the pick points in Figure 13.144.

Select **Color**, then enter **12** ↵
Select **MAIN MENU** → **Create** → **Surface** → **Ruled** → **Single**
Define contour 1: pick **P1**
Define contour 2: pick **P2**
Select **Done**

Select **Do it** to complete the ruled surface
The ruled surface should resemble Figure 13.145.

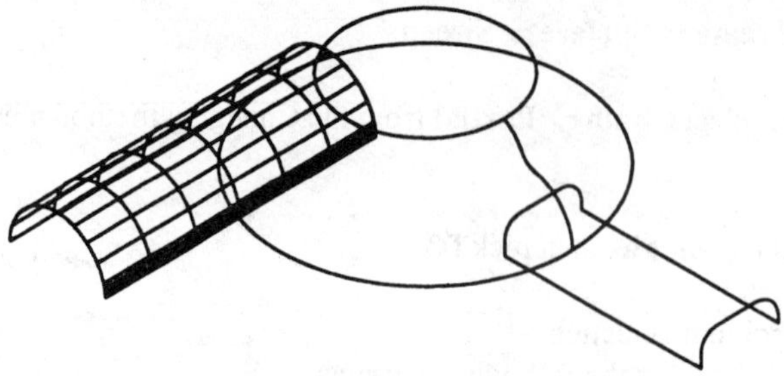

Figure 13.145

Step 5. Change to level 4 and make level 3 invisible.

Select **Level**, then enter **4** in the Main level box
Toggle the checkmark in level 3 to invisible
Select **OK** to return to graphic mode
The drawing now should appear as Figure 13.146.

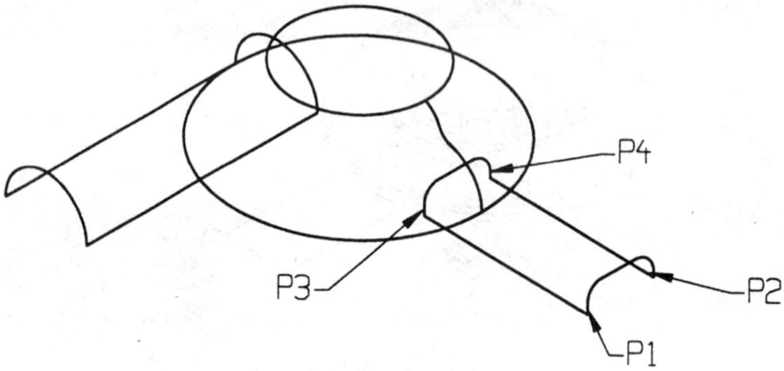

Figure 13.146

Step 6. Create a ruled surface for the handle using pick points in Figure 13.146.

Select **Color,** then enter **13** ↵
Select **BACKUP → Ruled**
Define contour 1: select **Chain → Partial**
Pick **P1** and **P2**
Define contour 2: select **Partial**, then pick **P3** and **P4**
Select **Done**
Select **Do it** to complete the surface
The new ruled surface should resemble Figure 13.147.

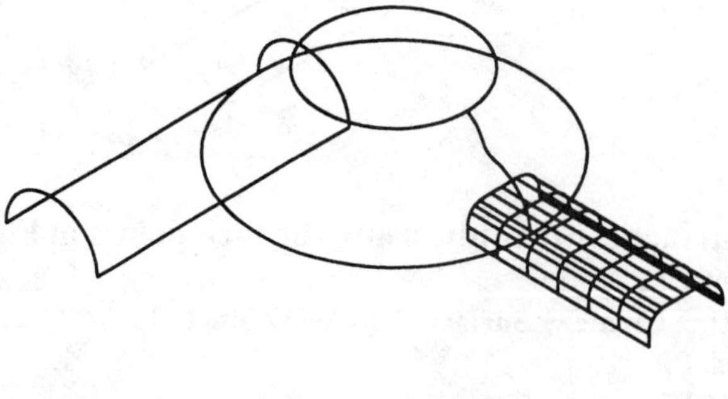

Figure 13.147

Step 7. Make levels 2 and 3 visible.

Select **Level**
Toggle levels 2 and 3 to visible (checkmarks in the Visible column)
Select **OK** to return to graphic mode

The drawing becomes Figure 13.148.

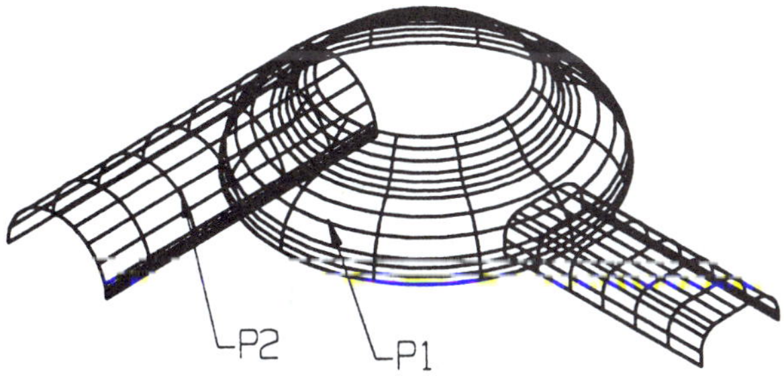

Figure 13.148

Step 8. Create a surface curve at the intersection between the frame surface and the tube surface.

Use the pick points in Figure 13.148.
Select **Level**, then enter **5** → OK
Select **Color**, then enter **14** ↵
Select **MAIN MENU** → **Create** → **Curve** → **Intersect**
Pick **P1**, then select **Done**
Pick **P2**, then select **Done**
Select **Options**
Set Intersection curve parameters as shown here:

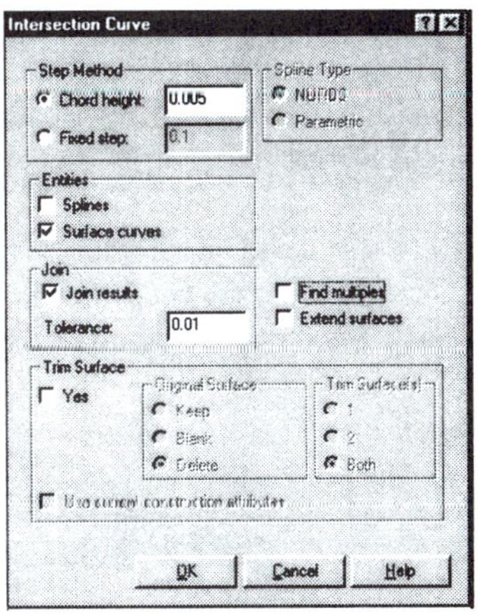

Select **OK** → **Do it**

The surface curve should appear as Figure 13.149.

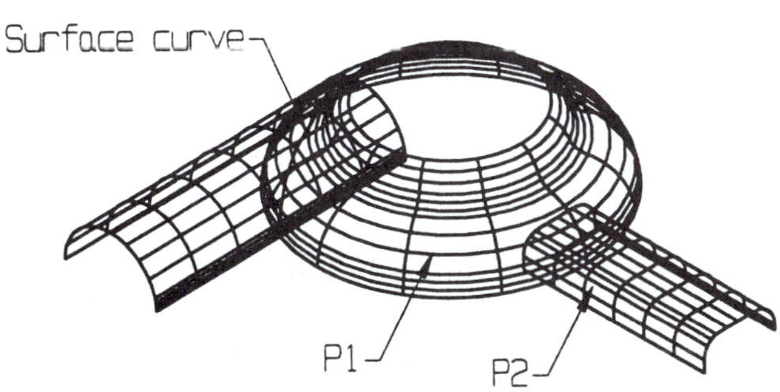

Figure 13.149

Step 9. Create a surface curve at the intersection between the frame surface and the handle surface.

Use the pick points in Figure 13.149.
Select **BACKUP → Intersect**
Pick **P1**, then **Done** to select the first set of the surfaces
Pick **P2**, then **Done** to select the second set of the surfaces
Select **Do it** to complete the surface curve
Both surface curves should appear as Figure 13.150.

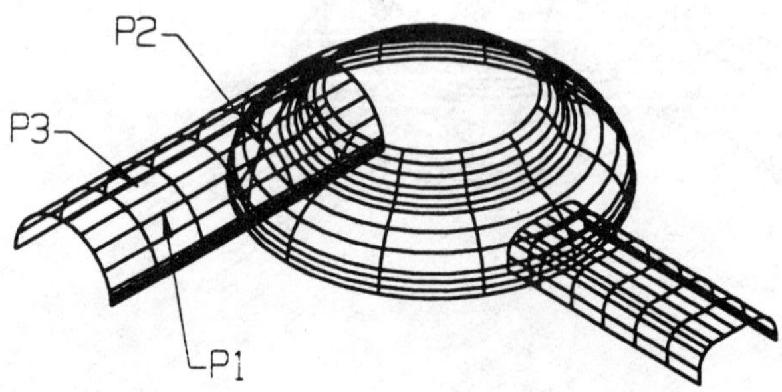

Figure 13.150

Step 10. Trim the tube surface using the pick points in Figure 13.150.

Select **Level**, then enter **6** → OK
Select **Color**, then enter **15** ↵
Select **MAIN MENU → Create → Surface → Trim/extend → To curves**
Pick **P1**, then select **Done** to select the surface to trim
Select **BACKUP,** then set **View/Norm** to **N**
Select **Surf crvs**
Pick **P2**, then select **Done**
Select **Do it**
Pick **P1** to select a surface to be trimmed
Pick **P3** to indicate a location to keep after trimming
The trimmed surface is shown in Figure 13.151.

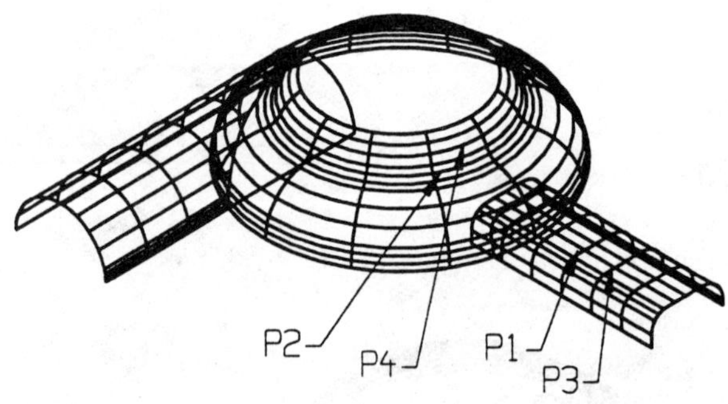

Figure 13.151

Step 11. Trim the handle surface using the pick points in Figure 13.151.

Select **BACKUP → To Surfaces**
Pick **P1**, then select **Done** to select the first set of surfaces
Pick **P2**, then select **Done** to select the second set of surfaces
Select **Options**

Set Trim Surfaces to Surfaces parameters as below

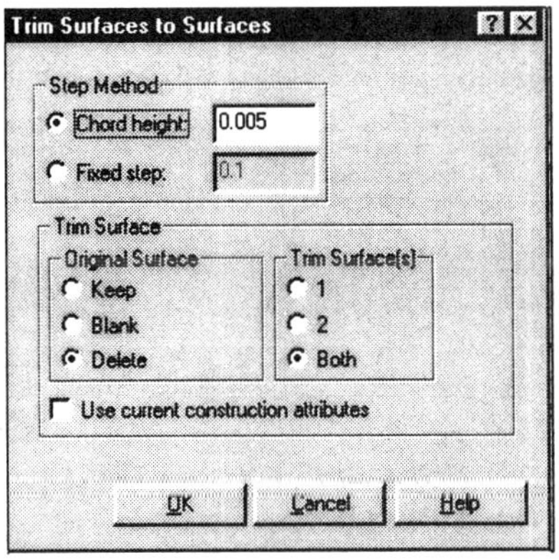

Select **OK** → **Do it**
Pick **P1** to select a surface to be trimmed
Pick **P3** to indicate the portion to keep after trimming
Pick **P2** to select a surface to be trimmed
Pick **P4** to indicate the kept portion after trimming
The trimmed surface should appear as Figure 13.152.

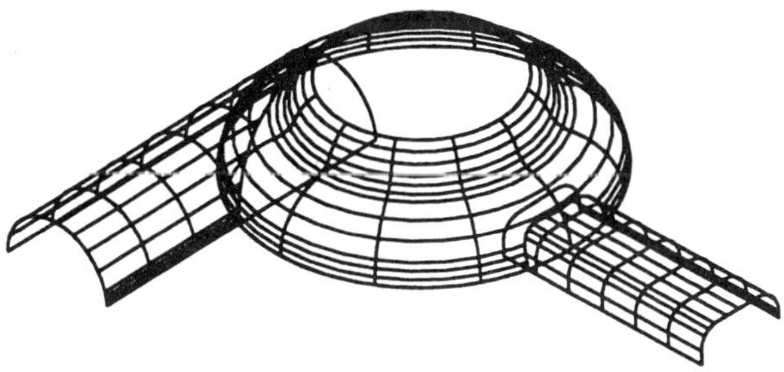

Figure 13.152

Step 12. Change to level 7 and make levels 2 to 6 invisible.

Select **Level**, then enter 7 in the Main Level box
Toggle the checkmarks for levels 2 to 6 invisible (dimmed)
Select **OK** to return to graphic mode

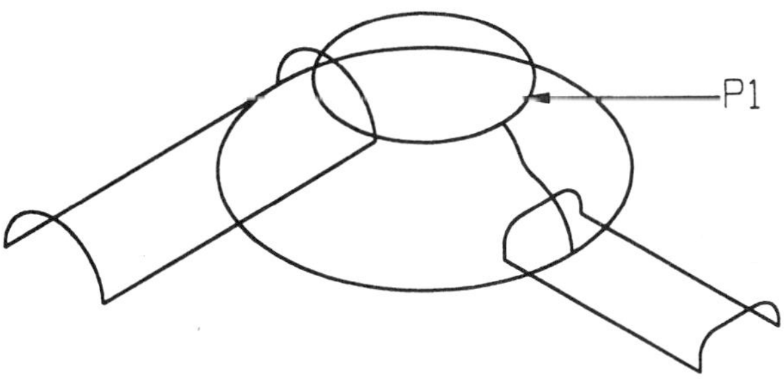

Figure 13.153

Step 13. Add a line to the top of the frame using the pick points in Figure 13.153.

Select **Color**, then enter **12** ↵
Select **Cplane → Top** if necessary
Select **Z → Endpoint**
Pick **P1** to obtain the Z value
Z1.0 should appear in the Secondary menu
Select **MAIN MENU → Create → Line → Endpoints**
Specify the first endpoint: **0, 0**
Specify the second endpoint: select **Endpoint**, then pick **P1**
The line is added to the drawing as shown in Figure 13.154.

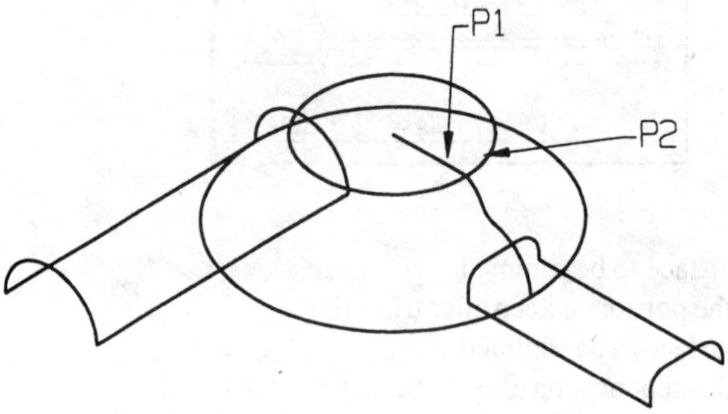

Figure 13.154

Step 14. Create a swept surface on the top frame.

Using the pick points in Figure 13.154.
Select **MAIN MENU → Create → Surface → Sweep**
Select **Single**
Define the across contour: pick **P1**, select **Done**
Define along contour 1: pick **P2**
Select **Done** to complete contour selection
Set the Swept surface parameters to the following settings:

Surface Error tolerance = **0.005** Surface Type = **N (Nurbs)** Trans/Rot = **R**

Select **Do it** to complete the surface
The top swept surface should look like Figure 13.155.

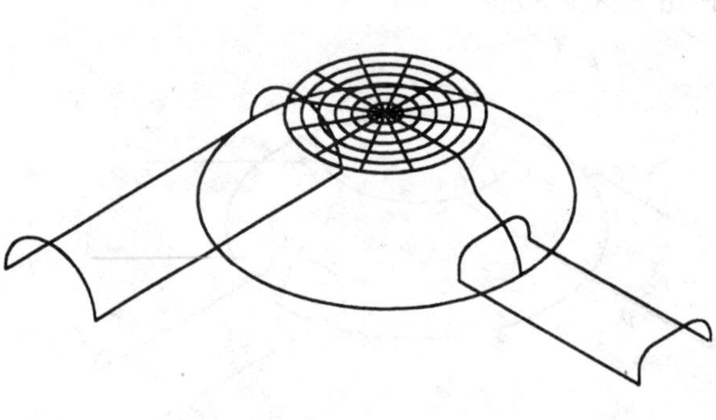

Figure 13.155

Step 15. Make all levels visible, except level 1

Select **Level → All On**
Toggle the check mark in level 1 to invisible
Select **OK** to return to graphic mode
The drawing now appears as Figure 13.156.

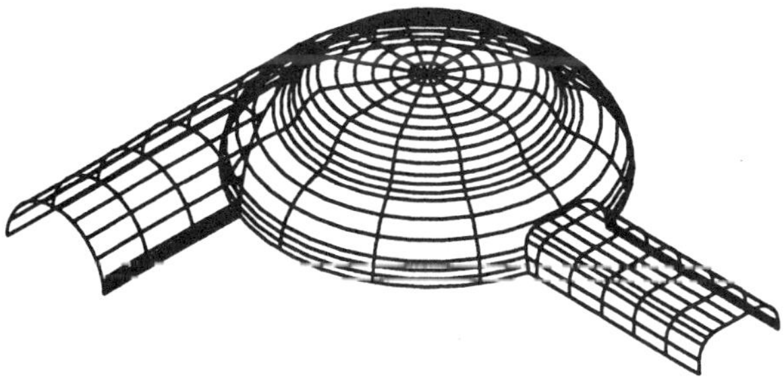

Figure 13.156

Step 16. Save the surface model.

Select **MAIN MENU → File → Save**
Enter file name: **dryers** ↵

Step 17. Mirror the surface model about the X axis.

Use the Front Cplane.
Select **Cplane → Front**
Select **Level**, then enter **8 → OK**
Select **Color**, then enter **13** ↵
Select **MAIN MENU → Xform → Mirror → All → Surfaces → Done → X axis**
Set the Mirror parameters to **Copy**
Select **OK**
The complete surface model should appear as Figure 13.157.

Figure 13.157

Project 11. Fan surface model

This surface model consists of six basic surfaces: one flat surface of the hub, one inner rim surface, one outer rim surface, and three surfaces for the blade. The three surfaces of the blade are copied to six locations to generate the surfaces of the other six blades. The wireframe model and surface model are shown in Figure 13.158a and Figure 13.158b.

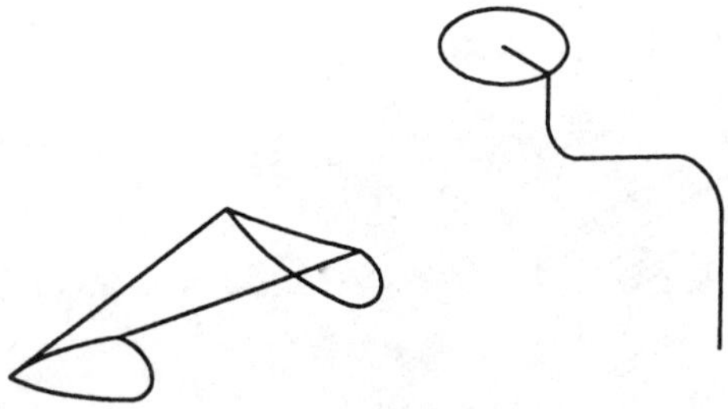

Figure 13.158a Wireframe model

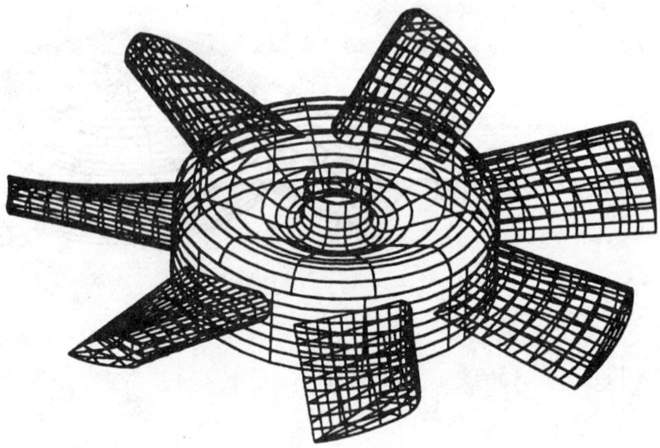

Figure 13.158b Surface model

Tips
1. The hub, rim and outer rim can be modeled as a single surface entity. However, we use three surface entities to model them to facilitate the generation of the toolpath.
2. The flat surface of the hub is created as a swept surface.
3. The inner rim surface of the hub is created as a swept surface. The across contour consists of four entities.
4. The outer rim surface can be modeled as a swept surface.
5. Both top and bottom surfaces of the blade are modeled by Coons surfacing technique. The number of patches in both along direction and across direction is one for both surfaces.
6. The outer end edge surface is modeled by the ruled surfacing technique.
7. Use Xform → Rotate commands to copy the three surfaces of the blade to six locations.
8. Use a different level and color for each surface.

Step 1. Load the wireframe model file (fan).

Select **MAIN MENU → File → Get**
Enter file name: **fan** ↵
The wireframe model of the fan should look like Figure 13.159.

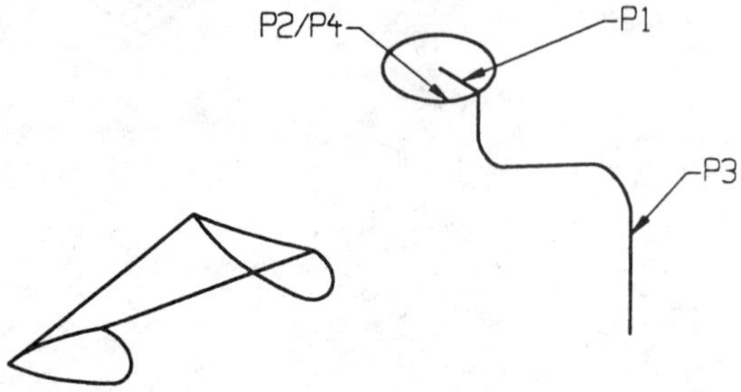

Figure 13.159

Step 2. Create two swept surfaces for the flat surface of the hub and the outer rim surface. 11

Use the pick points in Figure 13.159.
Select **Level,** then enter **6** →**OK**
Select **Color**, then enter **14** ↵
Select **MAIN MENU** → **Create** → **Surface** → **Sweep**
Define the across contour: select **Single**, then pick **P1**, select **Done**
Define along contour 1: pick **P2**
Select **Done** to complete contours selection
Set the Swept surface parameters to the following settings:

Surface Error Tolerance = **0.005** Surface Type = **N (Nurbs)** Trans/Rot = **R**

Select **Do it** to complete the flat surface
Define the across contour: pick **P3**, select **Done**
Define the along contour 1: pick **P4**
Select **Done** → **Do it** to complete the outer rim surface
The flat swept surface and the outer rim surface are shown in Figure 13.160.

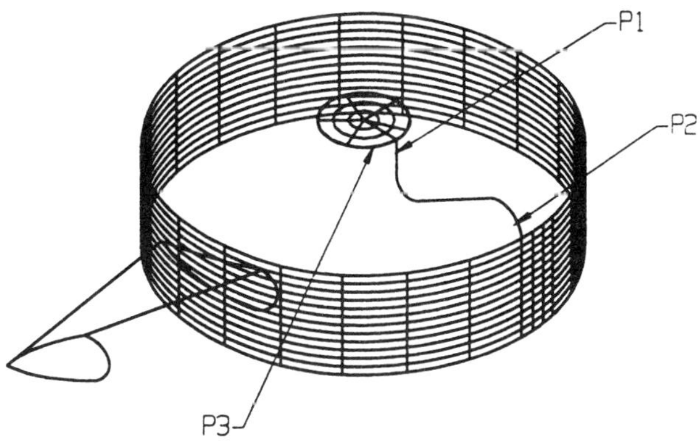

Figure 13.160

Step 3. Create a swept surface for the rim using the pick points in Figure 13.160.

Select **Color,** then enter **15** ↵
Select **BACKUP** → **Sweep**
Define the across contour: select **Chain** → **Partial**, then pick **P1** and **P2**
Select **Done**
Define along contour 1: select **Single**, then pick **P3**
Select **Done** to complete contours selection
Set the Swept surface parameters to the following settings:

Surface Error Tolerance = **0.01** Surface Type = **N (Nurbs)** Trans/Rot = **R**

Select **Do it** to complete the surface

The surface should resemble Figure 13.161.

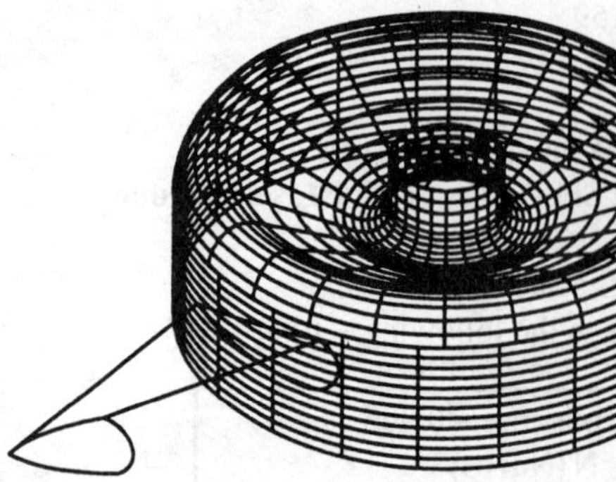

Figure 13.161

Step 4. Change to level 7 and make levels 3 and 6 invisible.

Select **Level,** enter 7 ↵
Toggle levels 3 and 6 to invisible (no checkmark in the Visible column)
Select **OK** to return to graphic mode
The drawing should look like Figure 13.162.

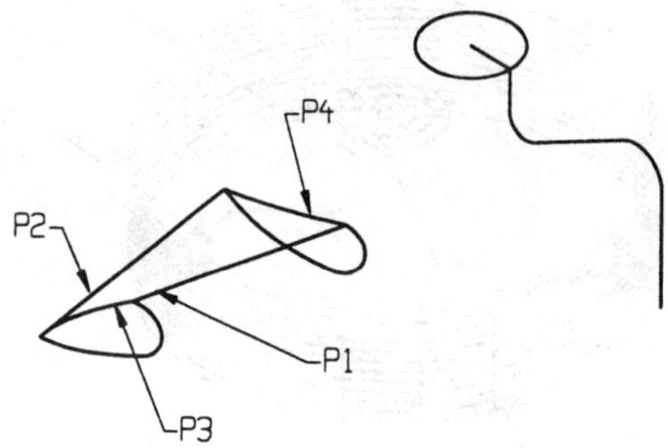

Figure 13.162

Step 5. Create a Coons surface for the top blade face

Use the pick points in Figure 13.162.
Select **Color,** then enter **11** ↵
Select **BACKUP → Coons**
Select **NO** to "Use automatic Coons chaining ?"
Enter number of patches in the along direction: **1** ↵
Enter number of patches in the across direction: **1** ↵
Define along contour 1 of row 1: select **Single**, then pick **P1**
Define along contour 1 of row 2: pick **P2**
Define across contour 1 of column 1: pick **P3**
Define across contour 1 of column 2: pick **P4**
Select **Done** to complete contours selection
Set the Coons surface parameters to the following settings:

Surface Error Tolerance =	**0.01**
Across cut distance =	**N (Nurbs)**
Blending =	**L (Linear)**

Select **Do it** to complete the surface
The surface should resemble Figure 13.163.

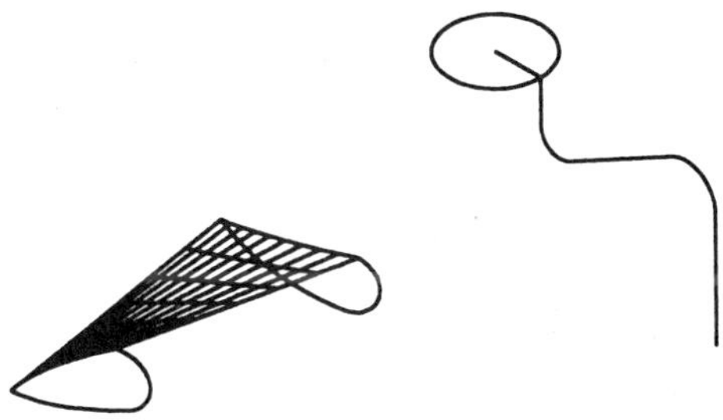

Figure 13.163

Step 6. Change to level 8 and make level 7 invisible.

Select **Level**, then enter **8** in the Main Level box
Toggle level 7 to invisible (no checkmark in the Visible column)
Select **OK** to return to graphic mode
The drawing appears as Figure 13.164.

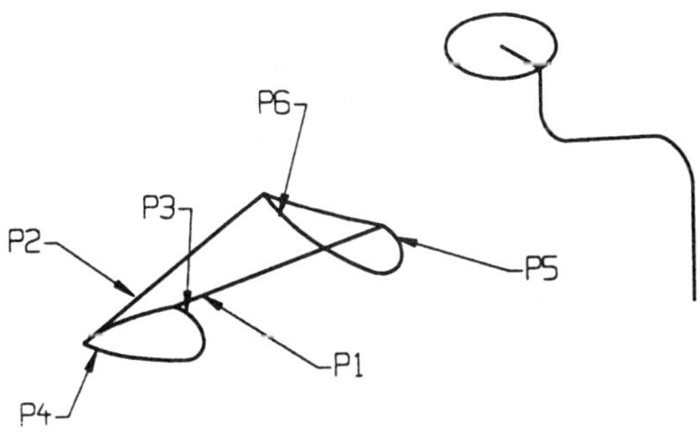

Figure 13.164

Step 7. Create a Coons surface for the bottom blade face.

Use the pick points in Figure 13.164.
Select **Color,** then enter **12** ↵
Select **BACKUP** → **Coons**
Select **NO** to "Use automatic Coons chaining ?"
Enter number of patches in the along direction: **1** ↵
Enter number of patches in the across direction: **1** ↵
Define along contour 1 of row 1: select **Single**, then pick **P1**
Define along contour 1 of row 2: pick **P2**
Define across contour 1 of column 1: select **Mode** → **Chain** → **Partial**
Pick **P3** and **P4**
Define across contour 1 of column 2: select **Partial**, then pick **P5** and **P6**
Select **Done** to complete contours selection
Set the Coons surface parameters to the following settings:

Surface Error Tolerance = **0.005** Surface Type = **N (Nurbs)** Blending = **P (Parabolic)**

Select **Do it** to complete the surface

The bottom Coons surface should appear s Figure 13.165.

Figure 13.165

Step 8. Change to level 9 and make level8 invisible.

Select **Level**, then enter **9** ↵
Toggle level 8 to invisible
Select **OK** to return to graphic mode
The drawing now appears as Figure 13.166.

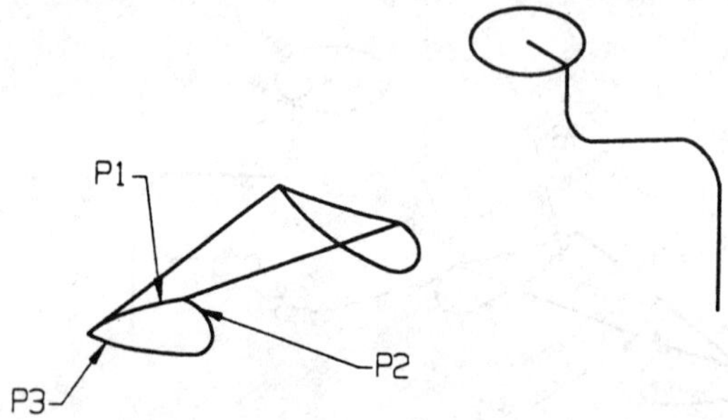

Figure 13.166

Step 9. Create a ruled surface for the outer end edge of the blade.

Use the pick points in Figure 13.166.
Select **Color**, then enter **14** ↵
Select **BACKUP → Ruled → Single**
Define contour 1: pick **P1**
Define contour 2: select **Mode → Chain → Partial**
Pick **P2** and **P3** (Note: the sync mode should be on "None")
Select **Done → Do it** to complete the ruled surface
The end edge surface should look like Figure 13.167.

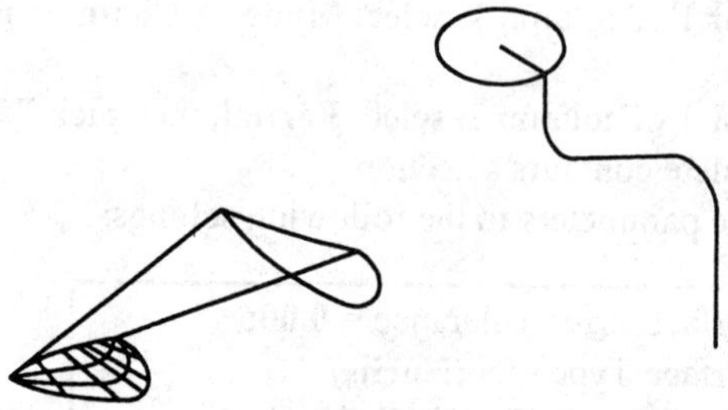

Figure 13.167

Step 10. Make levels 7 and 8 back to visible.

Select **Level**
Toggle levels 7 and 8 to visible (has checkmarks in the Visible Column)
Select **OK** to return to graphic mode
The three blade surfaces should resemble Figure 13.168.

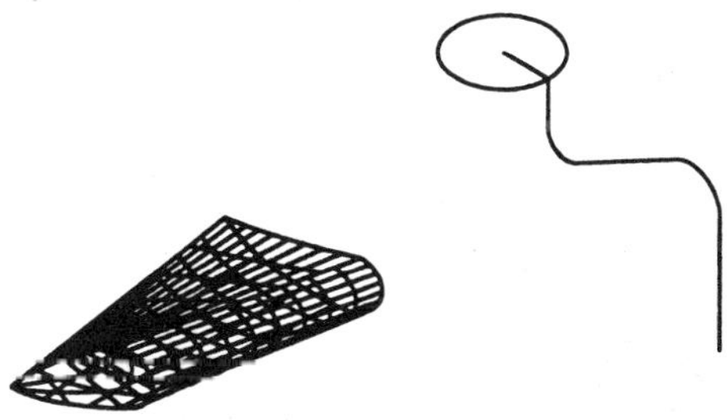

Figure 13.168

Step 11. Copy the blade surfaces to six locations using the Xform → Rotate commands.

Select **Level**, then enter **10 → OK**
Select **Color**, then enter **15 → OK**
Select **MAIN MENU → Xform → Rotate → All → Surfaces → Done → Origin**
Set the Rotate parameters as below:

Copy
Number of Steps = **6**
Rotation angle = **360/7**

Select **OK**
The three surfaces are copied to six locations as shown in Figure 13.169.

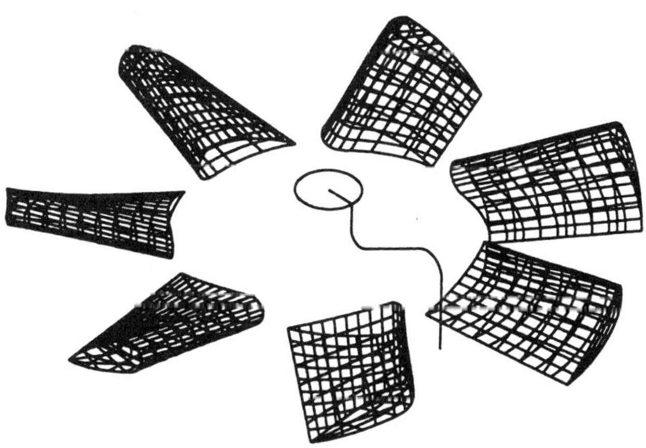

Figure 13.169

Step 12. Make levels 3 and 6 back to visible.

Select **Level**
Toggle levels 3 and 6 to visible (with checkmarks)
Select **OK** to return to graphic mode

The complete surface model should resemble Figure 13.170.

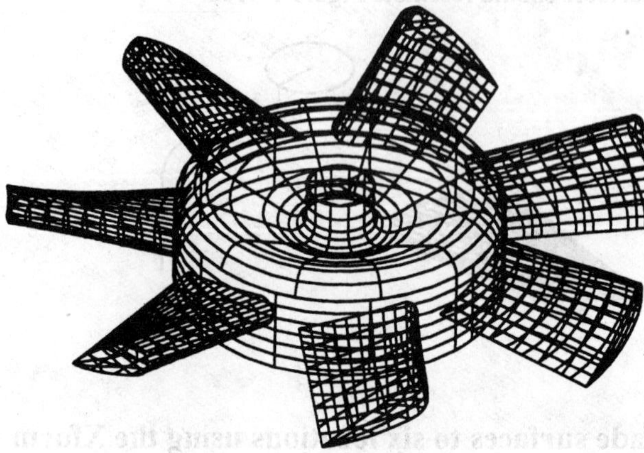

Figure 13.170

Step 13. Save the surface model in a file named fans.

Select **MAIN MENU → File → Save**
Enter file name: **fans**

Project 12. Car wheel hub 12

This example creates a surface model of a car wheel from the wireframe model of project 16 in chapter 11. The wireframe model and the completed surface model are shown in Figure 13.171. This is a rather complicated surface model which consists of many surfaces. The tips given on this page should help to complete the surface model.

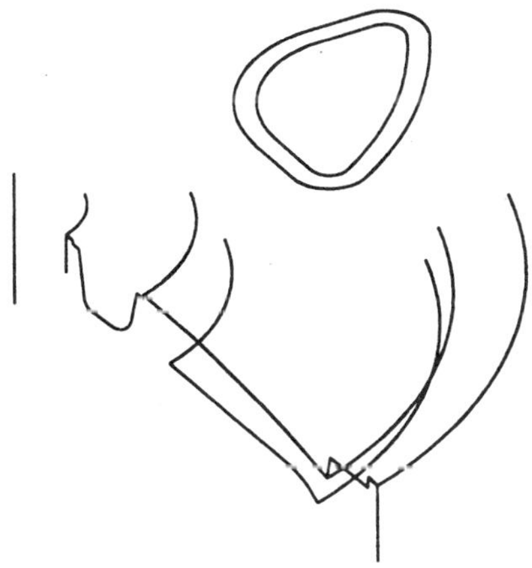

Figure 13.171a Wireframe model

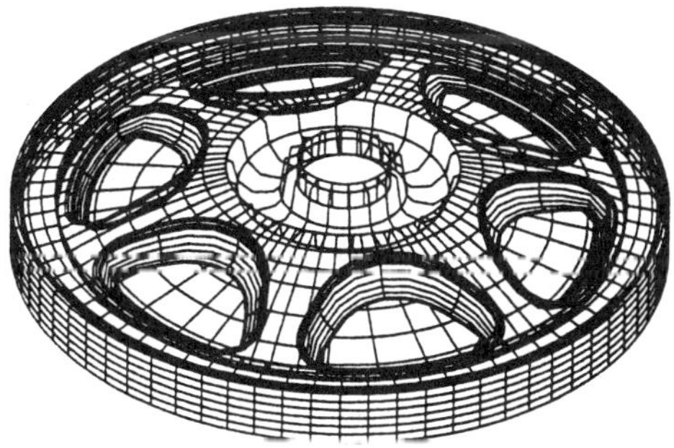

Figure 13.171b Surface model

Tips

1. Create the upper and lower surface using the swept surfacing technique.
2. The outer pocket profile projects onto the upper swept surface to generate a surface curve.
3. The inner pocket profile is projected onto the lower swept surface to generate another surface curve.
4. Create two construction lines for defining a Cplane using the "2 lines" command. This Cplane is used to create an arc as the across contour for the pocket surface.
5. Create the pocket surface using the two surface curves as the two along contours and an arc as the across contour
6. Create a fillet surface between the pocket surface and the upper swept surface.
7. Trim the upper surface to the fillet surface boundary.
8. Trim the lower surface to the pocket surface boundary.
9. Create two swept surfaces, one for the hub and the other for the rim.
10. Create two revolved surfaces, one for the inner hole and the other for the outer profile.
11. Copy all surface to five locations by using Xform → Rotate commands to complete the surface model

Step 1. Load the wireframe model (wheel).

Select **MAIN MENU → File → Get**

Enter file name: **wheel** ↵

The wireframe model drawing should appear as Figure 13.172.

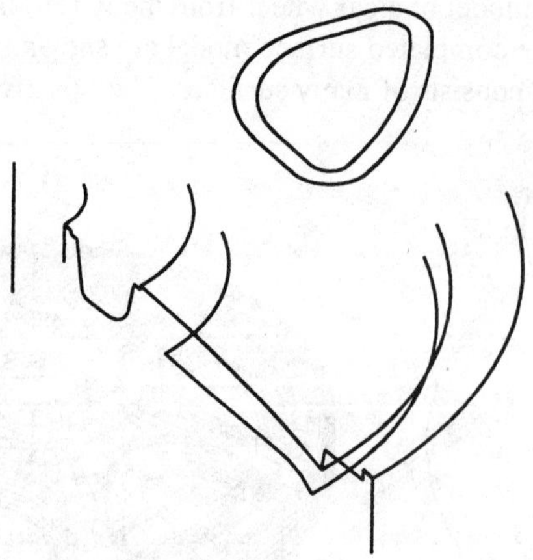

Figure 13.172

Step 2. Make level 2 invisible. Change level to 3 and color 13.

Select **Level**, then enter **3** ↵
Toggle level 2 to invisible (dimmed)
Select **OK** to return to graphic mode
Select **Color, then enter 13** ↵

The drawing should look like Figure 13.173.

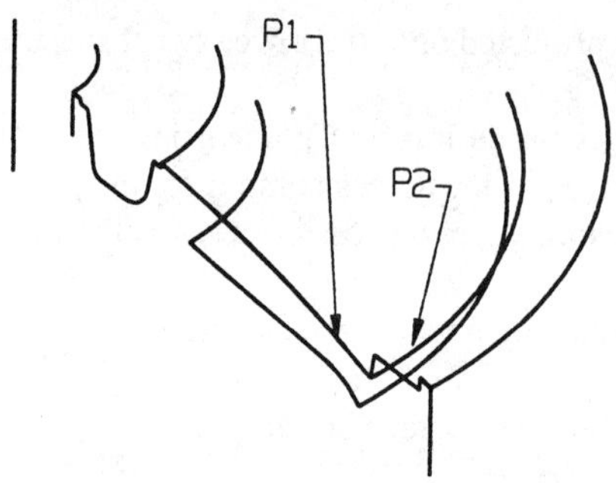

Figure 13.173

Step 3. Create the upper surface using the pick points in Figure 13.173.

Select **MAIN MENU → Create → Surface → Sweep**
Define the across contour : select **Single**, then pick **P1**, select **Done**
Define along contour 1: pick **P2**
Select **Done** to complete contours selection
Set the Swept surface parameters to the following settings:

Surface Error Tolerance =	**0.005**
Surface Type =	**N (Nurbs)**
Trans/Rot =	**R**

Select **Do it**
The surface should appear as Figure 13.174.

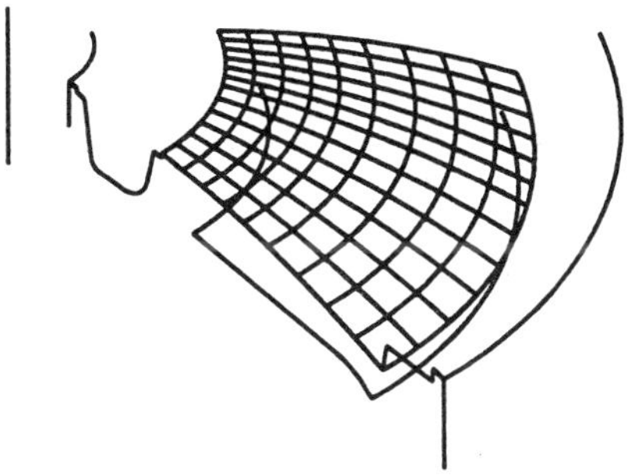

Figure 13.174

Step 4. Make level 3 invisible.

Select **Level**, then enter **4** ↵
Toggle level 3 to invisible (no checkmark in the Visible Column)
Select **OK** to return to graphic mode
Select **Color**, then enter **14** ↵

The drawing becomes Figure 13.175.

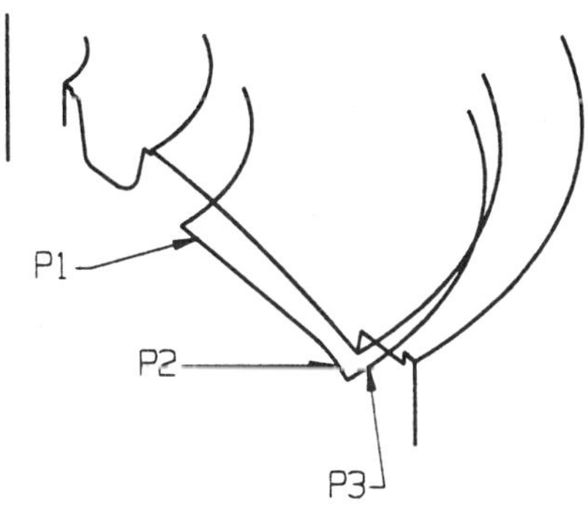

Figure 13.175

Step 5. Create the lower surface using swept surfacing technique.

Use the pick points in Figure 13.175.
Select **BACKUP → Sweep**
Define the across contour: select **Chain → Partial**
Pick **P1** and **P2,** select **Done**
Define along contour 1: select **Single**
Pick **P3**
Select **Done** to complete the contour selection
Select **Do it** to complete the surface

The new created surface should resemble Figure 13.176.

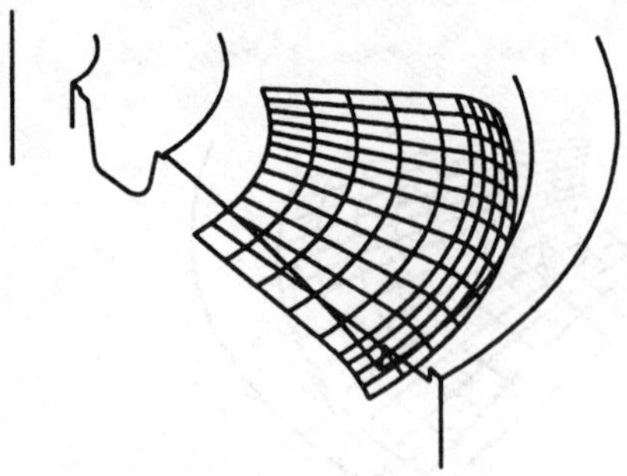

Figure 13.176

Step 6. Make level 2 visible. Change level to 5 and color to 15.

Select **Level**, then enter **5** ↵
Toggle level 2 to visible (has checkmark in the Visible Column)
Select **OK** to return to graphic mode
Select **Color,** then enter **15** ↵
The drawing now should look like Figure 13.177.

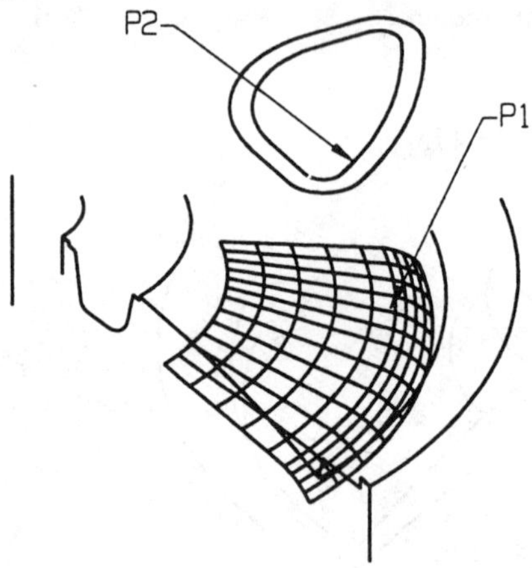

Figure 13.177

Step 7. Project the inner pocket profile to the lower surface to generate a surface curve.

Use the pick points in Figure 13.177.
Select **MAIN MENU → Create → Curve → Project**
Pick **P1** to select the surface
Select **Done**
Select **Chain,** then pick **P2**
Select **Done**
Toggle View/Norm to **V**
Select **Options**
Set the Project Curve parameters as shown here:

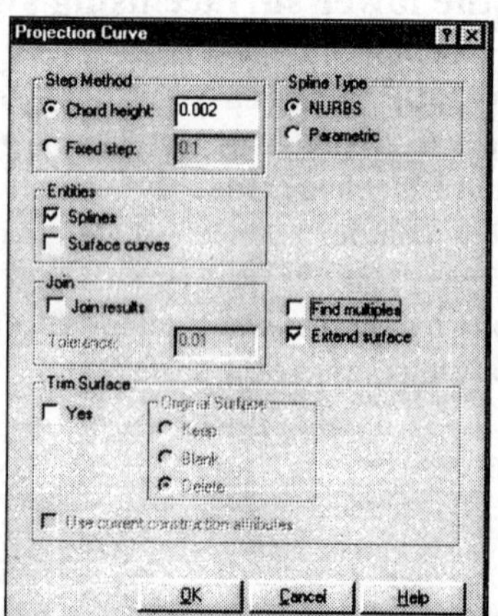

Select **OK → Do it**

The first surface curve should appear as in Figure 13.178.

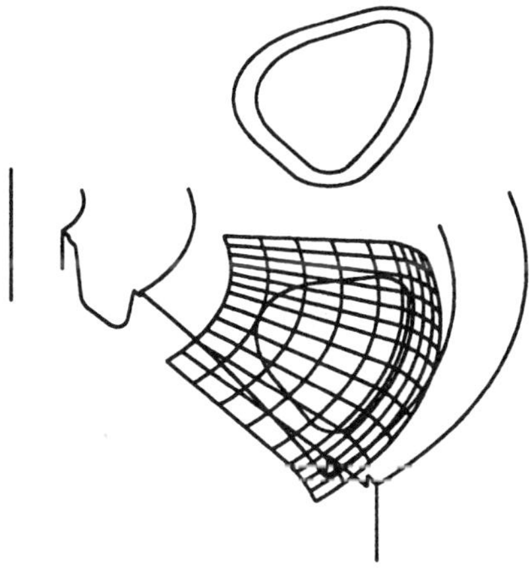

Figure 13.178

Step 8. Make level 4 invisible and level 3 visible.

Select **Level**
Toggle level 4 to invisible (no checkmark) and level 3 to visible (has a checkmark)
Select **OK** to return to graphic mode
The drawing now should look like Figure 13.179.

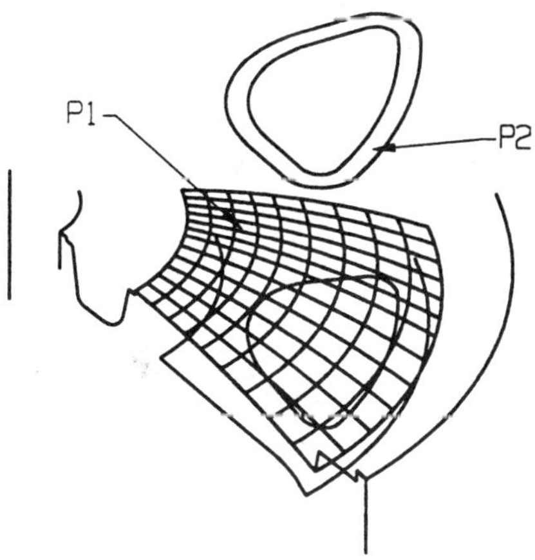

Figure 13.179

Step 9. Project the outer pocket profile to the supper surface to generate the second surface curve.

Use the pick points in Figure 13.179.
Select **BACKUP → Project**
Pick **P1** to select the surface → **DONE**
Select **Chain**, then pick **P2**
Select **Done → Do it**

The second surface curve is added as shown in Figure 13.180.

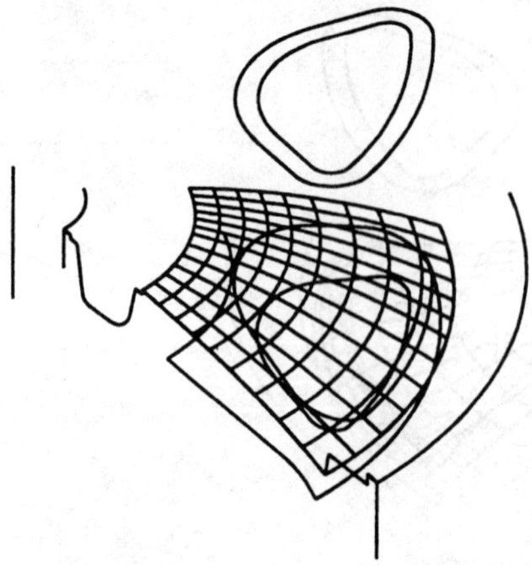

Figure 13.180

Step 10. Make levels 1,2 and 3 invisible.

Select **Level**
Toggle levels 1, 2 and 3 to invisible (no check marks)
Select **OK** to return to graphic mode

The drawing appears on the screen should now become Figure 13.181.

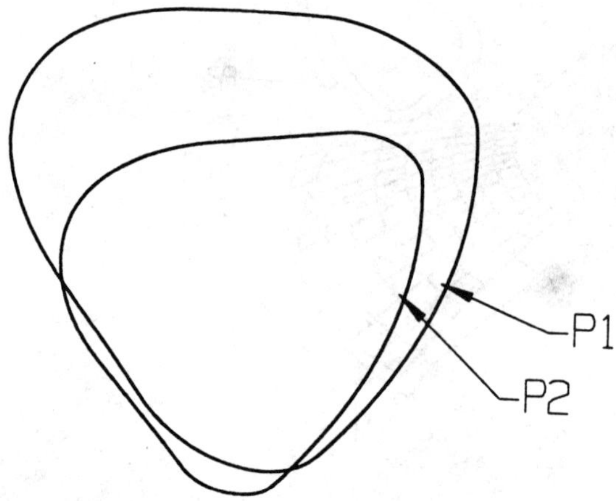

Figure 13.181

Step 11. Create a construction line using the pick points in Figure 13.181.

Select **Cplane → 3D**
Select **MAIN MENU → Create → Line → Endpoints → Midpoint**
Pick **P1**
Select **Midpoint**, then pick **P2**

The line is added as shown in Figure 13.182.

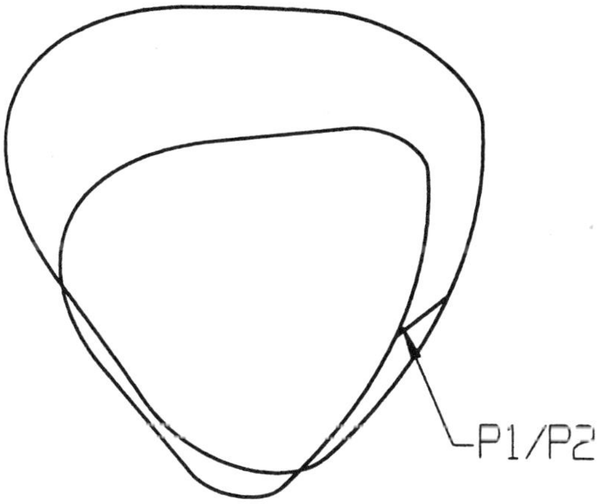

Figure 13.182

Step 12. Create another construction line using the pick points marked in Figure 13.182.

Select **Cplane** → **Top**
Select **Z** → **Endpoint**, then pick **P1**
(A value of approximately Z 0.5561 should appear in the Secondary menu)
Select **MAIN MENU** → **Create** → **Line** → **Endpoints** → **Endpoint**
Specify the first point: pick **P2**
Specify the second point: **0,0**

The drawing should appear as Figure 13.183.

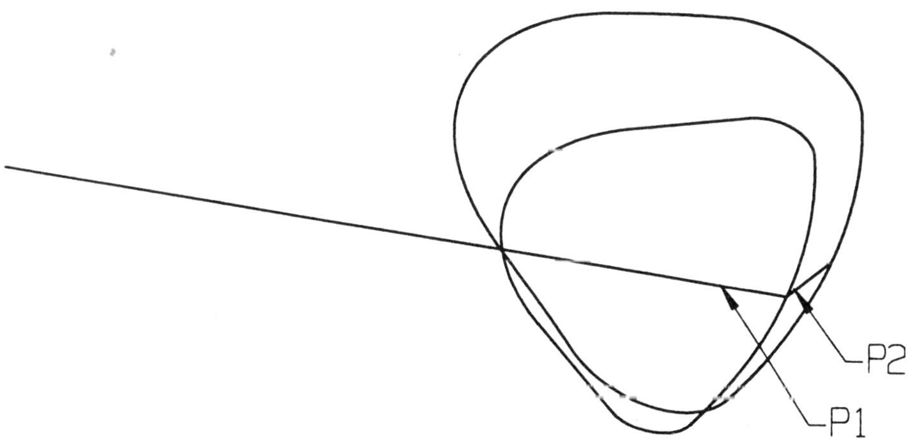

Figure 13.183

Step 13. Use the two construction lines to define a Cplane.

Use the pick points labeled in Figure 13.183.
Select **Cplane** → **Entity** → **Only** → **Lines**
Pick **P1** and **P2** to select the two lines
Select **Save** to accept the new Cplane

The drawing should look like Figure 13.184. (Note: the same as Figure 13.183).

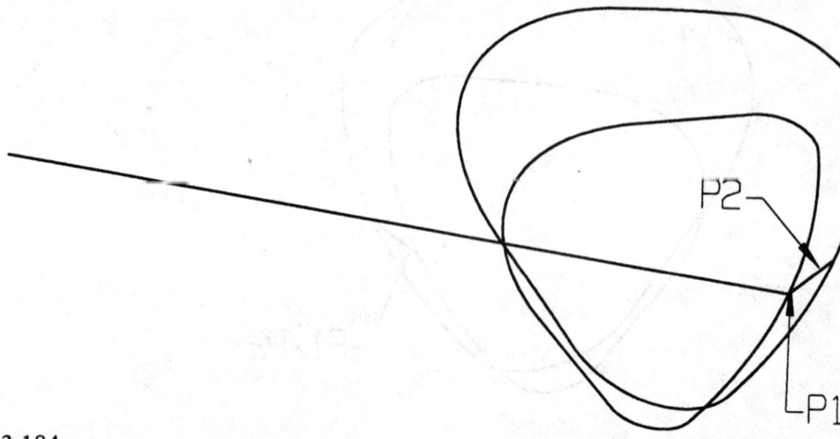

Figure 13.184

Step 14. Create an arc between two surface curves.

Use the pick points in Figure 13.184.
Select **MAIN MENU → Create → Arc → Endpoints → Endpoint**
Pick **P1** and **P2**
Enter the radius: **0.25 ↵**
Pick the desired arc (2nd arc from right)

The arc is added as shown in Figure 13.185.

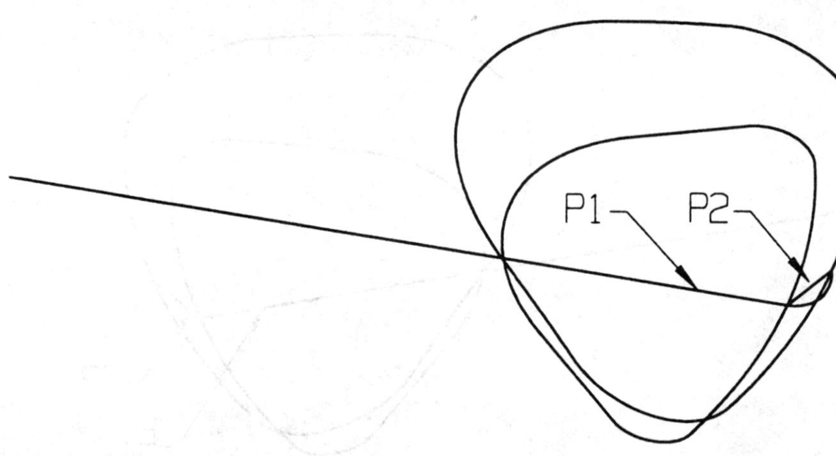

Figure 13.185

Step 15. Delete two construction lines using the pick points in Figure 13.185.

Select **MAIN MENU → Delete**
Pick **P1** and **P2**

The drawing now should resemble Figure 13.186.

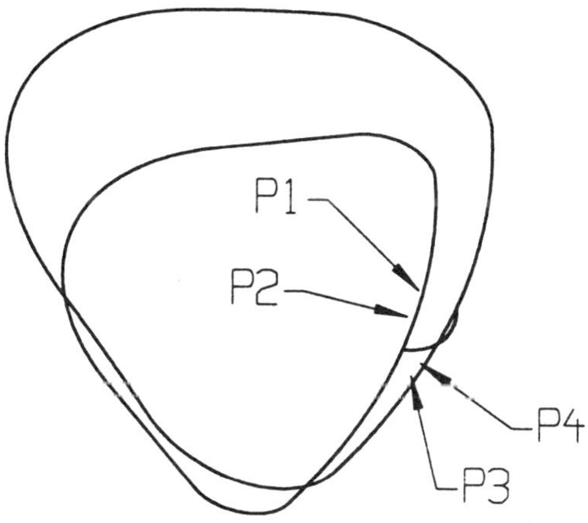

Figure 13.186

Step 16. Break two arcs into two pieces using the pick points in Figure 13.186.

Select **Cplane → Top**
Select **MAIN MENU → Modify → Break → 2 pieces**
Pick **P1** to select an entity
Select **Midpoint,** then pick **P2** to break the entity
Pick **P3** to select another entity
Select **Midpoint,** then pick **P4** to break the entity

The drawing should appear on the screen as Figure 13.187.

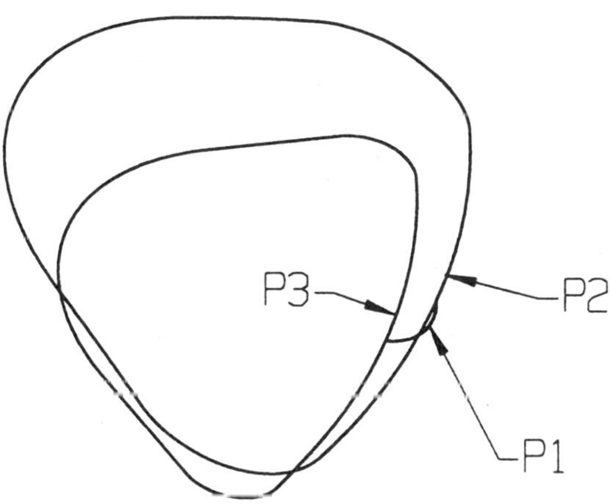

Figure 13.187

Step 17. Create the pocket surface by sweeping the arc along two surface curves.

Use the pick points in Figure 13.187.
Select **Color,** then enter **14** ↵
Select **MAIN MENU → Create → Surface → Sweep**
Define the across contour: select **Single**, then pick **P1**
Select **Done**

Define along contour 1: select **Chain** then pick **P2**
Define along contour 2: pick **P3**
Set the Swept surface parameters to the following settings:

Surface Error Tolerance = **0.005** Surface Type = **N (Nurbs)**

Select **Do it** to complete the surface
The pocket surface should look like Figure 13.188.

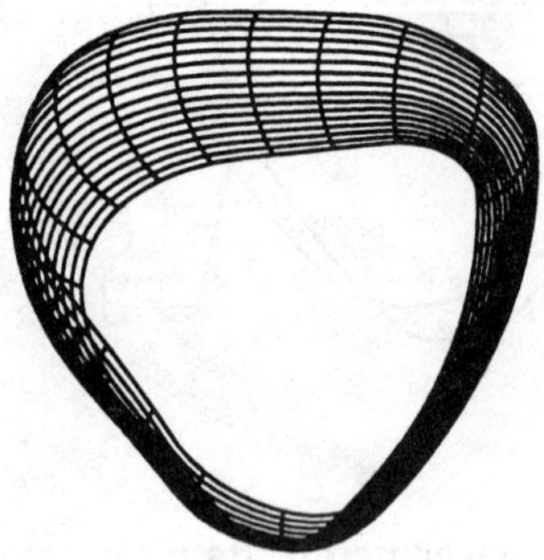

Figure 13.188

Step 18. Make level 3 visible.

Select **Level**
Toggle level 3 to visible
Select **OK** to return to graphic mode
The drawing now becomes Figure 13.189.

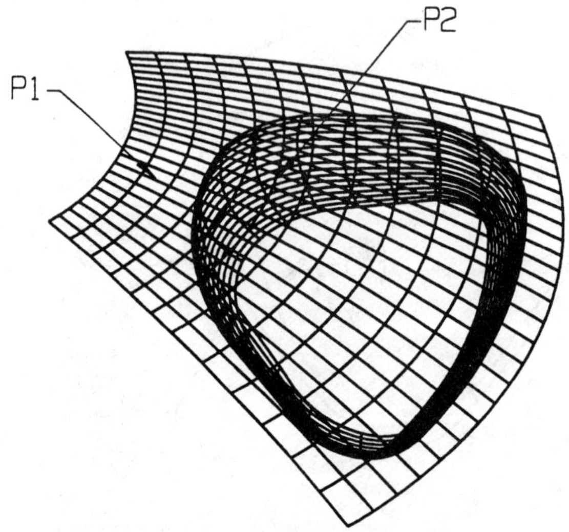

Figure 13.189

Step 19. Change the normal direction of the upper surface and the pocket surface

Use the pick points in Figure 13.189.
Select **MAIN MENU → Modify → Normal → Dynamic**
Pick **P1** and click the mouse to locate the arrow
Select **Flip** (the arrow should point downward)
Select **OK** to the normal direction for the upper surface

Pick **P2** to select the pocket surface and click the mouse to locate the arrow (the arrow should point outward), if necessary
Select **OK** for the normal direction for the pocket surface
The drawing is redisplayed in Figure 13.190.

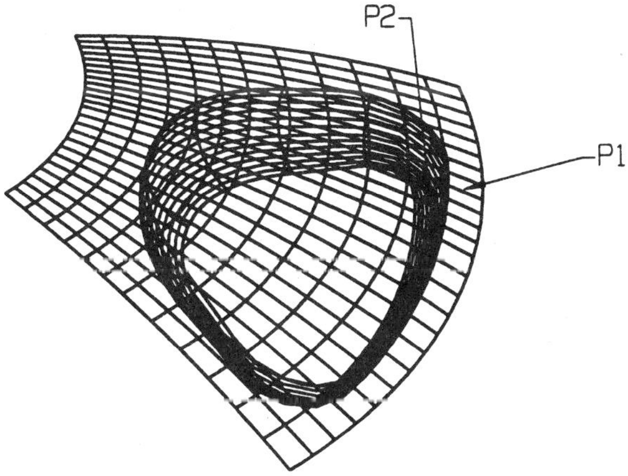

Figure 13.190

Step 20. Create a fillet surface between the upper surface and the pocket surface.

Use the pick points in Figure 13.190.
Select **Level**, then enter **6** in the Main level box → **OK**
Select **Color**, then enter **11**↵
Select **MAIN MENU** → **Create** → **Surface** → **Fillet** → **Surf/surf**
Pick **P1** on the upper surface, then select **Done** for 1st set of surfaces
Pick **P2** to select the pocket surface, then select **Done** for 2nd set of surfaces
Enter the radius = **0.1** ↵
Select **Options**
Set Surface-surface fillet parameters as shown here:

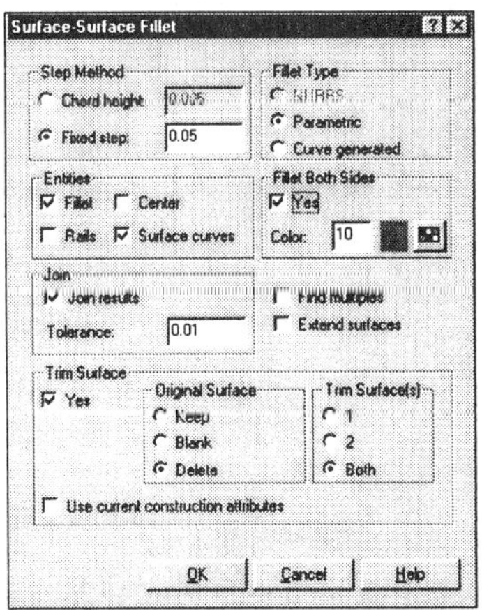

Select **OK** → **Do it**

The fillet surface should appear as Figure 13.191.

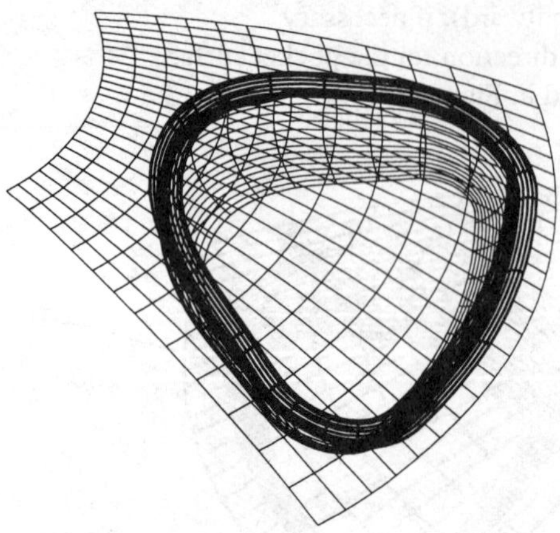

Figure 13.191

Step 21. Make only levels 4 and 5 visible.

Select **Color,** then **12** ↵
Select **Level**, then enter **7** ↵
Toggle levels 4 and 5 to visible
Note: levels 1, 2, 3 and 6 are not visible
The new drawing becomes Figure 13.192.

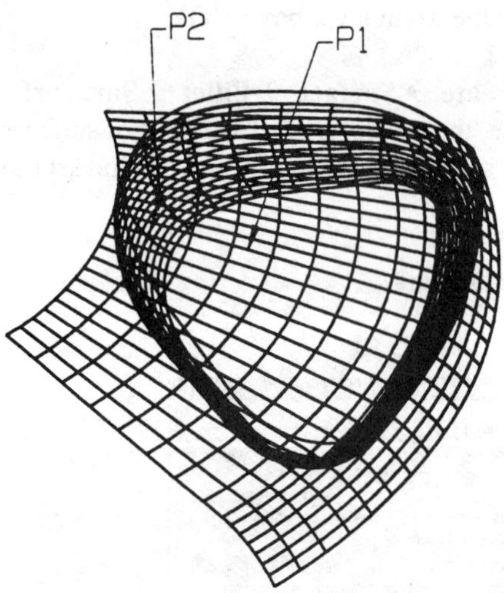

Figure 13.192

Step 22. Add a fillet surface between the lower surface and the pocket surface.

Use the pick points in Figure 13.192.
Select **MAIN MENU → Create → Surface → Fillet → Surf/surf**
Pick **P1** to select the lower surface
Select **Done**
Pick **P2** to select the pocket surface
Select **Done**
Enter radius = **0.15** ↵
Set **Trim** to **Y**
Select **Do it**
Note: Turn off "Yes" for the fillet both sides in the option menu

The fillet surface is added and the lower surface is trimmed in Figure 13.193.

Figure 13.193

Step 23. Make levels 5, 6 and 7 to visible to show trimmed surfaces.

Select **Level**
Toggle levels 3, 4, 5, 6 and 7 to visible (has checkmark)
Note: levels 1 and 2 are invisible
Select **OK** to return to graphic mode
The new drawing should resemble Figure 13.194.

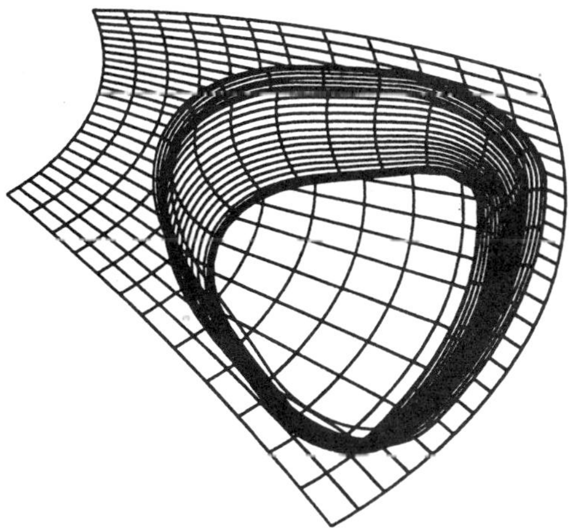

Figure 13.194

Step 24. Make only level 1 visible.

Select **Level**, then enter **8** in the Main Level box
Toggle level **1** to visible (levels 2-7 are invisible)
Select **OK** to return to graphic mode
The drawing should look like Figure 13.195.

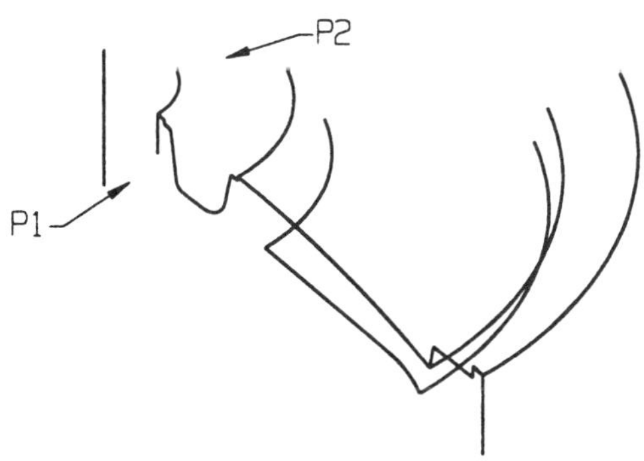

Figure 13.195

Step 25. Zoom the section profile for the hub.

Use the pick points in Figure 13.195.
Press **F1** to select the Z command
Pick **P1** and **P2** to zoom the hub profile

The zoomed drawing should appear as Figure 13.196.

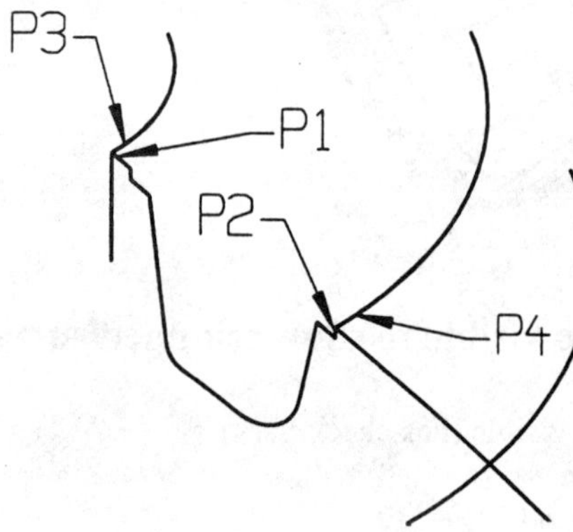

Figure 13.196

Step 26. Create a swept surface for the hub using the pick points in Figure 13.196.

Select **Color**, then enter **14** ↵
Select **MAIN MENU → Create → Surface → Sweep**
Define the across contour: select **Chain → Partial**
Pick **P1** and **P2,** select **Done**
Define along contour 1: select **Single**, then pick **P3**
Define along contour 2: pick **P4**
Set the Swept surface parameters as below

Surface Error Tolerance =	**0.002**
Surface Type =	**N (Nurbs)**

Select **Do it** to complete the surface
Press **Enter** to ignore the shape corners
Press **Alt+F1** to fit the drawing
The new hub surface should look like Figure 13.197.

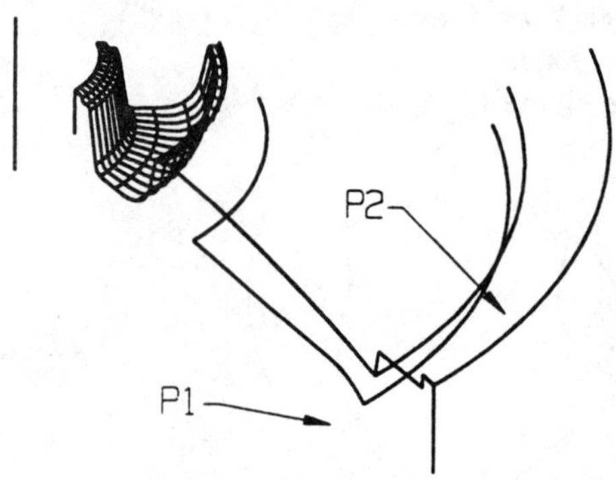

Figure 13.197

Step 27. Zoom the rim profile using the pick points in Figure 13.197.

Press **F1** to select the Zoom command
Pick **P1** and **P2** to define the zoom area
The zoomed drawing should resemble Figure 13.198.

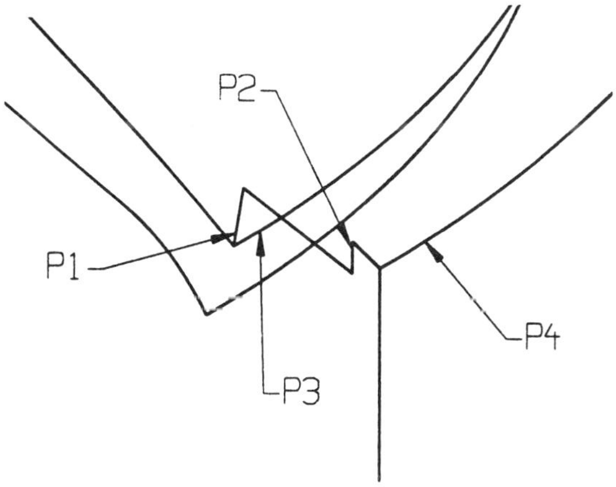

Figure 13.198

Step 28. Create a swept surface for the rim using the pick points in Figure 13.198.

Select **Sweep**
Define the across contour: select **Chain → Partial**
Pick **P1** and **P2,** select **Done**
Define along contour 1: select **Single**, then pick **P3**
Define along contour 2: pick **P4**
Select **Done → Do it**
Press **Enter** to ignore sharp corners
Press **Alt+F1** to fit the drawing
The rim surface should appear as Figure 13.199.

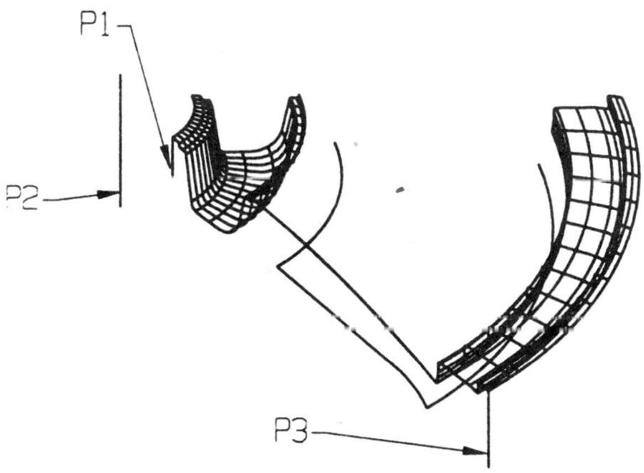

Figure 13.199

Step 29. Create two revolved surfaces using the pick points in Figure 13.199.

Select **Level**, then enter **9 → OK**
Select **Color**, then enter **15** ↵
Select **BACKUP → Revolve**
Select the profile entities: select **Single**, then pick **P1 → Done**

Select the axis of rotation: pick **P2**
Enter the **Starting angle: 0** ↵
Enter the **End angle: 60** to complete the first surface
Select **Do it**
Select **BACKUP → Revolve**
Select the profile entities: select **Single**, then pick **P3**
Select **Done**

Select the axis of rotation: pick **P2**
Enter the **Starting angle: 0** ↵
Enter the **End angle: 60**
Select **Do it** to complete the second surface
The two surfaces should resemble Figure 13.200.

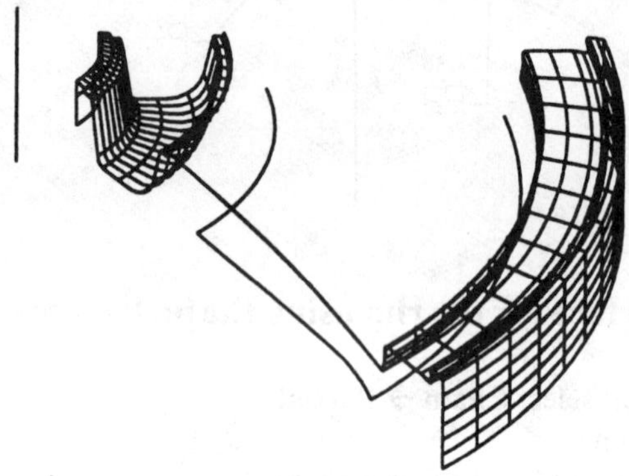

Figure 13.200

Step 30. Make levels 3 through 9 visible.

Select **Level**
Toggle levels 3-9 to visible
Select **OK** to return to graphic mode
The complete sectional surfaces should look like Figure 13.201.

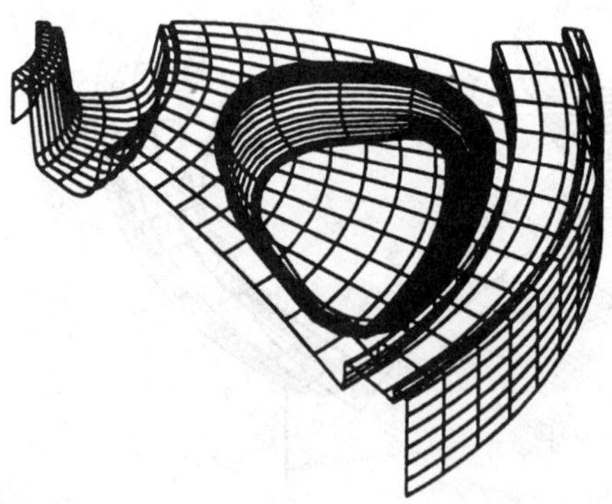

Figure 13.201

Step 31. Save the surface file wheel.

Select **MAIN MENU → File → Save**
Enter file name: **wheel**

Step 32. Copy the surfaces to five locations using Xform → Rotate commands.

Select **MAIN MENU → Xform → Rotate → All → Surfaces → Done → Origin**
Set the Rotate parameters as below:

Copy
Number of steps = **5**
Rotation angle = **60**

Select **OK** to complete the surface model
The final drawing should resemble Figure 13.202.

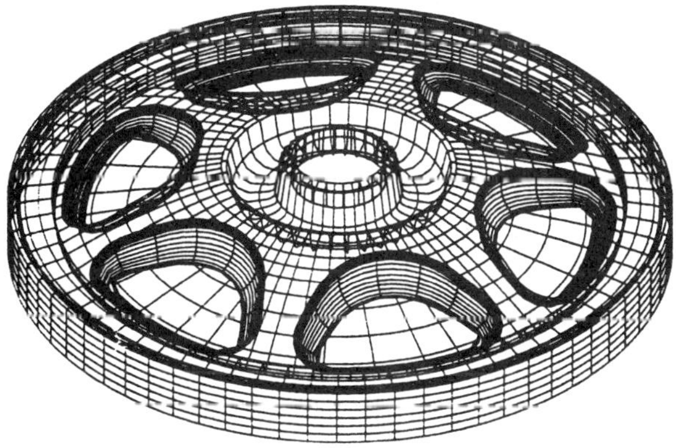

Figure 13.202

Ex Exercises

1. What are derived surfaces ?
2. What are the three derived surface modeling techniques available in Mastercam ?
3. Explain when to use fillet surfaces ?
4. What are the two types of fillet surfaces ?
5. What are the six patterns of variable radius fillet surfaces ?
6. List the two stepping methods for specifying the stepping distance of the surface.
7. What are the three types of information to be generated during the generating of a fillet surface ?
8. What is a trimmed surface ?
9. Under what conditions does surface trimming require you to redefine the outer boundary ?
10. What is an offset surface ?
11. What are composite surface models ?

Problems

12. Create two fillet surface from the surface model created in problem 12.17. The original surface model file is **ES1**. Save the fillet surface model as **ES14**. The two fillet surfaces have a constant radius of 0.25". The fillet surfaces with the base surfaces are shown in Figure 13.203. A similar example is project 1 of this chapter.

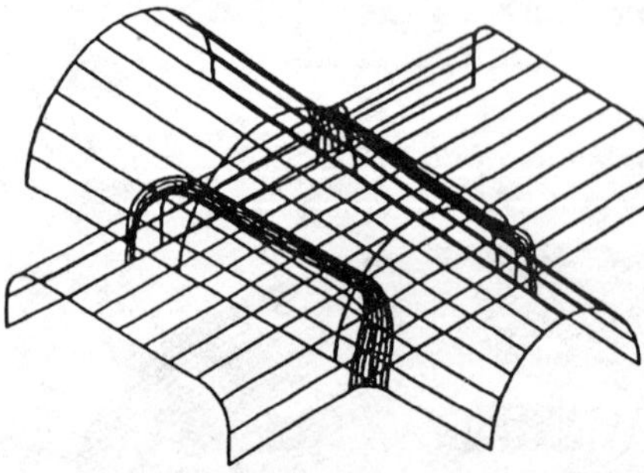

Figure 13.203.

13. Create a fillet surface at the intersection of two ruled surfaces created in problem 12.18. The radius of the fillet surface varies in a linear pattern, which starts at 0.5" at the right end to 0.35" at the other end. The fillet surface with the two base surfaces are shown in Figure 13.204. The original surface model file is **ES2**. Save the fillet surface model **ES15**. A similar example is project 2 in this chapter.

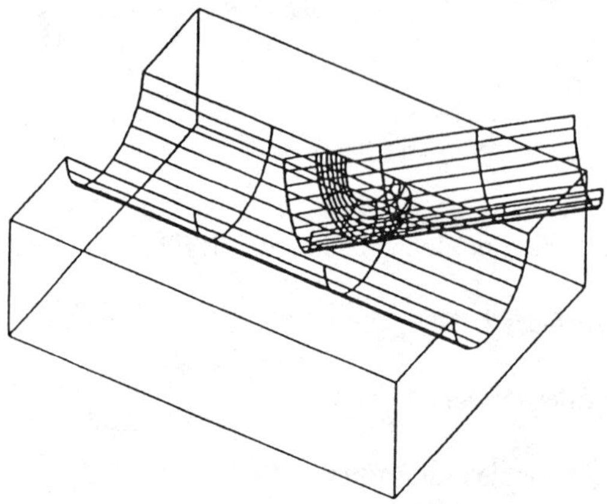

Figure 13.204

14. Create two trimmed surfaces from the surface model created in problem 12.17. The original surface model is **ES1**. Two surface curves should be created at the intersection between two ruled surfaces. These two surface curves are then used as the trimming boundary to trim two ruled surfaces. The trimmed surfaces are shown in Figure 13.205. Save the trimmed surfaces as **ES16**. A similar example is project 3 of this chapter.

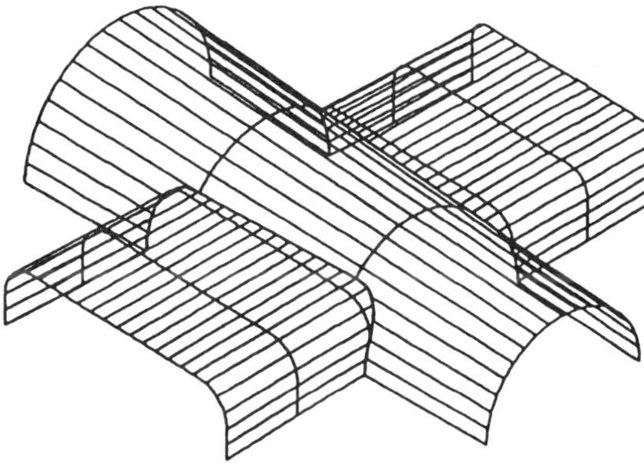

Figure 13.205

15. Create two trimmed surfaces from the surface model created in problem 13 of this chapter. The surface curves of the fillet surface are used as the trimming boundary. The base surface model file is **ES15**. Save the trimmed surfaces as **ES17**. The trimmed surfaces should look like Figure 13.206. A similar example is project 4 in this chapter.

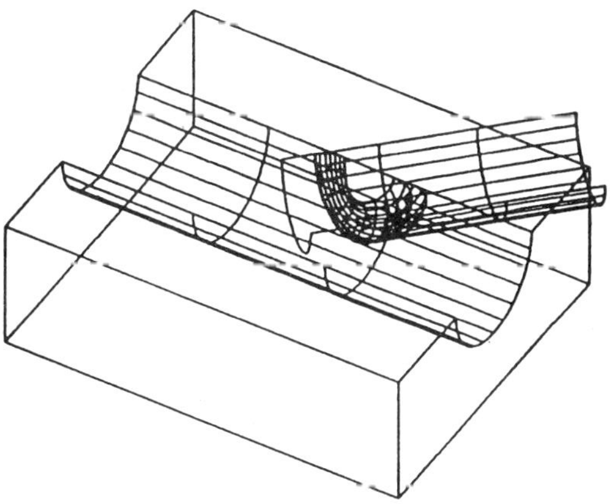

Figure 13.206

16. Generate an offset surface from the surface model created in problem 12.21. The original surface model file is **ES5**. The Coons surface is offset by 0.375" in the outward direction. The offset surface should resemble Figure 13.207. Save the offset surface as **ES18**. A similar example is project 6 of this chapter.

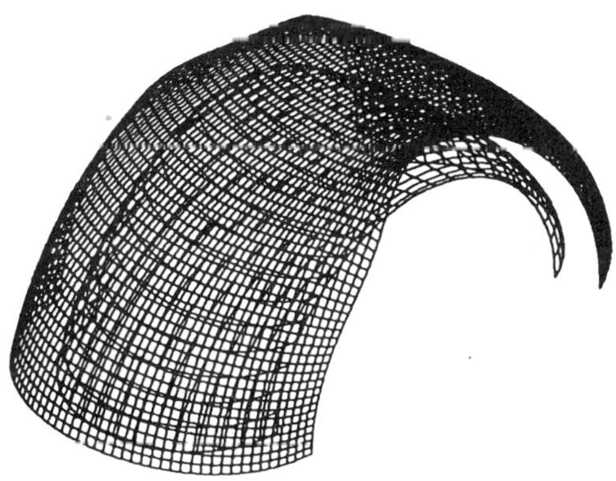

Figure 13.207

17. Create a composite surface model from the wireframe model given in problem 11.20. The wireframe model file is **E11**. The surface model consists of four surfaces: a ruled surface at the bottom, a swept surface for wall and top rim, and a fillet surface between the two surfaces as shown in Figure 13.208. Save the surface model as **ES19**. A similar example is project 7 in this chapter.

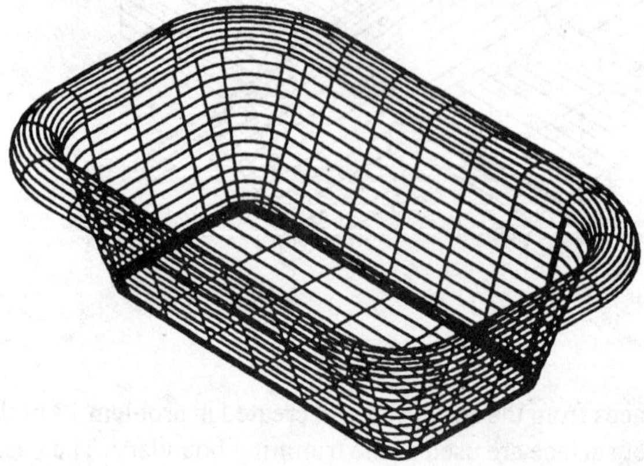

Figure 13.208

18. Create a composite surface model from the wireframe model given in problem 11.21. The wireframe model file is **E12**. This surface model consists of four surfaces including one swept surface on the top, one swept surface of the middle frame, and four ruled surfaces for the handles. Save the surface model file as **ES20**. The surface model should look like Figure 13.209. A similar example is project 9 in this chapter.

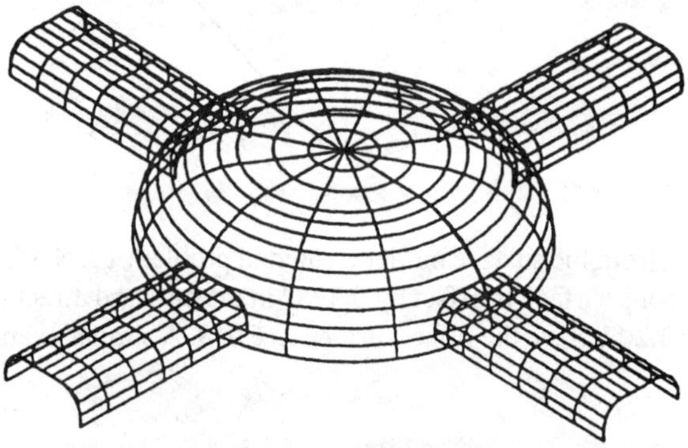

Figure 13.209

Chapter 14

3D Toolpaths I:Generated from Wireframe Models

Objectives:

1.Know two methods of generating toolpaths to cut surfaces.
2. Understand 3-d toolpath common parameters.
3. Know 3-d toolpath modules used to generate toolpaths from wireframe models.
4. Apply 3-d toolpath modules.

14.1 Two Surface Toolpath Generation Methods

Mastercam provides **two** methods to generate toolpaths for machining various forms of surfaces: wireframe and surface. Using the wireframe method, the wireframe model is used in a 3-d toolpath module to generate the toolpaths which machine the surface. However, the surface method takes an extra step to generate the surfacing toolpaths. The wireframe model is used to create the surface model first, then this surface model is used to generate the toolpaths by the various surfacing toolpath modules. Figure 14.1 shows a flow chart of these two methods of generating toolpaths for machining surfaces.

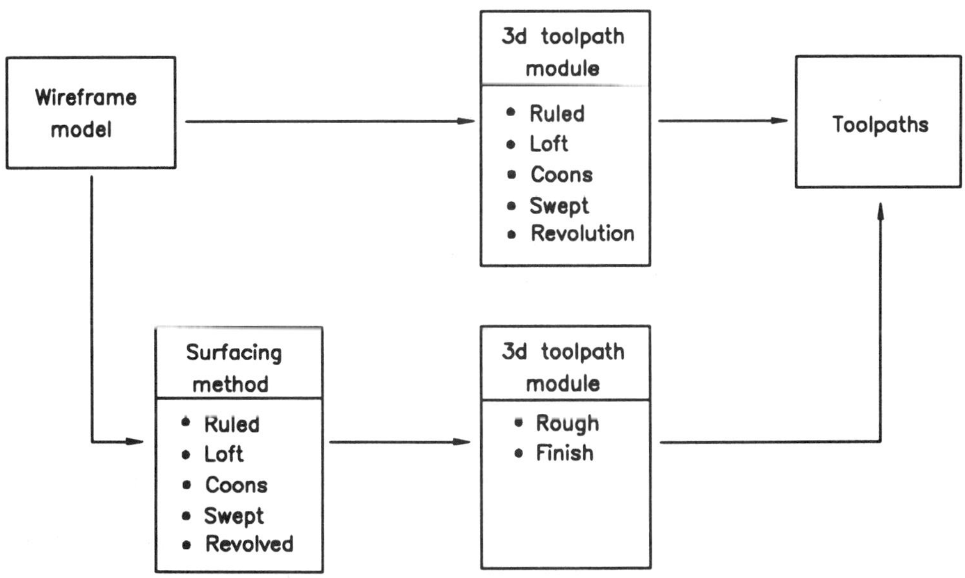

Figure 14.1

At the first glance, the wireframe method seems more straight forward and easy to use. However, we recommend using the surface method except for machining very simple surfaces. The reasons are elaborated in Table 14.1 which compares the two methods of generating surfacing toolpaths.

Table 14.1 Comparing two methods of generating 3-d surfacing toolpaths

Method	Advantages	Disadvantages
Wireframe method	1. Do not require creating a surface before generating toolpaths.	1. Can generate toolpaths for only a single surface. 2. Do not give the surface skin before toolpaths are created. 3. No surface model to be analyzed before generating toolpaths. 4. Required to define more parameters.
Surface method	1. Can generate toolpaths for multiple surfaces simultaneously. 2. Has the surface to be analyzed, examined, and edited before generating toolpaths. 3. Fewer parameters to define. 4. More flexible and easier to be edited.	1. Require an existing surface model to generate the toolpaths.

The wireframe method in generating surfacing toolpaths is presented in this chapter and the surface method is in chapter 15.

14.2 3D Toolpaths Common Parameters

As indicated in chapter 7, Mastercam uses two groups of parameters, common and module specific, to define machining and tooling data. Most common parameters presented in chapter 7 are applicable to 3-d cases. However, a number of additional parameters should be added for 3-d toolpath modules including; *along* and *across*, cutting method, stepping over distances (along cut distance, across cut distance), cutting direction, and cutter compensation.

Along and Across

Surfaces are defined by a series of joined or non-connected contours. These contours are arranged into two groups, along and across, according to their orientations. In other words, along and across are used to indicate the direction of a group of contours (Figure 14.2). Normally, the *along* direction follows the longer contours of the two directions. The *across* direction is the shorter contours.

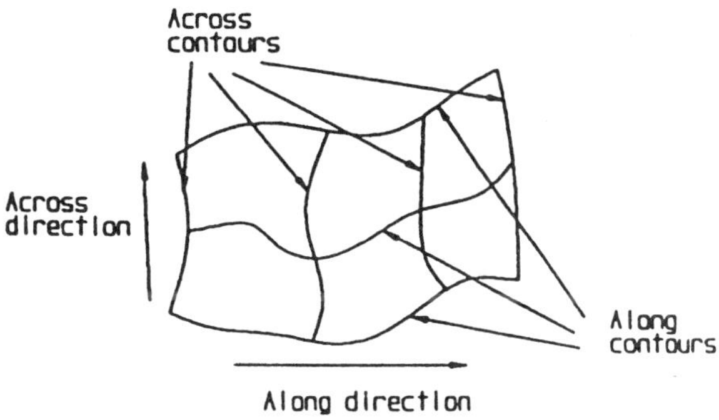

Figure 14.2

Cutting Methods

The cutting method determines the toolpath pattern Mastercam used to generate toolpaths in cutting a surface. There are **four** cutting methods: zig-zag, one way, circular and 5-axis. Each method has its unique features and uses. Table 14.2 summaries the features of each cutting method.

Table 14.2 Cutting methods in 3-d surfacing

Type	Features	Illustration
Zig- zag	• Cutter moves back and forth across the part to cut the surface. The cutter makes constant contact with the surface. • Takes shorter time. • Conventional milling in one direction and climb milling in the other direction This alternate milling pattern is not desirable.	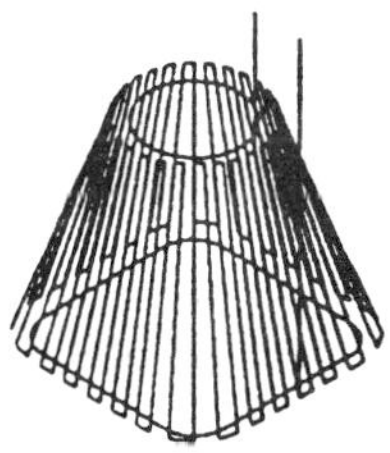
One way	• Cutter takes all passes on the surface in the same direction. It makes a pass, then retracts in Z direction, rapids to another starting point, takes another pass in the specified direction. Repeat the toolpath until completing the surface cutting. • Keep the same milling type (climb or conventional) • Take longer time due to retracting and plunging for each cutting pass.	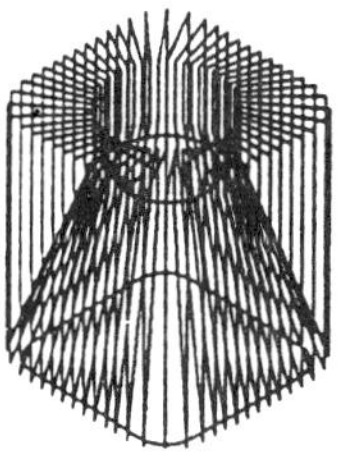
Circular	• Cutter moves along a spiral pattern to machine a surface. • Circular should only be used when closed contours are used. This means that the first and last contour are identical.	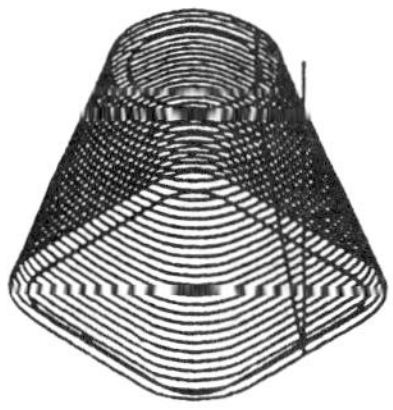
5-axis	• Cutter moves in the specified direction to machine a surface. • The tool axis is in the surface normal direction.	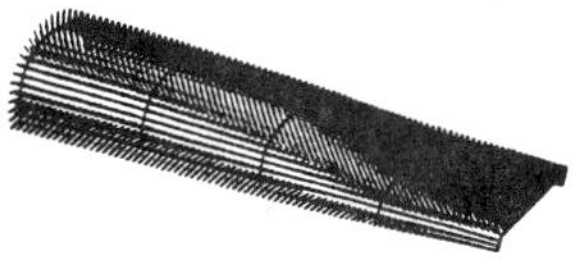

Cutting Direction

This parameter can be toggled to along or across which specifies the cutting direction of the toolpaths. In the **along** mode, the cutter cuts in the along direction while stepping over in the across direction as shown in Figure 14.3 . In the **across** mode, the cutter cuts in the across direction while stepping over in the along direction (Figure 14.4).

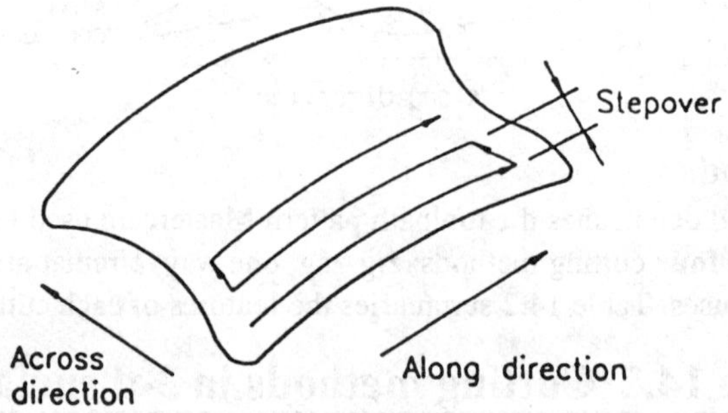

Figure 14.3

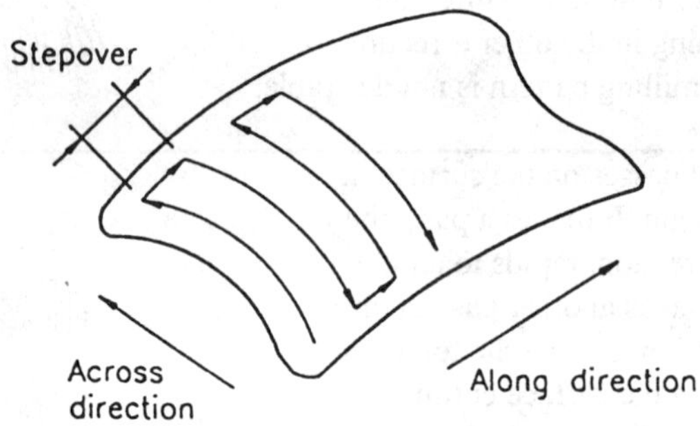

Figure 14.4

Stepping Over Distances

Surface cuttings are normally implemented in linear interpolation mode. In fact, the surface is approximated by a set of linear interpolation motion commands which step over the surface skin. Therefore, the system requires two stepping over values, one in along direction and the other in the across direction, to determine the actual coordinates of toolpaths. Mastercam uses two terms, along cut distance and across cut distance, to indicate these two stepping over values. The **along cut distance** is the cutter step-over distance in each along pass. The **across cut distance** is the cutter step-over distance between each along cut. Figure 14.5 illustrates the use of along cut distance and across cut distance in surface cutting. It should be noted that these two distances determine the cutting accuracy and the program size. The larger the distance, the bigger the surface positional error and the shorter the program size. Conversely, the smaller the distance, the smaller the surface positional error and the larger the program size.

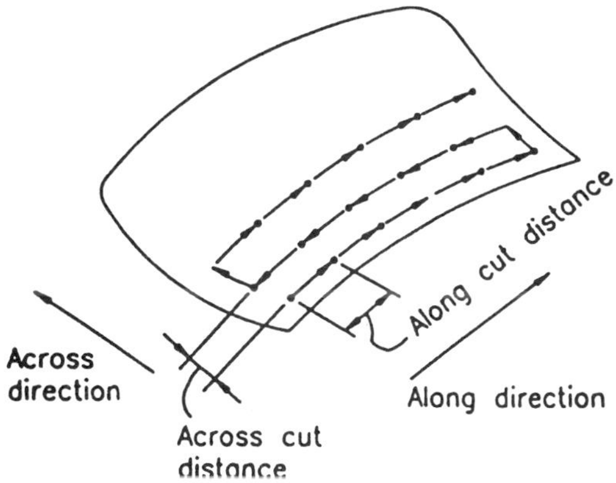

Figure 14.5

Cutter Compensation

Cutter compensation in a 3-d machining is more difficult to be determined than those in 2-d machining. The "cutter compensation in computer" parameter can be toggled to one of **five modes**: left center, left tip, right center, right tip, and off. It should be noted that ball-end mills or bull-nose mills are normally used in 3-d machining. The definition of cutter tip and cutter center for ball-end, bull-nose, and straight-end mills are illustrated in Figure 14.6. The selection of tip and center of the cutter has a significant effect on the toolpaths as shown in Figure 14.7.

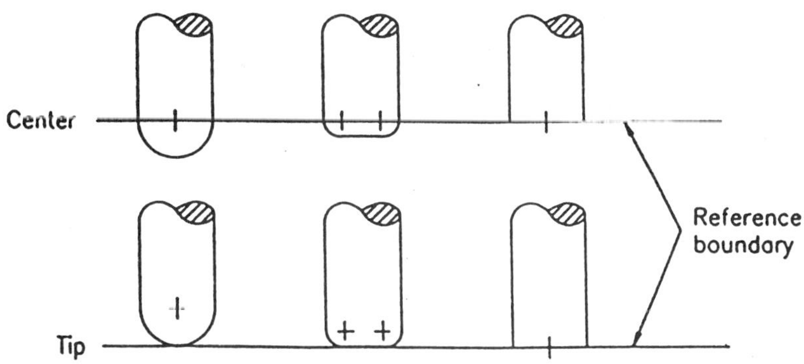

Figures 14.6

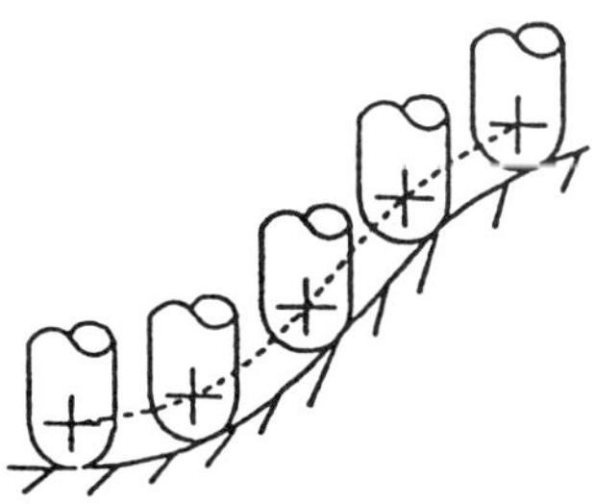

Figure 14.7a Center

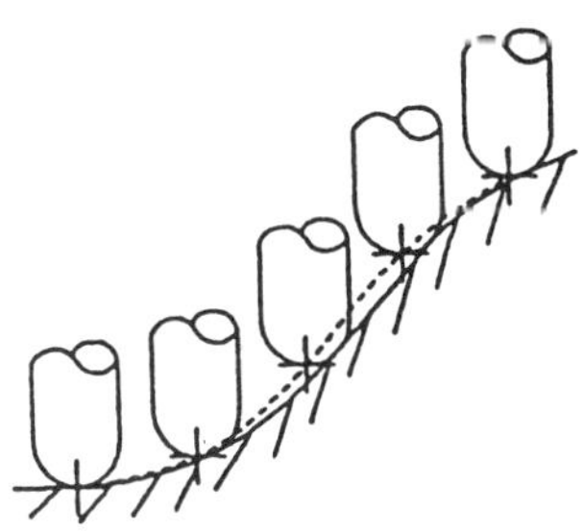

Figure 14.7b Tip

Tip	Mastercam actually calculates for a sphere when you specify a ball end mill so one could use a special shaped cutter if necessary.

The direction of cutter compensation can be left, right, or off. The offset direction is determined as followed:

Viewing from the first contour toward the last contour in the along direction:

Left:	The contours used to define the surface are located at the left side of the toolpaths (Figure 14.8a).
Right:	The contours used to define the surface are located at the right side of the toolpaths (Figure 14.8b).

Note: the cutter compensation in Figure 14.8b produces undercut throughout the surface.

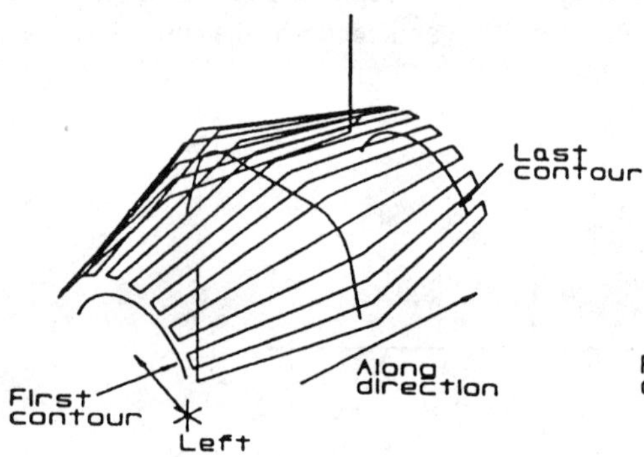

Figure 14.8a. Cutter compensation to the left

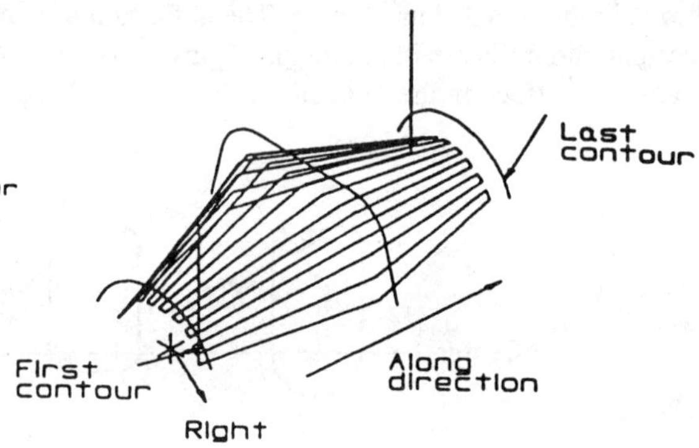

Figure 14.8b. Cutter compensation to the right

Figure 14.9 shows an example of picking the contour order reversed from that in Figure 14.8.

Note: when the picking order of the contours is reversed, the direction for cutter compensation should be changed accordingly.

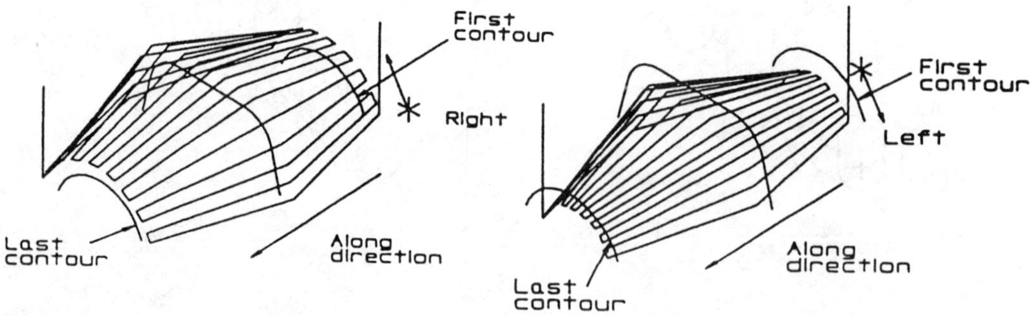

Figure 14.9

When cutter compensation is applied to the across direction, the viewing direction follows the across contour from the picking end to the other end. Then the direction of left and right is determined with the same principle as in the along direction. Figure 14.10 shows an example of cutter compensation in the across direction.

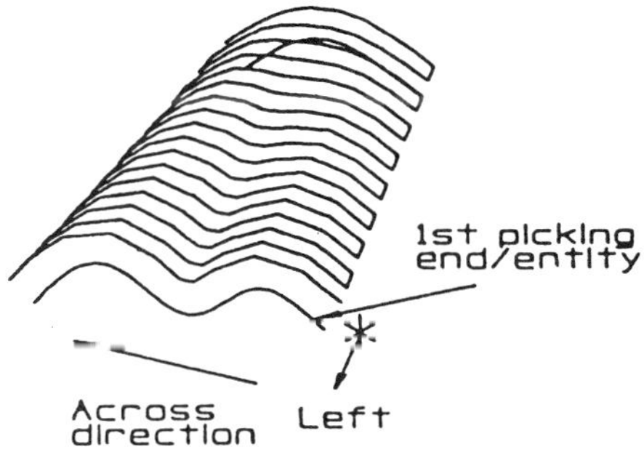

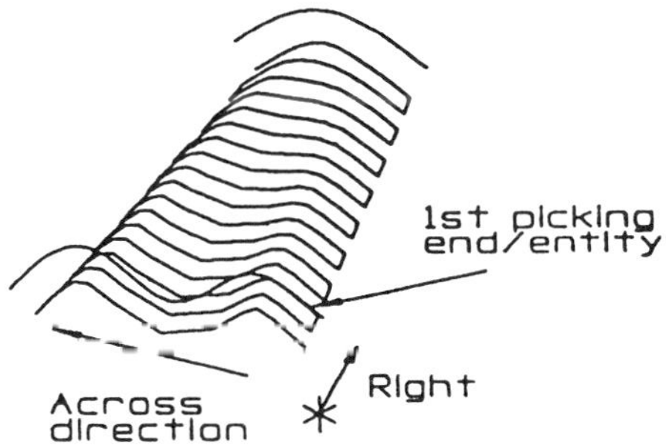

Figure 14.10a Cutter compensation to **left** Figure 14.10b Cutter compensation to **right**

14.3 3D Toolpath Modules

Mastercam has two groups of 3-d toolpath modules. The **first group** has **five** toolpath modules which are used to generate toolpaths for cutting a single surface from a wireframe model. The **second group** has **two** subgroups oftoolpath modules that are used to generate toolpaths to rough cut or finish cut an existing surface model. In this chapter we only present the first group. The second group is covered in chapter 15.

The **five 3-d toolpath modules** for working with wireframe models include ruled, loft, Coons, swept, and revolution. The selection of a proper 3-d toolpath module mainly depends on the nature of the surface to be cut and the type and number of surface profiles available in the wireframe model. On the next page, Table 14.3 summarizes the features of these five modules.

These five toolpath modules are presented in the following five sections. Each section begins with a brief discussion of the features of the module, module specific parameters, and concluded with one or two examples.

14.4 Ruled Toolpath Module

This ruled module is used for blending two to one hundred contours to produce a linear 3D surface as shown in Figure 14.11.

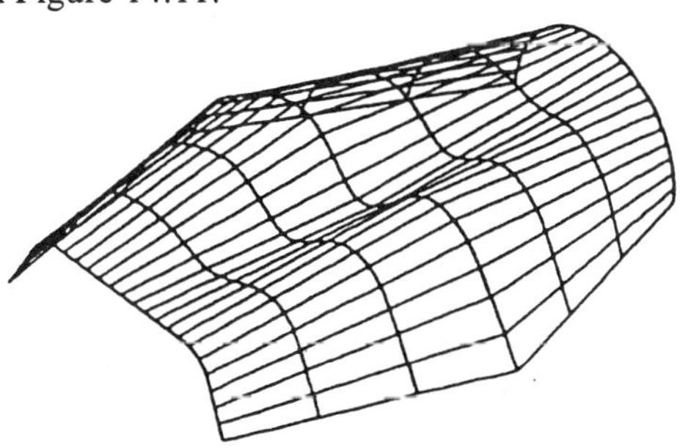

Figure 14.11

Table 14.3 3-d toolpath modules for machining surfaces from a wireframe model

Module type	Description	Illustration
Ruled	Creates the toolpaths to produce a surface formed by linearly blending at least two contours.	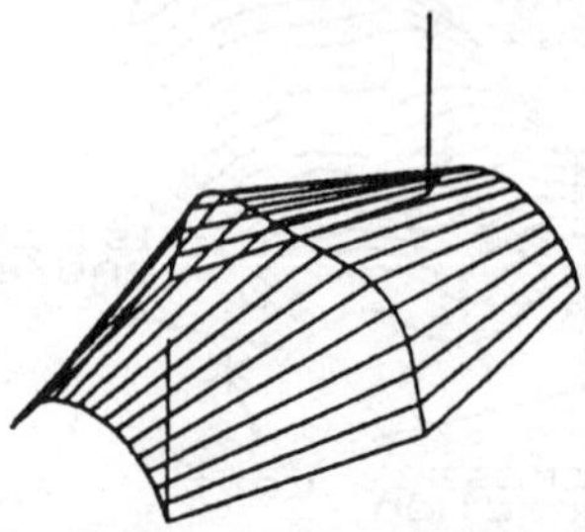
Loft	Creates the toolpaths to produce a surface formed by blending parabolically more than two contours.	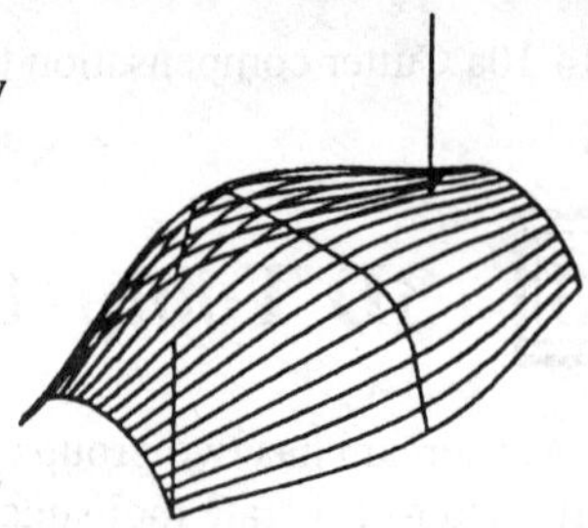
Coons	Creates the toolpaths to produce a surface that is formed by blending a grid of closed boundaries (patches).	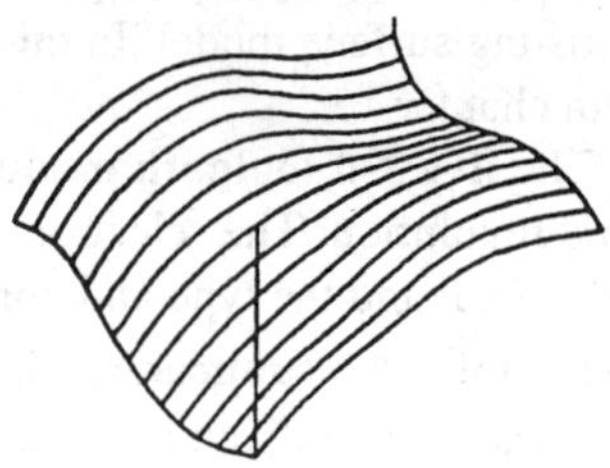
Swept 3D	Creates the toolpaths to cut a surface that is formed by sweeping one or two across contours along one or two rails (along contours).	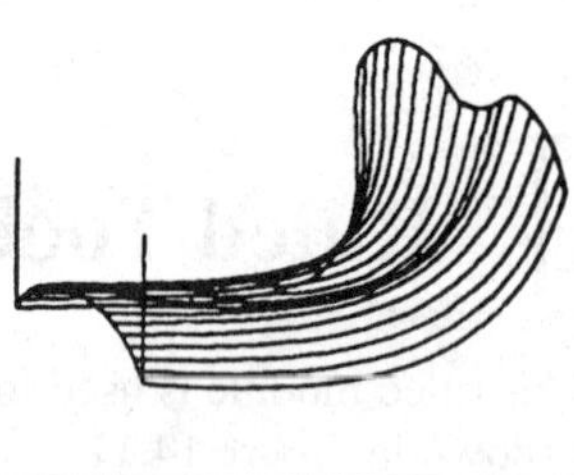
Revolution	Creates the toolpaths to produce a surface by rotating a contour about an axis of rotation.	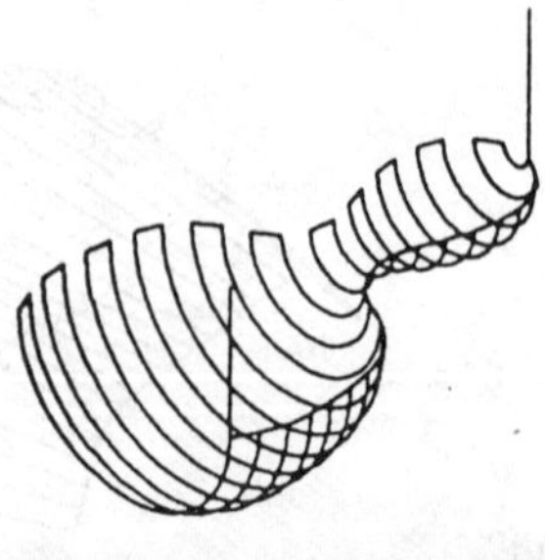

Ruled Parameters

The ruled parameters appear as below:

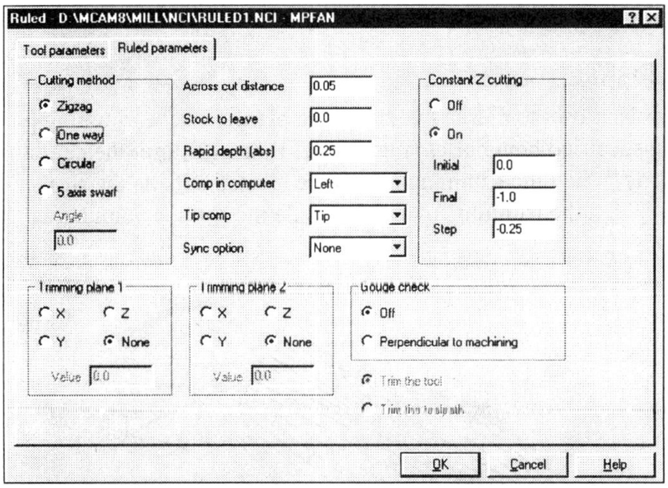

Constant Z Cutting

This parameter can be set to On or Off. When set to On, the cutter will be kept at a constant Z depth for each cut pass. The following three parameters will appear when the Constant Z cutting is set to On:

Initial	specifies the Z value of top boundary
Final	specifies the Z value of bottom boundary
Step	specifies the stepover value in Z direction of each pass

The Initial and Final define the constant Z cutting boundaries. These boundaries can be used to extend the toolpath beyond the defined surface or cut only a portion of the defined surface. Figure 14.12 illustrates the three parameters in constant Z cutting.

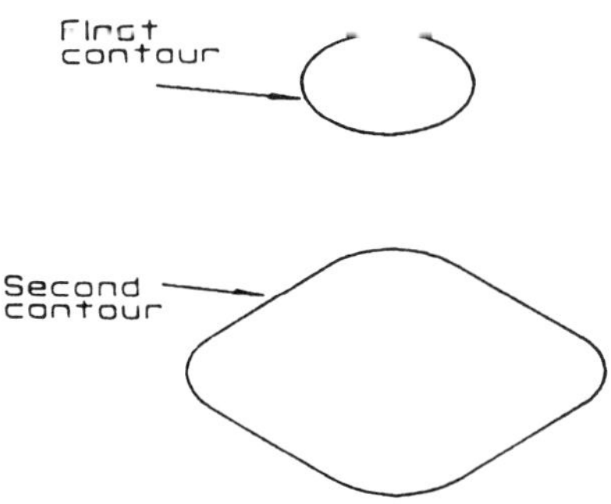

Figure 14.12a Isometric view

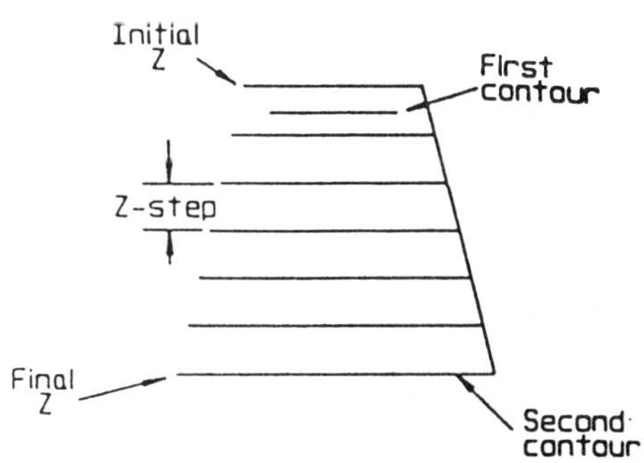

Figure 14.12b Front view

Taper Angle

This parameter specifies the angle of the surface slope for the cutting tool. It is only available for 5 axis cutting.

Trimming Planes

The ruled module allows to define two trimming planes. These trimming planes can be used to (1) extend the cut to the specified boundaries (Figure 14.13) and (2) limit the cut to pass the specified boundaries (Figure 14.14). When the trimming planes are located outside the surface boundaries, the toolpaths are extended. When the trimming planes fit inside the surface boundaries, the toolpaths are trimmed.

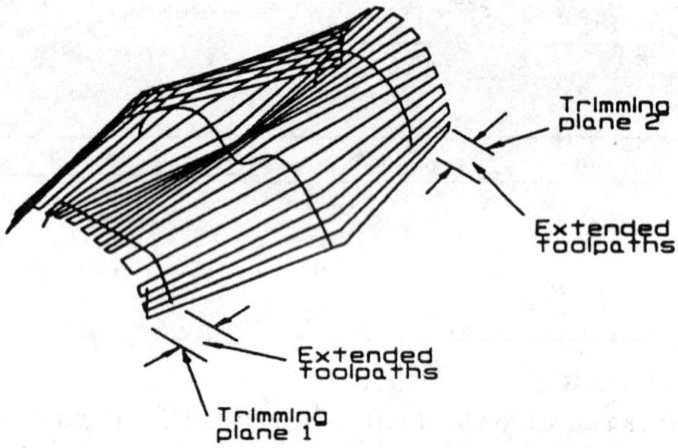

Figure 14.13 Extending

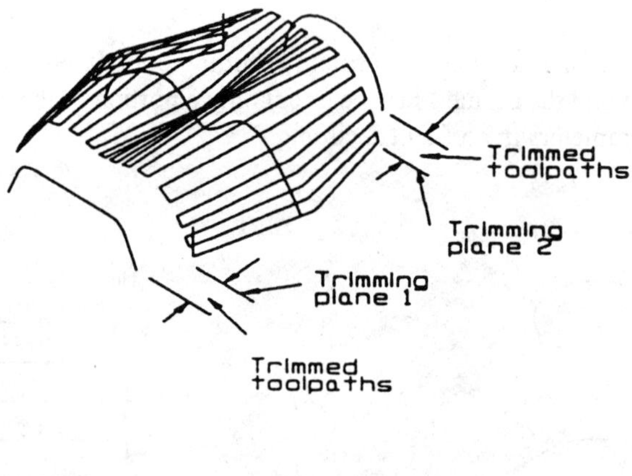

Figure 14.14 Trimming

Gouge Check Direction

This parameter can be toggled to one of two modes to determine whether the gouge check is to be performed. Gouge checking is ignored when off mode is selected.

Project 1. Machining a ruled surface formed by two contours

The ruled toolpath module is used to generate toolpaths for machining two ruled surfaces as shown in Figure 14.15. The wireframe model file is **ruled1** which is created in chapter 11. These two ruled surfaces intersect in the middle. Therefore, their toolpaths can not be used without modification. Actually, we can not machine these two ruled surfaces using the toolpaths generated from this project because the toolpath in one surface cuts into the other surface. In this project we can only illustrate generating toolpaths for machining ruled surfaces. We also assume that two fillet surfaces are to be added at the two places where the ruled surfaces intersect. This is done in chapter 15. Here we create two sets of toolpaths to machine two ruled surfaces. One file is saved as Surf1 and the other as Surf2.

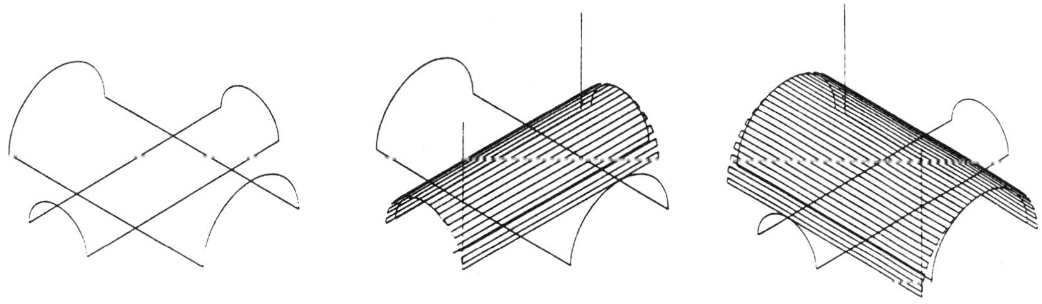

Figure 14.15

Tips 1. Cutter compensation in computer is set to **left** center for the first ruled surface and set to **right** center for the second ruled surface.

2. Cutter is 0.5" ball-end mill.

3. Save the toolpaths for each surface in a separate file, **surf1** for the first ruled surface and **surf2** for the second. These two toolpaths files can not be used without modification. They will cut through each other in the middle.

Step 1. Load the wireframe model file (ruled1.ge3) or create one by following the instructions in project 1 of chapter 11. The wireframe model should appear as in Figure 14.16.

Select **MAIN MENU → File → Get**

Enter file name: **ruled1** ↵

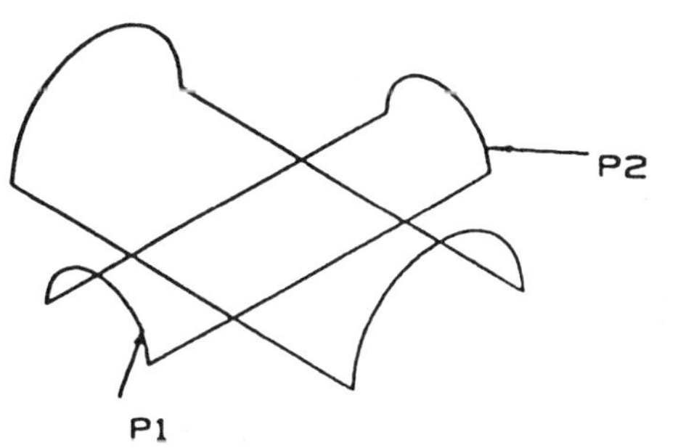

Figure 14.16

Step 2. Initiate ruled toolpath module.

Select **MAIN MENU → Toolpaths → Next menu → Wireframe → Ruled**

Step 3. Define the contours. Use the pick points in Figure 14.16 on the previous page .

Select **Single** then pick **P1**
Select **Mode → Single** then pick **P2**
Select **Done**

Step 4. Set the ruled parameters to the following settings.

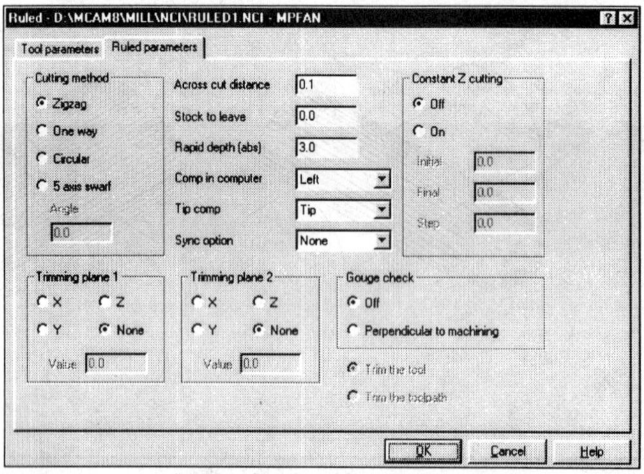

Click the **Tool parameters** tab to advance to the Tool parameters menu.

Step 5. Define Tool parameters to the following settings.

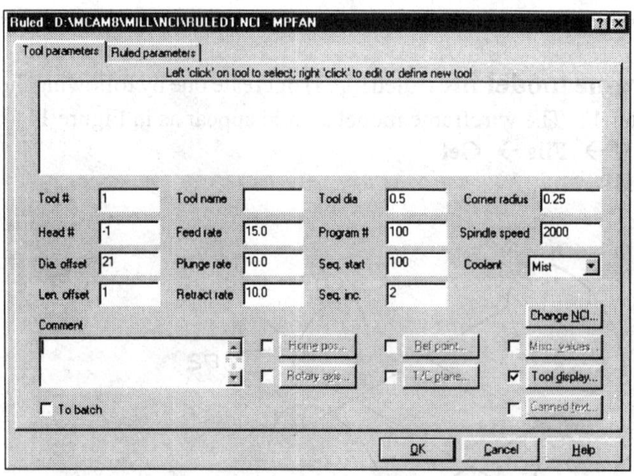

Click on the **Change NCI** and change the file name to **surf1→ OK**
Click on the **OK** button to complete the parameter settings.

Step 6. Write and save the toolpaths.

The toolpaths should display on the screen as Figure 14.17.
Select **MAIN MENU → Operations → Post**
Toggle **Save NCI file** to on (with check mark) **→ OK**
file name: **surf1**

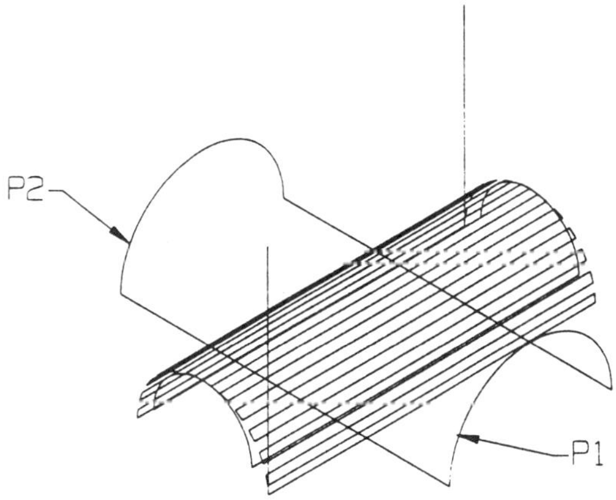

Figure 14.17

Step 7. Use ruled toolpath module again. Generate second ruled surface toolpaths.

Select **Toolpaths → Operations**
Click the "Ruled" toolpath with the right mouse button
Select **Delete** to delete the current toolpath **→ OK**

Step 8. Define ruled surface contours using the pick points (Figure 14.17).

Select **Next Menu → Wireframe → Ruled**
Select **Single** then pick **P1**
Select **Mode → Single** then pick **P2**
Select **Done**

Step 9. Define the ruled toolpath parameters to the following settings.

The Tool parameters for this surface are the same as those in step 5.
Click the **Ruled parameters** tab to advance to the Ruled parameters menu.

Step 10. Define NC parameters to the following settings.

Set the Ruled parameters as those given in step 4, with the exception of

Set Ruled Compensation to

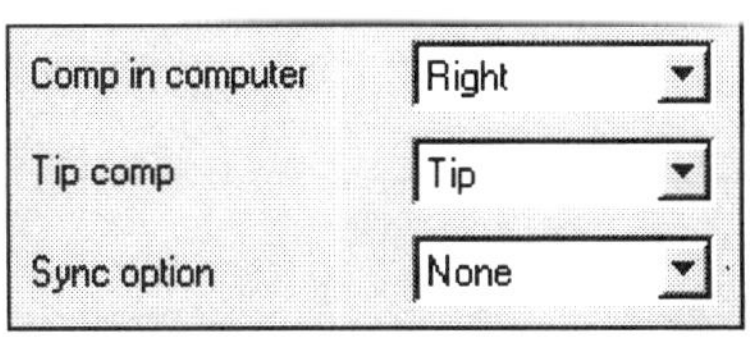

Select the **OK** button to complete the parameter settings.

Step 11. Write and accept the toolpaths.

Select **MAIN MENU → Toolpaths → Operations → Post**
Toggle **Save NCI file** to on (with check mark) **→ OK**
Enter filename: **surf2 → Save**
Select **OK** to leave the operations Manager dialog
The toolpaths should resemble Figure 14.18.

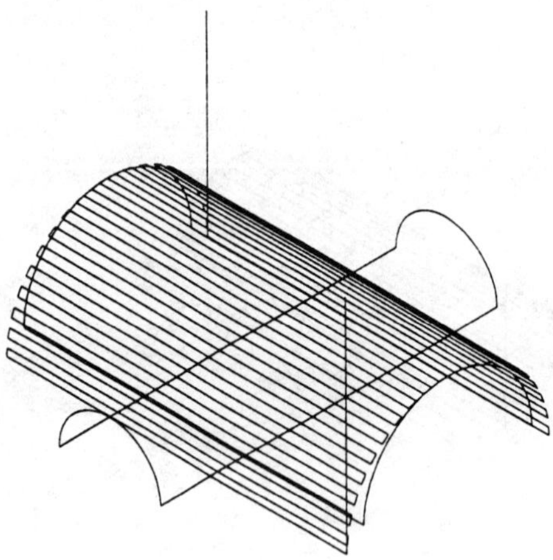

Figure 14.18

Project 2. Machining a ruled surface formed by three contours

A ruled surface is defined by a wireframe model of three contours as created in project 3 of chapter 11. The wireframe model and finished toolpaths are illustrated in Figure 14.19.

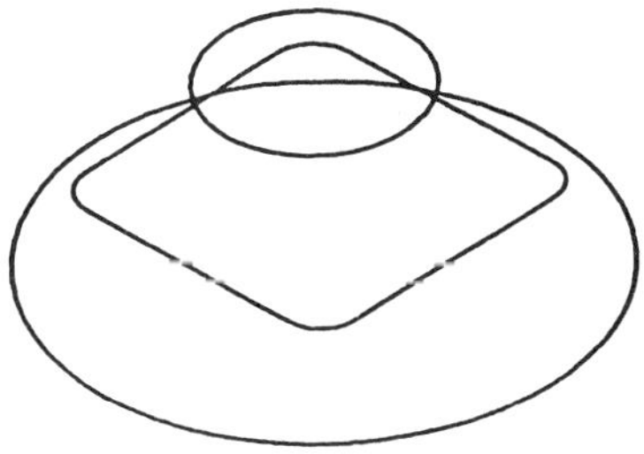

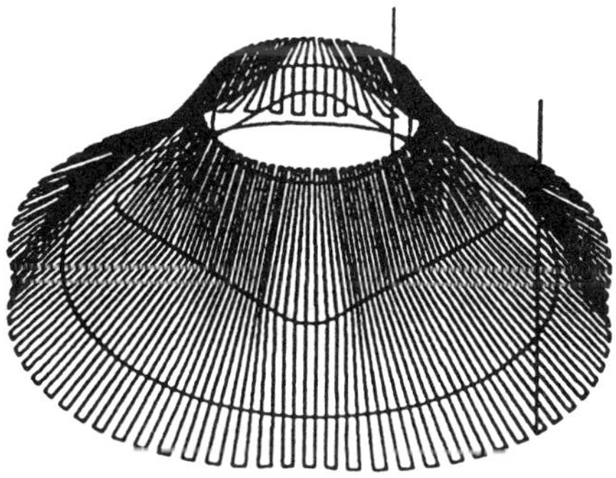

Figure 14.19

Tips 1. Use trimming planes to extend the cutting paths. The first trim plane is Z0.25 and the second plane Z-2.0.
2. The right vertical line of the rectangular contour must be broken into two pieces at the middle. This allows the alignment of the start points of three contours.
3. Picking sequence of the contours starts from the top downward. This determines the direction of toolpaths to go from top to bottom.

Step 1. Load the wireframe model file 3contour.ge3.

(or create one by following the instructions in project 3 of chapter 11.)
Select **MAIN MENU** → **File** → **Get**
Enter file name: **3contour** ↵

The wireframe model should appear as Figure 14.20.

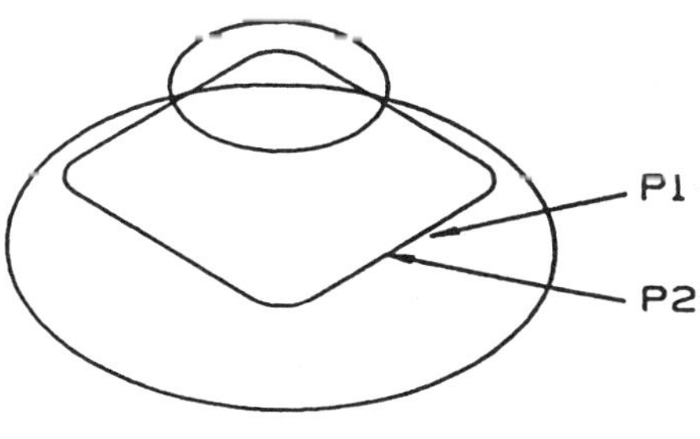

Figure 14.20

Step 2. Break the right vertical line of the rectangular contour into two pieces in the middle. Use the pick points in Figure 14.20.

Select **MAIN MENU → Modify → Break → 2 pieces**
Pick **P1** to select the entity to break
Select **Midpoint** from the Point menu
Pick **P2** to break the entity

The drawing does not look different before and after breaking. The drawing is redisplayed as in Figure 14.21.

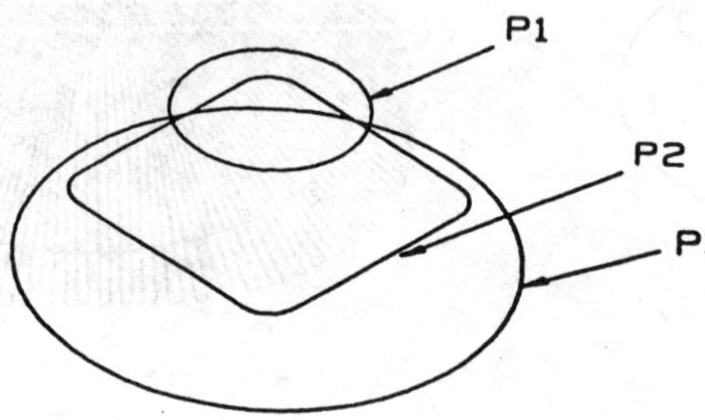

Figure 14.21

Step 3. Initiate ruled toolpath module.

Select **MAIN MENU → Toolpaths → Next menu → Wireframe → Ruled**

Step 4. Define the contours using the pick points in Figure 14.21.

Select **Single** then pick **P1** for contour 1
Select **Mode → Chain** then pick **P2**
Select **Mode → Single** then pick **P3**
Select **Done** to complete defining contours

Step 5. Define ruled parameters to the following settings.

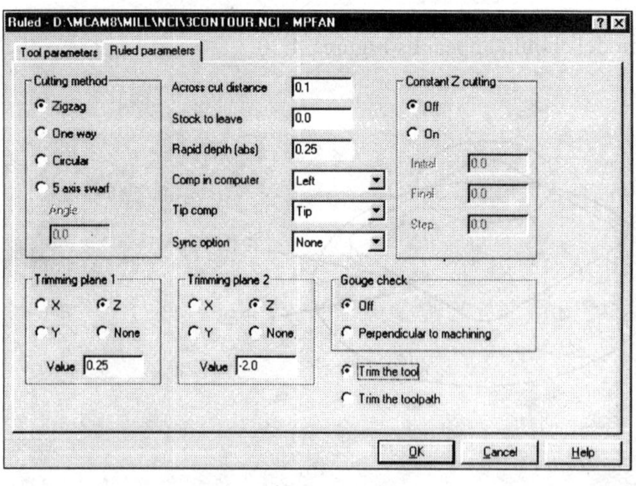

Select the **Tool parameters** tab to advance to the Tool parameters menu.

Step 6. Define Tool parameters to the following settings.

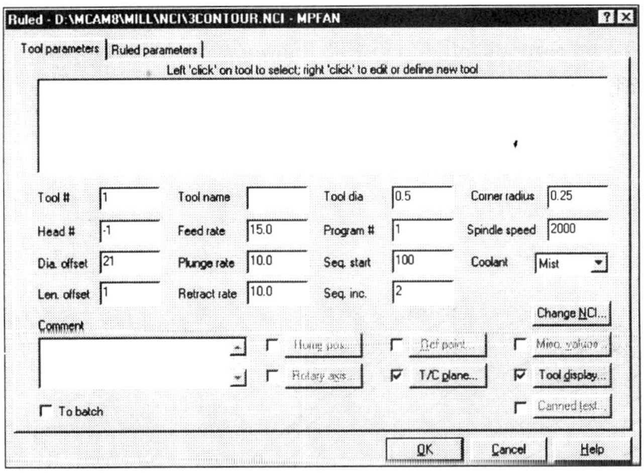

Click on **Change NCI** and change the filename to **ruledt2 → OK**
Select the **OK** to complete the parameter settings.

Step 7. Write and save the toolpaths.

Select **MAIN MENU → Toolpaths → Operations → Post**
Toggle **Save NCI file** to on (with check mark) **→ OK**
Enter filename: **ruledt2 → Save**
Select **OK** to leave the operations Manager dialog
The toolpaths should resemble Figure 14.22

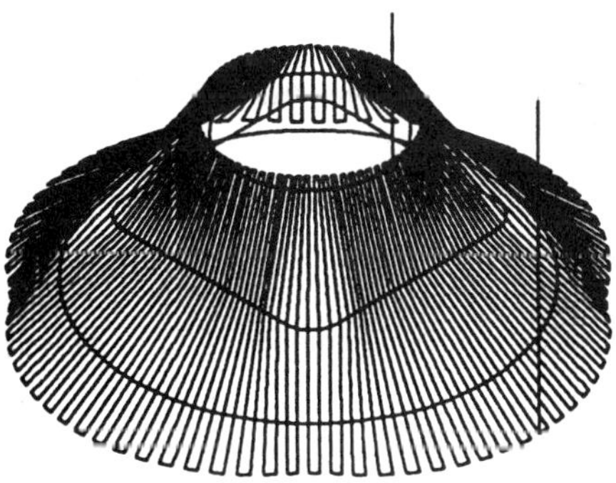

Figure 14.22

14.5 Loft Toolpath Module

This module is used to blend parabolically up to 100 contours which can be points, lines, arcs and splines or any combination of entity types. Figure 14.23 shows an example of the toolpaths generated by using the loft toolpath module.

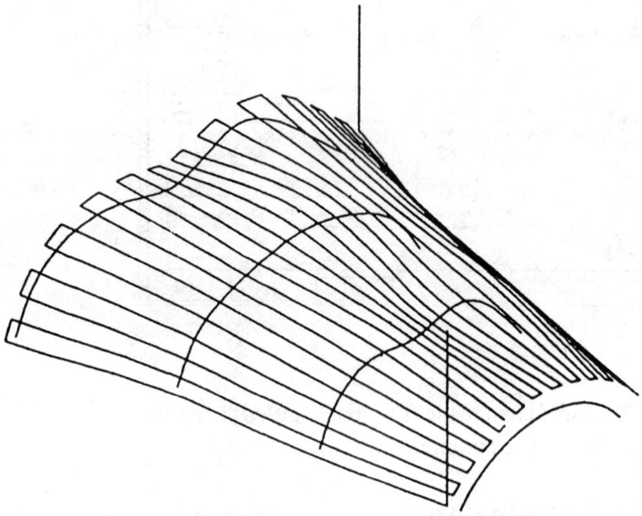

Figure 14.23

Lofted Parameters

The five loft parameters are listed below:

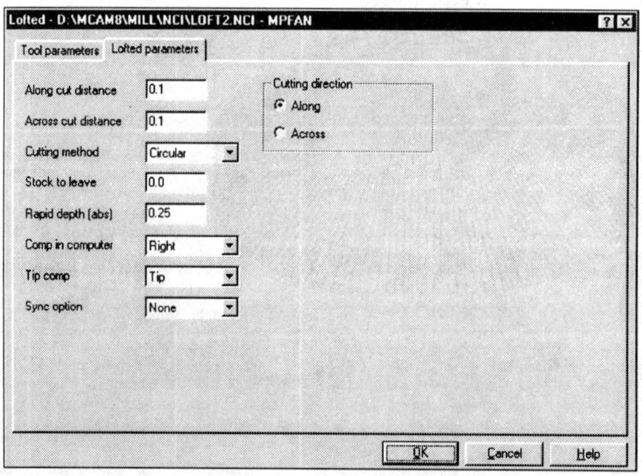

These five parameters have been discussed in previous sections.

Project 3. Machining a loft surface

The loft toolpath module is used to generate a set of toolpaths to machine a loft surface defined by 19 contours. The wireframe model for this surface is the file loft2 created in chapter 11. Figure 14.24 shows both the wireframe model and the toolpaths to cut this surface.

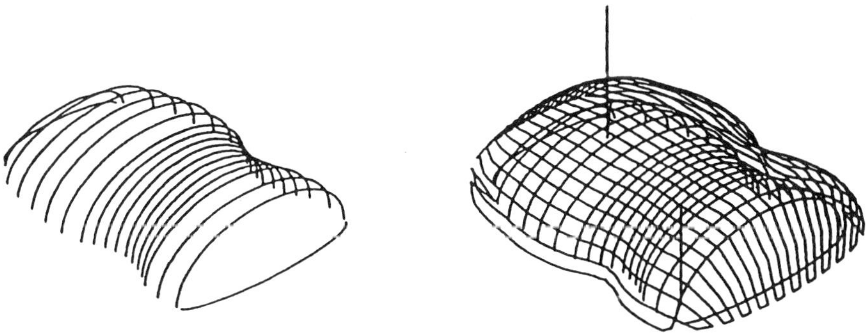

Figure 14.24

Tips 1. Wireframe model file is loft2.ge3.

2. Use Window → One Way → CW commands to orderly select contours.

3. Cutter compensation in computer should be set to right center.

Step 1. Load the part wireframe model file (loft2.ge3) or create one by following the instructions in project 4 of chapter 11.

Select **MAIN MENU → File → Get**
Enter file name: **loft2** ↵

The wireframe model should appear as Figure 14.25.

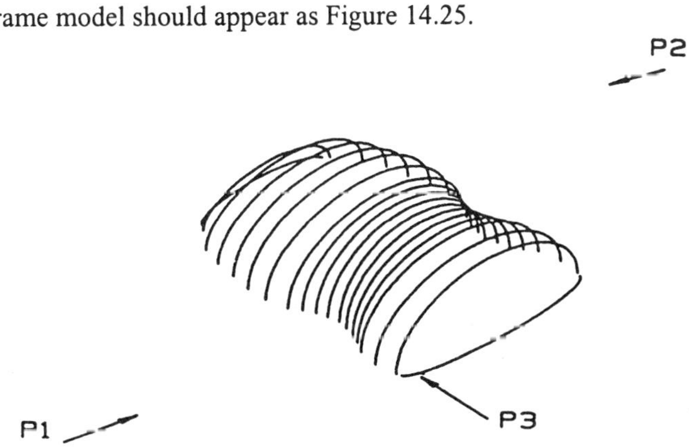

Figure 14.25

Step 2. Initiate loft toolpath module.

Select **MAIN MENU → Toolpaths → Next menu → Wireframe → Loft**

Step 3. Define the contours using the pick points in Figure 14.25.

Select **Window → Options → CW → One Way → OK**
Pick **P1** and **P2** to include all contours in the window
Select **Endpoint** then pick **P3**
Select **Done** to complete contours selection

Step 4. Define lofted parameters to the following settings.

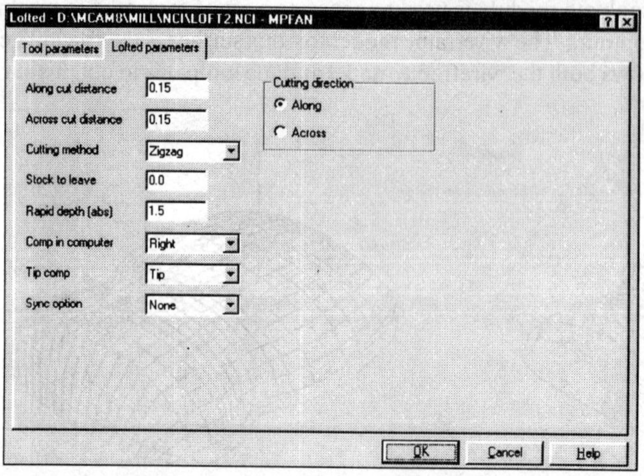

Select the **Tool parameters** tab to advance to the Tool parameters menu.

Step 5. Define Tool parameters to the following settings.

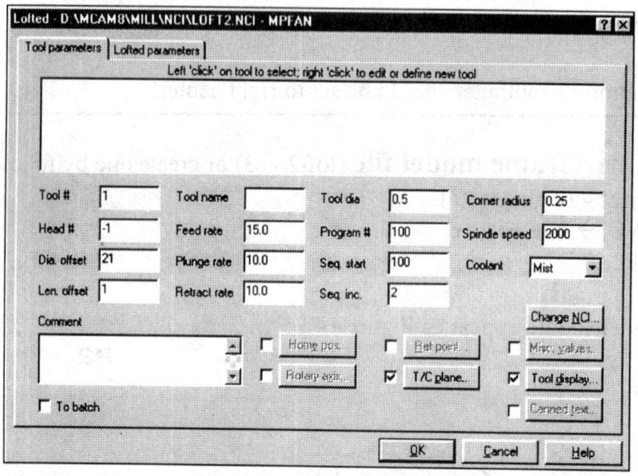

Click on the **Change NCI** button and change the file name to **loftt → OK**
Select **OK** to complete the parameter settings.

Step 6. Write and save the toolpath file.

Note: The system will issue a warning to indicate that there is an undercut on 4 of 851 points, and the largest undercut = -0.25.

Press **Enter** to display the toolpaths
Select **MAIN MENU → Toolpaths**
Select **Operations → Post**
Toggle **Save NCI file** to on (with check mark) **→ OK**
Enter filename: **loftt → Save**
Select **OK** to leave the operations Manager dialog
The toolpaths should resemble Figure 14.26.

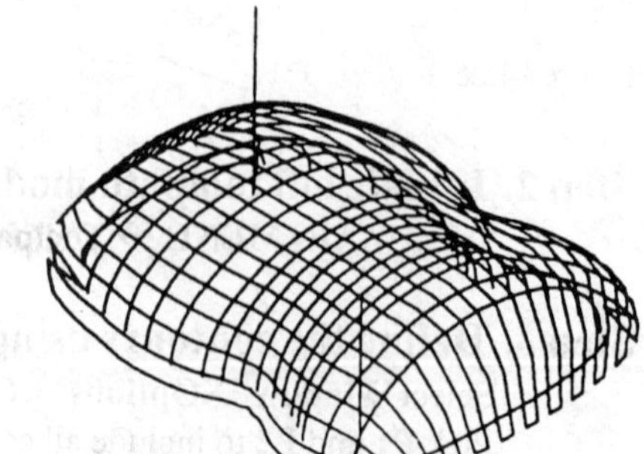

Figure 14.26

14.6 Coons Toolpath Module

The Coons module is used to generate a series of toolpaths to machine a surface defined by a single patch or multiple-patch model. Each patch normally consists of four contours. Figure 14.27 shows a surface produced by the toolpaths generated from Coons module.

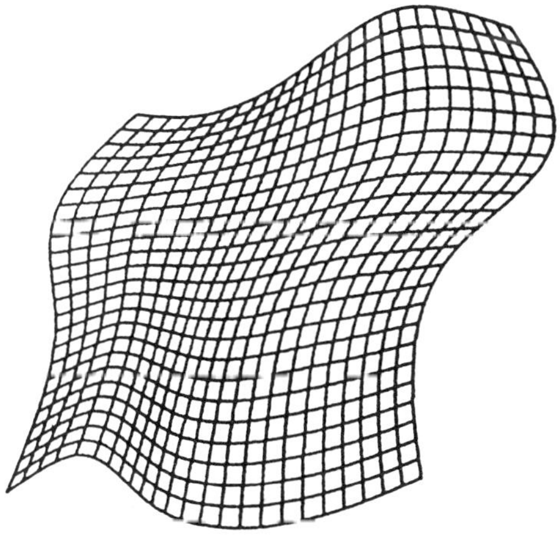

Figure 14.27

Coons Parameters

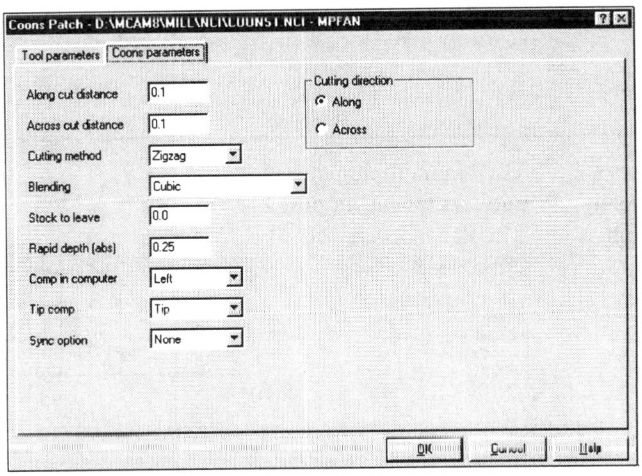

All parameters listed above, excepting the blending method, have been discussed in previous sections. Table 14.4 on the following page summarizes the features and applications of four blending methods used in Coons surfaces.

Tips
1. Refer to the instructions given for Coons surfaces in section 12.7 of chapter 12.
2. Select the starting point, along direction, and across direction.
3. Determine the number of along contours and the number of across contours.
4. Determine the number of along patches and the number of across patches.
5. Observe the picking order of selecting contours.

Table 14.4 Blending methods of Coons surfaces

Blending	Description	Application	Illustration
Linear	Patch contours are blended linearly to form a surface.	Use in single patch surfaces.	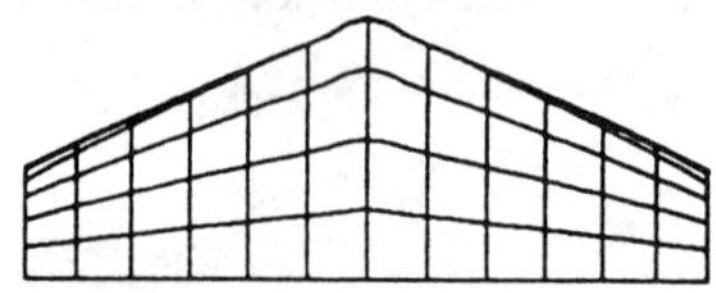
Parabolic	Patch contours are blended parabolically (2nd order) to form a surface.	Used in multiple-patch surfaces. These surfaces tend to produce flat spots on the surface.	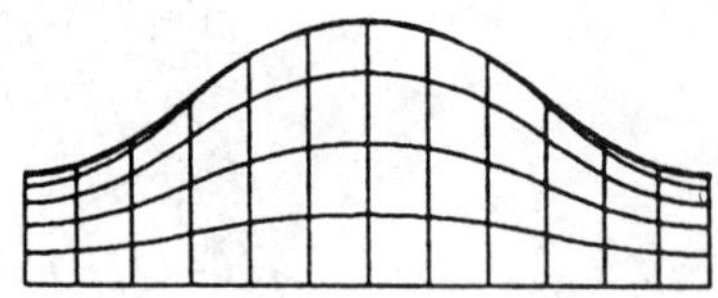
Cubic	Patch contours are blended cubically (3rd order) to form a surface.	Used in multiple-patch surfaces. These surfaces tend to produce flat spots on the surface.	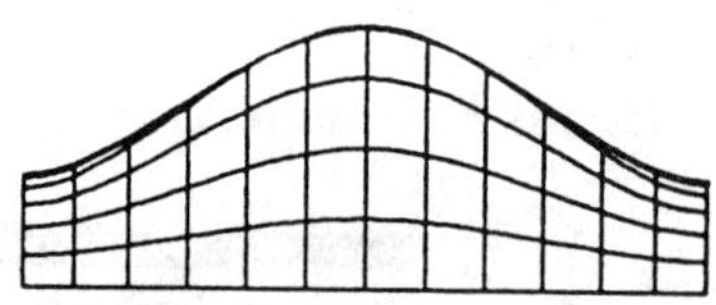
Cubic with slope matching	Patch contours are blended cubically (3rd order) with matching slope at the boundaries.	Used in multiple-patch surfaces whenever possible. The flat spots are eliminated.	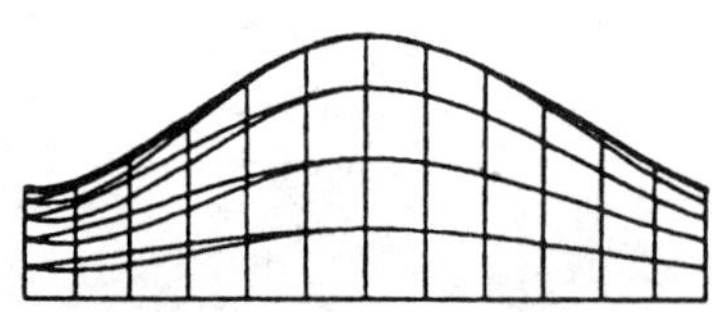

Row and Column

Mastercam uses rows and columns to identify the patch boundary grid. Along contours are assigned in rows and across contours in columns. Each contour in the grid is identified by an *along* row number and an *across* column number as shown in Figure 14.28.

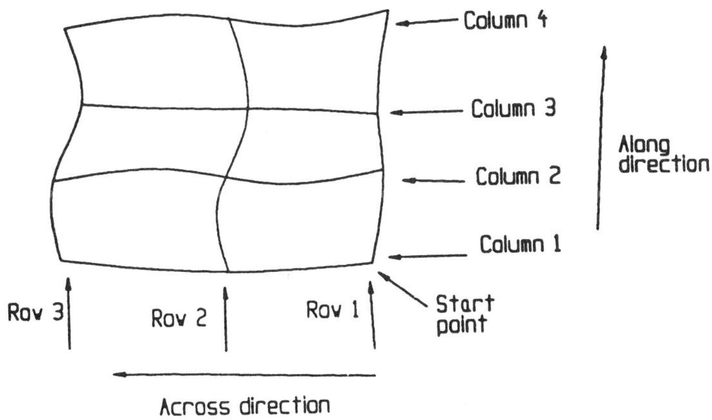

Figure 14.28

Number of Patches in Along and Across Directions

The system will ask you to enter the number of patches in the along and across directions, respectively. Whether the boundaries are closed affects your counting the number of patches. In open boundary cases, where the first and the last contour are not connected, the number of patches in the along direction is the number of across contours minus 1 and the number of patches in across direction is the number of along contours minus 1.

Figure 14.29 shows the contour profiles having an open boundary for defining a Coons surface. In this model, the start point is selected at point A and the along and across direction are as shown in the figure.

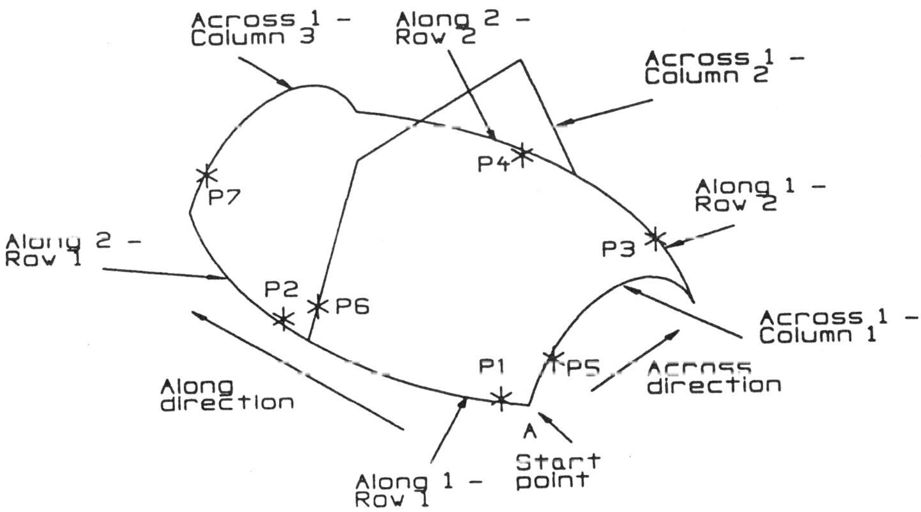

Figure 14.29

The number of along contours = 2
The number of across contours = 3
The number of along patches = The number of across contours - 1 = 3 - 1 = 2
The number of across patches = The number of along contours - 1 = 2 - 1 = 1

In close boundary cases where the first and the last contours are connected, the number of patches in the along direction is equal to the number of the across contours and the number of patches in the across direction is the number of along contours minus 1. Figure 14.30 shows an example of a closed boundary Coons surface.

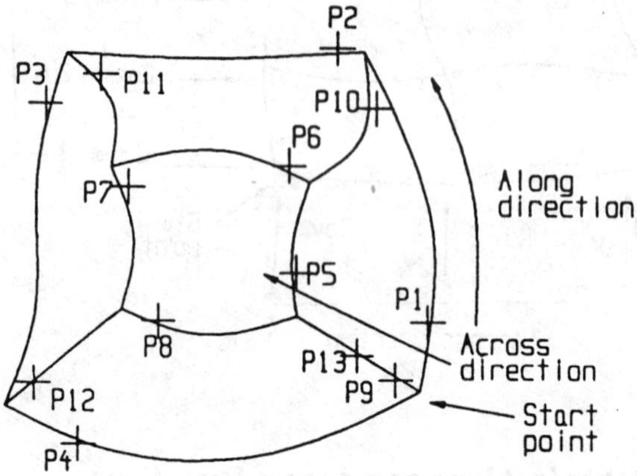

Figure 14.30

Number of along contours = 2
Number of across contours = 4
The number of patches in along direction = number of across contours = 4
The number of patches in across direction = number of along contours - 1 = 2 - 1 = 1

The Order of Contour Selection

The contours selection must follow a predetermined order that is along contours that are sequentially selected first, followed by the across contours as follows:

Selection order	Entity to be picked
1st selection	along row 1 - across column 1
2nd selection	along row 1 - across column 2
-	-
-	-
nth selection	along row 1 - across column n
n+1 selection	along row 2 - across column 1
n+2 selection	along row 2 - across column 2
-	-
-	-
2n selection	along row 2 - across column n
-	-
-	-
mn selection	along row m - across column n

Figure 14.29 on the previous page shows the contours selection sequence for an open boundary case and Figure 14.30 shows a closed boundary case.

Project 4. Machining a Coons surface of a single patch 4

The Coons toolpath module is used to generate the toolpaths for machining a surface defined by a single patch of four contours. The wireframe model and the toolpaths are illustrated in Figure 14.31.

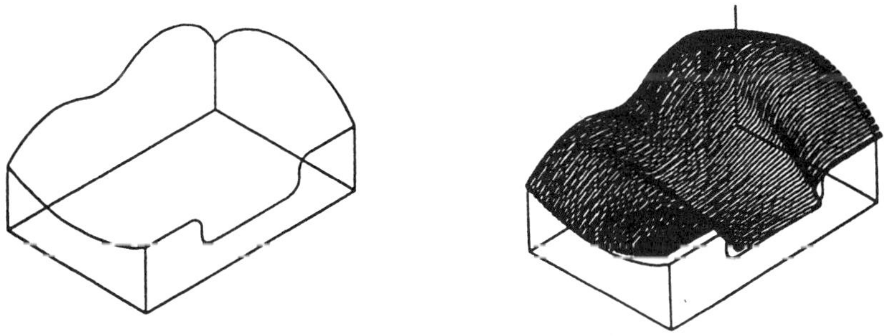

Figure 14.31

Tips 1. Use wireframe model file (coons1.ge3).

2. This is an open boundary case. The number of *along* contours is 2 and the number of *across* contours is 2. The number of patches in both along and across directions is 1 (or 2 - 1).
3. Use linear blending method because this is a single patch surface.

4. Cutter compensation in computer = left tip.

Step 1. Load the wireframe model file (coons1.ge3) or create one by following the instructions in project 5 of chapter 11.
Select **MAIN MENU → File → Get**
Enter file name: **coons1** ↵

The wireframe model should appear as Figure 14.32.

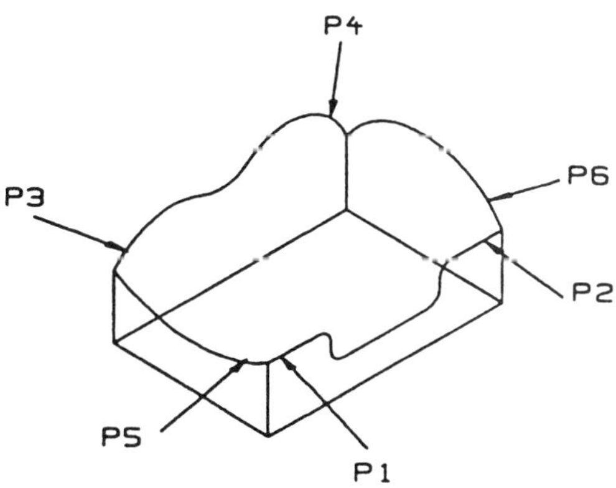

Figure 14.32

Step 2. Initiate the Coons toolpath module.

Select **MAIN MENU → Toolpaths → Next menu → Wireframe → Coons**

Step 3. Specify number of patches in along and across direction.

Enter **1** for the number of patches in the along direction
Enter **1** for the number of patches in the across direction

Step 4. Define contours using the pick points in Figure 14.32.

Select **Chain → Partial** then pick **P1** and **P2** to complete along contour 1 of row 1
then pick **P3** and **P4** to complete along contour 1 of row 2
Select **Mode →Single** then pick **P5** to define across contour 1 of column 1
Pick **P6** to define across contour 1 of column 2
Select **Done**

Step 5. Define Coons parameters to the following settings.

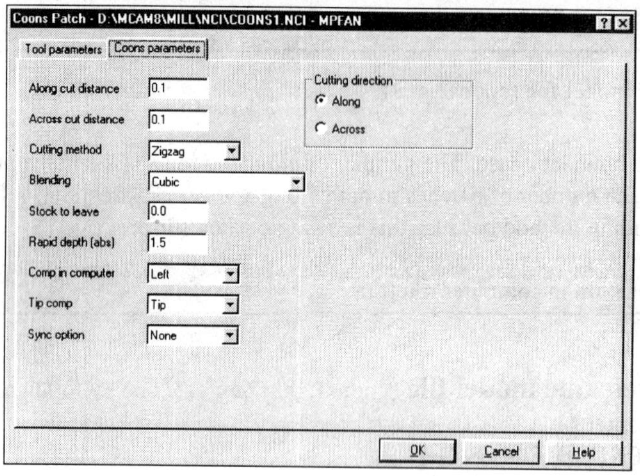

Select the **Tool parameters** tab to advance to the Tool parameters menu.

Step 6. Define Tool parameters to the following settings.

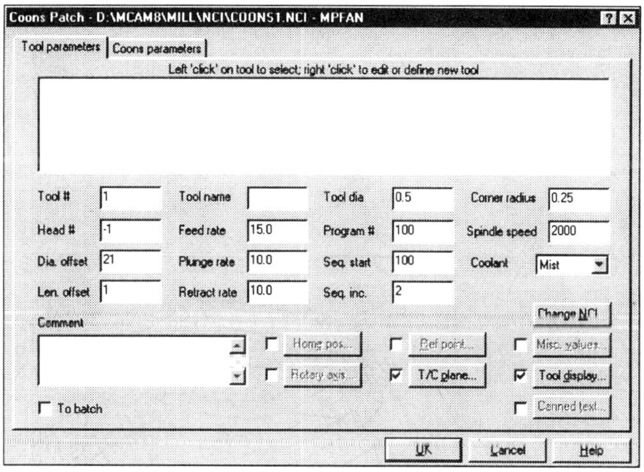

Click on **Change NCI** and change the file name to **coonst1** → **OK**
Select **OK** to complete the parameter settings.

Step 7. Write and save the toolpaths.

Select **MAIN MENU** → **Toolpaths** → **Operations** → **Post**
Toggle **Save NCI file** to on (with check mark) → **OK**
Enter filename: **coonst1** → **Save**
Select **OK** to leave the operations Manager dialog
The toolpaths should resemble Figure 14.33.

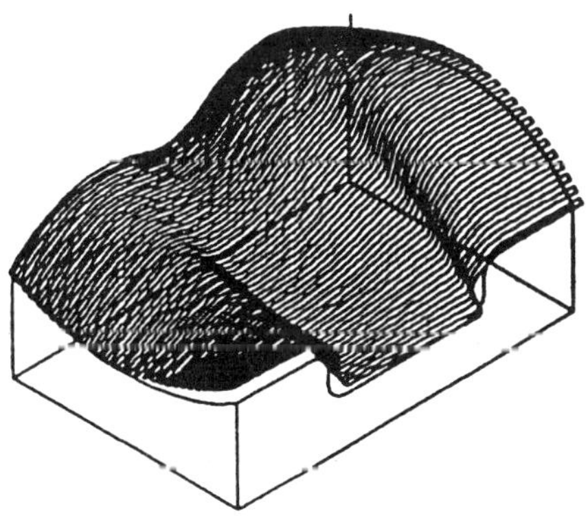

Figure 14.33

Project 5. Machining a Coons surface formed by multiple-patch

The Coons module is used to generate toolpaths to machine a Coons surface defined by a total of 12 patches. The wireframe model file is **coons4.ge3** created in project 7 of chapter 11. Figure 14.34 shows both the wireframe model and the toolpaths.

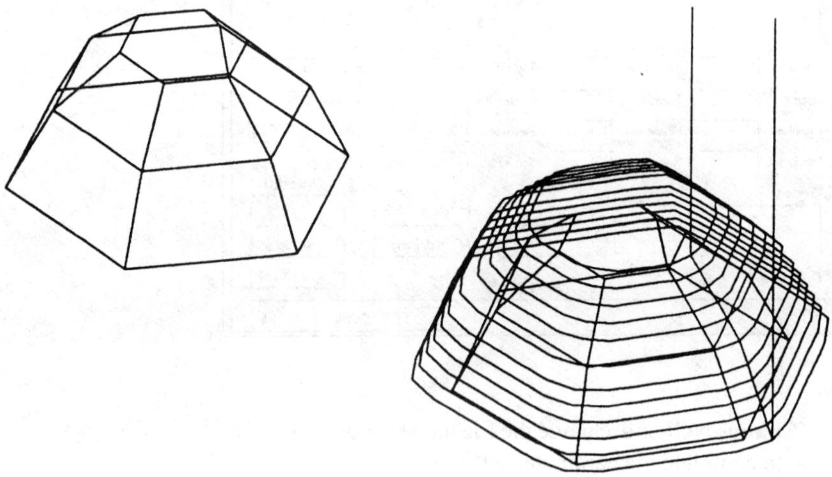

Figure 14.34

Tips 1. Use top Gview to facilitate the picking of contours.

2. The number of along contours = 3
   The number of across contours = 6
   The number of patches in along direction = 6
   The number of patches in across direction = 3 - 1 = 2

3. Use circular cutting method to reduce the part program size.

4. Set the cutting direction to along mode.

5. Cutter compensation in computer = left tip

6. Use the filter function to significantly reduce the toolpath points.

Step 1. Load the wireframe model file (coons4.ge3) or create one by following the instructions in project 7 of chapter 11.

Select **MAIN MENU → File → Get**

Enter file name: **coons4** ↵

The wireframe model should appear as in Figure 14.35.

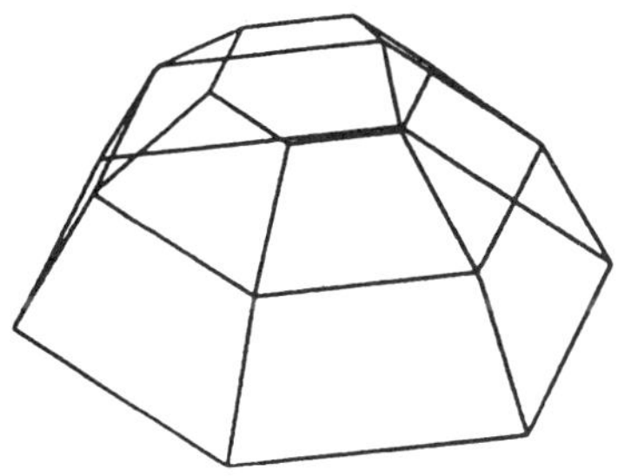

Figure 14.35

Step 2. Change Gview to top view.

Select **Gview** → **Top**

The wireframe model in the top view looks like Figure 14.36.

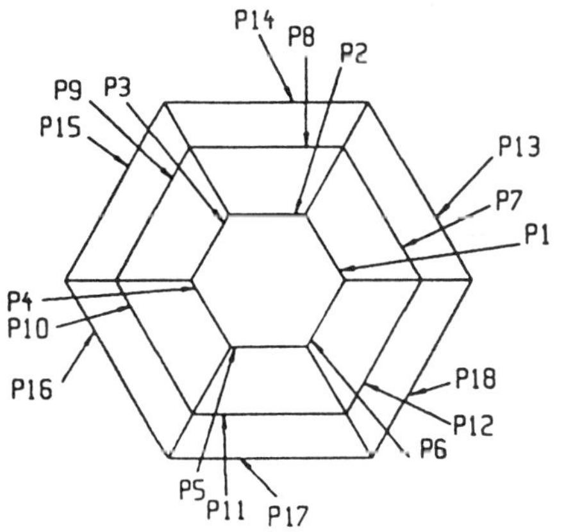

Figure 14.36a Along

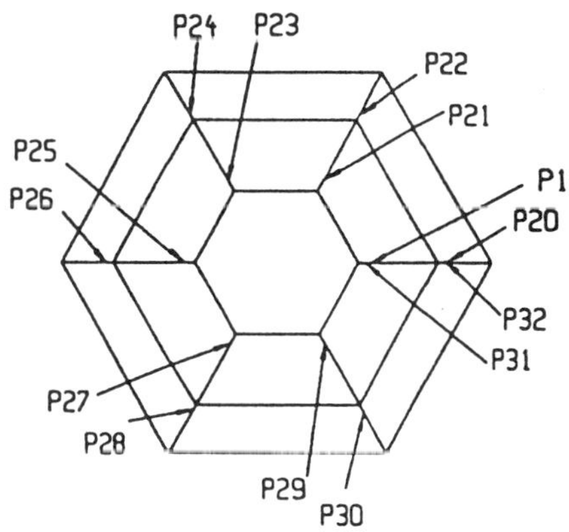

Figure 14.36b Across

Step 3. Initiate the Coons toolpath module.

Select **MAIN MENU** → **Toolpaths** → **Next menu** → **Wireframe** → **Coons**

Step 4. Specify the number of patches in along and across directions.

Enter **6** for the number of patches in the along direction
Enter **2** for the number of patches in the across direction

Step 5. Define the contours using the pick points in Figure 14.36.

Select **Single** then pick **P1**
Sequentially pick **P2 - P32**
Select **Done** to complete the contour definition

Step 6. Define Coons parameters to the following settings.

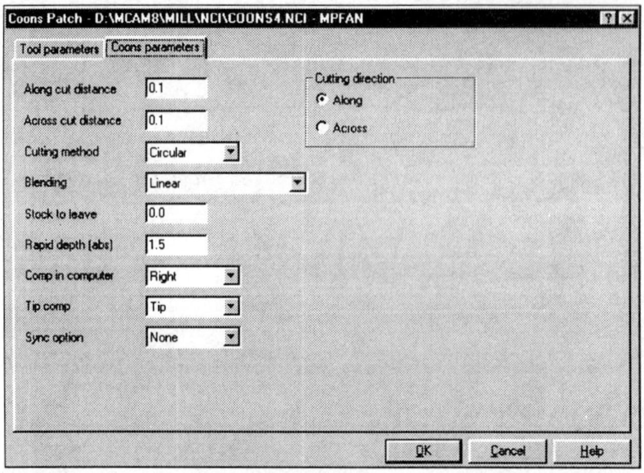

Select the **Tool parameters** tab to advance to the Tool parameters menu.

Step 7. Define Tool parameters to the following settings.

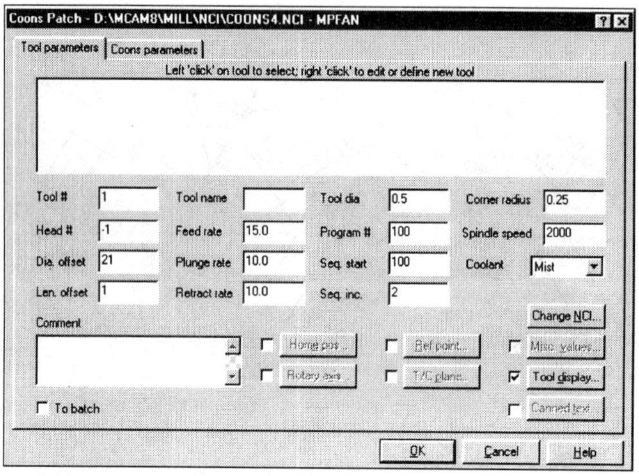

Click on **Change NCI**
Change the file name to **coonst2 → OK**
Select **OK** to complete the parameters settings.

The toolpaths shown in top Gview should look like Figure 14.37.

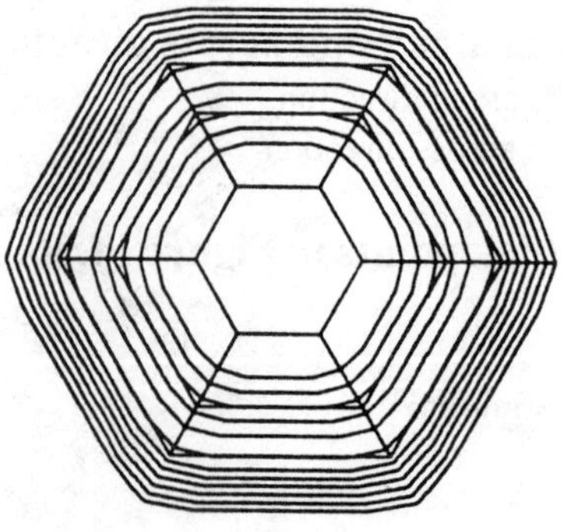

Figure 14.37

Step 8. Change Gview to Isometric.

Select **Gview → Isometric**

The toolpaths are shown in isometric view as in Figure 14.38.

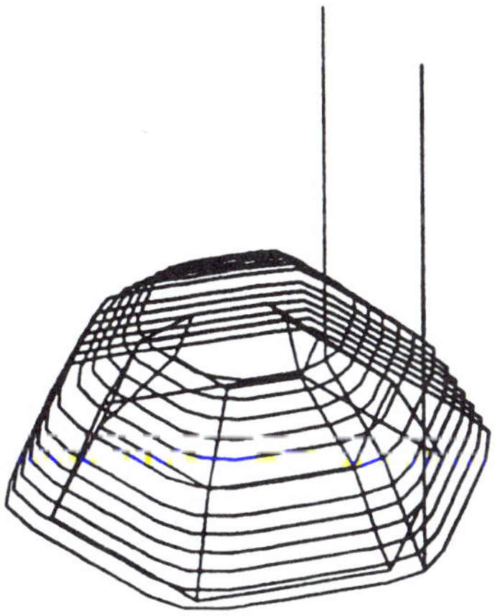

Figure 14.38

Step 9. Run the post processor.

Select **MAIN MENU → Toolpaths → Operations → Post**

In the Post processor dialog box, toggle **Save NCI file**, **Save NC file** and **Edit (NC)**

Select **OK** then enter file name: **coonst2.nci → Save**

enterfile name: **coonst2.nc → Save**

The part program steps are listed on the screen.

The last line is N1730 M30. This part program has a total of 822 lines.

Double click the upper left corner to exit the Edit utility.

Click **OK** from the "Operations Manager" menu.

Step 10. Run the filter function.

Select **MAIN MENU → NC utils**

Select **Filter → Settings**

Set the Filter settings as shown here:

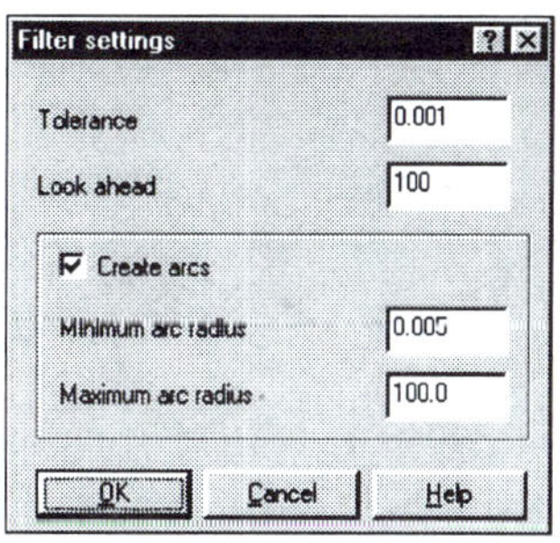

Select **OK → Do it**

File name: **coonst2.NCI → Open**

The system will perform the filtering to remove those unwanted program blocks.

It will indicate "Filter: 806 lines filtered to 247 lines. Reduction = 69.4%. Want to save changes?"

Select **Yes**

File name to write: **coonst2.NCI → Save**

Select **Yes** to "Delete old C:\m7\nci\coonst2.NCI ?"

Step 11. Repost process the filtered file

Select **Post proc → Run**

Filename: **coonst2.nci** for the NCI file **→ Open**

Filename: **coonst2.nc** for the NC file **→ Save**

Select **Yes** to delete the old NC file

The filtered program should be listed on the screen and the last line of the file is **N612M30**. This file contains a total of **263** lines (or blocks).

Step 12. Exit the Edit utility.

Double click the upper left corner to exit the Edit utility.

14.7 Swept Toolpath Module

The swept module is used to generate toolpaths for cutting surfaces that are formed by either translating a sectional profile along one or two rail contours or translating two sectional profiles along a rail contour. Mastercam provides the following three modes of swept toolpath module:

One across/ one along:	translate or rotate an across contour while following the along contour.
One across/ two along:	proportionally scale the across contour between the two along contours.
Two across/ one along:	perform a linear blend between the two across contours while following the along contour.

Swept 2D

The one across/one along mode is referred to as **2d swept in** Mastercam. In 2d mode, the along contour must lie parallel or perpendicular to the current tool plane if a tool plane is defined. Otherwise, it must parallel or perpendicular to the XY-plane. Any cross section taken normal to any part of the along contour remains constant (Figure 14.39).

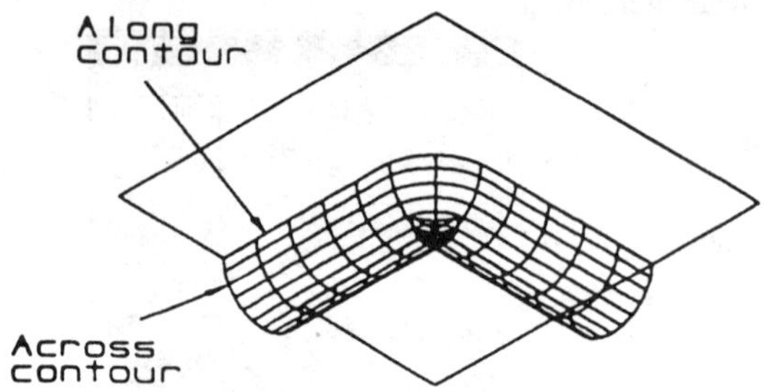

Figure 14.39

The dialog box of Swept 2D parameters is shown below.

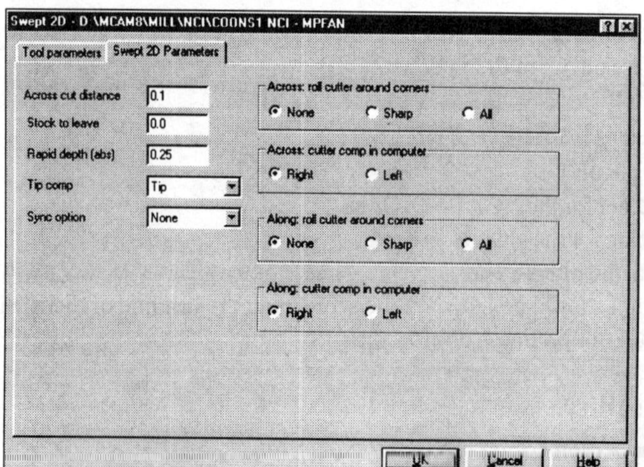

Swept 3D

The other two modes (two across/ one along and one across/ two along) are referred to as **3d swept**. In 3d mode, contours can be in any plane, and in any orientation. Figures 14.40 and 14.41 illustrate one across/two along, and two across/one along swept surface, respectively. The dialog box of Swept 3D parameter is shown below.

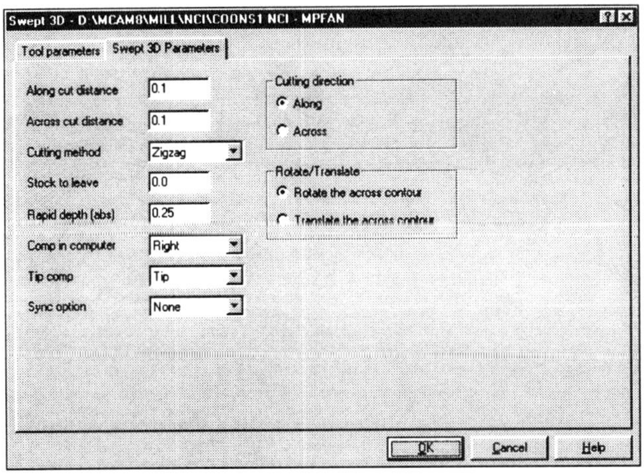

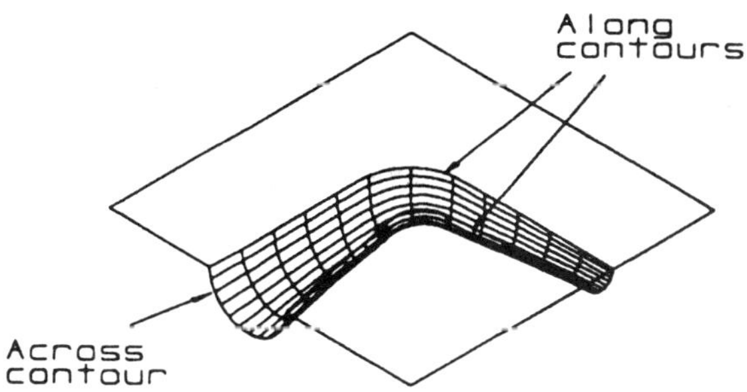

Figures 14.40

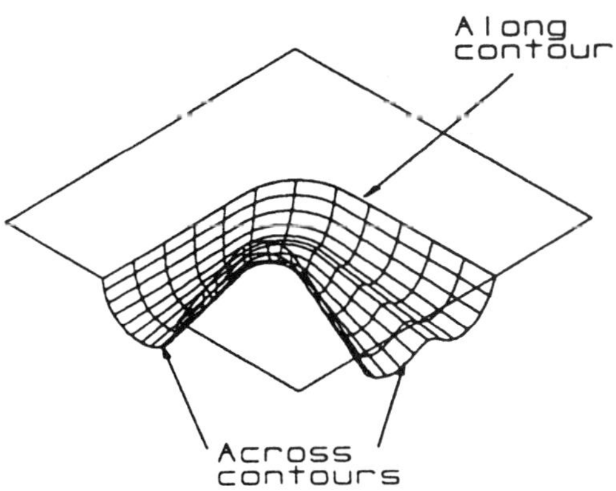

Figure 14.41

Project 6. Machining a 2D swept surface

Use a 2D swept module to generate toolpaths for cutting a swept surface. Figure 14.42 shows both the wireframe model and the toolpaths.

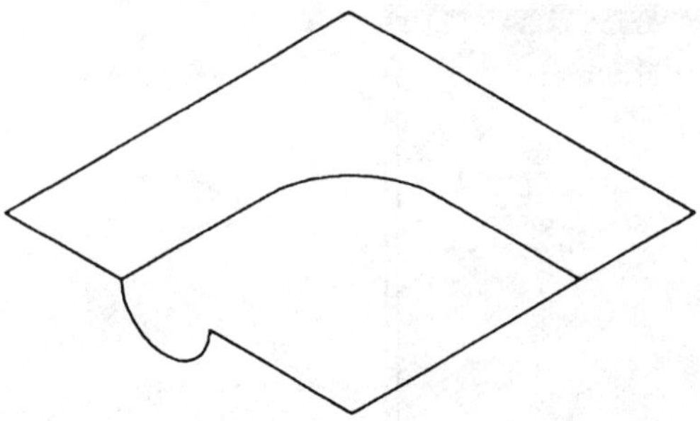

Figure 14.42a Wireframe

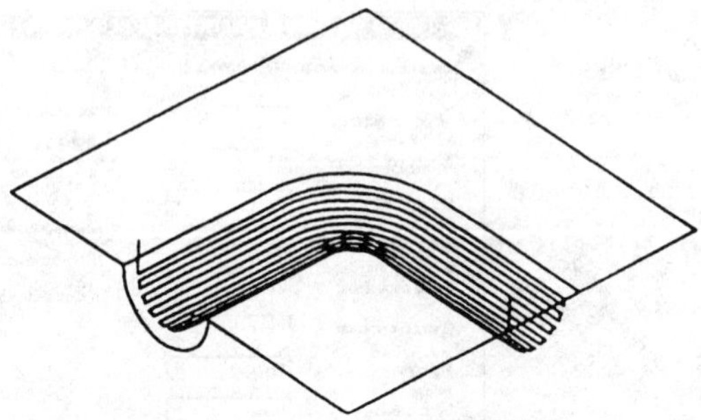

Figure 14.42b Toolpaths

Tips 1. Construct a wireframe model as shown in Figure 14.42.

2. Use the Front Cplane to create an arc for across contour.

3. The front horizontal line must be broken into two pieces in the middle. This allows the line to be trimmed to the two intersection points with the arc.

Step 1. Create a rectangle using the isometric Gview.

Select **Gview → Isometric**
Select **Cplane → Top** if necessary
Select **MAIN MENU → Create → Rectangle → 1 point**
Enter the width: **6** ↵
Enter the height: **6** ↵
Select the **lower left corner → OK**
Enter coordinate: **0,0** ↵
Press **Alt** + **F1** simultaneously then press **F2** to fit the drawing on the screen

The rectangle should appear as Figure 14.43.

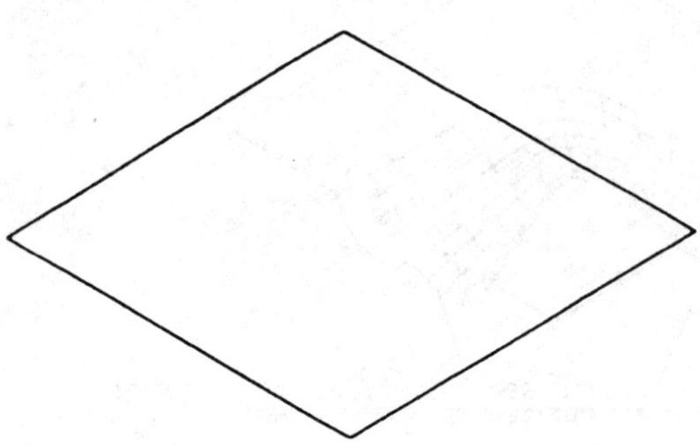

Figure 14.43

Step 2. Create two lines. 🖳6

Select **MAIN MENU → Create → Line → Endpoints**
Specify the first endpoint: **2,0** ↵
Specify the second endpoint: **2,5** ↵ for the vertical line
Specify the first endpoint: **6,4** ↵
Specify the second endpoint: **1,4** ↵ for the horizontal line

The two lines are added as shown in Figure 14.44.

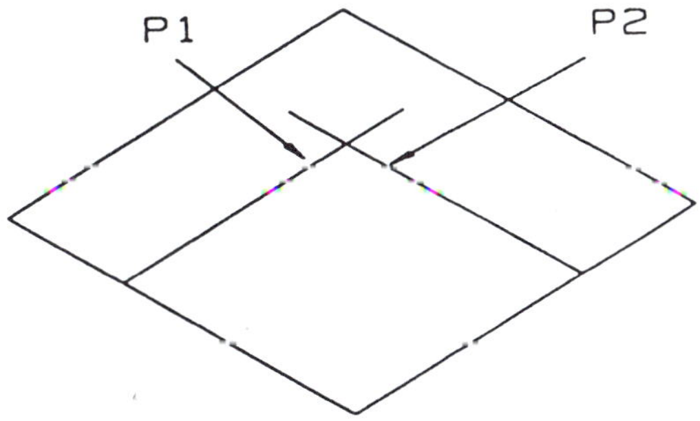

Figure 14.44

Step 3. Add a fillet to the two lines using the pick points in Figure 14.44.

Select **MAIN MENU → Modify → Fillet → Radius**
Enter radius: **1.5** ↵
Pick **P1** and **P2**

The fillet is added to the drawing as shown in Figure 14.45.

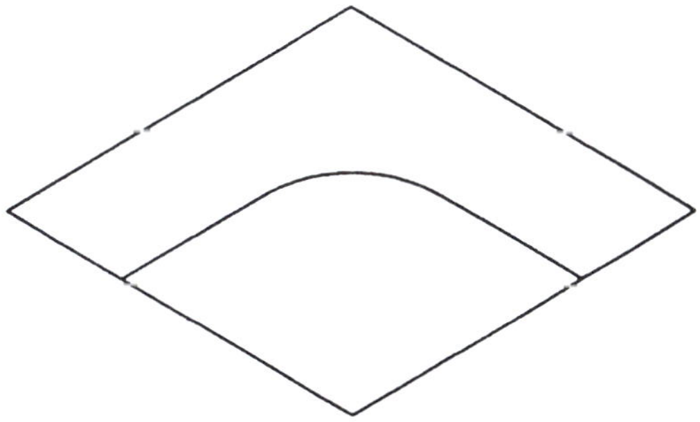

Figure 14.45

Step 4. Create an arc using the Front Cplane.

Select **Cplane → Front**
Select **MAIN MENU → Create → Arc → Endpoints**
Enter the first point: **2,0** ↵
Enter the second point: **3.5,0** ↵
Enter the radius: **0.75** ↵
Select arc: pick at the lower arc of the two

The arc is added to the drawing as shown in Figure 14.46.

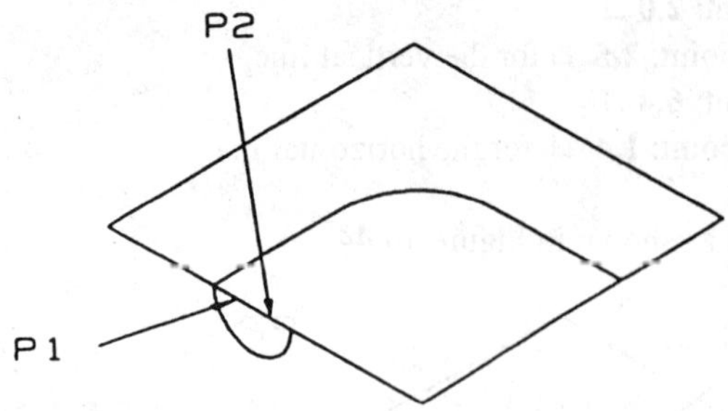

Figure 14.46

Step 5. Break the front line of the rectangle into two pieces using the pick points in Figure 14.46.

Select **MAIN MENU → Modify → Break → 2 pieces**
Pick **P1** to select an entity
Select **Midpoint**
Pick **P2** to enter the breakpoint

The front line is broken into two pieces but the drawing does not look different. The drawing is redrawn in Figure 14.47.

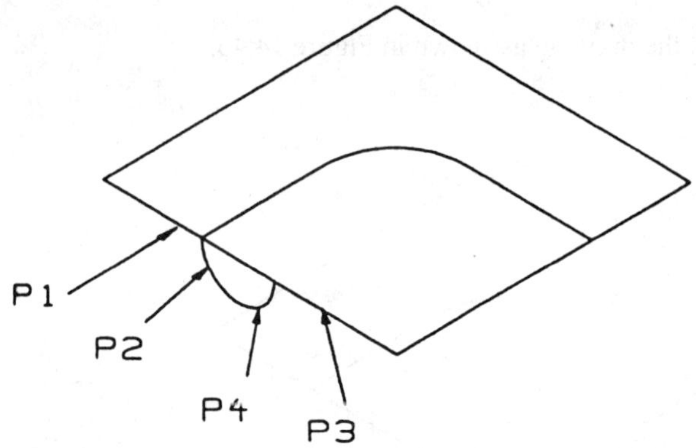

Figure 14.47

Step 6. Trim the front line using the pick points in Figure 14.47.

Change Cplane to 3D.
Select **Cplane → 3D**
Select **MAIN MENU → Modify → Trim → 2 entities**
Pick **P1** to select the entity to trim
Pick **P2** to select the entity to trim to
Pick **P3** to select the entity to trim
Pick **P4** to select the entity to trim to

The new drawing becomes Figures 14.48.

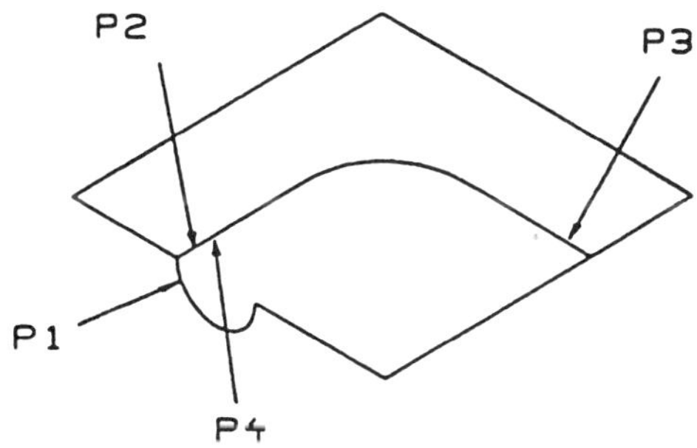

Figure 14.48

Step 7. Initiate swept toolpath module.

Select **MAIN MENU** → **Toolpaths** → **Next menu** → **Wireframe** → **Swept 2D**

Step 8. Define contours using the pick points in Figure 14.48.

Select **Single,**
then pick **P1** to define the across contour
Select **Mode** → **Chain** → **Partial** then pick **P2** and **P3**
Select **Done** to complete contour selection
Select **Endpoint** then pick **P4** to enter the intersection of the across and along contours

Step 9. Define Swept 2D parameters to the following settings.

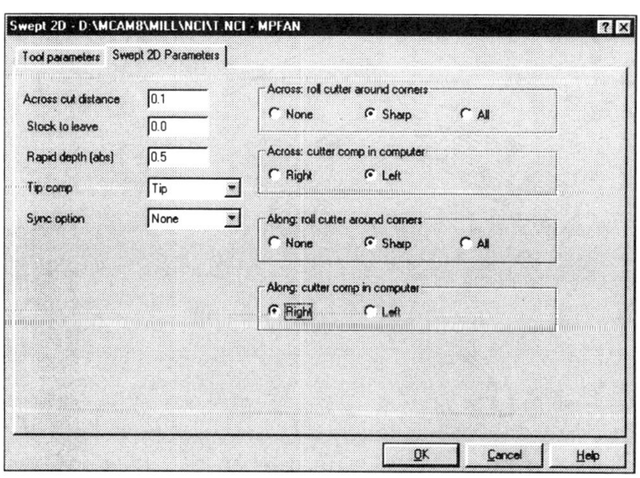

Select the **Tool parameters** tab to advance to the Tool parameters menu.

Step 10. Define Tool parameters to the following settings.

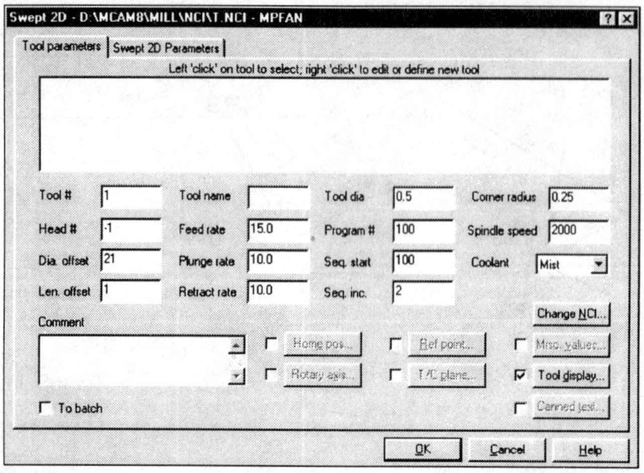

Click on **Change NCI**
Change the file name to **swepttl → OK**
Select **OK** to complete the parameter settings.

Step 11. Accept and save the toolpaths.

Select **MAIN MENU → Toolpaths → Operations → Post**
Toggle **Save NCI file** to on (with check mark) **→ OK**
Enter filename: **swepttl → Save**
Select **OK** to leave the operations Manager dialog
The toolpaths for cutting the swept surface are shown in Figure 14.49.

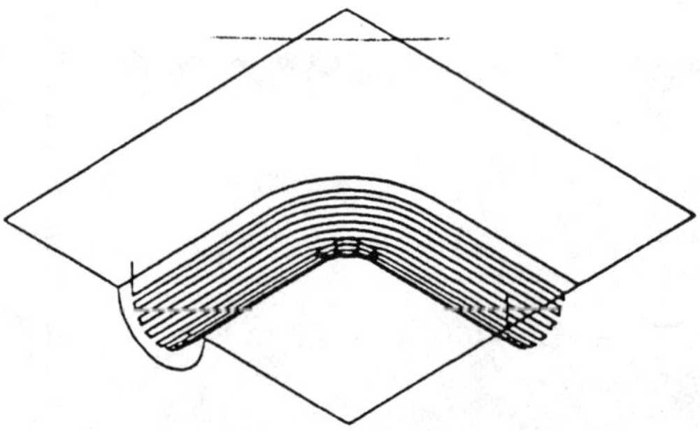

Figure 14.49

💻Project 7. Machining a swept surface defined by one across contour and two along contours 💻7

Use the swept toolpath module to generate a set of toolpaths to machine a swept surface defined by an across contour and two along contours. The wireframe model and the toolpaths are shown in Figure 14.50.

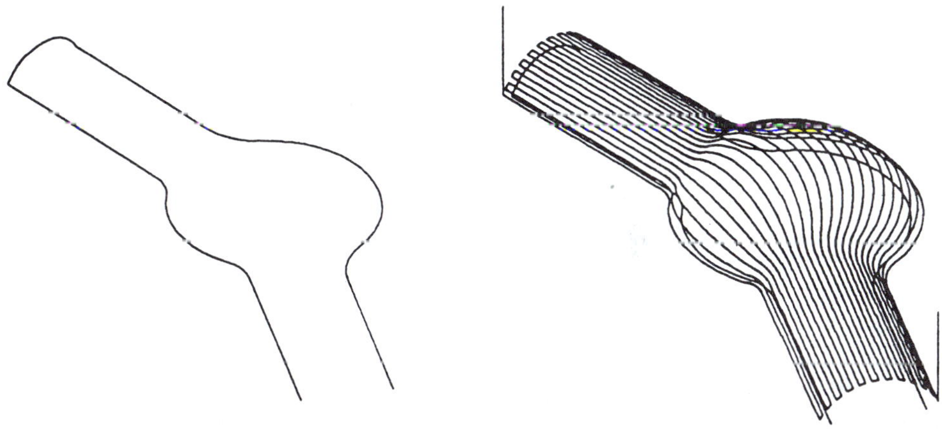

Figure 14.50

> ⌛**Tips** 1. Use the wireframe model file swept3.ge3.
>
> 2. Use 3d swept with one across/ two along commands.
>
> 3. The syncs command is used to change the density of cutting steps of the two fillets in the first along contour. The cutting density is a ratio used to determine the step from one sync to another. One sync should be designated as the reference sync. This reference sync is defined with a cutting density of 1. Other syncs are determined by the value given to the cutting density. The section with a cutting density of 2, for example, has twice the density of the reference sync. In this project, we assign a cutting density of 5 to the two fillets, and all other sections have the density of 1.
>
> 4. Cutter compensation in computer should be set to right tip.

Step 1. Load the wireframe model file (swept3.ge3) or create one by following the instructions in project 10 of chapter 11.

Select **MAIN MENU → File → Get**

Enter file name: **swept3** ↵

The wireframe model should look like Figure 14.51 on the next page.

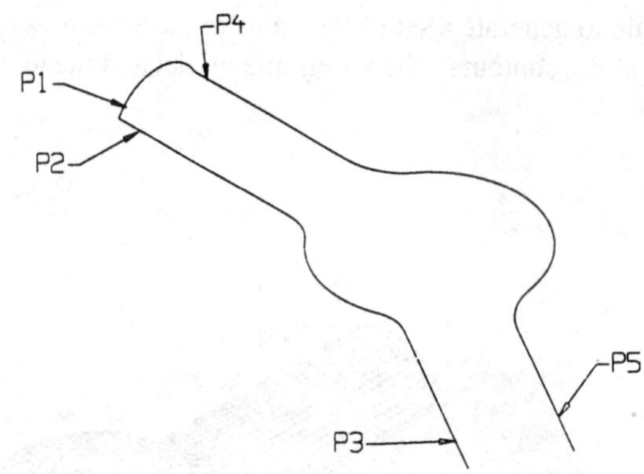

Figure 14.51

Step 2. Initiate swept toolpath module.

Select **MAIN MENU → Toolpaths → Next menu → Wireframe → Swept 3D**
Enter the number of across contours: **1** ↵

Step 3. Define the across contour using the pick points in Figure 14.51.

Define the across contour: Select **Single** then pick **P1**

Step 4. Define the two along contours.

Still use the pick points in Figure 14.51.
Select **Mode → Chain → Partial**
Pick **P2** and **P3** to define the along contour 1
Select **Partial**
Pick **P4** and **P5** to define the along contour 2
Select **Done**

Step 5. Define swept 3D parameters to the following settings.

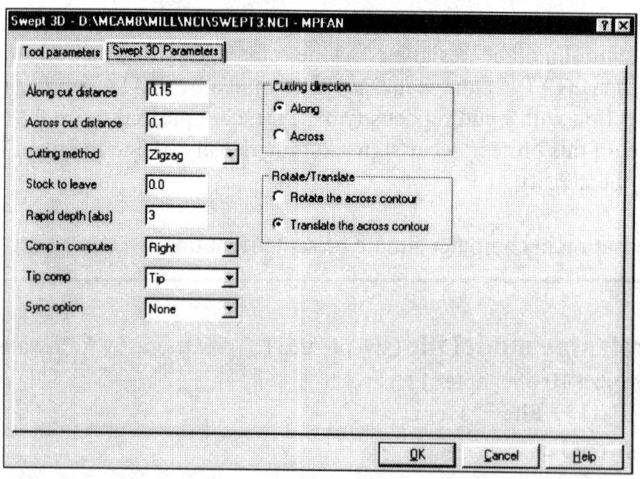

Select the **Tool parameters** tab to advance to the Tool parameters menu.

Step 6. Define Tool parameters to the following settings.

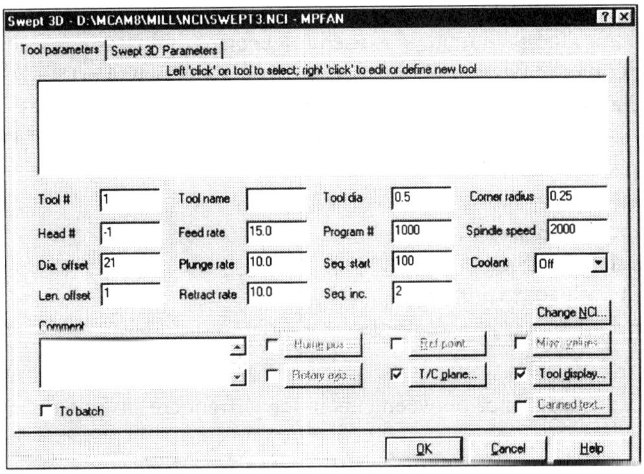

Click **Change NCI**
Select the file name as: **sweptt2 → OK**
Select **OK** to complete the parameter settings.

Step 7. Write and save the toolpaths.

Select **MAIN MENU → Toolpaths → Operations → Post**
Toggle **Save NCI file** to on (with check mark) **→ OK**
Enter filename: **sweptt2 → Save**
Select **OK** to leave the operations Manager dialog
The toolpaths should resemble Figure 14.52.

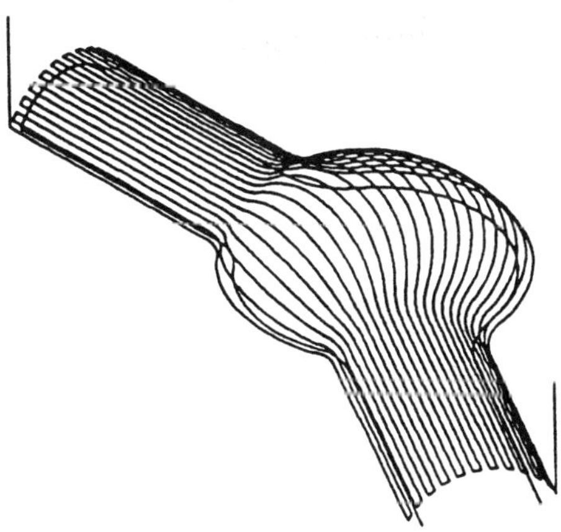

Figure 14.52

14.8 Surface of Revolution Toolpath Module

The surface of a revolution toolpath module is used to generate toolpaths to machine a surface that is defined by revolving a geometric contour about an axis. This is a very powerful tool for cutting any surface that is symmetrical about an axis. The surface of revolution parameters are:

Step size = 0.1 Axial depth = 0.0 Shape = Concave/Convex Retract to nothing Trim toolpath to nothing

Step size

This parameter specifies the distance between cuts in the current construction plane.

Axis depth

This parameter specifies the Z-coordinate of the axis of rotation. This Z value automatically determines the depth of the plane at which the toolpath starts being generated. Figures 14.53 and 14.54 show how the axial depth affects the toolpaths.

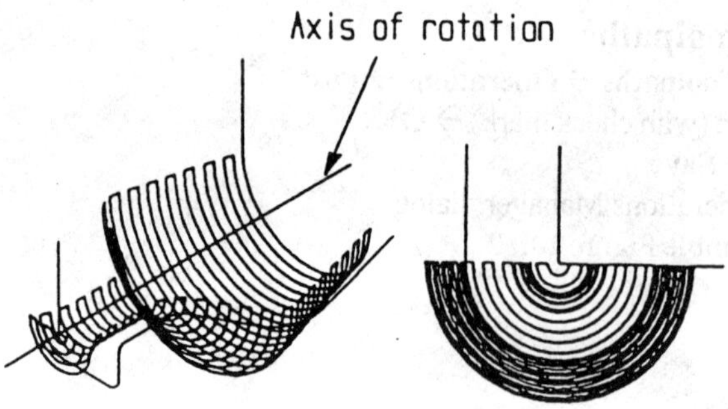

Figure 14.53 Axial depth = 0.0

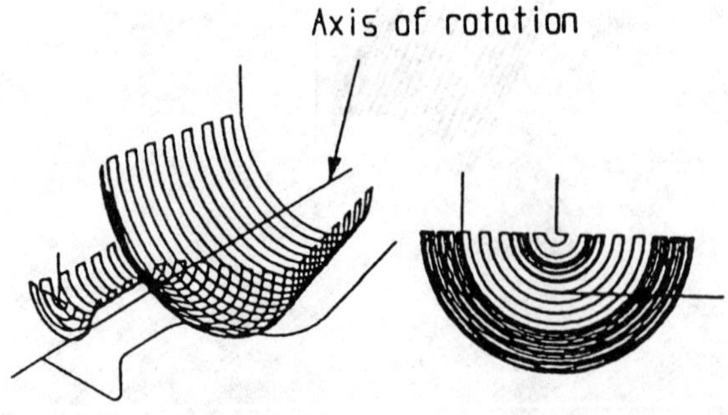

Figure 14.54 Axial depth= 0.5

Shape

This parameter allows us to select the shape of the revolved surface to be the concave or convex type. Figure 14.55 shows the toolpaths for cutting a cup in concave and convex shape.

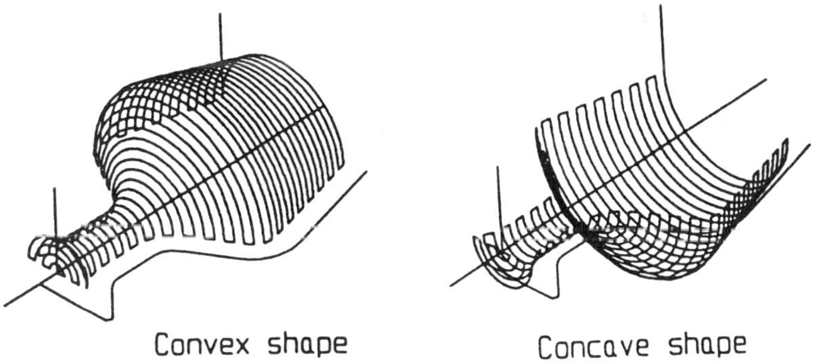

Figure 14.55

Retract to

This parameter adds a vertical wall to the surface. The system will generate a series of extended toolpaths normal to the current construction plane at surface's endpoints. At each of the surface endpoints, the tool retracts to the level specified by the Retract to parameter, then moves a stepover distance, moves down to the surface endpoint, and moves over the surface. Figure 14.56 shows the toolpath pattern of retract to parameter.

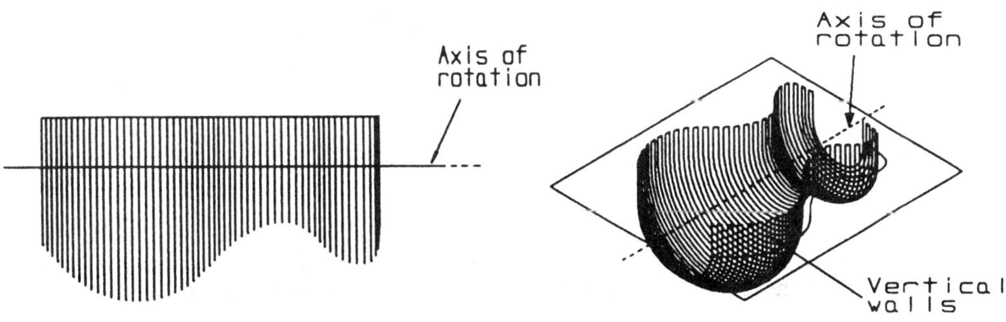

Figure 14.56

Trim to

This parameter allows the toolpaths to be trimmed or extended to a specified plane or boundary. There are two trim to modes: height and width. In trim to height mode, the toolpaths are extended to the specified height if this height is above the axis depth (axis of rotation) shown on the next page in Figure 14.57a, or the toolpaths are trimmed to the specified height if this height is below the axis depth shown in Figure 14.57b.

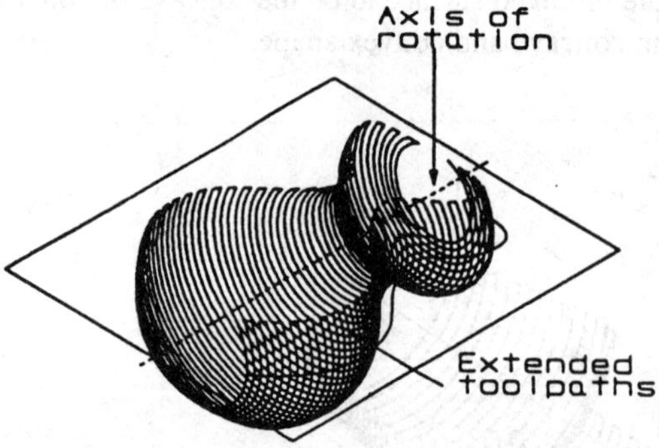

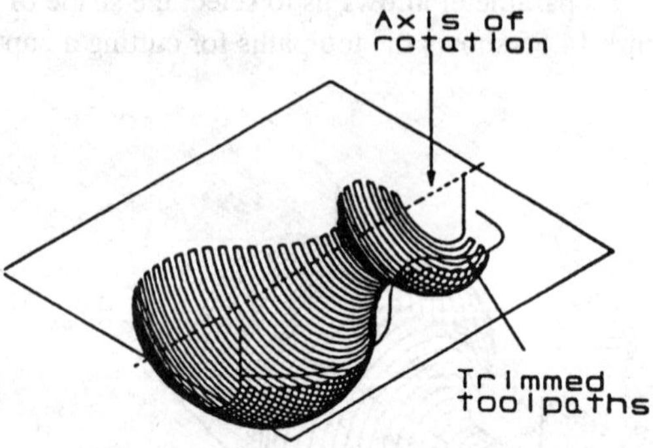

Figure 14.57a

Figure 14.57b

Note: When the toolpaths are extended above the axis depth, undercuts occur in most cases.

In the **convex cases,** the toolpaths will be trimmed when the trimming height is above the axis of rotation (Figure 14.58a), or the toolpaths will be extended when the trimming height is below the axis of rotation (Figure 14.58b).

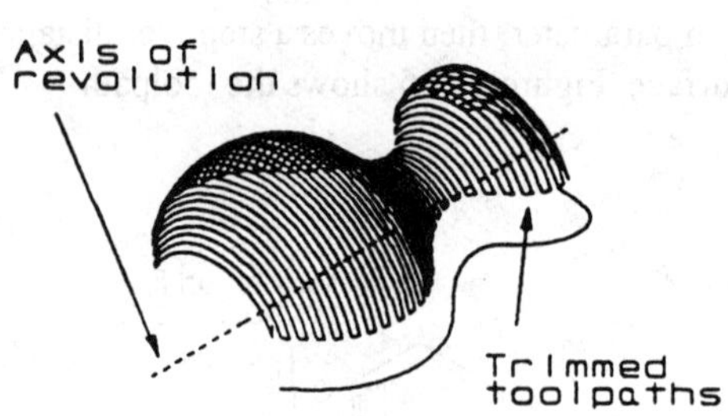

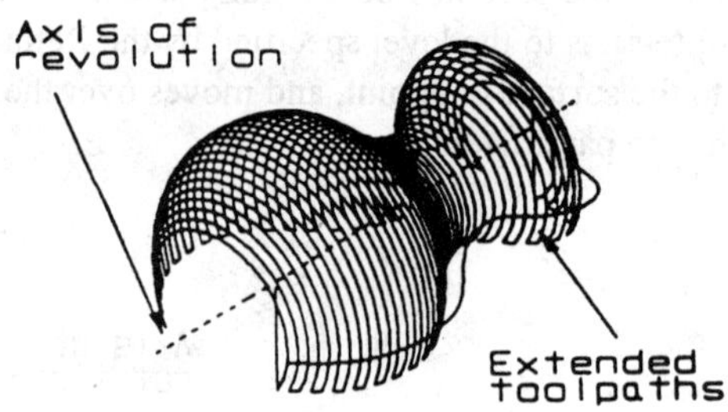

Figure 14.58a

Figure 14.58b

In trim to width mode, the toolpaths are to be trimmed to a fixed width specified by two parallel lines. Note that the toolpaths are trimmed to the tool center instead of the edge. Figure 14.59 shows a trim to width example.

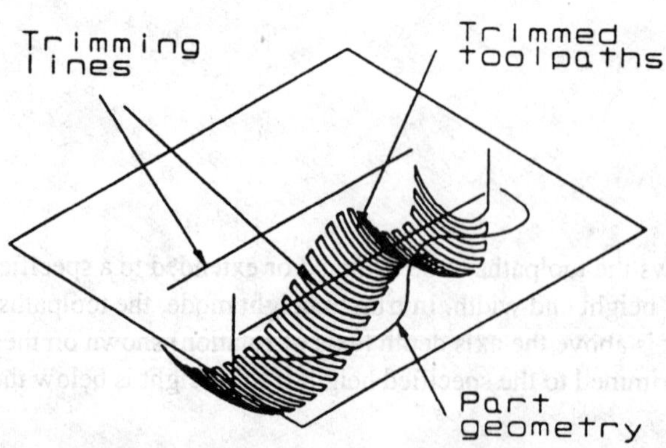

Figure 14.59

Project 8. Machining a surface of revolution

The revolution module is used to generate toolpaths to machine a cup with a convex shape. The wireframe model file is cup.ge3 created in project 8 of chapter 11. The wireframe model and the toolpaths are shown in Figure 14.60.

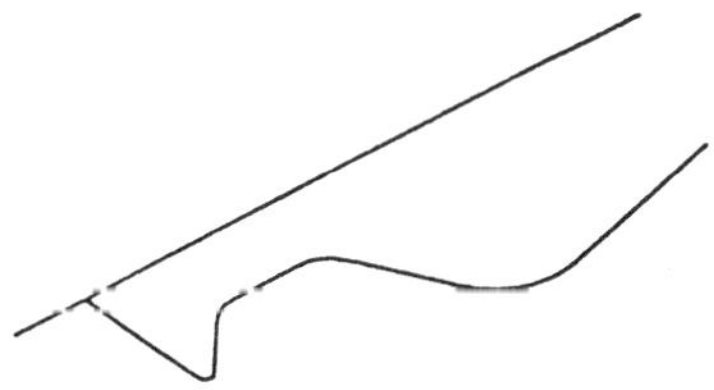

Figure 14.60a Wireframe model

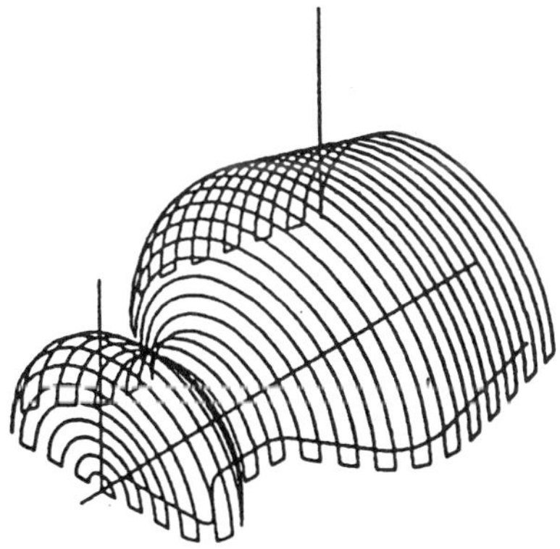

Figure 14.60b Toolpaths

Tips 1. Wireframe model file is cup.ge3.

2. Axis of rotation is Y axis.

3. Shape = Convex

Step 1. Load the wireframe model file cup.ge3.

(or create one by following the instructions in project 8 of chapter 11.)
Select **MAIN MENU** → **File** → **Get**
Enter file name: **cup** ↵
Select **Gview** → **Isometric**
The wireframe model of the cup should appear as Figure 14.61.

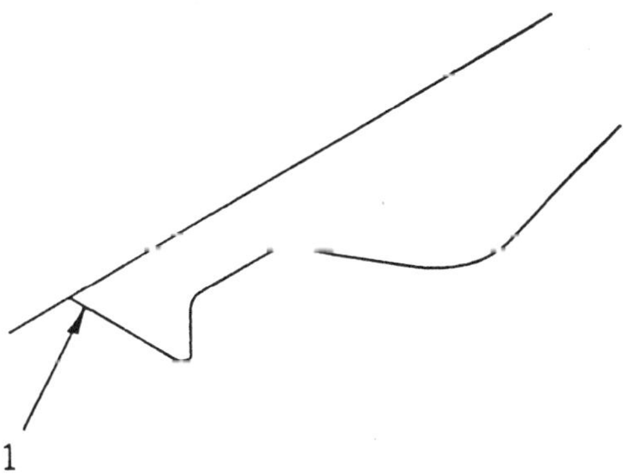

Figure 14.61

Step 2. Initiate the revolution toolpath module.

Select **MAIN MENU** → **Toolpaths** → **Next menu** → **Wireframe** → **Revolution**

Step 3. Define the contours using the pick point in Figure 14.61.

Select the edge of the surface: Select **Chain** then pick **P1**
Select **Done**
Select **Origin**

Step 4. Define the surface of revolution parameters to the following settings.

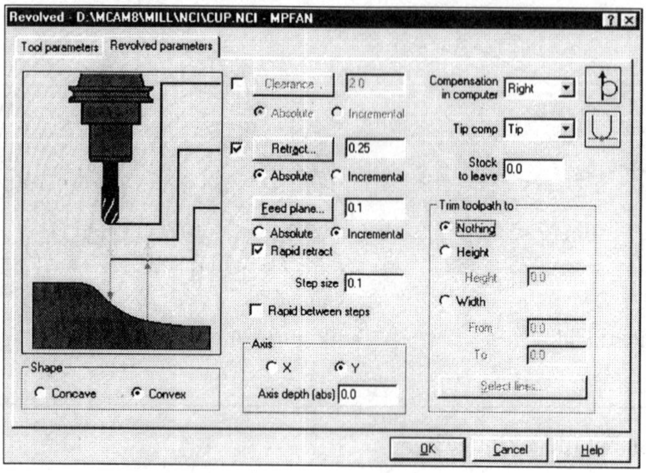

Select the **Tool parameters** tab to advance to the Tool parameters menu.

Step 5. Define the Tool parameters to the following settings.

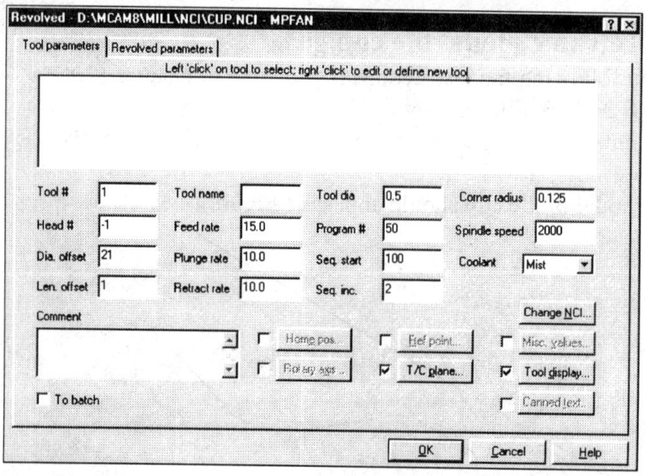

Click on **Change NCI**
Change the file name to **revolt1 OK**
Select **OK** to complete the parameters settings.

Step 6. Save and close the toolpath file.

Select **MAIN MENU → Toolpaths→ Operations → Post**
Toggle **Save NCI file** to on (with check mark) → **OK**
Enter filename: **revolt1 → Save**
Select **OK** to leave the operations Manager dialog

The toolpaths should resemble Figure 14.62.

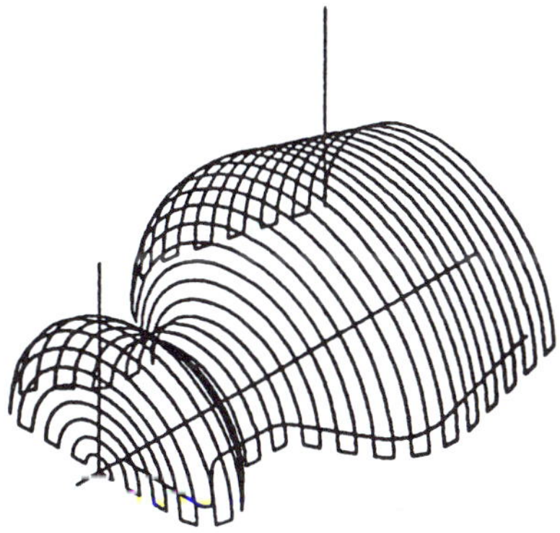

Figure 14.62

Ex Exercises

1. What are the two methods used to generate toolpaths to cut surfaces in Mastercam? Describe the advantages and disadvantages of using these two methods, respectively.

2. Define along and across directions.

3. What are the four cutting methods in 3d surfacing?

4. Describe, with a drawing, the main features of the Zig zag cutting method.

5. Describe, with a drawing, the main features of the one way cutting method.

6. Describe, with a drawing, the main features of the circular cutting method.

7. What are the two modes of cutting direction?

8. What are the two stepping over distances used in surfacing cutting? Use drawings to illustrate these two distances.

9. Describe how the stepping over distances affects the dimensional accuracy and part program size of surface machining.

10. What are the five modes of cutter compensation in computer?

11. What are two common types of cutters used in cutting surfaces?

12. Use drawings to show how the selection of cutter tip and cutter center affect the toolpaths?

13. Describe the two groups of 3d toolpath modules in Mastercam. Explain their differences.

14. List the five 3d toolpath modules that generate toolpaths from a wireframe model.

15. What is constant Z cutting in ruled module?

16. What do initial Z and final Z parameters perform in setting constant Z cutting?

17. Describe the functions of trimming planes in ruled module.

18. What are the four blending methods used in Coons module?

Problems

19. Use the ruled toolpath module to generate the toolpaths for machining two ruled surfaces from the wireframe model created in problem 11.10. The wireframe model file is **E1.** The wireframe model and the toolpaths are illustrated in Figure 14.63.

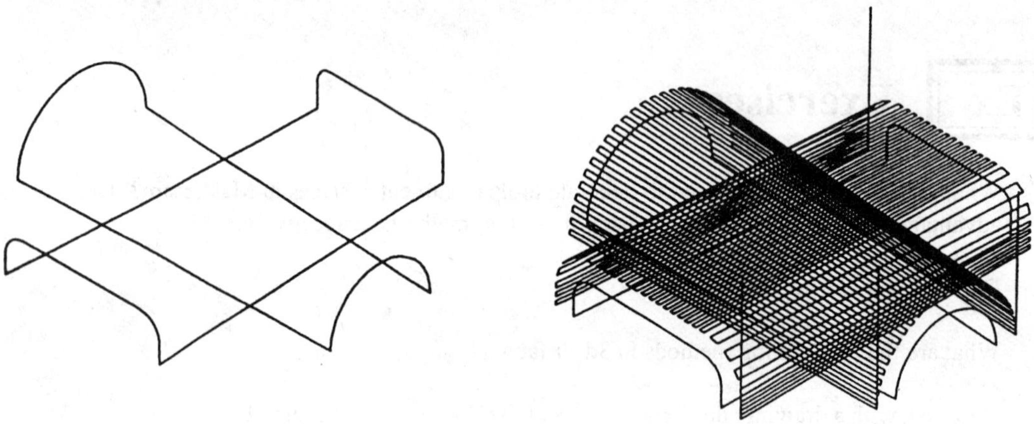

Figure 14.63

Tips 1. Wireframe model file is **E1**.

2. Save the toolpaths for cutting two ruled surfaces in two separate files **ET1** and **ET2**.

3.. Cutter is 0.75" ball-end mill.

4. Cutting method = Zig zag

20. Use the loft toolpath module to generate toolpaths for cutting a loft surface defined by the wireframe model created in problem 11.12. The wireframe model file is **E3**. Both the wireframe model and toolpaths are illustrated in Figure 14.64.

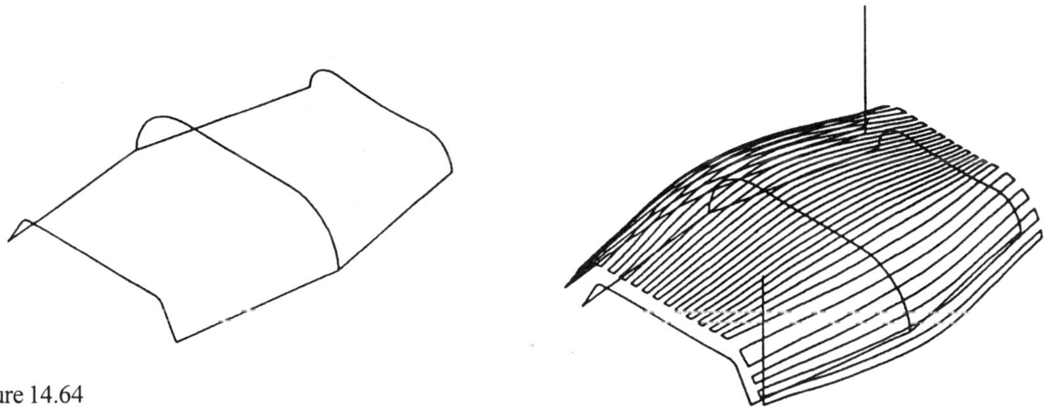

Figure 14.64

Tips 1. Wireframe model file is **E3.**

2. Pick the contours at the right end and start at contour A.

3. Set cutter compensation in computer to left tip.

21. Use the Coons toolpath module to generate toolpaths to cut the surface created from the wireframe model given in problem 11.14. This is a single patch Coons surface. The wireframe model file is **E5**. Both the wireframe model and toolpaths are shown in Figure 14.65.

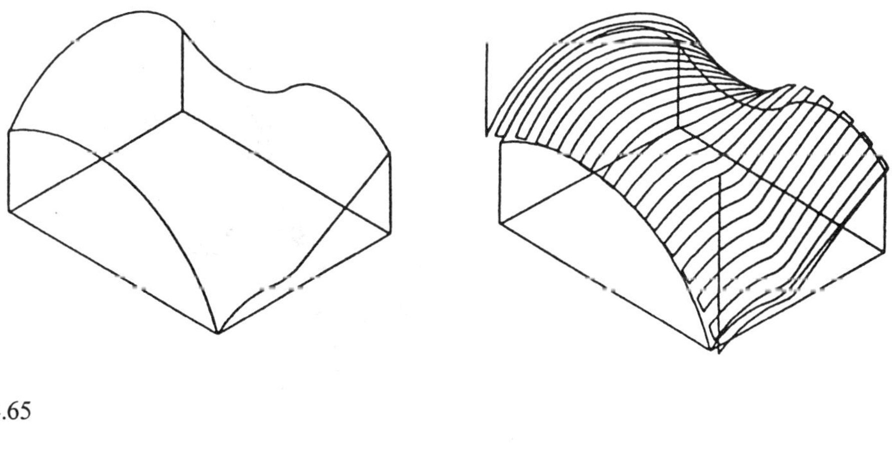

Figure 14.65

Tips 1. Wireframe model file is **E5.**

2. The number of patches in the along direction is 1.
   The number of patches in the across direction is 1.
3. Use the linear blending method because this is a single patch surface.

22. The Coons toolpath module is used to generate the toolpaths for machining a multiple-patch Coons surface. The wireframe model is created in problem 11.15 and has the name **E6**. Figure 14.66 shows both the wireframe model and the toolpaths.

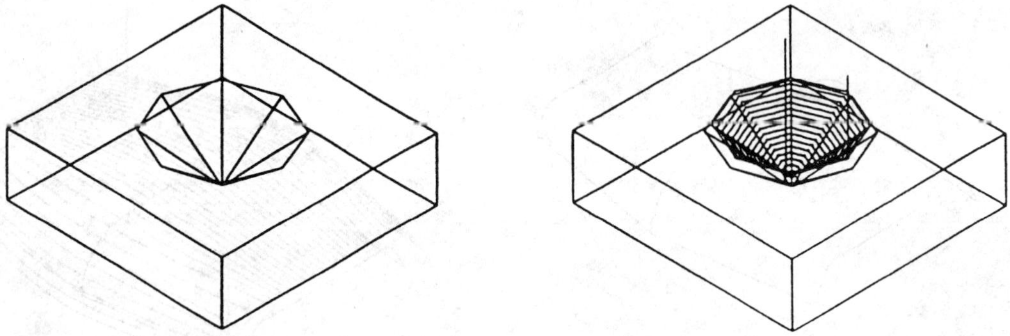

Figure 14.66

Tips 1. Wireframe model file is **E6.**

2. The number of patches in the along direction is 8.
   The number of patches in the across direction is 1.
3. The second along contours are a common point. This point serves as the contours for the second along contour rows.
4. Use linear blending method because all patches are flat surfaces.

23. The revolution toolpath module is used to generate the toolpaths for machining the cup defined by the wireframe model **E8** in problem 11.17. The cup model is made using the concave shape. Figure 14.67 shows both wireframe model and toolpaths.

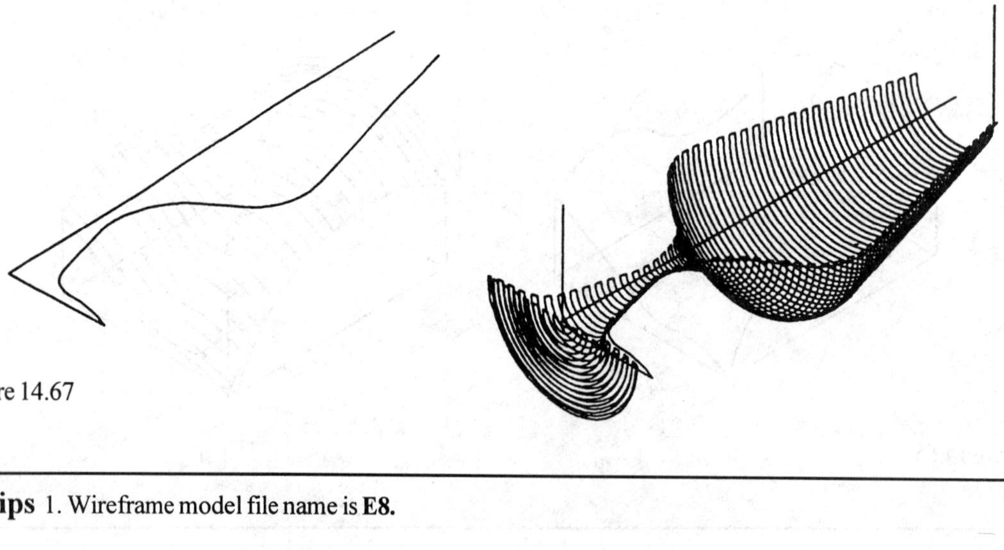

Figure 14.67

Tips 1. Wireframe model file name is **E8.**

2. The axis of rotation is Y axis.

3. Surface shape is concave.

4. Set both *retraction to* and *trim to* parameters to nothing.

24. Use the swept toolpath module to generate the toolpaths to cut a fly disk as shown in Figure 14.68. The wireframe model is created in problem 11.19 and has the name **E10**. The toolpaths for cutting the upper section of the model can be obtained by revolving the upper section profile about the Z axis. However, the bottom half of the model can not be machined in the same machine setup as the upper half. We need to flip the workpiece over and has the second setup for machining the bottom half. Therefore, it requires two toolpath files, one for the upper half and the other for the bottom half.

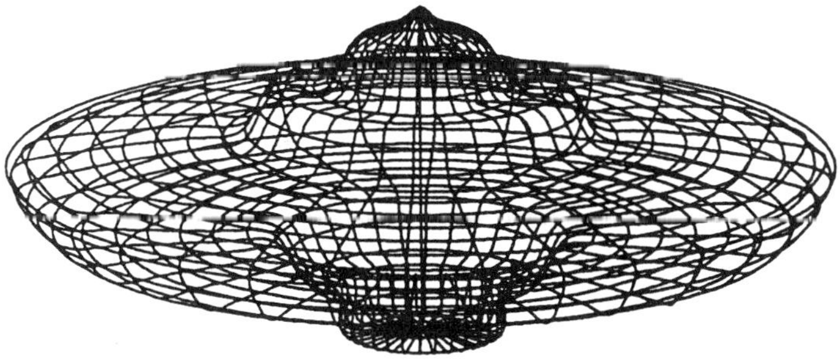

Figure 14.68

Tips
1. Use the contour profile of the upper half in the swept module to generate toolpaths and save it under one file name.
2. Change the contour profile in the bottom half to level 2. This allows the upper half contour (level 1) to be made invisible.
3. Rotate the contours in the bottom half about the X axis by 180°.
4. Use swept module to generate toolpaths for the bottom half and save under another file name.

Chapter 15

3D Toolpaths II: Generated from Surface Models

Objectives:

1. Features of seven surface roughing functions.
2. Features of eight surface finishing functions.
3. Common parameters used in surfacing toolpath functions.
4. Applying various surface toolpath functions to generate NC programs to machine surfaces.

Overview

Mastercam provides a variety of toolpath functions to generate toolpaths from existing surface models. There are two main groups of toolpath functions for cutting surfaces; **roughing functions** and **finishing functions**. There are **seven** roughing toolpath functions and **ten** finishing toolpath functions. Each toolpath function has its unique features and parameters. The intent of this chapter is to provide Mastercam users with the essential concepts and skills required to use various surfacing toolpath functions to generate roughing and finishing toolpaths to machine surface models.

15.1 Surface Toolpath Functions

All surfacing toolpath functions are grouped under the surface command. Its menu appears as below. The two surface options are briefly summarized below.

Rough: select one rough function to generate roughing toolpaths for a surface model.

Finish: select one finish function to generate finishing toolpaths for a surface model.

15.2 Rough Functions

Most surface models require two sets of toolpaths to complete their machining; roughing and finishing. A roughing cut must be implemented prior to a finishing cut. Mastercam provides seven functions to generate roughing toolpaths for cutting surface models. These seven functions can be divided into **two main types** of roughing: **roughing around surfaces** and **roughing a pocket.** Only the pocket function is used to generate toolpaths to rough cut the material between the surfaces and material boundary. The remaining six rough functions are used to generate toolpaths to rough cut the surface profiles. Table 15.1 summaries these seven surface roughing functions. These seven roughing functions are presented, in order, after the common parameters section.

15.3 Common Parameters

Mastercam uses various types of parameters to define information required to generate toolpaths. These parameters can be classified into **two groups; common parameters** and **toolpath function specific parameters**. As their names imply, common parameters are commonly used in all toolpath functions, while function specific parameters are unique to the particular function and are not applicable to any other functions. Common parameters used in rough functions consist of two parts; tool parameters and rough parameters. Tool parameters are common to all toolpath functions including 2D and 3D surface roughing and finishing toolpath functions. Rough parameters are common to all seven rough functions.

Tool Parameters

The tool parameters dialog box for roughing surfaces is identical to the one used in 2D toolpath functions. It is redisplayed below for reference.

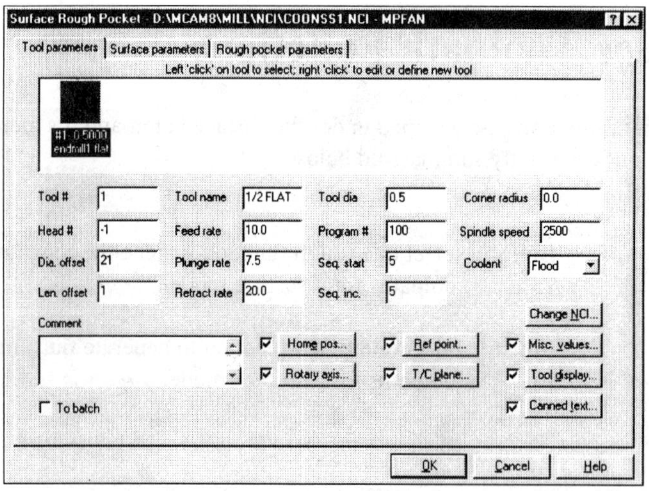

Rouging Function	Description	Illustration
Parallel	Generate roughing toolpaths that run in parallel direction specified by the machining angle parameter.	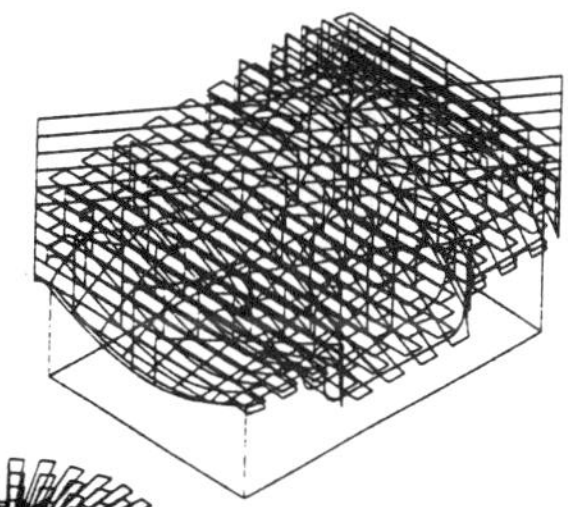
Radial	Generate roughing toolpaths that run in radial direction.	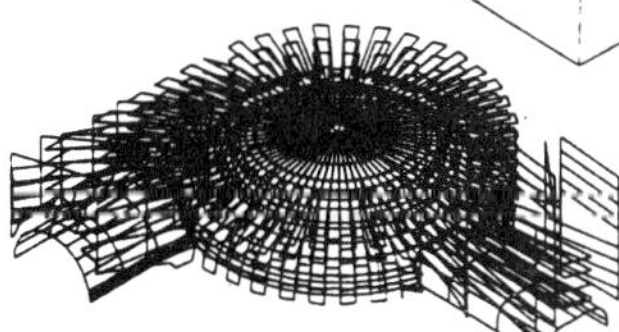
Project	Generate roughing toolpaths by projecting a set of existing toolpaths or geometry entities onto the selected surfaces.	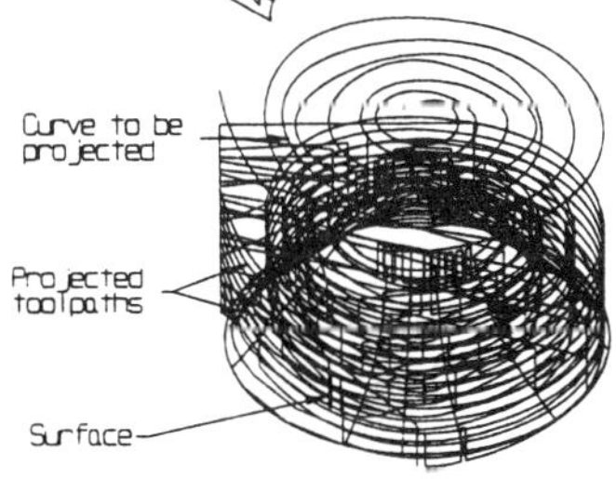
Flowline	Generate roughing toolpaths along the direction in the surface flowlines for roughing cut surface profile.	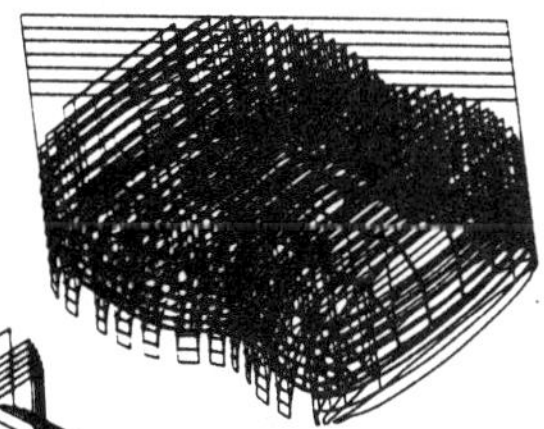
Contour	Generate roughing toolpaths along the surface contours.	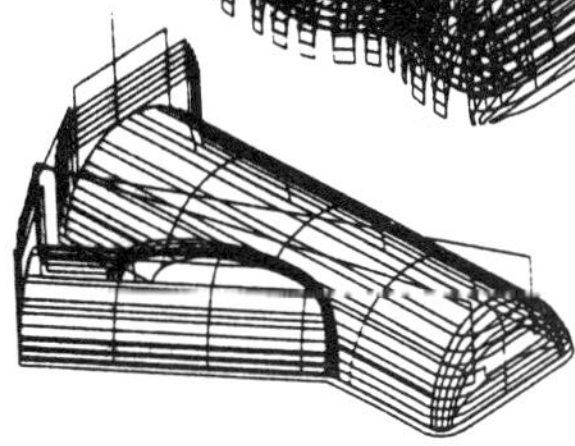
Pocket	Generate roughing toolpaths to rough out all stock between surfaces and pocket boundaries.	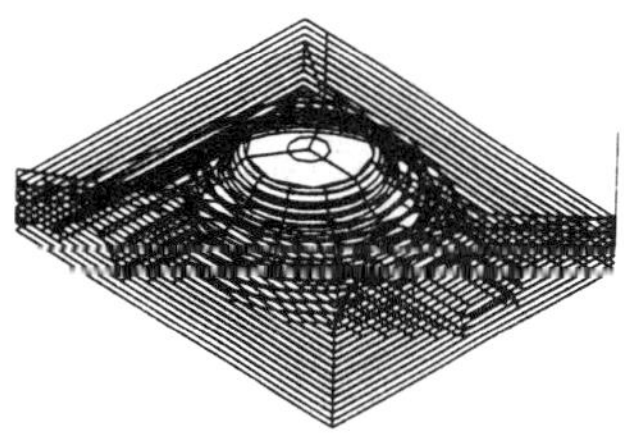
Plunge	Generate roughing toolpaths that plunge along the surface profiles in the Z direction.	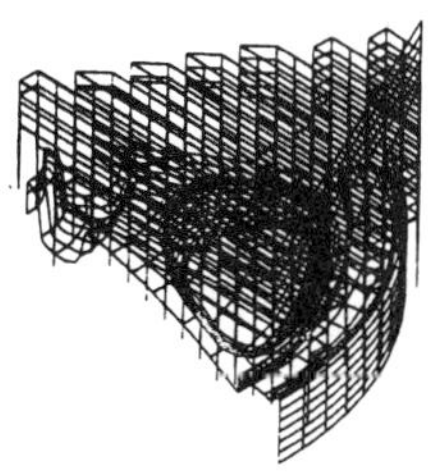

Surface Parameters

The rough parameters dialog box is identical to all seven roughing functions. It appears as below.

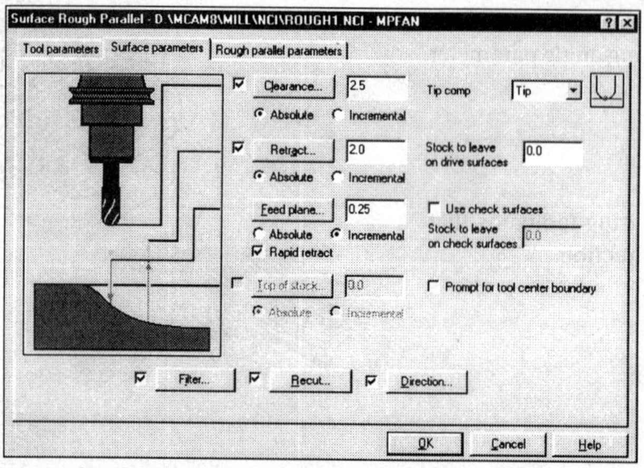

The roughing parameters can be categorized into the following eight categories: **Z depth parameters, Filter parameters, Direction parameters, Recut parameters, Tip/center compensation, Stock, Check surfaces,** and **Tool center boundary.**

Z depth parameters Mastercam uses four Z depth parameters to define the toolpaths in the Z direction. These four parameters; **Clearance height, Retract height, Feed plane,** and **Top of stock** are listed below and are shown in Figure 15.1.

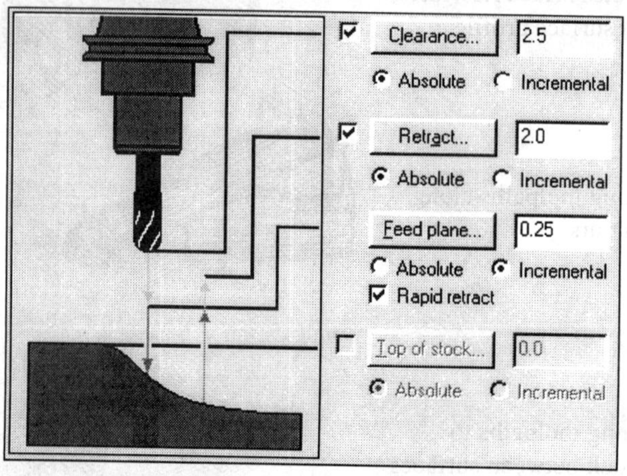

Figure 15.1

Clearance height The Clearance parameter specifies the Z-depth at which the tool moves to and from each toolpath operation. It can be set to Absolute or Incremental mode. In Absolute mode, the system places all the clearance heights at the given value by the Clearance parameter (Figure 15.2a). With Incremental mode, the system places each clearance height at a Z depth relative to the current top of the stock (Figure 15.2b).

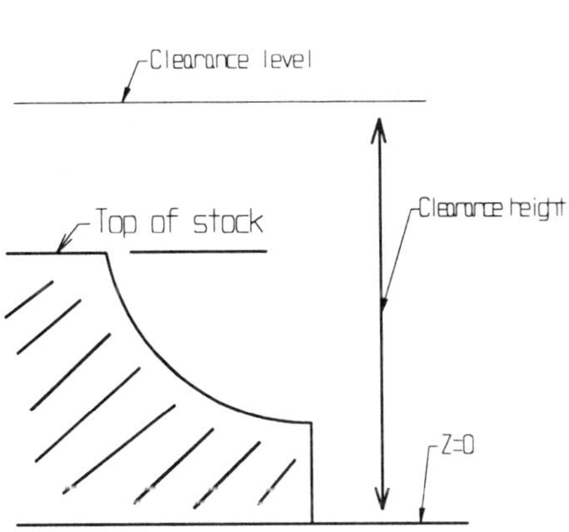

Figure 15.2a

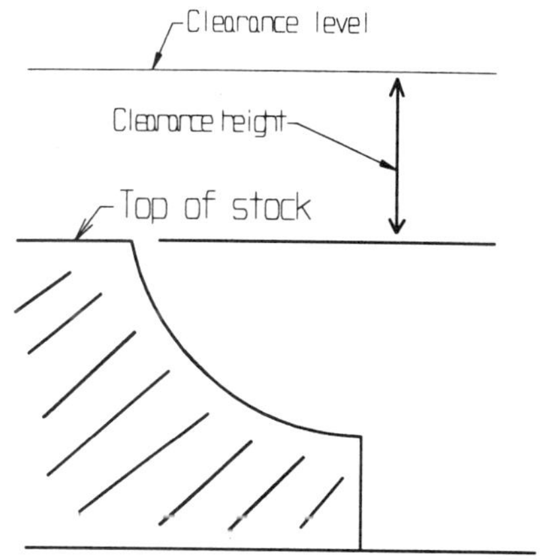

Figure 15.2b

Retract height The Retract parameter specifies the Z-depth at which the tool retracts to prior to the next tool pass. The Retract height must be above the feed height in order to make it efftive. It also can be set to either Absolute mode or Incremental mode. The way to determine the Retract height in these two modes are the same as in Clearance height.

Feed plane The Feed parameter specifies the Z-depth that the tool moves to at a rapid rate before it changes to the plunge rate to enter the workpiece. The tool plunges to this Z-level when traveling between separate passes when the Clearance parameter is not active. This parameter also has absolute mode and incremental mode.

Top of stock The Top of stock parameter specifies the highest Z-level of the material. It has two modes to enter the value for top of stock; absolute and incremental. This parameter is only available in the Pocket function.

Filter parameters This group of parameters defines the tolerance for the system to eliminate those unnecessary toolpath segments. Its dialog box appears as shown here.

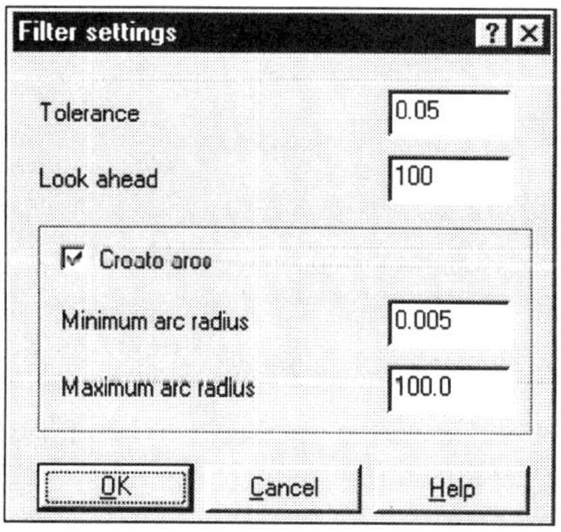

The four filter parameters are briefly described as below.

Tolerance:	specify the tolerance value for roughing toolpaths.
Look ahead:	specify the number of toolpath segments to be included in the filtering.
Minimum arc radius:	specify the minimum arc radius of the toolpath arcs.
Maximum arc radius:	specify the maximum arc radius of the toolpath arcs.

Direction parameters This group of parameters define the entry move and exit move of surface roughing toolpaths. Its dialog box appears as below.

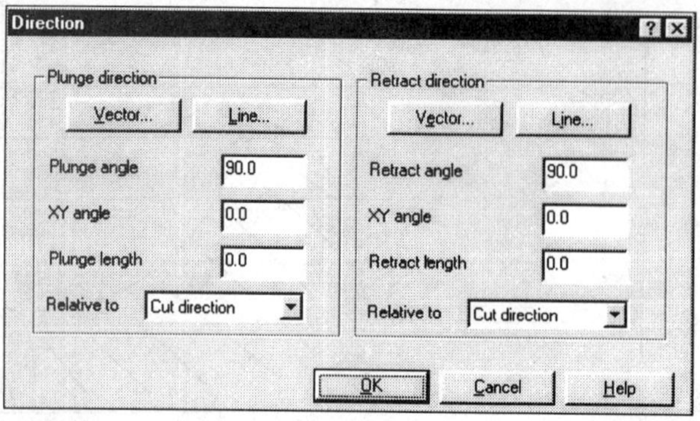

The direction of entry move and exit move can be specified in one of three ways: angle values, a vector or a line. The direction vector is defined by three direction parameters as shown here.

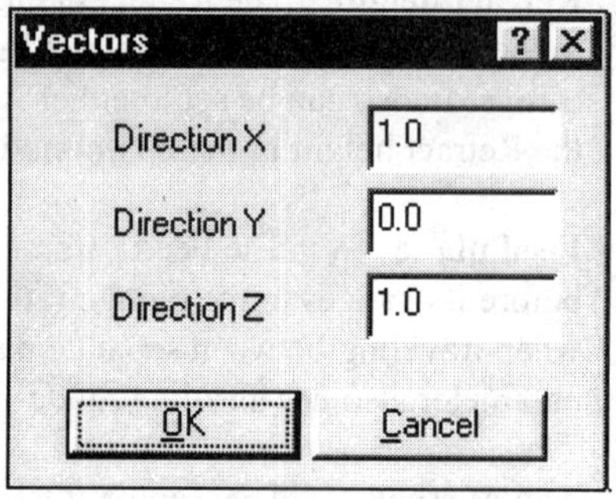

The values given to these three parameters will be reflected onto the plunge angle and XY angle in the direction dialog box. A "1.0" given to both Direction X and Direction Z as shown below makes the "Plunge angle" and "XY angle" value become 45.0 degrees and 0.0 degrees, respectively as shown.

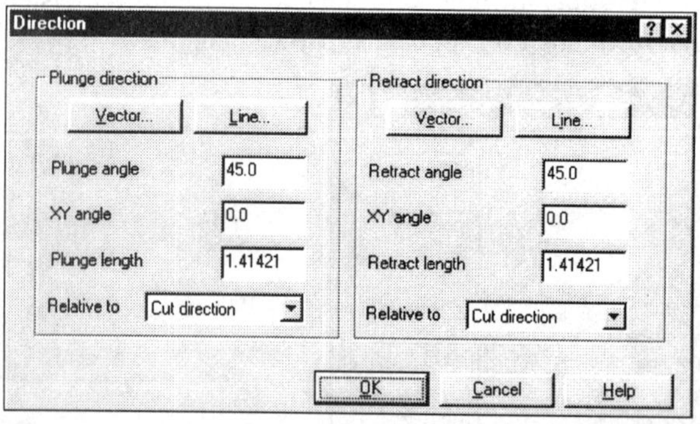

Click the Line button, the system will goes to the graphics window for you to select a line for the direction of entry move. After selecting the line, the system will return to the Direction dialog box.

When the Direction button is toggled to Off (no check mark), the system will set the direction angle to the default value which is 90.0 degrees.

Figure 15.3 shows the effect of direction angle values on the entry/exit moves. Figure 15.3a has the direction angle of 45.0derees, and Figure 15.3b shows the direction angle of 90.0 degrees.

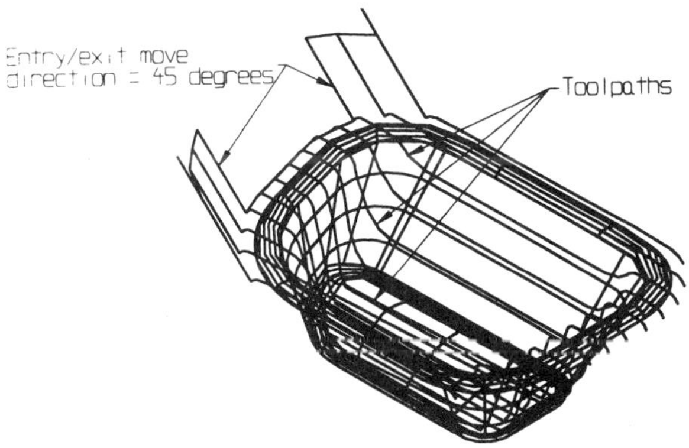

Figure 15.3a

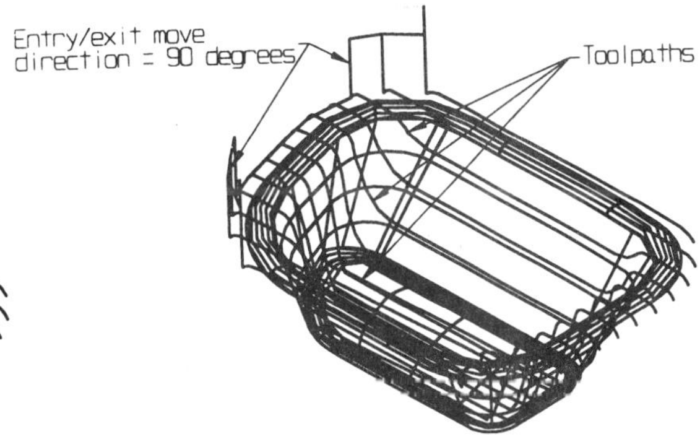

Figure 15.3b

Recut Parameters This parameter creates a recut toolpath file. Recut files are used to speed up regeneration of complicated surface toolpaths. They can also be used to archive surface toolpaths.

Tip/Center Compensation This parameter specifies the cutter compensation in Z direction either to cutter tip or cutter center. Figure 15.4 shows the compensation of these two modes.

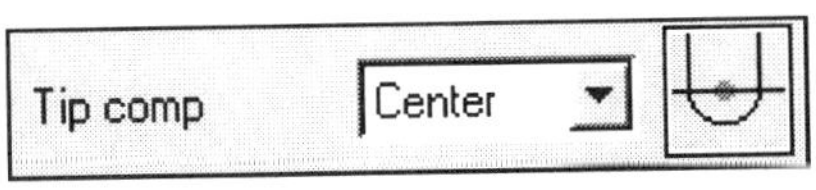

Figure 15.4a

Figure 15.4b

Drive/check surfaces Surfaces can be designated as the drive surface or the check surface. The drive surfaces are those surfaces that will be subjected to the machining operations. In other words, those surfaces wanted to be cut should be selected as the drive surfaces. The check surfaces are those surfaces that are not intended to be cut during toolpath generation for drive surfaces. This means that the system will avoid the cutting over check surfaces. Figure 15.5 shows an example of using drive/check surface function.

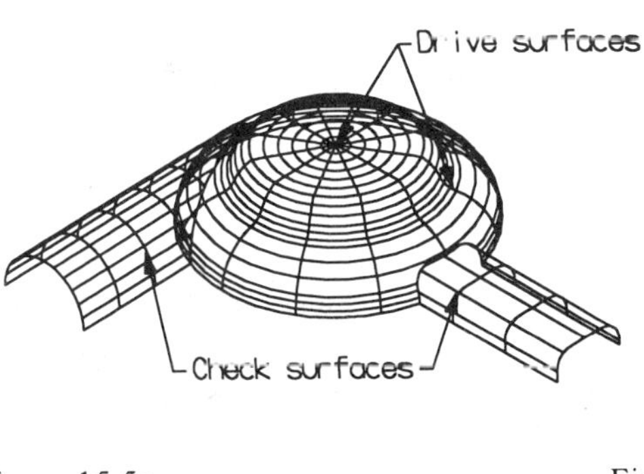

Figure 15.5a

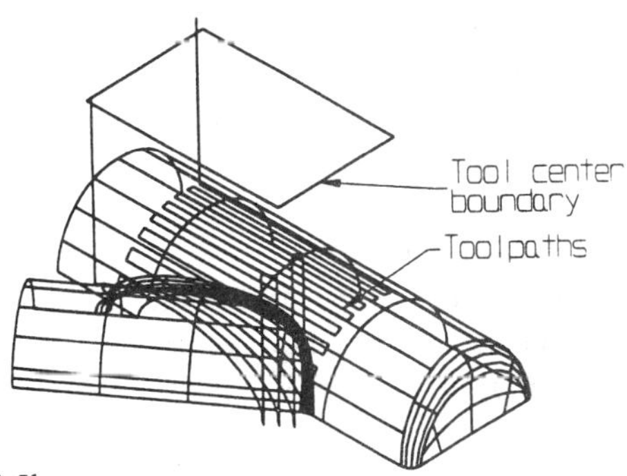

Figure 15.5b

Mastercam uses the following two parameters to specify the stock for drive surfaces and check surfaces:

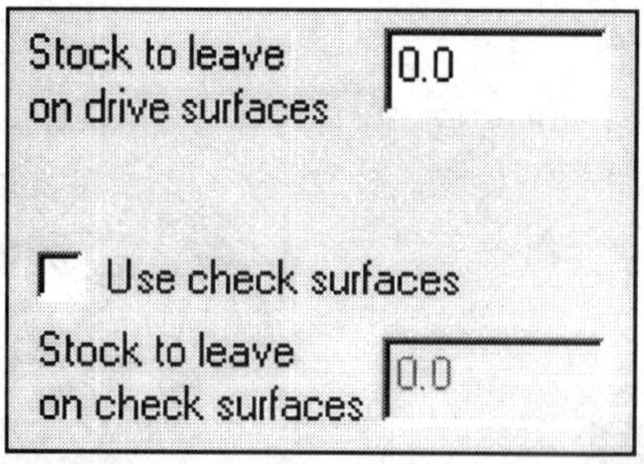

Click the "Use check surfaces" to On to cause the system to issue the prompt for you to select the check surfaces.

Tool center boundary This parameter allows for the selection of a closed contour on or near the selected surfaces as the limited boundary. The tool center will be confined within the boundary during toolpath generation. Multiple confinement boundaries are allowed. Toggle the "Prompt for tool center boundary" to On to make the system prompts you to select the boundaries. When this parameter is not activated the system will not prompt you for selecting the boundaries. Figure 15.6 shows an example of using the tool center boundary.

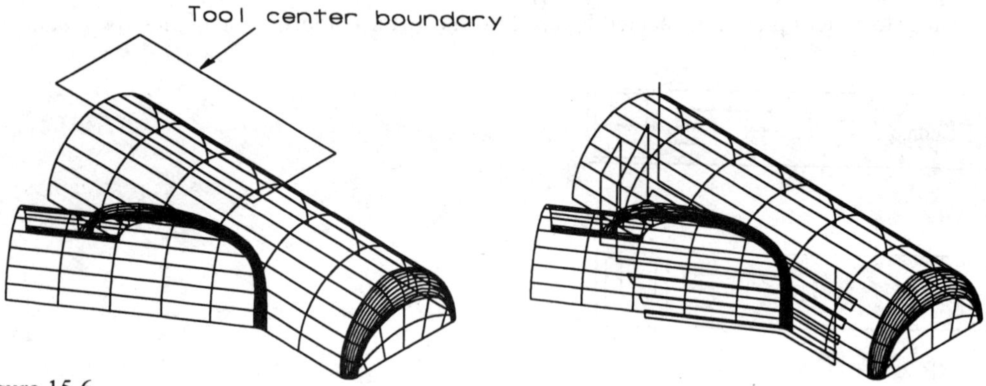

Figure 15.6

15.4 Rough Specific Parameters

Mastercam uses four additional parameters to define the roughing toolpaths in some rough functions. They are cut tolerance, cutting method, plunge control, and Z-motion along surface. They are applicable to some rough functions only. Each rough function has its own unique parameters that are presented in their respective function.

Cut tolerance

This parameter specifies the accuracy of the surface toolpath. The smaller the cut tolerance, the more accurate the toolpath, however, it generates a longer part program. For roughing surfaces, a cut tolerance of 0.05" may be adequate for most cases. Figure 15.7 contrasts the roughing toolpaths in using different values for cut tolerance.

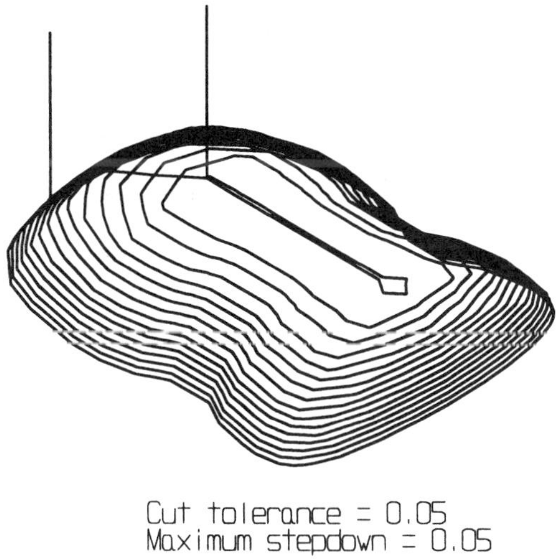

Figure 15.7a

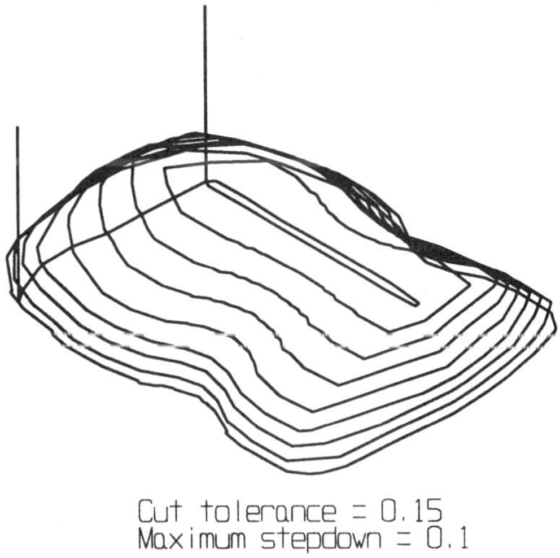

Figure 15.7b

Cutting Method

Two cutting methods are available in the roughing cut: zigzag and one way. Figure 15.8 shows the difference between these two cutting methods using the same surface model. In the zigzag mode, the cutter moves back and forth across the surfaces. In the one way mode, the cutter takes a pass, rapids up, moves back to the start of the cut, and takes another pass in the same direction.

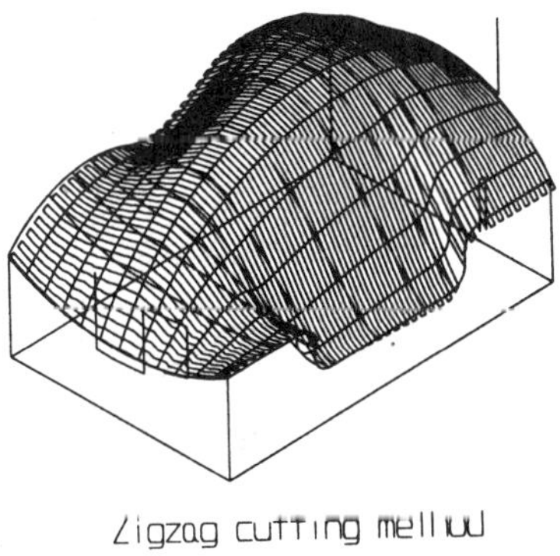

Figure 15.8a

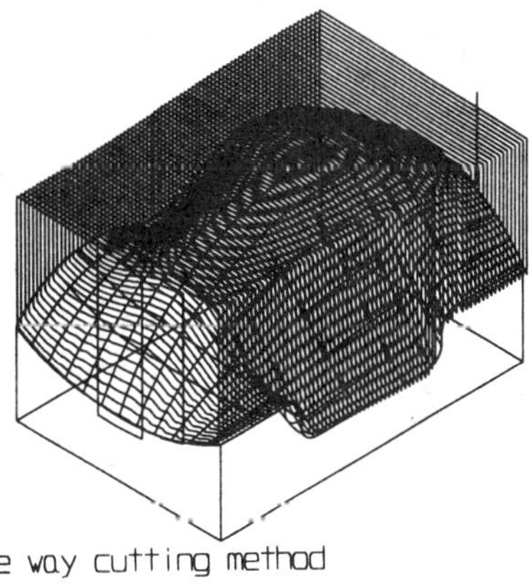

Figure 15.8b

Max stepdown This parameter specifies the maximum distance between two adjacent cuts in Z-direction (Figure 15.9). A larger stepdown value produces a smaller number of roughing levels and a rougher finish. A smaller stepdown value produces a larger number of roughing levels and a smoother finish.

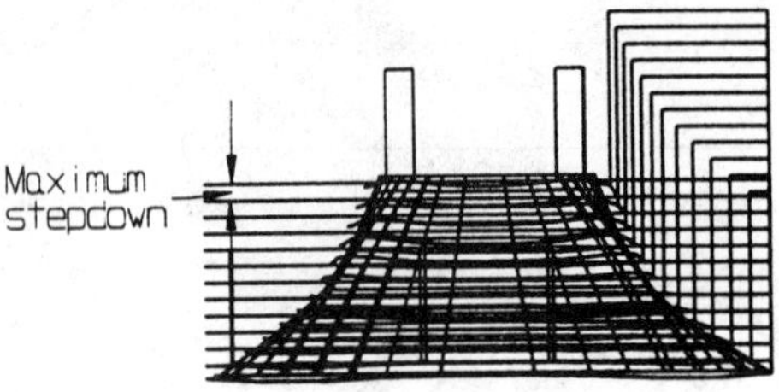

Maximum stepdown = 0.15

Figure 15.9a

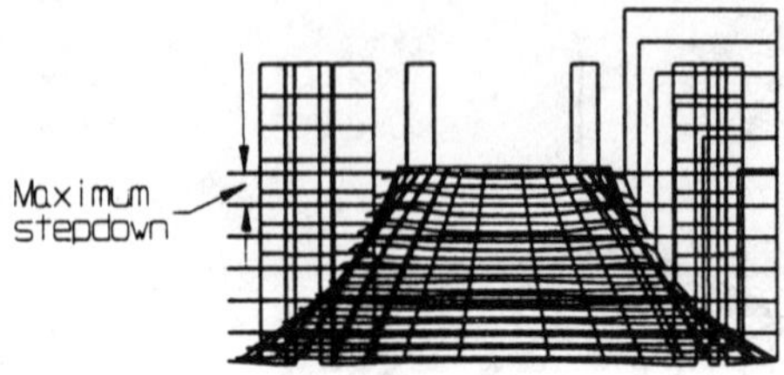

Maximum stepdown = 0.3

Figure 15.9b

Plunge Control

The plunge control parameters allow to select the method of plunging the tool to rough cut a multiple-surface part. The three plunge control methods are (Figure 15.10):

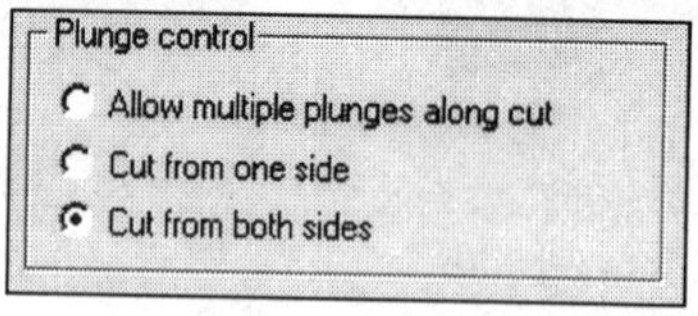

Allow multiple plunges along cut: perform any number of tool plunges along a surface model (Figure 15.10a). Used in multiple cavities parts.

Cut from one side: only plunge along one side of the part (Figure 15.10b).

Cut from both sides: plunge along each side of the part (Figure 15.10c).

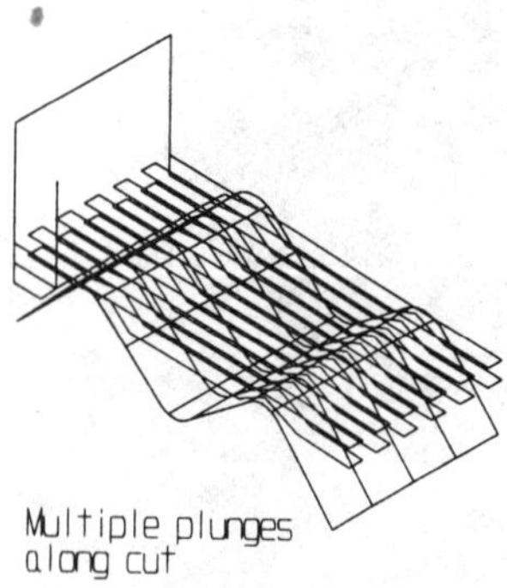

Figure 15.10a

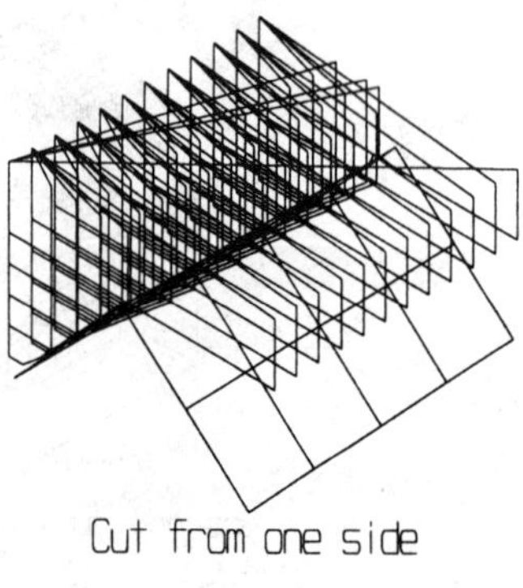

Figure 15.10b

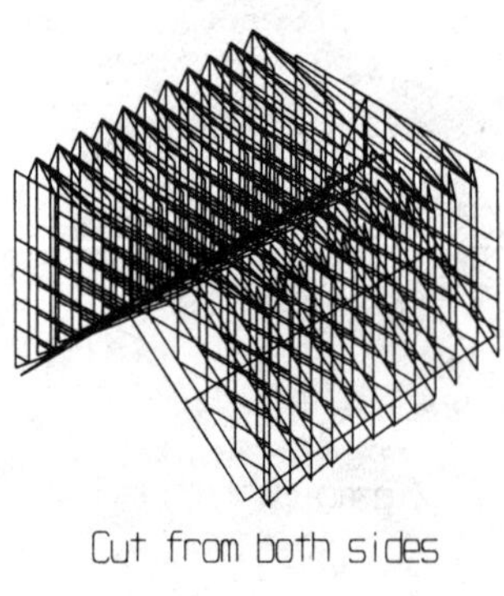

Figure 15.10c

Z Motion Control

Mastercam uses the following two parameters to control the Z motion along the surface while performing roughing cut:

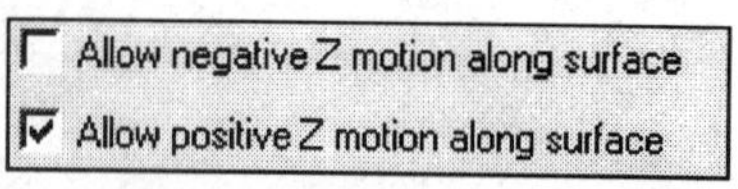

Toggle on the "Allow negative Z motion along surface" parameter makes the tool cut along the surface while plunging (Figure 15.11a). Toggle this parameter to "Off" causes the tool not to cut along the surface while plunging (Figure 15.11b).

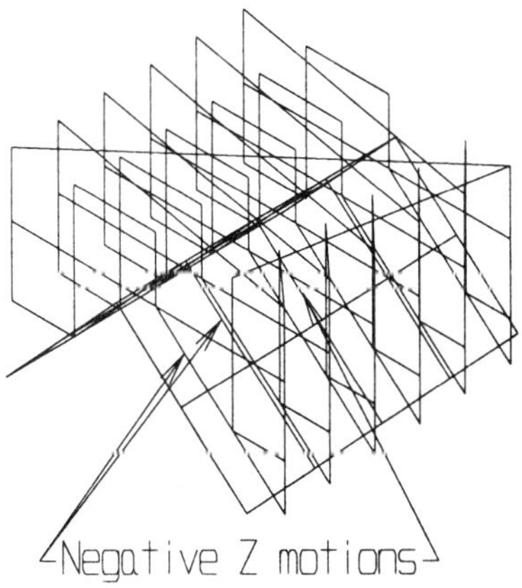

Figure 15.11a

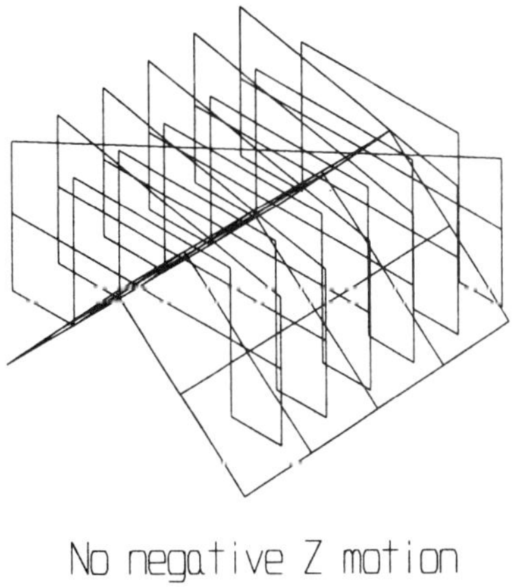

Figure 15.11b

Toggle on the "Allow positive Z motion along surface" parameter makes the tool cut along the surface while rising (Figure 15.12a). Toggle this parameter to "Off" causes the tool not to cut along the surface while rising (Figure 15.12b).

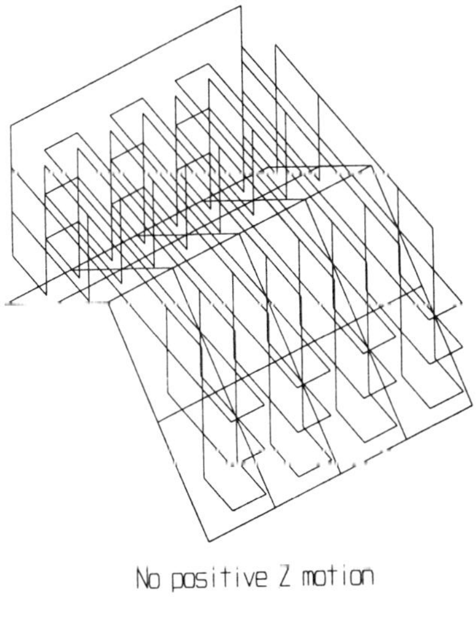

Figure 15.12a

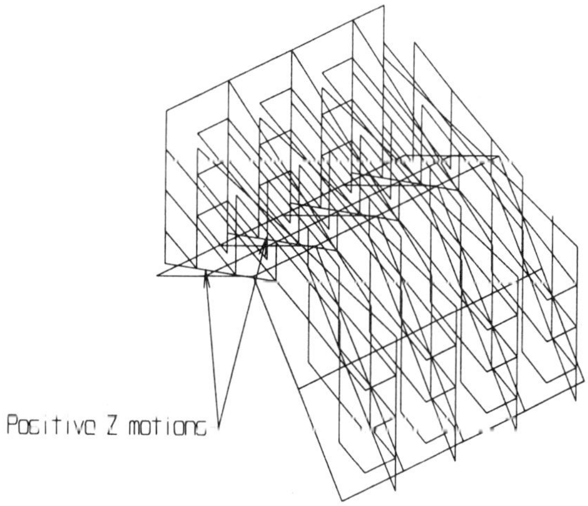

Figure 15.12b

These two Z motion control parameters can be independently set to their desired setting. Figure 15.13 shows the toolpaths that allow both positive and negative Z motions.

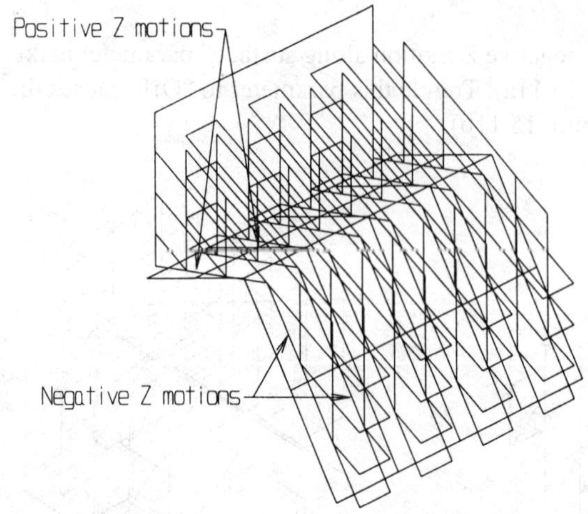

Figure 15.13

Part Shape Four surface rough functions: parallel, radial, project and flowline, require the selection of part shape for generating roughing toolpaths. The three part shape options are described below.

Boss: The surface to rough forms a bell-shape or extruded out configuration as one shown in Figure 15.14a.
Cavity: The surface to rough forms a recess style configuration as one shown in Figure 15.14b.
Unspecified: Surface shape style is defined. Mastercam will use the default surface toolpath parameters.

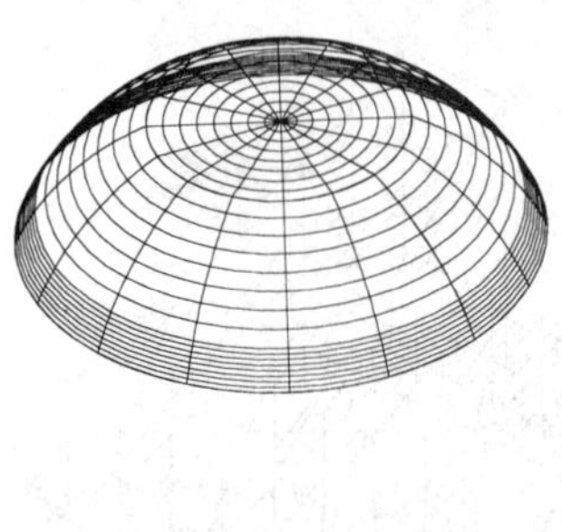

Figure 15.14 Bell shape

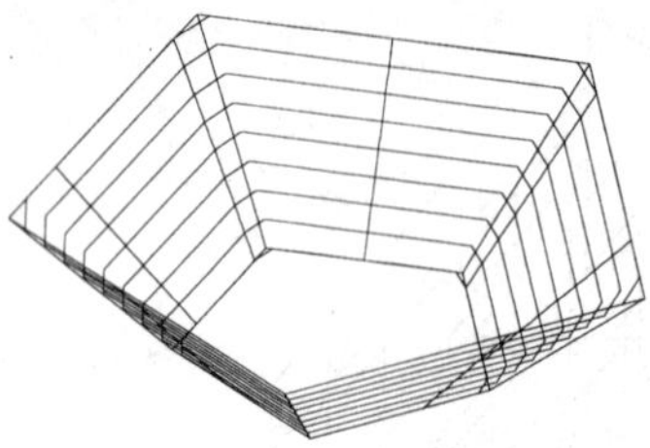

Figure 15.14b Recess style

15.5 Cut Depths, Gap Settings and Edge Settings

Cut depths

This group of parameters defines the critical cut depths during roughing. These parameters make sure that certain specified depths are cut during roughing. The cut depths can be defined in absolute mode or in incremental mode. The dialog box appears different for these two modes as next.

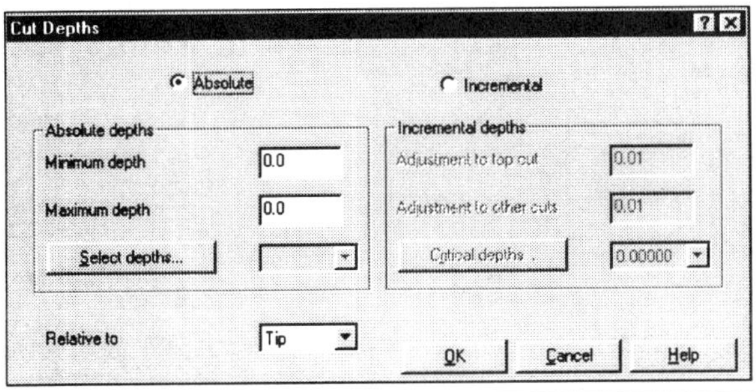

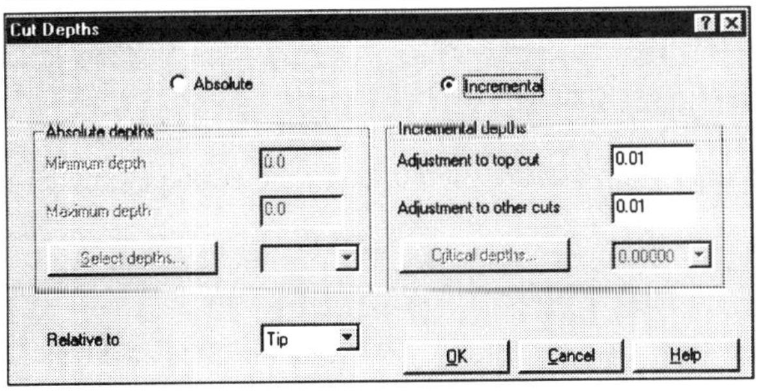

In Absolute mode, these two parameters define the critical depth (Figure 15.15):

Minimum depth:	the highest point that the tool will rise to while cutting material.
Maximum depth:	the lowest point that the tool will descend to while cutting material.

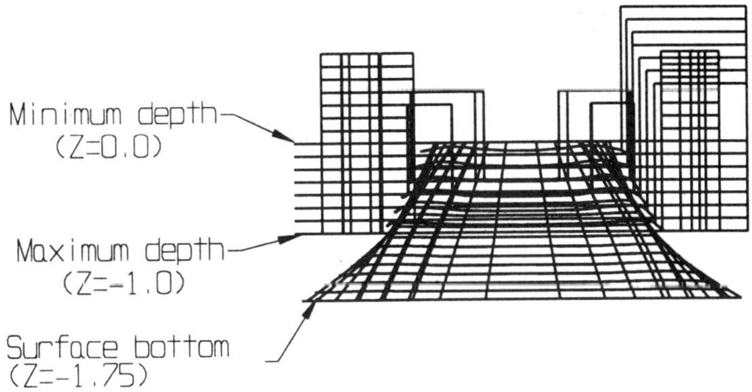

Figure 15.15

The Select depths button allows you to select graphically the minimum depth and maximum depth. Click this button, the system will move to graphic window for you to define the Z-depth.

In Incremental mode, the system places each cut at a Z-depth relative to the current surface depth. The system automatically determines the minimum and maximum depths of the toolpath based on the following three parameters (Figure 15.16):

Relative to: set whether the cut depths are referred to the tip or the center of the tool.

Adjustment to top cut: determine the distance between the minimum depth that the system calculates and where the first cut of the toolpath occurs. A positive value moves the cut to a lower level on the Z axis and a negative value moves it to a higher level on the Z axis.

Adjustment to other cuts: determine the distance to adjust the maximum depth and all critical depth. A positive value moves the cut to a higher position on the Z axis and a negative value moves it to a lower position on the Z axis.

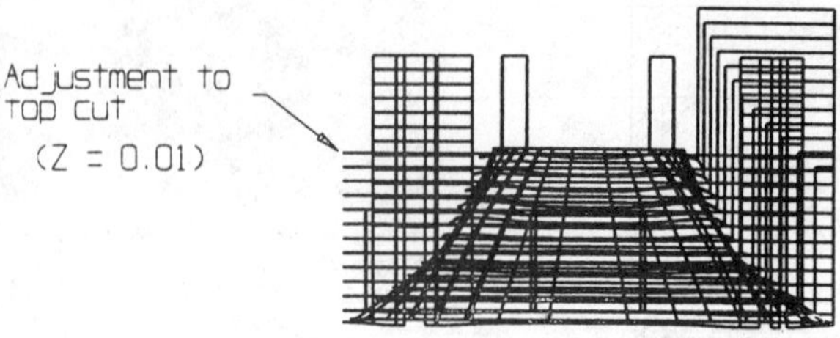

Figure 15.16a

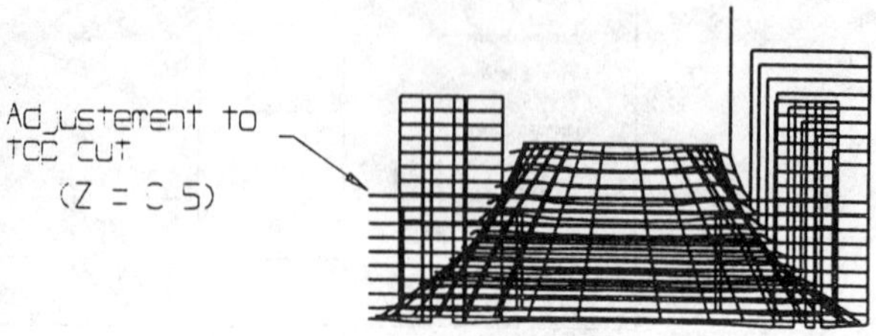

Figure 15.16b

There are two groups of parameters that are used to control the toolpath pattern when gaps and edges are encountered.

Gap Settings

Gaps are an opening or any break in the continuity of surfaces. Gaps are normally caused by:

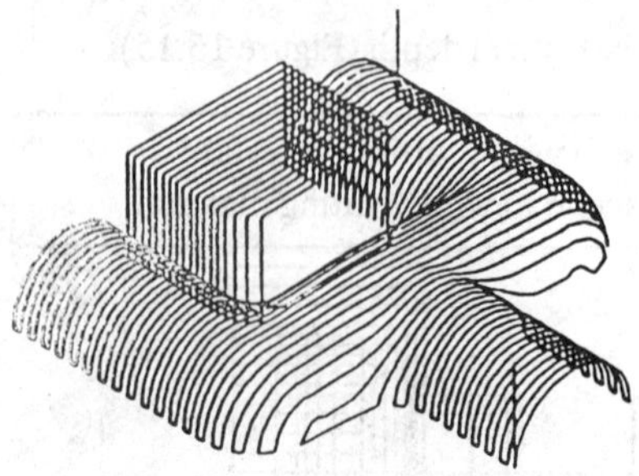

(1) adjacent surfaces that are not directly connected (Figure 15.17a)
(2) trimmed areas where gaps are produced (Figure 15.17b)
(3) gouge removed areas (Figure 15.17c).

Figure 15.17a

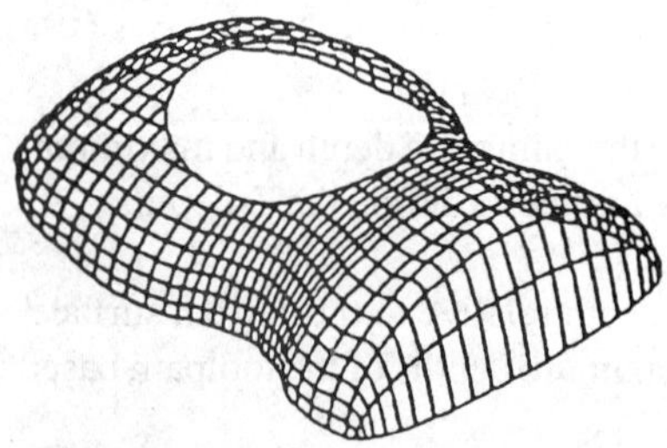

Figure 15.17b

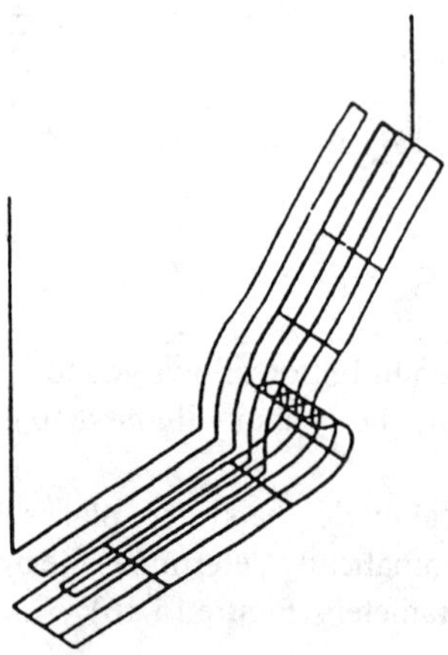

Figure 15.17c

Another term you should know about is motion. **Motion** is the projected length of each cutter move onto the Cplane. A gap size is referred to as the **given gap value.** It is used to determine whether the gap is a short gap or long gap. A long gap occurs when the motion is greater than the gap size. A short gap exists when the motion is equal to, or shorter than, the gap size.

Short gap	if motion < gap size
Long gap	if motion > gap size

The value of gap size is expressed in one of the following two ways:

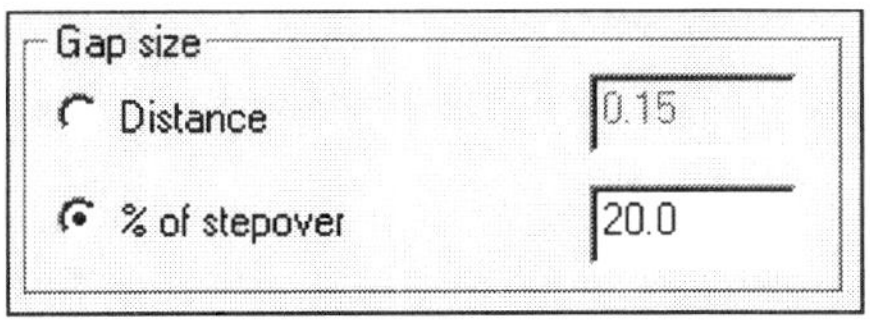

Distance:	directly specify the gap distance.
% of stepover:	specify the gap size in the percentage of the given stepover value.

Toolpath mode for short gaps (Motion < Gap Size)

Mastercam provides **four toolpath modes** for short gaps. The short gap toolpath mode menu appears as below.

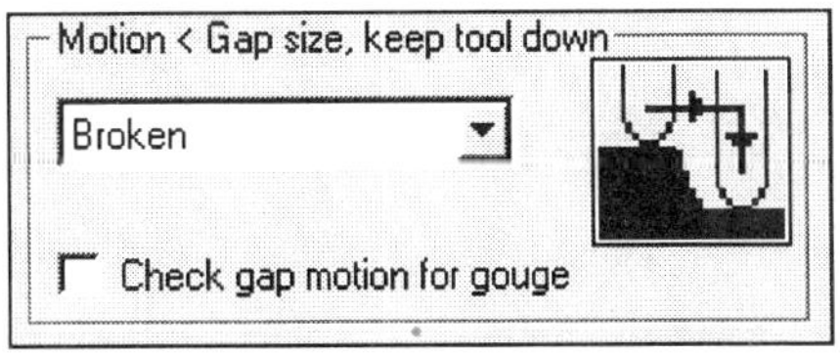

Direct Mode In the Direct mode, the cutter moves straight over the gaps in feed speed from position to position (Figure 15.18). In other words, the cutter moves from the end point of the toolpath on one surface (or move) to the start point of the toolpath on the adjacent surface (or move).

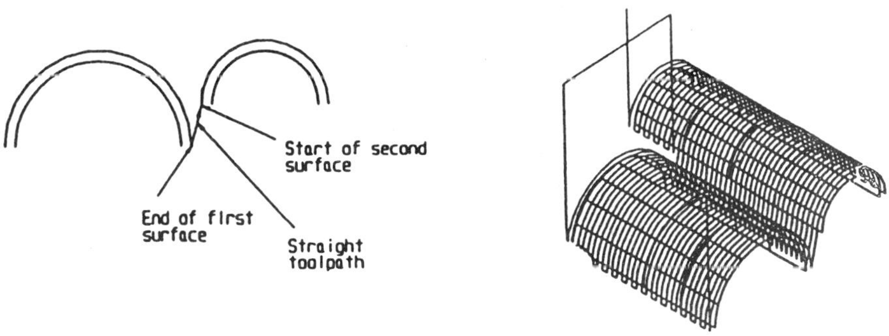

Figure 15.18

Broken Mode In the Broken mode, the toolpaths which move over gaps are broken into two segments; one with Z movement only and the other with movement in the X and/or Y direction (Figure 15.19). In other words, the cutter moves up (in the Z direction), then moves over (in the X and/or Y direction). The cutter moves over first, then moves down.

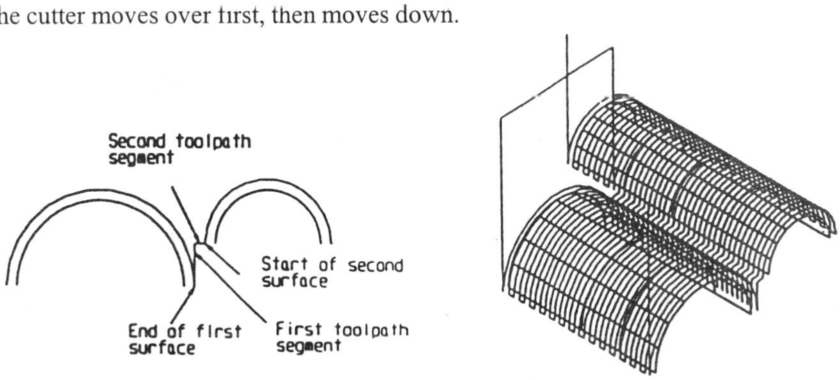

Figure 15.19

Smooth Mode In the Smooth mode, the toolpaths which move over gaps follow the fluid (smooth) motion (Figure 15.20). It is commonly used in high-speed machining.

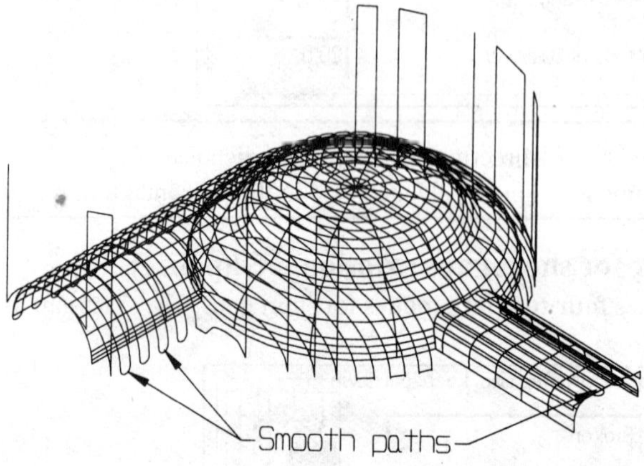

Figure 15.20

In the following surface(s) mode, the toolpaths which move over gaps follow the Z-motion of the surfaces (Figure 15.21).

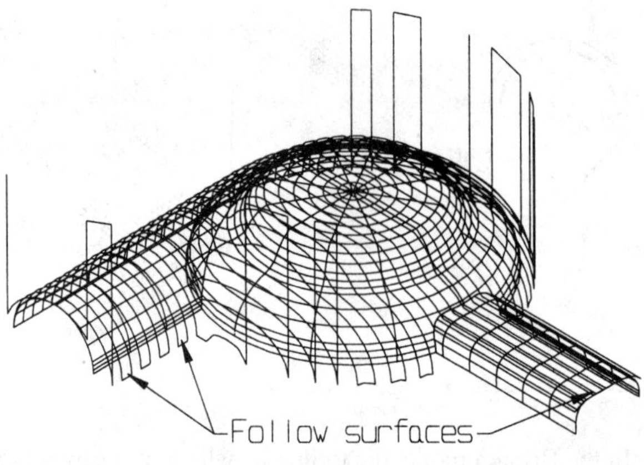

Figure 15.21

Toolpath Pattern for Long Gaps (Motion > Gap Size)

If a tool motion becomes larger than the given gap size, the system adds a retract motion to the toolpath. The toolpath pattern for long gaps following the following five steps (Figure 15.22):

(1) Cut over the first surface to one end in the specified direction.
(2) Rapidly retract to the rapid plane.
(3) Rapidly move over the gap to the start end of the second surface.
(4) Plunge to the start point of the second surface.
(5) Cut the second surface in the specified direction.

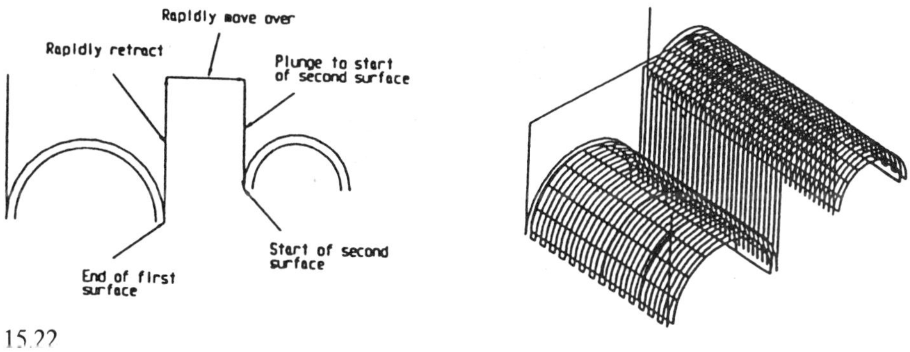

Figure 15.22

The remaining **five gap setting parameters** are briefly described below:

Optimize cut order: place the tool in an area and keeps it there until all cuts in the area are made.
Plunge into previously cut area: make the tool to plunge into an area of the part that was previously cleared by another cut.
Follow tool center boundary at gap: allow the tool to follow the boundary at a gap if a tool center boundary has been selected for the surface toolpath. The tool moves in XY directions to stay on the boundary.
Tangential arc radius: add an arc to the entry and exit points of a gap (Figure 15.23).

Tangential arc angle: specify the angle of the arc placed at the entry and exit points of a gap (Figure 15.24).

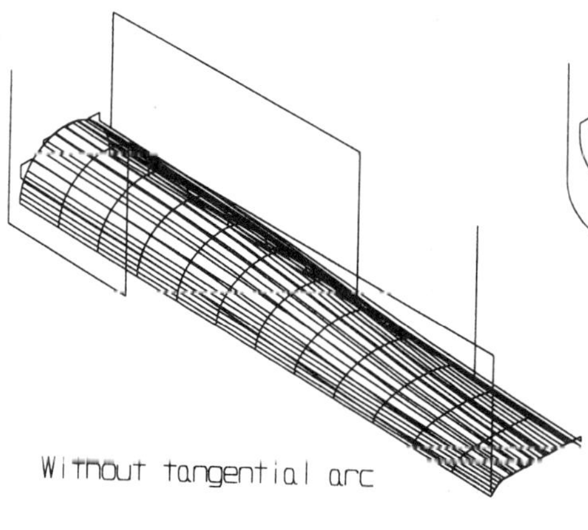

Figure 15.23

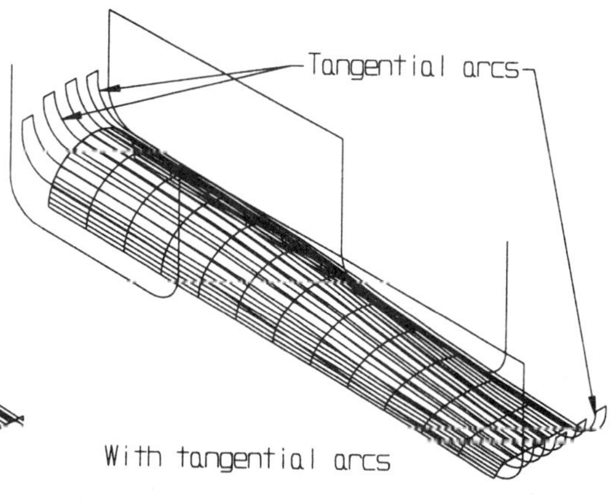

Figure 15.24

Edge Settings

In composite surface models, some surfaces may have open edges in which the surface skin is not fully extended to cover the edges of the surfaces. Mastercam classifies the surface open edges into two categories: **open edges between surfaces** and **open edges in single surfaces** (Figure 15.25). In the between surface group, the open edges are located at the intersection of two surfaces. In a single surface group, the open edges are on a surface that is not intersected with other surfaces at the open edge boundaries.

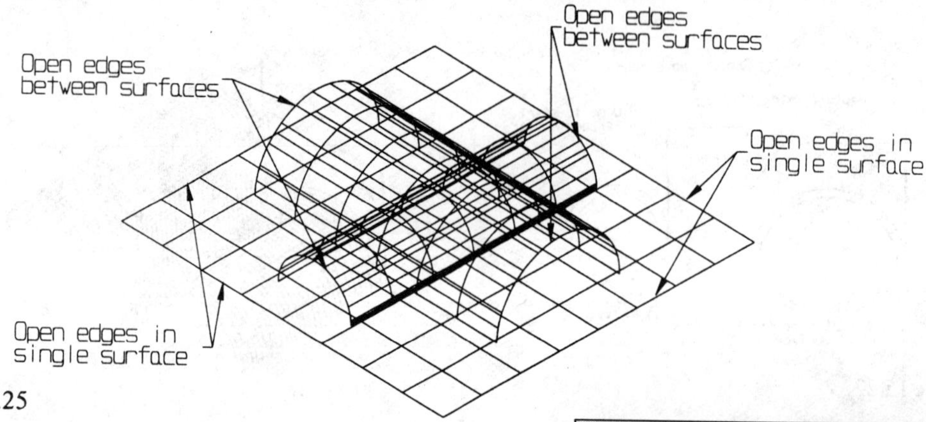

Figure 15.25

The edge settings dialog box appears as shown here.

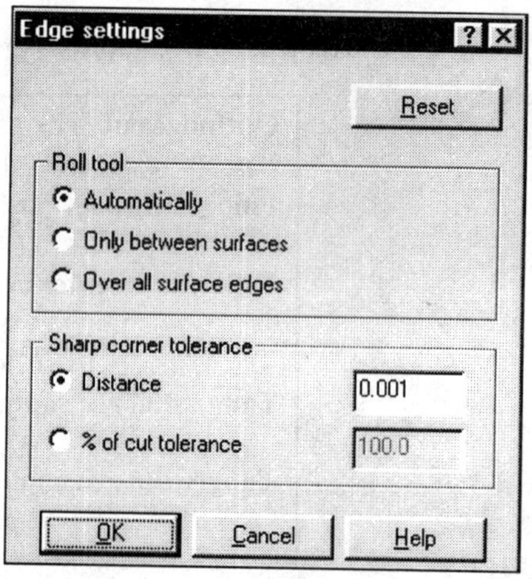

There are two parameters in the edge settings dialog box. They are: **Roll tool** and **Sharp corner tolerance.**

Roll tool Mastercam uses a "Roll tool" parameter to select the edge setting option. This parameter can be set to one of the three options as below.

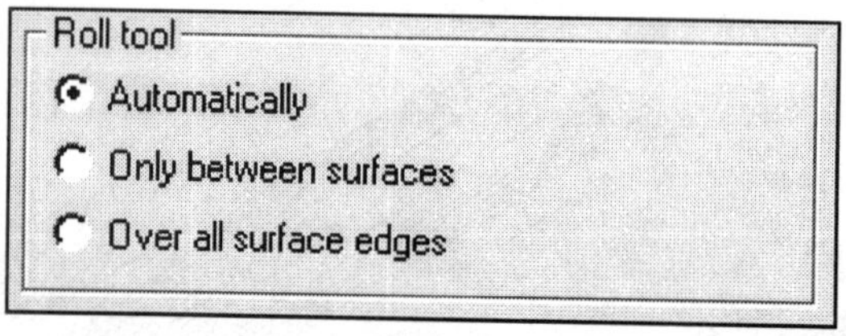

Automatically: The system automatically decides whether to roll tool at the surface edges. The tool rolls only between surfaces if no "tool center boundary" is used. This means the cutter center lies at the open edges of all surfaces (Figure 15.26a). With a tool center boundary being used, the tool rolls over all surface edges (Figure 15.26b). The "tool center boundary" parameter appears in the Rough parameters dialog box.

Only between surfaces: Roll the tool between surfaces only. Edge gougings will be removed in surfaces that are intersected with other surfaces. However, the cutter center lies at the open edges of single surfaces (Figure 15.27).

Over all surface edges: Roll the tool over all edges of the surface. Edge gougings will be removed in all surfaces including between surfaces and single surfaces (Figure 15.28).

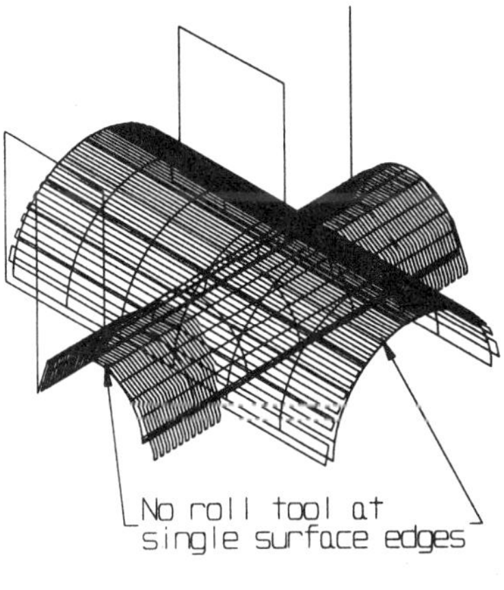

Figure 15.26a

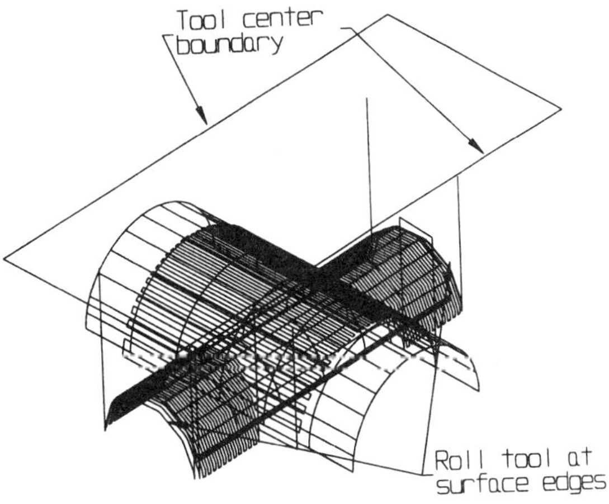

Figure 15.26b

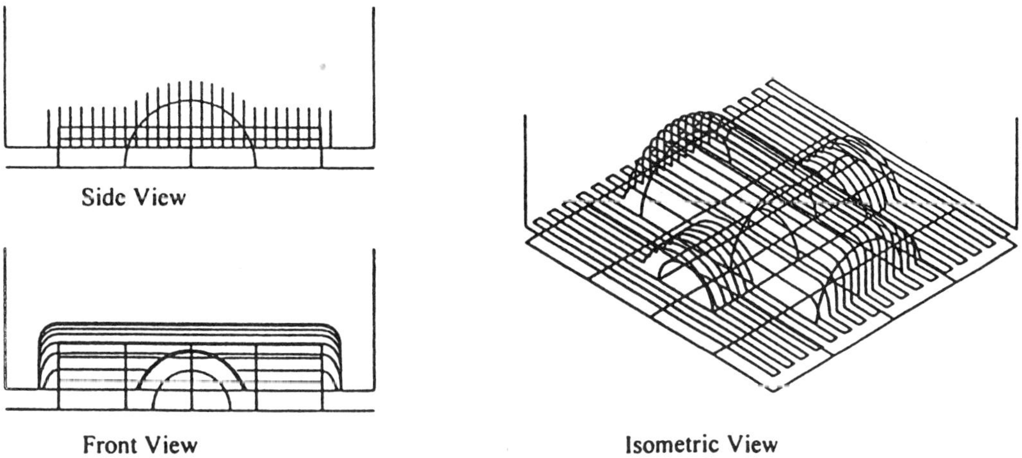

Figure 15.27

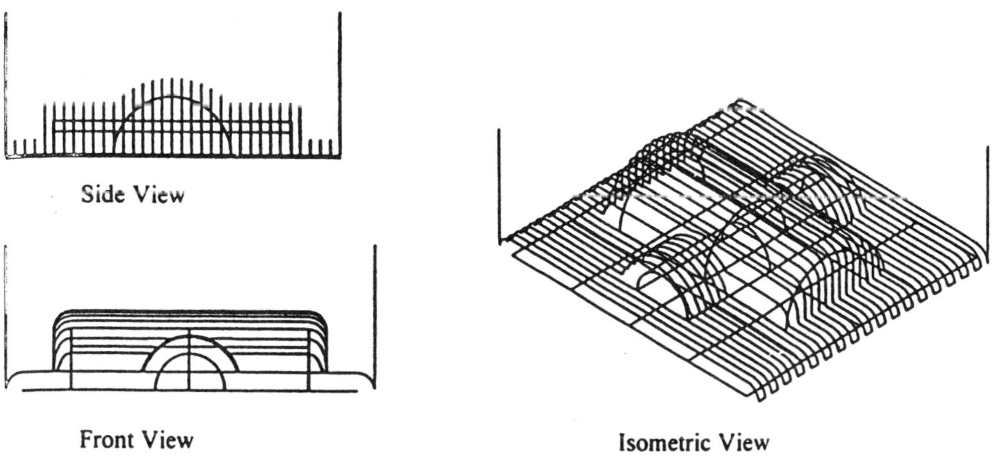

Figure 15.28

Sharp corner tolerance This parameter specifies the distance value for breaking the rolling tool motion into a set of smaller increments. A larger tolerance produces sharper corner increments (Figure 15.29a). A smaller tolerance has rounder corner increments (Figure 15.29b). The two options to specify the sharp corner tolerance are:

> **Distance:** specify a specific distance value as the sharp corner tolerance.
> **% of cut tolerance:** specify the tolerance value as a percentage of the cut tolerance for the toolpath.

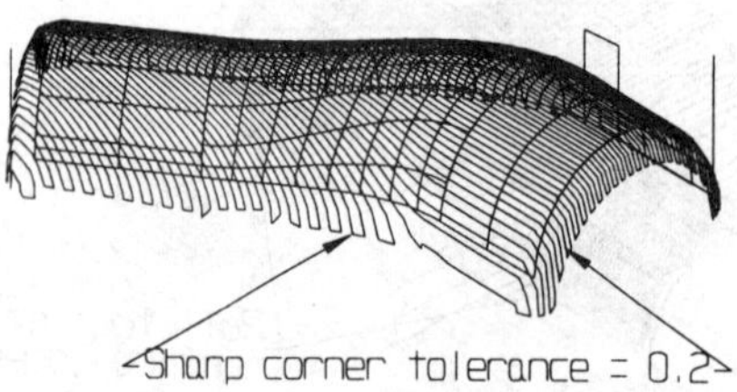

Figure 15.29a

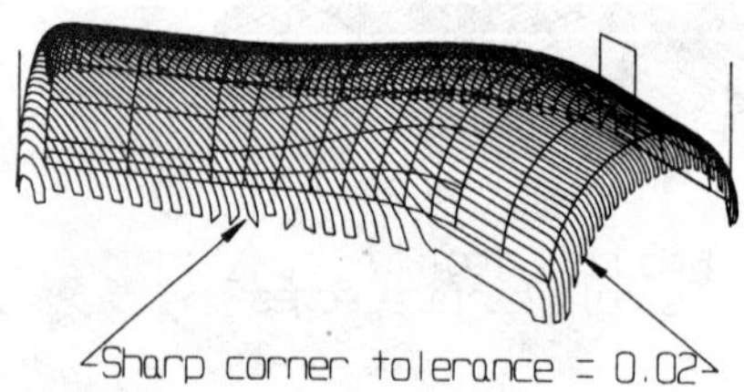

Figure 15.29b

15.6 Rough Parallel Function

This roughing function generates roughing toolpaths to cut along the selected surfaces in the specified direction (Figure 15.30). The parallel parameters dialog box appears as below.

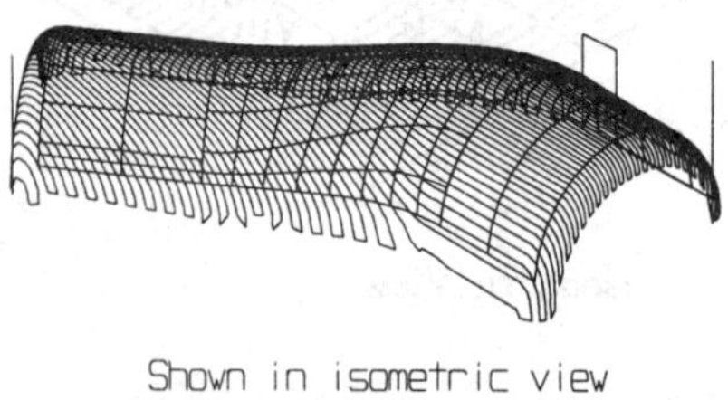

Figure 15.30a

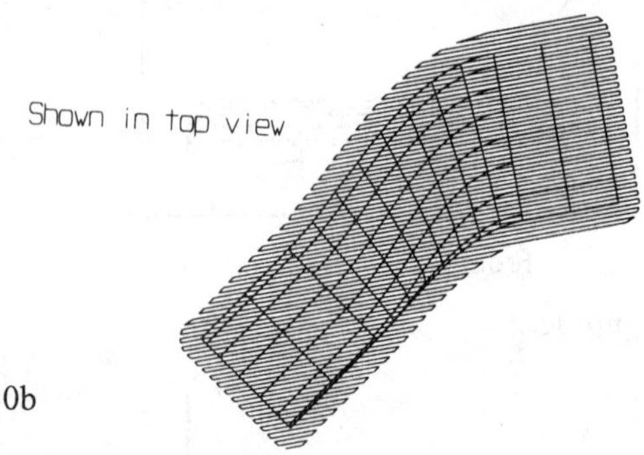

Figure 15.30b

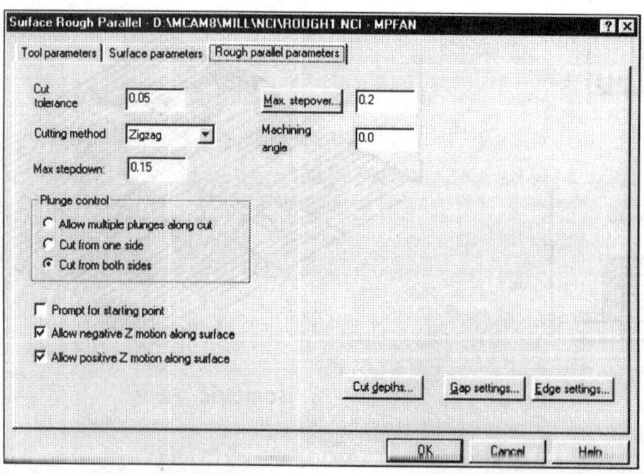

The unique parameter to this parallel function is machining angle. The machining angle is measured from the +X axis direction and is a positive value in the counterclockwise direction. Figure 15.31 shows two examples of machining angles; one in 0 degrees and the other in 45 degrees.

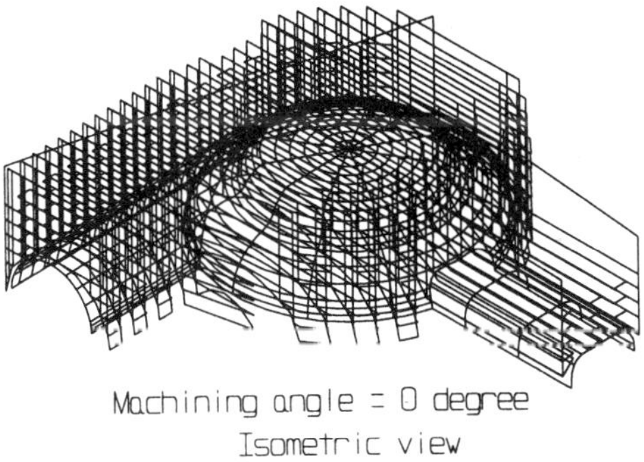

Figure 15.31a

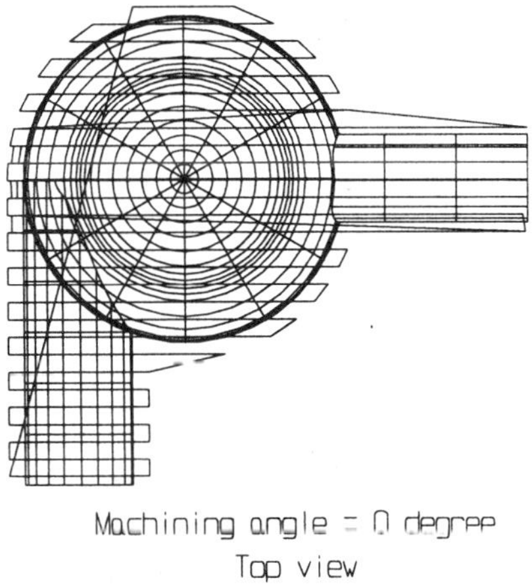

Figure 15.31a'

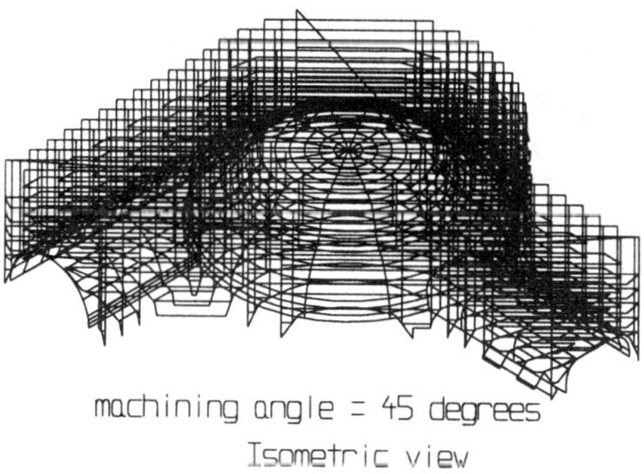

Figure 15.31b

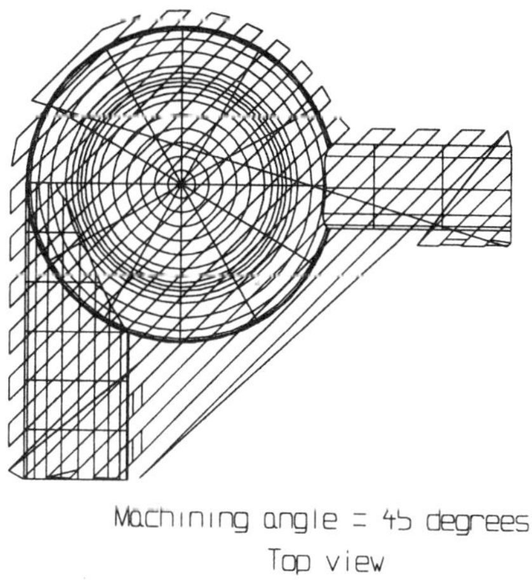

Figure 15.31b'

The maximum stepover parameter specifies the size of the stepover distance between two adjacent cuts. Click the "Max. stepover" button to open its dialog box as shown below.

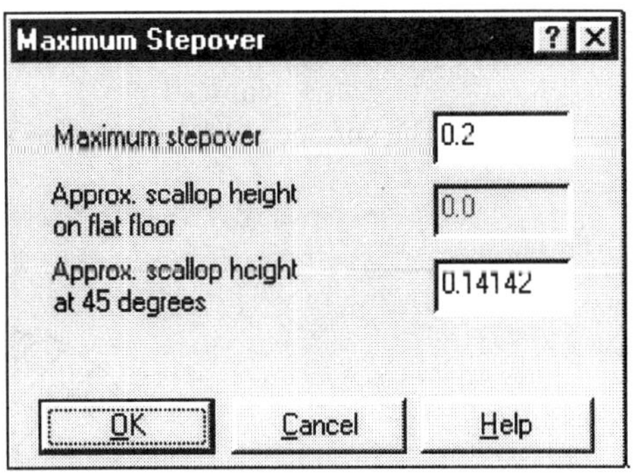

Changing the Maximum stepover value will automatically update the value for the approximate scallop height at a flat floor and the approximate scallop height at 45 degrees.

The "max stepdown" parameters specify the maximum stepdown distance from one level cut to the next level cut in the Z-direction.

Project 1. Generating toolpaths for rouging cut a surface model using the parallel function

The surface rough-parallel function is used to generate the roughing toolpaths to rough cut the Coons surface shown in Figure 15.32. Both toolpath model and verification model are shown.

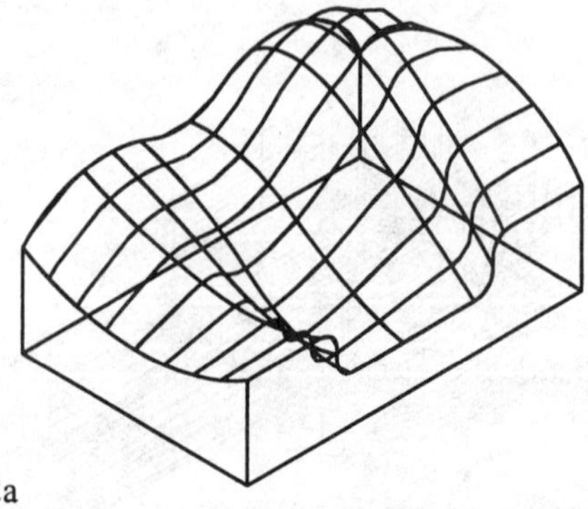

Figure 15.32a

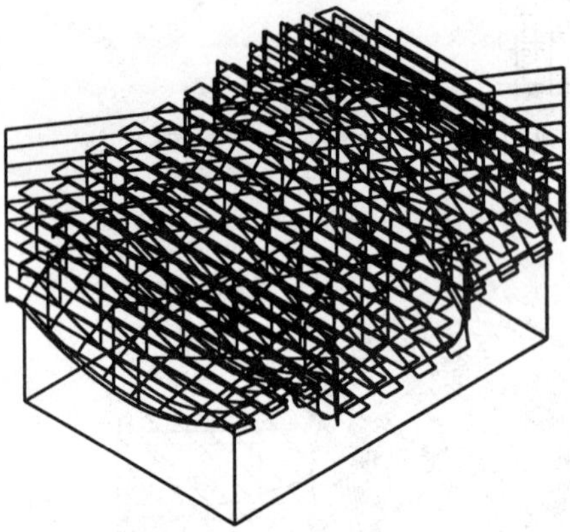

Figure 15.32b

Figure 15.32c

Tips 1. Use the surface model file coonss1.

2. Use Surface-Rough-Parallel function to generate roughing toolpaths.

3. Verify the roughing toolpaths.

Step 1. Open the surface model file coonss1.

Select **File → Get**

File name: **coonss1** ↵

The surface model appears as in Figure 15.33.

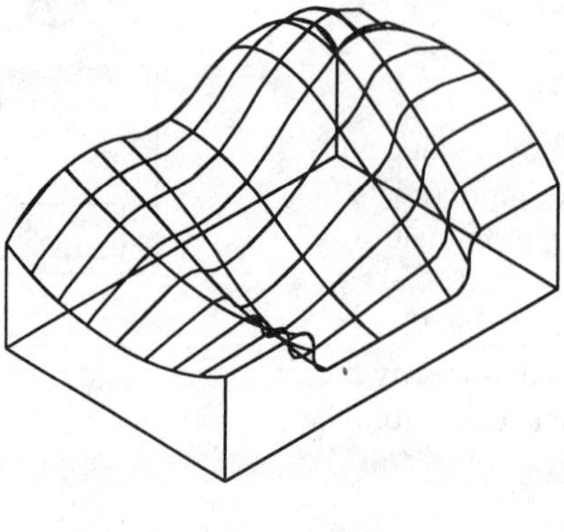

Figure 15.33

Step 2. Initiate the surface rough-parallel function. 1

Select **Cplane → Top**
Select **MAIN MENU → Toolpaths → Surface → Rough → Parallel → Unspecified**
Pick the surface → **Done**
Click right mouse button to open the tool library
Select **tool number 235** for (1/4 flat end mill)
Select **OK**
Set the tool parameters as below.
Click **Change NCI** and change the file name to **rough1 → OK**

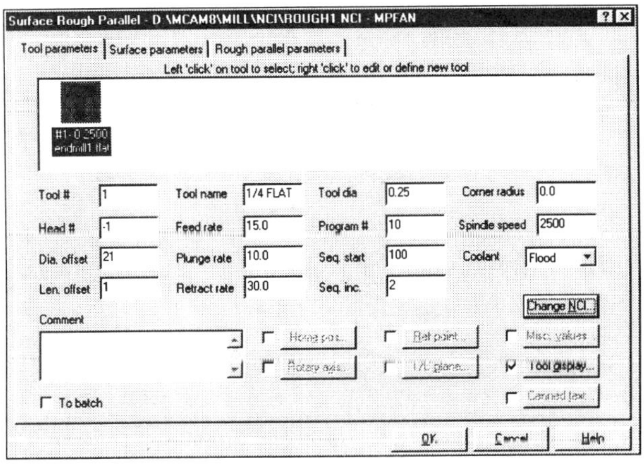

Step 3. Define the rough surface.

Click the "**Surface Parameters**" button to open rough parameters dialog box
Set surface parameters as below.

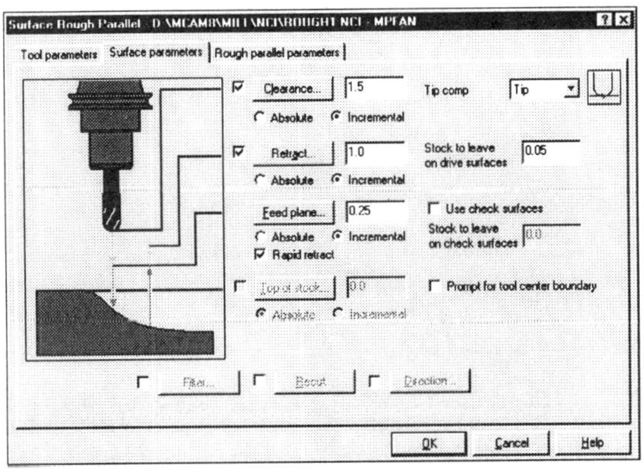

Step 4. Define the rough parallel parameters.

Click the "**Rough parallel parameters**" button

Step 5. Define the cut depth parameters.

Click the "**Cut Depths**" button to open the Cut Depths dialog box
Set cut depth parameters as shown here.

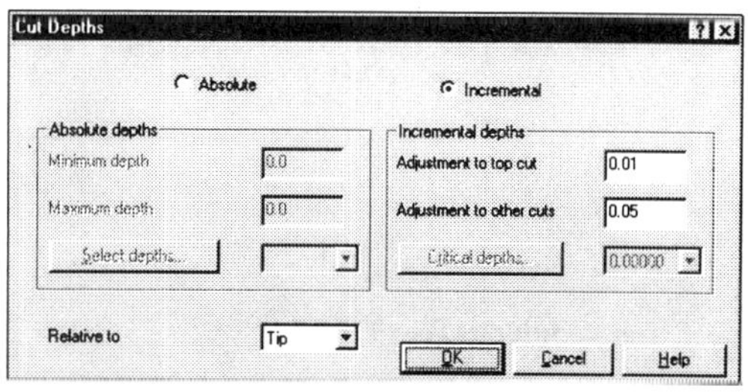

Select **OK** to return to rough parameters dialog box

Set the parameter values as below.

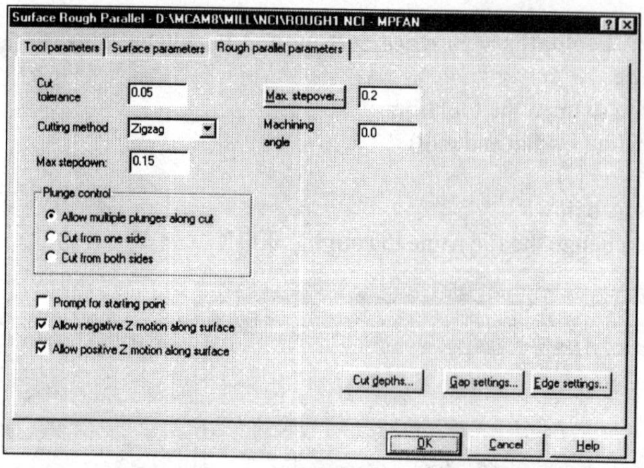

Step 6. Define the gap setting parameters.

Click the "**Gap settings**" button to open its dialog box

Set gap setting parameters as here.

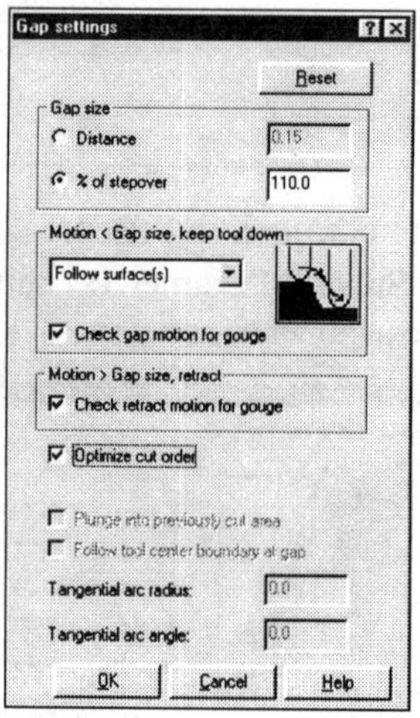

Select **OK**

Step 7. Define the edge setting parameters.

Click the "**Edge settings**" button to open its dialog box

Set edge setting parameters as below.

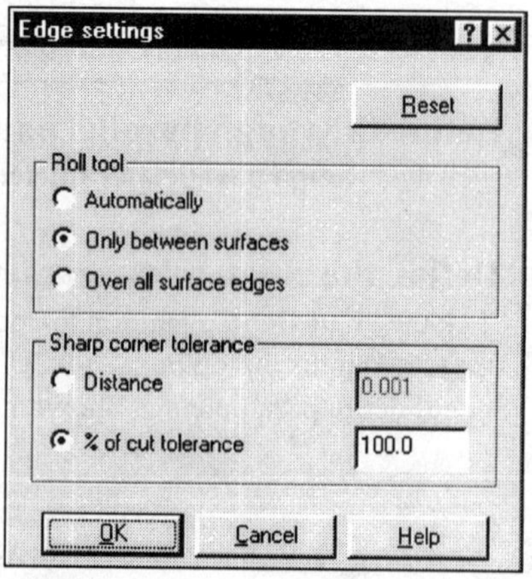

Select **OK → OK**

The roughing toolpaths are added to the model as shown in Figure 15.34.

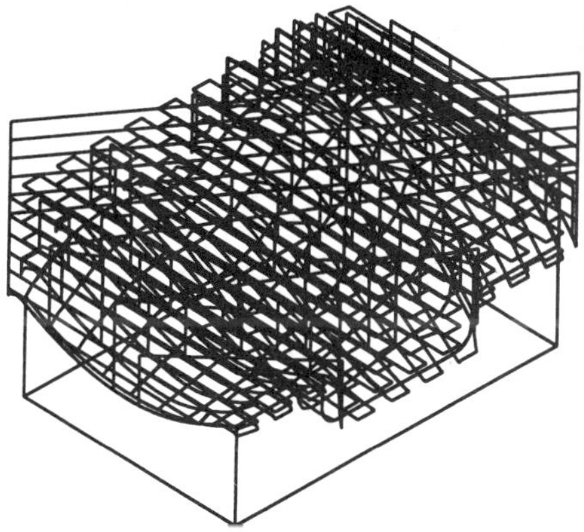

Figure 15.34

Step 8. Verify the roughing toolpaths.

Select **MAIN MENU → Toolpaths → Operations**
The Operations Manager dialog box should appear as below.

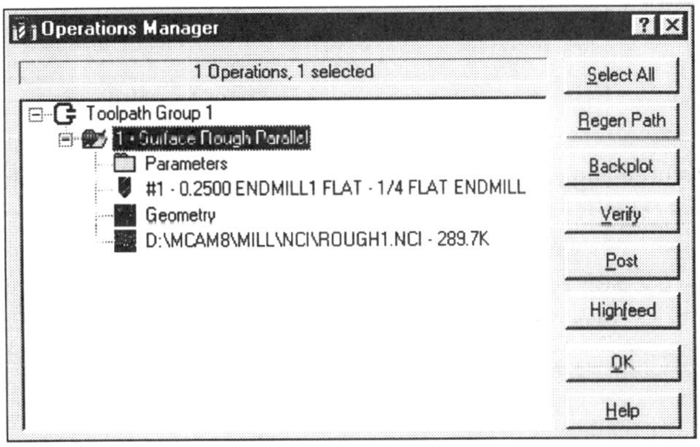

Click the **Verify** button
Select **Configure in Verify**
Click on **Scan NCI files**
Select **turbo** (no tool)

Select **OK**
Select **Machine**
The verification model should resemble Figure 15.35.

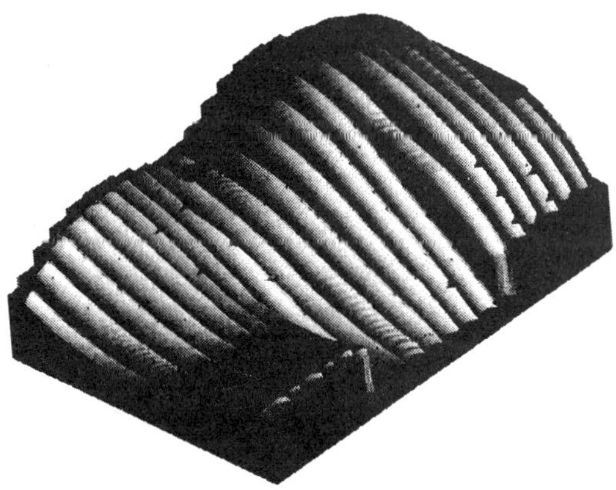

Figure 15.35

Step 9. Complete the roughing operation.

Select **BACKUP**
Select **OK** from the Operations Manager dialog box

15.7 Rough Radial Function

The radial function generates a set of toolpaths for roughing cut the surface model. The tool-paths are arranged in the radial pattern. The radial parameters dialog box is shown below.

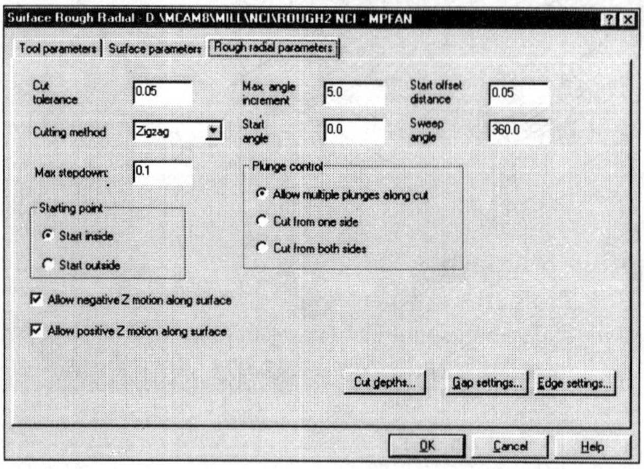

The three angle parameters to be defined in this roughing option are (Figure 15.36):

Maximum angle increment: specify the angle value to be incremented for each path.
Start angle: specify the starting angle of roughing paths.
Sweep angle: specify the sweep angle range of roughing paths.

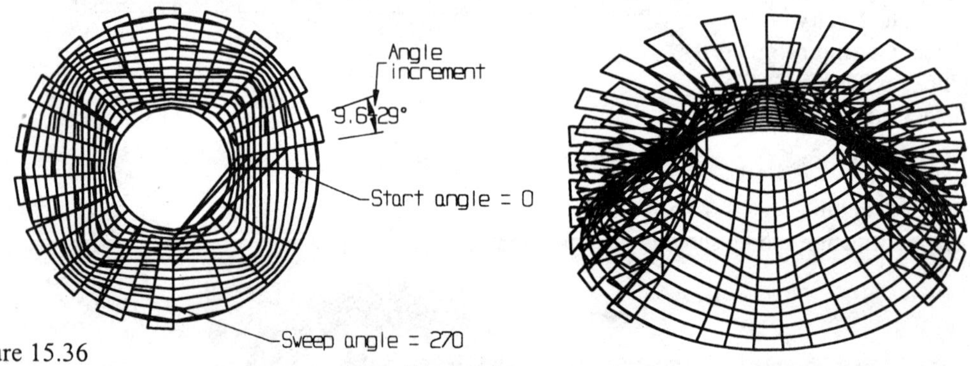

Figure 15.36

The "Starting point" parameter is used to specify the starting point and its direction of roughing paths. It has two the following two options:

Start inside: The roughing paths starts from the start point and cuts toward outside.

Start outside: The roughing paths starts from outside boundary of the starting angle and cuts toward inside.

Project 2. Generating roughing toolpaths for a surface model using radial function

This project uses the surface radial-rough function to generate toolpaths for roughing the dryer surface model as shown in Figure 15.37. The incremental angle is 5 degrees and maximum stepover distance is 0.2".

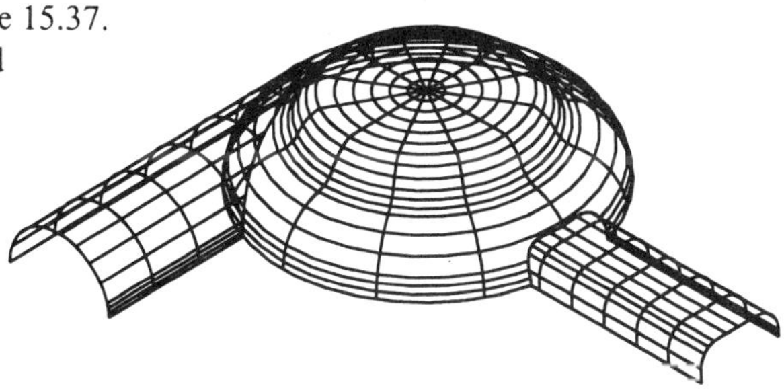

Figure 15.37a

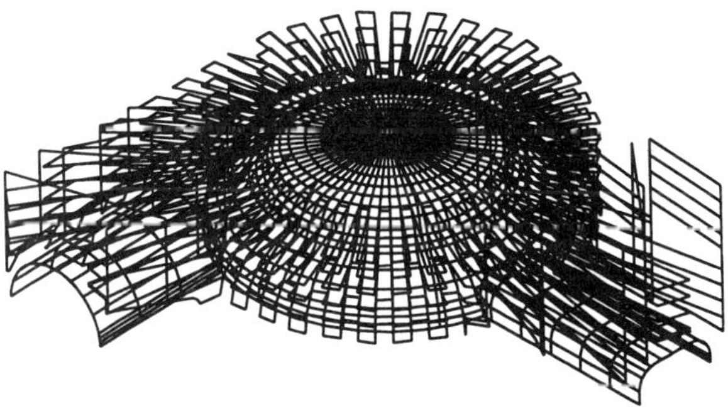

Figure 15.37b

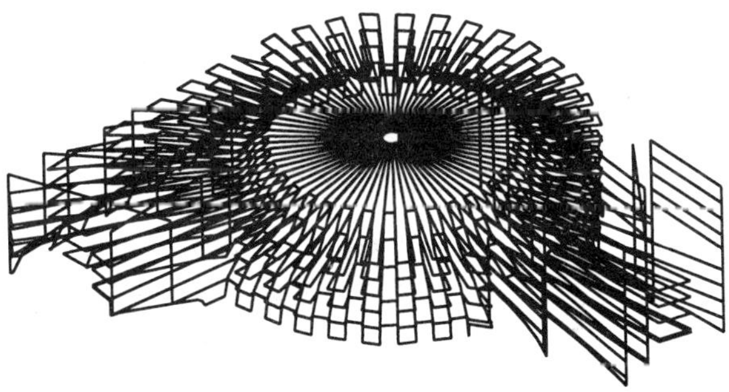

Figure 15.31c

Tips 1. Open the surface model file dryers.

2. Use the surface radial-rough function to generate the roughing toolpaths.

3. Use a ½" flat end mill.

Step 1. Open the surface model file "dryers".

Select **MAIN MENU → File → Get**

File name: **dryers** ↵

The dryer surface model appears as in Figure 15.38.

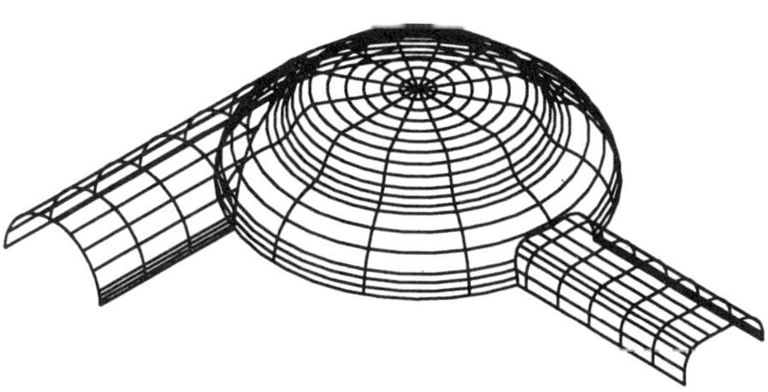

Figure 15.38

Step 2. Initiate the radial roughing function.

Select **Cplane → Top**

Select **MAIN MENU → Toolpaths → Surface → Rough → Radial → Boss**

Select **All → Surfaces → Done**

The Surface Rough Radial dialog box should appear.

Click the right mouse button, then select **Get** from the library

Select **tool number 239** (for ½" flat endmill)

Select **OK** to return back to the Tool parameters dialog box. Set tool parameters as below.

Select **Change NCI** and change the file name to **rough2**

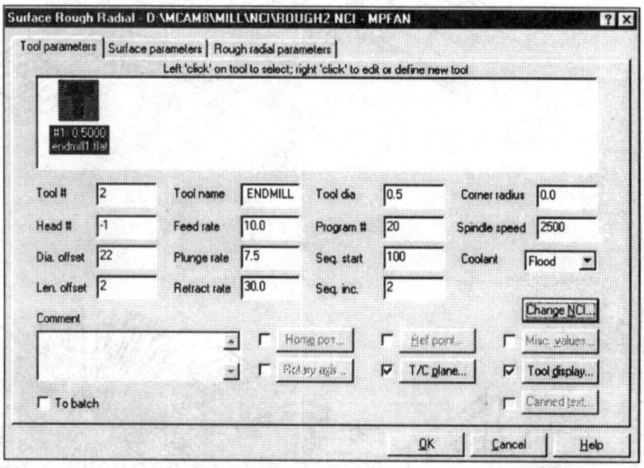

Step 3. Define surface rough parameters.

Click the "**Surface parameters**" button

Set surface parameters as below.

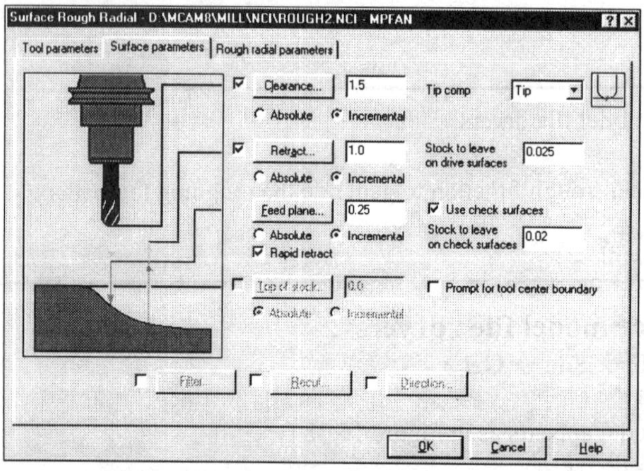

Step 4. Define Rough radial parameters.

Click the "**Rough radial parameters**" button

Set rough radial parameters to the following settings.

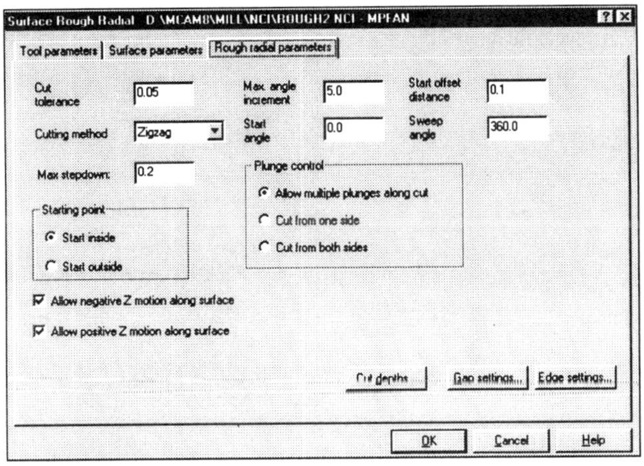

Step 5. Define the cut depth parameters.

Click the "**Cut depths**" button

Set the cut depth parameters as here.

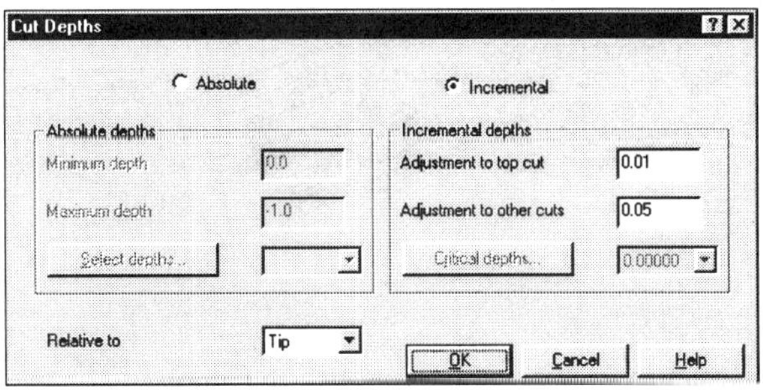

Select **OK**

Step 6. Set gap setting parameters.

Click the "**Gap settings**" button

Set gap setting parameters as below.

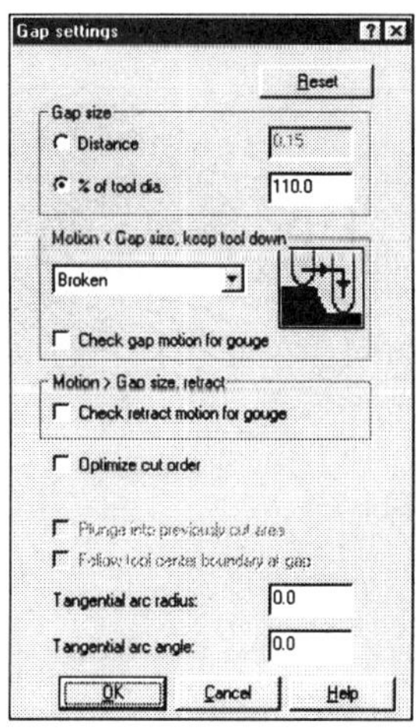

Select **OK**

Step 7. Define edge setting parameters.

Click the "**Edge settings**" button

Set edge setting parameters as below.

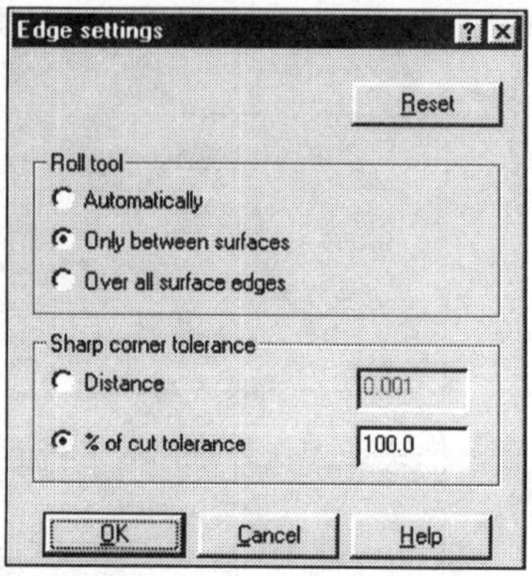

Select **OK → OK**

Step 8. Specify the rotation point.

Select **Endpoint**, then pick a line entity on the top flat surface of the model

The roughing toolpaths run in radial pattern are generated as in Figure 15.39.

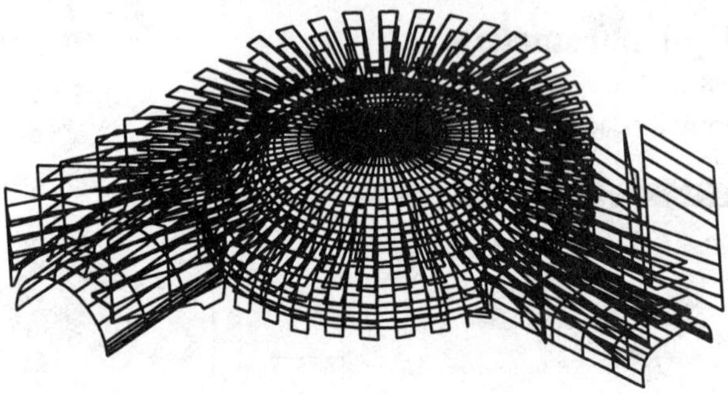

Figure 15.39

Figure 15.40 shows the roughing toolpaths without the surface model.

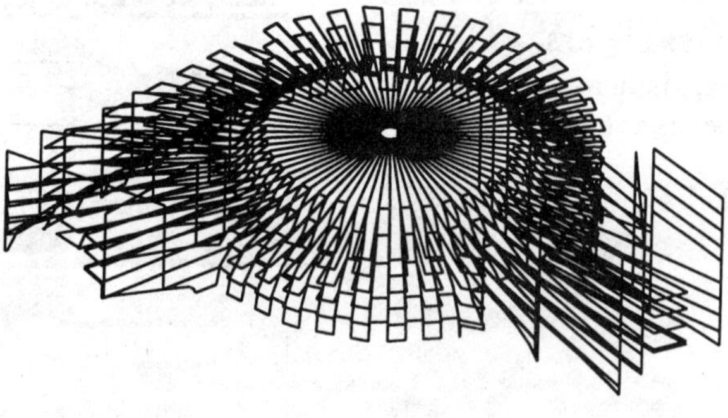

Figure 15.40

15.8 Rough Project Function

This rough function projects an existing set of toolpath files or geometry entities onto a surface model to generate the roughing toolpaths for cutting the model. This function provides free-form tool motion and excellent tool control. Three types of entities can be used for projection; **NCI**, **curves**, and **points**. They are described below:

NCI:	use an existing NCI file to project (Figure 15.41).
Curves:	use a curve or set of curves to project. Valid curves include splines and surface curves (Figure 15.42).
Points:	use a point or set of points to project (Figure 15.43).

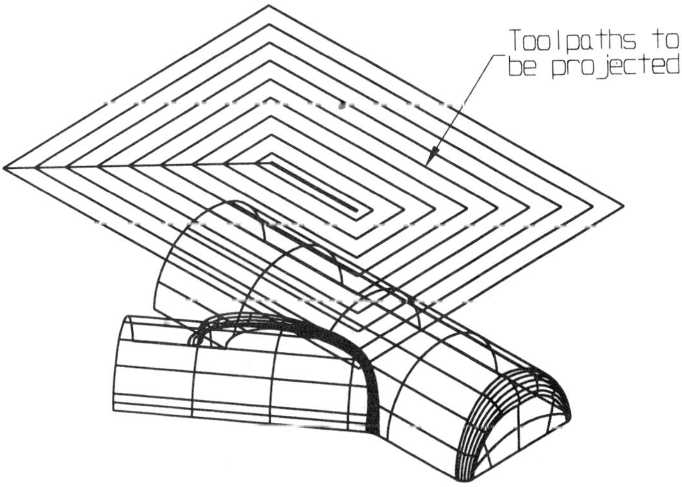

Figure 15.41a

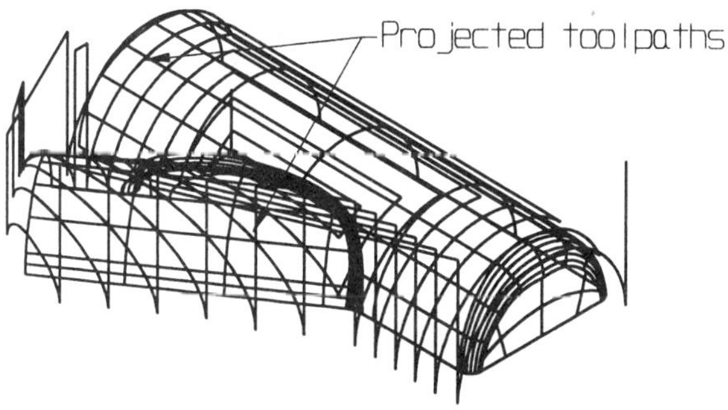

Figure 15.41b

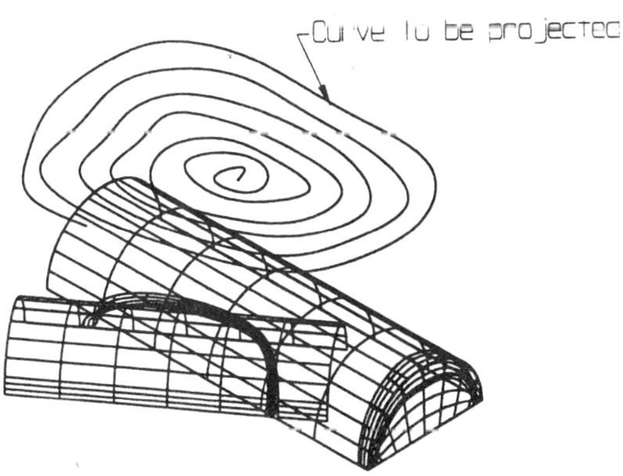

Figure 15.42a

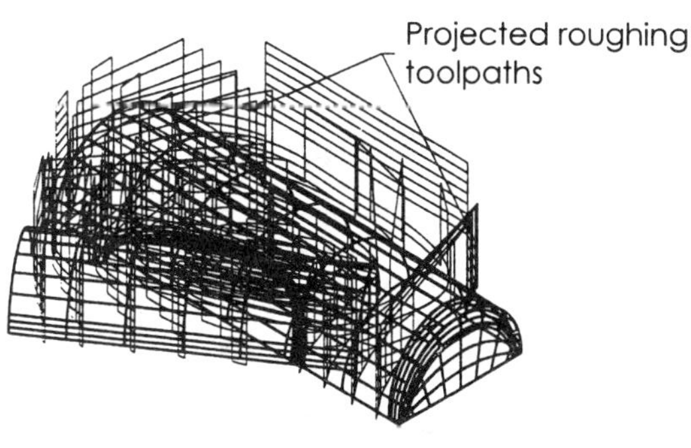

Figure 15.42b

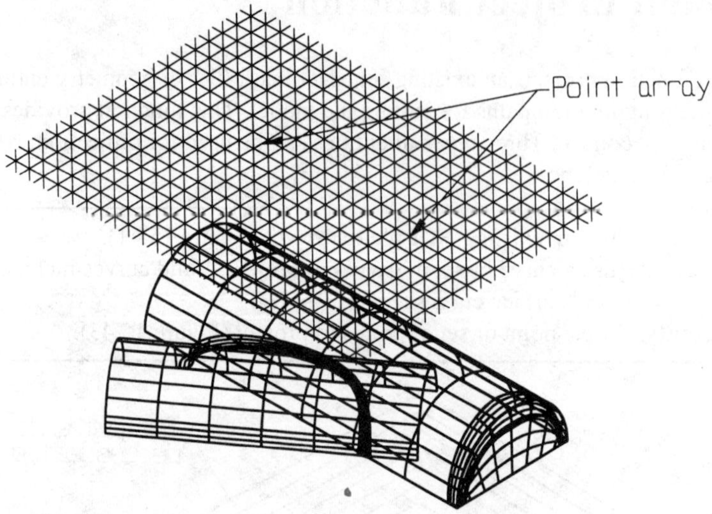

Figure 15.43a

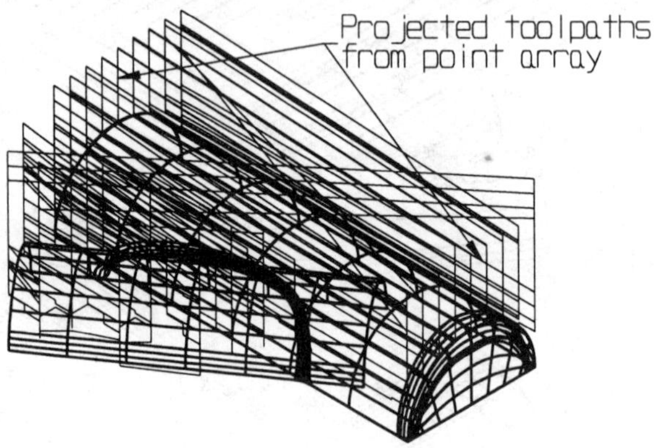

Figure 15.43b

The above three entity types used for projection must be created prior to using the project function. The dialog box for rough project function is shown below.

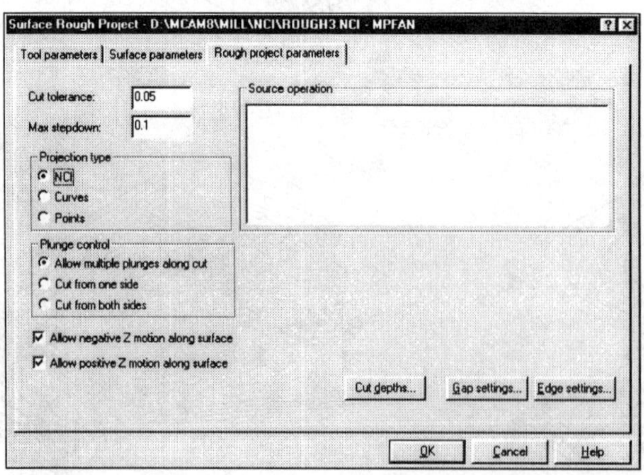

Project 3. Generating roughing toolpaths using project function

A point array is used as the projection entities to generate the toolpaths for doing a roughing cut of a Coons surface model (Figure 15.44).

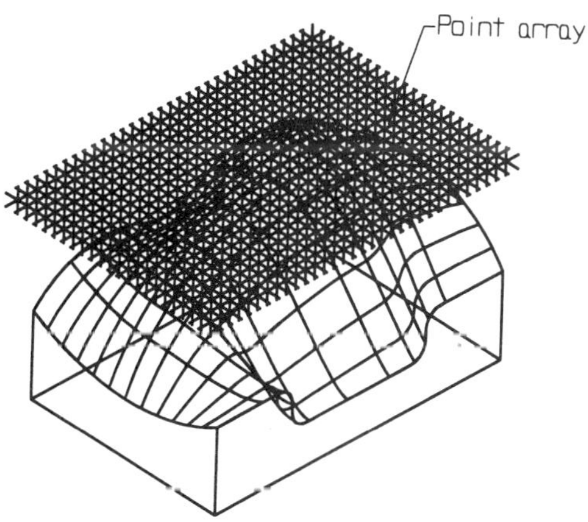

Figure 15.44a

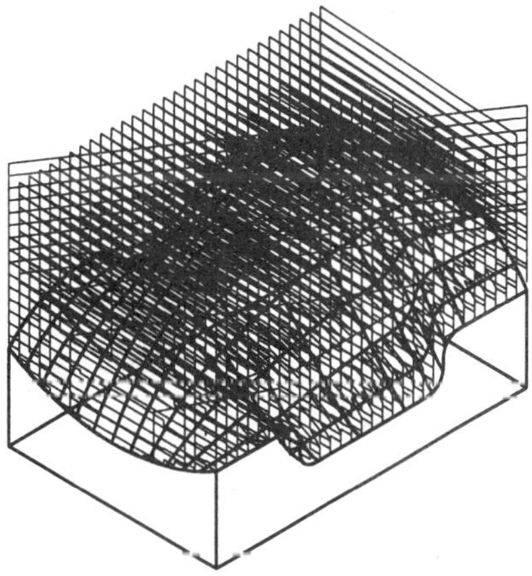

Figure 15.44b

Tips
1. Use the surface model file coonss2.
2. Create a point array with an increment of 0.25" in both X and Y directions. The number of points in horizontal direction is 22 and in vertical direction is 32.
3. Use the rough-project – point function to generate roughing toolpaths.
4. Use a ¼" flat end mill.

Step 1. Open the surface model file coonss2.

Select **MAIN MENU → File → Get**
File name: **coonss2** ↵
The surface model appears as in Figure 15.45.

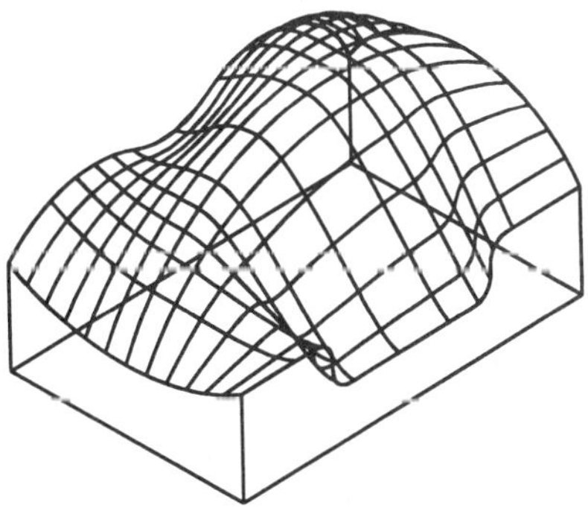

Figure 15.45

Step 2. Create a point array.

Select **Cplane → Top**
Select **Level**, then enter **3** ↵
Select **Z**, then enter **2.5** ↵
Select **MAIN MENU → Create → Point → Grid**

Enter Xstep: **0.25** ↵
Enter Ystep: **0.25** ↵
Enter angle: **0** ↵
Enter Num in X: **22** ↵
Enter Num in Y: **32** ↵
Select **Do it**
Enter lower left corner: **-0.25, -0.25** ↵
The point array is added to the model as shown in Figure 15.46.

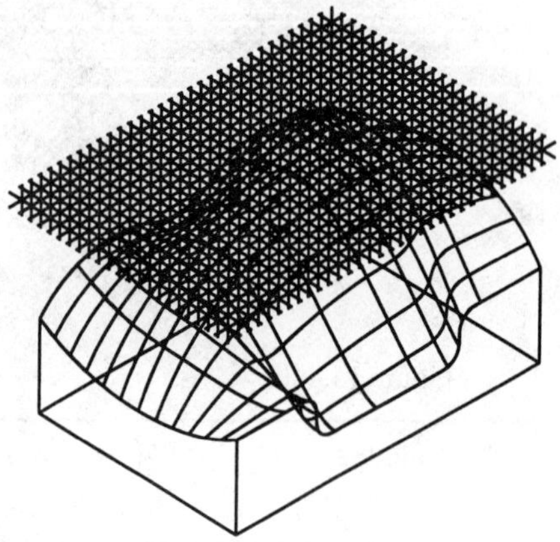

Figure 15.46

Step 3. Initiate the project function.

Select **MAIN MENU → Toolpaths → Surface → Rough → Project → Unspecified**
Select **All → Surfaces → Done**
The Tool parameters dialog box should appear on the screen.
Click the right mouse button, then select **Get tool from library**
Select **tool number 235** (1/4 end mill)
Select **OK**
Set Tool parameters as below.

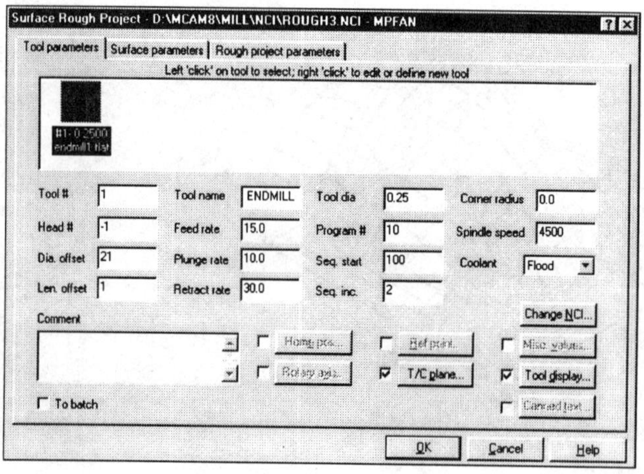

Select **Change NCI** and change the file name to **rough3**

p 4. Define surface rough parameters.

Click the "**Surface parameters**" button
Set surface parameters as below.

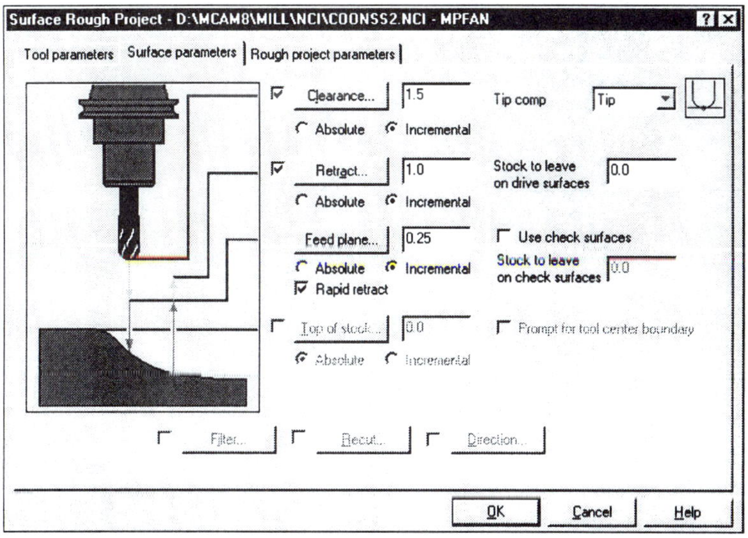

ep 5. Define rough project parameters.

Click the "**Rough project parameters**" button
Set rough project parameters as below.

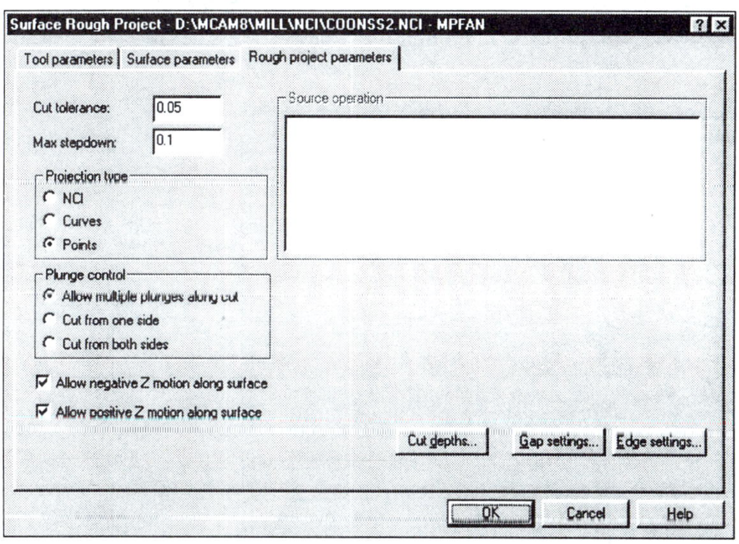

ep 6. Generate roughing toolpaths.

Select **OK**
Select **All → Points → Done**

The roughing toolpaths are generated as shown in Figure 15.47.

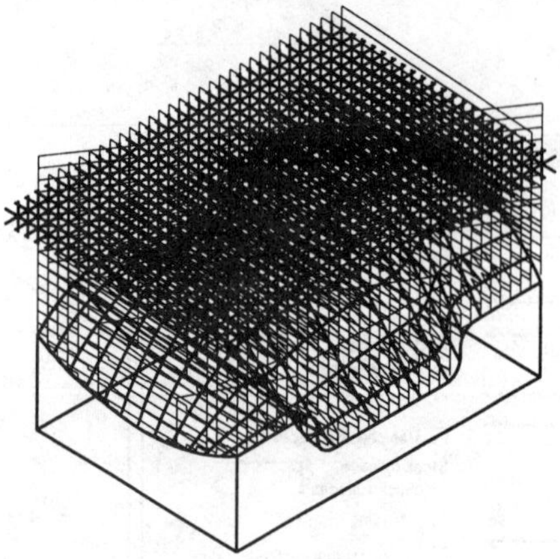

Figure 15.47

15.9 Rough Flowline Function

Rough flowline function generates a set of toolpaths for roughing a surface or set of surfaces. This surface roughing function allows precise control of the scallop height left on the surface(s). It can be used to create a smooth finish. The dialog box for flowline rough function is shown below.

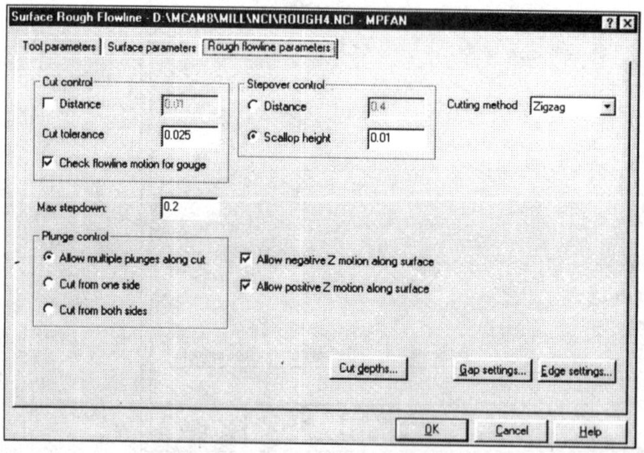

Tolerances

Surface cutting uses the principle of linear interpolation to approximate a surface. Its toolpaths can be controlled in two directions using the flowline method: **along direction** and **across direction**. Mastercam uses two parameters in this roughing function to define the tolerances in these two cutting directions: **cut control** and **stepover control**. The cut control is used to control the tool motion in the along direction, while the stepover control is used to control the tool motion in the across direction (Figure 15.49).

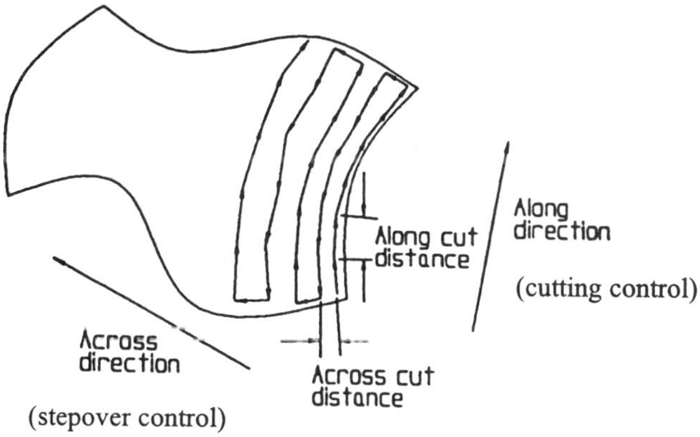

Figure 15.49

Each tolerance parameter has two methods in determining the stepping distance of the toolpath over the surfaces: **distance increment method** and **cut tolerance** (or scallop height) **method**.

Distance increment method: The "Distance in cut control" parameter specifies the stepover interval between two adjacent paths in the along direction. The "Distance in stepover control" parameter decides the stepover interval in the across direction.

Cut tolerance and scallop height method: The cut tolerance is the distance between the actual toolpath and the true surface in the along direction (Figure 15.50). This parameter is referred to as cut tolerance in Mastercam and is also commonly called as chordal deviation. The given cut tolerance value is the maximum allowable dimensional error between the toolpath and the surface. It is used to calculate the cutting increment in the along direction.

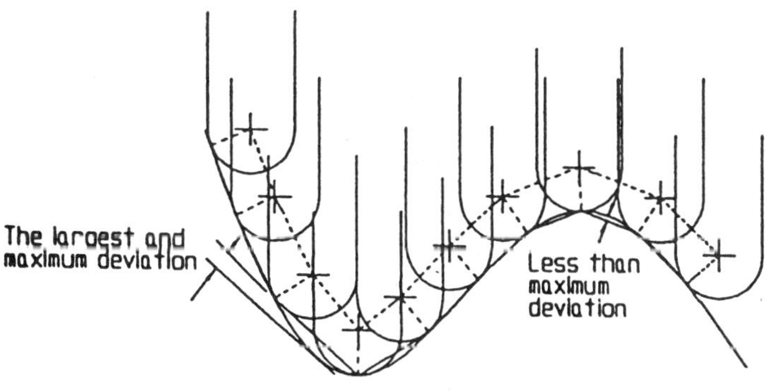

Figure 15.50

When a cutter with a non-flat end, such as a spherical end mill, is used to cut a surface in a zigzag pattern, an uncut strip results between the two adjacent cutting passes as shown in Figure 15.51. The height of these undesirable strips is called scallop height. The larger the stepover value between the two cutting passes, the bigger the scallop height. The given maximum scallop height value is used to calculate the cutter stepover distance in the across direction (or between each along cut). Mastercam uses scallop height to determine the stepping distance over surfaces.

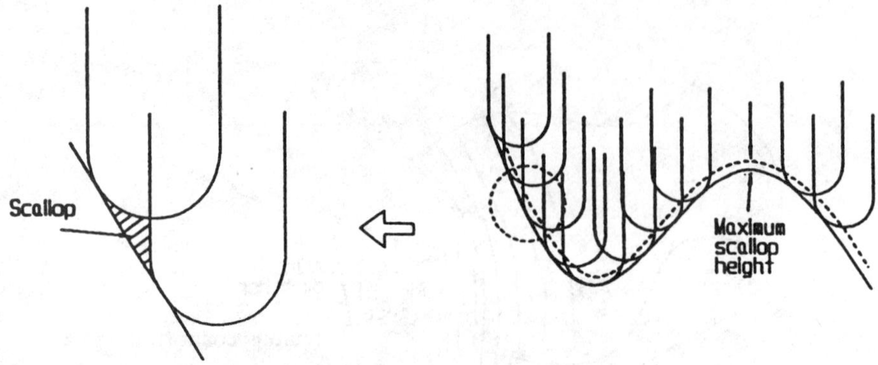

Figure 15.51

⌛Tips for selecting the stepping over methods:

1. Use the distance increment method when the surface has relatively large curvature radii, has no sharp shapes, or does not require a close dimensional accuracy (Figure 15.52).

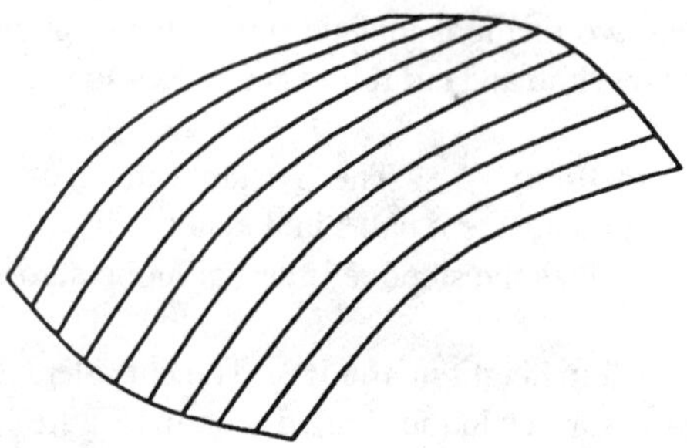

Figure 15.52

2. Use cut tolerance and scallop height method for those surfaces that have small curvature radii, have sharp shapes, or require a close tolerance (Figure 15.53). This method can accurately produce the surface within the specified dimensional accuracy.

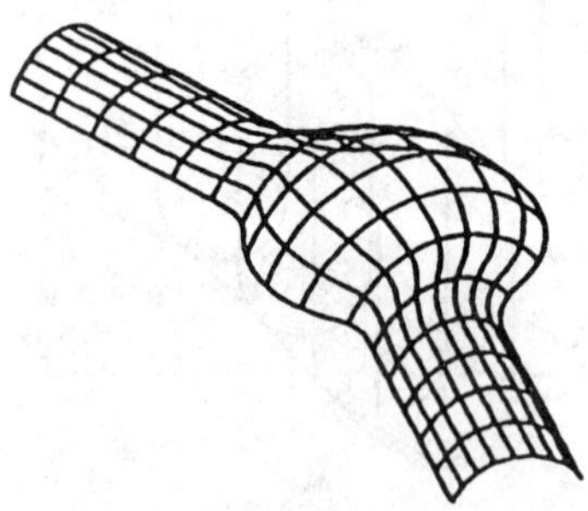

Figure 15.53

3. Computer processing time is significantly shorter when using the distance increment method than with the cut tolerance and scallop height method.

There are four flip options in flowline roughing function that allow to specify the offset direction, cut and step directions, and start point of the cutting. They are briefly described next.

Offset: flip the tool radius offset direction between the two direction of surface normal (Figure 15.54).
Cut dir: flip the toolpath direction between two cut directions, along or across (Figure 15.55).
Step dir: flip the toolpath starting corner of each surface to set the direction in which the tool movements of the flowline toolpath occur (Figure 15.56).
Start: flip the toolpath start point for each surface between two ends of cut direction of flowline (Figure 15.57).

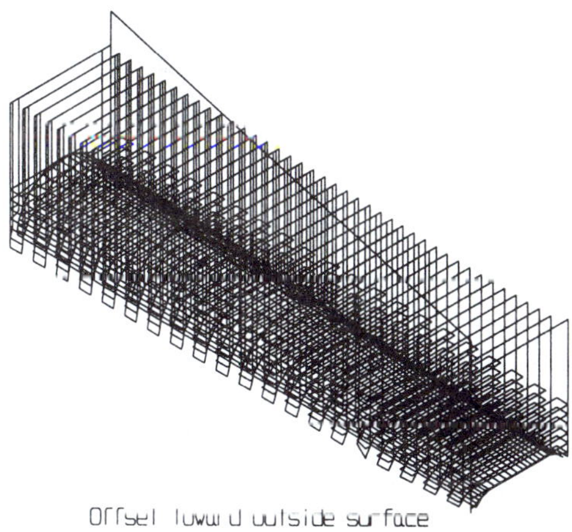

Figure 15.54a

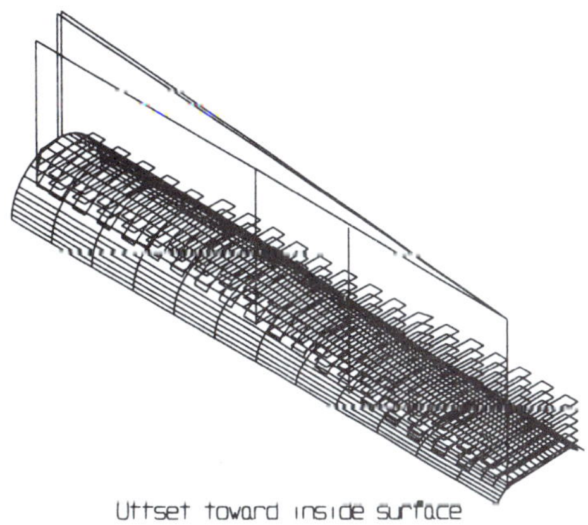

Figure 15.54b

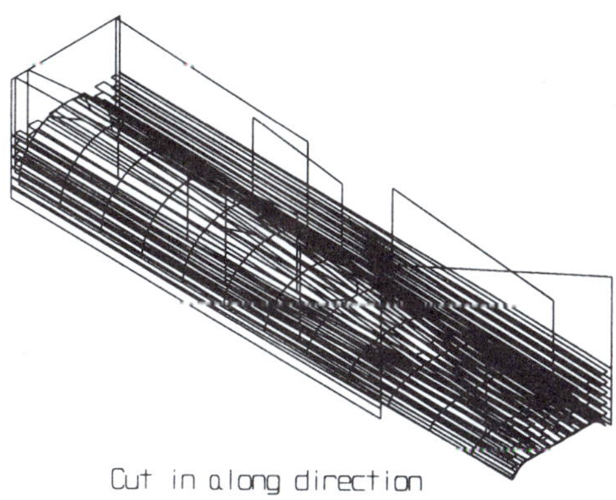

Figure 15.55a

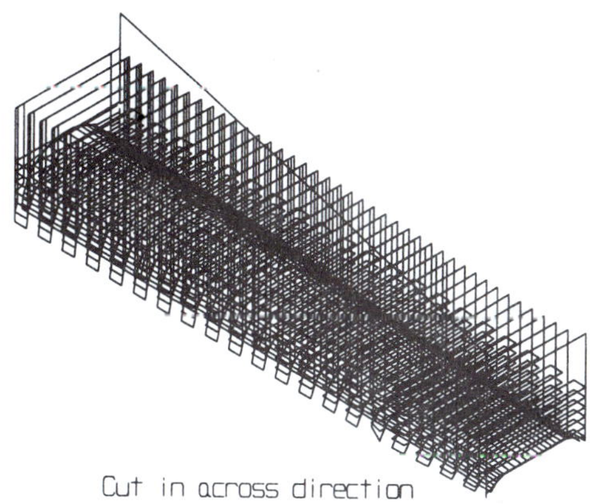

Figure 15.55b

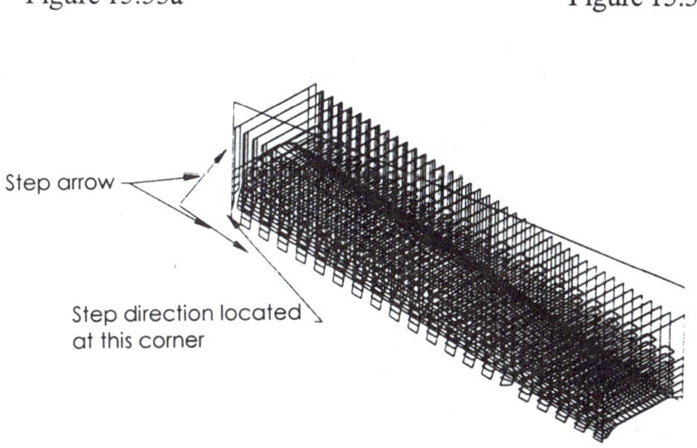

Figure 15.56a

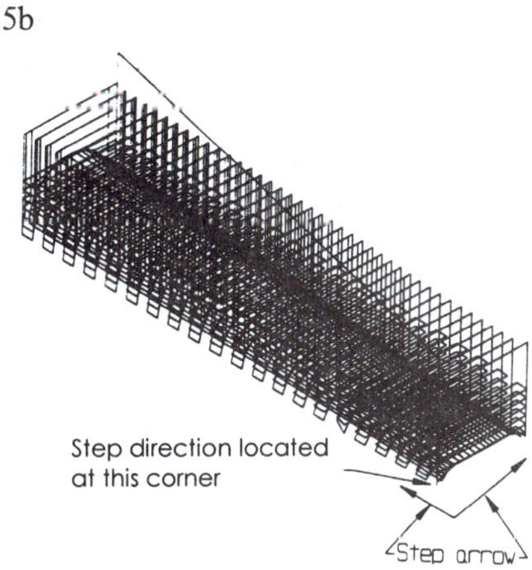

Figure 15.56b

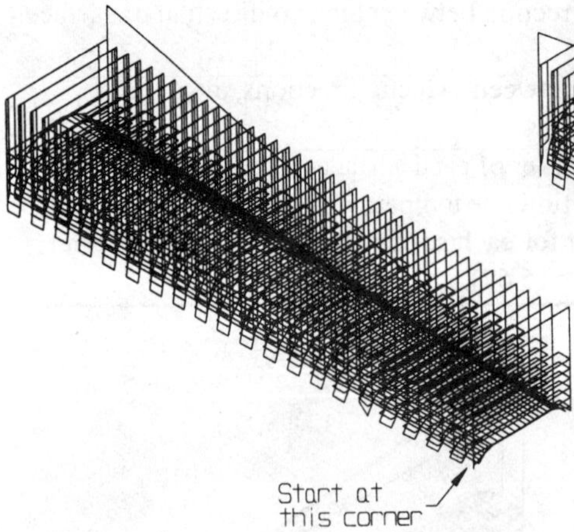

Figure 15.57a

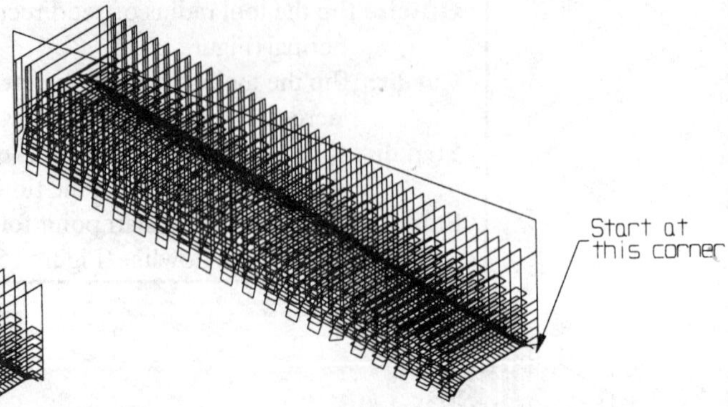

Figure 15.57b

The other parameter "Plot edges" is used to show shared surface edges and touch points using the following colors:

Color	Edges or points
Light blue lines	Free edges
Light cyan lines	Partially shared edges
Light red lines	Fully shared edges
Light blue points	Touch point projected onto adjacent surface

It is possible to simultaneously generate roughing toolpaths for multiple-surface model in one operation (Figure 15.58).

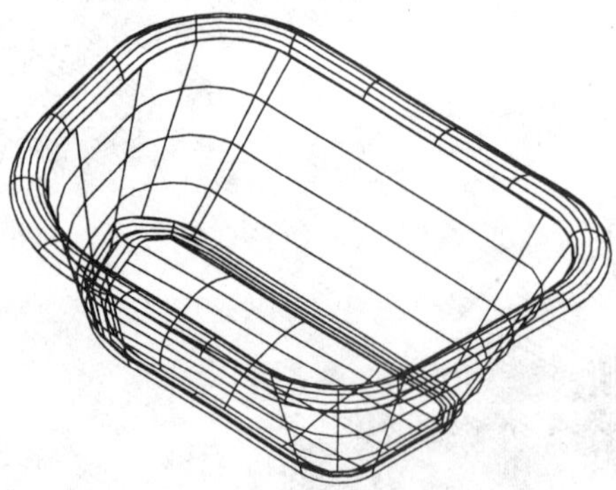

Figure 15.58a

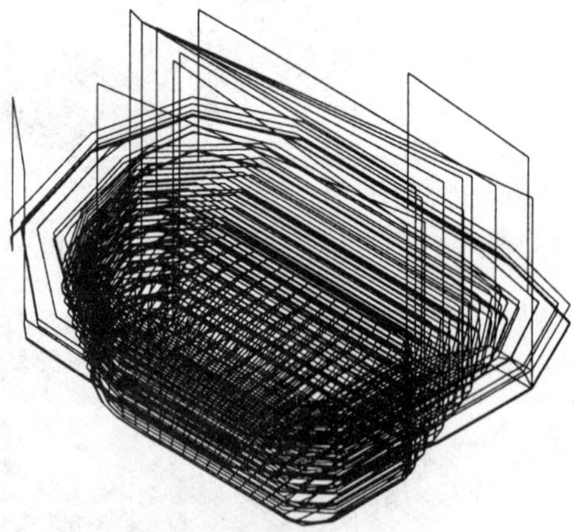

Figure 15.58b

Project 4. Generating roughing toolpaths using flowline function

The surface model to be rough cut consists of four surfaces including two ruled surfaces and two fillet surfaces (Figure 15.59). The rough-flowline function is used to generate toolpaths to rough cut these four surfaces simultaneously.

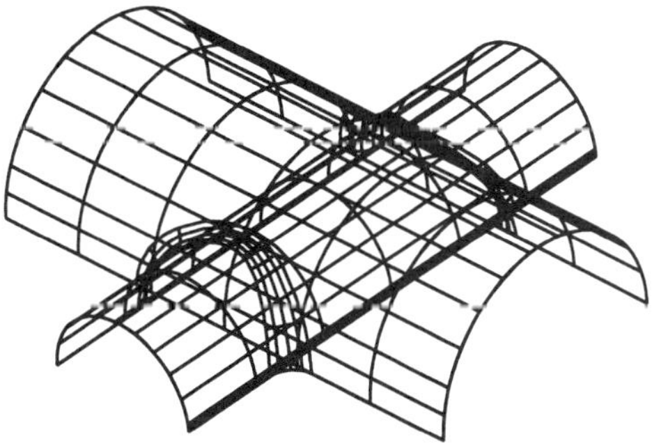

Figure 15.59a

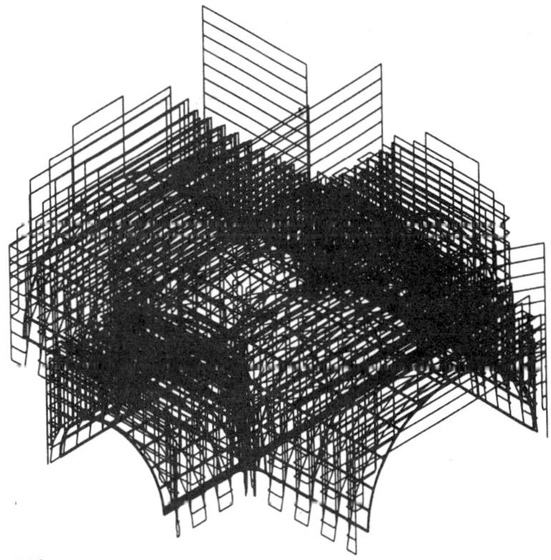

Figure 15.59b

Tips 1. Use the surface model file fillets1.

2. Use a 3/8" spherical end mill.

3. Use surface rough-flowline function.

4. Set the cut tolerance to 0.02" and maximum stepdown value 0.2".

Step 1. Open the surface model file fillets1.

Select **MAIN MENU → File → Get**
File name: **fillets1** ↵
The surface model appears as in Figure 15.60.

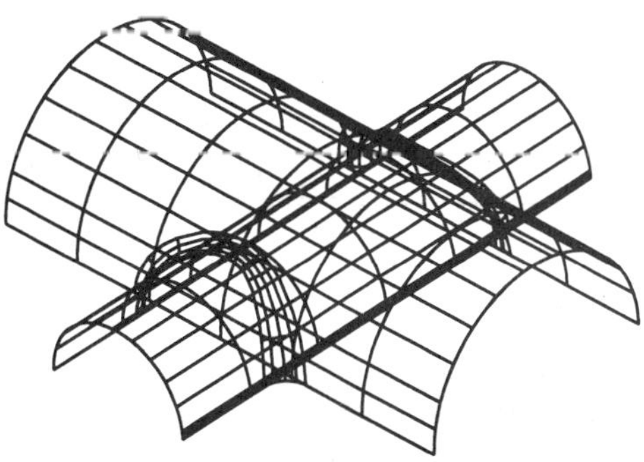

Figure 15.60

Step 2. Initiate the rough-flowline function.

Select **Cplane → Top**

Select **MAIN MENU → Toolpaths → Surface → Rough → Flowline → Boss**

Select **All → Surfaces → Done**

Step 3. Define the tool parameters as below.

Follow the procedure to select a **0.375" sphere endmill**

Set the tool parameters as below.

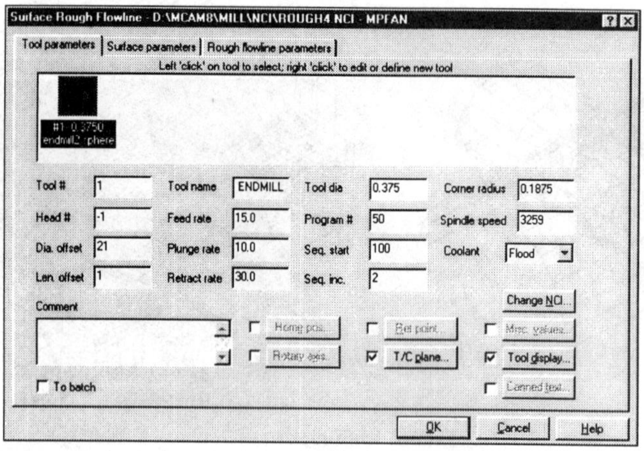

Select **Change NCI** and change the file name to **rough4**

Step 4. Define the surface rough parameters.

Click the "**Surface parameters**" button

Define the surface parameters as below.

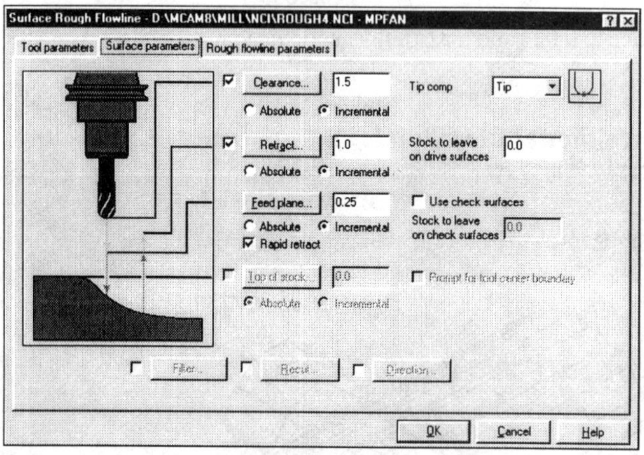

Step 5. Define the rough flowline parameters.

Select the "**Rough flowline Parameters**" button

Set the rough flowline parameters as below.

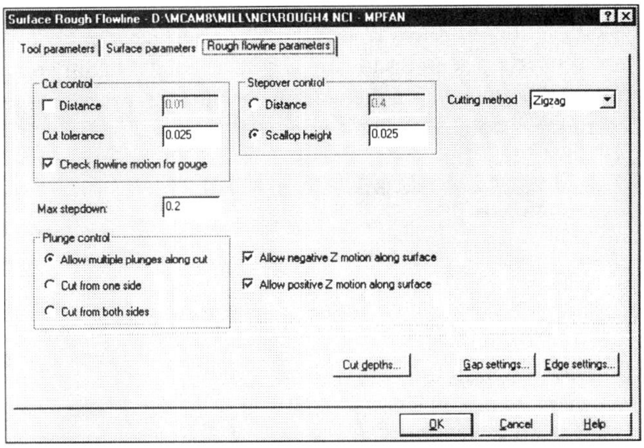

Select **OK → Done**
The roughing toolpaths are generated as in Figure 15.61.

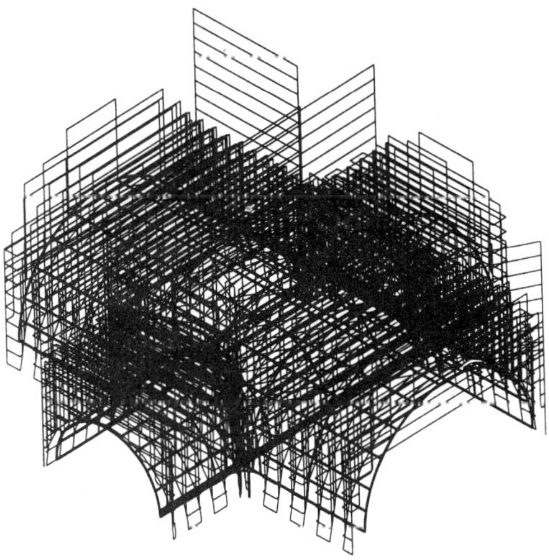

Figure 15.61

Step 6. Save the roughing toolpaths.

Select **MAIN MENU → Toolpath → Operations → Post**
Select **Save NC file → OK**
filename: **rough4 → Save**
Select **OK** to leave the Operations manager

15.10 Rough Contour Function

The contour rough function generates toolpaths to rough cut a surface model around its contour (Figure 15.62). This rough function generates toolpaths to cut the surface model in only one level. It is best suited for roughing those surface models in which the workpiece has been cast or forged to approximated shape and size. The rough contour dialog box is shown below.

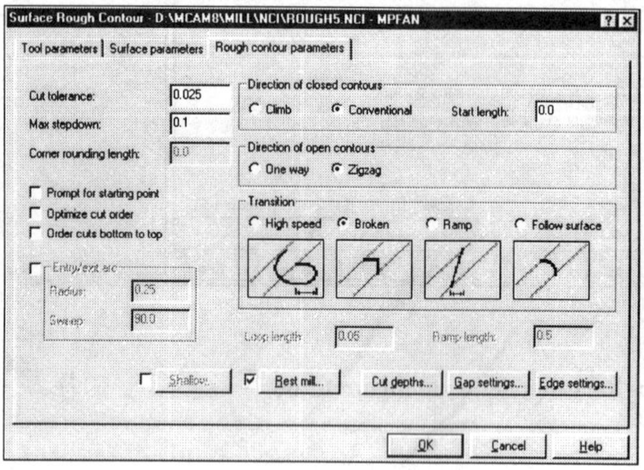

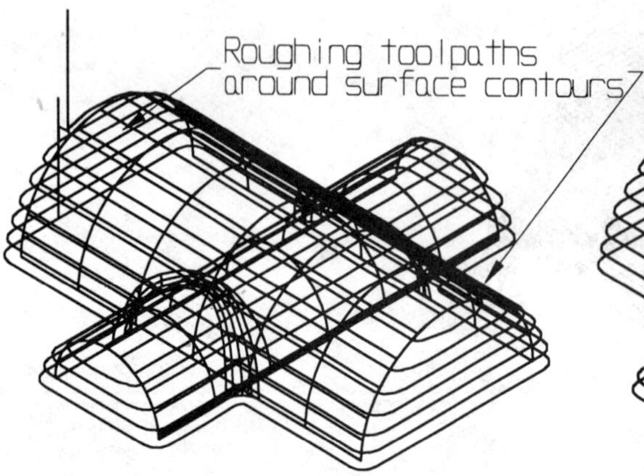

Figure 15.62a

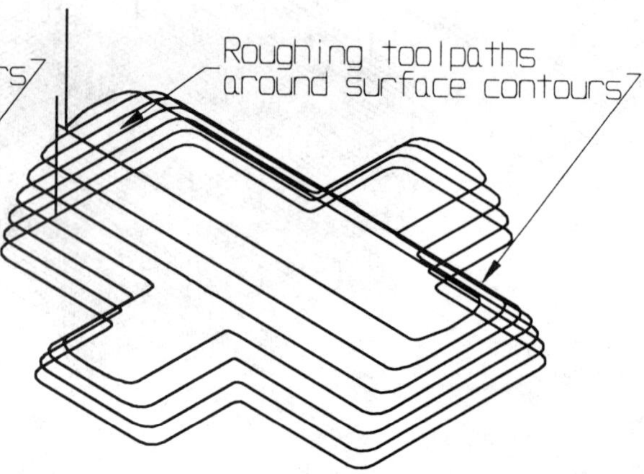

Figure 15.62b

Three parameters that are unique to this contour rough function are:

- **Direction of closed contours**
- **Direction of open contours**
- **Rest mill**

The system will create a set of contours around the surfaces to generate toolpaths based on the given conditions. There are two types of contours: **closed contour** and **open contour**. A closed contour has its first element and last element connected (Figure 15.63a). The first element and last element are not connected in an open contour (Figure 15.63b). The "Roll tool" parameter in the Edge settings dialog box is the parameter which determines whether closed contours or open contours are generated.

Roll tool option	Contour type
Automatically	Open contours
Only between surfaces	Open contours
Over all surface edges	Closed contours

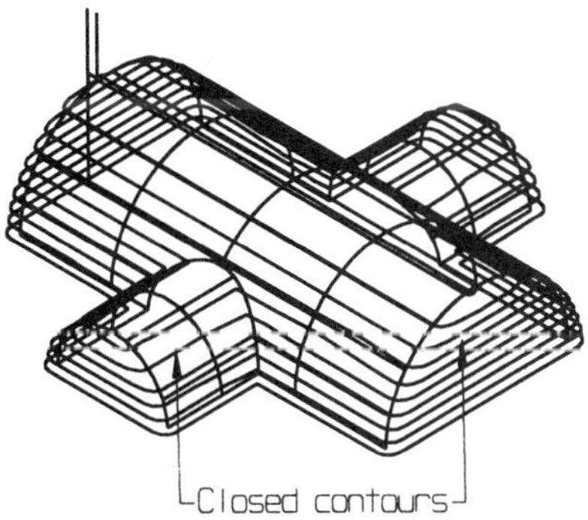

Figure 15.63a

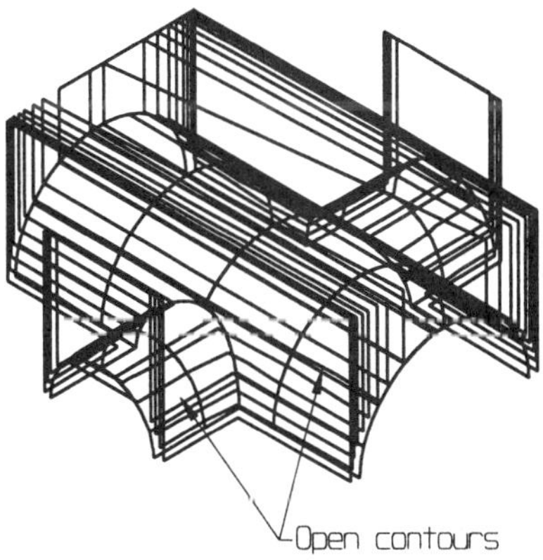

Figure 15.63b

Direction of closed contours

This parameter specifies the cutting directions of the surface contour toolpaths for closed contours. It has two options: **climb** and **conventional**. In climb cuts, the tool cuts the surface contours in the direction in which the tool rotating in a direction opposite of the direction of the cutter travels. In conventional cuts, the tool cuts the surface contours in the direction in which the tool rotating in the same direction as the cutter travels.

Direction of open contours

This parameter specifies the cutting patterns of the surface contour toolpaths for open contours. It has two options: one way and zigzag.

Transition

The transition parameters specify the toolpath pattern between two adjacent cuts. The menu shown below has these four patterns:

High speed:	The cutter moves at high speed from one cut to the next cut in looping and ramping mode.
Broken:	The cutter moves from one cut to the next in two segments; one movement in the X and/or Y direction and the other with Z movement only.
Ramp:	The cutter moves from one cut to the next in ramping mode.
Follow surface:	The cutter moves from one cut to the next along the surface profile.

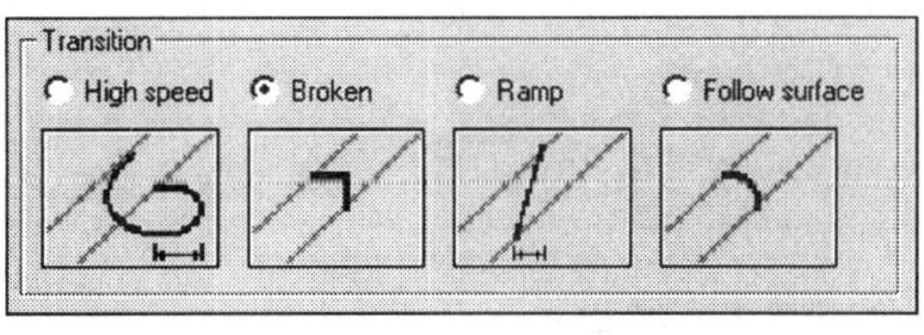

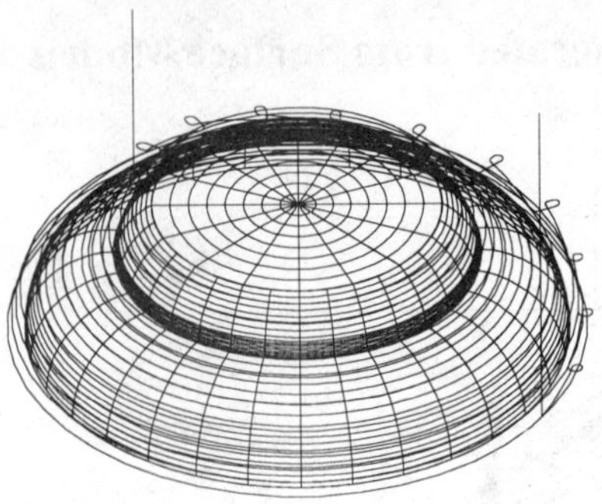

Figure 15.64a High speed transition

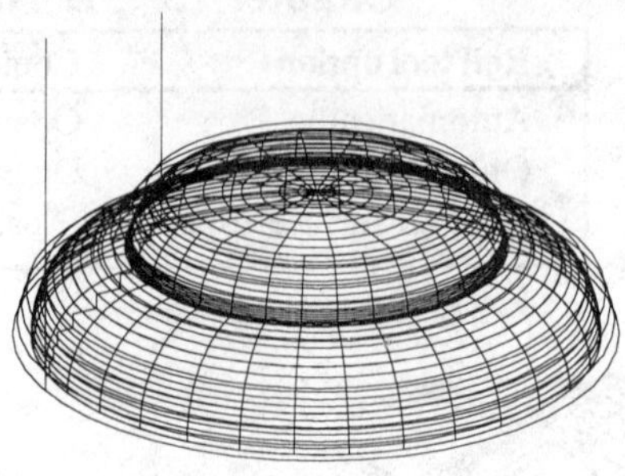

Figure 15.64b Broken transition

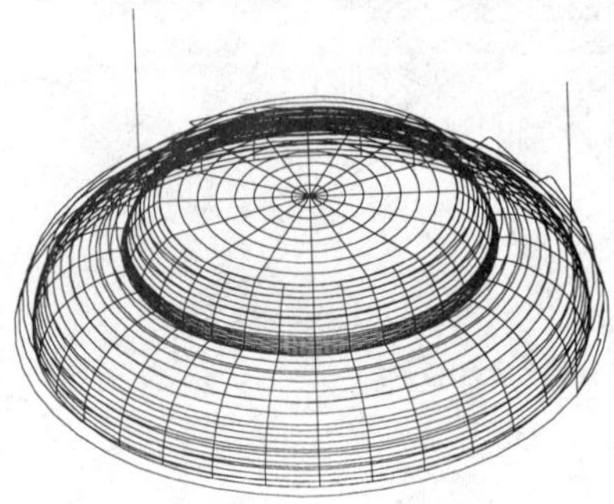

Figure 15.64c Ramp transition

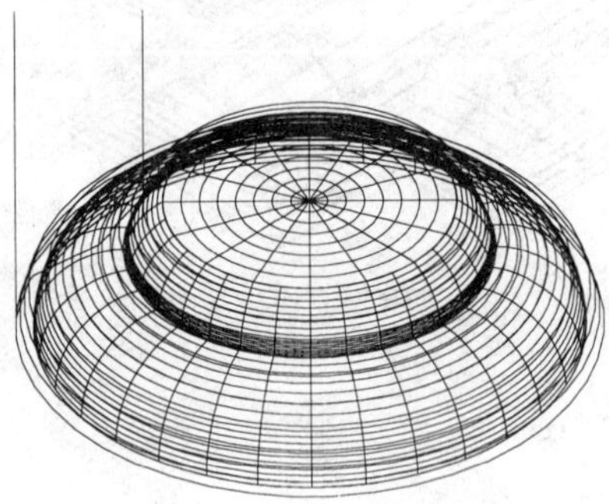

Figure 15.64d Follow surface transition

Contour shallow parameters

Mastercam provides a group of parameters to eliminate moves or add moves to shallow areas in a rough or finish contour toolpath with a constant Z value. The limiting stepover value becomes the **maximum stepover** when removing cuts from shallow areas. If adjacent cuts are further apart than the limiting stepover value, then one of the cuts is removed. The limiting stepover value becomes the **minimum stepover** when adding cuts to shallow areas. If adjacent cuts are further apart than the limiting stepover value, then additional cuts are added between the adjacent cuts.

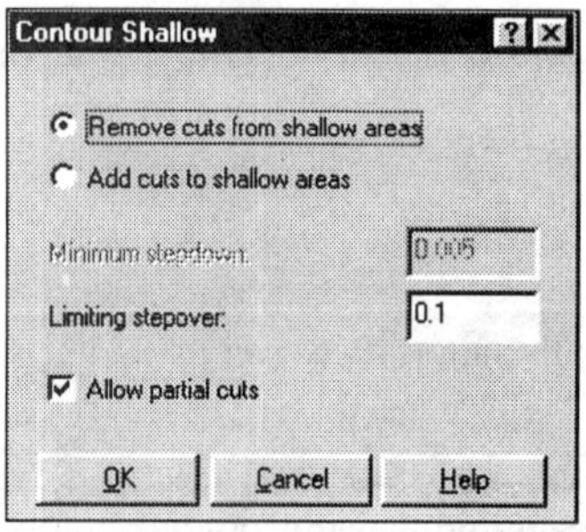

Rest mill

This parameter provides options for cutting previously machined areas of a surface contour toolpaths. Click "Rest mill" button to open "Rest mill" dialog box as shown below.

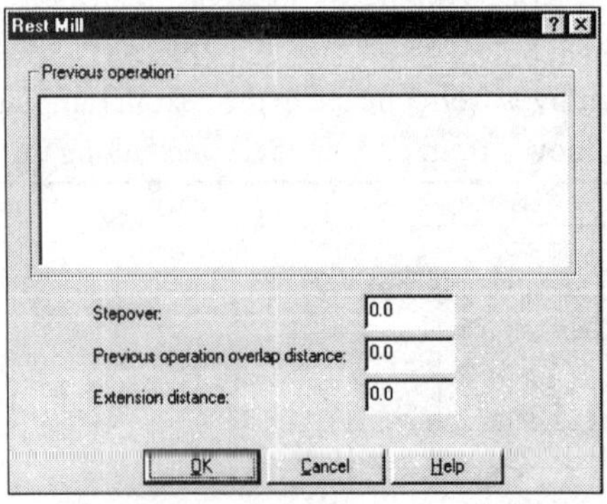

Project 5. Generating roughing toolpaths using rough-contour function 5

The rough-contour function is used to generate toolpaths for roughing a loft surface (Figure 15.65). The roughing toolpaths consist of only one level as shown in Figure 15.65c.

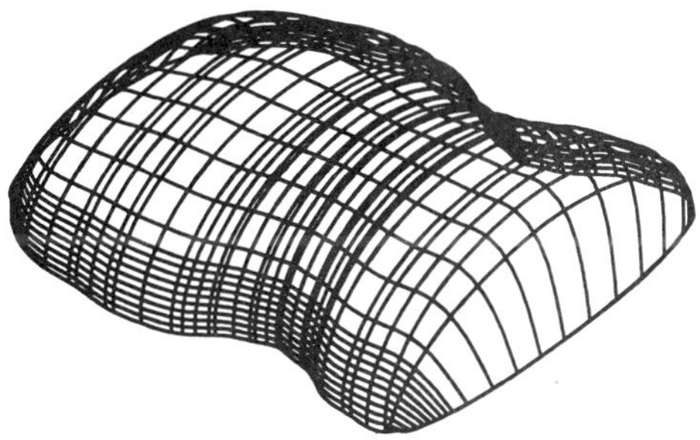

Figure 15.65a

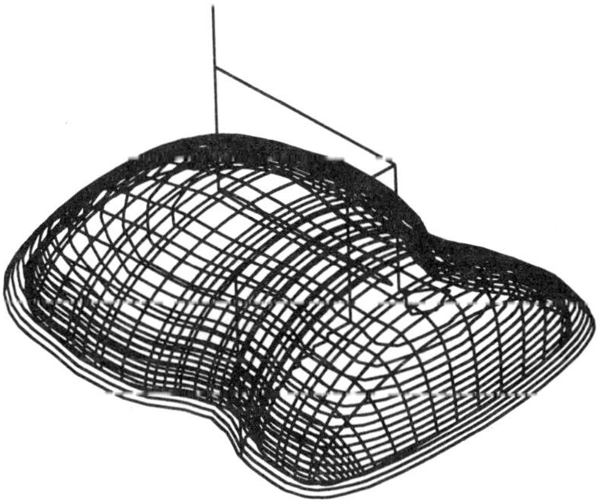

Figure 15.65b

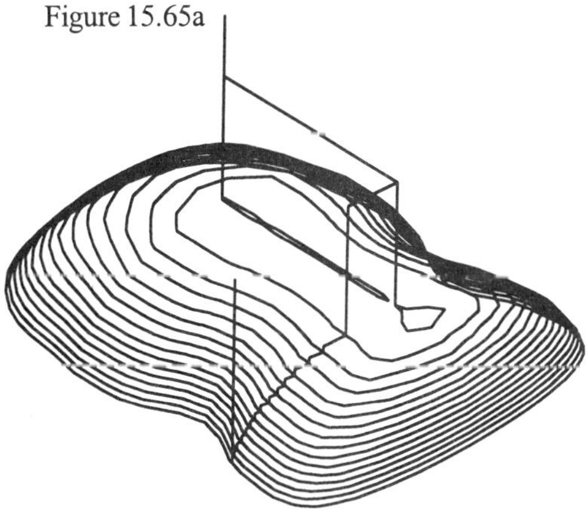

Figure 15.65c

Tips

1. Use the surface model file lofts2.
2. Use a 3/8" spherical end mill.
3. Use rough-contour function to generate roughing toolpaths.
4. Set cut tolerance to 0.025" and maximum stepdown to 0.05".

Step 1. Open the surface model file "lofts2".

Select **MAIN MENU → File → Get**
File name: **lofts2**
The loft surface model appears as in Figure 15.66.

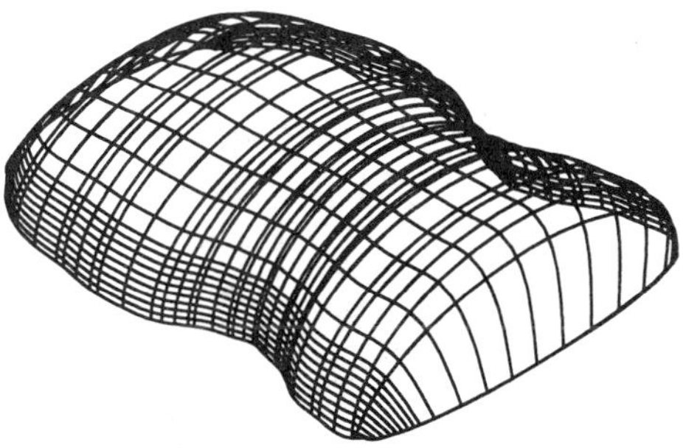

Figure 15.66

Step 2. Initiate the contour-rough function.

Select **Cplane → Top**
Select **MAIN MENU → Toolpaths → Surface → Rough → Contour**
Select **All → Surfaces → Done**

Step 3. Select 3/8" sphere end mill.

Click the right mouse button , then select "**Get tool from library**"
Select **tool number 254** (3/8-sphere endmill)
Select **OK**
Set tool parameters as below.

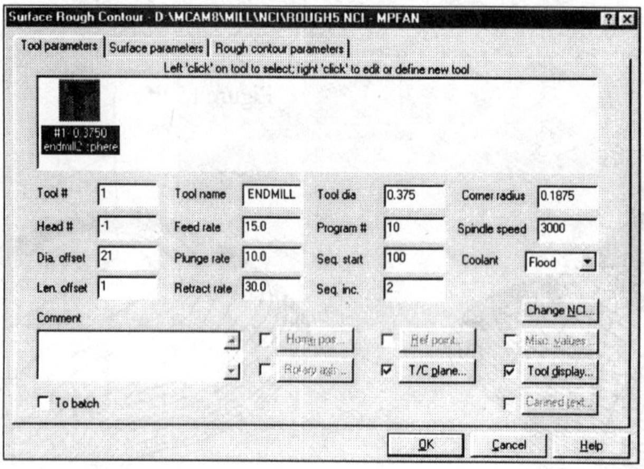

Click **Change NCI** and change the file name to **rough5**

Step 4. Define surface rough parameters.

Click the "**Surface parameters**" button
Set the surface parameters as below.

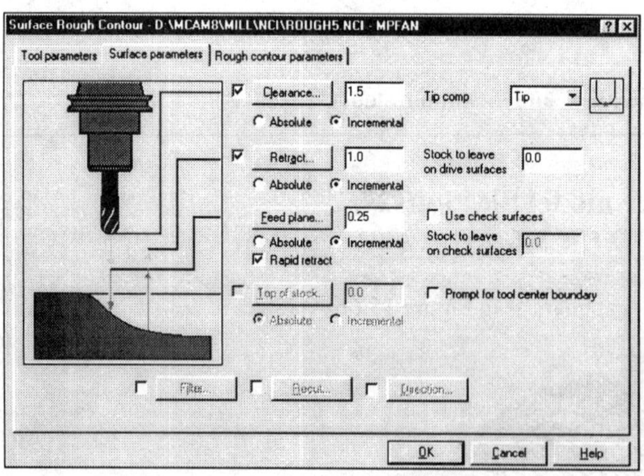

Step 5. Define the rough contour parameters.

Click the "**Rough contour parameters**" button
Set the rough contour parameters as below.

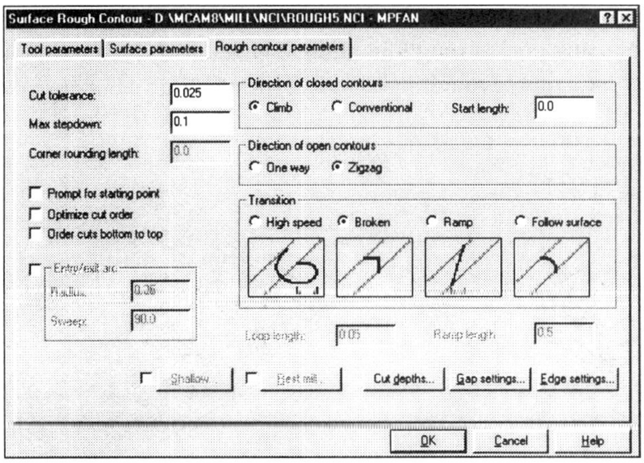

Select **OK**

The roughing toolpaths are generated as in Figure 15.67a. Figure 15.67b shows only the roughing toolpaths.

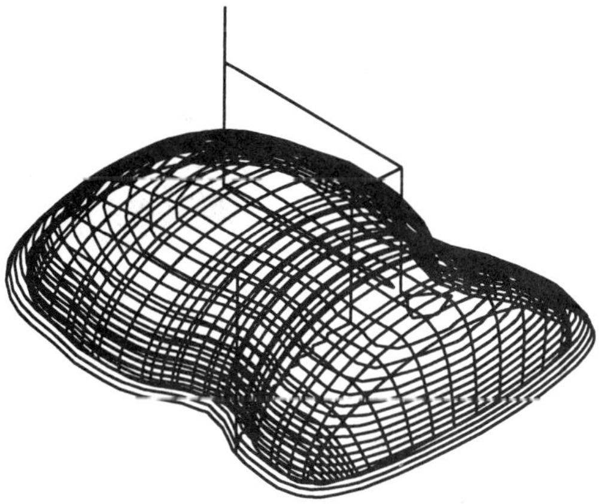

Figure 15.67a

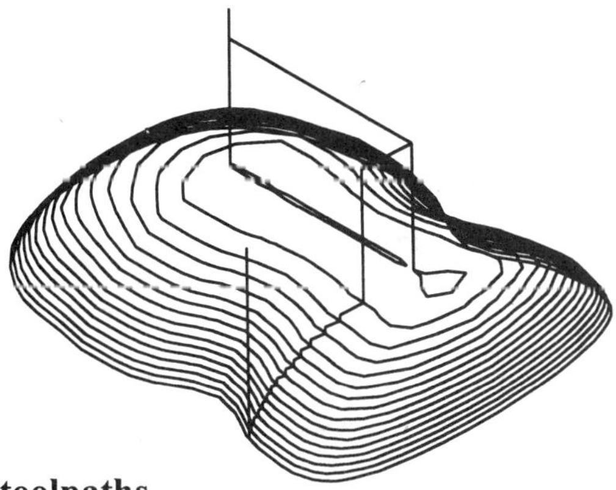

Figure 15.67b

Step 6. Save the toolpaths.

Select **MAIN MENU → Toolpaths → Operations → Post**
Select **Save NCI file → OK**
File name: rough5 → Save
Select **OK** to leave the Operations Manager

15.11 Pocket Rough Function

The pocket rough function generates a series of toolpaths to rough cut the surface model for further finish machining. This function requires a pocketing boundary to determine the pocketing rough. Figure 15.68 shows an example of using pocket rough function to generate a set of roughing toolpaths for a surface model. Figure 15.69 is an example of roughing a cavity type of surface model.

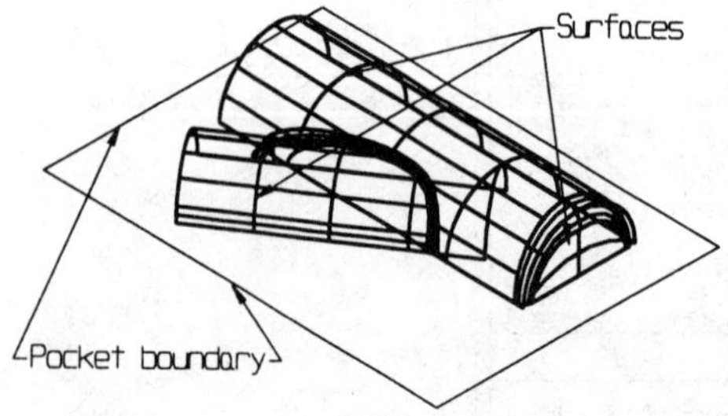

Figure 15.68a

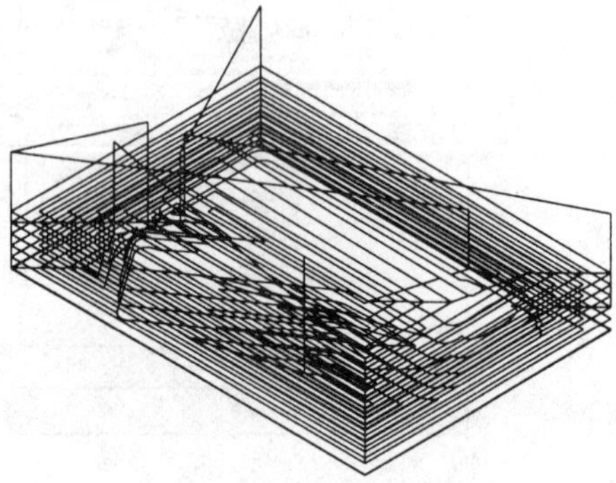

Figure 15.68b Roughing toolpaths

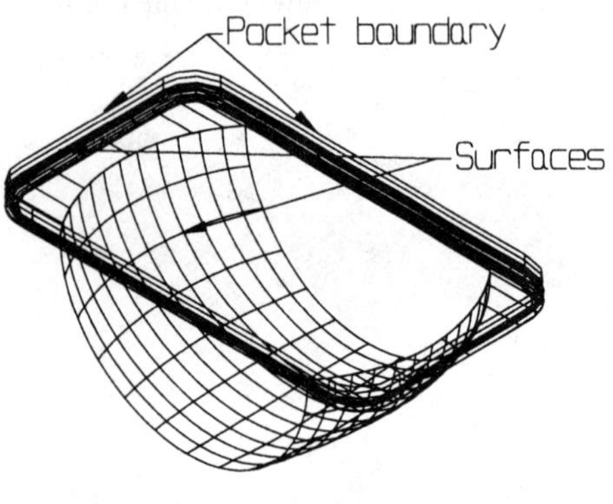

Figure 15.69a

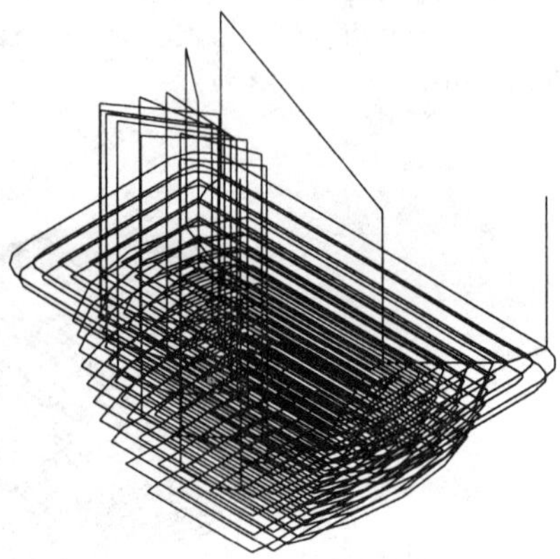

Figure 15.69b

The surface rough pocket parameters dialog box appears as below.

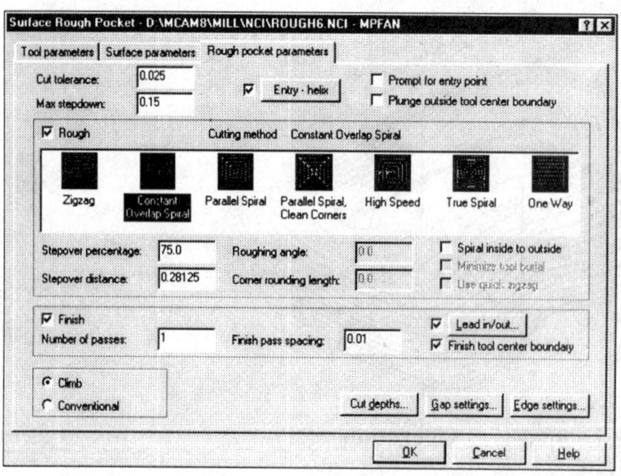

Cutting method

Mastercam provides **seven cutting methods** for generating toolpaths to rough a surface model:

Zigzag: rough the pocket in back and forth linear, parallel pattern according to the specified roughing angle.

Constant overlap spiral: the system calculates the stepover value based on the given stepover distance value and the remaining stock to be removed. The toolpaths are given in small linear moves.

Parallel spiral: rough the pocket in a spiral pattern that offsets the outer boundary by the stepover amount each time.

Parallel spiral, clean corners: rough the pocket in a spiral pattern that offsets the outer boundary by the stepover amount each time. In addition, it adds small cleanout moves in the corners of the pocket to remove leftover stock.

Quick zigzag: rough the pocket in a linear motion in the specified roughing angle. It is only available in surface pocket roughing function.

True spiral: rough the pocket in a circular toolpath pattern with tangent arcs. It provides a smooth motion for the tool, a short NC program, and good cleanout.

One way: rough the pocket in a linear pattern in only one direction.

Most parameters used in this rough function are identical to those parameters in the 2D pocket function presented in chapter 7. The four parameters that are unique to this pocket rough function are briefly described below.

Cut tolerance: specify the accuracy of the roughing toolpaths.

Entry Helixes: A helix or ramp movement can be added to the pocket toolpath entry. An entry helix uses the maximum possible radius to use more of the side of the end mill and less plunging. Figure 15.70 shows the entry helix.

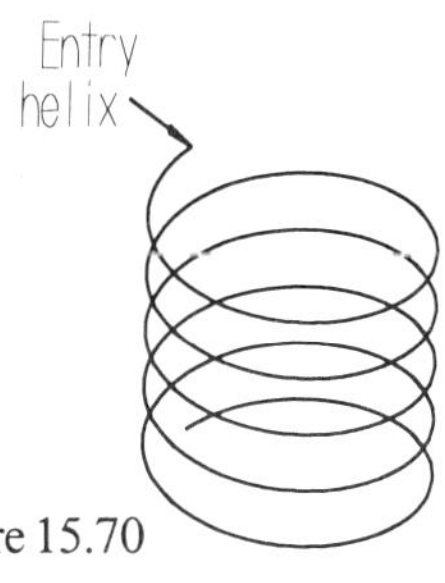

Figure 15.70

Helix parameters and the ramp parameters are displayed here for reference.

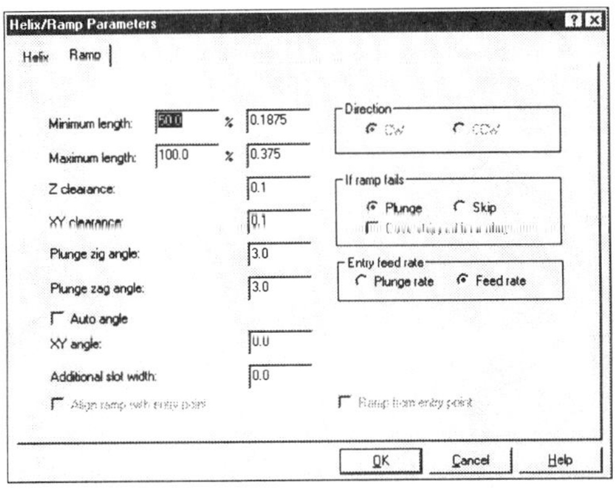

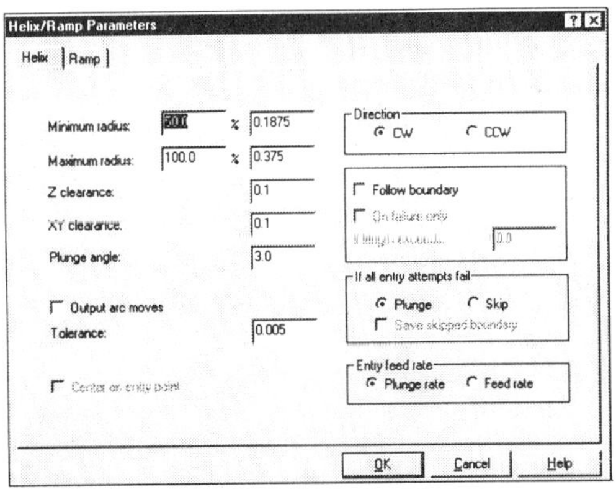

Prompt for entry point: ask for an approximate starting point for the toolpaths.

Plunge outside tool center boundary: specify a boundary from which the entry point of tool center to be placed its outside.

Project 6. Generating rough toolpaths using rough pocket function

A rectangle is created as the pocketing boundary. Use the rough pocket function to generate roughing toolpaths to rough out all material between the pocket boundary and the surface model as shown in Figure 15.71.

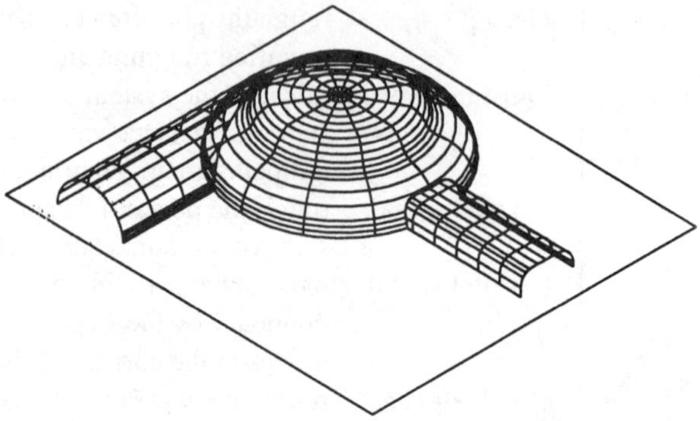

Figure 15.71a

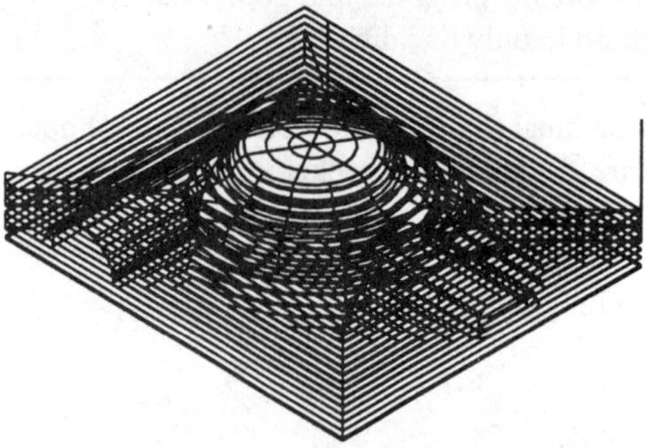

Figure 15.71b

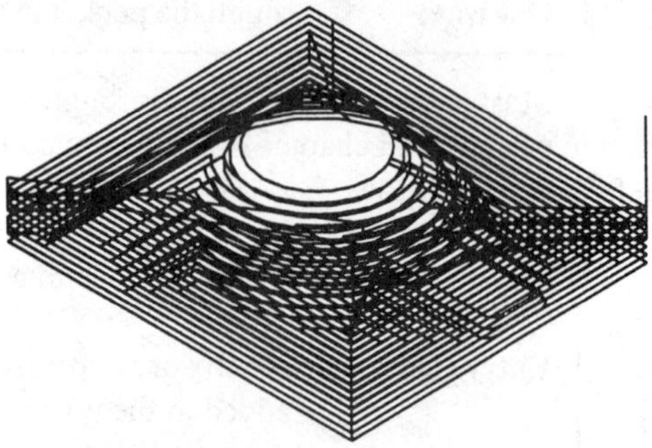

Figure 15.71c

Tips 1. Open the surface model file dryers.

2. Create a rectangle as the pocket boundary.

3. Use surface rough-pocket function to generate roughing toolpaths.

4. Use 3/8" spherical end mill..

Step 1. Open a surface model file dryers.

Select **MAIN MENU → File → Get**
File name: **dryers**
The dryer surface model appears as in Figure 15.72.

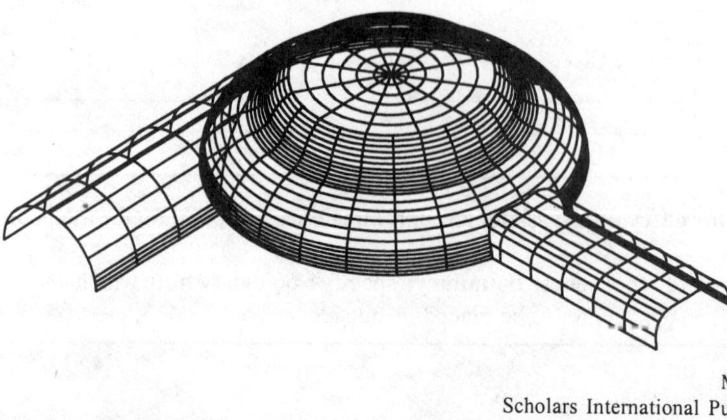

Figure 15.72

Step 2. Create a rectangle as the pocketing boundary. 6

Select **Cplane → Top**
Select **Level**, then enter **8** ↵
Select **Z**, then enter **0** ↵
Select **Create → Rectangle → 2 points**
Enter the lower left corner: **-2.5, -3.85** ↵
Enter the upper right corner: **4.5, 2.35** ↵

The rectangle is added as in Figure 15.73.

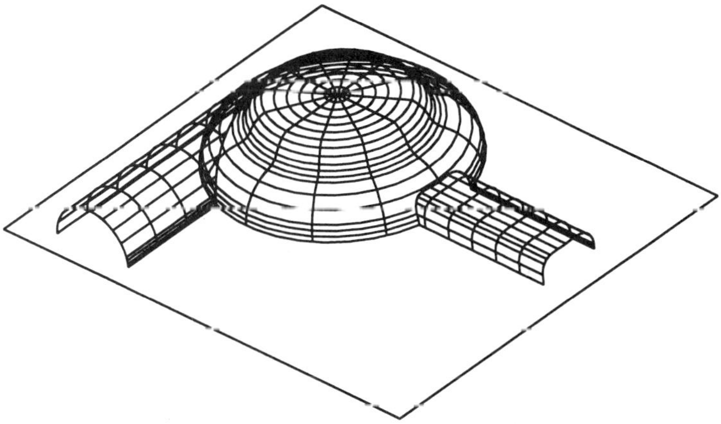

Figure 15.73

Step 3. Initiate the rough-pocket function.

Select **MAIN MENU → Toolpaths → Surface → Rough → Pocket**
Select **All → Surfaces → Done**

Step 4. Select a cutting tool.

Click at the right mouse button, then select "**Get tool from library**" to open the tool library
Select **tool number 254** (3/8" sphere end mill)
Select **OK**
Set rough parameters as below.

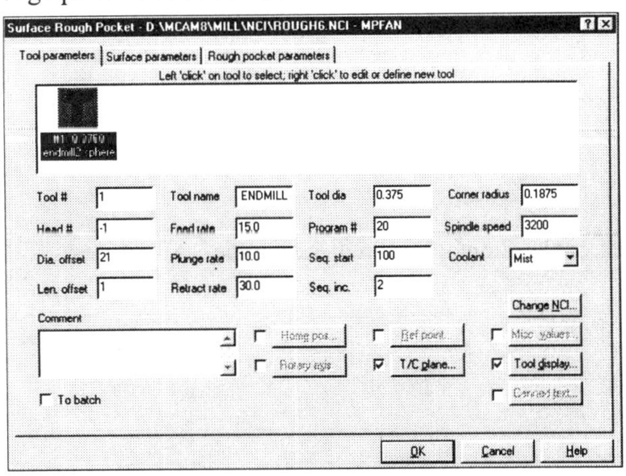

Click **Change NCI** and change the file name to **rough6**

Step 5. Define the surface rough parameters.

Click the "**Surface rough parameters**" button
Set the surface parameters as next.

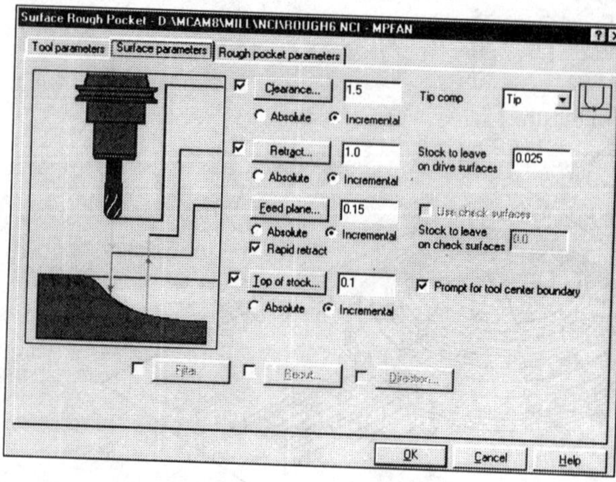

Step 6. Define the rough pocket parameters.

Click the "**Rough pocket parameters**" button
Set the rough pocket parameters as below.

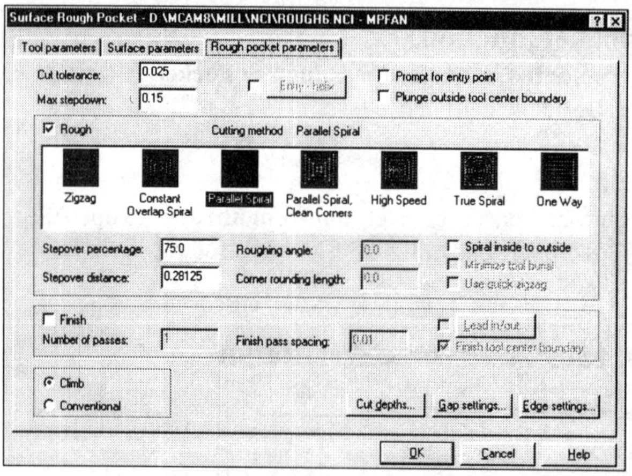

Select **OK**
Select **Chain**, then pick the front horizontal line on the rectangle
Select **Done**

The roughing toolpaths are generated as in Figure 15.74.

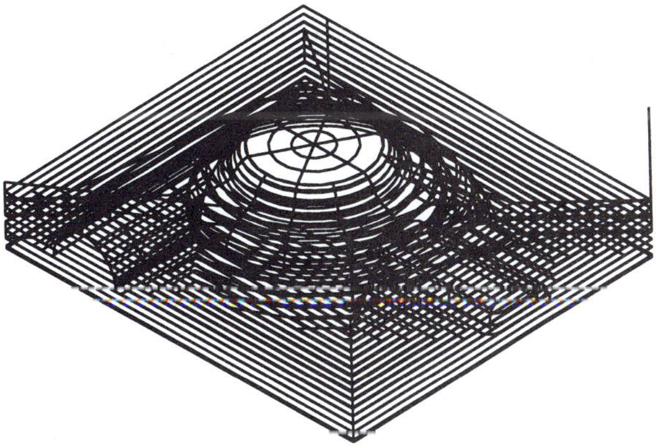

Figure 15.74

Figure 15.75 shows only the roughing toolpaths.

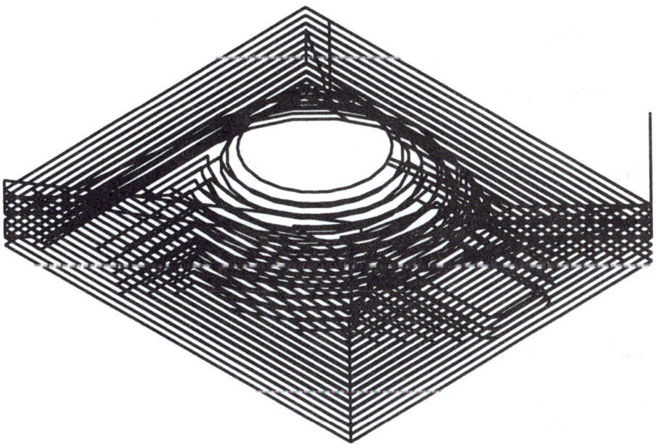

Figure 15.75

Step 7. Save the roughing toolpaths.

Select **MAIN MENU → Toolpaths→ Operations→ Post**
Select **Save NCI file → OK**
filename: **rough6 → Save**

💻 Project 7. Generating toolpaths to rough a surface model using the rough-pocket function

This project uses the outside profile of the rim as the pocket boundary to generate roughing toolpaths for a basket surface model with rough-pocket function. Figure 15.76 shows the surface model and toolpaths.

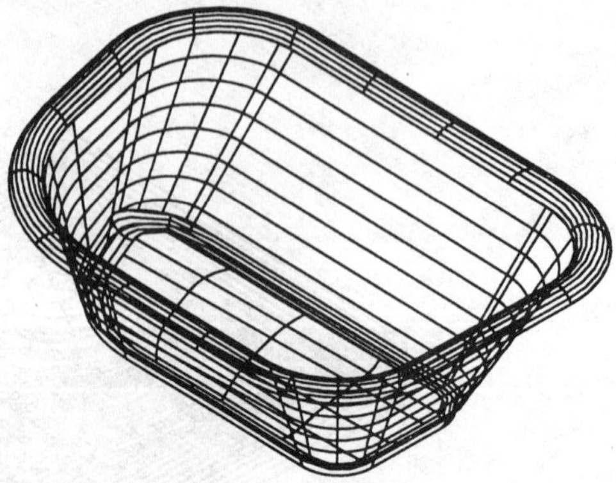

Figure 15.76a

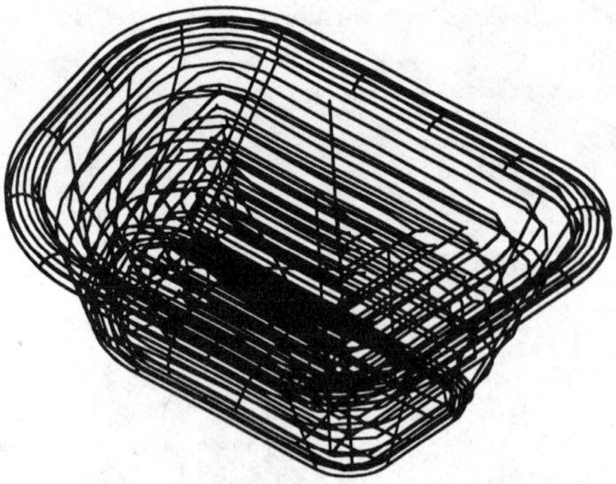

Figure 15.76b

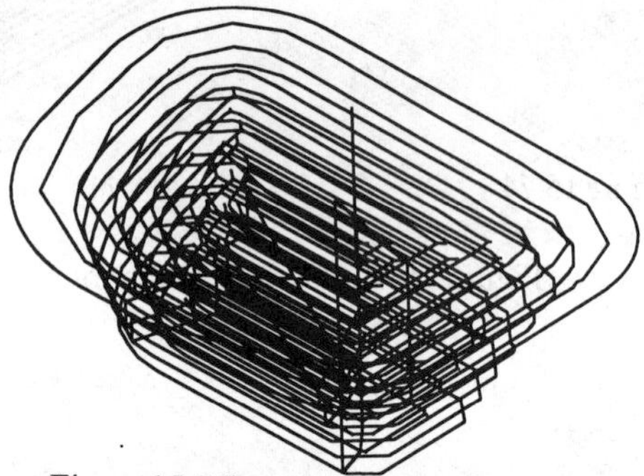

Figure 15.76b

⌛**Tips** 1. Open the surface model file baskets.

2. Use the surface rough-pocket function to generate roughing toolpaths.

3. Use ½" sphere end mill.

Step 1. Open the surface model file baskets.

Select **MAIN MENU → File → Get**
File name: **baskets**
The basket surface model appears as in Figure 15.77.

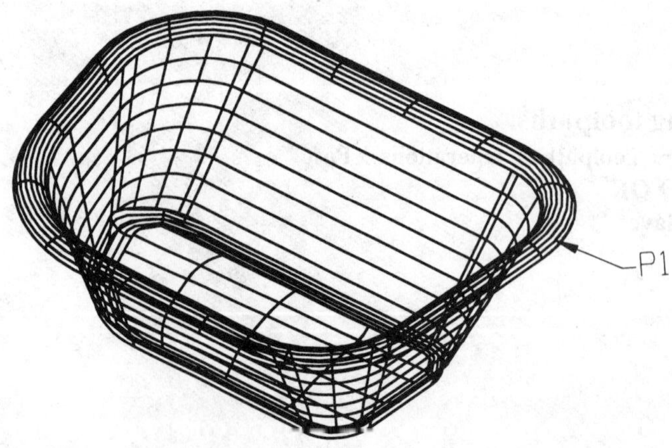

Figure 15.77

Step 2. Initiate the rough-pocket function. 7

Select **MAIN MENU → Toolpaths → Surface → Rough → Pocket**
Select **All → Surfaces → Done**
Click the right mouse button, then select "**Get tool from library**" to open tool library

Step 3. Select a tool.

Select **tool number 256** (1/2" sphere end mill)
Select **OK**
Define the tool parameters as below.

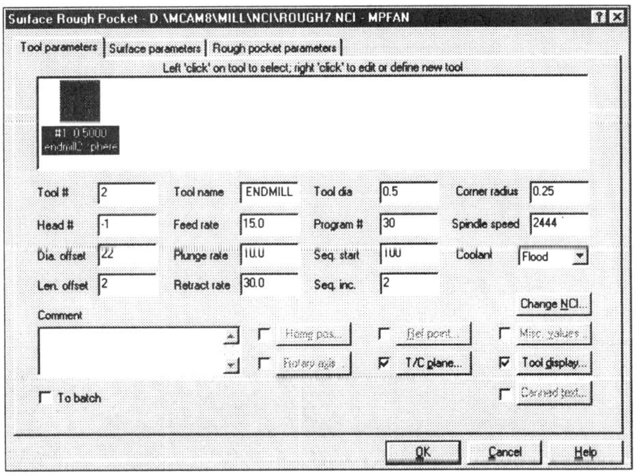

Click Change NCI and change the file name to rough7.

Step 4. Define the surface rough parameters.

Click the "**Surface rough parameters**" button
Set the surface parameters as below.

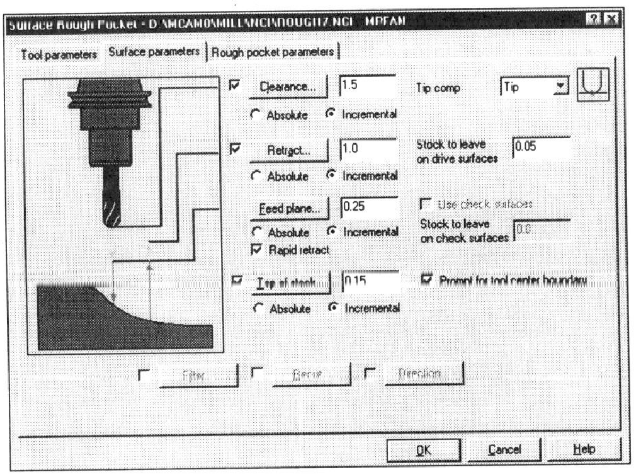

Step 5. Define the rough pocket parameters.

Click the "**Rough pocket parameters**" button

Set the rough pocket parameters as below.

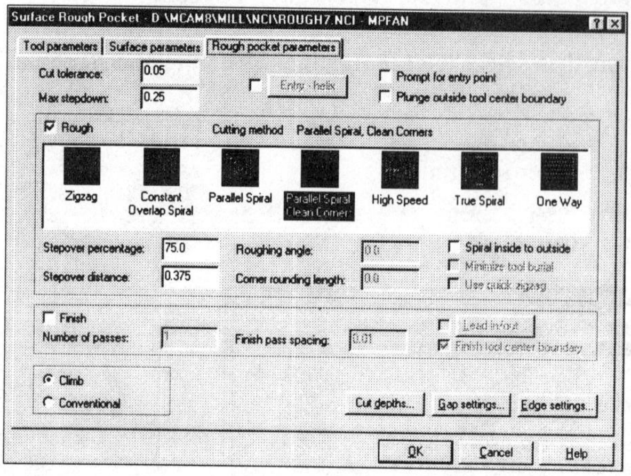

Select **OK**

Step 6. Define the outside boundary.

Select **Chain**, then pick **P1** as shown in Figure 15.77
Select **Done**
Roughing toolpaths are generated as in Figure 15.78.

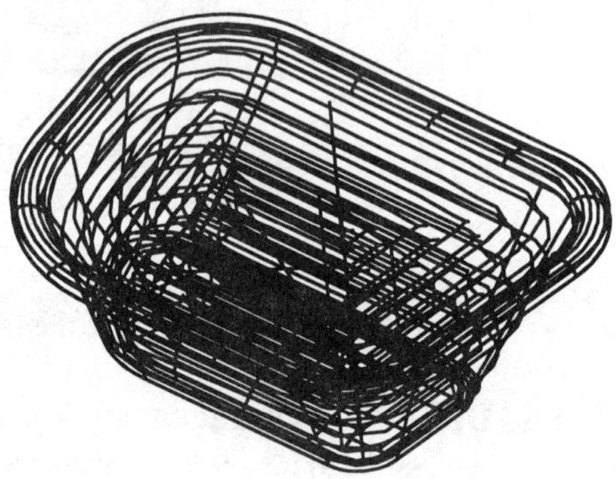

Figure 15.78

Figure 15.79 shows only the roughing toolpaths.

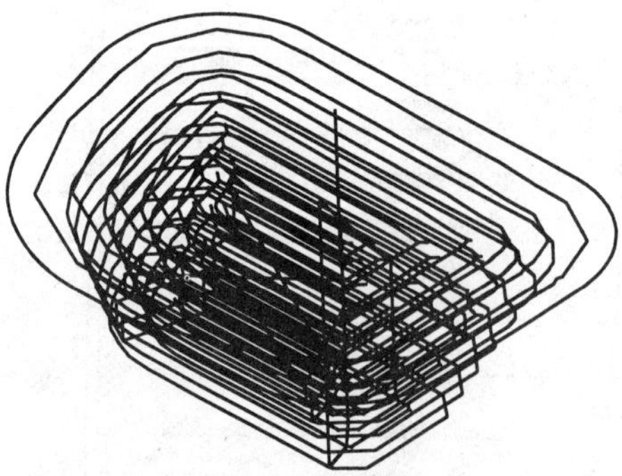

Figure 15.79

Step 7. Save the toolpath file.

Select **MAIN MENU → Toolpaths→ Operations→ Post**
Select **Save NCI file → OK**
File name: **rough7 → Save**
Select **OK** to exit the Operations Manager

15.12 Rough Plunge Function

This surface rough function generates a set of plunging toolpaths for roughing a surface model (Figure 15.80).

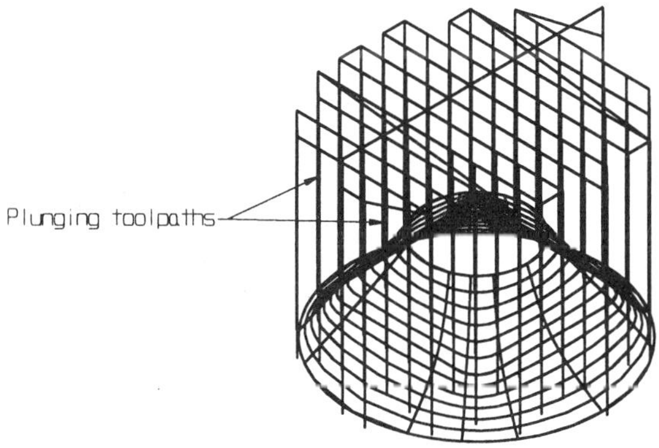

Figure 15.80

The plunge function dialog box appears as below.

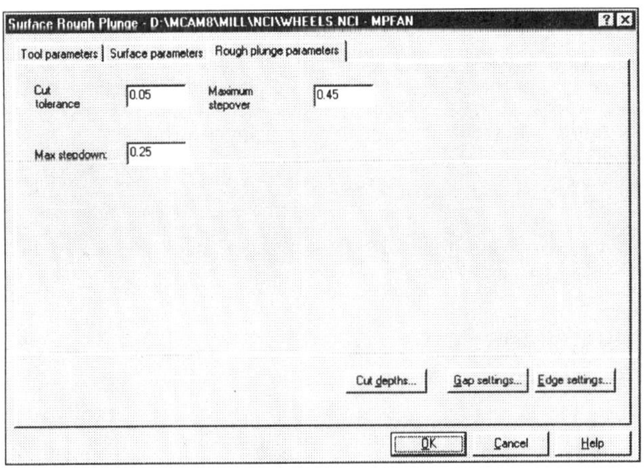

The system will prompt for the selection of two plunge points at the lower left corner and at upper right corner (Figure 15.81). These two points define the surface range to be roughed.

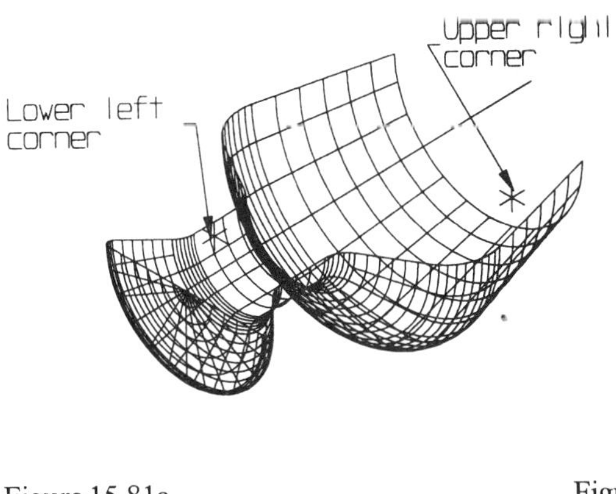

Figure 15.81a

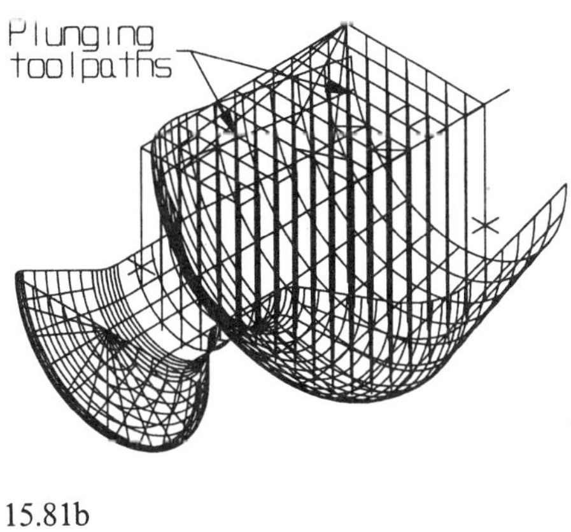

Figure 15.81b

Project 8. Generating roughing toolpaths using plunge function

The rough-plunge function is used to generate roughing toolpaths to cut the car wheel surface model as shown in Figure 15.82. Two corner points (-0.25, -0.5) and (6.0, 5.5) are used as the plunge boundary.

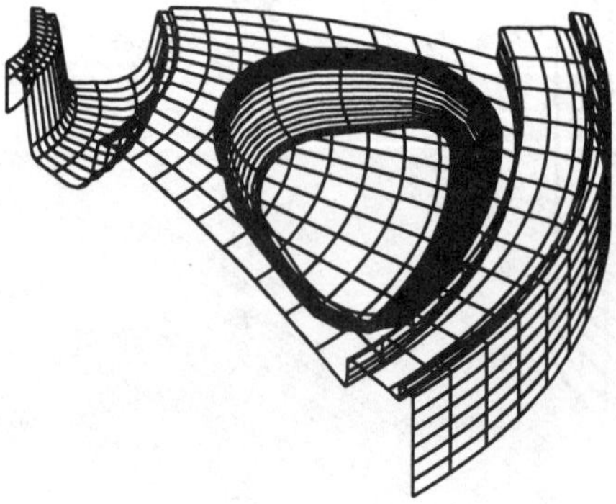

Figure 15.82a

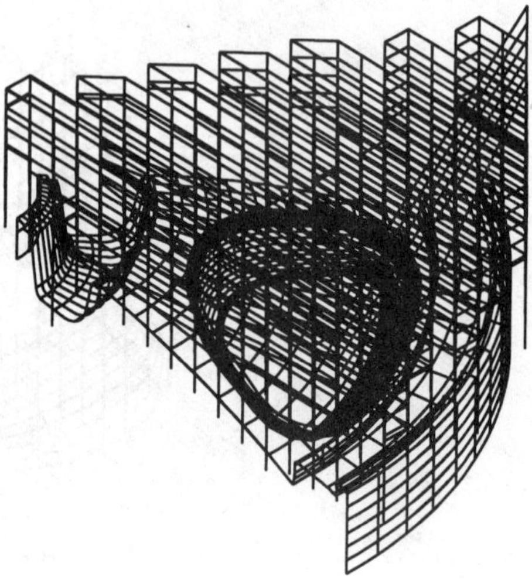

Figure 15.82b

Tips
1. Use the surface model file wheels.
2. Use the surface rough-plunge function to generate roughing toolpaths.
3. Define two corner points at (-0.25, -0.5) and (6.0, 5.5).
4. Use a ¾" spherical end mill.

Step 1. Open the surface model file wheels.

Select **MAIN MENU → File → Get**
File name: **wheels**
The wheel surface model appears as Figure 15.83.

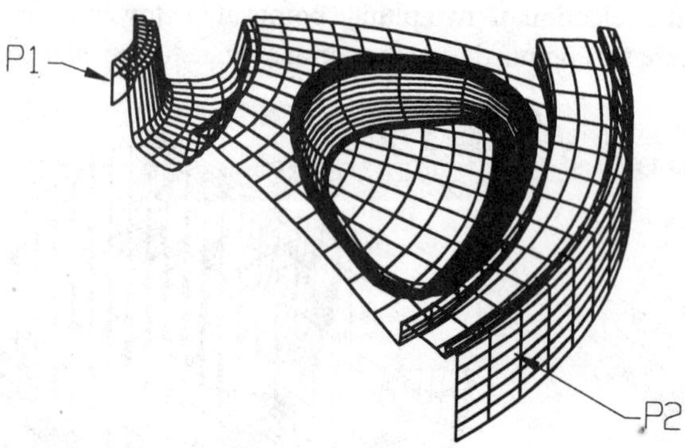

Figure 15.83

Step 2. Initiate the plunge rough function.

8

Use two pick points in Figure 15.83.
Select **Cplane → Top**
Select **MAIN MENU → Toolpaths → Surface → Rough → Plunge**
Select **All → Surfaces**
Select **Unselect**, then pick **P1** and **P2** to omit these two vertical surfaces
Select **BACKUP → Done**

Step 3. Select a tool.

Click the right mouse button, then select "**Get** tool from library"
Select **tool number 258** (3/4 sphere end mill)
Select **OK**
Define the tool parameters as below.

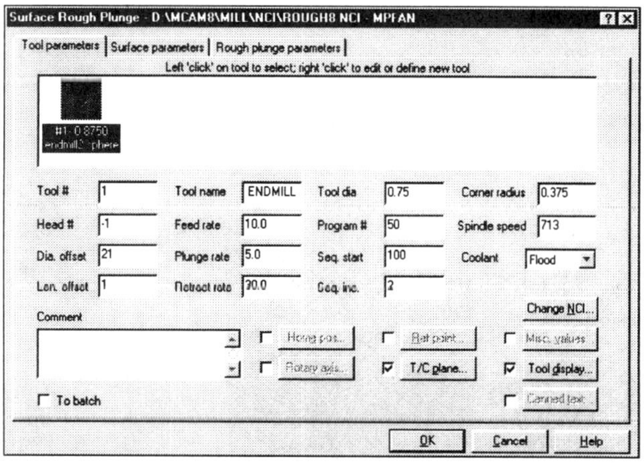

Click Change NCI and change the file name to rough8.

Step 4. Define the surface rough parameters.

Click the "**Surface parameters**" button
Set the surface parameters as below.

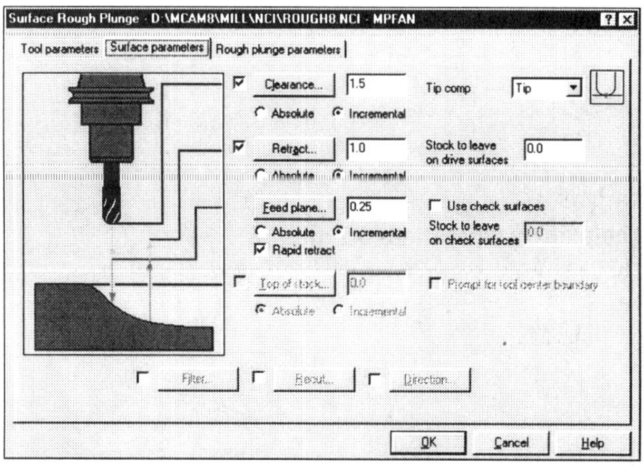

Step 5. Define the rough plunge parameters.

Click the "**Rough plunge parameters**" button

Set the rough plunge parameters as below.

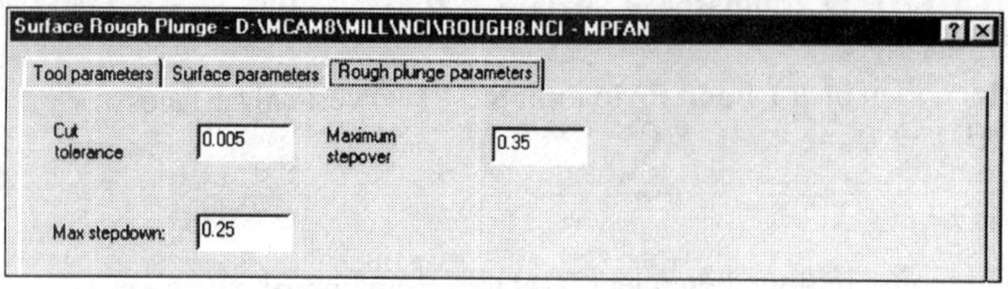

Step 6. Define two corner points.

Select **OK**

Select plunge point at lower left: **-0.25, -0.5** ↵

Select plunge point at upper right: **6.0, 5.5** ↵

The plunging toolpaths are generated as in Figure 15.84.

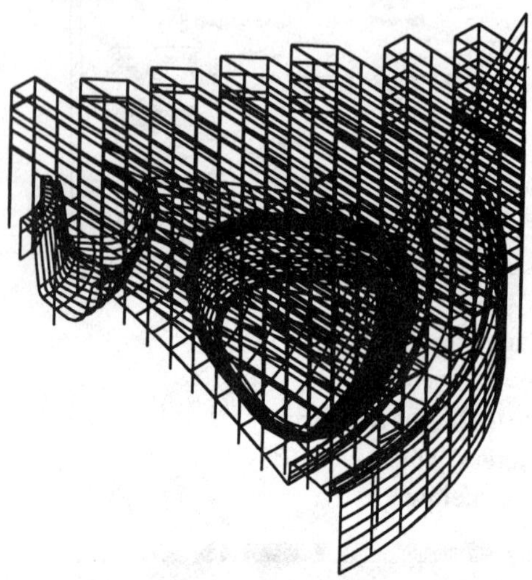

Figure 15.84

Step 7. Save the plunging toolpaths.

Select **MAIN MENU → Toolpaths→ Operations→ Post**

Select **Save NCI file → OK**

File name: **rough7 → Save**

Select **OK** to exit the Operations Manager

15.13 Finish Functions

Mastercam provides ten functions to generate toolpaths for finishing cut a surface model. These ten functions are tabulated in table 15.2 and listed below here.

Table 15.2 Ten surface finishing functions

Finish Function	Description	Illustration
Parallel	Generate finishing toolpaths that run in parallel direction specified by the machining angle parameter.	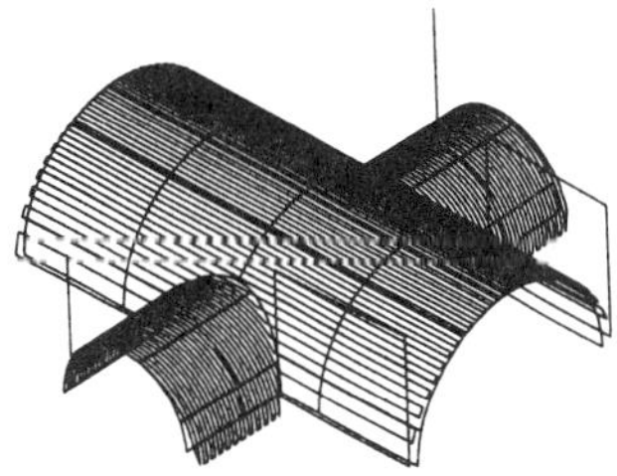
Par. Steep	Generate finishing toolpaths to clean remaining stock in the steep areas of the part. Steep areas are determined by two slope angles.	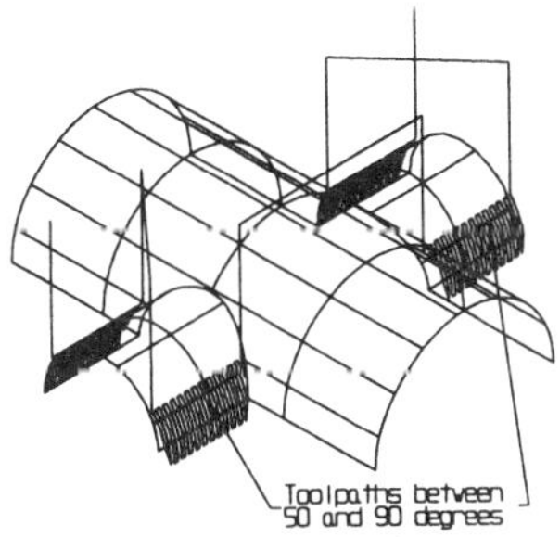
Radial	Generate finishing toolpaths that run in radial direction for cutting surfaces.	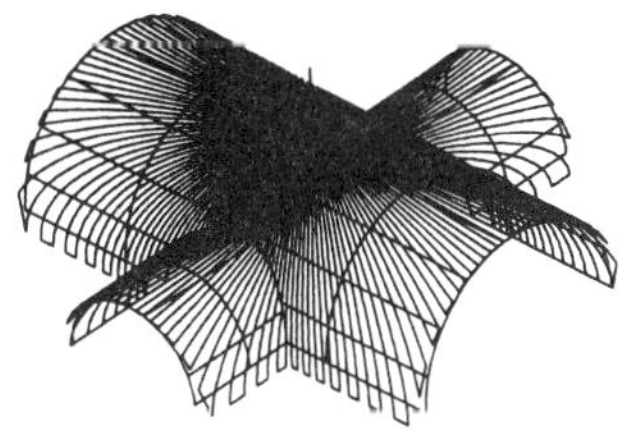
Project	Generate finishing toolpaths by projecting a set of existing toolpaths or geometry entities onto the selected surfaces.	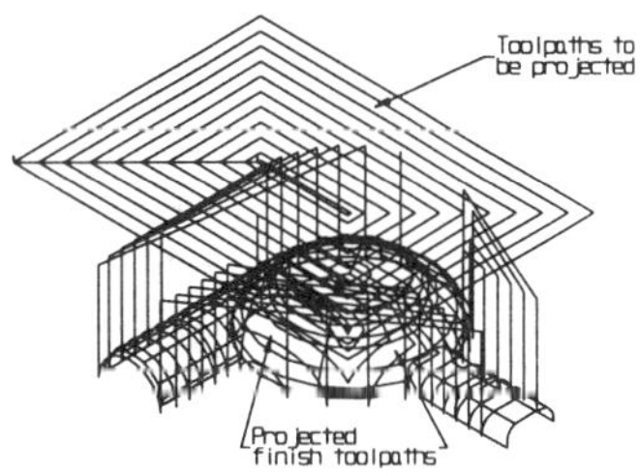
Flowline	Generate finishing toolpaths along the direction of the surface flow lines. Multiple surfaces can be used.	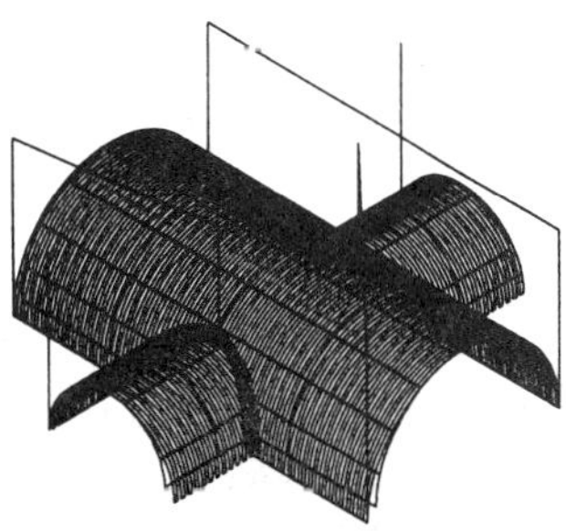

Table 15.2, continued.

Contour	Generate finishing toolpaths along the surface contours.	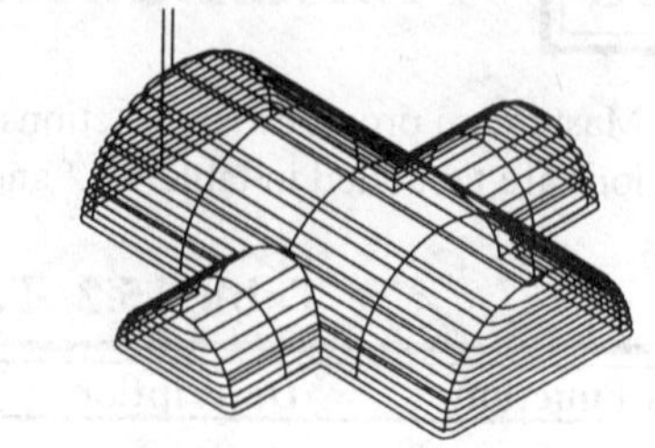
Shallow	Generate finishing toolpaths to clean remaining stock from shallow areas of the part. Shallow areas are determined by two slope angles.	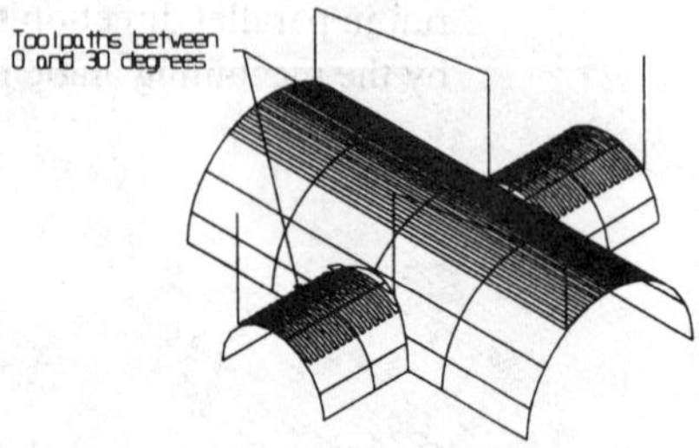
Pencil	Generate toolpaths to remove material in corners between surfaces.	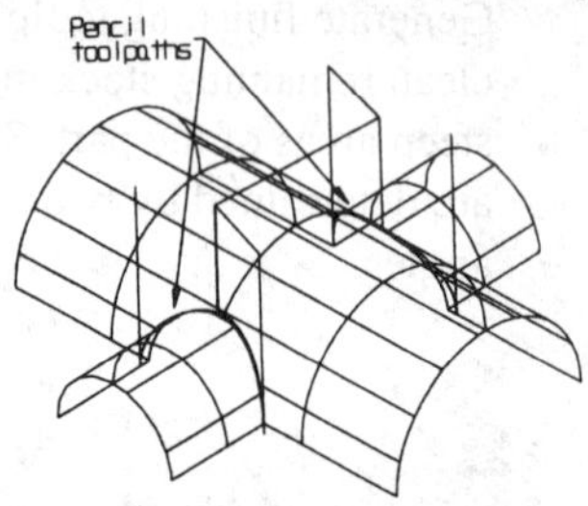
Leftover	Generate toolpaths to remove material left by a larger tool in a previous operation.	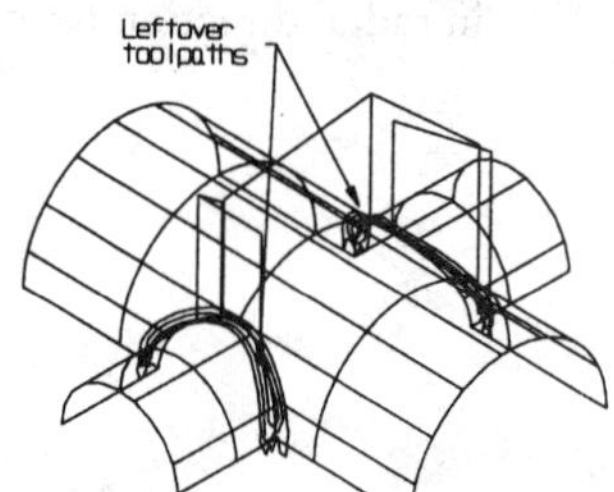 (Tool for previous operation is 1/2", new tool is 1/8")
Scallop	Generate finishing toolpaths that have consistent scallop heights over the entire set of surfaces.	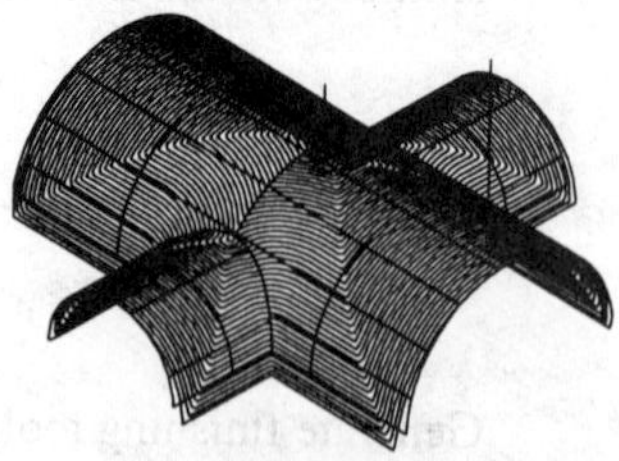

There are five finish functions that have their rough counterparts presented in previous sections. Actually, these five finish functions use the same parameters as in their rough counterparts. Rough functions uses more parameters than finish functions because they need to generate toolpaths for each roughing level. Only those five finish functions that are not covered in rough functions are discussed here in detail.

15.14 Parallel Finish Function

This function generates a set of linear, parallel toolpaths in a specified direction for the finish cut of a surface model (Figure 15.85). Its parameters dialog box appears as below.

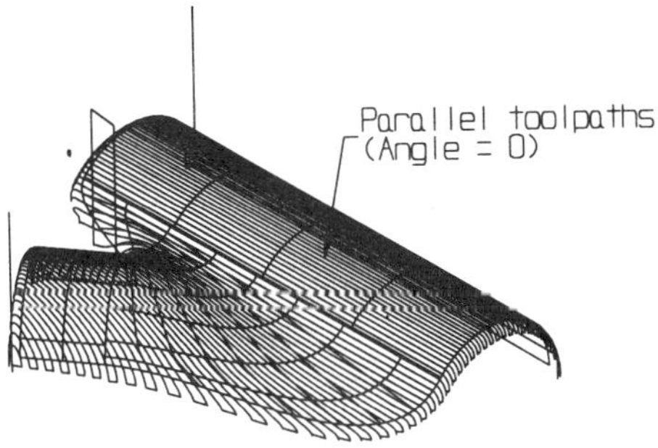

Figure 15.85a

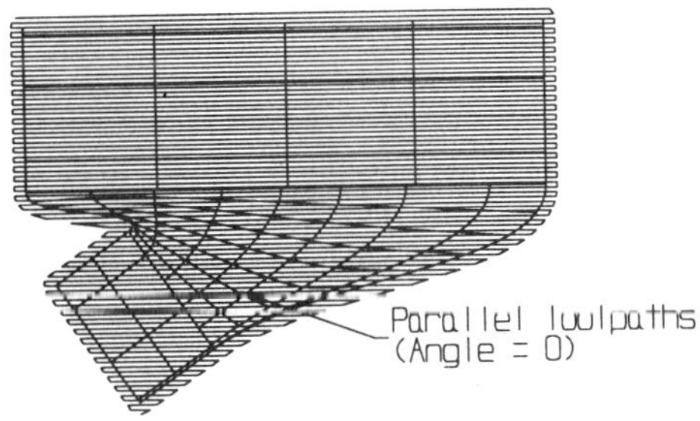

Figure 15.85b

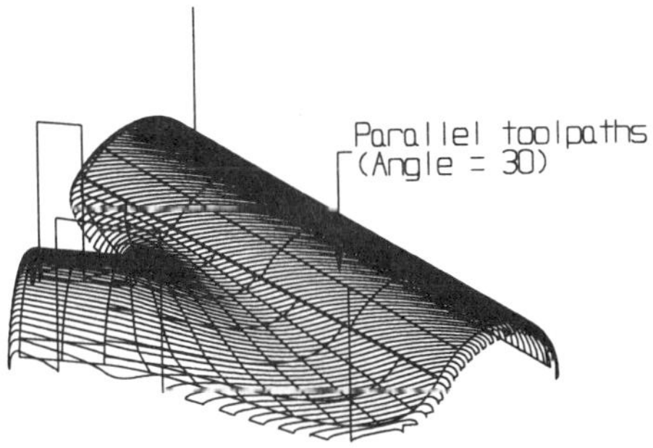

Figure 15.85c

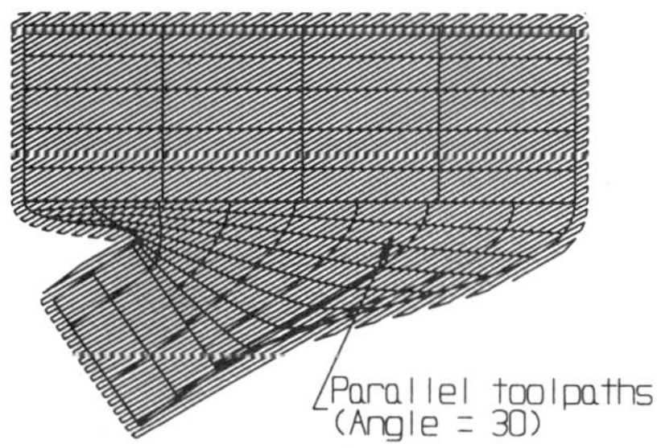

Figure 15.85d

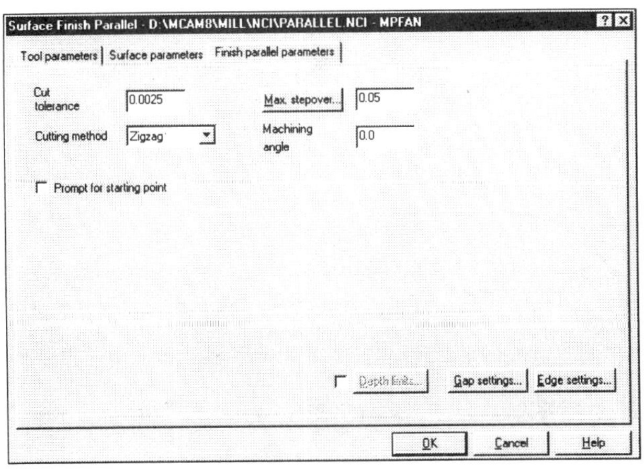

The **Depth parameters** opens a dialog box as shown here to determine where the Z-axis cutes are placed for all finish surface toolpaths except finish contour. All cuts are placed between the minimum and maximum depths.

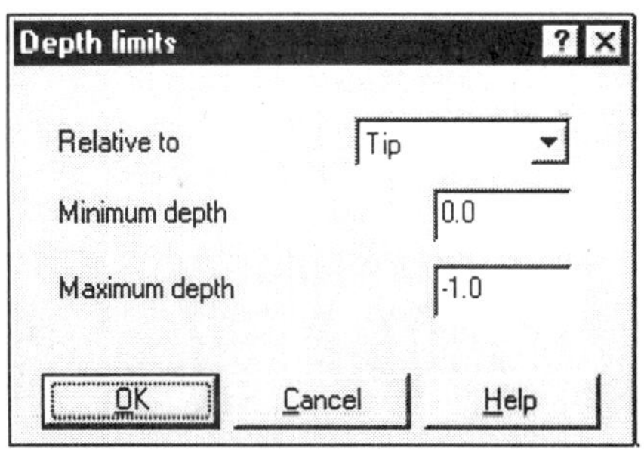

Project 9. Using parallel function

The surface finish-parallel function is used to generate finishing toolpaths to cut a flash light surface model. The external vertical wall surface is not included in the machining. Figure 15.86 shows the surface model and its finishing toolpaths.

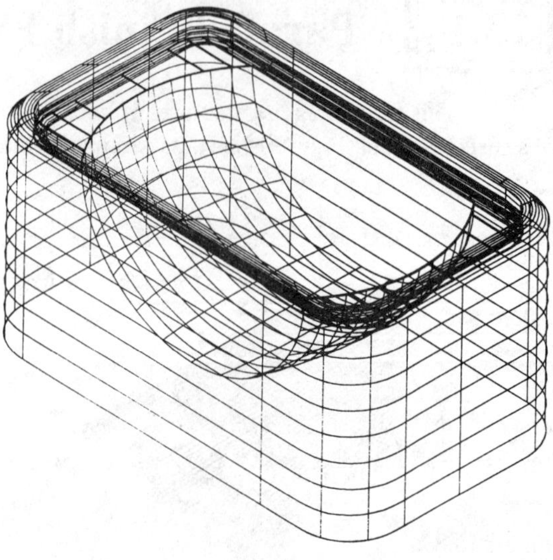

Figure 15.86a

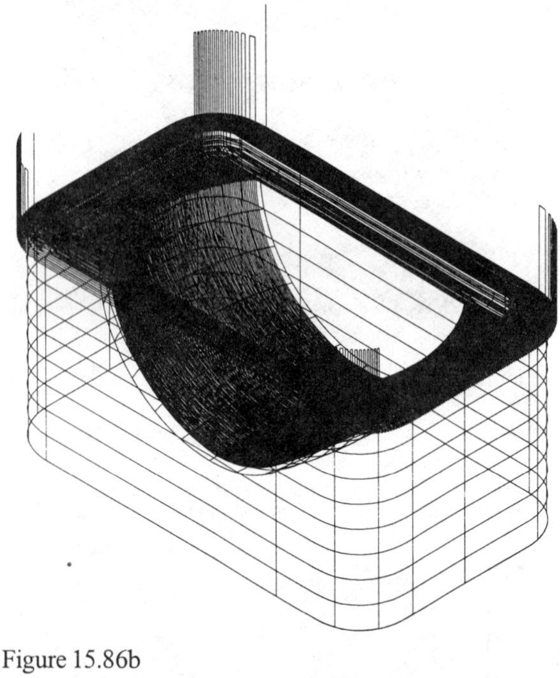

Figure 15.86b

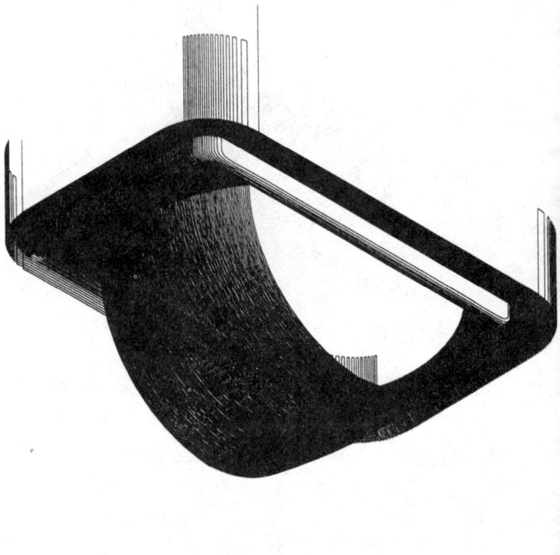

Figure 15.86c

Tips

1. Open the surface model file flashs.
2. Use surface finish-parallel function to generate finishing toolpaths.
3. Do not include the external vertical wall surface in machining.
4. Use a 3/16" spherical end mill.

Step 1. Open the surface model file flashs.

Select **MAIN MENU → File → Get**

File name: **flashs**

9

The flash light model appears as in Figure 15.87.

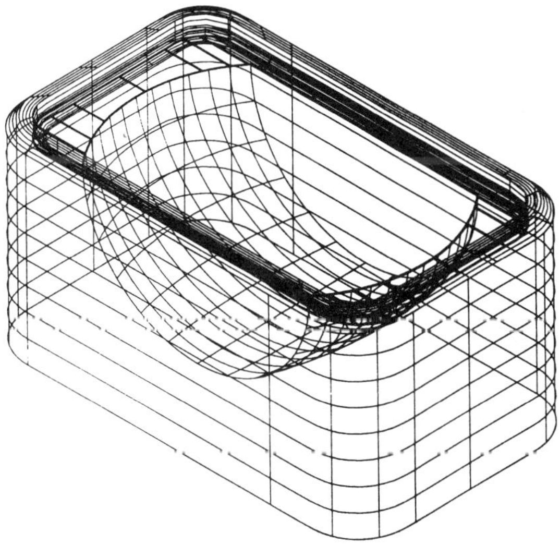

Figure 15.87

Step 2. Initiate the parallel function.

Select **MAIN MENU → Toolpaths → Surface → Finish → Parallel**
Select **All → Surfaces → Unselect**
Pick the external vertical wall surface
Select **BACKUP → Done**

Step 3. Define the tool parameters.

Click the right hand button then select "**Get** tool from library"
Select **tool number 251** for (3/16 sphere end mill)
Select **OK**
Set the tool parameters as below.

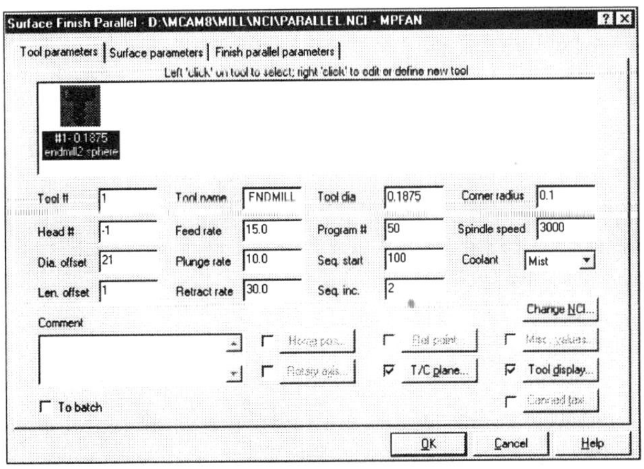

Click **Change NCI** and change the file name to **parallel**

Step 4. Define the surface finish parameters.

Click the "**Surface parameters**" button

Define the surface parameters as below.

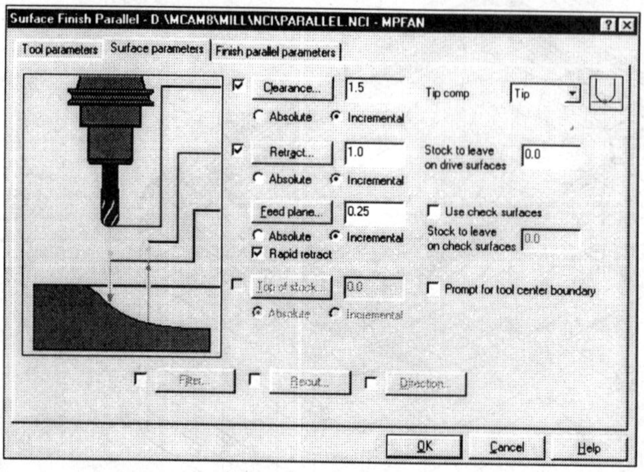

Step 5. Define the finish parallel parameters.

Click the "**Finish parallel parameters**" button

Set the finish parallel parameters as below.

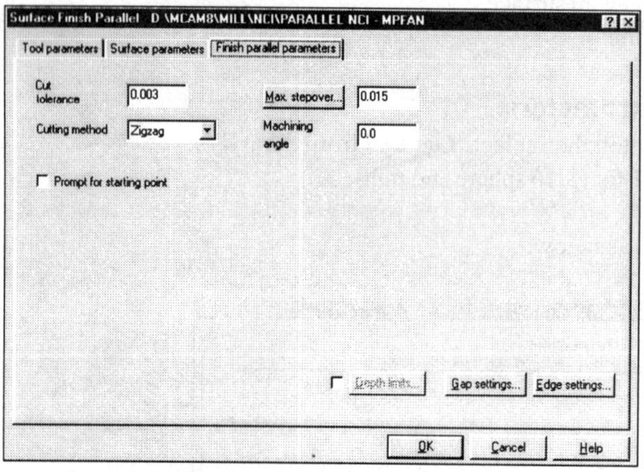

Step 6. Define gap and edge parameters.

Click the "**Gap settings**" button

Select **Smooth** for Motion < Gap size, keep tool down parameter

Select **OK**

Click the "**Edge settings**" button

Select "**Over all surface edges**" for Roll tool parameter

Select **OK → OK** to generate finishing toolpaths as Figure 15.88.

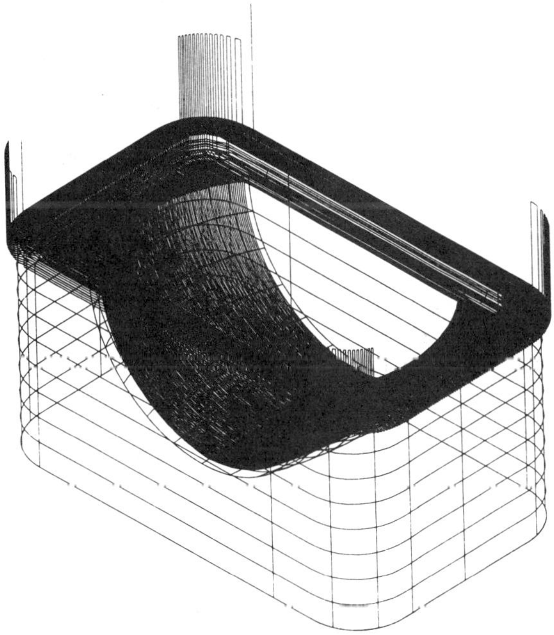

Figure 15.88

The toolpaths without showing the surface model appear as in Figure 15.89.

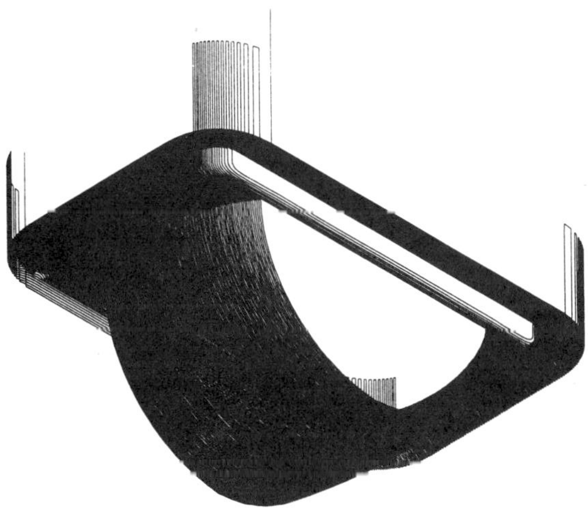

Figure 15.89

Step 7. Save the toolpaths.

Select **MAIN MENU → Toolpaths→ Operations→ Post**
Select **Save NCI file → Edit → OK**
File name: **parallel → Save**
Double click the upper left corner or the Programmer's File Editor to exit the edit NCI window

15.15 Parallel Steep Finish Function

This function is intended to generate a set of parallel toolpaths for the steep area of the part (Figure 15.90). The steep area is defined by two slope angles on the surface. Parallel steep parallel dialog box appears as below.

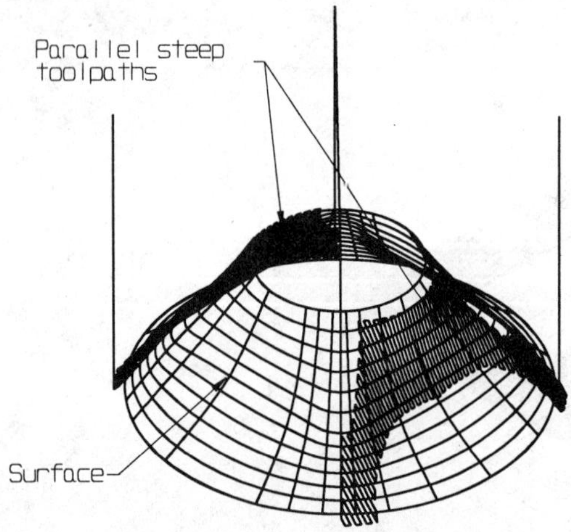

Figure 15.90

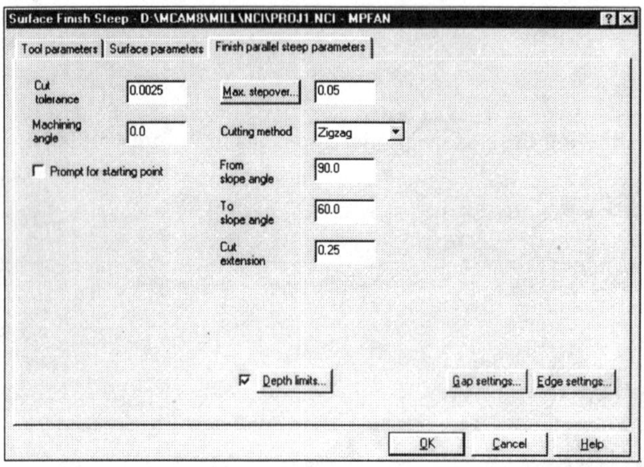

Mastercam uses two angles to define the steep area of the part; from slope angle and to slope angle. **From slope angle** specifies the minimum slope angle of the surface and **to slope angle** sets the maximum slope angle of the surface. Areas between from slope angle and to slope angle are machined (Figure 15.91).

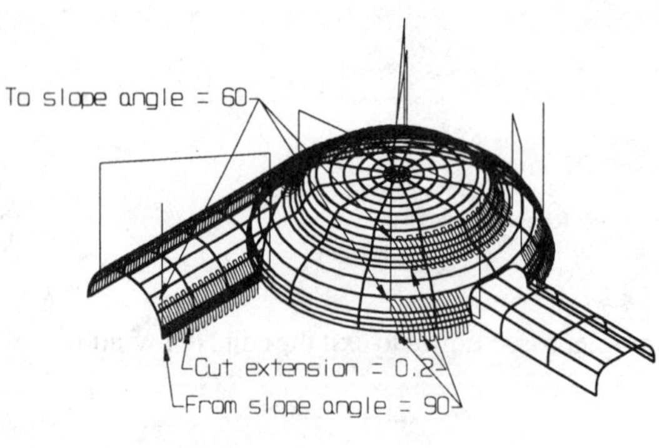

Figure 15.91a

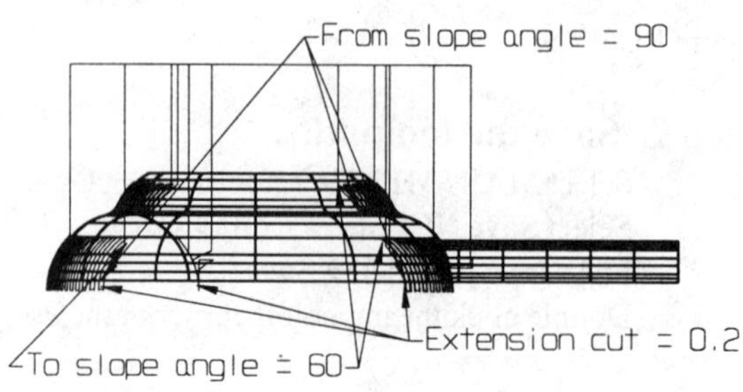

Figure 15.91b

The “Cut extension” parameter is used to extend the cut so that the tool can plunge into a previously cut area before machining the leftover stock. The given cut extension distance is added to both ends of the toolpath and follows the curvature of the surface (Figure 15.92).

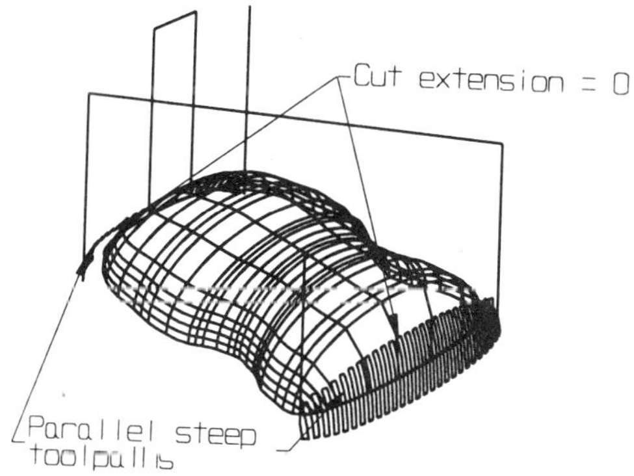

Figure 15.92a

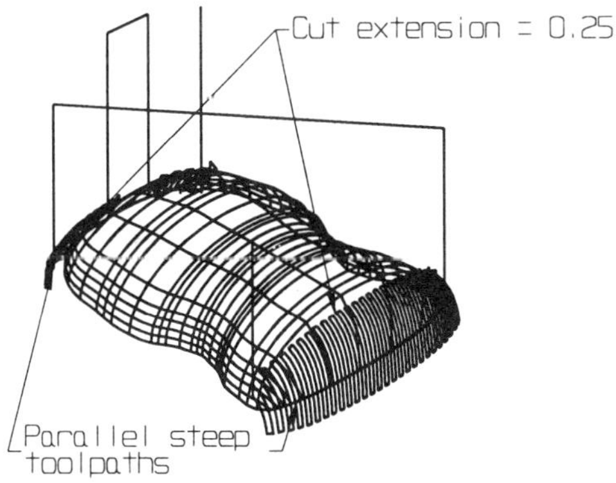

Figure 15.92b

15.16 Finish Leftover Function

The finish leftover function generates toolpaths for removing material left by a larger tool in a previous operation (Figure 15.93). The leftover parameters dialog box appears as below.

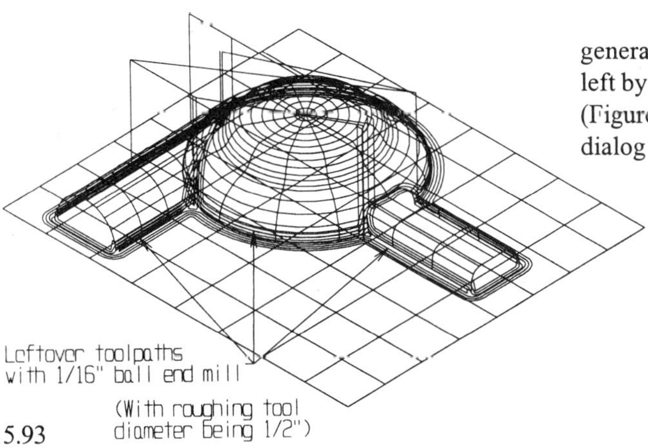

Figure 15.93

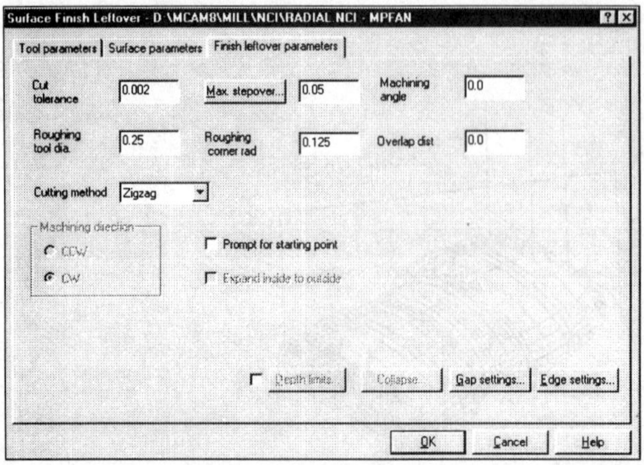

These two parameters are used to describe the cutting tool used in the previously operations:

Roughing tool dia.: specify the diameter of the tool used in the previous machining operation. **Roughing corner rad:** specify the corner radius of the tool used in the previous machining operation.

The system uses these two tooling parameters to compare to the corner radius of the finishing tool to determine the leftover amount for this operation. The tool diameter for the finish leftover operation must be smaller than the roughing tool diameter.

The "Overlap distance" parameter is used to add a distance to the roughing tool's corner radius to define a larger machined area than the roughing tool diameter would allow (Figure 15.94).

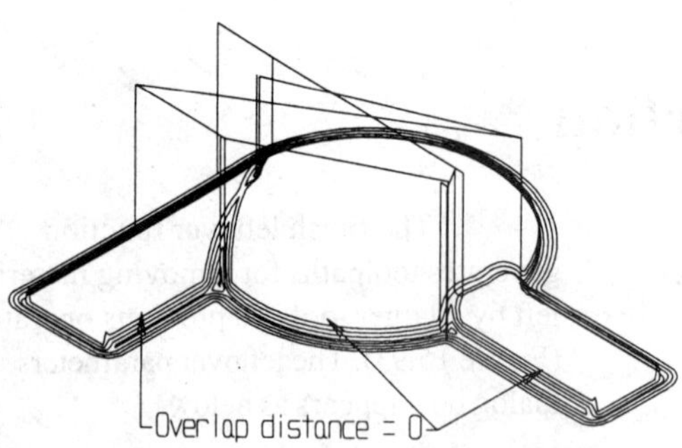

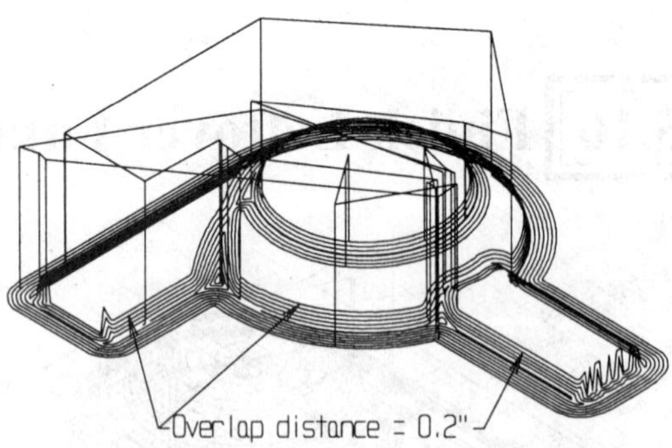

Figure 15.94a

Figure 15.94b

15.17 Finish Radial Function

This function generates a set of toolpaths that run in the radial direction from a given point for the finish cut of a surface model. Its parameter dialog box appears as below. Figure 15.95 shows an example using the radial finish function for generating finish toolpaths.

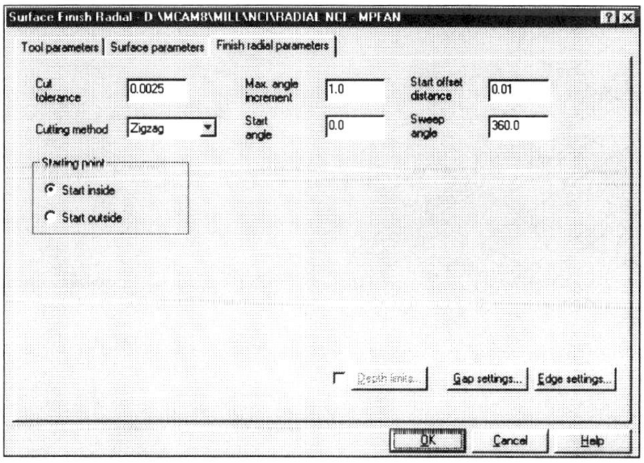

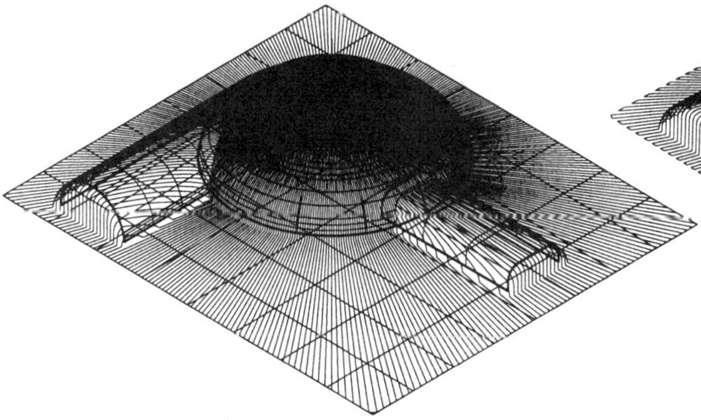

Figure 15.95a

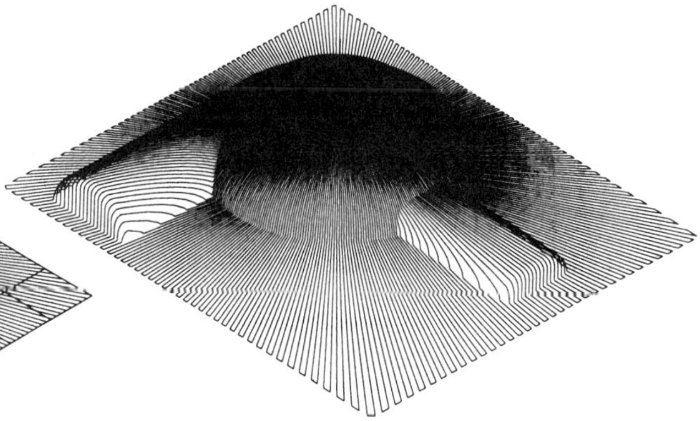

Figure 15.95b

Project 10. Using radial and leftover functions

The surface model shown in Figure 15.96a consists of three surfaces that are intersected each other. Leftover stocks will be found at intersecting corners if a spherical end mill is used. This project uses two surface finish functions to generate finishing toolpaths to machine the surface model. Radial function with a ¼" spherical end mill is used to generate finishing toolpaths. Leftover function with a 5/32" spherical end mill is used to generate toolpaths to remove leftover stock. Figure 15.96 shows toolpaths and verification model.

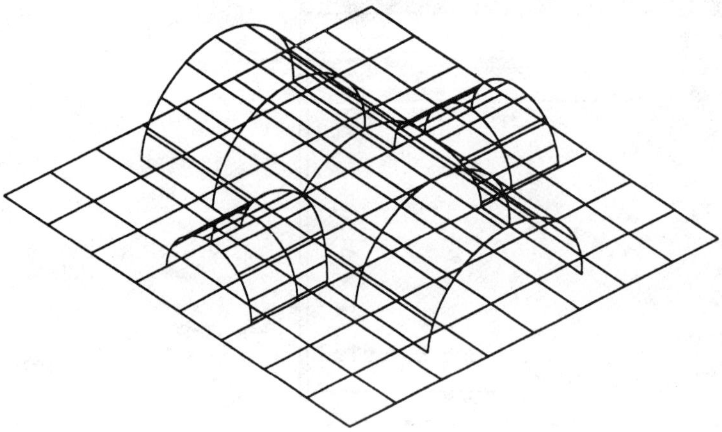

Figure 15.96a

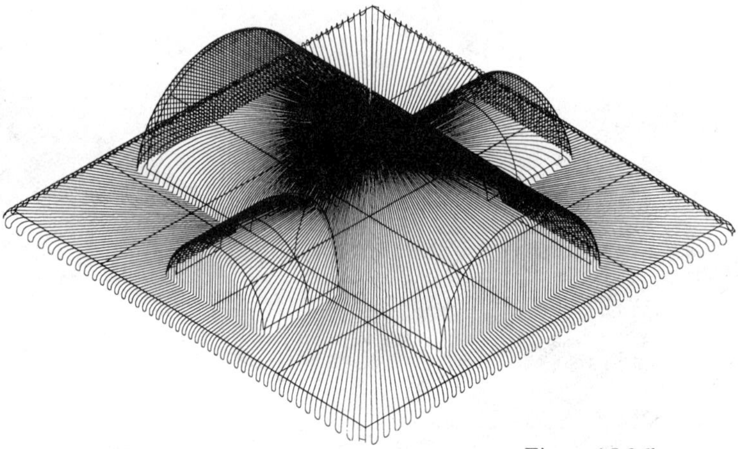

Figure 15.96b

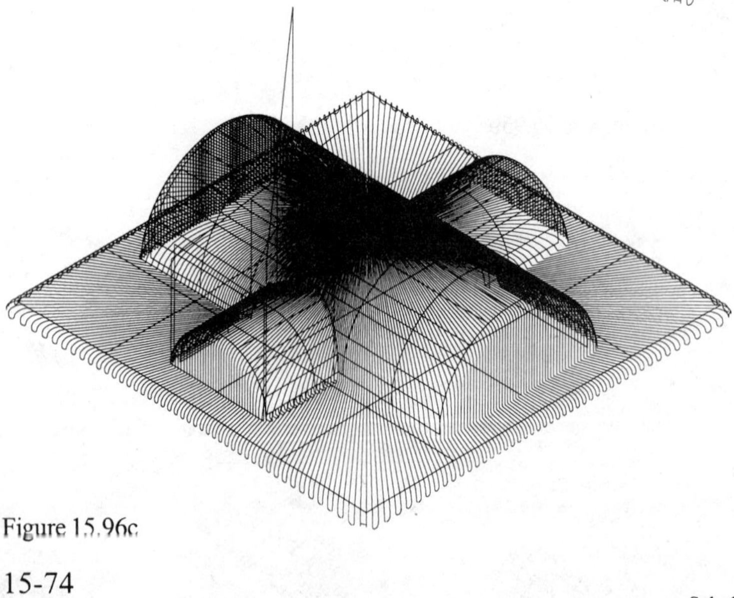

Figure 15.96c

10

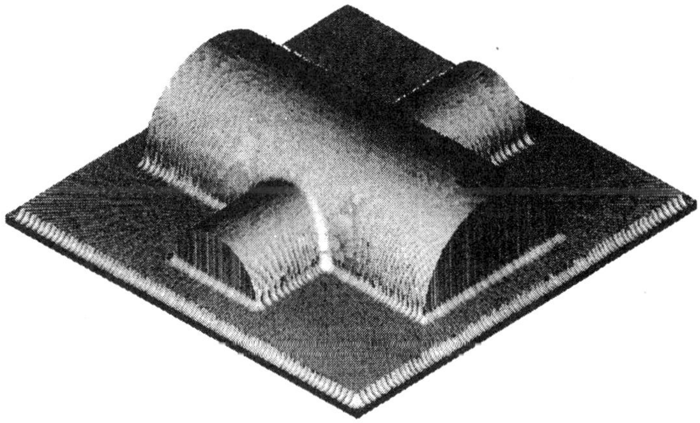

Figure 15.96d

Tips
1. Open the surface model file trims1.
2. Create a flat ruled surface.
3. Use the surface finish-radial function to generate finishing toolpaths.
4. Use a ¼" spherical end mill with the radial function.
5. Use the finish-leftover function to remove leftover stock.
6. Use a 5/32" spherical end mill with the leftover function.
7. Run Verify to verify the toolpaths.

Step 1. Open the surface model file trims1.

Select **MAIN MENU → File → Get**
File name: **trims1**
The surface model appears as in Figure 15.97.

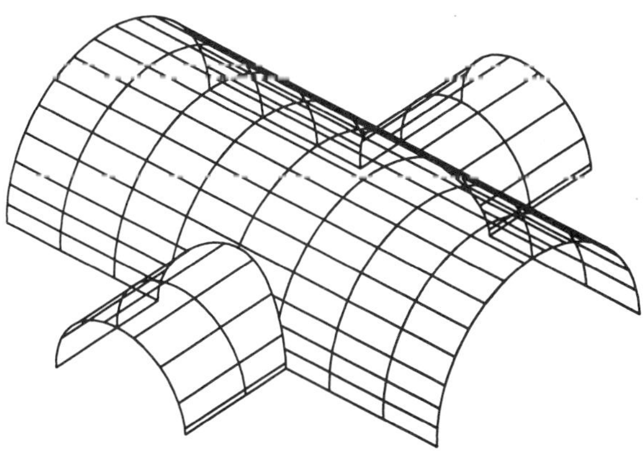

Figure 15.97

Step 2. Create a rectangle.

Select **Cplane → Top**
Select **Z**, then enter **0** ↵
Select **Level**, then enter **3** ↵
Select **Color**, then enter **13** ↵
Select **MAIN MENU → Create → Rectangle → 2 points**
Enter the lower left corner: **-3, -3** ↵
Enter the upper right corner: **3, 3** ↵
The rectangle is added to the model as in Figure 15.98.

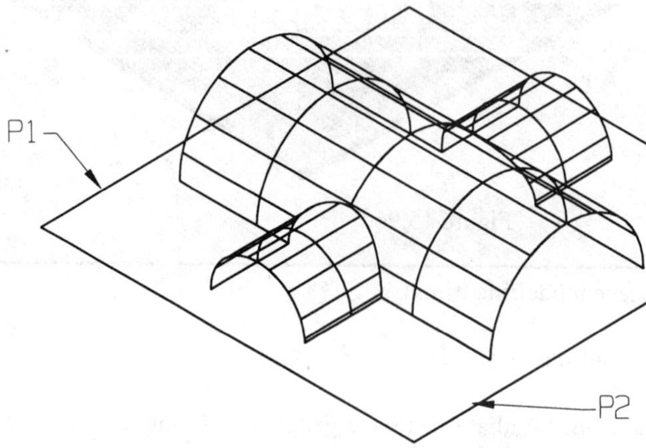

Figure 15.98

Step 3. Create a ruled surface.

Use the pick points in Figure 15.98.
Select **MAIN MENU → Create → Surface → Ruled → Single**
Pick **P1** and **P2**
Select **Done → Do it**
The ruled surface appears as in Figure 15.99.

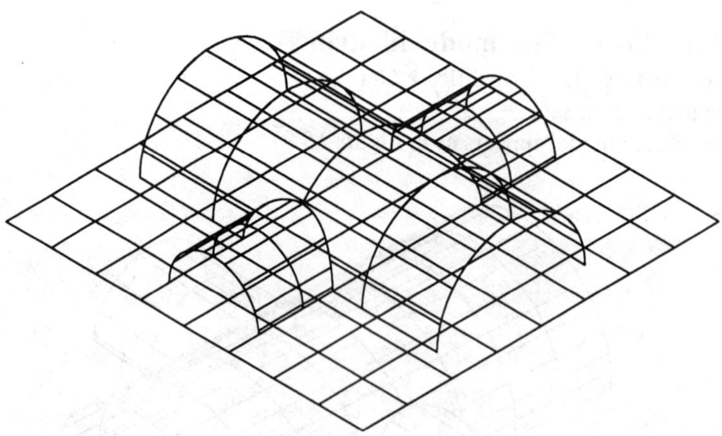

Figure 15.99

Step 4. Initiate the radial function.

Select **MAIN MENU → Toolpaths → Surface → Finish → Radial**
Select **All → Surfaces → Done**
Click the right mouse button, then select "**Get tool from library**"
Select **tool number 252** (1/4 sphere end mill), then select **OK**

Set the tool parameters as below.

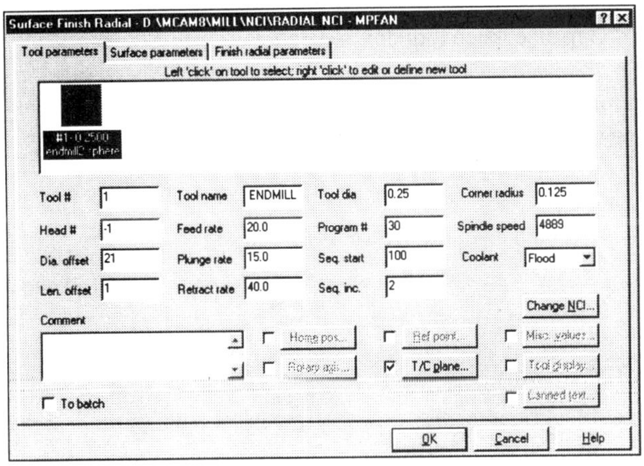

Step 5. Define the surface finish parameters.

Click the "**Surface parameters**" button

Set the surface parameters as below.

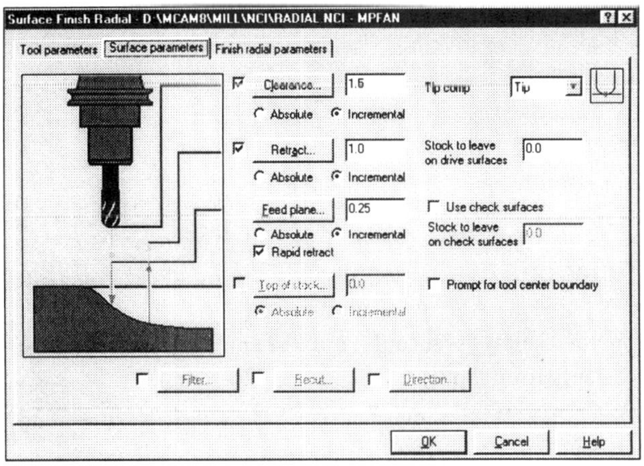

Step 6. Define the finish radial parameters.

Click the "**Finish radial parameters**" button

Set the finish radial parameters as below.

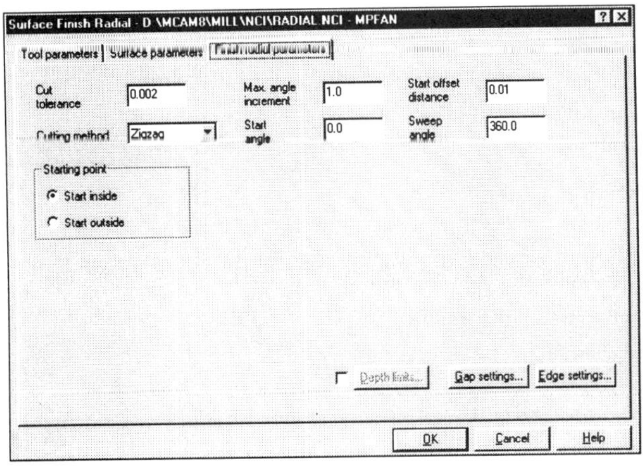

Step 7. Define gap and edge parameters.

Click the "**Gap settings**" button
Select **Smooth** for Motion < Gap size, keep tool down parameter
Select **OK**
Click the **Edge settings** button
Select the "**Over all surface edges**" for Roll tool parameter
Select **OK → OK**
Enter rotation point: **0, 0** ↵
The finishing toolpaths are generated as in Figure 15.100.

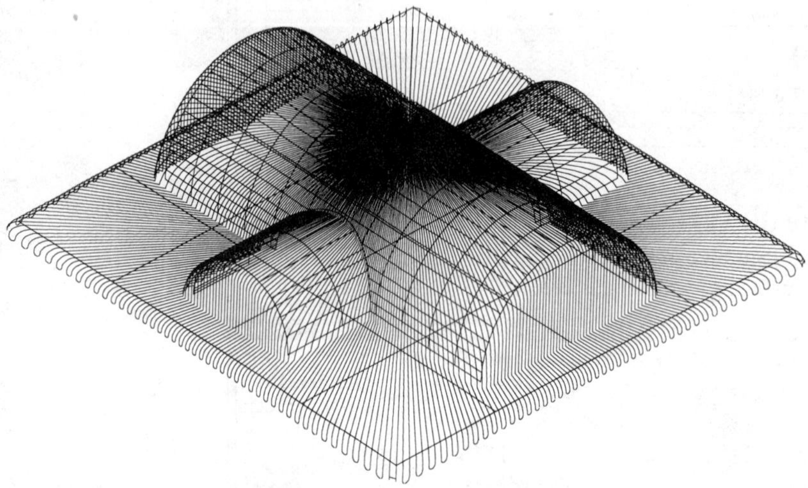

Figure 15.100

Step 8. Initiate the leftover function.

Select **Finish → Leftover → All → Surfaces → Done**
Click the right mouse button, then select "**Get tool from library**"
Select **tool number 250** (5/32 sphere end mill)
Select **OK**
Set the tool parameters as below.

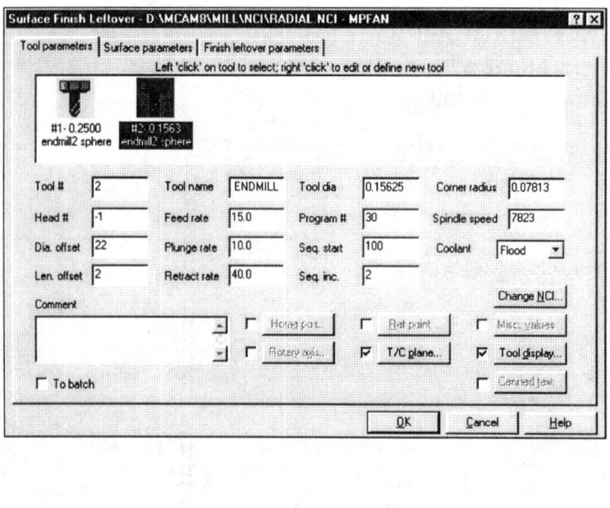

Step 9. Define the surface finish parameters.

Click the "**Surface parameters**" button
Set the surface parameters as below.

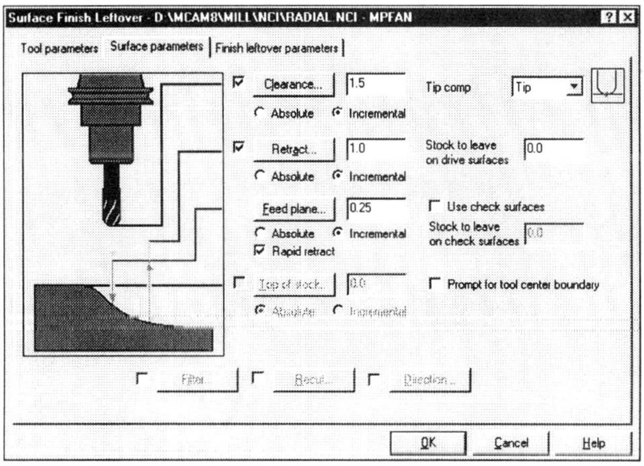

Step 10. Define the finish leftover parameters.

Click the "**Finish leftover parameters**" button
Set the finish leftover parameters as below.

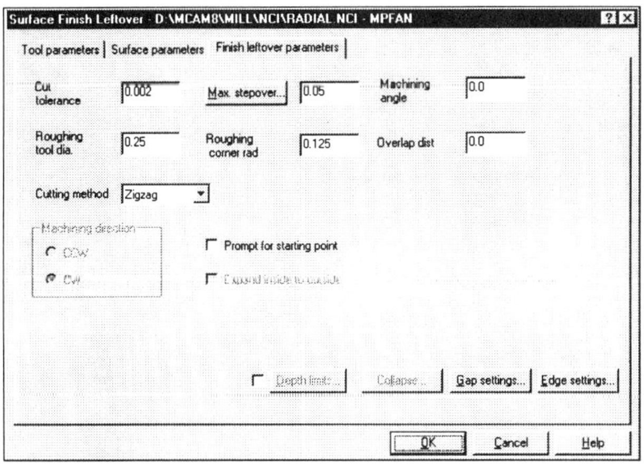

Step 11. Define gap and edge parameters.

Click the "**Gap settings**" button
Select **Smooth** for Motion < Gap size, keep tool down parameter
Select **OK**
Click the "**Edge settings**" button
Select "**Over all surface edges**" for Roll tool parameter
Select **OK** → **OK** to generate leftover toolpaths as shown in Figure 15.101.

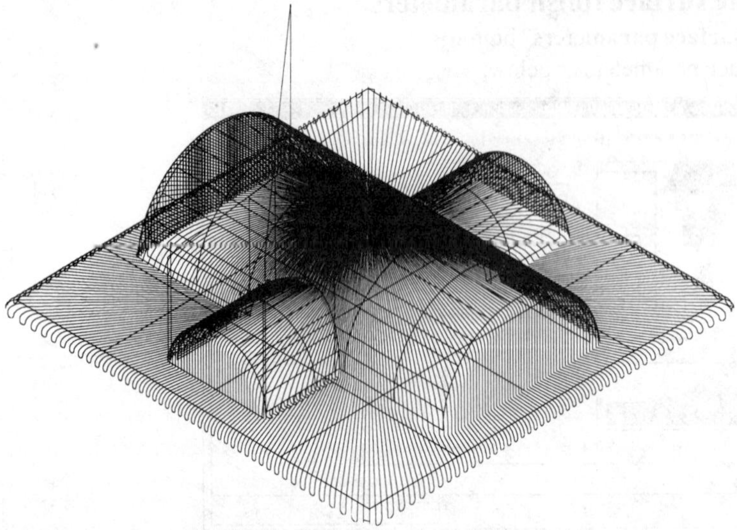

Figure 15.101

Step 12. Verify the toolpaths.

Select **BACKUP → Operations → Select All → Verify**
Select **Configure** in Verify dialog
Set the select mode parameters as below.

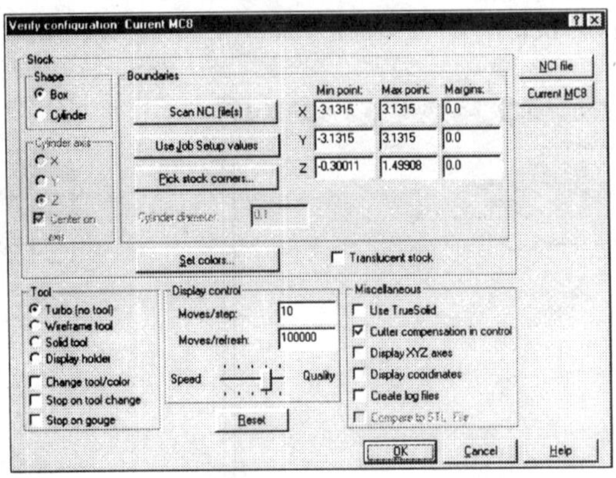

Click on the **Scan NCI file(s) to determine stock size**
Select **OK**
Select **Machine** to verify the toolpaths
The verify model should resemble Figure 15.102.

Figure 15.102

Step 13. Save the toolpaths file.

Select **BACKUP** to return to Operations Manager dialog box
Select **Post** from Operations Manager dialog box
Select **Save NCI file → OK**
File name: **radial**

15.18 Project Finish Function

This function generates a set of toolpaths by projecting an existing set of toolpaths for finish cutting a surface model (Figure 15.103). In addition to existing toolpaths, curves and points are also valid entities to be used for projection to obtain finish toolpaths. The project parameters dialog box appears as below.

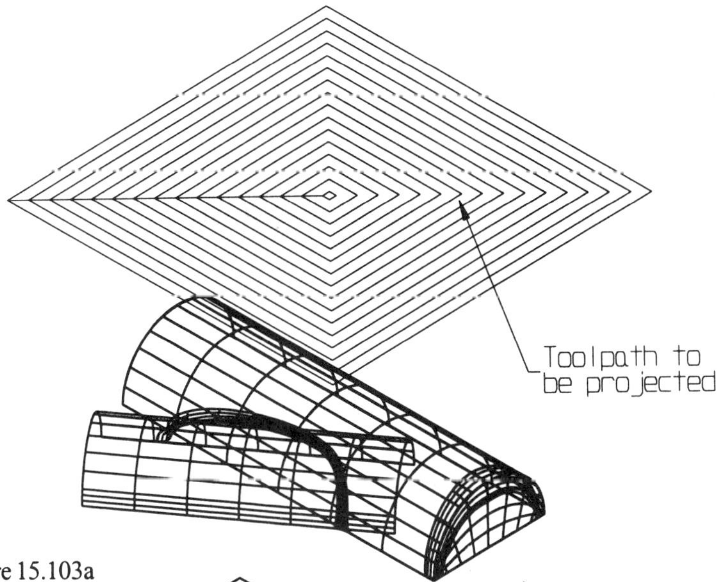

Figure 15.103a

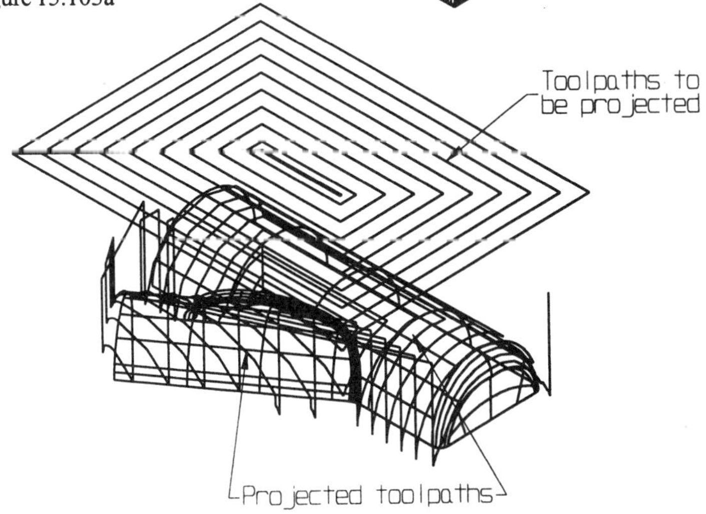

Figure 15.103b

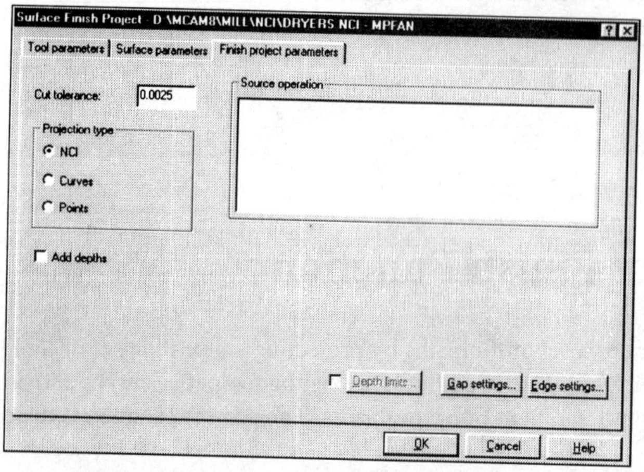

This function provides users better control of tool motions and cut pattern and orientation. The toolpaths to be projected control the spacing of cut passes and their X and Y coordinates. The surfaces to be projected onto control the Z-depth and X and Y boundary of the cut.

Add Depths

The "Add depths" parameter takes the depths from the selected NCI file and applies them to the toolpath. This means that the Z-depth of toolpaths are shifted to the existing toolpaths, rather than on the surfaces (Figure 15.104).

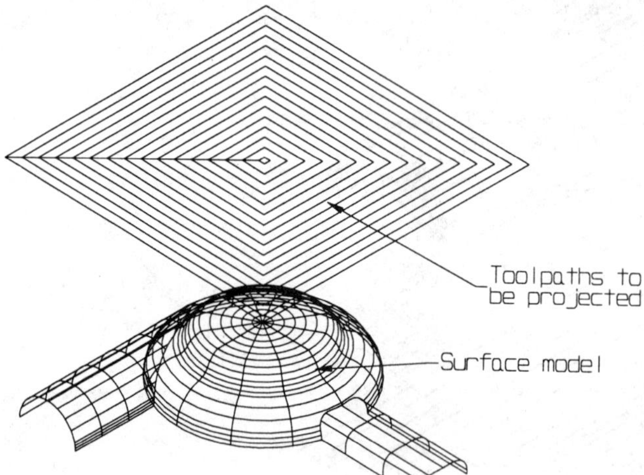

Figure 15.104a

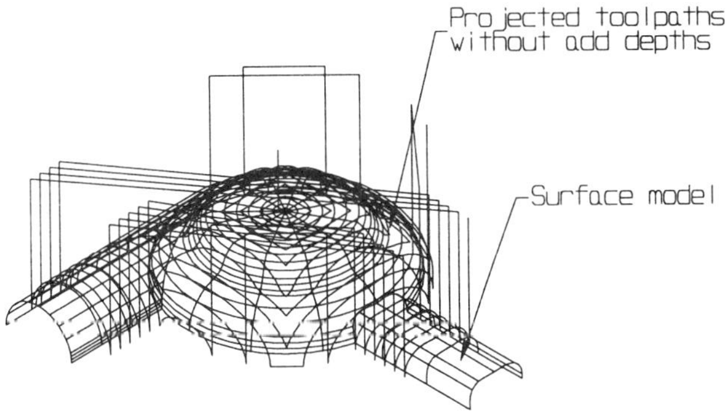

Figure 15.104b

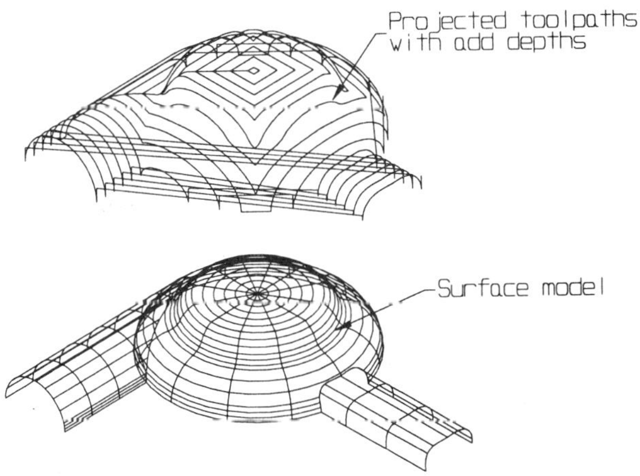

Figure 15.104c

Project 11. Using project function

This project shows how to generate finishing toolpaths to machine a surface model from an existing toolpath. A flat ruled surface is added to generate the toolpaths to be projected as shown in Figure 15.105b. This set of toolpaths is then projected onto the dryer surface model to generate the finishing toolpaths as shown in Figure 15.105c. Figure 15.105d is the verification model.

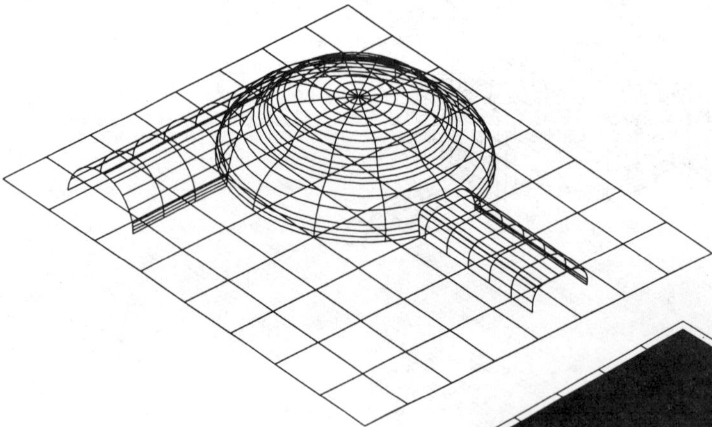

Figure 15.105a

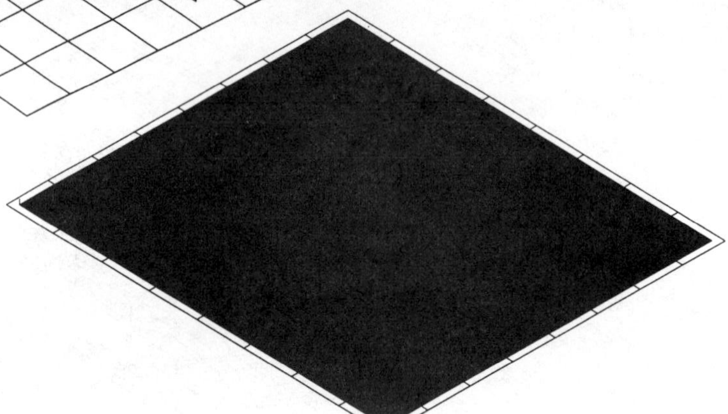

Figure 15.105b

Figure 15.105c

Figuer 15.105d

⌛Tips	
	1. Open the surface model file dryers.
	2. Create a ruled surface from a rectangle.
	3. Use the 2D pocket function to generate pocketing toolpaths with a ¼" flat end mill.
	4. Save the pocketing toolpaths as proj1.
	5. Use surface finish-project function to generate finish toolpaths.
	6. Use a ¼" sphere end mill.
	7. Verify the toolpaths using Verify.

💻11

Step 1. Open the surface model dryers.

Select **MAIN MENU → File → Get**
File name: **dryers**
The dryer surface model appears as in Figure 15.106.

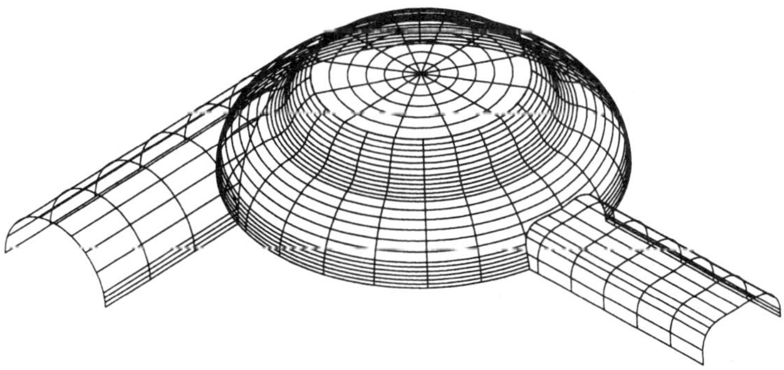

Figure 15.106

Step 2. Change graphic view to Top and set Z value to 0.0.

Select **Gview → Top**
Select **Cplane → Top**
Select **Z**, then enter **0**
The surface model shown in isometric view becomes Figure 15.107.

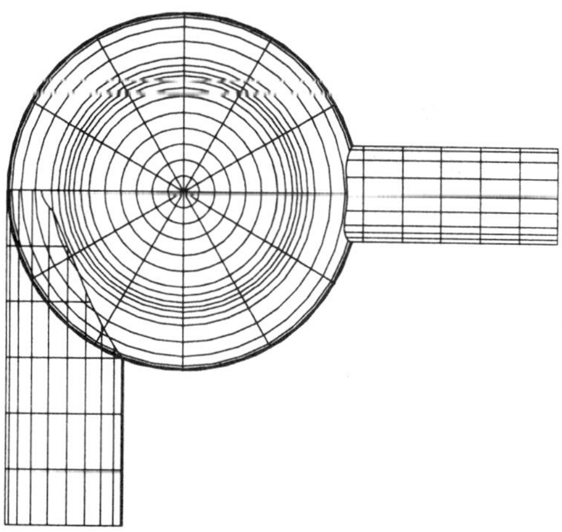

Figure 15.107

Step 3. Create a rectangle.

Select **Level**, then enter **10**
Select **MAIN MENU → Create → Rectangle → 2 points**
Enter the lower left corner: **-2.6, -4.0 ↵**
Enter the upper right corner: **4.5, 2.3 ↵**
Select **Gview → Isometric**
The rectangle is added to the model as in Figure 15.108.

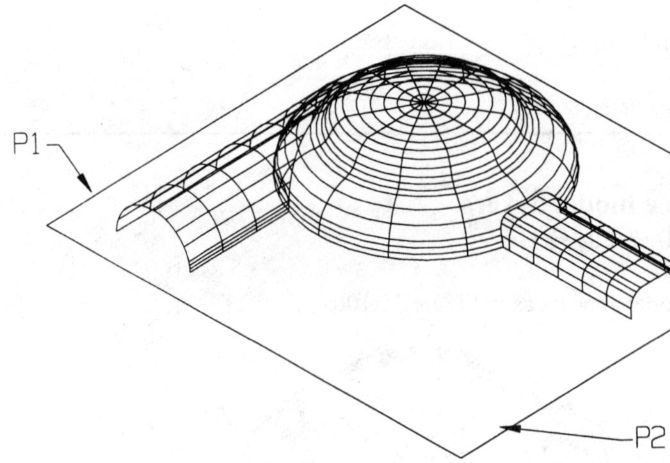

Figure 15.108

Step 4. Create a ruled surface.

Use the pick points in Figure 15.108.
Select **MAIN MENU → Create → Surface → Ruled → Single**
Pick **P1** and **P2** as shown in Figure 15.108
Select **Done → Do it**
The ruled surface is created as in Figure 15.109.

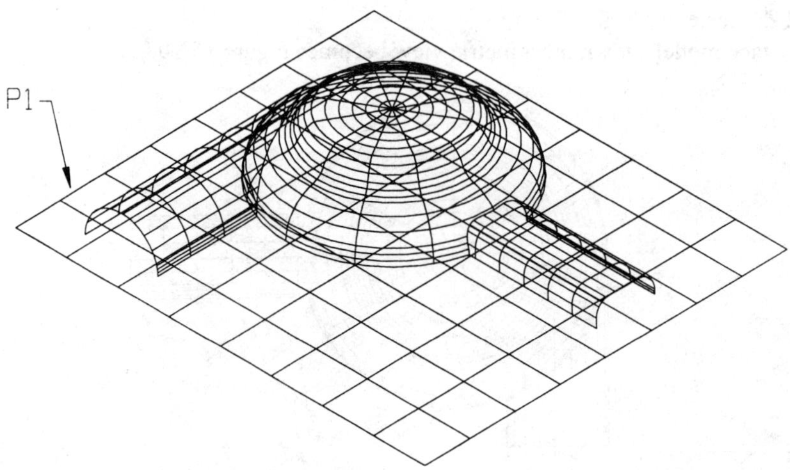

Figure 15.109

Step 5. Initiate the pocket function.

Use the pick point in Figure 15.109.

Select **MAIN MENU → Toolpaths → Pocket**

Select **Chain**, then pick **P1**

Select **Done**

The tool parameters dialog box should appear.

Click the right mouse button, then select "**Get tool from library**"

Pick **tool number 235** (¼ flat end mill)

Select **OK**

Set the tool parameters as below.

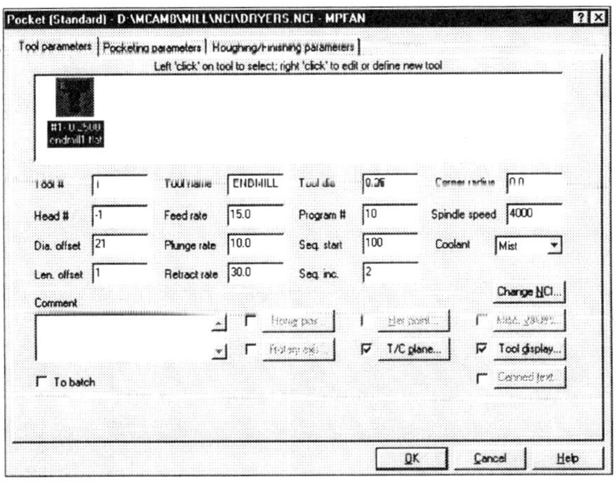

Click **Change NCI** and change the file name to **proj1**

Step 6. Define pocketing parameters.

Click the "**Pocketing parameters**" button

Set pocketing parameters as below.

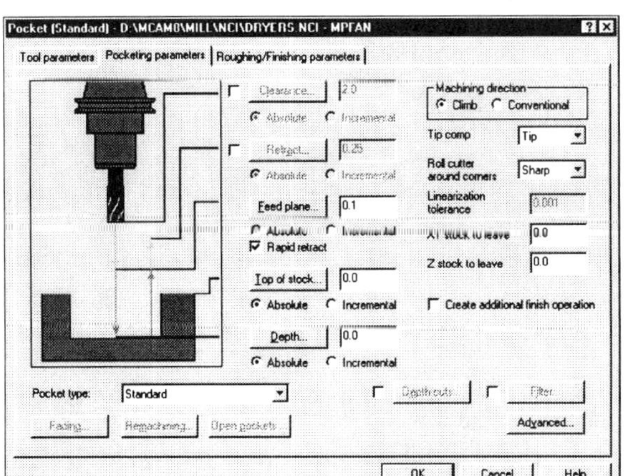

Step 7. Define the roughing/finishing parameters.

Click the "**Roughing/finishing parameters**" button

Set roughing parameters as below.

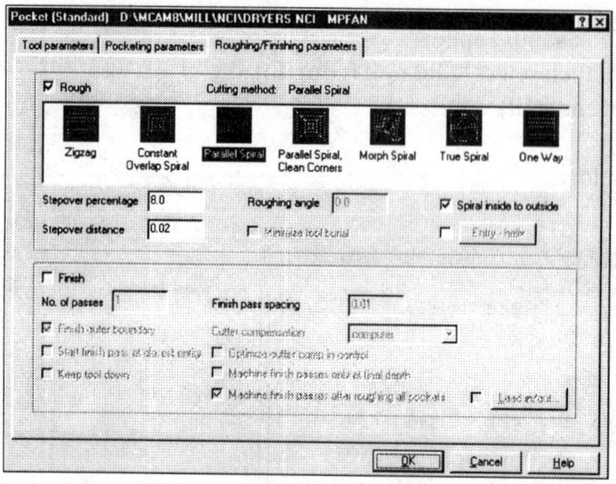

Select **OK**

The pocketing toolpaths are generated as in Figure 15.110.

Figure 15.110

Step 8. Save the toolpath file.

Select **MAIN MENU → Toolpaths → Operations → Post**

Select **Save NCI file → OK**

Filename: **proj1 → Save**

Select **File → Exit** from Progammer's File Editor

Step 9. Initiate the finish project function.

Select **MAIN MENU → Toolpaths → Surface → Finish → Project**

Select **All → Surfaces → Done**

Step 10. Define the tool parameters.

Click the right mouse button, then select "**Get tool from library**"
Pick **tool number 252** (1/4 sphere endmill)
Select **OK**
Define the tool parameters as below.

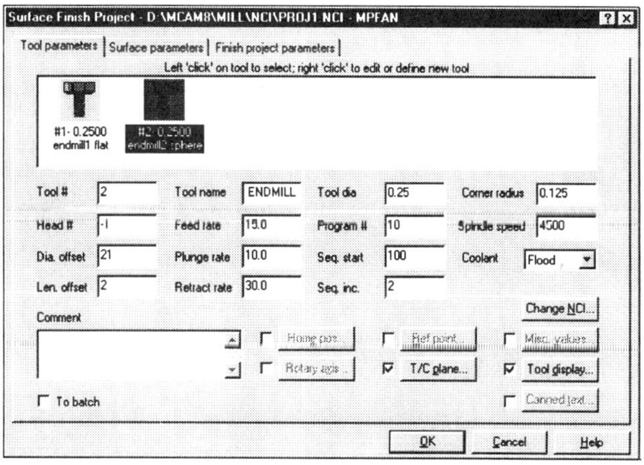

Step 11. Define the surface finish parameters.

Click the "**Surface finish parameters**" button
Define the surface parameters as below.

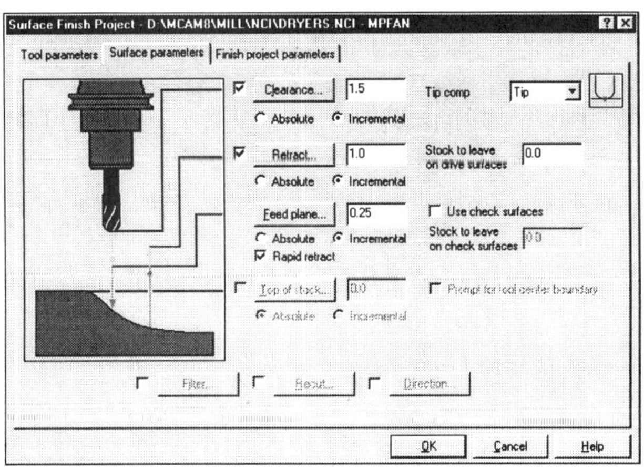

Step 12. Define the finish project parameters.

Click the "**Finish project parameters**" button
Click "**NCI**" from Projection type

The finish project parameters dialog box appears as below.

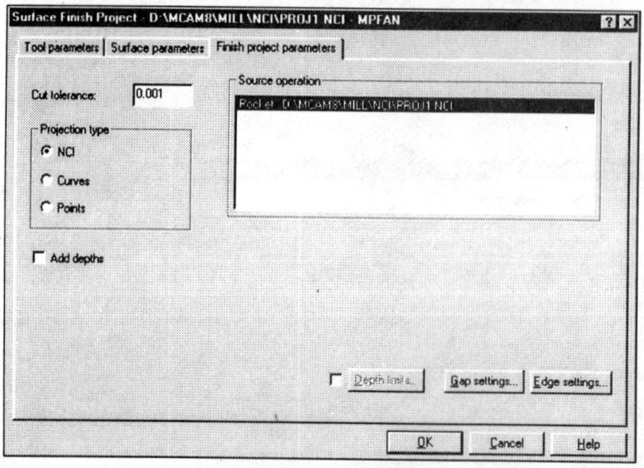

Select **OK** to generate finishing toolpaths

It takes several minutes for the computer to generate the toolpaths as shown in Figure 15.111.

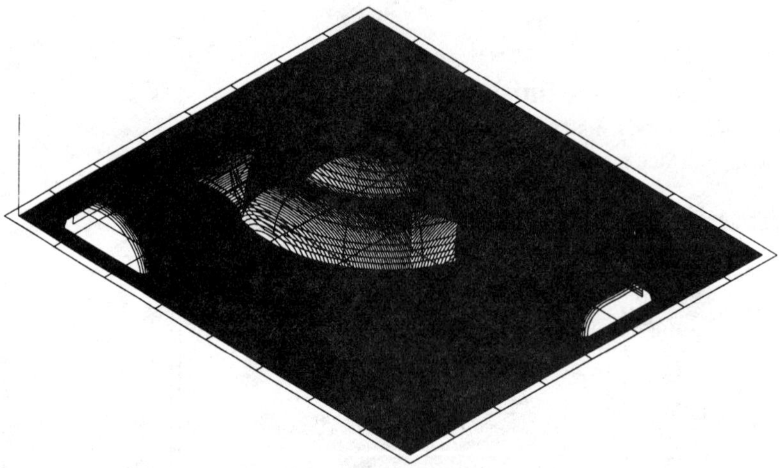

Figure 15.111

Step 13. Verify the model.

Select **BACKUP → Operations**
Select **Z-surface finish project → Verify**
Select **Configure** from Verify dialog
Set the Verify configuration as here:
Click **Scan NCI files**

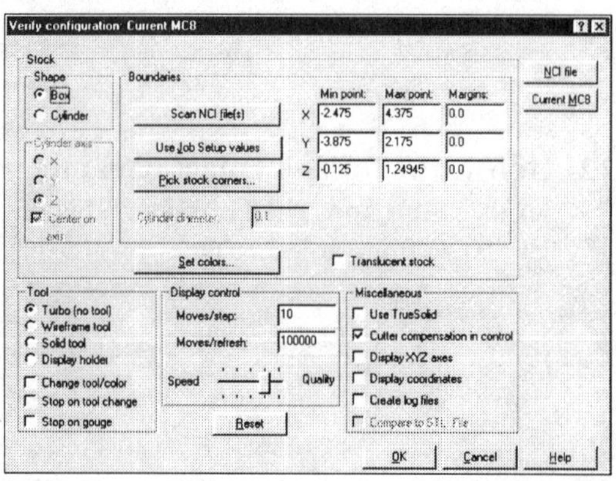

Select **OK**
Select **Machine** to verify the toolpaths

The verification model should resemble Figure 15.112.

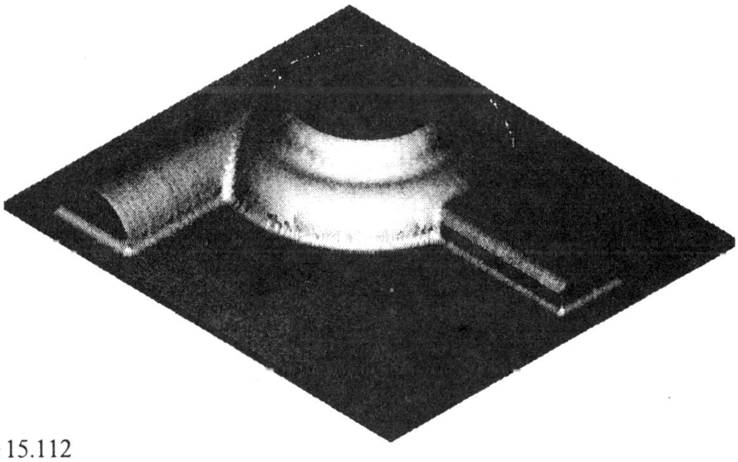

Figure 15.112

Step 14. Save the toolpath file.

Select **BACKUP** to return to Operations Manager dialog box
Select **OK** to exit Operations Manager dialog box
Select **MAIN MENU → File → Save**

15.19 Flowline Function

This function generates toolpaths to finish cut a surface model. The toolpaths run in the direction of surface flowline. The flowline parameters dialog box appears as below.

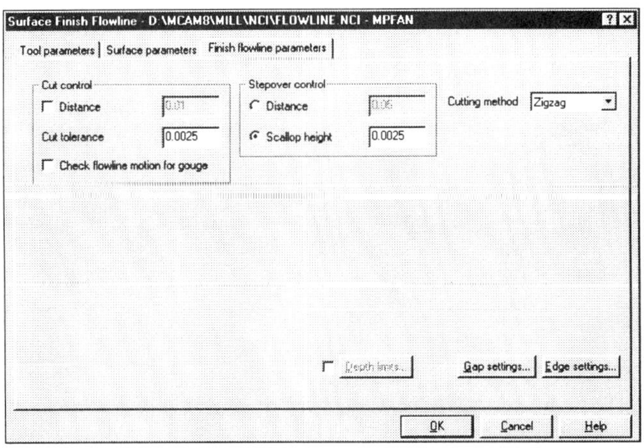

The "Check flowline motion for gouge" parameter is very important when multiple surfaces are included in generating toolpaths. When this parameter is turned to Off, gouges may occur if surfaces are not properly trimmed (Figure 15.113). When this parameter is turned to On, all potential gouges are removed (Figure 15.114).

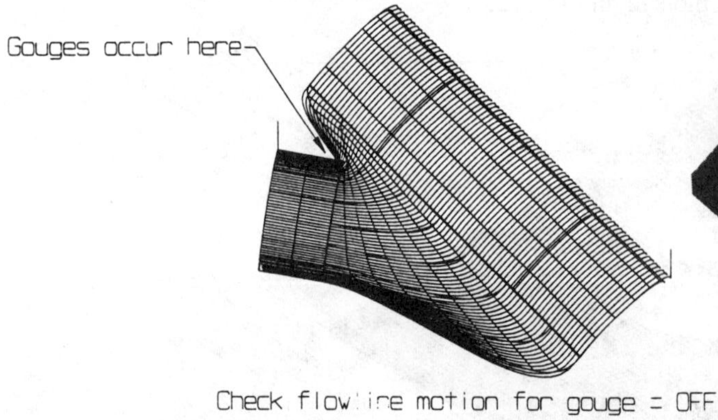

Figure 15.113a

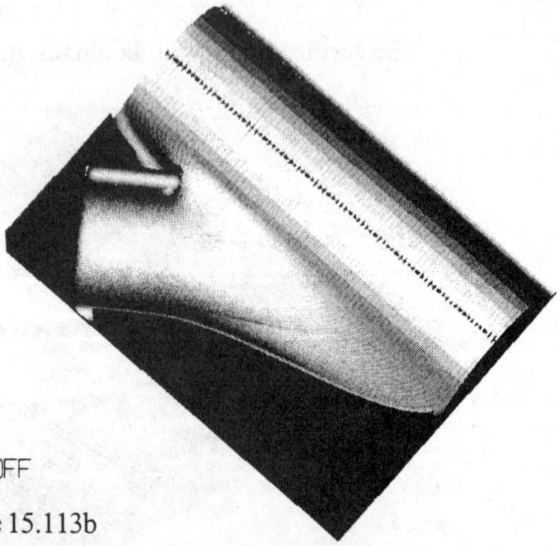

Figure 15.113b

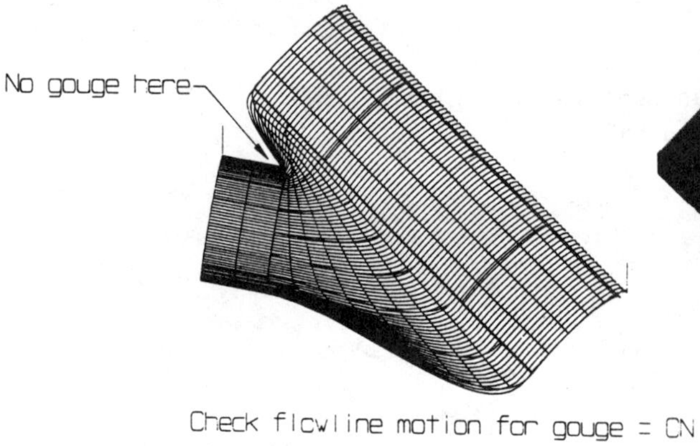

Figure 15.114a

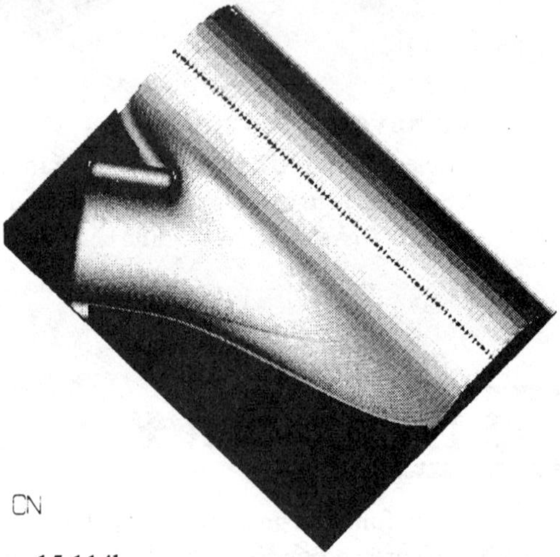

Figure 15.114b

Project 12. Using flowline function

Use the flowline function generates finishing toolpaths to cut a Coons surface as shown in Figure 15.115.

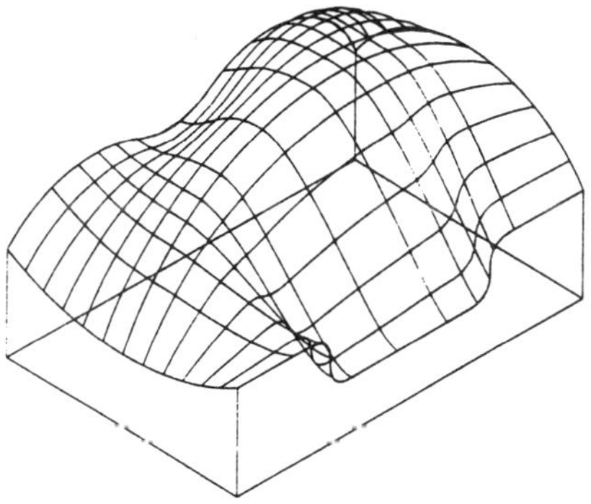

Figure 15.115a

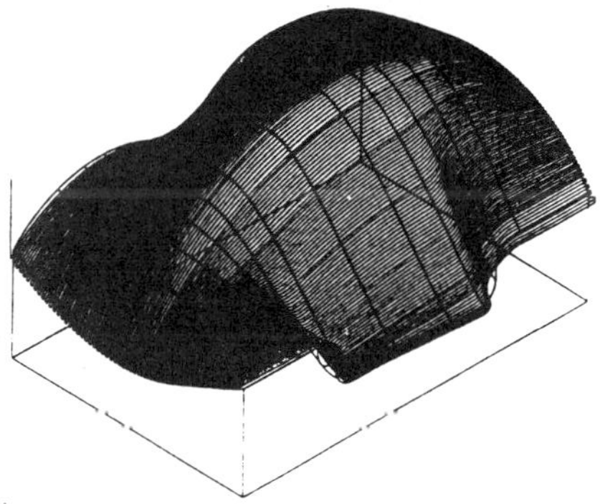

Figure 15.115b

Tips 1. Open the Coons surface model file coonnss2.

2. Use the surface finish-flowline function to generate toolpaths to cut the surface.

3. Use 3/8" sphere end mill.

Step 1. Open the coons surface model file "coonss2".

Select **MAIN MENU → File → Get**
File name: **coonss2**
The surface model appears as in Figure 15.116.

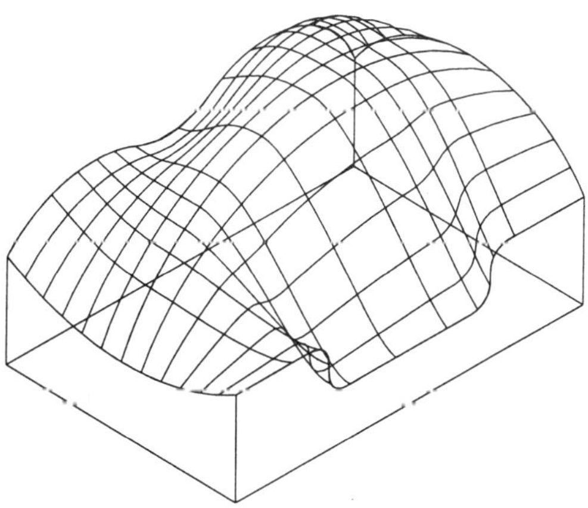

Figure 15.116

Step 2. Initiate the flowline function.

Select **Cplane →Top**
Select **MAIN MENU → Toolpaths → Surface → Finish → Flowline**
Select **All → Surfaces → Done**
Click the right mouse button, then select "**Get tool from library**"
Select **tool number 254** (3/8 sphere end mill)
Select **OK**

Set the tool parameters as below.

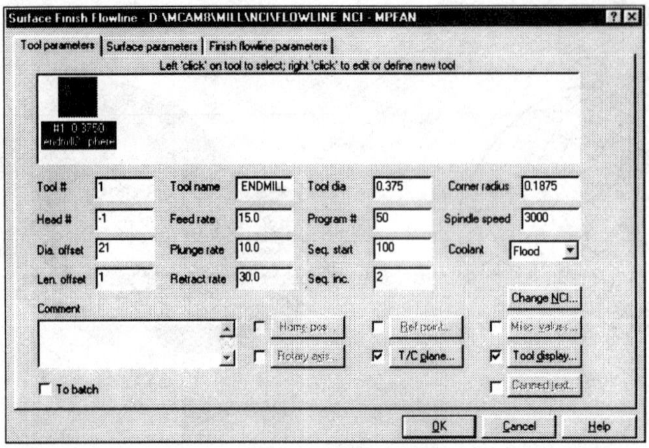

Step 3. Define the surface finish parameters.

Click the "**Surface parameters**" button

Set the surface parameters as below.

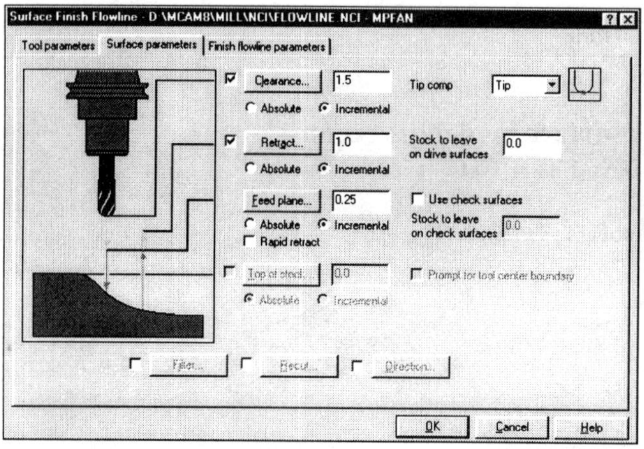

Step 4. Define the finish flowline parameters.

Click the "**Finish flowline parameters**" button

Set the finish flowline parameters as below.

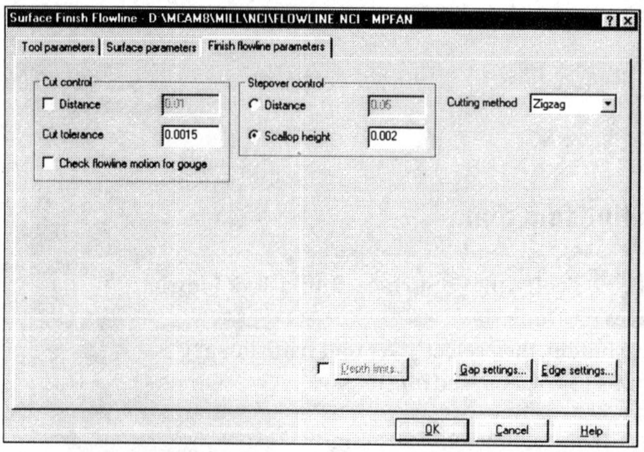

Step 5. Define gap and edge parameters.

Click the "**Gap settings**" button
Select **Direct** for Motion < Gap size, keep tool down parameter
Select **OK**
Select **OK**
The arrow to show the direction and starting location of toolpaths is initially located at the upper-right corner of the surface. The cut direction is in the X direction.
Select "**Cut dir**" to change the cut direction to the Y direction
Select "**Start**" to move the starting location to the upper-left corner
Select **Done** to generate the toolpaths as shown in Figure 15.117.

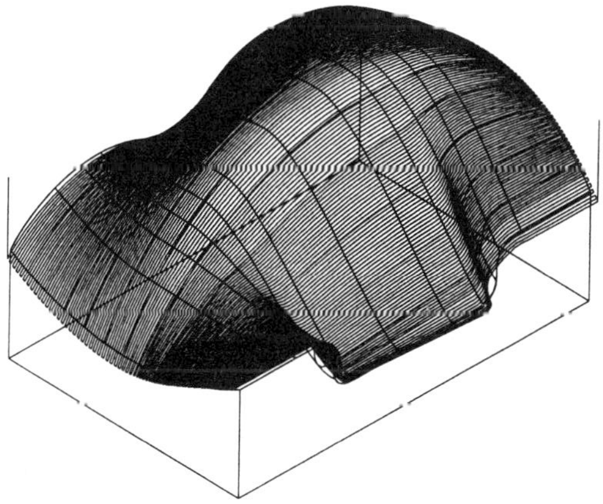

Figure 15.117

Step 6. Save the toolpath file.

Select **BACKUP →Operations**
Select **Post** from Operations Manager dialog box
Select **Save NC files → OK**
File name: **flowline**

15.20 Contour Function

This function generates a set of toolpaths to cut a surface model along their surface contours (Figure 15.118). The finish contour parameters dialog box appears as below.

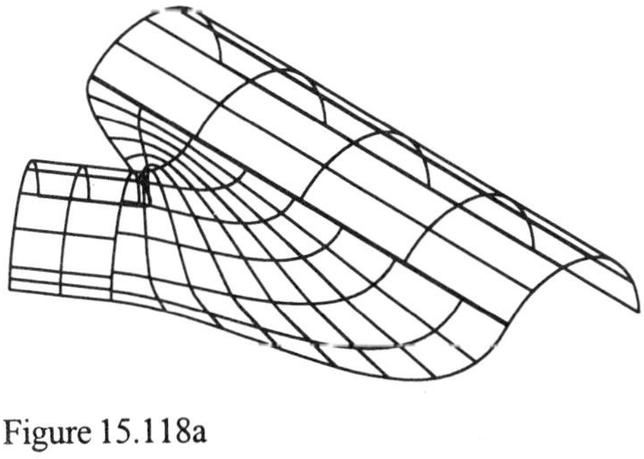

Figure 15.118a

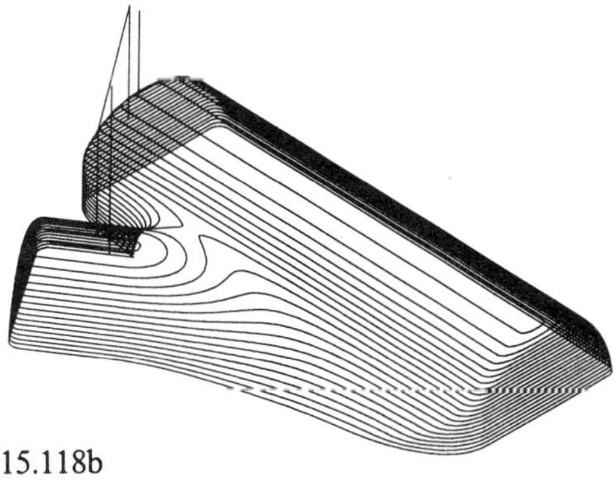

Figure 15.118b

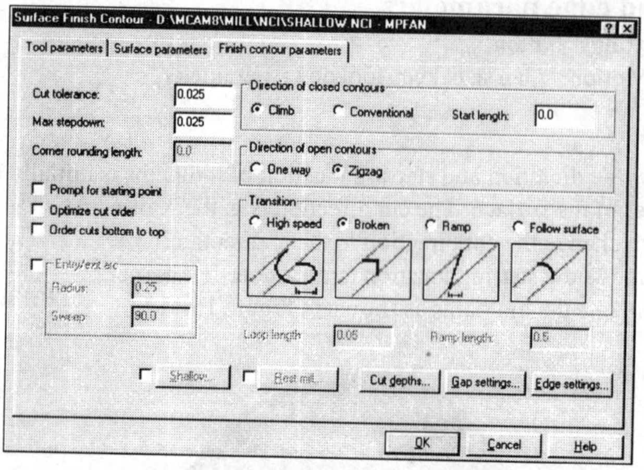

The transition parameter is same as in Rough contour function.

A potential problem with using the contour function is that the top flat or curve surface may not be cut and leaves a strip of uncut material as shown in Figure 15.119. The shallow function is used to generate toolpaths to remove these uncut areas.

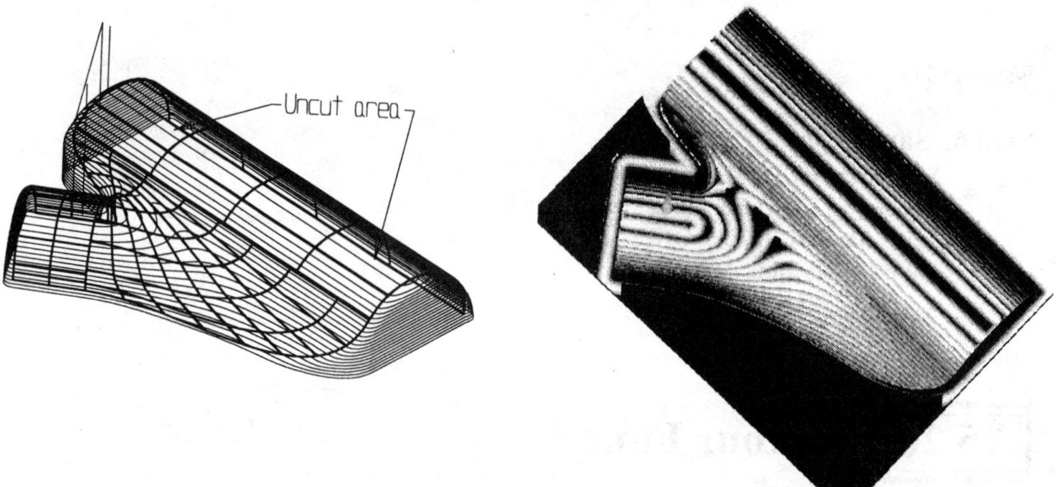

Figure 15.119

15.21 Finish Shallow Function

The shallow function generates a set of toolpaths to clean the remaining stock from shallow areas defined by two slope angles. This function is particularly useful to remove materials that are left from using a finish contour function. The finish shallow parameters dialog box appears as below.

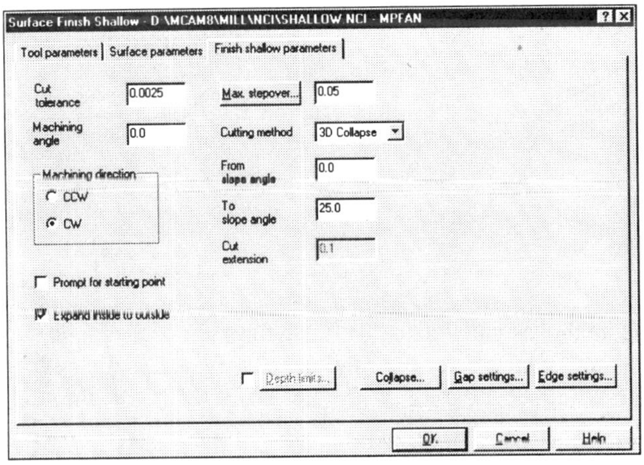

The following two angle parameters define the shallow areas (Figure 15.120):

From slope angle: specify the minimum slope angle of the shallow areas on the surfaces.

To slope angle: specify the maximum slope angle of the shallow areas on the surfaces.

The angles are measured from horizontal plane and going downward being positive angle. The horizontal plane has 0 degrees.

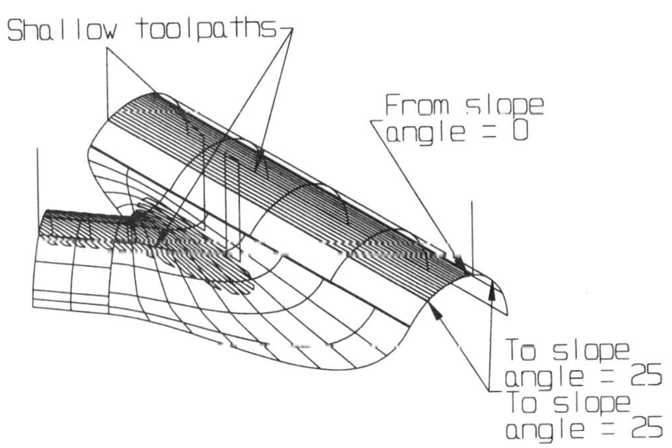

Figure 15.120

The "Cut extension" parameter is used to extend the cut in such a way that the tool can plunge into a previously cut area before machining the leftover stock. The cut extension distance adds to both ends of the toolpath and follows the curvature of the surface. Figure 15.121 shows the effect of adding cut extension.

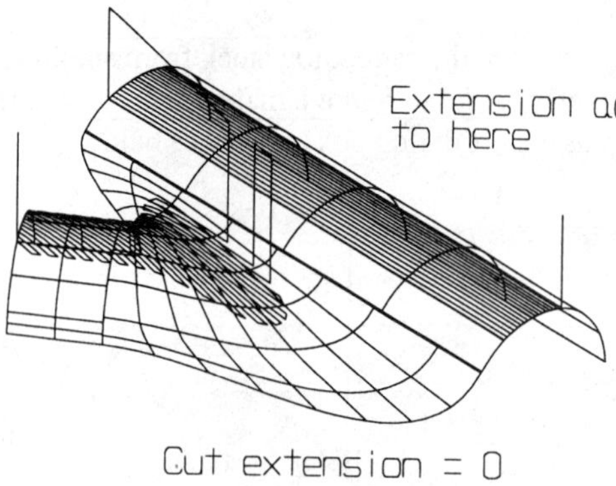

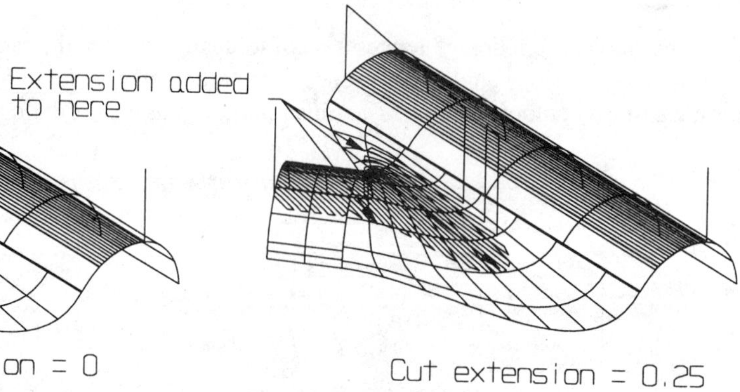

Figure 15.121a

Figure 15.121b

There are three cutting methods available in this finish function: zigzag, one way, and 3D collapse. The "3D collapse" method creates a zone around the cutting area, cuts the boundary of the zone, and then steps in to create a cut that offsets the outer boundary by the maximum stepover (Figure 15.122).

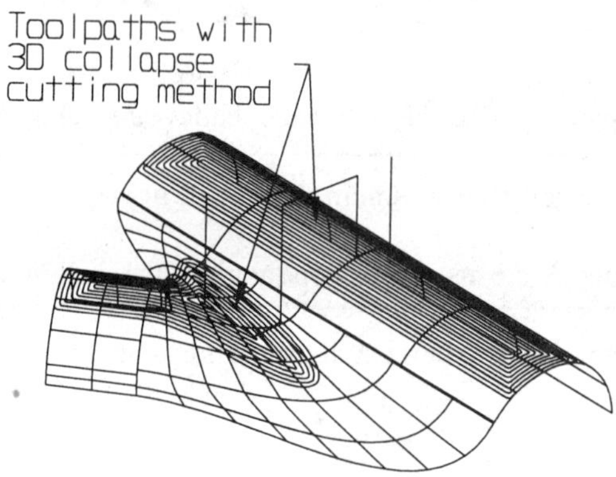

Figure 15.122

When 3D collapse cutting method is selected, the "Collapse" button becomes active to open Collapse parameters dialog box as below.

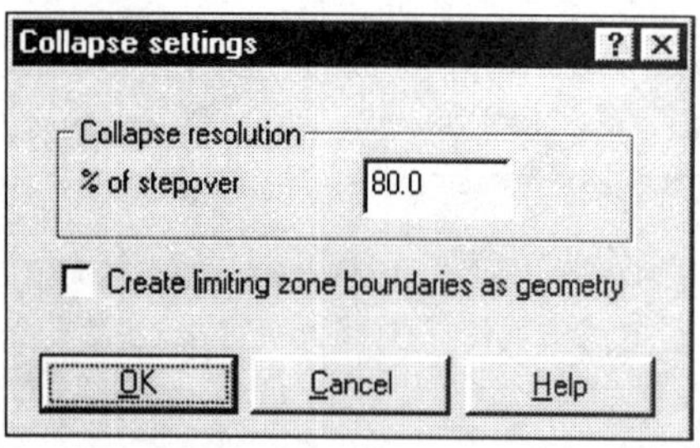

The "Collapse settings" defines how smoothly the collapse zones of a 3D collapse are created. The smaller the collapse resolution, the more accurate the toolpath. The collapse resolution is expressed in the percentage of the maximum stepover.

The "Create limiting zone boundaries as geometry" parameter is used to create geometry from the tool center boundaries of the 3D collapse.

Project 13. Using shallow and contour functions

This project uses two toolpath functions to generate two set of finishing toolpaths to machine a surface model. The shallow function is used to generate toolpaths to cut the areas that left from the contouring toolpaths. Figure 15.123 shows the surface model and two sets of finishing toolpaths.

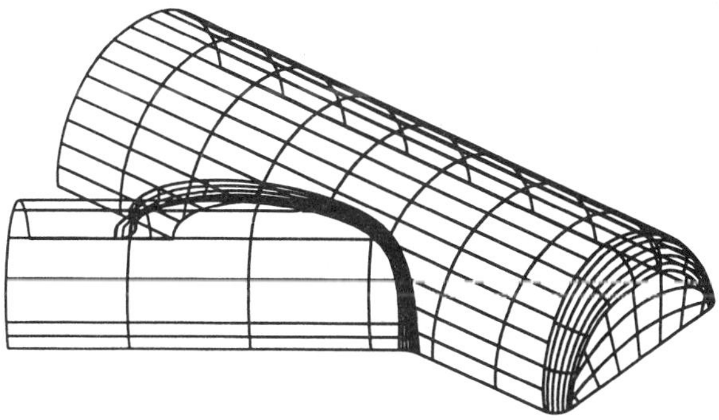

Figure 15.123a

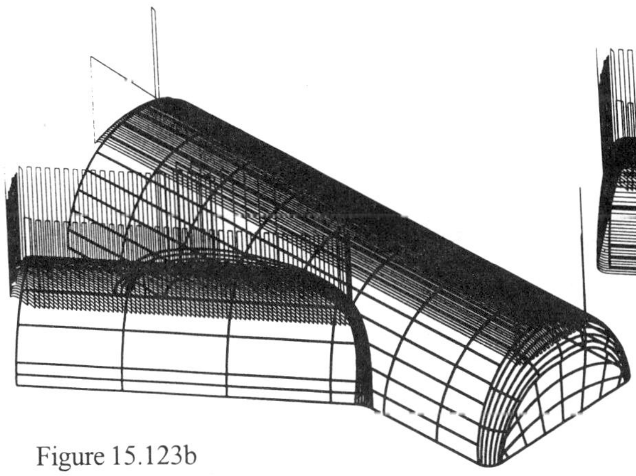

Figure 15.123b

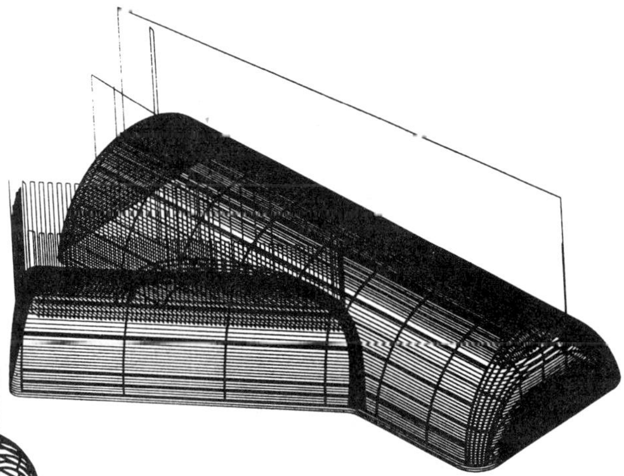

Figure 15.123c

> **Tips** 1. Open the surface model file trims2.
>
> 2. Use the shallow function to generate toolpaths for cutting surfaces between 0° and 25°.
>
> 3. Use a ¼" sphere end mill.
>
> 4. Use the surface finish-contour function to generate toolpaths.
>
> 5. Use the same ¼" sphere end mill.

Step 1. Open the surface model file trims2.

Select **MAIN MENU → File → Get**

File name: **trims2**

The fillet surface appears as Figure 15.124.

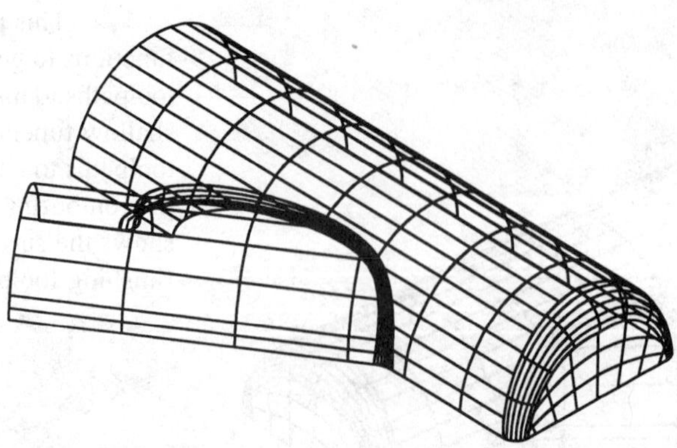

Figure 15.124

Step 2. Initiate the shallow function.

Select **Cplane → Top**
Select **MAIN MENU → Toolpaths → Surface → Finish → Shallow**
Select **All → Surfaces → Done**
The tool parameters dialog box should appear on the screen.
Click the right mouse button, then select "**Get tool from library**"
Select **tool number 252** (1/4 sphere end mill)
Select **OK**
Set the tool parameters as below.

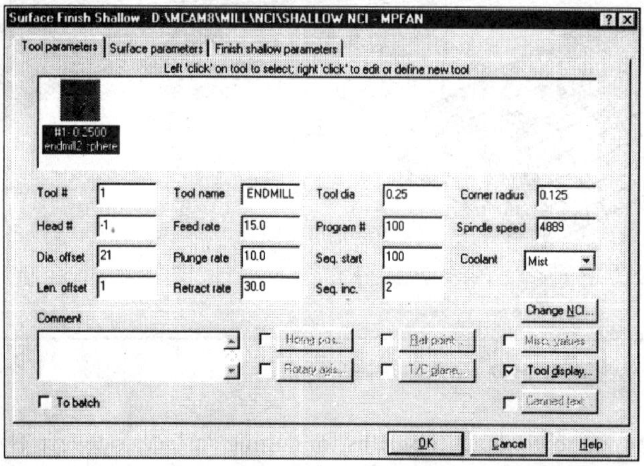

Step 3. Define the surface finish parameters.

Click the "**Surface parameters**" button

Set the surface parameters as below.

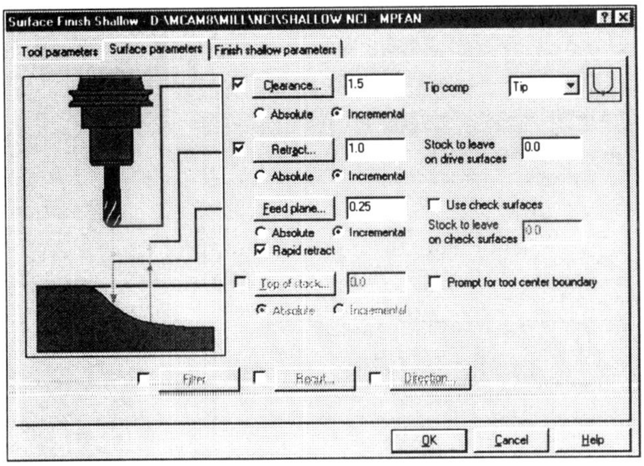

Step 4. Define the finish shallow parameters.

Click the "**Finish shallow parameters**" button

Set the finish shallow parameters as below.

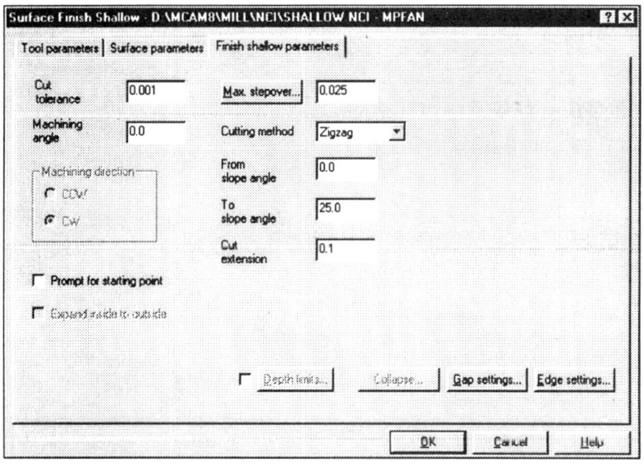

Step 5. Define the edge setting parameters.

Click the "**Edge settings**" button

Click "**Over all surface edges**" for Roll tool parameter

Select **OK** to return back to Shallow parameters dialog box

Select **OK** to generate toolpaths

The shallowing toolpaths between 0 and 25 degrees are generated as in Figure 15.125.

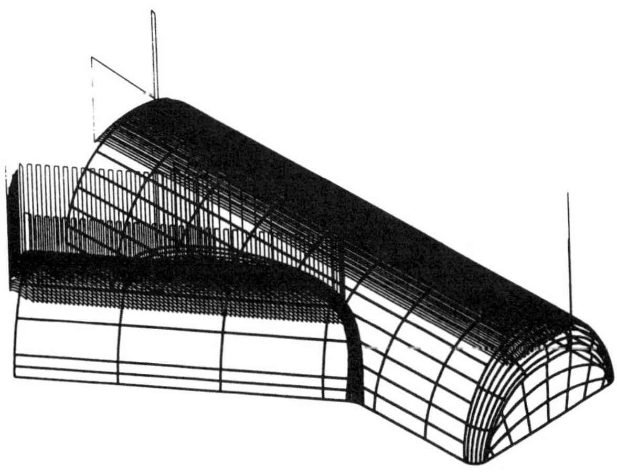

Figure 15.125

Step 6. Initiate the contour function.

Select **BACKUP → Surface → Finish → Contour**
Select **All → Surfaces → Done**
Set the tool parameters as below.

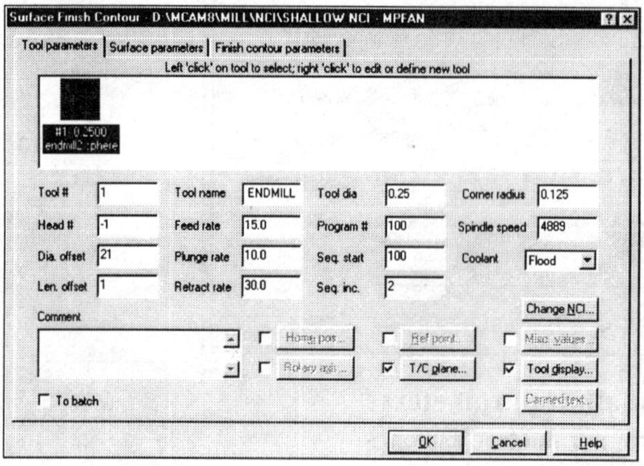

Step 7. Define the surface finish parameters.

Click the "**Surface parameters**" button
Set the surface parameters as below.

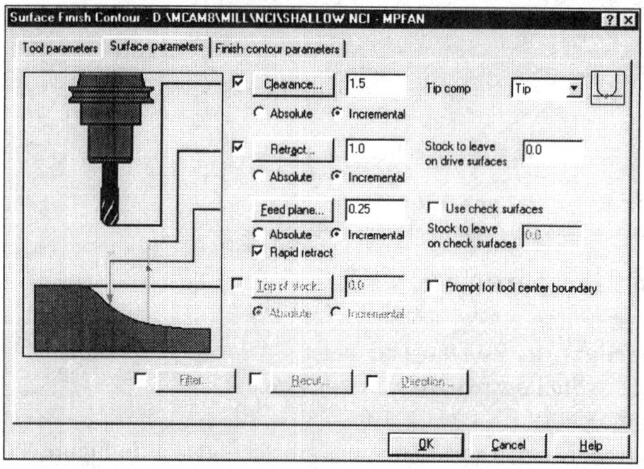

Step 8. Define the finish contour parameters.

Click the "**Finish contour parameters**" button

Set the finish contour parameters as below.

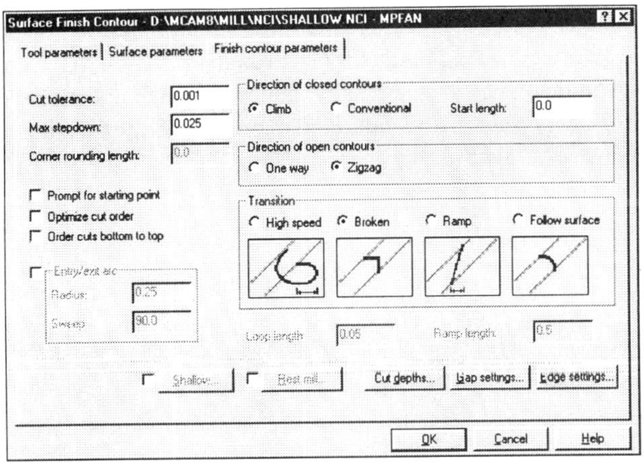

Step 9. Define the edge setting parameters.

Click the "**Edge settings**" button

Click "**Over all surface edges**" for Roll tool parameter

Select **OK → OK** to generate contouring toolpaths

It will take a few minutes for computer to generate the toolpaths as shown in Figure 15.126.

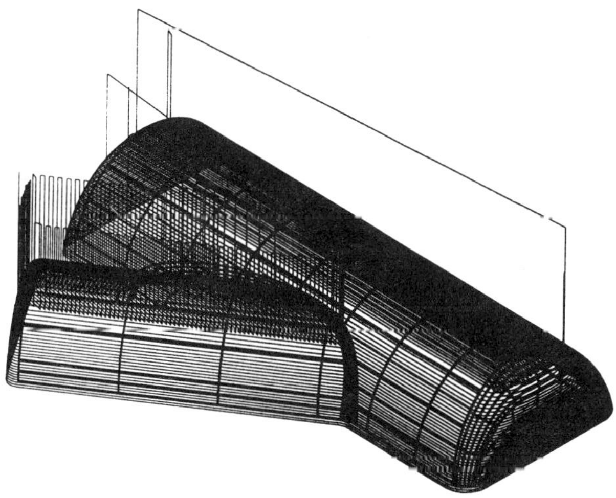

Figure 15.126

Step 10. Save the toolpaths.

Select **BACKUP → Operations → Select All → Post**

Select **Save NCI file → OK**

File name: **shallow → Save → OK**

15.22 Finish Pencil Function

The pencil function generates a set of toolpaths for (1) a rough operation to remove material in corners so subsequent operations can machine surfaces easily, and (2) a finish operation to clean leftover material from corners (Figure 15.127). Corners are encountered mainly at the intersection of surfaces. The pencil parameters dialog box appears as below.

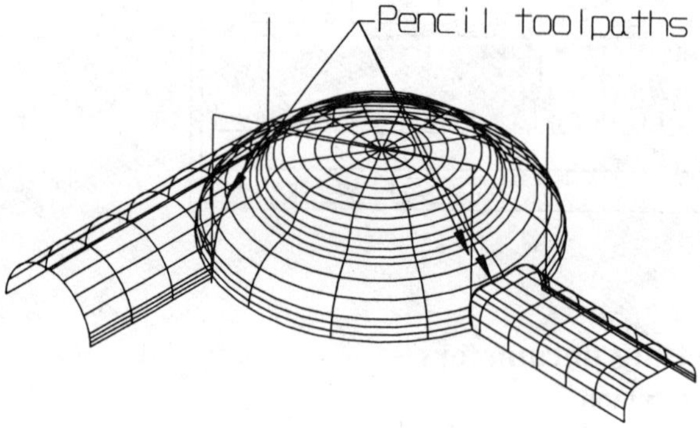

Figure 15.127

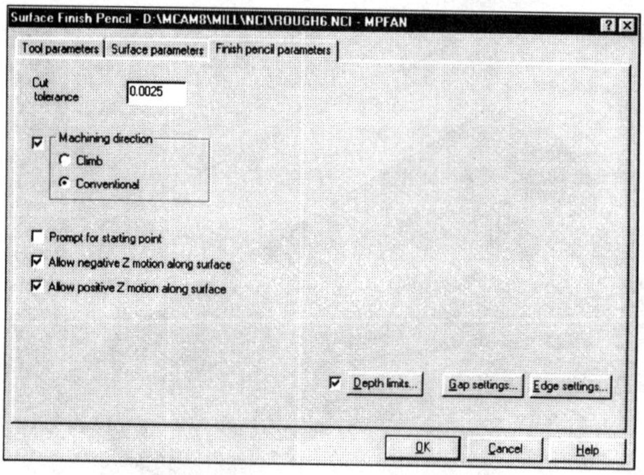

15.23 Finish Scallop Function

The scallop function generates toolpaths for machining selected surfaces. The toolpaths generated from this function have the following three distinct features (Figure 15.128):

(1) They have consistent scallop heights over the entire set of surfaces.
(2) They consistently touch the surfaces to minimize the retract motions.
(3) They have a spiral pattern generated from collapse 3D cutting method.

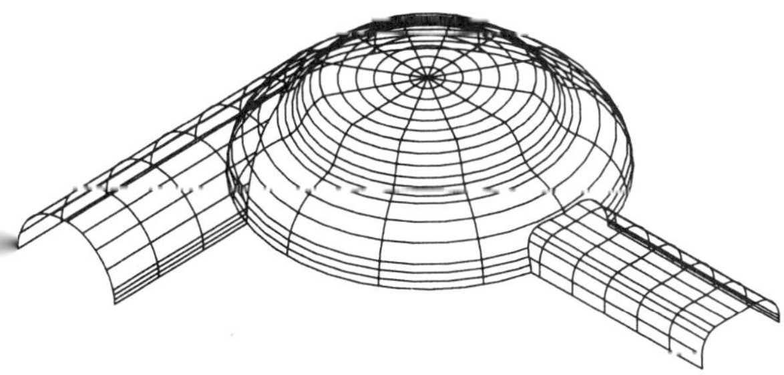

Figurc 15.128a

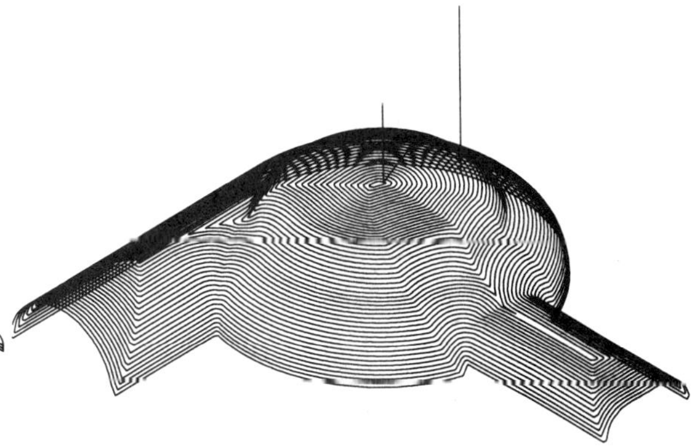

Figure 15.128b

The scallop parameters dialog box appears as below.

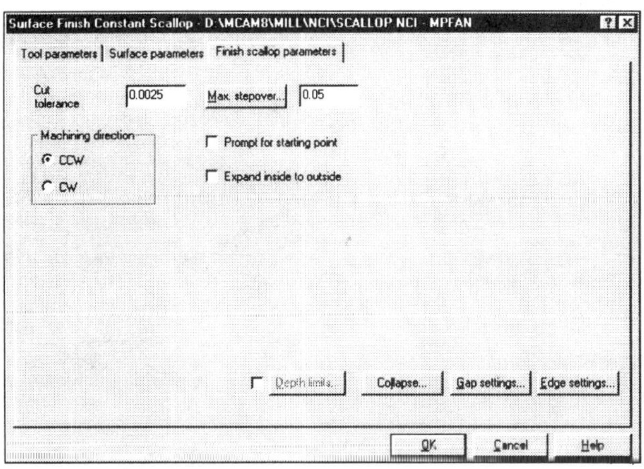

The toolpaths can be control by the following two parameters:

Machining direction: specify the cutting direction either in clockwise (CW) direction or counterclockwise (CCW) direction.

Expand inside to outside: specify the start of cutting motion
(1) at the center of the geometry and spiraling to the outer boundary, or
(2) at the outer boundary and spiraling toward the center.

💻 Project 14. Using scallop function

The scallop function is used to generate finishing toolpaths to cut the basket surface model as shown in Figure 15.129.

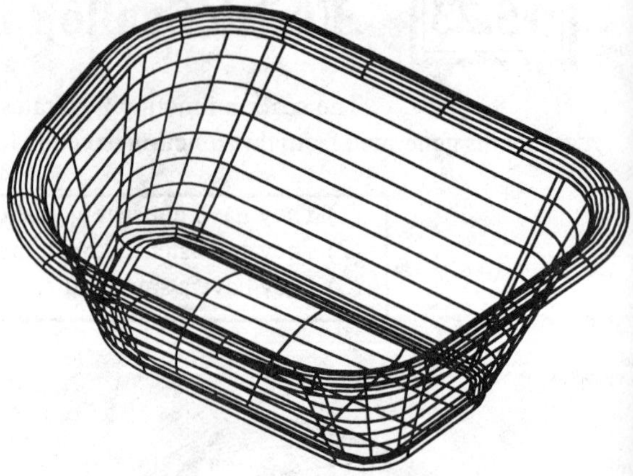

Figure 15.129a

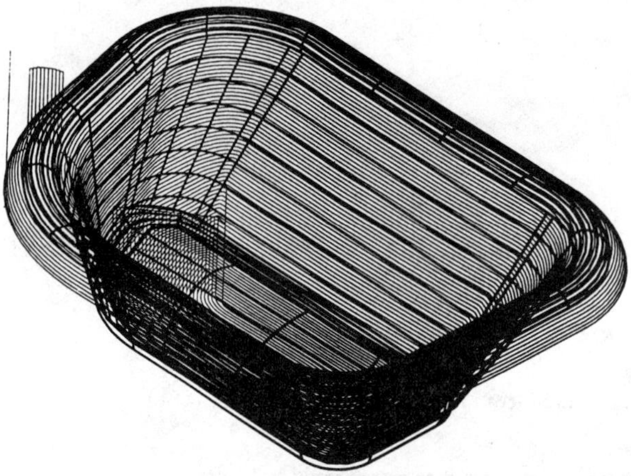

Figure 15.129b

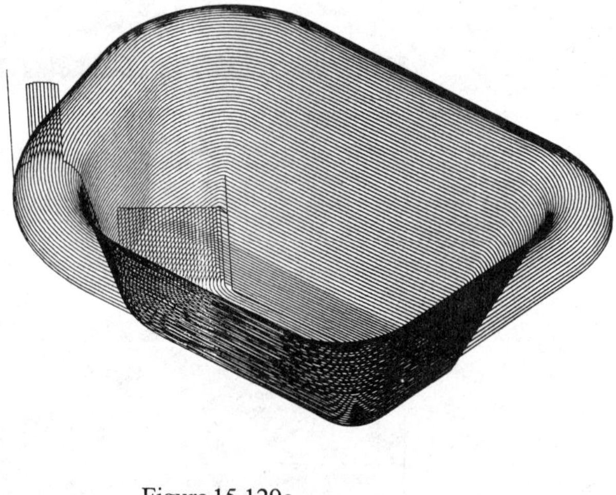

Figure 15.129c

⌛**Tips**	1. Open the surface model file baskets.
	2. Use the scallop function to generate finishing toolpaths.
	3. Use a 3/8" sphere end mill.

Step 1. Open the surface model file baskets.

Select **MAIN MENU → File → Get**
File name: **baskets**

The basket surface model appears as in Figure 15.130.

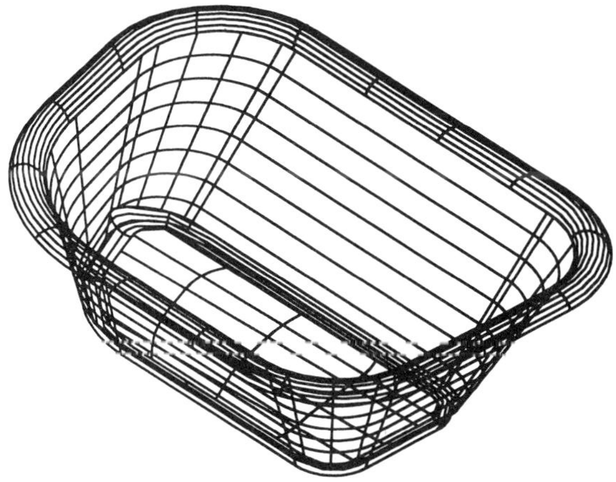

Figure 15.130

Step 2. Initiate the scallop function.

Select **MAIN MENU → Toolpaths → Surface → Finish → Scallop**
Select **All → Surfaces → Done**
Click the right mouse button then select "**Get tool from library**"
Select **tool number 254** (3/8 sphere end mill)
Select **OK**
Set tool parameters as below.

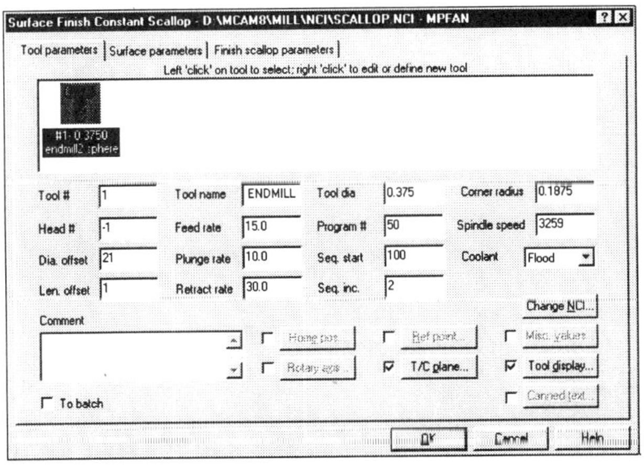

Step 3. Define the surface finish parameters.

Click the "**Surface parameters**" button
Set the surface parameters as on the next page.

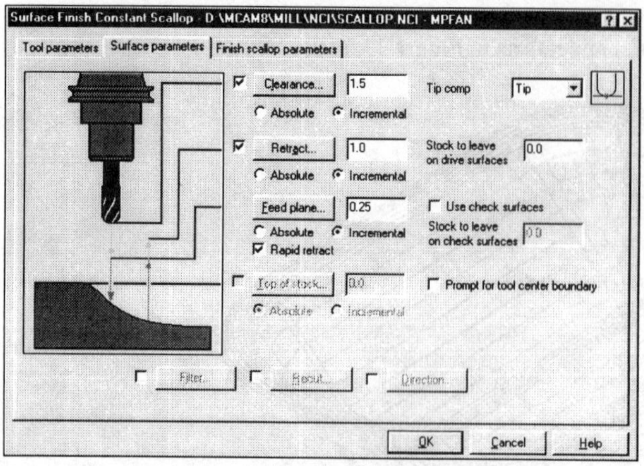

Step 4. Define the finish scallop parameters.

Click the "**Finish scallop parameters**" button
Set the finish scallop parameters as below.

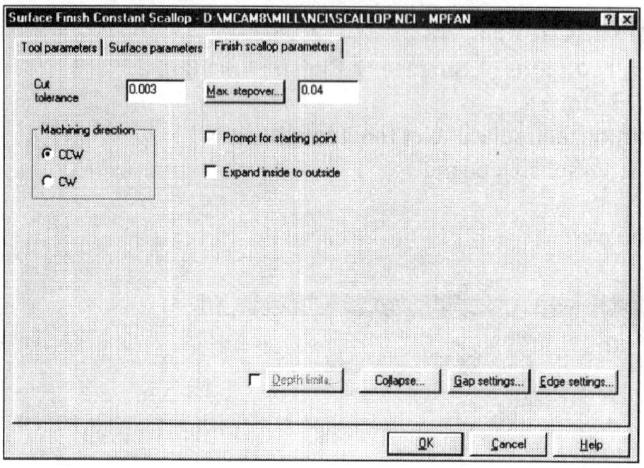

Step 5. Define the edge setting parameters.

Click the "**Edge settings**" button
Click "**Over all surface edges**" on Roll tool parameter
Select **OK → OK** to generate finishing toolpaths as shown in Figure 15.131.

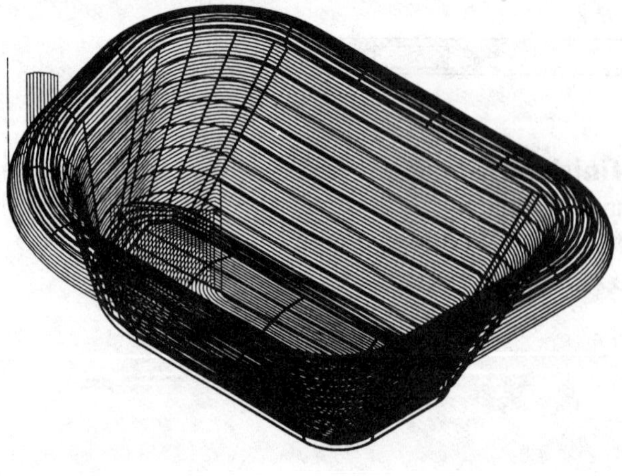

Figure 15.131

Figure 15.132 shows the toolpaths without the surface model.

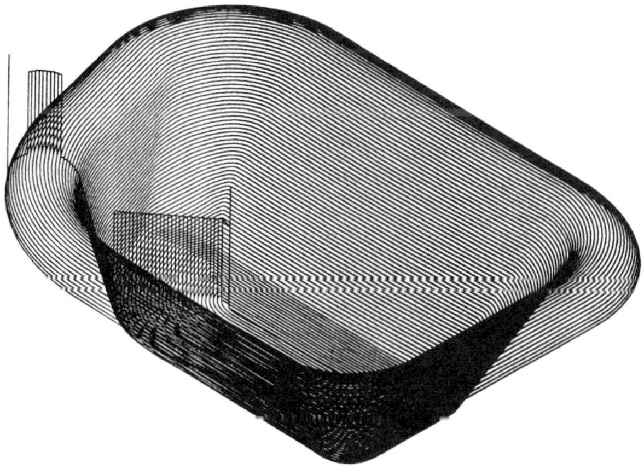

Figure 15.132

Step 6. Save the toolpath file.

Select **BACKUP → Operations → Post**
Select **Save NCI file → OK**
File name: **scallop → Save → OK**

Project 15. Using parallel function with copy-rotate command

Generating a set of toolpaths to cut the car wheel surface model is a challenge for a Mastercam user. The complete surface model consists of 60 surfaces (some surfaces are hidden in the model.) If one of the surface finish functions is used to generate the toolpaths for the entire surface model, it may take a much longer time to complete the process of generating the toolpaths. The approach we use here is to generate the toolpaths for a partial surface model consisting of only six surfaces. This set of toolpaths is then copied to the other five locations. By doing so, the system needs only a few minutes to complete the toolpaths for the entire model. The partial surface model and complete toolpaths are shown in Figure 15.133.

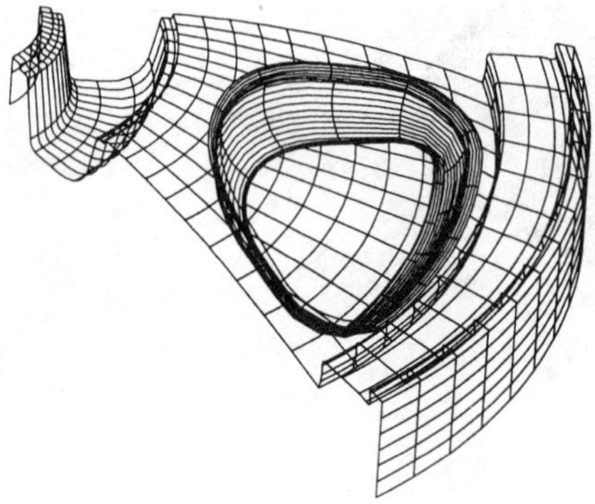

Figure 15.133a

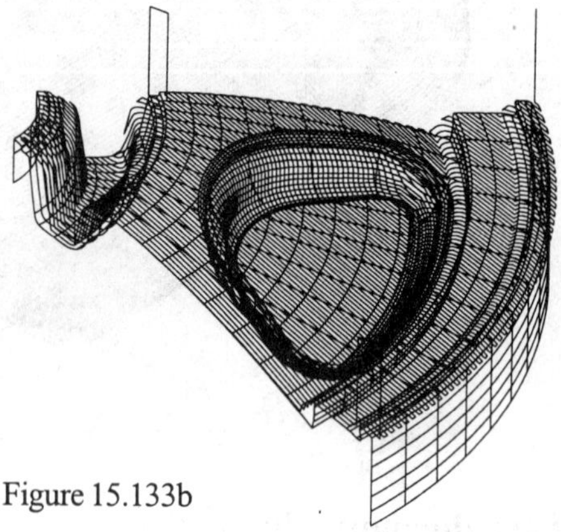

Figure 15.133b

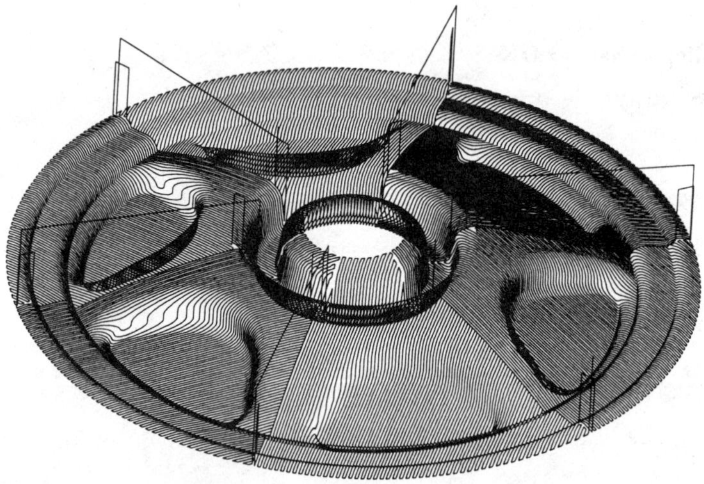

Figure 15.133c

Tips

1. Only a section of the surface model is used to generate toolpaths. This set of toolpaths is used to copy to five locations by using NC utils → Xform → Rotate commands.
2. The inner and outer rim surfaces can be cut by using a 2D toolpath function such as contour or pocket. They do no include using the surface finish-parallel function.
3. The surface model file is wheels.
4. Use surface finish-parallel function to generate the finishing toolpaths.
5. Use 3/8" sphere end mill.
6. Use Toolpaths → Next menu → Transform → Rotate commands with these parameters to copy the toolpaths to five locations:

   Rotation angle = **60** Number of steps = **5** Leave the original entities

Step 1. Open the wheel surface model.

Select **MAIN MENU → File → Get**
File name: **wheels**
The wheel surface model appears as in Figure 15.134.

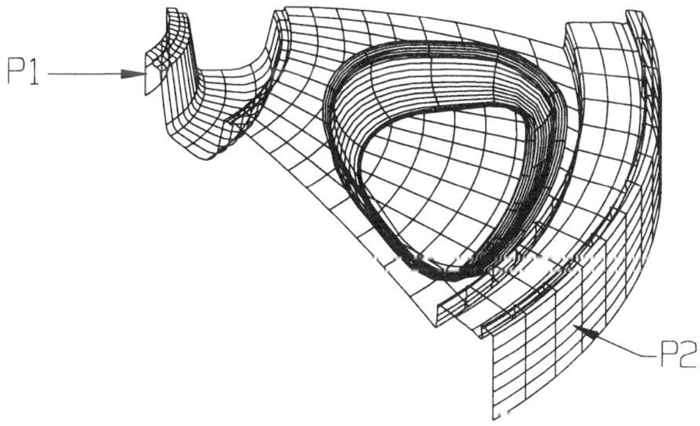

Figure 15.134

Step 2. Initiate the parallel function.

Use the pick points in Figure 15.134.
Select **Cplane → Top**
Select **MAIN MENU → Toolpaths → Surface → Finish → Parallel**
Select **All → Surfaces → Unselect**
Pick **P1** and **P2** to unselect two vertical wall surfaces
Select **BACKUP → Done**

Step 3. Define the tool parameters.

Click the right mouse button, then select "**Get tool from library**"
Select **tool number 254** (3/8 sphere end mill)
Select **OK**
Set the tool parameters as below.

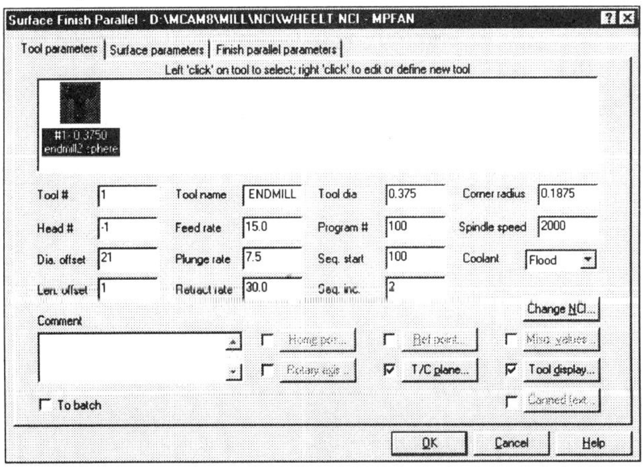

Click **Change NCI** and change the file name to **wheelt**

Step 4. Define the surface finish parameters.

Click the "**Surface parameters**" button
Set the surface parameters as next.

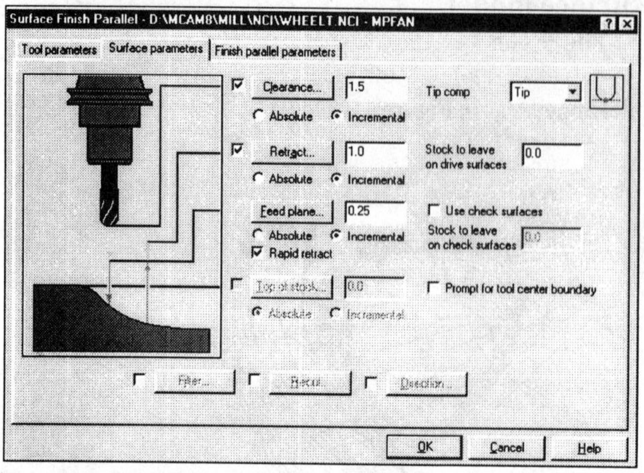

Step 5. Define the finish parallel parameters.

Click the "**Finish parallel parameters**" button

Define the finish parallel parameters as below.

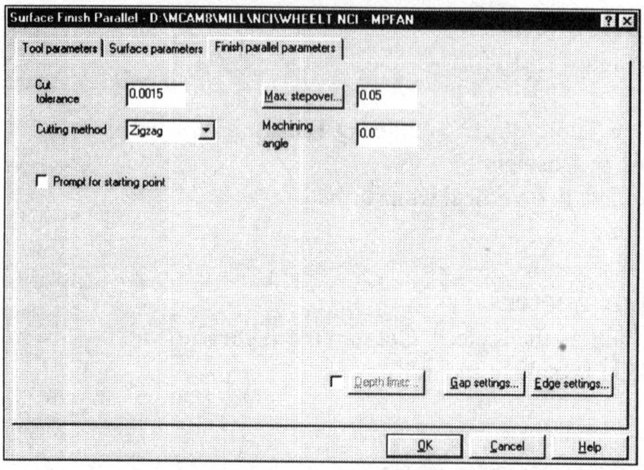

Step 6. Define the gap and edge parameters.

Click the "**Gap settings**" button

Set % of stepover to **200.0**

Select **Direct** for Motion < Gap size, keep tool down parameter

Select **OK**

Click the "**Edge settings**" button

Select **automatically** for Roll tool parameter

Select **OK** → **OK** to generate the toolpaths as shown in Figure 15.135.

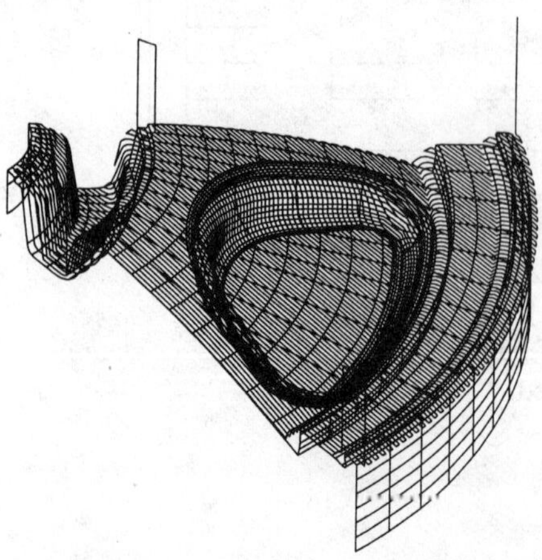

Figure 15.135

Step 7. Copy toolpaths five times using the Toolpaths → Transform commands

Select **MAIN MENU → Toolpaths → Next menu → Transform**

The transform Operation Parameters box should appear as below.

Set the parameters as shown:

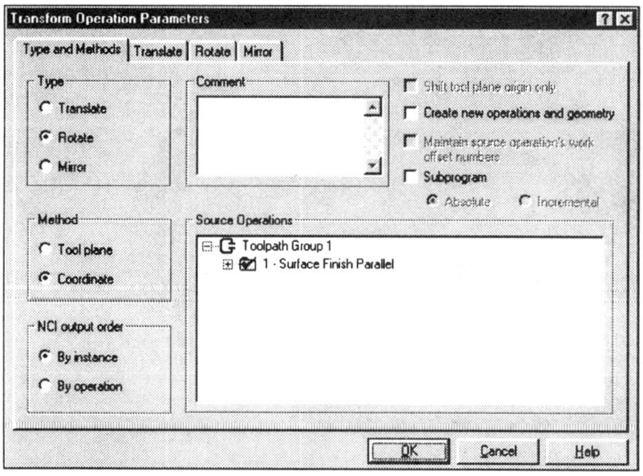

Select **Rotate** tab

Set the Rotate parameters as below.

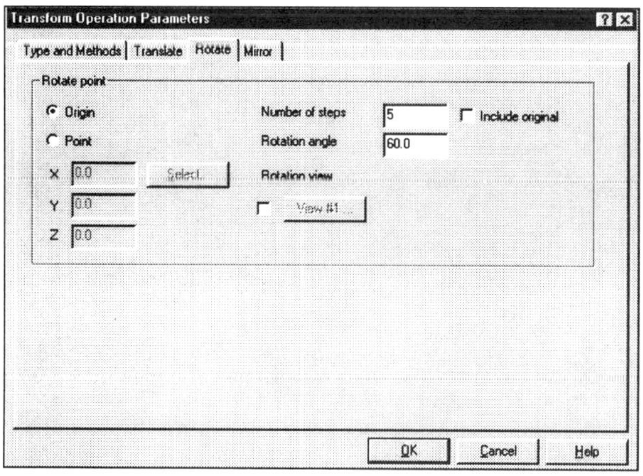

Select **OK** to copy the toolpaths to five locations

The five toolpath sections are added to the file as shown below.

The toolpaths are plotted as in Figure 15.136.

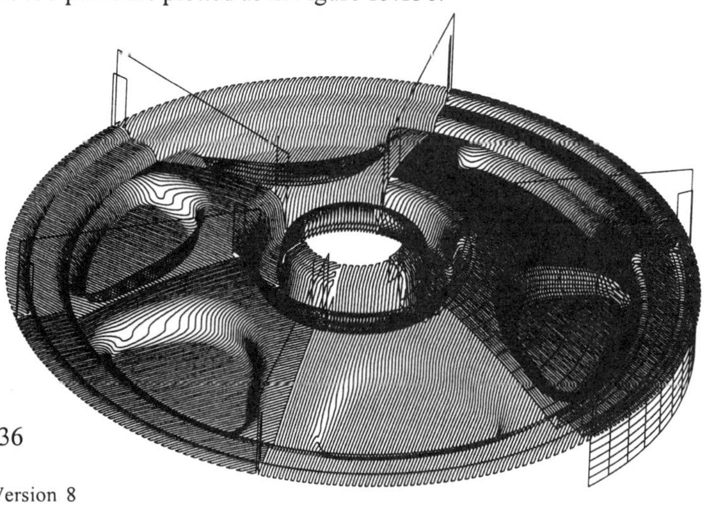

Figure 15.136

The toolpaths without showing surfaces appear as in Figure 15.137.

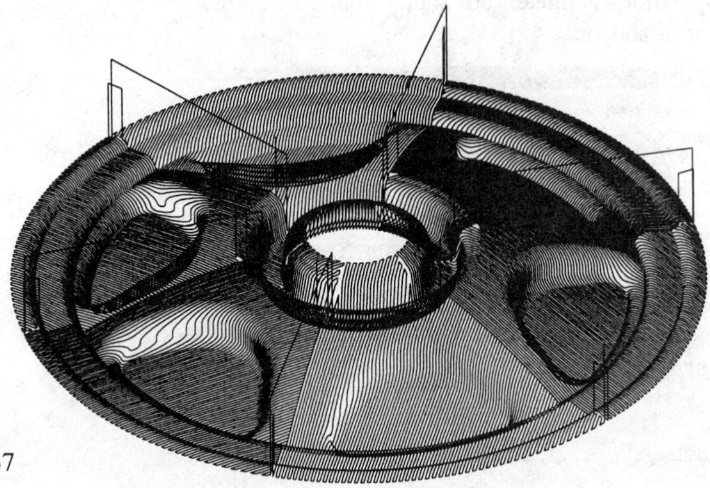

Figure 15.137

Step 8. Save the copied toolpath sections to the toolpath file.

Select **BACKUP → Operations → Post**
Select **Save NCI files → OK**
File name: **wheelt**

Project 16. Using flowline and radial functions with rotate-copy command 16

The fan surface model shown in Figure 15.138 has seven blades. Each blade consists of three surfaces; end ruled surface, top surface, and bottom surface. The bottom surface has a hook-shape that extends from top to bottom. In other words, we can not cut the bottom surface in one operation. This project uses the flowline function to generate toolpaths for cutting two blade surfaces from one direction. Use the vertical wall surface and the hub surface as the check surfaces. The radial function is used to cut the remaining three surfaces. The toolpaths for the blade is copied to six locations to complete the toolpaths. Figure 15.138 shows surface model, toolpaths, and verification model of this project.

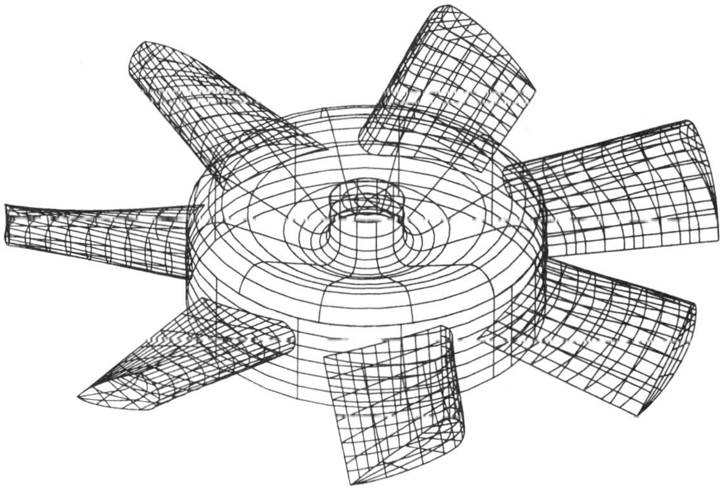

Figure 15.138a

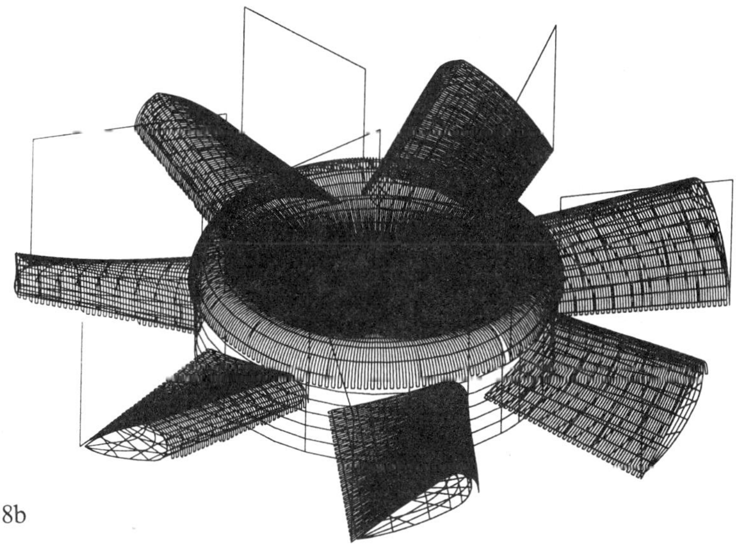

Figure 15.138b

Figure 138c

⌛**Tips** 1. Open the surface model file fans.

2. Change the direction normal for two surfaces, vertical wall surface and rim surface.

3. Use the flowline function to generate toolpaths for cutting the top section of a fan blade.

4. Use a ¼" sphere end mill.

5. Use the radial function to generate toolpaths for cutting three surfaces.

6. Use Toolpaths → Next menu → Transform commands to copy the blade toolpaths to six locations.

7. Verify the toolpaths.

Step 1. Open the fan surface model.

Select **MAIN MENU → File → Get**

File name: **fans**

The fan surface model appears as Figure 15.139.

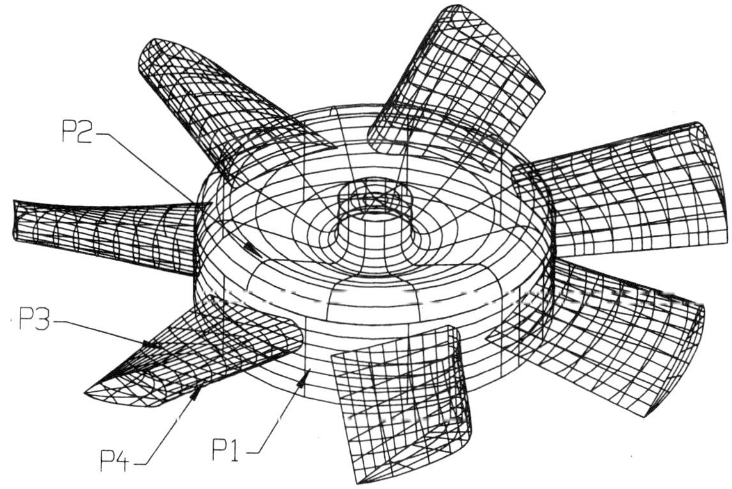

Figure 15.139

Step 2. Change the direction normal for two surfaces.

Use the pick points in Figure 15.139.
Select **MAIN MENU → Modify → Normal → Reverse**
Pick **P1** and **P2** to change the normal direction of two surfaces

Step 3. Initiate the flowline function.

Use the pick points in Figure 15.139.
Select **MAIN MENU → Toolpaths → Surface → Drive/check → On**
Pick **P1** and **P2** as two check surfaces
Select **Done → Done**
Select **Finish → Flowline**
Pick **P3** and **P4** to select two drive surfaces
Select **Done**

Step 4. Define the tool parameters.

Click the right mouse button, then select "**Get tool from library**"
Select **tool number 252** (1/4 sphere end mill)
Select **OK**

Click **Change NCI** and change the file name to: **fanst**

Set the tool parameters as below.

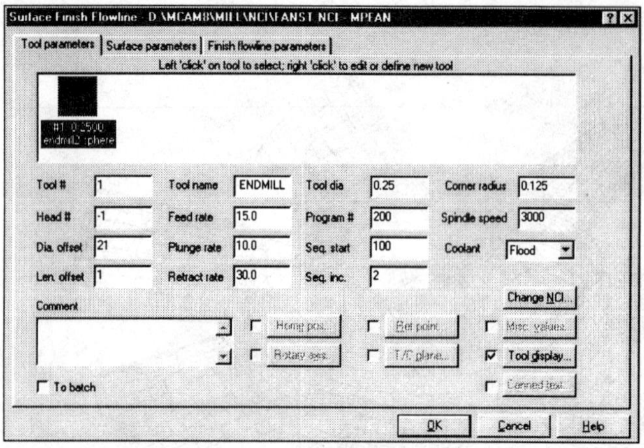

Step 5. Define the surface finish parameters.

Click the "**Surface parameters**" button

Define the surface parameters as below.

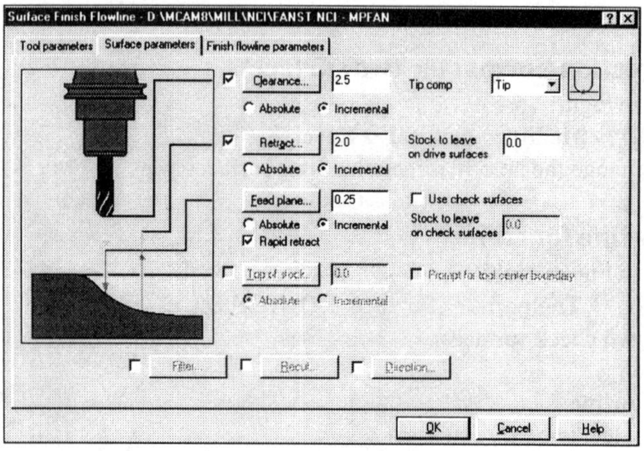

Step 6. Define the finish flowline parameters.

Click the "**Finish flowline Parameters**" button

Set the finish flowline parameters as below.

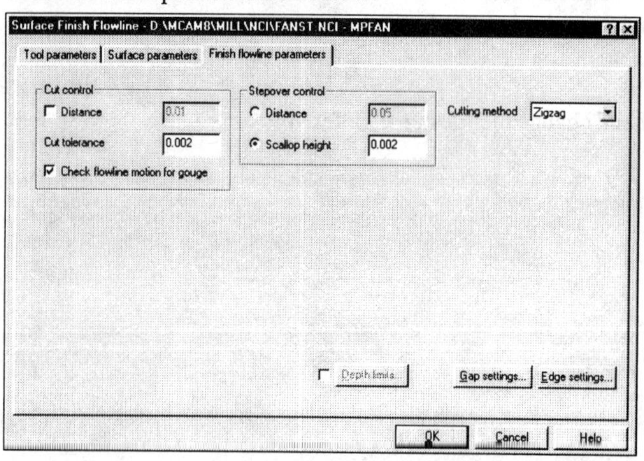

Step 7. Define the gap and edge parameters.

Click the "**Gap settings**" button
Set the gap parameters as below.

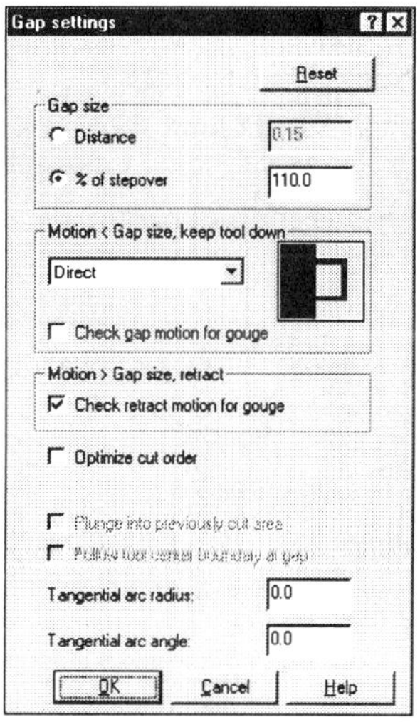

Select **OK**

Click the **"Edge settings"** button
Set the edge parameters as below.

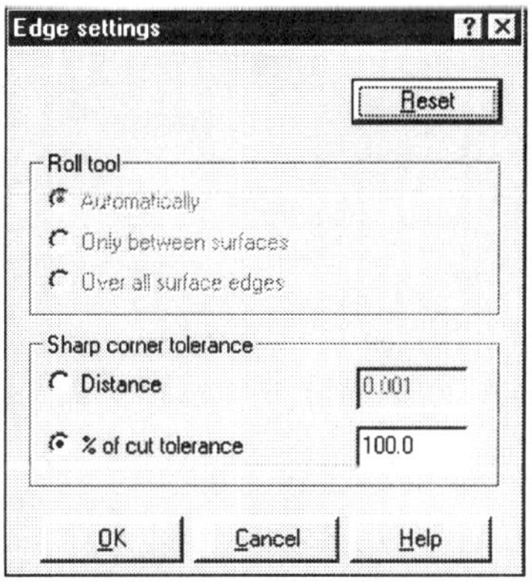

Select **OK → OK → Done** to generate the toolpaths as shown in Figure 15.140.

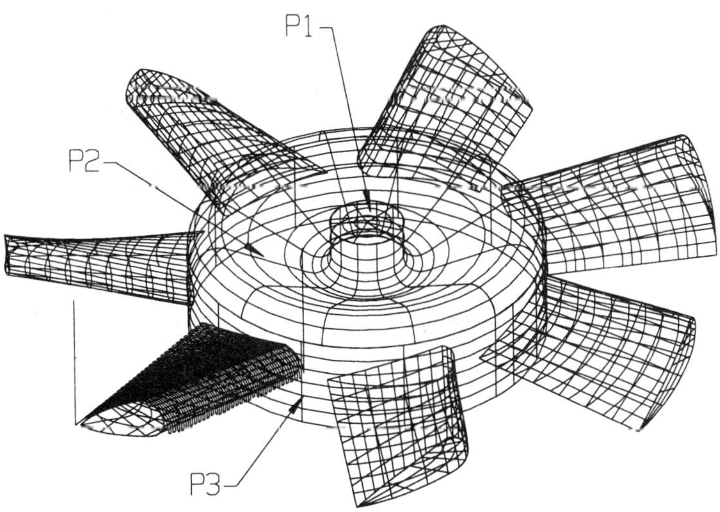

Figure 15.140

Step 8. Initiate the radial function.

Use the pick points in Figure 15.140.
Select **Finish → Radial**
Pick **P1**, **P2**, and **P3** to select three surfaces
Select **Done**
Define the tool parameters same as in step 4.

Step 9. Define the surface finish parameters.

Click the "**Surface parameters**" button
Set the surface parameters same as in step 5.

Step 10. Define the finish radial parameters.

Click the "**Finish radial parameters**" button
Set the finish radial parameters as below.

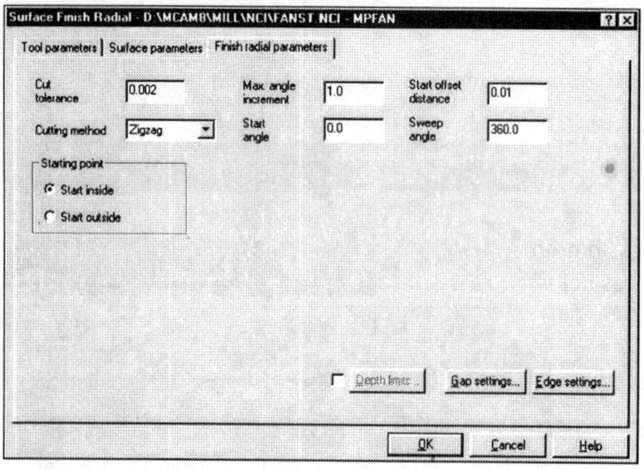

Step 11. Define the gap and edge parameters.

Set gap and edge parameters same as in step 7.
Select **OK → OK**
Enter the starting point: **0,0**
The toolpaths are generated as in Figure 15.141.

Figure 15.141

Step 12. Copy the blade toolpaths to six locations.

Select **MAIN MENU → Toolpaths → Next menu→Transform**
Select Type and Methods from the Transform Operation Parameter
Set the parameters as below.

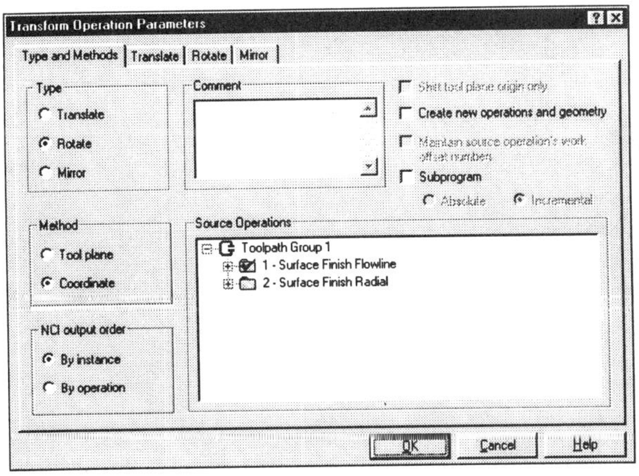

Select **Rotate** and set the parameters as below.

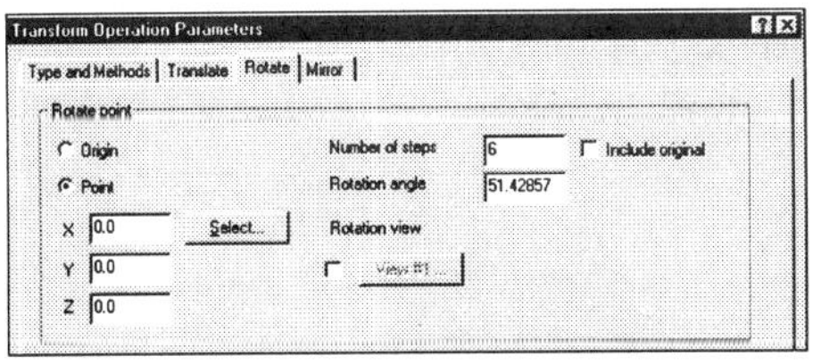

Select **OK** to copy toolpaths as shown in Figure 15.142.

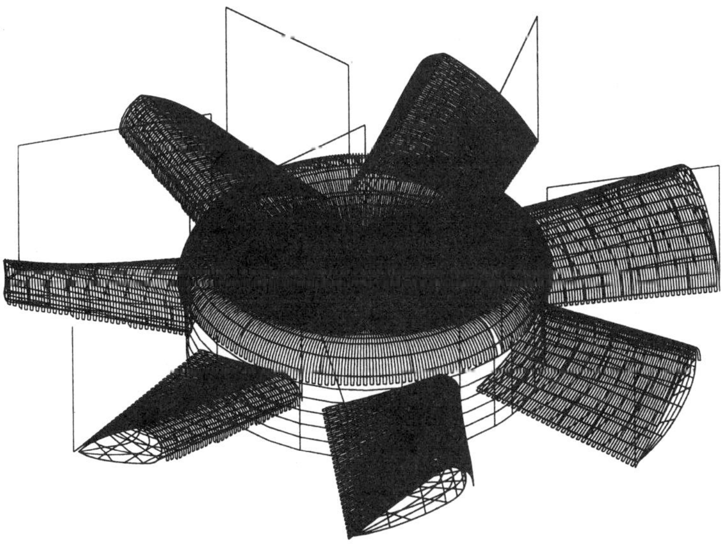

Figure 15.142

Step 13. Verify the toolpaths.

Directly select **BACKUP → Operations → Select All → Verify**
Select **Machine**

The verification model should resemble Figure 15.143.

Figure 15.143

Step 14. Save the surface model

Select **BACKUP** to return to Operations Manager dialog box
Select **Post** from Operations Manager dialog box
Toggle **NCI file** to on → **OK**
File name: **fanst** → **Save**
Select **OK** to leave the Operations Manager dialog box

Ex Exercises

1. List the five surface toolpath functions and briefly describe their functions.
2. What are the two groups of parameters used in surface toolpath functions?
3. List the seven roughing functions.
4. What are the drive surfaces?
5. What are check surfaces?
6. Describe the purpose of a tool center boundary.
7. What are two cutting methods in the roughing cut?
8. What are gaps?
9. What are the motions?
10. Explain how to determine whether a gap should be a short gap or a long gap.
11. What are two categories of surface open edges?
12. Describe the features of the rough parallel function.
13. Describe the features of the rough radial function.
14. Use a drawing to describe the three angle parameters used in the rough radial function.
15. Describe the features of the rough project function.
16. What are the three types of entities that can be used in the rough project function?
17. Describe the features of the rough flowline function.
18. Describe the features of the rough contour function.
19. Explain when you should use a rough contour function.
20. Describe the features of the pocket rough function.
21. Describe the features of the rough plunge function.
22. List the ten surface finish functions.
23. Describe the features of the parallel finish function.
24. Describe the features of the parallel steep finish function.
25. When should the finish leftover function be used?

26. Describe the features of the project finish function.

27. Describe the features of the finish shallow function and when to use it.

28. Describe the features of the finish pencil function and when to use it.

29. Describe the features of the finish scallop function.

Problems

30. Use the appropriate roughing and finish functions to generate the toolpaths for cutting the surface shown in Figure 15.144. The surface file name is ES3.

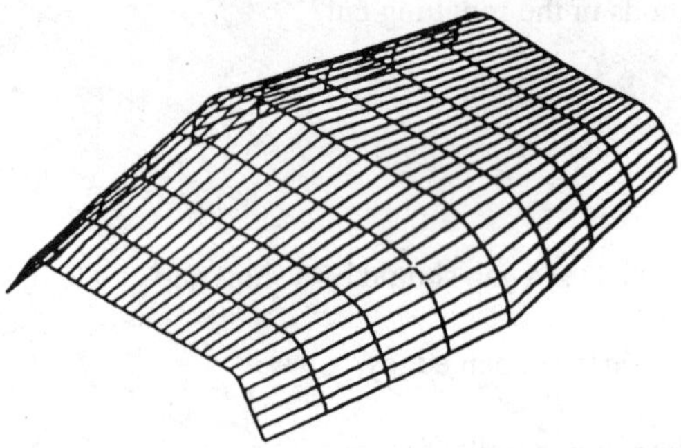

Figure 15.144

31. Use the appropriate roughing and finish functions to generate the toolpaths for cutting the surface model shown in Figure 15.145. The surface file name is ES6.

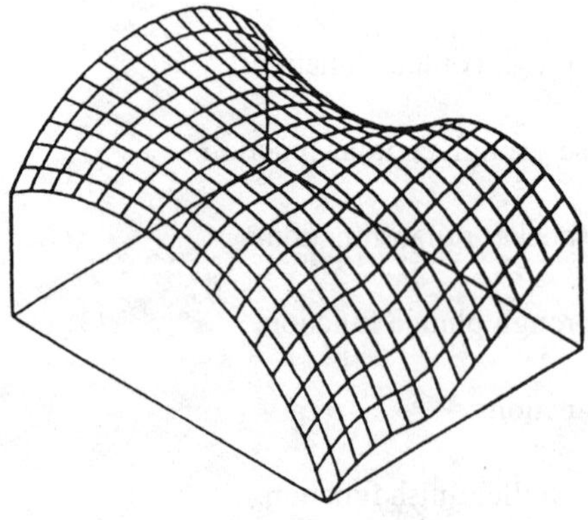

Figure 15.145

32. Use a finish function to generate the toolpaths for cutting a Cons surface with multiple patches. The surface file name is ES8. The surface model is shown in Figure 15.146.

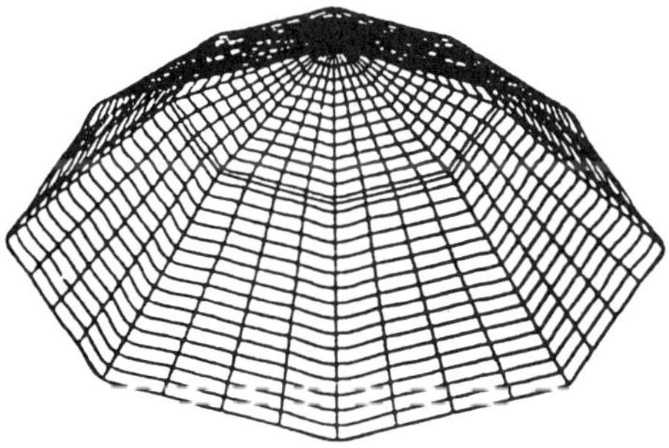

Figure 15.146

33. Use a finish function to generate the toolpaths for the fillet surface model as shown in Figure 15.147. The surface model file is ES14.

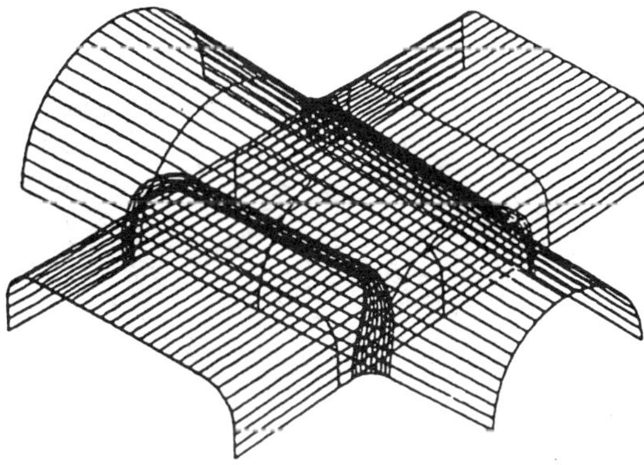

Figure 15.147

34. Use a finish function to generate the toolpaths for the surface model as shown in Figure 15.148. The surface model file is ES15.

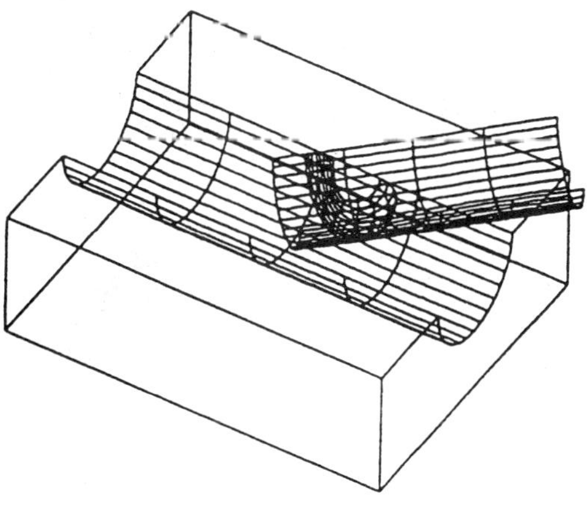

Figure 15.148

35. Use a rough and a finish function to generate the toolpaths for cutting the trimmed surface model as shown in Figure 15.149. The surface model file is ES16.

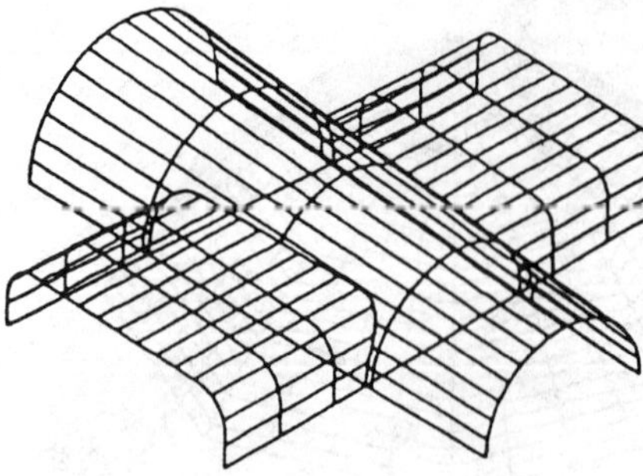

Figure 15.149

36. Use a rough and a finish function to generate the toolpaths for cutting a composite surface model as shown in Figure 15.150. The surface model file is ES19.

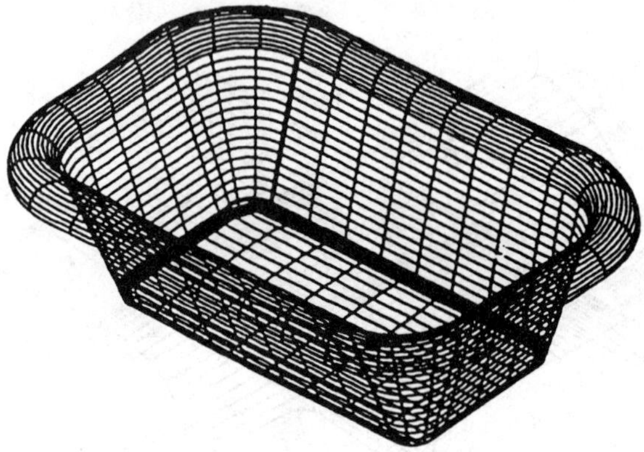

Figure 15.150

37. Generate a set of toolpaths to cut a composite surface model as shown in Figure 15.151. The surface model file is ES20.

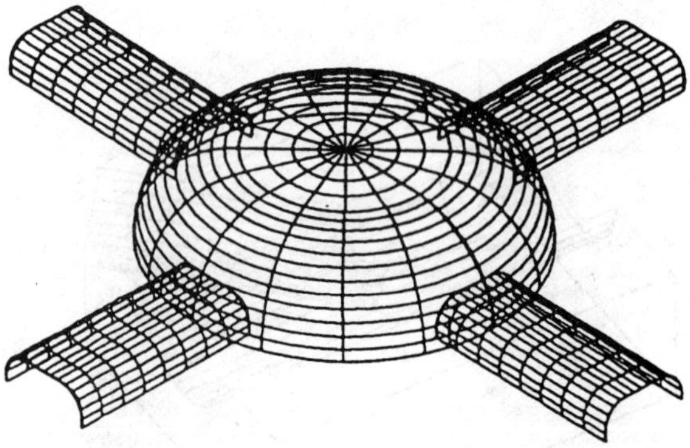

Figure 15.151

Chapter 16

Multiaxis Machining

Objectives:

1. Know four 5-axis toolpath functions.
2. Know rotary 4-axis toolpath function.
3. Apply multiaxis toolpath functions to cut surface models.

Overview

Most machining projects can be done with 3-axis machines. However, 3-axis machines may encounter difficulties or be unable to machine some complicated parts which have features such as slope planes, surfaces, undercuts, or multiple faces. In those cases, a 4-axis or 5-axis machine is more suitable to use. The programming for 4-axis and 5-axis machines is more complicated than 3-axis programming.

Mastercam is capable of generating toolpaths for 4-axis or 5-axis machining. The 4-axis machining has only one function, **Rotary 4-axis**. There are four 5-axis machining functions including **Curve 5-axis, Drill 5-axis, Swarf 5-axis**, and **Flowline 5-axis**. These multiaxis toolpath functions are used to generate toolpaths for cutting a surface model. This chapter presents these five multiaxis toolpath functions for cutting surfaces. The working principles and defining parameters of each function are covered. These are followed by several projects with step-by-step instructions.

16.1 Rotary Axes and Directions

The Electronic Industries Association has established a CNC machine axes identification standard, **EIA-267-B**. This standard defines 14 different axes, including 9 linear axes and 5 rotary axes, to describe all CNC machines, from simple to complex types. The linear axes on a machine may include 3 primary linear axes, 3 secondary linear axes, and 3 tertiary linear axes. The rotary axes may include 3 primary rotary axes and 2 secondary rotary axes. However, most CNC machines require only 3 linear axes. Some machines have one or two rotary axes in addition to the three linear axes.

Three primary rotary axes designated by the characters A, B, and C are used to indicate rotary motions about the X, Y, and Z axes, respectively in Figure 16.1. Rotary motion about the X axis is labeled with an A; rotary motion about the Y axis with B; and rotary motion about the Z axis with C.

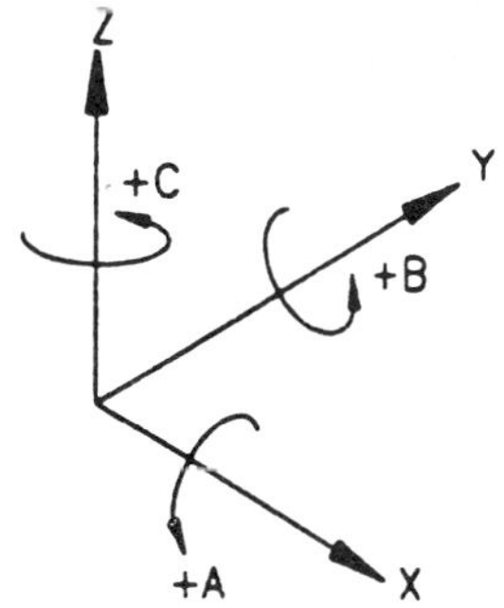

Figure 16.1

The thumb rule is used to determine the direction of the rotation. For example, with the thumb of the right hand pointing in the direction of the positive X axis, the four fingers will curl in the positive direction of the rotary A axis.

16.2 4-Axis and 5-Axis Machines

4th and 5th axis control can be implemented either on the machine tables or the spindle heads. Rotary indexing tables are common devices used to position the 4th and 5th axis on machine tables. The machine table is still controlled by three primary linear axes; X, Y, and Z. The indexing table provides 4th or 5th -axis positioning control. Figure 16.2 shows two examples using 4-axis positioning on a machine table. Figure 16.3 illustrates 5-axis machining. Rotary axes can be applied to the spindle head of machines (Figure 16.4). Profilers are the typical machines of this category.

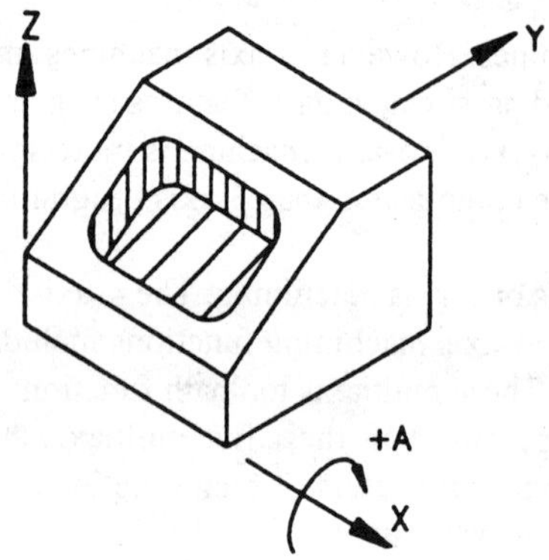

Figure 16.2a

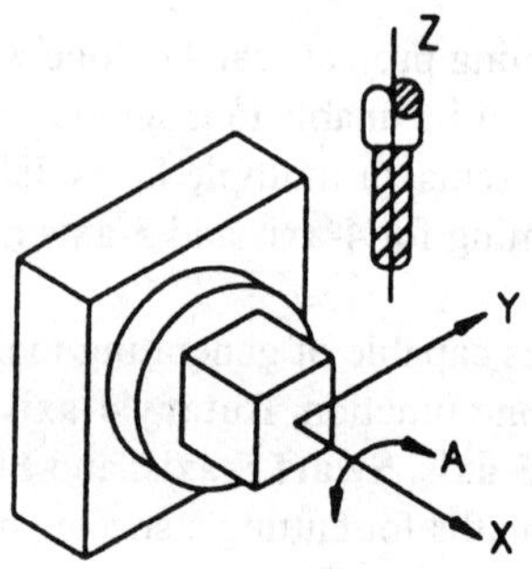

Figure 16.2b

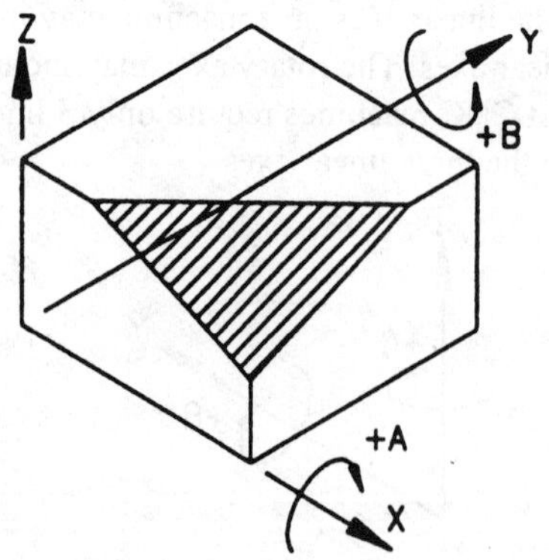

Figure 16.3

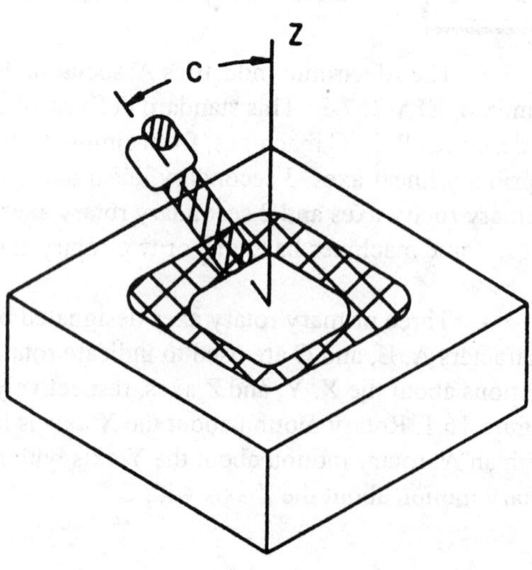

Figure 16.4

16.3 Part Features for 4th and 5th Axis Machining

A part feature is the distinctive geometric form or shape being produced from raw material. Typical part features include holes, slots, pockets, shoulders, profiles, angles, threads and surfaces. Those features that are defined in the XY-plane normally can be machined by 3-axis machines. Those features that are not lying in the XY-plane normally require using a 4- or 5-axis machine depending on the orientation of plane normal. Figure 16.5 shows an example of 4-axis machining and Figure 16.6 is an example of 5-axis machining.

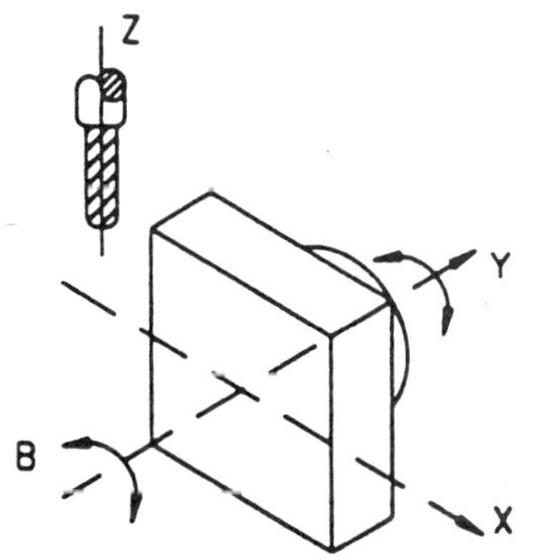

Figure 16.5

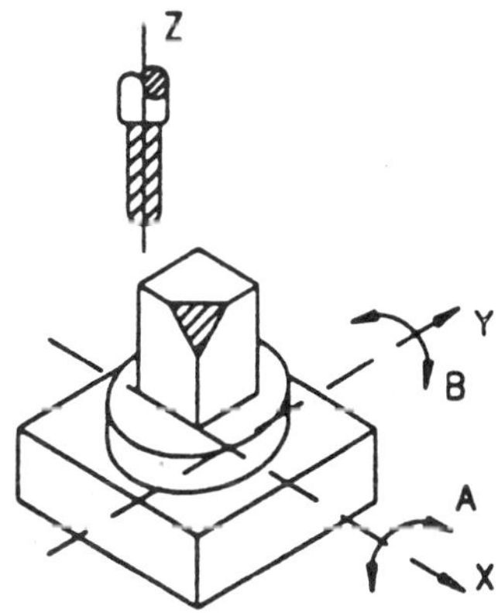

Figure 16.6

16.4 Rotary 4-Axis Function

The rotary 4-axis function generates toolpaths for cutting a surface model in a 4-axis CNC machine (Figure 16.7). Multiple-surface model can be used in rotary 4-axis function for generating toolpaths simultaneously (Figure 16.8). The rotary 4-axis parameter dialog box appears as below.

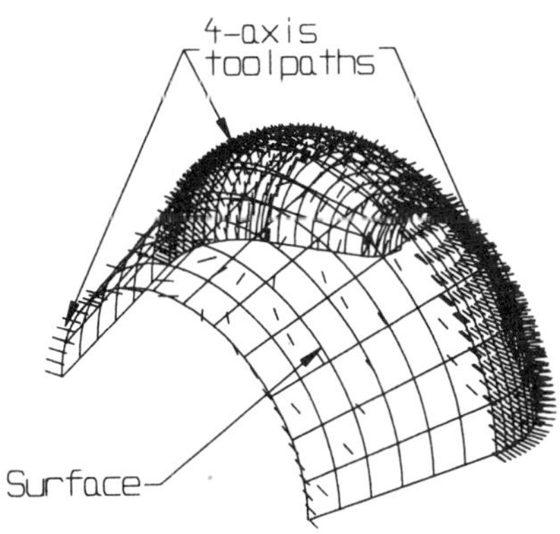

Figure 16.7

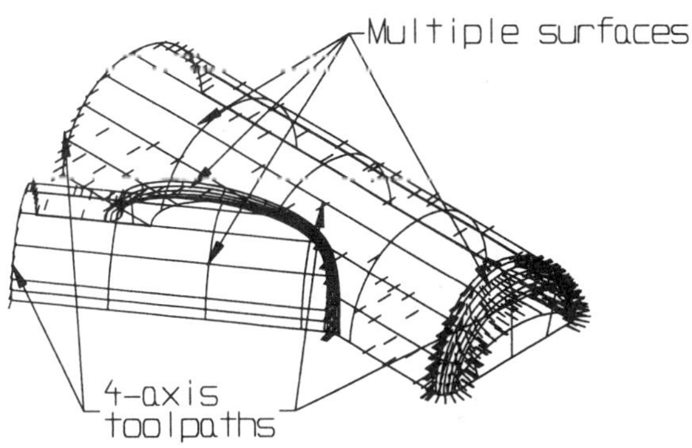

Figure 16.8

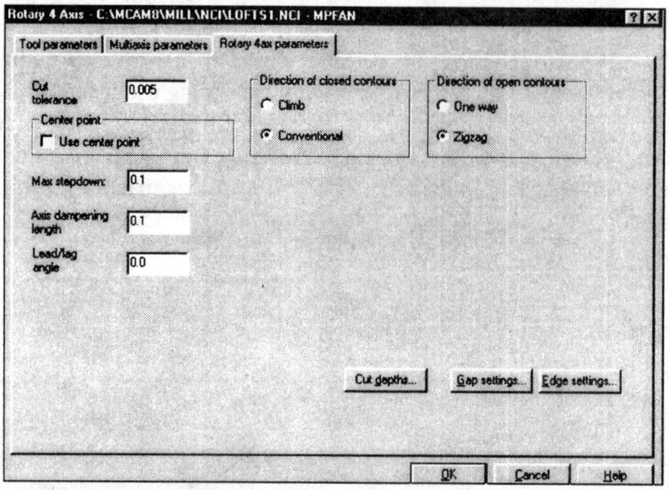

Three parameters that are unique to this toolpath function include: **Use center point, Axis dampening length,** and **Lead/lag angle**.

Use center point

This parameter uses a point at the center of the part to orient the tool axis (Figure 16.9). Mastercam will output the tool axis relative to the center point. When this parameter is set to **Off** (no check mark), the system will output the tool axis relative to the surface.

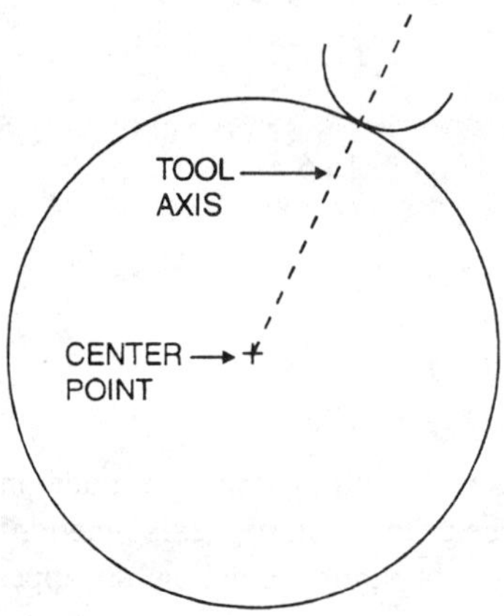

Figure 16.9

Maximum stepdown

This parameter specifies the maximum distance between two adjacent cuts in the Z-direction.

Axis dampening length

This parameter decides the position of the tool axis based on the given length along the surface of the part. This parameter becomes available only when the "Use center point" parameter is set to Off. A shorter dampening length produces more tool movement and a toolpath that adheres closely to the surface. A longer length provides less tool movement. Figure 16.10 shows the effect of axis dampening length on the toolpaths.

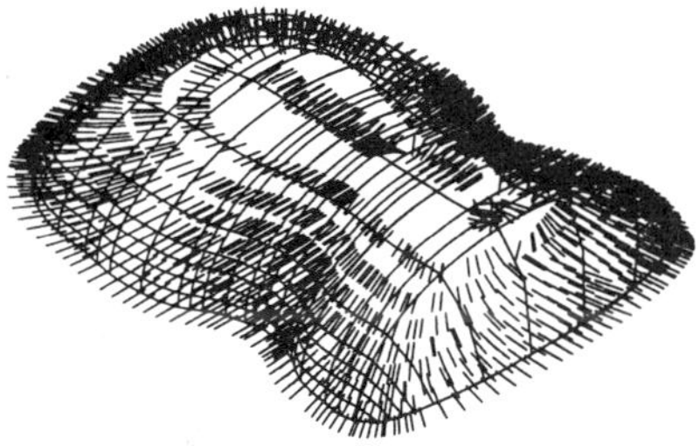

Figure 16.10a Axis dampening length = 1.0

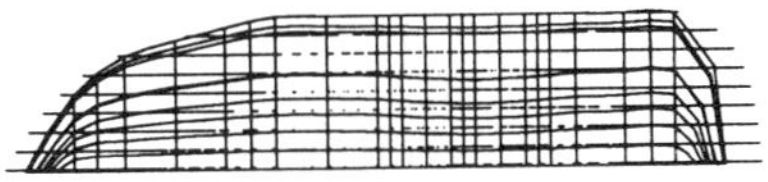

Figure 16.10b Axis dampening length = 1.0

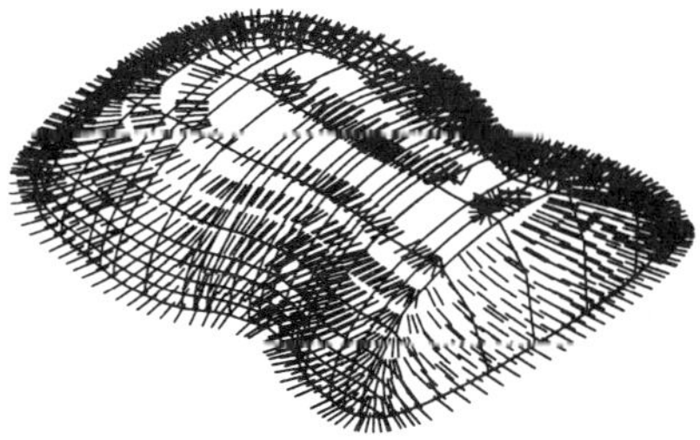

Figure 16.10c Axis dampening length = 0.1

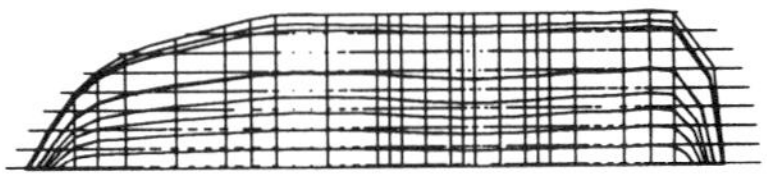

Figure 16.10d Axis dampening length = 0.1

Lead/lag angle

The "lead/lag angle" parameter specifies the relationship between tool axis and surface by an angle value. This angle can be the lead angle or lag angle. The lead angle is defined as the angle at which the tool passes over the part measured from the surface normal to the shank of the tool (Figure 16.11).

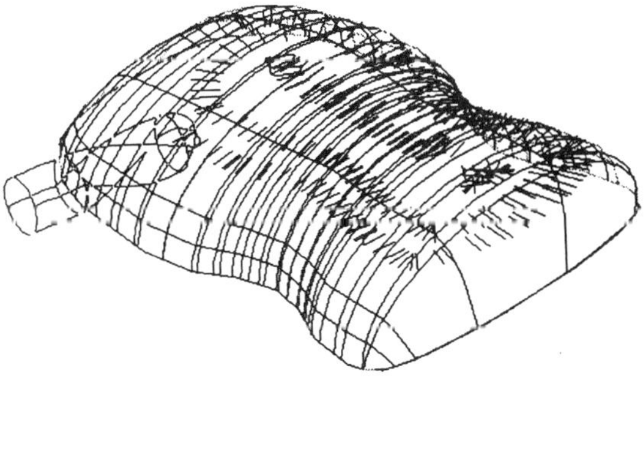

Figure 16.11a Lead angle = 0

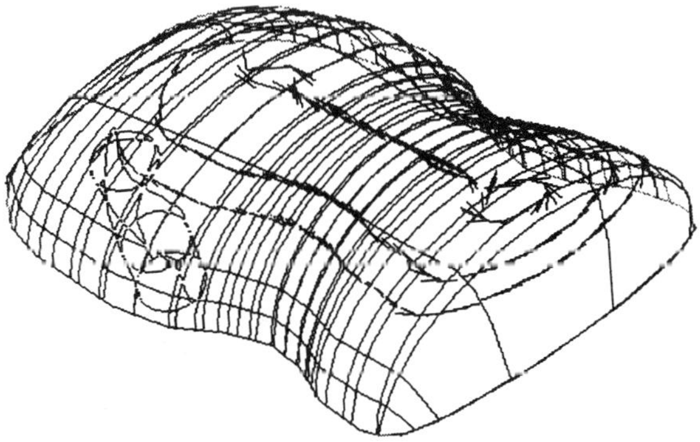

Figure 16.11b Lead angle = 30°

💻 Project 1. Using rotary 4-axis function to cut a single-surface model

This project shows how to create a set of rotary 4-axis toolpaths to cut a single-surface model. The loft surface to be used and its 4-axis toolpath are shown in Figure 16.12.

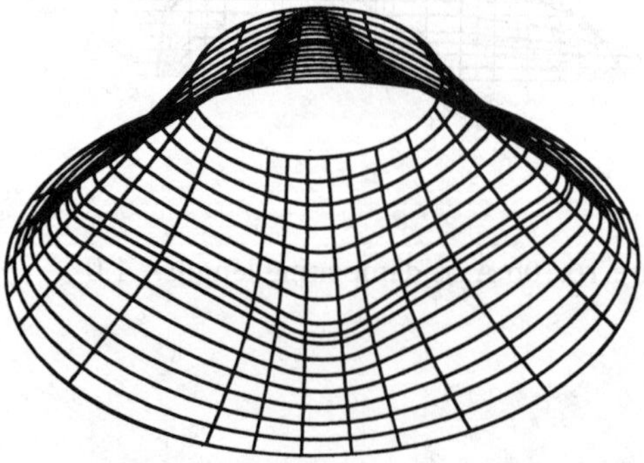

Figure 16.12a

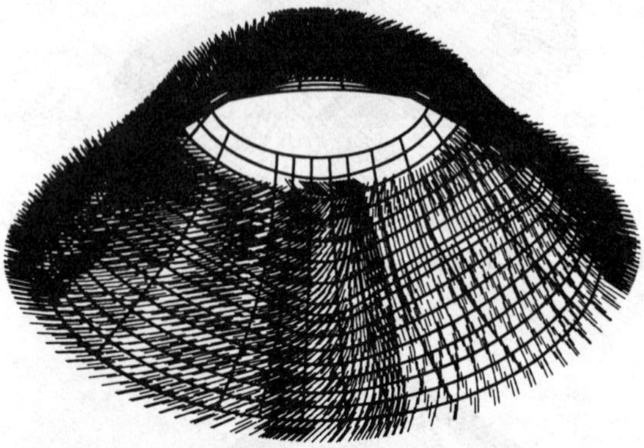

Figure 16.12b

⌛**Tips**	1. Use the surface model file lofts1.
	2. Use the rotary 4-axis function to generate toolpaths.
	3. Use a ½" sphere end mill.

Step 1. Open the surface model file lofts1.

Select **MAIN MENU → File → Get**
File name: **lofts1** ↵
The loft surface appears as in Figure 16.13.

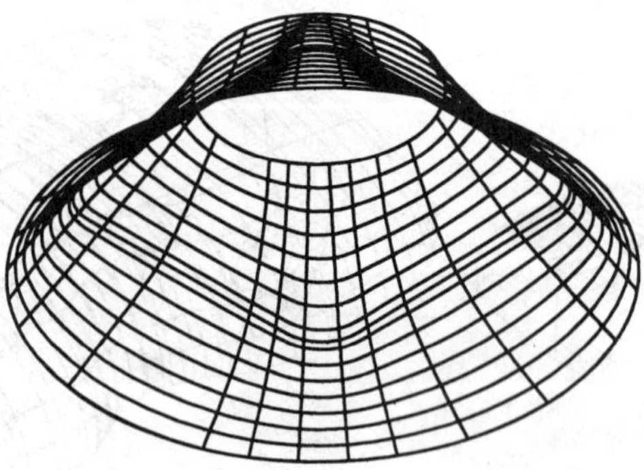

Figure 16.13

Step 2. Initiate the rotary 4-axis function.

Select **MAIN MENU → Toolpaths → Multiaxis → Rotary4ax**
Select output NCI file: **4ax1** ↵

Pick the loft surface, then select **Done**
Click the right mouse button, then select **Get tool from library**
Select **tool number 256** (1/2 sphere endmill)
Select **OK**
Set the Tool parameters menu as shown next.

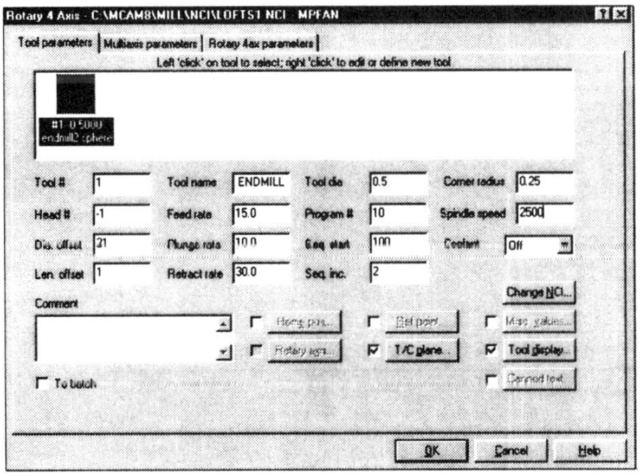

Step 3. Define the multiaxis parameters.

Click the **Multiaxis parameters** tab.
Set the multiaxis parameters as below.

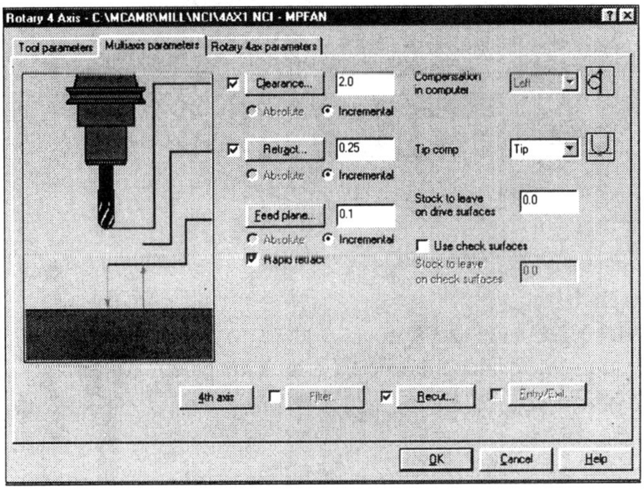

Step 4. Define the rotary 4ax parameters.

Click on the **Rotary 4ax parameters** tab.

Set the rotary 4ax parameters as below.

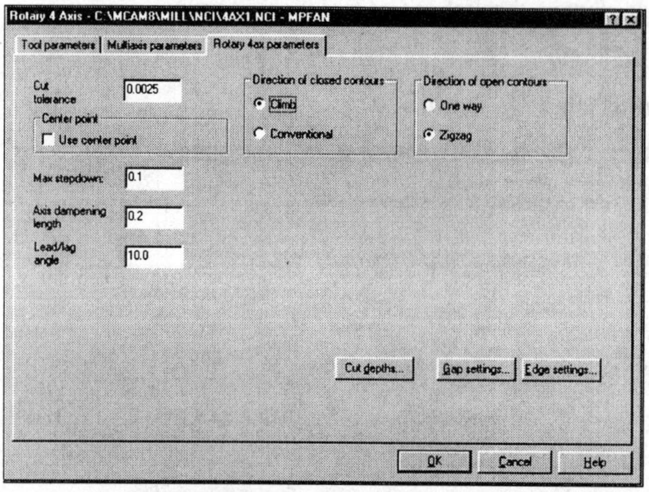

Select **OK** to generate toolpaths

The 4-axis toolpaths are generated as shown in Figure 16.14.

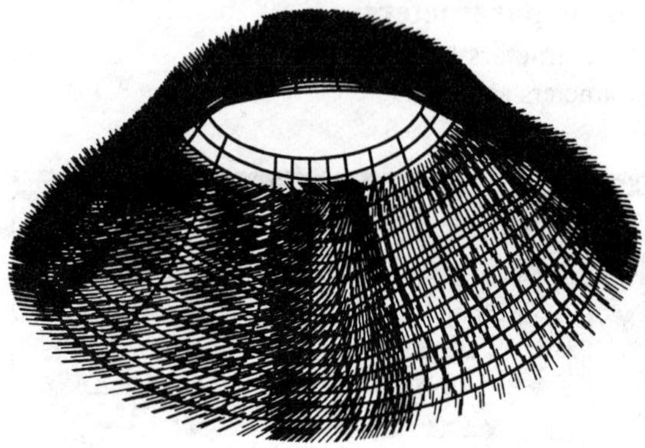

Figure 16.14

Step 5. Save the toolpath file.

Select **MAIN MENU → NC utils → Filter**

Select **Yes** to "Operations have been modified. Created the NCI text file?"

Select **Do it → Cancel**

Project 2. Using rotary 4-axis function for a multiple-surface model 2

This project use rotary 4-axis function to generate toolpaths for cutting the dryer surface model. Figure 16.15 shows both surface model and toolpaths.

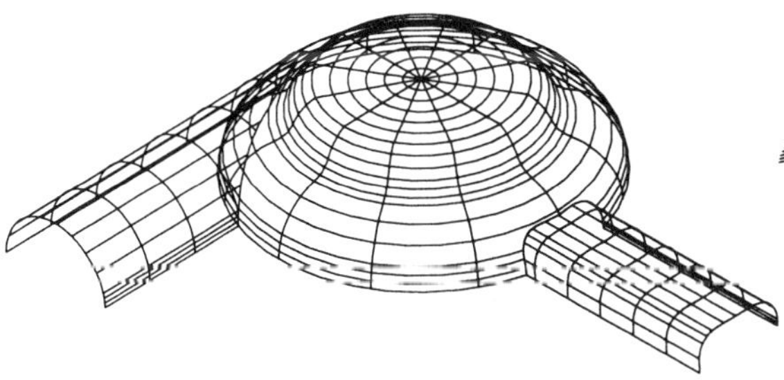

Figure 16.15a

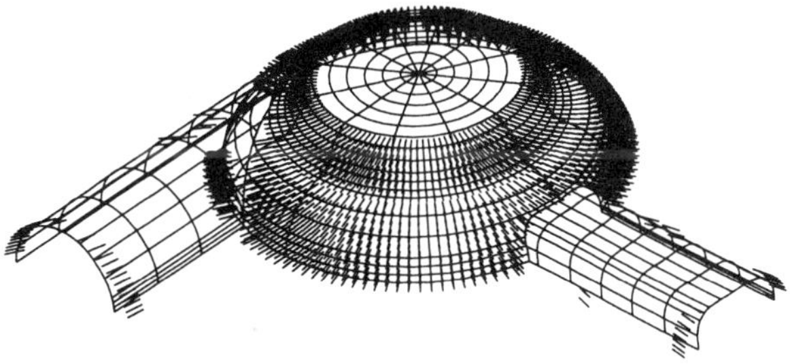

Figure 16.15b

Tips	1. Use the surface model file dryers.
	2. Use the rotary 4-axis function to generate toolpaths.
	3. Use a 3/8" sphere end mill.

Step 1. Open the surface model file dryers.

Select **MAIN MENU → File → Get**
File name: **dryers** ↵
The surface model appears as Figure 16.16.

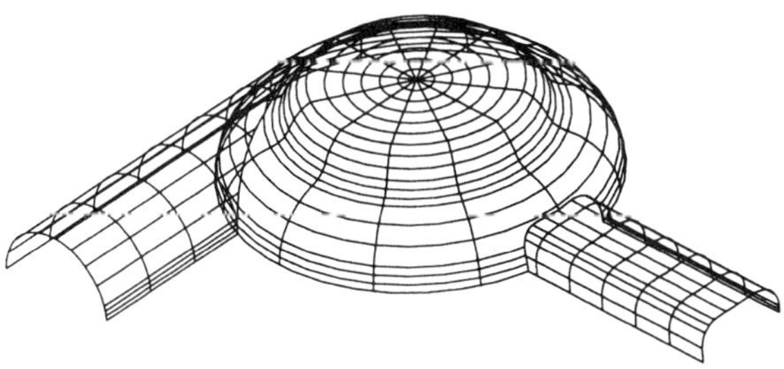

Figure 16.16

Step 2. Initiate the rotary 4-axis function.

Select **MAIN MENU → Toolpaths → Multiaxis → Rotary4ax**
File name for NCI file: **4ax2** ↵
Select **All → Surfaces → Done**
Click the right mouse button, then select **Get tool from library**
Select **tool number 254** (3/8 sphere endmill)
Select **OK**

Set the Tool parameters as below.

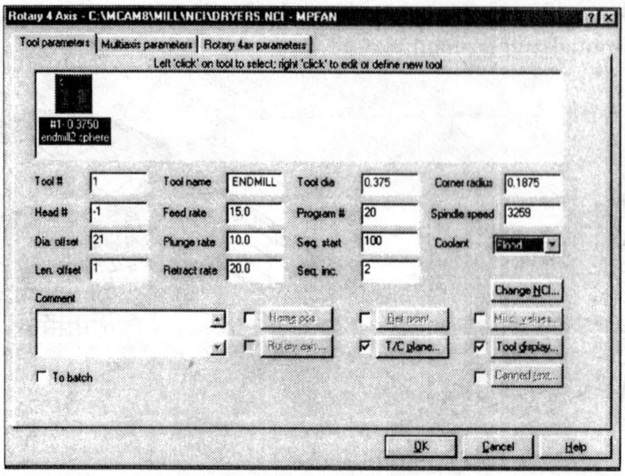

Step 3. Define the multiaxis parameters.

Click on the **Multiaxis parameters** tab.

Set the multiaxis parameters as below.

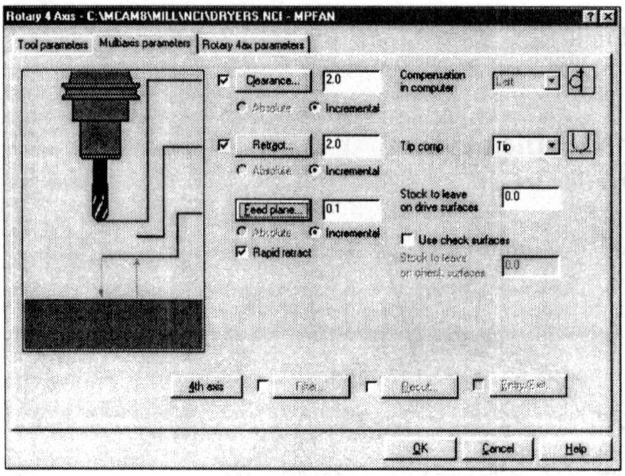

Step 4. Define the rotary 4-axis parameters.

Click on the **Rotary 4ax parameters** tab.

Set the rotary 4-axis parameters as below.

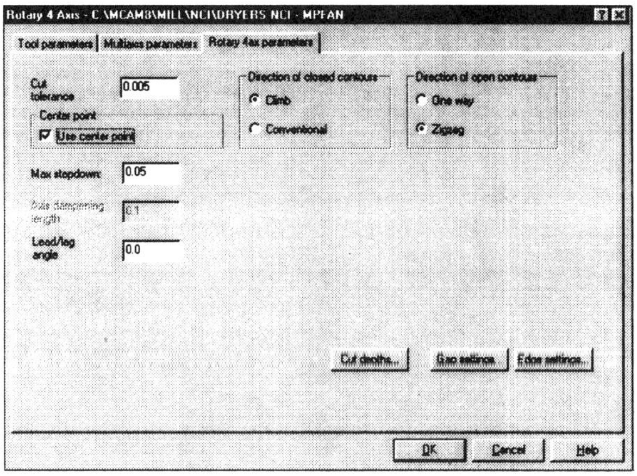

Select **OK**
Enter an approximate starting point: **0,0,0**
The 4-axis rotary toolpaths are generated as in Figure 16.17.

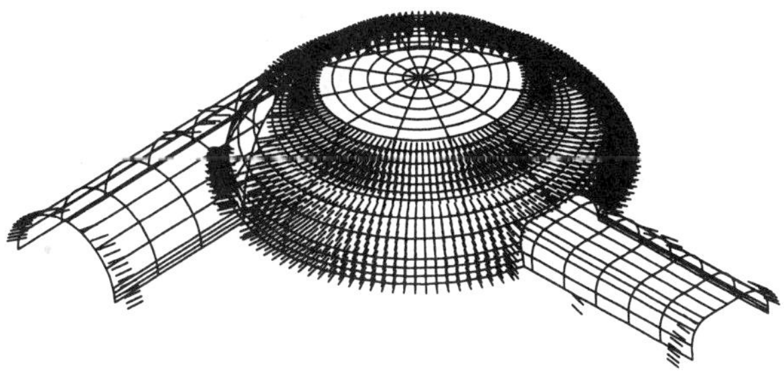

Figure 16.17

Step 5. Save the toolpath file.

Select **MAIN MENU → NC utils → Filter**
Select **Yes** to "Operations have been modified. Created the NCI text file?"
Select **Do it → Cancel**

16.5 5-Axis Toolpath Functions

There are four 5-axis toolpath functions. They are summarized in Table 16.1.

Table 16.1 Four 5-axis toolpath functions

Function	Description	Illustration
Curve5ax	Generate 5-axis toolpaths along surface edges, chained curves, or surface curves.	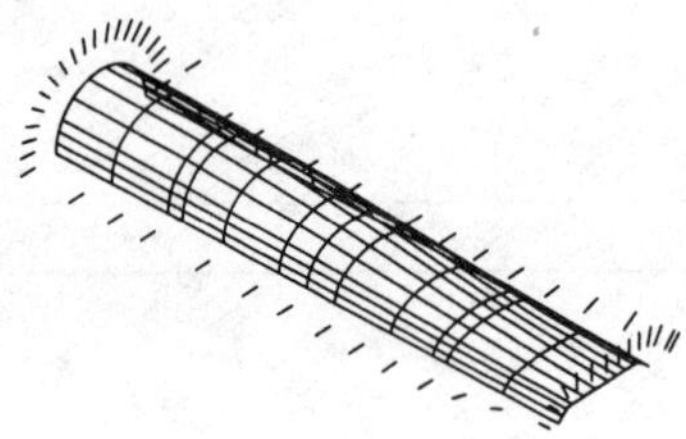
Drill5ax	Generate 5-axis drilling toolpaths that run in a specified direction and depth.	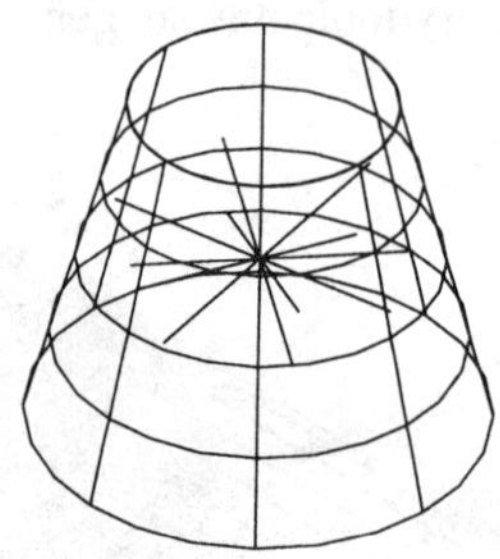
Swarf5ax	Generate 5-axis toolpaths for cutting a surface with the side of the tool.	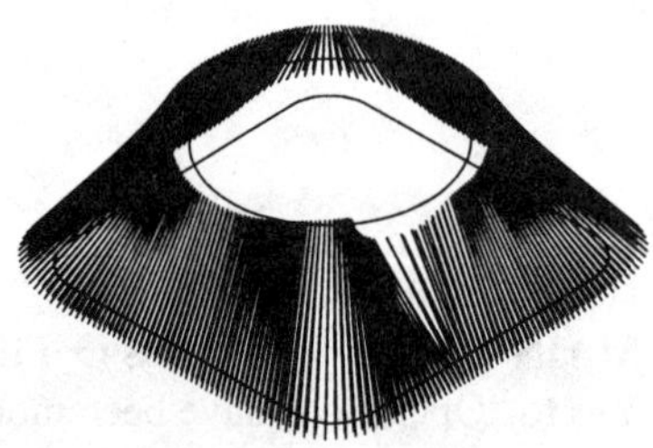
Flow5ax	Generate 5-axis toolpaths for cutting over the entire surface model.	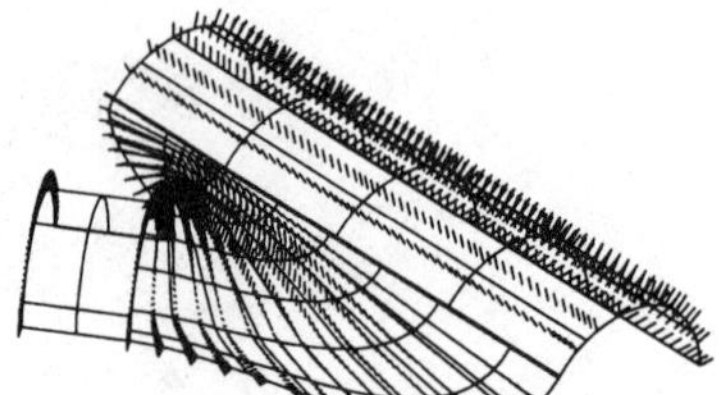

16.6 Curve 5-Axis Common Parameters

There are several aspects to consider when selecting geometry for curve 5-axis toolpaths. The output format, curve type, tool axis control, and tip control can all affect the resulting toolpath. Those parameters are grouped under the Curve 5-axis dialog box as shown below.

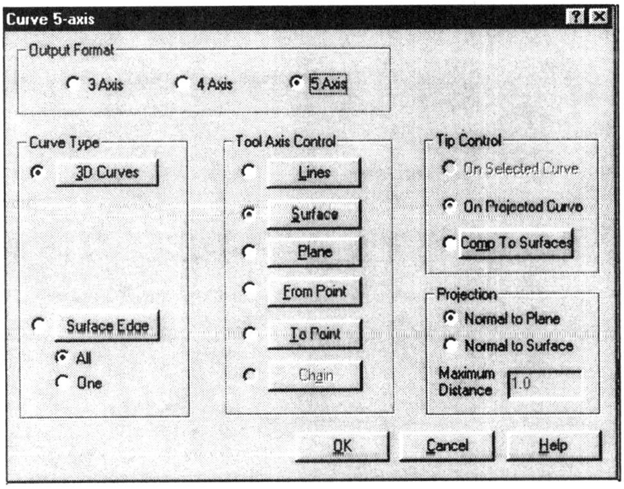

Output Format

This parameter selects the toolpath format for defining the direction vectors and coordinate values of toolpaths. It has the following three options:

3-axis: This option limits the tool positions to a single vector or direction. This output type drags the contact point of the tool over the selected curves. The 3-axis toolpath always has its tool axis perpendicular to the Cplane (Figure 16.18a).

4-axis: This option generates toolpaths for three linear axes (X, Y, Z) and one rotary axis (C). The tool vector are created parallel to a plane that is perpendicular to the rotary axis (Figure 16.18b).

5-axis: This option generates toolpaths for three linear axes (X, Y, Z) and two rotary axes that can be in any direction (Figure 16.18c).

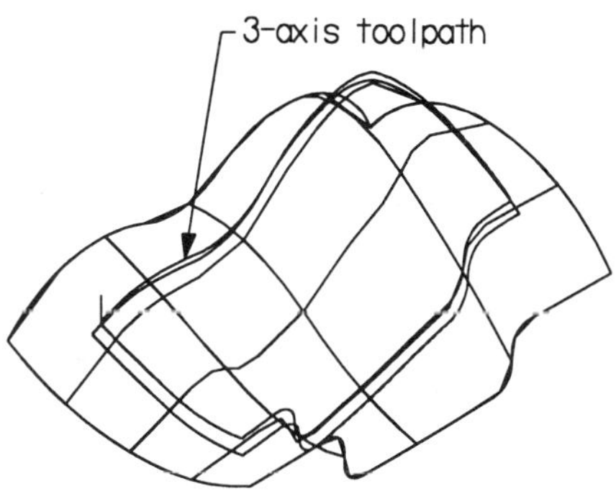

Figure 16.18a

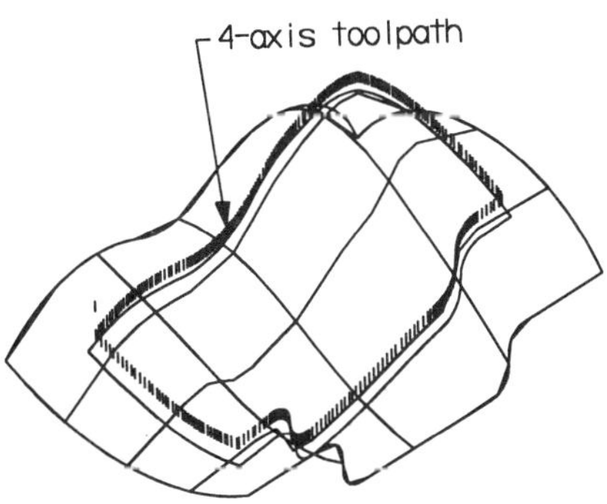

Figure 16.18b

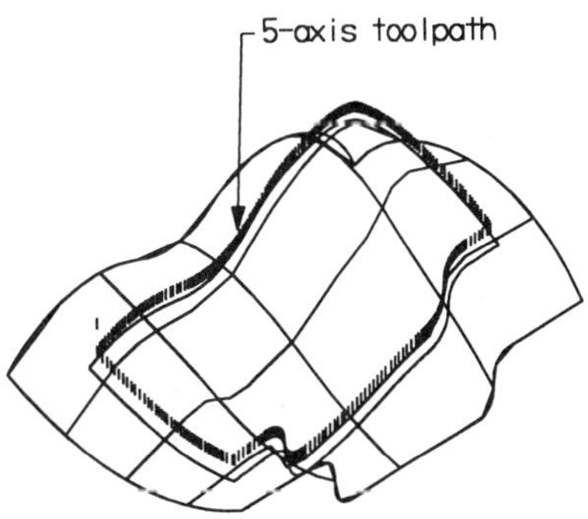

Figure 16.18c

Curve type

This parameter selects the toolpaths generated either from 3D curves or from surface edge.

3D curves:	generates toolpaths along all selected 3D curves (Figure 16.19a).
Surface edges:	(A) All edges: generates toolpaths along all surface edges (Figure 16.19b). (B) One edge: generates toolpaths along one selected surface edge (Figure 16.19c).

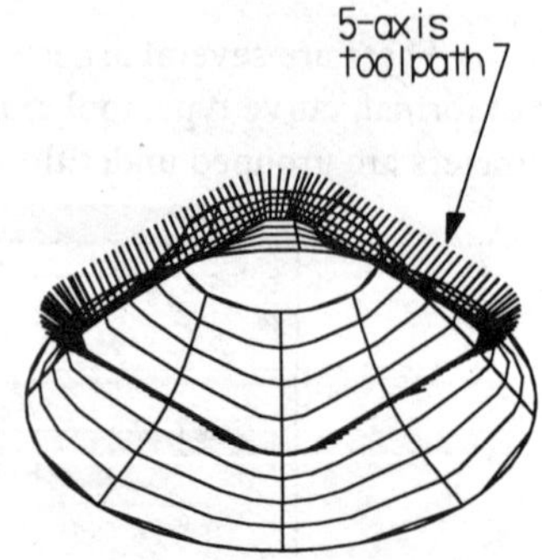

Figure 16.19a

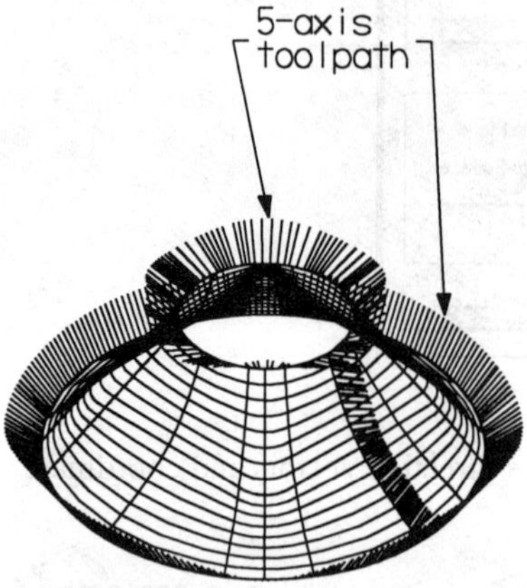

Figure 16.19b

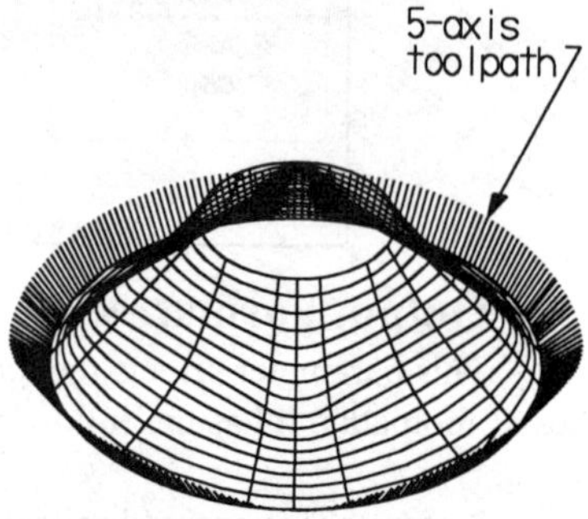

Figure 16.19c

Tool axis control

The tool axis control parameter determines how the tool adjusts its axis along the toolpath. It has the following **six** options:

Lines:	tool axes are always aligned with selected lines. The transition type between selected line directions must be specified if using more than one line.
Surface:	the tool axis is set to the normals of the selected surface.
Plane:	the tool axis is kept constant to a selected plane or entity.
From point:	the tool axis is always aimed from and passed from a selected point.
To point:	the tool axis is always aimed to and passed through a selected point.
Chain:	not available yet.

Tip Control

This parameter specifies how to control the tool tip. It has the following **three** options:

On selected curve:	the tool tip always lies on the selected curves.
On projected curve:	the tool tip is always in contact with the projected curves.
Comp to surface:	the tool tip is offset to the specified side of the surfaces.

Projection

The following are two ways to project chained entities onto the surface(s):

Normal to plane:	the chained 3D curves are projected in the direction perpendicular to the current construction plane.
Normal to surface:	the chained 3D curves are projected in the direction perpendicular to the surface.

The Curve 5ax Parameters

These parameters are used to control the position of the tool and accuracy of the tool motion during a curve 5-axis toolpath. The Curve5ax parameters tab is available after selecting geometry for the curve 5-axis toolpath.

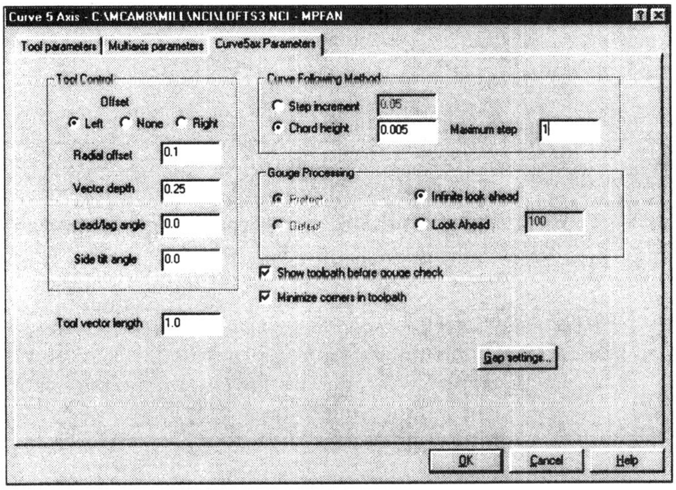

Tool Control

Offset direction This group of parameters are used to define the offset value and direction of the toolpaths. The Offset Direction parameters are used to set the direction for the toolpath offset from the surface edges, surface curves, or projected curves. This parameter can be set to one of the following three options (Figure 16.20).

None:	the tool lies on the surface edges, surface curves, or projected curves (Figure 16.20a)
Left:	the tool is offset from the left side by a given distance based on the toolpath direction(Figure 16.20b).
Right:	the tool is offset from the right side by a given distance based on the toolpath direction (Figure 16.20c).

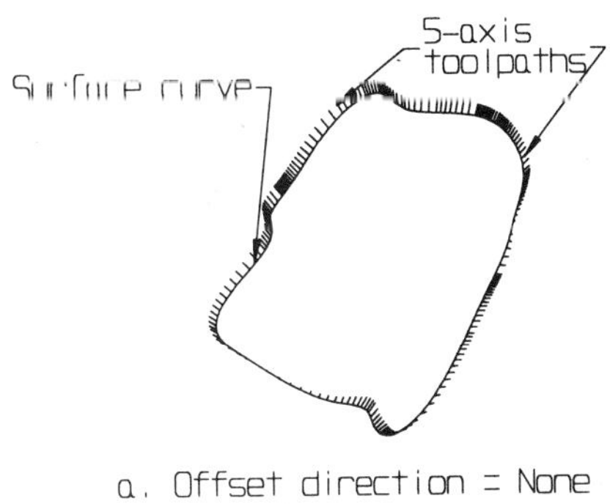

Figure 16.20a Offset direction = None

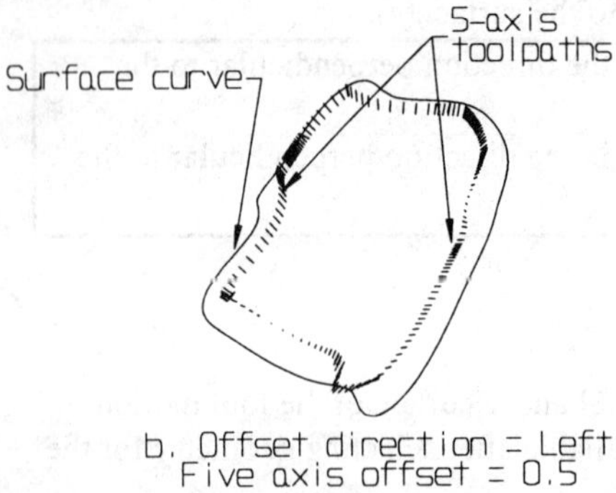

Figure 16.20b Offset direction = Left
Five axis offset = 0.5

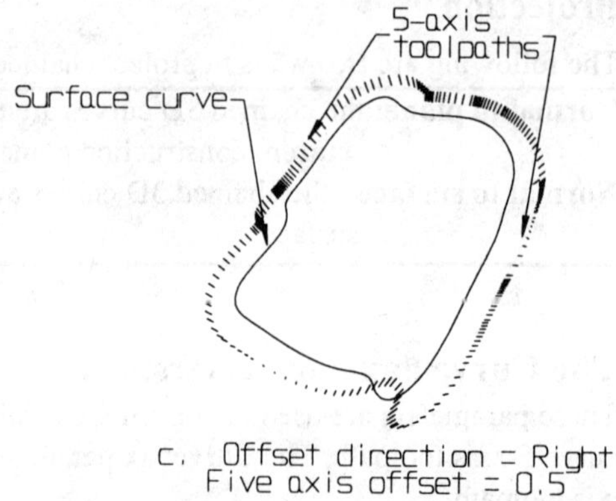

Figure 16.20c Offset direction = Right
Five axis offset = 0.5

Offset distances

Offset and depth: The cutter can be offset in two directions: XY-plane and Z-direction. Mastercam uses the "**Radial offset**" parameter to specify the offset value in the XY-plane and "**Vector angle**" parameter to specify the offset value in the Z-direction.

Side tilt angle and lead/lag angle: Two angle parameters also offset the tool axis orientation. The side tilt angle tilts the tool axis to the right or left by a given angle. A positive angle tilts the tool axis to the left and a negative angle tilts it to the right (Figure 16.21).

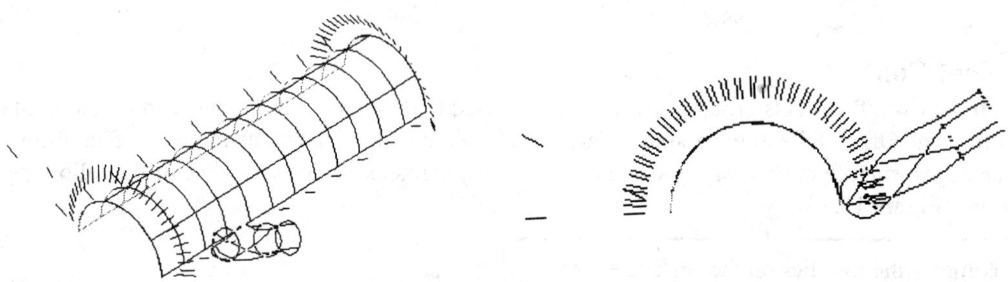

Figure 16.21a. Side tilt angle = 30°

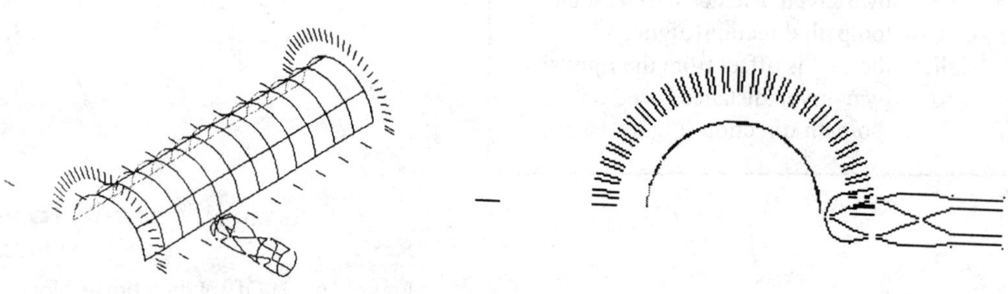

Figure 16.21b. Side tilt angle = 0°

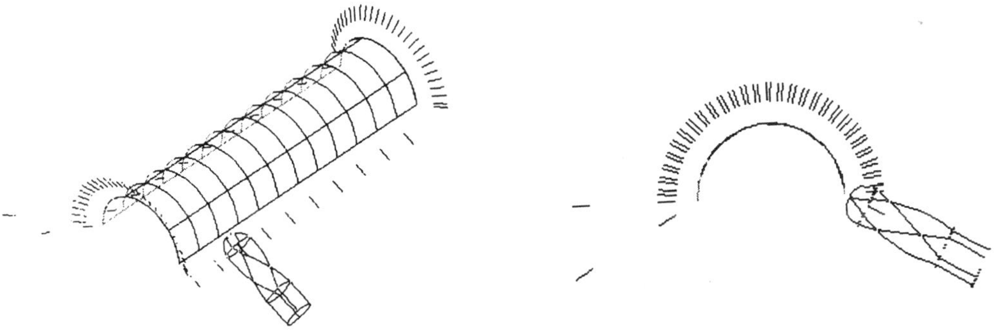

Figure 16.21c. Side tilt angle = -30°

The lead/lag angle tilts the tool to the front or back. A positive lead/lag angle tilts the top of the tool forward and a negative angle tilts it backward (Figure 16.22).

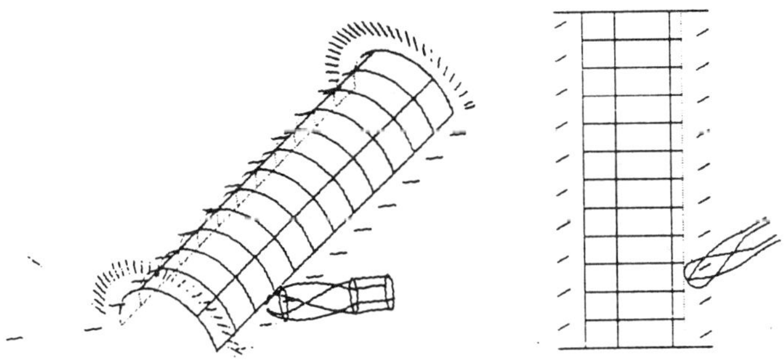

Figure 16.22a. Lead/lag angle = 30°

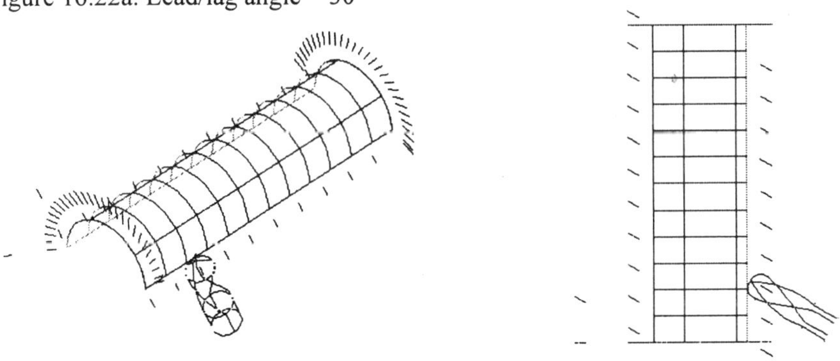

Figure 16.22b. Lead/lag angle = 0°

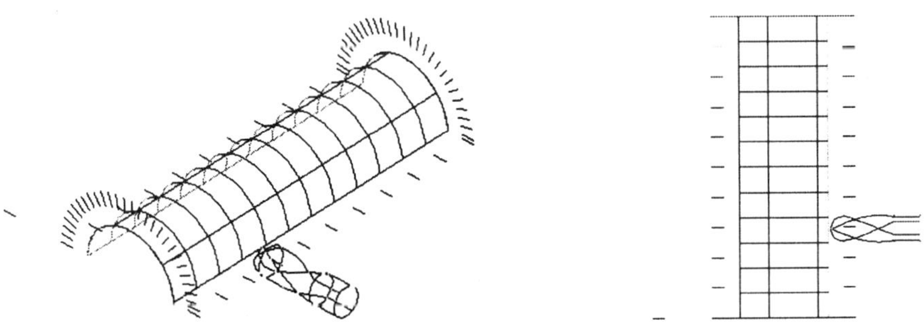

Figure 16.22c. Lead/lag angle = -30°

Curve Following Method

Mastercam uses two methods to determine the stepping distance along the cutting surface curves: **step increment** and **chord height**. With the step increment method, the cutter advances a given distance for each of the toolpath segments disregarding the tolerance of the toolpath. This method is often used for surfaces that are relatively flat and simple.

Using the chord height method, a cutter move is determined by the following two parameters:

Chord height:	specifies the maximum distance that the toolpath can deviate from the surface.
Maximum step:	specifies the maximum distance between toolpath segments.

Gouge Processing

The gouge check feature in the Curve 5-Axis functions only checks for gouges on the offset toolpath. It will not check for those non-offset toolpaths. This parameter can be set to one of the following four options:

Protect:	protects the selected surfaces while checking gouges.
Default:	use the default setting for checking gouges.
Infinite look ahead:	evaluates the entire toolpath when looking for gouges.
Look ahead:	evaluates a given number of toolpath moves ahead while looking for gouges.

Show toolpath before gouge check

This instructs Mastercam to show the toolpath before making any gouge check changes.

Minimize corners in toolpath

Selecting this option to remove the toolpath move immediately before and the toolpath move immediately after a corner in a toolpath that is offset to the outside.

Project 3. 5-axis outer edge toolpaths

This project generates the toolpaths to machine the outer edge of a loft surface. Both 5-axis and 3-axis toolpath modes are used, respectively (Figure 16.23).

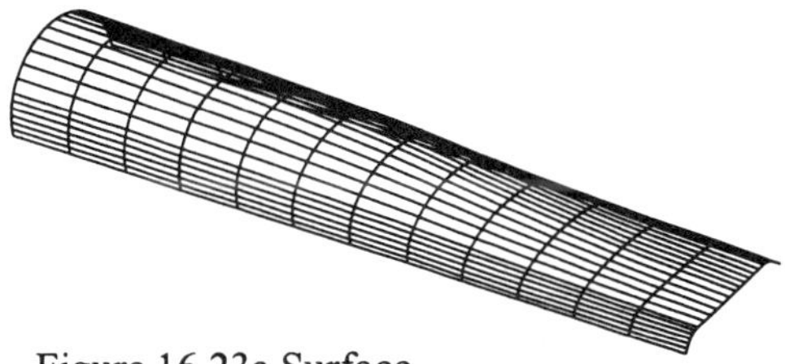

Figure 16.23a Surface

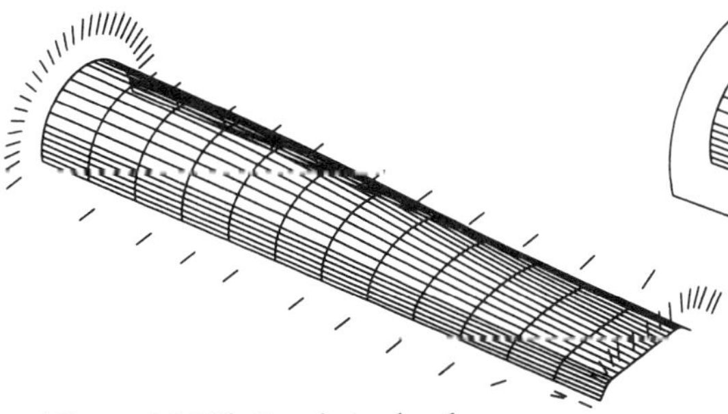

Figure 16.23b 5-axis toolpath

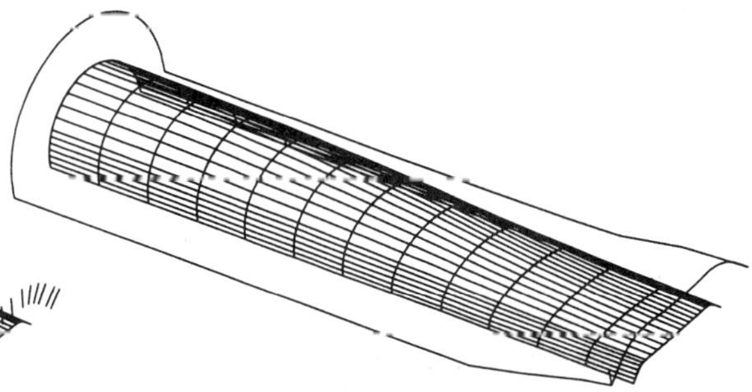

Figure 16.23c 3-axis toolpath

Tips 1. Use the loft surface file lofts3.

2. Save the 5-axis outer edge toolpath file as 5oe.

3. Save the 3-axis outer edge toolpath file as 3oe.

Step 1. Open the surface model file lofts3.

Select **MAIN MENU → File → Get**
File name: **lofts3** ↵
The drawing of lofts3 will appear as Figure 16.24.

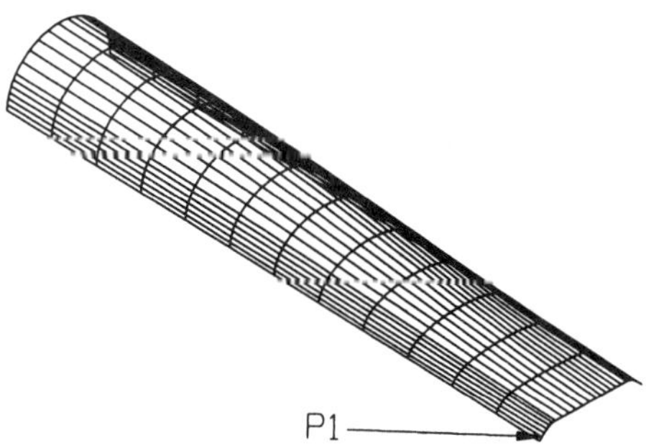

Figure 16.24

Step 2. Initiate the curve 5-axis function. Use the pick point in Figure 16.24.

Select **Cplane → Top**
Select **MAIN MENU → Toolpaths → Multiaxis → Curve5ax**

Set the Curve 5-axis parameters as below.

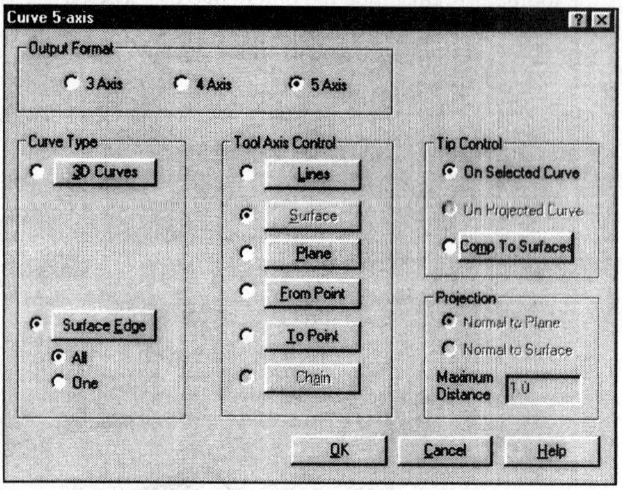

Select **OK**

Select Tool Axis Surface(s): pick any **point** on the surface to select it

Select **Done**

Move the cursor to the left-front corner and click **P1** as shown in Figure 16.24

The direction arrow should point toward the +Y direction on the screen, otherwise select **Flip** to change it

Select **OK** to accept this default direction.

Step 3. Define the tool parameters.

Set the tool parameters as below.

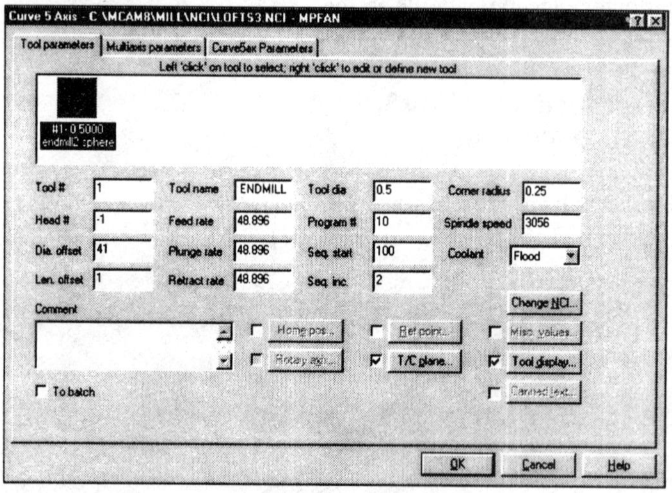

Step 4. Define the Multiaxis parameters.

Click the **"Multiaxis parameters"** tab

Set the multiaxis parameters as below.

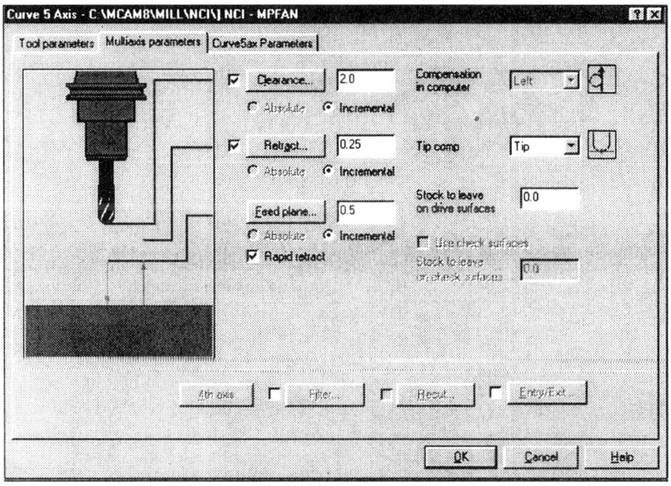

Step 5. Define the curve5ax parameters.

Click the **"Curve5ax Parameters"** button

Set the curve5ax parameters as below.

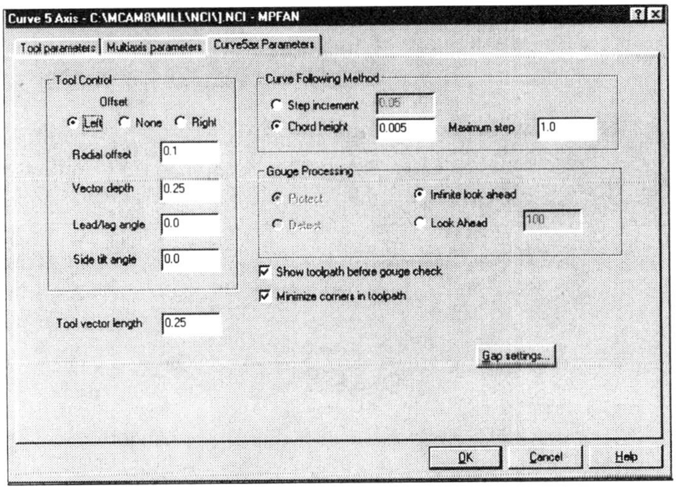

Select **OK**

The toolpaths are generated as in Figure 16.25.

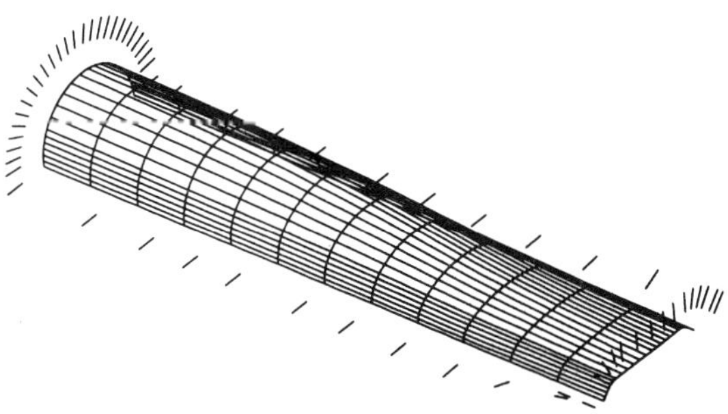

Figure 16.25

Step 6. Save the toolpath file.

Select **MAIN MENU → NC utils → Filter**

Select **Yes** to "Operations have been modified. Create the NCI text file?"

Select **Do it → Cancel**

Step 7. Generate the surface outer edge toolpath for the 3-axis mode.

Follow all procedure steps 1-5 except for step 2. This time, in step 2 set the Curve 5-Axis parameters as shown below.

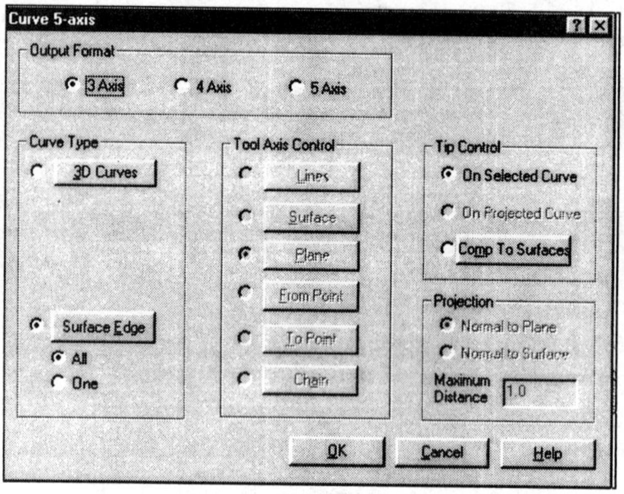

The toolpaths in 3-axis mode will appear as Figure 16.26.

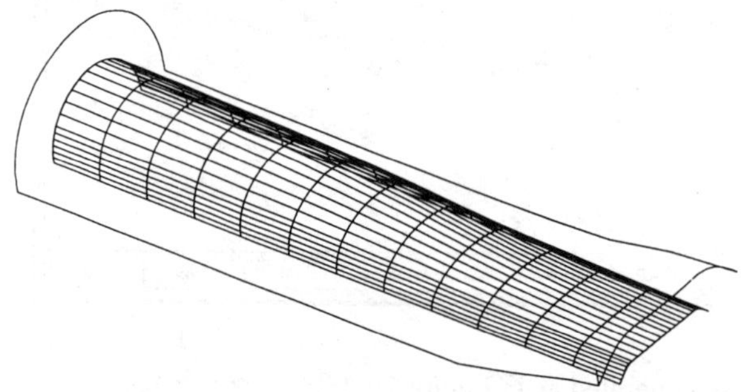

Figure 16.26

Project 4. 5-Axis chain curve

This project generates 5-axis toolpaths to machine a curve that is created by projecting a circle onto a Coons surface. Figure 16.27a shows the surface model and a circle. Figure 16.27b shows the toolpaths generated from projecting the circle onto the surface using the normal to plane method.

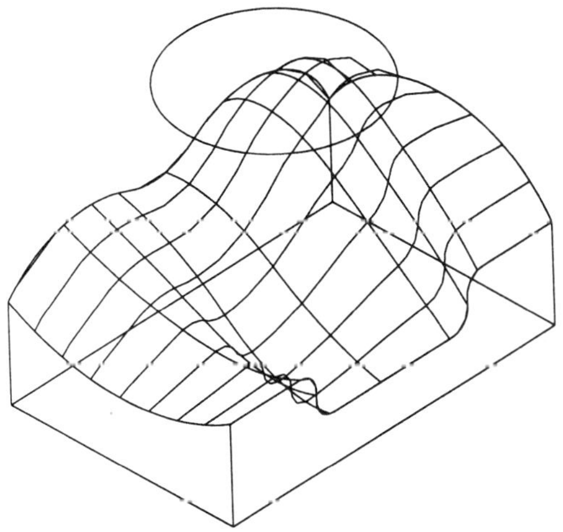

Figure 16.27a Surface and curve

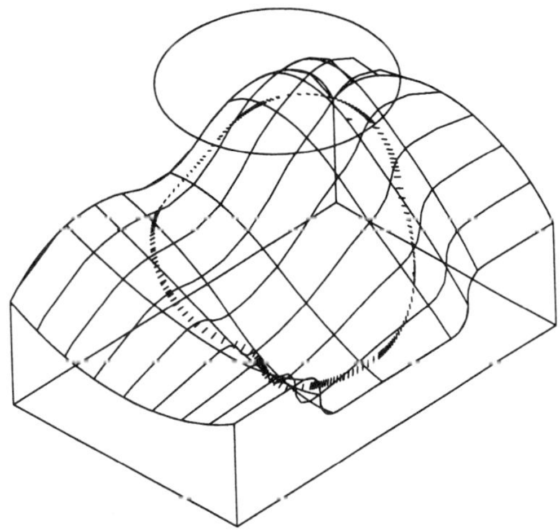

Figure 16.27b Toolpaths

Tips 1. Use the Coons surface file coonss1 as the base surface to be projected onto.

2. Create a circle having its center on (2.5, 3.75) with a diameter of 4" to use as the chain curve.

3. Use the Backplot function to visualize and verify the toolpaths.

Step 1. Open the surface model file coonss1.

Select **MAIN MENU → File → Get**
File name: **coonss1**↵
The Coons surface appears as Figure 16.28.

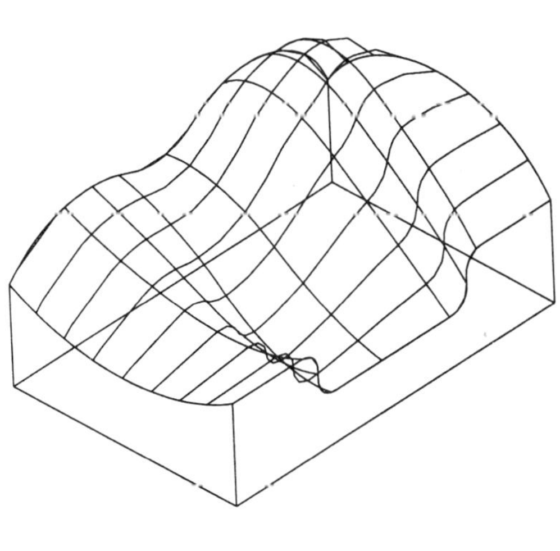

Figure 16.28

Step 2. Create a circle in level 3.

Select **Cplane → Top**
Select **Level**, then enter **3 → OK**
Select **Z**, then enter **3.5** ↵
Select **MAIN MENU → Create → Arc → Cir pt+dia**
Enter the diameter: **4** ↵
Enter coordinates: **2.5, 3.75** ↵
The circle is added as in Figure 16.29.

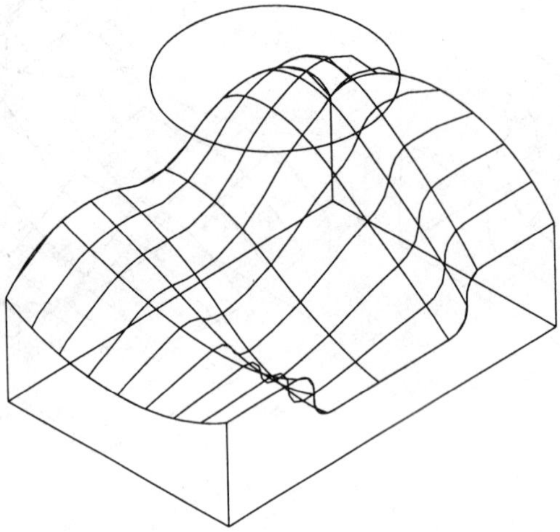

Figure 16.29

Step 3. Initiate the Curve 5-axis function.

Select **MAIN MENU → Toolpaths → Multiaxis → Curve5ax**
File name for NCI: **5cc** ↵
Set the Curve 5-axis parameters as below.

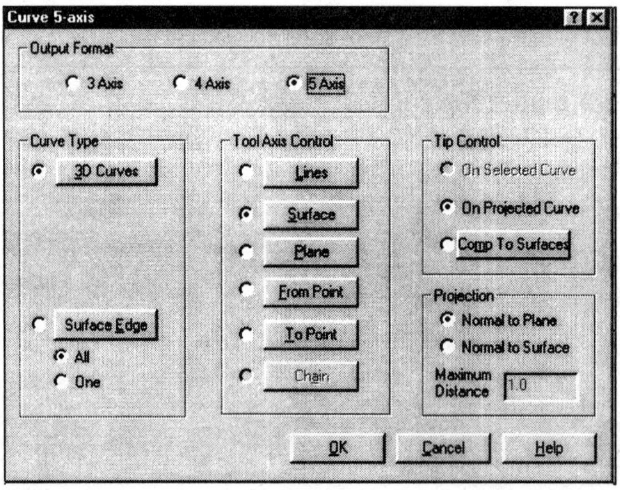

Select **OK**
Set Tool Axis Surface(s): pick any point on the Coons surface
Select **Done**
Select Chain boundaries1: pick the circle as the boundary
Select **Done**

Step 4. Define the tool parameters.

Set the tool parameters as shown next.

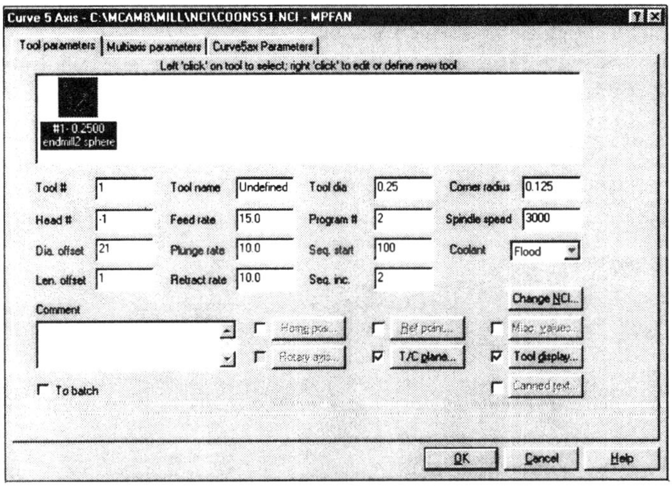

Step 5. Define the multiaxis parameters.

Click the **"Multiaxis parameters"** tab

Set the multiaxis parameters as below.

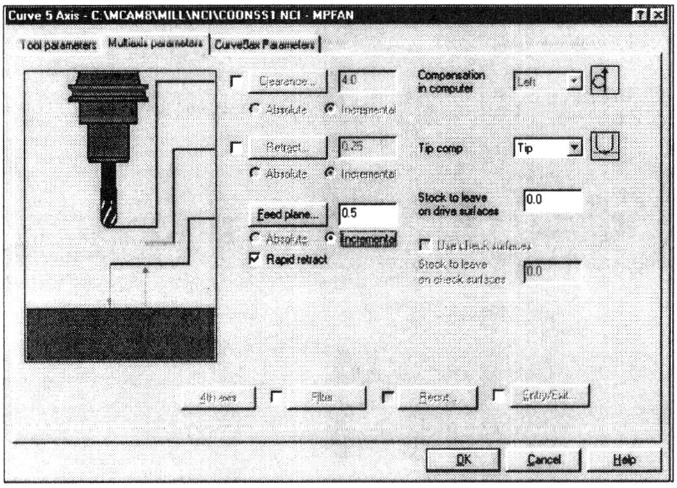

Step 6. Define the curve5ax parameters.

Click the **"Curve5ax Parameters"** button

Set the curve5ax parameters as below.

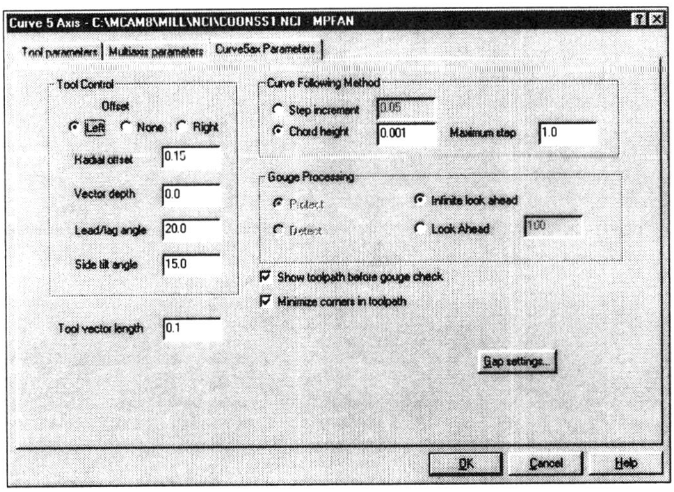

Select **OK** to generate the toolpaths
The toolpaths are shown in Figure 16.30.

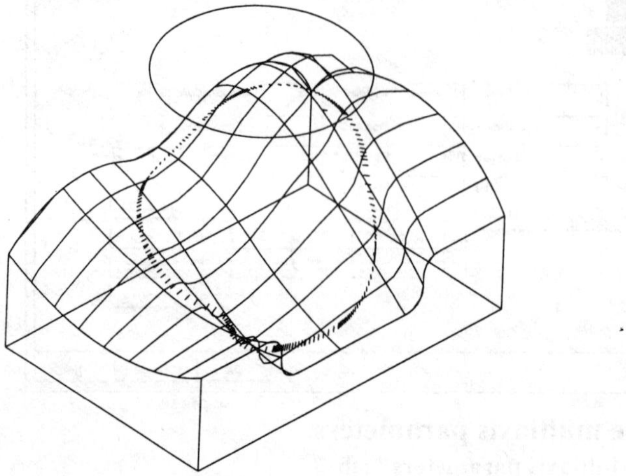

Figure 16.30

Step 7. Save the toolpath file.

Select **MAIN MENU → NC utils → Filter**
Select **Yes** to "Operations have been modified. Create the NCI text file?"
Select **Do it → Cancel**

Step 8. Backplot the toolpaths.

Select **MAIN MENU → NC utils → Backplot → Display**
Set the backplot display parameters as below.

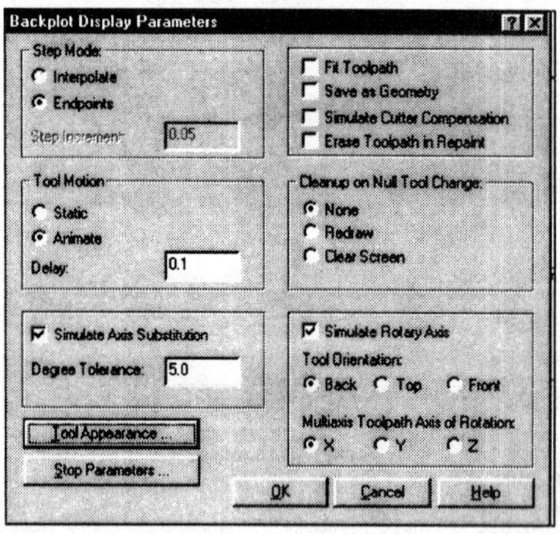

Select **OK**
Select **Run**
The toolpaths are animated on the screen.

Project 5. Curve 5-axis-surface curve 5

Generate 5-axis toolpaths to machine a series of surface curves on a surface (Figure 16.31). The surface curves are created by projecting a rectangle onto a surface. Then use the Curv5ax-surf crvs function to generate 5-axis toolpaths.

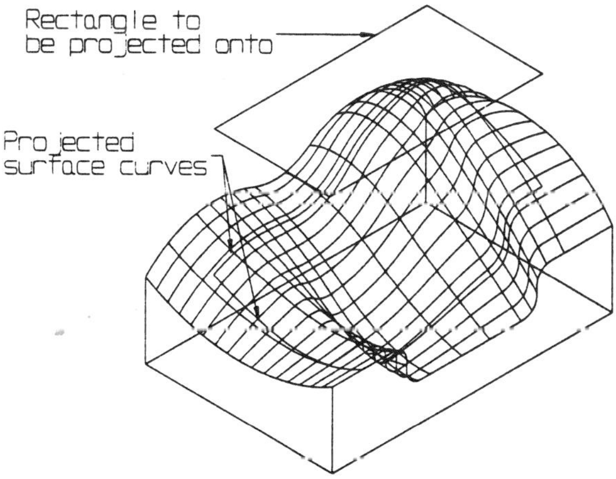

Figure 16.31a Surface curves

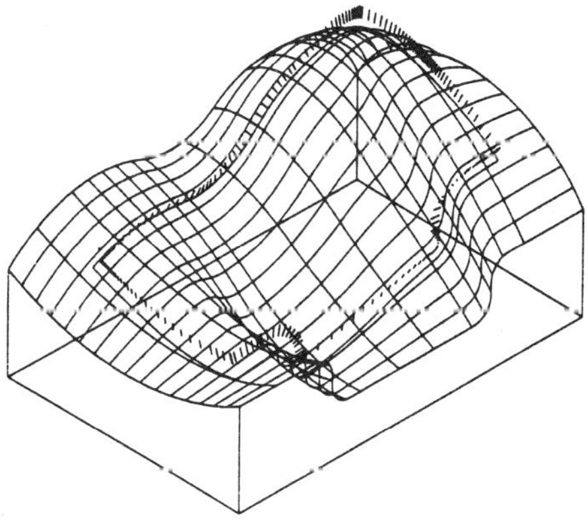

Figure 16.31b Toolpaths

Tips
1. Use the Coons surface coonss1 as the base surface.
2. Create a rectangle.
3. Project the rectangle onto the Coons surface to generate surface curves.
4. Use the Curv5ax-surf crvs function to generate toolpaths to cut surface file coonss1.

Step 1. Open the surface model file coonss1.

Select **MAIN MENU → File → Get**

File name: **coonss1** ↵

The surface model coonss1 will appear as Figure 16.32.

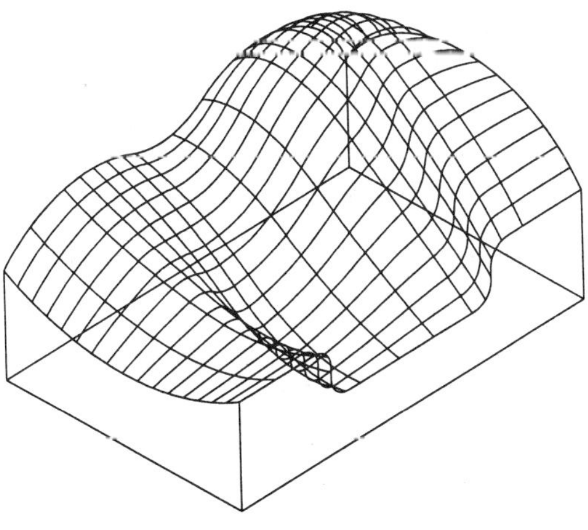

Figure 16.32

Step 2. Set the drawing environments for creating a rectangle.

Select **Level**, then enter **3 → OK**
Select **Z**, then enter **3.5** ↵
Select **Gview → Top**
Select **Cplane → Top**
The model shown in the top view will look like Figure 16.33.

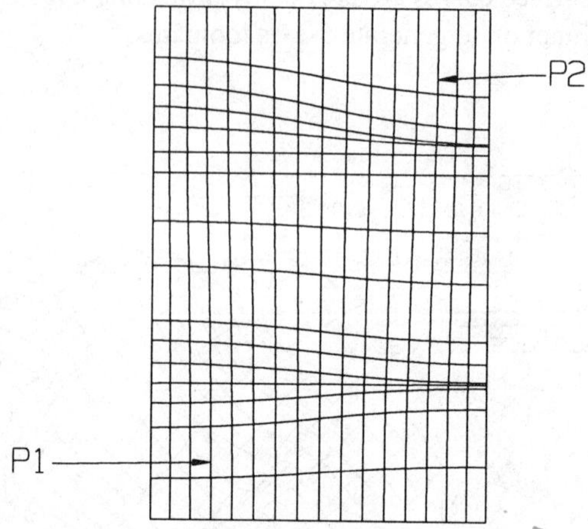

Figure 16.33

Step 3. Create a rectangle using the pick points in Figure 16.33.

Select **MAIN MENU → Create → Rectangle → 2 Points → Sketch**
Enter the lower left corner: pick **P1**
Enter the upper right corner: pick **P2**
Select **Gview → Isometric**
A rectangle is added to the model as in Figure 16.34.

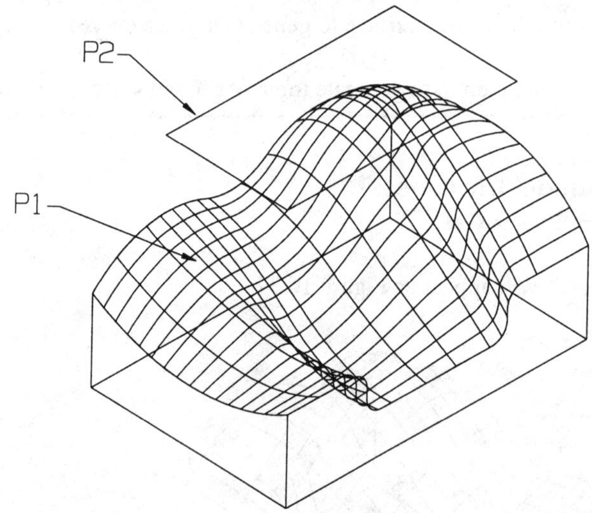

Figure 16.34

Step 4. Project the rectangle onto the surface to create surface curves.

Use the pick points in Figure 16.34.
Select **Level**, then enter **4 → OK**
Select **MAIN MENU → Create → Curve → Project**
Pick **P1** to select a surface
Select **Done**
Select **Chain**, then pick **P2**
Select **Done → Options**

Set projection curve parameters as below.

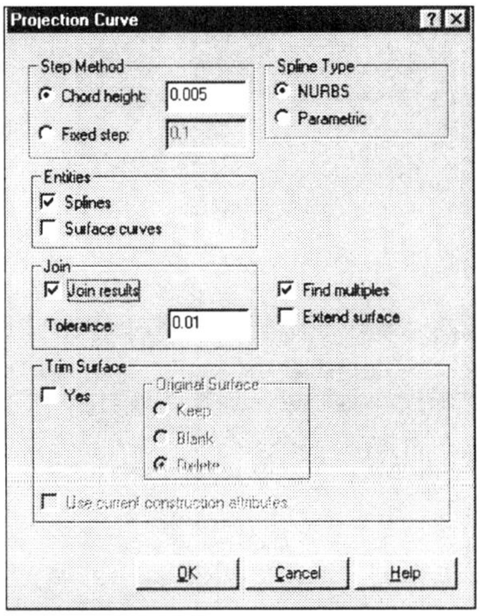

Select **OK**
Set **View/norm** to **V**
Select **Do it** to generate surface curves
Select **Level**
  toggle **3** to invisible (no check mark)
Select **OK**
The surface curves are added as in Figure 16.35.

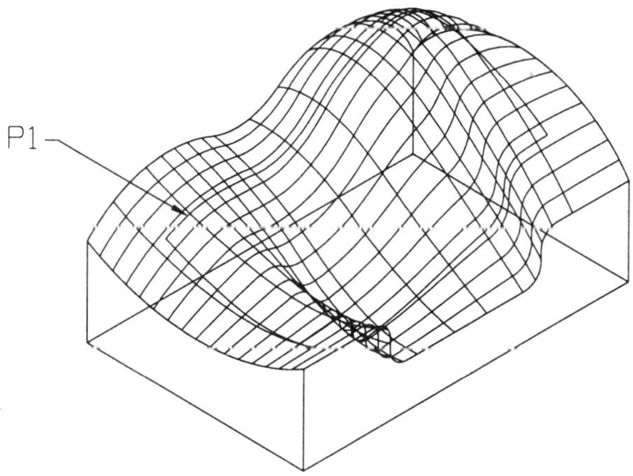

Figure 16.35

Step 5. Generate toolpaths for surface curves.

Use the pick point in Figure 16.35.
Select **MAIN MENU → Toolpaths → Multiaxis → Curve5ax**
File name for NCI: **psc** ↵

Set the Curve 5-axis parameters as below.

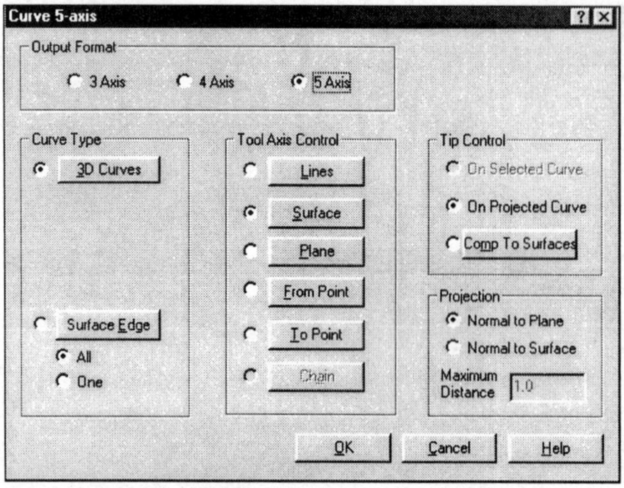

Select **OK**
Select Tool Axis Surface(s): pick the surface, then select **Done**
Select **Chain** boundaries: pick **P1**
Select **Done**

Step 6. Define the tool parameters.

Set the tool parameters as below.

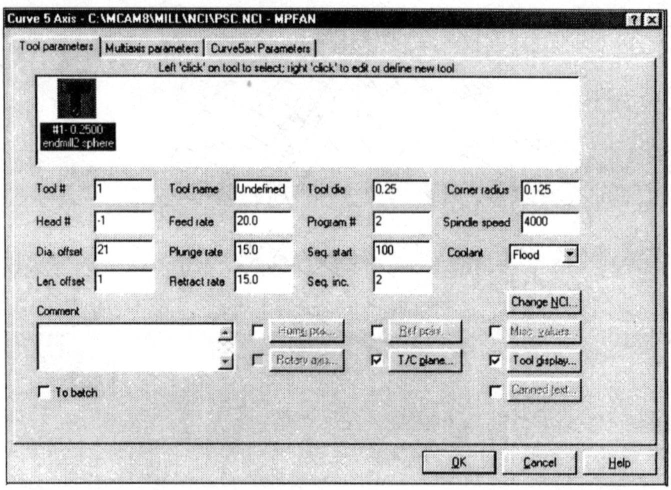

Step 7. Define the multiaxis parameters.

Click the **"Multiaxis parameters"** tab
Set the multiaxis parameters as shown next.

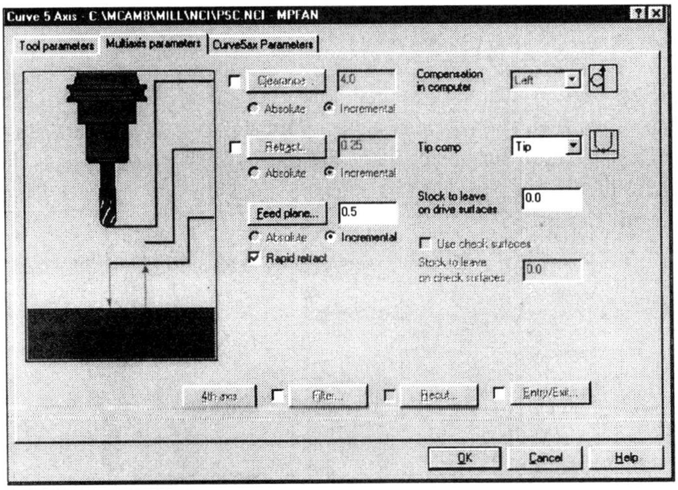

Step 8. Define the curve5ax parameters.

Click the **"Curve5ax Parameters"** button

Set the curve5ax parameters as below.

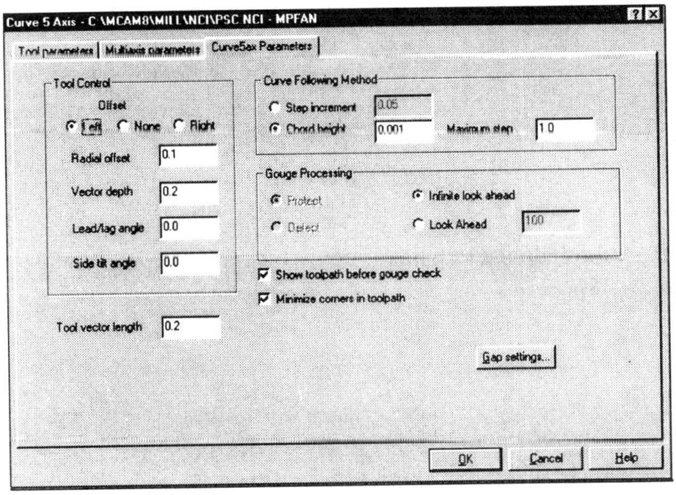

Select **OK**

The toolpaths are generated as shown in Figure 16.36.

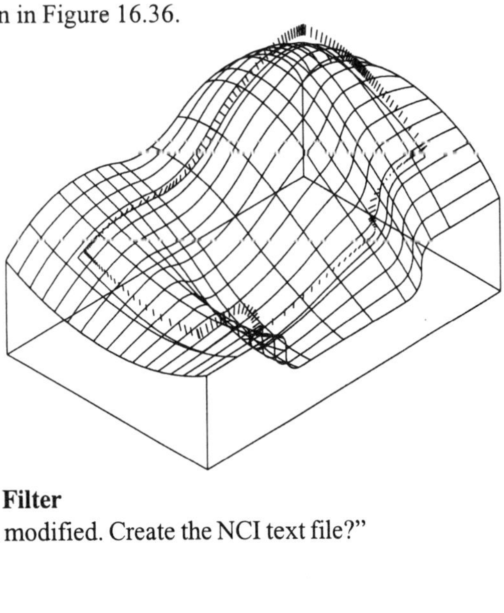

Figure 16.36

Step 9. Save the toolpath file.

Select **MAIN MENU → NC utils → Filter**

Select **Yes** to "Operations have been modified. Create the NCI text file?"

Select **Do it → Cancel**

16.7 Drill 5-Axis Function

The drill 5-axis function is used to drill holes in a specified direction. The location and direction of the drilling can be specified by two entity types; points and points/lines. With the Points option, a reference point and a projection surface or plane are used. The system projects the reference point onto the surface to obtain the drilling point on the surface, then it uses a normal vector as a reference to set the drilling direction (Figure 16.37).

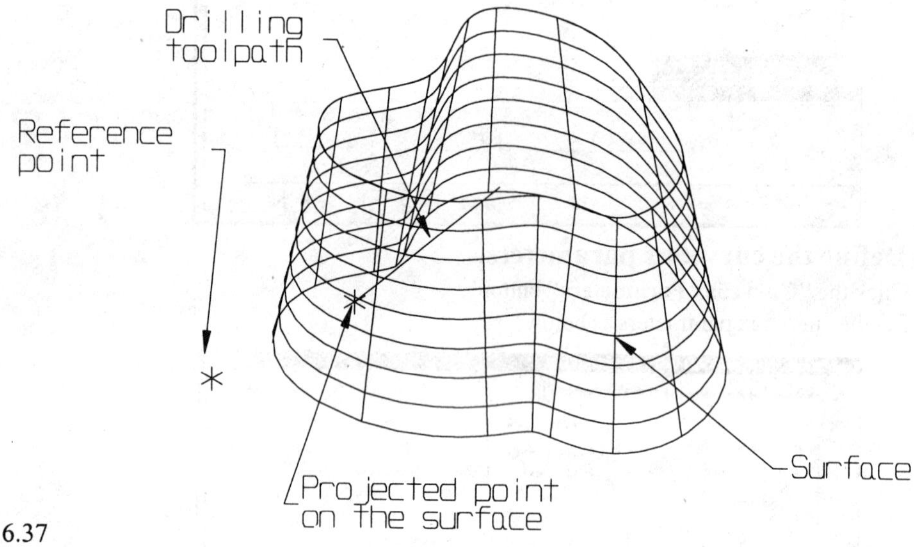

Figure 16.37

In Points/lines method, the endpoint of a line is used as the reference point and the line defines the drilling direction (Figure 16.38).

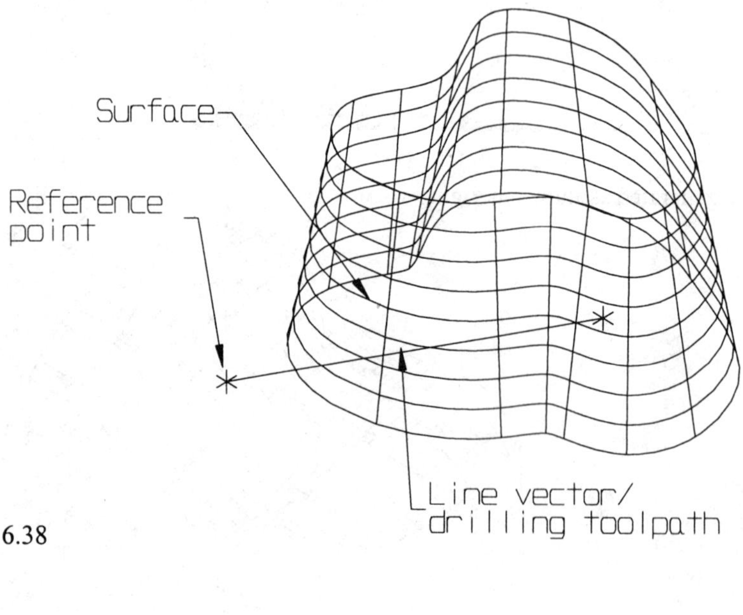

Figure 16.38

Point selection methods

The point Manager menu includes nine option for selecting and placing drilling points.

Manual:	manually selects or creates points for generating drilling toolpaths.
Automatic:	uses three points to automatically select a group of points for generating drilling toolpaths. The first selected point is used as the first point, the second selected point sets the search direction, and the third selected point is the stop point.
Entities:	places all drill points relative to selected entities.
Window pts:	selects a series of points within the window for generating drilling toolpaths.
Last:	selects drill points from the last drill operation
Mask on arc:	selects drill points at center points of arcs.
Patterns:	positions drill points in a bolt circle pattern or a grid pattern.
Options:	sorts drill points.
Subpgm ops:	repeats drill point pattern.

Drill 5-axis parameters

Drilling parameters are grouped under drill 5-axis parameters menu as shown below.

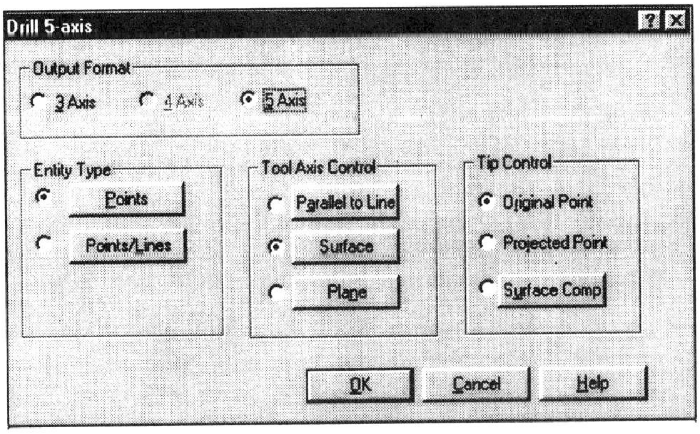

Tool Axis Control This parameter selects one of the following three method for the projection of the drill point:

Parallel to line:	projects the points parallel to a selected line
Surface:	projects the points normal to a selected surface.
Plane:	projects the points normal to the current construction plane.

Tip Control This parameter specifies how the selected point Mastercam uses as the reference point for drilling. It has the following three options:

Original point:	uses the original point above the surface as the reference (Figure 16.39a).
Projected point:	uses the projected point on the surface as the reference point (Figure 16.39b).
Surface Comp:	uses the surface composition point as the reference point.

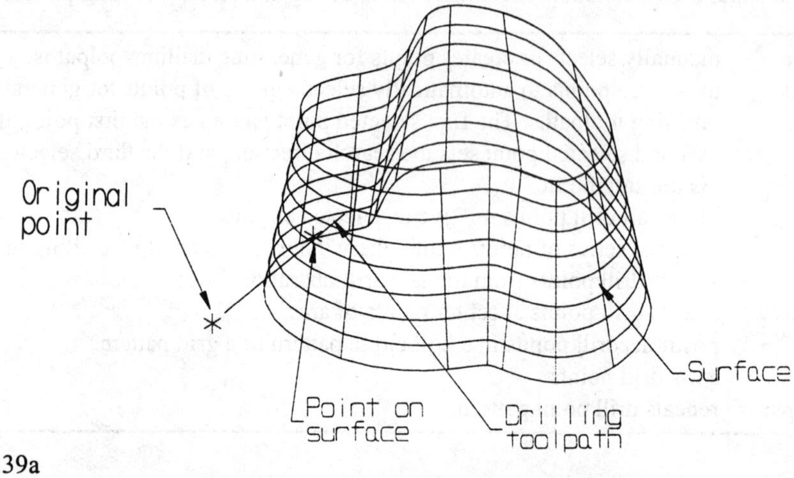

Figure 16.39a

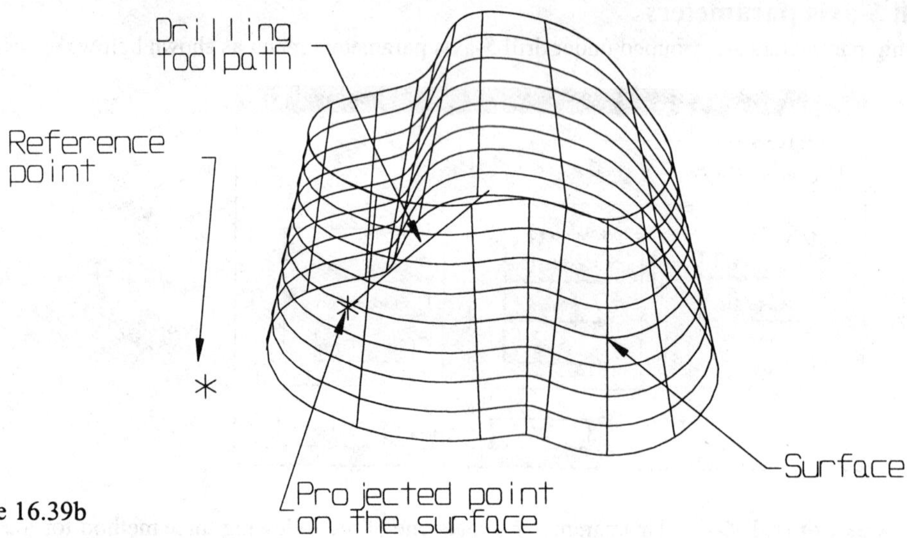

Figure 16.39b

Two projects are presented in this section to demonstrate how to use two functions of the Drill 5-axis. The first project uses the points method to generate a drilling toolpath that is normal to a draft surface, then copy this toolpath to five locations around the Z axis. The second project uses the Point/Line method to generate the toolpaths to drill two holes along the line orientation.

💻 Project 6. Drill 5-axis with points option 💻6

This project uses the Drill 5-axis function to generate a toolpath for a point and is perpendicular to the surface. This drilling toolpath is then copied to 5 locations by using the Toolpaths-Transform-Rotate function. Figure 16.40 shows surface model and drilling toolpaths.

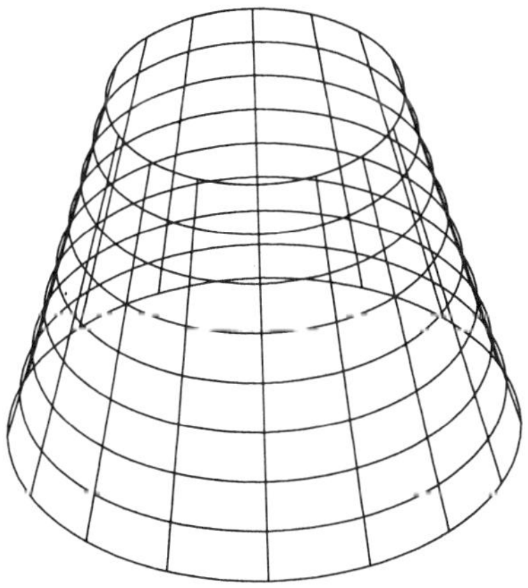

Figure 16.40a Surface

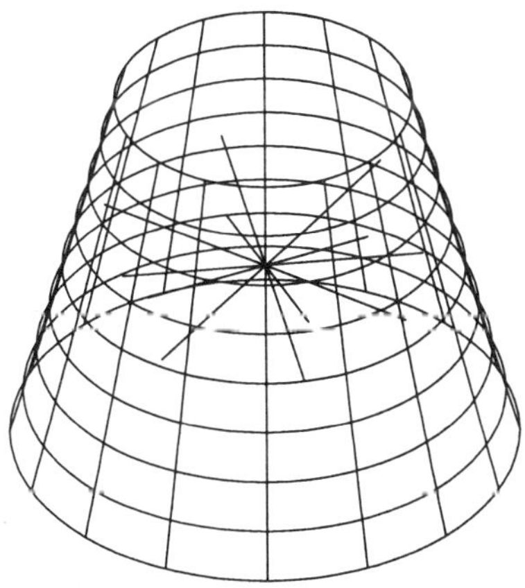

Figure 16.40b Drilling toolpaths

⌛**Tips**
1. Create a cone-shaped draft surface.
2. Use the front view to define a point as the drilling location.
3. Use the Toolpath → Next menu → Transform → Rotate function to copy the drilling toolpath to five locations around the cone-shaped surface.
4. Use the Backplot function to verify the toolpaths.

Step 1. Create a circle.

Select **Cplane → Top**
Select **Gview → Isometric**
Select **Z**, then enter **0** ↵
Select **MAIN MENU → Create → Arc → Cir pt+dia**
Enter radius: **3** ↵
Enter the center point: **0, 0**
The circle is created as in Figure 16.41.

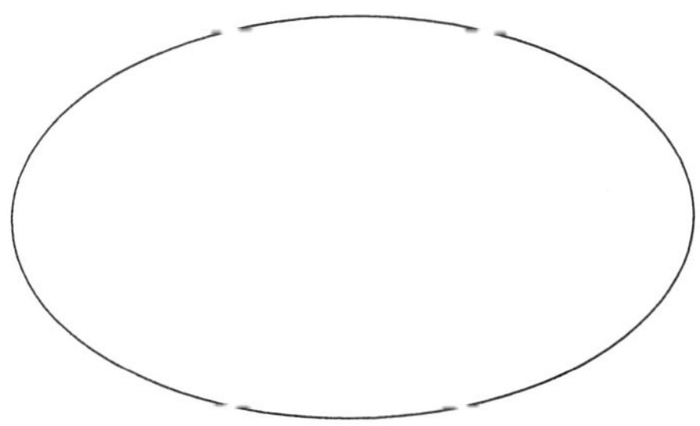

Figure 16.41

Step 2. Create a draft surface.

Select **MAIN MENU → Create → Surface → Draft**
Pick the circle to select the profile entity
Select **Done**
An arrow pointing upward will appear to indicate the extending direction.
Select **Length**, then enter **–4** ↵
Select **Angle**, then enter **–15** ↵
Select **Do it**
The draft surface is created as in Figure 16.42.

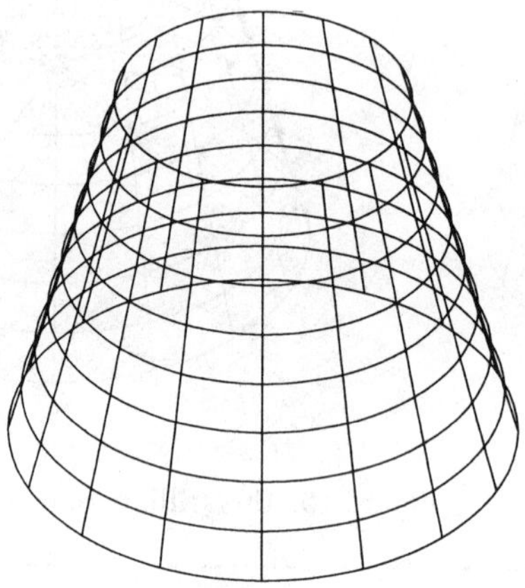

Figure 16.42

Select **MAIN MENU → File → Save**
File name: **5drl** ↵

Step 3. Define the drilling location.

Select **Cplane → Front**
Select **MAIN MENU → Toolpaths → Multiaxis → Drill5ax**
File name for NCI: **5drl** ↵
Set the Drill 5-axis parameter as below.

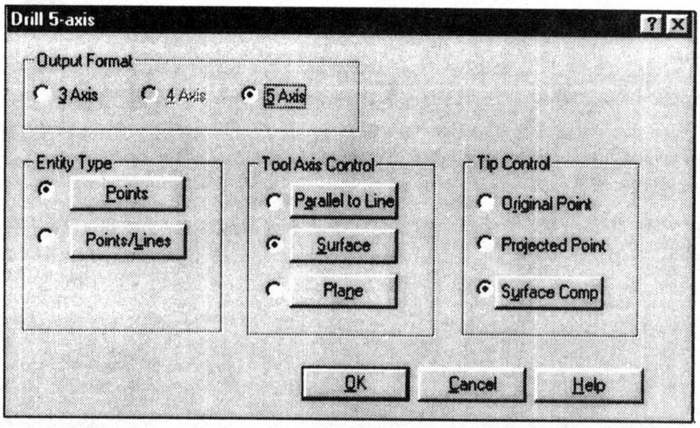

Select **OK**

Select **Manual**
Enter coordinates: **0, -1.5, 6**
A point will appear as in Figure 16.43.

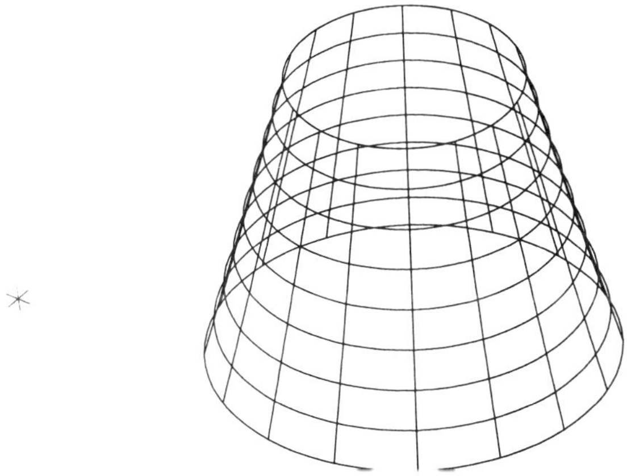

Figure 16.43

Press the **Esc** key to complete point selection, then select **OK**
Select Tool Axis surface(s): pick any point on the surface to select it
Select **OK**

Step 4. Define the drilling parameters.

Set the tool parameters as below.

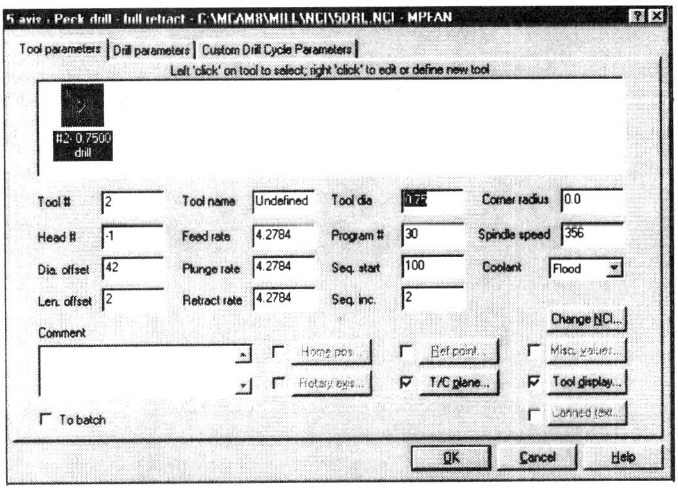

Click the **"Drill parameters"** tab
Set the drill parameters as below.

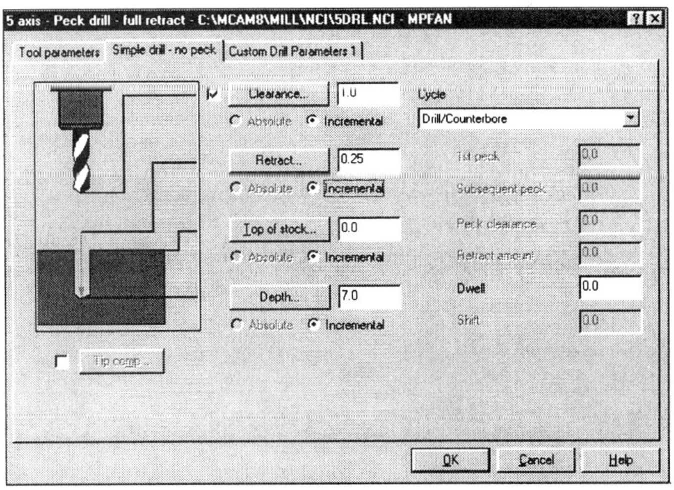

Select **OK**

The drilling path is shown in Figure 16.44.

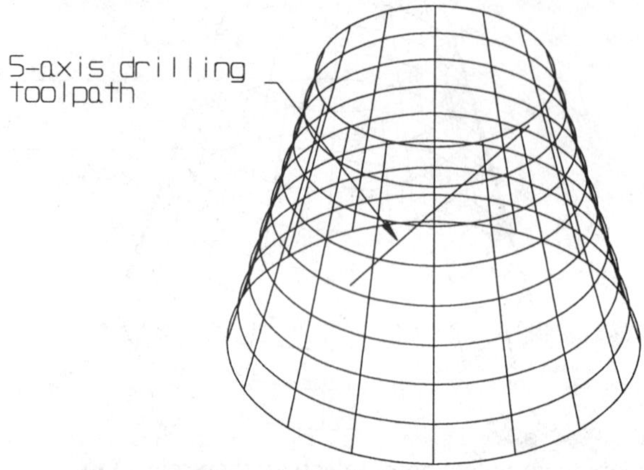

Figure 16.44

Step 5. Generate five drilling toolpaths by using Xform-Rotate function.

Select **Cplane → Top**

Select **MAIN MENU → Toolpaths → Next menu → Transform**

Set the Transform Operating Parameters as below.

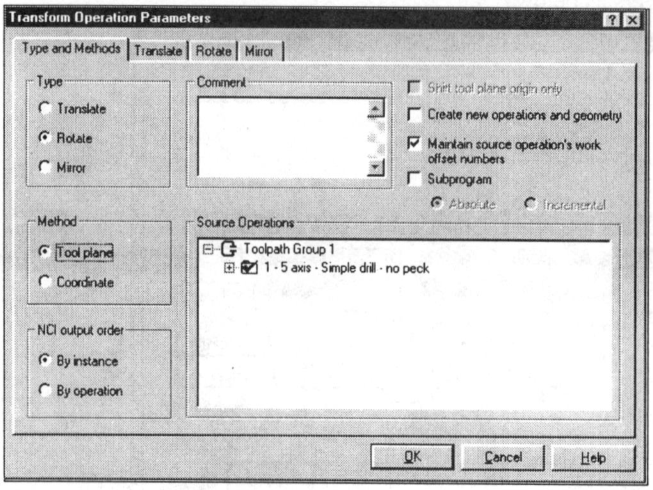

Click **"Rotate"** tag and set the parameters as below.

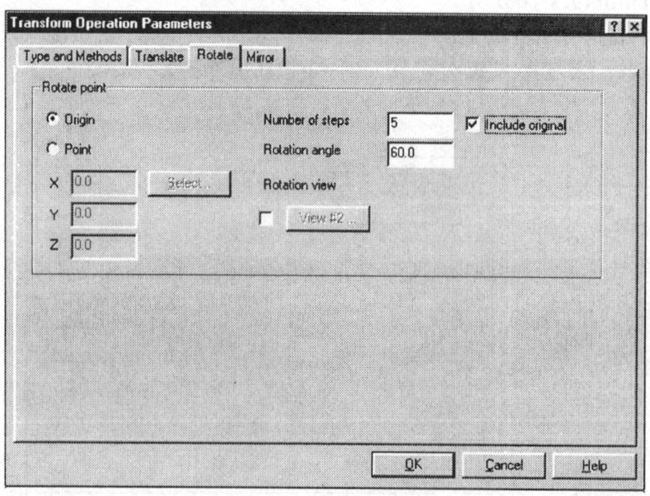

Select **OK**

The six drilling toolpaths are shown in the model as in Figure 16.45.

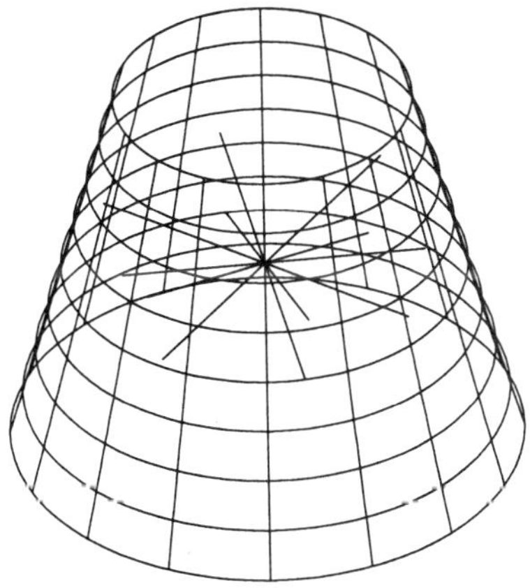

Figure 16.45

Step 7. Backplot the toolpath.

Select **BACKUP → Operations → Select All → Backplot → Run**

The toolpaths are backplot on the screen.

Project 7. Drill 5-axis using point/line option

Generate two drilling toolpaths to produce two holes on a cone-shaped surface along two lines (Figure 16.46). The cone-shaped surface is created in project 6 of this chapter.

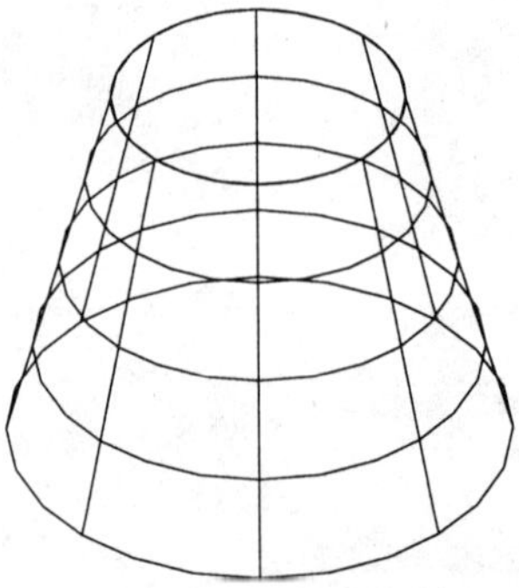

Figure 16.46a Surface

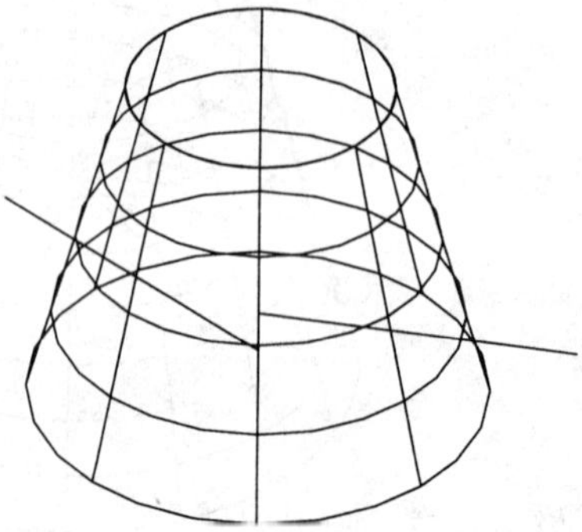

Figure 16.46b Toolpaths

Tips 1. Use the cone-shaped draft surface file 5drl.

2. Create two lines to use as the drilling direction for two holes.

3. Use Drill – pts/lines functions to generate toolpaths for two holes.

4. Backplot the toolpaths to verify results.

Step 1. Open the draft surface file 5drl.

(or create one by following the instructions in steps 1 and 2 in project 6.)
Select **MAIN MENU → File → Get**
File name: **5drl** ↵
The draft surface appears as Figure 16.47.

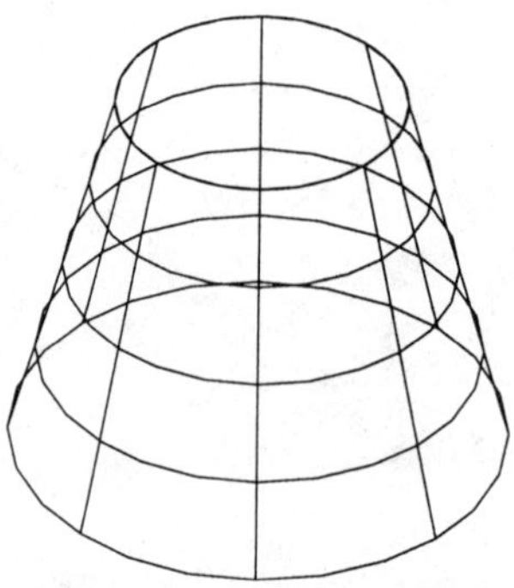

Figure 16.47

Step 2. Create two lines.

Select **MAIN MENU → Create → Line → Endpoints**

Enter the following four sets of coordinate values:

5,	0,	-1	
0,	0,	-3	for the first line
-4,	0,	-3.5	
0,	0,	-3.5	for the second line

The two lines are added as in Figure 16.48.

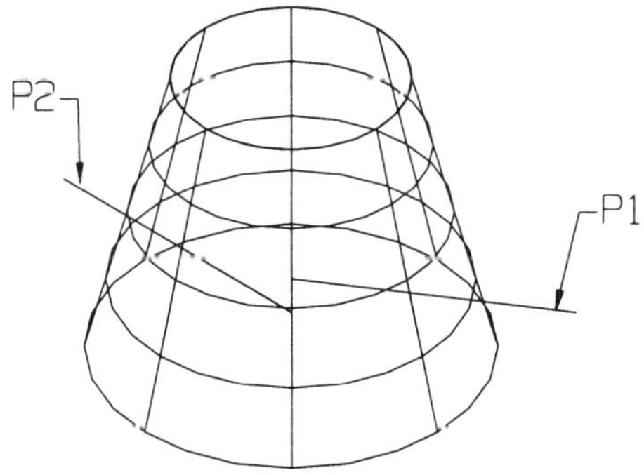

Figure 16.48

Step 3. Initiate Drill5ax – pts/lines function.

Use the pick points in Figure 16.48.
Select **MAIN MENU → Toolpaths → Multiaxis → Drill5ax**
File name for NCI: **5drll** ↵
Set the Drill 5-axis parameters as below.

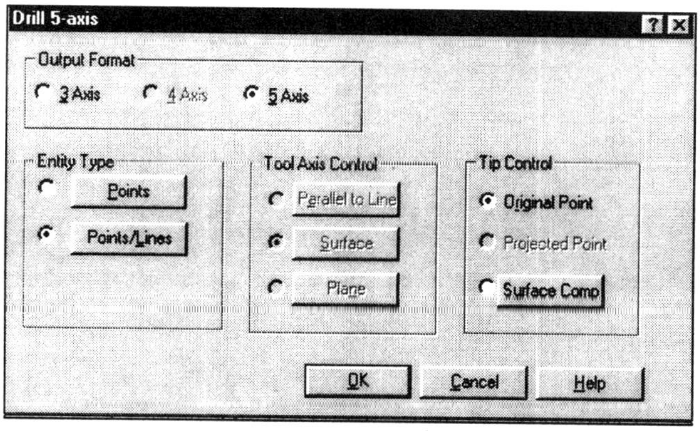

Select **OK**
Select **Manual → Endpoint**
Pick **P1** and **P2** to select two endpoints
Press **Esc** to complete point selection, then select **Done**
Sclcct **OK**

Step 4. Define the drilling parameters.

Set the tool parameters as below.

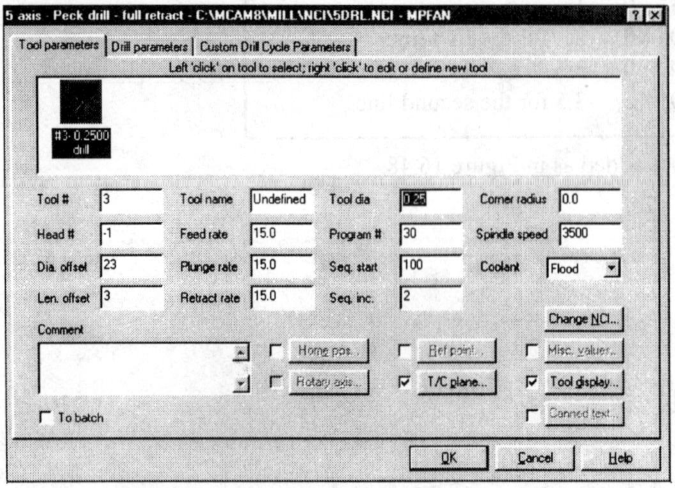

Select the **"Peck drill-full retract"** button

Set the peck drill-full retract parameters as below.

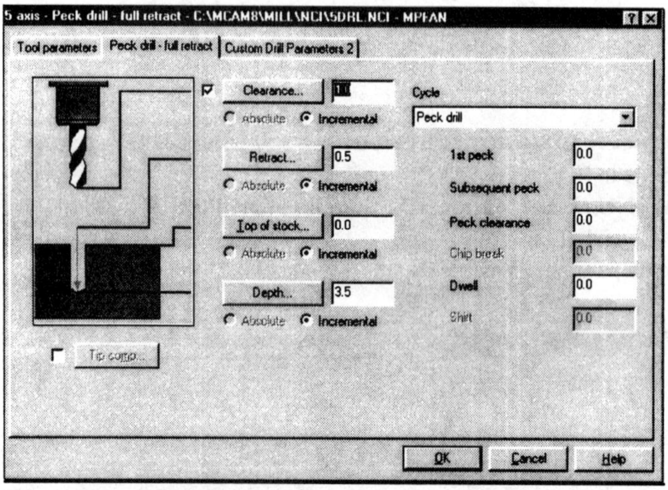

Select **OK** to generate the drilling toolpaths along two given lines

Step 5. Backplot the toolpaths.

Select **MAIN MENU → NC utils → Backplot → Run**

Two drilling toolpaths will be animated on the screen.

16.8 Swarf 5-Axis Function

The Swarf 5-axis function generates 5-axis toolpaths for cutting a selected surface with the side of the tool (Figure 16.49). The tool axis (shank) is oriented parallel to the surface.

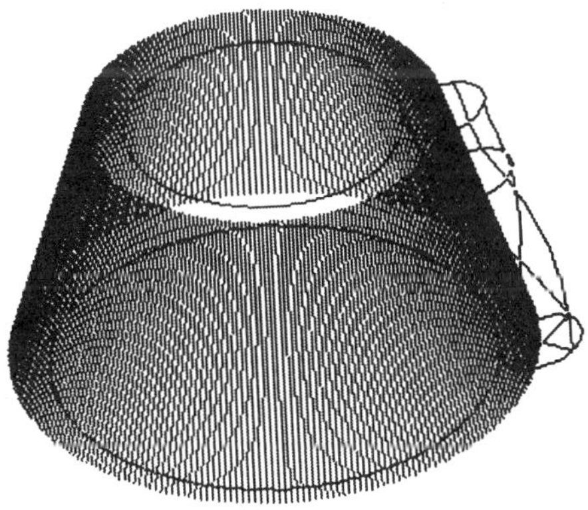

Figure 16.49

Swarf 5 axis

The Swarf 5-axis dialog box consists of **four** parameters; output format, walls, tool axis control, and tip control.

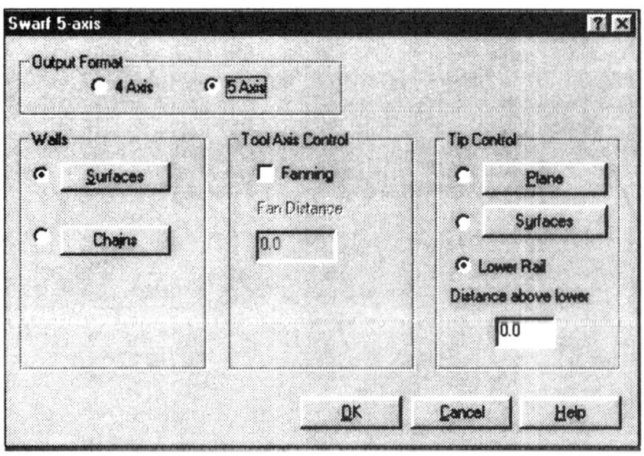

Output Format

There are two output formats for Swarf 5-axis; 4 Axis and 5 Axis. With the 4 Axis format, the output data contains toolpaths for controlling three linear axes and one rotary axis. In the 5 Axis format, the toolpath data is used to control three linear axes and two rotary axes.

Walls

This parameter specifies the element type to be used as the driving elements for generating Swarf 5-axis toolpaths. There two element types: surfaces and chained contour.

Surfaces:	uses the selected surfaces as the driving elements for generating swarf 5-axis toolpaths (Figure 16.50)
Chain:	uses two chained contours to define the driving wall for cutting; lower contour and upper contour (Figure 16.51). The lower chain must be defined first for the toolpaths to generate properly.

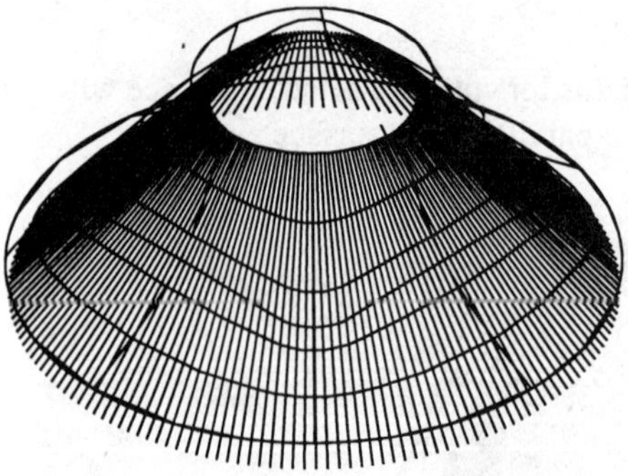

Figure 16.50

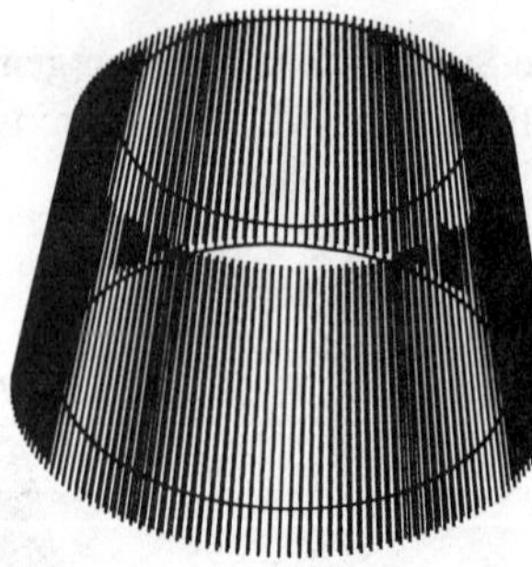

Figure 16.51

Tool Axis Control

The tool axis control is implemented by the **"Fanning"** parameter that decides whether to place fans at the end of each wall of the distance. The **"Fan Distance"** parameter specifies the minimum distance that the tool travels between the corner position and a position where the tool sits perpendicular to the floor (Figure 16.52). Fans are only used along flat walls. A larger fan distance creates a wider fan.

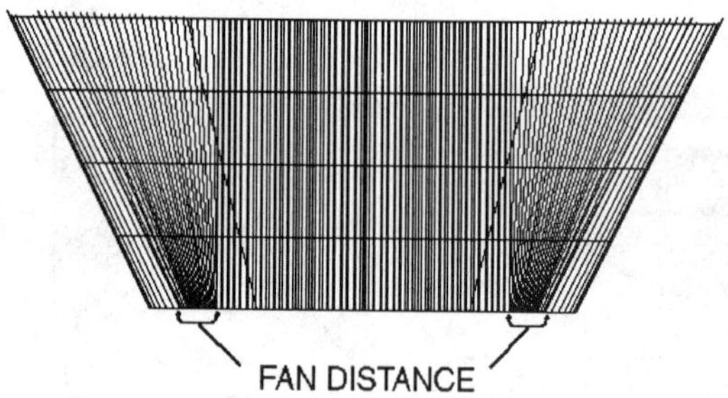

Figure 16.52

Tip Control

The tip control parameter specifies how the lowest depth of swarf toolpaths calculate. It has the following three options:

Plane:	places the lowest point of the tool on the selected surfaces for the toolpath floor (Figure 16.53).
Surface:	places the lowest point of the tool on the selected surfaces for the toolpath floor (Figure 16.54).
Lower Rail:	places the center of the tool in line with the lower trail when the tool rests against the wall (Figure 16.55). The "Distance **above lower"** input field specifies how far the center of the tool descends above or below the lower boundary.

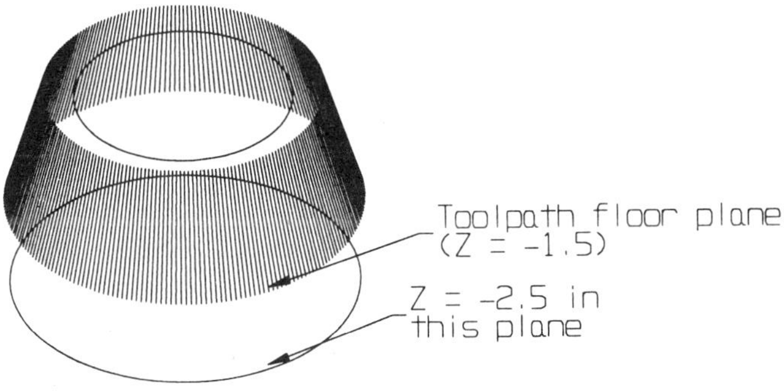

Figure 16.53

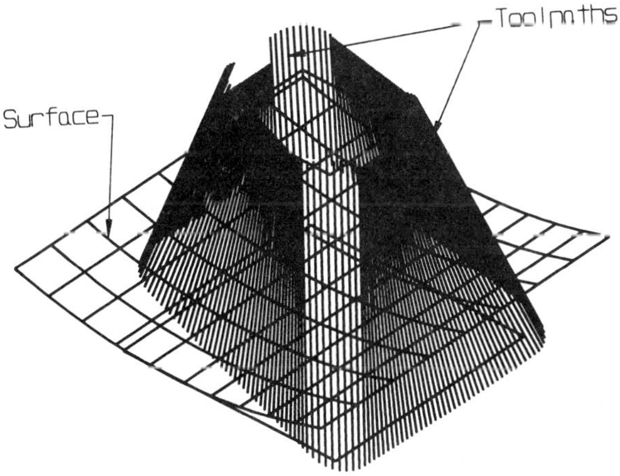

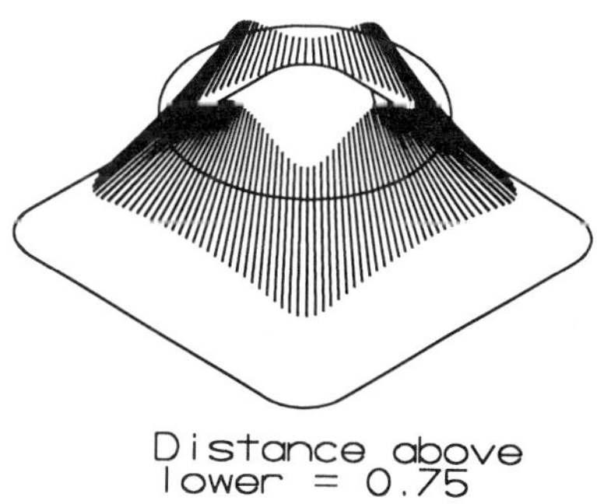

Figure 16.54

Figure 16.55

Swarf 5axis parameters

Those parameters related to swarf5ax function are grouped under Swarf 5ax parameters dialog box as shown below.

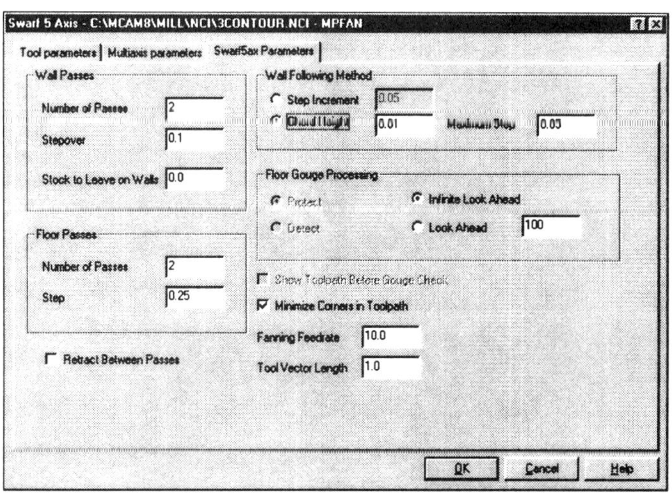

Wall Passes

Three parameters are used to define the cutting conditions for wall passes.

Number of passes:	the number of cutting passes along the wall.
Stepover:	the distance between two adjacent wall passes.
Stock to leave on wall:	the amount of stock to leave on wall.

Floor Passes

Mastercam uses two parameters to define the cutting passes in the floor direction.

Number of passes:	the number of cutting passes in the floor.
Step:	the depth between two adjacent floor passes.

The total number of toolpath passes is the product of passes on wall and number of passes on floor. Mastercam will generate four passes of toolpaths if both numbers of passes are set to 2. When the number of passes becomes greater than one, the stepover parameters becomes active for entering proper value. Figure 16.56 shows an example of having both numbers of passes equal to 2.

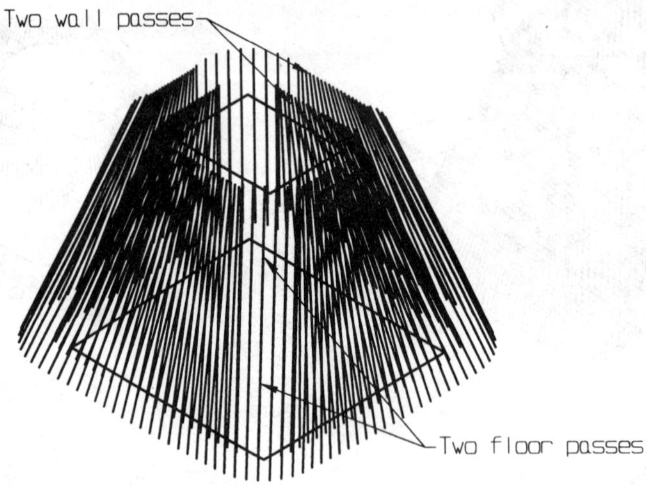

Figure 16.56

Minimize Corners in Toolpath

This parameter minimizes the cutting passes in the corners.

Tool Vector Length

This parameter sets all tool vectors in the toolpath to a specified length.

Two projects are presented in this section to show how to generate 5-axis swarf toolpaths. The first project uses a wireframe model as the wall for generating swarf toolpaths, and the second project uses a draft surface as the wall.

🖳 Project 8. Using 5-axis swarf function with wireframe model 🖳8

This project uses the 5-axis swarf function to generate toolpaths for cutting a slope surface defined by using two wireframe contours. Figure 16.57 shows two wireframe contours and the associated swarf toolpaths.

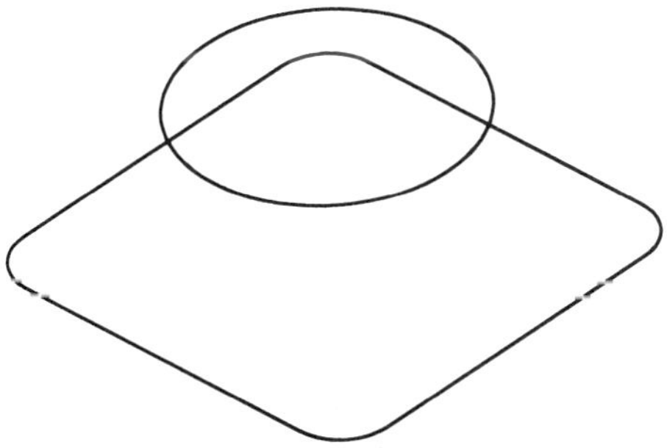

Figure 16.57a Wireframe

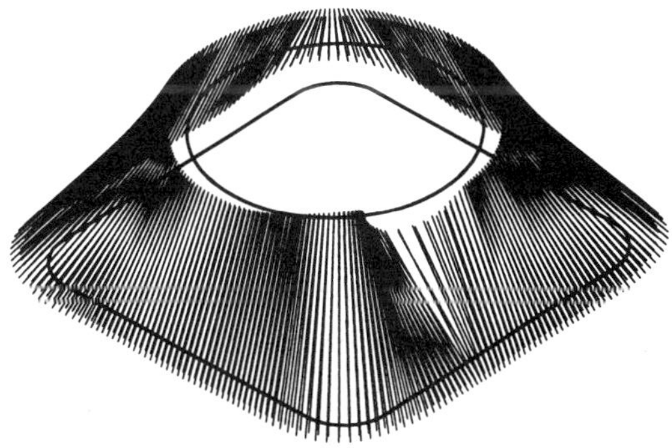

Figure 16.57b Toolpaths

Tips	1. Use the wireframe model 3contour. 2. Delete the bottom circle. 3. Break the right vertical line of the rectangle into two pieces. 4. Use Swarf5ax function to generate swarf toolpaths. 5. Backplot the toolpaths.

Step 1. Open the wireframe model 3contour.

Select **MAIN MENU → File → Get**
File name: **3contour** ↵
The wireframe model consisting of three contours appears as in Figure 16.58.

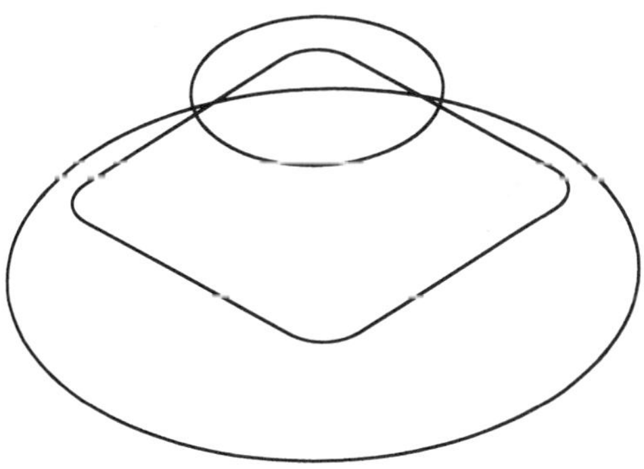

Figure 16.58

Step 2. Delete the bottom circle.

Select **MAIN MENU → Delete**
Pick the bottom circle to delete it

The new drawing becomes Figure 16.59.

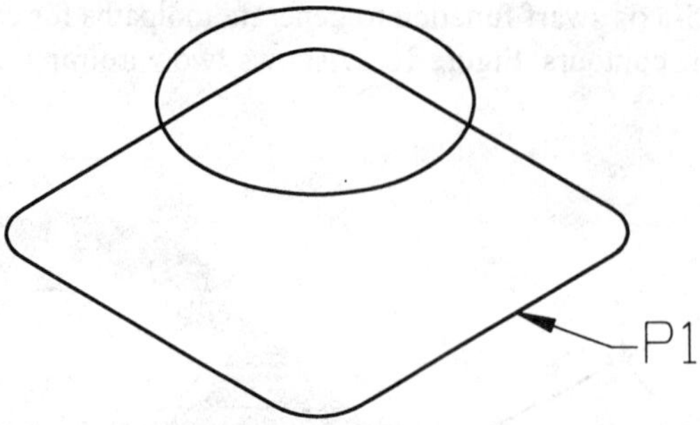

Figure 16.59

Step 3. Break the right vertical line of rectangle into two entities.

Use the pick point in Figure 16.59.
Select **MAIN MENU → Modify → Break → 2 pieces**
Pick **P1** to select the entity to break
Select **Midpoint**, then pick **P1** to break the line into 2 entities
The model is redrawn in Figure 16.60.

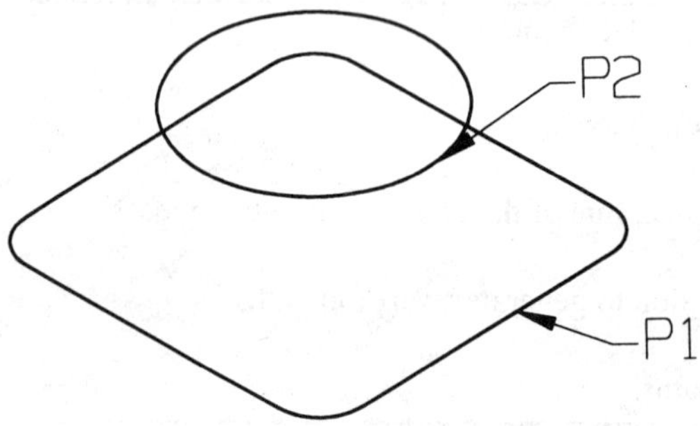

Figure 16.60

Step 4. Initiate the Swarf5ax function.

Use the pick points in Figure 16.60.
Select **MAIN MENU → Toolpaths → Multiaxis → Swarf5ax**
File name for NCI: **swarf ↵**
Set the Swarf 5-axis parameters as below.

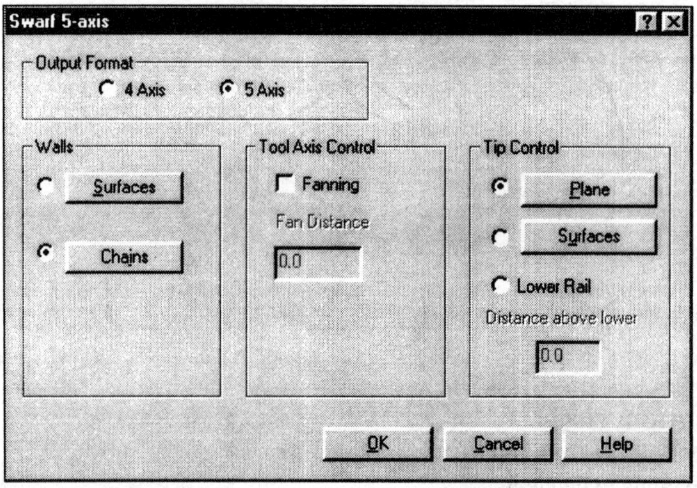

Select **OK**

Pick **P1** as the lower contour
Pick **P2** as the upper contour
Select **Done**
Select **Z =const**
Enter Z-coordinate of plane: **-1**

Step 5. Define the tool and other parameters.

Set the tool parameters as below.

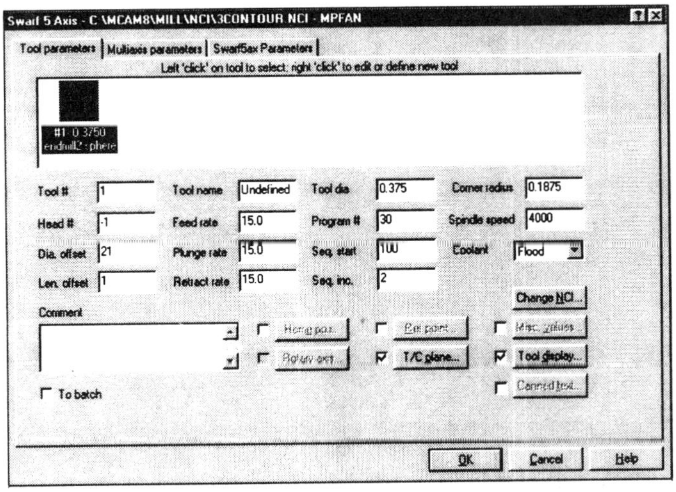

Click the "Multiaxis parameters" button
Set the multiaxis parameters as below.

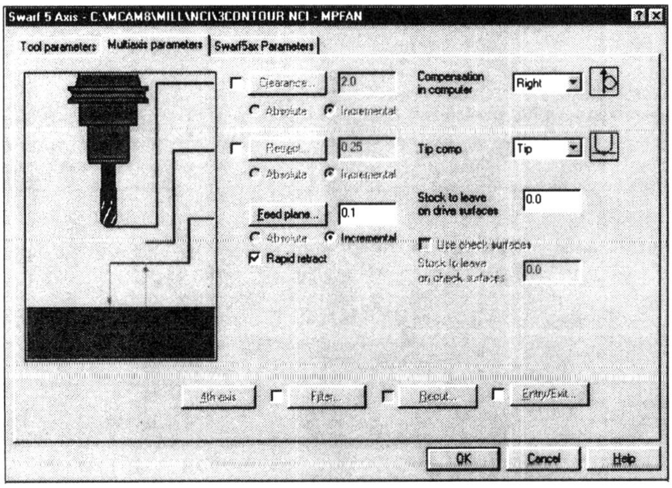

Click the "Swarf5ax Parameters" button

Set the swarf5ax parameters as below.

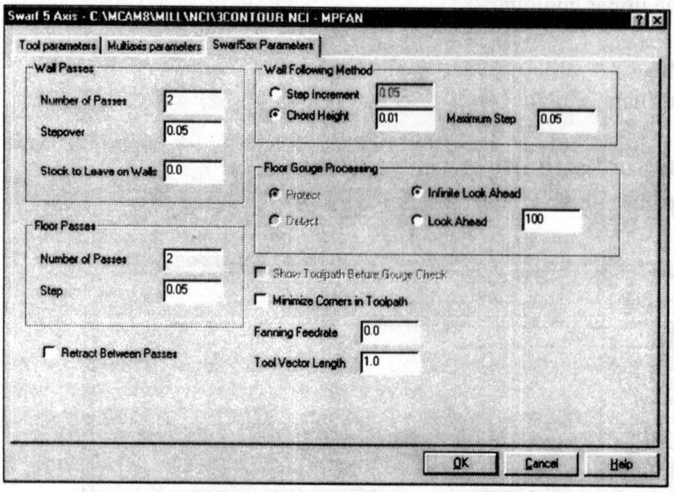

Select OK to generate the toolpaths as Figure 16.61.

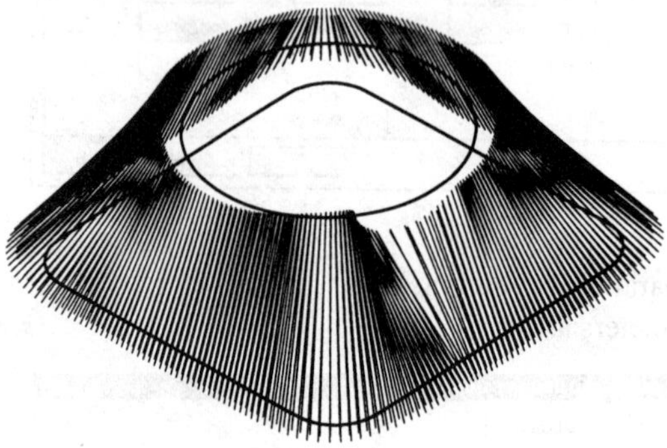

Figure 16.61

Step 6. Backplot the toolpaths.

Select **MAIN MENU → NC utils → Backplot**
Select **Run** to backplot the toolpaths on the screen

Note that there are four toolpath passes in this operation.

💻 Project 9. Using 5-axis swarf function with a surface model

This project creates swarf toolpaths to cut a draft surface (Figure 16.62). The draft surface is created in chapter 12 and has a file name drafts2.

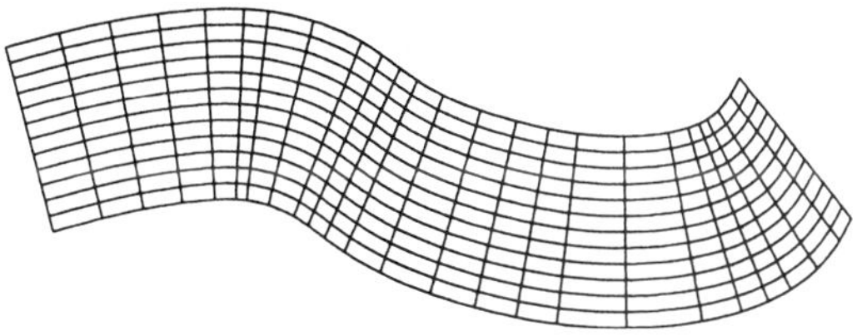

Figure 16.62a Surface

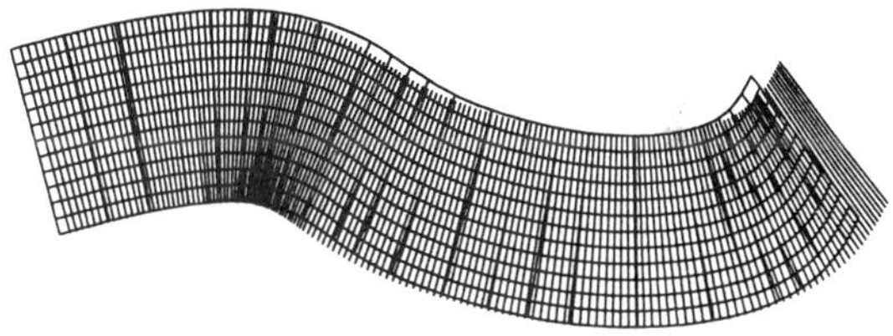

Figure 16.62b Toolpaths

⌛**Tips**	
	1. Open the draft surface model drafts2.
	2. Use the Swarf5ax function to generate toolpaths.
	3. Use a ½" end mill.
	4. Backplot the toolpaths to verify on the screen.

Step 1. Open the draft surface model drafts2.

Select **MAIN MENU → File → Get**

File name: **drafts2** ↵

The draft surface appears as in Figure 16.63.

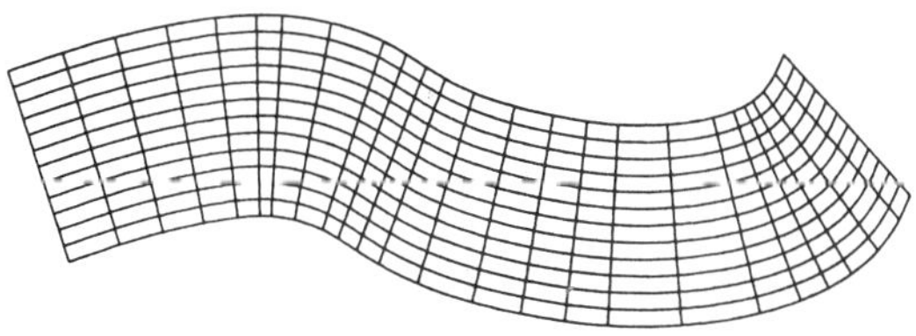

Figure 16.63

Step 2. Initiate the Swarf5ax function.

Select **MAIN MENU → Toolpaths → Multiaxis → Swarf5ax**

Set Swarf 5-axis parameters as below

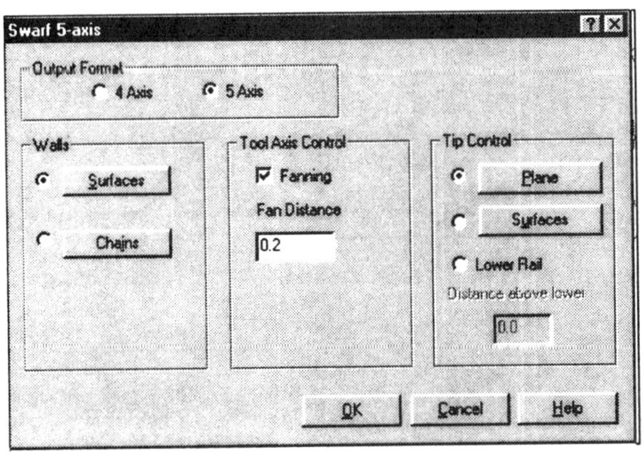

Select **OK**

Pick on the surface as the wall surface
Select **Done**
Pick the upper left corner of the surface as the 1st surface
An arrow will appear at the upper left corner.
Select **OK** if the arrow's direction is pointing to the right, otherwise select **Flip** to change it.
Select **Z = const**
Enter the Z-coordinate of plane = **-1**

Step 3. Define the tool parameters.

Click the right mouse button, then select **Get tool from library**
Select **tool #239** (1/2 flat endmill)
Select **OK**
Set the tool parameters as below.

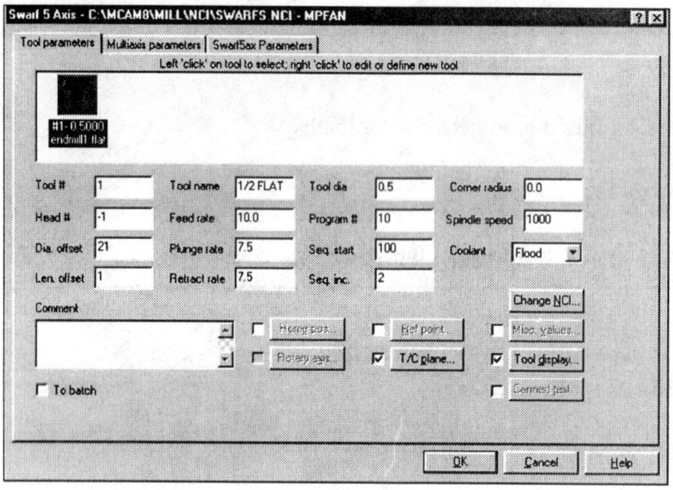

Step 4. Define the multiaxis parameters.

Click **"Multiaxis parameters"** tag and set its parameters as below.

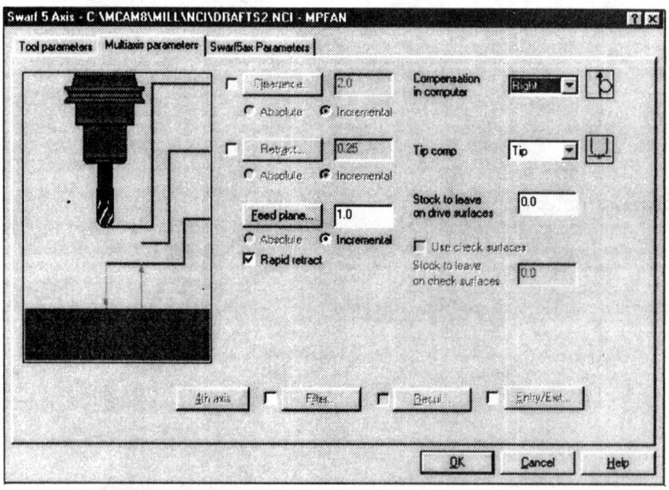

Step 5. Define the Swarf5ax parameters.

Click **"Swarf5ax Parameters"** tag and set its parameters as below.

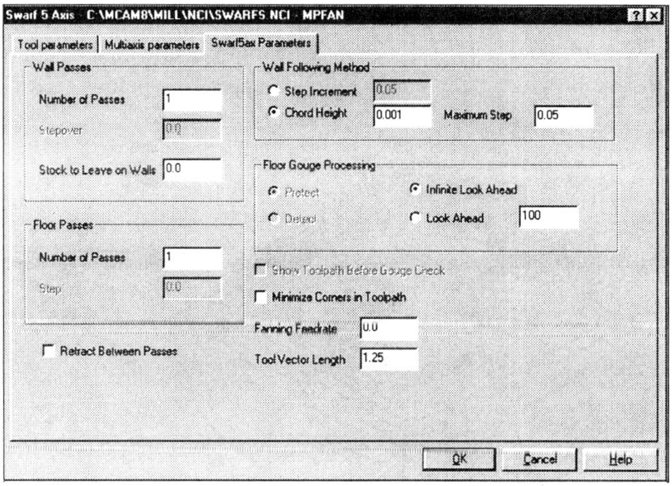

Select **OK** to generate toolpaths as shown in Figure 16.64.

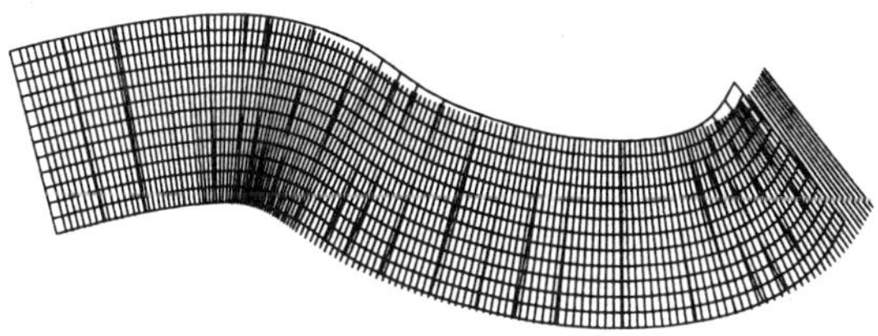

Figure 16.64

Step 4. Backplot the toolpath.

Select **MAIN MENU → NC utils → Backplot**

Select **Run** to verify the toolpaths on the screen

16.9 Flowline 5-Axis Function

The Flowline 5-axis function generates 5-axis toolpaths for cutting a surface model (Figure 16.65). This function can produce a very precise and smooth finish with accurate control of the scallop height left on the part. The flowline parameter dialog box appears as below.

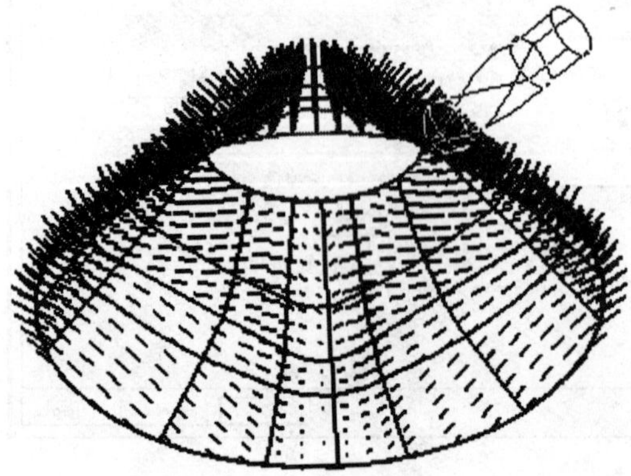

Figure 16.65

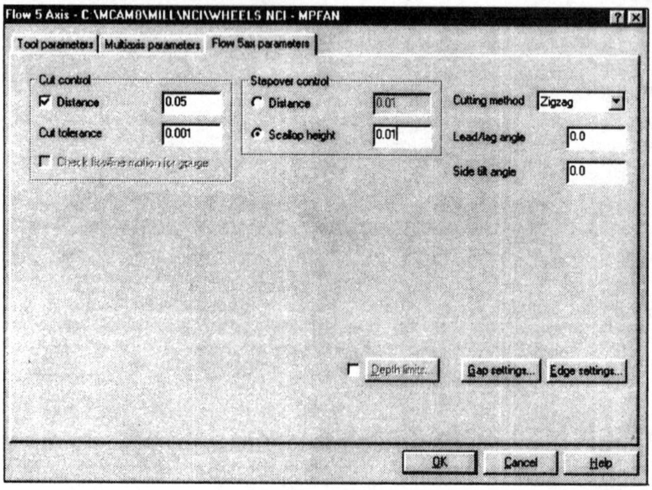

Side tilt angle

The side tilt angle is measured between the surface normal and the tool axis when the tool tilts to the left or right (Figure 16.66). A positive value sets the side tilt angle to the right of the motion of the initial pass. A negative value sets the angle to the left of the motion of the initial pass.

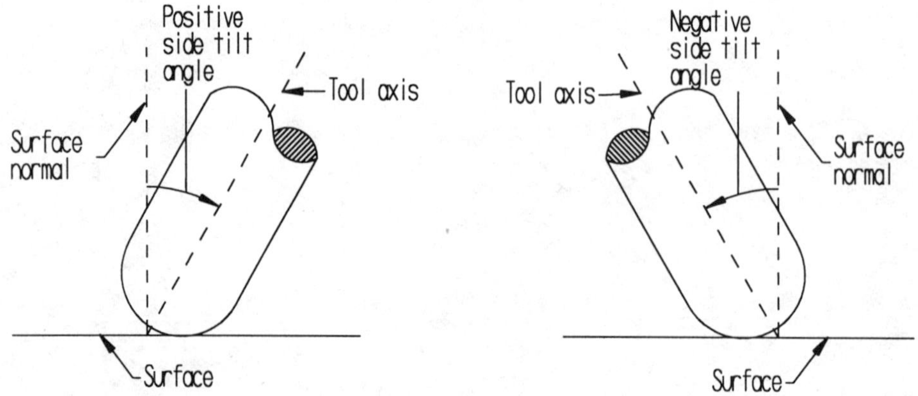

Figure 16.66 Side tilt angle

Lead/lag angle

The lead/lag angle is measured between the surface normal and the tool axis when the tool tilts forward or backward in the cutting direction. (Figure 16.67). A positive value tilts the tool forward in the cutting direction. A negative value tilts the tool backward in the cutting direction. A positive tilt angle is referred to as the lead angle and the negative tilt angle is called lag angle.

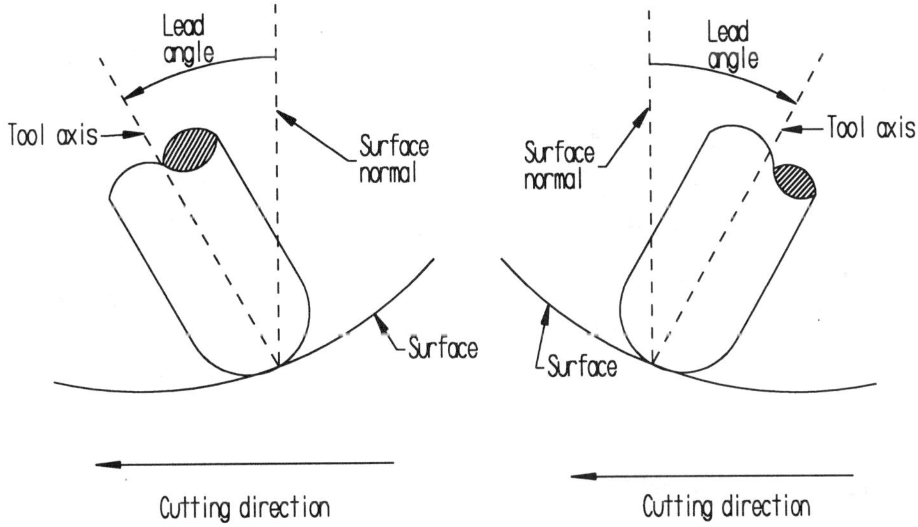

Figure 16.67

You can use a combination of side tile angle and lead/lag angle to control the orientation of tool axis during a flowline 5-axis toolpath.

Project 10. Generating 5-axis flowline toolpaths

This project uses the 5-axis flowline function to generate 5-axis toolpaths to cut three surfaces in the pocket of the car wheel model. These three surfaces include two fillet surfaces and one swept surface. Figure 16.68 shows the surface model and flowline toolpaths.

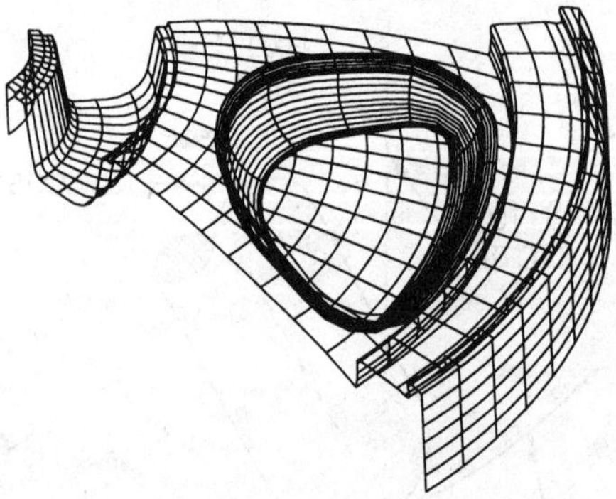

Figure 16.68a Surface model

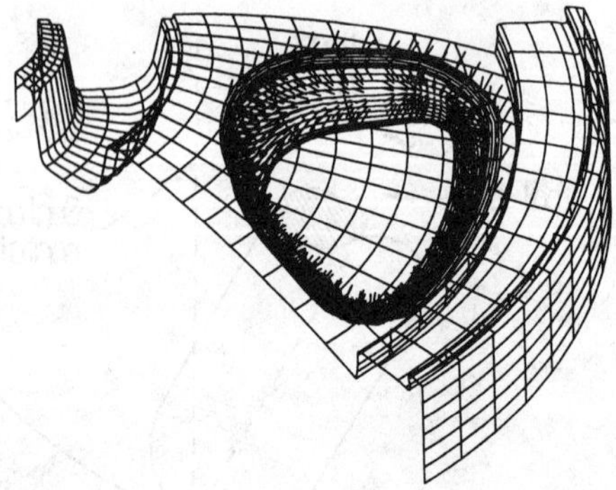

Figure 16.68b Toolpaths

Tips	1. Open the surface model file wheels.
	2. Use the flow5ax function to generate toolpaths.
	3. Select three surfaces in the concave pocket.
	4. Backplot the toolpaths to verify on the screen.

Step 1. Open the surface model file wheels.

Select **MAIN MENU → File → Get**
File name: **wheels** ↵
The car wheel surface model appears as Figure 16.69.

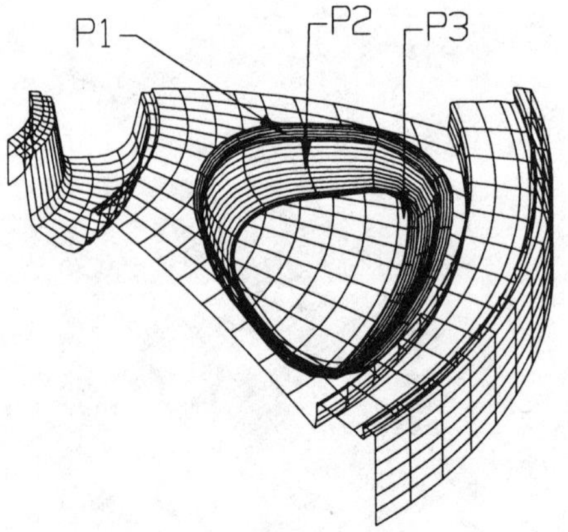

Figure 16.69

Step 2. Initiate the flow5ax function.

Use the pick points in Figure 16.75.
Select **Cplane → Top**
Select **MAIN MENU → Toolpaths → Multiaxis → Flow5ax**
File name for NCI: **flow5ax** ↵
Pick **P1**, **P2**, and **P3** to select three surfaces
Select **Done**
Click the right mouse button, then select **Get tool from library**
Select **tool #254** (3/8 sphere endmill)
Select **OK**

Set the tool parameters as below.

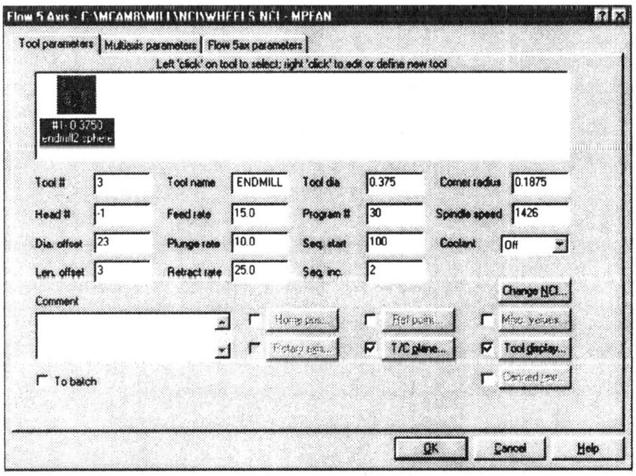

Step 3. Define the multiaxis parameters.

Click **"Multiaxis parameters"** button
Set the multiaxis parameters as below.

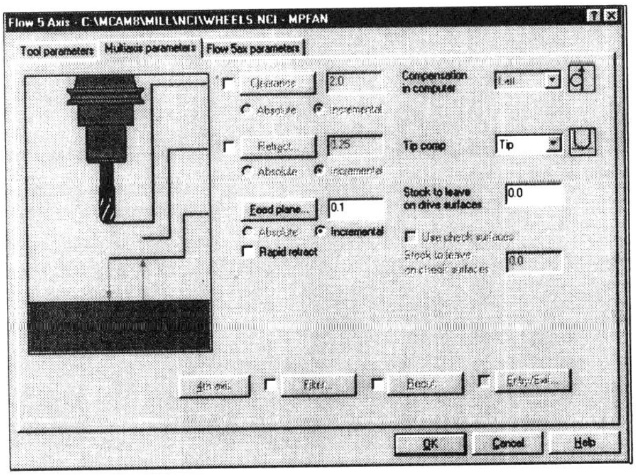

Step 4. Define the flow 5ax parameters.

Click **"Flow 5ax Parameters"** button

Set the flow 5ax parameters as below.

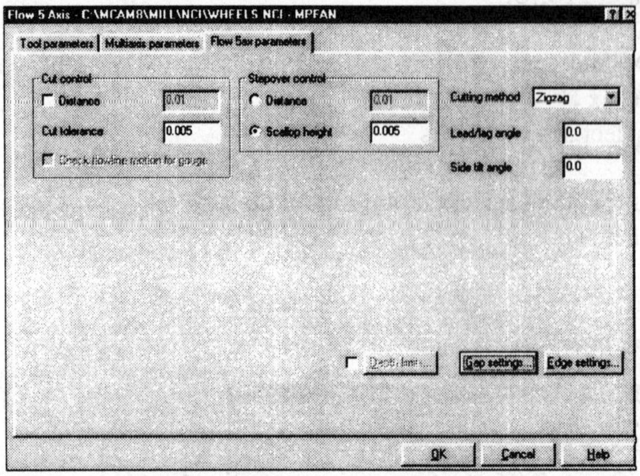

Select **OK**

Select **Done** to generate toolpaths as shown in Figure 16.70.

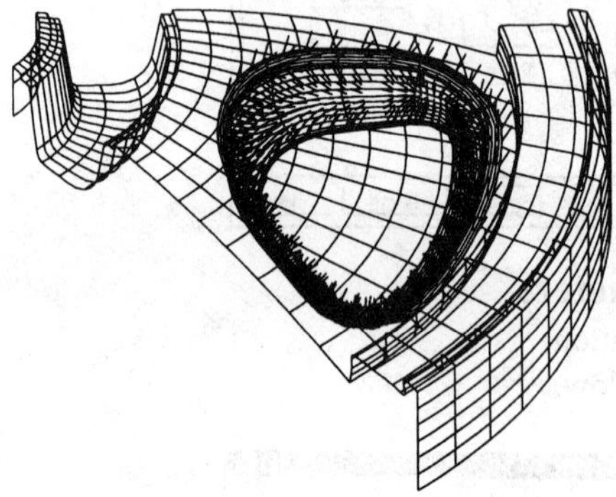

Figure 16.70

Step 5. Backplot the toolpaths.

Select **MAIN MENU → NC utils → Backplot**

Select **Run** to verify the toolpaths on the screen

Ex Exercises

1. List the four 5-axis machining functions available in Mastercam.
2. How many axes are defined by the EIA-267-B standard?
3. Use a drawing to explain how to define the three primary rotary axes and their rotation directions.
4. Use a drawing to describe the thumb rule for determining the direction of the rotation.
5. Can the rotary 4-axis function cut multiple surfaces in one operation?
6. Use a drawing to define the lead/lag angle in rotary 4-axis function.
7. When to use curve 5-axis function?
8. List the two curve types of curve 5-axis function and describe what they are.
9. Describe the difference of three output formats, 3-axis, 4 axis and 5-axis, in curve 5-axis function.
10. Use drawings to describe how the side tilt angle affecting the tool axis orientation.
11. Use drawings to describe how the lead/lag angle affecting the tool axis orientation.
12. List the two curve following methods used in curve 5-axis function and describe what they are.
13. What are the two methods of projecting chained entities onto the surface(s)?
14. List the two entity types for specifying the location and direction of the drilling in drill 5-axis function.
15. What are the main features of swarf 5-axis function?
16. List the three options of specifying the toolpath floor in using swarf 5-axis function.
17. What is the flowline 5-axis function?

Chapter 17

3D Toolpath Editing

Objectives:

1. Know two toolpath editing functions to modify toolpaths for machining 3d surfaces: project and trim.
2. Understand the features of these toolpath editing functions and know when to apply them.
3. Apply these editing functions to 3d surfacing toolpath projects.

Overview

Toolpaths for cutting some surface models can be significantly simplified by using toolpath editing functions. Those toolpath editing functions given in chapter 8 are applicable to editing 3d surfacing toolpaths. Two additional editing functions that are particularly designed for 3d surfacing toolpaths are presented in this chapter. They are project and trim.

17.1 Project Function

Project function allows toolpaths to be projected onto a plane, cylinder, cone, sphere, cross section or 3d surface. The projected toolpaths only change the depth (Z-coordinate) of the original toolpaths; both X and Y coordinates remain the same (Figure 17.1).

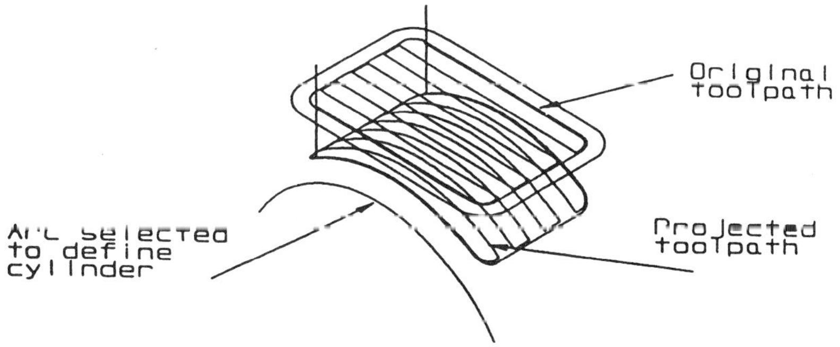

Figure 17.1

The following toolpath types can **not** be projected:

1. Drilling, boring, and taping.
2. Five axis moves.
3. Arcs in the ZX-plane and YZ-plane.

Note: that arcs in the ZX-plane or YZ-plane are normally generated from surface of revolution, 2-D contouring and 2-D swept surface.

Table 17.1 Six Types of Toolpath Projection

Project type	Description	Illustration
Plane	Project a toolpath file onto any 3d plane defined by the construction plane.	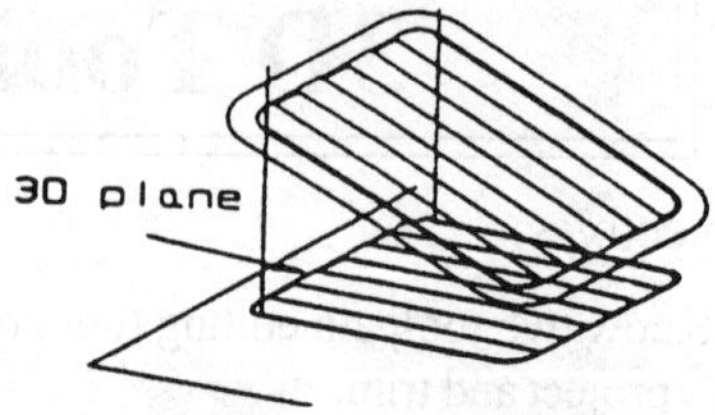
Cylinder	Project a toolpath file onto any cylinder that is defined by an arc. The axis of cylinder must be parallel to XY-plane. Concave or convex cylinders can be selected.	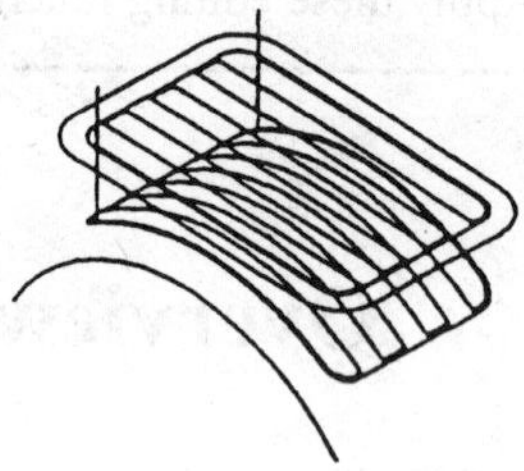
Sphere	Project a toolpath file onto any sphere. The sphere is defined by an arc. Concave or convex sphere is possible.	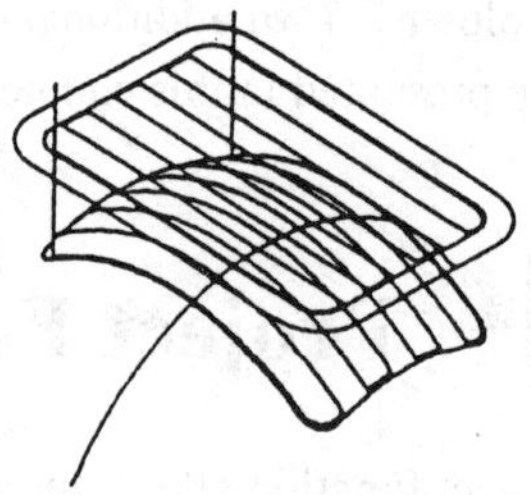
Cone	Project a toolpath file onto any cone. The cone is defined by two lines, one for the axis and the other for edge of the cone.	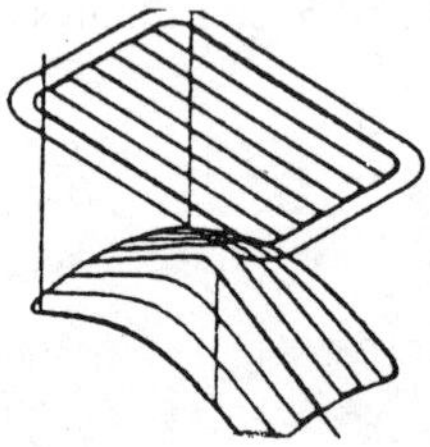
X-section	Project a toolpath file onto any cross section which is perpendicular to XY-plane or the current tool plane.	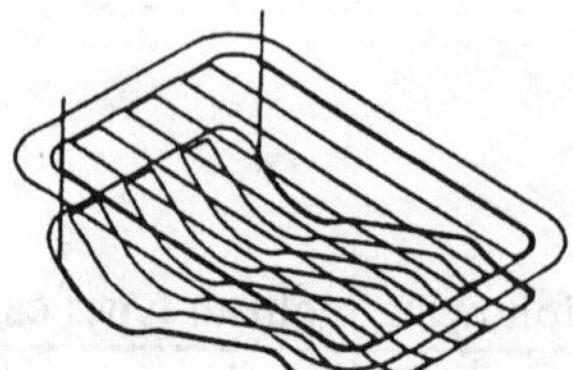

Steps for Implementing Toolpath Projects: 1

1. Create the profile or surface for defining the shape onto which the toolpaths are to be projected.
2. Generate the original toolpath file.
   (1) This file defines the X and Y coordinates of the toolpaths
   (2) Also the boundaries in the X and Y directions of the final toolpaths.
   (3) End program
   (4) Make sure the geometry to be projected fits on the surface.
3. Initiate the project function. Give a new name for projected path file.
4. Define the project parameters.
5. Accept the projected toolpaths.

Project 1. Projecting a set of lettering toolpaths to a surface

The toolpaths of a letter string which is arranged in an angular form are projected onto a sphere. Figure 17.2 shows the letter string, lettering toolpath and projected toolpath.

Figure 17.2a.

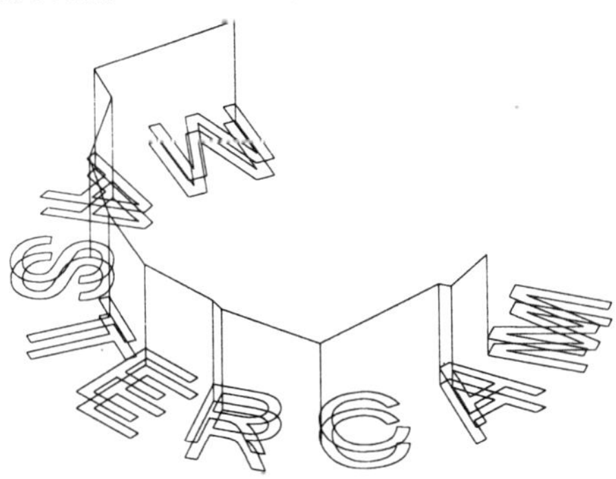

Figure 17.2b.

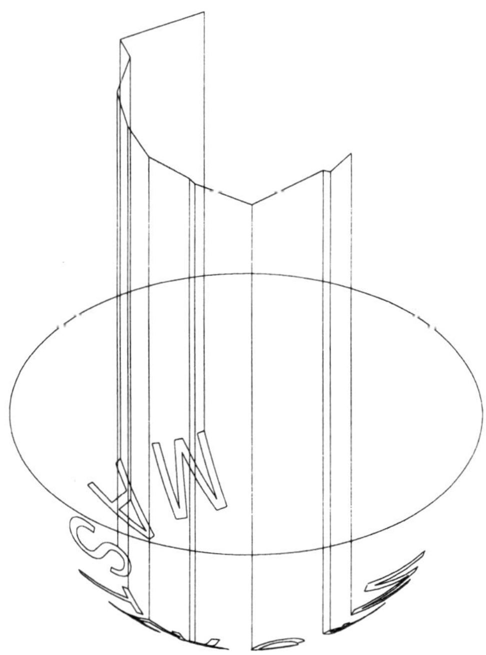

Figure 17.2c

Tips 1. Create three circles to form the wireframe model of the swept surface.

2. Create the swept surface.

3. Create a string of letters: MASTERCAM

4. Use the Contour module to generate the toolpaths for engraving letters.

5. Use the project module to project the lettering toolpaths onto the swept surface.

Step 1. Create a string of letters.

Select **Gview → Isometric**
Select **Z,** then enter **1.5** ↵
Select **MAIN MENU →Create → Next menu → Letters → True Type(R)**
Set the font parameters as shown below

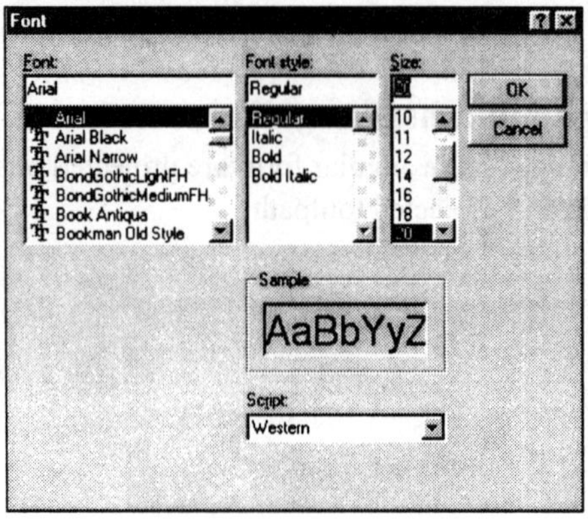

Select **OK**
Enter letters: **MASTERCAME**
Enter letter height: **0.5**↵
Select **Btm of Arc** for the "direction to write True Type(R) letters?"
Enter the letter spacing: **0.15** ↵
Enter coordinates: **0,0** ↵
Enter arc radius: **1** ↵
The letter string is added as in Figure 17.3

Figure 17.3

Step 2. Generate the toolpaths to cut the contours of the letters.

Select **MAIN MENU → Toolpaths → Contour**
Enter File name: **t1.NCI**, select **Save**
Select **Window**
Pick two points to define the window for including all entities
Select **Endpoint**
Pick the upper left corner of the first letter M
Select **Done**

Step 3. Select a tool and define the tool parameters.

Click the **right mouse button**,
then select "**Get tool from library**"
Select **tool #232** (1/8" flat end mill)
Select **Done**
Set the tool parameters as below.

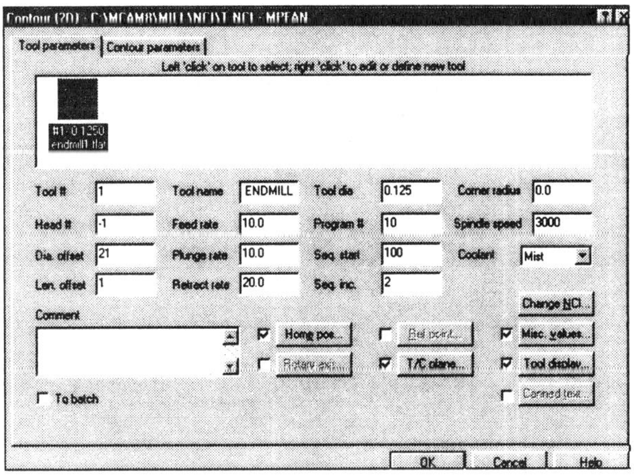

Step 4. Define the contour parameters.

Click on the "**Contour parameters**" tab
Set the contour parameters as shown here:

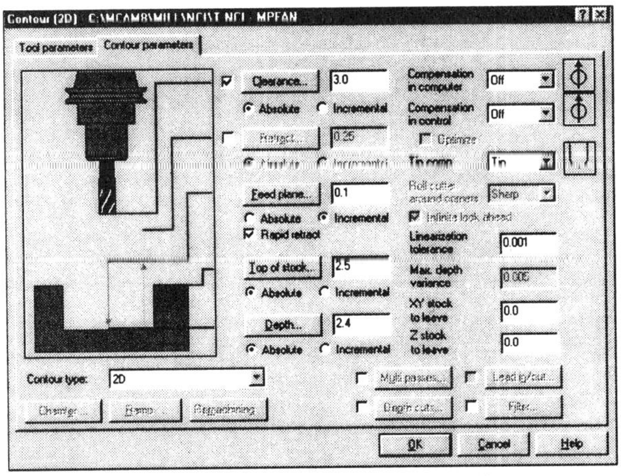

Select **OK**
The toolpaths are generated as in Figure 17.4

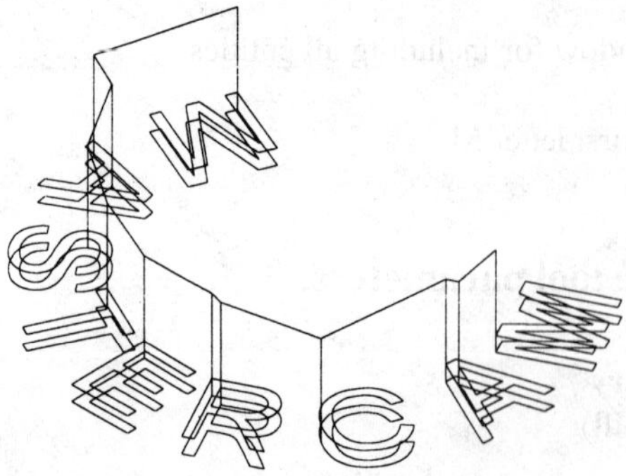

Figure 17.4

Step 5. Save the NCI file t1.

Select **MAIN MENU → NC utils → Filter**
Select **Yes** to "Operations have been modified. Create the NCI text file?"
Select **Do it → Cancel**

Select **MAIN MENU → File → Save**
Enter file name: **t1.MC8**

Step 6. Create a new file

Select **MAIN MENU → File → New**
Select **Yes** to "Are you sure you want to initialize geometry and operations?"

Step 7. Create a circle

Select **MAIN MENU → Create → Arc → Cir pt+dia**
Enter the diameter: **4** ↵
Enter coordinates: **0,0**
Select **View → Isometric**
The circle appears as in Figure 17.5.

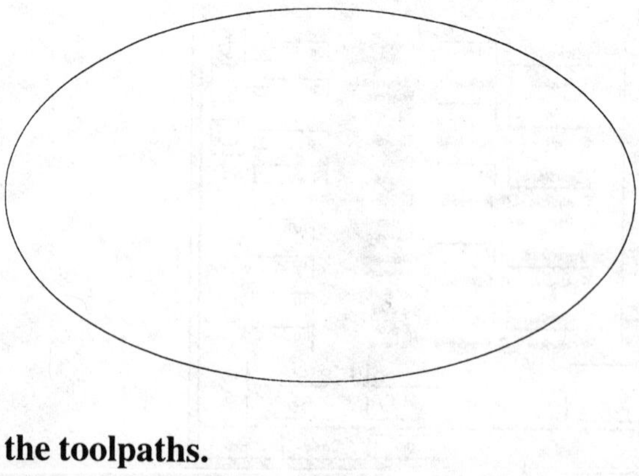

Figure 17.5

Select 8. Project the toolpaths.

Select **MAIN MENU → Toolpaths → Next menu → Project → Sphere**
Pick the circle to define the sphere
Select the "**Lower**" half

Set thte project parameters as below.

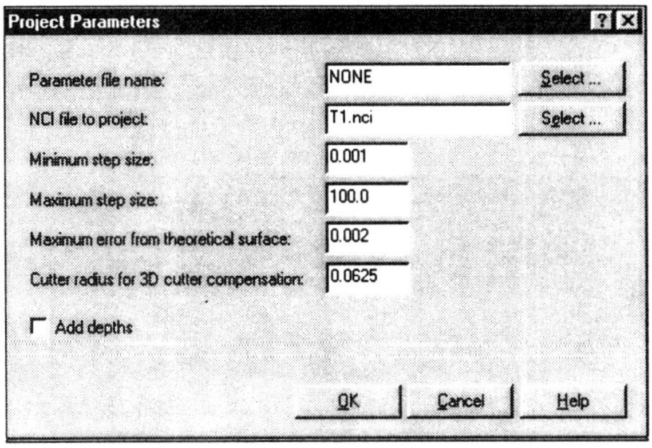

Select **OK**

Select **OK** to "#1-0.125 ENDMILL FLAT -1/8 FLAT ENDMILL has been created and added to your tool list"

The projected toolpaths are shown in Figure 17.6.

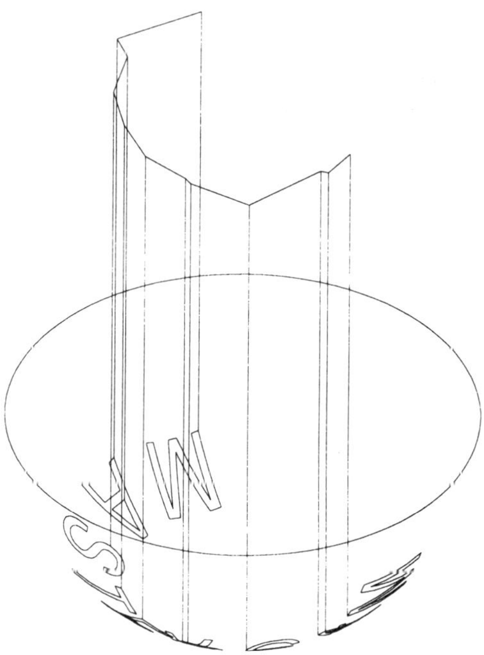

Figure 17.6

Step 9. Specify the NCI output file name.

File name to save: **proje-1.NCI**, select **Save**

17.2 Trim Function

The trim function is used to create a new set of toolpaths file by trimming an existing toolpath file to the specified boundaries (Figure 17.7). The original toolpath remains unchanged.

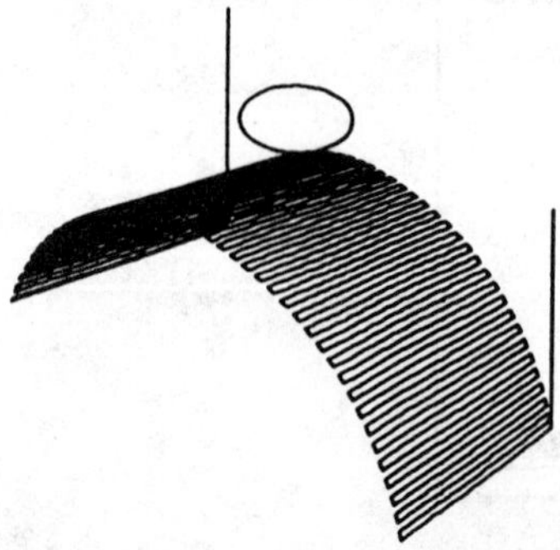

Figure 17.7a Before trimming

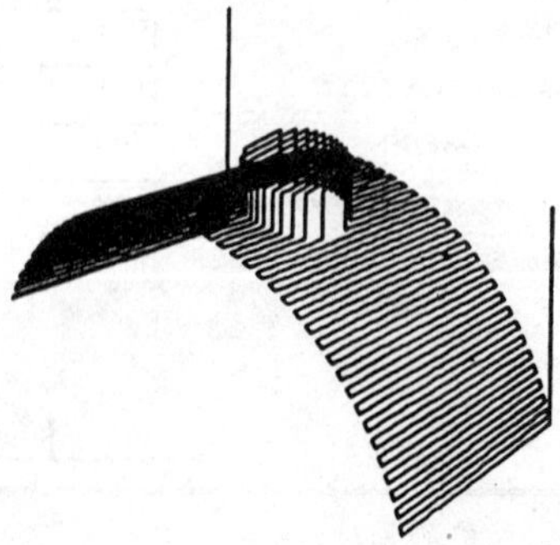

Figure 17.7b After trimming

Trimming is normally used in the following two applications:

1. To avoid islands or interferences (boss avoidance). This is especially useful in pocketing and surfacing.
2. To trim irregular boundaries at outside edges.

Trimming Boundaries

Mastercam allows us to use multiple trimming boundaries. The maximum number of boundaries is 50. The trimming boundaries must be **closed contours.** The trimming boundaries can be any shape and size and it is not necessary that they completely fall inside the toolpath range. **The trim function does not incorporate any cutter compensation. Therefore, the trimming contours should be created to reflect the center line of the cutter.**

Trimming Procedure

1. Generate the toolpath file to be trimmed and create the trimming boundaries. The toolpath (.NCI) file to be trimmed must exist before entering the Trim function.

2. Initiate the Trim function using the following commands:
   MAIN MENU → Toolpaths → Next Menu → Trim

3. Enter a new name for the trimmed file name.

4. Define trimming boundaries using the chain option.

5. Specify a point to indicate the side of the toolpath to keep.

6. Indicate whether the tool is up or down in the trimmed areas.

7. Select the NCI file to trim.

8. Accept the trimmed toolpath segment.

Project 2. Generating toolpaths for a surface and trimming the toolpaths to a rectangular boundary 2

The intent of this project is to trim the surfacing toolpaths to avoid an island of a rectangle as shown in Figure 17.8. The toolpaths are generated by using the flowline module.

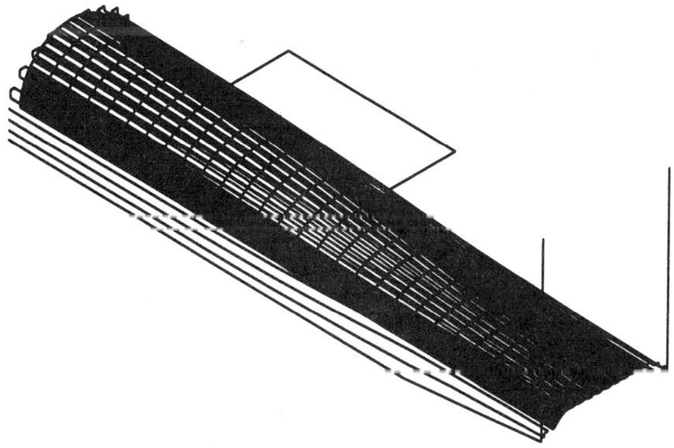

Figure 17.8a Before trimming

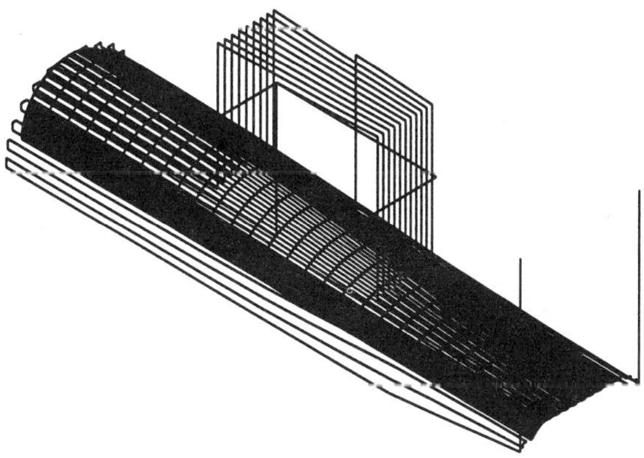

Figure 17.8b After trimming

Tips 1. The surface model used in this project is **lofts3.**

2. The island is a rectangle of 2"x 0.5". The trimming boundary for this rectangle should be 2.5"x1" because no cutter compensation is allowed in trimming. Therefore, we need to add the dimension of one-half of the cutter diameter to all sides of trimming boundary. The rectangle is centered at (-4,0) and has a height of Z1.5".

3. Use the flowline 3d toolpath module to generate the toolpaths for cutting the loft surface with a 0.5" ball end mill.

4. Initiate the trim function to trim the toolpaths to the rectangular boundary.

Step 1. Load the surface model file lofts3.

Select **MAIN MENU → File → Get**

Enter file pattern: **lofts3** ↵

The surface model should appear on screen as in Figure 17.9.

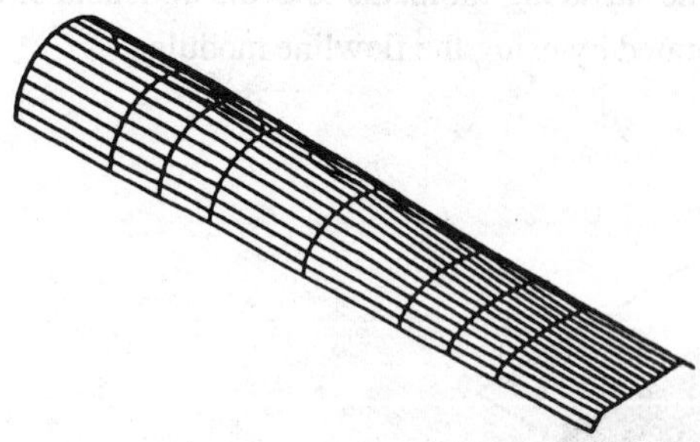

Figure 17.9

Step 2. Create a rectangle as the trimming boundary.

Select **Cplane → Top**
Select **Z** then enter **1.5** ↵
Select **MAIN MENU → Create → Rectangle → 2 points**
Enter the lower left corner: **-5.25,-0.5**
Enter the upper right corner: **-2.75,0.5**

The rectangle is added to the drawing as shown in Figure 17.10 on the next page.

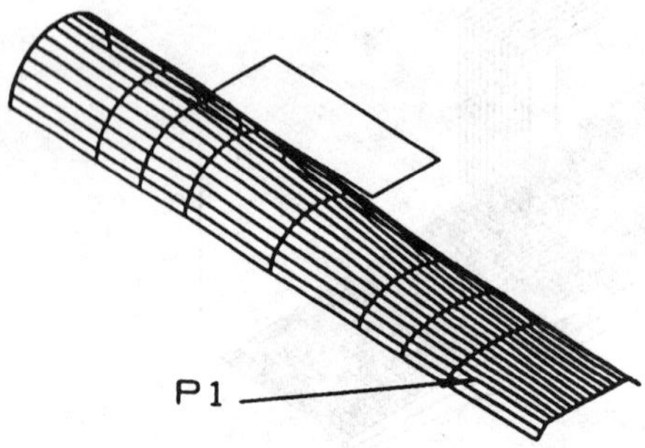

Figure 17.10

Step 3. Initiate the flowline toolpath module. Use the pick points in Figure 17.10.

Select **MAIN MENU → Toolpaths → Surface → Finish → Flowline**
Enter File name: **lofts3.NCI**, select **Save**
Select a surface: pick **P1**
Select **Done**

Step 4. Select a tool and define tool parameters.

Click the right mouse button, then select "Get tool from library"
Select **tool #256** (1/2 sphere end mill)
Select **OK**
Set the tool parameters as shown next.

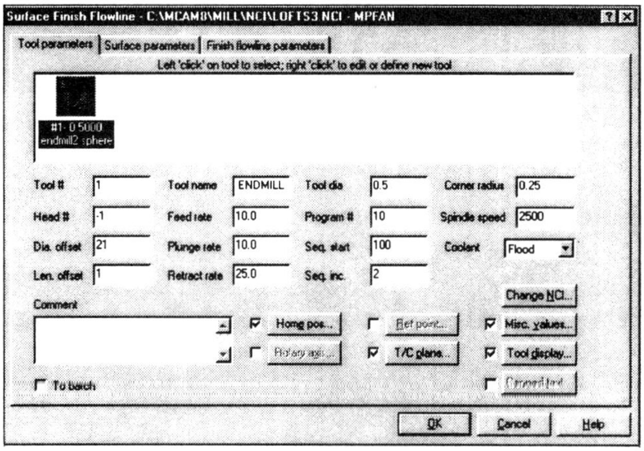

Step 5. Define the Surface parameters.

Click on the "**Surface parameters**" tab

Set the Surface parameters as below.

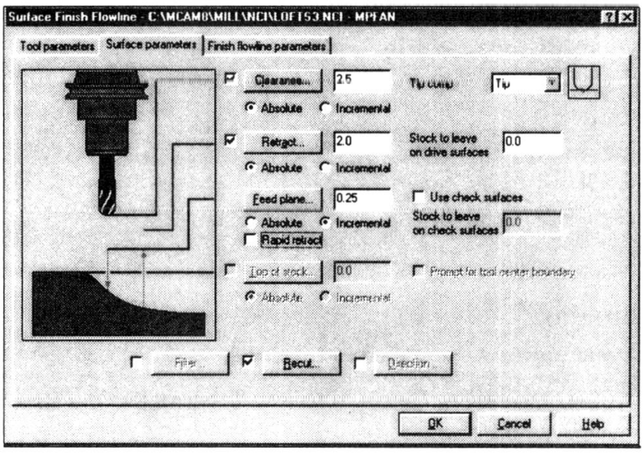

Select the **Finish flowline parameters** tab to advance to the flowline menu.

Step 6. Define the Finish flowline parameters.

Set the Finish flowline parameters as shown below.

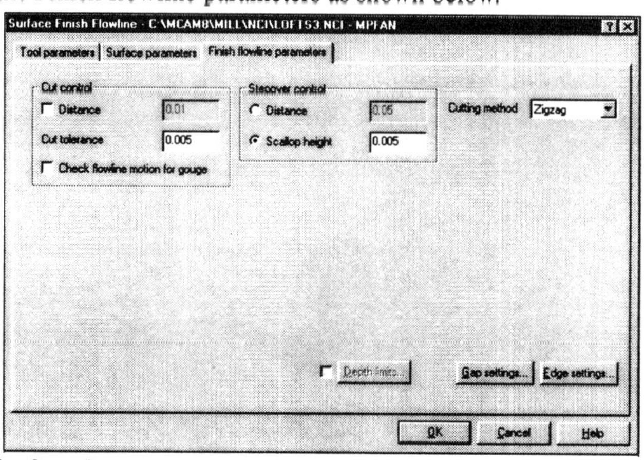

Select **OK**
Select **Cut dir**
Select **Done**
The toolpath is generated as in Figure 17.11.

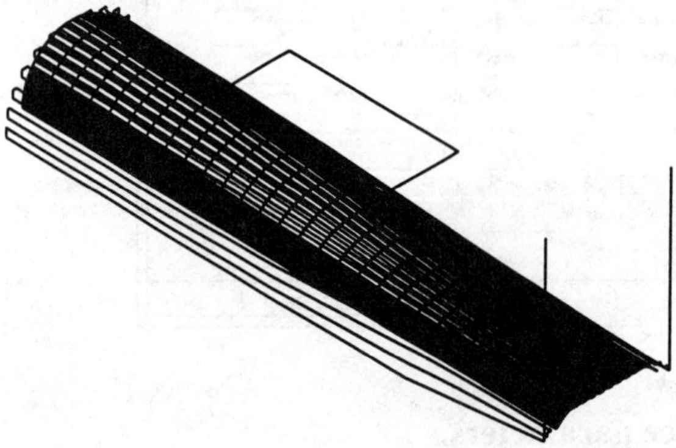

Figure 7.11

Step 7. Save the project file and toolpath file.

Select **MAIN MENU → File → Save**
Enter file name: **lofts3.MC8**
Select **Yes** to "Delete old lofts3.mc8"
Select **MAIN MENU → NC utils → Filter**
Select **Yes** to "Operations have been modified. Create the NC text file?"
Select **Do it → Cancel**

Step 8. Initiate the Trim function.

Select **MAIN MENU → Toolpaths → Next menu → Trim**
Define the trimming boundaries 1: Select **Chain,** then pick any line on the rectangle
Select **Done**
Enter a point on the side to keep: pick the lower left corner of the toolpath
Keep the tool? select **Up**
Enter the file name: **lofts3**
Select **Open**
The trimmed toolpaths should resemble Figure 17.12.

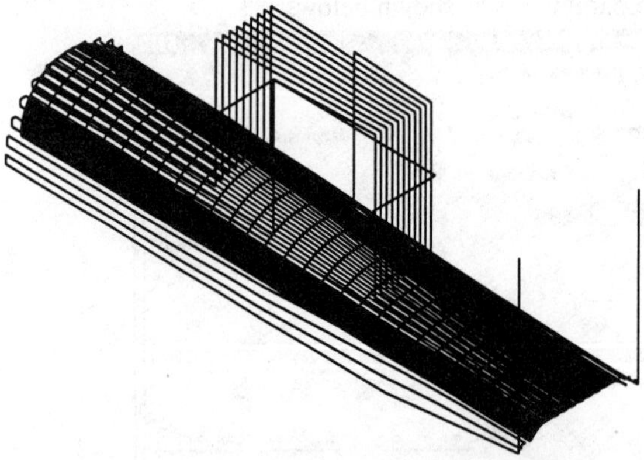

Figure 17.12

Ex Exercises

1. What are the five toolpath editing functions commonly used in editing 3d surfacing toolpaths?
2. How does the project function affect the X, Y, and Z coordinate values of the toolpath?
3. List three types of toolpaths that can not be projected.
4. Explain the main features of the trim function.
5. Identify two typical applications of the trim function.
6. What is the requirement of a trimming boundary?

Chapter 18

3D Toolpath Planning

Objectives:
1. Understand the toolpath generation procedure for 3D surfaces.
2. Identify features and surfaces of the parts.
3. Determine edge and skin profiles of a wireframe model for a surface model.
4. Select the surface modeling module and toolpath module for each surface.
5. Select proper tooling and machining parameter

Overview

The procedure of process planning for 2D projects is presented in chapter 10. Most of the material covered in chapter 10 is applicable to 3D surfacing projects. However, there are unique features in 3D surfacing toolpath planning that warrant the discussion of this topic in a separate chapter. This chapter focuses on surface identification, wireframe model construction, surfacing module selection, toolpath generation, toolpath editing, tools and machining data selection, and NC files management. The flow chart for planning 3D surfacing toolpaths is illustrated in Figure 18.1 on the following page.

18.1 Identifying Features and Surfaces

A part feature is the distinctive shape and size to be produced in a part. Part features can be generalized as 2D and 3D features. Flat surfaces, external and internal profiles, pockets, holes, etc., are typical 2D features. Surfaces are 3D features. It is very common to have a combination of both 2D features and 3D features in a part. In this case, we need to treat 2D features and 3D features separately.

The 3D features are identified according to their types; geometric surfaces or free-form surfaces, and single surface or composite surfaces. The surface type dictates the complexity of the required wireframe model. Some surface models require a single patch edge profile, while some need multiple patches or multiple profile sections. Geometric surfaces provide an exact surface skin, while the free-form surfaces furnish approximated surface texture. In most cases, a surface can be modeled by more than one surfacing technique. The answers to the following questions should help in selecting the proper surfacing techniques which in turn determine the required wireframe model:

Is the surface aesthetic or toleranced?
Is it a single surface model or a composite surface model?
How accurate is the surface skin required to be?

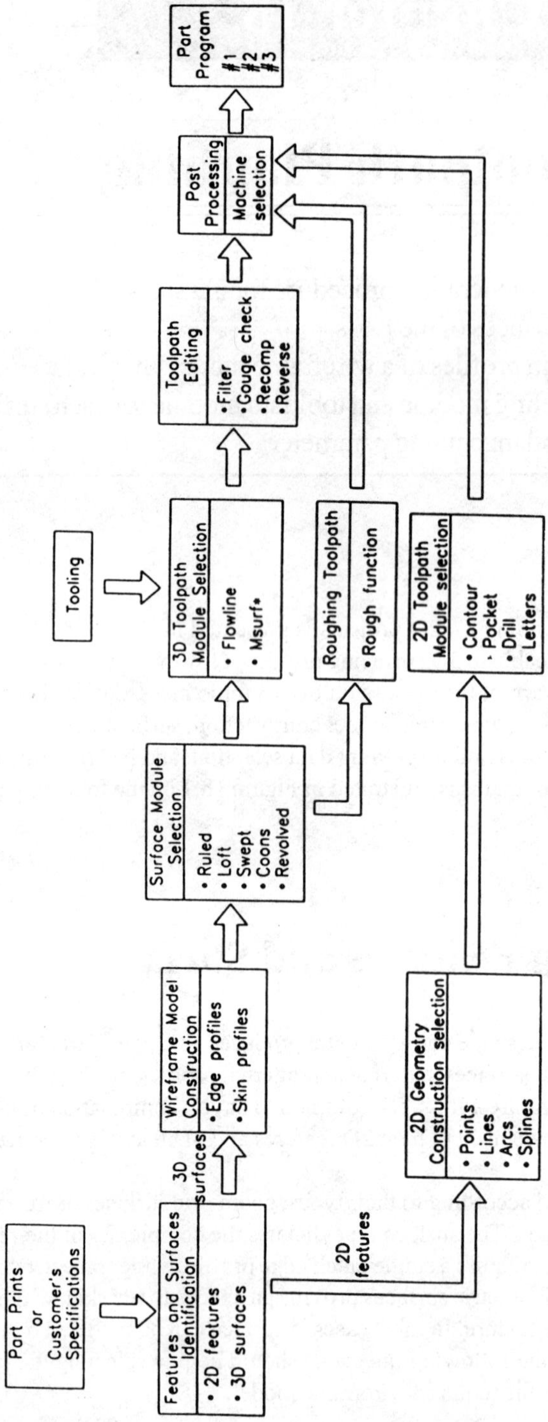
Part Prints
or
Customer's
Specifications
Features and Surfaces
Identification
• 2D features
• 3D surfaces
3D
surfaces
2D
features
Wireframe Model
Construction
•Edge profiles
•Skin profiles
Surface Module
Selection
• Ruled
• Loft
• Swept
• Coons
• Revolved
Tooling
3D Toolpath
Module Selection
• Flowline
• Msurf•
Roughing Toolpath
• Rough function
2D Geometry
Construction selection
• Points
• Lines
• Arcs
• Splines
2D Toolpath
Module selection
• Contour
• Pocket
• Drill
• Letters
Toolpath
Editing
•Filter
•Gouge check
•Recomp
•Reverse
Post
Processing
Machine
selection
Part
Program
#1
#2
#3

Figure 18.1

18.2 Wireframe Model Construction

A CAD system uses a set of edge and skin profiles to create a surface. The complete set of edge and skin profiles for a part is often referred to as the wireframe model. Actually, in most surface modeling cases only a partial wireframe model is required. The following two guidelines should help to determine how many edge and skin profiles are needed and where they are located:

> **Edge profiles** should be defined at the outer boundaries for all sides
> **Skin profiles** should be used to represent significant features in the surface skin

The edge profiles define the shape of the surface outer boundaries. They are definitely required. The skin profiles define the detailed texture of the surface skin. The more skin profiles used, the more accurate the surface produced.

The typical elements of edge profiles and skin profiles are points, lines, arcs, splines, and surface curves.

18.3 Surface Module Selection

Choosing proper surface modeling methods is very crucial for successfully defining surfaces. The analysis of surface features should reveal the proper surface modeling techniques to be used. The six surface modeling modules Mastercam provides to create various forms of surfaces are:

Surface Type	Description
Lofted	at least three profiles created by fitting parabolically through a set of cross sectional curves
Coons	a single patch of four profiles or multiple patches created by blending a patch of three or four prescribed intersecting curves or points which form a closed boundary, or multiple patches
Ruled	at least two profiles created by connecting straight lines between profiles
Revolved	a sectional profile and a line to revolve about created by rotating a sectional shape around an axis or a line
Sweep	(1) an along contour and an across contour created by translating or rotating a sectional profile along a drive curve (2) three profiles (two along and one across, or one along and two across) created by (a) translating an across profile along two drive curves (b) translating two across profiles along a drive curve
Draft	a sectional shape created by extruding a sectional shape straight along a line

There are four secondary surfacing techniques used to generate surfaces from existing surfaces.

Surface Type	Description
Offset	an existing surface created by offsetting an existing surface by a distance
Trimmed/ Extended	an existing surface created by trimming or extending an existing surface to a specified boundary
Fillet	two existing surfaces created by generating arc cross sections that are tangent to two existing surfaces
Blend	two or three existing surfaces created by blending a smooth surface between two or three existing surfaces.

18.4 Toolpath Modules Selection

There are two ways of generating toolpaths to cut surfaces. One is directly using 3D surfacing toolpath modules to generate the toolpath from the wireframe model. The other method is to define the surface model first, then use the flowline or multisurf module to generate the toolpaths from the surface model. It is recommended that the toolpaths be generated from the surface models.

Flowline module:	generates toolpaths for cutting single surfaces
Multisurf module:	generates toolpaths for cutting multiple surfaces

18.5 Toolpath Planning

The toolpaths used to machine a part having 3D surfaces normally consists of three types: 2D toolpaths, roughing toolpaths for surfaces, and finishing toolpaths for surfaces. These three types of toolpaths should be handled separately.

1. Use the 2D toolpath modules whenever possible

The 2D toolpath modules are often used in the following operations:

- contours/profiles
- pockets
- holes
- horizontal and vertical flat surfaces

Note: Many flat planes can be defined as surfaces. But their toolpaths should be generated from 2D modules such as pocket or contour. Sloped flat planes should be treated as surfaces in generating their toolpaths.

2. Roughing toolpaths for surfaces

The roughing toolpaths for cutting surfaces normally are 2D in nature. Therefore, their part programs are relatively much shorter than the finishing toolpaths. The workpiece should be cut to approximate size and shape by roughing toolpaths. This allows the use of one single pass of finishing toolpaths to complete the surface(s). Consequently, it helps reduce the part program size and machining time.

3. Finishing toolpaths for surfaces

Make one single pass if possible

Use the largest ball end mill that the surface curvature allows.

When the surface features are symmetrical, generate the toolpaths based on the selected surface segments. Then use toolpath editing functions such as mirror, rotate, and translate to simplify the process. The larger the number of surfaces included in the multisurf function, the longer the time needed by the system to generate the toolpaths. It may take many hours for the system to generate the finishing toolpaths for cutting a composite surface model of 60 surfaces that are formed by 10 symmetrical segments about the center. The process time can be reduced to merely 20 minutes if the primary toolpaths for cutting one of ten surfacing segments is generated, and then rotated to the other nine locations.

The machining sequence for surface(s) starts with 2D machining, then is followed by roughing and finishing.

18.6 Tooling

Two types of cutters that are used extensively in machining 3D surfaces are ball-end mills and bull-corner mills. The radius of ball-end mills are one-half of the cutter diameter. The radius of the corner arc for bull-corner mills is smaller than one-half of the cutter diameter. The following tips can be used to select proper tools for machining 3D surfaces:

- Use the larger cutter. The larger cutter reduces the cusp height, allows bigger stepover values, and shortens program size.

- The largest cutter usable is limited by the size of the surface curvatures and surface gaps. The cutter radius must be at least slightly smaller that the smallest surface curvature or its diameter should be smaller than the smallest surface gap in the model. A gouging or undercut may occur when the cutter size is too large.

- Cusp height is one of the main factors determining the roughness and tolerance of the machined surfaces. The formula given below can be used to calculate the cusp height:

$$Hc = R - [R2 - (S/2)2]\ \tfrac{1}{2}$$

or

$$S = 2[R2 - (r\text{-}Hc)2]1/2$$

where Hc = cusp height
R = tool nose radius
S = stepover value between two cutting passes

Note: The cutting speed and feedrate for cutting surfaces are the same as that used in 2D cases.

18.7 Accuracy Requirement

Surface roughness and tolerance are the two major factors to be considered in determining the accuracy requirement. The tips given below can be used to obtain the required surface quality:

Tips

1. Use increment mode when dimensional accuracy is not crucial or surfaces are rather flat (large curvature radius).
2. Use chordal mode when dimensional accuracy is important or surfaces are irregular.
3. When chordal mode is used, the value for chordal deviation should be somewhat smaller than the required dimensional accuracy.

Use a smaller stepover value or chordal deviation value to generate the toolpaths for cutting surfaces. Then use the filter function to remove those unnecessary toolpath points. The filter function allows setting the allowed deviation or error. Any two adjacent toolpath segments that do not deviate by a value that is larger than the allowed value will be combined into one segment. This significantly shortens the part program while meeting the accuracy and tolerance requirements.

18.8 Toolpath File Management

Here are two tips toward better file management.

Tips

1. Do not combine 2D toolpaths, roughing toolpaths, and finishing toolpaths altogether in one part program.
2. The memory size of the controller needs to be known. The program size can not be larger than the available memory size of the controller. Divide the program into several subprograms if the part program is larger than controller memory.

3D Toolpath Planning Examples

Two projects are given in this section to show how to perform toolpath planning for cutting 3D surfacing models.

Project 1.

Prepare a toolpath plan for cutting a composite surface model as shown in Figure 18.2. This surface model is also project 7 of chapter 13.

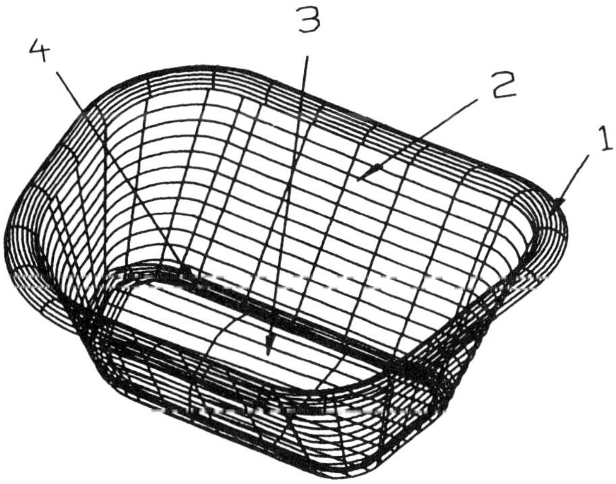

Figure 18.2

Step 1. Identify the part features and surfaces to be machined.

The following four surfaces can be identified in this model. Together they form a composite surface model that can be used to generate roughing toolpaths and finish toolpaths.

1. Top rim surface
2. Wall surface
3. Bottom flat surface
4. Fillet surface

Step 2. Select the surface modeling techniques for each surface.

The surface modeling techniques used for the four surfaces are:

1. **Top rim surface**	swept surface module with 2 along and 1 across
2. **Wall surface**	coons surface model or ruled surface module
3. **Bottom flat surface**	ruled surface
4. **Fillet surface**	fillet surface model

Step 3. Construct the wireframe model.

The complexity of the required wireframe model dictates the type of modeling techniques used and the required accuracy on the surface skin. The edge profiles an skin profiles of each surface are listed below and indicated in Figure 18.3.

Top rim surface	Edge profiles: contours 1 and 2 as well as arc 4 Skin profiles: arc 4
Wall surface	Edge profiles: contours 2 and 3 Skin profiles: lines 5-12
Bottom flat surface	Edge profile: contour 3 Skin profile: none
Fillet surface	No profile is required. Use the two existing surfaces (wall and bottom flat surfaces)

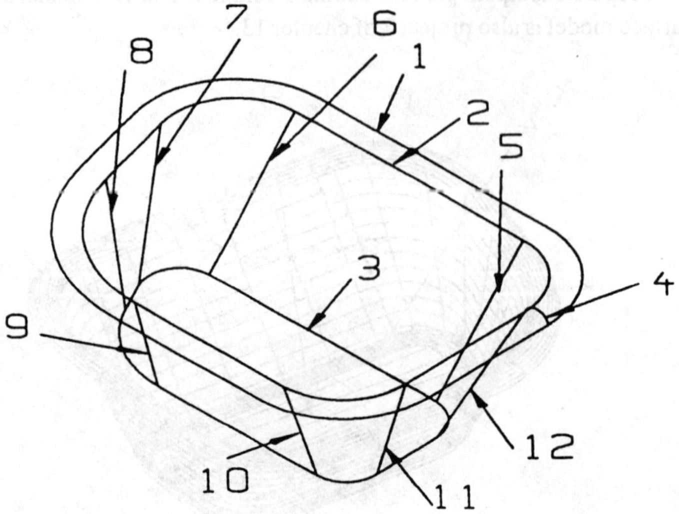

Figure 18.3

Step 4. Select toolpath modules.

The toolpaths required to machine this project consist of two parts; roughing toolpaths and finish toolpaths. Since this is a model with multiple surfaces, the best toolpath module is the Multisurf toolpath module. Use the rough function of the Multisurf module to generate the roughing toolpaths and the finish function of the Multisurf module to generate the finish toolpaths for the surface model, respectively.

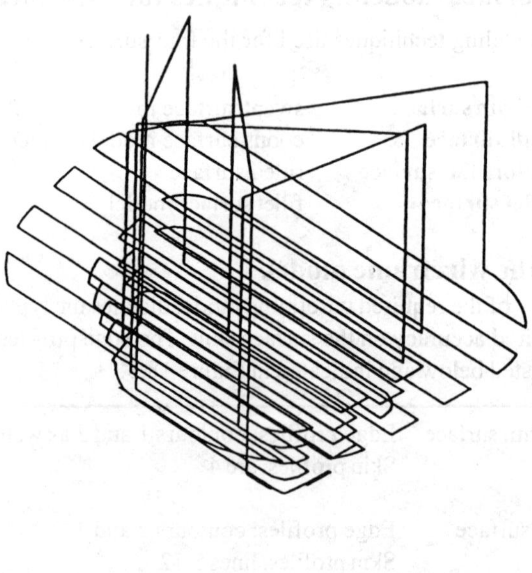

Figure 18.4

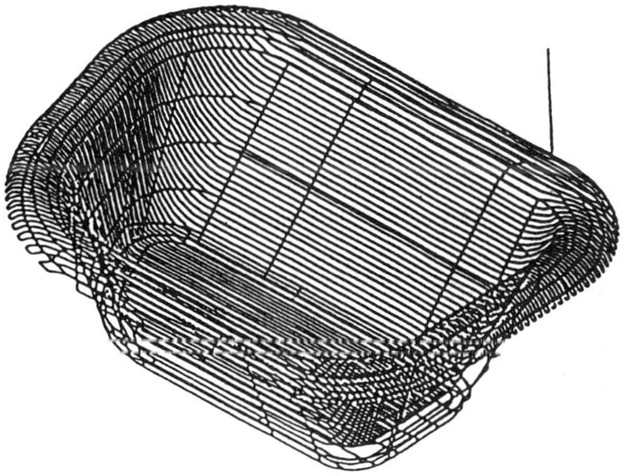

Figure 18.5

Step 5. Select the tooling and machining information.

Cutters: Roughing	¾" end mill	
	Finishing	3/8" ball end mill
Machining data:	Roughing:	Cutting speed= 350 fpm (or 2670RPM) Feedrate = 10 inches/min Depth of cut = 0.15 inches/pass
	Finishing:	Cutting speed= 250fpm (or 2500RPM) Feedrate = 15 inches/min Chordal Deviation= 0.01 inches

Project 2.

Prepare a toolpath plan for cutting a very complicated surface model as shown in Figure 18.6. This surface model is project 11 of chapter 13. The finish toolpaths for the surface model are given in project 8 of chapter 15.

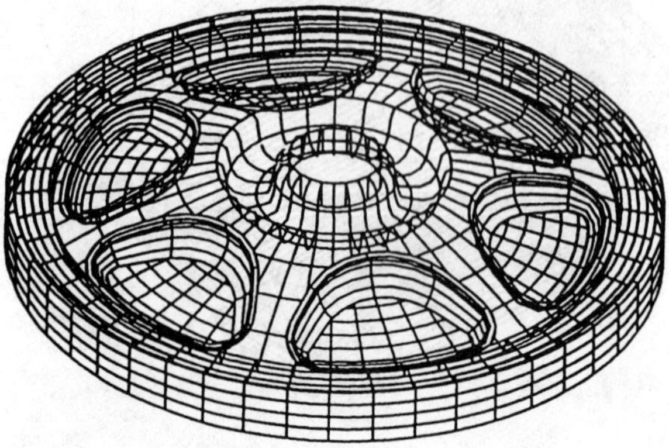

Figure 18.6

Step 1. Identify the part features and surfaces.

The complete surface model consists of 48 surfaces that are formed by six segments that are symmetric about the origin. This model can be generated by modeling a surface segment as shown in Figure 18.7 and then copying this surface segment onto five locations by rotating about the origin. Therefore, we need to define only the following eight surfaces:

1. Inner hole surface (straight circular surface)
2. Hub surface
3. Upper surface
4. Lower surface (pocket bottom surface)
5. Pocket wall surface
6. Fillet surface
7. Rim surface
8. Outer surface (straight circular surface)

Note: The upper and lower surfaces are trimmed surfaces.

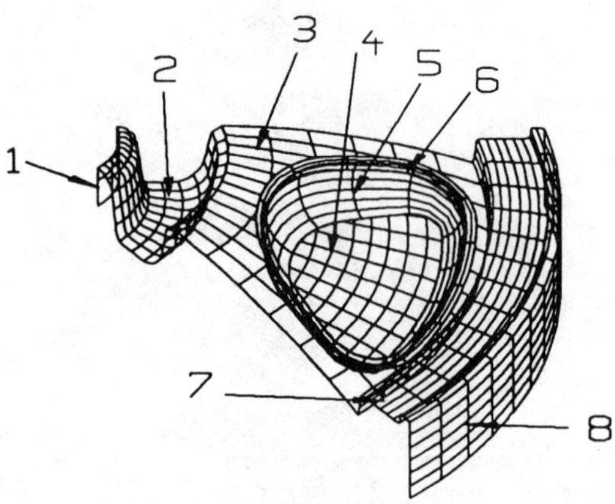

Figure 18.7

Step 2. Select the surface modeling techniques for each surface.

2

The surface modeling techniques used for the eight surfaces are listed below. Some surfaces can be modeled by more than one technique.

1. **Inner hole surface:** revolved or swept surface module
2. **Hub surface:** swept surface module (2 along and 1 across)
3. **Upper surface:** swept surface module (2 along and 1 across) and trim function (trimmed to fillet surface)
4. **Lower surface:** swept surface module (2 along and 1 across) and trim function (trimmed to pocket wall surface)
5. **Pocket wall surface:** swept surface module (2 along and 1 across)
6. **Fillet surface:** fillet surface module (between upper surface and pocket wall surface)
7. **Rim surface:** swept surface (2 along and 1 across)
8. **Outer surface:** revolved surface module

Step 3. Construct the wireframe model.

The required wireframe model consists of lines and arcs that are used to model the surface segment.

The two defining along contours for the pocket wall surface are the two surface curves that are obtained by projecting the inner and outer pocket profiles onto the upper and lower surfaces.

The required wireframe model for the basic surface segment is shown in Figure 18.8.

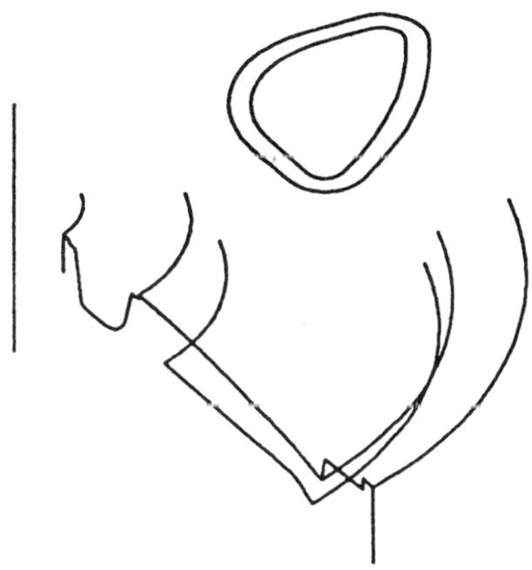

Figure 18.8

Step 4. Select the toolpath modules.

2D toolpaths: 2D pocket module to cut the inner hole surface
2D contour module to cut the outer surface

Roughing: Use the Multisurf Rough commands to generate toolpaths for roughing the following three surfaces; hub surface, upper surface, and pocket surface.
Note: The roughing toolpaths for the three surfaces listed above are copied to five locations by using the rotating function.

Finishing: Use the Multisurf Finish commands to generate toolpaths for finish cutting the composite surface model that consists of six surfaces as shown in Figure 18.9.

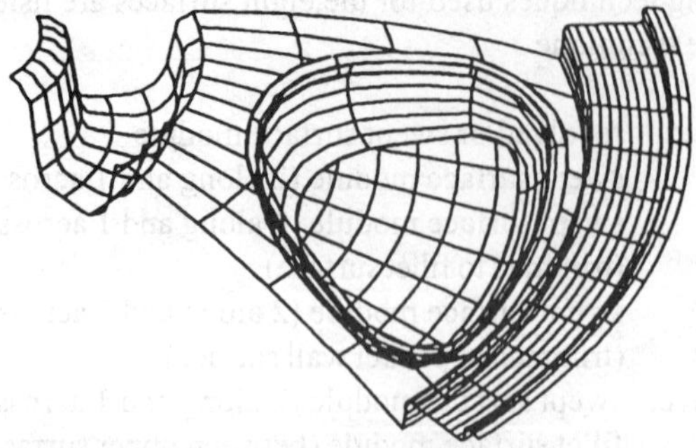

Figure 18.9

The finish toolpaths for the six surfaces should look like Figure 18.10. These finish toolpaths are then copied to five locations by using the rotating command. The finish toolpaths for the complete model are shown in Figure 18.11.

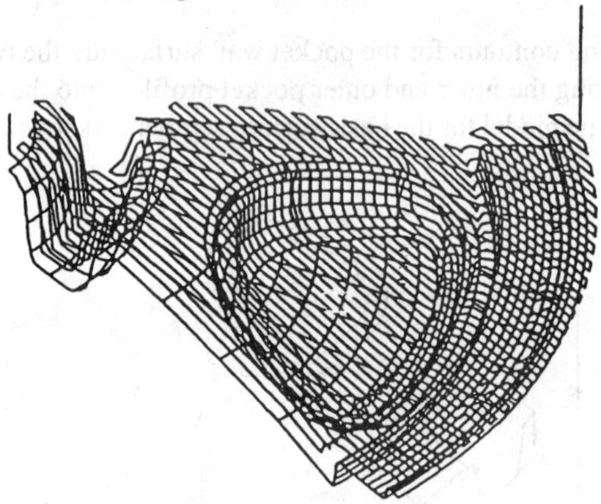

Figure 18.10

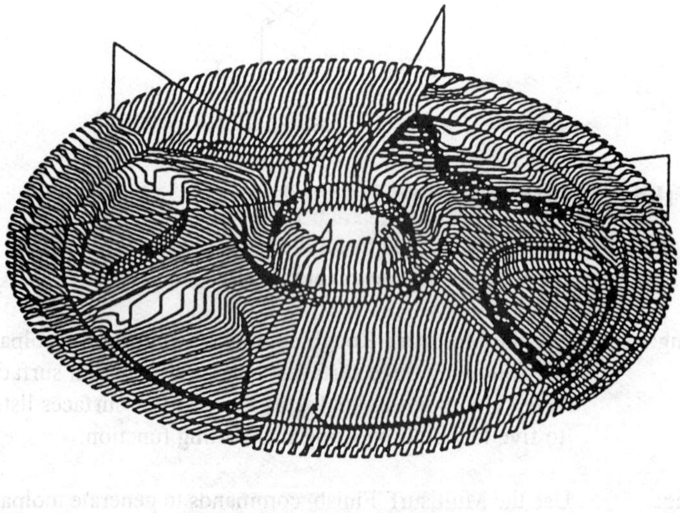

Figure 18.11

Note: It is possible to include all surfaces in a composite model to generate the finish toolpaths. However, it may take a very long time for the system to generate the toolpaths because it involves many more surfaces in the model.

Step 5. Select the tooling and machining information.

Cutters:	Roughing	1/2" end mill
	Finishing	3/8" ball end mill
Machining data:	Roughing:	Cutting speed= 350 fpm (or 2670RPM) Feedrate = 10 inches/min Depth of cut = 0.15 inches/pass
	Finishing:	Cutting speed= 250fpm (or 2500RPM) Feedrate = 15 inches/min Chordal Deviation= 0.01 inches

Ex Exercises

1. What are two types of part features? Describe their differences.
2. What is the difference between geometric surfaces and free-form surfaces in terms of the accuracy of the surface skin?
3. What is the prime factor in determining the number of skin profiles needed in a surface model?
4. What are typical elements of edge profiles and skin profiles?
5. List the six surface modeling modules in Mastercam. What is the required minimum number of profiles for each surface modeling module?
6. List the four secondary surfacing techniques.
7. Describe the two ways to generate toolpaths for cutting surfaces.
8. Explain when you should use the flowline and multisurf modules, respectively.
9. Explain why the 2D toolpaths, roughing toolpaths for surfaces, and finish toolpaths for surfaces should be generated separately and stored in different files.
10. What are two types of cutters that are extensively used in machining 3D surfaces?
11. Why is the larger cutter recommended in cutting surfaces? What are the limiting factors for the largest size of the cutters?
12. What are the two major factors to be considered in determining the accuracy of surfaces?

Chapter 19

Engraving Artworks

Objectives:

1. Scanning or obtaining artworks.
2. Converting artworks to vector format using Adobe Streamline programs.
3. Reducing the number of geometric entities using Interflux program.
4. Importing artworks to Mastercam.
5. Merging files in Mastercam.

Overview

Engraving is a major application in CNC machining. Letters and artworks are often engraved onto the parts. Artworks can be scanned and stored using the Bit Map Pixel (BMP) or other file format. These BMP files are picture image and can not be directly used in Mastercam for machining. They must be converted into the vector format. A number of software programs can be used to convert picture images to their equivalent vector form. Adobe Streamline and Corel Draw are two programs commonly used to convert images into line vector forms. The initial file normally consists of a large number of vector lines. It is impractical, if not impossible, to engrave all of the vector lines. They must be reduced to a manageable size. Adobe Streamline has various functions which smooth vector entities and reduce the number of entities. The Interflux program also can be used to reduce the large number of vector entities to a smaller number of vector lines while not significantly sacrificing image quality.

This chapter covers the procedure for converting artworks to the vector format and generating engraving toolpaths using Mastercam. Emphasis is given on to how to prepare artworks, converting drawing images to vector format using the Streamline program, reducing vector entities using the Interflux program, importing vector drawings into Mastercam, and generating engraving toolpaths to cut artworks.

19.1 Artworks and Bitmap Images

Artworks are pictorial illustrations that can be created in a wide variety of ways. Typical computer artworks include paintings, drawings, photos, sketches, and calligraphies. Artworks in any form can be readily converted into bitmap image files. These bitmap image files then can be manipulated and become readable to Mastercam for engraving. Bitmap images, also referred to raster images, use a grid of small squares known as pixels to represent graphics. A pixel, (from picture element) is the smallest visual element on a computer screen. Each pixel in a bitmap image has a specific location and color value assigned to it. When working with bitmap images, you edit a collection of pixels rather than shapes or objects.

Bitmap images can be created in one of the following ways:

- Create an image using an image-processing application software program
- Import an image from a clip-art collection
- Obtain an image by using a scanner or video digitizer

The digital bitmap image files can be saved in several formats. Some commonly used image file formats are:

BMP (Bit Map Pixel)
PCX (Windows PaintBrush)
TIFF (Tagged-Image File Format)
PSD (Photoshop)
PNT (MacPaint)

19.2 Vector Formats

The geometry types allowed in Mastercam include points, lines, arcs, splines, and surfaces. Picture image files can not be directly used in Mastercam. One way to make picture files usable in Mastercam is to convert images into the vector format. In vector format, images are represented by a series of short line elements. The vector representation of an image often requires more than ten thousand short line and arc elements. We need to carefully control the setting parameters to reduce the large number of vector elements. Figure 19.1 shows an example of bitmap image to vector drawing conversion. A comparison between bitmap images and vector artworks is summarized below

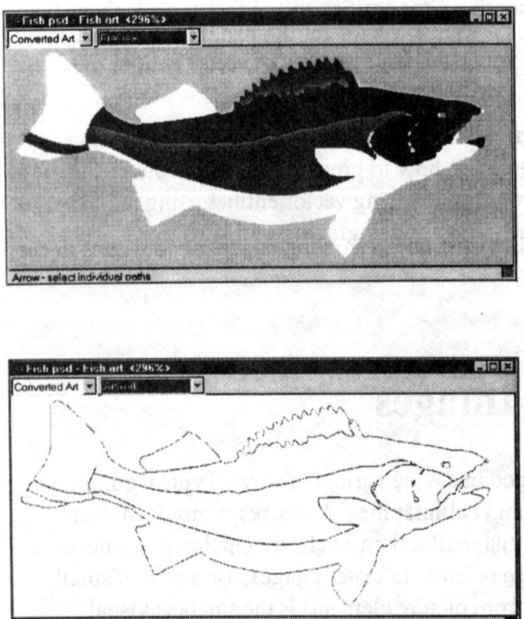

Bitmap Images

- Raster images.
- Use pixels, small square grids, to represent graphics.
- Can be distorted, lose details if they are manipulated.

Vector Artworks

- Consisting of lines and curves defined by mathematical objects called vectors.
- Vectors describe graphics according to their geometric characteristics.
- Can be moved or re-sized without losing the quality of the artwork.

Figure 19.1

The image file formats used depend on the conversion program used. You can save a converted image in one of the following file formats:

DXF	Metafile (Windows)	Adobe Illustrator

Two commonly used image to vector conversion programs are Adobe Streamline and Corel Draw. We only present the necessary information required to perform conversion using the Adobe Streamline program in the next section.

19.3 Adobe Streamline Program

Adobe Streamline is a computer graphic tool used for converting bitmap images into high quality vector drawings. It produces a much smaller file size than their bitmap counterparts. Adobe Streamline also offers various editing tools for changing the original image and the converted images.

You can save a converted image in one of the following file formats:

DXF	Metafile (Windows)	Adobe Illustrator

Entering Adobe Streamline

Follow these commands to open the Adobe Streamline program:

Select Start → Programs → Adobe → Adobe Streamline 4.0

The initial menu of Streamline appears as below.

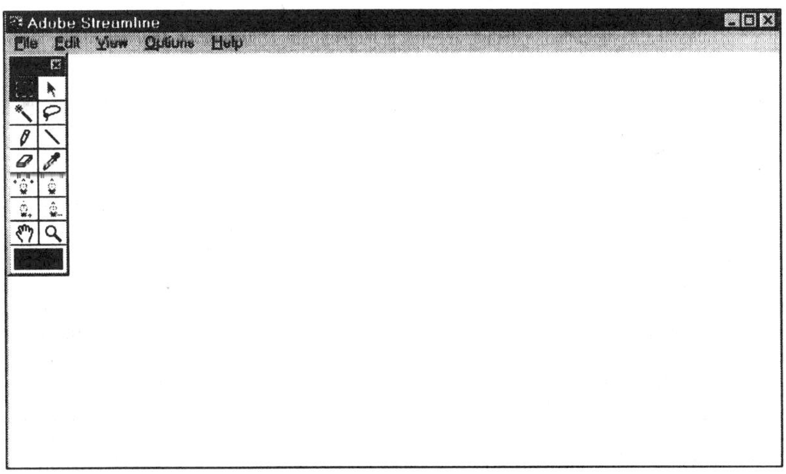

Adobe Streamline program provides three options menus for you to editing your images. They are **settings, color/B&W setup,** and **conversion setup**.

Settings menu

The Settings menu selects the image type to be converted and default parameters for each selected image type. The Settings menu appears as below.

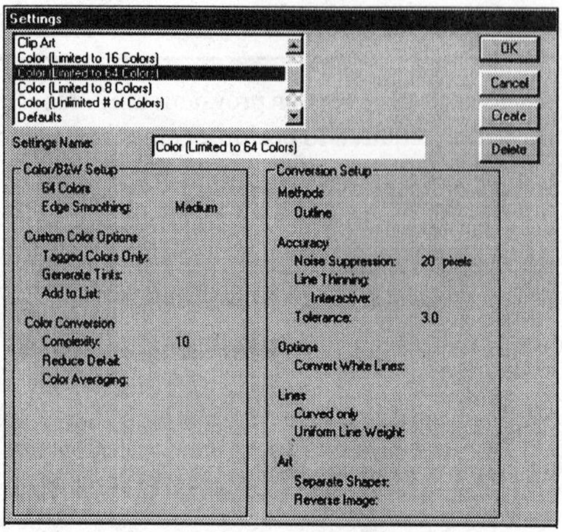

You can choose one of the following twelve image types in the list:

Blueprints	Business forms
Clip art	Color (Limited to 16 colors)
Color (Limited to 64 colors)	Color (Limited to 8 colors)
Color (Unlimited # of colors)	Defaults
Hand drawn sketches	Inked drawings
Technical illustration	New option

The parameters associated in this menu have default settings for each image type. You select an image type, the system automatically displays the default settings for relevant parameters.

Color/B&W Setup menu

This menu selects conversion settings and options for converting black-and-white, grayscale, and color bitmap images into vector line art. Active parameters will be highlighted when an option is selected with a Posterization parameter. The parameters menu for "Limited Colors" and "Black & White Only" options are given below.

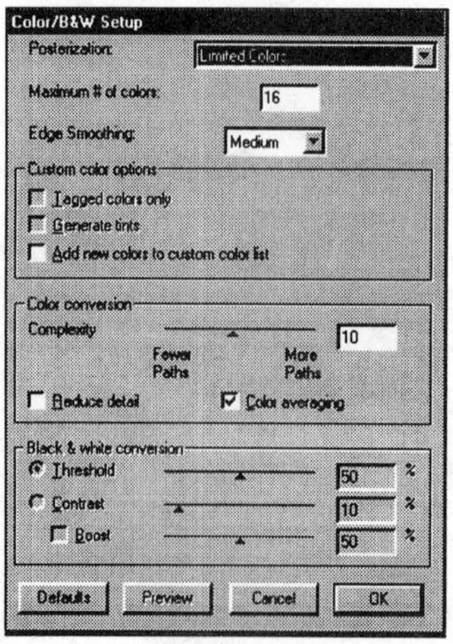

menu for limited colors

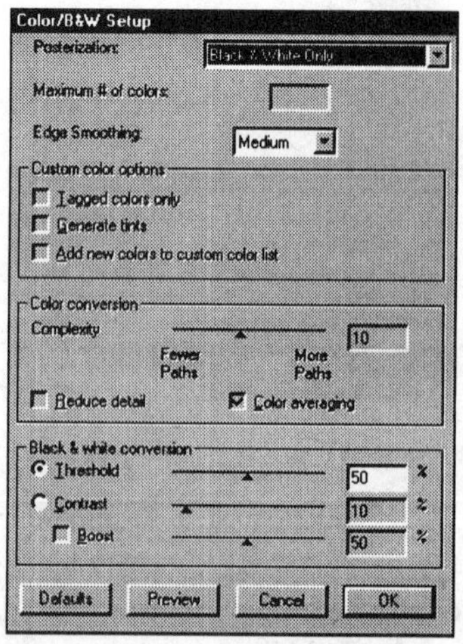

menu for black & white

Posterization This parameter selects the image mode to be converted. It has the following four types as shown in the screen capture here.

Edge smoothing This parameter allows you to control the level of edge smoothing in the converted image by limiting anti-aliasing in the original image. Anti-aliasing converts jagged edges in a bitmap image into clean edges. The higher the level of Edge Smoothing, the smoother are the paths in the converted image. Smoothing edges more than necessary can result in distorted paths.

This parameter has the following three options:

None:	no edge smoothing.
Medium:	perform average degree of edge smoothing.
Maximum:	perform maximum degree of edge smoothing.

Black & White Conversion The following three parameters are included in this group:

Threshold:	specify as a percentage the gray level above which Streamline will convert a pixel to black. For example, an 8-bit grayscale image has 256 (or 2^8) levels of gray, numbered 0 (black) to 255 (white). A threshold of 50% causes all pixels with gray-level values above 128 to be converted to black. The higher the percentage, the lower is the number of black pixels that remain.
Contrast:	specify as a percentage the contrast level above which Streamline will convert a pixel to black. Streamline compares how much each pixel contrasts with its neighboring pixels. Pixels exceeding the specified percentage are converted to black. The higher the percentage specified, the smaller is the resulting number of black pixels.
Boost:	enhance the details in the light or dark areas. It is useful when you convert color or grayscale images in which the stroke contrast is not pronounced.

Limited Colors Conversion The following parameters are used in the Limited Colors menu:

Maximum # of colors:	specify the maximum number of colors or grayscale levels to use in converting an image.
Edge smoothing:	control the level of edge smoothing in the converted image.
Color conversion:	control the way Streamline creates paths in color conversion

Color conversion has three parameters; complexity, reduce detail, and color averaging.

Complexity: This parameter defines how closely Streamline examines adjacent colors in an image to determine whether they require separate paths. A higher complexity setting creates more paths and more color variation in the converted image.

Reduce detail: This parameter reduces the level of detail that Streamline creates in a converted image. Streamline will double the resolution of an image before conversion when this parameter is toggled to Off (no √ mark). The image resolution is not doubled if this parameter is set to On (with √ mark).

Color averaging: This parameter controls how Streamline assigns colors to paths in a converted image. It is best suited for bitmap images consisting of solid areas of color. Color averaging will be disabled when convert ing continuous-tone images such as photographs or when perform ing multiple conversions with overlapping selections.

Conversion setup

The Conversion Setup menu allows you choose conversion methods, set line options, or reverse the bitmap image. It appears below.

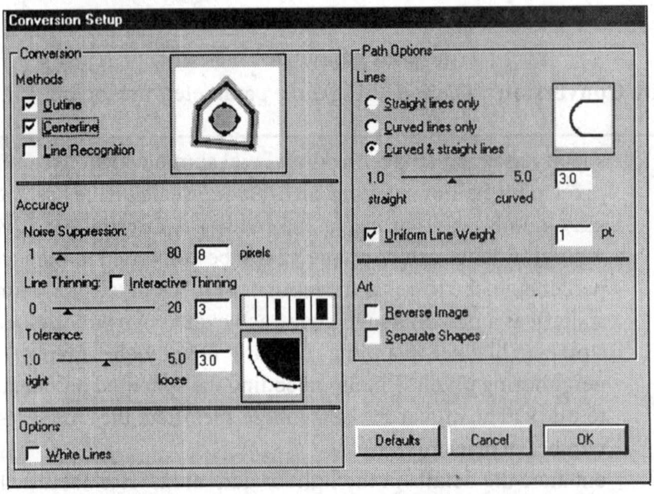

Conversion method Streamline provides the following three conversion methods:

Outline: convert images that contain filled areas and lines that vary in weight. It must be used for color images or grayscale conversions such as clip art, hand-drawn images, or photographs.

Centerline: convert images that contain consistent line weights and have no filled areas.

Line recognition: convert images that contain horizontal and vertical lines such as forms, charts, and graphs. It only recognizes and converts straight lines that are within 5% of the vertical or horizontal axis.

Path options

This group of parameters allows you to select the tolerance at which a line segment becomes straight or curved in the converted image.

Lines This parameter specifies the line type to be straight, curved, or combination of straight and curved in the converted image. It has the following three options:

Straight lines only:	all entities are represented by straight lines. Use this if the original image includes only straight lines.
Curved lines only:	all entities are represented by curved lines. Use this if the original image includes only curved lines.
Curved & straight lines:	creates both straight lines and curved lines based on the given curved scale. The curved scale sets the ratio of curved to straight lines in the converted artwork. The smaller the scale value, the more **straight line** segments. The larger the scale value, the more **curved** segments.

Accuracy

Three parameters in this group are used to select the general conversion options that determine the accuracy of the conversion. They are noise suppression, line thinning, and tolerance.

Noise suppression The Noise Suppression parameter is available only when the Outline conversion method is selected. It eliminates the stray pixels (noise) introduced by scanning a poor-quality original. Areas that are smaller than the Noise Suppression pixels settings are ignored when the image is converted.

Line thinning This parameter changes the way Streamline calculates the center of the line when it converts the line to a stroked path. Increasing the line thinning value results in more pixels being shaved off of variable-weight lines, resulting in more accurately rendered artwork and a reduction in the number of junction points. However, it will shorten lines that don't meet other lines or objects. The "Interactive Thinning" option allows you to adjust the level of line thinning during the conversion process and to preview the results of line thinning as it is performed.

Tolerance This parameter allows you to control how closely Streamline converts paths that follow curved and straight lines in the original image. A loose tolerance setting creates longer line segments and fewer anchor points. Inversely, a tight tolerance setting generates shorter line segments and more anchor points to maintain the exact detail of the original image.

Art

The following two parameters are included in this group; reverse image and separate shapes.

Reverse image:	reverses the black-and-white areas of an image before it is converted.
Separate shapes:	creates a unique path for each area in the bitmap image that is completely surrounded by a stroked line.

Two projects are presented in this section. The first project converts a clip art image to vector drawing using Adobe Streamline. The second project converts a grayscale image to a vector drawing. Both vector drawing files are saved in DXF format.

Project 1. Converting a clip art image to vector drawing

A clip art image in black and white are imported to Adobe Streamline and converted to a vector drawing. The clip art (pilot) used in this project is directly obtained from the tutorial files that come with Adobe Streamline. The clip art image and its vector drawing are shown in Figure 19.2.

Figure 19.2

Step 1. Import the clip art file.

Select **File → Open**

Change file folder and select the file as below.

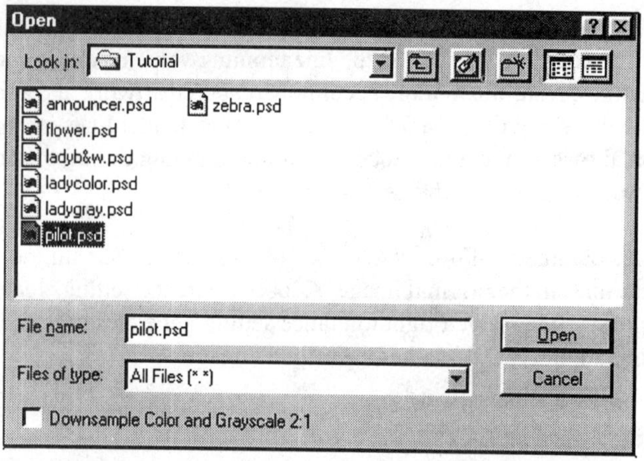

Select **Open** to import the image as shown in Figure 19.3.

Figure 19.3

Step 2. Define the setting parameters.

Select **Options → Settings**

The settings menu should appear as below.

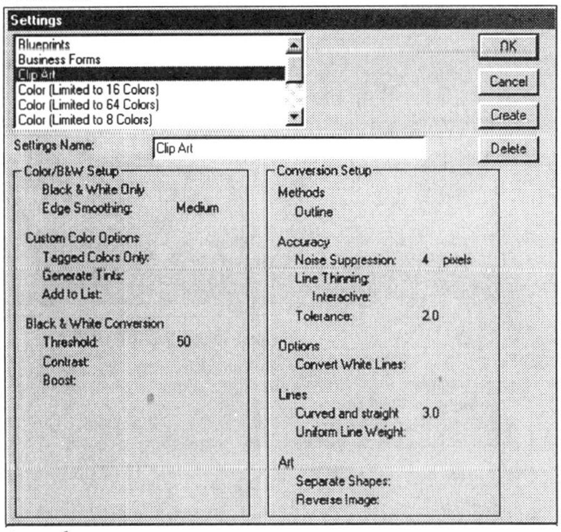

Select **Clip Art** from the settings list as above.

Select **OK**

Select **Options → Conversion Setup**

Set the conversion setup parameters as below.

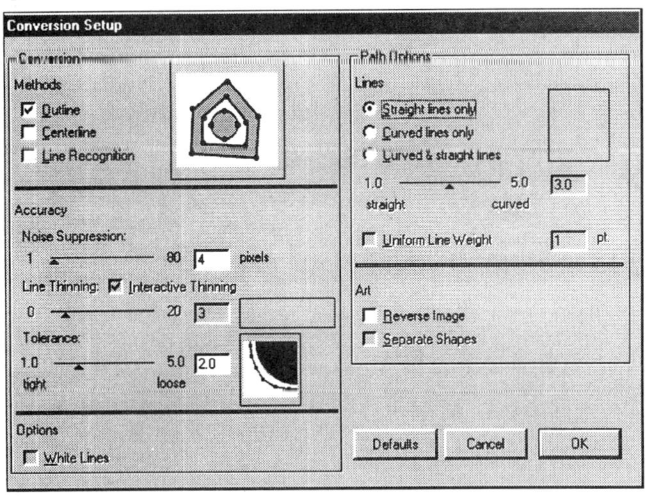

Select **OK**

Step 3. Convert and Display the artwork drawing.

Select **File → Convert** to convert the image to vector drawing

Click the pull down icon to open the pull down menu as below.

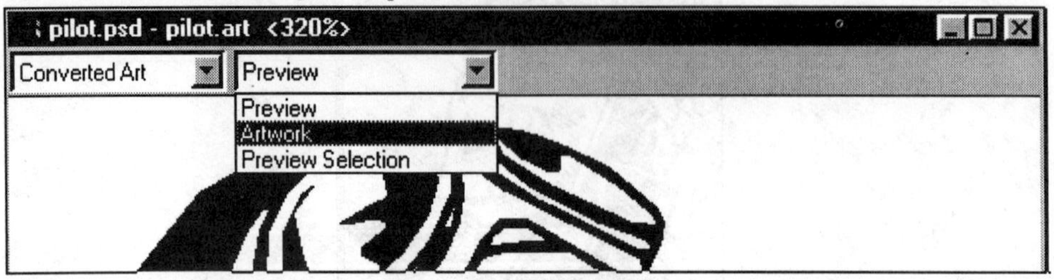

Select **Artwork** from the list

The artwork of the image should appear as in Figure 19.4.

Figure 19.4

Step 4. Save the vector drawing.

Select **File → Save Art As**

Change the file type to DXF(*.dxf) and save the file as below.

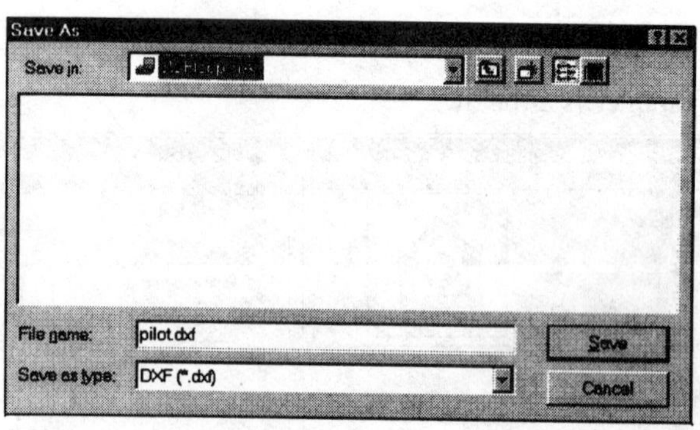

Project 2. Converting a grayscale image to vector drawing 2

A grayscale type bitmap image is converted to a vector drawing in this project. The bitmap image can be found in the project disk with drawing file "buck.psd". Figure 19.5 shows the bitmap image and its converted vector drawing.

Figure 19.5

Step 1. Import an image file "buck.psd".

Select **File → Open**
File name to open: **buck.psd**
The imported image appears as in Figure 19.6.

Figure 19.6

Step 2. Define setup parameters.

Select **Options → Color/B & W Setup**

Set the Color/B & W Setup parameters as below.

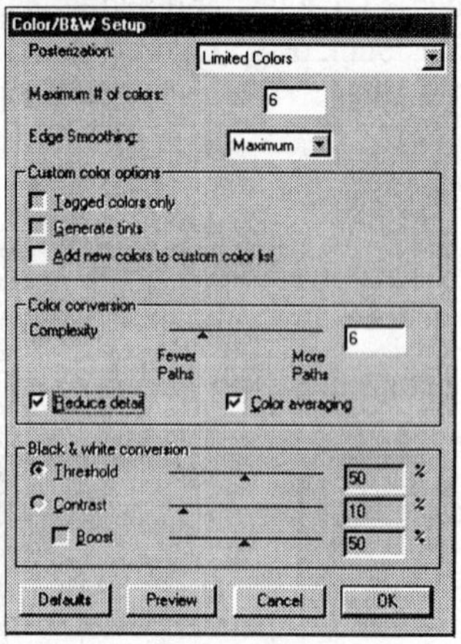

Select **OK**

Step 3. Define conversion setup parameters.

Select **Options → Conversion Setup**

Define the conversion setup parameters as below.

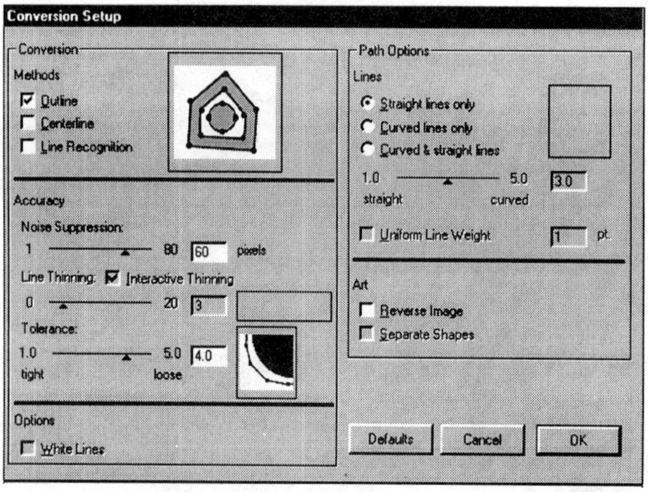

Select **OK**

Step 4. Convert the image to vector drawing.

Select **File → Convert** to convert the image to vector drawing

Select **Artwork** display Select Pull-down icon, then select Artwork from the list

The artwork drawing appears as in Figure 19.7.

Figure 19.7

Step 5. Save the artwork file.

Select **File → Save Art As**

Set the Save As parameters as below.

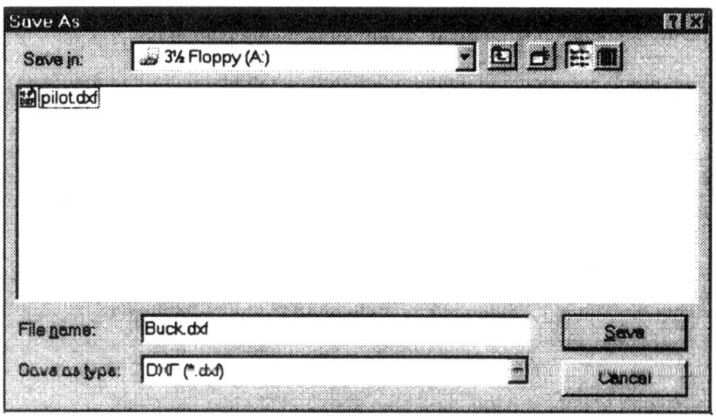

Select **Save** to save the file

19.4 Importing Vector Drawings to Mastercam

This section presents the directions for importing a vector drawing into Mastercam. The vector drawing will be temporarily placed at a location. Its size and location can be easily modified. Use the following tips to properly manipulate the imported vector drawings;

Tips
1. Place the vector drawing in a separate level and with a separate color, so it can be readily selected by level for further manipulation.

2. Use the following Xform commands to manipulate the drawing:
   a. Use the Translate function to move the drawing to proper location.
   b. Use the Scale or ScaleXYZ function to enlarge or reduce the drawing size.
   c Use the Rotate function to adjust the drawing position angularly.

3. It is possible to combine (or merge) the vector drawing with an existing Mastercam project.

4. It is possible to import more than one vector drawing file into the same project.

The procedure for importing a vector drawing to Mastercam is:

Select **MAIN MENU → File → Converters → DXF → Read File**

The vector drawings created from using Streamline may contain multiple-duplicated lines in the same area. This may create problems during generating toolpaths for engraving in Mastercam. We can use the following commands in Mastercam to eliminate the duplicated entities:

Select **MAIN MENU → Delete → Duplicate → Entities**

Project 3. Importing a vector drawing to Mastercam 3

This project imports a vector drawing file created in project 1 into Mastercam. The drawing is scaled to fit in a 2" x 4" rectangular envelop. The contour module is then used to engrave the artwork. Figure 19.8 shows the artwork and toolpath verification model.

Figure 19.8a

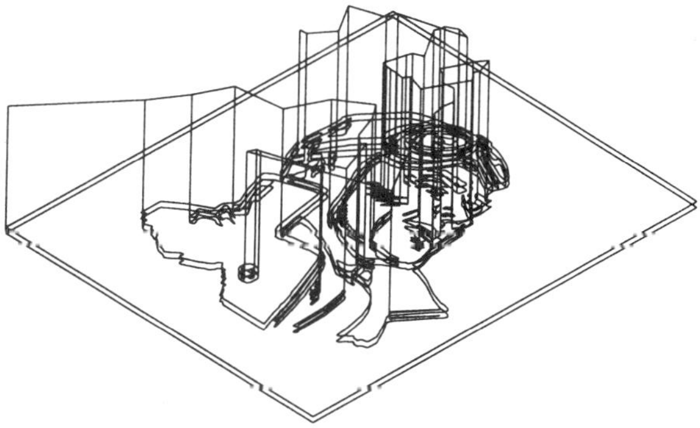

Figure 19.8b

Figure 19.8c

Step 1. Open a vector drawing file (pilot).

Select **MAIN MENU → File → Converters → DXF → Read file**

Specify File Name to Read: **pilot → Open**

Set the DXF Read Parameters as below.

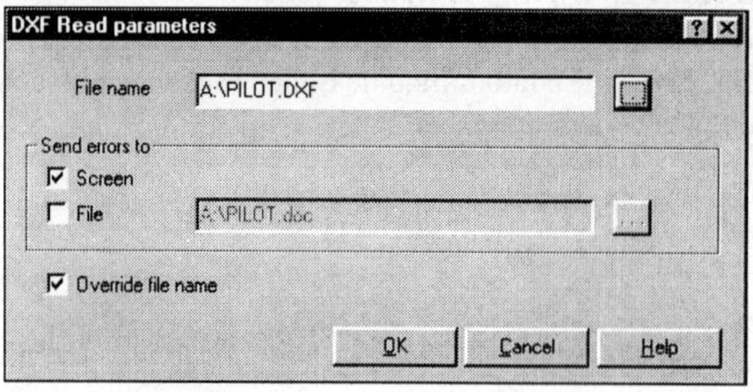

Select **OK**

The initial drawing starts as Figure 19.9.

Figure 19.9

Step 2. Create a rectangle in level 2.

Select **Level**, then enter **2**

Select **Color**, then select **Red** (12)

Select **MAIN MENU → Create → Rectangle → 2 Points**

Enter (**0,0**) and (**3.0,3.7**) as two corner points to define a rectangle

The rectangle is added as in Figure 19.10.

Figure 19.10

Step 3. Translate entities in level 1 to a new location.

Select **MAIN MENU → Xfrom → Translate → All → Color**
Select **White** (15) for color
Select **OK → Done → Rectang**
Enter the translation vector: **x0.5, y0.5**
Select **Move** and set Number of steps to **1**
Select **OK**
The new drawing becomes Figure 19.11.

Figure 19.11

Step 4. Initiate the contour function.

Select **MAIN MENU → Toolpaths → Contour**
File name for NCI: **pilot**
Select **Window**, then pick two points to form a window that includes all entities
Select the left-front corner as the search point
Select **Done**

Step 5. Select a 1/32" flat end mill and set tool parameters.

Click the right mouse button, then select "Get tool from library"
Select **tool #229** (1/32" flat end mill) from the list
Select **OK**
Set the tool parameters as below.

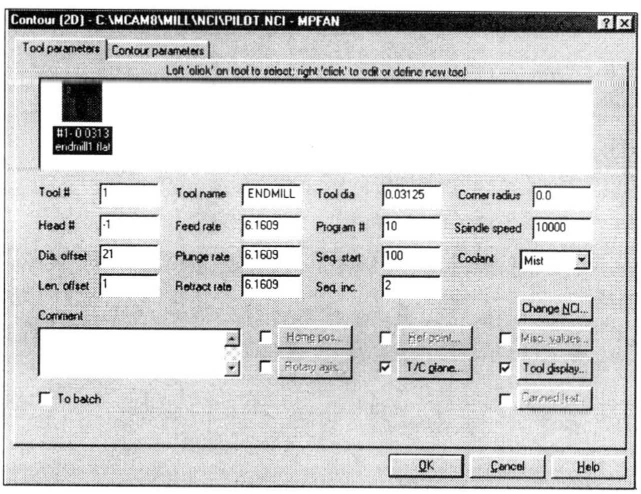

Step 6. Define the contour parameters.

Select the "Contour parameters" button

Set the contour parameters as below.

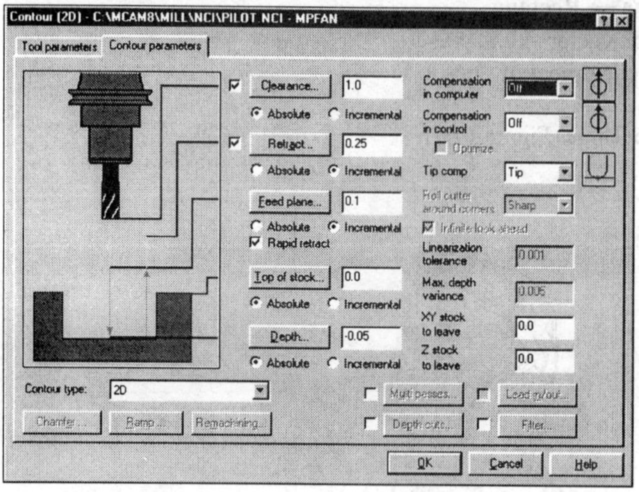

Select **OK**

Select **Gview → Isometric**

The engraving toolpaths are generated as in Figure 19.12.

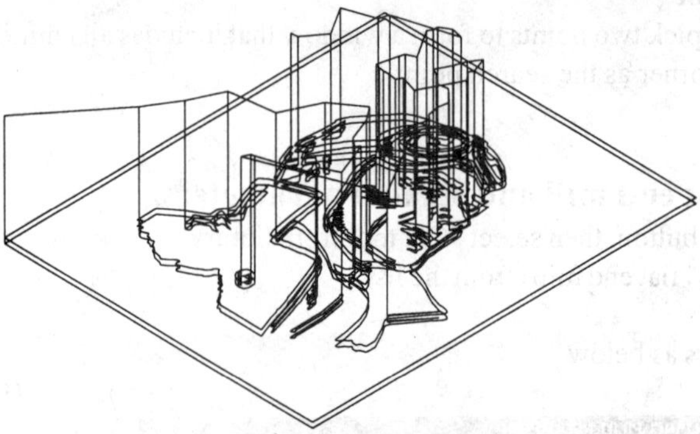

Figure 19.12

Step 7. Verify the toolpaths.

Select **Operations** to open the Operations Manager menu

Select **Verify**

Select **Configure** button on the Verify toolbar

Set the Verify configuration parameter as below

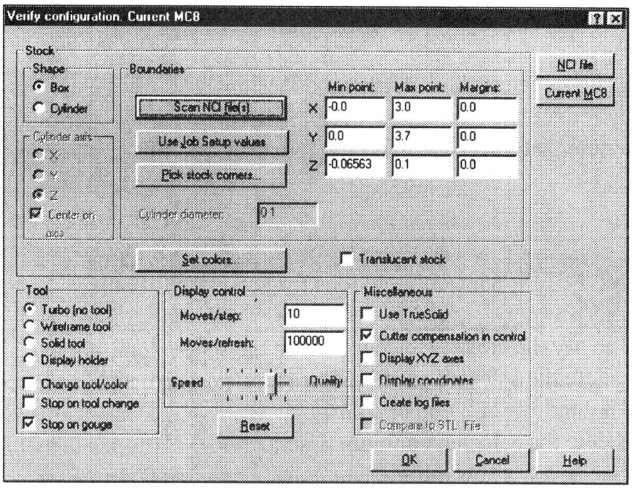

Select **OK**

Select **Machine** button on the Verify toolbar to begin verification

The toolpaths are animated on the screen.

The verification model should appear as Figure 19.13.

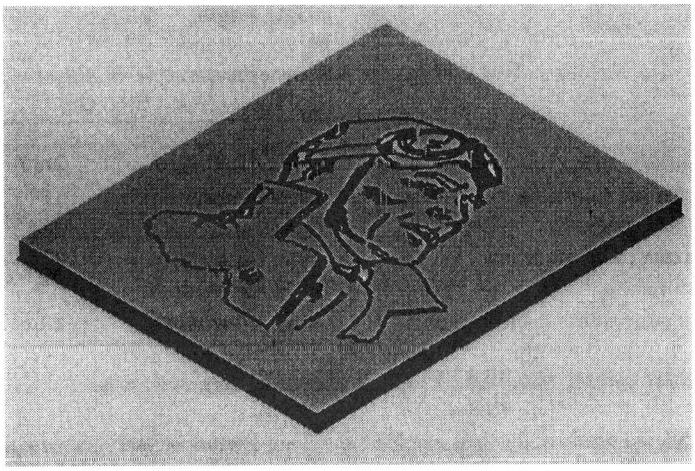

Figure 19.13

Select **BACKUP → OK** to exit the Operation Manager menu

Step 8. Save the toolpath file.

Select **MAIN MENU → File → Save**

File name to save: **pilot**

19.5 InterFlux Program

The InterFlux program developed by Northwood Designs, Inc. can be used to edit vector drawings. It can significantly reduce the number of line and arc segments by controlling the arc tolerance value and selecting the parameter settings. The main functions used in this text are grouped under Modify and Transform commands.

Modify

The Modify includes the following six functions for you to modify the vector drawing:

Arcs:	specify the arc tolerance to reduce the segment number.
Delete:	delete the selected entities. Use to delete **entities** that are specified by using a window, polygon or color.
dElete contour:	delete the selected contours. Use to delete **contours** that are specified by using a window, polygon or color.
Clean-up:	close open contours, merge between contours, or collapse small contours to points or delete them.
Reassign colors:	assign a color to selected entities.
create Polyline:	create a polyline from a series of points.

Arcs This is one of most useful functions in InterFlux for reducing the number of entities. It has these parameters:

Arc tolerance:	0.1
jaggie Cleanup:	ON/OFF
jaGgie length:	0.1
Jaggie tolerance:	0.1
Show endpoint:	ON/OFF
max arc Radius:	1000.000

The most significant parameter is "Arc tolerance". Use the larger arc tolerance value to reduce the number of segments. InterFlux will display the summary of modified results as shown here:

Original entities:	2000
Current lines:	121
Current arcs:	234
Current entities:	355
Tolerance used:	0.1
Entity reduction:	82.25%

Clean-up offers these choices:

cLose open contours:	make open contours becoming closed contours.
close Between contours:	merge adjacent contours. This function merges adjacent contours that are selected within a window, a polygon, or a color.
Collapse small contours:	shrink small contours to points or totally eliminate them. This function can be used to reduce those small contours that are smaller than the specified bounding tolerance to point or completely eliminate them. Its two parameters are: **Bounding tolerance:** 0.1000 **Modification type:** To Point/Delete
clean Move lines:	remove move lines.
Close open contours	This function makes those open contours that have a gap within the specified tolerance to become closed contours. The tolerance values are specified by the two parameters below: **Auto close tolerance:** 0.2000 **Manual close tolerance:** 0.2500

Transform

The following four parameters are used to modify the size and location of the drawing:

Scale: resize the drawing based on the given scale factors for X and Y directions. This function allows you to scale the drawing based on the given scale factors in the X and Y direction. The system will prompt "% to scale X and Y axis <X, Y>:" for you to specify scaling factors.

Force: resize the drawing to fit the drawing to a given rectangular envelop. This function allows you to resize the drawing to fit in a rectangular envelop. The system will prompt "Size to force X and Y axis to <X, Y>:" for you to specify the X and Y dimensions of the rectangle.

Translate: change the origin, move the drawing, and mirror or rotate the drawing.

Group: group the selected entities.

Translate The following seven functions are included in the Translate command:

Force to origin: force the left-front corner of the rectangular drawing envelop to move to the origin.

Center on origin: force the center of the rectangular drawing envelop to move to the origin.

Absolute move: move the left-front corner of the rectangular drawing envelop to the specified X and Y location.

Relative move: move the drawing by the given X and Y distances.

Between points: move the drawing by the distance specified by two points.

Mirror/Rotate: rotate and/or mirror the drawing.

Three sub-functions are under the Mirror/Rotate function:

Rotation angle: rotate the drawing by the specified angle.
Vertical mirror: flip the drawing in right-left direction.
Horizontal mirror: flip the drawing in up-down direction.

Leave original: make the original drawing remained and create a new drawing from rotate and/or mirror operation.

⌛ Tips for using InterFlux

1. Acceptable import file formats: HPGL (.PLT), EPSF (.EPS), AISS (.SI), DXF (.DXF)
2. Use Transform → Force functions to fix the size of the drawing.
3. Use Transform → Translate functions to relocate the origin of the drawing.
4. Use Transform → Mirror/Rotate functions to change the drawing orientation.
5. Use Modify → Arcs → Arc tolerance functions to reduce the segment number.
6. Use Modify → Clean-up functions to edit contours
7. Acceptable export file formats: NCI, NC, DXF, CDL, INC

Project 4. Using InterFlux program to edit a vector drawing

This project uses a vector drawing provided on the project disk to show how to edit drawing using InterFlux program. The Force function is used to change the size of the drawing to a 2"x 3.5" rectangle. Both shape and size have been changed. The Modify → Arcs commands are used to reduce the number of entities. Figure 19.14 shows the original drawing, drawing after forced, and drawing after edited using the Arts command.

a. Original drawing b. Drawing after forced c. Drawing after editing

Figure 19.14

Step 1. Import a DXF file buck.dxf.

Select **File → Import → DXF**

File name: **buck**

The buck drawing appears as in Figure 19.15.

Figure 19.15

Step 2. Force the size to 2"x 3.5".

Select **Transform → Force**

Size to force X and Y axis to (X, Y): **2,3.5**

The drawing size has been forced to 2"x 3.5" and the shape is modified accordingly in Figure 19.16.

Figure 19.16

Step 3. Reduce the number of entities.

Select **Modify → Arcs**

Set the arc parameters as below:

Arc tolerance:	**0.025**
jaggie Cleanup:	**ON**
jaGgie length:	**0.05**
Jaggie tolerance:	**0.05**
Show endpoints:	**ON**
Max arc Radius:	**1000.0**

Press the **Enter** key to accept the parameters

The system will prompt the following menu:

Original entities:	**768**
Current lines:	**370**
Current arcs:	**106**
Current entities:	**476**
Tolerance used:	**0.025**
Entity reduction:	**38.02%**

Select **Yes** to accept this conversion

The new drawing after conversion becomes Figure 19.17.

Figure 19.17

Step 4. Export the converted file buck-new.

Select **File → Export → DXF**

Select **No** to "This file already exists. Overwrite?"

Enter a new name: **buck-new**

Step 5. Exit InterFlux program.

Select **File → Exit**

💻 Project 5. Engraving the drawing of a buck image

This project uses the edited drawing (buck-new) in project 4 to engrave the buck image on a rectangular block. Figure 19.18 shows the drawing, toolpath and verification model of the project.

Figure 19.18a

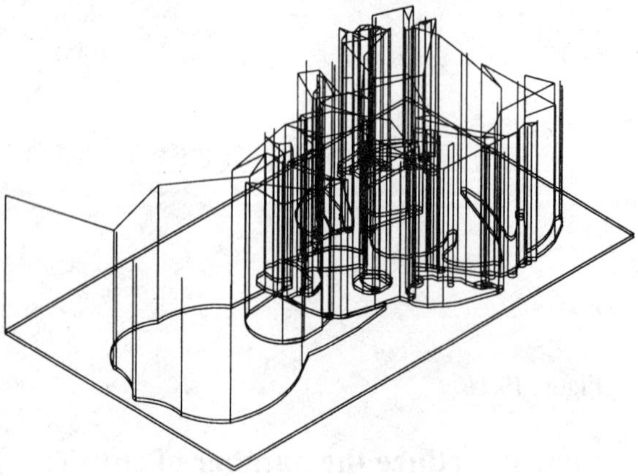

Figure 19.18b

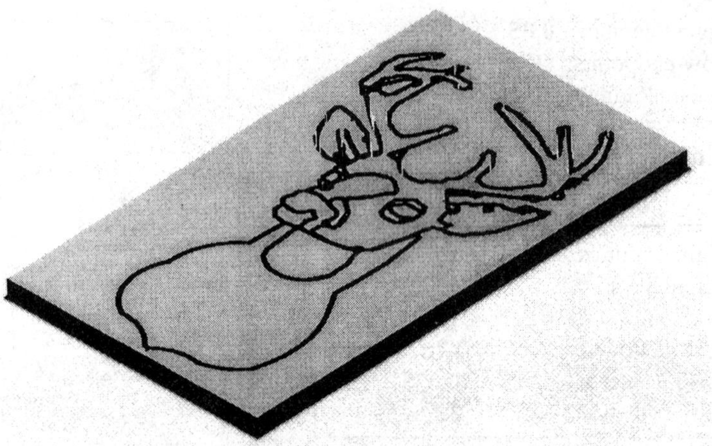

Figure 19.18c

Step 1. Import a DXF file buck-new.

Select **MAIN MENU → File → Converters → DXF → Read file**
File name to read: **buck-new**
Select **OK** to the DXF Read Parameters.
The vector drawing is imported as in Figure 19.19.

Figure 19.19

Step 2. Delete the duplicate entities.

Select **MAIN MENU → Delete → Duplicate → Entities**
The system will prompt "0 points, 48 lines, 2 arcs, 0 splines, 0 surfaces deleted"
Press the **Enter** key to continue

Step 3. Initiate the contour function.

Select **MAIN MENU → Toolpaths → Contour**
Enter file name for NCI: **buck**
Select **Window**, then pick two points to include all entities
Pick the lower-left corner to select the search point
Select **Done**

Step 4. Select a 1/32" ball-end mill and define the tool parameters.

Click the right mouse button, then select "Get tool from library"
Select **tool #246** (1/32" sphere end mill)
Select **OK**
Set the tool parameters as below.

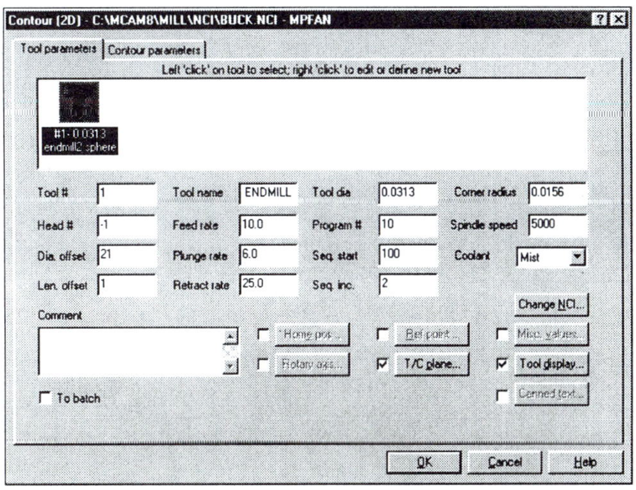

Step 5. Define the contour parameters.

Select the "Contour parameters" button

Define the contour parameters as below.

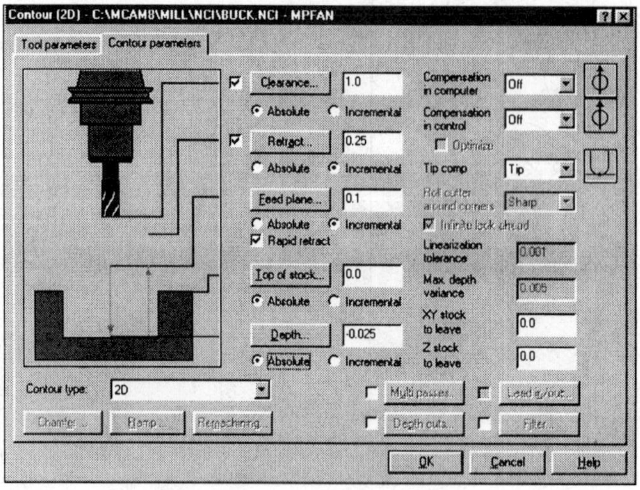

Select **OK** to generate contouring toolpaths

Select **Gview → Isometric**

The engraving toolpaths are shown in Figure 19.20.

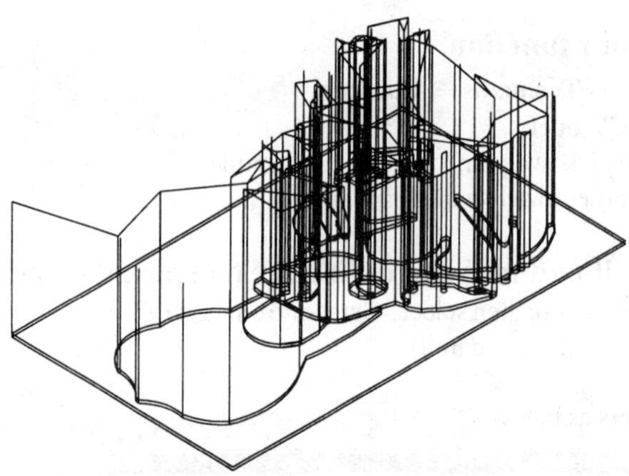

Figure 19.20

Step 6. Verify the toolpaths.

Select **Operations**

Select **Verify → Configure**

Select **Turbo (no tool)**

Select **OK**

Select **Machine** button on the Verify toolbar to begin verification

The toolpaths are animated on the screen and its final model should appear as Figure 19.21.

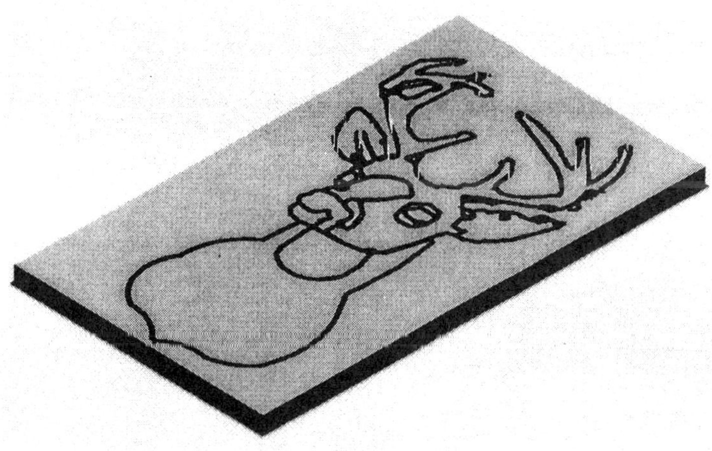

Figure 19.21

Select **BACKUP** → **OK** to return to graphic mode

Step 7. Save the toolpath model.

Select **MAIN MENU** → **File** → **Save**
File name to save: **buck**

Ex Exercises

1. What are bitmap images?
2. What are the two commonly used programs for converting bitmap images into vector drawings?
3. Explain how to represent graphics in the bitmap form.
4. List at least three ways for creating bitmap images.
5. What are vector drawings?
6. Describe the contrast between bitmap images and vector artworks.
7. What is the main function of Adobe Streamline?
8. Explain the effect of three edge smoothing options.
9. Describe the function of Threshold parameter.
10. Describe the function of Boost parameter.
11. List the three conversion methods used in Adobe Streamline.
12. List the commands used to import a vector drawing to Mastercam.
13. List the commands used to delete those duplicated entities.
14. Describe the main function of using InterFlux program.
15. What is the main modify function to reduce the number of entities in InterFlux?
16. Describe the function of "close open contours".
17. Describe the function of "close between contours".
18. Describe the function of "Collapse small contours."
19. Describe the following four parameters under Transform function in InterFlux:
    Scale
    Force
    Translate
    Group

Chapter 20

3D Digitizing: from Art to Part

Objectives:

1. Understand 3D digitizing and reverse engineering process.
2. Capture data from physical parts.
3. Build wireframe, surface, and solid models from digitizing data.
4. Generate tool paths to cut parts.

Overview

3D digitizing enables you to construct detailed computer models by simply tracing the feature surfaces of real physical objects. The 3D digitizing process is fast, accurate, and easy. There are many commercially available digitizing tools (coordinate measurement machines) including digitizers and scanners. You can have a manual 3D digitizer for the price of $2,500 that can provide you with a great digitizing accuracy. An interface software program is needed to link the coordinate measurement machine to a CAD/CAM program. The interface software program introduced in this chapter is HighRES Mastertool developed by HighRES, Inc. in La Jolla, CA. This is a powerful tool for engineers, designers, and anyone working in 3D to construct complex 3D models. HighRES Mastertool works by reporting the exact XYZ coordinates of the CMM stylus tip to the computer via the serial port. It works by simply holding the CMM probe stylus tip against the surface of the object and pressing either a footswitch, or a keyboard key to capture each data point. MasterTool software allows the operator to tell Mastercam what entity to build from each data set. You can create 2D points, lines, and splines, as well as 3D open or closed splines. The data can then be manipulated to build surfaces or solids for CNC machining. Figure 20.1 shows an example of 3D digitizing.

Figure 20.1

20.1 Reverse Engineering

Reverse engineering is a process that involves collecting the geometry data of an existing part, then using the collected data to recreate the CAD part model. Digitizing and CAD modeling are the two main techniques used in reverse engineering. Digitizing uses a coordinate measuring machine (CMM) to collect the point data from the surface skin from the physical part. These data points can be used to create wireframe, surface, and solid models of the part in a 3D CAD software.

A wide variety of coordinate measuring machines are commercially available. Some are 3 axis while others are 5 or 6 axis machines. Coordinate measurement machines can use a manual digitizer, laser scanner, optical scanner or sonar scanner. The manual digitizer enables a skilled operator to get efficient, complete surfaces where a scanner can't. Most scanners have some problems with line of sight and undercuts.

There are **two types** of digitizing; 2D digitizing and 3D digitizing. 2D digitizing produces various 2D geometry entities such as points, lines, closed lines, splines, closed splines, rectangle, and circle. 3D digitizing forms 3D spline curves. The selection of 2D digitizing or 3D digitizing depends on the complexity of the part shape, intended use, and machining requirements. The characteristics and applications of 2D digitizing and 3D digitizing are tabulated below.

2D Digitizing	
Characteristics	**Applications**
Produce planerized profiles readily to create solids.	Create extrude solids.
Produce exact profiles.	Create revolve surface.
Keep the data from out of plane.	
Slice and dice the object in a series of 2D profiles.	

3D Digitizing	
Characteristics	**Applications**
Obtain 3D point data of complex models.	Create 3D open or closed splines.
Represent parts in great detail and high accuracy.	Create loft and Coons surfaces.
Harder to create a line from 3D digitizing data.	

For more detailed information beyond the scope of this chapter, you can contact HighRes at: HighRES, Inc., PO Box 2746, La Jolla, CA 92038, Tel: (858) 459-1493.

All figures used in this chapter are provided by HighRes, Inc.

20.2 Square up Digital Part for Digitizing

Before the digitizing begins, the digitizer and part must be properly placed on the worktable and aligned with the CAD coordinate system. The procedure for placing the part and aligning with a CAD system is referred to "square up". This section presents the three step procedure for squaring up a part for Mastercam.

The Procedure for Squaring up a Part

1. Prepare the part for digitizing
Before start digitizing, you need to fix the digitizer and the part firmly to your work surface. The first step in preparing a part for digitizing is to think carefully about what you will be doing with the final model. If all you need is a 3D wireframe for trim lines, you won't need to capture many points. On the other hand, if machining surfaces or solids are needed, more digitizing points are needed to capture many details of the model.

2. Set the coordinate system for digitizing on Mastercam
The second step is to use a master square and mark 3 points on the desktop that will represent 0,0,0 along the X direction and XY-plane in Mastercam. One point in the lower left corner is normally used as the origin (0,0,0). The origin point and the point to the right define the X-axis of the coordinate system. The third point with the X-axis defines the XY-plane. The critical profile of the model is the centerline profile. Place the object on the desktop to allow for 3 points to square up the centerline of the part to Mastercam default XY, ZX, and YZ planes.

3. Square up the part
Select track and move the probe stylus to the 0,0,0 position and verify that you have squared up the part and your digitizer is working correctly. Figure 20.2 shows an example of 3-point axis of 3D digitizing.

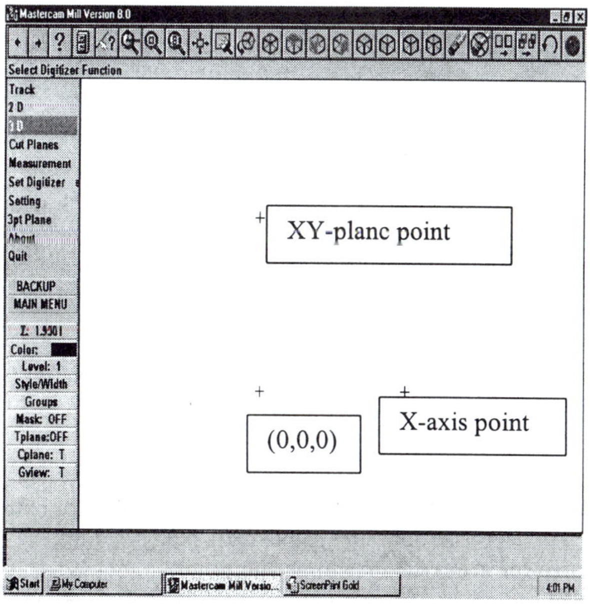

Figure 20.2

20.3 3D Manual Digitizer Usage

The most significant advantage of 3D manual digitizers over laser, optical, or sonar scanners is that manual digitizing enables a skilled operator to get efficient, complete surfaces where a scanner can't. For example, most scanners have serious problems with line of sight and undercuts. HighRES MasterTool allows for the operator to pick 3D digitized open and closed splines to generate freeform wireframe models that would be extremely difficult to create with calipers and micrometers. Care must be exercised when using any of the 3D digitizing functions, as any slip or skip of the point stylus will generate data points in the wrong direction, making an inaccurate model. Figure 20.3 is an example of a 3D wireframe model generated from 3D digitizing.

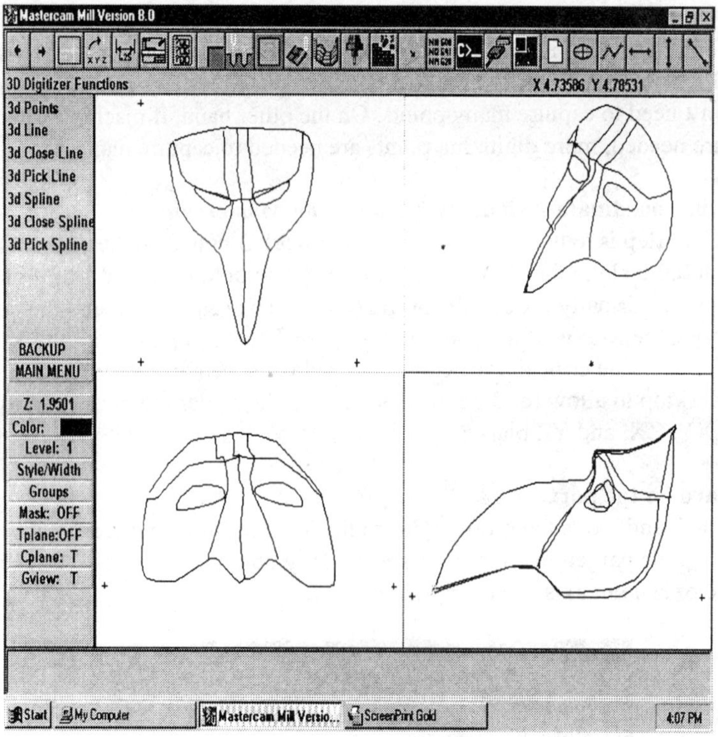

Figure 20.3

20.4 Creating Revolve Surfaces Using 2D Digitized Data

2D digitizing data can be readily used to create revolve surfaces or extruded solids. Revolve surfaces have a common characteristic, they are symmetrical about their axis of revolution. The profile needed for creating a revolve surface is 2D in nature. This section presents an example of digitizing a stemmed glass to obtain a 2D contour profile, then using Mastercam's revolve surface function to generate a final model.

Example: Digitizing using the Revolve Surface function:

Step 1. Set 3-point axis around base circle of glass.

Digitize a 3-point circle to represent the glass base.

Step 2. Set the Cplane to Side in Mastercam.

Rotate the Mastercam Cplane from Top to Side.

Step 3. Select Depth with digitizer from the MasterTool menu

Pick the stylus point on the glass that represents the centerline plane.
The default plane in Mastercam will be set to that point.
Figure 20.4 is an example of the 2D digitizing menu.

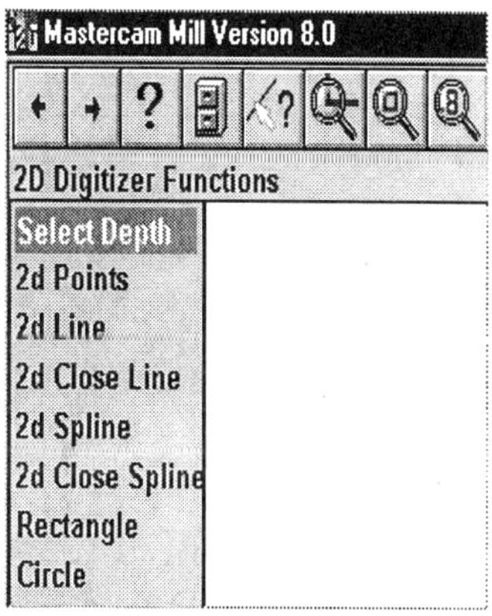

Figure 20.4

Step 4. Digitize the object

Select Digitize 2D open line and select points from the top to the bottom that represent the centerline profile for surface creation.
Figure 20.5 is an example of the 2D digitized centerline profile.

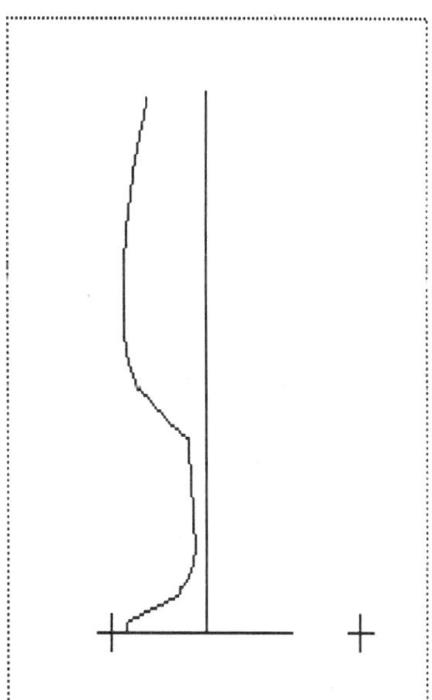

Figure 20.5

Step 5. Create the revolve surface

Use the Mastercam revolve surface function to revolve the centerline profile around the center point of the base circle for 360 degrees.

The revolved surface is shown in Figure 20.6.

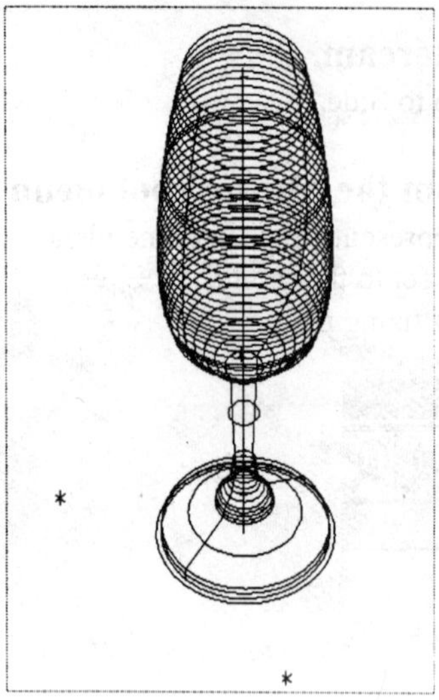

Figure 20.6

20.5 Extruded Solids

An extruded surface or solid requires a 2D closed profile. Mastercam extrudes the selected 2D closed profile in the specified direction by a given distance. Figure 20.7 shows the extruded surface of a guitar neck head created from a 2D closed profile.

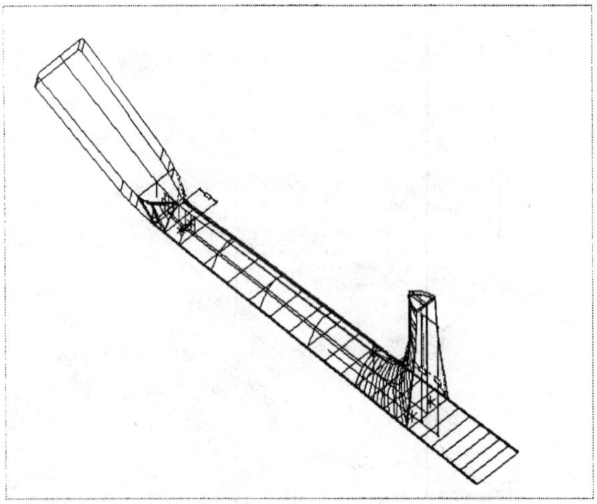

Figure 20.7

20.6 Loft Surfaces

In addition to the standard 2D and 3D digitizing menu features, MasterTool allows you to directly take slices through the part and filters out inaccurate data points that do not fall within a user specified distance to the Mastercam Cplane. Each slice is a readily formed planar profile. The loft surface is formed by smoothly blending a series of planar profiles. This section presents an example of creating a loft surface of the guitar neck from a series of sliced sections.

Example: Digitizing using the Loft function:

Step 1. Square up the guitar neck to 3-point axis

Figure 20.8 shows the wireframe of the guitar neck in 2D digitizing.

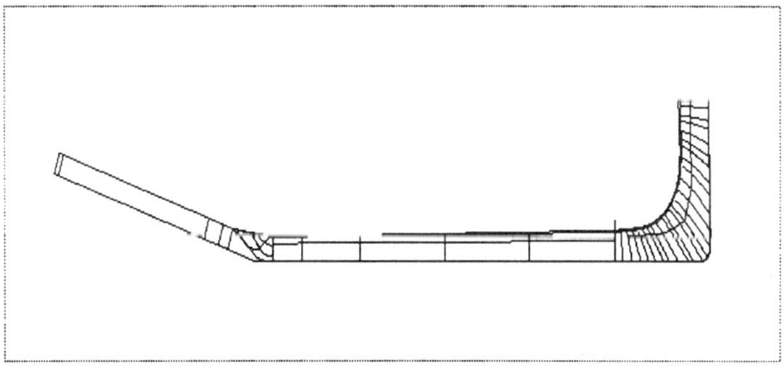

Figure 20.8

Step 2. Digitize the part

Set Cplane to Side view in Mastercam.
Digitize 3-point arcs at different depths that represent the guitar neck.
Figure 20.9 shows the wireframe of the digitized part.

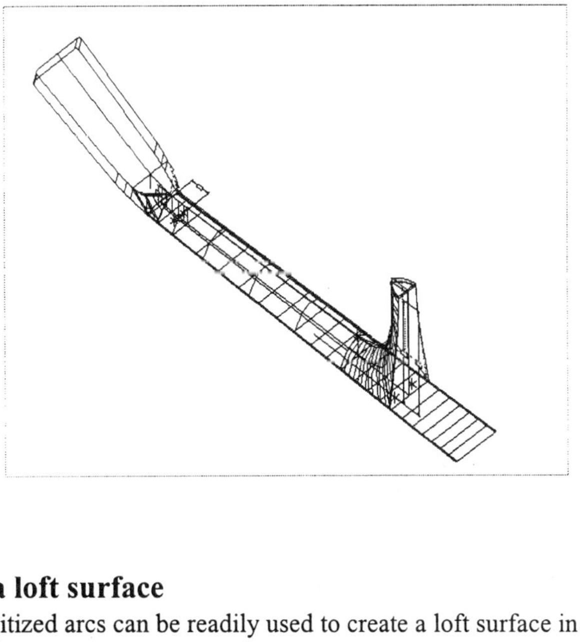

Figure 20.9

Step 3. Create a loft surface

The 3D digitized arcs can be readily used to create a loft surface in Mastercam.

20.7 Coons Surfaces

A Coons surface is created by blending four contours to form a patch surface. Multiple patches in a Coons surface are allowed. The advantage of using the Coons surface function is that you can capture complex geometry of the part. Figure 20.10 shows an example of a Coons surface of a guitar neck created from a number of 3D digitized open splines.

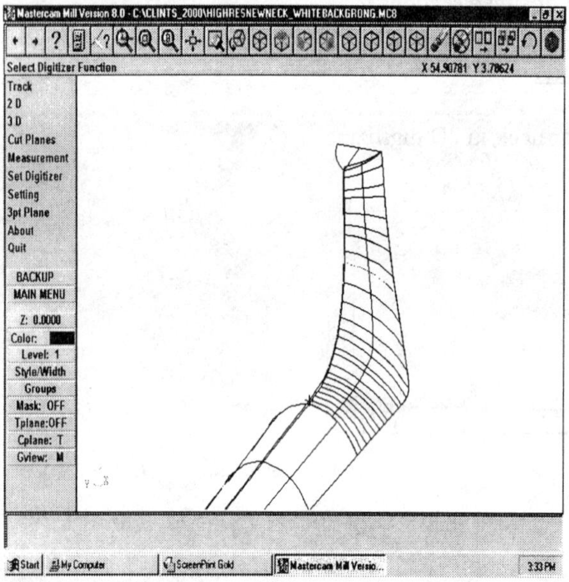

Figure 20.10a

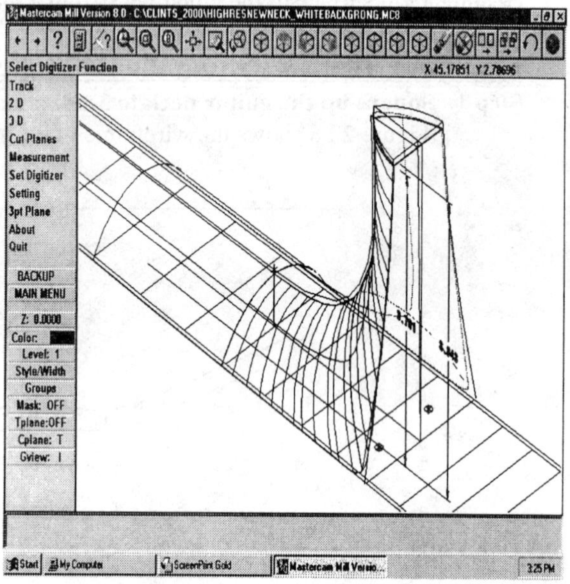

Figure 20.10b

20.8 Generating Toolpaths

After the surface models have been completed using the digitized point data in Mastercam, you can use all surface toolpath functions to generate roughing and finishing toolpaths to machine the part. See Chapter 15 for specifics on generating toolpaths for cutting various surfaces.

Ex Exercises

1. What is reverse engineering?
2. Describe the pros and cons of 2D digitizing.
3. Describe the pros and cons of 3D digitizing.
4. Explain how to square off the part for digitizing.
5. What surface functions can be used in using 2D digitized profiles?
6. What surface functions can be used in using 3D digitized profiles?

Mastercam 8

Index

2D Digitizing, 20-1~8
2D toolpath module
  Circ tlpths, 7-2
    Circlemill, 7-2, 7-123, 7-124
    Thread mill, 7-2
  Contour, 7-2, 7-38~49
  Drill, 7-2, 7-99~109
  Face, 7-2
  Point, 7-2, 7-127
2-line plane, 11-4
3D Digitizing, 20-1~8
3D Rough toolpath models
  Contour, 15-3, 15-44
  Flowline, 15-3, 15-36
  Parallel, 15-3, 15-20, 15-21
  Plunge, 15-3, 15-59
  Pocket, 15-3, 15-50
  Project, 15-3, 15-31
  Radial, 15-3, 15-26
3D toolpath common parameters, 14-2 ~ 14-7
  Along and across, 14-2
  Cutter compensation, 14-5, 14-6
  Cutting direction, 14-4
  Cutting method, 14-3
  Stepping over distances, 14-4
3D toolpath modules, 14-7
4-Axis machines, 16-2
5-Axis machines, 16-2
5-Axis toolpath functions, 16-12
  Curve5ax, 16-12, 16-13
  Drill5ax, 16-12
  Flow5ax, 16-12
  Swarf5ax, 16-12

- A -

Adobe streamline , 19-3 ~ 19-7
  Color/B&W set up, 19-3 ~ 19-6
  Conversion setup, 19-3, 19-6 ~ 19-7
  Settings, 19-3, 19-4
Advanced parameters, 7-66, 7-69, 7-70
  Linearization tolerance, 7-70
  Roll cutter around corners, 7-70
  Tip comp, 7-70
  XY stock to leave, 7-70
  Z stock to leave, 7-70
Allocations, 3-12
Analyze, 3-4
ANSI System 2-7
Arc, 5-13
  3 points, 5-13, 5-16
  Circ 2 pts, 5-13, 5-19
  Circ 3 pts, 5-13, 5-19
  Circ + dia, 5-13, 5-20
  Circ + edg, 5-13, 5-20
  Circ + rad, 5-13, 5-20
  Endpoint, 5-13, 5-15
  Polar, 5-13-15
  Tangent, 5-13, 5-16~19
Arc center words, 1-15
Artworks, 19-1, 19-2
Assign, 3-11
Associativity, 8-1

- B -

Backplot, 7-15~19
  Display, 7-17
    Cleanup on null tool change, 7-18
    Erase toolpath in repaint, 7-18
    Fit toolpath, 7-18
    Save as geometry, 7-18
    Simulate axis substitution, 7-18
    Simulate rotary axis, 7-18
    Step mode, 7-17
    Stop parameters, 7-18
    Tool appearance, 7-18
    Tool motion, 7-17
  MC8 file, 7-16
  Run, 7-15

- B - continued

Show hold, 7-16
Show tool, 7-16
Show path, 7-16
Step, 7-15
Verify, 7-16

BACKUP, 3-4, 3-6
Bazier surface, 12-2
Bitmap, 19-1, 19-2

BMP, 19-2
PCX, 19-2
PNT, 19-2
PSD, 19-2
TIFF, 19-2

Blend surface modeling, 13-1, 13-38

2 surf blnd, 13-38~43
3 surf blnd, 13-38, 13-48
Fillet blnd, 13-38

Boring Operations, 2-39~40

Feed and depth of cut, 2-40
Multiple-stage, 2-40
Single-stage, 2-39

Break, 6-3, 6-10

2 pieces, 6-10
At length, 6-10
At inters, 6-10
Break cir, 6-10
Cdata/line, 6-10
Draft/line, 6-10
Hatch/line, 6-10
Mny pieces, 6-10
Spl to arcs, 6-10
B-spline surface, 12-3

-C-

CAD, 4-1
CAD setting, 3-16
CAM, 4-1

Machining date, 4-1
Part geometry, 4-1

Cancel, 3-11
Career opportunity, 1-4, 1-5
Chain manager, 8-24

Add chain, 8-24, 8-25
Change at point, 8-15, 8-26
Change side, 8-24, 8-25
Delete chain, 8-25
Rechain all, 8-24
Rechain all of solid, 8-24
Rechain single, 8-25
Rename, 8-25
Resync all, 8-25
Reverse chain, 8-25, 8-26
Start point, 8-25

Chaining methods, 7-26~28

Area, 7-27
Chain, 7-27
Last, 7-28, 7-33
Point, 7-28, 7-33
Section 7-28, 7-33
Single, 7-28, 7-33
Window, 7-27, 7-31, 7-32

Chaining option, 7-29, 7-30

Move back, 7-29
Move fwd, 7-29
Reverse, 7-29
select str, 7-29

Chamfer, 5-29

Distance, 5-29, 5-30

Change the size of the window, 3-2
Circle mill module, 7-2, 7-123, 7-124
Circular interpolation, 1-27, 1-28
Closed loop system, 1-24, 1-25
CNC control systems, 1-13
CNC drive systems, 1-25
CNC interpolations, 1-27
CNC Milling Processes, 2-1~3
CNC operations, 1-4
CNC system elements, 1-6
CNC Turning Processes, 2-1, 2-4~5
Cnv to arcs, 6-3, 6-12
Collapse all, 8-13
Color, 3-5
Color/B&W setup menu, 19-4

Black and white conversion, 19-5
Edge smoothing, 19-5
Limited colors conversion, 19-5
Posterization, 19-5

Communication, 3-13
Compensations, 7-43~46

in computer, 7-44
in control, 7-44
Tip compensation, 7-46
Tool left, 7-43
Tool on, 7-43
Tool right, 7-43
Composite surfaces models, 13-63
Computer numerical control (CNC), 1-1, 1-2, 1-3

Construction plane, 11-3
Continuous path system, 1-22
Contour definition, 7-26

Chaining direction, 7-26
Chaining methods, 7-26~28
Chaining option, 7-29,7-30

Contour module, 7-38~49
Compensations, 7-43~46
Depth cuts, 7-39, 40
Lead in/out, 7-47~49
Multi passes, 7-39, 7-41, 7-42
Roll cutter around corners, 7-46, 7-47
Stock to leave, 7-39, 7-41
Z-depth parameters, 7-39
Contour shallow parameters, 15-46
Contouring system, 1-22
2-D contouring, 1-22, 1-23
2½-D contouring, 1-22, 1-23
3-D contouring, 1-22, 1-24
4-D contouring, 1-22, 1-24
Conversion setup, 19-3, 19-6 ~ 7
Accuracy, 19-7
Art, 19-7
Conversion method, 19-6
Path options, 19-7
Coons surface, 12-2, 12-24, 18-3
Coons surfaces modeling, 12-24 ~ 31
Coons toolpath module, 14-8, 14-21 ~ 24
Coons parameters, 14-21
Number of patches in along and across directions, 14-23
Row and column, 14-22
Order of contour selection, 14-24
Coordinate setting, 7-34
Home position, 7-34
Reference point, 7-35
Tool origin and tool plane, 7-35~38
Rotary axis, 7-38
Copying geometry, 8-7
Copying operations, 8-5 ~ 7
Copy after, 8-5, 8-6
Copy before, 8-5
Copying parameters, 8-7
Copying Tools, 8-7
Cplane, 3-5
Cpts NURBS, 6-3, 6-11
Dynamic, 6-11
Point entry, 6-11
Create, 3-4, 5-1
Creating a fillet surface, 13-10~15
between a plane and a surface, 13-10,13-12
between a curve and a surface, 13-12~13
between two surfaces, 13-14, 13-15
Cubic interpolation, 1-27, 1-29
Current configuration file options, 3-10, 3-17
Curve 5ax parameters, 16-15
Curve following method, 16-18
Gouge processing, 16-18
Minimize corners in toolpath, 16-18
Offset distances, 16-16 ~ 17
Show toolpath before gouge check, 16-18
Tool control, 16-15
Curve 5-Axis common parameters, 16-13 ~ 18
Curve type, 16-14
Output format, 16-13
Projection, 16-15
Tip control, 16-14
Tool axis control, 16-14
Curve following method, 16-18
Chord height, 16-18
Maximum step, 16-18
Curve type, 16-14
3D curves, 16-14
Surface edges, 16-14
Curve, 5-26
Cut depth, 15-12
Adjustment to other cuts, 15-13
Adjustment to top cut, 15-13
Maximum depth, 15-13
Minimum depth, 15-13
Relative to, 15-13
Cutter compensation, 14-5
Left, 14-6
Right, 14-6
Cutting method, 7-70~73
One way method, 7-71
Spiral method, 7-72
Zigzag method, 7-70, 7-71
Cutting method - other, 15-51
Constant overlap spiral, 15-51
One way, 15-51
Parallel spiral, 15-51
parallel spiral, clean corners, 15-51
Quick zigzag, 15-51
True spiral, 15-51
Zigzag, 15-51
Cutting method in 3D surfacing, 14-3
5-axis, 14-3
Circular, 14-3
One way, 14-3
Zig-zag, 14-3
Cutting Tool Material, 2-6
Selection, 2-9

-D-
Default value, 3-6
Delete, 3-4, 6-2
All, 6-2
Area, 6-2
Chain, 6-2
Duplicate, 6-2
Group, 6-2
Only, 6-2
Result, 6-2
Undelete, 6-2
Window, 6-2
Deleting operations, 8-9, 8-12, 8-13, 9-2, 9-6
Depth cuts, 7-39, 40
# of roughing passes, 7-40
Keep tool down, 7-41
Last finish cut, 7-40
Last roughing cut, 7-40
Next to last roughing cut, 7-40
Roughing step, 7-41
Second to last finish cut, 7-40
Subsequent finish cut, 7-40
Subsequent roughing cuts, 7-40
Derived surfaces modeling, 13-1
Blend surface modeling, 13-1, 13-38~43
Fillet surfaces modeling, 13-1~15
Offset surface modeling, 13-1, 13-35
Trim/Extend surface modeling, 13-1, 13-23~24
Derived surfaces, 12-4, 12-5
Digital feedback systems, 1-26
Dimension words, 1-15
Dimensions, 10-3
Direct numerical (DNC), 1-1, 1-2
Direction of closed contours, 15-45
climb, 15-45
conventional, 15-45
Direction of machine axes, 1-31
+X direction, 1-31
-X direction, 1-31
+Y direction, 1-31
-Y direction, 1-31
+Z direction, 1-31
-Z direction, 1-31
Direction of open contours, 15-45
Direction parameters, 15-4, 15-5, 15-6
Display control, 7-22
Moves/refresh, 7-22
Moves/step, 7-22
Speed-quality, 7-22
Distributive numerical control (DNC), 1-1, 1-3
Doc file, 8-9, 8-14, 8-15
Draft surfaces modeling, 12-46, 12-47
Draft, 12-46, 18-3
Drag, 6-3, 6-12
Drill 5-axis function, 16-32
Points and points/lines, 16-32
Drill 5-axis parameters, 16-33, 16-34
Tool axis control, 16-33
Tip control, 16-33
Drill module, 7-99~109
Cycle mode, 7-99, 7-101, 7-102
Pecking parameters, 7-99,7-102
Point selection, 7-103~107
Tip compensation, 7-99, 7-103
Z-depth, 7-99
Drilling operation, 2-37~39
Drill lip distance, 2-38
Penetration distance, 2-38
Safety distance, 2-38
Drive system, 1-6, 1-7
Drive/check surfaces, 15-7

-E-
Edge Settings, 15-17
open edges between surfaces, 15-17
open edges in single surfaces, 15-17
Roll tool, 15-18
Sharp corner tolerance, 15-18
Editing, 9-2
Edit NCI C-Hook method, 9-1, 9-5
EIA-267-B, 16-1
Ellipse, 5-35
A radius, 5-35
B radius, 5-35
End angle, 5-35
Rot angle, 5-35
Start angle, 5-35
Engraving Letters, 7-127
Edit note method, 7-127
Letter function, 7-127
Entity selection option, 6-13
All, 6-13
Area, 6-13
Chain, 6-13
Done, 6-13
Group, 6-13
Only, 6-13
Result, 6-13
Window, 6-13
Unselect, 6-13

Entity selection option, 6-13
- All, 6-13
- Area, 6-13
- Chain, 6-13
- Done, 6-13
- Group, 6-13
- Only, 6-13
- Result, 6-13
- Window, 6-13
- Unselect, 6-13

Entry-helix/ramp, 7-78~79
- Helix mode, 7-80
- Off patter, 7-79
- Ramp mode, 7-81

EOF, 9-2
Exiting Mastercam, 3-6
Expand all, 8-13
Extend, 6-3, 6-12

-F-

Face Milling, 2-32~33
Feed word, 1-15
Feedback loop, 1-26
Feedback system, 1-6, 1-7
File, 3-4
Files, 3-13
File structure of toolpaths, 9-2 ~4
Fillet, 5-21, 6-3
- Angle<180, 5-21
- Chain, 5-21
- Radius, 5-21
- Trim, 5-21

Fillet surface modeling, 13-1~15
- Color, 13-4
- Curve/surf, 13-2
- Entity to be generated, 13-3
- Extend surfaces, 13-5
- Fillet both sides, 13-4
- Fillet type, 13-4
- Find multiples, 13-5
- Joint Results, 13-4
- Joint Tolerance, 13-4
- Plane/surf, 13-2
- Surf/surf, 13-2
- Step method, 13-3
- Trim surface, 13-5
- Variable radius, 13-6

Fillet surface, 18-4
Fillet type, 13-4
- Curve-generated, 13-4
- NURBS, 13-4
- Parametric, 13-4

Filter parameters, 15-5
- Look ahead, 15-5
- Maximum arc radius, 15-5
- Minimum arc radius, 15-5
- Tolerance, 15-5

Finish functions, 15-63
- Contour, 15-64
- Flowline, 15-63, 15-91
- Leftover, 15-63, 15-71
- Parallel, 15-63
- Par. steep, 15-63
- Pencil, 15-63, 15-104
- Project, 15-63, 15-81
- Radial, 15-63, 15-73
- Scallop, 15-63, 15-105
- Shallow, 15-63, 15-97

Finish leftover function, 15-71
- Overlap distance, 15-72
- Roughing corner rad, 15-72
- Roughing tool dia, 15-72

Finish pencil function, 15-104
Finish radial function, 15-73
Finish scallop function, 15-105
- Expand inside to outside, 15-105
- Machining direction, 15-105

Finish shallow function, 15-97
- From slope angle, 15-97
- To slope angle, 15-97
- Collapse cutting method, 15-98
- Collapse settings, 15-98
- Create limited zone boundaries as geometry, 15-98

Floor passes, 16-46
- Number of passes, 16-46
- Step, 16-46

Flowline 5-axis function, 16-54
- Lead/lag angle, 16-55
- Parameters, 16-54
- Side tilt angle, 16-54

Flowline function, 15-91
Free-form surfaces, 12-4, 12-5

-G-

Gap settings, 15-14
- Gap size, 15-15
- Long gap, 15-14
- Short gap, 15-14

Gap size, 15-15
- Distance, 15-15
- % of stepover, 15-15

G-codes for milling, 1-15 ~19
Geometrical surfaces, 12-3

Geometry entities, 10-5
true entities, 10-5
construction entities, 10-5
Gouge processing, 16-18
Default, 16-18
Infinite look ahead, 16-18
Look ahead, 16-18
Protect, 16-18
Graphics display area, 3-3
Groups, 3-5, 6-44
Add to, 6-44
Colors, 6-44
Delete, 6-44
New, 6-44
Remove from, 6-44
Select, 6-44
Subgroup, 6-44
Undo sub, 6-44
View, 6-44
Gview, 3-5

-H-
Helical interpolation, 1-27, 1-28
Help, 3-8, 3-9, 3-11
Holder size, 7-6
Holder, 7-6
Holder diameter, 7-6
Tool number, 7-6

-I-
Inserts, 2-16~21
Chip breakers, 2-21
Nose radius, 2-15
Shape, 2-18
Size, 2-18
Thickness, 2-19
InterFlux program, 19-20
Modify, 19-20
Transform, 19-21
Tips, 19-21
ISO System, 2-7~8

-J-
Job setup, 7-24 ~ 26, 8-2
Feed calculation parameters, 7-26
Material selection, 7-25
Stock origin, 7-24
Stock size, 7-24
Tool configuration parameters, 7-25
Tool Offset registers, 7-25
Join, 6-3, 6-11

-L-
Lead in/out, 7-47~49
Entry/exit arc, 7-48
Entry/exit at midpoint in closed contours, 7-49
Entry/Exit line, 7-48
Enter on first depth cut only, 7-49
Exit on last depth cut only, 7-49
Use entry point, 7-49
Use point depth, 7-49
Lead/lag angle, 16-16, 16-7, 16-55
Letters, 5-30~34
Drafting, 5-30
File, 5-30, 5-32
Modify, 5-33, 5-34
Note, 5-33
TrueType(R), 5-30~31
Btm of arc, 5-31
Horizontal, 5-31
Top of arc, 5-31
Vertical, 5-31
Level, 3-5
Line, 5-6~12
Bisect, 5-7
Closest, 5-7
Endpoints, 5-7, 5-9
Horizontal, 5-7, 5-8
Multi, 5-7, 5-9
Perpendclr, 5-7, 5-11~12
Polar, 5-7, 5-9
Tangent, 5-7, 9-11
Vertical, 5-7, 5-8
Linear interpolation, 1-27, 1-28
Loft surfaces modeling, 12-16
Loft toolpath module, 14-8, 14-18
Lofted parameters, 14-18
Lofted surface, 12-16, 18-3

-M-
Machine control unit, 1-6, 1-7
Machine direction, 7-66, 7-69
Climb, 7-69
Conventional, 7-69
Machines axes designation, 1-31
Machine tool, 1-6, 1-7
Machine type, 7-6
Both, 7-6
Finish, 7-6
Rough, 7-6
Machine zero point, 1-32
Machining data, 10-8

Machining parameters, 2-24~31
Cutting speed, 2-24, 27
Depth of cut, 2-28
Feed rate, 2-27-28
Horsepower requirement, 2-29
Material removal rate, 2-28
Drilling, 2-28
Milling, 2-28
Turning, 2-28
Spindle speed, 2-24, 27
MAIN MENU, 3-4, 3-6
Mask, 3-5
Mastercam function keys, 3-8
Mastercam navigation commands, 3-6
Mastercam screen, 3-3
Mastercam short-cut keys, 3-7
Mastercam surfaces, 12-6
Maximize the window, 3-2
Merge, 3-11, 9-2
Milling operations (process selection), 10-3
Boring, 10-3
Drilling, 10-3
Facing, 10-3
Lettering, 10-3
Pocketing, 10-3
Process, 10-3
Profiling, 10-3
Slot cutting, 10-3
Shoulder, 10-3
Surface cutting, 10-3
Tapping, 10-3
Milling with ball end mills, 2-36~37
Minimize the window, 3-2
Mirror, 6-13, 6-14
2 points, 6-14
Line, 6-14
X axis, 6-14
Y axis, 6-14
Mirroring Parameters, 9-35 ~ 36
Mirror method, 9-36
Entity, 9-36
X axis, 9-36
Y axis, 9-36
Mirror points, 9-36
Reverse toolpath, 9-36
Select, 9-36
View #, 9-36
Mirroring toolpaths, 9-35 ~ 36
Miscellaneous words, 1-15, 1-20
Modify, 3-4, 6-2
Moving a window, 3-3
Moving operations, 8-3 ~ 8-5
Move after, 8-4, 8-5
Move before, 8-4, 8-5
Multi passes 7-39, 7-41, 7-42
Machine finish passes at, 7-42

-N-
NC address, 1-13, 1-14
NC coding system, 1-12
ASCII standard, 1-12
EIA standard, 1-12
NC functional blocks, 1-21
NC programming methods, 1-21
Computer programming, 1-21
Manual programming, 1-21
NC settings, 3-15
NC utils, 3-4
NC words, 1-15
Normal plane, 11-4
Normal, 6-3, 6-11
Numerical control (NC), 1-1
NURB surface, 12-3

-O-
Offs ctour, 6-13, 6-43
Offset distances, 16-16 ~ 17
Lead/lag angle, 16-16, 16-17
Radial offset, 16-16
Side tilt angle, 16-16
Vector angle, 16-16
Offset surface, 18-4
Offset, 6-13, 6-43
OK, 3-11
Open loop system, 1-25
Operations Manager, 7-15, 8-2, 8-3, 9-6
Backplot, 7-15 ~19, 8-43
Highspeed, 7-15, 8-3
OK, 8-3
Post, 7-15, 8-3
Regen path, 7-15, 8-3
Select all, 8-3
Verify, 7-15, 8-3
Options (in the right-click menu), 8-8
Change NCI destination, 8-8
Edit common parameters, 8-8
Filter, 8-8
Locking, 8-8
Posting, 8-8
calculate speeds/feeds, 8-8
Reverse toolpath, 8-8
Select by geometry, 8-8

- O - continued
Select all invalid, 8-8
Setup sheet, 8-8, 8-9, 8-10
Toolpath display, 8-8, 8-10
Toolpath Editor, 8-8

-P-
Parabolic interpolation, 1-27, 1-29
Parallel finish function, 15-65
Depth parameters, 15-65
Parallel steep finish function, 15-70
Cut extension, 15-71
From slop angle, 15-70
To slope angle, 15-70
Part drawings, 10-1
Part features, 10-2, 16-3, 18-1
for milling operations, 10-2
for turning operations, 10-2
Part program, 1-6, 1-7
Part shape, 15-12
Cavity, 15-12
Boss, 15-12
Unspecified, 15-12
Plane defining methods, 13-11
3-point, 13-11
C-plane, 13-11
Entity, 13-11
Line, 13-11
Normal, 13-11
X = const, 13-11
Y = const, 13-11
Z = const, 13-11
Plotter settings, 3-14
Pocket Module, 7-66~82
Advanced parameters, 7-66, 7-69, 7-70
Depth cuts parameters, 7-66, 7-67
Facing parameters, 7-66~68
Machine direction, 7-66, 7-69
Z-depth parameters, 7-66
Pocket rough function, 15-50
Cutting method, 15-51
Cut tolerance, 15-51
Entry helixes, 15-51
Plunge outside tool center boundary, 15-51
Prompt for entry point, 15-51
Point, 5-2 ~ 5
Along ent, 5-2, 5-4
Boltcircle, 5-2
Cpts NURBS, 5-2, 5-5
Dynamic, 5-2, 5-5
Grid, 5-2
Length, 5-2, 5-6
Node pts, 5-2, 5-4
Position, 5-2, 5-3
Slice, 5-2
srf project, 5-2
Point module, 7-2, 7-127
Backup, 7-127
Depth, 7-127
Feed rate, 7-127
GotoXY, 7-127
Goto XYZ, 7-127
Jump ht, 7-127
Tool down, 7-127
Tool up, 7-127
Point selection (for drill module), 7-103~107
Automatic, 7-103, 7-104
Entities, 7-103, 7-104
Last, 7-103
Manual, 7-103
Mask on arc, 7-103
Patterns, 7-103, 7-105
Window pts, 7-103~105
Point selection methods (for selecting drilling points), 16-33
Automatic, 16-33
Entities, 16-33
Last, 16-33
Manual, 16-33
Mask on arc, 16-33
Options, 16-33
Patterns16-33
Subpgm, 16-33
Window pts, 16-33
Point-to-point system (PTP), 1-22
Polygon, 5-36
Make NURBS,5-36
Meas crnr, 5-36
No. sides, 5-36
Radius, 5-36
Start angle, 5-36
Position loop, 1-26
Positioning system, 1-35
absolute positioning system, 1-35, 1-36
incremental positional system, 1-35, 1-36
selection of the positioning system, 1-37
Postprocessor, 4-1
Preparatory words, 1-15
Primary linear axes, 1-30
Process plan sheet preparation, 10-8 ~14
Process sequencing, 10-4
Profile elements of surfaces, 11-2
Program input device, 1-6, 1-7
Program zero points, 1-32, 1-34
Project finish function, 15-81
Add depths, 15-82

Project function, 17-1
Cone, 17-2
Cylinder, 17-2
Plane, 17-2
Sphere, 17-2
X-section, 17-2
Step implement toolpaths projects, 17-3
Projection, 16-15
Normal to plane, 16-15
Normal to surface, 16-15

-R-
Raw material drawing, 10-1,10-3
Rectangle, 5-27~29
1 point, 5-27
2 point, 5-28
Options, 5-28
Corner center point, 5-28
Corner fillets, 5-28
Rectangular shape, 5-28
Rotation, 5-28
Surface creation, 5-28, 5-29
Recut parameters, 15-7
Reference return point, 1-32, 1-33
Reference zero point, 1-32
Rest mill, 15-46
Revolution toolpath module, 14-42 ~44
Axis depth, 14-42
Retract to, 14-43
Shape, 14-43
Step size, 14-42
Trim to, 14-43
Revolved surfaces modeling, 12-44
Revolved, 12-44, 18-3
Right-click menu, 8-7 ~15, 9-6
Batch, 8-9
Collapse all, 8-9
Collision check, 8-9
Copy, 8-9
Cut, 8-9
Delete, 8-9, 9-6
Doc file, 8-9
Display options, 8-9
Expand all, 8-9
Get from library, 8-9
Groups, 8-9
Job setup, 8-9
Options, 8-8
Paste, 8-9
Renumber all, 8-9
Sort operations, 8-9
Save to library, 8-9
Toolpaths, 8-9
Undelete, 8-9
Right-hand rule, 1-31
Roll cutter around corners, 7-46, 7-47
All corners, 7-47
No corners, 7-47
Sharp corners, 7-47
Roll tool, 15-18
Automatically, 15-18
Only between surface, 15-18
Over all surface edges, 15-18
Roll, 6-13
Rotary 4-Axis function, 16-3 ~ 5
Axis dampening length, 16-4, 16-5
Lead/lag angle, 16-5
Maximum stepdown, 16-4
Parameters, 16-4
Use center point, 16-4
Rotary axes, 1-30, 16-1
Axis A, 1-30
Axis B, 1-30
Axis C, 1-30
Axis D, 1-3
Axis E, 1-20
Rotary directions, 16-1
Rotate, 6-13, 6-29
Rotating toolpaths, 9-24 ~ 25
Parameters, 9-25
Procedure, 9-25
Rough contour function, 15-44
Direction of closed contours, 15-44
Direction of open contours, 15-44
Rest mill, 15-44
Rough flowline function, 15-36
Tolerance, 15-36
Rough parallel function, 15-20, 15-21
Approx. scallop height at 45 degrees, 15-21
Approx. scallop height on flat floor, 15-21
Maximum stepover, 15-21
Rough plunge function, 15-59
Rough project function, 15-31
Curves, 15-31
NCI, 15-31
Points, 15-31
Rough radial function, 15-26
Maximum angle increment, 15-26
Start angle, 15-21
Start inside, 15-26
Start outside, 15-26
Sweep angle, 15-21
Rough specific parameters, 15-8~11
Cut tolerance, 15-8, 15-9
Cutting method, 15-9, 15-10
Max stepdown, 15-9

- R - continued
Part shape, 15-12
Plunge control, 15-10
Z motion control, 15-10
Roughing/Finishing parameters, 7-70~82
Cutting method, 7-70
Entry-helix/ramp, 7-78-79
Islands and pocket loops, 7-73~78
Stepover, 7-73
Ruled surface, 12-17, 18-3
Ruled surfacing modeling, 12-7, 12-8
Ruled toolpath module, 14-7 ~ 11
Constant Z cutting, 14-9
Gouge check direction, 14-10
Ruled parameters, 14-9
Taper Angle, 14-10
Trimming planes, 14-10

-S-
Save As, 3-11
Scale XYZ, 6-13, 6-40
Scale, 6-13, 6-40
Screen menu area, 3-3
Screen, 3-4, 3-17
Second menu, 3-5
Secondary linear axes, 1-20
Selecting a menu option, 3-4
Setup sheet, 8-8, 8-10, 8-11
Sharp corner tolerance, 15-20
Distance, 15-20
% of cut tolerance, 15-20
Side tilt angle, 16-16, 16-17, 16-54
Solids, 3-4
Sort operations, 8-9, 8-14
Ascending and descending, 8-14
Creation order, 8-14
NCI destination, 8-14
Tool number, 8-14
Tool plane, 8-14
Work offset, 8-14
Spindle words, 1-15
Spiral method, 7-72
Constant overlap spiral, 7-72
Morph spiral, 7-72, 7-73
Parallel spiral, 7-72
Parallel spiral, clean corners, 7-72
True spiral, 7-72, 7-73
Spline, 5-23
Automatic, 5-23, 5-24
Blend, 5-23
Curves, 5-23, 5-25
Manual, 5-23, 5-24
Start/Exit, 3-16
Status, 3-11
Stepover control, 15-36
Stretch, 6-13
Style/Width, 3-5
Surface mathematics, 12-2
Surface method, 14-2
Surface models, 11-2
Surface module selection, 18-3
Surface parameters, 15-4
Check surfaces, 15-4
Direction parameters, 15-4, 15-5 Drive
check surfaces, 15-7
Filter parameters, 15-4, 15-5
Recut parameters, 15-4
Stock parameters, 15-4
Tip/center compensation, 15-4, 15-7
Tool center boundary, 15-4, 15-8
Z depth parameters, 15-4
Surface trim options, 13-6
Surface types, 12-3
Surfaces roughnesses, 10-3
Surfaces, 5-26, 12-1
Surfacing mathematics principles, 12-6
Blend, 12-6
NURBS, 12-6
Parametric, 12-6
Surfacing project, 12-6
Swarf 5axis parameters, 16-45
Floor passes, 16-46
Minimize Corners in toolpath, 16-46
Tool Vector Length, 16-46
Wall passes, 16-46
Swarf 5-axis, 16-43
Output format, 16-43
Tip control, 16-44
Tool axis control, 16-44
Walls, 16-43
Sweep, 18-3
Swept 2D, 14-32
Swept 3D, 14-33
Swept surfaces modeling, 12-54
one across/one along, 12-54
one across/ two along, 12-54
Two across/one along, 12-54
Swept toolpath modules, 14-8, 14-32 ~ 34
one across/one along, 14-32
one across/ two along, 14-32
two across/ one along, 14-32
System configuration, 3-10
Button options, 3-10, 3-11
Current configuration file options, 3-10, 3-17
Tab options, 3-10, 3-12
System response area, 3-4

-T-
Tapping operations, 2-41~43
Depth, 2-43
Drill size, 2-41~43
Unified threads, 2-43
Matric threads, 2-43
Tertiary linear axes, 1-30
Tip compensation, 7-99, 7-103
Breakthrough, 7-103
Tip angle, 7-103
Tip length, 7-103
Tool diameter, 7-103
Tip control(for Curve 5ax), 16-14
On selected curve, 16-14
On projected curve, 16-14
Comp to surface, 16-14
Tip control (for Drill 5-axis), 16-33
Original point, 16-33
Projected point, 16-33
Surface Comp, 16-33
Tip control (for Swarf 5-axis), 16-44
Lower rail, 16-44
Plane, 16-44
Surface, 16-44
Tip/center compensation, 15-7
Tolerance, 15-36
Cut control, 15-36
Cut tolerance, scallop height method, 15-37
Distance increment method, 15-37
Tolerances, 3-12, 10-3
Tool axis control (for Curve 5ax), 16-14
Chain, 16-14
From point, 16-14
Lines, 16-14
Plane, 16-14
Surface, 16-14
To point, 16-14
Tool axis control (for Drill 5-axis), 16-33
Parallel to line, 16-33
Plane, 16-33
Surface, 16-33
Tool center boundary, 15-4, 15-8
Tool control, 16-15
Left, 16-15
None, 16-15
Right, 16-15
Tool definition, 7-3~14
Holder size, 7-6
Machine type, 7-6
Both, 7-6
Finish, 7-6
Rough, 7-6
Tool/Holder definition, 7-5
Tools manager, 7-3
Tool Parameters, 7-6, 7-7
Tool Size, 7-6
Tool type, 7-5
Tool display, 7-22
Change tool/color, 7-22
Display holder, 7-22
Solid tool, 7-22
Stop on gouge, 7-22
Stop on tool change, 7-22
Turbo(no tool), 7-22
Wireframe tool, 7-22
Tool manager, 8-2
Tool parameters, 7-6, 7-7, 8-2
% of matl. cutting speed, 7-7
% of matl. feed per tooth, 7-7
coolant, 7-8
Finish XY step, 7-7
Finish Z step, 7-7
Material, 7-7
Required pilot dia., 7-7
Rough XY step(%), 7-7
Rough Z step, 7-7
Spindle rotation, 7-8
Tool file name, 7-8
Tool name, 7-8
Tool plane, 7-35~37
2 lines, 7-37
Arc, 7-37
Front, 7-37
Normal, 7-37
Number, 7-37
Off, 7-37
Rotate, 7-37
Side, 7-37
Top, 7-37
Tool size, 7-6
Arbor diameter, 7-6
Corner radius, 7-6
Diameter, 7-6
Flute, 7-6
Overall, 7-6
Shoulder, 7-6
Tool words, 1-15
Toolbar area, 3-3
Toolbar/keys, 3-15
Toolholders, 2-21~24
Boring bar identification system, 2-23
Identification system, 2-22
Lead angle, 2-21~23
Profile angle, 2-23

Tooling, 18-5
Tooling data, 10-8
Tooling for milling, 2-10-14
  Automatic Tool Changer, 2-10
  Toolholders, 2-11
  Flange Type, 2-12
  Tapered shank, 2-12
  Adaptors, 2-13
  B-flange, 2-12
  Retention Knob, 2-13
  V-flange, 2-12
Tooling system for turning,2-13, 15
Toolpath display on/off, 8-8, 8-10
Toolpath editing, 9-1
  Edit C-Hook method, 9-1
  Operation manager method, 9-1
  Transform toolpaths method, 9-1
Toolpath file management, 18-6
Toolpath mode for short gaps, 15-15
  Direct mode, 15-15
  Broke mode, 15-15
  Smooth mode, 15-16
Toolpath modules selection, 18-4
  Flowline module, 18-4
  Mutisurf module, 18-4
Toolpath modules, 10-6, 10-7
Toolpath pattern for long gaps, 15-16, 15-17
  Follow tool center boundary at gap, 15-17
  Optimize cut order, 15-17
  Plunge into previously cut area, 15-17
  Tangential arc angle, 15-17
  Tangential arc radius, 15-17
Toolpath planning, 18-4
Toolpaths, 3-4, 8-8, 9-2 ~ 4
  File structure, 9-2 ~ 4
  Transform, 9-10 ~ 42
Tools manager, 7-3
  Change library, 7-3, 7-4
  Convert a library to text, 7-3, 7-4
  Create a library, 7-3, 7-4
  Create new tool, 7-3, 7-4, 7-8 ~10
  Delete tool, 7-3, 7-4
  Detail doc file, 7-3, 7-4
  Doc file, 7-3-7-4
  Edit tool, 7-3, 7-4, 7-12-14
  Get from library, 7-3, 7-4, 7-11, 7-12
  Save to library, 7-3, 7-4
Tplane, 3-5
Transform toolpaths, 9-10 ~ 42
Transition, 15-45
  Broken, 15-45
  Follow surface, 15-45
  High speed, 15-45
  Ramp, 15-45
Translate, 6-13, 6-41
  Rectang, 6-41
  Polar, 6-41
  Between pts, 6-41
  Between vws, 6-41
Translating toolpaths, 9–12 ~ 15
  Applications, 9-15
  Between points, 9-12
  Between veiws, 9-12
  Polar, 9-12
  Rectang, 9-12 ~ 14
    Number of X steps, 9-13 ~ 14
    Number of Y steps, 9-13 ~ 14
    X spacing, 9-13
    Y spacing, 9-13
  Transform, 9-10 ~ 9-42
  Procedure, 9-10
  Subprogram, 9-10
  Types, 9-10
Transform operation parameters, 9-10
Transform types, 9-10
  Mirror, 9-10, 9-35 ~ 36
  Rotate, 9-10, 9-24 ~ 25
  Translate, 9-10, 9-12 ~ 15
Trim, 6-3
  1 entity, 6-3, 6-4
  2 entities, 6-3, 6-4, 6-5
  3 entities, 6-3, 6-5
  Close arc, 6-3, 6-7
  Divide, 6-3, 6-7
  Many 6-3, 6-6
  Surface, 6-3
  To point, 6-3, 6-6
Trim function(3D toolpaths editing), 17-8
Trimming boundaries, 17-8
Trimming procedure, 10-8
Trim surfaces, 13-5
  Blank, 13-5, 13-6
  Delete, 13-5, 13-6
  Keep, 13-5
  Use current construction attributes, 13-6
Trimmed/Extended, 18-4

Trim/Extend surface modeling, 13-1, 13-23
Extend, 13-25
Flat bndy, 13-25
Remove bndy, 13-25
Split, 13-25
To curves, 13-23
To plane, 13-23
To surfaces, 13-24
Untrim, 13-25
Turning operation, 2-44~45
Chip breaker, 2-44
Depth of cut and deflection, 2-44
Feed selection, 2-44
Surface roughness, 2-44
Turning operations (process selection), 10-4
Boring, 10-4
Drilling, 10-4
Facing, 10-4
Grooving, 10-4
Process, 10-4
Roughing, 10-4
Tapping, 10-4
Threading, 10-4

-U-

Undelete, 6-2
All, 6-2
Number, 6-2
Single, 6-2

-V-

Variable radius, 13-6
Insert dyn, 13-7-9
Insert mid, 13-7, 13-9, 13-10
Modify radius value at radius markers, 13-10
Vector formats, 19-2
Velocity loop, 1-26
Verify, 7-20-23
Standard turbo dialog box, 7-20
Verify configuration, 7-20~23
Stock shape, 7-21
Tooldisplay, 7-22
Display control, 7-22
Miscellaneous, 7-22
File selection, 7-22

-W-

Wall passes, 16-46
Number of passes, 16-46
Stepover, 16-46
Stock to leave on wall, 16-46
Walls, 16-43
Chain, 16-43
Surfaces, 16-43
Wireframe method, 14-2
Wireframe model construction, 18-3
Edge profiles, 18-3
Skin profiles, 18-3
Wireframe models, 11-1
Work zero point, 1-32, 1-34

-X-

X to NURBS, 6-3, 6-12
Xform, 3-4, 6-12
Xform parameters, 6-13
Copy, 6-14
Join, 6-14
Move, 6-14
Number of steps, 6-14
Rotation angle, 6-14

-Z-

Z, 3-5
Z-depth, 7-99, 7-100
Clearance, 7-99
Depth, 7-99
Retract, 7-99
Top of stock, 7-99
Z-depth control, 11-5
Z-depth parameters, 7-39, 15-4
Clearance, 7-39
Clearance height, 15-4
Depth, 7-39
Feed plane, 7-39, 15-4, 15-5
Retract, 7-39
Retract height, 15-4, 15-5
Top of stock, 7-39, 15-4, 15-5